QUESTIONING MATTERS

Questioning Matters

AN INTRODUCTION TO PHILOSOPHICAL INQUIRY

DANIEL KOLAK

The William Patterson University of New Jersey

MAYFIELD PUBLISHING COMPANY

Mountain View, California

London • Toronto

Library of Congress Cataloging-in-Publication Data

Questioning matters : an introduction to philosophical inquiry /
   [compiled by] Daniel Kolak.
      p.   cm.
    ISBN 0-7674-0447-5
    1. Philosophy Introductions.   I. Kolak, Daniel.
  BD21.Q47 1999
  100—dc21   99-23104
                                          CIP

Manufactured in the United States of America
10 9 8 7 6 5 4 3 2 1

Mayfield Publishing Company
1280 Villa Street
Mountain View, California 94041

Sponsoring editor, Kenneth King; *production editor,* Carla White Kirschenbaum;
manuscript editor, Jennifer Gordon; *text and cover designer,* Joan Greenfield; *design
manager,* Jean Mailander; *manufacturing manager,* Randy Hurst. The text was set
in 9.5/12 New Baskerville by G&S Typesetters, Inc. and printed on 45# Custom
LG by Banta Book Group.

Cover image: The Metropolitan Museum of Art, Gift of Reante Hofmann, 1975
(1975.323). Photograph ©1996 The Metropolitan Museum of Art. ©Estate of
Hans Hofmann/Licensed by VAGA, New York, NY

Contents

JUSTICE AND LAW   610

Part 7: Art, Beauty, and the Meaning of Life   654

ART AND BEAUTY   658

MEANING   698

Appendix A

Preface

There are many fine philosophy anthologies out there. Why another one? Because we can—and must—strive to do a little better.

For a majority of students, this will be the only philosophy course they will ever take. This means that for many of them philosophy lives or dies by the book—the one book that in a single semester must do at least three things. It must pull them out of the comfort of ready-made answers and paint-by-numbers thinking. It must show them the wisdom of *re*thinking their conditioned beliefs and start them on the path of thinking for themselves, and it must, above all else, show that *questioning matters*. It is not just questioning: It's knowing how to ask the *right* questions that matters most. This puts a great burden on the philosophical thinking process, which involves reasoning, argumentation, and argument analysis. But philosophy also happens to be a subject area that students have not been exposed to before college. So all this needs to be introduced in a semester, and there is small margin for error.

Questioning Matters: An Introduction to Philosophical Inquiry contains the most proven classical foundations and contemporary sources, either in their entirety or carefully edited, all properly arranged and in the right doses. Its opening section contains a primer on logic and argument, as well as point-by-point instructions on how to read a work of philosophy. Every part of the book bridges past classics with carefully selected recent works in which the tools and methods of asking the right questions are applied in ways that students can emulate. Original commissioned articles by and dialogs with noted philosophers exemplify the very methods of reasoning and thinking we are trying to teach.

What this book does more than any other anthology is to model philosophical reasoning processes and methodologies. It provides an accessible, provocative collection of readings organized around a few central topics that are solidly grounded in the classical foundational issues; at the same time, this book makes philosophy not just relevant but essential. The focus is on learning to ask the right questions and analyzing and formulating arguments. The underlying theme is that philosophy is not merely a collection of views and theories but a critical activity as relevant to the timeless issues of existence as to the practical concerns of today.

FEATURES AND BENEFITS

- The anthology's overall theme stresses the activity of philosophy as an integrated method of reasoning over acceptance or rejection of various doctrines.

- "Tools of the Philosopher" in Part 1 introduces principles of reasoning as it demonstrates to students how to read a philosophical article.

- The text contains complete, or nearly complete, texts of Plato's *Euthyphro* and *Republic,* Descartes's *Meditations,* Berkeley's *Dialogues,* Hume's *Dialogues* and *Inquiry,* and Mill's *Utilitarianism.*

- There are specially commissioned articles by and dialogs between the author and such distinguished philosophers as Steven Stich, Daniel Dennett, Alvin Plantinga, Bernard Williams, and Jerrold Levinson. These readings directly address the overall themes and methods of the book, making *Questioning Matters* an exceptionally integrated anthology.

- The text includes high-interest topics, relating philosophy to recent developments in scientific disciplines, as well as to today's social, political, and moral problems.

- There are separate sections devoted to "Art and Beauty" and "Meaning."

- The section introductions with headnotes to each article supply historical material for the topical study of a problem, as well as developing in students an awareness and appreciation of process and method.

- Other useful pedagogical aids include a detailed appendix on writing a philosophy paper.

- There is a detailed Instructor's Manual.

I thank all the contributors and the many people who have helped bring this book into existence, especially: Dan Dennett, Alvin Plantinga, Jaakko Hintikka, Steve Stich, Bernard Williams, Ray Martin, Susan Leigh Anderson, Jerry Levinson, Marie Friquegnon, Stephen Layman, Garrett Thomson, and Hope May. I also thank my reviewers for their many excellent comments: Paul Bloomfield, University of Arizona; Heather J. Gert, Texas A&M University; Anthony Hanson, De Anza College; Sally Haslanger, Massachusetts Institute of Technology; William Heald, University of Iowa; Ralph Kennedy, Wake Forest University; Rhoda Hadassah Kotzin, Michigan State University; Norvin Richards, University of Alabama; Tad M. Schmaltz, Duke University; Larry Shapiro, University of Wisconsin at Madison; Robert A. Stecker, Central Michigan University; Mary Stevenson, University of Colorado at Denver; P. A. Woodward, East Carolina University; and Dr. Robert Zeuschner, Pasadena City College.

Finally, I thank my wonderful long-time editor and friend, Ken King, without whom this project would neither have gotten off the ground nor reached completion. He is the best.

QUESTIONING MATTERS

Tools of the Philosopher

Socrates lived in Athens, a city-state in ancient Greece, from 425–399 B.C.E.* While still a young man, Socrates—like many a young person at the time—traveled about seeking wisdom by asking questions of everyone who would talk to him, questions about anything and everything. Socrates thereby got a reputation for being extremely wise. One day, a friend of his went to the official oracle (the high priestess through whom supposedly the gods spoke) and asked whether anyone in Athens was wiser than Socrates. The Delphic prophetess answered that there was no one wiser.

How did Socrates react to this? According to his testimony, as told to us by his student Plato, Socrates did not believe the oracle. So he set out to prove the gods wrong. His method was simple: Go to those who you think are wiser than you and question them until you demonstrate to yourself their superiority. In the *Apology* he gives a moving and eloquent statement about how he thereby stumbled upon the true meaning of wisdom: All the supposedly wise people whom Socrates questioned invariably pretended to know more than they actually knew. Unlike them, Socrates knew what he did not know and—unlike them—he did not pretend to know more than he actually did. In this experience, he explains, he found the true meaning of wisdom.

Logic, making arguments, and argument analysis are among the most important tools of the philosopher. The second selection, "A Logic Primer: Reason and Argument" by C. Stephen Layman, will teach you everything you need to know to get started. It is, in fact, a minicourse in the art of logical thinking. If you study it carefully and learn its techniques, you will be well prepared to undertake the reading and study of philosophy provided in this book. With that same goal in mind, Hope May's "How to Read Philosophy" offers detailed advice, with lots of specific examples, on how to apply the philosopher's tools to reading some of the selections in this book.

---

*Before the Common Era, which coincides with "B.C."

Apology

PLATO

Plato (427–347 B.C.E.) lived in Athens and was a student of Socrates. Most of his surviving works, written in dialog form, feature the character of Socrates. Plato is generally regarded as one of the greatest philosophers of all times. He founded the Academy, the world's first university.

How you have felt, O men of Athens, at hearing the speeches of my accusers, I cannot tell; but I know that their persuasive words almost made me forget who I was, such was the effect of them; and yet they have hardly spoken a word of truth. But many as their falsehoods were, there was one of them which quite amazed me: I mean when they told you to be upon your guard, and not to let yourself be deceived by the force of my eloquence. They ought to have been ashamed of saying this, because they were sure to be detected as soon as I opened my lips and displayed my deficiency; they certainly did appear to be most shameless in saying this, unless by the force of eloquence they mean the force of truth: for then I do indeed admit that I am eloquent. But in how different a way from theirs! . . .

Well, then, I will make my defence, and I will endeavor in the short time which is allowed to do away with this evil opinion of me which you have held for such a long time; and I hope I may succeed, if this be well for you and me, and that my words may find favor with you. But I know that to accomplish this is not easy—I quite see the nature of the task. Let the event be as God wills: in obedience to the law I make my defence.

I will begin at the beginning, and ask what the accusation is which has given rise to this slander of me, and which has encouraged Meletus to proceed against me. What do the slanderers say? They shall be my prosecutors, and I will sum up their words in an affidavit: "Socrates is an evil-doer, and a curious person, who searches into things under the earth and in heaven, and he makes the worse appear the

better cause; and he teaches the aforesaid doctrines to others." That is the nature of the accusation. . . . But the simple truth is, O Athenians, that I have nothing to do with these studies. Very many of those here present are witnesses to the truth of this, and to them I appeal. . . . As little foundation is there for the report that I am a teacher, and take money; that is no more true than the other. . . .

I dare say that someone will ask the question, "Why is this, Socrates, and what is the origin of these accusations of you: for there must have been something strange which you have been doing? All this great fame and talk about you would never have arisen if you had been like other men: tell us, then, why this is, as we should be sorry to judge hastily of you." Now I regard this as a fair challenge, and I will endeavor to explain to you the origin of this name of "wise," and of this evil fame. Please to attend them. And although some of you may think I am joking, I declare that I will tell you the entire truth. Men of Athens, this reputation of mine has come of a certain sort of wisdom which I possess. If you ask me what kind of wisdom, I reply, such wisdom as is attainable by man, for to that extent I am inclined to believe that I am wise; whereas the persons of whom I was speaking have a superhuman wisdom, which I may fail to describe, because I have it not myself; and he who says that I have, speaks falsely, and is taking away my character. And here, O men of Athens, I must beg you not to interrupt me, even if I seem to say something extravagant. For the word which I will speak is not mine. I will refer you to a witness who is worthy of credit, and will tell you about my wisdom—whether I have any, and of what sort—and that witness shall be the god of Delphi. . . . [A] friend of mine . . . went to Delphi and boldly asked the oracle to tell him whether—as I was saying, I must beg

From "Apology," in *The Dialogue of Plato,* translated by Benjamin Jowett (Oxford: Clarendon Press, 1892).

you not to interrupt—he asked the oracle to tell him whether there was anyone wiser than I was, and the Pythian prophetess answered that there was no man wiser. . . .

Why do I mention this? Because I am going to explain to you why I have such an evil name. When I heard the answer, I said to myself, What can the god mean? and what is the interpretation of this riddle? for I know that I have no wisdom, small or great. What can he mean when he says that I am the wisest of men? And yet he is a god and cannot lie; that would be against his nature. After a long consideration, I at last thought of a method of trying the question. I reflected that if I could only find a man wiser than myself, then I might go to the god with a refutation in my hand. I should say to him, "Here is a man who is wiser than I am; but you said that I was the wisest." Accordingly I went to one who had the reputation of wisdom, and observed to him—his name I need not mention; he was a politician whom I selected for examination—and the result was as follows: When I began to talk with him, I could not help thinking that he was not really wise, although he was thought wise by many, and wiser still by himself; and I went and tried to explain to him that he thought himself wise, but was not really wise; and the consequence was that he hated me, and his enmity was shared by several who were present and heard me. So I left him, saying to myself, as I went away: Well, although I do not suppose that either of us knows anything really beautiful and good, I am better off than he is—for he knows nothing, and thinks that he knows. I neither know nor think that I know. In this latter particular, then, I seem to have slightly the advantage of him. Then I went to another, who had still higher philosophical pretensions, and my conclusion was exactly the same. I made another enemy of him, and of many others besides him.

After this I went to one man after another, being not unconscious of the enmity which I provoked, and I lamented and feared this: but necessity was laid upon me—the word of God, I thought, ought to be considered first. And I said to myself, Go I must to all who appear to know, and find out the meaning of the oracle. And I swear to you, Athenians, by the dog I swear!—for I must tell you the truth—the result of my mission was just this: I found that the men

most in repute were all but the most foolish; and that some inferior men were really wiser and better. I will tell you the tale of my wanderings and of the "Herculean" labors, as I may call them, which I endured only to find at last the oracle irrefutable. When I left the politicians, I went to the poets; tragic, dithyrambic, and all sorts. And there, I said to myself, you will be detected; now you will find out that you are more ignorant than they are. Accordingly, I took them some of the most elaborate passages in their own writings, and asked what was the meaning of them—thinking that they would teach me something. Will you believe me? I am almost ashamed to speak of this, but still I must say that there is hardly a person present who would not have talked better about their poetry than they did themselves. That showed me in an instant that not by wisdom do poets write poetry, but by a sort of genius and inspiration; they are like diviners or soothsayers who also say many fine things, but do not understand the meaning of them. And the poets appeared to me to be much in the same case; and I further observed that upon the strength of their poetry they believed themselves to be the wisest of men in other things in which they were not wise. So I departed, conceiving myself to be superior to them for the same reason that I was superior to the politicians.

At last I went to the artisans, for I was conscious that I knew nothing at all, as I may say, and I was sure that they knew many fine things; and in this I was not mistaken, for they did know many things of which I was ignorant, and in this they certainly were wiser than I was. But I observed that even the good artisans fell into the same error as the poets; because they were good workmen they thought that they also knew all sorts of high matters, and this defect in them overshadowed their wisdom—therefore I asked myself on behalf of the oracle, whether I would like to be as I was, neither having their knowledge nor their ignorance, or like them in both; and I made answer to myself and the oracle that I was better off as I was.

This investigation has led to my having many enemies of the worst and most dangerous kind, and has given occasion also to many calumnies, and I am called wise, for my hearers always imagine that I myself possess the wisdom which I find wanting in others; but the truth is, O men of Athens, that God only is wise; and in this oracle he means to say that the wisdom of men is little or nothing; he is not speaking of Socrates, he is only using my name as an illustration, as if he said, He, O men, is the wisest, who, like Socrates, knows that his wisdom is in truth worth nothing. And so I go my way, obedient to the god, and make inquisition into the wisdom of any-one, whether citizen or stranger, who appears to be wise; and if he is not wise, then in vindication of the oracle I show him that he is not wise; and this occu-pation quite absorbs me, and I have no time to give either to any public matter of interest or to any con-cern of my own, but I am in utter poverty by reason of my devotion to the god. . . .

A Logic Primer
Reason and Argument

C. STEPHEN LAYMAN

C. Stephen Layman teaches philosophy at Seattle Pacific University.

Part 1: Basic Concepts

Everyone thinks. Everyone reasons. Everyone ar-gues. And everyone is subjected to the reasoning and arguing of others. We are daily bombarded with reasoning from many sources: books, speeches, ra-dio, TV, newspapers, employers, friends, and family.

Some people think well, reason well, and ar-gue well. Some do not. The ability to think, reason, and argue well is partly a matter of natural gifts. But whatever our natural gifts, they can be refined and sharpened. The study of logic is one of the best ways to refine our natural ability to reason and ar-gue. Through the study of logic, we learn strategies for thinking well, ways to avoid common errors in reasoning, and effective techniques for evaluating arguments.

What is logic? Roughly speaking, logic is the study of methods for evaluating arguments. More precisely, **logic** is the study of methods for evaluating whether the premises of an argument adequately support (or provide good evidence for) its conclu-sion. To get a better grasp of what logic is, then, we need to understand the key concepts involved in this definition: argument, premise, conclusion, and support. This section of the article is designed to give you an initial understanding of these basic concepts.

An **argument** is a set of statements—one of which, the *conclusion,* is affirmed *on the basis of* the others, the *premises.* The premises of an argument are offered as support or evidence for the conclu-sion, and that support or evidence may be adequate or inadequate in a given case. The set of statements counts as an argument as long as one statement is affirmed on the basis of others. Here is an example of an argument:

1. All Quakers are pacifists. Jane is a Quaker. So, Jane is a pacifist.

The word *so* indicates that the conclusion of this ar-gument is "Jane is a pacifist." And the argument has two premises: "All Quakers are pacifists" and "Jane is a Quaker."

What is a statement? A **statement** is a sentence that is either true or false. For example,

2. Some dogs are collies.
3. No dogs are collies.
4. Some dogs weigh exactly 124.379 pounds.

Statement (2) is true, that is, it describes things as they are. And (3) is false for it describes things as otherwise than they are. Truth and falsehood are the two possible **truth values.** So, we can say that a state-ment is a sentence that has truth value. The truth value of (2) is true, whereas the truth value of (3) is false, but (2) and (3) are both statements. Is (4) a statement? Yes. You may not know its truth value, and perhaps no one does, but (4) is either true or false, and hence it is a statement.

Are any of the following items statements?

5. Get your dog off my lawn!
6. How many dogs do you own?
7. Let's get a dog.

No. Sentence (5) is a *command,* and one may obey or disobey a command, but it makes no sense to pronounce it true or false. So, although (5) is a sentence, it is not a statement. Sentence (6) is a *question,* and as such it is neither true nor false; hence, it is not a statement. Finally, (7) is a *proposal,* and proposals are neither true nor false, so (7) is not a statement.

The **premises** of an argument are the statements on the basis of which the conclusion is affirmed. To put it the other way around, the **conclusion** is the statement that is affirmed on the basis of the premises. In a well-constructed argument, the premises *give good reasons for believing that the conclusion is true.* But a poorly constructed argument is still an argument. For example, compare the following arguments:

8. All uncles are male. Chris is an uncle. So, Chris is male.
9. Some uncles are skinny. Chris is an uncle. So, Chris is skinny.

The premises of (8) support (or provide a basis for) the conclusion in this sense: If they are true, then the conclusion must be true. But the premises of (9) fail to support the conclusion adequately: Even if true, they do not provide good reason to believe that the conclusion is true. So, (9) is a bad argument, but it is still an argument.

Arguments are used very frequently in our verbal and written interactions with others. We also use arguments either to persuade others or to discover truth. For example, we often use arguments to persuade others to believe our political or ethical views, but we also use arguments as tools for discovering truth. For example, suppose a detective is investigating a crime: Who shot Alvin Smith? There are just two suspects, Griggs and Brooks. The detective es-

tablishes that Brooks was out of town at the time of the shooting, and argues as follows:

10. Either Brooks or Griggs shot Smith. Brooks did not shoot Smith. So, Griggs shot Smith.

In this case, the argument is used to discover truth. Of course, a given argument can be used *both* for the purpose of discovering truth and for the purpose of persuading others to believe the conclusion. Persuasion and truthseeking are often compatible goals. Sometimes, however, one of these goals interferes with the other. For example, in a political campaign one candidate might try to persuade the voters that his opponent is dishonest, even though he knows his opponent is honest.

We now have a preliminary understanding of what logic is. We can gain more insight by taking a closer look at what it means for the conclusion of an argument to be adequately based on or supported by the premises. To do this, we must explore the important concepts of validity and strength.

VALIDITY AND DEDUCTIVE SOUNDNESS

A valid argument is one in which the premises support the conclusion completely. More formally, a **valid argument** is one such that *it is impossible that its conclusion is false while its premises are true.* In other words, a valid argument has the following essential feature: Assuming its premises are true, its conclusion *must* be true. Each of the following arguments is valid:

11. All biologists are scientists. John is not a scientist. So, John is not a biologist.
12. If Alice stole the diamonds, then she is a thief. And Alice did steal the diamonds. So, Alice is a thief.
13. Either Bill has a poor memory or he is lying. Bill does not have a poor memory. So, Bill is lying.

In each case it is impossible for the conclusion to be false *while* (given that) the premises are true. Notice that one doesn't have to know whether the premises of an argument actually *are* true in order to determine its validity. One simply has to ascertain that the conclusion must be true *assuming* the premises are true.

In ordinary English, the word *valid* is often used simply to indicate one's overall approval of an argument. But logicians focus their attention on the link between the premises and the conclusion, rather than on the actual truth or falsity of the statements comprising the argument. Thus, *valid* has a more precise meaning for logicians.

The following observations about validity may help to prevent some common misunderstandings. First, notice that an argument can have one or more false premises and still be valid. For instance,

14. All birds have beaks. Some cats are birds. So, some cats have beaks.

Here the second premise is plainly false, and yet the argument is valid. It is impossible for the conclusion of (14) to be false, assuming that its premises are true. In the following argument both premises are false, but the argument is still valid:

15. All sharks are birds. All birds are politicians. So, all sharks are politicians.

Although the premises of (15) are in fact false, if they *were* true, the conclusion would have to be true also. It is impossible for the conclusion to be false assuming that the premises are true. So, the argument is valid.

Second, we cannot rightly conclude that an argument is valid simply on the grounds that its premises are all true. For example,

16. Some Americans are women. Bill Clinton is an American. So, Bill Clinton is a woman.

The premises here are true, but the conclusion is in fact false. So, obviously, it is possible that the conclusion of (16) is false while its premises are true; hence, (16) is not valid. Is the following argument valid?

17. Some Americans are Democrats. Bill Clinton is an American. So, Bill Clinton is a Democrat.

Here we have true premises and a true conclusion. Nevertheless, it is possible that the conclusion is false *while* the premises are true. (Clinton could switch political parties while remaining an Ameri-

can.) So, even if an argument has true premises and a true conclusion, it isn't necessarily valid, for the premises may not support the conclusion in the right way. (In many cases we simply do not know whether the premises of an argument are true or false, and yet we may know that the argument is valid.) Thus, the question, Are the premises actually true? is distinct from the question, Is the argument valid?

Third, suppose an argument is valid and has a false conclusion. Does it necessarily have at least one false premise? Yes. For if it had true premises, it would have to have a true conclusion, because it is valid. *Validity preserves truth,* that is, if we start with truth and reason in a valid fashion, we will always wind up with truth.

Fourth, does validity also preserve falsehood? That is, if we start with false premises and reason validly, are we bound to wind up with a false conclusion? It is tempting to answer yes, for "error in its own right breeds error—if the first step in an argument is wrong, everything that follows will be wrong." But the correct answer is no. Consider the following argument:

18. All dogs are ants. All ants are mammals. So, all dogs are mammals.

Is (18) valid? Yes. It is impossible that the conclusion of (18) is false, assuming that its premises are true. However, the premises here are false, while the conclusion is true. So, *validity does not preserve falsehood.* As a matter of fact, false premises plus valid reasoning may lead to either truth or falsity, depending on the case. Here is a valid argument with false premises and a false conclusion:

19. All birds are cats. Some dogs are birds. So, some dogs are cats.

The lesson here is that while valid reasoning guarantees that we will end up with truth if we start with it, we may wind up with either truth or falsehood if we reason validly from false premises.

An **invalid** argument has the following essential feature: It is *possible* for its conclusion to be false while its premises are true. Each of the following arguments is invalid:

20. All dogs are animals. All cats are animals. Hence, all dogs are cats.
21. If Pat is a wife, then Pat is a woman. But Pat is not a wife. So, Pat is not a woman.
22. Bill likes Sue. Therefore, Sue likes Bill.

The premises of (20) are in fact true, but its conclusion is false; so (20) is obviously invalid. Argument (21) is invalid because its premises leave open the possibility that Pat is an unmarried woman. And (22) is invalid, because even if Bill does like Sue, that is no guarantee that she likes him. In each of these cases, then, the conclusion could be false while (that is, assuming that) the premises are true.

Validity matters because true premises by themselves do not make good arguments. But, obviously we want our arguments to have true premises. A **deductively sound argument** has two essential features: *It is valid, and all its premises are true.* Notice that a deductively sound argument cannot have a false conclusion. Because a sound argument is valid and has only true premises, it must have a true conclusion. Here are two deductively sound arguments:

23. All collies are dogs. All dogs are animals. So, all collies are animals.
24. If Akron is in Ohio, then Akron is in the United States. Akron is in Ohio. So, Akron is in the United States.

A **deductively unsound argument** falls into one of the following three categories:

a. It is a valid but has at least one false premise.
b. It is invalid, but all its premises are true.
c. It is invalid *and* has at least one false premise.

In other words, a deductively unsound argument is one that is either invalid or has at least one false premise. For example, both of the following arguments are deductively unsound:

25. All birds are animals. Some grizzly bears are not animals. So, some grizzly bears are not birds.
26. All birds are animals. All grizzly bears are animals. So, all grizzly bears are birds.

Argument (25) is unsound, for although it is valid, it has a false (second) premise. Argument (26) is unsound, for although it has true premises, it is invalid. We can easily construct an unsound argument of the third type, that is, one that is both invalid *and* has at least one false premise, by replacing "birds" in argument (26) with "trees":

27. All trees are animals. All grizzly bears are animals. So, all grizzly bears are trees.

Deductive logic is the part of logic that is concerned with tests for validity and invalidity. Much of this article is devoted to an exploration of deductive logic. In fact, the next section will provide us with our first set of methods establishing the validity and invalidity of arguments.

A note on terminology is in order at the close of this section. Given our definitions, *arguments* are neither true nor false. But each *statement* is either true or false. On the other hand, *arguments* can be valid, invalid, deductively sound, or deductively unsound; but *statements* cannot be valid, invalid, deductively sound, or deductively unsound. Therefore, a given premise (or conclusion) is either true or false, but it cannot be valid, invalid, deductively sound, or deductively unsound.

STRENGTH AND INDUCTIVE SOUNDNESS

Even if an argument is not valid, its premises may still provide significant support for its conclusion. A strong argument is one in which the premises provide *partial* support for the conclusion. More precisely, a **strong argument** is one such that *it is unlikely (though possible) that its conclusion is false while its premises are true.* In other words, a strong argument has the following essential feature: It is probable (but not necessary) that if its premises are true, then its conclusion is true. For example,

28. Ninety percent of American males over fifty years of age cannot run a mile in less than six minutes. Thomas is an American male over fifty years of age. So, Thomas cannot run a mile in less than six minutes.

The premises of (28) do not absolutely guarantee the truth of the conclusion. Possibly Thomas belongs to that small percentage of American men over fifty who can run a mile in less than six minutes. Nevertheless, it is unlikely that the conclusion of (28) is false assuming its premises are true.

Now, let's alter (28) systematically to better understand the concept of strength. Suppose we replace "ninety" with "ninety-nine." Does the argument remain strong? Yes. In fact, it is even stronger. This indicates that strength, unlike validity, is very much a matter of degree. Suppose we replace "ninety" with "fifty-one." Is the argument then strong? Strictly speaking, yes, because the conclusion remains slightly more probable than not. Of course, once we replace "ninety" with "fifty-one," the argument is of little value: The amount of support given to the conclusion is scarcely worth mentioning. The point to bear in mind is that because strength comes in degrees, we may intelligibly speak of arguments that are *slightly* strong, *moderately* strong, or *very* strong. By way of contrast, it wouldn't make any sense at all to speak of slightly valid or moderately valid arguments. Validity is an all-or-nothing affair.

What if we replace "ninety" with "fifty" in argument (28)? Then the argument is not strong, but weak. A **weak argument** has the following essential feature: *It is not likely that if its premises are true, then its conclusion is true.* If we replace "ninety" with "fifty" in argument (28), then it is just as likely, given the premises, that Thomas *can* run the mile in less than six minutes as that he *cannot.* So, the argument is weak. The argument becomes even weaker if we replace "ninety" with "forty," "thirty," and so on.

At the other end of the scale, what if we replace "ninety percent of" with "all" in argument (28)? Does the argument remain strong? No. For at that point the argument becomes *valid*—it is impossible for the conclusion to be false while the premises are true. But, by definition, in a strong argument, it is *possible* that the conclusion is false while the premises are true. Thus, no valid argument is strong, and no strong argument is valid.

We shall explore the concept of strength more fully in later sections, but it will be helpful at this point to consider some additional examples of strong arguments, to underscore the fact that they come in very different types. For instance, **arguments from authority** can be strong. They have the following structure:

29. 1. **R** is a reliable authority regarding **S.**
     2. **R** sincerely asserts that **S.**
     So, **S.**

Here **R** stands for a person or reference work, while **S** stands for any statement. For instance,

30. According to historian Howard Zinn, by 1933, the worst year of America's Great Depression, one fourth to one third of America's labor force was out of work. So, a fourth or more of American workers are unemployed in 1933.— Howard Zinn, *A People's History of the United States* (New York: HarperCollins, 1995), p. 378.

This appeal to authority is legitimate, but authorities can make mistakes, so it is possible that the conclusion of (30) is false while its premises are true—possible, but unlikely; hence, the argument is strong. Yet it would be impossible to state the degree of strength with numerical precision.

Like arguments from authority, **arguments from analogy** are very common, and they too can be strong. The structure of an argument from analogy is as follows:

31. 1. Object (event or situation) **A** is similar to object (event or situation) **B** in certain relevant respects.
     2. **B** has property **P.**
     So, **A** has property **P** also.

Here is an example. Suppose Jack and Jill are riding horseback. Jill's horse jumps a fence. Jack is unsure if his horse can jump the fence, so Jill points out that his horse is very similar to hers in size, speed, strength, and training. She adds that, because Jack is an experienced rider and weighs no more than she does, Jack's horse is not operating with a handicap. She concludes that Jack's horse can jump the fence, too. We could outline Jill's reasoning as follows:

32. Jack's horse is similar in relevant respects to Jill's horse (and is similarly situated). Jill's horse was able to jump the fence. So, Jack's horse is able to jump the fence also.

This argument is not valid, because its conclusion can be false while its premises are true. For example, unknown to Jill, Jack's horse may have been given a drug that renders it unable to jump well today. Still, it is more probable than not that if the premises of (32) are true, then the conclusion is true, and hence the argument is at least slightly strong.

We said earlier that deductive logic is the part of logic that concerns tests for validity and invalidity. **Inductive logic** is the part of logic that concerns tests for the strength and weakness of arguments. An **inductively sound argument** is one that has two essential features: It is strong, and all its premises are true. Here is an example:

33. All or nearly all lemons that have been tasted were sour. So, all or nearly all lemons are sour.

This argument is not valid because the conclusion concerns not only lemons that have been tasted but lemons in general—*including those that have not been tasted.* And the premise does not rule out the *possibility* that a large percentage of untasted lemons are not sour. Nevertheless, it is unlikely that the conclusion is false given that the premise is true. And the premise is true. So, the argument is inductively sound.

An inductively sound argument can have a false conclusion, for its premises do not absolutely guarantee the truth of its conclusion. In this respect *inductively* sound arguments differ markedly from *deductively* sound arguments. A deductively sound argument cannot have a false conclusion, because it is valid, and all its premises are true (and if a valid argument has only true premises, its conclusion must be true also). An **inductively unsound argument** is one that is either (a) weak or (b) strong with at least one false premise. (Note that, by this definition, a weak argument with a false premise counts as inductively unsound.) Here is an example of an argument that is inductively unsound because it is weak:

34. Slightly less than fifty percent of Americans are men. Julia Roberts is an American. So, Julia Roberts is a man.

Although (34) has true premises, the premises do not provide even partial support (in our technical sense) for the conclusion: It is *not* likely that if the premises are true, then the conclusion is true. (Note: This is not because Julia Roberts is a woman. If we replace "Julia Roberts" with "Woody Allen," the argument is still weak, even though its conclusion is true.)

Here is an example of an argument that is inductively unsound because it is strong but has a false premise:

35. There is intelligent life on all of the following planets: Mercury, Venus, Earth, Jupiter, Uranus, Neptune, and Pluto. So, there is intelligent life on Mars.[4]

As far as we know, the premise of (35) is false, and so is the conclusion. But it is unlikely that the conclusion is false *given that* the premise is true. So, the argument is strong, but inductively unsound. Note that, by our definitions, no deductively sound argument is inductively sound, for no valid argument is strong. Similarly, no inductively sound argument is deductively sound, because no strong argument is valid. Note also that a valid argument with a false premise is deductively unsound, but it is not inductively unsound, for a valid argument is neither strong nor weak.

We now have many of the basic concepts of logic before us. But because it is easy to become confused about the relationships among these basic concepts, let's review the ground we have covered. We defined logic as the study of methods for evaluating whether the premises of an argument adequately *support* its conclusion. We have seen that arguments can be evaluated in terms of two different standards: validity and strength. Deductive logic is the branch of logic concerned with methods of evaluating arguments for validity and invalidity. Inductive logic is the branch of logic concerned with methods of evaluating arguments for strength and weakness.

Some logic texts state that there are two different kinds of *arguments,* deductive and inductive, and that deductive logic is about deductive arguments while inductive logic is about inductive arguments. These texts provide the following classification of arguments:

	Deductive Arguments	Inductive Arguments
Logically correct	valid	strong
Logically incorrect	invalid	weak

However, from the standpoint of this article the above picture is misleading.[5] For example, given our definitions, every inductively sound argument is invalid and hence deductively unsound. And every inductively unsound argument is also deductively unsound, because every inductively unsound argument is invalid. From the standpoint of this article, *deductive and inductive logic do not differ according to the kinds of arguments they treat but according to the different standards by which they evaluate arguments, namely, validity and strength.* From this point of view, arguments may be classified as shown here:

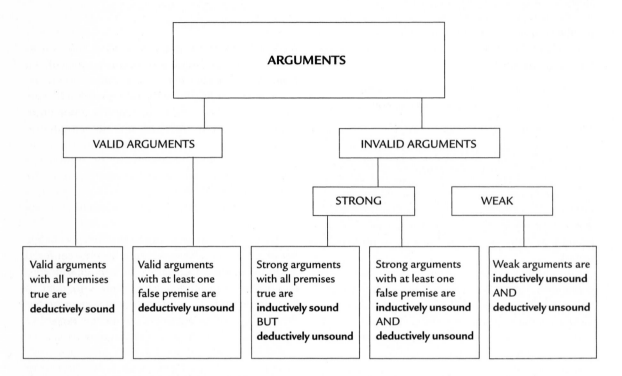

Note that, in this scheme, any argument that is not deductively sound is deductively unsound. For example, all *inductively sound* arguments are *deductively unsound* because they are invalid. Strong arguments with false premises are inductively unsound, but they are also deductively unsound for two reasons: (a) they are invalid, and (b) they have false premises. All weak arguments are inductively unsound (whether or not they have a false premise). And all weak arguments are also deductively unsound, because all weak arguments are invalid.

Some general remarks on terminology are in order at the close of this section. Notice that, given our definitions, *arguments* can be strong, weak, inductively sound, or inductively unsound. But *arguments* are never true, and they are never false. *Premises* are either true or false. *Conclusions* are either true or false. On the other hand, *premises* are never strong, weak, inductively sound, or inductively unsound.

And *conclusions* are never strong, weak, inductively sound, or inductively unsound.

Part 2: Argument Forms

We have seen that deductive logic is the part of logic that concerns tests for validity and invalidity. This section introduces the concept of argument forms and explains how an understanding of argument forms can establish that an argument is valid or invalid.

FORMS AND COUNTEREXAMPLES

Consider the following two arguments:

1. 1. All oaks are trees.
   2. All trees are plants.
   So, all oaks are plants.

2. 1. All monauli are flageolets.
    2. All flageolets are fipple-flutes.
    So, all monauli are fipple-flutes.

These two arguments have the same *form,* that is, they exemplify the same pattern of reasoning. We can represent the form as follows:

Form One
    1. All *A* are *B.*
    2. All *B* are *C.*
    So, all *A* are *C.*

Here the letters *A, B,* and *C* stand for *terms.* Let's say that a **term** is a word or phrase that stands for a class (that is, a collection or set) of things, such as the class of oaks or the class of trees. Thus, the words *oaks, trees,* and *plants* are terms in argument (1). (Certain descriptive phrases such as "oak trees less than two years old" also count as terms in the sense defined.) Form One provides a picture of the pattern of reasoning common to arguments (1) and (2). In regard to argument (1), *A* stands for the term "oaks," *B* for the term "trees," and *C* for the term "plants." In regard to argument (2), *A* stands for term "monauli," *B* stands for the term "flageolets," and *C* stands for the term "fipple-flutes."

Argument (1) is clearly valid: If all members of class *A* (oaks) are members of class *B* (trees), and all members of class *B* (trees) are members of class *C* (plants), then all members of *A* (oaks) are members of *C* (plants). We can diagram this logic as follows:

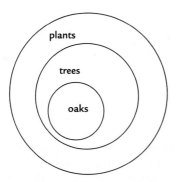

And regarding argument (2), while you may not have any idea whether the premises are true, you can see that (2) is valid because it has the same form

as (1). Any argument having Form One has the following feature: Its conclusion cannot be false while its premises are true. So, *the validity of the argument is guaranteed by its form and does not depend on its content* (that is, its specific subject matter).

Using Form One, we can generate valid arguments at will by substituting terms for the letters *A, B,* and *C.* An argument that results from uniformly replacing letters with terms (or statements) in an argument form is called a **substitution instance** of that form. Note that the replacement must be uniform, for example, if "oaks" replaces *A* in one instance, "oaks" must replace *A* all instances. Here is another valid form of argument, along with two substitution instances:

Form Two
    1. All *A* are *B.*
    2. Some *C* are not *B.*
    So, some *C* are not *A.*

Substitution Instances

3. 1. All emeralds
       are gems.
    2. Some rocks
       are not gems.
    So, some rocks
    are not emeralds.

4. 1. All collies
       are dogs.
    2. Some animals
       are not dogs.
    So, some animals
    are not collies.

In (3), "emeralds" replaces *A,* "gems" replaces *B,* and "rocks" replaces *C.* In (4), "collies" replaces *A,* "dogs" replaces *B,* and "animals" replaces *C.* Every argument having this form is valid. We can diagram the logic as follows:

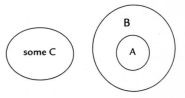

Clearly, if all members of class *A* are members of class *B,* and some members of class *C* are not members of *B,* then some members of *C* are not members of *A.* Thus, it is impossible for an argument having this form to have a false conclusion given that its premises are true.

Let's now consider the relationship between form and invalidity. The following argument has true premises and a false conclusion, so it is plainly invalid:

5. 1. All birds are animals.
    2. All dogs are animals.
    So, all birds are dogs.

If we let *A* stand for "birds," *B* for "animals," and *C* for "dogs," we can represent the form of the argument as follows:

Form Three
1. All *A* are *B*.
2. All *C* are *B*.
So, all *A* are *C*.

This argument form is invalid, for it allows us to move from true premises to a false conclusion. Argument (5) proves this, for it is a substitution instance of Form Three.

The relationship between argument (5) and Form Three suggests a procedure for showing that an argument is invalid. First, identify the form of the argument. Second, if the validity of the argument is suspect, produce a substitution instance of the argument form in which the premises are true and the conclusion is false. This will show that the argument form is invalid. Third, given that the validity of the argument depends on the form we have identified, we may conclude that the argument itself is invalid. Let's now make this procedure a bit more explicit and note some complications that may arise.

Consider the following argument:

6. 1. All determinists are fatalists.
    2. Some fatalists are not Calvinists.
    So, some Calvinists are not determinists.

Argument (6) has this form:

Form Four
1. All *A* are *B*.
2. Some *B* are not *C*.
So, some *C* are not *A*.

We can prove that this form is invalid by producing a substitution instance that has premises known to be true and a conclusion known to be false. For example,

7. 1. All dogs are animals. (true)
    2. Some animals are not collies. (true)
    So, some collies are not dogs. (false)

A substitution instance with premises known to be true and a conclusion known to be false is a **counterexample** to the form in question. A counterexample demonstrates the invalidity of an argument form by showing that the form does not preserve truth, that is, that the form can lead from true premises to a false conclusion. A good counterexample must have the following features:

a. It must have the correct form.
b. Its premises must be *well-known* truths.
c. Its conclusion must be a *well-known* falsehood.

Counterexample (7) shows that Form Four is invalid: "All *A* are *B*. Some *B* are not *C*. So, some *C* are not *A*." And argument (6)—"All determinists are fatalists. Some fatalists are not Calvinists. So, some Calvinists are not determinists."—has Form Four. Therefore, we may provisionally conclude that (6) is invalid. (The provisional nature of the conclusion will be explained momentarily.)

Now, let's break down the process of finding a counterexample into steps. We begin with an argument:

8. 1. No capitalists are philanthropists.
    2. All philanthropists are altruists.
    So, no capitalists are altruists.

If we let *A* stand for "capitalists," *B* for "philanthropists," and *C* for "altruists," we can represent the form as follows:

Form Five
1. No *A* are *B*.
2. All *B* are *C*.
So, no *A* are *C*.

Next we construct a substitution instance whose premises are well-known truths and whose conclusion is a well-known falsehood. It is best to employ terms whose interrelations are well understood, for example, simple biological terms such as "dog," "collie," "mammal," "cat," and "animal." Or simple geometrical terms such as "square," "figure," "rectangle," and "circle." It often helps to begin by writing a blatantly false conclusion. Then work backward. For instance,

9. 1. No dogs are *B*.
    2. All *B* are animals.
    So, no dogs are animals.

Notice that because "dogs" replaces *A* in the conclusion, it must also replace *A* in the first premise; and because "animals" replaces *C* in the conclusion, it must replace *C* in the second premise. Now we merely need to find a term to replace *B* with—a term that will make the premises well-known truths. "Cats" is an obvious choice. So, our completed counterexample looks like this:

10. 1. No dogs are cats.
     2. All cats are animals.
     So, no dogs are animals.

Because the premises are well-known truths, but the conclusion is a well-known falsehood, Form Five is invalid ("No *A* are *B;* all *B* are *C;* so, no *A* are *C*"). And we may provisionally conclude that argument (8) is invalid.

The counterexample method has some limitations and complications that we should note at this time. First, while the counterexample method can be used to prove that an invalid argument form is invalid, it cannot show that a valid form is valid. For example, suppose we show that a given argument form has a substitution instance that has true premises and a true conclusion. Does that show that the argument form is valid? No. Invalid forms often have such substitution instances. Here is one for Form Five ("No *A* are *B;* all *B* are *C;* so, no *A* are *C*):

11. 1. No cats are collies. (true)
     2. All collies are dogs. (true)
     So, no cats are dogs. (true)

Nevertheless, the argument form remains invalid because it *can* lead from true premises to a false conclusion, as counterexample (10) illustrates. Again, the point is that the counterexample method cannot establish validity—only invalidity.

Of course, it is impossible to construct a counterexample to a valid form. For if an argument form is valid, then any substitution instance with true premises is bound to have a true conclusion. This indicates a second limitation of the counterexample method. What if we suspect that an argument form is invalid, but we have difficulty constructing a counterexample? Perhaps the form is valid after all, or perhaps we just need to be more creative in thinking of substitution instances. How do we tell which? The counterexample method does not answer this question.

A third limitation of the counterexample method is that it cannot be used to show that an argument is either strong or weak, for the strength and weakness of an argument depends only partly on its form.

A minor complication that arises when constructing counterexamples concerns the word *some*. In logic, the word *some* means "at least one." Hence, the statement "Some dogs are animals" is true: *At least one* dog is an animal. And "Some dogs are animals" does *not* imply that some dogs are not animals. Both of the following are true statements: "Some dogs are animals" and "All dogs are animals."

A more interesting complication regarding counterexamples stems from the fact that an argument can have more than one form. This complication explains why the counterexample method allows us to draw only *provisional* conclusions regarding the invalidity of *arguments* (as opposed to argument *forms*). Let's consider an argument having Form One:

12. 1. All cats are mammals.
     2. All mammals are animals.
     So, all cats are animals.

Like all arguments having Form One, argument (12) is valid. But suppose we let the letters *A, B,* and *C* stand for *statements* (instead of terms, as we have been doing). Such a use of letters is entirely legitimate. And if we let *A* stand for the first premise, *B* for the second premise, and *C* for the conclusion, we can rightly say that argument (12) has the following form: "*A. B.* So, *C.*" This form, however, is invalid. Here is a counterexample:

13. 1. Trees exist.
     2. Frogs exist.
     So, unicorns exist.

To obtain the counterexample, simply substitute "Trees exists" for *A*, "Frogs exist" for *B*, and "Unicorns exist" for *C*. Have we shown that argument (12) is invalid? No. We have merely shown that it has *one* form that is invalid. We may add that, as a matter of fact, every argument has at least one invalid form.

For we can represent *any* argument as a series of statements, followed by a conclusion, along these lines: "*A. B. C. D.* So, *E*" (where the letters stand for *statements*). It is easy to construct a counterexample similar to (13) above to prove that any such form is invalid.

A single argument can have both valid and invalid forms. But here is a key point to remember: *An argument is valid if any of its forms is valid.* For if an argument has a valid form, then it is impossible for its conclusion to be false if its premises are true. To illustrate, argument (12) above is valid because it has a valid form, namely, Form One.

We can now see why the counterexample method yields only provisional results. For suppose we have correctly identified one of an argument's forms, and shown *that* form to be invalid by means of a counterexample. It remains possible—at least in theory—that the argument has an additional form that is valid. And, as we have just seen, it is not the possession of an invalid form that makes an argument invalid; rather, it is the lack of a valid form that makes an argument invalid.

What good is it, then, to show that an argument has a form that is invalid? Generally speaking, if we identify the form of an argument *with due sensitivity to its key logical words and phrases,* and if the form thus identified is invalid, then the argument has no further valid form and so it is invalid. This is why the counterexample method is a powerful tool for evaluating arguments, even though it cannot rigorously prove that a given *argument* is invalid. In addition, bear in mind that the counterexample method *can* be used to prove rigorously that invalid forms are invalid, and it is of great value for this reason also.

SOME FORMS WITH NAMES

We have seen how the concept of an argument form can be used to establish that an argument is invalid. And we have seen that if an argument has a valid form, then it is valid. In this section we shall identify some basic valid forms that occur so often that they have been given names by logicians. We shall also identify the names of two invalid forms that occur frequently. Prior to identifying these forms, however, we need to understand conditional ("if-then") state-

ments, because some of the most important argument forms centrally involve conditional statements.

Understanding Conditional Statements

Each of the following are conditional statements—often called simply *conditionals* by logicians:

14. If it is snowing, then the mail will be late.
15. If Abraham Lincoln was born in 1709, then he was born before the American Civil War.
16. If Abraham Lincoln was born in 1809, then he was born after the American Civil War.

Several points about conditionals should be noted. First, take note of the components of conditionals. The if-clause of a conditional is called its **antecedent.** The then-clause is called the **consequent.** The antecedent does not include the word *if*. Hence, the antecedent of (14) is "It is snowing," not "If it is snowing." Similarly, the consequent is the statement following the word *then* but does not include it. So, the consequent of (14) is "The mail will be late," not "then the mail will be late."

Second, conditionals are hypothetical in nature. Thus, in asserting a conditional, one does not assert that its antecedent is true. Nor does one assert that its consequent is true. Rather, one asserts that *if* the antecedent is true, *then* the consequent is true. Thus, (15) is a true conditional, even though its antecedent is false. (Lincoln was born in 1809, not 1709). For if Lincoln was born in 1709, then of course his birth preceded the American Civil War, which began in 1860. And (16) is false, even though its antecedent is true. For if Lincoln was born in 1809, then he certainly was not born *after* the American Civil War.

Third, there are many ways to express a conditional in ordinary English. Consider the following conditional statement:

17. If it is raining, then the ground is wet.

Items (a) through (f) below are all stylistic variants of (17), that is, alternate ways of saying the same thing:

a. *Given that* it is raining, the ground is wet.
b. *Assuming that* it is raining, the ground is wet.
c. The ground is wet *if* it is raining.

   d. The ground is wet *given that* it is raining.

   e. The ground is wet *assuming that* it is raining.

   f. It is raining *only if* the ground is wet.

A knowledge of such stylistic variants is an aid to identifying argument forms so a close look at these variants is warranted. Consider (c): Note that "if" comes not at the beginning, but in the middle of (c). Yet, (c) has the same underlying logical meaning as (17). And the phrase "given that" in (d) plays a role exactly analogous to "if" in (c). We might generalize from these examples by saying that "if" and its stylistic variants (for example, "given that" and "assuming that") *introduce an antecedent.* But we must hasten to add that this generalization applies only when "if" or its stylistic variants appear by themselves. When combined with "only," as in (f), the situation alters dramatically. Variant (f) has the same logical force as (17), but the phrase "only if" is confusing to many people and bears close examination.

To get clear about the logical force of "only if," it is helpful to consider very simple conditionals, such as

   18. Rex is a dog *only if* Rex is an animal.

   19. Rex is an animal *only if* Rex is a dog.

Obviously, (18) and (19) say different things. Conditional (19) is false. Rex may well be an animal even if Rex isn't a dog. Thus, (19) says, in effect, that "If Rex is an animal, Rex is a dog." But (18) says something entirely different, something true—namely, that if Rex is a dog, then Rex is an animal. In general, statements of the form "*A* only if *B*" are logically equivalent to statements of the form "If *A*, then *B.*" They are *not* logically equivalent to statements of the form "If *B*, then *A.*" Another way to generalize the point is to say that "only if" (unlike "if") *introduces a consequent,* that is, a then-clause.

Basic Argument Forms

We are now ready to examine some basic argument forms. Let's begin with **modus ponens.** Consider the following argument:

   20. 1. If it is raining, then the ground is wet.
         2. It is raining.
         So, the ground is wet.

This argument is obviously valid: Its conclusion cannot be false while its premises are true. Using letters to stand for statements, the form of the argument is as follows:

> *Modus Ponens*
>   1. If *A,* then *B.*
>   2. *A.*
>   So, *B.*

A stands for "It is raining"; *B* stands for "The ground is wet." This form of argument is always valid. It is called *modus ponens* ("the mode of positing") because the second premise posits (sets down as fact) the antecedent of the conditional (first) premise.

Two points about *modus ponens* are worth noting. First, the order of the premises does not matter. For example, both of the following count as *modus ponens:*

   21. If Einstein was a physicist, then he was a scientist. Einstein was a physicist. So, Einstein was a scientist.

   22. Einstein was a physicist. If Einstein was a physicist, then he was a scientist. So, Einstein was a scientist.

In other words, arguments of the form, "*A;* if *A,* then *B;* so, *B*" count as examples of *modus ponens.*

Second, the conditionals involved in *modus ponens* can be rather long and complex. For example,

   23. If every right can be waived and each person has a right to life, then euthanasia is permitted in those cases in which the person to be "euthanized" waives his or her right to life. Moreover, every right can be waived and each person has a right to life. So, euthanasia is permitted in those cases in which the person to be "euthanized" waives his or her right to life.

The conditional premise in argument (23) is relatively long and complex, but the form is still *modus ponens.* ("Every right can be waived and each person has a right to life" replaces *A;* "Euthanasia is permitted in those cases in which the person euthanized waives his or her right to life" replaces *B.*)

A second basic argument form is called **modus tollens.** Like *modus ponens,* one of its key premises is a conditional:

24. 1. If it is raining, then the ground is wet.
    2. The ground is not wet.
    So, it is not raining.

Modus tollens means "the mode or way of removing." The argument form gets its name from the second premise, which denies (removes the truth of) the consequent of the first premise. The form is as follows:

Modus Tollens
    1. If *A*, then *B*.
    2. Not *B*.
    So, not *A*.

"Not *A*" and "not *B*" stand for negations. A **negation** of a statement is its denial. For example, in argument (24), "The ground is not wet" plays the role of "Not *B*." The negation of a statement can be formed in various ways. Take the statement, "The ground is wet." Each of the following are negations of it:

    a. *It is not the case that* the ground is wet.
    b. *It's false that* the ground is wet.
    c. *It is not true that* the ground is wet.
    d. The ground is *not wet.*

As with *modus ponens,* the order of the premises does not matter. In other words, arguments of the form "Not *B*; if *A*, then *B*; so, not *A*" count as *modus tollens.*

    Consider a more complicated example of *modus tollens.* According to some physicists who endorse the Big Bang theory, the universe cannot be infinitely old, for the second law of thermodynamics tells us that in a closed physical system entropy always tends to increase; that is, energy gets diffused over time. (For instance, the radiant energy of a star will gradually become spread out evenly into the space surrounding it.) According to these physicists, if the physical universe has existed for an infinite period, there are now no concentrations of energy, for example, no stars or planets. But obviously, there are stars and planets, so the physical universe has not existed for an infinite period. We can put this reasoning explicitly into the *modus tollens* form as follows:

25. 1. If the physical universe has existed for an infinite period, then all the energy in the universe is spread out evenly (as opposed to being concentrated in such bodies as planets and stars).
    2. It is not true that all the energy in the universe is spread out evenly (as opposed to being concentrated in such bodies as planets and stars).
    So, it is not true that the physical universe has existed for an infinite period.

Notice how putting the argument into explicit form helps to focus attention on the key issues. There is no debate whatsoever about the second premise of this argument. There are stars and planets, and hence energy is not in fact spread out evenly throughout the physical universe. Nor is there any debate about the validity of the argument. Every argument having the form *modus tollens* is valid. The focus of the debate must therefore be upon the first premise, and that is just where physicists have placed it. For example, some physicists think that the universe oscillates, that is, goes through a cycle of Big Bangs and Big Crunches. And if the universe can oscillate, then its diffuse energy can be reconcentrated into usable forms, in which case the first premise is doubtful.

    Having examined two valid forms of argument, let's now take note of two invalid forms with which they are often confused. These invalid forms are called *fallacies.* A fallacy is an error in reasoning. Let's begin with **the fallacy of denying the antecedent,** which is often confused with *modus tollens.* Consider:

26. 1. If it is raining, then the ground is wet.
    2. It is not raining.
    So, the ground is not wet.

The first premise here is a conditional, as in the case of *modus tollens.* However, whereas the second premise of *modus tollens* denies the consequent of the conditional, the second premise of this argument denies the antecedent. This difference in form makes all the difference in the world. For even if the premises of this argument were true, the conclusion could still be false. For example, let us suppose that the ground is soaking wet due to the sprinkler's being left on all night. Then, even if it is not raining, the ground is wet. And remember that the first premise, being hypothetical, does not assert or imply that it is raining. Denying the antecedent is an invalid form of argument. We can picture its form as follows:

Fallacy of Denying the Antecedent
1. If *A,* then *B.*
2. Not *A.*
So, not *B.*

The order of the premises does not matter; hence, arguments of the form "Not *A;* if *A,* then *B;* so, not *B*" count as examples of denying the antecedent. Here is a counterexample that shows that denying the antecedent is invalid:

27. 1. If lemons are red, then lemons have a color. (true)
    2. Lemons are not red. (true)
    So, lemons do not have a color. (false)

In thinking about this counterexample, it is important to recall that conditionals are hypothetical statements. Thus, premise (1) does not say that lemons *are* red; it merely says that *if* lemons are red, *then* they have a color.

A second fallacy, often confused with *modus ponens,* is **the fallacy of affirming the consequent.** Here is an example:

28. 1. If it is raining, then the ground is wet.
    2. The ground is wet.
    So, it is raining.

The form is as follows:

Fallacy of Affirming the Consequent
1. If *A,* then *B.*
2. *B.*
So, *A.*

The order of the premises does not matter; hence, arguments of the form "*B;* if *A,* then *B;* so, *A*" are examples of affirming the consequent. Again, the example of a sprinkler left on overnight reveals the invalidity of the argument. One cannot assume that rain is the only thing that will make the ground wet. The fallacy of affirming the consequent gets its name from its second premise, which affirms the consequent of the conditional premise. Here is a counterexample that shows that the form is invalid:

29. 1. If lemons are red, then lemons have a color. (true)
    2. Lemons have a color. (true)
    So, lemons are red. (false)

Again, in thinking about this counterexample, bear in mind that the conditional premise is hypothetical in nature.

Two issues should be considered here before going on. First, it is sometimes alleged that we can imagine circumstances in which *modus ponens* or *modus tollens* fail, that is, in which the premises are true and the conclusion is false. For example, let's go back to *modus ponens:* "If it's raining, then the ground is wet. It's raining. So, the ground is wet." What if the ground is covered? What if the whole Earth were enclosed in a plastic bag? Then, even if it's raining, the ground won't be wet. Wouldn't *modus ponens* fail in such (admittedly far-fetched) circumstances? No. These are not circumstances in which the premises are true and the conclusion is false. Rather, they are circumstances in which the conditional premise ("If it's raining, the ground is wet") is false. Remember that when we are testing for validity we must assume the premises are true and consider whether this assumption forces us to assume the conclusion is true also.

Second, while the invalidity of denying the antecedent and affirming the consequent is readily apparent in the examples used thus far, the error isn't always quite so obvious. Consider the following example of affirming the consequent:

30. If lying causes ill feeling, then it is wrong. And lying is wrong. So, it causes ill feeling.

Example (30) is invalid because it overlooks the possibility that an act might be wrong for some reason other than its causing ill feeling. For instance, some say lying is wrong simply because society disapproves of it or simply because the liar violates a moral rule. The following example of the fallacy of denying the antecedent involves a similar error:

31. If using placebos causes harm, then it is wrong. But using placebos does not cause harm. Hence, using placebos is not wrong.

Example (31) overlooks the possibility that an act might be wrong even if it doesn't harm anyone. For example, some say that acts are wrong simply because God disapproves of them and regardless of the effects the actions have on other people.

Let us now return to valid forms. Consider the following argument:

32.   1. If tuition continues to increase, then only the wealthy will be able to afford a college education.
2. If only the wealthy will be able to afford a college education, then class divisions will be strengthened.
So, if tuition continues to increase, then class divisions will be strengthened.

We can represent the form as follows; it is called **hypothetical syllogism:**

Hypothetical Syllogism
1. If *A,* then *B.*
2. If *B,* then *C.*
So, if *A,* then *C.*

The order of the premises does not matter; hence, arguments of the form "If *B,* then *C; if A,* then *B;* so, if *A,* then *C*" are examples of hypothetical syllogism. The argument is called hypothetical syllogism because it involves only hypothetical (conditional) statements. "Syllogism" comes from Greek roots meaning "to reason together," that is, to put statements together into a pattern of reasoning. Every argument that exemplifies the form hypothetical syllogism is valid. Here is another example of this form:

33. If I am morally responsible, then I can choose between good and evil. If I can choose between good and evil, then some of my actions are free. Therefore, if I am morally responsible, then some of my actions are free.

Note that the conclusion of a hypothetical syllogism is a conditional statement.

So far we have focused on argument forms that centrally involve conditional statements. Not all argument forms are like this. Some make central use of **disjunctions,** that is, statements of the form, "Either *A* or *B.*" For example,

34.   1. Either Michelangelo painted *Guernica* or Picasso painted it.

2. Michelangelo did not paint *Guernica.*
So, Picasso painted *Guernica.*

The argument has the following form, which is called **disjunctive syllogism,** because of its either-or premise:

Disjunctive Syllogism
1. Either *A* or *B.*
2. Not *A.*
So, *B.*

Arguments having this form are *always* valid. The order of the premises does not matter; hence, arguments of the form "Not *A;* either *A* or *B;* so, *B*" are examples of disjunctive syllogism.

Some brief remarks about disjunctions are in order here. First, some terminology: The statements comprising a disjunction are called its **disjuncts.** For instance, the disjuncts of premise (1) in argument (34) are "Michelangelo painted *Guernica*" and "Picasso painted *Guernica.*"

Second, we shall take "Either *A* or *B*" to mean "Either *A* or *B* (or both)." This is called the **inclusive** sense of "or." For instance, suppose a job announcement reads: "Applicants must have either work experience or a bachelor's degree in the field." Obviously, an applicant with both work experience and a bachelor's degree is not excluded from applying.

Third, some authors speak of an **exclusive** sense of "or," claiming that "Either *A* or *B*" sometimes means "Either *A* or *B* (but not both)." For example, in commenting on a presidential election, one might say, "Either Smith or Jones will win the election," the assumption being that both will not (indeed, cannot) win. However, it is a matter of controversy whether there are really two different meanings of "or" *as opposed to* there simply being cases in which the context indicates that *A* and *B* are not (or cannot) both be true. Instead of letting this controversy detain us, let's simply assume that the locution "Either *A* or *B*" means "Either *A* or *B* (or both)."

Having made this assumption, however, we must immediately add that arguers are free to use the locution "Either *A* or *B* (but not both)." This locution is equivalent to two statements: "Either *A* or *B.* Not both *A* and *B.*" Consider the following argument:

35. Either Millard Fillmore was the thirteenth president of the United States or Zachary Tay-

lor was the thirteenth president of the United States (but not both). Millard Fillmore was the thirteenth president. So, Zachary Taylor was not the thirteenth president.

We may represent the form of argument (35) as follows: "Either *A* or *B*. Not both *A* and *B*. *A*. So, not *B*." This form is valid, but notice that it differs from disjunctive syllogism.

Also note that disjunctive syllogism differs from the following form of argument:

36. Either Hitler was a Nazi or Himmler was a Nazi (or both were). Hitler was a Nazi. Therefore, it is not the case that Himmler was a Nazi.

The form of argument (36) can best be represented as "Either *A* or *B* (or both). *A*. Therefore, not *B*." As a matter of historical fact, the premises of (36) are true, but its conclusion is false, so this argument form is definitely invalid.

What is the form of the following argument?

37. Either Bloggs is guilty or Brennan is guilty. It is false that Bloggs is guilty. So, Brennan is guilty.

The form is disjunctive syllogism, and the argument is valid.

One last form and our initial list of basic argument forms is complete. This form is called the **constructive dilemma,** and it combines both conditional and disjunctive statements. Here is an example:

38. 1. Either Donna knew the information on her tax returns was inaccurate or she did not know it.
     2. If Donna knew the information was inaccurate, she was lying.
     3. If Donna did not know the information was inaccurate, then she was negligent.
     So, either Donna was lying or she was negligent.

The form of this argument is as follows:

Constructive Dilemma
     1. Either *A* or *B*.
     2. If *A*, then *C*.
     3. If *B*, then *D*.
     So, either *C* or *D*.

Arguments of this form are always valid. The order of the premises in a constructive dilemma does not matter. For example, sometimes the conditional premises are given first, followed by the disjunctive premise. The traditional problem of evil can be put in the form of a constructive dilemma:

39. If God cannot prevent suffering, then God is not omnipotent. If God does not want to prevent suffering, then God is not perfectly good. But either God cannot prevent suffering or God does not want to prevent suffering. So, either God is not omnipotent or God is not perfectly good.

This dilemma nicely illustrates how logic can be used to formulate a problem in a revealing way. Because argument (39) is valid, the conclusion must be true if the premises are true. And the first premise seems undeniable. Moreover, theists, against whom the argument is directed, can hardly deny the third (disjunctive) premise. (If God *can* prevent suffering, then God must not want to prevent it, for some reason.) Historically speaking, the second premise has been the focus of debate, with theologians suggesting that God does not want to eliminate all suffering because suffering is the necessary means to certain good ends, for example, the spiritual maturity of free creatures.

Part 3: Identifying Arguments

The arguments we examined in the previous sections were short and simple. Moreover, it was quite obvious which statements were premises and which conclusions. But, as you probably already realize, authors do not commonly put their arguments in such a simple textbook form. The conclusion may be given first or sandwiched in between various premises. And a long argument may actually be a chain of shorter arguments—in which case it becomes vital to distinguish between the final (or overall) conclusion of the argument and various subconclusions that lead up to it.

This section tells you how to identify arguments as they appear in ordinary language, how to distinguish extraneous verbiage from premises and conclusions, and how to identify the structure of the argument (that is, which statements support which).

ARGUMENTS AND NONARGUMENTS

We must first learn to distinguish arguments from nonarguments. Recall that an argument is a set of statements, one of which, called the *conclusion*, is affirmed on the basis of the others, which are called *premises*. Obviously, one can do many things with language besides argue: extend greetings, tell a story, make a request, express feelings, provide information, tell a joke, pray, and so on. In this section we shall take note of some nonargumentative uses of statements that are sometimes confused with arguments.

In general, it is important to distinguish between **unsupported assertions** and arguments. For example,

1. From 1964 to 1972, the wealthiest and most powerful nation in the history of the world made a maximum military effort, with everything short of atomic bombs, to defeat a nationalist revolutionary movement in a tiny, peasant country (Vietnam)—and failed.

As it stands, this passage is not an argument but simply a statement about the war in Vietnam. No supporting statements (that is, premises) are provided here, and no inferences are drawn. Of course, supporting statements could be supplied, but because they do not appear in the quoted passage, it is not an argument taken as it stands.

Unsupported assertions come in a variety of types, and some of these may be confused with arguments. For example, a **report** is a set of statements intended to provide information about a situation, topic, or event. A report may contain many informational statements without containing any arguments. For instance,

2. Total global advertising expenditures multiplied nearly sevenfold from 1950 to 1990. They grew one-third faster than the world economy and three times faster than world population. In real terms, spending rose from $39 billion in 1950 to $256 billion in 1990—more than the gross national product of India or than all Third World governments spent on health and education.

Again, these statements could be backed up with further statements, but the passage, as it stands, is a report and not an argument. No inferences are drawn; the passage merely contains a series of informational statements.

An **illustration** is a statement together with an explanatory or clarifying example:

3. Mammals are vertebrate animals that nourish their young with milk. For example, cats, horses, goats, monkeys, and humans are mammals.

Because the word *thus* is often used to indicate the conclusion of an argument, illustrations are easily confused with arguments when the word *thus* is used to introduce the examples:

4. Whole numbers can be represented as fractions. Thus, 2 can be represented as 8/4, and 5 can be represented as 15/3.

In (4) the examples seem merely illustrative. But sometimes examples are given not merely to explain or clarify but to support (provide evidence for) a thesis, in which case the passage in question is an argument rather than an illustration:

5. You just said that no mammal can fly, but that is inaccurate. At least one mammal has wings and can fly. For example, bats are mammals.

And sometimes a passage can be reasonably interpreted either as an illustration or as an argument. It all depends on this question: Do the examples merely clarify (or explain) a statement, or are they used to *provide evidence* for it? If the examples are used to provide evidence, then the passage is an argument.

Sometimes statements are used not to provide evidence for another statement, but to provide reasons or explanations for the occurrence of some phenomenon. For example,

6. Judy got sick because she ate too much.
7. The dinosaurs are extinct because a "large comet or asteroid struck the earth some 65 million years ago, lofting a cloud of dust into the sky and blocking sunlight, thereby suppressing photosynthesis and . . . drastically lowering world temperatures . . ."

Such passages are easily confused with arguments because the word *because* is often used to indicate a premise. (We will discuss this further in the next section.) But consider each case carefully. Is (6) best construed as an argument for the conclusion that Judy got sick? More likely it is already accepted that Judy got sick, and the question is, Why did she get sick? or What caused her sickness? So, (6) appears to be simply an assertion about what caused Judy's sickness and not an argument. Similarly, (7) doesn't seem to be an argument for the conclusion that dinosaurs are extinct. That is a widely accepted fact. The question is, What explains it? And (7) states one possible explanation.

A complication should be mentioned at this point. Some arguments are arguments to the effect that a certain statement or hypothesis is the *best explanation* of some phenomenon (or that some statement is probably true *because* it is the best explanation of some phenomenon). These are arguments rather than mere assertions because premises are provided. For instance,

8. Three explanations have been offered for the extinction of the dinosaurs. First, that a global rise in temperature caused the testes of male dinosaurs to stop functioning. Second, that certain flowering plants (namely, angiosperms) evolved *after* the dinosaurs evolved. These plants were toxic for the dinosaurs, the dinosaurs ate the plants and died. Third, that a large comet struck the Earth, causing a cloud of dust that blocked out the sunlight, which in turn created a frigid climate for which the dinosaurs were ill suited. Now, there is no way to get any evidence either for or against the first hypothesis. And the second hypothesis is unlikely because it is probable that angiosperms were in existence 10 million years before the dinosaurs became extinct. There is, however, some evidence in favor of the third hypothesis. If the Earth was struck by a large comet at the time the dinosaurs became extinct (some 65 million years ago), then there should be unusually large amounts of iridium (a rare metal) in the sediments of that period, for most of the iridium on Earth comes from comets and other objects from outer space. And as a matter of fact unusually large amounts of iridium have been found in the sediments of that period. So, the third explanation seems best.

Passage (8) is an argument because evidence is given to support the claim that one of the three explanations is best.

Conditional statements, taken by themselves, are typically not arguments. For instance,

9. If Lucy works hard, then she will get a promotion.

There is some temptation to think that the antecedent (if-clause) of a conditional is a premise, and the consequent (then-clause) is a conclusion. But this is typically not the case. Remember that a conditional statement is hypothetical in nature. Thus, (9) merely asserts that if Lucy works hard, then she will get a promotion. Statement (9) does not assert that Lucy works hard. Nor does it assert that she will get a promotion. By contrast, consider the following argument:

10. Lucy works hard. Therefore, Lucy will get a promotion.

Here we clearly have a premise-conclusion structure. And the conclusion is asserted on the basis of the premise, which is also asserted.

Although conditionals, taken by themselves, are not arguments, in context they may serve to express an argument. For example, during a tournament a tennis coach might give the following advice to one of the players: "If you want to win, you should hit to your opponent's backhand." In this context, "you want to win" need not be explicitly stated; it can be assumed. So, in context, by expressing a conditional the coach may in effect offer a *modus ponens*-type argument: "If you want to win, then you should hit to your opponent's backhand. You want to win. So, you should hit to your opponent's backhand." However, adding unstated premises (and conclusions) to arguments is a bit tricky, and we shall return to it in a later section. The main point here is that outside of special contexts, conditionals by themselves are not arguments.

PUTTING AN ARGUMENT INTO TEXTBOOK FORM

Putting an argument into **textbook form** involves identifying an argument's premises and conclusion, eliminating inessential verbiage, and putting the steps of the argument (that is, the premises and conclusion) in proper order. This section describes and illustrates the basic principles involved in putting arguments into textbook form. Being able to put arguments into textbook form is a powerful tool for evaluating arguments.

Principle 1. Identify the Premises and the Conclusion.

The **premises** of an argument are the statements on the basis of which the conclusion is affirmed. Recall that **statements** are sentences that are either true or false. Each step of an argument, whether premise or conclusion, must be a statement. Consider the following simple example:

> 11. We should abolish the death penalty because it does not deter crime.

Example (11) is an argument. The word *because* often indicates a premise, and it does so in this case. Thus, we can be put (11) into textbook form as follows:

> 12. 1. The death penalty does not deter crime.
> So, 2. We should abolish the death penalty.

Whenever we put arguments into textbook form, let's adopt the convention of making the conclusion of the argument the last step. We shall also write "So" to mark a conclusion, as I have done here. Further, let's adopt the convention of placing a number before each step of the argument (whether premise or conclusion). A step of an argument without the word *So* in front of it will be understood to be a premise. In this case (1) is the only premise. We can drop the word *because* as our convention tells us that (1) is a premise.

Short as it is, argument (11) illustrates at least two noteworthy things. First, the conclusion of an argument often comes first in English prose. For example, the thesis sentence in a paragraph is often a conclusion that is supported by the statements appearing later in the paragraph. Thus, one cannot assume that an author will state his or her premises first and then draw a conclusion later on. In ordinary prose, the order is often reversed.

Second, argument (11) illustrates a typical use of premise indicators—in this case, the word *be-*

cause. **Premise indicators** are frequently followed by a premise, that is, a supporting reason. Common premise indicator words or phrases include:

because	after all
since	the reason is that
for	in light of the fact that
as	based on the fact that

We cannot assume that these words and phrases indicate premises on every occasion of their use. As we have already seen, the word *because* is often used in explanations. But the point here is that these words are frequently used as premise indicators, and knowing this is a great aid when putting arguments into textbook form.

Just as premise indicators typically signal premises, **conclusion indicators** typically signal conclusions. Common conclusion indicators include:

so	thus
therefore	accordingly
hence	consequently
implies that	we may infer that
it follows that	which proves that

Consider the following argument:

> 13. I was bitten by several dogs when I was a child. Therefore, dogs are dangerous.

In textbook form, argument (13) looks like this:

> 14. 1. I was bitten by several dogs when I was a child.
> So, 2. Dogs are dangerous.

Of course, this argument is weak, but a weak argument is still an argument.

At this point you know what premise and conclusion indicators are. The good news is that authors frequently use such words and phrases to clarify their intentions. The bad news is that authors often rely on more subtle methods (for instance, context, order, emphasis) to identify the structure of their reasoning. There is no substitute in such cases for logical and linguistic insight. *A good rule of thumb is to identify the conclusion first.* Once you figure out what the author is trying to prove, the rest of the argument often falls into place.

Let's now consider a slightly more complicated argument:

15. Since the average American consumes thirty times the amount of the Earth's resources as does the average Asian, Americans (taken as a group) are selfish. After all, excessive consumption is a form of greed. And greed is selfish desire.

What is the conclusion of the argument? That Americans (taken as a group) are selfish. "Since" is a premise indicator, and so is "after all." Thus, in textbook form, the argument looks like this:

16. 1. The average American consumes thirty times the amount of the Earth's resources as does the average Asian.
    2. Excessive consumption is a form of greed.
    3. Greed is selfish desire.
    So, 4. Americans (taken as a group) are selfish.

You may be wondering whether the order of the premises matters. From the standpoint of logic, the order makes no difference, so we simply list the premises in the order in which they appear in the original. Note, however, that the premises must precede the conclusion in the textbook form of an argument, for our conventions tell us that the last statement in the textbook form is the conclusion of the argument.

As we saw in Part 2, conditional statements have a number of stylistic variants. When putting an argument into textbook form, you should put any conditional premises or conclusions into **standard form,** that is, "If A, then B." This is for two reasons: First, most people find it easier to grasp the logical meaning of conditionals when they are in standard form; second, putting conditionals into standard form facilitates the recognition of argument forms. Consider the following example:

17. It is not permissible to eat cows and pigs. For it is permissible to eat cows and pigs only if it is permissible to eat dogs and cats. But it is not permissible to eat dogs and cats.

The textbook form is as follows:

18. 1. If it is permissible to eat cows and pigs, then it is permissible to eat dogs and cats.
    2. It is not permissible to eat dogs and cats.
    So, 3. It is not permissible to eat cows and pigs.

The argument form is *modus tollens*. Recall that common stylistic variants of "If A, then B" include these: "B if A," "B assuming that A," "B given that A," "A only if B," "Given that A, B," and "Assuming that A, B."

Before leaving the topic of identifying premises and conclusions, we need to take note of two slight complications involving rhetorical questions and commands. As we noted in Part 1, not all sentences are statements. For example, questions are sentences but questions are not statements. There is, however, one kind of question that serves as a disguised statement, namely, the so-called rhetorical question. A rhetorical question is used to emphasize a point. No answer is expected because the answer is considered apparent in the context. For example,

19. The common assumption that welfare recipients like being on welfare is false. Does anyone like to be poor and unemployed? Does anyone like to be regarded as a parasite?

In context it is clear that the arguer expects a no answer to both questions. So, these questions are in effect statements. In putting the argument into textbook form, we change them into statements, like this:

20. 1. No one likes to be poor and unemployed.
    2. No one likes to be regarded as a parasite.
    So, 3. The common assumption that welfare recipients like being on welfare is false.

Commands (or imperatives) are also sentences but not statements. If someone issues the command, "Shut the door!" it makes no sense to reply "That's true" (or "That's false"). No truth-claim has been made. However, imperatives sometimes turn up as premises or conclusions in arguments. Such imperatives are disguised "ought" statements. For example, consider the following argument:

21. Be a doctor! You've got the talent. You would enjoy the work. You could help many people. And you could make a lot of money!

In this type of case, the imperative "Be a doctor!" is naturally interpreted as "You ought to be a doctor," and this latter sentence expresses something either true or false. When an imperative is a disguised ought statement, you should make this explicit when putting the argument into textbook form:

22. 1. You've got the talent.
    2. You would enjoy the work.

3. You could help many people.

4. You could make a lot of money.

So, 5. You ought to be a doctor.

It would be equally correct to write the conclusion this way: "You should be a doctor."

Principle 2. Eliminate Excess Verbiage.

Four types of excess verbiage are extremely common in arguments. The first is **discount,** which is an acknowledgment of a fact or possibility that might be thought to render the argument invalid, weak, or otherwise unsound. For example, consider:

23. Although certain events in the subatomic realm occur at random, I still say that the universe as a whole displays a marvelous order. Perhaps the best evidence for this is the fact that scientists continue to discover regularities that can be formulated as laws.

The conclusion of this argument is "The universe as a whole displays a marvelous order." The premise is "Scientists continue to discover regularities that can be formulated as laws." But what are we to do with "Although certain events in the subatomic realm occur at random"? It does not seem to be a premise, for events that occur at random are not evidence of order. In fact, the statement "Certain events in the subatomic realm occur at random" seems to be evidence *against* the conclusion of the argument. And that is why it is best regarded, not as a premise, but as a discount.

Discounts are very important rhetorically. Roughly speaking, **rhetorical elements** in an argument are ones that increase its psychological persuasiveness without affecting its validity, strength, or soundness. And discounts often increase the psychological persuasiveness of an argument by anticipating potential objections. An audience is often disarmed to some degree by the realization that the arguer has already considered a potential objection and rejected it. But discounts aren't premises, because they don't support the conclusion. Therefore, we shall omit them from our textbook forms. To illustrate, the textbook form of argument (23) is as follows:

24.   1. Scientists continue to discover regularities that can be formulated as laws.

So, 2. The universe as a whole displays a marvelous order.

Words or phrases often used as **discount indicators** include:

although	while it may be true that
even though	while I admit that
in spite of the fact that	I realize that . . . , but
despite the fact that	I know that . . . , but

A second type of excess verbiage is **repetition.** Authors and speakers may repeat a premise or conclusion, perhaps altering the wording slightly. When this occurs, select the formulation that seems to put the argument in its best light and drop the others. Here's an example:

25. The study of logic will increase both your attention span and your patience with difficult concepts. In other words, if you apply yourself to the subject of logic, you'll find yourself able to concentrate for longer periods of time. You will also find yourself increasingly able to approach complex material without feeling frustrated or anxious. Therefore, a course in logic is well worth the effort.

A textbook version of argument (25) might look like this:

26.   1. The study of logic will increase both your attention span and your patience with difficult concepts.

So, 2. A course in logic is well worth the effort.

You may feel that something is lost in dropping the repetition in a case like this, and indeed something of rhetorical importance *is* lost. Repetition itself aids the memory. And a slight alteration of terminology can correct possible misunderstandings and make an idea more vivid. But our streamlined textbook version has advantages of its own; in particular, it enables us to focus on the argument's essential logical features.

A third type of excess verbiage is the assurance. An **assurance** is a statement, word, or phrase that indicates that the author is confident of a premise or inference. For example,

27. Ben will do well in the marathon for he is obviously in excellent condition.

Here is the textbook form:

28.   1. Ben is in excellent condition.
   So, 2. Ben will do well in the marathon.

The word *obviously* indicates the author's confidence in the premise, but it does not contribute to the validity, strength, or soundness of the argument. Typical assurances include:

obviously	everyone knows that
no doubt	it is well known that
certainly	no one will deny that
plainly	this is undeniable
clearly	this is a fact

Assurances are rhetorically important, because confidence often helps to win over an audience. But they seldom affect the validity, strength, or soundness of an argument, so we are usually free to omit them from our textbook forms.

A fourth type of excess verbiage is the hedge, which is just the opposite of an assurance. A **hedge** is a statement, word, or phrase that indicates that the arguer is tentative about a premise or inference. For instance,

29. In my opinion, we have lost the war on drugs. Accordingly, drugs should be legalized.

"In my opinion" is a hedge, so the textbook form would be:

30.   1. We have lost the war on drugs.
   So, 2. Drugs should be legalized.

Typical hedges include:

I think that	I believe that
it seems that	I guess that
perhaps	it is reasonable to suppose that
maybe	this seems reasonable
in my opinion	this is plausible

Hedges are rhetorically important, because without them one sounds dogmatic and close-minded. But hedges usually do not contribute to the validity, strength, or soundness of an argument, so we normally omit them from our textbook forms.

While assurances and hedges can usually be dropped when putting an argument into textbook form, they cannot always be dropped, for sometimes they contribute to the validity, strength, or soundness of the argument. To illustrate:

31. I am in pain if it seems to me that I am in pain. And it seems to me that I am in pain. Therefore, I am in pain.

The textbook form is as follows:

32.   1. If it seems to me that I am in pain, then I am in pain.
   2. It seems to me that I am in pain.
   So, 3. I am in pain.

The main point of this argument is that, in the case of pain, there is a special connection between what *seems* to be so and what *is* so. Hence, while we can usually drop "it seems to me that" as a hedge, in this case we cannot. This example underscores the fact that there is no substitute for vigilance when putting arguments into textbook form. The role of a word or phrase must be carefully evaluated in context.

Principle 3. Employ Uniform Language.

Compare the following two arguments:

33. If God is omniscient, then God knows whether or not you will steal a car tomorrow. And in fact God is all-knowing. So, God is cognizant of whether or not you will commit car theft tomorrow.

34. If God is omniscient, then God knows whether you will steal a car tomorrow. And in fact God is omniscient. So, God knows whether you will steal a car tomorrow.

The logical links between premises and conclusions in these arguments depend crucially on the terms involved: "omniscient," "steal," "all-knowing," and so forth. Argument (33) appears to have been written by someone using a thesaurus, substituting "omniscient" for "all-knowing," and "commit car theft," for "steal a car," "is cognizant of" for "knows." In short, the language in argument (33) is not uniform, but varied. The result is that the linkage between premises and conclusion is obscured in (33). By way of contrast, the premise-conclusion link is crystal clear in (34). And yet the underlying form of ument is the same in both cases, namely, *modus ponens*.

One good textbook version of (33) would be:

35. 1. If God is all-knowing, then God knows
        whether you will steal a car tomorrow.
     2. God is all-knowing.
  So, 3. God knows whether you will steal a car
        tomorrow.

Of course, you might just as well have used the term "omniscient" in place of "all-knowing." The important thing is to stick with one term throughout the argument, so as to highlight the logical form or pattern of reasoning.

Before leaving the topic of uniform language, let's consider one further example:

36. If you study other cultures, then you realize
    what a variety of human customs there is. If
    you understand the diversity of social practices,
    then you question your own customs. If you
    acquire doubts about the way you do things,
    then you become more tolerant. Therefore, if
    you expand your knowledge of anthropology,
    then you become more likely to accept other
    people and practices without criticism.

Once again, the lack of uniform language makes it very difficult to see whether (and how) the premises logically connect with the conclusion. A good textbook version of the argument would be:

37. 1. If you study other cultures, then you realize
        what a variety of human customs there is.
     2. If you realize what a variety of human customs there is, then you question your own
        customs.
     3. If you question your own customs, then
        you become more tolerant.
  So, 4. If you study other cultures, then you become more tolerant.

Now it is apparent that the argument is a tightly linked chain of reasoning. For the purpose of exhibiting the logical structure of an argument, the use of uniform language is enormously beneficial. By clarifying the linkages between premises and conclusions, uniform language helps us to avoid fuzzy thinking, which frequently stems from a careless use of words with *similar but slightly different* meanings.

Principle 4. Be Fair and Charitable in Interpreting an Argument.

Fairness involves being loyal to the original, not distorting the clear meaning. Charity is needed when the original is not clear in some respect but is ambiguous. And charity involves selecting an interpretation that puts the argument in its best possible light. Both of these concepts need to be explained in some detail.

With regard to fairness, many people tend to read more into an argument than they should. Instead of letting the author speak for herself, the argument is re-created in the reader's image. Key statements may be loosely reworded or couched in emotionally loaded terms. Important premises may be omitted. New premises, not provided in the original, may be added. And so on. There is indeed a place for identifying assumed but unstated premises in evaluating an argument. But before one can usefully identify unstated assumptions, one must first accurately represent the stated or explicit version of the argument, without distorting the meaning.

Fairness demands that we not let our biases interfere with providing a textbook form that is true to the author's original intent. For example, if someone argues in favor of euthanasia for permanently comatose patients, it almost certainly distorts the author's intent to describe him as in favor of "playing God." Similarly, a person who argues against promiscuity does not necessarily believe that all sex is evil and should not be so represented in the absence of solid evidence. Or again, one who advocates affirmative action isn't necessarily advocating the use of strict quotas to achieve greater equality. It is unfair to interpret such a person as advocating strict quotas unless he or she has clearly stated or implied this.

On the other hand, one must not conceive of fairness in too wooden a fashion. To interpret well, we must take into account various rhetorical devices, such as irony and deliberate exaggeration. Suppose an American newspaper reporter argues as follows:

38. Oh, yes, we are all deeply appreciative of the
    full and accurate information we received
    from our government during the Vietnam
    War. So, how can anyone doubt that we received full and accurate information during
    the war in the Persian Gulf?

Because it is well known that Americans were sometimes not told the truth by their own government during the Vietnam War, the reporter's real meaning is probably the exact opposite of the surface meaning of her words. A good textbook version of the argument would therefore have to make some changes, perhaps along the following lines:

> 39. 1. Americans did not receive full and accurate information from their government during the Vietnam War.
> So, 2. Americans possibly (or probably) did not receive full and accurate information from their government during the war in the Persian Gulf.

Incidentally, notice that in the textbook version the rhetorical question appears as a statement.

Charity enters the picture when an argument has been presented unclearly. Perhaps a premise can be understood in either of two ways. Or perhaps the structure of the argument is unclear: Which statement is supposed to support which? Where such ambiguities occur, charity demands that we put the argument in its best possible light. In other words, when we are confronted with an interpretive choice, we should try to select an interpretation that makes the argument valid, strong, or sound (as the case may be), rather than invalid, weak, or unsound. For instance,

> 40. Flag burning should be outlawed. I realize that there are worse things than flag burning, such as murder or kidnapping, but it ought to be illegal. Many people are disturbed by it. And it is unpatriotic. How important is freedom of expression, anyway?

Consider the following attempt to put the argument into textbook form:

> 41. 1. Many people are disturbed by flag burning.
>   2. Flag burning is unpatriotic.
>   3. Freedom of expression is not important.
> So, 4. Flag burning should be outlawed.

Premise (3) is stated in an uncharitable fashion. Admittedly, the meaning of the question, "How important is freedom of expression, anyway?" is unclear. But as stated, premise (3) is an easy target. Charity demands that we rephrase premise (3), per-

haps along the following lines: "Freedom of expression is not the most important thing" or "Freedom of expression is not the highest value."

Principle 5. Don't Confuse Subconclusions with Final Conclusions.

Some arguments proceed by establishing subconclusions, which in turn become premises supporting the final conclusion of the argument. A **subconclusion,** then, has a dual role: It is supported by a premise (or premises), but it also supports at least one further statement, which may be either the conclusion or another subconclusion. Consider an example:

> 42. It is not always moral to save five lives at the cost of one life. For if it is always moral to save five lives at the cost of one life, then it is moral to remove the organs of a healthy person against his wishes and transplant them in five people who need organ transplants. But it is not moral to perform such transplants because doing so violates the rights of the healthy person. Therefore, it is not always morally right to save five lives at the cost of one life.

The textbook form runs as follows:

> 43. 1. If it is always moral to save five lives at the cost of one life, then it is moral to remove the organs of a healthy person against his wishes and transplant them in five people who need organ transplants.
>   2. Removing the organs of a healthy person against his wishes and transplanting them in five people who need organ transplants violates the rights of the healthy person.
> So, 3. It is not moral to remove the organs of a healthy person against his wishes and transplant them in five people who need organ transplants.
> So, 4. It is not always moral to save five lives at the cost of one life.

Note that premise (2) supports subconclusion (3). This structure is required by the premise indicator "because" in argument (42). And the final conclusion (4) follows form (3) and (1), which work together as a logical unit (the form is *modus tollens*). To make the structure of the argument clear, shorthand expressions in the original such as "doing so" are here expanded and made explicit. (The extent to which this is helpful in a given case is a matter of judgment.)

Let's adopt the convention of always listing the final conclusion of the argument as the last step in the textbook form, marked by the word *So*. Subconclusions are also marked by the word *So* and are distinguished from final conclusions because they have a dual role, that is, they are supposed to follow from earlier steps in the argument and are supposed to support later steps. Of course, a subconclusion may in fact not be adequately supported by earlier steps, and it may not adequately support any later steps. But the textbook version is supposed to represent the arguer's intentions, even if those intentions are logically flawed.

Let's consider another argument that contains subconclusions:

44. Murder victims X, Y, and Z were apparently killed by the same person, whom police call "the Golden Gunner," for victims X, Y, and Z were all shot with a gold-plated bullet from the same .38 caliber pistol. Now, we know that most serial killers selected members of their own ethnic group as victims. And X, Y, and Z are White. Finally, nearly all serial killers are men. We may infer that the Golden Gunner is a White male.

The textbook form is as follows:

45.   1. Murder victims X, Y, and Z were all shot with a gold-plated bullet from the same .38 caliber pistol.
So, 2. Victims X, Y, and Z were killed by the same person, whom police call "the Golden Gunner."
   3. Most serial killers select members of their own ethnic group as victims.
   4. Victims X, Y, and Z are White.
   5. Nearly all serial killers are men.
So, 6. The Golden Gunner is a White male.

Here (2) is supported by (1). And steps (2), (3), (4), and (5) combine to support the final conclusion (6).

When evaluating an argument with subconclusions, we must evaluate the support for each subconclusion as well as the support for the final conclu-

sion of the argument. For example, if the argument for a given subconclusion fails by being weak or invalid, the overall argument is logically flawed. However, even if a given subconclusion is poorly supported by a premise that is supposed to support it, the overall argument may still retain merit under two conditions: (a) The subconclusion may be adequately supported by other premises in the argument, and/or (b) the subconclusion may be plausible taken all by itself.

You now have five principles in hand for identifying arguments and putting them into textbook form.

ENTHYMEMES

An **enthymeme** is an argument with an unstated premise, an unstated subconclusion, and/or an unstated conclusion. If we use the more general term "step" to refer to premises, subconclusions, and/or conclusions, we can say that an enthymeme is an argument with one or more unstated steps. Unstated steps are also referred to as *missing* or *implicit* steps. Enthymemes complicate the attempt to identify arguments, because the missing steps must be supplied. This section explains how to supply the unstated steps in enthymemes.

It is common for arguers to provide the premises of an argument and leave it up to their audience to draw the obvious conclusion or subconclusions. For instance,

46. If you want to win this election, you should respond to your critics. And I know you want to win this election.

Here the unstated conclusion is "You should respond publicly to your critics." Note that, if we add this step to the original, the form of the argument is *modus ponens*.

It is also common for arguers to leave a premise unstated. For instance,

47. The rich will get richer if the Republicans win. And taxes will increase if the Democrats win. Hence, either the rich will get richer or taxes will increase.

The unstated premise here is "Either the Republicans win or the Democrats win." Note that if this premise is added to the original, the argument has the form of a constructive dilemma.

In dealing with enthymemes, it will be helpful to keep in mind a distinction between the textbook form, which does not fill in the missing steps, and an **elaborated textbook form,** which does fill in the missing steps. In evaluating an enthymeme, we begin by constructing the textbook form—listing just those premises, subconclusions, and conclusions that are actually stated. Then, to arrive at the *elaborated* textbook form, we add such steps as are needed to render the argument valid (or strong). To illustrate, the textbook form for argument (47) is as follows:

48. 1. If the Republicans win, then the rich will get richer.
     2. If the Democrats win, then taxes will increase.
  So, 3. Either the rich will get richer or taxes will increase.

By contrast, the *elaborated textbook form* for argument (47) looks like this:

49. [1. Either the Republicans win or the Democrats win.]
     2. If the Republicans win, then the rich will get richer.
     3. If the Democrats win, then taxes will increase.
  So, 4. Either the rich will get richer or taxes will increase.

Note the use of brackets to indicate the unstated (or implicit) step that has been added.

When constructing an elaborated textbook form for an enthymeme, it is easy to get carried away by listing possible background assumptions the original author may have been making. However, it is important to avoid getting carried away, because there is a great risk of misrepresenting an author when we attempt to fill in unstated steps in an argument. Here are some principles of charity to bear in mind when constructing elaborated textbook forms:

Principle A An elaborated textbook form should be a *valid* argument unless one of the following conditions holds: (i) The argument is clearly presented as invalid or strong, or (ii) one cannot make the original argument valid without adding a false (or doubtful) premise, but one *can* make the original argument strong without adding a false (or doubtful) premise.

Principle B If you intend for an elaborated textbook form to be valid, add only those steps to the original argument that are needed to give it a form known to be valid, such as *modus ponens*. (Note: A good working knowledge of argument forms is indispensable for the construction of elaborated textbook forms.)

Principle C If you intend for the elaborated textbook form to be strong, add only those steps needed to make the original argument strong.

Now, let's apply these principles to some examples. Consider:

50. One often hears left-leaning critics say that the United States pursued a genocidal policy during the Vietnam War. But if the United States pursued a genocidal policy in Vietnam, the major cities of North Vietnam were utterly annihilated by bombing. Thus, the only reasonable conclusion is that the United States did not aim at genocide in Vietnam.

The elaborated textbook form of (50) is as follows:

51. 1. If the United States pursued a genocidal policy in Vietnam, then the major cities in North Vietnam were utterly annihilated by bombing.
     [2. It is not true that the major cities in North Vietnam were utterly annihilated by bombing.]
  So, 3. The United States did not pursue a genocidal policy in Vietnam.

Following Principle A, we have constructed a valid argument. Following Principle B, we have added just one step that is needed to give the argument a form known to be valid, namely, *modus tollens*. Again, observe that brackets are used to indicate the missing step.

Here it should be noted that it is quite common for the conditional premise of the *modus ponens* or *modus tollens* forms to be left unstated. Consider the following examples:

52. Since Henry can run a mile in under five minutes, he is in excellent physical condition.

53. Since this stone will not scratch glass, this stone is not a diamond.

The elaborated textbook form for argument (52) is:

54. [1. If Henry can run a mile in under five minutes, then he is in excellent physical condition.]
  2. Henry can run a mile in under five minutes.
  So, 3. Henry is in excellent physical condition.

Here the form is *modus ponens*. Note the brackets around the conditional premise to indicate that it is not explicit in the original. The elaborated textbook form for argument (53) is:

55. [1. If this stone is a diamond, this stone will scratch glass.]
  2. This stone will not scratch glass.
  So, 3. This stone is not a diamond.

Here the form is *modus tollens*.

Occasionally an enthymeme is clearly presented as invalid. For instance,

56. If people respect the boss, then the boss is talented. My fellow employees, we are forced to conclude that the boss is not talented.

Plainly, the unstated premise is "People do not respect the boss." So, Principle A tells us that the elaborated textbook form will exemplify the fallacy of denying the antecedent:

57. 1. If people respect the boss, then the boss is talented.
  [2. People do not respect the boss.]
  So, 3. The boss is not talented.

It is rather rare, however, for an enthymeme to be clearly presented as a fallacy. An elaborated textbook form should not contain fallacies unless the original argument is clearly presented as such.

Arguments may be presented as strong rather than valid. For example:

58. Judy Smith is an American. So, it is likely that Judy disapproves of communism.

The important phrase "it is likely that" indicates that the argument is claimed to be strong. So, the elaborated textbook form looks like this:

59. [1. Most Americans disapprove of communism.]
  2. Judy Smith is an American.
  So, 3. Judy Smith disapproves of communism.

Notice that if we try to turn (58) into a *valid* argument, we run into certain difficulties. Consider the following two attempts:

60. [1. All Americans disapprove of communism.]
  2. Judy Smith is an American.
  So, 3. Judy Smith disapproves of communism.

61. [1. If Judy Smith is an American, then she disapproves of communism.]
  2. Judy Smith is an American.
  So, 3. Judy disapproves of communism.

Although (60) and (61) are both valid, in each case the first premise is false or doubtful. These examples are included here simply to illustrate clause ii of Principle A.

Subconclusions are also frequently left unstated. For example, consider the following argument:

62. Pollution will increase dramatically if the population continues to grow at the current rate. And the environment will be destroyed if pollution increases dramatically. Unfortunately, the population will continue to grow at the current rate. Accordingly, the environment will be destroyed.

To cut down on writing, let's use capital letters to stand for the statements in (62) as follows: *P* is pollution will increase dramatically. *G* is the population continues to grow at the current rate. *E* is the environment will be destroyed. Using this abbreviation scheme, the textbook form runs as follows:

63. 1. If *G*, then *P*.
  2. If *P*, then *E*.
  3. *G*.
  So, 4. *E*.

A subconclusion has been left unstated, but we make it explicit when constructing an *elaborated* textbook form:

64.   1. If *G*, then *P*.
      2. If *P*, then *E*.
      [So, 3. If *G*, then *E*.]   1, 2, hypothetical syllogism
      4. *G*.
      So, 5. *E*.   3, 4, *modus ponens*

Now the argument is a tightly linked chain exemplifying two valid argument forms. In the case of arguments with subconclusions, it is helpful to indicate which steps support which, and to indicate which argument forms are exemplified, as above. For example, "1, 2, hypothetical syllogism" written to the right of the third step means that subconclusion (3) is supported by premises (1) and (2), and the argument form involved is hypothetical syllogism.

A brief word about the background assumptions of an argument may be helpful at this point. The background assumptions of an argument are often called its presuppositions. A **presupposition** of an argument is a statement which is *implied* by one or more premises of the argument but that is not itself a step in the argument (that is, not a premise, not a subconclusion, and not the conclusion). In identifying arguments, it is important not to confuse premises and presuppositions. For instance, consider the following argument:

65. Pruning trees is wrong because it involves torturing trees.

Here is a correct, elaborated textbook form of (65):

66.   1. Pruning trees involves torturing them.
      [2. If pruning trees involves torturing them, then it is wrong.]
      So, 3. Pruning trees is wrong.

Because torture necessarily involves inflicting pain, the first premise of this argument implies that trees can feel pain. Thus, the argument *presupposes* that trees can feel pain. But notice that this presupposition does not appear in our elaborated textbook form. We have added only a single step that is needed to give the argument a form known to be valid, namely, *modus ponens*.

Identifying an argument's presuppositions is useful in evaluating the truth of its premises, for any statement that implies something false is itself false. Thus, if it is false that trees can feel pain, then premise (1) of argument (66) is false, because premise (1)

implies that trees *can* feel pain. But while identifying an argument's presuppositions is often helpful when evaluating for soundness, two common errors regarding presuppositions must be avoided.

First, presuppositions must not be confused with unstated premises. Typically, one adds unstated premises in order to render an argument valid or strong. (The only exception is when the argument is clearly presented as invalid or weak.) But adding presuppositions will not render an argument valid or strong. Again, a presupposition of an argument is a statement that is not a step in the argument (not even an unstated step) but that is implied by one or more premises of the argument.

Second, it is notoriously easy to think that an argument presupposes something when it really doesn't. Indeed, one of the most common errors of reasoning among well-educated people could be generalized as follows: "Your argument presupposes statement *S* (when the argument doesn't *necessarily* presuppose *S*), and because *S* is false or dubious, your argument is unsound." For example, consider the following argument:

67. The choices a human being makes are influenced by his past because a person's upbringing limits the options that occur to him.

Through carelessness or inattention, one might suppose that the premise of this argument, "A person's upbringing limits the options that occur to him," implies determinism with respect to human acts, that is, the view that the past causally necessitates a unique future. (According to determinists, I may *think* I can choose either option A or option B, but factors in the past cause me to select A rather than B, or vice versa.) Note, however, that the premise of (67) doesn't really imply determinism. The premise says only that our choices are limited by our upbringing. For instance, a person deprived of an education might be unaware that certain alternatives are open to him (for example, that he could enroll in a particular government program), and yet he still has alternatives to choose from (such as, get a job, live on the streets, or enter a life of crime). The lesson here is to take care when claiming that an argument presupposes something; be sure that a premise (or premises) really imply the statement in question.

How to Read Philosophy

HOPE MAY

Hope May (1971–   ) is a member of the Department of Philosophy and Religion at Central Michigan University.

It is one thing to run your eyes over the printed words on a page, and it is quite another thing to understand what is signified by those words. Only the latter activity constitutes reading. You are probably accustomed to reading in a manner that requires little effort. For instance, when reading a newspaper article, a work of fiction, or even a textbook, your comprehension is virtually automatic. Most likely, you rarely ponder each word, or even each sentence, in order to understand what you are reading. Typically, you are accustomed to reading as a passive activity.

Reading a philosophical text, however, requires you to read *actively* and hence to think about, to contemplate, and to scrutinize what you are reading. Properly reading a philosophical text will require you to stop and reread a sentence several times before you fully understand it. Many times, you will have to reread an entire selection in order to completely grasp it. This in no way impugns your level of reading comprehension, however. As it happens, most professional philosophers also ponder over sentences and even individual words. On many occasions I have heard professional philosophers say things like "I have read it only once" in order to indicate that they have not mastered the material.

One of the chief obstacles faced by students beginning to read philosophy is the completely different kind of reading style that it requires. So, when you sit down to read a philosophical work, do not expect to be told a story. Nor should you expect to be given a body of facts that you are to memorize. Properly reading a philosophical text requires you to stop and think, to step back from what you are reading, to look up words that you do not understand, and to reread certain passages. Reading a

philosophical text takes work, and is much more like writing a book than it is like passively reading one.

Before turning to some specific strategies for reading a philosophical text, let me first give some preliminary remarks about the subject matter of philosophy. As you will see, philosophy demands extra effort from its reader because its subject matter is so very different from the subject matter of many of the academic disciplines with which you are familiar.

FAMILIARIZING YOURSELF WITH THE TERRAIN

How many electrons does an arsenic atom have? What is the distance from the Earth to its nearest star? What is the length of the hypotenuse with sides of 3 and 4 inches? These are questions that can be answered, respectively, by performing experiments, taking measurements, and solving equations. What is communism? and When was the battle of Yorktown?, on the other hand, are questions that are not answered by resorting to scientific or quantitative methods but by consulting the relevant reference books. All of these questions, regardless of the different methods used to answer them, have only a single answer. Philosophical questions are very different. Philosophical questions are not answered in any of the aforementioned ways, and a single philosophical question has many possible answers.

A philosophical question is answered by constructing a point of view. Think of a point of view (P.O.V.) as a reasoned position on an issue about which there is disagreement, or, alternatively, as a reasoned answer to a question to which there are many possible answers. Importantly, a certain point of view is not *the* answer to a philosophical question but is rather a *possible* answer. Each philosophical question has several possible answers that comprise several possible points of view. Consider the

I would like to thank Dillon Moorehead and Joseph Salerno for their thoughtful comments and valuable criticisms on earlier drafts of this essay.

philosophical question, What makes certain actions morally right? There are several possible answers to this question; three of them are:

1. An action is morally right if my religion says so.
2. An action is morally right if it makes me happy.
3. An action is morally right if my society says so.

Although all of these statements answer the question What makes an action morally right?, not one of them is a completely developed point of view. A point of view is much more than a blunt assertion of some statement such as "an action is morally right if my religion says so." A P.O.V. is a *reasoned* answer. A reasoned answer is simply one in which reasons are given in support of that answer. Three reasoned answers to the question What makes certain actions morally right? are:

1. An action is morally right if my religion says so. This is because the God of my religion is the true God, and an action is morally right if it conforms to the standards of rightness that are defined by the true God.
2. An action is morally right if it makes an individual happy. This is because the purpose of life is to be happy, and an action is right if it helps an individual achieve that purpose.
3. An action is morally right if my society says so. This is because the standards of right and wrong are determined completely by my society, and an action is morally right if it conforms to the standards that are defined by one's society.

These are all reasoned answers, but philosophers give reasoned answers that are much lengthier and developed than the ones above.

The fact that an answer is reasoned does not mean that it is a *good* answer. Philosophers say that a point of view is better than another if it has superior *logical properties*. I will explain what this means more fully in a later section. For now, it is important to realize that the logical properties of a P.O.V. are *objective;* they do not depend on one's mere taste. Being invalid, being internally inconsistent, begging the question, having false premises, having undesirable consequences, and being subject to counterexamples are all *undesirable* logical properties. On the other hand, *desirable* logical properties include being valid, being internally consistent, being an

answer to the philosophical question, having true premises, having favorable consequences, and being free from counterexamples. Whether a P.O.V. has desirable or undesirable logical properties is independent of the feelings that you have about it. Selecting a P.O.V. from a number of competing points of view, then, is not an arbitrary matter. Some points of view possess better logical properties than others.

Philosophers construct points of view as well as describe their logical properties. In fact, a philosopher will often try to "sell" you her P.O.V. by arguing that it has better logical properties than its competitors. This is why philosophy requires a heightened attentiveness from its reader. Philosophers are not simply presenting facts but are using ideas and logic to construct points of view on concepts like morality, truth, and beauty. This is why understanding what is signified by the words in a philosophical text requires a very different ability than the one that enables you to comprehend newspaper articles, for instance. For the words in a philosophical text denote ideas that comprise a sort of geometric structure— a conceptual space in which a point of view on a certain term such as "morality" consists. You cannot see the contours of this space by passively reading. Only when you reflect on what you are reading will you begin see the conceptual space created by the philosopher. And only when you see this space will you be able to understand the text that you are reading. Below, I describe some specific strategies that will help you to do this.

GENERAL STRATEGIES

There are three main obstacles that beginning philosophy students encounter. The first concerns the *content* of the philosophical work, the second concerns its *argumentative structure,* and the third concerns its *evaluation.* Let's look at these obstacles and some strategies for dealing with each.

CONTENT

Technical Terms in Philosophy

Before you start reading, make sure you have a notebook, a writing implement of some kind, and a dictionary. For philosophy, just as any other discipline, has its own vocabulary. Just as the term "molecule" is peculiar to chemistry, and just as the term "hypotenuse" is peculiar to geometry, there are certain terms that are peculiar to philosophy. In order to understand your text, you will need to look up these words (in addition to any nontechnical words that you do not understand).

Often, a good dictionary will have entries for philosophical terms, but typically, these entries are not very helpful because the philosophical meaning of a term is different from the standard meaning. For instance, "a priori" and "a posteriori" are technical philosophical terms that are used to describe statements and/or concepts. Philosophers distinguish *a priori* statements that can be known independently of sense experience from *a posteriori* statements that can only be known through sense experience. Thus, philosophers say that the statement "0 = 0" is *a priori* because it can only be known through reason (we do not experience zero, or any other number, for that matter, with our senses), whereas the statement "fire is hot" is *a posteriori* because it can only be known through sense experience.

You can see that the entries for "a priori" and "a posteriori" in Webster's *New World Dictionary* do not help us to understand the philosophical meanings of these terms:

> **a priori:** 1. from cause to effect or from a generalization to particular instances; deductively; 2. of such reasonings; deductive. 3. based on theory instead of experience or experiment. 4. before examination or analysis. Opposed to A POSTERIORI.

> **a posteriori:** 1. from effect to cause, or from particular instances to a generalization; inductive or inductively. 2. based on observation or experience; empirical. Opposed to A PRIORI.

None of these definitions informs you of the way in which philosophers use these terms. Only the third definition of "a priori" comes close to the philosophical meaning of the term, but philosophers do not generally regard a priori statements as being "based on theory." Rather, a priori statements are ones that are known through *reason*. It is true that the second definition of "a posteriori" comes close to the philosophical definition of this term, but

there are two definitions offered of this term, and it is not made clear which definition is the philosophical one.

Because standard dictionaries often lack the philosophical definition of a term, it is most effective to read philosophy with a philosophical dictionary (such as the *Cambridge Philosophical Dictionary*). If you are using a standard dictionary, make sure that you write down the term and ask your instructor about it in class. Because standard dictionaries often provide several definitions of a single term, you may not know which of these definitions is the philosophical one.

Determining Your Author's Point of View

Now that you have a notebook, a writing implement, and a dictionary of some sort, the next thing that you need to do is to determine the focus and scope of your author's P.O.V. Doing so involves first understanding the questions that your author is trying to answer. Your author may be answering a general philosophical question such as, What makes an action morally right? or What is knowledge? If so, her point of view will have a relatively broad scope. On the other hand, your author may be answering a more specific philosophical question such as, Is a priori knowledge possible? and To what do theoretical terms such as "atom" refer? If so, her point of view will have a relatively narrow scope. If you have a sense of the questions that your author is trying to answer, you will have a sense of what the text is *about*. And if you have a sense of what the text is about, you will be in a much better position to interact with it.

There are several things that you can do to help you understand the philosophical questions for which your author tries to provide answers. First, look at the title of the essay or the book that you are reading. Usually, authors title their works so that their readers have a general idea of the subject of the work. For instance, the title of one of David Hume's works is *An Inquiry Concerning Human Understanding*. Although somewhat general, the title lets us know that the focus of Hume's P.O.V. is human understanding or, in other words, human knowledge. One may reasonably conclude from this title that the question for which Hume provides an answer is, What is knowledge? But there are other things that we do to get even more clarity on the questions that are important to your author.

Usually, philosophers state the purpose of their essay in the first few paragraphs of their work and state their conclusions in the last few paragraphs. So, scanning the beginning and the end of your work can give you a more precise idea of the philosophical questions that are important to your author. For instance, the final paragraph of Hume's *Inquiry* reads as follows:

> When we run over libraries, persuaded of these principles, what havoc must we make? If we take in our hand any volume; of divinity or school metaphysics, for instance, let us ask, Does it contain any abstract reasoning concerning quantity or number? No. Does it contain any experimental reasoning concerning matter of fact or existence? No. Commit it then to the flames; for it can contain nothing but sophistry and illusion.

The passage clearly states that certain books contain false reasoning and consequently hinder humans from true understanding. This paragraph also tells us that Hume believes that true understanding involves "abstract reasoning concerning quantity or number" or "experimental reasoning concerning matter of fact or existence." From reading just this single paragraph, we can realize that Hume believes that the subject of his essay, human understanding, can only be achieved by following these very specific methods. If we look at the above in conjunction with the title of Hume's work, we can reasonably conclude that these elements indicate that the question that Hume is trying to answer is, By what methods can humans achieve knowledge? This is indeed a more precise question than the question that we formulated by looking at Hume's title alone.

One last thing that you should do in order to help you understand the questions your author is trying to answer is to see if the text is divided into sections. Often, the author tries to aid readers' comprehension by dividing the work into sections; looking at the section headings can usually help you determine the scope of your author's P.O.V. You can usually determine what kinds of questions an author is trying to answer if you have some idea of the scope of that author's P.O.V. Hume, for instance, divides his *Inquiry* as follows:

Section I: Of the Different Species of Philosophy

Section II: Of the Origin of Ideas

Section III: Of the Association of Ideas

Section IV: Sceptical Doubts Concerning the Operations of the Understanding

Section V: Sceptical Solution of These Doubts

Section VI: Of Probability

Section VII: Of the Idea of Necessary Connexion

Section VIII: Of Liberty and Necessity

Section IX: Of the Reason of Animals

Section X: Of Miracles

Section XI: Of a Particular Providence and of a Future State

Section XII: Of the Academical or Sceptical Philosophy

We stated above that Hume seems to be concerned with the question, By what methods can humans achieve knowledge? If we consider this in conjunction with the above sections, we have reason to believe that Hume is asking whether certain methods can provide us with knowledge about "probability," "the idea of necessary connexion," "liberty and necessity," and so on. So the scope of Hume's P.O.V. reaches out, it seems, to each of these particular issues. Moreover, Sections IV, V, and XII use the word *sceptical* in their titles, and given this in conjunction with Hume's last paragraph, which you read above, it is reasonable to conclude that Hume's P.O.V. involves "sceptical philosophy" (whatever that is). By looking at a text's title and section headings in conjunction with its first and last few paragraphs, you can determine a lot about the questions with which your author is concerned. Write down all of the section headings in your notebook.

Once you think you have discovered the questions that your author is trying to answer, write them down. Also write down *why* you think these are the questions. Was it the title that helped you? The section headings? The first few paragraphs? A combination of these elements? If you cannot discover the questions that your author is trying to answer, try rereading the first and last few pages very slowly.

Summing up our strategies dealing with content, then, make sure you have a notebook and dictionary so that you can take notes and write down the definitions of unfamiliar words as you are reading. Then, determine the questions that your author is trying to answer by (1) looking at the title of the work, (2) scanning its first and last few paragraphs, and (3) writing down the titles of the sections or chapters within that work. Consider all of these different elements when trying to hone in on these questions. After you have found the relevant questions, write them down, in addition to the reasons that you have for believing that these are the questions with which your author is concerned.

Recall that a P.O.V. is a reasoned answer to a question to which there are several possible reasoned answers. A reasoned answer to a question contains an *argument* for that answer. An argument is not just a dispute between two people but can also be understood as one's reasons for believing something. This brings us to our second obstacle encountered by students beginning to read philosophy—the obstacle concerning argumentative structure.

ARGUMENTATIVE STRUCTURE

Philosophers construct points of view, and points of view contain arguments. Arguments, however, have structure. Some arguments have very simple structures; other arguments have structures that are more complex. An argument that has a simple structure has only one conclusion. Three different arguments with simple structures are

G 1. The God of my religion is the true God.
  2. An action is morally right if it conforms to the standards of rightness that are defined by the true God.
  An action is morally right if my religion says so.

H 1. The purpose of life is to be happy.
  2. An action is right if it helps an individual to achieve his or her purpose.
  An action is morally right if it makes me happy.

S 1. The standards of right and wrong are determined completely by my society.
  2. An action is morally right if it conforms to the standards of rightness that are defined by one's society.
  An action is morally right if my society says so.

All of these arguments have very simple structures. They have at most two premises and one conclusion (the horizontal line separates the premises from the conclusion; think of this line as meaning "therefore"). On the other hand, an argument that has a complex structure has more than one conclusion. In an argument with complex structure, reasons are given in support of reasons.

To illustrate, look at argument G above. Note that there are no reasons given in support of premises (1) and (2); these premises are just bluntly asserted. But we can imagine someone arguing for premise (1) by claiming: (a) my parents told me that the God of my religion is the true God, and (b) my parents never lie. Thus, one way of arguing for the claim that "the God of my religion is the true God" is

P a. My parents told me that the God of my religion is the true God.
  b. My parents never lie.
  1. The God of my religion is the true God.

The conclusion of argument P is the first premise in argument G. We say that arguments P and G form an argument chain P + G. The full argument looks like

P a. My parents told me that the God of my religion is the true God.
  b. My parents never lie
  1. The God of my religion is the true God.
G 2. An action is morally right if it conforms to the standards of rightness that are defined by the true God.
  3. An action is morally right if my religion says so.

It is clear that argument P + G has a more complex structure than argument G, for P + G has two conclusions, whereas argument G has only one.

Some points of view have argumentative structures that are simple, whereas other points of view have argumentative structures that are complex. In order to understand a philosophical text, you need to understand its structure. And in order to understand the structure of a P.O.V., you need to do two things. First, you need to find your author's main conclusion. Then, you need to find the premises that your author provides in support of that conclusion.

Finding the Main Conclusion

Philosophers try to convince their readers of certain statements. The *main conclusion* is the chief statement of which your author is trying to convince you. Look at argument P + G above. Note that although this argument has two conclusions, one of the conclusions, statement (3), is the main conclusion. The main conclusion is the claim for which one ultimately argues; it is the statement for which one's reasons are ultimately offered.

A philosophical P.O.V. is usually an argument with a complex structure. But no matter how complex the structure, every argument has one, and only one, main conclusion. In order to determine the argumentative structure of your author's P.O.V., you must first find its main conclusion. The main conclusion of a P.O.V. is always formulable in one sharp sentence.

Formulating a Hypothesis About the Conclusion

In order to determine the main conclusion of a philosophical work, it is useful to first limit the possibilities of what the conclusion may be. Doing so amounts to honing in the main conclusion, or, in other words, knowing in a *general* sense what kinds of claims for which you are and are not looking. You can hone in on the main conclusion by looking at the text's title, its first and last few paragraphs, and its section headings. Thus, using the techniques that help you to determine the questions with which your author is concerned can help you to get some sense of what her main conclusion is.

For instance, from the title, the first and last few paragraphs, and the section titles of Hume's *Inquiry Concerning Human Understanding,* we can estimate that Hume is concerned with the topic of human knowledge, that he thinks that knowledge can be achieved only by following very specific methods, and that he discusses "scepticism." It is reasonable to assume, then, that Hume's main conclusion will be about knowledge, rather than about the nature of morality or the existence of God (though he may discuss these issues in order to arrive at his conclusion about human knowledge). It is also reasonable to assume that Hume's main conclusion will specify the methods by which knowledge can be attained. Of course, we have not determined Hume's main conclusion with certainty (we need to read the whole text to do that), but we do have a general idea

of the kind of claim for which he will be arguing. And having a general idea of the main conclusion will surely help us in our search to find it.

When you think you have a general idea of the main conclusion of your text, write it down. This is your *hypothesis* about the main conclusion. In addition to writing down your hypothesis about the main conclusion, write down the reasons that led you to formulate this hypothesis.

Forming Paragraph Summaries

After you write down your hypothesis about the main conclusion, you then need to sharpen your focus and to look for the main conclusion *paragraph by paragraph.* You do this by summarizing each paragraph and then looking at your paragraph summaries in order to determine the main conclusion. So, move on to the next paragraph only when you can state in a clear, concise statement the main point of the paragraph that you have just read. If you cannot clearly state the main point of a paragraph, reread it until you can. Make sure you write down each of your paragraph summaries because you will need them in order to determine the argumentative structure of the text. These summaries will be very useful to you later, especially for the purposes of an exam or a writing assignment.

Determining Argumentative Structure

Often, a *single paragraph* of a philosophical text contains one or more arguments. These are subarguments of the main argument of the text. These subarguments may be simple or complex. As you read each paragraph, you need to determine whether the paragraph contains an argument. To do so, ask, What is the point of this paragraph? What is it asking me to believe? and Does the author provide a basis on which I am supposed to believe the main point of the paragraph? If you answer yes to this last question, then the paragraph has an argumentative structure. If you answer no, the paragraph does not.

If your paragraph has an argumentative structure, you need to determine whether it is simple or complex. If you think that you have found a claim in your paragraph (call it "a") that is used to support another claim that is *not* the main point of the paragraph (call it "b"), but "b" is used to support the main point of the paragraph (call it "c"), write down "c" as the conclusion of an argument, "b" as its premise, and "a" as a premise for "b." Separate the premises from the conclusions by drawing a horizontal line between them—like so:

<u>a</u>
<u>b</u>
c

In such a situation, your paragraph has a complex argumentative structure.

If you find that your paragraph contains an argument that is either simple or complex, write the argument down. The argument may or may not be the main point of the paragraph. If it is, your paragraph summary should include something about the argument. It will take you some time to summarize all of the paragraphs. I do not recommend summarizing all of them in one sitting. Give yourself at least two days to do this.

Pinpointing the Main Conclusion

When you are done summarizing each paragraph of your text, look for the main conclusion by looking at *all* of your summaries. As you are reading over these summaries, keep the question in mind: Given all of these summaries, what is the author's main conclusion? What is the author ultimately trying to show? Use the title and section headings to help you. Also use your hypothesis about the main conclusion. Write in a complete sentence what the author is trying to say. Make sure that the conclusion is clear and concise. If it takes you a large paragraph to express the author's central thesis, then you probably have not pinpointed it. The main conclusion should be formulable in one sharp sentence.

Finding the Reasons for the Main Conclusion

After finding the main conclusion, now you need to find the premises—the reasons—that your author offers in support of the main conclusion. The question to keep in mind as you are looking for the reasons for the main conclusion is, On what basis am I supposed to believe the main conclusion? If your text has sections, you may want to look at them in or-

der to answer this question because authors sometimes devote a section to each of the premises in their overall argument; look at the titles that you have written down and after every section ask, What is the point of this section? How is it related to the main conclusion? Is this section used to support any other section?

Another thing to do in order to find the reasons for the main conclusion is to look at your paragraph summaries. Look at each summary and ask, Is the author writing this paragraph in order to give support to the main conclusion? Is the author writing this paragraph in order to give support to the *premises* that are offered in support of the main conclusion?

When you think you have found the reasons that your author gives in support of the main conclusion, write them above the horizontal line above the main conclusion and number each premise. For instance, if the main conclusion of your work is "an action is morally right if my religion says so," and if the reasons used to support this claim are (1) the God of my religion is the true God and (2) an action is morally right if it conforms to the standards of rightness that are defined by the true God, then you would write:

1. The God of my religion is the true God.
2. An action is morally right if it conforms to the standards of rightness that are defined by the <u>true God.</u>

An action is morally right if my religion says so.

If your author provides reasons for any of her premises, make sure you include these as well. So if your author argued for premise (1) by claiming (a) my parents told me that the God of my religion is the true God, and (b) my parents never lie, then you would write:

a. My parents told me that the God of my religion is the true God.
b. <u>My parents never lie.</u>
1. The God of my religion is the true God.
2. An action is morally right if it conforms to the standards of rightness that are defined by the <u>true God.</u>

An action is morally right if my religion says so.

Once you have written down the reasons for the main conclusion, you have determined the argumentative structure of your work. The structure of the above argument is complex.

Summing up our strategies dealing with argumentative structure, then, hone in on the main conclusion by looking at the title, skimming the beginning and end of the text, and looking at section headings. Next, form a hypothesis about the main conclusion, and write it down. Then read the text one paragraph at a time. Determine whether a paragraph contains an argument by asking, What is point of this paragraph? and Is this point argued for or is it bluntly stated? Summarize the main point of each paragraph in a clear, concise statement. Use your paragraph summaries along with your other strategies and your hypothesis about the main conclusion in order to pinpoint the main conclusion. Once you determine the main conclusion, write it down and draw a horizontal line above it. Then, use section headings in conjunction with your paragraph summaries in order to determine the premises that your author uses in support of the conclusion. Write down the premises above the conclusion in addition to any reasons that are offered in support of these premises.

I have provided some exercises below in which you can practice identifying the argumentative structure of a paragraph. Try to determine the argumentative structure of the following excerpts from some classic works of philosophy.

Exercises for Finding the Main Conclusion

Summarize the main point in the following excerpts from some classic works of philosophy. Ask yourself these questions about each.

1. What is the author trying to show? Can you formulate the main conclusion in one sharp sentence?

2. On what basis am I supposed to believe this claim? What are the reasons that the philosopher offers in support of his main point? Does the philosopher offer reasons for believing any of his reasons?

   All reasonings concerning matter of fact seem to be founded on the relation of Cause and Effect. . . . I shall venture to affirm, as a general proposition, which admits of no exception, that the knowledge of this relation is not, in any instance, attained by reasonings a priori; but arises entirely from experience, when we find that any particular objects are constantly conjoined with each other. Let an object be presented to a man of ever so strong natural reason and abilities; if that object be entirely new to him, he will not be able, by the most accurate examination of its sensible qualities, to discover any of its causes or effects. Adam, though his rational faculties be supposed, at the very first, entirely perfect, could have not inferred from the fluidity and transparency of water that it would suffocate him, or from the light and warmth of fire that it would consume him. No object ever discovers, by the qualities which appear to the senses, either the causes which produced it, or the effects which will arise from it; nor can our reason, unassisted by experience, ever draw any inference concerning real existence and matter of fact.

   (Hume, *An Inquiry Concerning Human Understanding*)

   I shall further add that, after the same manner as modern philosophers prove certain sensible qualities to have no existence in matter, or without the mind, the same thing may be likewise proved of all other sensible qualities whatsoever. Thus, for instance, it is said that heat and cold are affections only of the mind, and not all patterns of real beings existing in the corporeal substances which excite them. For that the same body which appears cold to one hand seems warm to another. Now, why may we not as well argue that figure and extension are not patterns or resemblances of qualities existing in matter, because to the same eye at different stations, or eyes of a different texture at the same station, they appear various and cannot, therefore, be the images of anything settled and determinate without the mind? Again, it is proved that sweetness is not really in the sapid thing, because, the thing remaining unaltered, the sweetness is changed into bitter, as in the case of a fever or otherwise vitiated palate. Is it not as reasonable to say that motion is not without the mind, since if the succession of ideas in the mind become swifter, the motion, it is acknowledged, shall appear slower without any alteration in any external object?

   In short, let anyone consider those arguments which are thought manifestly to prove that colors and tastes exist only in the mind, and he shall find that they may with equal force be brought to prove that there is no extension or color in an outward object as that we do not know by sense which is the true extension or color of the object. But the arguments foregoing plainly show it to be impossible that any color or extension at all, or other sensible quality whatsoever, should exist in an unthinking subject without the mind.

(Berkeley, *A Treatise Concerning the Principles of Human Knowledge*)

The general opinion of men is supposed to be, that the natural vocation of a woman is that of a wife and mother. I say, is supposed to be, because, judging from acts—from the whole of the present constitution of society—one might infer that their opinion was the direct contrary. They might be supposed to think that the alleged natural vocation of women was of all things the most repugnant to their nature; insomuch that if they are free to anything else—if any other means of living, or occupation of their time and faculties, is open, which has any chance of appearing desirable to them—there will not be enough of them who will be willing to accept the condition said to be natural to them. If this is the real opinion of men in general, it would be well that it should be spoken out. I should like to hear somebody openly enunciating the doctrine (it is already implied in much that is written on the subject)—"It is necessary to society that women should marry and produce children. They will not do so unless they are compelled. Therefore, it is necessary to compel them." The merits of the case would then be clearly defined. . . . Those who attempt to force women into marriage by closing all other doors against them, lay themselves open to a . . . retort. If they mean what they say, their opinion must evidently be, that men do not render the marriage condition so desirable to women, as to induce them to accept it for its own recommendations. It is not a sign of one's thinking the boon one offers very attractive, when one allows only . . . "that or none."

(Mill, *On the Subjection of Women*)

Hume's Line of Reasoning   The conclusion of Hume's

argument is "the cause–effect relation is known only through sense experience." Hume is taking issue with those who believe that the cause–effect relation is known a priori, that is, independently of sense experience.

Hume states the conclusion in the beginning of this passage, and gives his reasons for this claim immediately afterward. Thus, every thing after the word *Let* is a reason that Hume gives for his conclusion. Paraphrased, his argument is that no matter how strong someone's reasoning abilities, one cannot use reason alone to infer the causes or effects of an object from the qualities of that object. Hence, the cause–effect relationship must be known through sense experience. Summarized, the argument looks like this:

> 1. No matter how powerful one's reasoning ability, one cannot use reason alone to infer the causes and effects of an object from its qualities.
> _____
> The cause–effect relationship is known not through reason, but through sense experience.

The above is a simple argument; it has only one conclusion. But look at Hume's first premise. Do you think that he offers reasons for his claim that "no matter how powerful one's reasoning ability, one cannot use reason alone to infer the causes and effects of an object from its qualities"? He seems to. His remarks about Adam appear to support premise (1). If one looks at the argument in this way, then Hume's argument is complex, because he offers reasons for his reasons. Hume claims that Adam, even with perfect rational faculties, was unable to infer from the qualities of fire that it would consume him. And because Adam could not infer the causes and effects of an object from its qualities, then no person, no matter how powerful their reasoning ability, could infer the causes and effects of an object from its qualities. So Hume's argument stated in full is:

> 2. Adam had perfect reasoning abilities.
> 3. Adam could not infer from the qualities of fire, that it would consume him.
> _____
> 1. No matter how powerful one's reasoning ability, one cannot use reason alone to infer the causes and effects of an object from its qualities.
> _____
> The cause–effect relationship is known not through reason, but through sense experience.

Berkeley's Line of Reasoning Berkeley's main conclusion is that "it is impossible for the qualities of an object to exist without the mind." Berkeley is taking issue with those philosophers who make a distinction between primary and secondary qualities. *Primary qualities* are qualities that belong to the object, and it was assumed that figure, motion, and extension were such qualities. Secondary qualities, on the other hand, were considered to be qualities that did not belong to the object but to the subject who was perceiving the object. The quality of sweetness, for example, was considered to be a secondary quality because two individuals could disagree about whether an object was, in fact, sweet. Someone who eats an apple after drinking wine does not perceive the apple as sweet but as bitter. On the other hand, someone who eats an apple after drinking water might perceive the same apple as sweet. Philosophers reasoned that because there is disagreement about whether an object is sweet or bitter, these qualities are secondary qualities, that is, they do not belong to the object but to the subject perceiving the subject. Berkeley claims that all qualities are secondary qualities.

Crucial to Berkeley's argument is his reliance on a particular line of reasoning that "modern philosophers" use to "prove certain sensible qualities to have no existence in matter." In other words, these philosophers use a certain method of proof to determine that certain qualities are secondary and hence are mind dependent. Berkeley's claim is that this method of proof also establishes that it is impossible for any quality to exist without the mind and, hence, that all qualities are secondary. As mentioned above, philosophers reasoned that because the same thing can seem both sweet and bitter to two different people, these qualities do not belong to the object but to the subject and, hence, are secondary. This particular method of proof is used when Berkeley mentions "the same body which appears cold to one hand appears warm to another" and when he mentions "sweetness is changed into bitter, as in the case of a fever." Stated explicitly, this method to prove the existence of secondary qualities is:

1. If there is disagreement about what qualities an object has, then those qualities are only in the mind (that is, are mind dependent).

2. People disagree about whether an object is cold or warm, sweet or bitter.

Therefore, coldness, warmness, sweetness, and bitterness are mind dependent.

The same method of proof, according to Berkeley, establishes that all qualities are mind dependent. Even the quality of shape, for instance, which "modern philosophers" believed was "primary" or mind independent, is also a quality about which there is disagreement. For, someone standing near a tree sees rounded edges, whereas someone standing far away does not. If we accept the premises of the above argument, then we must accept the conclusion that all qualities are mind dependent. Berkeley's argument is:

1. If there is disagreement about what qualities an object has, then those qualities are mind dependent.
2. People disagree about all qualities that an object has.

All qualities are mind dependent.

Do you think that Berkeley offers reasons for believing either premise (1) or premise (2)? If not, can you think of any reasons that would support these claims?

Mill's Line of Reasoning The conclusion of Mill's argument is "men believe that women would find marriage and motherhood undesirable, if women were to have other options." Mill takes the fact that women are forced into marriage as evidence for the fact that men believe that they must be forced to do so. But, claims Mill, this is at odds with men's claim that the roles of wife and mother are the "natural vocations" of a woman. For if the roles of wife and mother are the "natural vocations" of a woman, then why do women need to be forced into these roles? According to Mill, the fact that men force women into these roles by denying them any other option (save death or ostracism), shows that men tacitly believe that women find these roles undesirable. Mill assumes several premises in his argument:

1. If men force women into marriage and motherhood, then men believe that women would find marriage and motherhood undesirable, if women were to have other options.

2. Currently, men force women into marriage and
   motherhood.
Men believe that women would find marriage and
motherhood undesirable, if women were to have
other options.

Premise (2) was a known fact of Mill's day, and so he
did not need to give reasons for it. Do you think that
Mill gives any reasons for premise (1), though? If
not, can you think of any reasons that would support
this claim?

EVALUATION

After you determine the argumentative structure of
your author's P.O.V., the next step is to evaluate it.
It is very important for you to formulate your own
opinions on the topic on which your author's P.O.V.
is focused. Do not be afraid or intimidated to do so
just because you are reading the work of a professional philosopher! Maybe your gut is telling you
that a certain claim cannot be right. If so, ask yourself, Why do I have this gut feeling? But if you do not
have such an immediate reaction to a philosophical text, there are ways of evaluating your author's
P.O.V., for whether a P.O.V. is good or bad depends
on its logical properties. Below, I show how you can
determine whether your author's P.O.V. possesses
some of the more important logical properties.

Determining Whether the Argument Is Valid

Being valid is a desirable logical property. Being
invalid, on the other hand, is an undesirable logical property. Arguments, not premises, are valid or
invalid. So, being valid and being invalid are properties that belong to the argument—the P.O.V. as
a whole—not the individual statements that comprise it.

It is crucial that you realize that a valid argument
does not *necessarily* have true premises. Nor does an
invalid argument necessarily have false premises. A
valid argument could have false premises, such as

All women are idiots.
I am a woman.
I am an idiot.

If the premises are true, the conclusion must be
true. So the argument is valid. But the first premise

is not true. So the argument is *valid with a false premise*. An example of an invalid argument with false
premises is

All men are six feet or taller.
All gymnasts are six feet or taller.
All gymnasts are men.

The above argument is invalid because, even if the
premises were true, the conclusion would not necessarily be true. Just because two groups have the
same property (in this case, being six feet or taller),
this does not mean that one group belongs to another. All dogs are mortal and all cats are mortal, but
this does not mean that all cats are dogs.

In order to determine whether your author's
P.O.V. is valid or invalid, ask, *If* the premises are true,
must the conclusion be true? If you answer no, then
the argument is invalid. If you discover that your author's argument is invalid, you may need to supply
missing premises that your author is tacitly assuming. Adding missing premises can turn an invalid argument into a valid one. For instance, look at one of
Hume's arguments from his *Inquiry Concerning Human Understanding*:

1. No matter how powerful one's reasoning ability,
   one cannot use reason alone to infer the causes
   and effects of an object from its qualities.
The cause–effect relationship is known through
sense experience.

Strictly speaking, this argument is invalid. Just because we cannot know the causal properties of an object by using reason, this does not mean that we must
know these properties through sense experience. It
could be the case that we know causal properties
through some other method (this is, in fact, what
Kant believed). In any case, when Hume was writing,
everyone assumed that knowledge either arises out
of sense experience or is acquired through reason.
Hume tacitly assumes this premise in his argument.
If we add this premise, his argument is valid:

1. No matter how powerful one's reasoning ability,
   one cannot use reason alone to infer the causes
   and effects of an object from its qualities.
[2.] All knowledge comes from either reason or
   from sense experience.
The cause–effect relationship is known through
sense experience.

Note how the second premise is bracketed. A premise that is bracketed indicates that it is not explicitly stated in the text. If you think that your author is assuming claims that are relevant for his or her argument, make sure that you include these claims as bracketed premises in your argument.

If you discover that your author's argument is valid, then your author's P.O.V. possesses a desirable logical property. A P.O.V. that is valid is *somewhat* good but is by no means perfect, for a P.O.V. can simultaneously possess desirable and undesirable logical properties. For instance, a P.O.V. could be *valid but have false premises.* Being valid is, as you know, a desirable logical property. Having false premises, on the other hand, is not. This brings us to another question that you should ask in order to determine some of the logical properties of your author's P.O.V., namely, Are the premises true?

Determining the Truth of the Premises

Recall the argument mentioned earlier:

1. The standards of right and wrong are determined completely by my society.
2. An action is morally right if it conforms to the standards of rightness that are defined by one's society.
   An action is morally right if my society says so.

The above P.O.V. is valid, but are the premises true? These premises are philosophical claims, and it is not immediately clear whether they are true or false. Nevertheless, there are techniques that one can use in order to determine whether premises such as these are false. One can argue that a premise is false by showing that it implies undesirable consequences, and one can argue that a premise is false by showing that there are counterexamples to the premise.

Determining Whether the Premises Imply Undesirable Consequences

In order to determine whether your author's premises are false, then, first look at each one and ask, Does this claim imply any undesirable consequences? A consequence of a P.O.V. is just a statement that must be true if that P.O.V. is true. If, for ex-

ample, the statement "all men are mortal" is true, then it also must be true that "no men are not mortal." Thus "no men are not mortal" is a consequence of "all men are mortal." If one of your author's premises implies an *undesirable* consequence, then your author's P.O.V. possesses an undesirable logical property. If none of your author's premises imply undesirable consequences, then your author's P.O.V. possesses a *desirable* logical property.

Consider one of the premises of the above argument, "the standards of right and wrong are determined completely by my society." Let us determine whether this statement implies any undesirable consequences. Indeed it does. For if it is true that the standards of right and wrong are determined completely by one's society, then the standards of one's society could never be wrong. For these standards *define* rightness and wrongness. But if this is true, then if a society states that child molesting is right, it is. But this, of course, is an undesirable consequence and is a good reason for thinking that the claim is false.

Determining Whether There are Counterexamples to the Premises

Another way of showing that a premise is false is by showing that it is subject to a counterexample. Consider the claim "all men are six feet tall." Are there any counterexamples to this claim? A counterexample is simply an instance that shows that some claim is false. If you can find just one man who is not six feet tall, you have found a counterexample to this claim. If you find that one of your author's premises is subject to a counterexample, then you have discovered that her P.O.V. has an undesirable logical property.

Summing up our remarks on evaluation, then, when evaluating your author's P.O.V., ask these questions: Is the argument valid? Are the premises true? (Do they imply undesirable consequences? Are they subject to counterexamples?) Answering these questions will disclose some of the logical properties of your author's P.O.V., thereby enabling you to evaluate it as philosophers do.

Exercises follow to allow you to practice argument evaluation on some classic works of philosophy. Answers are provided at the end of each section.

EVALUATION PRACTICE

Look at the following arguments and ask yourself, Is this argument valid? Are the premises true?

Evaluating Hume's Line of Reasoning

    3. Adam had perfect reasoning abilities.

    4. <u>Adam could not infer from the qualities of fire, that it would consume him.</u>

    1. No matter how powerful one's reasoning ability, one cannot use reason alone to infer the causes and effects of an object from its qualities.

   [2]. Facts can only be known through sense experi-<u>ence or through reason.</u>

Therefore, the cause–effect relationship is known not through reason, but through sense experience.

1. Do you think premises (4) and (5) are good reasons for believing the conclusion (1)? If so, why? If not, why not?
2. Do you think premises (1) and (2) are good reasons for believing the conclusion? If so, why? If not, why not?
3. Do you believe that the premises are true? If so, why? If not, why not?

Except for the argument that Hume uses to establish his first conclusion, all of the above arguments contain premises that provide good reasons for believing the conclusion. Hume makes a generalization about the power of reason by looking at a single case wherein an individual's reasoning ability is supposed to be perfect. But one could object that, just because one person with perfect reasoning ability could not infer the causal properties of fire, this does not mean that no person with sufficient rational powers could make the inference. Maybe there is something about Adam that is preventing his perfect rational faculty from inferring the causal properties of an object. One cannot infer something about all persons simply by looking at only one individual. One could object that Hume does not provide good reasons for his first conclusion and hence that his first argument is invalid.

Philosophers have disagreed with some of Hume's premises. Immanuel Kant, for example, disagrees with Hume's implicit assumption that "facts can only be known through experience or through reason." According to Kant, there is another mode by which we apprehend facts, namely, the *synthetic a priori*. Kant, then, raises a counterexample to Hume's claim that "facts can be known only through experience or through reason."

Evaluating Berkeley's Line of Reasoning

    1. If there is disagreement about what qualities an object has, then those qualities are mind dependent.

    2. <u>People disagree about all qualities that an object has.</u>

All qualities are mind dependent.

1. Do you think premises (1) and (2) are good reasons for believing the conclusion? If so, why? If not, why not?
2. Do you believe that the premises are true? If so, why? If not, why not?

Berkeley's argument is valid. If his premises are true, his conclusion must be true. However, issue has been taken with both of Berkeley's assumptions. First, it has been noted that the fact that people disagree about what qualities an object has does not mean that these qualities are just "in the mind." At one point people disagreed about the shape of the Earth, but this does not mean that the shape of the Earth is mind dependent. The Earth has its shape regardless of what people think it is. This is a counterexample to Berkeley's claim.

Second, philosophers have claimed, in response to Berkeley's second premise, that people in the same condition will agree on the qualities of an object. Certainly someone who ingests orange juice upon waking will taste something different than the person who drinks orange juice after brushing her teeth, but this is because these two individuals are in different conditions. If we put two individuals in the same conditions, it is argued, they will experience the same qualities. If two people brush their teeth after drinking orange juice, they will have the same sensation of bitterness. Similarly, if two people stand far away from a tree, they will see its contours as straight and so on. People in the same condition do not disagree about the qualities that an object has then. This is a counterexample to Berkeley's second premise.

Evaluating Mill's Line of Reasoning

1. If men force women into marriage and motherhood, then men believe that women would find
   marriage and motherhood undesirable, if
   women were to have other options.
2. Currently, men force women into marriage and
   motherhood.

Men believe that women would find marriage and
motherhood undesirable, if women were to have
other options.

1. Do you think premises (1) and (2) are good
   reasons for believing the conclusion? If so, why?
   If not, why not?
2. Do you believe that the premises are true? If so,
   why? If not, why not?

Mill's argument is valid. However, because men
do not currently force women into marriage, Mill's
second premise is false. He assumes the following
principle in his first premise: "If A forces B into C,
then A believes that B would find C undesirable, if
B had other options." One might argue that this
premise is false. Imagine, for instance, that a coach
forces an Olympic athlete to train for twelve hours
a day. This does not mean that the coach believes
that the athlete would find this undesirable, if the
athlete had other options. So, one may argue that
Mill's first premise is subject to counterexamples.
This objection seems unfair, however. The Olympic
athlete *chose* to do so, and in so choosing, is "forced"
to do things to achieve her goal. Women in Mill's
day, however, did not choose to be wives and mothers, so they cannot be compared with Olympic ath-
letes. Mill could respond by stating that the objection seems misplaced.

SUMMARY

This essay has given you strategies for conquering
the three main obstacles that students encounter
when beginning to read philosophy. Regarding content, make sure you have a notebook and dictionary
so that you can take notes and write down the definitions of unfamiliar words as you are reading. Then,
determine the questions that your author is trying
to answer by (1) looking at the title of the work,
(2) scanning its first and last few paragraphs, and
(3) writing down the titles of the sections or chapters
within that work. After you have found these questions, write them down, in addition to the reasons
that you have for believing that these are the questions with which your author is concerned. Regarding argumentative structure, hone in on the main
conclusion by (1) looking at the title, (2) skimming
the beginning and end of the text, and (3) looking
at section headings. Next, form a hypothesis about
the main conclusion and write it down. Read the text
one paragraph at a time. Determine whether a paragraph contains an argument by asking, What is point
of this paragraph? and Is this point argued for or
is it bluntly stated? Summarize the main point of
each paragraph in a clear, concise statement. Use
your paragraph summaries along with steps 1–3
and your hypothesis about the main conclusion
in order to pinpoint the main conclusion. Once
you determine the main conclusion, write it down
and draw a horizontal line above it. Then, use section headings in conjunction with your paragraph
summaries in order to determine the premises that
your author uses in support of the conclusion. Write
down the premises above the conclusion in addition
to any reasons that are offered in support of these
premises.

Regarding evaluation, you should formulate your
own opinion about the topic, and ask: (1) Is the argument valid? and (2) Are the premises true? (Do
they imply undesirable consequences? Are they subject to counterexamples?)

Finally, if you have trouble with any of these
obstacles, reread the text. Professional philosophers
often have to read something at least two times before they fully understand it. A flowchart summarizing the above steps is provided here.

How to Read Philosophy

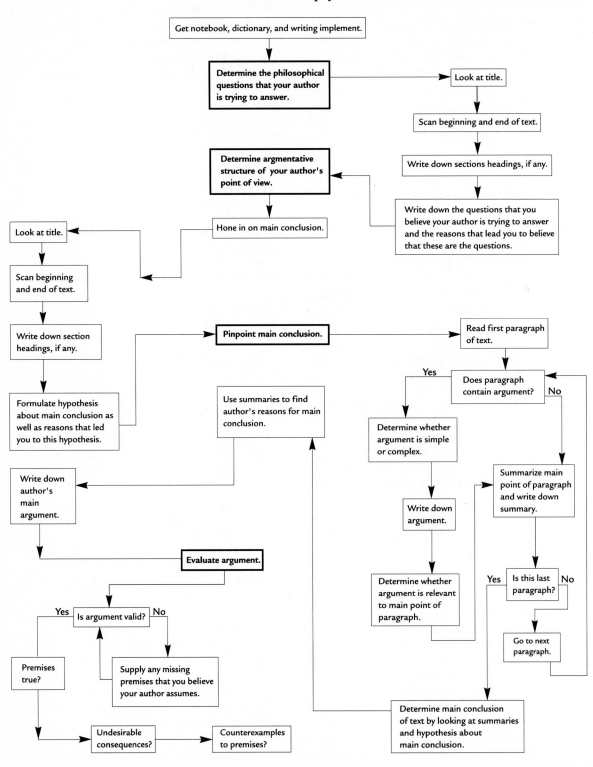

Get notebook, dictionary, and writing implement.

Determine the philosophical questions that your author is trying to answer.

Look at title.

Scan beginning and end of text.

Write down sections headings, if any.

Write down the questions that you believe your author is trying to answer and the reasons that lead you to believe that these are the questions.

Determine argmentative structure of your author's point of view.

Hone in on main conclusion.

Look at title.

Scan beginning and end of text.

Write down section headings, if any.

Formulate hypothesis about main conclusion as well as reasons that led you to this hypothesis.

Pinpoint main conclusion.

Read first paragraph of text.

Yes

Does paragraph contain argument?

No

Determine whether argument is simple or complex.

Use summaries to find author's reasons for main conclusion.

Summarize main point of paragraph and write down summary.

Write down author's main argument.

Write down argument.

Determine whether argument is relevant to main point of paragraph.

Yes Is this last paragraph? No

Evaluate argument.

Go to next paragraph.

Yes Is argument valid? No

Premises true?

Supply any missing premises that you believe your author assumes.

Undesirable consequences?

Counterexamples to premises?

Determine main conclusion of text by looking at summaries and hypothesis about main conclusion.

PART 2

Knowledge and Reality

KNOWLEDGE AND REALITY

Many people claim to know many things. But *how* do they know what they *claim* to know? What *is* knowledge? Epistemology, or the theory of knowledge, is a branch of philosophy that is concerned with this question.

In the first selection, taken from two of Plato's main dialogs—*Meno* and *the Republic*—Plato presents his theory of innate knowledge. According to Plato, the objects of our knowledge do not exist among the appearances. Indeed, the objects that appear to us only obscure the true nature of the real objects that are themselves nowhere to be seen. Real objects exist beyond appearances, in the world of pure ideas, or forms, to which the soul has direct access before birth and to which, after we are born, we have an inborn capacity to recall. Plato explains this relationship between appearance and reality allegorically. He argues that the objects we perceive are at best but shadows of real things and that the most real things are not *things* but *ideas*. Using the allegory of the cave, the simile of the sun, and the divided line, he presents his Theory of Ideas, or Forms, in what many regard to be his greatest dialog, *The Republic*. Set during a pause in the Peloponnesian War, ten or so years before Socrates was put on trial for corrupting the youth and while Athens was still a democracy, it is a work he kept revising for the rest of his life.

Descartes begins his famous *Meditations* by taking stock of all his acquired opinions and then asking, *How do I know that what I believe to be true, is true?* He wonders how he came to his beliefs. He notices that, although it would be impossible to examine each of his beliefs individually, there are only a few methods by which his beliefs were acquired. Most of his beliefs came about through conditioning by various religious, political, and educational authorities. Descartes now asks, *Have I ever been deceived by any of these methods?* If so, then I must throw out all beliefs derived from that method. His method, in other words, is to find the general principles on the basis of which some set of beliefs is acquired and then to test not the individual beliefs but the principles on which they are based—the method by which they were acquired. If the principles and methods are bad, any beliefs thus acquired are not knowledge.

Descartes was a rationalist who, like Plato, held that knowledge must be attained by the light of reason. Locke was an empiricist who claimed that all knowledge comes from experience. However, he fully agreed with Descartes that the mind and our ideas are better and more directly known than physical objects, which are known only indirectly. In many ways, Locke's *Essay Concerning Human Understanding* (1690), from which the third selection in Part 2 is taken, is a critical response to and development of Descartes's views—only it moves in a different direction. Locke attacks the idea of innate knowledge, arguing that all ideas in the mind can be accounted for through experience— either via sensation (mental events derived from the outer senses) or reflection (mental events evoked through introspection).

Berkeley developed his philosophy in part as a reaction to Locke. Locke had shown that secondary qualities exist only in the mind, leaving the primary qualities in the things themselves. Berkeley argues that even primary qualities exist only in the mind. Locke's mistake, he claims, is that he derived the objective existence of extension, hardness, weight, motion, and the other primary qualities of sensible objects, through the (bogus) principle of abstraction. That is, Locke, according to Berkeley, mistakenly thinks he has an abstract idea of substance and extension—matter—as a something "I know not what" to which the mind adheres the secondary qualities of color, texture, and so on. A closer scrutiny of such notions and careful inspection of the actual contents of the mind, along with an analysis of language—the "curtain of words" that deceives us—reveals, Berkeley argues, that there really are no such things as abstract ideas. If we do not allow ourselves to be deceived by our language and analyze the actual notions themselves, we shall see that the mind contains only particular ideas. What Locke called the "primary qualities" of sensible objects thus have no existence beyond the conscious mind. Each and every property of a sensible object exists only as a sensation within the perception of a conscious being.

In his *Inquiry Concerning Human Understanding,* Hume pushes Locke and Berkeley's empiricism to its logical conclusion. Whereas Locke's views were tempered by common-sense notions of reality, often inconsistently, and Berkeley made an exception to his empiricist principles by relying on the concept of "a transcendental other"—God—Hume refuses to make his philosophy bow either to common sense—for which he was criticized by Thomas Reid (1710–1796)—or to transcendental metaphysics. In trying to create a fully consistent but purely empirical philosophy, not only does Hume deny the existence of a Berkeleyian or Cartesian self, he provides devastating empirical criticisms of many metaphysical concepts, such as causation, morality, space, time, and freedom, formulating skeptical objections to all inferences that go beyond immediate experience. Even impressions of the "external" senses exist only in the sensing mind, and he rejects all attempts to argue from the senses to the existence of continuing physical substances outside the mind. By developing Berkeley's criticism of abstract ideas and general entities to their extreme, Hume sets out, as did Berkeley, to improve Locke's theory of knowledge. In some ways he does not go as far as Berkeley; in others he goes even farther. Like Berkeley, Hume is an ultranominalist in that he denies the possibility of there being any sorts of abstract ideas. He does not, however, deny the existence of an "external" reality, although he does claim that it cannot be known with certainty.

In making his arguments, Hume invokes his famous distinction, now called "Hume's fork," between (a) inquiry into relations of ideas and (b) inquiry into matters of fact, which is also called the analytic-synthetic distinction. Analytic propositions are expressed by a priori sentences, whose negation leads to self-contradiction; these sentences are true by definition and therefore are necessarily true. Synthetic propositions, on the other hand, are expressed by a posteriori sentences that are not necessarily true and whose negation is not self-contradictory; thus, they are not necessarily true. Following Leibniz, Spinoza, and Descartes, Hume accepts that there are a priori necessary truths, but he argues that they are tautological. Tautologies are empty—merely verbal truths that provide information only about the conventional meaning of words. They do not provide any new information about the world.

Kant read Hume's criticisms of a priori necessary truths (found in the domain of "relations of ideas," versus "matters of fact"). He tried to solve the problem of knowledge with the notion of a posteriori synthetic truths. These come to the mind in the form of perceptions that, as Hume showed, exist only as momentary, flickering sensations, or—even worse—as fictional abstract ideas in the mind. So how can we have knowledge of reality? For Kant, this is not only the central problem of metaphysics but of the whole of philosophy. Every attempt to solve the problem of metaphysics, Kant argues, has thus far been thwarted not so much by lack of available solutions but by the presence of *too many* solutions. That is, for every solution to the problem of metaphysics, philosophers have constructed competing solutions in terms of a completely different method for acquiring true knowledge of reality. What we need, he claims, is to be able to take the all-important first step in the right direction—but which way could that possibly be? Rationalist systems of pure reason, built using a priori analytic truths, have given rise to dogmatic beliefs such as Berkeley's omniperceiving God, Descartes's self, and Descartes's nondeceiving God. Meanwhile, empiricist systems of pure experience, built using a posteriori synthetic truths, have fostered skeptical doubts, such as Hume's no-self, no-God, no-world. So Kant sets out to find an alternative to both empiricism and rationalism as a way of avoiding both dogmatism and skepticism.

According to Kant's philosophy, there are two distinct realities: the phenomenal world of appearance and representation and the noumenal world of things-in-themselves. The noumenal world cannot be known by the mind; we can only know the world as it is interpreted and structured through the mind's categories and as it is represented as phenomena. The key to his "transcendental" philosophy consists in the mind's coming to be aware that the phenomenal world of appearances consists not of objects in the world as they exist in themselves but of the mind's own representations of things as interpreted through and structured by its own categories. This means that when I open my eyes and am confronted by all the visible objects in my field of vision (the manifold of intuition) I must learn to recognize that what I am looking at is a sort of virtual reality, a world of my own ideas, representations of objects in the world and not the objects in the world as they exist in themselves. And yet Kant claims not to be an idealist (at least not in Berkeley's sense) because a phenomenon experienced as a representation of an object—say, the chair I see—is in fact the product of two causes: the mind and the chair-in-itself. In other words, as a phenomenal object the chair represented to me as a phenomenon exists as an interface between the mind and the world. Kant's phenomenal world is, therefore, real. It can be studied formally by science and mathematics. That is how, given the necessary, Transcendental Illusion (in which we mistake phenomena for things in themselves), the science of nature is, nevertheless, possible.

SKEPTICISM AND SCIENCE

Bertrand Russell, a sympathetic critic of Hume, remarked that by making the empirical philosophy of Berkeley and Locke consistent, Hume "made it incredible." In "Science and Induction" from his *Problems of Philosophy,* Russell explains why there are problems with basing knowledge on experience. However, Russell then revamps and elaborates the sort of foundationalism that was advocated not just by the empiricists Locke, Berkeley, and Hume but also by the rationalist Descartes; Russell, though, avoids the transcendental philosophy of Kant, which, like most of Kant's nineteenth-century critics, he saw as deeply problematic and inconsistent—the chief problem, in Russell's view, being Kant's notion of a noumenal world beyond our reach. Russell presents a theory of how we can get to science from what he regards as the ultimate data of empirical knowledge, sense data, to all of the things we think we know about the world and ourselves; this task leads him to try to solve the problem of skepticism and induction through a theory of inductive inferences of the sort he claims are actually made in science.

Charles Sanders Peirce, who initiated the movement in American philosophy known as *pragmatism,* presents a pragmatist answer to the problem of knowledge with a new theory of truth. According to his *pragmatic principle,* we must "Consider what effects, that conceivable might have practical bearings, we conceive the object of our conception to have. Then our conception of these effects is the whole of our conception of the object." What this means is that beliefs, according to Peirce, are psychological habits predisposing us to respond in specific ways to specific situations, similar to the way that Hume supposed. Any situation in our experience causes either physical movement of the body or psychological expectation in the mind. In his classic article, "The Fixation of Beliefs," he claims there are four basic ways for our habits, customs, traditions, and "folkways" to become "fixed" in our minds. These apply to everything from personal convictions to metaphysical philosophical systems, and they are used for both settling opinions and resolving doubt: tenacity, authority, the a priori method, and the method of science. The only reliable method, however, is the latter scientific method in which one does not know in advance where one is going. This concept is closely aligned with Darwin's analysis of how evolution works. Evolution works precisely because there is nothing guiding it. In this way, Peirce sought to develop a new scientific method in which our beliefs are a response to something independent of ourselves, in terms of both our desires and our opinions. Moreover, this is a publicly verifiable method and thus markedly influenced by the positivist philosophy of the subsequent logical positivist movement.

Peirce's follow-up to "Fixation of Belief," called "How to Make Our Ideas Clear," is a criticism of Descartes's theory of knowledge in general and, in particular, Descartes's notion of "clear and distinct ideas," which Peirce claims is itself not clear and distinct. Peirce's complaint against Descartes is that he relies solely on the a priori method, which he rejects on grounds that it appeals, ultimately, to nonverifiable self-evidence. Peirce thus calls for a third grade of clearness, itself predicated upon and identical with his pragmatic maxim, which renders as meaningless any terms or concepts that go beyond the possible effects on observable objects: Beliefs must be judged solely by the habits they produce, the practical rules of action that they govern. His system thus comes full circle and completes itself.

The philosopher of science Paul Feyerabend, on the other hand, is deeply critical of science. In fact, he claims that science today has replaced religion in its indoctrination by authority into a particular belief system. Part of the problem is that when we examine the scientific revolutions since the seventeenth century—for instance, nearly every view that has ever been held to be the one and only true and correct view—they have turned out by the end of the twentieth century to be either false or deeply questionable. At the time the view was held, however, people took the (now-defunct) view to be the final truth. The scientists of the time claimed, although their theories might not be absolutely perfect and account for everything, that they were the best and most reliable theory. Furthermore, whereas science once had to fight off the repression of religious authority, it has now become an even more repressive authority because it has become too rigid. Feyerabend argues that science has neither achieved a correct and sound method for its results nor have its results proven the validity of its method.

In his "Infinite Regress of Reasons," D. M. Armstrong gives an unusually clear, systematic, and concise explanation of the problems facing all traditional theories of knowledge, including foundationalism and coherence theories, and then suggests a reliability theory of knowledge to replace them. The logical symbolism is quite natural once you get used to it. The letter "A" (capital or lowercase) stands for any *person,* and the letters "p," "q," and "r" stand for any statements. For instance, in "A knows that p," "A" could stand for "Einstein," "Joe," or "God" and "p" for the statement "Space and time are relative," "$E = mc^2$," or "George Washington was the first president of the United States." (Later in the selection, however, he also uses "A," "B," and "C" to stand for *events,* such as the ending of World War II or a clap of thunder.) The expression "Kap" stands for "A knows that p." "Bap" stands for "A believes that p." "~Kap" and "~Bap" stand for "A does not know that p" and "A does not believe that p," respectively. Finally, *punter,* which appears in the first paragraph, is Australian for "someone who gambles on horses."

In "Is Man a Rational Animal?" a leading contemporary philosopher, Stephen Stich, asks the age-old question of whether we are rational beings—that Aristotle famously answered in the positive but that Stich answers largely in the negative. Written from the standpoint of naturalized epistemology, the selection shows how empirical sciences today shed light on philosophical questions and includes some fascinating data from recent psychological studies. It also involves not only evolutionary psychology, a very important new branch of cognitive studies, but offers insights into recent interdisciplinary work on theory acceptance, the nature of scientific facts, and the role of evolutionary biology in ethics. Stich brings out a number of fallacies that he claims points collectively to the conclusion that, even at our best, we are not nearly as rational as we may like to think.

Knowledge

PLATO

Plato (428–348 B.C.E.), Socrates's most prolific student, wrote more than two dozen dialogs on nearly every philosophical topic. He lived and taught philosophy in ancient Athens and founded the Academy, the world's first university.

FROM *MENO*

MENO: Yes, Socrates; but what do you mean by saying that we do not learn, and that what we call learning is only a process of recollection? Can you teach me how this is?

SOCRATES: I told you, Meno, just now that you were a rogue, and now you ask whether I can teach you, when I am saying that there is no teaching, but only recollection; and thus you imagine that you will involve me in a contradiction.

MEN.: Indeed, Socrates, I protest that I had no such intention. I only asked the question from habit; but if you can prove to me that what you say is true, I wish that you would.

SOC.: It will be no easy matter, but I will try to please you to the utmost of my power. Suppose that you call one of your numerous attendants, that I may demonstrate on him.

MEN.: Certainly. Come hither, boy.

SOC.: He is Greek, and speaks Greek, does he not?

MEN.: Yes, indeed; he was born in the house.

SOC.: Attend now to the questions which I ask him, and observe whether he learns of me or only remembers.

MEN.: I will.

SOC.: Tell me, boy, do you know that a figure like this is a square?

BOY: I do.

SOC.: And you know that a square figure has these four lines equal?

BOY: Certainly.

SOC.: And these lines which I have drawn through the middle of the square are also equal?

BOY: Yes.

SOC.: A square may be of any size?

BOY: Certainly.

SOC.: And if one side of the figure be of two feet, and the other side be of two feet, how much will the whole be? Let me explain: if in one direction the space was of two feet, and in the other direction of one foot, the whole would be of two feet taken once?

BOY: Yes.

SOC.: But since this side is also of two feet, there are twice two feet?

BOY: There are.

SOC.: Then the square is of twice two feet?

BOY: Yes.

SOC.: And how many are twice two feet? Count and tell me.

BOY: Four, Socrates.

SOC.: And might there not be another square twice as large as this, and having like this the lines equal?

BOY: Yes.

SOC.: And of how many feet will that be?

BOY: Of eight feet.

SOC.: And now try and tell me the length of the line

From *The Dialogues of Plato*, 3rd ed., translated by Benjamin Jowett (Oxford: Oxford University Press, 1896).

which forms the side of that double square: this is two feet—what will that be?

Boy: Clearly, Socrates, it will be double.

Soc.: Do you observe, Meno, that I am not teaching the boy anything, but only asking him questions; and now he fancies that he knows how long a line is necessary in order to produce a figure of eight square feet; does he not?

Men.: Yes.

Soc.: And does he really know?

Men.: Certainly not.

Soc.: He only guesses that because the square is double, the line is double.

Men.: True.

Soc.: Observe him while he recalls the steps in regular order. (*To the Boy.*) Tell me, boy, do you assert that a double space comes from a double line? Remember that I am not speaking of an oblong, but of a figure equal every way, and twice the size of this—that is to say of eight feet; and I want to know whether you still say that a double square comes from a double line?

Boy: Yes.

Soc.: But does not this line become doubled if we add another such line here?

Boy: Certainly.

Soc.: And four such lines will make a space containing eight feet?

Boy: Yes.

Soc.: Let us describe such a figure: Would you not say that this is the figure of eight feet?

Boy: Yes.

Soc.: And are there not these four divisions in the figure, each of which is equal to the figure of four feet?

Boy: True.

Soc.: And is not that four times four?

Boy: Certainly.

Soc.: And four times is not double?

Boy: No, indeed.

Soc.: But how much?

Boy: Four times as much.

Soc.: Therefore the double line, boy, has given a space, not twice, but four times as much.

Boy: True.

Soc.: Four times four are sixteen—are they not?

Boy: Yes.

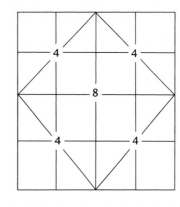

Soc.: What line would give you a space of eight feet, as this gives one of sixteen feet;—do you see?

Boy: Yes.

Soc.: And the space of four feet is made from this half line?

Boy: Yes.

Soc.: Good; and is not a space of eight feet twice the size of this, and half the size of the other?

Boy: Certainly.

Soc.: Such a space, then, will be made out of a line greater than this one, and less than that one?

Boy: Yes; I think so.

Soc.: Very good; I like to hear you say what you think. And now tell me, is not this a line of two feet and that of four?

Boy: Yes.

Soc.: Then the line which forms the side of eight feet ought to be more than this line of two feet, and less than the other of four feet?

Boy: It ought.

Soc.: Try and see if you can tell me how much it will be.

Boy: Three feet.

Soc.: Then if we add a half to this line of two, that will be the line of three. Here are two and there is one; and on the other side here are two also and there is one: and that makes the figure of which you speak?

Boy: Yes.

Soc.: But if there are three feet this way and three feet that way, the whole space will be three times three feet?

Boy: That is evident.

Soc.: And how much are three times three feet?

Boy: Nine.

SOC.: And how much is the double of four?

BOY: Eight.

SOC.: Then the figure of eight is not made out of a line of three?

BOY: No.

SOC.: But from what line?—tell me exactly; and if you would rather not reckon, try and show me the line.

BOY: Indeed, Socrates, I do not know.

SOC.: Do you see, Meno, what advances he has made in his power of recollection? He did not know at first, and he does not know now, what is the side of a figure of eight feet: but then he thought that he knew, and answered confidently as if he knew, and had no difficulty; now he has a difficulty, and neither knows nor fancies that he knows.

MEN.: True.

SOC.: Is he not better off in knowing his ignorance?

MEN.: I think that he is.

SOC.: If we have made him doubt, and given him the "torpedo's shock," have we done him any harm?

MEN.: I think not.

SOC.: We have certainly, as would seem, assisted him in some degree to the discovery of the truth: and now he will wish to remedy his ignorance, but then he would have been ready to tell all the world again and again that the double space should have a double side.

MEN.: True.

SOC.: But do you suppose that he would ever have enquired into or learned what he fancied that he knew, though he was really ignorant of it, until he had fallen into perplexity under the idea that he did not know, and had desired to know?

MEN.: I think not, Socrates.

SOC.: Then he was the better for the torpedo's touch?

MEN.: I think so.

SOC.: Mark now the farther development. I shall only ask him, and not teach him, and he shall share the enquiry with me: and do you watch and see if you find me telling or explaining anything to him, instead of eliciting his opinion. Tell me, boy, is not this a square of four feet which I have drawn?

BOY: Yes.

SOC.: And now I add another square equal to the former one?

BOY: Yes.

SOC.: And a third, which is equal to either of them?

BOY: Yes.

SOC.: Suppose that we fill up the vacant corner?

BOY: Very good.

SOC.: Here, then, there are four equal spaces?

BOY: Yes.

SOC.: And how many times larger is this space than this other?

BOY: Four times.

SOC.: But it ought to have been twice only, as you will remember.

BOY: True.

SOC.: And does not this line, reaching from corner to corner, bisect each of these spaces?

BOY: Yes.

SOC.: And are there not here four equal lines which contain this space?

BOY: There are.

SOC.: Look and see how much this space is.

BOY: I do not understand.

SOC.: Has not each interior line cut off half of the four spaces?

BOY: Yes.

SOC.: And how many spaces are there in this section?

BOY: Four.

SOC.: And how many in this?

BOY: Two.

SOC.: And four is how many times two?

BOY: Twice.

SOC.: And this space is of how many feet?

BOY: Of eight feet.

SOC.: And from what line do you get this figure?

BOY: From this.

SOC.: That is, from the line which extends from corner to corner of the figure of four feet?

BOY: Yes.

SOC.: And that is the line which the learned call the diagonal. And if this is the proper name, then you, Meno's slave, are prepared to affirm that the double space is the square of the diagonal?

BOY: Certainly, Socrates.

SOC.: What do you say of him, Meno? Were not all these answers given out of his own head?

MEN.: Yes, they were all his own.

SOC.: And yet, we were just now saying, he did not know?

MEN.: True.

SOC.: But still he had in him those notions of his—had he not?

MEN.: Yes.

SOC.: Then he who does not know may still have the true notions of that which he does not know?

MEN.: He has.

SOC.: And at present these notions have just been stirred up in him, as in a dream; but if he were frequently asked the same questions, in different forms, he would know as well as any one at last?

MEN.: I dare say.

SOC.: Without any one teaching him he will recover his knowledge for himself, if he is only asked questions?

MEN.: Yes.

SOC.: And this spontaneous recovery of knowledge in him is recollection?

MEN.: True.

SOC.: And this knowledge which he now has must he not either have acquired or always possessed?

MEN.: Yes.

SOC.: But if he always possessed this knowledge he would always have known; or if he has acquired the knowledge he could not have acquired it in this life, unless he has been taught geometry; for he may be made to do the same with all geometry and every other branch of knowledge. Now, has any one ever taught him all this? You must know about him, if, as you say, he was born and bred in your house.

MEN.: And I am certain that no one ever did teach him.

SOC.: And yet he has the knowledge?

MEN.: The fact, Socrates, is undeniable.

SOC.: But if he did not acquire the knowledge in this life, then he must have had and learned it at some other time?

MEN.: Clearly he must.

SOC.: Which must have been the time when he was not a man?

MEN.: Yes.

SOC.: And if there have been always true thoughts in him, both at the time when he was and was not a man, which only need to be awakened into knowledge by putting questions to him, his soul must have always possessed this knowledge, for he always either was or was not a man?

MEN.: Obviously.

SOC.: And if the truth of all things always existed in the soul, then the soul is immortal. Wherefore be of good cheer, and try to recollect what you do know, or rather what you do not remember.

FROM *PHAEDO*

SOCRATES: Now consider this question. We affirm, do we not, that there is such a thing as equality, not of one piece of wood or stone or similar material thing with another, but that, over and above this, there is absolute equality? Shall we say so?

Say so, yes, replied Simmias, and swear to it, with all the confidence in life.

And do we know the nature of this absolute existence?

To be sure, he said.

And whence did we obtain our knowledge? Did we not see equalities of material things, such as pieces of wood and stones, and conceive from them the idea of an equality which is different from them? For you will acknowledge that there is a difference? Or look at the matter in another way:—Do not the same pieces of wood or stone appear to one man equal, and to another unequal?

That is certain.

But did pure equals ever appear to you unequal? or equality the same as inequality?

Never, Socrates.

Then these equal objects are not the same with the idea of equality?

I should say, clearly not, Socrates.

And yet from these equals, although differing from the idea of equality, you obtained the knowledge of that idea?

Very true, he said.

Which might be like, or might be unlike them? Yes.

But that makes no difference: so long as from seeing one thing you conceive another, whether like or unlike, there must surely have been an act of recollection?

Very true.

But what would you say of equal portions of wood or other material equals? and what is the impression produced by them? Are they equals in the same sense in which absolute equality is equal? or do they fall short of this perfect equality in a measure.

Yes, he said, in a very great measure too.

And must we not allow, that when a man, looking at any object, reflects "the thing which I see aims at being like some other thing, but falls short of and cannot be like that other thing, and is inferior," he who so reflects must have had a previous knowledge of that to which the other, although similar, was inferior?

Certainly.

And has not this been our own case in the matter of equals and of absolute equality?

Precisely.

Then we must have known equality previously to the time when we first saw the material equals, and reflected that they all strive to attain absolute equality, but fall short of it?

Very true.

And we recognize also that we have only derived this conception of absolute equality, and can only derive it, from sight or touch, or from some other of the senses, which are all alike in this respect?

Yes, Socrates, for the purposes of the present argument, one of them is the same as the other.

From the senses then is derived the conception that all sensible equals aim at an absolute equality of which they fall short?

Yes.

Then before we began to see or hear or perceive in any way, we must have had a knowledge of absolute equality, or we could not have referred to that standard the equals which are derived from the senses?—for to that they all aspire, and of that they fall short.

No other inference can be drawn from the previous statements.

And did we now begin to see and hear and have the use of our other senses as soon as we were born?

Certainly.

Then we must have acquired the knowledge of equality at some previous time?

Yes.

That is to say, before we were born, I suppose?

It seems so.

And if we acquired this knowledge before we were born, and were born having the use of it, then we also knew before we were born and at the instant of birth not only the equal or the greater or the less, but all other such ideas; for we are not speaking only of equality, but of beauty, goodness, justice, holiness, and of all which we stamp with the name of absolute being in the dialectical process, both when we affirm with certainty that we acquired the knowledge before birth?

We do.

But, if after having acquired, we have not on each occasion forgotten what we acquired, then we must always come into life having this knowledge, and shall have it always as long as life lasts—for knowing is the acquiring and retaining knowledge and not losing it. Is not the loss of knowledge, Simmias, just what we call forgetting?

Quite true, Socrates.

But if this knowledge which we acquired before birth was lost by us at birth, and if afterwards by the use of the senses we recovered what we previously knew, will not the process which we call learning be a recovering of knowledge which is natural to us, and may not this be rightly termed recollection?

Very true.

So much is clear—that when we perceive something, either by the help of sight, or hearing, or some other sense, that perception can lead us to think of some other thing like or unlike which is associated with it but has been forgotten. Whence, as I was saying, one of two alternatives follows:— either we all have this knowledge at birth, and continue to know through life; or, after birth, those who are said to learn only recollect, and learning is simply recollection.

Yes, that is quite true, Socrates.

And which alternative, Simmias, do you prefer? Have we the knowledge at our birth, or do we recollect afterwards things which we knew previously to our birth?

I cannot decide at the moment.

At any rate you can decide whether he who has knowledge will or will not be able to render an account of his knowledge? What do you say?

Certainly, he will.

But do you think that every man is able to give an account of the matters about which we were speaking a moment ago?

Would that they could, Socrates, but I much rather fear that tomorrow, at this time, there will no longer be anyone alive who is able to give an account of them such as ought to be given.

Then you are not of opinion, Simmias, that all men know these things.

Certainly not.

They are in the process of recollecting that which they learned before?

Certainly.

But when did our souls acquire this knowledge? —clearly not since we were born as men?

Certainly not.

And therefore, previously?

Yes.

Then, Simmias, our souls must also have existed without bodies before they were in the form of man, and must have had intelligence.

Unless indeed you suppose, Socrates, that all knowledge is given us at the very moment of birth; for this is the only time which remains.

Yes, my friend, but if so, when, pray, do we lose it? for it is not in us when we are born—that is admitted. Do we lose it at the moment of receiving it, or if not at what other time?

No, Socrates, I perceive that I was unconsciously talking nonsense.

Then may we not say, Simmias, that if there do exist these things of which we are always talking, absolute beauty and goodness, and all that class of realities; and if to this we refer all our sensations and with this compare them, finding the realities to be pre-existent and our own possession—then just as surely as these exist, so surely must our souls have existed before our birth? Otherwise our whole argument would be worthless. By an equal compulsion we must believe both that these realities exist, and that our souls existed before our birth; and if not the realities, then not the souls.

Yes, Socrates; I am convinced that there is precisely the same necessity for the one as for the other; and the argument finds a safe refuge in the position that the existence of the soul before birth cannot be separated from the existence of the reality of which you speak. For there is nothing which to my mind is so patent as that beauty, goodness, and the other realities of which you were just now speaking, exist in the fullest possible measure; and I am satisfied with the proof.

FROM *REPUBLIC*

SOCRATES: Yes, I said, but I must first come to an understanding with you, and remind you of what I have mentioned in the course of this discussion, and at many other times.

GLAUCON: What?

The old story, that there is a many beautiful and a many good, and so of other things which we describe and define; to all of them "many" is applied.

True, he said.

And there is an absolute beauty and an absolute good, and of other things to which the term "many" is applied there is an absolute; for they may be brought under a single idea, which is called the essence of each.

Very true.

The many, as we say, are seen but not known, and the ideas are known but not seen.

Exactly.

And what is the organ with which we see the visible things?

The sight, he said.

And with the hearing, I said, we hear, and with the other senses perceive the other objects of sense?

True.

But have you remarked that sight is by far the most costly and complex piece of workmanship which the artificer of the senses ever contrived?

No, I never have, he said.

Then reflect: has the ear or voice need of any third or additional nature in order that the one may be able to hear and the other to be heard?

Nothing of the sort.

No, indeed, I replied; and the same is true of most, if not all, the other senses—you would not say that any of them requires such an addition?

Certainly not.

But you see that without the addition of some other nature there is no seeing or being seen?

How do you mean?

Sight being, as I conceive, in the eyes, and he who has eyes wanting to see; colour being also present in them, still unless there be a third nature specially adapted to the purpose, the owner of the eyes will see nothing and the colours will be invisible.

Of what nature are you speaking?

Of that which you term light, I replied.

True, he said.

Noble, then, is the bond which links together sight and visibility, and great beyond other bonds by no small difference of nature; for light is their bond, and light is no ignoble thing?

Nay, he said, the reverse of ignoble.

And which, I said, of the gods in heaven would you say was the lord of this element? Whose is that light which makes the eye to see perfectly and the visible to appear?

You mean the sun, as you and all mankind say.

May not the relation of sight to this deity be described as follows:

How?

Neither sight nor the eye in which sight resides is the sun?

No.

Yet of all the organs of sense the eye is the most like the sun?

By far the most like.

And the power which the eye possesses is a sort of effluence which is dispensed from the sun?

Exactly.

Then the sun is not sight, but the author of sight who is recognized by sight.

True, he said.

And this is he whom I call the child of the good, whom the good begat in his own likeness, to be in the visible world, in relation to sight and the things of sight, what the good is in the intellectual world in relation to mind and the things of mind.

Will you be a little more explicit? he said.

Why, you know, I said, that the eyes, when a person directs them towards objects on which the light of day is no longer shining, but the moon and stars only, see dimly, and are nearly blind; they seem to have no clearness of vision in them?

Very true.

But when they are directed towards objects on which the sun shines, they see clearly and there is sight in them?

Certainly.

And the soul is like the eye: when resting upon that on which truth and being shine, the soul perceives and understands and is radiant with intelligence; but when turned towards the twilight of becoming and perishing, then she has opinion only, and goes blinking about, and is first of one opinion and then of another, and seems to have no intelligence?

Just so.

Now, that which imports truth to the known and the power of knowing to the knower is what I would have you term the idea of good, and this you will deem to be the cause of science, and of truth in so far as the latter becomes the subject of knowledge; beautiful too, as are both truth and knowledge, you will be right in esteeming this other nature as more beautiful than either; and, as in the previous instance, light and sight may be truly said to be like the sun, and yet not to be the sun, so in this other sphere, science and truth may be deemed to be like the good, but not the good; the good has a place of honour yet higher.

What a wonder of beauty that must be, he said, which is the author of science and truth, and yet surpasses them in beauty; for you surely cannot mean to say that pleasure is the good?

God forbid, I replied; but may I ask you to consider the image in another point of view?

In what point of view?

You would say, would you not, that the sun is not only the author of visibility in all visible things, but of generation and nourishment and growth, though he himself is not generation?

Certainly.

In like manner the good may be said to be not only the author of knowledge to all things known, but of their being and essence, and yet the good is not essence, but far exceeds essence in dignity and power.

Glaucon said, with a ludicrous earnestness: By the light of heaven, how amazing!

Yes, I said, and the exaggeration may be set down to you; for you made me utter my fancies.

And pray continue to utter them; at any rate let us hear if there is anything more to be said about the similitude of the sun.

Yes, I said, there is a great deal more.

Then omit nothing, however slight.

I will do my best, I said; but I should think that a great deal will have to be omitted.

You have to imagine, then, that there are two ruling powers, and that one of them is set over the intellectual world, the other over the visible. I do not say heaven, lest you should fancy that I am playing upon the name. May I suppose that you have this distinction of the visible and intelligible fixed in your mind?

I have.

Now take a line which has been cut into two unequal parts, and divide each of them again in the same proportion, and suppose the two main divisions to answer, one to the visible and the other to the intelligible, and then compare the subdivisions in respect of their clearness and want of clearness, and you will find that the first section in the sphere of the visible consists of images. And by images I mean, in the first place, shadows, and in the second place, reflections in water and in solid, smooth and polished bodies and the like: Do you understand?

Yes, I understand.

Imagine, now, the other section, of which this is only the resemblance, to include the animals which we see, and everything that grows or is made.

Very good.

Would you not admit that both the sections of this division have different degrees of truth, and that the copy is to the original as the sphere of opinion is to the sphere of knowledge?

Most undoubtedly.

Next proceed to consider the manner in which the sphere of the intellectual is to be divided.

In what manner?

Thus:—There are two subdivisions, in the lower of which the soul uses the figures given by the former division as images; the enquiry can only be hypothetical, and instead of going upwards to a principle descends to the other end; in the higher of the two, the soul passes out of hypotheses, and goes up to a principle which is above hypotheses, making no use of images as in the former case, but proceeding only in and through the ideas themselves.

I do not quite understand your meaning, he said.

Then I will try again; you will understand me better when I have made some preliminary remarks. You are aware that students of geometry, arithmetic, and the kindred sciences assume the odd and the even and the figures and three kinds of angles and the like in their several branches of science; these are their hypotheses, which they and every body are supposed to know, and therefore they do not deign to give any account of them either to themselves or others; but they begin with them, and go on until they arrive at last, and in a consistent manner, at their conclusion?

Yes, he said, I know.

And do you not know also that although they make use of the visible forms and reason about them, they are thinking not of these, but of the ideals which they resemble; not of the figures which they draw, but of the absolute square and the absolute diameter, and so on—the forms which they draw or make, and which have shadows and reflections in water of their own, are converted by them into images, but they are really seeking to behold the things themselves, which can only be seen with the eye of the mind?

That is true.

And of this kind I spoke as the intelligible, although in the search after it the soul is compelled to use hypotheses; not ascending to a first principle, because she is unable to rise above the region of hypothesis, but employing the objects of which the shadows below are resemblances in their turn as images, they having in relation to the shadows and reflections of them a greater distinctness, and therefore a higher value.

I understand, he said, that you are speaking of the province of geometry and the sister arts.

And when I speak of the other division of the intelligible, you will understand me to speak of that other sort of knowledge which reason herself attains by the power of dialectic, using the hypotheses not as first principles, but only as hypotheses—that is to say, as steps and points of departure into a world which is above hypotheses, in order that she may soar beyond them to the first principle of the whole; and clinging to this and then to that which depends on this, by successive steps she descends again without the aid of any sensible object, from ideas, through ideas, and in ideas she ends.

I understand you, he replied; not perfectly, for you seem to me to be describing a task which is really tremendous; but, at any rate, I understand you to say that knowledge and being, which the science of dialectic contemplates, are clearer than the notions of the arts, as they are termed, which proceed from hypotheses only: these are also contemplated by the understanding, and not by the senses; yet, because they start from hypotheses and do not ascend to a principle, those who contemplate them appear to you not to exercise the higher reason upon them, although when a first principle is added to them they are cognizable by the higher reason. And the habit which is concerned with geometry and the cognate sciences I suppose that you would term understanding and not reason, as being intermediate between opinion and reason.

You have quite conceived my meaning, I said; and now, corresponding to these four divisions, let there be four faculties in the soul—reason answering to the highest, understanding to the second, faith (or conviction) to the third, and perception of shadows to the last—and let there be a scale of them, and let us suppose that the several faculties have clearness in the same degree that their objects have truths.

I understand, he replied, and give my assent, and accept your arrangement.

* * *

And now, I said, let me show in a figure how far our nature is enlightened or unenlightened:— Behold! human beings living in an underground den, which has a mouth open towards the light and reaching all along the den; here they have been from their childhood, and have their legs and necks chained so that they cannot move, and can only see before them, being prevented by the chains from turning round their heads. Above and behind them a fire is blazing at a distance, and between the fire and the prisoners there is a raised way; and you will see, if you look, a low wall built along the way, like the screen which marionette players have in front of them, over which they show the puppets.

I see.

And do you see, I said, men passing along the wall carrying all sorts of vessels, and statues and figures of animals made of wood and stone and various materials, which appear over the wall? Some of them are talking, others silent.

You have shown me a strange image, and they are strange prisoners.

Like ourselves, I replied; and they see only their own shadows, or the shadows of one another which the fire throws on the opposite wall of the cave?

True, he said; how could they see anything but the shadows if they were never allowed to move their heads?

And of the objects which are being carried in like manner they would only see the shadows?

Yes, he said.

And if they were able to converse with one another, would they not suppose that they were naming what was actually before them?

Very true.

And suppose further that the prison had an echo which came from the other side, would they not be sure to fancy when one of the passers-by spoke that the voice which they heard came from the passing shadow?

No question, he replied.

To them, I said, the truth would be literally nothing but the shadows of the images.

That is certain.

And now look again, and see what will naturally follow if the prisoners are released and disabused of their error. At first, when any of them is liberated and compelled suddenly to stand up and turn his neck round and walk and look towards the light, he will suffer sharp pains; the glare will distress him, and he will be unable to see the realities of which in his former state he had seen the shadows; and then conceive some one saying to him, that what he saw before was an illusion, but that now, when he is approaching nearer to being and his eye is turned towards more real existence, he has a clearer vision,— what will be his reply? And you may further imagine that his instructor is pointing to the objects as they pass and requiring him to name them,—will he not be perplexed? Will he not fancy that the shadows which he formerly saw are truer than the objects which are now shown to him?

Far truer.

And if he is compelled to look straight at the light, will he not have a pain in his eyes which will make him turn away to take refuge in the objects of vision which he can see, and which he will conceive to be in reality clearer than the things which are now being shown to him?

True, he said.

And suppose once more, that he is reluctantly dragged up a steep and rugged ascent, and held fast until he is forced into the presence of the sun himself, is he not likely to be pained and irritated? When he approaches the light his eyes will be dazzled, and he will not be able to see anything at all of what are now called realities.

Not all in a moment, he said.

He will require to grow accustomed to the sight

of the upper world. And first he will see the shadows best, next the reelections of men and other objects in the water, and then the objects themselves; then he will gaze upon the light of the moon and the stars and the spangled heaven; and he will see the sky and the stars by night better than the sun or the light of the sun by day?

Certainly.

Last of all he will be able to see the sun, and not mere reflections of him in the water, but he will see him in his own proper place, and not in another; and he will contemplate him as he is.

Certainly.

He will then proceed to argue that this is he who gives the season and the years, and is the guardian of all that is in the visible world, and in a certain way the cause of all things which he and his fellows have been accustomed to behold?

Clearly, he said, he would first see the sun and then reason about him.

And when he remembered his old habitation, and the wisdom of the den and his fellow-prisoners, do you not suppose that he would felicitate himself on the change, and pity them?

Certainly, he would.

And if they were in the habit of conferring honours among themselves on those who were quickest to observe the passing shadows and to remark which of them went before, and which followed after, and which were together; and who were therefore best able to draw conclusions as to the future, do you think that he would care for such honours and glories, or envy the possessors of them? Would he not say with Homer,

"Better to be the poor servant of a poor master,"

and to endure anything, rather than think as they do and live after their manner?

Yes, he said, I think that he would rather suffer anything than entertain these false notions and live in this miserable manner.

Imagine once more, I said, such a one coming suddenly out of the sun to be replaced in his old situation; would he not be certain to have his eyes full of darkness?

To be sure, he said.

And if there were a contest, and he had to compete in measuring the shadows with the prisoners who had never moved out of the den, while his sight was still weak, and before his eyes had become steady (and the time which would be needed to acquire this new habit of sight might be very considerable), would he not be ridiculous? Men would say of him that up he went and down he came without his eyes; and that it was better not even to think of ascending; and if any one tried to loose another and lead him up to the light, let them only catch the offender, and they would put him to death.

No question, he said.

This entire allegory, I said, you may now append, dear Glaucon, to the previous argument; the prison-house is the world of sight, the light of the fire is the sun, and you will not misapprehend me if you interpret the journey upwards to be the ascent of the soul into the intellectual world according to my poor belief, which, at your desire, I have expressed—whether rightly or wrongly God knows. But, whether true or false, my opinion is that in the world of knowledge the idea of good appears last of all, and is seen only with an effort; and, when seen, is also inferred to be the universal author of all things beautiful and right, parent of light and of the lord of light in this visible world, and the immediate source of reason and truth in the intellectual; and that this is the power upon which he who would act rationally either in public or private life must have his eye fixed.

I agree, he said, as far as I am able to understand you.

Moreover, I said, you must not wonder that those who attain to this beatific vision are unwilling to descend to human affairs; for their souls are ever hastening into the upper world where they desire to dwell; which desire of theirs is very natural, if our allegory may be trusted.

Yes, very natural.

And is there anything surprising in one who passes from divine contemplations to the evil state of man, misbehaving himself in a ridiculous manner; if, while his eyes are blinking and before he has become accustomed to the surrounding darkness, he is compelled to fight in courts of law, or in other places, about the images or the shadows of images of justice, and is endeavouring to meet the conceptions of those who have never yet seen absolute justice?

Anything but surprising, he replied.

Any one who has common sense will remember

that the bewilderments of the eyes are of two kinds, and arise from two causes, either from coming out of the light or from going into the light, which is true of the mind's eye, quite as much as of the bodily eye; and he who remembers this when he sees any one whose vision is perplexed and weak, will not be too ready to laugh; he will first ask whether that soul of man has come out of the brighter life, and is unable to see because unaccustomed to the dark, or having turned from darkness to the day is dazzled by excess of light. And he will count the one happy in his condition and state of being, and he will pity the other; or, if he have a mind to laugh at the soul which comes from below into the light, there will be more reason in this than in the laugh which greets him who returns from above out of the light into the den.

That, he said, is a very just distinction.

But then, if I am right, certain professors of education must be wrong when they say that they can put a knowledge into the soul which was not there before, like sight into blind eyes.

They undoubtedly say this, he replied.

Whereas, our argument shows that the power and capacity of learning exists in the soul already; and that just as the eye was unable to turn from darkness to light without the whole body, so too the instrument of knowledge can only by the movement of the whole soul be turned from the world of becoming into that of being, and learn by degrees to endure the sight of being, and of the brightest and best of being, or in other words, of the good.

Very true.

And must there not be some art which will effect conversion in the easiest and quickest manner; not implanting the faculty of sight, for that exists already, but has been turned in the wrong direction, and is looking away from the truth?

Meditations on First Philosophy

RENÉ DESCARTES

French philosopher René Descartes (1596–1650) is generally regarded as the founder of modern philosophy. Among his many achievements is analytic geometry, which he invented; the "Cartesian coordinate system" carries his name.

Meditation I
Of the things of which we may doubt

Several years have now elapsed since I first became aware that I had accepted, even from my youth, many false opinions for true, and that consequently what I afterwards based on such principles was highly doubtful; and from that time I was convinced of the necessity of undertaking once in my life to rid myself of all the opinions I had adopted, and of commencing anew the work of building from the foundation, if I desired to establish a firm and abiding superstructure in the sciences. But as this enter-prise appeared to me to be one of great magnitude, I waited until I had attained an age so mature as to leave me no hope that at any stage of life more advanced I should be better able to execute my design. On this account, I have delayed so long that I should henceforth consider I was doing wrong were I still to consume in deliberation any of the time that now remains for action. To-day, then, since I have opportunely freed my mind from all cares, [and am happily disturbed by no passions], and since I am in the secure possession of leisure in a peaceable retirement, I will at length apply myself earnestly and freely to the general overthrow of all my former opinions. But, to this end, it will not be necessary for me to show that the whole of these are false—a

Translated by John Veitch.

point, perhaps, which I shall never reach; but as even now my reason convinces me that I ought not the less carefully to withhold belief from what is not entirely certain and indubitable, than from what is manifestly false, it will be sufficient to justify the rejection of the whole if I shall find in each some ground for doubt. Nor for this purpose will it be necessary even to deal with each belief individually, which would be truly an endless labour; but, as the removal from below of the foundation necessarily involves the downfall of the whole edifice, I will at once approach the criticism of the principles on which all my former beliefs rested.

All that I have, up to this moment, accepted as possessed of the highest truth and certainty, I received either from or through the senses. I observed, however, that these sometimes misled us; and it is the part of prudence not to place absolute confidence in that by which we have even once been deceived.

But it may be said, perhaps, that, although the senses occasionally mislead us respecting minute objects, and such as are so far removed from us as to be beyond the reach of close observation, there are yet many other of their informations (presentations), of the truth of which it is manifestly impossible to doubt; as for example, that I am in this place, seated by the fire, clothed in a winter dressing-gown, that I hold in my hands this piece of paper, with other intimations of the same nature. But how could I deny that I possess these hands and this body, and withal escape being classed with persons in a state of insanity, whose brains are so disordered and clouded by dark bilious vapours as to cause them pertinaciously to assert that they are monarchs when they are in the greatest poverty; or clothed [in gold] and purple when destitute of any covering; or that their head is made of clay, their body of glass, or that they are gourds? I should certainly be not less insane than they, were I to regulate my procedure according to examples so extravagant.

Though this be true, I must nevertheless here consider that I am a man, and that, consequently, I am in the habit of sleeping, and representing to myself in dreams those same things, or even sometimes others less probable, which the insane think are presented to them in their waking moments. How often have I dreamt that I was in these familiar circumstances—that I was dressed, and occupied this place by the fire, when I was lying undressed in bed? At the present moment, however, I certainly look upon this paper with eyes wide awake; the head which I now move is not asleep; I extend this hand consciously and with express purpose, and I perceive it; the occurrences in sleep are not so distinct as all this. But I cannot forget that, at other times, I have been deceived in sleep by similar illusions; and, attentively considering those cases, I perceive so clearly that there exist no certain marks by which the state of waking can ever be distinguished from sleep, that I feel greatly astonished; and in amazement I almost persuade myself that I am now dreaming.

Let us suppose, then, that we are dreaming, and that all these particulars—namely, the opening of the eyes, the motion of the head, the forth-putting of the hands—are merely illusions; and even that we really possess neither an entire body nor hands such as we see. Nevertheless, it must be admitted at least that the objects which appear to us in sleep are, as it were, painted representations which could not have been formed unless in the likeness of realities; and, therefore, that those general objects, at all events,—namely, eyes, a head, hands, and an entire body—are not simply imaginary, but really existent. For, in truth, painters themselves, even when they study to represent sirens and satyrs by forms the most fantastic and extraordinary, cannot bestow upon them natures absolutely new, but can only make a certain medley of the members of different animals; or if they chance to imagine something so novel that nothing at all similar has ever been seen before, and such as is, therefore, purely fictitious and absolutely false, it is at least certain that the colours of which this is composed are real.

And on the same principle, although these general objects, viz. a body, eyes, a head, hands, and the like, be imaginary, we are nevertheless absolutely necessitated to admit the reality at least of some other objects still more simple and universal than these, of which, just as of certain real colours, all those images of things, whether true and real, or false and fantastic, that are found in our consciousness (*cogitatio*), are formed.

To this class of objects seem to belong corporeal nature in general and its extension; the figure of extended things, their quantity or magnitude, and their number, as also the place in, and the time during, which they exist, and other things of the same sort. We will not, therefore, perhaps reason illegitimately if we conclude from this that Physics, Astronomy, Medicine, and all the other sciences that have for their end the consideration of composite objects, are indeed of a doubtful character; but that Arithmetic, Geometry, and the other sciences of the same class, which regard merely the simplest and most general objects, and scarcely inquire whether or not these are really existent, contain somewhat that is certain and indubitable: for whether I am awake or dreaming, it remains true that two and three make five, and that a square has but four sides; nor does it seem possible that truths so apparent can ever fall under a suspicion of falsity [or incertitude].

Nevertheless, the belief that there is a God who is all-powerful, and who created me, such as I am, has, for a long time, obtained steady possession of my mind. How, then, do I know that he has not arranged that there should be neither earth, nor sky, nor any extended thing, nor figure, nor magnitude, nor place, providing at the same time, however, for [the rise in me of the perceptions of all these objects, and] the persuasion that these do not exist otherwise than as I perceive them? And further, as I sometimes think that others are in error respecting matters of which they believe themselves to possess a perfect knowledge, how do I know that I am not also deceived each time I add together two and three, or number the sides of a square, or form some judgment still more simple, if more simple indeed can be imagined? But perhaps Deity has not been willing that I should be thus deceived, for He is said to be supremely good. If, however, it were repugnant to the goodness of Deity to have created me subject to constant deception, it would seem likewise to be contrary to his goodness to allow me to be occasionally deceived; and yet it is clear that this is permitted. Some, indeed, might perhaps be found who would be disposed rather to deny the existence of a Being so powerful than to believe that there is nothing certain. But let us for the present refrain from opposing this opinion, and grant that all which is here said of a Deity is fabulous; nevertheless in whatever way it be supposed that I reached the state in which I exist, whether by fate, or chance, or by an endless series of antecedents and consequents, or by

any other means, it is clear (since to be deceived and to err is a certain defect) that the probability of my being so imperfect as to be the constant victim of deception, will be increased exactly in proportion as the power possessed by the cause, to which they assign my origin, is lessened. To these reasonings I have assuredly nothing to reply, but am constrained at last to avow that there is nothing of all that I formerly believed to be true of which it is impossible to doubt, and that not through thoughtlessness or levity, but from cogent and maturely considered reasons; so that henceforward, if I desire to discover anything certain, I ought not the less carefully to refrain from assenting to those same opinions than to what might be shown to be manifestly false.

But it is not sufficient to have made these observations; care must be taken likewise to keep them in remembrance. For those old and customary opinions perpetually recur—long and familiar usage giving them the right of occupying my mind, even almost against my will, and subduing my belief; nor will I lose the habit of deferring to them and confiding in them so long as I shall consider them to be what in truth they are, viz., opinions to some extent doubtful, as I have already shown, but still highly probable, and such as it is much more reasonable to believe than deny. It is for this reason I am persuaded that I shall not be doing wrong, if, taking an opposite judgment of deliberate design, I become my own deceiver, by supposing, for a time, that all those opinions are entirely false and imaginary, until at length, having thus balanced my old by my new prejudices, my judgment shall no longer be turned aside by perverted usage from the path that may conduct to the perception of truth. For I am assured that, meanwhile, there will arise neither peril nor error from this course, and that I cannot for the present yield too much to distrust, since the end I now seek is not action but knowledge.

I will suppose, then, not that Deity, who is sovereignly good and the fountain of truth, but that some malignant demon, who is at once exceedingly potent and deceitful, has employed all his artifice to deceive me; I will suppose that the sky, the air, the earth, colours, figures, sounds, and all external things, are nothing better than the illusions of dreams, by means of which this being has laid snares for my credulity; I will consider myself as without hands, eyes, flesh, blood, or any of the senses, and as falsely believing that I am possessed of these; I will continue resolutely fixed in this belief, and if indeed by this means it be not in my power to arrive at the knowledge of truth, I shall at least do what is in my power, viz., [suspend my judgment], and guard with settled purpose against giving my assent to what is false, and being imposed upon by this deceiver, whatever be his power and artifice.

But this undertaking is arduous, and a certain indolence insensibly leads me back to my ordinary course of life; and just as the captive, who, perchance, was enjoying in his dreams an imaginary liberty, when he begins to suspect that it is but a vision, dreads awakening, and conspires with the agreeable illusions that the deception may be prolonged; so I, of my own accord, fall back into the train of my former beliefs, and fear to arouse myself from my slumber, lest the time of laborious wakefulness that would succeed this quiet rest, in place of bringing any light of day, should prove inadequate to dispel the darkness that will arise from the difficulties that have now been raised.

Meditation II
Of the nature of the human mind; and that it is more easily known than the body

The Meditation of yesterday has filled my mind with so many doubts, that it is no longer in my power to forget them. Nor do I see, meanwhile, any principle on which they can be resolved; and, just as if I had fallen all of a sudden into very deep water, I am so greatly disconcerted as to be unable either to plant my feet firmly on the bottom or sustain myself by swimming on the surface. I will, nevertheless, make an effort, and try anew the same path on which I had entered yesterday, that is, proceed by casting aside all that admits of the slightest doubt, not less than if I had discovered it to be absolutely false; and I will continue always in this track until I shall find something that is certain, or at least, if I can do nothing more, until I shall know with certainty that there is nothing certain. Archimedes, that he might transport the entire globe from the place it occupied to another, demanded only a point that was firm and immoveable; so also, I shall be entitled to entertain the highest expectations, if I am fortunate enough to discover only one thing that is certain and indubitable.

I suppose, accordingly, that all the things which I see are false (fictitious); I believe that none of those objects which my fallacious memory represents ever existed; I suppose that I possess no senses; I believe that body, figure, extension, motion, and place are merely fictions of my mind. What is there, then, that can be esteemed true? Perhaps this only, that there is absolutely nothing certain.

But how do I know that there is not something different altogether from the objects I have now enumerated, of which it is impossible to entertain the slightest doubt? Is there not a God, or some being, by whatever name I may designate him, who causes these thoughts to arise in my mind? But why suppose such a being, for it may be I myself am capable of producing them? Am I, then, at least not something? But I before denied that I possessed senses or a body; I hesitate, however, for what follows from that? Am I so dependent on the body and the senses that without these I cannot exist? But I had the persuasion that there was absolutely nothing in the world, that there was no sky and no earth, neither minds nor bodies; was I not, therefore, at the same time, persuaded that I did not exist? Far from it; I assuredly existed, since I was persuaded. But there is I know not what being, who is possessed at once of the highest power and the deepest cunning, who is constantly employing all his ingenuity in deceiving me. Doubtless, then, I exist, since I am deceived; and, let him deceive me as he may, he can never bring it about that I am nothing, so long as I shall be conscious that I am something. So that it must, in fine, be maintained, all things being maturely and carefully considered, that this proposition (*pronunciatum*) I am, I exist, is necessarily true each time it is expressed by me, or conceived in my mind.

But I do not yet know with sufficient clearness what I am, though assured that I am; and hence, in the next place, I must take care, lest perchance I inconsiderately substitute some other object in room of what is properly myself, and thus wander from truth, even in that knowledge (cognition) which I hold to be of all others the most certain and evident. For this reason, I will now consider anew what I formerly believed myself to be, before I entered on the present train of thought; and of my previous opinion I will retrench all that can in the least be invalidated by the grounds of doubt I have adduced, in order that there may at length remain nothing but what is certain and indubitable. What then did I formerly think I was? Undoubtedly I judged that I was a man. But what is a man? Shall I say a rational animal? Assuredly not; for it would be necessary forthwith to inquire into what is meant by animal, and what by rational, and thus, from a single question, I should insensibly glide into others, and these more difficult than the first; nor do I now possess enough of leisure to warrant me in wasting my time amid subtleties of this sort. I prefer here to attend to the thoughts that sprang up of themselves in my mind, and were inspired by my own nature alone, when I applied myself to the consideration of what I was. In the first place, then, I thought that I possessed a countenance, hands, arms, and all the fabric of members that appears in a corpse, and which I called by the name of body. It further occurred to me that I was nourished, that I walked, perceived, and thought, and all those actions I referred to the soul; but what the soul itself was I either did not stay to consider, or, if I did, I imagined that it was something extremely rare and subtle, like wind, or flame, or ether, spread through my grosser parts. As regarded the body, I did not even doubt of its nature, but thought I distinctly knew it, and if I had wished to describe it according to the notions I then entertained, I should have explained myself in this manner: By body I understand all that can be terminated by a certain figure; that can be comprised in a certain place, and so fill a certain space as therefrom to exclude every other body; that can be perceived either by touch, sight, hearing, taste, or smell; that can be moved in different ways, not indeed of itself, but by something foreign to it by which it is touched [and from which it receives the impression]; for the power of self-motion, as likewise that of perceiving and thinking, I held as by no means pertaining to the nature of body; on the contrary, I was somewhat astonished to find such faculties existing in some bodies.

But [as to myself, what can I now say that I am], since I suppose there exists an extremely powerful, and, if I may so speak, malignant being, whose whole endeavours are directed towards deceiving me? Can I affirm that I possess any one of all those attributes of which I have lately spoken as belonging to the nature of body? After attentively considering them in my own mind, I find none of them that can properly be said to belong to myself. To recount them were idle and tedious. Let us pass, then, to the attributes of the soul. The first mentioned were the powers of nutrition and walking; but, if it be true that I have no body, it is true likewise that I am capable neither of walking nor of being nourished. Perception is another attribute of the soul; but perception too is impossible without the body: besides, I have frequently, during sleep, believed that I perceived objects which I afterwards observed I did not in reality perceive. Thinking is another attribute of the soul; and here I discover what properly belongs to myself. This alone is inseparable from me. I am—I exist: this is certain; but how often? As often as I think; for perhaps it would even happen, if I should wholly cease to think, that I should at the same time altogether cease to be. I now admit nothing that is not necessarily true: I am therefore, precisely speaking, only a thinking thing, that is, a mind (*mens sive animus*), understanding, or reason,—terms whose signification was before unknown to me. I am, however, a real thing, and really existent; but what thing? The answer was, a thinking thing. The question now arises, am I aught besides? I will stimulate my imagination with a view to discovering whether I am not still something more than a thinking being. Now it is plain I am not the assemblage of members called the human body; I am not a thin and penetrating air diffused through all these members, or wind, or flame, or vapour, or breath, or any of all the things I can imagine; for I supposed that all these were not, and, without changing the supposition, I find that I still feel assured of my existence.

But it is true, perhaps, that those very things which I suppose to be non-existent, because they are unknown to me, are not in truth different from myself whom I know. This is a point I cannot determine, and do not now enter into any dispute regarding it. I can only judge of things that are known to me: I am conscious that I exist, and I who know that I exist inquire into what I am. It is, however, perfectly certain that the knowledge of my existence, thus precisely taken, is not dependent on things, the existence of which is as yet unknown to me: and consequently it is not dependent on any of the things I can feign in imagination. Moreover, the phrase itself,

I frame an image (*effingo*), reminds me of my error; for I should in truth frame one if I were to imagine myself to be anything, since to imagine is nothing more than to contemplate the figure or image of a corporeal thing; but I already know that I exist, and that it is possible at the same time that all those images, and in general all that relates to the nature of body, are merely dreams [or chimeras]. From this I discover that it is not more reasonable to say, I will excite my imagination that I may know more distinctly what I am, than to express myself as follows: I am now awake, and perceive something real; but because my perception is not sufficiently clear, I will of express purpose go to sleep that my dreams may represent to me the object of my perception with more truth and clearness. And, therefore, I know that nothing of all that I can embrace in imagination belongs to the knowledge which I have of myself, and that there is need to recall with the utmost care the mind from this mode of thinking, that it may be able to know its own nature with perfect distinctness.

But what, then, am I? A thinking thing, it has been said. But what is a thinking thing? It is a thing that doubts, understands, [conceives], affirms, denies, wills, refuses, that imagines also, and perceives. Assuredly it is not little, if all these properties belong to my nature. But why should they not belong to it? Am I not that very being who now doubts of almost everything; who, for all that, understands and conceives certain things; who affirms one alone as true, and denies the others; who desires to know more of them, and does not wish to be deceived; who imagines many things, sometimes even despite his will; and is likewise percipient of many, as if through the medium of the senses. Is there nothing of all this as true as that I am, even although I should be always dreaming, and although he who gave me being employed all his ingenuity to deceive me? Is there also any one of these attributes that can be properly distinguished from my thought, or that can be said to be separate from myself? For it is of itself so evident that it is I who doubt, I who understand, and I who desire, that it is here unnecessary to add anything by way of rendering it more clear. And I am as certainly the same being who imagines; for, although it may be (as I before supposed) that nothing I imagine is true, still the power of imagination does not cease really to exist in me and to form part of my thought.

In fine, I am the same being who perceives, that is, who apprehends certain objects as by the organs of sense, since, in truth, I see light, hear a noise, and feel heat. But it will be said that these presentations are false, and that I am dreaming. Let it be so. At all events it is certain that I seem to see light, hear a noise, and feel heat; this cannot be false, and this is what in me is properly called perceiving (*sentire*), which is nothing else than thinking. From this I begin to know what I am with somewhat greater clearness and distinctness than heretofore.

But, nevertheless, it still seems to me, and I cannot help believing, that corporeal things, whose images are formed by thought, [which fall under the senses], and are examined by the same, are known with much greater distinctness than that I know not what part of myself which is not imaginable; although, in truth, it may seem strange to say that I know and comprehend with greater distinctness things whose existence appears to me doubtful, that are unknown, and do not belong to me, than others of whose reality I am persuaded, that are known to me, and appertain to my proper nature; in a word, than myself. But I see clearly what is the state of the case. My mind is apt to wander, and will not yet submit to be restrained within the limits of truth. Let us therefore leave the mind to itself once more, and, according to it every kind of liberty, [permit it to consider the objects that appear to it from without], in order that, having afterwards withdrawn it from these gently and opportunely, [and fixed it on the consideration of its being and the properties it finds in itself], it may then be the more easily controlled.

Let us now accordingly consider the objects that are commonly thought to be [the most easily, and likewise] the most distinctly known, viz., the bodies we touch and see; not, indeed, bodies in general, for these general notions are usually somewhat more confused, but one body in particular. Take, for example, this piece of wax; it is quite fresh, having been but recently taken from the bee-hive; it has not yet lost the sweetness of the honey it contained; it still retains somewhat of the odour of the flowers from which it was gathered; its colour, figure, size, are apparent (to the sight); it is hard, cold, easily handled; and sounds when struck upon with the finger. In fine, all that contributes to make a body as distinctly known as possible, is found in the one before us. But, while I am speaking, let it be placed near the fire—what remained of the taste exhales, the smell evaporates, the colour changes, its figure is destroyed, its size increases, it becomes liquid, it grows hot, it can hardly be handled, and, although struck upon, it emits no sound. Does the same wax still remain after this change? It must be admitted that it does remain; no one doubts it, or judges otherwise. What, then, was it I knew with so much distinctness in the piece of wax? Assuredly, it could be nothing of all that I observed by means of the senses, since all the things that fell under taste, smell, sight, touch, and hearing are changed, and yet the same wax remains. It was perhaps what I now think, viz., that this wax was neither the sweetness of honey, the pleasant odour of flowers, the whiteness, the figure, nor the sound, but only a body that a little before appeared to me conspicuous under these forms, and which is now perceived under others. But, to speak precisely, what is it that I imagine when I think of it in this way? Let it be attentively considered, and, retrenching all that does not belong to the wax, let us see what remains. There certainly remains nothing, except something extended, flexible, and movable. But what is meant by flexible and movable? Is it not that I imagine that the piece of wax, being round, is capable of becoming square, or of passing from a square into a triangular figure? Assuredly such is not the case, because I conceive that it admits of an infinity of similar changes; and I am, moreover, unable to compass this infinity by imagination, and consequently this conception which I have of the wax is not the product of the faculty of imagination. But what now is this extension? Is it not also unknown? for it becomes greater when the wax is melted, greater when it is boiled, and greater still when the heat increases; and I should not conceive [clearly and] according to truth, the wax as it is, if I did not suppose that the piece we are considering admitted even of a wider variety of extension than I ever imagined. I must, therefore, admit that I cannot even comprehend by imagination what the piece of wax is, and that it is the mind alone (*mens*, Lat., *entendement*, F.) which perceives it. I speak of one piece in particular; for, as to wax in general, this is still more evident. But what is the piece of wax that can be perceived only by the [understanding or] mind? It is certainly the same which I see, touch, imagine; and,

in fine, it is the same which, from the beginning, I believed it to be. But (and this it is of moment to observe) the perception of it is neither an act of sight, of touch, nor of imagination, and never was either of these, though it might formerly seem so, but is simply an intuition (*inspectio*) of the mind, which may be imperfect and confused, as it formerly was, or very clear and distinct, as it is at present, according as the attention is more or less directed to the elements which it contains, and of which it is composed.

But, meanwhile, I feel greatly astonished when I observe [the weakness of my mind, and] its proneness to error. For although, without at all giving expression to what I think, I consider all this in my own mind, words yet occasionally impede my progress, and I am almost led into error by the terms of ordinary language. We say, for example, that we see the same wax when it is before us, and not that we judge it to be the same from its retaining the same colour and figure: whence I should forthwith be disposed to conclude that the wax is known by the act of sight, and not by the intuition of the mind alone, were it not for the analogous instance of human beings passing on in the street below, as observed from a window. In this case I do not fail to say that I see the men themselves, just as I say that I see the wax; and yet what do I see from the window beyond hats and cloaks that might cover artificial machines, whose motions might be determined by springs? But I judge that there are human beings from these appearances, and thus I comprehend, by the faculty of judgment alone which is in the mind, what I believed I saw with my eyes.

The man who makes it his aim to rise to knowledge superior to the common, ought to be ashamed to seek occasions of doubting from the vulgar forms of speech: instead, therefore, of doing this, I shall proceed with the matter in hand, and inquire whether I had a clearer and more perfect perception of the piece of wax when I first saw it, and when I thought I knew it by means of the external sense itself, or, at all events, by the common sense (*sensus communis*), as it is called, that is, by the imaginative faculty; or whether I rather apprehend it more clearly at present, after having examined with greater care, both what it is, and in what way it can be known. It would certainly be ridiculous to entertain any doubt on this point. For what, in that first perception, was there distinct? What did I perceive which any animal might not have perceived? But when I distinguish the wax from its exterior forms, and when, as if I had stripped it of its vestments, I consider it quite naked, it is certain, although some error may still be found in my judgment, that I cannot, nevertheless, thus apprehend it without possessing a human mind.

But, finally, what shall I say of the mind itself, that is, of myself? for as yet I do not admit that I am anything but mind. What, then! I who seem to possess so distinct an apprehension of the piece of wax,—do I not know myself, both with greater truth and certitude, and also much more distinctly and clearly? For if I judge that the wax exists because I see it, it assuredly follows, much more evidently, that I myself am or exist, for the same reason: for it is possible that what I see may not in truth be wax, and that I do not even possess eyes with which to see anything; but it cannot be that when I see, or, which comes to the same thing, when I think I see, I myself who think am nothing. So likewise, if I judge that the wax exists because I touch it, it will still also follow that I am; and if I determine that my imagination, or any other cause, whatever it be, persuades me of the existence of the wax, I will still draw the same conclusion. And what is here remarked of the piece of wax, is applicable to all the other things that are external to me. And further, if the [notion or] perception of wax appeared to me more precise and distinct, after that not only sight and touch, but many other causes besides, rendered it manifest to my apprehension, with how much greater distinctness must I now know myself, since all the reasons that contribute to the knowledge of the nature of wax, or of any body whatever, manifest still better the nature of my mind? And there are besides so many other things in the mind itself that contribute to the illustration of its nature, that those dependent on the body, to which I have here referred, scarcely merit to be taken into account.

But, in conclusion, I find I have insensibly reverted to the point I desired; for, since it is now manifest to me that bodies themselves are not properly perceived by the senses nor by the faculty of imagination, but by the intellect alone; and since they are not perceived because they are seen and touched,

but only because they are understood [or rightly comprehended by thought], I readily discover that there is nothing more easily or clearly apprehended than my own mind. But because it is difficult to rid one's self so promptly of an opinion to which one has been long accustomed, it will be desirable to tarry for some time at this stage, that, by long continued meditation, I may more deeply impress upon my memory this new knowledge.

Meditation III
Of God: that He exists

I will now close my eyes, I will stop my ears, I will turn away my senses from their objects, I will even efface from my consciousness all the images of corporeal things; or at least, because this can hardly be accomplished, I will consider them as empty and false; and thus, holding converse only with myself, and closely examining my nature, I will endeavour to obtain by degrees a more intimate and familiar knowledge of myself. I am a thinking (conscious) thing, that is, a being who doubts, affirms, denies, knows a few objects, and is ignorant of many,—[who loves, hates], wills, refuses,—who imagines likewise, and perceives; for, as I before remarked, although the things which I perceive or imagine are perhaps nothing at all apart from me [and in themselves], I am nevertheless assured that those modes of consciousness which I call perceptions and imaginations, in as far only as they are modes of consciousness, exist in me. And in the little I have said I think I have summed up all that I really know, or at least all that up to this time I was aware I knew. Now, as I am endeavouring to extend my knowledge more widely, I will use circumspection, and consider with care whether I can still discover in myself anything further which I have not yet hitherto observed. I am certain that I am a thinking thing; but do I not therefore likewise know what is required to render me certain of a truth? In this first knowledge, doubtless, there is nothing that gives me assurance of its truth except the clear and distinct perception of what I affirm, which would not indeed be sufficient to give me the assurance that what I say is true, if it could ever happen that anything I thus clearly and distinctly perceived should prove false; and accordingly it seems to me that I may now take as a general rule, that all that is very clearly and distinctly apprehended (conceived) is true.

Nevertheless I before received and admitted many things as wholly certain and manifest, which yet I afterwards found to be doubtful. What, then, were those? They were the earth, the sky, the stars, and all the other objects which I was in the habit of perceiving by the senses. But what was it that I clearly [and distinctly] perceived in them? Nothing more than that the ideas and the thoughts of those objects were presented to my mind. And even now I do not deny that these ideas are found in my mind. But there was yet another thing which I affirmed, and which, from having been accustomed to believe it, I thought I clearly perceived, although, in truth, I did not perceive it at all; I mean the existence of objects external to me, from which those ideas proceeded, and to which they had a perfect resemblance; and it was here I was mistaken, or if I judged correctly, this assuredly was not to be traced to any knowledge I possessed (the force of my perception, Lat.).

But when I considered any matter in arithmetic and geometry, that was very simple and easy, as, for example, that two and three added together make five, and things of this sort, did I not view them with at least sufficient clearness to warrant me in affirming their truth? Indeed, if I afterwards judged that we ought to doubt of these things, it was for no other reason than because it occurred to me that a God might perhaps have given me such a nature as that I should be deceived, even respecting the matters that appeared to me the most evidently true. But as often as this preconceived opinion of the sovereign power of a God presents itself to my mind, I am constrained to admit that it is easy for him, if he wishes it, to cause me to err, even in matters where I think I possess the highest evidence; and, on the other hand, as often as I direct my attention to things which I think I apprehend with great clearness, I am so persuaded of their truth that I naturally break out into expressions such as these: Deceive me who may, no one will yet ever be able to bring it about that I am not, so long as I shall be conscious that I am, or at any future time cause it to be true that I have never been, it being now true that I am, or make two and three more or less than five, in supposing which, and other like absurdities, I discover a manifest contradiction.

And in truth, as I have no ground for believing that Deity is deceitful, and as, indeed, I have not even considered the reasons by which the existence of a Deity of any kind is established, the ground of doubt that rests only on this supposition is very slight, and, so to speak, metaphysical. But, that I may be able wholly to remove it, I must inquire whether there is a God, as soon as an opportunity of doing so shall present itself; and if I find that there is a God, I must examine likewise whether he can be a deceiver: for, without the knowledge of these two truths, I do not see that I can ever be certain of anything. And that I may be enabled to examine this without interrupting the order of meditation I have proposed to myself [which is, to pass by degrees from the notions that I shall find first in my mind to those I shall afterwards discover in it], it is necessary at this stage to divide all my thoughts into certain classes, and to consider in which of these classes truth and error are, strictly speaking, to be found.

Of my thoughts some are, as it were, images of things, and to these alone properly belongs the name *idea;* as when I think [represent to my mind] a man, a chimera, the sky, an angel, or God. Others, again, have certain other forms; as when I will, fear, affirm, or deny, I always, indeed, apprehend something as the object of my thought, but I also embrace in thought something more than the representation of the object; and of this class of thoughts some are called volitions or affections, and others judgments.

Now, with respect to ideas, if these are considered only in themselves, and are not referred to any object beyond them, they cannot, properly speaking, be false; for, whether I imagine a goat or a chimera, it is not less true that I imagine the one than the other. Nor need we fear that falsity may exist in the will or affections; for, although I may desire objects that are wrong, and even that never existed, it is still true that I desire them. There thus only remain our judgments, in which we must take diligent heed that we be not deceived. But the chief and most ordinary error that arises in them consists in judging that the ideas which are in us are like or conformed to the things that are external to us; for assuredly, if we but considered the ideas themselves as certain modes of our thought (consciousness), without referring them to anything beyond, they would hardly afford any occasion of error.

But, among these ideas, some appear to me to be

innate, others adventitious, and others to be made by myself (factitious); for, as I have the power of conceiving what is called a thing, or a truth, or a thought, it seems to me that I hold this power from no other source than my own nature; but if I now hear a noise, if I see the sun, or if I feel heat, I have all along judged that these sensations proceeded from certain objects existing out of myself; and, in fine, it appears to me that sirens, hippogryphs, and the like, are inventions of my own mind. But I may even perhaps come to be of opinion that all my ideas are of the class which I call adventitious, or that they are all innate, or that they are all factitious, for I have not yet clearly discovered their true origin; and what I have here principally to do is to consider, with reference to those that appear to come from certain objects without me, what grounds there are for thinking them like these objects.

The first of these grounds is that it seems to me I am so taught by nature; and the second that I am conscious that those ideas are not dependent on my will, and therefore not on myself, for they are frequently presented to me against my will,—as at present, whether I will or not, I feel heat; and I am thus persuaded that this sensation or idea (*sensum vel ideam*) of heat is produced in me by something different from myself, viz., by the heat of the fire by which I sit. And it is very reasonable to suppose that this object impresses me with its own likeness rather than any other thing.

But I must consider whether these reasons are sufficiently strong and convincing. When I speak of being taught by nature in this matter, I understand by the word nature only a certain spontaneous impetus that impels me to believe in a resemblance between ideas and their objects, and not a natural light that affords a knowledge of its truth. But these two things are widely different; for what the natural light shows to be true can be in no degree doubtful, as, for example, that I am because I doubt, and other truths of the like kind: inasmuch as I possess no other faculty whereby to distinguish truth from error, which can teach me the falsity of what the natural light declares to be true, and which is equally trustworthy; but with respect to [seemingly] natural impulses, I have observed, when the question related to the choice of right or wrong in action, that they frequently led me to take the worse part; nor do I see that I have any better ground for following them in what relates to truth and error. Then, with respect to the other reason, which is that because these ideas do not depend on my will, they must arise from objects existing without me, I do not find it more convincing than the former; for, just as those natural impulses, of which I have lately spoken, are found in me, notwithstanding that they are not always in harmony with my will, so likewise it may be that I possess some power not sufficiently known to myself capable of producing ideas without the aid of external objects, and, indeed, it has always hitherto appeared to me that they are formed during sleep, by some power of this nature, without the aid of aught external. And, in fine, although I should grant that they proceeded from those objects, it is not a necessary consequence that they must be like them. On the contrary, I have observed, in a number of instances, that there was a great difference between the object and its idea. Thus, for example, I find in my mind two wholly diverse ideas of the sun; the one, by which it appears to me extremely small, draws its origin from the senses, and should be placed in the class of adventitious ideas; the other, by which it seems to be many times larger than the whole earth, is taken up on astronomical grounds, that is, elicited from certain notions born with me, or is framed by myself in some other manner. These two ideas cannot certainly both resemble the same sun; and reason teaches me that the one which seems to have immediately emanated from it is the most unlike. And these things sufficiently prove that hitherto it has not been from a certain and deliberate judgment, but only from a sort of blind impulse, that I believed in the existence of certain things different from myself, which, by the organs of sense, or by whatever other means it might be, conveyed their ideas or images into my mind [and impressed it with their likenesses].

But there is still another way of inquiring whether, of the objects whose ideas are in my mind, there are any that exist out of me. If ideas are taken in so far only as they are certain modes of consciousness, I do not remark any difference or inequality among them, and all seem, in the same manner, to proceed from myself; but, considering them as images, of which one represents one thing and another a different, it is evident that a great diversity obtains among them. For, without doubt, those that represent substances are something more, and contain in themselves, so to speak, more objective reality [that is, participate by representation in higher degrees of being or perfection], than those that represent only modes or accidents; and again, the idea by which I conceive a God [sovereign], eternal, infinite, [immutable], all-knowing, all-powerful, and the creator of all things that are out of himself,—this, I say, has certainly in it more objective reality than those ideas by which finite substances are represented.

Now, it is manifest by the natural light that there must at least be as much reality in the efficient and total cause as in its effect; for whence can the effect draw its reality if not from its cause? and how could the cause communicate to it this reality unless it possessed it in itself? And hence it follows, not only that what is cannot be produced by what is not, but likewise that the more perfect,—in other words, that which contains in itself more reality,—cannot be the effect of the less perfect: and this is not only evidently true of those effects, whose reality is actual or formal, but likewise of ideas, whose reality is only considered as objective. Thus, for example, the stone that is not yet in existence, not only cannot now commence to be, unless it be produced by that which possesses in itself, formally or eminently, all that enters into its composition, [in other words, by that which contains in itself the same properties that are in the stone, or others superior to them]; and heat can only be produced in a subject that was before devoid of it, by a cause that is of an order [degree or kind], at least as perfect as heat; and so of the others. But further, even the idea of the heat, or of the stone, cannot exist in me unless it be put there by a cause that contains, at least, as much reality as I conceive existent in the heat or in the stone: for, although that cause may not transmit into my idea anything of its actual or formal reality, we ought not on this account to imagine that it is less real; but we ought to consider that, [as every idea is a work of the mind], its nature is such as of itself to demand no other formal reality than that which it borrows from our consciousness, of which it is but a mode, [that is, a manner or way of thinking]. But in order that an idea may contain this objective reality rather than that, it must doubtless derive it from some cause in which is found at least as much formal reality as the

idea contains of objective; for, if we suppose that there is found in an idea anything which was not in its cause, it must of course derive this from nothing. But, however imperfect may be the mode of existence by which a thing is objectively [or by representation] in the understanding by its idea, we certainly cannot, for all that, allege that this mode of existence is nothing, nor, consequently, that the idea owes its origin to nothing. Nor must it be imagined that, since the reality which is considered in these ideas is only objective, the same reality need not be formally (actually) in the causes of these ideas, but only objectively: for, just as the mode of existing objectively belongs to ideas by their peculiar nature, so likewise the mode of existing formally appertains to the causes of these ideas (at least to the first and principal), by their peculiar nature. And although an idea may give rise to another idea, this regress cannot, nevertheless, be infinite; we must in the end reach a first idea, the cause of which is, as it were, the archetype in which all the reality [or perfection] that is found objectively [or by representation] in these ideas is contained formally [and in act]. I am thus clearly taught by the natural light that ideas exist in me as pictures or images, which may in truth readily fall short of the perfection of the objects from which they are taken, but can never contain anything greater or more perfect.

And in proportion to the time and care with which I examine all those matters, the conviction of their truth brightens and becomes distinct. But, to sum up, what conclusion shall I draw from it all? It is this;—if the objective reality [or perfection] of any one of my ideas be such as clearly to convince me, that this same reality exists in me neither formally nor eminently, and if, as follows from this, I myself cannot be the cause of it, it is a necessary consequence that I am not alone in the world, but that there is besides myself some other being who exists as the cause of that idea; while, on the contrary, if no such idea be found in my mind, I shall have no sufficient ground of assurance of the existence of any other being besides myself; for, after a most careful search, I have, up to this moment, been unable to discover any other ground.

But, among these my ideas, besides that which represents myself, respecting which there can be here no difficulty, there is one that represents a

God; others that represent corporeal and inanimate things; others angels; others animals; and, finally, there are some that represent men like myself. But with respect to the ideas that represent other men, or animals, or angels, I can easily suppose that they were formed by the mingling and composition of the other ideas which I have of myself, of corporeal things, and of God, although there were, apart from myself, neither men, animals, nor angels. And with regard to the ideas of corporeal objects, I never discovered in them anything so great or excellent which I myself did not appear capable of originating; for, by considering these ideas closely and scrutinising them individually, in the same way that I yesterday examined the idea of wax, I find that there is but little in them that is clearly and distinctly perceived. As belonging to the class of things that are clearly apprehended, I recognise the following, viz., magnitude or extension in length, breadth, and depth; figure, which results from the termination of extension; situation, which bodies of diverse figures preserve with reference to each other; and motion or the change of situation; to which may be added substance, duration, and number. But with regard to light, colours, sounds, odours, tastes, heat, cold, and the other tactile qualities, they are thought with so much obscurity and confusion, that I cannot determine even whether they are true or false; in other words, whether or not the ideas I have of these qualities are in truth the ideas of real objects. For although I before remarked that it is only in judgments that formal falsity, or falsity properly so called, can be met with, there may nevertheless be found in ideas a certain material falsity, which arises when they represent what is nothing as if it were something. Thus, for example, the ideas I have of cold and heat are so far from being clear and distinct, that I am unable from them to discover whether cold is only the privation of heat, or heat the privation of cold; or whether they are not real qualities: and since, ideas being as it were images, there can be none that does not seem to us to represent some object, the idea which represents cold as something real and positive will not improperly be called false, if it be correct to say that cold is nothing but a privation of heat; and so in other cases. To ideas of this kind, indeed, it is not necessary that I should assign any author besides myself: for if they are false, that is, represent objects that are unreal, the natural light teaches me that they proceed from nothing; in other words, that they are in me only because something is wanting to the perfection of my nature; but if these ideas are true, yet because they exhibit to me so little reality that I cannot even distinguish the object represented from non-being, I do not see why I should not be the author of them.

With reference to those ideas of corporeal things that are clear and distinct, there are some which, as appears to me, might have been taken from the idea I have of myself, as those of substance, duration, number, and the like. For when I think that a stone is a substance, or a thing capable of existing of itself, and that I am likewise a substance, although I conceive that I am a thinking and non-extended thing, and that the stone, on the contrary, is extended and unconscious, there being thus the greatest diversity between the two concepts,—yet these two ideas seem to have this in common that they both represent substances. In the same way, when I think of myself as now existing, and recollect besides that I existed some time ago, and when I am conscious of various thoughts whose number I know, I then acquire the ideas of duration and number, which I can afterwards transfer to as many objects as I please. With respect to the other qualities that go to make up the ideas of corporeal objects, viz., extension, figure, situation, and motion, it is true that they are not formally in me, since I am merely a thinking being; but because they are only certain modes of substance, and because I myself am a substance, it seems possible that they may be contained in me eminently.

There only remains, therefore, the idea of God, in which I must consider whether there is anything that cannot be supposed to originate with myself. By the name God, I understand a substance infinite, [eternal, immutable], independent, all-knowing, allpowerful, and by which I myself, and every other thing that exists, if any such there be, were created. But these properties are so great and excellent, that the more attentively I consider them the less I feel persuaded that the idea I have of them owes its origin to myself alone. And thus it is absolutely necessary to conclude, from all that I have before said, that God exists: for though the idea of substance be in my mind owing to this, that I myself am a substance, I should not, however, have the idea of an infinite substance, seeing I am a finite being, unless it were given me by some substance in reality infinite.

And I must not imagine that I do not apprehend the infinite by a true idea, but only by the negation of the finite, in the same way that I comprehend repose and darkness by the negation of motion and light: since, on the contrary, I clearly perceive that there is more reality in the infinite substance than in the finite, and therefore that in some way I possess the perception (notion) of the infinite before that of the finite, that is, the perception of God before that of myself, for how could I know that I doubt, desire, or that something is wanting to me, and that I am not wholly perfect, if I possessed no idea of a being more perfect than myself, by comparison of which I knew the deficiencies of my nature?

And it cannot be said that this idea of God is perhaps materially false, and consequently that it may have arisen from nothing, [in other words, that it may exist in me from my imperfection], as I before said of the ideas of heat and cold, and the like: for, on the contrary, as this idea is very clear and distinct, and contains in itself more objective reality than any other, there can be no one of itself more true, or less open to the suspicion of falsity.

The idea, I say, of a being supremely perfect, and infinite, is in the highest degree true; for although, perhaps, we may imagine that such a being does not exist, we cannot, nevertheless, suppose that his idea represents nothing real, as I have already said of the idea of cold. It is likewise clear and distinct in the highest degree, since whatever the mind clearly and distinctly conceives as real or true, and as implying any perfection, is contained entire in this idea. And this is true, nevertheless, although I do not comprehend the infinite, and although there may be in God an infinity of things that I cannot comprehend, nor perhaps even compass by thought in any way; for it is of the nature of the infinite that it should not be comprehended by the finite; and it is enough that I rightly understand this, and judge that all which I clearly perceive, and in which I know there is some perfection, and perhaps also an infinity of properties of which I am ignorant, are formally or eminently in God, in order that the idea I have of him may become the most true, clear, and distinct of all the ideas in my mind.

But perhaps I am something more than I suppose myself to be, and it may be that all those perfections which I attribute to God, in some way exist potentially in me, although they do not yet show themselves, and are not reduced to act. Indeed, I am already conscious that my knowledge is being increased [and perfected] by degrees; and I see nothing to prevent it from thus gradually increasing to infinity, nor any reason why, after such increase and perfection, I should not be able thereby to acquire all the other perfections of the Divine nature; nor, in fine, why the power I possess of acquiring those perfections, if it really now exist in me, should not be sufficient to produce the ideas of them. Yet, on looking more closely into the matter, I discover that this cannot be; for, in the first place, although it were true that my knowledge daily acquired new degrees of perfection, and although there were potentially in my nature much that was not as yet actually in it, still all these excellences make not the slightest approach to the idea I have of the Deity, in whom there is no perfection merely potentially [but all actually] existent; for it is even an unmistakable token of imperfection in my knowledge, that it is augmented by degrees. Further, although my knowledge increase more and more, nevertheless I am not, therefore, induced to think that it will ever be actually infinite, since it can never reach that point beyond which it shall be incapable of further increase. But I conceive God as actually infinite, so that nothing can be added to his perfection. And, in fine, I readily perceive that the objective being of an idea cannot be produced by a being that is merely potentially existent, which, properly speaking, is nothing, but only by a being existing formally or actually.

And, truly, I see nothing in all that I have now said which it is not easy for any one, who shall carefully consider it, to discern by the natural light; but when I allow my attention in some degree to relax, the vision of my mind being obscured, and, as it were, blinded by the images of sensible objects, I do not readily remember the reason why the idea of a being more perfect than myself, must of necessity have proceeded from a being in reality more perfect. On this account I am here desirous to inquire further, whether I, who possess this idea of God, could exist supposing there were no God. And I ask, from whom could I, in that case, derive my existence?

Perhaps from myself, or from my parents, or from some other causes less perfect than God; for anything more perfect, or even equal to God, cannot be thought or imagined. But if I [were independent of every other existence, and] were myself the author of my being, I should doubt of nothing, I should desire nothing, and, in fine, no perfection would be awanting to me; for I should have bestowed upon myself every perfection of which I possess the idea, and I should thus be God. And it must not be imagined that what is now wanting to me is perhaps of more difficult acquisition than that of which I am already possessed; for, on the contrary, it is quite manifest that it was a matter of much higher difficulty that I, a thinking being, should arise from nothing, than it would be for me to acquire the knowledge of many things of which I am ignorant, and which are merely the accidents of a thinking substance; and certainly, if I possessed of myself the greater perfection of which I have now spoken, [in other words, if I were the author of my own existence], I would not at least have denied to myself things that may be more easily obtained, [as that infinite variety of knowledge of which I am at present destitute]. I could not, indeed, have denied to myself any property which I perceive is contained in the idea of God, because there is none of these that seems to me to be more difficult to make or acquire; and if there were any that should happen to be more difficult to acquire, they would certainly appear so to me (supposing that I myself were the source of the other things I possess), because I should discover in them a limit to my power. And though I were to suppose that I always was as I now am, I should not, on this ground, escape the force of these reasonings, since it would not follow, even on this supposition, that no author of my existence needed to be sought after. For the whole time of my life may be divided into an infinity of parts, each of which is in no way dependent on any other; and, accordingly, because I was in existence a short time ago, it does not follow that I must now exist, unless in this moment some cause create me anew as it were,—that is, conserve me. In truth, it is perfectly clear and evident to all who will attentively consider the nature of duration, that the conservation of a substance, in each moment of its duration, requires the same power and act that would be necessary to create it, supposing it were not yet in existence; so that it is manifestly a dictate of the natural light that conservation and creation differ merely in respect of our mode of thinking [and not in reality]. All that is here required, therefore, is that I interrogate myself to discover whether I possess any power by means of which I can bring it about that I, who now am, shall exist a moment afterwards; for, since I am merely a thinking thing (or since, at least, the precise question, in the meantime, is only of that part of myself), if such a power resided in me, I should, without doubt, be conscious of it; but I am conscious of no such power, and thereby I manifestly know that I am dependent upon some being different from myself.

But perhaps the being upon whom I am dependent, is not God, and I have been produced either by my parents, or by some causes less perfect than Deity. This cannot be: for, as I before said, it is perfectly evident that there must at least be as much reality in the cause as in its effect; and accordingly, since I am a thinking thing, and possess in myself an idea of God, whatever in the end be the cause of my existence, it must of necessity be admitted that it is likewise a thinking being, and that it possesses in itself the idea and all the perfections I attribute to Deity. Then it may again be inquired whether this cause owes its origin and existence to itself, or to some other cause. For if it be self-existent, it follows, from what I have before laid down, that this cause is God; for, since it possesses the perfection of self-existence, it must likewise, without doubt, have the power of actually possessing every perfection of which it has the idea,—in other words, all the perfections I conceive to belong to God. But if it owe its existence to another cause than itself, we demand again, for a similar reason, whether this second cause exists of itself or through some other, until, from stage to stage, we at length arrive at an ultimate cause, which will be God. And it is quite manifest that in this matter there can be no infinite regress of causes, seeing that the question raised respects not so much the cause which once produced me, as that by which I am at this present moment conserved.

Nor can it be supposed that several causes concurred in my production, and that from one I received the idea of one of the perfections I attribute to Deity, and from another the idea of some other, and thus that all those perfections are indeed found somewhere in the universe, but do not all exist together in a single being who is God; for, on the contrary, the unity, the simplicity or inseparability of all the properties of Deity, is one of the chief perfections I conceive him to possess; and the idea of this unity of all the perfections of Deity could certainly not be put into my mind by any cause from which I did not likewise receive the ideas of all the other perfections; for no power could enable me to embrace them in an inseparable unity, without at the same time giving me the knowledge of what they were [and of their existence in a particular mode].

Finally, with regard to my parents [from whom it appears I sprung], although all that I believed respecting them be true, it does not, nevertheless, follow that I am conserved by them, or even that I was produced by them, in so far as I am a thinking being. All that, at the most, they contributed to my origin was the giving of certain dispositions (modifications) to the matter in which I have hitherto judged that I or my mind, which is what alone I now consider to be myself, is enclosed; and thus there can here be no difficulty with respect to them, and it is absolutely necessary to conclude from this alone that I am, and possess the idea of a being absolutely perfect, that is, of God, that his existence is most clearly demonstrated.

There remains only the inquiry as to the way in which I received this idea from God; for I have not drawn it from the senses, nor is it even presented to me unexpectedly, as is usual with the ideas of sensible objects, when these are presented or appear to be presented to the external organs of the senses; it is not even a pure production or fiction of my mind, for it is not in my power to take from or add to it; and consequently there but remains the alternative that it is innate, in the same way as is the idea of myself. And, in truth, it is not to be wondered at that God, at my creation, implanted this idea in me, that it might serve, as it were, for the mark of the workman impressed on his work; and it is not also necessary that the mark should be something different from the work itself; but considering only that God is my creator, it is highly probable that he in some way fashioned me after his own image and likeness, and that I perceive this likeness, in which is contained the idea of God, by the same faculty by which I apprehend myself,—in other words, when I make my-

self the object of reflection, I not only find that I am an incomplete, [imperfect] and dependent being, and one who unceasingly aspires after something better and greater than he is; but, at the same time, I am assured likewise that he upon whom I am dependent possesses in himself all the goods after which I aspire, [and the ideas of which I find in my mind], and that not merely indefinitely and potentially, but infinitely and actually, and that he is thus God. And the whole force of the argument of which I have here availed myself to establish the existence of God, consists in this, that I perceive I could not possibly be of such a nature as I am, and yet have in my mind the idea of a God, if God did not in reality exist,—this same God, I say, whose idea is in my mind—that is, a being who possesses all those lofty perfections, of which the mind may have some slight conception, without, however, being able fully to comprehend them—and who is wholly superior to all defect, [and has nothing that marks imperfection]: whence it is sufficiently manifest that he cannot be a deceiver, since it is a dictate of the natural light that all fraud and deception spring from some defect.

But before I examine this with more attention, and pass on to the consideration of other truths that may be evolved out of it, I think it proper to remain here for some time in the contemplation of God himself—that I may ponder at leisure his marvellous attributes—and behold, admire, and adore the beauty of this light so unspeakably great, as far, at least, as the strength of my mind, which is to some degree dazzled by the sight, will permit. For just as we learn by faith that the supreme felicity of another life consists in the contemplation of the Divine majesty alone, so even now we learn from experience that a like meditation, though incomparably less perfect, is the source of the highest satisfaction of which we are susceptible in this life.

Meditation IV
Of truth and error

I have been habituated these bygone days to detach my mind from the senses, and I have accurately observed that there is exceedingly little which is known with certainty respecting corporeal objects,—that we know much more of the human mind, and still more of God himself. I am thus able now without difficulty to abstract my mind from the contemplation of [sensible of] imaginable objects, and apply it to those which, as disengaged from all matter, are purely intelligible. And certainly the idea I have of the human mind in so far as it is a thinking thing, and not extended in length, breadth, and depth, and participating in none of the properties of body, is incomparably more distinct than the idea of any corporeal object; and when I consider that I doubt, in other words, that I am an incomplete and dependent being, the idea of a complete and independent being, that is to say of God, occurs to my mind with so much clearness and distinctness,—and from the fact alone that this idea is found in me, or that I who possess it exist, the conclusions that God exists, and that my own existence, each moment of its continuance, is absolutely dependent upon him, are so manifest,—as to lead me to believe it impossible that the human mind can know anything with more clearness and certitude. And now I seem to discover a path that will conduct us from the contemplation of the true God, in whom are contained all the treasures of science and wisdom, to the knowledge of the other things in the universe.

For, in the first place, I discover that it is impossible for him ever to deceive me, for in all fraud and deceit there is a certain imperfection: and although it may seem that the ability to deceive is a mark of subtlety or power, yet the will testifies without doubt of malice and weakness; and such, accordingly, cannot be found in God. In the next place, I am conscious that I possess a certain faculty of judging [or discerning truth from error], which I doubtless received from God, along with whatever else is mine; and since it is impossible that he should will to deceive me, it is likewise certain that he has not given me a faculty that will ever lead me into error, provided I use it aright.

And there would remain no doubt on this head, did it not seem to follow from this, that I can never therefore be deceived; for if all I possess be from God, and if he planted in me no faculty that is deceitful, it seems to follow that I can never fall into error. Accordingly, it is true that when I think only of God (when I look upon myself as coming from God, Fr.), and turn wholly to him, I discover [in myself] no cause of error or falsity: but immediately there-

after, recurring to myself, experience assures me that I am nevertheless subject to innumerable errors. When I come to inquire into the cause of these, I observe that there is not only present to my consciousness a real and positive idea of God, or of a being supremely perfect, but also, so to speak, a certain negative idea of nothing,—in other words, of that which is at an infinite distance from every sort of perfection, and that I am, as it were, a mean between God and nothing, or placed in such a way between absolute existence and non-existence, that there is in truth nothing in me to lead me into error, in so far as an absolute being is my creator; but that, on the other hand, as I thus likewise participate in some degree of nothing or of non-being, in other words, as I am not myself the supreme Being, and as I am wanting in many perfections, it is not surprising I should fall into error. And I hence discern that error, so far as error is not something real, which depends for its existence on God, but is simply defect; and therefore that, in order to fall into it, it is not necessary God should have given me a faculty expressly for this end, but that my being deceived arises from the circumstance that the power which God has given me of discerning truth from error is not infinite.

Nevertheless this is not yet quite satisfactory; for error is not a pure negation, [in other words, it is not the simple deficiency or want of some knowledge which is not due], but the privation or want of some knowledge which it would seem I ought to possess. But, on considering the nature of God, it seems impossible that he should have planted in his creature any faculty not perfect in its kind, that is, wanting in some perfection due to it: for if it be true, that in proportion to the skill of the maker the perfection of his work is greater, what thing can have been produced by the supreme Creator of the universe that is not absolutely perfect in all its parts? And assuredly there is no doubt that God could have created me such as that I should never be deceived; it is certain, likewise, that he always wills what is best; is it better, then, that I should be capable of being deceived than that I should not?

Considering this more attentively, the first thing that occurs to me is the reflection that I must not be surprised if I am not always capable of comprehending the reasons why God acts as he does; nor must I doubt of his existence because I find, perhaps, that there are several other things besides the present respecting which I understand neither why nor how they were created by him; for, knowing already that my nature is extremely weak and limited, and that the nature of God, on the other hand, is immense, incomprehensible, and infinite, I have no longer any difficulty in discerning that there is an infinity of things in his power whose causes transcend the grasp of my mind: and this consideration alone is sufficient to convince me, that the whole class of final causes is of no avail in physical [or natural] things; for it appears to me that I cannot, without exposing myself to the charge of temerity, seek to discover the [impenetrable] ends of Deity.

It further occurs to me that we must not consider only one creature apart from the others, if we wish to determine the perfection of the works of Deity, but generally all his creatures together; for the same object that might perhaps, with some show of reason, be deemed highly imperfect if it were alone in the world, may for all that be the most perfect possible, considered as forming part of the whole universe: and although, as it was my purpose to doubt of everything, I only as yet know with certainty my own existence and that of God, nevertheless, after having remarked the infinite power of Deity, I cannot deny that he may have produced many other objects, or at least that he is able to produce them, so that I may occupy a place in the relation of a part to the great whole of his creatures.

Whereupon, regarding myself more closely, and considering what my errors are (which alone testify to the existence of imperfection in me), I observe that these depend on the concurrence of two causes, viz., the faculty of cognition which I possess, and that of election or the power of free choice,—in other words, the understanding and the will. For by the understanding alone, I [neither affirm nor deny anything, but] merely apprehend (*percipio*) the ideas regarding which I may form a judgment; nor is any error, properly so called, found in it thus accurately taken. And although there are perhaps innumerable objects in the world of which I have no idea in my understanding, it cannot, on that account, be said that I am deprived of those ideas [as of something that is due to my nature], but simply that I do not possess them, because, in truth, there is no ground to prove that Deity ought to have endowed me with

a larger faculty of cognition than he has actually bestowed upon me; and however skilful a workman I suppose him to be, I have no reason, on that account, to think that it was obligatory on him to give to each of his works all the perfections he is able to bestow upon some. Nor, moreover, can I complain that God has not given me freedom of choice, or a will sufficiently ample and perfect, since, in truth, I am conscious of will so ample and extended as to be superior to all limits. And what appears to me here to be highly remarkable is that, of all the other properties I possess, there is none so great and perfect as that I do not clearly discern it could be still greater and more perfect. For, to take an example, if I consider the faculty of understanding which I possess, I find that it is of very small extent, and greatly limited, and at the same time I form the idea of another faculty of the same nature, much more ample and even infinite; and seeing that I can frame the idea of it, I discover, from this circumstance alone, that it pertains to the nature of God. In the same way, if I examine the faculty of memory or imagination, or any other faculty I possess, I find none that is not small and circumscribed, and in God immense [and infinite]. It is the faculty of will only, or freedom of choice, which I experience to be so great that I am unable to conceive the idea of another that shall be more ample and extended; so that it is chiefly my will which leads me to discern that I bear a certain image and similitude of Deity. For although the faculty of will is incomparably greater in God than in myself, as well in respect of the knowledge and power that are conjoined with it, and that render it stronger and more efficacious, as in respect of the object, since in him it extends to a greater number of things, it does not, nevertheless, appear to me greater, considered in itself formally and precisely: for the power of will consists only in this, that we are able to do or not to do the same thing (that is, to affirm or deny, to pursue or shun it), or rather in this alone, that in affirming or denying, pursuing or shunning, what is proposed to us by the understanding, we so act that we are not conscious of being determined to a particular action by any external force. For, to the possession of freedom, it is not necessary that I be alike indifferent towards each of two contraries; but, on the contrary, the more I am inclined towards the one, whether because I clearly know that in it there is the reason of truth and goodness, or because God thus internally disposes my thought, the more freely do I choose and embrace it; and assuredly divine grace and natural knowledge, very far from diminishing liberty, rather augment and fortify it. But the indifference of which I am conscious when I am not impelled to one side rather than to another for want of a reason, is the lowest grade of liberty, and manifests defect or negation of knowledge rather than perfection of will; for if I always clearly knew what was true and good, I should never have any difficulty in determining what judgment I ought to come to, and what choice I ought to make, and I should thus be entirely free without ever being indifferent.

From all this I discover, however, that neither the power of willing, which I have received from God, is of itself the source of my errors, for it is exceedingly ample and perfect in its kind; nor even the power of understanding, for as I conceive no object unless by means of the faculty that God bestowed upon me, all that I conceive is doubtless rightly conceived by me, and it is impossible for me to be deceived in it.

Whence, then, spring my errors? They arise from this cause alone, that I do not restrain the will, which is of much wider range than the understanding, within the same limits, but extend it even to things I do not understand, and as the will is of itself indifferent to such, it readily falls into error and sin by choosing the false in room of the true, and evil instead of good.

For example, when I lately considered whether aught really existed in the world, and found that because I considered this question, it very manifestly followed that I myself existed, I could not but judge that what I so clearly conceived was true, not that I was forced to this judgment by any external cause, but simply because great clearness of the understanding was succeeded by strong inclination in the will; and I believed this the more freely and spontaneously in proportion as I was less indifferent with respect to it. But now I not only know that I exist, in so far as I am a thinking being, but there is likewise presented to my mind a certain idea of corporeal nature; hence I am in doubt as to whether the thinking nature which is in me, or rather which I myself am, is different from that corporeal nature, or whether both are merely one and the same thing, and I here suppose that I am as yet ignorant of any

reason that would determine me to adopt the one belief in preference to the other: whence it happens that it is a matter of perfect indifference to me which of the two suppositions I affirm or deny, or whether I form any judgment at all in the matter.

This indifference, moreover, extends not only to things of which the understanding has no knowledge at all, but in general also to all those which it does not discover with perfect clearness at the moment the will is deliberating upon them; for, however probable the conjectures may be that dispose me to form a judgment in a particular matter, the simple knowledge that these are merely conjectures, and not certain and indubitable reasons, is sufficient to lead me to form one that is directly the opposite. Of this I lately had abundant experience, when I laid aside as false all that I had before held for true, on the single ground that I could in some degree doubt of it. But if I abstain from judging of a thing when I do not conceive it with sufficient clearness and distinctness, it is plain that I act rightly, and am not deceived; but if I resolve to deny or affirm, I then do not make a right use of my free will; and if I affirm what is false, it is evident that I am deceived: moreover, even although I judge according to truth, I stumble upon it by chance, and do not therefore escape the imputation of a wrong use of my freedom; for it is a dictate of the natural light, that the knowledge of the understanding ought always to precede the determination of the will.

And it is this wrong use of the freedom of the will in which is found the privation that constitutes the form of error. Privation, I say, is found in the act, in so far as it proceeds from myself, but it does not exist in the faculty which I received from God, nor even in the act, in so far as it depends on him; for I have assuredly no reason to complain that God has not given me a greater power of intelligence or more perfect natural light than he has actually bestowed, since it is of the nature of a finite understanding not to comprehend many things, and of the nature of a created understanding to be finite; on the contrary, I have every reason to render thanks to God, who owed me nothing, for having given me all the perfections I possess, and I should be far from thinking that he has unjustly deprived me of, or kept back, the other perfections which he has not bestowed upon me.

I have no reason, moreover, to complain because

he has given me a will more ample than my under-standing, since, as the will consists only of a single el-ement, and that indivisible, it would appear that this faculty is of such a nature that nothing could be taken from it [without destroying it]: and certainly, the more extensive it is, the more cause I have to thank the goodness of him who bestowed it upon me.

And, finally, I ought not also to complain that God concurs with me in forming the acts of this will, or the judgments in which I am deceived, because those acts are wholly true and good, in so far as they depend on God; and the ability to form them is a higher degree of perfection in my nature than the want of it would be. With regard to privation, in which alone consists the formal reason of error and sin, this does not require the concurrence of Deity, because it is not a thing [or existence], and if it be referred to God as to its cause, it ought not to be called privation, but negation, [according to the sig-nification of these words in the schools]. For in truth it is no imperfection in Deity that he has accorded to me the power of giving or withholding my assent from certain things of which he has not put a clear and distinct knowledge in my understanding; but it is doubtless an imperfection in me that I do not use my freedom aright, and readily give my judg-ment on matters which I only obscurely and confus-edly conceive.

I perceive, nevertheless, that it was easy for Deity so to have constituted me as that I should never be deceived, although I still remained free and pos-sessed of a limited knowledge, viz., by implanting in my understanding a clear and distinct knowledge of all the objects respecting which I should ever have to deliberate; or simply by so deeply engraving on my memory the resolution to judge of nothing without previously possessing a clear and distinct conception of it, that I should never forget it. And I easily un-derstand that, in so far as I consider myself as a single whole, without reference to any other being in the universe, I should have been much more perfect than I now am, had Deity created me superior to er-ror; but I cannot therefore deny that it is not some-how a greater perfection in the universe, that cer-tain of its parts are not exempt from defect, as others are, than if they were all perfectly alike. And I have no right to complain because God, who placed me in the world, was not willing that I

should sustain that character which of all others is the chief and most perfect; I have even good reason to re-main satisfied on the ground that, if he has not given me the perfection of being superior to error by the first means I have pointed out above, which depends on a clear and evident knowledge of all the matters regarding which I can deliberate, he has at least left in my power the other means, which is, firmly to re-tain the resolution never to judge where the truth is not clearly known to me: for, although I am conscious of the weakness of not being able to keep my mind continually fixed on the same thought, I can never-theless, by attentive and oft-repeated meditation, impress it so strongly on my memory that I shall never fail to recollect it as often as I require it, and I can acquire in this way the habitude of not erring; and since it is in being superior to error that the highest and chief perfection of man consists, I deem that I have not gained little by this day's meditation, in having discovered the source of error and falsity.

And certainly this can be no other than what I have now explained: for as often as I so restrain my will within the limits of my knowledge, that it forms no judgment except regarding objects which are clearly and distinctly represented to it by the under-standing, I can never be deceived; because every clear and distinct conception is doubtless some-thing, and as such cannot owe its origin to nothing, but must of necessity have God for its author — God, I say, who, as supremely perfect, cannot, without a contradiction, be the cause of any error; and conse-quently it is necessary to conclude that every such conception [or judgment] is true. Nor have I merely learned to-day what I must avoid to escape error, but also what I must do to arrive at the knowledge of truth; for I will assuredly reach truth if I only fix my attention sufficiently on all the things I conceive perfectly, and separate these from others which I conceive more confusedly and obscurely: to which for the future I shall give diligent heed.

Meditation V
Of the essence of material things; and, again, of God; that He exists

Several other questions remain for consideration respecting the attributes of God and my own nature or mind. I will, however, on some other occasion perhaps resume the investigation of these. Meanwhile, as I have discovered what must be done and what avoided to arrive at the knowledge of truth, what I have chiefly to do is to essay to emerge from the state of doubt in which I have for some time been, and to discover whether anything can be known with certainty regarding material objects. But before considering whether such objects as I conceive exist without me, I must examine their ideas in so far as these are to be found in my consciousness, and discover which of them are distinct and which confused.

In the first place, I distinctly imagine that quantity which the philosophers commonly call continuous, or the extension in length, breadth, and depth that is in this quantity, or rather in the object to which it is attributed. Further, I can enumerate in it many diverse parts, and attribute to each of these all sorts of sizes, figures, situations, and local motions; and, in fine, I can assign to each of these motions all degrees of duration. And I not only distinctly know these things when I thus consider them in general; but besides, by a little attention, I discover innumerable particulars respecting figures, numbers, motion, and the like, which are so evidently true, and so accordant with my nature, that when I now discover them I do not so much appear to learn anything new, as to call to remembrance what I before knew, or for the first time to remark what was before in my mind, but to which I had not hitherto directed my attention. And what I here find of most importance is, that I discover in my mind innumerable ideas of certain objects, which cannot be esteemed pure negations, although perhaps they possess no reality beyond my thought, and which are not framed by me though it may be in my power to think, or not to think them, but possess true and immutable natures of their own. As, for example, when I imagine a triangle, although there is not perhaps and never was in any place in the universe apart from my thought one such figure, it remains true nevertheless that this figure possesses a certain determinate nature, form, or essence, which is immutable and eternal, and not framed by me, nor in any degree dependent on my thought; as appears from the circumstance, that diverse properties of the triangle may be demonstrated, viz., that its three angles are equal to two right, that its greatest side is subtended by its greatest angle, and the like, which, whether I will or not, I now clearly discern to

belong to it, although before I did not at all think of them, when, for the first time, I imagined a triangle, and which accordingly cannot be said to have been invented by me. Nor is it a valid objection to allege, that perhaps this idea of a triangle came into my mind by the medium of the senses, through my having seen bodies of a triangular figure; for I am able to form in thought an innumerable variety of figures with regard to which it cannot be supposed that they were ever objects of sense, and I can nevertheless demonstrate diverse properties of their nature no less than of the triangle, all of which are assuredly true since I clearly conceive them: and they are therefore something, and not mere negations; for it is highly evident that all that is true is something, [truth being identical with existence]; and I have already fully shown the truth of the principle, that whatever is clearly and distinctly known is true. And although this had not been demonstrated, yet the nature of my mind is such as to compel me to assent to what I clearly conceive while I so conceive it; and I recollect that even when I still strongly adhered to the objects of sense, I reckoned among the number of the most certain truths those I clearly conceived relating to figures, numbers, and other matters that pertain to arithmetic and geometry, and in general to the pure mathematics.

But now if because I can draw from my thought the idea of an object, it follows that all I clearly and distinctly apprehend to pertain to this object, does in truth belong to it, may I not from this derive an argument for the existence of God? It is certain that I no less find the idea of a God in my consciousness, that is, the idea of a being supremely perfect, than that of any figure or number whatever: and I know with not less clearness and distinctness that an [actual and] eternal existence pertains to his nature than that all which is demonstrable of any figure or number really belongs to the nature of that figure or number; and, therefore, although all the conclusions of the preceding Meditations were false, the existence of God would pass with me for a truth at least as certain as I ever judged any truth of mathematics to be, although indeed such a doctrine may at first sight appear to contain more sophistry than truth. For, as I have been accustomed in every other matter to distinguish between existence and essence, I easily believe that the existence can be separated from the essence of God, and that thus God may be conceived as not actually existing. But, nevertheless, when I think of it more attentively, it appears that the existence can no more be separated from the essence of God, than the idea of a mountain from that of a valley, or the equality of its three angles to two right angles, from the essence of a [rectilineal] triangle; so that it is not less impossible to conceive a God, that is, a being supremely perfect, to whom existence is awanting, or who is devoid of a certain perfection, than to conceive a mountain without a valley.

But though, in truth, I cannot conceive a God unless as existing, any more than I can a mountain without a valley, yet, just as it does not follow that there is any mountain in the world merely because I conceive a mountain with a valley, so likewise, though I conceive God as existing, it does not seem to follow on that account that God exists; for my thought imposes no necessity on things; and as I may imagine a winged horse, though there be none such, so I could perhaps attribute existence to God, though no God existed. But the cases are not analogous, and a fallacy lurks under the semblance of this objection: for because I cannot conceive a mountain without a valley, it does not follow that there is any mountain or valley in existence, but simply that the mountain or valley, whether they do or do not exist, are inseparable from each other; whereas, on the other hand, because I cannot conceive God unless as existing, it follows that existence is inseparable from him, and therefore that he really exists: not that this is brought about by my thought, or that it imposes any necessity on things, but, on the contrary, the necessity which lies in the thing itself, that is, the necessity of the existence of God, determines me to think in this way: for it is not in my power to conceive a God without existence, that is, a being supremely perfect, and yet devoid of an absolute perfection, as I am free to imagine a horse with or without wings.

Nor must it be alleged here as an objection, that it is in truth necessary to admit that God exists, after having supposed him to possess all perfections, since existence is one of them, but that my original supposition was not necessary; just as it is not necessary to think that all quadrilateral figures can be inscribed in the circle, since, if I supposed this, I should be constrained to admit that the rhombus, being a figure of four sides, can be therein inscribed, which,

however, is manifestly false. This objection is, I say, incompetent; for although it may not be necessary that I shall at any time entertain the notion of Deity, yet each time I happen to think of a first and sovereign being, and to draw, so to speak, the idea of him from the storehouse of the mind, I am necessitated to attribute to him all kinds of perfections, though I may not then enumerate them all, nor think of each of them in particular. And this necessity is sufficient, as soon as I discover that existence is a perfection, to cause me to infer the existence of this first and sovereign being: just as it is not necessary that I should ever imagine any triangle, but whenever I am desirous of considering a rectilineal figure composed of only three angles, it is absolutely necessary to attribute those properties to it from which it is correctly inferred that its three angles are not greater than two right angles, although perhaps I may not then advert to this relation in particular. But when I consider what figures are capable of being inscribed in the circle, it is by no means necessary to hold that all quadrilateral figures are of this number; on the contrary, I cannot even imagine such to be the case, so long as I shall be unwilling to accept in thought aught that I do not clearly and distinctly conceive: and consequently there is a vast difference between false suppositions, as is the one in question, and the true ideas that were born with me, the first and chief of which is the idea of God. For indeed I discern on many grounds that this idea is not factitious, depending simply on my thought, but that it is the representation of a true and immutable nature: in the first place, because I can conceive no other being, except God, to whose essence existence [necessarily] pertains; in the second, because it is impossible to conceive two or more gods of this kind; and it being supposed that one such God exists, I clearly see that he must have existed from all eternity, and will exist to all eternity; and finally, because I apprehend many other properties in God, none of which I can either diminish or change.

But, indeed, whatever mode of probation I in the end adopt, it always returns to this, that it is only the things I clearly and distinctly conceive which have the power of completely persuading me. And although, of the objects I conceive in this manner, some, indeed, are obvious to every one, while others are only discovered after close and careful investigation; nevertheless, after they are once discovered, the latter are not esteemed less certain than the former. Thus, for example, to take the case of a right-angled triangle, although it is not so manifest at first that the square of the base is equal to the squares of the other two sides, as that the base is opposite to the greatest angle; nevertheless, after it is once apprehended, we are as firmly persuaded of the truth of the former as of the latter. And, with respect to God, if I were not pre-occupied by prejudices, and my thought beset on all sides by the continual presence of the images of sensible objects, I should know nothing sooner or more easily than the fact of his being. For is there any truth more clear than the existence of a Supreme Being, or of God, seeing it is to his essence alone that [necessary and eternal] existence pertains? And although the right conception of this truth has cost me much close thinking, nevertheless at present I feel not only as assured of it as of what I deem most certain, but I remark further that the certitude of all other truths is so absolutely dependent on it, that without this knowledge it is impossible ever to know anything perfectly.

For although I am of such a nature as to be unable, while I possess a very clear and distinct apprehension of a matter, to resist the conviction of its truth, yet because my constitution is also such as to incapacitate me from keeping my mind continually fixed on the same object, and as I frequently recollect a past judgment without at the same time being able to recall the grounds of it, it may happen meanwhile that other reasons are presented to me which would readily cause me to change my opinion, if I did not know that God existed; and thus I should possess no true and certain knowledge, but merely vague and vacillating opinions. Thus, for example, when I consider the nature of the [rectilineal] triangle, it most clearly appears to me, who have been instructed in the principles of geometry, that its three angles are equal to two right angles, and I find it impossible to believe otherwise, while I apply my mind to the demonstration; but as soon as I cease from attending to the process of proof, although I still remember that I had a clear comprehension of it, yet I may readily come to doubt of the truth demonstrated, if I do not know that there is a God: for I may persuade myself that I have been so constituted by nature as to be sometimes deceived, even in mat-

ters which I think I apprehend with the greatest evidence and certitude, especially when I recollect that I frequently considered many things to be true and certain which other reasons afterwards constrained me to reckon as wholly false.

But after I have discovered that God exists, seeing I also at the same time observed that all things depend on him, and that he is no deceiver, and thence inferred that all which I clearly and distinctly perceive is of necessity true: although I no longer attend to the grounds of a judgment, no opposite reason can be alleged sufficient to lead me to doubt of its truth, provided only I remember that I once possessed a clear and distinct comprehension of it. My knowledge of it thus becomes true and certain. And this same knowledge extends likewise to whatever I remember to have formerly demonstrated, as the truths of geometry and the like: for what can be alleged against them to lead me to doubt of them? Will it be that my nature is such that I may be frequently deceived? But I already know that I cannot be deceived in judgments of the grounds of which I possess a clear knowledge. Will it be that I formerly deemed things to be true and certain which I afterwards discovered to be false? But I had no clear and distinct knowledge of any of those things, and, being as yet ignorant of the rule by which I am assured of the truth of a judgment, I was led to give my assent to them on grounds which I afterwards discovered were less strong than at the time I imagined them to be. What further objection, then, is there? Will it be said that perhaps I am dreaming (an objection I lately myself raised), or that all the thoughts of which I am now conscious have no more truth than the reveries of my dreams? But although, in truth, I should be dreaming, the rule still holds that all which is clearly presented to my intellect is indisputably true.

And thus I very clearly see that the certitude and truth of all science depends on the knowledge alone of the true God, insomuch that, before I knew him, I could have no perfect knowledge of any other thing. And now that I know him, I possess the means of acquiring a perfect knowledge respecting innumerable matters, as well relative to God himself and other intellectual objects as to corporeal nature, in so far as it is the object of pure mathematics [which do not consider whether it exists or not].

Meditation VI
Of the existence of material things, and of the real distinction between the mind and body of man

There now only remains the inquiry as to whether material things exist. With regard to this question, I at least know with certainty that such things may exist, in as far as they constitute the object of the pure mathematics, since, regarding them in this aspect, I can conceive them clearly and distinctly. For there can be no doubt that God possesses the power of producing all the objects I am able distinctly to conceive, and I never considered anything impossible to him, unless when I experienced a contradiction in the attempt to conceive it aright. Further, the faculty of imagination which I possess, and of which I am conscious that I make use when I apply myself to the consideration of material things, is sufficient to persuade me of their existence: for, when I attentively consider what imagination is, I find that it is simply a certain application of the cognitive faculty (*facultas cognoscitiva*) to a body which is immediately present to it, and which therefore exists.

And to render this quite clear, I remark, in the first place, the difference that subsists between imagination and pure intellection [or conception]. For example, when I imagine a triangle I not only conceive (*intelligo*) that it is a figure comprehended by three lines, but at the same time also I look upon (*intueor*) these three lines as present by the power and internal application of my mind (*acie mentis*), and this is what I call imagining. But if I desire to think of a chiliogon, I indeed rightly conceive that it is a figure composed of a thousand sides, as easily as I conceive that a triangle is a figure composed of only three sides; but I cannot imagine the thousand sides of a chiliogon as I do the three sides of a triangle, nor, so to speak, view them as present [with the eyes of my mind]. And although, in accordance with the habit I have of always imagining something when I think of corporeal things, it may happen that, in conceiving a chiliogon, I confusedly represent some figure to myself, yet it is quite evident that this is not a chiliogon, since it in no wise differs from that which I would represent to myself, if I were to think of a myriogon, or any other figure of many sides; nor would this representation be of any use in discovering and unfolding the properties that constitute the

difference between a chiliogon and other polygons. But if the question turns on a pentagon, it is quite true that I can conceive its figure, as well as that of a chiliogon, without the aid of imagination; but I can likewise imagine it by applying the attention of my mind to its five sides, and at the same time to the area which they contain. Thus I observe that a special effort of mind is necessary to the act of imagination, which is not required to conceiving or understanding (*ad intelligendum*); and this special exertion of mind clearly shows the difference between imagination and pure intellection (*imaginatio et intellectio pura*). I remark, besides, that this power of imagination which I possess, in as far as it differs from the power of conceiving, is in no way necessary to my [nature or] essence, that is, to the essence of my mind; for although I did not possess it, I should still remain the same that I now am, from which it seems we may conclude that it depends on something different from the mind. And I easily understand that, if some body exists, with which my mind is so conjoined and united as to be able, as it were, to consider it when it chooses, it may thus imagine corporeal objects; so that this mode of thinking differs from pure intellection only in this respect, that the mind in conceiving turns in some way upon itself, and considers some one of the ideas it possesses within itself; but in imagining it turns towards the body, and contemplates in it some object conformed to the idea which it either of itself conceived or apprehended by sense. I easily understand, I say, that imagination may be thus formed, if it is true that there are bodies; and because I find no other obvious mode of explaining it, I thence, with probability, conjecture that they exist, but only with probability; and although I carefully examine all things, nevertheless I do not find that, from the distinct idea of corporeal nature I have in my imagination, I can necessarily infer the existence of any body.

But I am accustomed to imagine many other objects besides that corporeal nature which is the object of the pure mathematics, as, for example, colours, sounds, tastes, pain, and the like, although with less distinctness; and, inasmuch as I perceive these objects much better by the senses, through the medium of which and of memory, they seem to have reached the imagination, I believe that, in order the more advantageously to examine them, it is proper I should at the same time examine what sense-perception is, and inquire whether from those ideas that are apprehended by this mode of thinking (consciousness), I cannot obtain a certain proof of the existence of corporeal objects.

And, in the first place, I will recall to my mind the things I have hitherto held as true, because perceived by the senses, and the foundations upon which my belief in their truth rested; I will, in the second place, examine the reasons that afterwards constrained me to doubt of them; and, finally, I will consider what of them I ought now to believe.

Firstly, then, I perceived that I had a head, hands, feet, and other members composing that body which I considered as part, or perhaps even as a whole, of myself. I perceived further, that that body was placed among many others, by which it was capable of being affected in diverse ways, both beneficial and hurtful; and what was beneficial I remarked by a certain sensation of pleasure, and what was hurtful by a sensation of pain. And, besides this pleasure and pain, I was likewise conscious of hunger, thirst, and other appetites, as well as certain corporeal inclinations towards joy, sadness, anger, and similar passions. And, out of myself, besides the extension, figure, and motions of bodies, I likewise perceived in them hardness, heat, and the other tactile qualities, and, in addition, light, colours, odours, tastes, and sounds, the variety of which gave me the means of distinguishing the sky, the earth, the sea, and generally all the other bodies, from one another. And certainly, considering the ideas of all these qualities, which were presented to my mind, and which alone I properly and immediately perceived, it was not without reason that I thought I perceived certain objects wholly different from my thought, namely, bodies from which those ideas proceeded; for I was conscious that the ideas were presented to me without my consent being required, so that I could not perceive any object, however desirous I might be, unless it were present to the organ of sense; and it was wholly out of my power not to perceive it when it was thus present. And because the ideas I perceived by the senses were much more lively and clear, and even, in their own way, more distinct than any of those I could of myself frame by meditation, or which I found impressed on my memory, it seemed that they could not have proceeded from myself,

and must therefore have been caused in me by some other objects; and as of those objects I had no knowledge beyond what the ideas themselves gave me, nothing was so likely to occur to my mind as the supposition that the objects were similar to the ideas which they caused. And because I recollected also that I had formerly trusted to the senses, rather than to reason, and that the ideas which I myself formed were not so clear as those I perceived by sense, and that they were even for the most part composed of parts of the latter, I was readily persuaded that I had no idea in my intellect which had not formerly passed through the senses. Nor was I altogether wrong in likewise believing that that body which, by a special right, I called my own, pertained to me more properly and strictly than any of the others; for in truth, I could never be separated from it as from other bodies: I felt in it and on account of it all my appetites and affections, and in fine I was affected in its parts by pain and the titillation of pleasure, and not in the parts of the other bodies that were separated from it. But when I inquired into the reason why, from this I know not what sensation of pain, sadness of mind should follow, and why from the sensation of pleasure joy should arise, or why this indescribable twitching of the stomach, which I call hunger, should put me in mind of taking food, and the parchedness of the throat of drink, and so in other cases, I was unable to give any explanation, unless that I was so taught by nature; for there is assuredly no affinity, at least none that I am able to comprehend, between this irritation of the stomach and the desire of food, any more than between the perception of an object that causes pain and the consciousness of sadness which springs from the perception. And in the same way it seemed to me that all the other judgments I had formed regarding the objects of sense, were dictates of nature; because I remarked that those judgments were formed in me, before I had leisure to weight and consider the reasons that might constrain me to form them.

But, afterwards, a wide experience by degrees sapped the faith I had reposed in my senses; for I frequently observed that towers, which at a distance seemed round, appeared square when more closely viewed, and that colossal figures, raised on the summits of these towers, looked like small statues, when viewed from the bottom of them; and, in other instances without number, I also discovered error in judgments founded on the external senses; and not only in those founded on the external, but even in those that rested on the internal senses; for is there aught more internal than pain? and yet I have sometimes been informed by parties whose arm or leg had been amputated, that they still occasionally seemed to feel pain in that part of the body which they had lost,—a circumstance that led me to think that I could not be quite certain even that any one of my members was affected when I felt pain in it. And to these grounds of doubt I shortly afterwards also added two others of very wide generality: the first of them was that I believed I never perceived anything when awake which I could not occasionally think I also perceived when asleep, and as I do not believe that the ideas I seem to perceive in my sleep proceed from objects external to me, I did not any more observe any ground for believing this of such as I seem to perceive when awake; the second was that since I was as yet ignorant of the author of my being, or at least supposed myself to be so, I saw nothing to prevent my having been so constituted by nature as that I should be deceived even in matters that appeared to me to possess the greatest truth. And, with respect to the ground on which I had before been persuaded of the existence of sensible objects, I had no great difficulty in finding suitable answers to them; for as nature seemed to incline me to many things from which reason made me averse, I thought that I ought not to confide much in its teachings. And although the perceptions of the senses were not dependent on my will, I did not think that I ought on that ground to conclude that they proceeded from things different from myself, since perhaps there might be found in me some faculty, though hitherto unknown to me, which produced them.

But now that I begin to know myself better, and to discover more clearly the author of my being, I do not, indeed, think that I ought rashly to admit all which the senses seem to teach, nor, on the other hand, is it my conviction that I ought to doubt in general of their teachings.

And, firstly, because I know that all which I clearly and distinctly conceive can be produced by God exactly as I conceive it, it is sufficient that I am able clearly and distinctly to conceive one thing apart from another, in order to be certain that the one is different from the other, seeing they may at least be made to exist separately, by the omnipotence of God; and it matters not by what power this separation is made, in order to be compelled to judge them different; and, therefore, merely because I know with certitude that I exist, and because, in the meantime, I do not observe that aught necessarily belongs to my nature or essence beyond my being a thinking thing, I rightly conclude that my essence consists only in my being a thinking thing, [or a substance whose whole essence or nature is merely thinking]. And although I may, or rather, as I will shortly say, although I certainly do possess a body with which I am very closely conjoined; nevertheless, because, on the one hand, I have a clear and distinct idea of myself, in as far as I am only a thinking and unextended thing, and as, on the other hand, I possess a distinct idea of body, in as far as it is only an extended and unthinking thing, it is certain that I, [that is, my mind, by which I am what I am], is entirely and truly distinct from my body, and may exist without it.

Moreover, I find in myself diverse faculties of thinking that have each their special mode: for example, I find I possess the faculties of imagining and perceiving, without which I can indeed clearly and distinctly conceive myself as entire, but I cannot reciprocally conceive them without conceiving myself, that is to say, without an intelligent substance in which they reside, for [in the notion we have of them, or to use the terms of the schools] in their formal concept, they comprise some sort of intellection; whence I perceive that they are distinct from myself as modes are from things. I remark likewise certain other faculties, as the power of changing place, of assuming diverse figures, and the like, that cannot be conceived and cannot therefore exist, any more than the preceding, apart from a substance in which they inhere. It is very evident, however, that these faculties, if they really exist, must belong to some corporeal or extended substance, since in their clear and distinct concept there is contained some sort of extension, but no intellection at all. Farther, I cannot doubt but that there is in me a certain passive faculty of perception, that is, of receiving and taking knowledge of the ideas of sensible things; but this would be useless to me, if there did not also exist in me, or in some other thing, another active faculty capable of forming and producing those ideas. But this active faculty cannot be in me [in as far as I am but a thinking thing], seeing that it does not presuppose thought, and also that those ideas are frequently produced in my mind without my contributing to it in any way, and even frequently contrary to my will. This faculty must therefore exist in some substance different from me, in which all the objective reality of the ideas that are produced by this faculty, is contained formally or eminently, as I before remarked; and this substance is either a body, that is to say, a corporeal nature in which is contained formally [and in effect] all that is objectively [and by representation] in those ideas; or it is God himself, or some other creature, of a rank superior to body, in which the same is contained eminently. But as God is no deceiver, it is manifest that he does not of himself and immediately communicate those ideas to me, nor even by the intervention of any creature in which their objective reality is not formally, but only eminently, contained. For as he has given me no faculty whereby I can discover this to be the case, but, on the contrary, a very strong inclination to believe that those ideas arise from corporeal objects, I do not see how he could be vindicated from the charge of deceit, if in truth they proceeded from any other source, or were produced by other causes than corporeal things: and accordingly it must be concluded, that corporeal objects exist. Nevertheless they are not perhaps exactly such as we perceive by the senses, for their comprehension by the senses is, in many instances, very obscure and confused; but it is at least necessary to admit that all which I clearly and distinctly conceive as in them, that is, generally speaking, all that is comprehended in the object of speculative geometry, really exists external to me.

But with respect to other things which are either only particular, as, for example, that the sun is of such a size and figure, etc., or are conceived with less clearness and distinctness, as light, sound, pain, and the like, although they are highly dubious and uncertain, nevertheless on the ground alone that God is no deceiver, and that consequently he has permitted no falsity in my opinions which he has not likewise given me a faculty of correcting, I think I may with safety conclude that I possess in myself the means of arriving at the truth. And, in the first place, it cannot be doubted that in each of the dictates of

nature there is some truth: for by nature, considered in general, I now understand nothing more than God himself, or the order and disposition established by God in created things; and by my nature in particular I understand the assemblage of all that God has given me.

But there is nothing which that nature teaches me more expressly [or more sensibly] than that I have a body which is ill affected when I feel pain, and stands in need of food and drink when I experience the sensations of hunger and thirst, etc. And therefore I ought not to doubt but that there is some truth in these informations.

Nature likewise teaches me by these sensations of pain, hunger, thirst, etc., that I am not only lodged in my body as a pilot in a vessel, but that I am besides so intimately conjoined, and as it were intermixed with it, that my mind and body compose a certain unity. For if this were not the case, I should not feel pain when my body is hurt, seeing I am merely a thinking thing, but should perceive the wound by the understanding alone, just as a pilot perceives by sight when any part of his vessel is damaged; and when my body has need of food or drink, I should have a clear knowledge of this, and not be made aware of it by the confused sensations of hunger and thirst; for, in truth, all these sensations of hunger, thirst, pain, etc., are nothing more than certain confused modes of thinking, arising from the union and apparent fusion of mind and body.

Besides this, nature teaches me that my own body is surrounded by many other bodies, some of which I have to seek after, and others to shun. And indeed, as I perceive different sorts of colours, sounds, odours, tastes, heat, hardness, etc., I safely conclude that there are in the bodies from which the diverse perceptions of the senses proceed, certain varieties corresponding to them, although, perhaps, not in reality like them; and since, among these diverse perceptions of the senses, some are agreeable, and others disagreeable, there can be no doubt that my body, or rather my entire self, in as far as I am composed of body and mind, may be variously affected, both beneficially and hurtfully, by surrounding bodies.

But there are many other beliefs which, though seemingly the teaching of nature, are not in reality so, but which obtained a place in my mind through a habit of judging inconsiderately of things. It may thus easily happen that such judgments shall contain error: thus, for example, the opinion I have that all space in which there is nothing to affect [or make an impression on] my senses is void; that in a hot body there is something in every respect similar to the idea of heat in my mind; that in a white or green body there is the same whiteness or greenness which I perceive; that in a bitter or sweet body there is the same taste, and so in other instances; that the stars, towers, and all distant bodies, are of the same size and figure as they appear to our eyes, etc. But that I may avoid everything like indistinctness of conception, I must accurately define what I properly understand by being taught by nature. For nature is here taken in a narrower sense than when it signifies the sum of all the things which God has given me; seeing that in that meaning the notion comprehends much that belongs only to the mind [to which I am not here to be understood as referring when I use the term nature]; as, for example, the notion I have of the truth, that what is done cannot be undone, and all the other truths I discern by the natural light [without the aid of the body]; and seeing that it comprehends likewise much besides that belongs only to body, and is not here any more contained under the name nature, as the quality of heaviness, and the like, of which I do not speak,—the term being reserved exclusively to designate the things which God has given to me as a being composed of mind and body. But nature, taking the term in the sense explained, teaches me to shun what causes in me the sensation of pain, and to pursue what affords me the sensation of pleasure, and other things of this sort; but I do not discover that it teaches me, in addition to this, from these diverse perceptions of the senses, to draw any conclusions respecting external objects without a previous [careful and mature] consideration of them by the mind; for it is, as appears to me, the office of the mind alone, and not of the composite whole of mind and body, to discern the truth in those matters. Thus, although the impression a star makes on my eye is not larger than that from the flame of a candle, I do not, nevertheless, experience any real or positive impulse determining me to believe that the star is not greater than the flame; the true account of the matter being merely that I have so judged from my youth without any rational ground. And, though on approaching the fire I feel heat, and even pain on approaching it too closely, I have, however, from this no ground for holding that something resembling the heat I feel is in the fire, any more than that there is something similar to the pain; all that I have ground for believing is, that there is something in it, whatever it may be, which excites in me those sensations of heat or pain. So also, although there are spaces in which I find nothing to excite and affect my senses, I must not therefore conclude that those spaces contain in them no body; for I see that in this, as in many other similar matters, I have been accustomed to pervert the order of nature, because these perceptions of the senses, although given me by nature merely to signify to my mind what things are beneficial and hurtful to the composite whole of which it is a part, and being sufficiently clear and distinct for that purpose, are nevertheless used by me as infallible rules by which to determine immediately the essence of the bodies that exist out of me, of which they can of course afford me only the most obscure and confused knowledge.

But I have already sufficiently considered how it happens that, notwithstanding the supreme goodness of God, there is falsity in my judgments. A difficulty, however, here presents itself, respecting the things which I am taught by nature must be pursued or avoided, and also respecting the internal sensations in which I seem to have occasionally detected error, [and thus to be directly deceived by nature]: thus, for example, I may be so deceived by the agreeable taste of some viand with which poison has been mixed, as to be induced to take the poison. In this case, however, nature may be excused, for it simply leads me to desire the viand for its agreeable taste, and not the poison, which is unknown to it; and thus we can infer nothing from this circumstance beyond that our nature is not omniscient; at which there is assuredly no ground for surprise, since, man being of a finite nature, his knowledge must likewise be of limited perfection. But we also not unfrequently err in that to which we are directly impelled by nature, as is the case with invalids who desire drink or food that would be hurtful to them. It will here, perhaps, be alleged that the reason why such persons are deceived is that their nature is corrupted; but this leaves the difficulty untouched, for a sick man is not less really the creature of God than a man who is in full health; and therefore it is as repugnant to the goodness of God that the nature of the former should be deceitful as it is for that of the latter to be so. And, as a clock, composed of wheels and counter weights, observes not the less accurately all the laws of nature when it is ill made, and points out the hours incorrectly, than when it satisfies the desire of the maker in every respect; so likewise if the body of man be considered as a kind of machine, so made up and composed of bones, nerves, muscles, veins, blood, and skin, that although there were in it no mind, it would still exhibit the same motions which it at present manifests involuntarily, and therefore without the aid of the mind, [and simply by the dispositions of its organs], I easily discern that it would also be as natural for such a body, supposing it dropsical, for example, to experience the parchedness of the throat that is usually accompanied in the mind by the sensation of thirst, and to be disposed by this parchedness to move its nerves and its other parts in the way required for drinking, and thus increase its malady and do itself harm, as it is natural for it, when it is not indisposed to be stimulated to drink for its good by a similar cause; and although looking to the use for which a clock was destined by its maker, I may say that it is deflected from its proper nature when it incorrectly indicates the hours, and on the same principle, considering the machine of the human body as having been formed by God for the sake of the motions which it usually manifests, although I may likewise have ground for thinking that it does not follow the order of its nature when the throat is parched and drink does not tend to its preservation, nevertheless I yet plainly discern that this latter acceptation of the term nature is very different from the other; for this is nothing more than a certain denomination, depending entirely on my thought, and hence called extrinsic, by which I compare a sick man and an imperfectly constructed clock with the idea I have of a man in good health and a well made clock; while by the other acceptation of nature is understood something which is truly found in things, and therefore possessed of some truth.

But certainly, although in respect of a dropsical body, it is only by way of exterior denomination that

we say its nature is corrupted, when, without requiring drink, the throat is parched; yet, in respect of the composite whole, that is, of the mind in its union with the body, it is not a pure denomination, but really an error of nature, for it to feel thirst when drink would be hurtful to it: and, accordingly, it still remains to be considered why it is that the goodness of God does not prevent the nature of man thus taken from being fallacious.

To commence this examination accordingly, I here remark, in the first place, that there is a vast difference between mind and body, in respect that body, from its nature, is always divisible, and that mind is entirely indivisible. For in truth, when I consider the mind, that is, when I consider myself in so far only as I am a thinking thing, I can distinguish in myself no parts, but I very clearly discern that I am somewhat absolutely one and entire; and although the whole mind seems to be united to the whole body, yet, when a foot, an arm, or any other part is cut off, I am conscious that nothing has been taken from my mind; nor can the faculties of willing, perceiving, conceiving, etc., properly be called its parts, for it is the same mind that is exercises [all entire] in willing, in perceiving, and in conceiving, etc. But quite the opposite holds in corporeal or extended things; for I cannot imagine any one of them [how small soever it may be], which I cannot easily sunder in thought, and which, therefore, I do not know to be divisible. This would be sufficient to teach me that the mind or soul of man is entirely different from the body, if I had not already been apprised of it on other grounds.

I remark, in the next place, that the mind does not immediately receive the impression from all the parts of the body, but only from the brain, or perhaps even from one small part of it, viz., that in which the common sense (*sensus communis*) is said to be, which as often as it is affected in the same way, gives rise to the same perception in the mind, although meanwhile the other parts of the body may be diversely disposed, as is proved by innumerable experiments, which it is unnecessary here to enumerate.

I remark, besides, that the nature of body is such that none of its parts can be moved by another part a little removed from the other, which cannot likewise be moved in the same way by any one of the parts that lie between those two, although the most remote part does not act at all. As, for example, in the cord A, B, C, D, [which is in tension], if its last part D, be pulled, the first part A, will not be moved in a different way than it would be were one of the intermediate parts B or C to be pulled, and the last part D meanwhile to remain fixed. And in the same way, when I feel pain in the foot, the science of physics teaches me that this sensation is experienced by means of the nerves dispersed over the foot, which, extending like cords from it to the brain, when they are contracted, in the foot, contract at the same time the inmost parts of the brain in which they have their origin, and excite in these parts a certain motion appointed by nature to cause in the mind a sensation of pain, as if existing in the foot: but as these nerves must pass through the tibia, the leg, the loins, the back, and neck, in order to reach the brain, it may happen that although their extremities in the foot are not affected, but only certain of their parts that pass through the loins or neck, the same movements, nevertheless, are excited in the brain by this motion as would have been caused there by a hurt received in the foot, and hence the mind will necessarily feel pain in the foot, just as if it had been hurt; and the same is true of all the other perceptions of our senses.

I remark, finally, that as each of the movements that are made in the part of the brain by which the mind is immediately affected, impresses it with but a single sensation, the most likely supposition in the circumstances is, that this movement causes the mind to experience, among all the sensations which it is capable of impressing upon it, that one which is the best fitted, and generally the most useful for the preservation of the human body when it is in full health. But experience shows us that all the perceptions which nature has given us are of such a kind as I have mentioned; and accordingly, there is nothing found in them that does not manifest the power and goodness of God. Thus, for example, when the nerves of the foot are violently or more than usually shaken, the motion passing through the medulla of the spine to the innermost parts of the brain affords a sign to the mind on which it experiences a sensation, viz., of pain, as if it were in the foot, by which the mind is admonished and excited to do its utmost to remove the cause of it as dangerous and hurtful to the foot. It is

true that God could have so constituted the nature of man as that the same motion in the brain would have informed the mind of something altogether different: the motion might, for example, have been the occasion on which the mind became conscious of itself, in so far as it is in the brain, or in so far as it is in some place intermediate between the foot and the brain, or, finally, the occasion on which it perceived some other object quite different, whatever that might be; but nothing of all this would have so well contributed to the preservation of the body as that which the mind actually feels. In the same way, when we stand in need of drink, there arises from this want a certain parchedness in the throat that moves its nerves, and by means of them the internal parts of the brain; and this movement affects the mind with the sensation of thirst, because there is nothing on that occasion which is more useful for us than to be made aware that we have need of drink for the preservation of our health; and so in other instances.

Whence it is quite manifest that, notwithstanding the sovereign goodness of God, the nature of man, in so far as it is composed of mind and body, cannot but be sometimes fallacious. For, if there is any cause which excites, not in the foot, but in some one of the parts of the nerves that stretch from the foot to the brain, or even in the brain itself, the same movement that is ordinarily created when the foot is ill affected, pain will be felt, as it were, in the foot, and the sense will thus be naturally deceived; for as the same movement in the brain can but impress the mind with the same sensation, and as this sensation is much more frequently excited by a cause which hurts the foot than by one acting in a different quarter, it is reasonable that it should lead the mind to feel pain in the foot rather than in any other part of the body. And if it sometimes happens that the parchedness of the throat does not arise, as is usual, from drink being necessary for the health of the body, but from quite the opposite cause, as is the case with the dropsical, yet it is much better that it should be deceitful in that instance, than if, on the contrary, it were continually fallacious when the body is well-disposed; and the same holds true in other cases.

And certainly this consideration is of great service, not only in enabling me to recognize the errors to which my nature is liable, but likewise in rendering it more easy to avoid or correct them: for, knowing that all my senses more usually indicate to me what is true than what is false, in matters relating to the advantage of the body, and being able almost always to make use of more than a single sense in examining the same object, and besides this, being able to use my memory in connecting present with past knowledge, and my understanding which has already discovered all the causes of my errors, I ought no longer to fear that falsity may be met with in what is daily presented to me by the senses. And I ought to reject all the doubts of those bygone days, as hyperbolical and ridiculous, especially the general uncertainty respecting sleep, which I could not distinguish from the waking state: for I now find a very marked difference between the two states, in respect that our memory can never connect our dreams with each other and with the course of life, in the way it is in the habit of doing with events that occur when we are awake. And, in truth, if some one, when I am awake, appeared to me all of a sudden and as suddenly disappeared, as do the images I see in sleep, so that I could not observe either whence he came or whither he went, I should not without rea-

son esteem it either a spectre or phantom formed in my brain, rather than a real man. But when I perceive objects with regard to which I can distinctly determine both the place whence they come, and that in which they are, and the time at which they appear to me, and when, without interruption, I can connect the perception I have of them with the whole of the other parts of my life, I am perfectly sure that what I thus perceive occurs while I am awake and not during sleep. And I ought not in the least degree to doubt of the truth of those presentations, if, after having called together all my senses, my memory, and my understanding for the purpose of examining them, no deliverance is given by any one of these faculties which is repugnant to that of any other: for since God is no deceiver, it necessarily follows that I am not herein deceived. But because the necessities of action frequently oblige us to come to a determination before we have had leisure for so careful an examination, it must be confessed that the life of man is frequently obnoxious to error with respect to individual objects; and we must, in conclusion, acknowledge the weakness of our nature.

The Causal and Representational Theories of Perception

JOHN LOCKE

English empiricist philosopher John Locke (1632–1704) was deeply influential—not simply in epistemology and metaphysics but also in his natural rights political theory.

Some further considerations concerning our simple ideas of sensation

1. POSITIVE IDEAS FROM PRIVATIVE CAUSES.— Concerning the simple ideas of sensation it is to be considered, that whatsoever is so constituted in nature as to be able by affecting our senses to cause any

perception in the mind, does thereby produce in the understanding a simple idea; which, whatever be the external cause of it, when it comes to be taken notice of by our discerning faculty, it is by the mind looked on and considered there to be a real positive idea in the understanding, as much as any other whatsoever; though perhaps the cause of it be but a privation of the subject.

2. Thus the ideas of heat and cold, light and

From *An Essay Concerning Human Understanding*. First published in 1690.

darkness, white and black, motion and rest, are equally clear and positive ideas in the mind; though perhaps some of the causes which produce them are barely privations in those subjects from whence our senses derive those ideas. These the understanding, in its view of them, considers all as distinct positive ideas without taking notice of the causes that produce them: which is an inquiry not belonging to the idea as it is in the understanding, but to the nature of the things existing without us. These are two very different things, and carefully to be distinguished; it being one thing to perceive and know the idea of white or black, and quite another to examine what kind of particles they must be, and how ranged in the superficies, to make any object appear white or black.

3. A painter or dyer who never inquired into their causes, hath the ideas of white and black and other colours as clearly, perfectly, and distinctly in his understanding, and perhaps more distinctly than the philosopher who hath busied himself in considering their natures, and thinks he knows how far either of them is in its cause positive or privative; and the idea of black is no less positive in his mind than that of white, however the cause of that colour in the external object may be only a privation.

4. If it were the design of my present undertaking to inquire into the natural causes and manner of perception, I should offer this as a reason why a privative cause might, in some cases at least, produce a positive idea, viz., that all sensation being produced in us only by different degrees an modes of motion in our animal spirits, variously agitated by external objects, the abatement of any former motion must as necessarily produce a new sensation as the variation or increase of it; and so introduce a new idea, which depends only on a different motion of the animal spirits in that organ.

5. But whether this be so or not I will not here determine, but appeal to every one's own experience, whether the shadow of a man, though it consists of nothing but the absence of light (and the more the absence of light is, the more discernible is the shadow), does not, when a man looks on it, cause as clear and positive idea in his mind, as a man himself, though covered over with clear sunshine? And the picture of a shadow is a positive thing. Indeed, we have negative names, [which stand not directly for positive ideas, but for their absence, such as *insipid, silence, nihil, & c.,* which words denote positive ideas, *v.g., taste, sound, being,* with a signification of their absence].

6. *Positive ideas from privative causes.*—And thus one may truly be said to see darkness. For, supposing a hole perfectly dark, from whence no light is reflected, it is certain one may see the figure of it, or it may be painted; or whether the ink I write with makes any other idea, is a question. The privative causes I have here assigned of positive ideas are according to the common opinion; but, in truth, it will be hard to determine whether there be really any ideas from a privative cause, till it be determined whether rest be any more a privation than motion.

7. *Ideas in the mind, qualities in bodies.*—To discover the nature of our ideas the better, and to discourse of them intelligibly, it will be convenient to distinguish them, as they are ideas or perceptions in our minds, and as they are modifications of matter in the bodies that cause such perceptions in us; that so we may not think (as perhaps usually is done) that they are exactly the images and resemblances of something inherent in the subject; most of those of sensation being in the mind no more the likeness of something existing without us than the names that stand for them are the likeness of our ideas, which yet upon hearing they are apt to excite in us.

8. Whatsoever the mind perceives in itself, or is the immediate object of perception, thought, or understanding, that I call "idea"; and the power to produce any idea in our mind, I call "quality" of the subject wherein that power is. Thus a snowball having the power to produce in us the ideas of white, cold, and round, the powers to produce those ideas in us as they are in the snowball, I call "qualities"; and as they are sensations or perceptions in our understandings, I call them "ideas"; which ideas, if I speak of them sometimes as in the things themselves, I would be understood to mean those qualities in the objects which produce them in us.

9. *Primary qualities.*—[Qualities thus considered in bodies are, First, such as are utterly inseparable from the body, in what estate soever it be;] and such as, in all the alterations and changes it suffers, all the force can be used upon it, it constantly keeps; and such as sense constantly finds in every particle of matter which has bulk enough to be perceived, and the mind finds inseparable from every particle of matter, though less than to make itself singly be perceived by our senses: *v.g.*, take a grain of wheat, divide it into two parts, each part has still solidity, extension, figure, and mobility; divide it again, and it retains still the same qualities: and so divide it on till the parts become insensible, they must retain still each of them all those qualities. For, division (which is all that a mill or pestle or any other body does upon another, in reducing it to insensible parts) can never take away either solidity, extension, figure, or mobility from any body, but only makes two or more distinct separate masses of matter of that which was but one before; all which distinct masses, reckoned as so many distinct bodies, after division, make a certain number. [These I call *original* or *primary* qualities of body, which I think we may observe to produce simple ideas in us, viz., solidity, extension, figure, motion or rest, and number.]

10. *Secondary qualities.*—Secondly. Such qualities, which in truth are nothing in the objects themselves, but powers to produce various sensations in us by their primary qualities, *i.e.*, by the bulk, figure, texture, and motion of their insensible parts, as colours, sounds, tastes &c., these I call *secondary* qualities. To these might be added a third sort, which are allowed to be barely powers, though they are as much real qualities in the subject as those which I, to comply with the common way of speaking, call qualities, but, for distinction, *secondary* qualities. For, the power in fire to produce a new colour or consistency in wax or clay, by its primary qualities, is as much a quality in fire as the power it has to produce in me a new idea or sensation of warmth or burning, which I felt not before, by the same primary qualities, viz., the bulk, texture, and motion of its insensible parts.

11. [*How primary qualities produce their ideas.*—The next thing to be considered is, how bodies produce ideas in us; and that is manifestly by impulse, the only way which we can conceive bodies to operate in.]

12. If, then, external objects be not united to our minds when they produce ideas therein, and yet we perceive these original qualities in such of them as singly fall under our senses, it is evident that some motion must be thence continued by our nerves, or animal spirits, by some parts of our bodies, to the brains or the seat of sensation, there to produce in our minds the particular ideas we have of them. And since the extension, figure, number, and motion of

bodies of an observable bigness, may be perceived at a distance by the sight, it is evident some singly imperceptible bodies must come from them to the eyes, and thereby convey to the brain some motion which produces these ideas which we have of them in us.

13. *How secondary.*—After the same manner that the ideas of these original qualities are produced in us, we may conceive that the ideas of secondary qualities are also produced, viz., by the operation of insensible particles on our senses. For it being manifest that there are bodies, and good store of bodies, each whereof are so small that we cannot by any of our senses discover either their bulk, figure, or motion (as is evident in the particles of the air and water, and others extremely smaller than those, perhaps as much smaller than the particles of air or water as the particles of air or water are smaller than peas or hailstones): let us suppose at present that the different motions and figures, bulk and number, of such particles, affecting the several organs of our senses, produce in us those different sensations which we have from the colours and smells of bodies, *v.g.*, that a violet, by the impulse of such insensible particles of matter of peculiar figures and bulks, and in different degrees and modifications of their motions, causes the ideas of the blue colour and sweet scent of that flower to be produced in our minds; it being no more impossible to conceive that God should annex such ideas to such motions, with which they have no similitude, than that he should annex the idea of pain to the motion of a piece of steel dividing our flesh, with which the idea hath no resemblance.

14. What I have said concerning colours and smells may be understood also of tastes and sounds, and other the like sensible qualities; which, whatever reality we by mistake attribute to them, are in truth nothing in the objects themselves, but powers to produce various sensations in us, and depend on those primary qualities, viz., bulk, figure, texture, and motion of parts [as I have said].

15. *Ideas of primary qualities are resemblances; of secondary, not.*—From whence I think it is easy to draw this observation, that the ideas of primary qualities of bodies are resemblances of them, and their patterns do really exist in the bodies themselves; but the ideas produced in us by these secondary qualities have no resemblance of them at all. There is nothing like our ideas existing in the bodies themselves. They are, in the bodies we denominate from them, only a power to produce those sensations in us; and what is sweet, blue, or warm in idea, is but the certain bulk, figure, and motion of the insensible parts in the bodies themselves, which we call so.

16. Flame is denominated *hot* and *light;* snow, *white* and *cold;* and manna *white* and *sweet,* from the ideas they produce in us, which qualities are commonly thought to be the same in those bodies that those ideas are in us, the one the perfect resemblance of the other, as they are in a mirror; and it would by most men be judged very extravagant, if one should say otherwise. And yet he that will consider that the same fire that at one distance produces in us the sensation of warmth, does at a nearer approach produce in us the far different sensation of pain, ought to bethink himself what reason he has to say, that this idea of warmth which was produced in him the same way is not in the fire. Why is whiteness and coldness in snow and pain not, when it produces the one and the other idea in us, and can do neither but by the bulk, figure, number, and motion of its solid parts?

17. The particular bulk, number, figure, and motion of the parts of fire or snow are really in them, whether any one's senses perceive them or no; and therefore they may be called *real* qualities, because they really exist in those bodies. But light, heat, whiteness, or coldness, are no more really in them than sickness or pain is in manna. Take away the sensation of them; let not the eyes see light or colours, nor the ears hear sounds; let the palate not taste, nor the nose smell, and all colours, tastes, odours, and sounds, as they are such particular ideas, vanish and cease, and are reduced to their causes, *i.e.,* bulk, figure, and motion of parts.

18. A piece of manna of a sensible bulk is able to produce in us the idea of a round or square figure; and by being removed from one place to another, the idea of motion. This idea of motion represents it as it really is in manna moving: a circle or square are the same, whether in idea or existence, in the mind or in the manna. And this, both motion and figure, are really in the manna, whether we take notice of them or no: this everybody is ready to agree to. Besides, manna, by the bulk, figure, texture, and motion of its parts, has a power to produce the sensa-

tions of sickness, and sometimes of acute pains or gripings in us. That these ideas of sickness and pain are *not* in the manna, but effects of its operations on us, and are nowhere when we feel them not; this also every one readily agrees to. And yet men are hardly to be brought to think that sweetness and whiteness are not really in manna; which are but the effects of the operations of manna, by the motion, size, and figure of its particles, on the eyes and palate: as the pain and sickness caused by manna are confessedly nothing but the effects of its operations on the stomach and guts, by the size, motion, and figure of its insensible parts, (for by nothing else can a body operate, as has been proved): as if it could not operate on the eyes and palate, and thereby produce in the mind particular distinct ideas, which in itself it has not, as well as we allow it can operate on the guts and stomach, and thereby produce distinct ideas, which in itself it has not. These ideas, being all effects of the operations of manna on several parts of our bodies, by the size, figure, number, and motion of its parts;—why those produced by the eyes and palate should rather be thought to be really in the manna, than those produced by the stomach and guts; or why the pain and sickness, ideas that are the effect of manna, should be thought to be nowhere when they are not felt; and yet the sweetness and whiteness, effects of the same manna on other parts of the body, by ways equally as unknown, should be thought to exist in the manna, when they are not seen or tasted, would need some reason to explain.

19. Let us consider the red and white colours in porphyry. Hinder light from striking on it, and its colours vanish; it no longer produces any such ideas in us: upon the return of light it produces these appearances on us again. Can any one think any real alterations are made in the porphyry by the presence or absence of light; and that those ideas of whiteness and redness are really in porphyry in the light, when it is plain *it has no colour in the dark?* It has, indeed, such a configuration of particles, both night and day, as are apt, by the rays of light rebounding from some parts of that hard stone, to produce in us the idea of redness, and from others the idea of whiteness; but whiteness or redness are not in it at any time, but such a texture that hath the power to produce such a sensation in us.

20. Pound an almond, and the clear white colour

will be altered into a dirty one, and the sweet taste into an oily one. What real alteration can the beating of the pestle make in any body, but an alteration of the texture of it?

21. Ideas being thus distinguished and understood, we may be able to give an account how the same water, at the same time, may produce the idea of cold by one hand and of heat by the other: whereas it is impossible that the same water, if those ideas were really in it, should at the same time be both hot and cold. For, if we imagine *warmth,* as it is in our hands, to be nothing but a certain sort and degree of motion in the minute particles of our nerves or animal spirits, we may understand how it is possible that the same water may, at the same time, produce the sensations of heat in one hand and cold in the other; which yet *figure* never does, that never producing the idea of a square by one hand which has produced the idea of a globe by another. But if the sensation of heat and cold be nothing but the increase or diminution of the motion of the minute parts of our bodies, caused by the corpuscles of any other body, it is easy to be understood, that if that motion be greater in one hand than in the other; if a body be applied to the two hands, which has in its minute particles a greater motion than in those of one of the hands, and a less than in those of the other, it will increase the motion of the one hand and lessen it in the other; and so cause the different sensations of heat and cold that depend thereon.

22. I have in what just goes before been engaged in physical inquiries a little further than perhaps I intended. But, it being necessary to make the nature of sensation a little understood; and to make the difference between the *qualities* in bodies, and the *ideas* produced by them in the mind, to be distinctly conceived, without which it were impossible to discourse intelligibly of them;—I hope I shall be pardoned this little excursion into natural philosophy; it being necessary in our present inquiry to distinguish the *primary* and *real* qualities of bodies, which are always in them (viz. solidity, extension, figure, number, and motion, or rest, and are sometimes perceived by us, viz. when the bodies they are in are big enough singly to be discerned), from those *secondary* and *imputed* qualities, which are but the powers of several combinations of those primary ones, when they operate without being distinctly discerned;—whereby

we may also come to know what ideas are, and what are not, resemblances of something really existing in the bodies we denominate from them.

23. The qualities, then, that are in bodies, rightly considered, are of three sorts:—

First, The bulk, figure, number, situation, and motion or rest of their solid parts. Those are in them, whether we perceive them or not; and when they are of that size that we can discover them, we have by these an idea of the thing as it is in itself; as is plain in artificial things. These I call *primary qualities.*

Secondly, The power that is in any body, by reason of its insensible primary qualities, to operate after a peculiar manner on any of our senses, and thereby produce in *us* the different ideas of several colours, sounds, smells, tastes, &c. These are usually called *sensible qualities.*

Thirdly, The power that is in any body, by reason of the particular constitution of its primary qualities, to make such a change in the bulk, figure, texture, and motion of *another body,* as to make it operate on our senses differently from what it did before. Thus the sun has a power to make wax white, and fire to make lead fluid. [These are usually called *powers.*]

The first of these, as has been said, I think may be properly called real, original, or primary qualities; because they are in the things themselves, whether they are perceived or not: and upon their different modifications it is that the secondary qualities depend.

The other two are only powers to act differently upon other things: which powers result from the different modifications of those primary qualities.

24. But, though the two latter sorts of qualities are powers barely, and nothing but powers, relating to several other bodies, and resulting from the different modifications of the original qualities, yet they are generally otherwise thought of. For the *second* sort, viz. the powers to produce several ideas in us, by our senses, are looked upon as real qualities in the things thus affecting us: but the *third* sort are called and esteemed barely powers, e.g., the idea of heat or light, which we receive by our eyes, or touch, from the sun, are commonly thought real qualities existing in the sun, and something more than mere powers in it. But when we consider the sun in reference to wax, which it melts or blanches, we look on the whiteness and softness produced in the wax, not as qualities in the sun, but effects produced by powers in it. Whereas, if rightly considered, these qualities of light and warmth, which are perceptions in me when I am warmed or enlightened by the sun, are no otherwise in the sun, than the changes made in the wax, when it is blanched or melted, are in the sun. They are all of them equally *powers in the sun, depending on its primary qualities;* whereby it is able, in the one case, so to alter the bulk, figure, texture, or motion of some of the insensible parts of my eyes or hands, as thereby to produce in me the idea of light or heat; and in the other, it is able so to alter the bulk, figure, texture, or motion of the insensible parts of the wax, as to make them fit to produce in me the distinct ideas of white and fluid.

25. The reason why the one are ordinarily taken for real qualities, and the other only for bare powers, seems to be, because the ideas we have of distinct colours, sounds, &c., containing nothing at all in them of bulk, figure, or motion, we are not apt to think them the effects of these primary qualities; which appear not, to our senses, to operate in their production, and with which they have not any apparent congruity or conceivable connexion. Hence it is that we are so forward to imagine, that those ideas are the resemblances of something really existing in the objects themselves: since sensation discovers nothing of bulk, figure, or motion of parts in their production; nor can reason show how bodies, *by their bulk, figure, and motion,* should produce in the mind the ides of blue or yellow, &c. But, in the other case, in the operations of bodies changing the qualities one of another, we plainly discover that the quality produced hath commonly no resemblance with anything in the thing producing it; wherefore we look on it as a bare effect of power. For, through receiving the idea of heat or light from the sun, we are apt to think *it* is a perception and resemblance of such a quality in the sun; yet when we see wax, or a fair face, receive change of colour from the sun, we cannot imagine *that* to be the reception or resemblance of anything in the sun, because we find not those different colours in the sun itself. For, our senses being able to observe a likeness or unlikeness of sensible qualities in two different external objects, we forwardly enough conclude the production of any sensible quality in any subject to be an effect of bare power, and not the communication of any qual-

ity which was really in the efficient, when we find no such sensible quality in the thing that produced it. But our senses, not being able to discover any unlikeness between the idea produced in us, and the quality of the object producing it, we are apt to imagine that our ideas are resemblances of something in the objects, and not the effects of certain powers placed in the modification of their primary qualities, with which primary qualities the ideas produced in us have no resemblance.

26. To conclude. Beside those before-mentioned primary qualities in bodies, viz. bulk, figure, extension, number; and motion of their solid parts; all the rest, whereby we take notice of bodies, and distinguish them one from another, are nothing else but several powers in them, depending on those primary qualities; whereby they are fitted, either by immediately operating on our bodies to produce several different ideas in us; or else, by operating on other bodies, so to change their primary qualities as to render them capable of producing ideas in us different from what before they did. The former of these, I think, may be called secondary qualities *immediately perceivable:* the latter, secondary qualities, *mediately perceivable.*

Of our knowledge of the existence of other things

1. The knowledge of our own being we have by intuition. The existence of a God, reason clearly makes known to us, as has been shown.

The knowledge of the existence of *any other thing* we can have only by *sensation:* for there being no necessary connexion of real existence with any *idea* a man hath in his memory; nor of any other existence but that of God with the existence of any particular man: no particular man can know the existence of any other being, but only when, by actual operating upon him, it makes itself perceived by him. For, the having the idea of anything in our mind, no more proves the existence of that thing, than the picture of a man evidences his being in the world, or the visions of a dream make thereby a true history.

2. It is therefore the *actual receiving* of ideas from without that gives us notice of the existence of other things, and makes us know, that something doth exist at that time without us, which causes that idea in us; though perhaps we neither know nor consider how it does it. For it takes not from the certainty of our senses, and the ideas we receive by them, that we know not the manner wherein they are produced: e.g. whilst I write this, I have, by the paper affecting my eyes, that idea produced in my mind, which, whatever object causes, I call *white;* by which I know that that quality or accident (i.e. whose appearance before my eyes always causes that idea) both really exist, and hath a being without me. And of this, the greatest assurance I can possibly have, and to which my faculties can attain, is the testimony of my eyes, which are the proper and sole judges of this thing; whose testimony I have reason to rely on as so certain, that I can no more doubt, whilst I write this, that I see white and black, and that something really exists that causes that sensation in me, than that I write or move my hand; which is a certainty as great as human nature is capable of, concerning the existence of anything, but a man's self alone, and of God.

3. The notice we have by our senses of the existing of things without us, though it be not altogether so certain as our intuitive knowledge, or the deductions of our reason employed about the clear abstract ideas of our own minds; yet it is an assurance that deserves the name of *knowledge.* If we persuade ourselves that our faculties act and inform us right concerning the existence of those objects that affect them, it cannot pass for an ill-grounded confidence: for I think nobody can, in earnest, be so sceptical as to be uncertain of the existence of those things which he sees and feels. At least, he that can doubt so far, (whatever he may have with his own thoughts,) will never have any controversy with me; since he can never be sure I say anything contrary to his own opinion. As to myself, I think God has given me assurance enough of the existence of things without me: since, by their different application, I can produce in myself both pleasure and pain, which is one great concernment of my present state. This is certain: the confidence that our faculties do not herein deceive us, is the greatest assurance we are capable of concerning the existence of material beings. For we cannot act anything but by our faculties; nor talk of knowledge itself, but by the help of those faculties which are fitted to apprehend even what knowledge is.

But besides the assurance we have from our senses themselves, that they do not err in the information they give us of the existence of things without us, when they are affected by them, we are further confirmed in this assurance by other concurrent reasons:—

4. I. It is plain those perceptions are produced in us by exterior causes affecting our senses: because those that want the *organs* of any sense, never can have the ideas belonging to that sense produced in their minds. This is too evident to be doubted: and therefore we cannot but be assured that they come in by the organs of that sense, and no other way. The organs themselves, it is plain, do not produce them: for then the eyes of a man in the dark would produce colours, and his nose smell roses in the winter: but we see nobody gets the relish of a pineapple, till he goes to the Indies, where it is, and tastes it.

5. II. Because sometimes I find that *I cannot avoid the having those ideas produced in my mind.* For though, when my eyes are shut, or windows fast, I can at pleasure recall to my mind the ideas of light, or the sun, which former sensations had lodged in my memory; so I can at pleasure lay by *that* idea, and take into my view that of the smell of a rose, or taste of sugar. But, if I turn my eyes at noon towards the sun, I cannot avoid the ideas which the light or sun then produces in me. So that there is a manifest difference between the ideas laid up in my memory, (over which, if they were there only, I should have constantly the same power to dispose of them, and lay them by at pleasure,) and those which force themselves upon me, and I cannot avoid having. And therefore it must needs be some exterior cause, and the brisk acting of some objects without me, whose efficacy I cannot resist, that produces those ideas in my mind, whether I will or no. Besides, there is nobody who doth not perceive the difference in himself between contemplating the sun, as he hath the idea of it in his memory, and actually looking upon it: of which two, his perception is so distinct, that few of his ideas are more distinguishable one from another. And therefore he hath certain knowledge that they are not *both* memory, or the actions of his mind, and fancies only within him; but that actual seeing hath a cause without.

6. III. Add to this, that many of those ideas are *produced in us with pain,* which afterwards we remember without the least offence. Thus, the pain of heat or cold, when the idea of it is revived in our minds, gives us no disturbance; which, when felt, was very troublesome; and is again, when actually repeated: which is occasioned by the disorder the external object causes in our bodies when applied to them: and we remember the pains of hunger, thirst, or the headache, without any pain at all; which would either never disturb us, or else constantly do it, as often as we thought of it, were there nothing more but ideas floating in our minds, and appearances entertaining our fancies, without the real existence of things affecting us from abroad. The same may be said of *pleasure,* accompanying several actual sensations. And though mathematical demonstration depends not upon sense, yet the examining them by diagrams gives great credit to the evidence of our sight, and seems to give it a certainty approaching to that of demonstration itself. For, it would be very strange, that a man should allow it for an undeniable truth, that two angles of a figure, which he measures by lines and angles of a diagram, should be bigger one than the other, and yet doubt of the existence of those lines and angles, which by looking on he makes use of to measure that by.

7. IV. Our *senses* in many cases *bear witness to the truth of each other's report,* concerning the existence of sensible things without us. He that *sees* a fire, may, if he doubt whether it be anything more than a bare fancy, *feel* it too; and be convinced, by putting his hand in it. Which certainly could never be put into such exquisite pain by a bare idea or phantom, unless that the pain be a fancy too: which yet he cannot, when the burn is well, by raising the idea of it, bring upon himself again.

Thus I see, whilst I write this, I can change the appearance of the paper; and by designing the letters, tell *beforehand* what new idea it shall exhibit the very next moment, by barely drawing my pen over it: which will neither appear (let me fancy as much as I will) if my hands stand still; or though I move my pen, if my eyes be shut: nor, when those characters are once made on the paper, can I choose afterwards but see them as they are; that is, have the ideas of such letters as I have made. Whence it is manifest, that they are not barely the sport and play of my own imagination, when I find that the characters that were made at the pleasure of my own thoughts, do not obey them; nor yet cease to be, whenever I shall fancy it, but continue to affect my senses constantly

and regularly, according to the figures I made them. To which if we will add, that the sight of those shall, from another man, draw such sounds as I beforehand design they shall stand for, there will be little reason left to doubt that those words I write do really exist without me, when they cause a long series of regular sounds to affect my ears, which could not be the effect of my imagination, nor could my memory retain them in that order.

8. But yet, if after all this any one will be so sceptical as to distrust his senses, and to affirm that all we see and hear, feel and taste, think and do, during our whole being, is but the series and deluding appearances of a long dream, whereof there is no reality; and therefore will question the existence of all things, or our knowledge of anything: I must desire him to consider, that, if all be a dream, then he doth but dream that he makes the question, and so it is not much matter that a waking man should answer him. But yet, if he pleases, he may dream that I make him this answer. That the certainty of things existing in *rerun natura* when we have the testimony of our senses for it is not only as great as our frame can attain to, but as our condition needs. For, our faculties being suited not to the full extent of being, nor to a perfect, clear, comprehensive knowledge of things free from all doubt and scruple; but to the preservation of us, in whom they are; and accommodated to the use of life: they serve to our purpose well enough, if they will but give us certain notice of those things, which are convenient or inconvenient to us. For he that sees a candle burning, and hath experimented the force of its flame by putting his finger in it, will little doubt that this is something existing without him, which does him harm, and puts him to great pain: which is assurance enough, when no man requires greater certainty to govern his actions by than what is as certain as his actions themselves. And if our dreamer pleases to try whether the glowing heat of a glass furnace be barely a wandering imagination in a drowsy man's fancy, by putting his hand into it, he may perhaps be wakened into a certainty greater than he could wish, that it is something more than bare imagination. So that this evidence is as great as we can desire, being as certain to us as our pleasure or pain, i.e. happiness or misery; beyond which we have no concernment, either of knowing or being. Such an assurance of the existence of things without us is sufficient to direct us in the attaining the good and avoiding the evil which is caused by them, which is the important concernment we have of being made acquainted with them.

9. In fine, then, when our senses do actually convey into our understandings any idea, we cannot but be satisfied that there doth something *at that time* really exist without us, which doth affect our senses, and by them give notice of itself to our apprehensive faculties, and actually produce that idea which we then perceive: and we cannot so far distrust their testimony, as to doubt that such *collections* of simple ideas as we have observed by our senses to be united together, do really exist together. But this knowledge extends as far as the present testimony of our senses, employed about particular objects that do then affect them, and no further. For if I saw such a collection of simple ideas as it wont to be called *man,* existing together one minute since, and am now alone, I cannot be certain that the same man exists now, since there is no *necessary connexion* of his existence a minute since with his existence now: by a thousand ways he may cease to be, since I had the testimony of my senses for his existence. And if I cannot be certain that the man I saw last to-day is now in being, I can less be certain that he is so who hath been longer removed from my senses, and I have not seen since yesterday, or since the last year: and much less can I be certain of the existence of men that I never saw. And, therefore, though it be highly probable that millions of men do now exist, yet, whilst I am alone, writing this, I have not that certainty of it which we strictly call knowledge; though the great likelihood of it puts me past doubt, and it be reasonable for me to do several things upon the confidence that there are men (and men also of my acquaintance, with whom I have to do) now in the world: but this is but probability, not knowledge.

10. Whereby yet we may observe how foolish and vain a thing it is for a man of a narrow knowledge, who having reason given him to judge of the different evidence and probability of things, and to be swayed accordingly; how vain, I say, it is to expect demonstration and certainty in things not capable of it; and refuse assent to very rational propositions, and act contrary to very plain and clear truths, because they cannot be made out so evident, as to surmount every the least (I will not say reason, but) pretence of doubting. He that, in the ordinary affairs of life, would admit of nothing but direct plain demonstration, would be sure of nothing in this world, but of perishing quickly. The wholesomeness of his meat or drink would not give him reason to venture on it: and I would fain know what it is he could do upon such grounds as are capable of no doubt, no objection.

Three Dialogues Between Hylas and Philonous

GEORGE BERKELEY

The great British empiricist and idealist philosopher George Berkeley (1685–1753) was born in Ireland and served as the Anglican Bishop of Cloyne.

THE FIRST DIALOGUE

PHILONOUS: Good morning, Hylas. I did not expect to find you abroad so early.

HYLAS: It is indeed something unusual; but my thoughts were so taken up with a subject I was discoursing of last night that, finding I could not sleep, I resolved to rise and take a turn in the garden.

PHIL.: It happened well, to let you see what innocent

First published in 1713.

and agreeable pleasures you lose every morning. Can there be a pleasanter time of the day or a more delightful season of the year? That purple sky, those wild but sweet notes of birds, the fragrant bloom upon the trees and flowers, the gentle influence of the rising sun—these and a thousand nameless beauties of nature inspire the soul with secret transports; its faculties, too, being at this time fresh and lively, are fit for those meditations which the solitude of a garden and tranquility of the morning naturally dispose us to. But I am afraid I interrupt your thoughts, for you seemed very intent on something.

HYL.: It is true, I was, and shall be obliged to you if you will permit me to go on in the same vein; not that I would by any means deprive myself of your company, for my thoughts always flow more easily in conversation with a friend than when I am alone; but my request is that you would suffer me to impart my reflections to you.

PHIL.: With all my heart, it is what I should have requested myself if you had not prevented me.

HYL.: I was considering the old fate of those men who have in all ages, through an affectation of being distinguished from the vulgar, or some unaccountable turn of thought, pretended either to believe nothing at all or to believe the most extravagant things in the world. This, however, might be borne if their paradoxes and skepticism did not draw after them some consequences of general disadvantage to mankind. But the mischief lies here: that when men of less leisure see them who are supposed to have spent their whole time in the pursuits of knowledge professing an entire ignorance of all things or advancing such notions as are repugnant to plain and commonly received principles, they will be tempted to entertain suspicions concerning the most important truths, which they had hitherto held sacred and unquestionable.

PHIL.: I entirely agree with you as to the ill tendency of the affected doubts of some philosophers and fantastical conceits of others. I am even so far gone of late in this way of thinking that I have quitted several of the sublime notions I had got in their schools for vulgar opinions. And I give it you on my word, since this revolt from metaphysical notions to the plain dictates of nature and common sense, I find my understanding strangely enlightened, so that I can now easily comprehend a great many things which before were all mystery and riddle.

HYL.: I am glad to find there was nothing in the accounts I heard of you.

PHIL.: Pray, what were those?

HYL.: You were represented in last night's conversation as one who maintained the most extravagant opinion that ever entered into the mind of man, to wit, that there is no such thing as "material substance" in the world.

PHIL.: That there is no such thing as what philosophers call "material substance," I am seriously persuaded; but if I were made to see anything absurd or skeptical in this, I should then have the same reason to renounce this that I imagine I have now to reject the contrary opinion.

HYL.: What! Can anything be more fantastical, more repugnant to common sense or a more manifest piece of skepticism than to believe there is no such thing as matter?

PHIL.: Softly, good Hylas. What if it should prove that you, who hold there is, are, by virtue of that opinion, a greater skeptic and maintain more paradoxes and repugnances to common sense than I who believe no such thing?

HYL.: You may as soon persuade me the part is greater than the whole, as that, in order to avoid absurdity and skepticism, I should ever be obliged to give up my opinion in this point.

PHIL.: Well then, are you content to admit that opinion for true which, upon examination, shall appear most agreeable to common sense and remote from skepticism?

HYL.: With all my heart. Since you are for raising disputes about the plainest things in nature, I am content for once to hear what you have to say.

PHIL.: Pray, Hylas, what do you mean by a "skeptic"?

HYL.: I mean what all men mean, one that doubts of everything.

PHIL.: He then who entertains no doubt concerning some particular point, with regard to that point cannot be thought a skeptic.

HYL.: I agree with you.

PHIL.: Whether does doubting consist in embracing the affirmative or negative side of a question?

HYL.: In neither; for whoever understands English

cannot but know that *doubting* signifies a suspense between both.

PHIL.: He then that denies any point can no more be said to doubt of it than he who affirms it with the same degree of assurance.

HYL.: True.

PHIL.: And, consequently, for such his denial is no more to be esteemed a skeptic than the other.

HYL.: I acknowledge it.

PHIL.: How comes it to pass then, Hylas, that you pronounce me a skeptic because I deny what you affirm, to wit, the existence of matter? Since, for aught you can tell, I am as peremptory in my denial as you in your affirmation.

HYL.: Hold, Philonous, I have been a little out in my definition; but every false step a man makes in discourse is not to be insisted on. I said indeed that a "skeptic" was one who doubted of everything, but I should have added: or who denies the reality and truth of things.

PHIL.: What things? Do you mean the principles and theorems of sciences? But these you know are universal intellectual notions, and consequently independent of matter; the denial therefore of this does not imply the denying them.

HYL.: I grant it. But are there no other things? What think you of distrusting the senses, of denying the real existence of sensible things, or pretending to know nothing of them. Is not this sufficient to denominate a man a skeptic?

PHIL.: Shall we therefore examine which of us it is that denies the reality of sensible things or professes the greatest ignorance of them, since, if I take you rightly, he is to be esteemed the greatest skeptic?

HYL.: That is what I desire.

PHIL.: What mean you by "sensible things"?

HYL.: Those things which are perceived by the senses. Can you imagine that I mean anything else?

PHIL.: Pardon me, Hylas, if I am desirous clearly to apprehend your notions, since this may much shorten our inquiry. Suffer me then to ask you this further question. Are those things only perceived by the senses which are perceived immediately? Or may those things properly be said to be "sensible" which are perceived mediately, or not without the intervention of others?

HYL.: I do not sufficiently understand you.

PHIL.: In reading a book, what I immediately perceive are the letters, but mediately, or by means of these, are suggested to my mind the notions of God, virtue, truth, etc. Now, that the letters are truly sensible things, or perceived by sense, there is no doubt; but I would know whether you take the things suggested by them to be so too.

HYL.: No, certainly; it were absurd to think God or virtue sensible things, though they may be signified and suggested to the mind by sensible marks with which they have an arbitrary connection.

PHIL.: It seems, then, that by "sensible things" you mean those only which can be perceived immediately by sense.

HYL.: Right.

PHIL.: Does it not follow from this that, though I see one part of the sky red, and another blue, and that my reason does thence evidently conclude there must be some cause of that diversity of colors, yet that cause cannot be said to be a sensible thing or perceived by the sense of seeing?

HYL.: It does.

PHIL.: In like manner, though I hear variety of sounds, yet I cannot be said to hear the causes of those sounds?

HYL.: You cannot.

PHIL.: And when by my touch I perceive a thing to be hot and heavy, I cannot say, with any truth or propriety, that I feel the cause of its heat or weight?

HYL.: To prevent any more questions of this kind, I tell you once for all that by "sensible things" I mean those only which are perceived by sense, and that in truth the senses perceive nothing which they do not perceive immediately, for they make no inferences. The deducing therefore of causes or occasions from effects and appearances, which alone are perceived by sense, entirely relates to reason.

PHIL.: This point then is agreed between us—that *sensible things are those only which are immediately perceived by sense.* You will further inform me whether we immediately perceive by sight anything besides light and colors and figures; or by hearing, anything but sounds; by the palate, anything besides tastes; by the smell, besides odors; or by the touch, more than tangible qualities.

HYL.: We do not.

PHIL.: It seems, therefore, that if you take away all sensible qualities, there remains nothing sensible?

HYL.: I grant it.

PHIL.: Sensible things therefore are nothing else but so many sensible qualities or combinations of sensible qualities?

HYL.: Nothing else.

PHIL.: Heat is then a sensible thing?

HYL.: Certainly.

PHIL.: Does the reality of sensible things consist in being perceived, or is it something distinct from their being perceived, and that bears no relation to the mind?

HYL.: To *exist* is one thing, and to be *perceived* is another.

PHIL.: I speak with regard to sensible things only; and of these I ask, whether by their real existence you mean a subsistence exterior to the mind and distinct from their being perceived?

HYL.: I mean a real absolute being, distinct from and without any relation to their being perceived.

PHIL.: Heat therefore, if it be allowed a real being, must exist without the mind?

HYL.: It must.

PHIL.: Tell me, Hylas, is this real existence equally compatible to all degrees of heat, which we perceive, or is there any reason why we should attribute it to some and deny it to others? And if there be, pray, let me know that reason.

HYL.: Whatever degree of heat we perceive by sense, we may be sure the same exists in the object that occasions it.

PHIL.: What! the greatest as well as the least?

HYL.: I tell you, the reason is plainly the same in respect of both: they are both perceived by sense; nay, the greater degree of heat is more sensibly perceived; and consequently, if there is any difference, we are more certain of its real existence than we can be of the reality of a lesser degree.

PHIL.: But is not the most vehement and intense degree of heat a very great pain?

HYL.: No one can deny it.

PHIL.: And is any unperceiving thing capable of pain or pleasure?

HYL.: No, certainly.

PHIL.: Is your material substance a senseless being or a being endowed with sense and perception?

HYL.: It is senseless, without doubt.

PHIL.: It cannot, therefore, be the subject of pain?

HYL.: By no means.

PHIL.: Nor, consequently, of the greatest heat perceived by sense, since you acknowledge this to be no small pain?

HYL.: I grant it.

PHIL.: What shall we say then of your external object: is it a material substance, or no?

HYL.: It is a material substance with the sensible qualities inhering in it.

PHIL.: How then can a great heat exist in it, since you own it cannot in a material substance? I desire you would clear this point.

HYL.: Hold, Philonous, I fear I was out in yielding intense heat to be a pain. It should seem rather that pain is something distinct from heat, and the consequence or effect of it.

PHIL.: Upon putting your hand near the fire, do you perceive one simple uniform sensation or two distinct sensations?

HYL.: But one simple sensation.

PHIL.: Is not the heat immediately perceived?

HYL.: It is.

PHIL.: And the pain?

HYL.: True.

PHIL.: Seeing therefore they are both immediately perceived at the same time, and the fire affects you only with one simple or uncompounded idea, it follows that this same simple idea is both the intense heat immediately perceived and the pain; and, consequently, that the intense heat immediately perceived is nothing distinct from a particular sort of pain.

HYL.: It seems so.

PHIL.: Again, try in your thoughts, Hylas, if you can conceive a vehement sensation to be without pain or pleasure.

HYL.: I cannot.

PHIL.: Or can you frame to yourself an idea of sensible pain or pleasure, in general, abstracted from every particular idea of heat, cold, tastes, smells?

HYL.: I do not find that I can.

PHIL.: Does it not therefore follow that sensible pain is nothing distinct from those sensations or ideas —in an intense degree?

HYL.: It is undeniable; and, to speak the truth, I begin to suspect a very great heat cannot exist but in a mind perceiving it.

PHIL.: What! are you then in that *skeptical* state of suspense, between affirming and denying?

HYL.: I think I may be positive in the point. A very violent and painful heat cannot exist without the mind.

PHIL.: It has not therefore, according to you, any real being?

HYL.: I own it.

PHIL.: Is it therefore certain that there is no body in nature really hot?

HYL.: I have not denied there is any real heat in bodies. I only say there is no such thing as an intense real heat.

PHIL.: But did you not say before that all degrees of heat were equally real, or, if there was any difference, that the greater were more undoubtedly real than the lesser?

HYL.: True; but it was because I did not then consider the ground there is for distinguishing between them, which I now plainly see. And it is this: because intense heat is nothing else but a particular kind of painful sensation, and pain cannot exist but in a perceiving being, it follows that no intense heat can really exist in an unperceiving corporeal substance. But this is no reason why we should deny heat in an inferior degree to exist in such a substance.

PHIL.: But how shall we be able to discern those degrees of heat which exist only in the mind from those which exist without it?

HYL.: That is no difficult matter. You know the least pain cannot exist unperceived; whatever, therefore, degree of heat is a pain exists only in the mind. But as for all other degrees of heat nothing obliges us to think the same of them.

PHIL.: I think you granted before that no unperceiving being was capable of pleasure any more than of pain.

HYL.: I did.

PHIL.: And is not warmth, or a more gentle degree of heat than what causes uneasiness, a pleasure?

HYL.: What then?

PHIL.: Consequently, it cannot exist without the mind in an unperceiving substance, or body.

HYL.: So it seems.

PHIL.: Since, therefore, as well those degrees of heat that are not painful, as those that are, can exist only in a thinking substance, may we not conclude that external bodies are absolutely incapable of any degree of heat whatsoever?

HYL.: On second thoughts, I do not think it is so evident that warmth is a pleasure as that a great degree of heat is a pain.

PHIL.: I do not pretend that warmth is as great a pleasure as heat is a pain. But if you grant it to be even a small pleasure, it serves to make good my conclusion.

HYL.: I could rather call it an "indolence." It seems to be nothing more than a privation of both pain and pleasure. And that such a quality or state as this may agree to an unthinking substance, I hope you will not deny.

PHIL.: If you are resolved to maintain that warmth, or a gentle degree of heat, is no pleasure, I know not how to convince you otherwise than by appealing to your own sense. But what think you of cold?

HYL.: The same that I do of heat. An intense degree of cold is a pain; for to feel a very great cold is to perceive a great uneasiness; it cannot therefore exist without the mind; but a lesser degree of cold may, as well as a lesser degree of heat.

PHIL.: Those bodies, therefore, upon whose application to our own we perceive a moderate degree of heat must be concluded to have a moderate degree of heat or warmth in them; and those upon whose application we feel a like degree of cold must be thought to have cold in them.

HYL.: They must.

PHIL.: Can any doctrine be true that necessarily leads a man into an absurdity?

HYL.: Without doubt it cannot.

PHIL.: Is it not an absurdity to think that the same thing should be at the same time both cold and warm?

HYL.: It is.

PHIL.: Suppose now one of your hands is hot, and the other cold, and that they are both at once put into the same vessel of water, in an intermediate state, will not the water seem cold to one hand, and warm to the other?

HYL.: It will.

PHIL.: Ought we not therefore, by your principles, to

conclude it is really both cold and warm at the same time, that is, according to your own concession, to believe an absurdity?

HYL.: I confess it seems so.

PHIL.: Consequently, the principles themselves are false, since you have granted that no true principle leads to an absurdity.

HYL.: But, after all, can anything be more absurd than to say, *there is no heat in the fire?*

PHIL.: To make the point still clearer; tell me whether, in two cases exactly alike, we ought not to make the same judgment?

HYL.: We ought.

PHIL.: When a pin pricks your finger, does it not rend and divide the fibres of your flesh?

HYL.: It does.

PHIL.: And when a coal burns your finger, does it any more?

HYL.: It does not.

PHIL.: Since, therefore, you neither judge the sensation itself occasioned by the pin, nor anything like it to be in the pin, you should not, conformably to what you have now granted, judge the sensation occasioned by the fire, or anything like it, to be in the fire.

HYL.: Well, since it must be so, I am content to yield this point and acknowledge that heat and cold are only sensations existing in our minds. But there still remain qualities enough to secure the reality of external things.

PHIL.: But what will you say, Hylas, if it shall appear that the case is the same with regard to all other sensible qualities, and that they can no more be supposed to exist without the mind than heat and cold?

HYL.: Then, indeed, you will have done something to the purpose; but that is what I despair of seeing proved.

PHIL.: Let us examine them in order. What think you of tastes—do they exist without the mind, or no?

HYL.: Can any man in his senses doubt whether sugar is sweet or wormwood bitter?

PHIL.: Inform me, Hylas. Is a sweet taste a particular kind of pleasure or pleasant sensation, or is it not?

HYL.: It is.

PHIL.: And is not bitterness some kind of uneasiness or pain?

HYL.: I grant it.

PHIL.: If therefore, sugar and wormwood are unthinking corporeal substances existing without the mind, how can sweetness and bitterness, that is, pleasure and pain, agree to them?

HYL.: Hold, Philonous. I now see what it was [that] deluded me all this time. You asked whether heat and cold, sweetness and bitterness, were not particular sorts of pleasure and pain; to which I answered simply that they were. Whereas I should have thus distinguished: those qualities as perceived by us are pleasures or pains, but not as existing in the external objects. We must not therefore conclude absolutely that there is no heat in the fire or sweetness in the sugar, but only that heat or sweetness, as perceived by us, are not in the fire or sugar. What say you to this?

PHIL.: I say it is nothing to the purpose. Our discourse proceeded altogether concerning sensible things, which you defined to be "the things we immediately perceive by our senses." Whatever other qualities, therefore, you speak of, as distinct from these, I know nothing of them, neither do they at all belong to the point in dispute. You may, indeed, pretend to have discovered certain qualities which you do not perceive and assert those insensible qualities exist in fire and sugar. But what use can be made of this to your present purpose, I am at a loss to conceive. Tell me then once more, do you acknowledge that heat and cold, sweetness and bitterness (meaning those qualities which are perceived by the senses), do not exist without the mind?

HYL.: I see it is to no purpose to hold out, so I give up the cause as to those mentioned qualities, though I profess it sounds oddly to say that sugar is not sweet.

PHIL.: But, for your further satisfaction, take this along with you: that which at other times seems sweet shall, to a distempered palate, appear bitter, and nothing can be plainer than that divers persons perceive different tastes in the same food, since that which one man delights in, another abhors. And how could this be if the taste was something really inherent in the food?

HYL.: I acknowledge I know not how.

PHIL.: In the next place, odors are to be considered. And with regard to these I would fain know whether what has been said of tastes does not exactly agree to them? Are they not so many pleasing or displeasing sensations?

HYL.: They are.

PHIL.: Can you then conceive it possible that they should exist in an unperceiving thing?

HYL.: I cannot.

PHIL.: Or can you imagine that filth and ordure affect those brute animals that feed on them out of choice with the same smells which we perceive in them?

HYL.: By no means.

PHIL.: May we not therefore conclude of smells, as of the other forementioned qualities, that they cannot exist in any but a perceiving substance or mind?

HYL.: I think so.

PHIL.: Then as to sounds, what must we think of them, are they accidents really inherent in external bodies or not?

HYL.: That they inhere not in the sonorous bodies is plain from hence; because a bell struck in the exhausted receiver of an air-pump sends forth no sound. The air, therefore, must be thought the subject of sound.

PHIL.: What reason is there for that, Hylas?

HYL.: Because, when any motion is raised in the air, we perceive a sound greater or lesser, in proportion to the air's motion; but without some motion in the air we never hear any sound at all.

PHIL.: And granting that we never hear a sound but when some motion is produced in the air, yet I do not see how you can infer from thence that the sound itself is in the air.

HYL.: It is this very motion in the external air that produces in the mind the sensation of sound. For, striking on the drum of the ear, it causes a vibration which by the auditory nerves being communicated to the brain, the soul is thereupon affected with the sensation called "sound."

PHIL.: What! is sound then a sensation?

HYL.: I tell you, as perceived by us it is a particular sensation in the mind.

PHIL.: And can any sensation exist without the mind?

HYL.: No, certainly.

PHIL.: How then can sound, being a sensation, exist in the air if by the "air" you mean a senseless substance existing without the mind?

HYL.: You must distinguish, Philonous, between sound as it is perceived by us, and as it is in itself; or (which is the same thing) between the sound we immediately perceive and that which exists without us. The former, indeed, is a particular kind of sensation, but the latter is merely a vibrative or undulatory motion in the air.

PHIL.: I thought I had already obviated that distinction by the answer I gave when you were applying it in a like case before. But, to say no more of that, are you sure then that sound is really nothing but motion?

HYL.: I am.

PHIL.: Whatever, therefore, agrees to real sound may with truth be attributed to motion?

HYL.: It may.

PHIL.: It is then good sense to speak of "motion" as of a thing that is *loud, sweet, acute,* or *grave.*

HYL.: I see you are resolved not to understand me. Is it not evident those accidents or modes belong only to sensible sound, or sound in the common acceptation of the word, but not to sound in the real and philosophic sense, which, as I just now told you, is nothing but a certain motion of the air?

PHIL.: It seems then there are two sorts of sound—the one vulgar, or that which is heard, the other philosophical and real?

HYL.: Even so.

PHIL.: And the latter consists in motion?

HYL.: I told you so before.

PHIL.: Tell me, Hylas, to which of the senses, think you, the idea of motion belongs? To the hearing?

HYL.: No, certainly; but to the sight and touch.

PHIL.: It should follow then that, according to you, real sounds may possibly be *seen* or *felt,* but never *heard.*

HYL.: Look you, Philonous, you may, if you please, make a jest of my opinion, but that will not alter the truth of things. I own, indeed, the inferences you draw me into sound something oddly, but common language, you know, is framed by, and for the use of, the vulgar. We must not therefore wonder if expressions adapted to exact philosophic notions seem uncouth and out of the way.

PHIL.: Is it come to that? I assure you I imagine myself to have gained no small point since you make so light of departing from common phrases and opinions, it being a main part of our inquiry to examine whose notions are widest of the common road and most repugnant to the general sense of the world. But can you think it no more than a philosophical paradox to say that "real sounds are never heard," and that the idea of them is obtained by some other sense? And is there nothing in this contrary to nature and the truth of things?

HYL.: To deal ingenuously, I do not like it. And, after the concessions already made, I had as well grant that sounds, too, have no real being without the mind.

PHIL.: And I hope you will make no difficulty to acknowledge the same of colors.

HYL.: Pardon me; the case of colors is very different. Can anything be plainer than that we see them on the objects?

PHIL.: The objects you speak of are, I suppose, corporeal substances existing without the mind?

HYL.: They are.

PHIL.: And have true and real colors inhering in them?

HYL.: Each visible object has that color which we see in it.

PHIL.: How! is there anything visible but what we perceive by sight?

HYL.: There is not.

PHIL.: And do we perceive anything by sense which we do not perceive immediately?

HYL.: How often must I be obliged to repeat the same thing? I tell you, we do not.

PHIL.: Have patience, good Hylas, and tell me once more whether there is anything immediately perceived by the senses except sensible qualities. I know you asserted there was not; but I would now be informed whether you still persist in the same opinion.

HYL.: I do.

PHIL.: Pray, is your corporeal substance either a sensible quality or made up of sensible qualities?

HYL.: What a question that is! Who ever thought it was?

PHIL.: My reason for asking was, because in saying "each visible object has that color which we see in it," you make visible objects to be corporeal substances, which implies either that corporeal substances are sensible qualities or else that there is something besides sensible qualities perceived by sight; but as this point was formerly agreed between us, and is still maintained by you, it is a clear consequence that your corporeal substance is nothing distinct from sensible qualities.

HYL.: You may draw as many absurd consequences as you please and endeavor to perplex the plainest things, but you shall never persuade me out of my senses. I clearly understand my own meaning.

PHIL.: I wish you would make me understand it, too. But, since you are unwilling to have your notion of corporeal substance examined, I shall urge that point no further. Only be pleased to let me know whether the same colors which we see exist in external bodies or some other.

HYL.: The very same.

PHIL.: What! are then the beautiful red and purple we see on yonder clouds really in them? Or do you imagine they have in themselves any other form than that of a dark mist or vapor?

HYL.: I must own, Philonous, those colors are not really in the clouds as they seem to be at this distance. They are only apparent colors.

PHIL.: "Apparent" call you them? How shall we distinguish these apparent colors from real?

HYL.: Very easily. Those are to be thought apparent which, appearing only at a distance, vanish upon a nearer approach.

PHIL.: And those, I suppose, are to be thought real which are discovered by the most near and exact survey.

HYL.: Right.

PHIL.: Is the nearest and exactest survey made by the help of a microscope or by the naked eye?

HYL.: By a microscope, doubtless.

PHIL.: But a microscope often discovers colors in an object different from those perceived by the unassisted sight. And, in case we had microscopes magnifying to any assigned degree, it is certain that no object whatsoever, viewed through them, would appear in the same color which it exhibits to the naked eye.

HYL.: And what will you conclude from all this? You cannot argue that there are really and naturally no colors on objects because by artificial managements they may be altered or made to vanish.

PHIL.: I think it may evidently be concluded from your own concessions that all the colors we see with our naked eyes are only apparent as those on the clouds, since they vanish upon a more close and accurate inspection which is afforded us by a microscope. Then, as to what you say by way of prevention: I ask you whether the real and natural state of an object is better discovered by a very sharp and piercing sight or by one which is less sharp?

HYL.: By the former without doubt.

PHIL.: Is it not plain from dioptrics that microscopes make the sight more penetrating and represent objects as they would appear to the eye in case it were naturally endowed with a most exquisite sharpness?

HYL.: It is.

PHIL.: Consequently, the microscopical representation is to be thought that which best sets forth the real nature of the thing, or what it is in itself. The colors, therefore, by it perceived are more genuine and real than those perceived otherwise.

HYL.: I confess there is something in what you say.

PHIL.: Besides, it is not only possible but manifest that there actually are animals whose eyes are by nature framed to perceive those things which by reason of their minuteness escape our sight. What think you of those inconceivably small animals perceived by glasses? Must we suppose they are all stark blind? Or, in case they see, can it be imagined their sight has not the same use in preserving their bodies from injuries which appears in that of all other animals? And if it has, is it not evident they must see particles less than their own bodies, which will present them with a far different view in each object from that which strikes our senses? Even our own eyes do not always represent objects to us after the same manner. In the jaundice everyone knows that all things seem yellow. Is it not therefore highly probable those animals in whose eyes we discern a very different texture from that of ours, and whose bodies abound with different humors, do not see the same colors in every object that we do? From all which should it not seem to follow that all colors are equally apparent, and that none of those which we perceive are really inherent in any outward object?

HYL.: It should.

PHIL.: The point will be past all doubt if you consider that, in case colors were real properties or affections inherent in external bodies, they could admit of an alteration without some change wrought in the very bodies themselves; but is it not evident from what has been said that, upon the use of microscopes, upon a change happening in the humors of the eye, or a variation of distance, without any manner of real alteration in the thing itself, the colors of any object are either changed or totally disappear? Nay, all other circumstances remaining the same, change but the situation of some objects and they shall present different colors to the eye. The same thing happens upon viewing an object in various degrees of light. And what is more known than that the same bodies appear differently colored by candlelight from what they do in the open day? Add to these the experiment of a prism which, separating the heterogeneous rays of light alters the color of any object and will cause the whitest to appear of a deep blue or red to the naked eye. And now tell me whether you are still of opinion that every body has its true real color inhering in it; and if you think it has, I would fain know further from you what certain distance and position of the object, what peculiar texture and formation of the eye, what degree or kind of light is necessary for ascertaining that true color and distinguishing it from apparent ones.

HYL.: I own myself entirely satisfied that they are all equally apparent and that there is no such thing as color really inhering in external bodies, but that it is altogether in the light. And what confirms me in this opinion is that in proportion to the light colors are still more or less vivid; and if there be no light, then are there no colors perceived. Besides, allowing there are colors on external objects, yet, how is it possible for us to perceive them? For no external body affects the mind unless it acts first on our organs of sense. But the only action of bodies is motion, and motion cannot be communicated otherwise than by impulse. A distant object, therefore, cannot act on the eye, nor consequently make itself or its properties perceivable to the soul. Whence it plainly follows that it is immediately some contiguous substance which, operating on the eye, occasions a perception of colors; and such is light.

PHIL.: How! is light then a substance?

HYL.: I tell you, Philonous, external light is nothing but a thin fluid substance whose minute particles, being agitated with a brisk motion and in various manners reflected from the different surfaces of outward objects to the eyes, communicate different motions to the optic nerves; which, being propagated to the brain, cause therein various impressions, and these are attended with the sensations of red, blue, yellow, etc.

PHIL.: It seems, then, the light does no more than shake the optic nerves.

HYL.: Nothing else.

PHIL.: And, consequent to each particular motion of the nerves, the mind is affected with a sensation which is some particular color.

HYL.: Right.

PHIL.: And these sensations have no existence without the mind.

HYL.: They have not.

PHIL.: How then do you affirm that colors are in the light, since by "light" you understand a corporeal substance external to the mind?

HYL.: Light and colors, as immediately perceived by us, I grant cannot exist without the mind. But in themselves they are only the motions and configurations of certain insensible particles of matter.

PHIL.: Colors, then, in the vulgar sense, or taken for the immediate objects of sight, cannot agree to any but a perceiving substance.

HYL.: That is what I say.

PHIL.: Well then, since you give up the point as to those sensible qualities which are alone thought colors by all mankind besides, you may hold what you please with regard to those invisible ones of the philosophers. It is not my business to dispute about them; only I would advise you to bethink yourself whether, considering the inquiry we are upon, it be prudent for you to affirm—*the red and blue which we see are not real colors, but certain unknown motions and figures which no man ever did or can see are truly so.* Are not these shocking notions, and are not they subject to as many ridiculous inferences as those you were obliged to renounce before in the case of sounds?

HYL.: I frankly own, Philonous, that it is in vain to stand out any longer. Colors, sounds, tastes, in a word, all those termed "secondary qualities,"

have certainly no existence without the mind. But by this acknowledgment I must not be supposed to derogate anything from the reality of matter or external objects; seeing it is no more than several philosophers maintain, who nevertheless are the farthest imaginable from denying matter. For the clearer understanding of this you must know sensible qualities are by philosophers divided into "primary" and "secondary." The former are extension, figure, solidity, gravity, motion, and rest. And these they hold exist really in bodies. The latter are those above enumerated, or, briefly, all sensible qualities besides the primary, which they assert are only so many sensations or ideas existing nowhere but in the mind. But all this, I doubt not, you are apprised of. For my part I have been a long time sensible there was such an opinion current among philosophers, but was never thoroughly convinced of its truth until now.

PHIL.: You are still then of opinion that *extension* and *figures* are inherent in external unthinking substances?

HYL.: I am.

PHIL.: But what if the same arguments which are brought against secondary qualities will hold good against these also?

HYL.: Why then I shall be obliged to think they too exist only in the mind.

PHIL.: Is it your opinion the very figure and extension which you perceive by sense exist in the outward object or material substance?

HYL.: It is.

PHIL.: Have all other animals as good grounds to think the same of the figure and extension which they see and feel?

HYL.: Without doubt, if they have any thought at all.

PHIL.: Answer me, Hylas. Think you the senses were bestowed upon all animals for their preservation and well-being in life? Or were they given to men alone for this end?

HYL.: I make no question but they have the same use in all other animals.

PHIL.: If so, is it not necessary they should be enabled by them to perceive their own limbs and those bodies which are capable of harming them?

HYL.: Certainly.

PHIL.: A mite therefore must be supposed to see his

own foot, and things equal or even less than it, as bodies of some considerable dimension, though at the same time they appear to you scarce discernible or at best at so many visible points?

HYL.: I cannot deny it.

PHIL.: And to creatures less than the mite they will seem yet larger?

HYL.: They will.

PHIL.: Insomuch that what you can hardly discern will to another extremely minute animal appear as some huge mountain?

HYL.: All this I grant.

PHIL.: Can one and the same thing be at the same time in itself of different dimensions?

HYL.: That were absurd to imagine.

PHIL.: But from what you have laid down it follows that both the extension by you perceived and that perceived by the mite itself, as likewise all those perceived by lesser animals, are each of them the true extension of the mite's foot; that is to say, by your own principles you are led into an absurdity.

HYL.: There seems to be some difficulty in the point.

PHIL.: Again, have you not acknowledged that no real inherent property of any object can be changed without some change in the thing itself?

HYL.: I have.

PHIL.: But, as we approach to or recede from an object, the visible extension varies, being at one distance ten or a hundred times greater than at another. Does it not therefore follow from hence likewise that it is not really inherent in the object?

HYL.: I own I am at a loss what to think.

PHIL.: Your judgment will soon be determined if you will venture to think as freely concerning this quality as you have done concerning the rest. Was it not admitted as a good argument that neither heat nor cold was in the water because it seemed warm to one hand and cold to the other?

HYL.: It was.

PHIL.: Is it not the very same reasoning to conclude there is no extension or figure in an object because to one eye it shall seem little, smooth, and round, when at the same time it appears to the other great, uneven, and angular?

HYL.: The very same. But does this latter fact ever happen?

PHIL.: You may at any time make the experiment by looking with one eye bare and with the other through a microscope.

HYL.: I know not how to maintain it, and yet I am loath to give up *extension;* I see so many odd consequences following upon such a concession.

PHIL.: Odd, say you? After the concessions already made, I hope you will stick at nothing for its oddness [But, on the other hand, should it not seem very odd if the general reasoning which includes all other sensible qualities did not also include extension? If it be allowed that no idea nor anything like an idea can exist in an unperceiving substance, then surely it follows that no figure or mode of extension, which we can either perceive or imagine, or have any idea of, can be really inherent in matter, not to mention the peculiar difficulty there must be in conceiving a material substance, prior to and distinct from extension, to be the *substratum* of extension. Be the sensible quality what it will—figure or sound or color—it seems alike impossible it should subsist in that which does not perceive it.]

HYL.: I give up the point for the present, reserving still a right to retract my opinion in case I shall hereafter discover any false step in my progress to it.

PHIL.: That is a right you cannot be denied. Figures and extension being dispatched, we proceed next to *motion.* Can a real motion in any external body be at the same time both very swift and very slow?

HYL.: It cannot.

PHIL.: Is not the motion of a body swift in a reciprocal proportion to the time it takes up in describing any given space? Thus a body that describes a mile in an hour moves three times faster than it would in case it described only a mile in three hours.

HYL.: I agree with you.

PHIL.: And is not time measured by the succession of ideas in our minds?

HYL.: It is.

PHIL.: And is it not possible ideas should succeed one another twice as fast in your mind as they do in mine, or in that of some spirit of another kind?

HYL.: I own it.

PHIL.: Consequently, the same body may to another

seem to perform its motion over any space in half the time that it does to you. And the same reasoning will hold as to any other proportion; that is to say, according to your principles (since the motions perceived are both really in the object) it is possible one and the same body shall be really moved the same way at once, both very swift and very slow. How is this consistent either with common sense or with what you just now granted?

HYL.: I have nothing to say to it.

PHIL.: Then as for *solidity;* either you do not mean any sensible quality by that word, and so it is beside our inquiry; or if you do, it must be either hardness or resistance. But both the one and the other are plainly relative to our senses: it being evident that what seems hard to one animal may appear soft to another who has greater force and firmness of limbs. Nor is it less plain that the resistance I feel is not in the body.

HYL.: I own the very sensation of resistance, which is all you immediately perceive, is not in the *body,* but the cause of that sensation is.

PHIL.: But the causes of our sensations are not things immediately perceived, and therefore not sensible. This point I thought had been already determined.

HYL.: I own it was; but you will pardon me if I seem a little embarrassed; I know not how to quit my old notions.

PHIL.: To help you out, do but consider that if *extension* be once acknowledged to have no existence without the mind, the same must necessarily be granted of motion, solidity, and gravity, since they all evidently suppose extension. It is therefore superfluous to inquire particularly concerning each of them. In denying extension, you have denied them all to have any real existence.

HYL.: I wonder, Philonous, if what you say be true, why those philosophers who deny the secondary qualities any real existence should yet attribute it to the primary. If there is no difference between them, how can this be accounted for?

PHIL.: It is not my business to account for every opinion of the philosophers. But, among other reasons which may be assigned for this, it seems probable that pleasure and pain being rather annexed to the former than the latter may be one.

Heat and cold, tastes and smells have something more vividly pleasing or disagreeable than the ideas of extension, figure, and motion affect us with. And, it being too visibly absurd to hold that pain or pleasure can be in an unperceiving substance, men are more easily weaned from believing the external existence of the secondary than the primary qualities. You will be satisfied there is something in this if you recollect the difference you made between an intense and more moderate degree of heat, allowing the one a real existence while you denied it to the other. But, after all, there is no rational ground for that distinction, for surely an indifferent sensation is as truly a *sensation* as one more pleasing or painful, and consequently should not any more than they be supposed to exist in an unthinking subject.

HYL.: It is just come into my head, Philonous, that I have somewhere heard of a distinction between *absolute* and *sensible* extension. Now though it be acknowledged that *great* and *small,* consisting merely in the relation which other extended beings have to the parts of our own bodies, do not really inhere in the substances themselves, yet nothing obliges us to hold the same with regard to *absolute* extension, which is something abstracted from *great* and *small,* from this or that particular magnitude or figure. So likewise as to motion: *swift* and *slow* are altogether relative to the succession of ideas in our own minds. But it does not follow, because those modifications of motion exist not without the mind, that therefore absolute motion abstracted from them does not.

PHIL.: Pray what is it that distinguishes one motion, or one part of extension, from another? Is it not something sensible, as some degree of swiftness or slowness, some certain magnitude or figure peculiar to each?

HYL.: I think so.

PHIL.: These qualities, therefore, stripped of all sensible properties, are without all specific and numerical differences, as the schools call them.

HYL.: They are.

PHIL.: That is to say, they are extension in general, and motion in general.

HYL.: Let it be so.

PHIL.: But it is a universally received maxim that

everything which exists is particular. How then can motion in general, or extension in general, exist in any corporeal substance?

HYL.: I will take time to solve your difficulty.

PHIL.: But I think the point may be speedily decided. Without doubt you can tell whether you are able to frame this or that idea. Now I am content to put our dispute on this issue. If you can frame in your thoughts a distinct abstract idea of motion or extension divested of all those sensible modes as swift and slow, great and small, round and square, and the like, which are acknowledged to exist only in the mind, I will then yield the point you contend for. But if you cannot, it will be unreasonable on your side to insist any longer upon what you have no notion of.

HYL.: To confess ingenuously, I cannot.

PHIL.: Can you even separate the ideas of extension and motion from the ideas of all those qualities which they who make the distinction term "secondary"?

HYL.: What! is it not an easy matter to consider extension and motion by themselves, abstracted from all other sensible qualities? Pray how do the mathematicians treat of them?

PHIL.: I acknowledge, Hylas, it is not difficult to form general propositions and reasonings about those qualities without mentioning any other, and, in this sense, to consider or treat of them abstractedly. But how does it follow that, because I can pronounce the word "motion" by itself, I can form the idea of it in my mind exclusive of body? Or because theorems may be made of extension and figures, without any mention of *great* or *small,* or any other sensible mode or quality, that therefore it is possible such an abstract idea of extension, without any particular size or figure or sensible quality, should be distinctly formed and apprehended by the mind? Mathematicians treat of quantity without regarding what other sensible qualities it is attended with, as being altogether indifferent to their demonstrations. But when, laying aside the words, they contemplate the bare ideas, I believe you will find they are not the pure abstracted ideas of extension.

HYL.: But what say you to *pure intellect?* May not abstracted ideas be framed by that faculty?

PHIL.: Since I cannot frame abstract ideas at all, it is plain I cannot frame them by the help of pure intellect, whatsoever faculty you understand by those words. Besides, not to inquire into the nature of pure intellect and its spiritual objects, as *virtue, reason, God,* or the like, thus much seems manifest that sensible things are only to be perceived by sense or represented by the imagination. Figures, therefore, and extension, being originally perceived by sense, do not belong to pure intellect; but, for your further satisfaction, try if you can frame the idea of any figure abstracted from all particularities of size or even from other sensible qualities.

HYL.: Let me think a little—I do not find that I can.

PHIL.: And can you think it possible that [an idea] should really exist in nature which implies a repugnancy in its conception?

HYL.: By no means.

PHIL.: Since therefore it is impossible even for the mind to disunite the ideas of extension and motion from all other sensible qualities, does it not follow that where the one exist there necessarily the other exist likewise?

HYL.: It should seem so.

PHIL.: Consequently, the very same arguments which you admitted as conclusive against the secondary qualities are, without any further application of force, against the primary, too. Besides, if you will trust your senses, is it not plain all sensible qualities coexist, or to them appear as being in the same place? Do they ever represent a motion or figure as being divested of all other visible and tangible qualities?

HYL.: You need say no more on this head. I am free to own, if there be no secret error or oversight in our proceedings hitherto, that all sensible qualities are alike to be denied existence without the mind. But my fear is that I have been too liberal in my former concessions, or overlooked some fallacy or other. In short, I did not take time to think.

PHIL.: For that matter, Hylas, you may take what time you please in reviewing the progress of our inquiry. You are at liberty to recover any slips you might have made, or offer whatever you have omitted which makes for your first opinion.

HYL.: One great oversight I take to be this—that I did not sufficiently distinguish the *object* from the *sensation.* Now, though this latter may not exist without the mind, yet it will not thence follow that the former cannot.

PHIL.: What object do you mean? The object of the senses?

HYL.: The same.

PHIL.: It is then immediately perceived?

HYL.: Right.

PHIL.: Make me to understand the difference between what is immediately perceived and a sensation.

HYL.: The sensation I take to be an act of the mind perceiving; besides which there is something perceived, and this I call the "object." For example, there is red and yellow on that tulip. But then the act of perceiving those colors is in me only, and not in the tulip.

PHIL.: What tulip do you speak of? Is it that which you see?

HYL.: The same.

PHIL.: And what do you see besides color, figure, and extension?

HYL.: Nothing.

PHIL.: What you would say then is that the red and yellow are coexistent with the extension; is it not?

HYL.: That is not all; I would say they have a real existence without the mind, in some unthinking substance.

PHIL.: That the colors are really in the tulip which I see is manifest. Neither can it be denied that this tulip may exist independent of your mind or mine; but that any immediate object of the senses—that is, any idea, or combination of ideas—should exist in an unthinking substance, or exterior to all minds, is in itself an evident contradiction. Nor can I imagine how this follows from what you said just now, to wit, that the red and yellow were on the tulip *you saw,* since you do not pretend to *see* that unthinking substance.

HYL.: You have an artful way, Philonous, of diverting our inquiry from the subject.

PHIL.: I see you have no mind to be pressed that way. To return then to your distinction between *sensation* and *object;* if I take you right, you distinguish in every perception two things, the one an action of the mind, the other not.

HYL.: True.

PHIL.: And this action cannot exist in, or belong to, any unthinking thing, but whatever besides is implied in a perception may?

HYL.: That is my meaning.

PHIL.: So that if there was a perception without any act of the mind, it were possible such a perception should exist in an unthinking substance?

HYL.: I grant it. But it is impossible there should be such a perception.

PHIL.: When is the mind said to be active?

HYL.: When it produces, puts an end to, or changes anything.

PHIL.: Can the mind produce, discontinue, or change anything but by an act of the will?

HYL.: It cannot.

PHIL.: The mind therefore is to be accounted *active* in its perceptions so far forth as *volition* is included in them?

HYL.: It is.

PHIL.: In plucking this flower I am active, because I do it by the motion of my hand, which was consequent upon my volition; so likewise in applying it to my nose. But is either of these smelling?

HYL.: No.

PHIL.: I act, too, in drawing the air through my nose, because my breathing so rather than otherwise is the effect of my volition. But neither can this be called "smelling," for if it were I should smell every time I breathed in that manner?

HYL.: True.

PHIL.: Smelling then is somewhat consequent to all this?

HYL.: It is.

PHIL.: But I do not find my will concerned any further. Whatever more there is—as that I perceive such a particular smell, or any smell at all—this is independent of my will, and therein I am altogether passive. Do you find it otherwise with you, Hylas?

HYL.: No, the very same.

PHIL.: Then, as to seeing, is it not in your power to open your eyes or keep them shut, to turn them this or that way?

HYL.: Without doubt.

PHIL.: But does it in like manner depend on your will that in looking on this flower you perceive *white* rather than any other color? Or, directing your open eyes toward yonder part of the heaven, can you avoid seeing the sun? Or is light or darkness the effect of your volition?

HYL.: No, certainly.

PHIL.: You are then in these respects altogether passive?

HYL.: I am.

PHIL.: Tell me now whether *seeing* consists in perceiving light and colors or in opening and turning the eyes?

HYL.: Without doubt, in the former.

PHIL.: Since, therefore, you are in the very perception of light and colors altogether passive, what is become of that action you were speaking of as an ingredient in every sensation? And does it not follow from your own concessions that the perception of light and colors, including no action in it, may exist in an unperceiving substance? And is not this a plain contradiction?

HYL.: I know not what to think of it.

PHIL.: Besides, since you distinguish the *active* and *passive* in every perception, you must do it in that of pain. But how is it possible that pain, be it as little active as you please, should exist in an unperceiving substance? In short, do but consider the point and then confess ingenuously whether light and colors, tastes, sounds, etc., are not all equally passions or sensations in the soul. You may indeed call them "external objects" and give them in words what subsistence you please. But examine your own thoughts and then tell me whether it be not as I say?

HYL.: I acknowledge, Philonous, that, upon a fair observation of what passes in my mind, I can discover nothing else but that I am a thinking being affected with variety of sensations; neither is it possible to conceive how a sensation should exist in an unperceiving substance. But then, on the other hand, when I look on sensible things in a different view, considering them as so many modes and qualities, I find it necessary to suppose a material *substratum,* without which they cannot be conceived to exist.

PHIL.: "Material substratum" call you it? Pray, by which of your senses came you acquainted with that being?

HYL.: It is not itself sensible; its modes and qualities only being perceived by the senses.

PHIL.: I presume then it was by reflection and reason you obtained the idea of it?

HYL.: I do not pretend to any proper positive idea of it. However, I conclude it exists because qualities cannot be conceived to exist without a support.

PHIL.: It seems then you have only a relative notion of it, or that you conceive it not otherwise than by conceiving the relation it bears to sensible qualities?

HYL.: Right.

PHIL.: Be pleased, therefore, to let me know wherein that relation consists.

HYL.: Is it not sufficiently expressed in the term "substratum" or "substance"?

PHIL.: If so, the word "substratum" should import that it is spread under the sensible qualities or accidents?

HYL.: True.

PHIL.: And consequently under extension?

HYL.: I own it.

PHIL.: It is therefore somewhat in its own nature distinct from extension?

HYL.: I tell you extension is only a mode, and matter is something that supports modes. And is it not evident the thing supported is different from the thing supporting?

PHIL.: So that something distinct from, and exclusive of, extension is supposed to be the *substratum* of extension?

HYL.: Just so.

PHIL.: Answer me, Hylas, can a thing be spread without extension, or is not the idea of extension necessarily included in *spreading?*

HYL.: It is.

PHIL.: Whatsoever therefore you suppose spread under anything must have in itself an extension distinct from the extention of that thing under which it is spread?

HYL.: It must.

PHIL.: Consequently, every corporeal substance being the *substratum* of extension must have in itself another extention by which it is qualified to be a *substratum,* and so on to infinity? And I ask whether this be not absurd in itself and repugnant to what you granted just now, to wit, that the *substratum* was something distinct from and exclusive of extension?

HYL.: Aye, but, Philonous, you take me wrong. I do

not mean that matter is *spread* in a gross literal sense under extension. The word "substratum" is used only to express in general the same thing with "substance."

PHIL.: Well then, let us examine the relation implied in the term "substance." Is it not that it stands under accidents?

HYL.: The very same.

PHIL.: But that one thing may stand under or support another, must it not be extended?

HYL.: It must.

PHIL.: Is not therefore this supposition liable to the same absurdity with the former?

HYL.: You still take things in a strict literal sense; that is not fair, Philonous.

PHIL.: I am not for imposing any sense on your words; you are at liberty to explain them as you please. Only, I beseech you, make me understand something by them. You tell me matter supports or stands under accidents. How! is it as your legs support your body?

HYL.: No; that is the literal sense.

PHIL.: Pray let me know any sense, literal or not literal, that you understand it in.—How long must I wait for an answer, Hylas?

HYL.: I declare I know not what to say. I once thought I understood well enough what was meant by matter's supporting accidents. But now, the more I think on it, the less can I comprehend it; in short, I find that I know nothing of it.

PHIL.: It seems then you have no idea at all, neither relative nor positive, of matter? you know neither what it is in itself nor what relation it bears to accidents?

HYL.: I acknowledge it.

PHIL.: And yet you asserted that you could not conceive how qualities or accidents should really exist without conceiving at the same time a material support of them?

HYL.: I did.

PHIL.: That is to say, when you conceive the real existence of qualities, you do withal conceive something which you cannot conceive?

HYL.: It was wrong I own. But still I fear there is some fallacy or other. Pray, what think you of this? It is just come into my head that the ground of all our mistake lies in your treating of each quality by itself. Now I grant that each quality cannot singly subsist without the mind. Color cannot without extension, neither can figure without some other sensible quality. But, as the several qualities united or blended together form entire sensible things, nothing hinders why such things may not be supposed to exist without the mind.

PHIL.: Either, Hylas, you are jesting or have a very bad memory. Though, indeed, we went through all the qualities by name one after another, yet my arguments, or rather your concessions, nowhere tended to prove that the secondary qualities did not subsist each alone by itself, but that they were not *at all* without the mind. Indeed, in treating of figure and motion we concluded they could not exist without the mind, because it was impossible even in thought to separate them from all secondary qualities, so as to conceive them existing by themselves. But then this was not the only argument made use of upon that occasion. But (to pass by all that has been hitherto said and reckon it for nothing, if you will have it so) I am content to put the whole upon this issue. If you can conceive it possible for any mixture or combination of qualities, or any sensible object whatever, to exist without the mind, then I will grant it actually to be so.

HYL.: If it comes to that the point will soon be decided. What more easy than to conceive a tree or house existing by itself, independent of, and unperceived by, any mind whatsoever? I do at this present time conceive them existing after that manner.

PHIL.: How say you, Hylas, can you see a thing which is at the same time unseen?

HYL.: No, that were a contradiction.

PHIL.: Is it not as great a contradiction to talk of *conceiving* a thing which is *unconceived*?

HYL.: It is.

PHIL.: The tree or house, therefore, which you think of is conceived by you?

HYL.: How should it be otherwise?

PHIL.: And what is conceived is surely in the mind?

HYL.: Without question, that which is conceived is in the mind.

PHIL.: How then came you to say you conceived a house or tree existing independent and out of all minds whatsoever?

HYL.: That was I own an oversight, but stay, let me

consider what let me into it.—It is a pleasant mistake enough. As I was thinking of a tree in a solitary place where no one was present to see it, methought that was to conceive a tree as existing unperceived or unthought of, not considering that I myself conceived it all the while. But now I plainly see that all I can do is to frame ideas in my own mind. I may indeed conceive in my own thoughts the idea of a tree, or a house, or a mountain, but that is all. And this is far from proving that I can conceive them *existing out of the mind of all spirits.*

PHIL.: You acknowledge then that you cannot possibly conceive how any one corporeal sensible thing should exist otherwise than in a mind?

HYL.: I do.

PHIL.: And yet you will earnestly contend for the truth of that which you cannot so much as conceive?

HYL.: I profess I know not what to think; but still there are some scruples remain with me. Is it not certain I see things at a distance? Do we not perceive the stars and moon, for example, to be a great way off? Is not this, I say, manifest to the senses?

PHIL.: Do you not in a dream, too, perceive those or the like objects?

HYL.: I do.

PHIL.: And have they not then the same appearance of being distant?

HYL.: They have.

PHIL.: But you do not thence conclude the apparitions in a dream to be without the mind?

HYL.: By no means.

PHIL.: You ought not therefore to conclude that sensible objects are without the mind, from their appearance or manner wherein they are perceived.

HYL.: I acknowledge it. But does not my sense deceive me in those cases?

PHIL.: By no means. The idea or thing which you immediately perceive, neither sense nor reason informs you that it actually exists without the mind. By sense you only know that you are affected with such certain sensations of light, colors, etc. And these you will not say are without the mind.

HYL.: True, but, beside all that, do you not think the sight suggests something of *outness* or *distance?*

PHIL.: Upon approaching a distant object, do the visible size and figure change perpetually or do they appear the same at all distances?

HYL.: They are in a continual change.

PHIL.: Sight, therefore, does not suggest or any way inform you that the visible object you immediately perceive exists at a distance, or will be perceived when you advance farther onward, there being a continued series of visible objects succeeding each other during the whole time of your approach.

HYL.: It does not; but still I know, upon seeing an object, what object I shall perceive after having passed over a certain distance: no matter whether it be exactly the same or no, there is still something of distance suggested in the case.

PHIL.: Good Hylas, do but reflect a little on the point, and then tell me whether there be any more in it than this. From the ideas you actually perceive by sight, you have by experience learned to collect what other ideas you will (according to the standing order of nature) be affected with, after such a certain succession of time and motion.

HYL.: Upon the whole, I take it to be nothing else.

PHIL.: Now is it not plain that if we suppose a man born blind was on a sudden made to see, he could at first have no experience of what may be suggested by sight?

HYL.: It is.

PHIL.: He would not then, according to you, have any notion of distance annexed to the things he saw, but would take them for a new set of sensations existing only in his mind?

HYL.: It is undeniable.

PHIL.: But to make it more plain: is not *distance* a line turned endwise to the eye?

HYL.: It is.

PHIL.: And can a line so situated be perceived by sight?

HYL.: It cannot.

PHIL.: Does it not therefore follow that distance is not properly and immediately perceived by sight?

HYL.: It should seem so.

PHIL.: Again, is it your opinion that colors are at a distance?

HYL.: It must be acknowledged they are only in the mind.

PHIL.: But do not colors appear to the eye as co-existing in the same place with extension and figures?

HYL.: They do.

PHIL.: How can you then conclude from sight that figures exist without, when you acknowledge colors do not; the sensible appearances being the very same with regard to both?

HYL.: I know not what to answer.

PHIL.: But allowing that distance was truly and immediately perceived by the mind, yet it would not thence follow it existed out of the mind. For whatever is immediately perceived is an idea; and can any *idea* exist out of the mind?

HYL.: To suppose that were absurd; but, inform me, Philonous, can we perceive or know nothing besides our ideas?

PHIL.: As for the rational deducing of causes from effects, that is beside our inquiry. And by the senses you can best tell whether you perceive anything which is not immediately perceived. And I ask you whether the things immediately perceived are other than your own sensations or ideas? You have indeed more than once, in the course of this conversation, declared yourself on those points, but you seem, by this last question, to have departed from what you then thought.

HYL.: To speak the truth, Philonous, I think there are two kinds of objects: the one perceived immediately, which are likewise called "ideas"; the other are real things or external objects, perceived by the mediation of ideas which are their images and representations. Now I own ideas do not exist without the mind, but the latter sort of objects do. I am sorry I did not think of this distinction sooner; it would probably have cut short your discourse.

PHIL.: Are those external objects perceived by sense or by some other faculty?

HYL.: They are perceived by sense.

PHIL.: How! is there anything perceived by sense which is not immediately perceived?

HYL.: Yes, Philonous, in some sort there is. For example, when I look on a picture or statue of Julius Caesar, I may be said, after a manner, to perceive him (though not immediately) by my senses.

PHIL.: It seems then you will have our ideas, which

alone are immediately perceived, to be pictures of external things: and that these also are perceived by sense inasmuch as they have a conformity or resemblance to our ideas?

HYL.: That is my meaning.

PHIL.: And in the same way that Julius Caesar, in himself invisible, is nevertheless perceived by sight, real things, in themselves imperceptible, are perceived by sense.

HYL.: In the very same.

PHIL.: Tell me, Hylas, when you behold the picture of Julius Caesar, do you see with your eyes any more than some colors and figures, with a certain symmetry and composition of the whole?

HYL.: Nothing else.

PHIL.: And would not a man who had never known anything of Julius Caesar see as much?

HYL.: He would.

PHIL.: Consequently, he has his sight and the use of it in as perfect a degree as you?

HYL.: I agree with you.

PHIL.: Whence comes it then that your thoughts are directed to the Roman emperor, and his are not? This cannot proceed from the sensations or ideas of sense by you then perceived, since you acknowledge you have no advantage over him in that respect. It should seem therefore to proceed from reason and memory, should it not?

HYL.: It should.

PHIL.: Consequently, it will not follow from that instance that anything is perceived by sense which is not immediately perceived. Though I grant we may, in one acceptation, be said to perceive sensible things mediately by sense—that is, when, from a frequently perceived connection, the immediate perception of ideas by one sense suggest to the mind others, perhaps belonging to another sense, which are wont to be connected with them. For instance, when I hear a coach drive along the streets, immediately I perceive only the sound; but from the experience I have had that such a sound is connected with a coach, I am said to hear the coach. It is nevertheless evident that, in truth and strictness, nothing can be *heard* but *sound:* and the coach is not then properly perceived by sense, but suggested from experience. So likewise when we are said to see a red-hot bar of iron; the solidity and heat of the iron are not the objects of sight, but suggested to the imagination by the color and figure which are properly perceived by that sense. In short, those things alone are actually and strictly perceived by any sense which would have been perceived in case that same sense had then been first conferred on us. As for other things, it is plain they are only suggested to the mind by experience grounded on former perceptions. But, to return to your comparison of Caesar's picture, it is plain, if you keep to that, you must hold the real things or archetypes of our ideas are not perceived by sense, but by some internal faculty of the soul, as reason or memory. I would, therefore, fain know what arguments you can draw from reason for the existence of what you call "real things" or "material objects," or whether you remember to have seen them formerly as they are in themselves, or if you have heard or read of anyone that did.

HYL.: Philonous, you are disposed to raillery; but that will never convince me.

PHIL.: My aim is only to learn from you the way to come at the knowledge of "material beings." Whatever we perceive is perceived either immediately or mediately—by sense, or by reason and reflection. But, as you have excluded sense, pray show me what reason you have to believe their existence, or what *medium* you can possibly make use of to prove it, either to mine or your own understanding.

HYL.: To deal ingenuously, Philonous, now [that] I consider the point, I do not find I can give you any good reason for it. But thus much seems pretty plain, that it is at least possible such things may really exist. And as long as there is no absurdity in supposing them, I am resolved to believe as I did, till you bring good reasons to the contrary.

PHIL.: What! is it come to this, that you only believe the existence of material objects, and that your belief is founded barely on the possibility of its being true? Then you will have me bring reasons against it, though another would think it reasonable the proof should lie on him who holds the affirmative. And, after all, this very point which you are now resolved to maintain, without any reason, is in effect what you have more than

once during this discourse seen good reason to give up. But to pass over all this—if I understand you rightly, you say our ideas do not exist without the mind, but that they are copies, images, or representations of certain originals that do?

HYL.: You take me right.

PHIL.: They are then like external things?

HYL.: They are.

PHIL.: Have those things a stable and permanent nature, independent of our senses, or are they in a perpetual change, upon our producing any motions in our bodies, suspending, exerting, or altering our faculties or organs of sense?

HYL.: Real things, it is plain, have a fixed and real nature, which remains the same notwithstanding any change in our senses or in the posture and motion of our bodies; which indeed may affect the ideas in our minds, but it were absurd to think they had the same effect on things existing without the mind.

PHIL.: How then is it possible that things perpetually fleeting and variable as our ideas should be copies or images of anything fixed and constant? Or, in other words, since all sensible qualities, as size, figure, color, etc., that is, our ideas, are continually changing upon every alteration in the distance, medium, or instruments of sensation—how can any determinate material objects be properly represented or painted forth by several distinct things each of which is so different from and unlike the rest? Or, if you say it resembles some one only of our ideas, how shall we be able to distinguish the true copy from all the false ones?

HYL.: I profess, Philonous, I am at a loss. I know not what to say to this.

PHIL.: But neither is this all. Which are material objects in themselves—perceptible or imperceptible?

HYL.: Properly and immediately nothing can be perceived but ideas. All material things, therefore, are in themselves insensible and to be perceived only by our ideas.

PHIL.: Ideas then are sensible, and their archetypes or originals insensible?

HYL.: Right.

PHIL.: But how can that which is sensible be like that which is insensible? Can a real thing, in itself *invisible,* be like a *color,* or a real thing which is not *audible* be like a *sound?* In a word, can anything be like a sensation or idea, but another sensation or idea?

HYL.: I must own, I think not.

PHIL.: Is it possible there should be any doubt on the point? Do you not perfectly know your own ideas?

HYL.: I know them perfectly, since what I do not perceive or know can be no part of my idea.

PHIL.: Consider, therefore, and examine them, and then tell me if there be anything in them which can exist without the mind, or if you can conceive anything like them existing without the mind?

HYL.: Upon inquiry I find it impossible for me to conceive or understand how anything but an idea can be like an idea. And it is most evident that *no idea can exist without the mind.*

PHIL.: You are, therefore, by your principles forced to deny the reality of sensible things, since you made it to consist in an absolute existence exterior to the mind. That is to say, you are a downright skeptic. So I have gained my point, which was to show your principles led to skepticism.

HYL.: For the present I am, if not entirely convinced, at least silenced.

PHIL.: I would fain know what more you would require in order to a perfect conviction. Have you not had the liberty of explaining yourself all manner of ways? Were any little slips in discourse laid hold and insisted on? Or were you not allowed to retract or reinforce anything you had offered, as best served your purpose? Has not everything you could say been heard and examined with all the fairness imaginable? In a word, have you not in every point been convinced out of your own mouth? And, if you can at present discover any flaw in any of your former concessions, or think of any remaining subterfuge, any new distinction, color, or comment whatsoever, why do you not produce it?

HYL.: A little patience, Philonous. I am at present so amazed to see myself ensnared, and as it were imprisoned in the labyrinths you have drawn me into, that on the sudden it cannot be expected I should find my way out. You must give me time to look about me and recollect myself.

PHIL.: Hark; is not this the college bell?

HYL.: It rings for prayers.

PHIL.: We will go in then, if you please, and meet here again tomorrow morning. In the meantime, you may employ your thoughts on this morning's discourse and try if you can find any fallacy in it, or invent any new means to extricate yourself.

HYL.: Agreed.

THE SECOND DIALOGUE

HYLAS: I beg your pardon, Philonous, for not meeting you sooner. All this morning my head was so filled with our late conversation that I had not leisure to think of the time of the day, or indeed of anything else.

PHILONOUS: I am glad you were so intent upon it, in hopes if there were any mistakes in your concessions, or fallacies in my reasonings from them, you will now discover them to me.

HYL.: I assure you I have done nothing ever since I saw you but search after mistakes and fallacies, and, with that [in] view, have minutely examined the whole series of yesterday's discourse; but all in vain, for the notions it led me into, upon review, appear still more clear and evident; and the more I consider them, the more irresistibly do they force my assent.

PHIL.: And is not this, think you, a sign that they are genuine, that they proceed from nature and are conformable to right reason? Truth and beauty are in this alike, that the strictest survey sets them both off to advantage, while the false luster of error and disguise cannot endure being reviewed or too nearly inspected.

HYL.: I own there is a great deal in what you say. Nor can anyone be more entirely satisfied of the truth of those odd consequences so long as I have in view the reasonings that lead to them. But when these are out of my thoughts, there seems, on the other hand, something so satisfactory, so natural and intelligible in the modern way of explaining things that I profess I know not how to reject it.

PHIL.: I know not what way you mean.

HYL.: I mean the way of accounting for our sensations or ideas.

PHIL.: How is that?

HYL.: It is supposed the soul makes her residence in

some part of the brain, from which the nerves take their rise, and are then extended to all parts of the body; and that outward objects, by the different impressions they make on the organs of sense, communicate certain vibrative motions to the nerves, and these, being filled with spirits, propagate them to the brain or seat of the soul, which, according to the various impressions or traces thereby made in the brain, is variously affected with ideas.

PHIL.: And call you this an explication of the manner whereby we are affected with ideas?

HYL.: Why not, Philonous; have you anything to object against it?

PHIL.: I would first know whether I rightly understand your hypothesis. You make certain traces in the brain to be the causes or occasions of our ideas. Pray tell me whether by the "brain" you mean any sensible thing.

HYL.: What else think you I could mean?

PHIL.: Sensible things are all immediately perceivable; and those things which are immediately perceivable are ideas, and these exist only in the mind. This much you have, if I mistake not, long since agreed to.

HYL.: I do not deny it.

PHIL.: The brain therefore you speak of, being a sensible thing, exists only in the mind. Now I would fain know whether you think it reasonable to suppose that one idea or thing existing in the mind occasions all other ideas. And if you think so, pray how do you account for the origin of that primary idea or brain itself?

HYL.: I do not explain the origin of our ideas by that brain which is perceivable to sense, this being itself only a combination of sensible ideas, but by another which I imagine.

PHIL.: But are not things imagined as truly *in the mind* as things perceived?

HYL.: I must confess they are.

PHIL.: It comes, therefore, to the same thing; and you have been all this while accounting for ideas by certain motions or impressions of the brain, that is, by some alteration in an idea, whether sensible or imaginable it matters not.

HYL.: I begin to suspect my hypothesis.

PHIL.: Besides spirits, all that we know or conceive are our own ideas. When, therefore, you say all

ideas are occasioned by impressions in the brain, do you conceive this brain or no? If you do, then you talk of ideas imprinted in an idea causing that same idea, which is absurd. If you do not conceive it, you talk unintelligibly, instead of forming a reasonable hypothesis.

HYL.: I now clearly see it was a mere dream. There is nothing in it.

PHIL.: You need not be much concerned at it, for, after all, this way of explaining things, as you called it, could never have satisfied any reasonable man. What connection is there between a motion in the nerves and the sensations of sound or color in the mind? Or how is it possible these should be the effect of that?

HYL.: But I could never think it had so little in it as now it seems to have.

PHIL.: Well then, are you at length satisfied that no sensible things have a real existence, and that you are in truth an arrant *skeptic*?

HYL.: It is too plain to be denied.

PHIL.: Look! are not the fields covered with a delightful verdure? Is there not something in the woods and groves, in the rivers and clear springs, that soothes, that delights, that transports the soul? At the prospect of the wide and deep ocean, or some huge mountain whose top is lost in the clouds, or of an old gloomy forest, are not our minds filled with a pleasing horror? Even in rocks and deserts is there not an agreeable wildness? How sincere a pleasure is it to behold the natural beauties of the earth! To preserve and renew our relish for them, is not the veil of night alternately drawn over her face, and does she not change her dress with the seasons? How aptly are the elements disposed! What variety and use in the meanest productions of nature! What delicacy, what beauty, what contrivance in animal and vegetable bodies! How exquisitely are all things suited, as well to their particular ends as to constitute apposite parts of the whole! And while they mutually aid and support, do they not also set off and illustrate each other? Raise now your thoughts from this ball of earth to all those glorious luminaries that adorn the high arch of heaven. The motion and situation of the planets, are they not admirable for use and order? Were those (miscalled "erratic") globes ever known to stray in their repeated journeys through the pathless void? Do they not measure areas round the sun ever proportioned to the times? So fixed, so immutable are the laws by which the unseen Author of nature actuates the universe. How vivid and radiant is the luster of the fixed stars! How magnificent and rich that negligent profusion with which they appear to be scattered throughout the whole azure vault! Yet, if you take the telescope, it brings into your sight a new host of stars that escape the naked eye. Here they seem contiguous and minute, but to a nearer view, immense orbs of light at various distances, far sunk in the abyss of space. Now you must call imagination to your aid. The feeble narrow sense cannot descry innumerable worlds revolving round the central fires, and in those worlds the energy of an all-perfect Mind displayed in endless forms. But neither sense nor imagination are big enough to comprehend the boundless extent with all its glittering furniture. Though the laboring mind exert and strain each power to its utmost reach, there still stands out ungrasped a surplusage immeasurable. Yet all the vast bodies that compose this mighty frame, how distant and remote soever, are by some secret mechanism, some divine art and force, linked in a mutual dependence and intercourse with each other, even with this earth, which was almost slipt from my thoughts and lost in the crowd of worlds. Is not the whole system immense, beautiful, glorious beyond expression and beyond thought! What treatment, then, do those philosophers deserve who would deprive these noble and delightful scenes of all reality? How should those principles be entertained that lead us to think all the visible beauty of the creation a false imaginary glare? To be plain, can you expect this skepticism of yours will not be thought extravagantly absurd by all men of sense?

HYL.: Other men may think as they please, but for your part you have nothing to reproach me with. My comfort is you are as much a skeptic as I am.

PHIL.: There, Hylas, I must beg leave to differ from you.

HYL.: What! have you all along agreed to the premises, and do you now deny the conclusion and leave me to maintain those paradoxes by myself which you led me into? This surely is not fair.

PHIL.: I deny that I agreed with you in those notions that led to skepticism. You indeed said the *reality* of sensible things consisted in an *absolute existence* out of the minds of spirits, or distinct from their being perceived. And, pursuant to this notion of reality, you are obliged to deny sensible things any real existence; that is, according to your own definition, you profess yourself a skeptic. But I neither said nor thought the reality of sensible things was to be defined after that manner. To me it is evident, for the reasons you allow of, that sensible things cannot exist otherwise than in a mind or spirit. Whence I conclude, not that they have no real existence, but that, seeing they depend not on my thought and have an existence distinct from being perceived by me, *there must be some other mind wherein they exist.* As sure, therefore, as the sensible world really exists, so sure is there an infinite omnipresent Spirit, who contains and supports it.

HYL.: What! this is no more than I and all Christians hold; nay, and all others, too, who believe there is a God and that He knows and comprehends all things.

PHIL.: Aye, but here lies the difference. Men commonly believe that all things are known or perceived by God, because they believe the being of a God; whereas I, on the other side, immediately and necessarily conclude the being of a God, because all sensible things must be perceived by him.

HYL.: But so long as we all believe the same thing, what matter is it how we come by that belief?

PHIL.: But neither do we agree in the same opinion. For philosophers, though they acknowledge all corporeal beings to be perceived by God, yet they attribute to them an absolute subsistence distinct from their being perceived by any mind whatever, which I do not. Besides, is there no difference between saying, *there is a God, therefore He perceives all things,* and saying, *sensible things do really exist; and if they really exist, they are necessarily perceived by an infinite mind: therefore there is an infinite mind, or God?* This furnishes you with a direct and immediate demonstration, from a most evident principle, of the *being of a God.* Divines and philosophers had proved beyond all controversy, from the beauty and usefulness of the several parts of the creation, that it was the workmanship of God. But that—setting aside all help of astronomy and natural philosophy, all contemplation of the contrivance, order and adjustment of things—an infinite mind should be necessarily inferred from the bare *existence* of the sensible world is an advantage to them only who have made this easy reflection, that the sensible world is that which we perceive by our several senses; and that nothing is perceived by the senses beside ideas; and that no idea or archetype of an idea can exist otherwise than in a mind. You may now, without any laborious search into the sciences, without any subtlety of reason or tedious length of discourse, oppose and baffle the most strenuous advocate for atheism, those miserable refuges, whether in an eternal succession of unthinking causes and effects or in a fortuitous concourse of atoms; those wild imaginations of Vanini, Hobbes, and Spinoza: in a word, the whole system of atheism, is it not entirely overthrown by this single reflection on the repugnancy included in supposing the whole or any part, even the most rude and shapeless, of the visible world to exist without a mind? Let any one of those abettors of impiety but look into his own thoughts, and there try if he can conceive how so much as a rock, a desert, a chaos, or confused jumble of atoms, how anything at all, either sensible or imaginable, can exist independent of a mind, and he need go no further to be convinced of his folly. Can anything be fairer than to put a dispute on such an issue and leave it to a man himself to see if he can conceive, even in thought, what he holds to be true in fact, and from a notional to allow it a real existence?

HYL.: It cannot be denied there is something highly serviceable to religion in what you advance. But do you not think it looks very like a notion entertained by some eminent moderns, of *seeing all things in God?*

PHIL.: I would gladly know that opinion; pray explain it to me.

HYL.: They conceive that the soul, being immaterial, is incapable of being united with material things so as to perceive them in themselves, but that she perceives them by her union with the substance of God, which, being spiritual, is therefore purely intelligible, or capable of being the immediate object of a spirit's thought. Besides, the divine essence contains in it perfections correspondent to each created being, and which are, for that reason, proper to exhibit or represent them to the mind.

PHIL.: I do not understand how our ideas, which are things altogether passive and inert, can be the essence or any part (or like any part) of the essence or substance of God, who is an impassive, indivisible, purely active being. Many more difficulties and objections there are which occur at first view against this hypothesis; but I shall only add that it is liable to all the absurdities of the common hypothesis, in making a created world exist otherwise than in the mind of a Spirit. Beside all which it has this peculiar to itself that it makes that material world serve to no purpose. And if it pass for a good argument against other hypotheses in the sciences that they suppose nature or the divine wisdom to make something in vain, or do that by tedious roundabout methods which might have been performed in a much more easy and compendious way, what shall we think of that hypothesis which supposes the whole world made in vain?

HYL.: But what say you, are not you too of opinion that we see all things in God? If I mistake not, what you advance comes near it.

PHIL.: [Few men think, yet all have opinions. Hence men's opinions are superficial and confused. It is nothing strange that tenets which in themselves are ever so different should nevertheless be confounded with each other by those who do not consider them attentively. I shall not therefore be surprised if some men imagine that I run into the enthusiasm of Malebranche, though in truth I am very remote from it. He builds on the most abstract general ideas, which I entirely disclaim. He asserts an absolute external world, which I deny. He maintains that we are deceived by our senses and know not the real natures or the true forms and figures of extended beings; of all which I hold the direct contrary. So that upon the whole there are no principles more fundamentally opposite than his and mine. It must be owned that,] I entirely agree with what the holy Scripture says, "That in God we live and move and have our being." But that we see things in His essence, after the manner above set forth, I am far from believing. Take here in brief my meaning: It is evident that the things I perceive are my own ideas, and that no idea can exist unless it be in a mind. Nor is it less plain that these ideas or things by me perceived, either themselves or their archetypes, exist independently of my mind; since I know myself not to be their author, it being out of my power to determine at pleasure what particular ideas I shall be affected with upon opening my eyes or ears. They must therefore exist in some other mind, whose will it is they should be exhibited to me. The things, I say, immediately perceived are ideas or sensations, call them which you will. But how can any idea or sensation exist in, or be produced by, anything but a mind or spirit? This indeed is inconceivable; and to assert that which is inconceivable is to talk nonsense, is it not?

HYL.: Without doubt.

PHIL.: But, on the other hand, it is very conceivable that they should exist in and be produced by a spirit, since this is no more than I daily experience in myself, inasmuch as I perceive numberless ideas, and, by an act of my will, can form a great variety of them and raise them up in my imagination; though, it must be confessed, these creatures of the fancy are not altogether so distinct, so strong, vivid, and permanent as those perceived by my senses, which latter are called "real things." From all which I conclude, *there is a Mind which affects me every moment with all the sensible impressions I perceive.* And from the variety, order, and manner of these I conclude the Author of them to be *wise, powerful, and good beyond comprehension.* Mark it well; I do not say I see things by perceiving that which represents them in the intelligible Substance of God. This I do not understand; but I say the things by me perceived are known by the understanding and produced by the will of an infinite Spirit. And is not all this most plain and evident? Is there any more in it than what a little observation of our own minds, and that which passes in them, not only enables us to conceive but also obliges us to acknowledge?

HYL.: I think I understand you very clearly and own the proof you give of a Deity seems no less evident than surprising. But allowing that God is the supreme and universal cause of all things, yet may there not be still a third nature besides spirits and ideas? May we not admit a subordinate and limited cause of our ideas? In a word, may there not for that be *matter?*

PHIL.: How often must I inculcate the same thing? You allow the things immediately perceived by sense to exist nowhere without the mind; but there is nothing perceived by sense which is not perceived immediately: therefore there is nothing sensible that exists without the mind. The matter, therefore, which you still insist on is something intelligible, I suppose something that may be discovered by reason, and not by sense.

HYL.: You are in the right.

PHIL.: Pray let me know what reasoning your belief of matter is grounded on, and what this matter is in your present sense of it.

HYL.: I find myself affected with various ideas whereof I know I am not the cause; neither are they the cause of themselves or of one another, or capable of subsisting by themselves, as being altogether inactive, fleeting, dependent beings. They have therefore some cause distinct from me and them, of which I pretend to know no more than that it is *the cause of my ideas.* And this thing, whatever it be, I call "matter."

PHIL.: Tell me, Hylas, has everyone a liberty to change the current proper signification attached to a common name in any language? For example, suppose a traveler should tell you that in a certain country men pass unhurt through the fire; and, upon explaining himself, you found he meant by the word "fire" that which others call "water"; or, if he should assert that there are trees that walk upon two legs, meaning men by the term "trees." Would you think this reasonable?

HYL.: No, I should think it very absurd. Common custom is the standard of property in language. And for any man to affect speaking improperly is to pervert the use of speech, and can never serve to a better purpose than to protract and multiply disputes where there is no difference in opinion.

PHIL.: And does not "matter," in the common current acceptation of the word, signify an extended, solid, movable, unthinking, inactive substance?

HYL.: It does.

PHIL.: And has it not been made evident that no such substance can possibly exist? And though it should be allowed to exist, yet how can that which is *inactive* be a *cause,* or that which is *unthinking* be a *cause of thought?* You may, indeed, if you please, annex to the word "matter" a contrary meaning to what is vulgarly received, and tell me you understand by it an unextended, thinking, active being which is the cause of our ideas. But what else is this than to play with words and run into that very fault you just now condemned with so much reason? I do by no means find fault with your reasoning, in that you collect a cause from the phenomena; but I deny that the cause deducible by reason can properly be termed "matter."

HYL.: There is indeed something in what you say. But I am afraid you do not thoroughly comprehend my meaning. I would by no means be thought to deny that God, or an infinite Spirit, is the Supreme Cause of all things. All I contend for is that, subordinate to the Supreme Agent, there is a cause of a limited and inferior nature which concurs in the production of our ideas, not by any act of will or spiritual efficiency, but by that kind of action which belongs to matter, viz., motion.

PHIL.: I find you are at every turn relapsing into your old exploded conceit, of a movable and consequently an extended substance existing without the mind. What! have you already forgotten you were convinced, or are you willing I should repeat what has been said on that head? In truth, this is not fair dealing in you still to suppose the being of that which you have so often acknowledged to have no being. But, not to insist further on what has been so largely handled, I ask whether all your ideas are not perfectly passive and inert, including nothing of action in them.

HYL.: They are.

PHIL.: And are sensible qualities anything else but ideas?

HYL.: How often have I acknowledged that they are not.

PHIL.: But is not motion a sensible quality?

HYL.: It is.

PHIL.: Consequently, it is no action?

HYL.: I agree with you. And indeed it is very plain that when I stir my finger it remains passive, but my will which produced the motion is active.

PHIL.: Now I desire to know, in the first place, whether, motion being allowed to be no action, you can conceive any action besides volition; and, in the second place, whether to say something and conceive nothing be not to talk nonsense; and, lastly, whether, having considered the premises, you do not perceive that to suppose any efficient or active cause of our ideas other than *spirit* is highly absurd and unreasonable.

HYL.: I give up the point entirely. But, though matter may not be a cause, yet what hinders it being an *instrument* subservient to the Supreme Agent in the production of our ideas?

PHIL.: An instrument say you; pray what may be the figure, springs, wheels, and motions of that instrument?

HYL.: Those I pretend to determine nothing of, both the substance and its qualities being entirely unknown to me.

PHIL.: What! You are then of opinion it is made up of unknown parts, that it has unknown motions and an unknown shape?

HYL.: I do not believe that it has any figure or motion at all, being already convinced that no sensible qualities can exist in an unperceiving substance.

PHIL.: But what notion is it possible to frame of an instrument void of all sensible qualities, even extension itself?

HYL.: I do not pretend to have any notion of it.

PHIL.: And what reason have you to think this unknown, this inconceivable somewhat does exist? Is it that you imagine God cannot act as well without it, or that you find by experience the use of some such thing when you form ideas in your own mind?

HYL.: You are always teasing me for reasons of my belief. Pray what reasons have you not to believe it?

PHIL.: It is to me a sufficient reason not to believe the existence of anything if I see no reason for believing it. But, not to insist on reasons for believing, you will not so much as let me know what it is you would have me believe, since you say you have no manner of notion of it. After all, let me entreat you to consider whether it be like a philosopher, or even like a man of common sense, to pretend to believe you know not what, and you know not why.

HYL.: Hold, Philonous. When I tell you matter is an *instrument,* I do not mean altogether nothing. It is true I know not the particular kind of instrument, but, however, I have some notion of *instrument in general,* which I apply to it.

PHIL.: But what if it should prove that there is something, even in the most general notion of *instrument,* as taken in a distinct sense from *cause,* which makes the use of it inconsistent with the divine attributes?

HYL.: Make that appear and I shall give up the point.

PHIL.: What mean you by the general nature or notion of instrument?

HYL.: That which is common to all particular instruments composes the general notion.

PHIL.: Is it not common to all instruments that they are applied to the doing those things only which cannot be performed by the mere act of our wills? Thus, for instance, I never use an instrument to move my finger, because it is done by a volition. But I should use one if I were to remove part of a rock or tear up a tree by the roots. Are you of the same mind? Or can you show any example where an instrument is made use of in producing an effect immediately depending on the will of the agent?

HYL.: I own I cannot.

PHIL.: How, therefore, can you suppose that an all-perfect Spirit, on whose will all things have an absolute and immediate dependence, should need an instrument in his operations or, not needing it, make use of it? Thus it seems to me that you are obliged to own the use of a lifeless inactive instrument to be incompatible with the infinite perfection of God, that is, by your own confession, to give up the point.

HYL.: It does not readily occur what I can answer you.

PHIL.: But methinks you should be ready to own the truth when it has been fairly proved to you. We, indeed, who are beings of finite powers, are forced to make use of instruments. And the use of an instrument shows the agent to be limited by rules of another's prescription, and that he cannot obtain his end but in such a way and by such conditions. Whence it seems a clear consequence that the Supreme Unlimited Agent uses no tool or instrument at all. The will of an Omnipotent Spirit is no sooner exerted than executed, without the application of means, which, if they are employed by inferior agents, it is not upon account of any real efficacy that is in them, or necessary aptitude to produce any effect, but merely in compliance with the laws of nature or those conditions prescribed to them by the First Cause, who is Himself above all limitation or prescription whatsoever.

HYL.: I will no longer maintain that matter is an instrument. However, I would not be understood to give up its existence neither, since, notwithstanding what has been said, it may still be an *occasion.*

PHIL.: How many shapes is your matter to take? Or how often must it be proved not to exist before you are content to part with it? But to say no more of this (though by all the laws of disputation I may justly blame you for so frequently changing the signification of the principal term), I would fain know what you mean by affirming that matter is an "occasion," having already denied it to be a cause. And when you have shown in what sense you understand occasion, pray, in the next place, be pleased to show me what reason induces you to believe there is such an occasion of our ideas?

HYL.: As to the first point: by "occasion" I mean an inactive unthinking being, at the presence whereof God excites ideas in our minds.

PHIL.: And what may be the nature of that inactive unthinking being?

HYL.: I know nothing of its nature.

PHIL.: Proceed then to the second point and assign some reason why we should allow an existence to this inactive, unthinking, unknown thing.

HYL.: When we see ideas produced in our minds after an orderly and constant manner, it is natural to think they have some fixed and regular occasions at the presence of which they are excited.

PHIL.: You acknowledge then God alone to be the cause of our ideas, and that He causes them at the presence of those occasions.

HYL.: That is my opinion.

PHIL.: Those things which you say are present to God, without doubt He perceives.

HYL.: Certainly; otherwise they could not be to Him an occasion of acting.

PHIL.: Not to insist now on your making sense of this hypothesis, or answering all the puzzling questions and difficulties it is liable to: I only ask whether the order and regularity observable in the series of our ideas, or the course of nature, be not sufficiently accounted for by the wisdom and power of God; and whether it does not derogate from those attributes to suppose. He is influenced, directed, or put in mind, when and what He is to act, by an unthinking substance? And, lastly, whether, in case I granted all you contend for, it would make anything to your purpose, it not being easy to conceive how the external or absolute existence of an unthinking substance, distinct from its being perceived, can be inferred from my allowing that there are certain things perceived by the mind of God which are to Him the occasion of producing ideas in us?

HYL.: I am perfectly at a loss what to think, this notion of occasion seeming now altogether as groundless as the rest.

PHIL.: Do you not at length perceive that in all these different acceptations of matter you have been only supposing you know not what, for no manner of reason and to no kind of use?

HYL.: I freely own myself less fond of my notions since they have been so accurately examined. But still, methinks, I have some confused perception that there is such a thing as matter.

PHIL.: Either you perceive the being of matter immediately or mediately: If immediately, pray inform me by which of the senses you perceive it. If mediately, let me know by what reasoning it is inferred from those things which you perceive immediately. So much for the perception. Then for the matter itself, I ask whether it is object, substratum, cause, instrument, or occasion? You have already pleaded for each of these, shifting your notions and making matter to appear sometimes in one shape, then in another. And what you have offered has been disapproved and rejected by yourself. If you have anything new to advance I would gladly hear it.

HYL.: I think I have already offered all I had to say on those heads. I am at a loss what more to urge.

PHIL.: And yet you are loath to part with your old prejudice. But to make you quit it more easily, I desire that, besides what has been hitherto suggested, you will further consider whether, upon supposition that matter exists, you can possibly conceive how you should be affected by it? Or, supposing it did not exist, whether it be not evident you might for all that be affected with the same ideas you now are, and consequently have the very same reason to believe its existence that you now can have?

HYL.: I acknowledge it is possible we might perceive all things just as we do now, though there was no matter in the world; neither can I conceive, if there be matter, how it should produce any idea in our minds. And I do further grant you have entirely satisfied me that it is impossible there should be such a thing as matter in any of the foregoing acceptations. But still I cannot help supposing that there is *matter* in some sense or other. What that is I do not indeed pretend to determine.

PHIL.: I do not expect you should define exactly the nature of that unknown being. Only be pleased to tell me whether it is a substance—and if so, whether you can suppose a substance without accidents; or in case you suppose it to have accidents or qualities, I desire you will let me know what those qualities are, at least what is meant by "matter's supporting them"?

HYL.: We have already argued on those points. I have no more to say to them. But, to prevent any further questions, let me tell you I at present understand by "matter" neither substance nor accident, thinking nor extended being, neither cause, instrument, nor occasion, but something entirely unknown, distinct from all these.

PHIL.: It seems then you include in your present notion of matter nothing but the general abstract idea of *entity*.

HYL.: Nothing else, save only that I superadd to this general idea the negation of all those particular things, qualities, or ideas that I perceive, imagine, or in anywise apprehend.

PHIL.: Pray where do you suppose this unknown matter to exist?

HYL.: Oh Philonous! now you think you have entangled me; for if I say it exists in place, then you will infer that it exists in the mind, since it is agreed that place or extension exists only in the mind; but I am not ashamed to own my ignorance. I know not where it exists; only I am sure it exists not in place. There is a negative answer for you. And you must expect no other to all the questions you put for the future about matter.

PHIL.: Since you will not tell me where it exists, be pleased to inform me after what manner you suppose it to exist, or what you mean by its "existence"?

HYL.: It neither thinks nor acts, neither perceives nor is perceived.

PHIL.: But what is there positive in your abstracted notion of its existence?

HYL.: Upon a nice observation, I do not find I have any positive notion or meaning at all. I tell you again, I am not ashamed to own my ignorance. I know not what is meant by its existence or how it exists.

PHIL.: Continue, good Hylas, to act the same ingenuous part and tell me sincerely whether you can frame a distinct idea of entity in general, prescinded from and exclusive of all thinking and corporeal beings, all particular things whatsoever.

HYL.: Hold, let me think a little—I profess, Philonous, I do not find that I can. At first glance methought I had some dilute and airy notion of pure entity in abstract, but, upon closer attention, it has quite vanished out of sight. The more I think on it, the more am I confirmed in my prudent resolution of giving none but negative answers and not pretending to the least degree of any positive knowledge or conception of matter, its *where*, its *how*, its *entity*, or anything belonging to it.

PHIL.: When, therefore, you speak of the existence of matter, you have not any notion in your mind?

HYL.: None at all.

PHIL.: Pray tell me if the case stands not thus: at first, from a belief of material substance, you would have it that the immediate objects existed without the mind; then, that they are archetypes; then, causes; next, instruments; then, occasions: lastly, *something in general,* which being interpreted proves *nothing.* So matter comes to nothing. What think you, Hylas, is not this a fair summary of your whole proceeding?

HYL.: Be that as it will, yet I still insist upon it, that our not being able to conceive a thing is no argument against its existence.

PHIL.: That from a cause, effect, operation, sign, or other circumstance there may reasonably be inferred the existence of a thing not immediately perceived; and that it were absurd for any man to argue against the existence of that thing, from his having no direct and positive notion of it, I freely own. But where there is nothing of all this, where neither reason nor revelation induces us to believe the existence of a thing, where we have not even a relative notion of it, where an abstraction is made from perceiving and being perceived, from spirit and idea, lastly, where there is not so much as the most inadequate or faint idea pretended to, I will not, indeed, thence conclude against the reality of any notion or existence of anything; but my inference shall be that you mean nothing at all, that you employ words to no matter of purpose, without any design or signification whatsoever. And I leave it to you to consider how mere jargon should be treated.

HYL.: To deal frankly with you, Philonous, your arguments seem in themselves unanswerable, but they have not so great an effect on me as to produce that entire conviction, that hearty acquiescence, which attends demonstration. I find myself still relapsing into an obscure surmise of I know not what—*matter.*

PHIL.: But are you not sensible, Hylas, that two things must concur to take away all scruple and work a plenary assent in the mind? Let a visible object be set in never so clear a light, yet, if there is any imperfection in the sight, or if the eye is not directed towards it, it will not be distinctly seen. And though a demonstration be never so well grounded and fairly proposed, yet, if there is withal a stain of prejudice or a wrong bias on the understanding, can it be expected on a sudden to perceive clearly and adhere firmly to the truth? No, there is need of time and pains: the attention must be awakened and detained by a frequent repetition of the same thing placed oft in the same, oft in different lights. I have said it already, and find I must still repeat and inculcate, that it is an unaccountable license you take in pretending to maintain you know not what, for you know not what reason, to you know not what purpose. Can this be paralleled in any art or science, any sect or profession of men? Or is there anything so barefacedly groundless and unreasonable to be met with even in the lowest of common conversation? But, perhaps, you will still say, matter may exist, though at the same time you neither know what is meant by "matter" or by its "existence." This indeed is surprising, and the more so because it is altogether voluntary, you not being led to it by any one reason, for I challenge you to show me that thing in nature which needs matter to explain or account for it.

HYL.: The reality of things cannot be maintained without supposing the existence of matter. And is not this, think you, a good reason why I should be earnest in its defense?

PHIL.: The reality of things! What things, sensible or intelligible?

HYL.: Sensible things.

PHIL.: My glove, for example?

HYL.: That or any other thing perceived by the senses.

PHIL.: But to fix on some particular thing, is it not a sufficient evidence to me of the existence of this *glove* that I see it and feel it and wear it? Or, if this will not do, how is it possible I should be assured of the reality of this thing which I actually see in this place by supposing that some unknown thing, which I never did or can see, exists after an unknown manner, in an unknown place, or in no place at all? How can the supposed reality of that which is intangible be a proof that anything tangible really exists? Or of that which is invisible, that any visible thing or, in general, of anything which is imperceptible, that a perceptible exists? Do but explain this and I shall think nothing too hard for you.

HYL.: Upon the whole, I am content to own the existence of matter is highly improbable; but the direct and absolute impossibility of it does not appear to me.

PHIL.: But granting matter to be possible, yet, upon that account merely, it can have no more claim to existence than a golden mountain or a centaur.

HYL.: I acknowledge it, but still you do not deny it is possible; and that which is possible, for aught you know, may actually exist.

PHIL.: I deny it to be possible; and have, if I mistake not, evidently proved, from your own concessions, that it is not. In the common sense of the word "matter," is there any more implied than an extended, solid, figured, movable substance existing without the mind? And have not you acknowledged, over and over, that you have seen evident reason for denying the possibility of such a substance?

HYL.: True, but that is only one sense of the term "matter."

PHIL.: But is it not the only proper genuine received sense? And if matter in such a sense be proved impossible, may it not be thought with good grounds absolutely impossible? Else how could anything be proved impossible? Or, indeed, how could there be any proof at all one way or other to a man who takes the liberty to unsettle and change the common signification of words?

HYL.: I thought philosophers might be allowed to speak more accurately than the vulgar, and were not always confined to the common acceptation of a term.

PHIL.: But this now mentioned is the common received sense among philosophers themselves. But, not to insist on that, have you not been allowed to take matter in what sense you pleased? And have you not used this privilege in the utmost extent, sometimes entirely changing, at others leaving out or putting into the definition of it whatever, for the present, best served your design, contrary to all the known rules of reason and logic? And has not this shifting, unfair method of yours spun out our dispute to an unnecessary length, matter having been particularly examined and by your own confession refuted in each of those senses? And can any more be required to prove the absolute impossibility of a thing than the proving it impossible in every particular sense that either you or anyone else understands it in?

HYL.: But I am not so thoroughly satisfied that you have proved the impossibility of matter in the last most obscure abstracted and indefinite sense.

PHIL.: When is a thing shown to be impossible?

HYL.: When a repugnancy is demonstrated between the ideas comprehended in its definition.

PHIL.: But where there are no ideas, there no repugnancy can be demonstrated between ideas?

HYL.: I agree with you.

PHIL.: Now, in that which you call the obscure indefinite sense of the word "matter," it is plain, by your own confession, there was included no idea at all, no sense except an unknown sense, which is the same thing as none. You are not, therefore, to expect I should prove a repugnancy between ideas where there are no ideas, or the impossibility of matter taken in an *unknown* sense, that is, no sense at all. My business was only to show you meant *nothing;* and this you were brought to own. So that, in all your various senses, you have been shown either to mean nothing at all or, if anything, an absurdity. And if this be not sufficient to prove the impossibility of a thing, I desire you will let me know what is.

HYL.: I acknowledge you have proved that matter is impossible, nor do I see what more can be said in defense of it. But, at the same time that I give up this, I suspect all my other notions. For surely none could be more seemingly evident than this once was; and yet it now seems as false and absurd as ever it did true before. But I think we have discussed the point sufficiently for the present. The remaining part of the day I would willingly spend in running over in my thoughts the several heads of this morning's conversation, and tomorrow shall be glad to meet you here again about the same time.

PHIL.: I will not fail to attend you.

THE THIRD DIALOGUE

PHILONOUS: Tell me, Hylas, what are the fruits of yesterday's meditation? Has it confirmed you in the same mind you were in at parting, or have you since seen cause to change your opinion?

HYLAS: Truly my opinion is that all our opinions are alike vain and uncertain. What we approve today, we condemn tomorrow. We keep a stir about knowledge and spend our lives in pursuit of it, when, alas! we know nothing all the while; nor do I think it possible for us ever to know anything in this life. Our faculties are too narrow and too few. Nature certainly never intended us for speculation.

PHIL.: What! say you we can know nothing, Hylas?

HYL.: There is not that single thing in the world whereof we can know the real nature, or what it is in itself.

PHIL.: Will you tell me I do not really know what fire or water is?

HYL.: You may indeed know that fire appears hot, and water fluid; but this is no more than knowing what sensations are produced in your own mind upon the application of fire and water to your organs of sense. Their internal constitution, their true and real nature, you are utterly in the dark as to *that*.

PHIL.: Do I not know this to be a real stone that I stand on, and that which I see before my eyes to be a real tree?

HYL.: *Know?* No, it is impossible you or any man alive should know it. All you know is that you have such a certain idea or appearance in your own mind. But what is this to the real tree or stone? I tell you that color, figure, and hardness, which you perceive, are not the real natures of those things, or in the least like them. The same may be said of all other real things or corporeal substances which compose the world. They have, none of them, anything in themselves, like those sensible qualities by us perceived. We should not, therefore, pretend to affirm or know anything of them, as they are in their own nature.

PHIL.: But surely, Hylas, I can distinguish gold, for example, from iron; and how could this be if I knew not what either truly was?

HYL.: Believe me, Philonous, you can only distinguish between your own ideas. That yellowness, that weight, and other sensible qualities, think you they are really in the gold? They are only relative to the senses and have no absolute existence in nature. And in pretending to distinguish the species of real things by the appearances in your mind, you may perhaps act as wisely as he that should conclude two men were of a different species because their clothes were not of the same color.

PHIL.: It seems, then, we are altogether put off with the appearances of things, and those false ones, too. The very meat I eat, and the cloth I wear, have nothing in them like what I see and feel.

HYL.: Even so.

PHIL.: But is it not strange the whole world should be thus imposed on and so foolish as to believe their senses? And yet I know not how it is, but men eat, and drink, and sleep, and perform all the offices of life as comfortably and conveniently as if they really knew the things they are conversant about.

HYL.: They do so; but you know ordinary practice does not require a nicety of speculative knowledge. Hence the vulgar retain their mistakes, and for all that make a shift to bustle through the affairs of life. But philosophers know better things.

PHIL.: You mean they know that they *know nothing*.

HYL.: That is the very top and perfection of human knowledge.

PHIL.: But are you all this while in earnest, Hylas; and are you seriously persuaded that you know nothing real in the world? Suppose you are going to write, would you not call for pen, ink, and paper, like another man; and do you not know what it is you call for?

HYL.: How often must I tell you that I know not the real nature of any one thing in the universe? I may indeed upon occasion make use of pen, ink, and paper. But what any one of them is in its own true nature, I declare positively I know not. And the same is true with regard to every other corporeal thing. And what is more, we are not only ignorant of the true and real nature of things, but even of their existence. It cannot be denied that we perceive such certain appearances or ideas, but it cannot be concluded from thence that bodies really exist. Nay, now I think on it, I must, agreeably to my former concessions, further declare that it is impossible any real corporeal thing should exist in nature.

PHIL.: You amaze me. Was ever anything more wild and extravagant than the notions you now maintain? And is it not evident you are led into all these extravagances by the belief of *material substance?* This makes you dream of those unknown natures in everything. It is this occasions your distinguishing between the reality and sensible appearances of things. It is to this you are indebted for being ignorant of what everybody else knows perfectly well. Nor is this all: you are not only ignorant of the true nature of everything, but you know not whether any thing really exists or whether there are any true natures at all, forasmuch as you attribute to your material beings an absolute or external existence wherein you suppose their reality consists. And as you are forced in the end to acknowledge such an existence means either a direct repugnancy or nothing at all, it follows that you are obliged to pull down your own hypothesis of material substance and positively to deny the real existence of any part of the universe. And so you are plunged into the deepest and most deplorable skepticism that ever man was. Tell me, Hylas, is it not as I say?

HYL.: I agree with you. "Material substance" was no more than a hypothesis, and a false and groundless one, too. I will no longer spend my breath in defense of it. But whatever hypothesis you advance or whatever scheme of things you introduce in its stead, I doubt not it will appear every whit as false; let me but be allowed to question you upon it. That is, suffer me to serve you in your own kind, and I warrant it shall conduct you through as many perplexities and contradictions to the very same state of skepticism that I myself am in at present.

PHIL.: I assure you, Hylas, I do not pretend to frame any hypothesis at all. I am of a vulgar cast, simple enough to believe my senses and leave things as I find them. To be plain, it is my opinion that the real things are those very things I see and feel, and perceive by my senses. These I know and, finding they answer all the necessities and purposes of life, have no reason to be solicitous about any other unknown beings. A piece of sensible bread, for instance, would stay my stomach better than ten thousand times as much of that insensible, unintelligible real bread you speak of. It is likewise my opinion that colors and other sensible qualities are on the objects. I cannot for my life help thinking that snow is white, and fire hot. You, indeed, who by "snow" and "fire" mean certain external, unperceived, unperceiving substances are in the right to deny whiteness or heat to be affections inherent in them. But I who understand by those words the things I see and feel am obliged to think like other folks. And as I am no skeptic with regard to the nature of things, so neither am I as to their existence. That a thing should be really perceived by my senses and at the same time not really exist is to me a plain contradiction, since I cannot prescind or abstract, even in thought, the existence of a sensible thing from its being perceived. Wood, stones, fire, water, flesh, iron, and the like things which I name and discourse of are things that I know. And I should not have known them but that I perceived them by my senses; and things perceived by the senses are immediately perceived; and things immediately perceived are ideas; and ideas cannot exist without the mind; their existence therefore consists in being perceived; when, therefore, they are actually perceived, there can be no doubt of their existence. Away then with all that skepticism, all those ridiculous philosophical doubts. What a jest is it for a philosopher to question the existence of sensible things till he has it proved to him from the veracity of God, or to pretend our knowledge in this point falls short of intuition or demonstration! I might as well doubt of my own being as of the being of those things I actually see and feel.

HYL.: Not so fast, Philonous: You say you cannot conceive how sensible things should exist without the mind. Do you not?

PHIL.: I do.

HYL.: Supposing you were annihilated, cannot you conceive it possible that things perceivable by sense may still exist?

PHIL.: I can, but then it must be in another mind. When I deny sensible things an existence out of the mind, I do not mean my mind in particular, but all minds. Now it is plain they have an existence exterior to my mind, since I find them by experience to be independent of it. There is therefore some other mind wherein they exist during the intervals between the times of my perceiving them, as likewise they did before my birth, and would do after my supposed annihilation. And as the same is true with regard to all other finite created spirits, it necessarily follows there is an *omnipresent external Mind* which knows and comprehends all things, and exhibits them to our view in such a manner and according to such rules as He Himself has ordained and are by us termed the "laws of nature."

HYL.: Answer me, Philonous. Are all our ideas perfectly inert beings? Or have they any agency included in them?

PHIL.: They are altogether passive and inert.

HYL.: And is not God an agent, a being purely active?

PHIL.: I acknowledge it.

HYL.: No idea, therefore, can be like unto or represent the nature of God.

PHIL.: It cannot.

HYL.: Since, therefore, you have no idea of the mind of God, how can you conceive it possible that things should exist in His mind? Or, if you can conceive the mind of God without having an idea of it, why may not I be allowed to conceive the existence of matter, notwithstanding I have no idea of it?

PHIL.: As to your first question: I own I have property no *idea* either of God or any other spirit; for these, being active, cannot be represented by things perfectly inert as our ideas are. I do nevertheless know that I, who am a spirit or thinking substance, exist as certainly as I know my ideas exist. Further, I know what I mean by the terms "I" and "myself"; and I know this immediately or intuitively, though I do not perceive it as I perceive a triangle, a color, or a sound. The mind, spirit, or soul is that indivisible unextended thing which thinks, acts, and perceives. I say "indivisible," because unextended; and "unextended," because extended, figured, movable things are ideas; and that which perceives ideas, which thinks and wills, is plainly itself no idea, nor like an idea. Ideas are things inactive and perceived. And spirits a sort of beings altogether different from them. I do not therefore say my soul is an idea, or like an idea. However, taking the word "idea" in a large sense, my soul may be said to furnish me with an idea, that is, an image or likeness of God, though indeed extremely inadequate. For all the notion I have of God is obtained by reflecting on my own soul, heightening its powers, and removing its imperfections. I have, therefore, though not an inactive idea, yet in *myself* some sort of an active thinking image of the Deity. And though I perceive Him not by sense, yet I have a notion of Him, or know Him by reflection and reasoning. My own mind and my own ideas I have an immediate knowledge of; and, by the help of these, do mediately apprehend the possibility of the existence of other spirits and ideas. Further, from my own being, and from the dependency I find in myself and my ideas, I do, by an act of reason, necessarily infer the existence of a God and of all created things in the mind of God. So much for your first question. For the second: I suppose by this time you can answer it yourself. For you neither perceive matter objectively, as you do an inactive being or idea, nor know it, as you do yourself by a reflex act; neither do you mediately apprehend it by similitude of the one or the other, nor yet collect it by reasoning from that which you know immediately. All which makes the case of *matter* widely different from that of the *Deity*.

[HYL.: You say your own soul supplies you with some sort of an idea or image of God. But, at the same time, you acknowledge you have, properly speaking, no idea of your own soul. You even affirm that spirits are a sort of beings altogether different from ideas. Consequently, that no idea can be like a spirit. We have, therefore, no idea of any spirit. You admit nevertheless that there is spiritual substance, although you have no idea of it, while you deny there can be such a thing as material substance, because you have no notion or idea of it. Is this fair dealing? To act consistently, you must either admit matter or reject spirit. What say you to this?

PHIL.: I say, in the first place, that I do not deny the existence of material substance merely because I have no notion of it, but because the notion of it is inconsistent, or, in other words, because it is repugnant that there should be a notion of it. Many things, for aught I know, may exist whereof neither I nor any other man has or can have any idea or notion whatsoever. But then those things must be possible, that is, nothing inconsistent must be included in their definition. I say, secondly, that, although we believe things to exist which we do not perceive, yet we may not believe that any particular thing exists without some reason for such belief; but I have no reason for believing the existence of matter. I have no immediate intuition thereof, neither can I immediately from my sensations, ideas, notions, actions, or passions infer an unthinking, unperceiving, inactive substance, either by probable deduction or necessary consequence. Whereas the being of my self, that is, my own soul, mind, or thinking principle, I evidently know by reflection. You will forgive me if I repeat the same things in answer to the same objections. In the very notion or definition of "material substance" there is included a manifest repugnance and inconsistency. But this cannot be said of the notion of spirit. That ideas should exist in what does not perceive, or be produced by what does not act, is repugnant. But it is no repugnancy to say that a perceiving thing should be the subject of ideas, or an active thing the cause of them. It is granted we have neither an immediate evidence nor a demonstrative knowledge of the existence of other finite spirits, but it will not thence follow that such spirits are on a foot with material substances, if to suppose the one be inconsistent, and it be not inconsistent to suppose the other; if the one can be inferred by no argument, and there is a probability for the other; if we see signs and effects indicating distinct finite agents like ourselves, and see no sign or symptom whatever that leads to a rational belief of matter. I say, lastly, that I have a notion of spirit, though I have not, strictly speaking, an idea of it. I do not perceive it as an idea, or by means of an idea, but know it by reflection.

HYL.: Notwithstanding all you have said, to me it seems that, according to your own way of thinking, and in consequence of your own principles, it should follow that you are only a system of floating ideas without any substance to support them. Words are not to be used without a meaning. And, as there is no more meaning in *spiritual* substance than in *material* substance, the one is to be exploded as well as the other.

PHIL.: How often must I repeat that I know or am conscious of my own being, and that I *myself* am not my ideas, but somewhat else, a thinking, active principle that perceives, knows, wills, and operates about ideas. I know that I, one and the same self, perceive both colors and sounds, that a color cannot perceive a sound, nor a sound a color, that I am therefore one individual principle distinct from color and sound, and, for the same reason, from all other sensible things and inert ideas. But I am not in like manner conscious either of the existence or essence of matter. On the contrary, I know that nothing inconsistent can exist, and that the existence of matter implies an inconsistency. Further, I know what I mean when I affirm that there is a spiritual substance or support of ideas, that is, that a spirit knows and perceives ideas. But I do not know what is meant when it is said that an unperceiving substance has inherent in it and supports either ideas or the archetypes of ideas. There is, therefore, upon the whole no parity of case between spirit and matter.]

HYL.: I own myself satisfied in this point. But do you in earnest think the real existence of sensible things consists in their being actually perceived? If so, how comes it that all mankind distinguish between them? Ask the first man you meet, and he shall tell you, "to be perceived" is one thing, and "to exist" is another.

PHIL.: I am content, Hylas, to appeal to the common sense of the world for the truth of my notion. Ask the gardener why he thinks yonder cherry tree exists in the garden, and he shall tell you, because he sees and feels it; in a word, because he perceives it by his senses. Ask him why he thinks an orange tree not to be there, and he shall tell you, because he does not perceive it. What he perceives by sense, that he terms a real being and says it "is" or "exists"; but that which is not perceivable, the same, he says, has no being.

HYL.: Yes, Philonous, I grant the existence of a sensible thing consists in being perceivable, but not in being actually perceived.

PHIL.: And what is perceivable but an idea? And can an idea exist without being actually perceived? These are points long since agreed between us.

HYL.: But be your opinion never so true, yet surely you will not deny it is shocking and contrary to the common sense of men. Ask the fellow whether yonder tree has an existence out of his mind; what answer think you he would make?

PHIL.: The same that I should myself, to wit, that it does exist out of his mind. But then to a Chris-

tian it cannot surely be shocking to say, the real tree, existing without his mind, is truly known and comprehended by (that is, *exists in*) the infinite mind of God. Probably he may not at first glance be aware of the direct and immediate proof there is of this, inasmuch as the very being of a tree, or any other sensible thing, implies a mind wherein it is. But the point itself he cannot deny. The question between the materialists and me is not whether things have a *real* existence out of the mind of this or that person, but, whether they have an *absolute* existence, distinct from being perceived by God, and exterior to all minds. This, indeed, some heathens and philosophers have affirmed, but whoever entertains notions of the Deity suitable to the Holy Scriptures will be of another opinion.

HYL.: But, according to your notions, what difference is there between real things and chimeras formed by the imagination or the visions of a dream, since they are all equally in the mind?

PHIL.: The ideas formed by the imagination are faint and indistinct; they have, besides, an entire dependence on the will. But the ideas perceived by sense, that is, real things, are more vivid and clear, and, being imprinted on the mind by a spirit distinct from us, have not the like dependence on our will. There is, therefore, no danger of confounding these with the foregoing, and there is as little of confounding them with the visions of a dream, which are dim, irregular, and confused. And though they should happen to be never so lively and natural, yet, by their not being connected and of a piece with the preceding and subsequent transaction of our lives, they might easily be distinguished from realities. In short, by whatever method you distinguish *things* from *chimeras* on your own scheme, the same, it is evident, will hold also upon mine. For it must be, I presume, by some perceived difference, and I am not for depriving you of any one thing that you perceive.

HYL.: But still, Philonous, you hold there is nothing in the world but spirits and ideas. And this you must needs acknowledge sounds very oddly.

PHIL.: I own the word "idea," not being commonly used for "thing," sounds something out of the way. My reason for using it was because a necessary relation to the mind is understood to be implied by the term; and it is now commonly used by philosophers to denote the immediate objects of the understanding. But however oddly the proposition may sound in words, yet it includes nothing so very strange or shocking in its sense, which in effect amounts to no more than this, to wit, that there are only things perceiving and things perceived, or that every unthinking being is necessarily, and from the very nature of its existence, perceived by some mind, if not by any finite created mind, yet certainly by the infinite mind of God, in whom "we live, and move, and have our being." Is this as strange as to say the sensible qualities are not on the object or that we cannot be sure of the existence of things, or know anything of their real natures, though we both see and feel them and perceive them by all our senses?

HYL.: And, in consequence of this, must we not think there are no such things as physical or corporeal causes, but that a spirit is the immediate cause of all the *phenomena* in nature? Can there be anything more extravagant than this?

PHIL.: Yes, it is infinitely more extravagant to say a thing which is inert operates on the mind, and which is unperceiving is the cause of our perceptions. Besides, that which to you I know not for what reason seems so extravagant is no more than the Holy Scriptures assert in a hundred places. In them God is represented as the sole and immediate Author of all those effects which some heathens and philosophers are wont to ascribe to Nature, Matter, Fate, or the like unthinking principle. This is so much the constant language of Scripture that it were needless to confirm it by citations.

HYL.: You are not aware, Philonous, that, in making God the immediate Author of all the motions in nature, you make Him the Author of murder, sacrilege, adultery, and the like heinous sins.

PHIL.: In answer to that I observe, first, that the imputation of guilt is the same whether a person commits an action with or without an instrument. In case, therefore, you suppose God to act by the mediation of an instrument or occasion called "matter," you as truly make Him the Author of sin as I, who think Him the immediate agent in all those operations vulgarly ascribed to Nature. I further observe that sin or moral turpitude does not consist in the outward physical action or motion, but in the internal deviation of the will from the laws of reason and religion. This is plain, in that the killing an enemy in a battle or putting a criminal legally to death is not thought sinful, though the outward act be the very same with that in the case of murder. Since, therefore, sin does not consist in the physical action, the making God an immediate cause of all such actions is not making Him the Author of sin. Lastly, I have nowhere said that God is the only agent who produces all the motions in bodies. It is true I have denied there are any other agents besides spirits, but this is very consistent with allowing to thinking rational beings, in the production of motions, the use of limited powers, ultimately, indeed, derived from God but immediately under the direction of their own wills, which is sufficient to entitle them to all the guilt of their actions.

HYL.: But the denying matter, Philonous, or corporeal substance, there is the point. You can never persuade me that this is not repugnant to the universal sense of mankind. Were our dispute to be determined by most voices, I am confident you would give up the point without gathering the votes.

PHIL.: I wish both our opinions were fairly stated and submitted to the judgment of men who had plain common sense, without the prejudices of a learned education. Let me be represented as one who trusts his senses, who thinks he knows the things he sees and feels, and entertains no doubts of their existence; and you fairly set forth with all your doubts, your paradoxes, and your skepticism about you, and I shall willingly acquiesce in the determination of any indifferent person. That there is no substance wherein ideas can exist besides spirit is to me evident, and that the objects immediately perceived are ideas is on all hands agreed. And that sensible qualities are objects immediately perceived no one can deny. It is therefore evident there can be no *substratum* of those qualities but spirit, in which they exist, not by way of mode or property, but as a thing perceived in that which perceives it. I deny, therefore, that there is any unthinking *substratum* of the objects of sense, and in that acceptation that there is any material substance. But if by "material substance" is meant only sensible body, that which is seen and felt (and the unphilosophical part of the world, I dare say, mean no more), then I am more certain of matter's existence than you or any other philosopher pretend to be. If there be anything which makes the generality of mankind averse from the notions I espouse, it is a misapprehension that I deny the reality of sensible things; but as it is you who are guilty of that and not I, it follows that in truth their aversion is against your notions and not mine. I do therefore assert that I am as certain as of my own being that there are bodies or corporeal substances (meaning the things I perceive by my senses), and that, granting this, the bulk of mankind will take no thought about, nor think themselves at all concerned in the fate of, those unknown natures and philosophical quiddities which some men are so fond of.

HYL.: What say you to this? Since, according to you, men judge of the reality of things by their senses, how can a man be mistaken in thinking the moon a plain lucid surface, about a foot in diameter, or a square tower, seen at a distance, round, or an oar, with one end in the water, crooked?

PHIL.: He is not mistaken with regard to the ideas he actually perceives, but in the inferences he makes from his present perceptions. Thus, in the case of the oar, what he immediately perceives by sight is certainly crooked, and so far he is in the right. But if he thence conclude that upon taking the oar out of the water he shall perceive the same crookedness, or that it would affect his touch as crooked things are wont to do, in that he is mistaken. In like manner, if he shall conclude, from what he perceives in one station, that, in case he advances toward the moon or tower, he should still be affected with the like ideas, he is mistaken. But his mistake lies not in what he perceives immediately and at present (it being a manifest contradiction to suppose he should err in respect of that), but in the wrong judgment he makes concerning the ideas he apprehends to be connected with those immediately perceived, or, concerning the ideas, that

from what he perceives at present he imagines would be perceived in other circumstances. The case is the same with regard to the Copernican system. We do not here perceive any motion of the earth, but it were erroneous thence to conclude that, in case we were placed at as great a distance from that as we are now from the other planets, we should not then perceive its motion.

HYL.: I understand you and must needs own you say things plausible enough, but give me leave to put you in mind of one thing. Pray, Philonous, were you not formerly as positive that matter existed as you are now that it does not?

PHIL.: I was. But here lies the difference. Before, my positiveness was founded, without examination, upon prejudice, but now, after inquiry, upon evidence.

HYL.: After all, it seems our dispute is rather about words than things. We agree in the thing, but differ in the name. That we are affected with ideas from without is evident; and it is no less evident that there must be (I will not say archetypes, but) powers without the mind corresponding to those ideas. And as these powers cannot subsist by themselves, there is some subject of them necessarily to be admitted, which I call "matter," and you call "spirit." This is all the difference.

PHIL.: Pray, Hylas, is that powerful being, or subject of powers, extended?

HYL.: It has not extension, but it has the power to raise in you the idea of extension.

PHIL.: It is therefore itself unextended?

HYL.: I grant it.

PHIL.: Is it not also active?

HYL.: Without doubt; otherwise, how could we attribute powers to it?

PHIL.: Now let me ask you two questions: *First,* whether it be agreeable to the usage either of philosophers or others to give the name "matter" to an unextended active being? And, secondly, whether it be not ridiculously absurd to misapply names contrary to the common use of language?

HYL.: Well then, let it not be called "matter," since you will have it so, but some "third nature," distinct from matter and spirit. For what reason is there why you should call it spirit? Does not the notion of spirit imply that it is thinking as well as active and unextended?

PHIL.: My reason is this: because I have a mind to have some notion or meaning in what I say, but I have no notion of any action distinct from volition, neither can I conceive volition to be anywhere but in a spirit; therefore, when I speak of an active being I am obliged to mean a spirit. Besides, what can be plainer than that a thing which has no ideas in itself cannot impart them to me; and, if it has ideas, surely it must be a spirit. To make you comprehend the point still more clearly, if it be possible: I assert as well as you that, since we are affected from without, we must allow powers to be without, in a being distinct from ourselves. So far we are agreed. But then we differ as to the kind of this powerful being. I will have it to be spirit, you matter or I know not what (I may add, too, you know not what) third nature. Thus I prove it to be spirit. From the effects I see produced I conclude there are actions; and because actions, volitions; and because there are volitions, there must be a will. Again, the things I perceive must have an existence, they or their archetypes, out of my mind; but, being ideas, neither they nor their archetypes can exist otherwise than in an understanding, there is therefore an understanding. But will and understanding constitute in the strictest sense a mind or spirit. The powerful cause, therefore, of my ideas is in strict propriety of speech a *spirit*.

HYL.: And now I warrant you think you have made the point very clear, little suspecting that what you advance leads directly to a contradiction. Is it not an absurdity to imagine any imperfection in God?

PHIL.: Without a doubt.

HYL.: To suffer pain is an imperfection?

PHIL.: It is.

HYL.: Are we not sometimes affected with pain and uneasiness by some other being?

PHIL.: We are.

HYL.: And have you not said that being is a spirit, and is not that spirit God?

PHIL.: I grant it.

HYL.: But you have asserted that whatever ideas we perceive from without are in the mind which affects us. The ideas, therefore, of pain and uneasiness are in God, or, in other words, God suffers pain; that is to say, there is an imperfection in the divine nature, which, you acknowledge, was absurd. So you are caught in a plain contradiction.

PHIL.: That God knows or understands all things, and that He knows, among other things, what pain is, even every sort of painful sensation, and what it is for His creatures to suffer pain, I make no question. But that God, though He knows and sometimes causes painful sensations in us, can Himself suffer pain I positively deny. We, who are limited and dependent spirits, are liable to impressions of sense, the effects of an external agent, which, being produced against our wills, are sometimes painful and uneasy. But God, whom no external being can affect, who perceives nothing by sense as we do, whose will is absolute and independent, causing all things, and liable to be thwarted or resisted by nothing, it is evident such a Being as this can suffer nothing, nor be affected with any painful sensation or, indeed, any sensation at all. We are chained to a body; that is to say, our perceptions are connected with corporeal motions. By the law of our nature we are affected upon every alteration in the nervous parts of our sensible body; which sensible body, rightly considered, is nothing but a complexion of such qualities or ideas as have no existence distinct from being perceived by a mind; so that this connection of sensations with corporeal motions means no more than a correspondence in the order of nature between two sets of ideas, or things immediately perceivable. But God is a pure spirit, disengaged from all such sympathy or natural ties. No corporeal motions are attended with the sensations of pain or pleasure in His mind. To know everything knowable is certainly a perfection, but to endure or suffer or feel anything by sense is an imperfection. The former, I say, agrees to God, but not the latter. God knows or has ideas, but His ideas are not conveyed to Him by sense, as ours are. Your not distinguishing where there is so manifest a difference makes you fancy you see an absurdity where there is none.

HYL.: But all this while you have not considered that

the quantity of matter has been demonstrated to be proportional to the gravity of bodies. And what can withstand demonstration?

PHIL.: Let me see how you demonstrate that point.

HYL.: I lay it down for a principle that the moments or quantities of motion in bodies are in a direct compound reason of the velocities and quantities of matter contained in them. Hence, where the velocities are equal, it follows the moments are directly as the quantity of matter in each. But it is found by experience that all bodies (bating the small inequalities arising from the resistance of the air) descend with an equal velocity; the motion therefore of descending bodies, and consequently their gravity, which is the cause or principle of that motion, is proportional to the quantity of matter, which was to be demonstrated.

PHIL.: You lay it down as a self-evident principle that the quantity of motion in any body is proportional to the velocity and matter taken together; and this is made use of to prove a proposition from whence the existence of matter is inferred. Pray is not this arguing in a circle?

HYL.: In the premise I only mean that the motion is proportional to the velocity, jointly with the extension and solidity.

PHIL.: But allowing this to be true, yet it will not thence follow that gravity is proportional to matter in your philosophic sense of the word, except you take it for granted that unknown *substratum,* or whatever else you call it, is proportional to those sensible qualities which to suppose is plainly begging the question. That there is magnitude and solidity or resistance perceived by sense I readily grant, as likewise, that gravity may be proportional to those qualities I will not dispute. But that either these qualities as perceived by us, or the powers producing them, do exist in a *material substratum*—this is what I deny, and you, indeed, affirm but, notwithstanding your demonstration, have not yet proved.

HYL.: I shall insist no longer on that point. Do you think, however, you shall persuade me the natural philosophers have been dreaming all this while? Pray what becomes of all their hypotheses and explications of the phenomena which suppose the existence of matter?

PHIL.: What mean you, Hylas, by the "phenomena"?

HYL.: I mean the appearances which I perceive by my senses.

PHIL.: And the appearances perceived by sense, are they not ideas?

HYL.: I have told you so a hundred times.

PHIL.: Therefore, to explain the phenomena is to show how we come to be affected with ideas in that manner and order wherein they are imprinted on our senses. Is it not?

HYL.: It is.

PHIL.: Now, if you can prove that any philosopher has explained the production of any one idea in our minds by the help of *matter,* I shall forever acquiesce and look on all that has been said against it as nothing; but if you cannot, it is vain to urge the explication of phenomena. That a being endowed with knowledge and will should produce or exhibit ideas is easily understood. But that a being which is utterly destitute of these faculties should be able to produce ideas, or in any sort to affect an intelligence, this I can never understand. This I say, though we had some positive conception of matter, though we knew its qualities and could comprehend its existence, would yet be so far from explaining things that it is itself the most inexplicable thing in the world. And yet, for all this, it will not follow that philosophers have been doing nothing; for by observing and reasoning upon the connection of ideas, they discover the laws and methods of nature, which is a part of knowledge both useful and entertaining.

HYL.: After all, can it be supposed God would deceive all mankind? Do you imagine He would have induced the whole world to believe the being of matter if there was no such thing?

PHIL.: That every epidemical opinion arising from prejudice, or passion, or thoughtlessness may be imputed to God, as the Author of it, I believe you will not affirm. Whatsoever opinion we father on Him, it must be either because He has discovered it to us by supernatural revelation or because it is so evident to our natural faculties, which were framed and given us by God, that it is impossible we should withhold our assent from it. But where is the revelation? Or where is the evidence that extorts the belief of matter? Nay, how does it appear that matter, taken for something distinct from what we perceive by our senses is thought to exist by all mankind, or, indeed, by any except a few philosophers who do not know what they would be at? Your question supposes these points are clear; and, when you have cleared them, I shall think myself obliged to give you another answer. In the meantime let it suffice that I tell you I do not suppose God has deceived mankind at all.

HYL.: But the novelty, Philonous, the novelty! There lies the danger. New notions should always be discountenanced; they unsettle men's minds, and nobody knows where they will end.

PHIL.: Why the rejecting a notion that has no foundation, either in sense or in reason or in Divine authority, should be thought to unsettle the belief of such opinions as are grounded on all or any of these, I cannot imagine. That innovations in government and religion are dangerous and ought to be discountenanced, I freely own. But is there the like reason why they should be discouraged in philosophy? The making anything known which was unknown before is an innovation in knowledge; and if all such innovations had been forbidden, men would [not] have made a notable progress in the arts and sciences. But it is none of my business to plead for novelties and paradoxes. That the qualities we perceive are not on the objects, that we must not believe our senses, that we know nothing of the real nature of things and can never be assured even of their existence, the real colors and sounds are nothing but certain unknown figures and motions, that motions are in themselves neither swift nor slow, that there are in bodies absolute extensions without any particular magnitude or figure, that a thing stupid, thoughtless, and inactive operates on a spirit, that the least particle of a body contains innumerable extended parts—these are the novelties, these are the strange notions which shock the genuine uncorrupted judgment of all mankind, and, being once admitted, embarrass the mind with endless doubts and difficulties. And it is against these and the like innovations I endeavor to vindicate Common Sense. It is true, in doing this I may, perhaps, be obliged to use some ambages and ways of speech not common. But if my notions are once thoroughly understood, that which is most singular in them will, in effect, be found to amount to no more than this—that it is absolutely impossible and a plain contradiction to suppose any unthinking being should exist without being perceived by a mind. And if this notion be singular, it is a shame it should be so at this time of day and in a Christian country.

HYL.: As for the difficulties other opinions may be liable to, those are out of the question. It is your business to defend your own opinion. Can anything be plainer than that you are for changing all things into ideas? You, I say, who are not ashamed to charge me with skepticism. This is so plain, there is no denying it.

PHIL.: You mistake me. I am not for changing things into ideas but rather ideas into things, since those immediate objects of perception, which, according to you, are only appearances of things, I take to be the real things themselves.

HYL.: Things! you may pretend what you please; but it is certain you leave us nothing but the empty forms of things, the outside only which strikes the senses.

PHIL.: What you call the empty forms and outside of things seem to me the very things themselves. Nor are they empty or incomplete otherwise than upon your supposition that matter is an essential part of all corporeal things. We both, therefore, agree in this, that we perceive only sensible forms; but herein we differ: you will have them to be empty appearances, I real beings. In short, you do not trust your senses, I do.

HYL.: You say you believe your senses, and seem to applaud yourself that in this you agree with the vulgar. According to you, therefore, the true nature of a thing is discovered by the senses. If so, whence comes that disagreement? Why, is not the same figure, and other sensible qualities, perceived all manner of ways? And why should we use a microscope the better to discover the true nature of a body, if it were discoverable to the naked eye?

PHIL.: Strictly speaking, Hylas, we do not see the same object that we feel; neither is the same object perceived by the microscope which was by the naked eye. But in case every variation was thought sufficient to constitute a new kind of individual, the endless number or confusion of names would render language impracticable. Therefore, to avoid this as well as other inconveniences which are obvious upon a little thought, men combine together several ideas, apprehended by divers senses, or by the same sense at different times or in different circumstances, but observed, however, to have some connection in nature, either with respect to coexistence or succession; all which they refer to one name and consider as one thing. Hence it follows that when I examine by my other senses a thing I have seen, it is not in order to understand better the same object which I had perceived by sight, the object of one sense not being perceived by the other senses. And when I look through a microscope, it is not that I may perceive more clearly that I perceived already with my bare eyes, the object perceived by the glass being quite different from the former. But in both cases my aim is only to know what ideas are connected together; and the more a man knows of the connection of ideas, the more he is said to know of the nature of things. What, therefore, if our ideas are variable, what if our senses are not in all circumstances affected with the same appearances? It will not thence follow they are not to be trusted or that they are inconsistent either with themselves or anything else, except it be with your preconceived notion of (I know not what) one single, unchanged, unperceivable, real nature, marked by each name; which prejudice seems to have taken its rise from not rightly understanding the common language of men speaking of several distinct ideas as united into one thing by the mind. And, indeed, there is cause to suspect several erroneous conceits of the philosophers are owing to the same original: while they began to build their schemes not so much on notions as words which are framed by the vulgar merely for convenience and dispatch in the common actions of life, without any regard to speculation.

HYL.: Methinks I apprehend your meaning.

PHIL.: It is your opinion the ideas we perceive by our senses are not real things, but images or copies of them. Our knowledge, therefore, is no further real than as our ideas are the true representa-

tions of those originals. But as these supposed originals are in themselves unknown, it is impossible to know how far our ideas resemble them, or whether they resemble them at all. We cannot, therefore, be sure we have any real knowledge. Further, as our ideas are perpetually varied, without any change in the supposed real things, it necessarily follows they cannot all be true copies of them, if some are and others are not, it is impossible to distinguish the former from the latter. And this plunges us yet deeper in uncertainty. Again, when we consider the point, we cannot conceive how any idea, or anything like an idea, should have an absolute existence out of a mind, nor consequently, according to you, how there should be any real thing in nature. The result of all which is that we are thrown into the most hopeless and abandoned skepticism. Now give me leave to ask you, *first*, whether your referring ideas to certain absolutely existing unperceived substances, as their originals, be not the source of all this skepticism? *Secondly*, whether you are informed, either by sense or reason, of the existence of those unknown originals? And in case you are not, whether it be not absurd to suppose them? *Thirdly*, whether, upon inquiry, you find there is anything distinctly conceived or meant by the "absolute or external existence of unperceiving substances"; *Lastly*, whether, the premises considered, it be not the wisest way to follow nature, trust your senses, and, laying aside all anxious thought about unknown natures or substances, admit with the vulgar those for real things which are perceived by the senses?

HYL.: For the present I have no inclination to the answering part. I would much rather see how you can get over what follows. Pray, are not the objects perceived by the senses of one likewise perceivable to others present? If there were a hundred more here, they would all see the garden, the trees and flowers, as I see them. But they are not in the same manner affected with the ideas I frame in my imagination. Does not this make a difference between the former sort of objects and the latter?

PHIL.: I grant it does. Nor have I ever denied a difference between the objects of sense and those of imagination. But what would you infer from thence? You cannot say that sensible objects exist unperceived because they are perceived by many.

HYL.: I own I can make nothing of that objection, but it has led me into another. Is it not your opinion that by our senses we perceive only the ideas existing in our minds?

PHIL.: It is.

HYL.: But the same idea which is in my mind cannot be in yours or in any other mind. Does it not, therefore, follow from your principles that no two can see the same thing? And is not this highly absurd?

PHIL.: If the term "same" be taken in the vulgar acceptation, it is certain (and not at all repugnant to the principles I maintain) that different persons may perceive the same thing, or the same thing or idea exist in different minds. Words are of arbitrary imposition; and since men are used to apply the word "same" where no distinction or variety is perceived, and I do not pretend to alter their perceptions, it follows that, as men have said before, *several saw the same thing,* so they may, upon like occasions, still continue to use the same phrase without any deviation either from propriety of language or the truth of things. But if the term "same" be used in the acceptation of philosophers who pretend to an abstracted notion of identity, then, according to their sundry definitions of this notion (for it is not yet agreed wherein that philosophic identity consists), it may or may not be possible for divers persons to perceive the same thing. But whether philosophers shall think fit to call a thing the "same" or no is, I conceive, of small importance. Let us suppose several men together, all endured with the same faculties, and consequently affected in like sort by their senses, and who had yet never known the use of language; they would without question agree in their perceptions. Though perhaps, when they came to the use of speech, some regarding the uniformness of what was perceived might call it the "same" thing; others, especially regarding the diversity of persons who perceived, might choose the denomination of "different" things. But who sees not that all the dispute is about a word, to wit, whether what is perceived by different persons may yet have the term "same" applied to it? Or suppose a house whose walls or outward shell remaining unaltered, the chambers are all pulled down, and new ones built in their place, and that you should call this the "same," and I should say it was not the "same" house—would we not, for all this, perfectly agree in our thoughts of the house considered in itself? And would not all the difference consist in a sound? If you should say we differed in our notions, for that you superadded to your idea of the house the simple abstracted idea of identity, whereas I did not, I would tell you I know not what you mean by that "abstracted idea of identity," and should desire you to look into your own thoughts and be sure you understood yourself.—Why so silent, Hylas? Are you not yet satisfied men may dispute about identity and diversity without any real difference in their thoughts and opinions abstracted from names? Take this further reflection with you—that, whether matter be allowed to exist or no, the case is exactly the same as to the point in hand. For the materialists themselves acknowledge what we immediately perceive by our senses to be our own ideas. Your difficulty, therefore, that no two see the same thing makes equally against the materialists and me.

HYL.: But they suppose an external archetype to which referring their several ideas they may truly be said to perceive the same thing.

PHIL.: And (not to mention your having discarded those archetypes) so may you suppose an external archetype on my principles; *external,* I mean, to your own mind, though, indeed, it must be supposed to exist in that mind which comprehends all things; but then, this serves all the ends of *identity,* as well as if it existed out of a mind. And I am sure you yourself will not say it is less intelligible.

HYL.: You have indeed clearly satisfied me either that there is no difficulty at bottom in this point or, if there be, that it makes equally against both opinions.

PHIL.: But that which makes equally against two contradictory opinions can be a proof against neither.

HYL.: I acknowledge it. But, after all, Philonous, when I consider the substance of what you advance against skepticism, it amounts to no more than this: we are sure that we really see, hear, feel, in a word, that we are affected with sensible impressions.

PHIL.: And how are we concerned any further? I see this cherry, I feel it, I taste it, and I am sure *nothing* cannot be seen or felt or tasted; it is therefore *real.* Take away the sensations of softness, moisture, redness, tartness, and you take away the cherry. Since it is not a being distinct from sensations, a cherry, I say, is nothing but a congeries of sensible impressions, or ideas perceived by various senses, which ideas are united into one thing (or have one name given them) by the mind because they are observed to attend each other. Thus, when the palate is affected with such a particular taste, the sight is affected with a red color, the touch with roundness, softness, etc. Hence, when I see and feel and taste in sundry certain manners, I am sure the cherry exists or is real, its reality being in my opinion nothing abstracted from those sensations. But if by the word "cherry" you mean an unknown nature distinct from all those sensible qualities, and by its "existence" something distinct from its being perceived, then, indeed, I own neither you nor I, nor anyone else, can be sure it exists.

HYL.: But what would you say, Philonous, if I should bring the very same reasons against the existence of sensible things in a mind which you have offered against their existing in a material *substratum?*

PHIL.: When I see your reasons, you shall hear what I have to say to them.

HYL.: Is the mind extended or unextended?

PHIL.: Unextended, without doubt.

HYL.: Do you say the things you perceive are in your mind?

PHIL.: They are.

HYL.: Again, have I not heard you speak of sensible impressions?

PHIL.: I believe you may.

HYL.: Explain to me now, O Philonous! how is it possible there should be room for all those trees and houses to exist in your mind. Can extended things be contained in that which is unextended? Or are we to imagine impressions made on a thing void of all solidity? You cannot say objects are in your mind, as books in your study, or that things are imprinted on it, as the figure of a seal upon wax. In what sense, therefore, are we to understand those expressions? Explain me this if you can, and I shall then be able to answer all those queries you formerly put to me about my *substratum.*

PHIL.: Look you, Hylas, when I speak of objects as existing in the mind or imprinted on the senses, I would not be understood in the gross literal sense—as when bodies are said to exist in a place or a seal to make an impression upon wax. My meaning is only that the mind comprehends or perceives them, and that it is affected from without or by some being distinct from itself. This is my explication of your difficulty; and how it can serve to make your tenet of an unperceiving material *substratum* intelligible, I would fain know.

HYL.: Nay, if that be all, I confess I do not see what use can be made of it. But are you not guilty of some abuse of language in this?

PHIL.: None at all. It is no more than common custom, which you know is the rule of language, has authorized, nothing being more usual than for philosophers to speak of the immediate objects of the understanding as things existing in the mind. Nor is there anything in this but what is conformable to the general analogy of language; most part of the mental operations being signified by words borrowed from sensible things, as is plain in the terms "comprehend," "reflect," "discourse," etc., which, being applied to the mind, must not be taken in their gross original sense.

HYL.: You have, I own, satisfied me in this point. But there still remains one great difficulty which I know not how you will get over. And, indeed, it is of such importance that if you could solve all others without being able to find a solution for this, you must never expect to make me a proselyte to your principles.

PHIL.: Let me know this mighty difficulty.

HYL.: The Scripture account of the creation is what appears to me utterly irreconcilable with your notions. Moses tells us of a creation—a creation of what? of ideas? No, certainly, but of things, of real things, solid corporeal substances. Bring your principles to agree with this and I shall perhaps agree with you.

PHIL.: Moses mentions the sun, moon, and stars, earth and sea, plants and animals. That all these do really exist and were in the beginning created by God, I make no question. If by "ideas" you mean fictions and fancies of the mind, then these are no ideas. If by "ideas" you mean immediate objects of the understanding, or sensible things which cannot exist unperceived, or out of a mind, then these things are ideas. But whether you do or do not call them "ideas," it matters little. The difference is only about a name. And whether that name be retained or rejected, the sense, the truth, and reality of things continues the same. In common talk, the objects of our senses are not termed "ideas" but "things." Call them so still, provided you do not attribute to them any absolute external existence, and I shall never quarrel with you for a word. The creation, therefore, I allow to have been a creation of things, of *real* things. Neither is this in the least inconsistent with my principles, as is evident from what I have now said; and would have been evident to you without this if you had not forgotten what had been so often said before. But as for solid corporeal substances, I desire you to show where Moses makes any mention of them; and if they should be mentioned by him or any other inspired writer, it would still be incumbent on you to show those words were not taken in the vulgar acceptation for things falling under our senses, but in the philosophic acceptation for matter or an unknown quiddity with an absolute existence. When you have proved these points, then (and not till then) may you bring the authority of Moses into our dispute.

HYL.: It is in vain to dispute about a point so clear. I am content to refer it to your own conscience. Are you not satisfied there is some peculiar repugnancy between the Mosaic account of the creation and your notions?

PHIL.: If all possible sense which can be put on the first chapter of Genesis may be conceived as consistently with my principles as any other, then it has no peculiar repugnancy with them. But there is no sense you may not as well conceive, believing as I do. Since, besides spirits, all you conceive are ideas, and the existence of these I do not deny. Neither do you pretend they exist without the mind.

HYL.: Pray let me see any sense you can understand it in.

PHIL.: Why, I imagine that if I had been present at the creation, I should have seen things produced into being—that is become perceptible—in the order prescribed by the sacred historian. I ever before believed the Mosaic account of the creation, and now find no alteration in my manner of believing it. When things are said to begin or end their existence, we do not mean this with regard to God, but His creatures. All objects are eternally known by God, or, which is the same thing, have an eternal existence in His mind; but when things, before imperceptible to creatures, are, by a decree of God, made perceptible to them, then are they said to begin a relative existence with respect to created minds. Upon reading therefore the Mosaic account of the creation, I understand that the several parts of the world became gradually perceivable to finite spirits endowed with proper faculties, so that, whoever such were present, they were in truth perceived by them. This is the literal obvious sense suggested to me by the words of the Holy Scripture, in which is included no mention or thought either of *substratum,* instrument, occasion, or absolute existence. And, upon inquiry, I doubt not it will be found that most plain honest men who believe the creation never think of those things any more than I. What metaphysical sense you may understand it in, you only can tell.

HYL.: But, Philonous, you do not seem to be aware that you allow created things in the beginning only a relative and consequently hypothetical being; that is to say, upon supposition there were men to perceive them, without which they have no actuality of absolute existence wherein creation might terminate. Is it not, therefore, according to you, plainly impossible the creation of any inanimate creatures should precede that of man? And is not this directly contrary to the Mosaic account?

PHIL.: In answer to that, I say, *first,* created beings might begin to exist in the mind of other created intelligences besides men. You will not, therefore, be able to prove any contradiction between Moses and my notions unless you first show there was no other order of finite created spirits in being before man. I say further, in case we conceive the creation as we should at this time a parcel of plants or vegetables of all sorts produced by an invisible power in a desert where nobody was present—that this way of explaining or conceiving it is consistent with my principles, since they deprive you of nothing, either sensible or imaginable; that it exactly suits with the common, natural, and undebauched notions of mankind; that it manifests the dependence of all things on God, and consequently has all the good effect or influence, which it is possible that important article of our faith should have in making men humble, thankful, and resigned to their Creator. I say, moreover, that, in this naked conception of things, divested of words, there will not be found any notion of what you call the "actuality of absolute existence." You may indeed raise a dust with those terms and so lengthen our dispute to no purpose. But I entreat you calmly to look into your own thoughts and then tell me if they are not a useless and unintelligible jargon.

HYL.: I own I have no very clear notion annexed to them. But what say you to this? Do you not make the existence of sensible things consist in their being in a mind? And were not all things externally in the mind of God? Did they not therefore exist from all eternity, according to you? And how could that which was eternal be created in time? Can anything be clearer or better connected than this?

PHIL.: And are not you too of opinion that God knew all things from eternity?

HYL.: I am.

PHIL.: Consequently, they always had a being in the Divine intellect.

HYL.: This I acknowledge.

PHIL.: By your own confession, therefore, nothing is new, or begins to be, in respect of the mind of God. So we are agreed in that point.

HYL.: What shall we make then of the creation?

PHIL.: May we not understand it to have been entirely in respect of finite spirits, so that things, with regard to us, may properly be said to begin their existence, or be created, when God decreed they should become perceptible to intelligent creatures in that order and manner which He then established and we now call the laws of nature? You may call this a "relative," or "hypothetical existence," if you please. But so long as it supplies us with the most natural, obvious, and literal sense of the Mosaic history of the creation, so long as it answers all the religious ends of that great article, in a word, so long as you can assign no other sense or meaning in its stead, why should we reject this? Is it to comply with a ridiculous skeptical humor of making everything nonsense and unintelligible? I am sure you cannot say it is for the glory of God. For allowing it to be a thing possible and conceivable that the corporeal world should have an absolute existence extrinsical to the mind of God, as well as to the minds of all created spirits, yet how could this set forth either the immensity or omniscience of the Deity or the necessary and immediate dependence of all things on Him? Nay, would it not rather seem to derogate from those attributes?

HYL.: Well, but as to this decree of God's for making things perceptible, what say you, Philonous, is it not plain God did either execute that decree from all eternity or at some certain time began to will what He had not actually willed before, but only designed to will? If the former, then there could be no creation or beginning of existence in finite things. If the latter, then we must acknowledge something new to befall the Deity, which implies a sort of change; and all change argues imperfection.

PHIL.: Pray consider what you are doing. Is it not evident this objection concludes equally against a creation in any sense, nay, against every other act of the Deity discoverable by the light of nature? None of which can we conceive otherwise than as performed in time and having a beginning.

God is a Being of transcendent and unlimited perfections; His Nature, therefore, is incomprehensible to finite spirits. It is not, therefore, to be expected that any man, whether *materialist* or *immaterialist,* should have exactly just notions of the Deity, His attributes, and ways of operation. If then you would infer anything against me, your difficulty must not be drawn from the inadequateness of our conceptions of the Divine nature, which is unavoidable on any scheme, but from the denial of matter, of which there is not one word, directly or indirectly, in what you have now objected.

HYL.: I must acknowledge the difficulties you are concerned to clear are such only as arise from the nonexistence of matter and are peculiar to that notion. So far you are in the right. But I cannot by any means bring myself to think there is no such peculiar repugnancy between the creation and your opinion, though, indeed, where to fix it I do not distinctly know.

PHIL.: What would you have? Do I not acknowledge a two-fold state of things, the one ectypal or nature, the other archetypal and eternal? The former was created in time, the latter existed from everlasting in the mind of God. Is not this agreeable to the common notions of divines? Or is any more than this necessary in order to conceive the creation? But you suspect some peculiar repugnancy, though you know not where it lies. To take away all possibility of scruple in the case, do but consider this one point: either you are not able to conceive the creation on any hypothesis whatsoever, and if so, there is no ground for dislike or complaint against my particular opinion on that score; or you are able to conceive it, and if so, why not on my principles, since thereby nothing conceivable is taken away? You have all along been allowed the full scope of sense, imagination, and reason. Whatever, therefore, you could before apprehend, either immediately or mediately by your senses, or by ratiocination from your senses, whatever you could perceive, imagine, or understand, remains still with you. If, therefore, the notion you have of the creation by other principles be intelligible, you have it still upon mine; if it be not intelligible, I conceive it to be no notion at all, and so there is no loss of it. And, indeed, it seems to me very plain that the supposition of matter, that is, a thing perfectly unknown and inconceivable, cannot serve to make us conceive anything. And I hope it need not be proved to you that if the existence of matter does not make the creation conceivable, the creation's being without it inconceivable can be no objection against its nonexistence.

HYL.: I confess, Philonous, you have almost satisfied me in this point of the creation.

PHIL.: I would fain know why you are not quite satisfied. You tell me indeed of a repugnancy between the Mosaic history and immaterialism, but you know not where it lies. Is this reasonable, Hylas? Can you expect I should solve a difficulty without knowing what it is? But, to pass by all that, would not a man think you were assured there is no repugnancy between the received notions of materialists and the inspired writings?

HYL.: And so I am.

PHIL.: Ought the historical part of Scripture to be understood in a plain obvious sense or in a sense which is metaphysical and out of the way?

HYL.: In the plain sense, doubtless.

PHIL.: When Moses speaks of herbs, earth, water, etc., as having been created by God, think you not the sensible things commonly signified by those words are suggested to every unphilosophical reader?

HYL.: I cannot help thinking so.

PHIL.: And are not all ideas, or things perceived by sense, to be denied a real existence by the doctrine of the materialists?

HYL.: This I have already acknowledged.

PHIL.: The creation, therefore, according to them, was not the creation of things sensible, which have only a relative being, but of certain unknown natures which have an absolute being wherein creation might terminate?

HYL.: True.

PHIL.: Is it not, therefore, evident the assertors of matter destroy the plain obvious sense of Moses, with which their notions are utterly inconsistent, and instead of it obtrude on us I know not what, something equally unintelligible to themselves and me?

HYL.: I cannot contradict you.

PHIL.: Moses tells us of a creation. A creation of what? of unknown quiddities, of occasions, or *substratum?* No, certainly, but of things obvious to the senses. You must first reconcile this with your notions if you expect I should be reconciled to them.

HYL.: I see you can assault me with my own weapons.

PHIL.: Then as to *absolute existence,* was there ever known a more jejune notion than that? Something it is so abstracted and unintelligible that you have frankly owned you could not conceive it, much less explain anything by it. But allowing matter to exist and the notion of absolute existence to be as clear as light, yet, was this ever known to make the creation more credible? Nay, has it not furnished the atheists and infidels of all ages with the most plausible arguments against a creation? That a corporeal substance which has an absolute existence without the minds of spirits should be produced out of nothing, by the mere will of a spirit, has been looked upon as a thing so contrary to all reason, so impossible and absurd, that not only the most celebrated among the ancients, but even divers modern and Christian philosophers have thought matter coeternal with the Deity. Lay these things together and then judge you whether materialism disposes men to believe the creation of things.

HYL.: I own, Philonous, I think it does not. This of the creation is the last objection I can think of; and I must needs own it has been sufficiently answered as well as the rest. Nothing now remains to be overcome but a sort of unaccountable backwardness that I find in myself toward your notions.

PHIL.: When a man is swayed, he knows not why, to one side of a question, can this, think you, be anything else but the effect of prejudice, which never fails to attend old and rooted notions? And, indeed, in this respect I cannot deny the belief of matter to have very much the advantage over the contrary opinion with men of a learned education.

HYL.: I confess it seems to be as you say.

PHIL.: As a balance, therefore, to this weight of prejudice, let us throw into the scale the great advantages that arise from the belief of immaterialism, both in regard to religion and human learning. The being of a God and incorruptibility of the soul, those great articles of religion, are they not proved with the clearest and most immediate evidence? When I say the being of a *God,* I do not mean an obscure general cause of things whereof we have no conception, but *God* in the strict and proper sense of the word, a Being whose spirituality, omnipresence, providence, omniscience, infinite power, and goodness are as conspicuous as the existence of sensible things, of which (notwithstanding the fallacious pretenses and affected scruples of skeptics) there is no more reason to doubt than of our own being. Then, with relation to human sciences: in Natural Philosophy, what intricacies, what obscurities, what contradictions has the belief of matter led men into! To say nothing of the numberless disputes about its extent, continuity, homogeneity, gravity, divisibility, etc.—do they not pretend to explain all things by bodies operating on bodies, according to the laws of motion? And yet, are they able to comprehend how any one body should move another? Nay, admitting there was no difficulty in reconciling the notion of an inert being with a cause, or in conceiving how an accident might pass from one body to another, yet, by all their strained thoughts and extravagant suppositions, have they been able to reach the mechanical production of any one animal or vegetable body? Can they account, by the laws of motion, for sounds, tastes, smells, or colors, or for the regular course of things? Have they accounted, by physical principles, for the aptitude and contrivance even of the most inconsiderable parts of the universe? But laying aside matter and corporeal causes and admitting only the efficiency of an All-perfect Mind, are not all the effects of nature easy and intelligible? If the *phenomena* are nothing else but *ideas,* God is a *spirit,* but matter an unintelligent, unperceiving being. If they demonstrate an unlimited power in their cause, God is active and omnipotent, but matter an inert mass. If the order, regularity, and usefulness of them can never be sufficiently admired, God is infinitely wise and provident, but matter destitute of all contrivance and design. These surely are great advantages in physics. Not to mention that the apprehension of a distant Deity naturally disposes men to a negligence of their moral actions, which they would be more cautious of, in case they thought him immediately present and acting on their minds without the interposition of matter or unthinking second causes. Then in metaphysics: what difficulties concerning entity in abstract, substantial forms, hylarchic principles, plastic natures, substance and accident, principle of individuation, possibility of matter's thinking, origin of ideas, the manner how two independent substances so widely different as *spirit* and *matter* should mutually operate on each other? What difficulties, I say, and endless disquisitions concerning these and innumerable other the like points do we escape by supposing only spirits and ideas? Even the mathematics themselves, if we take away the absolute existence of extended things, become much more clear and easy, the most shocking paradoxes and intricate speculations in those sciences depending on the infinite divisibility of finite extension, which depends on that supposition. But what need is there to insist on the particular sciences? Is not that opposition to all science whatsoever, that frenzy of the ancient and modern skeptics, built on the same foundation? Or can you produce so much as one argument against the reality of corporeal things or in behalf of that avowed utter ignorance of their natures which does not suppose their reality to consist in an external absolute existence? Upon this supposition, indeed, the objections from the change of colors in a pigeon's neck, or the appearance of the broken oar in the water, must be allowed to have weight. But these and the like objections vanish if we do not maintain the being of absolute external originals, but place the reality of things in ideas, fleeting, indeed, and changeable; however, not changed at random, but according to the fixed order of nature. For herein consists that constancy and truth of things which secures all the concerns of life, and distinguishes that which is real from the irregular visions of the fancy.

HYL.: I agree to all you have now said and must own that nothing can incline me to embrace your opinion more than the advantages I see it is attended with. I am by nature lazy, and this would be a mighty abridgment in knowledge. What doubts, what hypotheses, what labyrinths of amusements, what fields of disputation, what an ocean of false learning may be avoided by that single notion of *immaterialism!*

PHIL.: After all, is there anything further remaining to be done? You may remember you promised to embrace that opinion which upon examination should appear most agreeable to common sense and remote from skepticism. This, by your own confession, is that which denies matter or the absolute existence of corporeal things. Nor is this all; the same notion has been proved several ways, viewed in different lights, pursued in its consequences, and all objections against it cleared. Can there be a greater evidence of its truth? Or is it possible it should have all the marks of a true opinion and yet be false?

HYL.: I own myself entirely satisfied for the present in all respects. But what security can I have that I shall still continue the same full assent to your opinion and that no unthought-of-objection or difficulty will occur hereafter?

PHIL.: Pray, Hylas, do you in other cases, when a point is once evidently proved, withhold your assent on account of objections or difficulties it may be liable to? Are the difficulties that attend the doctrine of incommensurable quantities, of the angle of contact, of the asymptotes to curves, or the like, sufficient to make you hold out against mathematical demonstration? Or will you disbelieve the Providence of God because there may be some particular things which you know not how to reconcile with it? If there are difficulties attending immaterialism, there are at the same time direct and evident proofs of it. But for the existence of matter there is not one proof, and far more numerous and insurmountable objections lie against it. But where are those mighty difficulties you insist on? Alas! you know not where or what they are; something which may possibly occur hereafter. If this be a sufficient pretense for withholding your full assent, you should never yield it to any proposition, how free soever from exceptions, how clearly and solidly soever demonstrated.

HYL.: You have satisfied me, Philonous.

PHIL.: But to arm you against all future objections, do but consider that which bears equally hard on two contradictory opinions can be proof against neither. Whenever, therefore, any difficulty occurs, try if you can find a solution for it on the hypothesis of the materialists. Be not deceived by words, but sound your own thoughts. And in case you cannot conceive it easier by the help of materialism, it is plain it can be no objection against immaterialism. Had you proceeded all along by this rule, you would probably have spared yourself abundance of trouble in objecting, since of all your difficulties I challenge you to show one that is explained by matter, nay, which is not more unintelligible with than without that supposition, and consequently makes rather *against* than *for* it. You should consider, in each particular, whether the difficulty arises from the *nonexistence of matter*. If it does not, you might as well argue from the infinite divisibility of extension against the Divine prescience as from such a difficulty against immaterialism. And yet, upon recollection, I believe you will find this to have been often if not always the case. You should likewise take heed not to argue on a *petitio principii*. One is apt to say the unknown substances ought to be esteemed real things rather than the ideas in our minds; and who can tell but the unthinking external substance may concur as a cause or instrument in the productions of our ideas? But is not this proceeding on a supposition that there are such external substances? And to suppose this, is it not begging the question? But above all things, you should beware of imposing on yourself by that vulgar sophism which is called *ignoratio elenchi*. You talked often as if you thought I maintained the nonexistence of sensible things, whereas in truth no one can be more thoroughly assured of their existence than I am; and it is you who doubt, I should have said, positively deny it. Everything that is seen,

felt, heard, or any way perceived by the senses is, on the principles I embrace, a real being, but not on yours. Remember, the matter you contend for is an unknown somewhat (if indeed it may be termed "somewhat"), which is quite stripped of all sensible qualities, and can neither be perceived by sense, nor apprehended by the mind. Remember, I say that it is not any object which is hard or soft, hot or cold, blue or white, round or square, etc.—for all these things I affirm do exist. Though, indeed, I deny they have an existence distinct from being perceived, or that they exist out of all minds whatsoever. Think on these points; let them be attentively considered and still kept in view. Otherwise you will not comprehend the state of the question, without which your objections will always be wide of the mark and, instead of mine, may possibly be directed (as more than once they have been) against your own notions.

HYL.: I must needs own, Philonous, nothing seems to have kept me from agreeing with you more than this same *mistaking the question*. In denying matter, at first glimpse I am tempted to imagine you deny the things we see and feel, but, upon reflection, find there is no ground for it. What think you, therefore, of retaining the name "matter" and applying it to *sensible things*? This may be done without any change in your sentiments; and, believe me, it would be a means of reconciling them to some persons who may be more shocked at an innovation in words than in opinion.

PHIL.: With all my heart; retain the word "matter" and apply it to the objects of sense, if you please, provided you do not attribute to them any subsistence distinct from their being perceived. I shall never quarrel with you for an expression. "Matter" or "material substance" are terms introduced by philosophers, and, as used by them, imply a sort of independence, or a subsistence distinct from being perceived by a mind; but are never used by common people, or, if ever, it is to signify the immediate objects of sense. One would think, therefore, so long as the names of all particular things with the terms "sensible," "substance," "body," "stuff," and the like, are retained, the word "matter" should be never missed in common talk. And in philosophical discourses it seems the best way to leave it quite out, since there is not, perhaps, any one thing that has more favored and strengthened the depraved bent of the mind toward atheism than the use of that general confused term.

HYL.: Well, but, Philonous, since I am content to give up the notion of an unthinking substance exterior to the mind, I think you ought not to deny me the privilege of using the word "matter" as I please, and annexing it to a collection of sensible qualities subsisting only in the mind. I freely own there is no other substance, in a strict sense, than spirit. But I have been so long accustomed to the term "matter" that I know not how to part with it. To say there is no matter in the world is still shocking to me. Whereas to say there is no matter if by that term be meant an unthinking substance existing without the mind, but if by matter is meant some sensible thing whose existence consists in being perceived, then there is matter—this distinction gives it quite another turn; and men will come into your notions with small difficulty when they are proposed in that manner. For, after all, the controversy about matter in the strict acceptation of it lies altogether between you and the philosophers, whose principles, I acknowledge, are not near so natural or so agreeable to the common sense of mankind and the Holy Scripture as yours. There is nothing we either desire or shun but as it makes, or is apprehended to make, some part of our happiness or misery. But what has happiness or misery, joy or grief, pleasure or pain to do with absolute existence or with unknown entities abstracted from all relation to us? It is evident things regard us only as they are pleasing or displeasing; and they can please or displease only so far forth as they are perceived. Further, therefore, we are not concerned; and

thus far you leave things as you found them. Yet still there is something new in this doctrine. It is plain, I do not now think with the philosophers, nor yet altogether with the vulgar. I would know how the case stands in that respect, precisely what you have added to or altered in my former notions.

PHIL.: I do not pretend to be a setter-up of new notions. My endeavors tend only to unite and place in a clearer light that truth which was before shared between the vulgar and the philosophers, the former being of opinion that *those things they immediately perceive are the real things,* and the latter, that *the things immediately perceived are ideas which exist only in the mind.* Which two notions put together do, in effect, constitute the substance of what I advance.

HYL.: I have been a long time distrusting my senses; methought I saw things by a dim light and through false glasses. Now the glasses are removed and a new light breaks in upon my understanding. I am clearly convinced that I see things in their native forms and am no longer in pain about their *unknown natures* or *absolute existence.* This is the state I find myself in at present, though, indeed, the course that brought me to it I do not yet thoroughly comprehend. You set out upon the same principles that Academics, Cartesians, and the like sects usually do, and for a long time it looked as if you were advancing their philosophical skepticism; but, in the end, your conclusions are directly opposite to theirs.

PHIL.: You see, Hylas, the water of yonder fountain, how it is forced upwards, in a round column, to a certain height, at which it breaks and falls back into the basin from whence it rose, its ascent as well as descent proceeding from the same uniform law or principle of gravitation. Just so, the same principles which, at first view, lead to skepticism, pursued to a certain point, bring men back to common sense.

An Inquiry Concerning Human Understanding

DAVID HUME

The great British empiricist philosopher and skeptic David Hume (1711–1766) was born in Scotland.

Section II. Of the origin of ideas

Everyone will readily allow that there is a considerable difference between the perceptions of the mind when a man feels the pain of excessive heat or the pleasure of moderate warmth, and when he afterwards recalls to his memory this sensation or anticipates it by his imagination. These faculties may mimic or copy the perceptions of the senses, but they never can entirely reach the force and vivacity of the original sentiment. The utmost we say of them, even when they operate with greatest vigor, is that they represent their object in so lively a manner that we could *almost* say we feel or see it. But, except the mind be disordered by disease or madness, they never can arrive at such a pitch of vivacity, as to render these perceptions altogether undistinguishable. All the colors of poetry, however splendid, can never paint natural objects in such a manner as to make the description be taken for a real landscape. The most lively thought is still inferior to the dullest sensation.

We may observe a like distinction to run through all the other perceptions of the mind. A man in a fit of anger, is actuated in a very different manner from one who only thinks of that emotion. If you tell me that any person is in love, I easily understand your meaning and form a just conception of his situation, but never can mistake that conception for the real disorders and agitations of the passion. When we reflect on our past sentiments and affections, our thought is a faithful mirror and copies its objects truly, but the colors which it employs are faint and dull, in comparison of those in which our original

perceptions were clothed. It requires no nice discernment or metaphysical head to mark the distinction between them.

Here, therefore, we may divide all the perceptions of the mind into two classes or species, which are distinguished by their different degrees of force and vivacity. The less forcible and lively are commonly denominated "thoughts" or "ideas." The other species want a name in our language, and in most others; I suppose, because it was not requisite for any but philosophical purposes to rank them under a general term or appellation. Let us, therefore, use a little freedom and call them "impressions," employing that word in a sense somewhat different from the usual. By the term "impression," then, I mean all our more lively perceptions, when we hear, or see, or feel, or love, or hate, or desire, or will. And impressions are distinguished from ideas, which are the less lively perceptions of which we are conscious when we reflect on any of those sensations or movements above mentioned.

Nothing, at first view, may seem more unbounded than the thought of man, which not only escapes all human power and authority, but is not even restrained within the limits of nature and reality. To form monsters and join incongruous shapes and appearances costs the imagination no more trouble than to conceive the most natural and familiar objects. And while the body is confined to one planet, along which it creeps with pain and difficulty, the thought can in an instant transport us into the most distant regions of the universe, or even beyond the universe into the unbounded chaos where nature is supposed to lie in total confusion. What never was seen or heard of, may yet be con-

From *An Inquiry Concerning Human Understanding.* Sections II, IV–VII. First published in 1748.

ceived, nor is any thing beyond the power of thought except what implies an absolute contradiction.

But though our thought seems to possess this unbounded liberty, we shall find upon a nearer examination, that it is really confined within very narrow limits, and that all this creative power of the mind amounts to no more than the faculty of compounding, transposing, augmenting, or diminishing the materials afforded us by the senses and experience. When we think of a golden mountain, we only join two consistent ideas, "gold" and "mountain," with which we were formerly acquainted. A virtuous horse we can conceive, because, from our own feeling, we can conceive virtue; and this we may unite to the figure and shape of a horse, which is an animal familiar to us. In short, all the materials of thinking are derived either from our outward or inward sentiment, the mixture and composition of these belongs alone to the mind and will, or, to express myself in philosophical language, all our ideas or more feeble perceptions are copies of our impressions or more lively ones.

To prove this, the two following arguments will, I hope, be sufficient. *First,* when we analyze our thoughts or ideas, however compounded or sublime, we always find that they resolve themselves into such simple ideas as were copied from a precedent feeling or sentiment. Even those ideas which at first view seem the most wide of this origin are found, upon a nearer scrutiny, to be derived from it. The idea of God, as meaning an infinitely intelligent, wise, and good Being, arises from reflecting on the operations of our own mind, and augmenting, without limit, those qualities of goodness and wisdom. We may prosecute this inquiry to what length we please; where we shall always find that every idea which we examine is copied from a similar impression. Those who would assert that this position is not universally true, nor without exception, have only one, and that an easy, method of refuting it by producing that idea which, in their opinion, is not derived from this source. It will then be incumbent on us, if we would maintain our doctrine, to produce the impression or lively perception which corresponds to it.

Secondly, if it happen, from a defect of the organ, that a man is not susceptible of any species of sensation, we always find that he is as little susceptible of the correspondent ideas. A blind man can form no notion of colors, a deaf man of sounds. Restore either of them that sense in which he is deficient by opening this new inlet for his sensations, you also open an inlet for the ideas, and he finds no difficulty in conceiving these objects. The case is the same, if the object proper for exciting any sensation has never been applied to the organ. A Laplander . . . has no notion of the relish of wine. And though there are few or no instances of a like deficiency in the mind where a person has never felt or is wholly incapable of a sentiment or passion that belongs to his species, yet we find the same observation to take place in a less degree. A man of mild manners can form no idea of inveterate revenge or cruelty, nor can a selfish heart easily conceive the heights of friendship and generosity. It is readily allowed that other beings may possess many senses of which we can have no conception, because the ideas of them have never been introduced to us in the only manner by which an idea can have access to the mind, to wit, by the actual feeling and sensation.

There is, however, one contradictory phenomenon which may prove that it is not absolutely impossible for ideas to arise independent of their correspondent impressions. I believe it will readily be allowed that the several distinct ideas of color, which enter by the eye, or those of sound, which are conveyed by the ear, are really different from each other, though at the same time resembling. Now, if this be true of different colors, it must be no less so of the different shades of the same color; and each shade produces a distinct idea, independent of the rest. For if this should be denied, it is possible, by the continual gradation of shades, to run a color insensibly into what is most remote from it; and if you will not allow any of the means to be different, you cannot, without absurdity, deny the extremes to be the same. Suppose, therefore, a person to have enjoyed his sight for thirty years and to have become perfectly acquainted with colors of all kinds, except one particular shade of blue, for instance, which it never has been his fortune to meet with; let all the different shades of that color, except that single one, be placed before him, descending gradually from the deepest to the lightest, it is plain that he will perceive a blank, where that shade is wanting, and will be sensible that there is a greater distance in that place between the contiguous colors than in any other. Now I ask whether it be possible for him, from his own imagination, to supply this deficiency and raise up to himself the idea of that particular shade, though it had never been conveyed to him by his senses? I believe there are few but will be of opinion that he can; and this may serve as a proof that the simple ideas are not always, in every instance, derived from the correspondent impressions, though this instance is so singular that it is scarcely worth our observing, and does not merit that for it alone we should alter our general maxim.

Here, therefore, is a proposition which not only seems in itself simple and intelligible, but, if a proper use were made of it, might render every dispute equally intelligible, and banish all that jargon which has so long taken possession of metaphysical reasonings and drawn disgrace upon them. All ideas, especially abstract ones, are naturally faint and obscure. The mind has but a slender hold of them. They are apt to be confounded with other resembling ideas; and when we have often employed any term, though without a distinct meaning, we are apt to imagine it has a determinate idea annexed to it. On the contrary, all impressions, that is, all sensations either outward or inward, are strong and vivid. The limits between them are more exactly determined, nor is it easy to fall into any error or mistake with regard to them. When we entertain, therefore, any suspicion that a philosophical term is employed without any meaning or idea (as is but too frequent), we need but enquire, *from what impression is that supposed idea derived?* And if it be impossible to assign any, this will serve to confirm our suspicion. By bringing ideas in so clear a light, we may reasonably hope to remove all dispute which may arise concerning their nature and reality.[1]

Section IV. Skeptical doubts concerning the operations of the understanding

PART I

All the objects of human reason or inquiry may naturally be divided into two kinds, to wit, "Relations of Ideas," and "Matters of Fact." Of the first kind are the sciences of Geometry, Algebra, and Arithmetic, and, in short, every affirmation which is either intuitively or demonstratively certain. *That the square of the hypotenuse is equal to the square of the two sides* is a proposition which expresses a relation between these figures. *That three times five is equal to the half of thirty* expresses a relation between these numbers. Propositions of this kind are discoverable by the mere operation of thought, without dependence on what is anywhere existent in the universe. Though there never were a circle or triangle in nature, the truths demonstrated by Euclid would forever retain their certainty and evidence.

Matters of fact, which are the second objects of human reason, are not ascertained in the same manner, nor is our evidence of their truth, however great, of a like nature with the foregoing. The contrary of every matter of fact is still possible, because it can never imply a contradiction and is conceived by the mind with the same facility and distinctness as if ever so conformable to reality. *That the sun will not rise tomorrow* is no less intelligible a proposition and implies no more contradiction than the affirmation *that it will rise.* We should in vain, therefore, attempt to demonstrate its falsehood. Were it demonstratively false, it would imply a contradiction and could never be distinctly conceived by the mind.

It may, therefore, be a subject worthy of curiosity to inquire what is the nature of that evidence which assures us of any real existence and matter of fact beyond the present testimony of our senses or the records of our memory. This part of philosophy, it is observable, has been little cultivated either by the ancients or moderns; and, therefore, our doubts and errors in the prosecution of so important an inquiry may be the more excusable while we march through such difficult paths without any guide or direction. They may even prove useful by exciting curiosity and destroying that implicit faith and security which is the bane of all reasoning and free inquiry. The discovery of defects in the common philosophy if any such there be, will not, I presume, be a discouragement, but rather an incitement, as is usual, to attempt something more full and satisfactory than has yet been proposed to the public.

All reasonings concerning matter of fact seem to be founded on the relation of *cause* and *effect.* By means of that relation alone we can go beyond the evidence of our memory and senses. If you were to ask a man, why he believes any matter of fact which is absent, for instance, that his friend is in the country or in France, he would give you a reason, and this reason would be some other fact: as a letter received from him or the knowledge of his former resolutions and promises. A man finding a watch or any other machine in a desert island would conclude that there had once been men in that island. All our reasonings concerning fact are of the same nature. And here it is constantly supposed that there is a connection between the present fact and that which is inferred from it. Were there nothing to bind them together, the inference would be entirely precarious. The hearing of an articulate voice and rational discourse in the dark assures us of the presence of some person. Why? Because these are the effects of the human make and fabric, and closely connected with it. If we anatomize all the other reasonings of this nature, we shall find that they are founded on the relation of cause and effect, and that this relation is either near or remote, direct or collateral. Heat and light are collateral effects of fire, and the one effect may justly be inferred from the other.

If we would satisfy ourselves, therefore, concerning the nature of that evidence which assures us of matters of fact, we must inquire how we arrive at the knowledge of cause and effect.

I shall venture to affirm, as a general proposition which admits of no exception, that the knowledge of this relation is not, in any instance, attained by reasonings a priori, but arises entirely from experience, when we find that any particular objects are constantly conjoined with each other. Let an object be presented to a man of ever so strong natural reason and abilities—if that object be entirely new to him, he will not be able, by the most accurate examination of its sensible qualities, to discover any of its causes or effects. Adam, though his rational faculties be supposed, at the very first, entirely perfect, could not have inferred from the fluidity and transparency of water that it would suffocate him, or from the light and warmth of fire that it would consume him. No object ever discovers, by the qualities which appear to the senses, either the causes which produced it or the effects which will arise from it; nor can our reason, unassisted by experience, ever draw any inference concerning real existence and matter of fact.

This proposition, *that causes and effects are discoverable, not by reason, but by experience,* will readily be admitted with regard to such objects as we remember to have once been altogether unknown to us, since we must be conscious of the utter inability which we then lay under of foretelling what would arise from them. Present two smooth pieces of marble to a man who has no tincture of natural philosophy; he will never discover that they will adhere together in such a manner as to require great force to separate them in a direct line, while they make so small a resistance to a lateral pressure. Such events as bear little analogy to the common course of nature are also readily confessed to be known only by experience, nor does any man imagine that the explosion of gunpowder or the attraction of a loadstone could ever be discovered by arguments a priori. In like manner, when an effect is supposed to depend upon an intricate machinery or secret structure of parts, we make no difficulty in attributing all our knowledge of it to experience. Who will assert that he can give the ultimate reason why milk or bread is proper nourishment for a man, not for a lion or a tiger?

But the same truth may not appear at first sight to have the same evidence with regard to events which have become familiar to us from our first appearance in the world, which bear a close analogy to the whole course of nature, and which are supposed to depend on the simple qualities of objects without any secret structure of parts. We are apt to imagine that we could discover these effects by the mere operation of our reason without experience. We fancy that, were we brought on a sudden into this world, we could at first have inferred that one billiard ball would communicate motion to another upon impulse, and that we needed not to have waited for the event in order to pronounce with certainty concerning it. Such is the influence of custom that where it is strongest it not only covers our natural ignorance but even conceals itself, and seems not to take place, merely because it is found in the highest degree.

But to convince us that all the laws of nature and all the operations of bodies without exception are known only by experience, the following reflections may perhaps suffice. Were any object presented to us, and were we required to pronounce concerning the effect which will result from it without consulting past observation, after what manner, I beseech you, must the mind proceed in this operation? It must invent or imagine some event which it ascribes to the object as its effect; and it is plain that this invention must be entirely arbitrary. The mind can never possibly find the effect in the supposed cause by the most accurate scrutiny and examination. For the effect is totally different from the cause, and consequently can never be discovered in it. Motion in the second billiard ball is a quite distinct event from motion in the first, nor is there anything in the one to suggest the smallest hint of the other. A stone or piece of metal raised into the air and left without any support immediately falls. But to consider the matter *a priori*, is there anything we discover in this situation which can beget the idea of a downward rather than an upward or any other motion in the stone or metal?

And as the first imagination or invention of a particular effect in all natural operations is arbitrary where we consult not experience, so must we also esteem the supposed tie or connection between the cause and effect which binds them together and renders it impossible that any other effect could result from the operation of that cause. When I see, for instance, a billiard ball moving in a straight line towards another, even suppose motion in the second ball should by accident be suggested to me as the result of their contact or impulse, may I not conceive that a hundred different events might as well follow from that cause? May not both these balls remain at absolute rest? May not the first ball return in a straight line or leap off the second in any line or direction? All these suppositions are consistent and conceivable. Why, then, should we give the preference to one which is no more consistent or conceivable than the rest? All our reasonings *a priori* will never be able to show us any foundation for this preference.

In a word, then, every effect is a distinct event from its cause. It could not, therefore, be discovered in the cause, and the first invention or conception of it *a priori*, must be entirely arbitrary. And even after it is suggested, the conjunction of it with the cause must appear equally arbitrary, since there are always many other effects which, to reason, must seem fully as consistent and natural. In vain, therefore, should we pretend to determine any single event or infer any cause or effect without the assistance of observation and experience.

Hence we may discover the reason why no philosopher who is rational and modest has ever pretended to assign the ultimate cause of any natural operation, or to show distinctly the action of that power which produces any single effect in the universe. It is confessed that the utmost effort of human reason is to reduce the principles productive of natural phenomena to a greater simplicity, and to resolve the many particular effects into a few general causes, by means of reasonings from analogy, experience, and observation. But as to the causes of these general causes, we should in vain attempt their discovery, nor shall we ever be able to satisfy ourselves by any particular explication of them. These ultimate springs and principles are totally shut up from human curiosity and inquiry. Elasticity, gravity, cohesion of parts, communication of motion by impulse—these are probably the ultimate causes and principles which we ever discover in nature; and we may esteem ourselves sufficiently happy if, by accurate inquiry and reasoning, we can trace up the particular phenomena to, or near to, these general principles. The most perfect philosophy of the natural kind only staves off our ignorance a little longer, as perhaps the most perfect philosophy of the moral or metaphysical kind serves only to discover larger portions of it. Thus the observation of human blindness and weakness is the result of all philosophy, and meets us, at every turn, in spite of our endeavors to elude or avoid it.

Nor is geometry, when taken into the assistance of natural philosophy, ever able to remedy this defect or lead us into the knowledge of ultimate causes by all that accuracy of reasoning for which it is so justly celebrated. Every part of mixed mathematics proceeds upon the supposition that certain laws are established by nature in her operations, and abstract reasonings are employed either to assist experience in the discovery of these laws or to determine their influence in particular instances where it depends upon any precise degree of distance and quantity. Thus it is a law of motion, discovered by experience, that the moment or force of any body in motion is in the compound ratio or proportion of its solid contents and its velocity, and, consequently, that a small force may remove the greatest obstacle or raise the greatest weight if by any contrivance or machinery we can increase the velocity of that force so as to make it an overmatch for its antagonist. Geometry assists us in the application of this law by giving us the just dimensions of all the parts and figures which can enter into any species of machine, but still the discovery of the law itself is owing merely to experience; and all the abstract reasonings in the world could never lead us one step towards the knowledge of it. When we reason *a priori* and consider merely any object or cause as it appears to the mind, independent of all observation, it never could suggest to us the notion of any distinct object, such as its effect, much less show us the inseparable and inviolable connection between them. A man must be very sagacious who could discover by reasoning that crystal is the effect of heat, and ice of cold, without being previously acquainted with the operation of these qualities.

PART II

But we have not yet attained any tolerable satisfaction with regard to the question first proposed. Each solution still gives rise to a new question as difficult as the foregoing and leads us on to further inquiries. When it is asked, *What is the nature of all our reasonings concerning matter of fact?* the proper answer seems to be, That they are founded on the relation of cause and effect. When again it is asked, *What is the foundation of all our reasonings and conclusions concerning that relation?* it may be replied in one word, *experience*. But if we still carry on our sifting humor and ask, *What is the foundation of all conclusions from experience?* this implies a new question which may be of more difficult solution and explication. Philosophers that give themselves airs of superior wisdom and sufficiency have a hard task when they encounter persons of inquisitive dispositions, who push them from every corner to which they retreat, and who are sure at last to bring them to some dangerous dilemma. The best expedient to prevent this confusion is to be modest in our pretentions and even to discover the difficulty ourselves before it is objected to us. By this means, we may make a kind of merit of our very ignorance.

I shall content myself in this section with an easy task and shall pretend only to give a negative answer to the question here proposed. I say, then, that even after we have experience of the operations of cause and effect, our conclusions from that experience are not founded on reasoning or any process of understanding. This answer we must endeavor both to explain and to defend.

It must certainly be allowed that nature has kept us at a great distance from all her secrets and has afforded us only the knowledge of a few superficial qualities of objects, while she conceals from us those powers and principles on which the influence of those objects entirely depends. Our senses inform us of the color, weight, and consistency of bread, but neither sense nor reason can ever inform us of those qualities which fit it for the nourishment and support of a human body. Sight or feeling conveys an idea of the actual motion of bodies, but as to that wonderful force or power which would carry on a moving body forever in a continued change of place, and which bodies never lose but by communicating it to others, of this we cannot form the most distant conception. But notwithstanding this ignorance of natural powers[2] and principles, we always presume when we see like sensible qualities that they have like secret powers, and expect that effects similar to those which we have experienced will follow from them. If a body of like color and consistence with that bread which we have formerly eaten be presented to us, we make no scruple of repeating the experiment and foresee with certainty like nourishment and support. Now this is a process of the mind or thought of which I would willingly know the foundation. It is allowed on all hands that there is no known connection between the sensible qualities and the secret powers, and, consequently, that the mind is not led to form such a conclusion concerning their constant and regular conjunction by anything which it knows of their nature. As to past *experience*, it can be allowed to give *direct* and *certain* information of those precise objects only, and that precise period of time which fell under its cognizance: But why this experience should be extended to future times and to other objects which, for aught we know, may be only in appearance similar, this is the main question on which I would insist. The bread which I formerly ate nourished me; that is, a body of such sensible qualities was, at that time, endued with such secret powers. But does it follow that other bread must also nourish me at another time, and that like sensible qualities must always be attended with like secret powers? The consequence seems nowise necessary. At least, it must be acknowledged that there is here a consequence drawn by the mind, that there is a certain step taken, a process of thought, and an inference which wants to be explained. These two propositions are far from being the same: *I have found that such an object has always been attended with such an effect,* and *I foresee that other objects which are in appearance similar will be attended with similar effects.* I shall allow, if you please, that the one proposition may justly be inferred from the other: I know, in fact, that it always is inferred. But if you insist that the inference is made by a chain of reasoning, I desire you to produce that reasoning. The connection between these propositions is not intuitive. There is required a medium which may enable the mind to draw such an inference, if indeed it be drawn by reasoning and argument. What that medium is I must confess passes my comprehension; and it is incumbent on those to produce it who assert that it really exists and is the origin of all our conclusions concerning matter of fact.

This negative argument must certainly, in process of time, become altogether convincing if many penetrating and able philosophers shall turn their inquiries this way, and no one be ever able to discover any connecting proposition or intermediate step which supports the understanding in this conclusion. But as the question is yet new, every reader may not trust so far to his own penetration, as to conclude, because an argument escapes his inquiry, that therefore it does not really exist. For this reason it may be requisite to venture upon a more difficult task, and, enumerating all the branches of human knowledge, endeavor to show that none of them can afford such an argument.

All reasonings may be divided into two kinds, namely, demonstrative reasoning, or that concerning relations of ideas, and moral reasoning, or that concerning matter of fact and existence. That there are no demonstrative arguments in the case seems evident, since it implies no contradiction that the course of nature may change and that an object, seemingly like those which we have experienced, may be attended with different or contrary effects. May I not clearly and distinctly conceive that a body, falling from the clouds and which in all other respects resembles snow, has yet the taste of salt or feeling of fire? Is there any more intelligible proposition

than to affirm that all the trees will flourish in December and January, and will decay in May and June? Now, whatever is intelligible and can be distinctly conceived implies no contradiction and can never be proved false by any demonstrative argument or abstract reasoning *a priori.*

If we be, therefore, engaged by arguments to put trust in past experience and make it the standard of our future judgment, these arguments must be probable only, or such as regard matter of fact and real existence, according to the division above mentioned. But that there is no argument of this kind must appear if our explication of that species of reasoning be admitted as solid and satisfactory. We have said that all arguments concerning existence are founded on the relation of cause and effect, that our knowledge of that relation is derived entirely from experience, and that all our experimental conclusions proceed upon the supposition that the future will be conformable to the past. To endeavor, therefore, the proof of this last supposition by probable arguments, or arguments regarding existence, must be evidently going in a circle and taking that for granted which is the very point in question.

In reality, all arguments from experience are founded on the similarity which we discover among natural objects, and by which we are induced to expect effects similar to those which we have found to follow from such objects. And though none but a fool or madman will ever pretend to dispute the authority of experience or to reject that great guide of human life, it may surely be allowed a philosopher to have so much curiosity at least as to examine the principle of human nature which gives this mighty authority to experience and makes us draw advantage from that similarity which nature has placed among different objects. From causes which appear similar, we expect similar effects. This is the sum of all our experimental conclusions. Now it seems evident that, if this conclusion were formed by reason, it would be as perfect at first, and upon one instance, as after ever so long a course of experience; but the case is far otherwise. Nothing so like as eggs, yet no one, on account of this appearing similarity, expects the same taste and relish in all of them. It is only after a long course of uniform experiments in any kind that we attain a firm reliance and security with regard to a particular event. Now, where is that process of reasoning which, from one instance, draws a conclusion so different from that which it infers from a hundred instances that are nowise different from that single one? This question I propose as much for the sake of information as with an intention of raising difficulties. I cannot find, I cannot imagine any such reasoning. But I keep my mind still open to instruction if anyone will vouchsafe to bestow it on me.

Should it be said that, from a number of uniform experiments, we *infer* a connection between the sensible qualities and the secret powers, this, I must confess, seems the same difficulty, couched in different terms. The question still recurs, On what process of argument is this *inference* founded? Where is the medium, the interposing ideas which join propositions so very wide of each other? It is confessed that the color, consistence, and other sensible qualities of bread appear not of themselves to have any connection with the secret powers of nourishment and support; for otherwise we could infer these secret powers from the first appearance of these sensible qualities without the aid of experience, contrary to the sentiment of all philosophers, and contrary to plain matter of fact. Here, then, is our natural state of ignorance with regard to the powers and influence of all objects. How is this remedied by experience? It only shows us a number of uniform effects resulting from certain objects, and teaches us that those particular objects, at that particular time, were endowed with such powers and forces. When a new object endowed with similar sensible qualities is produced, we expect similar powers and forces, and look for a like effect. From a body of like color and consistence with bread, we expect like nourishment and support. But this surely is a step or progress of the mind which wants to be explained. When a man says, *I have found, in all past instances, such sensible qualities, conjoined with such secret powers,* and when he says, *similar sensible qualities will always be conjoined with similar secret powers,* he is not guilty of a tautology, nor are these propositions in any respect the same. You say that the one proposition is an inference from the other; but you must confess that the inference is not intuitive, neither is it demonstrative. Of what nature is it then? To say it is experimental is begging the question. For all inferences from experience suppose, as their foundation, that the future will resemble the past and that

similar powers will be conjoined with similar sensible qualities. If there be any suspicion that the course of nature may change, and that the past may be no rule for the future, all experience becomes useless and can give rise to no inference or conclusion. It is impossible, therefore, that any arguments from experience can prove this resemblance of the past to the future; since all these arguments are founded on the supposition of that resemblance. Let the course of things be allowed hitherto ever so regular, that alone, without some new argument or inference, proves not that for the future it will continue so. In vain do you pretend to have learned the nature of bodies from your past experience. Their secret nature and consequently all their effects and influence, may change without any change in their sensible qualities. This happens sometimes, and with regard to some objects. Why may it happen always, and with regard to all objects? What logic, what process of argument secures you against this supposition? My practice, you say, refutes my doubts. But you mistake the purport of my question. As an agent, I am quite satisfied in the point; but as a philosopher who has some share of curiosity, I will not say scepticism, I want to learn the foundation of this inference. No reading, no inquiry has yet been able to remove my difficulty or give me satisfaction in a matter of such importance. Can I do better than propose the difficulty to the public, even though, perhaps, I have small hopes of obtaining a solution? We shall at least, by this means, be sensible of our ignorance, if we do not augment our knowledge.

I must confess that a man is guilty of unpardonable arrogance who concludes, because an argument has escaped his own investigation, that therefore it does not really exist. I must also confess that, though all the learned, for several ages, should have employed themselves in fruitless search upon any subject, it may still, perhaps, be rash to conclude positively that the subject must therefore pass all human comprehension. Even though we examine all the sources of our knowledge and conclude them unfit for such a subject, there may still remain a suspicion that the enumeration is not complete, or the examination not accurate. But with regard to the present subject, there are some considerations which seem to remove all this accusation of arrogance or suspicion of mistake.

It is certain that the most ignorant and stupid peasants, nay infants, nay even brute beasts, improve by experience and learn the qualities of natural objects by observing the effects which result from them. When a child has felt the sensation of pain from touching the flame of a candle, he will be careful not to put his hand near any candle, but will expect a similar effect from a cause which is similar in its sensible qualities and appearance. If you assert, therefore, that the understanding of the child is led into this conclusion by any process of argument or ratiocination, I may justly require you to produce that argument, nor have you any pretense to refuse so equitable a demand. You cannot say that the argument is abstruse and may possibly escape your inquiry, since you confess that it is obvious to the capacity of a mere infant. If you hesitate, therefore, a moment or if, after reflection, you produce any intricate or profound argument, you, in a manner, give up the question and confess that it is not reasoning which engages us to suppose the past resembling the future, and to expect similar effects from causes which are to appearance similar. This is the proposition which I intended to enforce in the present section. If I be right, I pretend not to have made any mighty discovery. And if I be wrong, I must acknowledge myself to be indeed a very backward scholar, since I cannot now discover an argument which, it seems, was perfectly familiar to me long before I was out of my cradle.

Section V. Skeptical solution of these doubts

PART I

The passion for philosophy, like that for religion, seems liable to this inconvenience, that though it aims at the correction of our manners, and extirpation of our vices, it may only serve, by imprudent management, to foster a predominant inclination and push the mind with more determined resolution toward that side which already *draws* too much by the bias and propensity of the natural temper. It is certain that, while we aspire to the magnanimous firmness of the philosophic sage and endeavor to confine our pleasures altogether within our own minds, we may, at last, render our philosophy, like that of Epictetus and other Stoics, only a more re-

fined system of selfishness, and reason ourselves out of all virtue as well as social enjoyment. While we study with attention the vanity of human life and turn all our thoughts toward the empty and transitory nature of riches and honors, we are, perhaps, all the while flattering our natural indolence which, hating the bustle of the world and drudgery of business, seeks a pretense of reason to give itself a full and uncontrolled indulgence. There is, however, one species of philosophy which seems little liable to this inconvenience, and that because it strikes in with no disorderly passion of the human mind, nor can mingle itself with any natural affection or propensity; and that is the Academic or Skeptical philosophy. The Academics always talk of doubt and suspense of judgment, of danger in hasty determinations, of confining to very narrow bounds the inquiries of the understanding, and of renouncing all speculations which lie not within the limits of common life and practice. Nothing, therefore, can be more contrary than such a philosophy to the supine indolence of the mind, its rash arrogance, its lofty pretensions, and its superstitious credulity. Every passion is mortified by it, except the love of truth; and that passion never is nor can be carried to too high a degree. It is surprising, therefore, that this philosophy, which in almost every instance must be harmless and innocent, should be the subject of so much groundless reproach and obloquy. But, perhaps, the very circumstance which renders it so innocent is what chiefly exposes it to the public hatred and resentment. By flattering no irregular passion, it gains few partisans. By opposing so many vices and follies, it raises to itself abundance of enemies who stigmatize it as libertine, profane, and irreligious.

Nor need we fear that this philosophy, while it endeavors to limit our inquiries to common life, should ever undermine the reasonings of common life and carry its doubts so far as to destroy all action as well as speculation. Nature will always maintain her rights and prevail in the end over any abstract reasoning whatsoever. Though we should conclude, for instance, as in the foregoing section, that in all reasonings from experience there is a step taken by the mind which is not supported by any argument or process of the understanding, there is no danger that these reasonings, on which almost all knowledge depends, will ever be affected by such a discovery. If the mind be not engaged by argument to make this step, it must be induced by some other principle of equal weight and authority; and that principle will preserve its influence as long as human nature remains the same. What that principle is may well be worth the pains of inquiry.

Suppose a person, though endowed with the strongest faculties of reason and reflection, to be brought on a sudden into this world; he would, indeed, immediately observe a continual succession of objects and one event following another, but he would not be able to discover anything further. He would not at first, by any reasoning, be able to reach the idea of cause and effect, since the particular powers by which all natural operations are performed never appear to the senses; nor is it reasonable to conclude, merely because one event in one instance precedes another, that therefore the one is the cause, the other the effect. The conjunction may be arbitrary and casual. There may be no reason to infer the existence of one from the appearance of the other: and, in a word, such a person without more experience could never employ his conjecture or reasoning concerning any matter of fact or be assured of anything beyond what was immediately present to his memory or senses.

Suppose again that he has acquired more experience and has lived so long in the world as to have observed similar objects or events to be constantly conjoined together—what is the consequence of this experience? He immediately infers the existence of one object from the appearance of the other, yet he has not, by all his experience, acquired any idea or knowledge of the secret power by which the one object produces the other, nor is it by any process of reasoning he is engaged to draw this inference; but still he finds himself determined to draw it, and though he should be convinced that his understanding has no part in the operation, he would nevertheless continue in the same course of thinking. There is some other principle which determines him to form such a conclusion.

This principle is *custom* or *habit*. For whatever the repetition of any particular act or operation produces a propensity to renew the same act or operation without being impelled by any reasoning or process of the understanding, we always say that this propensity is the effect of *custom*. By employing that word we pretend not to have given the ultimate reason of such a propensity. We only point out a principle of human nature which is universally acknowledged, and which is well known by its effects. Perhaps we can push our inquiries no further or pretend to give the cause of this cause, but must rest contented with it as the ultimate principle which we can assign of all our conclusions from experience. It is sufficient satisfaction that we can go so far without repining at the narrowness of our faculties, because they will carry us no further. And it is certain we here advance a very intelligible proposition at least, if not a true one, when we assert that after the constant conjunction of two objects, heat and flame, for instance, weight and solidity, we are determined by custom alone to expect the one from the appearance of the other. This hypothesis seems even the only one which explains the difficulty why we draw from a thousand instances an inference which we are not able to draw from one instance that is in no respect different from them. Reason is incapable of any such variation. The conclusions which it draws from considering one circle are the same which it would form upon surveying all the circles in the universe. But no man, having seen only one body move after being impelled by another, could infer that every other body will move after a like impulse. All inferences from experience, therefore, are effects of custom, not of reasoning.[3]

Custom, then, is the great guide of human life. It is that principle alone which renders our experience useful to us and makes us expect, for the future, a similar train of events with those which have appeared in the past. Without the influence of custom we should be entirely ignorant of every matter of fact beyond what is immediately present to the memory and senses. We should never know how to adjust means to ends or to employ our natural powers in the production of any effect. There would be an end at once of all action as well as of the chief part of speculation.

But here it may be proper to remark that though our conclusions from experience carry us beyond our memory and senses and assure us of matters of fact which happened in the most distant places and most remote ages, yet some fact must always be present to the senses of memory from which we may first proceed in drawing these conclusions. A man who should find in a desert country the remains of pompous buildings would conclude that the country had, in ancient times, been cultivated by civilized inhabitants; but did nothing of this nature occur to him, he could never form such an inference. We learn the events of former ages from history, but then we must peruse the volume in which this instruction is contained, and thence carry up our inferences from one testimony to another, till we arrive at the eyewitnesses and spectators of these distant events. In a word, if we proceed not upon some fact present to the memory or senses, our reasonings would be merely hypothetical; and however the particular links might be connected with each other, the whole chain of inferences would have nothing to support it, nor could we ever, by its means, arrive at the knowledge of any real existence. If I ask why you believe any particular matter of fact which you relate, you must tell me some reason; and this reason will be some other fact connected with it. But as you cannot proceed after this manner *in infinitum,* you must at last terminate in some fact which is present to your memory or senses or must allow that your belief is entirely without foundation.

What, then, is the conclusion of the whole matter? A simple one, though, it must be confessed, pretty remote from the common theories of philosophy. All belief of matter of fact or real existence is derived merely from some object present to the memory or senses and a customary conjunction between that and some other object; or, in other words, having found, in many instances, that any two kinds of objects, flame and heat, snow and cold, have always been conjoined together: if flame or snow be presented anew to the senses, the mind is carried by custom to expect heat or cold, and to *believe* that such a quality does exist and will discover itself upon a nearer approach. This belief is the necessary result of placing the mind in such circumstances. It is an operation of the soul, when we are so situated, as unavoidable as to feel the passion of love, when we receive benefits; or hatred, when we meet with injuries. All these operations are a species of natural instincts, which no reasoning or process of the thought and understanding is able either to produce or to prevent. At this point it would be very allowable for us to stop our philosophical researches. In most questions we can never make a single step

further; and in all questions we must terminate here at last, after our most restless and curious inquiries. But still our curiosity will be pardonable, perhaps commendable, if it carry us on to still further researches and make us examine more accurately the nature of this *belief* and of the *customary conjunction* whence it is derived. By this means we may meet with some explications and analogies that will give satisfaction, at least to such as love the abstract sciences, and can be entertained with speculations which, however accurate, may still retain a degree of doubt and uncertainty. As to readers of a different taste, the remaining part of this Section is not calculated for them; and the following inquiries may well be understood, though it be neglected.

PART II

Nothing is more free than the imagination of man, and though it cannot exceed that original stock of ideas furnished by the internal and external senses, it has unlimited power of mixing, compounding, separating, and dividing these ideas in all the varieties of fiction and vision. It can feign a train of events with all the appearance of reality, ascribe to them a particular time and place, conceive them as existent, and paint them out to itself with every circumstance that belongs to any historical fact which it believes with the greatest certainty. Wherein, therefore, consists the difference between such a fiction and belief? It lies not merely in any peculiar idea which is annexed to such a conception as commands our assent, and which is wanting to every known fiction. For as the mind has authority over all its ideas, it could voluntarily annex this particular idea to any fiction, and consequently be able to believe whatever it pleases, contrary to what we find by daily experience. We can, in our conception, join the head of a man to the body of a horse, but it is not in our power to believe that such an animal has ever really existed.

It follows, therefore, that the difference between *fiction* and *belief* lies in some sentiment or feeling which is annexed to the latter, not to the former, and which depends not on the will, nor can be demanded at pleasure. It must be excited by nature like all other sentiments and must rise from the particular situation in which the mind is placed at any particular juncture. Whenever any object is presented to the memory or senses, it immediately, by the force of custom, carries the imagination to conceive that object which is usually conjoined to it; and this conception is attended with a feeling or sentiment different from the loose reveries of the fancy. In this consists the whole nature of belief. For as there is no matter of fact which we believe so firmly that we cannot conceive the contrary, there would be no difference between the conception as assented to and that which is rejected were it not for some sentiment which distinguishes the one from the other. If I see a billiard ball moving toward another on a smooth table, I can easily conceive it to stop upon contact. This conception implies no contradiction, but still it feels very differently from that conception by which I represent to myself the impulse and the communication of motion from one ball to another.

Were we to attempt a *definition* of this sentiment, we should, perhaps, find it a very difficult, if not an impossible, task; in the same manner as if we should endeavor to define the feeling of cold, or passion of anger, to a creature who never had any experience of these sentiments. Belief is the true and proper name of this feeling, and no one is ever at a loss to know the meaning of that term, because every man is every moment conscious of the sentiment represented by it. It may not, however, be improper to attempt a *description* of this sentiment, in hopes we may by that means arrive at some analogies which may afford a more perfect explication of it. I say that belief is nothing but a more vivid, lively, forcible, firm, steady conception of an object than what the imagination alone is ever able to attain. This variety of terms, which may seem so unphilosophical, is intended only to express that act of the mind which renders realities, or what is taken for such, more present to us than fictions, causes them to weigh more in the thought, and gives them a superior influence on the passions and imagination. Provided we agree about the thing, it is needless to dispute about the terms. The imagination has the command over all its ideas and can join and mix and vary them in all the ways possible. It may conceive fictitious objects with all the circumstances of place and time. It may set them in a manner before our eyes, in their true colors, just as they might have existed.

But as it is impossible that this faculty of imagination can ever, of itself, reach belief, it is evident that belief consists not in the peculiar nature or order of ideas, but in the *manner* of their conception and in their *feeling* to the mind. I confess that it is impossible perfectly to explain this feeling or manner of conception. We may make use of words which express something near it. But its true and proper name, as we observed before, is "belief," which is a term that everyone sufficiently understands in common life. And in philosophy we can go no further than assert that *belief* is something felt by the mind, which distinguishes the ideas of the judgment from the fictions of the imagination. It gives them more weight and influence, makes them appear of greater importance, enforces them in the mind, and renders them the governing principle of our actions. I hear at present, for instance, a person's voice with whom I am acquainted, and the sound comes as from the next room. This impression of my senses immediately conveys my thought to the person, together with all the surrounding objects. I paint them out to myself as existing at present, with the same qualities and relations of which I formerly knew them possessed. These ideas take faster hold of my mind than ideas of an enchanted castle. They are very different from the feeling and have a much greater influence of every kind, either to give pleasure or pain, joy or sorrow.

Let us, then, take in the whole compass of this doctrine and allow that the sentiment of belief is nothing, but a conception more intense and steady than what attends the mere fictions of the imagination, and that this *manner* of conception arises from a customary conjunction of the object with something present to the memory or senses. I believe that it will not be difficult, upon these suppositions, to find other operations of the mind analogous to it and to trace up these phenomena to principles still more general.

We have already observed that nature has established connections among particular ideas, and that no sooner one idea occurs to our thoughts than it introduces its correlative and carries our attention towards it by a gentle and insensible movement. These principles of connection or association we have reduced to three, namely, "resemblance," "contiguity," and "causation," which are the only bonds that unite our thoughts together and beget that regular train of reflection or discourse which, in a greater or less degree, takes place among mankind. Now here arises a question on which the solution of the present difficulty will depend. Does it happen in all these relations that when one of the objects is presented to the senses or memory, the mind is not only carried to the conception of the correlative, but reaches a steadier and stronger conception of it than what otherwise it would have been able to attain? This seems to be the case with that belief which arises from the relation of cause and effect. And if the case be the same with the other relations or principles of association, this may be established as a general law which takes place in all the operations of the mind.

We may, therefore, observe, as the first experiment to our present purpose, that upon the appearance of the picture of an absent friend our idea of him is evidently enlivened by the *resemblance,* and that every passion which that idea occasions, whether of joy or sorrow, acquires new force and vigor. In producing this effect there concur both a relation and a present impression. Where the picture bears him no resemblance, at least was not intended for him, it never so much as conveys our thought to him. And where it is absent, as well as the person, though the mind may pass from the thought of one to that of the other, it feels its idea to be rather weakened than enlivened by that transition. We take a pleasure in viewing the picture of a friend when it is set before us; but when it is removed, rather choose to consider him directly than by reflection on an image which is equally distant and obscure.

The ceremonies of the Roman Catholic religion may be considered as instances of the same nature. The devotees of that superstition usually plead, in excuse for the mummeries with which they are upbraided, that they feel the good effect of those external motions, and postures, and actions in enlivening their devotion and quickening their fervor, which otherwise would decay if directed entirely to distant and immaterial objects. We shadow out the objects of our faith, say they, in sensible types and images, and render them more present to us by the immediate presence of these types than it is possible for us to do merely by an intellectual view and contemplation. Sensible objects have always a greater

influence on the fancy than any other, and this influence they readily convey to those ideas to which they are related and which they resemble. I shall only infer from these practices and this reasoning that the effect of resemblance in enlivening the ideas is very common: and as in every case a resemblance and a present impression must concur, we are abundantly supplied with experiments to prove the reality of the foregoing principle.

We may add force to these experiments by others of a different kind, in considering the effects of *contiguity* as well as of *resemblance.* It is certain that distance diminishes the force of every idea and that, upon our approach to any object, though it does not discover itself to our senses, it operates upon the mind with an influence which imitates an immediate impression. The thinking on any object readily transports the mind to what is contiguous; but it is only the actual presence of an object that transports the mind to what is contiguous; but it is only the actual presence of an object that transports it with a superior vivacity. When I am a few miles from home, whatever relates to it touches me more nearly than when I am two hundred leagues distant, though even at that distance the reflecting of anything in the neighborhood of my friends or family naturally produces an idea of them. But, as in this latter case, both the objects of the mind are ideas, notwithstanding there is an easy transition between them; that transition alone is not able to give a superior vivacity to any of the ideas, for want of some immediate impression.[4]

No one can doubt but *causation* has the same influence as the other two relations of resemblance and contiguity. Superstitious people are fond of the relics of saints and holy men, for the same reason that they seek after types or images in order to enliven their devotion and give them a more intimate and strong conception of those exemplary lives which they desire to imitate. Now it is evident that one of the best relics which a devotee could procure would be the handiwork of a saint; and if his clothes and furniture are ever to be considered in this light, it is because they were once at his disposal and were moved and affected by him; in which respect they are to be considered as imperfect effects, and as connected with him by a shorter chain of consequences than any of those by which we learn the reality of his existence.

Suppose that the son of a friend who had been long dead or absent were presented to us; it is evident that this object would instantly revive its correlative idea and recall to our thoughts all past intimacies and familiarities in more lively color than they would otherwise have appeared to us. This is another phenomenon which seems to prove the principle above mentioned.

We may observe that in these phenomena the belief of the correlative object is always presupposed, without which the relation could have no effect. The influence of the picture supposes that we *believe* our friend to have once existed. Contiguity to home can never excite our ideas of home unless we *believe* that it really exists. Now I assert that this belief, where it reaches beyond the memory or senses, is of a similar nature and arises from similar causes with the transition of thought and vivacity of conception here explained. When I throw a piece of dry wood into a fire, my mind is immediately carried to conceive that it augments, not extinguishes, the flame. This transition of thought from the cause to the effect proceeds not from reason. It derives its origin altogether from custom and experience. And, as it first begins from an object present to the senses, it renders the idea or conception of flame more strong or lively than any loose floating reverie of the imagination. The idea arises immediately. The thought moves instantly toward it and conveys to it all that force of conception which is derived from the impression present to the senses. When a sword is leveled at my breast, does not the idea of wound and pain strike me more strongly than when a glass of wine is presented to me, even though by accident this idea should occur after the appearance of the latter object? But what is there in this whole matter to cause such a strong conception except only a present object and a customary transition to the idea of another object which we have been accustomed to conjoin with the former? This is the whole operation of the mind in all our conclusions concerning matter of fact and existence; and it is a satisfaction to find some analogies by which it may be explained. The transition from a present object does in all cases give strength and solidity to the related idea.

Here, then, is a kind of pre-established harmony between the course of nature and the succession of our ideas; and though the powers and forces by which the former is governed be wholly unknown to us, yet our thoughts and conceptions have still, we find, gone on in the same train with the other works of nature. Custom is that principle by which this correspondence has been effected, so necessary to the subsistence of our species and the regulation of our conduct in every circumstance and occurrence of human life. Had not the presence of an object instantly excited the idea of those objects commonly conjoined with it, all our knowledge must have been limited to the narrow sphere of our memory and senses, and we should never have been able to adjust means to ends or employ our natural powers either to the producing of good or avoiding of evil. Those who delight in the discovery and contemplation of *final causes* have here ample subject to employ their wonder and admiration.

I shall add, for a further confirmation of the foregoing theory, that as this operation of the mind, by which we infer like effects from like causes, and *vice versa,* is so essential to the subsistence of all human creatures, it is not probable that it could be trusted to the fallacious deductions of our reason, which is slow in its operations, appears not, in any degree, during the first years of infancy, and, at best, is in every age and period of human life extremely liable to error and mistake. It is more conformable to the ordinary wisdom of nature to secure so necessary an act of the mind by some instinct or mechanical tendency which may be infallible in its operations, may discover itself at the first appearance of life and thought, and may be independent of all the labored deductions of the understanding. As nature has taught us the use of our limbs without giving us the knowledge of the muscles and nerves by which they are actuated, so has she implanted in us an instinct which carries forward the thought in a correspondent course to that which she has established among external objects, though we are ignorant of those powers and forces on which this regular course and succession of objects totally depends.

Section VI. Of probability[5]

Though there be no such thing as *chance* in the world, our ignorance of the real cause of any event has the same influence on the understanding and begets a like species of belief or opinion.

There is certainly a probability which arises from a superiority of chances on any side; and, according as this superiority increases and surpasses the opposite chances, the probability receives a proportionable increase and begets still a higher degree of belief of assent to that side in which we discover the superiority. If a die were marked with one figure or number of spots on four sides, and with another figure or number of spots on the two remaining sides, it would be more probable that the former would turn up than the latter, though, if it had a thousand sides marked in the same manner, and only one side different, the probability would be much higher and our belief or expectation of the event more steady and secure. This process of the thought or reasoning may seem trivial and obvious; but to those who consider it more narrowly it may, perhaps, afford matter for curious speculation.

It seems evident that when the mind looks forward to discover the event which may result from the throw of such a die, it considers the turning up of each particular side as alike probable; and this is the very nature of chance, to render all the particular events comprehended in it entirely equal. But finding a greater number of sides concur in the one event than in the other, the mind is carried more frequently to that event and meets it oftener in revolving the various possibilities or chances on which the ultimate result depends. This concurrence of several views in one particular event begets immediately, by an explicable contrivance of nature, the sentiment of belief and gives that event the advantage over its antagonist which is supported by a smaller number of views and recurs less frequently to the mind. If we allow that belief is nothing but a firmer and stronger conception of an object than what attends the mere fictions of the imagination, this operation may, perhaps, in some measure be accounted for. The concurrence of these several views or glimpses imprints the idea more strongly on the imagination, gives it superior force and vigor, renders its influence on the passions and affections more sensible, and, in a word, begets that reliance or security which constitutes the nature of belief and opinion.

The case is the same with the probability of causes as with that of chance. There are some causes which are entirely uniform and constant in producing a particular effect, and no instance has ever yet been found of any failure or irregularity in their operation. Fire has always burned, and water suffocated, every human creature. The production of motion by impulse and gravity is a universal law which has hitherto admitted of no exception. But there are other causes which have been found more irregular and uncertain, nor has rhubarb always proved a purge, or opium a soporific, to everyone who has taken these medicines. It is true, when any cause fails of producing its usual effect, philosophers ascribe not this to any irregularity in nature, but suppose that some secret causes in the particular structure of parts have prevented the operation. Our reasonings, however, and conclusions concerning the event are the same as if this principle had no place. Being determined by custom to transfer the past to the future in all our inferences, where the past has been entirely regular and uniform we expect the event with the greatest assurance and leave no room for any contrary supposition. But where different effects have been found to follow from causes which are to *appearance* exactly similar, all these various effects must occur to the mind in transferring the past to the future, and enter into our consideration when we determine the probability of the event. Though we give the preference to that which has been found most usual, and believe that this effect will exist, we must not overlook the other effects, but must assign to each of them a particular weight and authority in proportion as we have found it to be more or less frequent. It is more probable, in almost every country of Europe, that there will be frost sometime in January than that the weather will continue open throughout the whole month, though this probability varies according to the different climates, and approaches to a certainty in the more northern kingdoms. Here, then, it seems evident that when we transfer the past to the future in order to determine the effect which will result from any cause, we transfer all the different events in the same proportion as they have appeared in the past, and conceive one to have existed a hundred times, for instance, another ten times, and another once. As a great number of views do here concur in one event, they fortify and confirm it to the imagination, beget that sentiment which we call "belief," and give its objects the preference above the contrary event which is not supported by an equal number of experiments and recurs not so frequently to the thought in transferring the past to the future. Let anyone try to account for this operation of the mind upon any of the received systems of philosophy, and he will be sensible of the difficulty. For my part, I shall think it sufficient if the present hints excite the curiosity of philosophers and make them sensible how defective all common theories are in treating of such curious and such sublime subjects.

Section VII. Of the idea of necessary connection

PART I

The great advantage of the mathematical sciences above the moral consists in this, that the ideas of the former, being sensible, are always clear and determinate, the smallest distinction between them is immediately perceptible, and the same terms are still expressive of the same ideas without ambiguity or variation. An oval is never mistaken for a circle, nor an hyperbola for an ellipsis. The isosceles and scalenum are distinguished by boundaries more exact than vice and virtue, right and wrong. If any term be defined in geometry, the mind readily, of itself substitutes on all occasions the definition for the term defined, or, even when no definition is employed, the object itself may be presented to the senses and by that means be steadily and clearly apprehended. But the finer sentiments of the mind, the operations of the understanding, the various agitations of the passions, though really in themselves distinct, easily escape us when surveyed by reflection, nor is it in our power to recall the original object as often as we have occasion to contemplate it. Ambiguity, by this means, is gradually introduced into our reasonings; similar objects are readily taken to be the same, and the conclusion becomes at last very wide of the premises.

One may safely, however, affirm that if we consider these sciences in a proper light, their advantages and disadvantages nearly compensate each other and reduce both of them to a state of equality. If the mind, with greater facility, retains the ideas of geometry clear and determinate, it must carry on a much longer and more intricate chain of reasoning and compare ideas much wider of each other in order to reach the abstruser truths of that science. And if moral ideas are apt, without extreme care, to fall into obscurity and confusion, the inferences are always much shorter in these disquisitions, and the intermediate steps which lead to the conclusion much fewer than in the sciences which treat of quantity and number. In reality, there is scarcely a proposition in Euclid so simple as not to consist of more parts than are to be found in any moral reasoning which runs not into chimera and conceit. Where we trace the principles of the human mind through a few steps, we may be very well satisfied with our progress, considering how soon nature throws a bar to all our inquiries concerning causes and reduces us to an acknowledgment of our ignorance. The chief obstacle, therefore, to our improvements in the moral or metaphysical sciences is the obscurity of the ideas and ambiguity of the terms. The principal difficulty in the mathematics is the length of inferences and compass of thought requisite to the forming of any conclusion. And, perhaps, our progress in natural philosophy is chiefly retarded by the want of proper experiments and phenomena, which are often discovered by chance and cannot always be found when requisite, even by the most diligent and prudent inquiry. As moral philosophy seems hitherto to have received less improvement than either geometry or physics, we may conclude that if there be any difference in this respect among these sciences, the difficulties which obstruct the progress of the former require superior care and capacity to be surmounted.

There are no ideas which occur in metaphysics more obscure and uncertain than those of "power," "force," "energy," or "necessary connection," of which it is every moment necessary for us to treat in all our disquisitions. We shall, therefore, endeavor in this Section to fix, if possible, the precise meaning of these terms and thereby remove some part of that obscurity which is so much complained of in this species of philosophy.

It seems a proposition which will not admit of much dispute that all our ideas are nothing but copies of our impressions, or, in other words, that it is impossible for us to *think* of anything which we have not antecedently *felt*, either by our external or internal senses. I have endeavored[6] to explain and prove this proposition, and have expressed my hopes that by a proper application of it men may reach a greater clearness and precision in philosophical reasonings than what they have hitherto been able to attain. Complex ideas may, perhaps, be well known by definition, which is nothing but an enumeration of those parts or simple ideas that compose them. But when we have pushed up definitions to the most simple ideas and find still some ambiguity and obscurity, what resources are we then possessed of? By what invention can we throw light upon these ideas and render them altogether precise and determinate to our intellectual view? Produce the impressions or original sentiments from which the ideas are copied. These impressions are all strong and sensible. They admit not of ambiguity. They are not only placed in a full light themselves, but may throw light on their correspondent ideas, which lie in obscurity. And by this means we may perhaps attain a new microscope or species of optics by which, in the moral sciences, the most minute and most simple ideas may be so enlarged as to fall readily under our apprehension and be equally known with the grossest and most sensible ideas that can be the object of our inquiry.

To be fully acquainted, therefore, with the idea of power or necessary connection, let us examine its impression and, in order to find the impression with greater certainty, let us search for it in all the sources from which it may possibly be derived.

When we look about us towards external objects, and consider the operation of causes, we are never able, in a single instance, to discover any power or necessary connection, any quality which binds the effect to the cause and renders the one an infallible consequence of the other. We only find that the one does actually in fact follow the other. The impulse of one billiard ball is attended with motion in the second. This is the whole that appears to the *outward* senses. The mind feels no sentiment or *inward* impression from this succession of objects: consequently, there is not, in any single particular instance of cause and effect, anything which can suggest the idea of power or necessary connection.

From the first appearance of an object we never can conjecture what effect will result from it. But were the power or energy of any cause discoverable by the mind, we could foresee the effect, even without experience, and might, at first, pronounce with

certainty concerning it by mere dint of thought and reasoning.

In reality, there is no part of matter that does ever, by its sensible qualities, discover any power or energy, or give us ground to imagine that it could produce anything, or be followed by any other object, which we could denominate its effect. Solidity, extension, motion—these qualities are all complete in themselves and never point out any other event which may result from them. The scenes of the universe are continually shifting, and one object follows another in an uninterrupted succession; but the power or force which actuates the whole machine is entirely concealed from us and never discovers itself in any of the sensible qualities of body. We know that, in fact, heat is a constant attendant of flame; but what is the connection between them we have no room so much as to conjecture or imagine. It is impossible, therefore, that the idea of power can be derived from the contemplation of bodies in single instances of their operation, because no bodies ever discover any power which can be the original of this idea.[7]

Since, therefore, external objects as they appear to the senses give us no idea of power or necessary connection by their operation in particular instances, let us see whether this idea be derived from reflection on the operations of our own minds and be copied from any internal impression. It may be said that we are every moment conscious of internal power while we feel that, by the simple command of our will, we can move the organs of our body or direct the faculties of our mind. An act of volition produces motion in our limbs or raises a new idea in our imagination. This influence of the will we know by consciousness. Hence we acquire the idea of power or energy, and are certain that we ourselves and all other intelligent beings are possessed of power. This idea, then, is an idea of reflection since it arises from reflecting on the operations of our own mind and on the command which is exercised by will both over the organs of the body and faculties of the soul.

We shall proceed to examine this pretension and, first, with regard to the influence of volition over the organs of the body. This influence, we may observe, is a fact which, like all other natural events, can be known only by experience, and can never be foreseen from any apparent energy or power in the cause which connects it with the effect and renders the one an infallible consequence of the other. The motion of our body follows upon the command of our will. Of this we are every moment conscious. But the means by which this is effected, the energy by which the will performs so extraordinary an operation—of this we are so far from being immediately conscious that it must forever escape our most diligent inquiry.

For, *first,* is there any principle in all nature more mysterious than the union of soul with body, by which a supposed spiritual substance acquires such an influence over a material one that the most refined thought is able to actuate the grossest matter? Were we empowered by a secret wish to remove mountains or control the planets in their orbit, this extensive authority would not be more extraordinary, nor more beyond our comprehension. But if, by consciousness, we perceived any power or energy in the will, we must know this power; we must know its connection with the effect; we must know the secret union of soul and body, and the nature of both these substances by which the one is able to operate in so many instances upon the other.

Secondly, we are not able to move all the organs of the body with a like authority, though we cannot assign any reason, besides experience, for so remarkable a difference between one and the other. Why has the will an influence over the tongue and fingers, not over the heart and liver? This question would never embarrass us were we conscious of a power in the former case, not in the latter. We should then perceive, independent of experience, why the authority of the will over organs of the body is circumscribed within such particular limits. Being in that case fully acquainted with the power or force by which it operates, we should also know why its influence reaches precisely to such boundaries, and no further.

A man suddenly struck with a palsy in the leg or arm, or who has newly lost those members, frequently endeavors, at first, to move them and employ them in their usual offices. Here he is as much conscious of power to command such limbs as a man in perfect health is conscious of power to actuate any member which remains in its natural state and condition. But consciousness never deceives. Consequently, neither in the one case nor in the other are we ever conscious of any power. We learn the influence of our will from experience alone. And experience only teaches us how one event constantly follows another, without instructing us in the secret connection which binds them together and renders them inseparable.

Thirdly, we learn from anatomy that the immediate object of power in voluntary motion is not the member itself which is moved, but certain muscles and nerves and animal spirits, and, perhaps, something still more minute and more unknown, through which the motion is successfully propagated ere it reach the member itself whose motion is the immediate object of volition. Can there be a more certain proof that the power by which this whole operation is performed, so far from being directly and fully known by an inward sentiment or consciousness, is to the last degree mysterious and unintelligible? Here the mind wills a certain event; immediately another event, unknown to ourselves and totally different from the one intended, is produced. This event produces another, equally unknown, till, at last, through a long succession the desired event is produced. But if the original power were felt, it must be known; were it known, its effect must also be known, since all power is relative to its effect. And, *vice versa,* if the effect be not known, the power cannot be known nor felt. How indeed can we be conscious of a power to move our limbs when we have no such power, but only that to move certain animal spirits which, though they produce at last the motion of our limbs, yet operate in such a manner as is wholly beyond our comprehension?

We may therefore conclude from the whole, I hope, without any temerity, though with assurance, that our idea of power is not copied from any sentiment or consciousness of power within ourselves when we give rise to animal motion or apply our limbs to their proper use and office. That their motion follows the command of the will is a matter of common experience, like other natural events; but the power or energy by which this is effected, like that in other natural events, is unknown and inconceivable.[8]

Shall we then assert that we are conscious of a power or energy in our own minds when, by an act or command of our will, we raise up a new idea, fix the mind to the contemplation of it, turn it on all sides, and at last dismiss it for some other idea when we think that we have surveyed it with sufficient accuracy? I believe the same arguments will prove that even this command of the will gives us no real idea of force or energy.

First, it must be allowed that when we know a power, we know that very circumstance in the cause by which it is enabled to produce the effect, for these are supposed to be synonymous. We must, therefore, know both the cause and effect and the relation between them. But do we pretend to be acquainted with the nature of the human soul and the nature of an idea, or the aptitude of the one to produce the other? This is a real creation, a production of something out of nothing, which implies a power so great that it may seem, at first sight, beyond the reach of any being less than infinite. At least it must be owned that such a power is not felt, nor known, nor even conceivable by the mind. We only feel the event, namely, the existence of an idea consequent to a command of the will; but the manner in which this operation is performed, the power by which it is produced, is entirely beyond our comprehension.

Secondly, the command of the mind over itself is limited, as well as its command over the body; and these limits are not known by reason or any acquaintance with the nature of cause and effect, but only by experience and observation, as in all other natural events and in the operation of external objects. Our authority over our sentiments and passions is much weaker than that over our ideas; and even the latter authority is circumscribed within very narrow boundaries. Will any one pretend to assign the ultimate reason of these boundaries, or show why the power is deficient in one case, not in another.

Thirdly, this self-command is very different at different times. A man in health possesses more of it than one languishing with sickness. We are more master of our thoughts in the morning than in the evening; fasting, than after a full meal. Can we give any reason for these variations except experience? Where then is the power of which we pretend to be conscious? Is there not here, either in a spiritual or material substance, or both, some secret mechanism or structure of parts upon which the effect depends, and which, being entirely unknown to us, renders the power or energy of the will equally unknown and incomprehensible?

Volition is surely an act of the mind with which we are sufficiently acquainted. Reflect upon it. Consider it on all sides. Do you find anything in it like this creative power by which it raises from nothing a new idea and, with a kind of *fiat,* imitates the omnipotence of its Maker, if I may be allowed so to speak, who called forth into existence all the various scenes of nature? So far from being conscious of this energy in the will, it requires as certain experience as that of which we are possessed to convince us that such extraordinary effects do ever result from a simple act of volition.

The generality of mankind never find any difficulty in accounting for the more common and familiar operations of nature, such as the descent of heavy bodies, the growth of plants, the generation of animals, or the nourishment of bodies by food; but suppose that in all these cases they perceive the very force or energy of the cause by which it is connected with its effect, and is forever infallible in its operation. They acquire, by long habit, such a turn of mind that upon the appearance of the cause they immediately expect, with assurance, its usual attendant, and hardly conceive it possible that any other event could result from it. It is only on the discovery of extraordinary phenomena, such as earthquakes, pestilence, and prodigies of any kind, that they find themselves at a loss to assign a proper cause and to explain the manner in which the effect is produced by it. It is usual for men, in such difficulties, to have recourse to some invisible intelligent principle as the immediate cause of that event which surprises them, and which they think cannot be accounted for from the common powers of nature. But philosophers, who carry their scrutiny a little further, immediately perceive that, even in the most familiar events, the energy of the cause is as unintelligible as in the most unusual, and that we only learn by experience the frequent conjunction of objects, without being ever able to comprehend anything like connection between them. Here, then, many philosophers think themselves obliged by reason to have recourse, on all occasions, to the same principle which the vulgar never appeal to but in cases that appear miraculous and supernatural. They acknowledge mind and intelligence to be, not only the ultimate and original cause of all things, but the immediate and sole cause of every event which appears in nature. They pretend that those objects which are commonly denominated "causes" are in reality nothing but "occasions," and that the true and direct principle of every effect is not any power or force in nature, but a volition of the Supreme Being, who wills that such particular objects should forever be conjoined with each other. Instead of saying that one billiard ball moves another by a force which it has derived from the author of nature, it is the Deity himself, they say, who, by a particular volition, moves the second ball, being determined to this operation by the impulse of the first ball, in consequence of those general laws which he has laid down to himself in the government of the universe. But philosophers, advancing still in their inquiries, discover that as we are totally ignorant of the power on which depends the mutual operation of bodies, we are no less ignorant of that power on which depends the operation of mind on body, or of body on mind; nor are we able, either from our senses or consciousness, to assign the ultimate principle in the one case more than in the other. The same ignorance, therefore, reduces them to the same conclusion. They assert that the Deity is the immediate cause of the union between soul and body, and that they are not the organs of sense which, being agitated by external objects, produce sensations in the mind; but that it is a particular volition of our omnipotent Maker which excites such a sensation in consequence of such a motion in the organ. In like manner, it is not any energy in the will that produces local motion in our members: It is God himself, who is pleased to second our will, in itself impotent, and to command that motion which we erroneously attribute to our own power and efficacy. Nor do philosophers stop at this conclusion. They sometimes extend the same inference to the mind itself in its internal operations. Our mental vision or conception of ideas is nothing but a revelation made to us by our Maker. When we voluntarily turn our thoughts to any object and raise up its image in the fancy, it is not the will which creates that idea, it is the universal Creator who discovers it to the mind and renders it present to us.

Thus, according to these philosophers, everything is full of God. Not content with the principle that nothing exists but by his will, that nothing possesses any power but by his concession, they rob nature and all created beings of every power in order to render their dependence on the Deity still more sensible and immediate. They consider not that by this theory they diminish, instead of magnifying, the grandeur of those attributes which they affect so much to celebrate. It argues, surely, more power in the Deity to delegate a certain degree of power to inferior creatures than to produce everything by his own immediate volition. It argues more wisdom to contrive at first the fabric of the world with such perfect foresight that of itself, and by its proper operation, it may serve all the purposes of Providence than if the great Creator were obliged every moment to adjust its parts and animate by his breath all the wheels of that stupendous machine.

But if we would have a more philosophical confutation of this theory, perhaps the two following reflections may suffice:

First, it seems to me that this theory of the universal energy and operation of the Supreme Being is too bold ever to carry conviction with it to a man sufficiently apprised of the weakness of human reason and the narrow limits to which it is confined in all its operations. Though the chain of arguments which conduct to it were ever so logical, there must arise a strong suspicion, if not an absolute assurance, that it has carried us quite beyond the reach of our faculties when it leads to conclusions so extraordinary and so remote from common life and experience. We are got into fairyland long ere we have reached the last steps of our theory; and *there* we have no reason to trust our common methods of arguments or to think that our usual analogies and probabilities have any authority. Our line is too short to fathom such immense abysses. And however we may flatter ourselves that we are guided, in every step which we take, by a kind of verisimilitude and experience, we may be assured that this fancied experience has no authority when we thus apply it to subjects that lie entirely out of the sphere of experience. But on this we shall have occasion to touch afterwards.[9]

Secondly, I cannot perceive any force in the arguments on which this theory is founded. We are ignorant, it is true, of the manner in which bodies operate on each other. Their force or energy is entirely incomprehensible. But are we not equally ignorant of the manner or force by which a mind, even the Supreme Mind, operates, either on itself or on body? Whence, I beseech you, do we acquire any idea of it? We have no sentiment or consciousness of this power in ourselves. We have no idea of the Supreme Being but what we learn from reflection on our own faculties. Were our ignorance, therefore, a good reason for rejecting anything, we should be led into that principle of denying all energy in the Supreme Being, as much as in the grossest matter. We surely comprehend as little the operations of the one as of the other. Is it more difficult to conceive that motion may arise from impulse than that it may arise from volition? All we know is our profound ignorance in both cases.[10]

PART II

But to hasten to a conclusion of this argument, which is already drawn out to too great a length: We have sought in vain for an idea of power or necessary connection in all the sources from which we could suppose it to be derived. It appears that in single instances of the operation of bodies we never can, by our utmost scrutiny, discover anything but one event following another, without being able to comprehend any force or power by which the cause operates or any connection between it and its supposed effect. The same difficulty occurs in contemplating the operations of mind on body, where we observe the motion of the latter to follow upon the volition of the former, but are not able to observe or conceive the tie which binds together the motion and volition, or the energy, by which the mind produces this effect. The authority of the will over its own faculties and ideas is not a whit more comprehensible, so that, upon the whole, there appears not, throughout all nature, any one instance of connection which is conceivable by us. All events seem entirely loose and separate. One event follows another, but we never can observe any tie between them. They seem *conjoined*, but never *connected*. And as we can have no idea of anything which never appeared to our outward sense or inward sentiment, the necessary conclusion *seems* to be that we have no idea of connection or power at all, and that these words are absolutely without any meaning when em-

ployed either in philosophical reasonings or common life.

But there still remains one method of avoiding this conclusion, and one source which we have not yet examined. When any natural object or event is presented, it is impossible for us, by any sagacity or penetration, to discover, or even conjecture, without experience, what event will result from it, or to carry our foresight beyond that object which is immediately present to the memory and senses. Even after one instance or experiment where we have observed a particular event to follow upon another, we are not entitled to form a general rule or foretell what will happen in like cases, it being justly esteemed an unpardonable temerity to judge the whole course of nature from one single experiment, however accurate or certain. But when one particular species of events has always, in all instances, been conjoined with another, we make no longer any scruple of foretelling one upon the appearance of the other, and of employing that reasoning which can alone assure us of any matter of fact or existence. We then call the one object "cause," the other "effect." We suppose that there is some connection between them, some power in the one by which it infallibly produces the other and operates with the greatest certainty and strongest necessity.

It appears, then, that this idea of a necessary connection among events arises from a number of similar instances which occur, of the constant conjunction of these events; nor can that idea ever be suggested by any one of these instances surveyed in all possible lights and positions. But there is nothing in a number of instances, different from every single instance, which is supposed to be exactly similar, except only that after a repetition of similar instances the mind is carried by habit, upon the appearance of one event, to expect its usual attendant and to believe that it will exist. This connection, therefore, which we *feel* in the mind, this customary transition of the imagination from one object to its usual attendant, is the sentiment or impression from which we form the idea of power or necessary connection. Nothing further is in the case. Contemplate the subject on all sides, you will never find any other origin of that idea. This is the sole difference between one instance, from which we can never receive the idea of connection, and a number of similar instances by which it is suggested. The first time a man saw the communication of motion by impulse, as by the shock of two billiard balls, he could not pronounce that the one event was *connected,* but only that it was *conjoined* with the other. After he has observed several instances of this nature, he then pronounces them to be *connected.* What alteration has happened to give rise to this new idea of *connection?* Nothing but that he now *feels* these events to be *connected* in his imagination, and can readily foretell the existence of one from the appearance of the other. When we say, therefore, that one object is connected with another, we mean only that they have acquired a connection in our thought and give rise to this inference by which they become proofs of each other's existence—a conclusion which is somewhat extraordinary, but which seems founded on sufficient evidence. Nor will its evidence be weakened by any general diffidence of the understanding or skeptical suspicion concerning every conclusion which is new and extraordinary. No conclusions can be more agreeable to skepticism than such as make discoveries concerning the weakness and narrow limits of human reason and capacity.

And what stronger instance can be produced of the surprising ignorance and weakness of the understanding than the present? For surely, if there be any relation among objects which it imports us to know perfectly, it is that of cause and effect. On this are founded all our reasonings concerning matter of fact or existence. By means of it alone we attain any assurance concerning objects which are removed from the present testimony of our memory and senses. The only immediate utility of all sciences is to teach us how to control and regulate future events by their causes. Our thoughts and inquiries are, therefore, every moment employed about this relation; yet so imperfect are the ideas which we form concerning it that it is impossible to give any just definition of cause, except what is drawn from something extraneous and foreign to it. Similar objects are always conjoined with similar. Of this we have experience. Suitably to this experience, therefore, we may define a cause to be *an object followed by another, and where all the objects, similar to the first, are followed by objects similar to the second.* Or, in other words, *where, if the first object had not been, the second never had existed.* The appearance of a cause always conveys the mind, by a customary transition, to the idea of the effect. Of this also we have experience. We may, therefore, suitably to this experience, form another definition of cause and call it *an object followed by another, and whose appearance always conveys the thought to that other.* But though both these definitions be drawn from circumstances foreign to the cause, we cannot remedy this inconvenience or attain any more perfect definition which may point out that circumstance in the cause which gives it a connection with its effect. We have no idea of this connection, nor even any distinct notion what it is we desire to know when we endeavour at a conception of it. We say, for instance, that the vibration of this string is the cause of this particular sound. But what do we mean by that affirmation? We either mean *that this vibration is followed by this sound, and that all similar vibrations have been followed by similar sounds; or, that this vibration is followed by this sound, and that, upon the appearance of one, the mind anticipates the senses and forms immediately an idea of the other.* We may consider the relation of cause and effect in either of these two lights; but beyond these we have no idea of it.[11]

To recapitulate, therefore, the reasonings of this Section: Every idea is copied from some preceding impression or sentiment; and where we cannot find any impression, we may be certain that there is no idea. In all single instances of the operation of bodies or minds there is nothing that produces any impression, nor consequently can suggest any idea, of power or necessary connection. But when many uniform instances appear, and the same object is always followed by the same event, we then begin to entertain the notion of cause and connection. We then *feel* a new sentiment or impression, to wit, a customary connection in the thought or imagination between one object and its usual attendant; and this sentiment is the original of that idea which we seek for. For as this idea arises from a number of similar instances, and not from any single instance, it must arise from that circumstance in which the number of instances differ from every individual instance. But this customary connection or transition of the imagination is the only circumstance in which they differ.

In every other particular they are alike. The first in- stance which we saw of motion, communicated by the shock of two billiard balls (to return to this obvi- ous illustration), is exactly similar to any instance that may at present occur to us, except only that we could not at first *infer* one event from the other, which we are enabled to do at present, after so long a course of uniform experience. I know not whether the reader will readily apprehend this reasoning. I am afraid that, should I multiply words about it or throw it into a greater variety of lights, it would only become more obscure and intricate. In all abstract reasonings there is one point of view which, if we can happily hit, we shall go farther towards illustrating the subject than by all the eloquence in the world. This point of view we should endeavor to reach, and reserve the flowers of rhetoric for subjects which are more adapted to them.

Notes

1. It is probable that no more was meant by those who denied innate ideas than that all ideas were copies of our impressions, though it must be confessed that the terms which they employed were not chosen with such caution, nor so exactly denied, as to prevent all mis- takes about their doctrine. For what is meant by "in- nate"? If "innate" be equivalent to "natural," then all the perceptions and ideas of the mind must be allowed to be innate or natural, in whatever sense we take the latter word, whether in opposition to what is uncom- mon, artificial, or miraculous. If by innate he meant contemporary to our birth, the dispute seems to be frivolous, nor is it worth while to inquire at what time thinking begins, whether before, at, or after our birth. Again, the word "idea" seems to be commonly taken in a very loose sense by Locke and others, as standing for any of our perceptions, our sensations and passions, as well as thoughts. Now, in this sense, I should desire to know what can be meant by asserting that self-love, or resentment of injuries, or the passion between the sexes is not innate?

But admitting these terms "impressions" and "ideas" in the sense above explained, and understanding by "innate" what is original or copies from no precedent perception, then may we assert that all our impres- sions are innate, and our ideas not innate.

To be ingenuous, I must own it to be my opinion that Locke was betrayed into this question by the schoolmen, who, making use of undefined terms,

draw out their disputes to a tedious length without ever touching the point in question. A like ambigu- ity and circumlocution seem to run through that phi- losopher's reasonings, on this as well as most other subjects.

2. The word "power" is here used in a loose and popular sense. The more accurate explication of it would give additional evidence to this argument. See Section VII.

3. Nothing is more usual than for writers, even on *moral, political,* or *physical* subjects, to distinguish between *rea- son* and *experience,* and to suppose that these species of argumentation are entirely different from each other. The former are taken for the mere result of our intel- lectual faculties, which, by considering *a priori* the nature of things, and examining the effects that must follow from their operation, establish particular prin- ciples of science and philosophy. The latter are sup- posed to be derived entirely from sense and observa- tion, by which we learn what has actually resulted from the operation of particular objects, and are thence able to infer what will for the future result from them. Thus, for instance, the limitations and restraints of civil government and a legal constitution may be de- fended, either from *reason,* which, reflecting on the great frailty and corruption of human nature, teaches that no man can safely be trusted with unlimited au- thority; or from *experience* and history, which inform us of the enormous abuses that ambition in every age and country has been found to make of so imprudent a confidence.

The same distinction between reason and experi- ence is maintained in all our deliberations concerning the conduct of life, while the experienced statesman, general physician, or merchant, is trusted and fol- lowed, and the unpracticed novice, with whatever nat- ural talents endowed, neglected and despised. Though it be allowed that reason may form very plausible con- jectures with regard to the consequences of such a particular conduct in such particular circumstances, it is still supposed imperfect without the assistance of ex- perience, which is alone able to give stability and cer- tainty to the maxim derived from study and reflection.

But notwithstanding that this distinction be thus universally received, both in the active and speculative scenes of life, I shall not scruple to pronounce that it is, at bottom, erroneous, or at least superficial.

If we examine those arguments which, in any of the sciences above mentioned, are supposed to be the mere effects of reasoning and reflection, they will be found to terminate at last in some general principle or conclusion for which we can assign no reason but ob- servation and experience. The only difference between them and those maxims which are vulgarly esteemed the result of pure experience is that the former cannot be established without some process of thought, and some reflection on what we have observed, in order to distinguish its circumstances and trace its consequences—whereas, in the latter, the experienced event is exactly and fully similar to that which we infer as the result of any particular situation. The history of a Tiberius or a Nero makes us dread a like tyranny, were our monarchs freed from the restraints of laws and senates: but the observation of any fraud or cruelty in private life is sufficient, with the aid of a little thought, to give us the same apprehension, while it serves as an instance of the general corruption of human nature, and shows us the danger which we must incur by reposing an entire confidence in mankind. In both cases, it is experience which is ultimately the foundation of our inference and conclusion.

There is no man so young and unexperienced as not to have formed from observation many general and just maxims concerning human affairs and the conduct of life; but it must be confessed that when a man comes to put these in practice he will be extremely liable to error, till time and further experience both enlarge these maxims, and teach him their proper use and application. In every situation or incident there are many particular and seemingly minute circumstances which the man of greatest talents is at first apt to overlook, though on them the justness of his conclusions, and consequently the prudence of his conduct, entirely depend. Not to mention that, to a young beginner, the general observations and maxims occur not always on the proper occasions, nor can be immediately applied with due calmness and distinction. The truth is, an unexperienced reasoner could be no reasoner at all were he absolutely inexperienced; and when we assign that character to anyone, we mean it only in a comparative sense, and suppose him possessed of experience in a smaller and more imperfect degree.

4. [A footnote containing a long quotation from Cicero, deleted.]

5. Mr. Locke divides all arguments into "demonstrative" and "probable." In this view, we must say that it is only probable that all men must die, or that the sun will rise tomorrow. But to conform our language more to common use, we ought to divide arguments into *demonstrations, proofs,* and *probabilities:* by proofs, meaning such arguments from experience as leave no room for doubt or opposition.

6. Section II.

7. Mr. Locke, in his chapter of Power, says that, finding from experience that there are several new productions in matter, and concluding that there must somewhere be a power capable of producing them, we arrive at last by this reasoning at the idea of power. But no reasoning can ever give us a new, original simple idea, as this philosopher himself confesses. This, therefore, can never be the origin of that idea.

8. It may be pretended, that the resistance which we meet with in bodies, obliging us frequently to exert our force and call up all our power, this gives us the idea of force and power. It is this *nisus* or strong endeavor of which we are conscious, that is the original impression from which this idea is copied. But, *first,* we attribute power to a vast number of objects where we never can suppose this resistance or exertion of force to take place: to the Supreme Being, who never meets with any resistance; to the mind in its command over its ideas and limbs, in common thinking and motion, where the effect follows immediately upon the will, without any exertion or summoning up of force; to inanimate matter, which is not capable of this sentiment. *Secondly,* this sentiment of an endeavor to overcome resistance has no known connection with any event: What follows it we know by experience, but could not know it *a priori.* It must, however, be confessed that the animal *nisus* which we experience, though it can afford no accurate precise idea of power, enters very much into that vulgar, inaccurate idea which is formed of it.

9. Section XII. [Not included here.]

10. I need not examine at length the *vis inertiae* which is so much talked of in the new philosophy, and which is ascribed to matter. We find by experience that a body at rest or in motion continues forever in its present state, till put from it by some new cause; and that a body impelled takes as much motion from the impelling body as it acquires itself. These are facts. When we call this a *vis inertiae,* we only mark these facts, without pretending to have any idea of the inert power, in the same manner as, when we talk of gravity, we mean certain effects without comprehending that active power. It was never the meaning of Sir Isaac Newton to rob second causes of all force or energy, though some of his followers have endeavored to establish that theory upon his authority. On the contrary, that great philosopher had recourse to an ethereal active fluid to explain his universal attraction, though he was so cautious and modest as to allow that it was a mere hypothesis not to be insisted on without more experiments. I must confess that there is something in the fate of opinions a little extraordinary. Descartes insinuated that doctrine of the universal and sole efficacy

of the Deity, without insisting on it. Malebranche and other Cartesians made it the foundation of all their philosophy. It had, however, no authority in England. Locke, Clarke, and Cudworth never so much as take notice of it, but suppose all along that matter has a real, though subordinate and derived, power. By what means has it become so prevalent among our modern metaphysicians?

11. According to these explications and definitions, the idea of *power* is relative as much as that of *cause;* and both have a reference to an effect, or some other event constantly conjoined with the former. When we consider the *unknown* circumstance of an object by which the degree or quantity of its effect is fixed and determined, we call that its power. And accordingly, it is allowed by all philosophers that the effect is the measure of the power. But if they had any idea of power as it is in itself, why could they not measure it in itself? The dispute, whether the force of a body in motion be as its velocity, or the square of its velocity; this dispute, I say, needed not be decided by comparing its effects in equal or unequal times, but by direct mensuration and comparison.

As to the frequent use of the words "force," "power," "energy," etc., which everywhere occur in common conversation as well as in philosophy, that is no proof that we are acquainted, in any instance, with the connecting principle between cause and effect, or can account ultimately for the production of one thing by another. These words, as commonly used, have very loose meanings annexed to them, and their ideas are very uncertain and confused. No animal can put external bodies in motion without the sentiment of a *nisus* or endeavor; and every animal has a sentiment or feeling from the stroke or blow of an external object that is in motion. These sensations, which are merely animal, and from which we can *a priori* draw no inference, we are apt to transfer to inanimate objects, and to suppose that they have some such feelings whenever they transfer or receive motion. With regard to energies, which are exerted without our annexing to them any idea of communicated motion, we consider only the constant experienced conjunction of the events; and as we *feel* a customary connection between the ideas, we transfer that feeling to the objects, as nothing is more usual than to apply to external bodies every internal sensation which they occasion.

How Is the Science of Nature Possible?

IMMANUEL KANT

Born in Köningsberg, East Prussia (now part of Russia), the great German philosopher Immanuel Kant (1724–1804) was one of the most influential of all modern thinkers.

. . . I openly confess, the suggestion of David Hume was the very thing, which many years ago first awoke me from my dogmatic slumber, and gave my investigations in the field of speculative philosophy quite a new direction. I was far from following him in the conclusions at which he arrived by regarding, not the whole of his problem, but a part, which by itself can give us no information. If we start from a well-founded, but undeveloped, thought, which another has bequeathed to us, we may well hope by con-

From *Prolegomena to Any Future Metaphysics,* translated by Paul Carus (Open Court, 1902). With emendations by Daniel Kolak.

tinued reflection to advance farther than the acute man, to whom we owe the first spark of light.

I therefore first tried whether Hume's objection could not be put into a general form, and soon found that the concept of the connection of cause and effect was by no means the only idea by which the understanding thinks the connection of things *a priori,* but rather that metaphysics consists altogether of such connections. I sought to ascertain their number, and when I had satisfactorily succeeded in this by starting from a single principle, I proceeded to the deduction of these concepts, which I was now certain were not deduced from experience, as Hume had apprehended, but sprang from the pure understanding. This deduction (which seemed impossible to my acute predecessor, which had never even occurred to any one else, though no one had hesitated to use the concepts without investigating the basis of their objective validity) was the most difficult task ever undertaken in the service of metaphysics; and the worst was that metaphysics, such as it then existed, could not assist me in the least, because this deduction alone can render metaphysics possible. But as soon as I had succeeded in solving Hume's problem not merely in a particular case, but with respect to the whole faculty of pure reason, I could proceed safely, though slowly, to determine the whole sphere of pure reason completely and from general principles, in its circumference as well as in its contents. This was required for metaphysics in order to construct its system according to a reliable method.

But I fear that the execution of Hume's problem in its widest extent (viz., my *Critique of Pure Reason*) will fare as the problem itself fared, when first proposed. It will be misjudged because it is misunderstood, and misunderstood because people choose to skim through the book, and not to think through it—a disagreeable task, because the work is dry, obscure, opposed to all ordinary notions, and moreover long-winded. I confess, however, I did not expect to hear from philosophers complaints of want of popularity, entertainment, and facility, when the existence of a highly prized and indispensable cognition is at stake, which cannot be established otherwise, than by the strictest rules of methodic precision. Popularity may follow, but is inadmissible at the beginning. Yet as regards a certain obscurity, arising partly from the diffuseness of the plan, owing to which the principal points of the investigation are easily lost sight of, the complaint is just, and I intend to remove it by the present *Prolegomena*. . . .

2. Concerning the Kind of Cognition Which Can Alone Be Called Metaphysical

a. Of the Distinction between Analytical and Synthetical Judgments in General.—The peculiarity of its sources demands that metaphysical cognition must consist of nothing but *a priori* judgments. But whatever be their origin, or their logical form, there is a distinction in judgments, as to their content, according to which they are either merely explicative, adding nothing to the content of the cognition, or expansive, increasing the given cognition: the former may be called analytical, the latter synthetical, judgments.

Analytical judgments express nothing in the predicate but what has been already actually thought in the concept of the subject, though not so distinctly or with the same (full) consciousness. When I say: All bodies are extended, I have not amplified in the least my concept of body, but have only analysed it, as extension was really thought to belong to that concept before the judgment was made, though it was not expressed; this judgment is therefore analytical. On the contrary, this judgment, All bodies have weight, contains in its predicate something not actually thought in the general concept of the body; it amplifies my knowledge by adding something to my concept, and must therefore be called synthetical.

b. The Common Principle of All Analytical Judgments Is the Law of Contradiction.—All analytical judgments depend wholly on the law of contradiction, and are in their nature *a priori* cognitions, whether the concepts that supply them with matter be empirical or not. For the predicate of an affirmative analytical judgment is already contained in the concept of the subject, of which it cannot be denied without contradiction. In the same way its opposite is necessarily denied of the subject in an analytical, but negative, judgment, by the same law of contradiction. Such is the nature of the judgments: all bodies are extended, and no bodies are unextended (i.e., simple).

For this very reason all analytical judgments are *a priori* even when the concepts are empirical, as, for example, gold is a yellow metal; for to know this I require no experience beyond my concept of gold as a yellow metal: it is, in fact, the very concept, and I need only analyse it, without looking beyond it elsewhere.

c. Synthetical Judgments Require a Different Principle from the Law of Contradiction.—There are synthetical *a posteriori* judgments of empirical origin; but there are also others which are proved to be certain *a priori*, and which spring from pure understanding and reason. Yet they both agree in this, that they cannot possibly spring from the principle of analysis, viz., the law of contradiction, alone; they require a quite different principle, though, from whatever they may be deduced, they must be subject to the law of contradiction, which must never be violated, even though everything cannot be deduced from it. I shall first classify synthetical judgments.

1. *Empirical Judgments* are always synthetical. For it would be absurd to base an analytical judgment on experience, as our concept suffices for the purpose without requiring any testimony from experience. That body is extended, is a judgment established *a priori,* and not an empirical judgment. For before appealing to experience, we already have all the conditions of the judgment in the concept, from which we have but to elicit the predicate according to the law of contradiction, and thereby to become conscious of the necessity of the judgment, which experience could not even teach us.

2. *Mathematical Judgments* are all synthetical. This fact seems hitherto to have altogether escaped the observation of those who have analysed human reason; it even seems directly opposed to all their conjectures, though incontestably certain, and most important in its consequences. For as it was found that the conclusions of mathematicians all proceed according to the law of contradiction (as is demanded by all apodeictic* certainty), men persuaded themselves that the fundamental principles were known from the same law. This was a great mistake, for a synthetical proposition can indeed be comprehended according to the law of contradiction, but only by presupposing another synthetical proposition from which it follows, but never in itself.

First of all, we must observe that all proper mathematical judgments are *a priori,* and not empirical, because they carry with them necessity, which cannot be obtained from experience. But if this be not conceded to me, very good; I shall confine my assertion to *pure mathematics,* the very notion of which implies that it contains pure *a priori* and not empirical cognitions.

It might at first be thought that the proposition $7 + 5 = 12$ is a mere analytical judgment, following from the concept of the sum of seven and five, according to the law of contradiction. But on closer examination it appears that the concept of the sum of $7 + 5$ contains merely their union in a single number, without its being at all thought what the particular number is that unites them. The concept of twelve is by no means thought by merely thinking of the combination of seven and five; and analyse this possible sum as we may, we shall not discover twelve in the concept. We must go beyond these concepts, by calling to our aid some concrete image, i.e., either our five fingers, or five points (as Segner has it in his arithmetic), and we must add successively the units of the five, given in some concrete image, to the concept of seven. Hence our concept is really amplified by the proposition $7 + 5 = 12$, and we add to the first a second, not thought in it. Arithmetical judgments are therefore synthetical, and the more plainly according as we take larger numbers; for in such cases it is clear that, however closely we analyse our concepts without calling visual images to our aid, we can never find the sum by such mere dissection.

All principles of geometry are no less analytical. That a straight line is the shortest path between two points, is a synthetical proposition. For my concept of straight contains nothing of quantity, but only a quality. The attribute of shortness is therefore altogether additional, and cannot be obtained by any analysis of the concept. Here, too, visualisation must come to aid us. It alone makes the synthesis possible.

Some other principles, assumed by geometers, are indeed actually analytical, and depend on the law of contradiction; but they only serve, as identical propositions, as a method of concatenation, and not as principles, e.g., $a = a$, the whole is equal to itself, or $a + b > a$, the whole is greater than its part. And yet even these, though they are recognised as valid from mere concepts, are only admitted in mathematics, because they can be represented in some visual form. What usually makes us believe that the predicate of such apodeictic judgments is already contained in our concept, and that the judgment is therefore analytical, is the duplicity of the expression, requesting us to think a certain predicate as of necessity implied in the thought of a given concept, which necessity attaches to the concept. But the question is not what we are requested to join in thought *to* the given concept, but what we actually think together with and in it, though obscurely; and so it appears that the predicate belongs to these con-

---

*"Certain beyond dispute."

cepts necessarily indeed, yet not directly but indirectly by an added visualisation.

4. *The General Question of the* Prolegomena—*Is Metaphysics at All Possible?*

Were a metaphysics, which could maintain its place as a science, really in existence; could we say, here is metaphysics, learn it, and it will convince you irresistibly and irrevocably of its truth: this question would be useless, and there would only remain that other question (which would rather be a test of our acuteness, than a proof of the existence of the thing itself), "How is the science possible, and how does reason come to attain it?" But human reason has not been so fortunate in this case. There is no single book to which you can point as you do to Euclid, and say: This is metaphysics; here you may find the noblest objects of this science, the knowledge of a highest being, and of a future existence, proved from principles of pure reason. We can be shown indeed many judgments, demonstrably certain, and never questioned; but these are all analytical, and rather concern the materials and the scaffolding for metaphysics, than the extension of knowledge, which is our proper object in studying it (§2). Even supposing you produce synthetical judgments (such as the law of sufficient reason, which you have never proved, as you ought to, from pure reason *a priori,* though we gladly concede its truth), you lapse when they come to be employed for your principal object, into such doubtful assertions, that in all ages one metaphysics has contradicted another, either in its assertions, or their proofs, and thus has itself destroyed its own claim to lasting assent. Nay, the very attempts to set up such a science are the main cause of the early appearance of scepticism, a mental attitude in which reason treats itself with such violence that it could never have arisen save from complete despair of ever satisfying our most important aspirations. For long before men began to inquire into nature methodically, they consulted abstract reason, which had to some extent been exercised by means of ordinary experience; for reason is ever present, while laws of nature must usually be discovered with labor. So metaphysics floated to the surface, like foam, which dissolved the moment it was scooped off. But immediately there appeared a new supply on the surface, to be ever eagerly gathered up by some, while others, instead of seeking in the depths the cause of the phenomenon, thought they showed their wisdom by ridiculing the idle labor of their neighbors.

The essential and distinguishing feature of pure mathematical cognition among all other *a priori* cognitions is, that it cannot at all proceed from concepts, but only by means of the construction of concepts. . . . As therefore in its judgments it must proceed beyond the concept to that which its corresponding visualisation contains, these judgments neither can, nor ought to, arise analytically, by dissecting the concept, but are all synthetical.

I cannot refrain from pointing out the disadvantage resulting to philosophy from the neglect of this easy and apparently insignificant observation. Hume being prompted (a task worthy of a philosopher) to cast his eye over the whole field of *a priori* cognitions in which human understanding claims such mighty possessions, heedlessly severed from it a whole, and indeed its most valuable, province, viz., pure mathematics; for he thought its nature, or, so to speak, the state-constitution of this empire, depended on totally different principles, namely, on the law of contradiction alone; and although he did not divide judgments in this manner formally and universally as I have done here, what he said was equivalent to this: that mathematics contains only analytical, but metaphysics synthetical, *a priori* judgments. In this, however, he was greatly mistaken, and the mistake had a decidedly injurious effect upon his whole conception. But for this, he would have extended his question concerning the origin of our synthetical judgments far beyond the metaphysical concept of causality, and included in it the possibility of mathematics *a priori* also, for this latter he must have assumed to be equally synthetical. And then he could not have based his metaphysical judgments on mere experience without subjecting the axioms of mathematics equally to experience, a thing which he was far too acute to do. The good company into which metaphysics would thus have been brought, would have saved it from the danger of a contemptuous ill-treatment, for the thrust intended for it must have reached mathematics, which was not and could not have been Hume's intention. Thus that acute writer would have been led into considerations which must needs be similar to those that now occupy us, but which would have gained inestimably by his inimitably elegant style.

Metaphysical judgments, properly so called, are all synthetical. We must distinguish judgments pertaining to metaphysics from metaphysical judgments properly so called. Many of the former are analytical, but they only afford the means for metaphysical judgments, which are the whole end of the science, and which are always synthetical. For if there be concepts pertaining to metaphysics (as, for example, that of substance), the judgments springing from simple analysis of them also pertain to metaphysics, as, for example, substance is that which only exists as subject; and by means of several such analytical judgments, we seek to approach the definition of the concept. But as the analysis of a pure concept of the understanding pertaining to metaphysics, does not proceed in any different manner from the dissection of any other, even empirical, concepts, not pertaining to metaphysics (such as: air is an elastic fluid, the elasticity of which is not destroyed by any known degree of cold), it follows that the concept indeed, but not the analytical judgment, is properly metaphysical. This science has something peculiar in the production of its *a priori* cognitions, which must therefore be distinguished from the features it has in common with other rational knowledge. Thus the judgment, that all the substance in things is permanent, is a synthetical and properly metaphysical judgment.

If the *a priori* principles, which constitute the materials of metaphysics, have first been collected according to fixed principles, then their analysis will be of great value; it might be taught as a particular part, containing nothing but analytical judgments pertaining to metaphysics, and could be treated separately from the synthetical which constitute metaphysics proper. For indeed these analyses are not elsewhere of much value, except in metaphysics, i.e., as regards the synthetical judgments, which are to be generated by these previously analysed concepts.

4. The General Question of the Prolegomena— Is Metaphysics at All Possible?

The conclusion drawn in this section then is, that metaphysics is properly concerned with synthetical propositions *a priori*, and these alone constitute its

end, for which it indeed requires various dissections of its concepts, viz., of its analytical judgments, but wherein the procedure is not different from that in every other kind of knowledge, in which we merely seek to render our concepts distinct by analysis. But the generation of *a priori* cognition by concrete images as well as by concepts, in fine of synthetical propositions *a priori* in philosophical cognition, constitutes the essential subject of metaphysics.

Weary therefore as well of dogmatism, which teaches us nothing, as of scepticism, which does not even promise us anything, not even the quiet state of a contented ignorance; disquieted by the importance of knowledge so much needed; and lastly, rendered suspicious by long experience of all knowledge, which we believe we possess, or which offers itself, under the title of pure reason: there remains but one critical question on the answer to which our future procedure depends, viz., *Is metaphysics at all possible?* But this question must be answered not by sceptical objections to the asseverations of some actual system of metaphysics (for we do not as yet admit such a thing to exist), but from the conception, as yet only problematical, of a science of this sort. . . .

The General Problem: How Is Cognition from Pure Reason Possible?

5. We have above learned the significant distinction between analytical and synthetical judgments. The possibility of analytical propositions was easily comprehended, being entirely founded on the law of contradiction. The possibility of synthetical *a posteriori* judgments, of those which are gathered from experience, also requires no particular explanation; for experience is nothing but a continual synthesis of perceptions. There remain therefore only synthetical propositions *a priori*, of which the possibility must be sought or investigated, because they must depend upon other principles than the law of contradiction.

But here we need not first establish the possibility of such propositions so as to ask whether they are possible. For there are enough of them which indeed are of undoubted certainty, and as our present method is analytical, we shall start from the fact, that such synthetical but purely rational cognition actually exists; but we must now inquire into the reason of this possibility, and ask, *how* such cognition is possible, in order that we may from the principles of its possibility be enabled to determine the conditions of its use, its sphere and its limits. The proper problem upon which all depends, when expressed with scholastic precision, is therefore:

How are Synthetic Propositions a priori possible?

For the sake of popularity I have above expressed this problem somewhat differently, as an inquiry into purely rational cognition, which I could do for once without detriment to the desired comprehension, because, as we have only to do here with metaphysics and its sources, the reader will, I hope, after the foregoing remarks, keep in mind that when we speak of purely rational cognition, we do not mean analytical, but synthetical cognition.

Metaphysics stands or falls with the solution of this problem: its very existence depends upon it. Let any one make metaphysical assertions with ever so much plausibility, let him overwhelm us with conclusions, if he has not previously proved able to answer this question satisfactorily, I have a right to say: this is all vain baseless philosophy and false wisdom. You speak through pure reason, and claim, as it were to create cognitions *a priori* by not only dissecting given concepts, but also by asserting connections which do not rest upon the law of contradiction, and which you believe you conceive quite independently of all experience; how do you arrive at this, and how will you justify your pretensions? An appeal to the consent of the common sense of mankind cannot be allowed; for that is a witness whose authority depends merely upon rumor. Says Horace:

Quodcunque ostendis mihi sic, incredulus odi.
[To all that which thou provest me thus, I refuse to give credence.]

The answer to this question, though indispensable, is difficult; and though the principal reason that it was not made long ago is, that the possibility of the question never occurred to anybody, there is yet another reason, which is this that a satisfactory answer to this one question requires a much more persistent, profound, and painstaking reflection, than the most diffuse work on metaphysics, which on its first appearance promised immortality to its author. And every intelligent reader, when he carefully reflects what this problem requires, must at first

be struck with its difficulty, and would regard it as insoluble and even impossible, did there not actually exist pure synthetical cognitions *a priori*. This actually happened to David Hume, though he did not conceive the question in its entire universality as is done here, and as must be done, should the answer be decisive for all Metaphysics. For how is it possible, says that acute man, that when a concept is given me, I can go beyond it and connect with it another, which is not contained in it, in such a manner as if the latter necessarily belonged to the former? Nothing but experience can furnish us with such connections (thus he concluded from the difficulty which he took to be an impossibility), and all that vaunted necessity, or, what is the same thing, all cognition assumed to be *a priori,* is nothing but a long habit of accepting something as true, and hence of mistaking subjective necessity for objective.

Should my reader complain of the difficulty and the trouble which I occasion him in the solution of this problem, he is at liberty to solve it himself in an easier way. Perhaps he will then feel under obligation to the person who has undertaken for him a labor of so profound research, and will rather be surprised at the facility with which, considering the nature of the subject, the solution has been attained. Yet it has cost years of work to solve the problem in its whole universality (using the term in the mathematical sense, viz., for that which is sufficient for all cases), and finally to exhibit it in the analytical form, as the reader finds it here.

All metaphysicians are therefore solemnly and legally suspended from their occupations till they shall have answered in a satisfactory manner the question, "How are synthetic cognitions *a priori* possible?" For the answer contains the only credentials which they must show when they have anything to offer in the name of pure reason. But if they do not possess these credentials, they can expect nothing else of reasonable people, who have been deceived so often, than to be dismissed without further ado.

If they on the other hand desire to carry on their business, not as a science, but as an art of wholesome oratory suited to the common sense of man, they cannot in justice be prevented. They will then speak the modest language of a rational belief, they will grant that they are not allowed even to conjecture, far less to know, anything which lies beyond the bounds of all possible experience, but only to assume (not for speculative use, which they must abandon, but for practical purposes only) the existence of something that is possible and even indispensable for the guidance of the understanding and of the will in life. In this manner alone can they be called useful and wise men, and the more so as they renounce the title of metaphysicians; for the latter profess to be speculative philosophers, and since, when judgments *a priori* are under discussion, poor probabilities cannot be admitted (for what is declared to be known *a priori* is thereby announced as necessary), such men cannot be permitted to play with conjectures, but their assertions must be either science, or are worth nothing at all.

It may be said, that the entire transcendental philosophy, which necessarily precedes all metaphysics, is nothing but the complete solution of the problem here propounded, in systematical order and completeness, and hitherto we have never had any transcendental philosophy; for what goes by its name is properly a part of metaphysics, whereas the former science is intended first to constitute the possibility of the latter, and must therefore precede all metaphysics. And it is not surprising that when a whole science, deprived of all help from other sciences, and consequently in itself quite new, is required to answer a single question satisfactorily, we should find the answer troublesome and difficult, nay even shrouded in obscurity. . . .

FIRST PART OF THE TRANSCENDENTAL PROBLEM

How Is Pure Mathematics Possible?

13.   Those who cannot yet rid themselves of the notion that space and time are actual qualities inhering in things in themselves, may exercise their acumen on the following paradox. When they have in vain attempted its solution, and are free from prejudices at least for a few moments, they will suspect that the degradation of space and of time to mere forms of our sensuous intuition may perhaps be well founded.

If two things are quite equal in all respects as much as can be ascertained by all means possible, quantitatively and qualitatively, it must follow, that the one can in all cases and under all circumstances replace the other, and this substitution would not occasion the least perceptible difference. This in fact is true of plane figures in geometry; but some spherical figures exhibit, notwithstanding a complete internal agreement, such a contrast in their external relation, that the one figure cannot possibly be put in the place of the other. For instance, two spherical triangles on opposite hemispheres, which have an arc of the equator as their common base, may be quite equal, both as regards sides and angles, so that nothing is to be found in either, if it be described for itself alone and completed, that would not equally be applicable to both; and yet the one cannot be put in the place of the other (being situated upon the opposite hemisphere). Here then is an internal difference between the two triangles, which difference our understanding cannot describe as internal, and which only manifests itself by external relations in space.

But I shall adduce examples, taken from common life, that are more obvious still.

What can be more similar in every respect and in every part more alike to my hand and to my ear, than their images in a mirror? And yet I cannot put such a hand as is seen in the glass in the place of its archetype; for if this is a right hand, that in the glass is a left one, and the image or reflection of the right ear is a left one which never can serve as a substitute for the other. There are in this case no internal differences which our understanding could determine by thinking alone. Yet the differences are internal as the senses teach, for, notwithstanding their complete equality and similarity, the left hand cannot be enclosed in the same bounds as the right one (they are not congruent); the glove of one hand cannot be used for the other. What is the solution? These objects are not representations of things as they are in themselves, and as the pure understanding would cognise them, but sensuous intuitions, that is, appearances, the possibility of which rests upon the relation of certain things unknown in themselves to something else, viz., to our sensibility. Space is the form of the external intuition of this sensibility, and the internal determination of every space is only possible by the determination of its external relation to the whole space, of which it is a part (in other words, by its relation to the external sense). That is to say, the part is only possible through the whole, which is never the case with things in themselves, as objects of the mere understanding, but with appearances only. Hence the difference between similar and equal things, which are yet not congruent (for instance, two symmetric helices), cannot be made intelligible by any concept, but only by the relation to the right and the left hands which immediately refers to intuition.

Remark I

Pure mathematics, and especially pure geometry, can only have objective reality on condition that they refer to objects of sense. But in regard to the latter the principle holds good, that our sense representation is not a representation of things in themselves, but of the way in which they appear to us. Hence it follows, that the propositions of geometry are not the results of a mere creation of our poetic imagination, and that therefore they cannot be referred with assurance to actual objects; but rather that they are necessarily valid of space, and consequently of all that may be found in space, because space is nothing else than the form of all external appearances, and it is this form alone in which objects of sense can be given. Sensibility, the form of which is the basis of geometry, is that upon which the possibility of external appearance depends. Therefore these appearances can never contain anything but what geometry prescribes to them.

It would be quite otherwise if the senses were so constituted as to represent objects as they are in themselves. For then it would not by any means follow from the conception of space, which with all its properties serves to the geometer as an *a priori* foundation, together with what is thence inferred, must be so in nature. The space of the geometer would be considered a mere fiction, and it would not be credited with objective validity, because we cannot see how things must of necessity agree with an image of them, which we make spontaneously and previous to our acquaintance with them. But if this image, or rather this formal intuition, is the essential property of our sensibility, by means of which alone objects are given to us, and if this sensibility represents not things in themselves, but their appearances: we shall easily comprehend, and at the same time indisputably prove, that all external objects of our world of

sense must necessarily coincide in the most rigorous way with the propositions of geometry; because sensibility by means of its form of external intuition, viz., by space, the same with which the geometer is occupied, makes those objects at all possible as mere appearances.

It will always remain a remarkable phenomenon in the history of philosophy, that there was a time, when even mathematicians, who at the same time were philosophers, began to doubt, not of the accuracy of their geometrical propositions so far as they concerned space, but of their objective validity and the applicability of this concept itself, and of all its corollaries, to nature. They showed much concern whether a line in nature might not consist of physical points, and consequently that true space in the object might consist of simple [discrete] parts, while the space which the geometer has in his mind [being continuous] cannot be such. They did not recognise that this mental space renders possible the physical space, i.e., the extension of matter; that this pure space is not at all a quality of things in themselves, but a form of our sensuous faculty of representation; and that all objects in space are mere appearances, i.e., not things in themselves but representations of our sensuous intuition. But such is the case, for the space of the geometer is exactly the form of sensuous intuition which we find *a priori* in us, and contains the ground of the possibility of all external appearances (according to their form), and the latter must necessarily and most rigidly agree with the propositions of the geometer, which he draws not from any fictitious concept, but from the subjective basis of all external phenomena, which is sensibility itself. In this and no other way can geometry be made secure as to the undoubted objective reality of its propositions against all the intrigues of a shallow metaphysics, which is surprised at them [the geometrical propositions], because it has not traced them to the sources of their concepts.

Remark II

Whatever is given us as object, must be given us in intuition. All our intuition however takes place by means of the senses only; the understanding intuits nothing, but only reflects. And as we have just shown that the senses never and in no manner enable us to know things in themselves, but only their appearances, which are mere representations of the sensibility, we conclude that "all bodies, together with the space in which they are, must be considered nothing but mere representations in us, and exist nowhere but in our thoughts." You will say: Is not this manifest idealism?

Idealism consists in the assertion, that there are none but thinking beings, all other things, which we think are perceived in intuition, being nothing but representations in the thinking beings, to which no object external to them corresponds in fact. Whereas I say, that things as objects of our senses existing outside us are given, but we know nothing of what they may be in themselves, knowing only their appearances, i.e., the representations which they cause in us by affecting our senses. Consequently I grant by all means that there are bodies without us, that is, things which, though quite unknown to us as to what they are in themselves, we yet know by the representations which their influence on our sensibility procures us, and which we call bodies, a term signifying merely the appearance of the thing which is unknown to us, but not therefore less actual. Can this be termed idealism? It is the very contrary.

Long before Locke's time, but assuredly since him, it has been generally assumed and granted without detriment to the actual existence of external things, that many of their predicates may be said to belong not to the things in themselves, but to their appearances, and to have no proper existence outside our representation. Heat, color, and taste, for instance, are of this kind. Now, if I go farther, and for weighty reasons rank as mere appearances the remaining qualities of bodies also, which are called primary, such as extension, place, and in general space, with all that which belongs to it (impenetrability or materiality, space, etc.)—no one in the least can adduce the reason of its being inadmissible. As little as the man who admits colors not to be properties of the object in itself, but only as modifications of the sense of sight, should on that account be called an idealist, so little can my system be named idealistic, merely because I find that more, nay,

All the properties which constitute the intuition of a body belong merely to its appearance.

The existence of the thing that appears is thereby not destroyed, as in genuine idealism, but it is only

shown, that we cannot possibly know it by the senses as it is in itself.

I should be glad to know what my assertions must be in order to avoid all idealism. Undoubtedly, I should say, that the representation of space is not only perfectly conformable to the relation which our sensibility has to objects—that I have said—but that it is quite similar to the object,—an assertion in which I can find as little meaning as if I said that the sensation of red has a similarity to the property of vermilion, which in me excites this sensation.

Remark III

Hence we may at once dismiss an easily foreseen but futile objection, "that by admitting the ideality of space and of time the whole sensible world would be turned into mere sham." At first all philosophical insight into the nature of sensuous cognition was spoiled, by making the sensibility merely a confused mode of representation, according to which we still know things as they are, but without being able to reduce everything in this our representation to a clear consciousness; whereas proof is offered by us that sensibility consists, not in this logical distinction of clearness and obscurity, but in the genetical one of the origin of cognition itself. For sensuous perception represents things not at all as they are, but only the mode in which they affect our senses, and consequently by sensuous perception appearances only and not things themselves are given to the understanding for reflection. After this necessary corrective, an objection rises from an unpardonable and almost intentional misconception, as if my doctrine turned all the things of the world of sense into mere illusion.

When an appearance is given us, we are still quite free as to how we should judge the matter. The appearance depends upon the senses, but the judgment upon the understanding, and the only question is, whether in the determination of the object there is truth or not. But the difference between truth and dreaming is not ascertained by the nature of the representations, which are referred to objects (for they are the same in both cases), but by their connection according to those rules, which determine the coherence of the representations in the concept of an object, and by ascertaining whether they can subsist together in experience or not. And it is not the fault of the appearances if our cognition takes illusion for truth, i.e., if the intuition, by which an object is given us, is considered a concept of the thing or of its existence also, which the understanding can only think. The senses represent to us the paths of the planets as now progressive, now retrogressive, and herein is neither falsehood nor truth, because as long as we hold this path to be nothing but appearance, we do not judge of the objective nature of their motion. But as a false judgment may easily arise when the understanding is not on its guard against this subjective mode of representation being considered objective, we say they appear to move backward; it is not the senses however which must be charged with the illusion, but the understanding, whose province alone it is to give an objective judgment on appearances.

Thus, even if we did not at all reflect on the origin of our representations, whenever we connect our intuitions of sense (whatever they may contain), in space and in time, according to the rules of the coherence of all cognition in experience, illusion or truth will arise according as we are negligent or careful. It is merely a question of the use of sensuous representations in the understanding, and not of their origin. In the same way, if I consider all the representations of the senses, together with their form, space and time, to be nothing but appearances, and space and time to be a mere form of the sensibility, which is not to be met with in objects out of it, and if I make use of these representations in reference to possible experience only, there is nothing in my regarding them as appearances that can lead astray or cause illusion. For all that they can correctly cohere according to rules of truth in experience. Thus all the propositions of geometry hold good of space as well as of all the objects of the senses, consequently of all possible experience, whether I consider space as a mere form of the sensibility, or as something cleaving to the things themselves. In the former case however I comprehend how I can know *a priori* these propositions concerning all the objects of external intuition. Otherwise, everything else as regards all possible experience remains just as if I had not departed from the vulgar view.

But if I venture to go beyond all possible experi-

ence with my notions of space and time, which I cannot refrain from doing if I proclaim them qualities inherent in things in themselves (for what should prevent me from letting them hold good of the same things, even though my senses might be different, and unsuited to them?), then a grave error may arise due to illusion, for thus I would proclaim to be universally valid what is merely a subjective condition of the intuition of things and sure only for all objects of sense, viz., for all possible experience; I would refer this condition to things in themselves, and do not limit it to the conditions of experience.

My doctrine of the ideality of space and of time, therefore, far from reducing the whole sensible world to mere illusion, is the only means of securing the application of one of the most important cognitions (that which mathematics propounds *a priori*) to actual objects, and of preventing its being regarded as mere illusion. For without this observation it would be quite impossible to make out whether the intuitions of space and time, which we borrow from no experience, and which yet lie in our representation *a priori,* are not mere phantasms of our brain, to which objects do not correspond, at least not adequately, and consequently, whether we have been able to show its unquestionable validity with regard to all the objects of the sensible world just because they are mere appearances.

Secondly, though these my principles make appearances of the representations of the senses, they are so far from turning the truth of experience into mere illusion, that they are rather the only means of preventing the transcendental illusion, by which metaphysics has hitherto been deceived, leading to the childish endeavor of catching at bubbles, because appearances, which are mere representations, were taken for things in themselves. Here originated the remarkable event of the antimony of reason which I shall mention by and by, and which is destroyed by the single observation, that appearance, as long as it is employed in experience, produces truth, but the moment it transgresses the bounds of experience, and consequently becomes transcendent, produces nothing but illusion.

Inasmuch, therefore, as I leave to things as we obtain them by the senses their actuality, and only limit our sensuous intuition of these things to this, that they represent in no respect, not even in the pure intuitions of space and of time, anything more than mere appearances of those things, but never their constitution in themselves, this is not a sweeping illusion invented for nature by me. My protestation too against all charges of idealism is so valid and clear as even to seem superfluous, were there not incompetent judges, who, while they would have an old name for every deviation from their perverse though common opinion, and never judge of the spirit of philosophic nomenclature, but cling to the letter only, are ready to put their own conceits in the place of well-defined notions, and thereby deform and distort them. I have myself given this my theory the name of transcendental idealism, but that cannot authorise any one to confound it either with the empirical idealism of Descartes, (indeed, his was only an insoluble problem, owing to which he thought every one at liberty to deny the existence of the corporeal world, because it could never be proved satisfactorily), or with the mystical and visionary idealism of Berkeley, against which and other similar phantasms our *Critique* contains the proper antidote. My idealism concerns not the existence of things (the doubting of which, however, constitutes idealism in the ordinary sense), since it never came into my head to doubt it, but it concerns the sensuous representation of things, to which space and time especially belong. Of these [viz., space and time], consequently of all appearances in general, I have only shown, that they are neither things (but mere modes of representation), nor determinations belonging to things in themselves. But the word "transcendental," which with me means a reference of our cognition, i.e., not to things, but only to the cognitive faculty, was meant to obviate this misconception. Yet rather than give further occasion to it by this word, I now retract it, and desire this idealism of mine to be called critical. But if it be really an objectionable idealism to convert actual things (not appearances) into mere representations, by what name shall we call him who conversely changes mere representations to things? It may, I think, be called "dreaming idealism," in contradistinction to the former, which may be called "visionary," both of which are to be refuted by my transcendental, or, better, critical idealism.

SECOND PART OF THE TRANSCENDENTAL PROBLEM

How Is the Science of Nature Possible?

14.   Nature is the existence of things, so far as it is determined according to universal laws. Should nature signify the existence of things in themselves, we could never cognise it either *a priori* or *a posteriori*. Not *a priori*, for how can we know what belongs to things in themselves, since this never can be done by the dissection of our concepts (in analytical judgments)? We do not want to know what is contained in our concept of a thing (for the [concept describes what] belongs to its logical being), but what is in the actuality of the thing superadded to our concept, and by what the thing itself is determined in its existence outside the concept. Our understanding, and the conditions on which alone it can connect the determinations of things in their existence, do not prescribe any rule to things themselves; these do not conform to our understanding, but it must conform itself to them; they must therefore be first given us in order to gather these determinations from them, wherefore they would not be cognised *a priori*.

A cognition of the nature of things in themselves *a posteriori* would be equally impossible. For, if experience is to teach us laws, to which the existence of things is subject, these laws, if they regard things in themselves, must belong to them of necessity even outside our experience. But experience teaches us what exists and how it exists, but never that it must necessarily exist so and not otherwise. Experience therefore can never teach us the nature of things in themselves.

15.   We nevertheless actually possess a pure science of nature in which are propounded, *a priori* and with all the necessity requisite to apodeictical propositions, laws to which nature is subject. I need only call to witness that propaedeutic of natural science which, under the title of the universal science of nature, precedes all physics (which is founded upon empirical principles). In it we have mathematics applied to appearance, and also merely discursive principles (or those derived from concepts), which constitute the philosophical part of the pure cognition of nature. But there are several things in

it, which are not quite pure and independent of empirical sources: such as the concept of *motion,* that of *impenetrability* (upon which the empirical concept of matter rests), that of *inertia,* and many others, which prevent its being called a perfectly pure science of nature. Besides, it only refers to objects of the external sense, and therefore does not give an example of a universal science of nature, in the strict sense, for such a science must reduce nature in general, whether it regards the object of the external or that of the internal sense (the object of physics as well as psychology), to universal laws. But among the principles of this universal physics there are a few which actually have the required universality; for instance, the propositions that "substance is permanent," and that "every event is determined by a cause according to constant laws," etc. These are actually universal laws of nature, which subsist completely *a priori.* There is then in fact a pure science of nature, and the question arises, *How is it possible?*

16. The word "nature" assumes yet another meaning, which determines the object, whereas in the former sense it only denotes the conformity to law of the determinations of the existence of things generally. If we consider it *materialiter* (i.e., in the matter that forms its objects) "nature is the complex of all the objects of experience." And with this only are we now concerned, for besides, things which can never be objects of experience, if they must be cognised as to their nature, would oblige us to have recourse to concepts whose meaning could never be given *in concreto* (by any example of possible experience). Consequently we must form for ourselves a list of concepts of their nature, the reality whereof (i.e., whether they actually refer to objects, or are mere creations of thought) could never be determined. The cognition of what cannot be an object of experience would be hyperphysical, and with things hyperphysical we are here not concerned, but only with the cognition of nature, the actuality of which can be confirmed by experience, though it [the cognition of nature] is possible *a priori* and precedes all experience.

17. The formal [aspect] of nature in this narrower sense is therefore the conformity to law of all the objects of experience, and so far as it is cognised *a priori,* their necessary conformity. But it has just been shown that the laws of nature can never be cognised *a priori* in objects so far as they are considered not in reference to possible experience, but as things in themselves. And our inquiry here extends not to things in themselves (the properties of which we pass by), but to things as objects of possible experience, and the complex of these is what we properly designate as nature. And now I ask, when the possibility of a cognition of nature *a priori* is in question, whether it is better to arrange the problem thus: How can we cognise *a priori* that things as objects of experience necessarily conform to law? or thus: How is it possible to cognise *a priori* the necessary conformity to law of experience itself as regards all its objects generally?

Closely considered, the solution of the problem, represented in either way, amounts, with regard to the pure cognition of nature (which is the point of the question at issue), entirely to the same thing. For the subjective laws, under which alone an empirical cognition of things is possible, hold good of these things, as objects of possible experience (not as things in themselves, which are not considered here). Either of the following statements means quite the same:

> A judgment of observation can never rank as experience, without the law, that "whenever an event is observed, it is always referred to some antecedent, which it follows according to a universal rule."
>
> "Everything, of which experience teaches that it happens, must have a cause."

It is, however, more commendable to choose the first formula. For we can *a priori* and previous to all given objects have a cognition of those conditions, on which alone experience is possible, but never of the laws to which things may in themselves be subject, without reference to possible experience. We cannot therefore study the nature of things *a priori* otherwise than by investigating the conditions and the universal (though subjective) laws, under which alone such a cognition as experience (as to mere form) is possible, and we determine accordingly the possibility of things, as objects of experience. For if I should choose the second formula, and seek the conditions *a priori,* on which nature as an object of experience is possible, I might easily fall into error, and fancy that I was speaking of nature as a thing in itself, and then move round in endless circles, in a vain search for laws concerning things of which nothing is given me.

Accordingly we shall here be concerned with experience only, and the universal conditions of its possibility which are given *a priori*. Thence we shall determine nature as the whole object of all possible experience. I think it will be understood that I here do not mean the rules of the observation of a nature that is already given, for these already presuppose experience. I do not mean how (through experience) we can study the laws of nature; for these would not then be laws *a priori*, and would yield us no pure science of nature; but [I mean to ask] how the conditions *a priori* of the possibility of experience are at the same time the sources from which all the universal laws of nature must be derived.

18.   In the first place we must state that, while all judgments of experience are empirical (i.e., have their ground in immediate sense-perception), *vice versa*, all empirical judgments are not judgments of experience, but, besides the empirical, and in general besides what is given to the sensuous intuition, particular concepts must yet be superadded—concepts which have their origin quite *a priori* in the pure understanding, and under which every perception must be first of all subsumed and then by their means changed into experience.

Empirical judgments, so far as they have objective validity, are **judgments of experience;** but those which are only subjectively valid, I name mere **judgments of perception.** The latter require no pure concept of the understanding, but only the logical connection of perception in a thinking subject. But the former always require, besides the representation of the sensuous intuition, particular *concepts originally begotten in the understanding*, which produce the objective validity of the judgment of experience.

All our judgments are at first merely judgments of perception; they hold good only for us (i.e., for our subject), and we do not till afterwards give them a new reference (to an object), and desire that they shall always hold good for us and in the same way for everybody else; for when a judgment agrees with an object, all judgments concerning the same object must likewise agree among themselves, and thus the objective validity of the judgment of experience signifies nothing else than its necessary universality of application. And conversely when we have reason to consider a judgment necessarily universal (which never depends upon perception, but upon the pure concept of the understanding, under which the perception is subsumed), we must consider it objective also, that is, that it expresses not merely a reference of our perception to a subject, but a quality of the object. For there would be no reason for the judgments of other men necessarily agreeing with mine, if it were not the unity of the object to which they all refer, and with which they accord; hence they must all agree with one another.

19.   Therefore objective validity and necessary universality (for everybody) are equivalent terms, and though we do not know the object in itself, yet when we consider a judgment as universal, and also necessary, we understand it to have objective validity. By this judgment we cognise the object (though it remains unknown as it is in itself) by the universal and necessary connection of the given perceptions. As this is the case with all objects of sense, judgments of experience take their objective validity not from the immediate cognition of the object (which is impossible), but from the condition of universal validity in empirical judgments, which, as already said, never rests upon empirical, or, in short, sensuous conditions, but upon a pure concept of the understanding. The object always remains unknown in itself; but when by the concept of the understanding the connection of the representations of the object, which are given to our sensibility, is determined as universally valid, the object is determined by this relation, and it is the judgment that is objective.

To illustrate the matter: When we say, "the room is warm, sugar sweet, and wormwood bitter,"—we have only subjectively valid judgments. I do not at all expect that I or any other person shall always find it as I now do; each of these sentences only expresses a relation of two sensations to the same subject, to myself, and that only in my present state of perception; consequently they are not valid of the object. Such are judgments of perception. Judgments of experience are of quite a different nature. What experience teaches me under certain circumstances, it must always teach me and everybody; and its validity is not limited to the subject nor to its state at a particular time. Hence I pronounce all such judgments as being objectively valid. For instance, when I say the air is elastic, this judgment is as yet a judgment of perception only—I do nothing but refer two of my sensations to one another. But, if I would have it called a judgment of experience, I require this connection to stand under a condition, which makes it universally valid. I desire therefore that I and everybody else should always connect necessarily the same perceptions under the same circumstances.

20. We must consequently analyse experience in order to see what is contained in this product of the senses and of the understanding, and how the judgment of experience itself is possible. The foundation is the intuition of which I become conscious, i.e., perception, which pertains merely to the senses. But in the next place, there are acts of judging (which belong only to the understanding). But this judging may be twofold—first, I may merely compare perceptions and connect them in a particular state of my consciousness; or, secondly, I may connect them in consciousness generally. The former judgment is merely a judgment of perception, and of subjective validity only: it is merely a connection of perceptions in my mental state, without reference to the object. Hence it is not, as is commonly imagined, enough for experience to compare perceptions and to connect them in consciousness through judgment; there arises no universality and necessity, for which alone judgments can become objectively valid and be called experience.

Quite another judgment therefore is required before perception can become experience. The given intuition must be subsumed under a concept, which determines the form of judging in general relatively to the intuition, connects its empirical consciousness in consciousness generally, and thereby procures universal validity for empirical judgments. A concept of this nature is a pure *a priori* concept of the understanding, which does nothing but determine for an intuition the general way in which it can be used for judgments. Let the concept be that of cause, then it determines the intuition which is subsumed under it, e.g., that of air, relative to judgments in general, viz., the concept of air serves with regard to its expansion in the relation of antecedent to consequent in a hypothetical judgment. The concept of cause accordingly is a pure concept of the understanding, which is totally disparate from all possible perception, and only serves to determine the representation subsumed under it, relatively to judgments in general, and so to make a universally valid judgment possible.

Before, therefore, a judgment of perception can become a judgment of experience, it is requisite that the perception should be subsumed under some such a concept of the understanding; for instance, air ranks under the concept of causes, which determines our judgment about it in regard to its expansion as hypothetical. Thereby the expansion of the air is represented not as merely belonging to the perception of the air in my present state or in several states of mine, or in the state of perception of others, but as belonging to it necessarily. The judgment, "the air is elastic," becomes universally valid, and a judgment of experience, only by certain judgments preceding it, which subsume the intuition of air under the concept of cause and effect: and they thereby determine the perceptions not merely as regards one another in me, but relatively to the form of judging in general, which is here hypothetical, and in this way they render the empirical judgment universally valid.

If all our synthetical judgments are analysed so far as they are objectively valid, it will be found that they never consist of mere intuitions connected only (as is commonly believed) by comparison into a judgment; but that they would be impossible were not a pure concept of the understanding superadded to the concepts abstracted from intuition, under which concept these latter are subsumed, and in this manner only combined into an objectively valid judgment. Even the judgments of pure mathematics in their simplest axioms are not exempt from this condition. The principle, "a straight line is the shortest between two points," presupposes that the line is subsumed under the concept of quantity, which certainly is no mere intuition, but has its seat in the understanding alone, and serves to determine the intuition (of the line) with regard to the judgments which may be made about it, relatively to their quantity, that is, to plurality. For under them it is understood that in a given intuition there is contained a plurality of homogeneous parts.

21. To prove, then, the possibility of experience so far as it rests upon pure concepts of the

Logical Table of Judgments

1.	2.
As to Quantity	*As to Quality*
Universal	Affirmative
Particular	Negative
Singular	Infinite
3.	4.
As to Relation	*As to Modality*
Categorical	Problematical
Hypothetical	Assertorical
Disjunctive	Apodeictical

Transcendental Table of the Pure Concepts
of the Understanding

1.	2.
As to Quantity	*As to Quality*
Unity (the Measure)	Reality
Plurality (the Quantity)	Negation
Totality (the Whole)	Limitation
3.	4.
As to Relation	*As to Modality*
Substance	Possibility
Cause	Existence
Community	Necessity

Pure Physiological Table of the Universal Principles
of the Science of Nature

1.	2.
Axioms of Intuition	Anticipations of Perception
3.	4.
Analogies of Experience	Postulates of Empirical Thinking Generally

understanding *a priori,* we must first represent what belongs to judgments in general and the various functions of the understanding, in a complete table. For the pure concepts of the understanding must run parallel to these functions, as such concepts are nothing more than concepts of intuitions in general, so far as these are determined by one or other of these functions of judging, in themselves, that is, necessarily and universally. Hereby also the *a priori* principles of the possibility of all experience, as of an objectively valid empirical cognition, will be precisely determined. For they are nothing but propositions by which all perception is (under cer-

tain universal conditions of intuition) subsumed under those pure concepts of the understanding.

21*a.*   In order to comprise the whole matter in one idea, it is first necessary to remind the reader that we are discussing not the origin of experience, but of that which lies in experience. The former pertains to empirical psychology, and would even then never be adequately explained without the latter, which belongs to the critique of cognition, and particularly of the understanding.

Experience consists of intuitions, which belong to the sensibility, and of judgments, which are entirely a work of the understanding. But the judgments, which the understanding forms alone from sensuous intuitions, are far from being judgments of experience. For in the one case the judgment connects only the perceptions as they are given in the sensuous intuition, while in the other the judgments must express what experience in general, and not what the mere perception (which possesses only subjective validity) contains. The judgment of experience must therefore add to the sensuous intuition and its logical connection in a judgment (after it has been rendered universal by comparison) something that determines the synthetical judgment as necessary and therefore as universally valid. This can be nothing else than that concept which represents the intuition as determined in itself with regard to one form of judgment rather than another, viz., a concept of that synthetical unity of intuitions which can only be represented by a given logical function of judgments.

22. The sum of the matter is this: the business of the senses is to intuit—that of the understanding is to think. But thinking is uniting representations in one consciousness. This union originates either merely relative to the subject, and is accidental and subjective, or is absolute, and is necessary or objective. The union of representations in one consciousness is judgment. Thinking therefore is the same as judging, or referring representations to judgments in general. Hence judgments are either merely subjective, when representations are referred to a consciousness in one subject only, and united in it, or objective, when they are united in a consciousness generally, that is, necessarily. The logical functions of all judgments are but various modes of uniting representations in consciousness. But if they serve for concepts, they are concepts of their necessary union in a consciousness, and so principles of objectively valid judgments. This union in a consciousness is either analytical, by identity, or synthetical, by the combination and addition of various representations one to another. Experience consists in the synthetical connection of phenomena (perceptions) in consciousness, so far as this connection is necessary. Hence the pure concepts of the understanding are those under which all perceptions must be subsumed ere they can serve for judgments of experience, in which the synthetical unity of the perceptions is represented as necessary and universally valid.

23. Judgments, when considered merely as the condition of the union of given representations in a consciousness, are rules. These rules, so far as they represent the union as necessary, are rules *a priori*, and so far as they cannot be deduced from higher rules, are fundamental principles. But in regard to the possibility of all experience, merely in relation to the form of thinking in it, no conditions of judgments of experience are higher than those which bring the phenomena, according to the various forms of their intuition, under pure concepts of the understanding, and render the empirical judgment objectively valid. These concepts are therefore the *a priori* principles of possible experience.

The principles of possible experience are then at the same time universal laws of nature, which can be cognised *a priori*. And thus the problem in our second question, "How is the pure science of nature possible?" is solved. For the system which is required for the form of a science is to be met with in perfection here, because, beyond the above-mentioned formal conditions of all judgments in general offered in logic, no others are possible, and these constitute a logical system. The concepts grounded thereupon, which contain the *a priori* conditions of all synthetical and necessary judgments, accordingly constitute a transcendental system. Finally the principles, by means of which all phenomena are subsumed under these concepts, constitute a physical system, that is, a system of nature, which precedes all empirical cognition of nature, makes it even possible, and hence may in strictness be denominated the universal and pure science of nature.

24. The first one of the physiological principles subsumes all phenomena, as intuitions in space and time, under the concept of quantity, and is so far a principle of the application of mathematics to experience. The second one subsumes the empirical element, viz., sensation, which denotes the real in intuitions, not indeed directly under the concept of quantity, because sensation is not an intuition that contains either space or time, though it places the respective object into both. But still there is between reality (sense-representation) and the zero, or total void of intuition in time, a difference which has a

quantity. For between every given degree of light and of darkness, between every degree of heat and of absolute cold, between every degree of weight and of absolute lightness, between every degree of occupied space and of totally void space, diminishing degrees can be conceived, in the same manner as between consciousness and total unconsciousness (the darkness of a psychological blank) ever diminishing degrees obtain. Hence there is no perception that can prove an absolute absence of it; for instance, no psychological darkness that cannot be considered as a kind of consciousness, which is only outbalanced by a stronger consciousness. This occurs in all cases of sensation, and so the understanding can anticipate even sensations, which constitute the peculiar quality of empirical representations (appearances), by means of the principle: "that they all have (consequently that what is real in all phenomena has) a degree." Here is the second application of mathematics to the science of nature.

25. Regarding the relation of appearances in terms of their existence, the determination is not mathematical but dynamical, and can never be objectively valid, consequently never fit for experience, if it does not come under *a priori* principles by which the cognition of experience relative to appearances becomes even possible. Hence appearances must be subsumed under the concept of substance, which is the foundation of all determination of existence, as a concept of the thing itself; or secondly—so far as a succession is found among phenomena, that is, an event—under the concept of an effect with reference to cause; or lastly—so far as coexistence is to be known objectively, that is, by a judgment of experience—under the concept of community (action and reaction). Thus *a priori* principles form the basis of objectively valid, though empirical judgments, that is, of the possibility of experience so far as it must connect objects as existing in nature. These principles are the proper laws of nature, which may be termed dynamical.

Finally the cognition of the agreement and connection not only of appearances among themselves in experience, but of their relation to experience in general, belongs to the judgments of experience. This relation contains either their agreement with the formal conditions, which the understanding cognises, or their coherence with the materials of the senses and of perception, or combines both into one concept. Consequently it contains possibility, actuality, and necessity according to universal laws of nature; and this constitutes the physical doctrine of method, or the distinction of truth and of hypotheses, and the bounds of the certainty of the latter.

26. The third table of Principles drawn from the nature of the understanding itself after the critical method, shows an inherent perfection, which raises it far above every other table which has hitherto though in vain been tried or may yet be tried by analysing the objects themselves dogmatically. It exhibits all synthetical *a priori* principles completely and according to one principle, viz., the faculty of judging in general, constituting the essence of experience as regards the understanding, so that we can be certain that there are no more such principles, which affords a satisfaction such as can never be attained by the dogmatical method. Yet is this not all: there is a still greater merit in it.

We must carefully bear in mind the proof which shows the possibility of this cognition *a priori,* and at the same time limits all such principles to a condition which must never be lost sight of, if we desire it not to be misunderstood, and extended in use beyond the original sense which the understanding attaches to it. This limit is that they contain nothing but the conditions of possible experience in general so far as it is subjected to laws *a priori.* Consequently I do not say, that things *in themselves* possess a quantity, that their actuality possesses a degree, their existence a connection of accidents in a substance, etc. This nobody can prove, because such a synthetical connection from mere concepts, without any reference to sensuous intuition on the one side, or connection of it in a possible experience on the other, is absolutely impossible. The essential limitation of the concepts in these principles then is: That all things stand necessarily *a priori* under the aforementioned conditions, as objects of experience only.

Hence there follows secondly a specifically peculiar mode of proof of these principles: they are not directly referred to appearances and to their relations, but to the possibility of experience, of which appearances constitute the matter only, not the form. Thus they are referred to objectively and universally valid synthetical propositions, in which we distinguish judgments of experience from those of perception. This takes place because appearances, as mere intuitions, occupying a part of space and time, come under the concept of quantity, which unites their multiplicity *a priori* according to rules synthetically. Again, so far as the perception contains, besides intuition, sensibility, and between the latter and nothing (i.e., the total disappearance of sensibility), there is an ever-decreasing transition, it is apparent that that which is in appearances must have a degree, so far as it (viz., the perception) does not itself occupy any part of space or of time. Still the transition to actuality from empty time or empty space is only possible in time; consequently though sensibility, as the quality of empirical intuition, can never be cognised *a priori,* by its specific difference from other sensibilities, yet it can, in a possible experience in general, as a quantity of perception be intensely distinguished from every other similar perception. Hence the application of mathematics to nature, as regards the sensuous intuition by which nature is given to us, becomes possible and is thus determined.

SKEPTICISM AND SCIENCE

Science and Induction

BERTRAND RUSSELL

English philosopher Bertrand Russell (1872–1970), famous for his scientific and logical realism, was born in Scotland and taught philosophy at Cambridge University. He published over a hundred dred books and won the Nobel Prize.

APPEARANCE AND REALITY

Is there any knowledge in the world which is so certain that no reasonable man could doubt it? This question, which at first sight might not seem difficult, is really one of the most difficult that can be asked. When we have realized the obstacles in the way of a straightforward and confident answer, we shall be well launched on the study of philosophy—for philosophy is merely the attempt to answer such ultimate questions, not carelessly and dogmatically, as we do in ordinary life and even in the sciences, but critically, after exploring all that makes such questions puzzling, and after realizing all the vagueness and confusion that underlie our ordinary ideas.

In daily life, we assume as certain many things which, on a closer scrutiny, are found to be so full of apparent contradictions that only a great amount of thought enables us to know what it is that we really may believe. In the search for certainty, it is natural to begin with our present experiences, and in some sense, no doubt, knowledge is to be derived from them. But any statement as to what it is that our immediate experiences make us know is very likely to be wrong. It seems to me that I am now sitting in a chair, at a table of a certain shape, on which I see sheets of paper with writing or print. By turning my head I see out of the window buildings and clouds and the sun. I believe that the sun is about ninety-three million miles from the earth; that it is a hot globe many times bigger than the earth; that, owing

to the earth's rotation, it rises every morning, and will continue to do so for an indefinite time in the future. I believe that, if any other normal person comes into my room, he will see the same chairs and tables and books and papers as I see, and that the table which I see is the same as the table which I feel pressing against my arm. All this seems to be so evident as to be hardly worth stating, except in answer to a man who doubts whether I know anything. Yet all this may be reasonably doubted, and all of it requires much careful discussion before we can be sure that we have stated it in a form that is wholly true.

To make our difficulties plain, let us concentrate attention on the table. To the eye it is oblong, brown and shiny, to the touch it is smooth and cool and hard; when I tap it, it gives out a wooden sound. Any one else who sees and feels and hears the table will agree with this description, so that it might seem as if no difficulty would arise; but as soon as we try to be more precise our troubles begin. Although I believe that the table is "really" of the same colour all over, the parts that reflect the light look much brighter than the other parts, and some parts look white because of reflected light. I know that, if I move, the parts that reflect the light will be different, so that the apparent distribution of colours on the table will change. It follows that if several people are looking at the table at the same moment, no two of them will see exactly the same distribution of colours, because no two can see it from exactly the same point

From *The Problems of Philosophy* (Oxford University Press, 1912).

of view, and any change in the point of view makes some change in the way the light is reflected.

For most practical purposes these differences are unimportant, but to the painter they are all-important: the painter has to unlearn the habit of thinking that things seem to have the colour which common sense says they "really" have, and to learn the habit of seeing things as they appear. Here we have already the beginning of one of the distinctions that cause most trouble in philosophy—the distinction between "appearance" and "reality," between what things seem to be and what they are. The painter wants to know what things seem to be, the practical man and the philosopher want to know what they are; but the philosopher's wish to know this is stronger than the practical man's, and is more troubled by knowledge as to the difficulties of answering the question.

To return to the table. It is evident from what we have found, that there is no colour which preeminently appears to be *the* colour of the table, or even of any one particular part of the table—it appears to be of different colours from different points of view, and there is no reason for regarding some of these as more really its colour than others. And we know that even from a given point of view the colour will seem different by artificial light, or to a colour-blind man, or to a man wearing blue spectacles, while in the dark there will be no colour at all, though to touch and hearing the table will be unchanged. This colour is not something which is inherent in the table, but something depending upon the table and the spectator and the way the light falls on the table. When, in ordinary life, we speak of *the* colour of the table, we only mean the sort of colour which it will seem to have to a normal spectator from an ordinary point of view under usual conditions of light. But the other colours which appear under other conditions have just as good a right to be considered real; and therefore, to avoid favouritism, we are compelled to deny that, in itself, the table has any one particular colour.

The same thing applies to the texture. With the naked eye one can see the grain, but otherwise the table looks smooth and even. If we looked at it through a microscope, we should see roughness and hills and valleys, and all sorts of differences that are imperceptible to the naked eye. Which of these is the "real" table? We are naturally tempted to say that what we see through the microscope is more real, but that in turn would be changed by a still more powerful microscope. If, then, we cannot trust what we see with the naked eye, why should we trust what we see through a microscope? Thus, again, the confidence in our senses with which we began deserts us.

The *shape* of the table is no better. We are all in the habit of judging as to the "real" shapes of things, and we do this so unreflectingly that we come to think we actually see the real shapes. But, in fact, as we all have to learn if we try to draw, a given thing looks different in shape from every different point of view. If our table is "really" rectangular, it will look, from almost all points of view, as if it had two acute angles and two obtuse angles. If opposite sides are parallel, they will look as if they converged to a point away from the spectator; if they are of equal length, they will look as if the nearer side were longer. All these things are not commonly noticed in looking at a table, because experience has taught us to construct the "real" shape from the apparent shape, and the "real" shape is what interests us as practical men. But the "real" shape is not what we see; it is something inferred from what we see. And what we see is constantly changing in shape as we move about the room; so that here again the senses seem not to give us the truth about the table itself, but only about the appearance of the table.

Similar difficulties arise when we consider the sense of touch. It is true that the table always gives us a sensation of hardness, and we feel that it resists pressure. But the sensation we obtain depends upon how hard we press the table and also upon what part of the body we press with; thus the various sensations due to various pressures or various parts of the body cannot be supposed to reveal *directly* any definite property of the table, but at most to be *signs* of some property which perhaps *causes* all the sensations, but is not actually apparent in any of them. And the same applies still more obviously to the sounds which can be elicited by rapping the table.

Thus it becomes evident that the real table, if there is one, is not the same as what we immediately experience by sight or touch or hearing. The real table, if there is one, is not *immediately* known to us at all, but must be an inference from what is immediately known. Hence, two very difficult questions at once arise; namely, (1) Is there a real table at all? (2) If so, what sort of object can it be?

It will help us in considering these questions to have a few simple terms of which the meaning is definite and clear. Let us give the name of "sense-data" to the things that are immediately known in sensation: such things as colours, sounds, smells, hardness roughness, and so on. We shall give the name "sensation" to the experience of being immediately aware of these things. Thus, whenever we see a colour, we have a sensation *of* the colour, but the colour itself is a sense-datum, not a sensation. The colour is that *of* which we are immediately aware, and the awareness itself is the sensation. It is plain that if we are to know anything about the table, it must be by means of the sense-data—brown colour, oblong shape, smoothness, etc.—which we associate with the table; but, for the reasons which have been given, we cannot say that the table *is* the sense-data, or even that the sense-data are directly properties of the table. Thus a problem arises as to the relation of the sense-data to the real table, supposing there is such a thing.

The real table, if it exists, we will call a "physical object." Thus we have to consider the relation of sense-data to physical objects. The collection of all physical objects is called "matter." Thus our two questions may be re-stated as follows: (1) Is there any such thing as matter? (2) If so, what is its nature?

The philosopher who first brought prominently forward the reasons for regarding the immediate objects of our senses as not existing independently of us was Bishop Berkeley (1685–1753). . . . [He tried] to prove that there is no such thing as matter at all, and that the world consists of nothing but minds and their ideas. . . . The arguments employed are of very different value: some are important and sound, others are confused or quibbling. But Berkeley retains the merit of having shown that the existence of matter is capable of being denied without absurdity, and that if there are any things that exist independently of us they cannot be the immediate objects of our sensations.

There are two different questions involved when we ask whether matter exists, and it is important to keep them clear. We commonly mean by "matter" something which is opposed to "mind," something which we think of as occupying space and as radically incapable of any sort of thought or consciousness. It is chiefly in this sense that Berkeley denies matter; that is to say, he does not deny that the sense-data which we commonly take as signs of the existence of the table are really signs of the existence of *something* independent of us, but he does deny that this something is nonmental, that it is neither mind nor ideas entertained by some mind. He admits that there must be something which continues to exist when we go out of the room or shut our eyes, and that what we call seeing the table does really give us reason for believing in something which persists even when we are not seeing it. But he thinks that this something cannot be radically different in nature from what we see, and cannot be independent of seeing altogether, though it must be independent of *our* seeing. He is thus led to regard the "real" table as an idea in the mind of God. Such an idea has the required permanence and independence of ourselves, without being—as matter would otherwise be—something quite unknowable, in the sense that we can only infer it, and can never be directly and immediately aware of it.

Other philosophers since Berkeley have also held that, although the table does not depend for its existence upon being seen by me, it does depend upon being seen (or otherwise apprehended in sensation) by *some* mind—not necessarily the mind of God, but more often the whole collective mind of the universe. This they hold, as Berkeley does, chiefly because they think there can be nothing real—or at any rate nothing known to be real—except minds and their thoughts and feelings. We might state the argument by which they support their view in some such way as this: "Whatever can be thought of is an idea in the mind of the person thinking of it; therefore nothing can be thought of except ideas in minds; therefore anything else is inconceivable, and what is inconceivable cannot exist."

Such an argument, in my opinion, is fallacious; and of course those who advance it do not put it so shortly or so crudely. But whether valid or not, the argument has been very widely advanced in one form or another; and very many philosophers, perhaps a majority, have held that there is nothing real except minds and their ideas. Such philosophers are called "idealists." When they come to explaining matter, they either say, like Berkeley, that matter is really nothing but a collection of ideas, or they say, like Leibniz (1646–1716), that what appears as matter is really a collection of more or less rudimentary minds.

But these philosophers, though they deny matter as opposed to mind, nevertheless, in another sense, admit matter. It will be remembered that we asked two questions; namely, (1) Is there a real table at all? (2) If so, what sort of object can it be? Now both Berkeley and Leibniz admit that there is a real table, but Berkeley says it is certain ideas in the mind of God, and Leibniz says it is a colony of souls. Thus both of them answer our first question in the affirmative, and only diverge from the views of ordinary mortals in their answer to our second question. In fact, almost all philosophers seem to be agreed that there is a real table: they almost all agree that, however much our sense-data—colour, shape, smoothness, etc.—may depend upon us, yet their occurrence is a sign of something existing independently of us, something differing, perhaps, completely from our sense-data, and yet to be regarded as causing those sense-data whenever we are in a suitable relation to the real table.

Now obviously this point in which the philosophers are agreed—the view that there *is* a real table, whatever its nature may be—is vitally important, and it will be worth while to consider what reasons there are for accepting this view before we go on to the further question as to the nature of the real table. Our next [section], therefore, will be concerned with the reasons for supposing that there is a real table at all.

Before we go farther it will be well to consider for a moment what it is that we have discovered so far. It has appeared that, if we take any common object of the sort that is supposed to be known by the senses, what the senses *immediately* tell us is not the truth about the object as it is apart from us, but only the truth about certain sense-data which, so far as we can see, depend upon the relations between us and the object. Thus what we directly see and feel is merely "appearance," which we believe to be a sign of some "reality" behind. But if the reality is not what appears, have we any means of knowing whether there is any reality at all? And if so, have we any means of finding out what it is like?

Such questions are bewildering, and it is difficult to know that even the strangest hypotheses may not be true. Thus our familiar table, which has roused but the slightest thoughts in us hitherto, has become a problem full of surprising possibilities. The one thing we know about it is that it is not what it seems. Beyond this modest result, so far, we have the most complete liberty of conjecture. Leibniz tells us it is a community of souls; Berkeley tells us it is an idea in the mind of God; sober science, scarcely less wonderful, tell us it is a vast collection of electric charges in violent motion.

Among these surprising possibilities, doubt suggests that perhaps there is no table at all. Philosophy, if it cannot *answer* so many questions as we could wish, has at least the power of *asking* questions which increase the interest of the world, and show the strangeness and wonder lying just below the surface even in the commonest things of daily life.

THE EXISTENCE OF MATTER

We have to ask ourselves whether, in any sense at all, there is such a thing as matter. Is there a table which has a certain intrinsic nature, and continues to exist when I am not looking, or is the table merely a product of my imagination, a dream-table in a very prolonged dream? This question is of the greatest importance. For if we cannot be sure of the independent existence of objects, we cannot be sure of the independent existence of other people's bodies, and therefore still less of other people's minds, since we have no grounds for believing in their minds except such as are derived from observing their bodies. Thus if we cannot be sure of the independent existence of objects, we shall be left alone in a desert—it may be that the whole outer world is nothing but a dream, and that we alone exist. This is an uncomfortable possibility; but although it cannot be strictly *proved* to be false, there is not the slightest reason to suppose that it is true. In this [section] we have to see why this is the case.

Before we embark upon doubtful matters, let us try to find some more or less fixed point from which to start. Although we are doubting the physical existence of the table, we are not doubting the existence of the sense-data which made us think there was a table; we are not doubting that, while we look, a certain colour and shape appear to us, and while we press, a certain sensation of hardness is experienced by us. All this, which is psychological, we are not calling in question. In fact, whatever else may be doubtful, some at least of our immediate experiences seem absolutely certain.

Descartes (1596–1650), the founder of modern philosophy, invented a method which may still be used with profit—the method of systematic doubt. He determined that he would believe nothing which he did not see quite clearly and distinctly to be true. Whatever he could bring himself to doubt, he would doubt, until he saw reason for not doubting it. By applying this method he gradually became convinced that the only existence of which he could be *quite* certain was his own. He imagined a deceitful demon, who presented unreal things to his senses in a perpetual phantasmagoria; it might be very improbable that such a demon existed, but still it was possible, and therefore doubt concerning things perceived by the senses was possible.

But doubt concerning his own existence was not possible, for if he did not exist, no demon could deceive him. If he doubted, he must exist; if he had any experiences whatever, he must exist. Thus, his own existence was an absolute certainty to him. "I think, therefore I am," he said (*Cogito, ergo sum*); and on the basis of this certainty he set to work to build up again the world of knowledge which his doubt had laid in ruins. By inventing the method of doubt, and by showing that subjective things are the most certain, Descartes performed a great service to philosophy, and one which makes him still useful to all students of the subject.

But some care is needed in using Descartes' argument. "*I* think, therefore *I* am" says rather more than is strictly certain. It might seem as though we were quite sure of being the same person to-day as we were yesterday, and this is no doubt true in some sense. But the real Self is as hard to arrive at as the real table, and does not seem to have that absolute, convincing certainty that belongs to particular experiences. When I look at my table and see a certain brown colour, what is quite certain at once is not "*I* am seeing a brown colour," but rather, "a brown colour is being seen." This of course involves something (or somebody) which (or who) sees the brown colour; but it does not of itself involve that more or less permanent person whom we call "I." So far as immediate certainty goes, it might be that the something which sees the brown colour is quite momentary, and not the same as the something which has some different experience the next moment.

Thus it is our particular thoughts and feelings that have primitive certainty. And this applies to dreams and hallucinations as well as to normal perceptions: when we dream or see a ghost, we certainly do have the sensations we think we have, but for various reasons it is held that no physical object corresponds to these sensations. Thus the certainty of our knowledge of our own experiences does not have to be limited in any way to allow for exceptional cases. Here, therefore, we have, for what it is worth, a solid basis from which to begin our pursuit of knowledge.

The problem we have to consider is this: Granted that we are certain of our own sense-data, have we any reason for regarding them as signs of the existence of something else, which we can call the physical object? When we have enumerated all the sense-data which we should naturally regard as connected with the table, have we said all there is to say about the table, or is there still something else—something not a sense-datum, something which persists when we go out of the room? Common sense unhesitatingly answers that there is. What can be bought and sold and pushed about and have a cloth laid on it, and so on, cannot be a *mere* collection of sense-data. If the cloth completely hides the table, we shall derive no sense-data from the table, and therefore, if the table were merely sense-data, it would have ceased to exist, and the cloth would be suspended in empty air, resting, by a miracle, in the place where the table formerly was. This seems plainly absurd; but whoever wishes to become a philosopher must learn not to be frightened by absurdities.

One great reason why it is felt that we must secure a physical object in addition to the sense-data, is that we want the *same* object for different people. When ten people are sitting round a dinner table, it seems preposterous to maintain that they are not seeing the same tablecloth, the same knives and forks and spoons and glasses. But the sense-data are private to each separate person; what is immediately present to the sight of one is not immediately present to the sight of another: they all see things from slightly different points of views, and therefore see them slightly differently. Thus, if there are to be public neutral objects, which can be in some sense known to many different people, there must be something over and above the private and particular sense-data which appear to various people. What reason, then, have we for believing that there are such public neutral objects?

The first answer that naturally occurs to one is that, although different people may see the table slightly differently, still they all see more or less similar things when they look at the table, and the variations in what they see follow the laws of perspective and reflection of light, so that it is easy to arrive at a permanent object underlying all the different people's sense-data. I bought my table from the former occupant of my room; I could not buy *his* sense-data, which died when he went away, but I could and did buy the confident expectation of more or less similar sense-data. Thus it is the fact that different people have similar sense-data, and that one person in a given place at different times has similar sense-data, which makes us suppose that over and above the sense-data there is a permanent public object which underlies or causes the sense-data of various people at various times.

Now in so far as the above considerations depend upon supposing that there are other people besides ourselves, they beg the very question at issue. Other people are represented to me by certain sense-data, such as the sight of them or the sound of their voices, and if I had no reason to believe that there were physical objects independent of my sense-data, I should have no reason to believe that other people exist except as part of my dream. Thus, when we are trying to show that there must be objects independent of our own sense-data, we cannot appeal to the testimony of other people, since this testimony itself consists of sense-data, and does not reveal other people's experiences unless our own sense-data are signs of things existing independently of us. We must therefore, if possible, find, in our own purely private experiences, characteristics which show, or tend to show, that there are in the world things other than ourselves and our private experiences.

In one sense it must be admitted that we can never *prove* the existence of things other than ourselves and our experiences. No logical absurdity results from the hypothesis that the world consists of myself and my thoughts and feelings and sensations, and that everything else is mere fancy. In dreams a very complicated world may seem to be present, and yet on waking we find it was a delusion; that is to say, we find that the sense-data in the dream do not appear to have corresponded with such physical objects as we should naturally infer from our sense-data. (It is true that, when the physical world is assumed, it is possible to find physical causes for the sense-data in dreams: a door banging, for instance, may cause us to dream of a naval engagement. But although, in this case, there is a physical *cause* for the sense-data, there is not a physical object *corresponding* to the sense-data in the way in which an actual naval battle would correspond.) There is no logical impossibility in the supposition that the whole of life is a dream, in which we ourselves create all the objects that come before us. But although this is not logically impossible, there is no reason whatever to suppose that it is true; and it is, in fact, a less simple hypothesis, viewed as a means of accounting for the facts of our own life, than the common-sense hypothesis that there really are objects independent of us, whose action on us causes our sensations.

The way in which simplicity comes in from supposing that there really are physical objects is easily seen. If the cat appears at one moment in one part of the room, and at another in another part, it is natural to suppose that it has moved from the one to the other, passing over a series of intermediate positions. But if it is merely a set of sense-data, it cannot have ever been in any place where I did not see it; thus we shall have to suppose that it did not exist at all while I was not looking, but suddenly sprang into being in a new place. If the cat exists whether I see it or not, we can understand from our own experience how it gets hungry between one meal and the next; but if it does not exist when I am not seeing it, it seems odd that appetite should grow during non-existence as fast as during existence. And if the cat consists only of sense-data, it cannot be *hungry*, since no hunger but my own can be a sense-datum to me. Thus the behaviour of the sense-data which represent the cat to me, though it seems quite natural when regarded as an expression of hunger, becomes utterly inexplicable when regarded as mere movements and changes of patches of colour, which are as incapable of hunger as a triangle is of playing football.

But the difficulty in the case of the cat is nothing compared to the difficulty in the case of human beings. When human beings speak—that is, when we hear certain noises which we associate with ideas, and simultaneously see certain motions of lips and expressions of face—it is very difficult to suppose that what we hear is not the expression of a thought, as we know it would be if we emitted the same sounds. Of course similar things happen in dreams, where we are mistaken as to the existence of other people. But dreams are more or less suggested by what we call waking life, and are capable of being more or less accounted for on scientific principles if we assume that there really is a physical world. Thus every principle of simplicity urges us to adopt the natural view, that there really are objects other than ourselves and our sense-data which have an existence not dependent upon our perceiving them.

Of course it is not by argument that we originally come by our belief in an independent external world. We find this belief ready in ourselves as soon as we begin to reflect: it is what may be called an *instinctive* belief. We should never have been led to question this belief but for the fact that, at any rate in the case of sight, it seems as if the sense-datum itself were instinctively believed to be the independent object, whereas argument shows that the object cannot be identical with the sense-datum. This discovery, however—which is not at all paradoxical in the case of taste and smell and sound, and only slightly so in the case of touch—leaves undiminished our instinctive belief that there *are* objects *corresponding* to our sense-data. Since this belief does not lead to any difficulties, but on the contrary tends to simplify and systematize our account of our experiences, there seems no good reason for rejecting it. We may therefore admit—though with a slight doubt derived from dreams—that the external world does not really exist, and is not wholly dependent for its existence upon our continuing to perceive it.

The argument which has led us to this conclusion is doubtless less strong than we could wish, but it is typical of many philosophical arguments, and it is therefore worth while to consider briefly its general character and validity. All knowledge, we find, must be built up upon our instinctive beliefs, and if these are rejected, nothing is left. But among our instinctive beliefs some are much stronger than others, while many have, by habit and association, become entangled with other beliefs, not really instinctive, but falsely supposed to be part of what is believed instinctively.

Philosophy should show us the hierarchy of our instinctive beliefs, beginning with those we hold most strongly, and presenting each as much isolated and as free from irrelevant additions as possible. It should take care to show that, in the form in which they are finally set forth, our instinctive beliefs do not clash, but form a harmonious system. There can never be any reason for rejecting one instinctive belief except that it clashes with others; thus, if they are found to harmonize, the whole system becomes worthy of acceptance.

It is of course *possible* that all or any of our beliefs may be mistaken, and therefore all ought to be held with at least some slight element of doubt. But we cannot have *reason* to reject a belief except on the ground of some other belief. Hence, by organizing our instinctive beliefs and their consequences, by considering which among them is most possible, if necessary, to modify or abandon, we can arrive, on the basis of accepting as our sole data what we instinctively believe, at an orderly systematic organization of our knowledge, in which, though the *possibility* of error remains, its likelihood is diminished by the interrelation of the parts and by the critical scrutiny which has preceded acquiescence.

This function, at least, philosophy can perform. Most philosophers, rightly or wrongly, believe that philosophy can do much more than this—that it can give us knowledge, not otherwise attainable, concerning the universe as a whole, and concerning the nature of ultimate reality. Whether this be the case or not, the more modest function we have spoken of can certainly be performed by philosophy, and certainly suffices, for those who have once begun to doubt the adequacy of common sense, to justify the arduous and difficult labours that philosophical problems involve.

THE NATURE OF MATTER

. . . We agreed, though without being able to find demonstrative reasons, that it is rational to believe that our sense-data—for example, those which we regard as associated with my table—are really signs of the existence of something independent of us and our perceptions. That is to say, over and above the sensations of colour, hardness, noise, and so on, which make up the appearance of the table to me, I assume that there is something else, *of* which these things are appearances. The colour ceases to exist if I shut my eyes, the sensation of hardness ceases to exist if I remove my arm from contact with the table, the sound ceases to exist if I cease to rap the table with my knuckles. But I do not believe that when all these things cease the table ceases. On the contrary, I believe that it is because the table exists continuously that all these sense-data will reappear when I open my eyes, replace my arm, and begin again to rap with my knuckles. The question we have to consider in this chapter is: What is the nature of this real table, which persists independently of my perception of it?

To this question physical science gives an answer, somewhat incomplete it is true, and in part still very hypothetical, but yet deserving of respect so far as it goes. Physical science, more or less unconsciously, has drifted into the view that all natural phenomena ought to be reduced to motions. Light and heat and sound are all due to wave-motions, which travel from the body emitting them to the person who sees light or feels heat or hears sound. That which has the wave-motion is either aether or "gross matter," but in either case is what the philosopher would call matter. The only properties which science assigns to it are position in space, and the power of motion according to the laws of motion. Science does not deny that it *may* have other properties; but if so, such other properties are not useful to the man of science, and in no way assist him in explaining the phenomena.

It is sometimes said that "light *is* a form of wave-motion," but this is misleading, for the light which we immediately see, which we know directly by means of our senses, is *not* a form of wave-motion, but something quite different—something which we all know if we are not blind, though we cannot describe it so as to convey our knowledge to a man who is blind. A wave-motion, on the contrary, could quite well be described to a blind man, since he can acquire a knowledge of space by the sense of touch; and he can experience a wave-motion by a sea voyage almost as well as we can. But this, which a blind man can understand, is not what we mean by *light:* we mean by *light* just that which a blind man can never understand, and which we can never describe to him.

Now this something, which all of us who are not blind know, is not, according to science, really to be found in the outer world: it is something caused by the action of certain waves upon the eyes and nerves and brain of the person who sees the light. When it is said that light *is* waves, what is really meant is that waves are the physical cause of our sensations of light. But light itself, the thing which seeing people experience and blind people do not, is not supposed by science to form any part of the world that is independent of us and our senses. And very similar remarks would apply to other kinds of sensations.

It is not only colours and sounds and so on that are absent from the scientific world of matter, but also *space* as we get it through sight or touch. It is essential to science that its matter should be in *a* space, but the space in which it is cannot be exactly the space we see or feel. To begin with, space as we see it is not the same as space as we get it by the sense of touch; it is only by experience in infancy that we learn how to touch things we see, or how to get a sight of things which we feel touching us. But the space of science is neutral as between touch and sight; thus it cannot be either the space of touch or the space of sight.

Again, different people see the same object as of different shapes, according to their point of view. A circular coin, for example, though we should always *judge* it to be circular, will *look* oval unless we are straight in front of it. When we judge that it *is* circular, we are judging that it has a real shape which is not its apparent shape, but belongs to it intrinsically apart from its appearance. But this real shape, which is what concerns science, must be in a real space, not the same as anybody's *apparent* space. The real space is public, the apparent space is private to the percipient. In different people's *private* spaces the same object seems to have different shapes; thus the real space, in which it has its real shape, must be different from the private spaces. The space of science, therefore, though *connected* with the spaces we see and feel, is not identical with them, and the manner of its connexion requires investigation.

We agreed provisionally that physical objects cannot be quite like our sense-data, but may be regarded as *causing* our sensations. These physical objects are in the space of science, which we may call "physical" space. It is important to notice that, if our sensations are to be caused by physical objects, there must be a physical space containing these objects and our sense-organs and nerves and brain. We get a sensation of touch from an object when we are in contact with it; that is to say, when some part of our body occupies a place in physical space quite close to the space occupied by the object. We see an object (roughly speaking) when no opaque body is between the object and our eyes in physical space. Similarly, we only hear or smell or taste an object when we are sufficiently near to it, or when it touches the tongue, or has some suitable position in physical space relative to our body. We cannot begin to state what different sensations we shall derive from a given object under different circumstances unless we regard the object and our body as both in one physical space, for it is mainly the relative positions of the object and our body that determine what sensations we shall derive from the object.

Now our sense-data are situated in our private spaces, either the space of sight or the space of touch or such vaguer spaces as other senses may give us. If, as science and common sense assume, there is one public all-embracing physical space in which physical objects are, the relative positions of physical objects in physical space must more or less correspond to the relative positions of sense-data in our private spaces. There is no difficulty in supposing this to be the case. If we see on a road one house nearer to us than another, our other senses will bear out the view that it is nearer; for example, it will be reached sooner if we walk along the road. Other people will agree that the house which looks nearer to us is nearer; the ordnance map will take the same view; and thus everything points to a spatial relation between the houses corresponding to the relation between the sense-data which we see when we look at the houses. Thus we may assume that there is a physical space in which physical objects have spatial relations corresponding to those which the corresponding sense-data have in our private spaces. It is this physical space which is dealt with in geometry and assumed in physics and astronomy.

Assuming that there is physical space, and that it does thus correspond to private spaces, what can we know about it? We can know *only* what is required in order to secure the correspondence. That is to say, we can know nothing of what it is like in itself, but we can know the sort of arrangement of physical objects which results from their spatial relations. We can know, for example, that the earth and moon and sun are in one straight line during an eclipse, though we cannot know what a physical straight line is in itself, as we know the look of a straight line in our visual space. Thus we come to know much more about the *relations* of distances in physical space than about the distances themselves; we may know that one distance is greater than another, or that it is along the same straight line as the other, but we cannot have that immediate acquaintance with physical distances that we have with distances in our private spaces, or with colours or sounds or other sense-data. We can know all those things about physical space which a man born blind might know through other people about the space of sight; but the kind of things which a man born blind could never know about the space of sight we also cannot know about physical space. We can know the properties of the relations required to preserve the correspondence with sense-data, but we cannot know the nature of the terms between which the relations hold.

With regard to time, our *feeling* of duration or of the lapse of time is notoriously an unsafe guide as to the time that has elapsed by the clock. Times when we are bored or suffering pain pass slowly, times when we are agreeably occupied pass quickly, and times when we are sleeping pass almost as if they did not exist. Thus, in so far as time is constituted by duration, there is the same necessity for distinguishing a public and a private time as there was in the case of space. But in so far as time consists in an *order* of before and after, there is no need to make such a distinction; the time-order which events seem to have is, so far as we can see, the same as the time-order which they do have. At any rate no reason can be given for supposing that the two orders are not the same. The same is usually true of space; if a regiment of men are marching along a road, the *shape* of the regiment will look different from different points of view, but the men will appear arranged in the same *order* from all points of view. Hence we regard the *order* as true also in physical space, whereas the shape is only supposed to correspond to the physical space so far as is required for the preservation of the order.

In saying that the time-order which events *seem to have* is the same as the time-order which they *really have*, it is necessary to guard against a possible misunderstanding. It must not be supposed that the various states of different physical objects have the same time-order as the sense-data which constitute the perceptions of those objects. Considered as physical objects, the thunder and lightning are simultaneous; that is to say, the lightning is simultaneous with the disturbance of the air in the place where the disturbance begins, namely, where the lightning is. But the sense-datum which we call hearing the thunder does not take place until the disturbance of the air has travelled as far as to where we are. Similarly, it takes about eight minutes for the sun's light to reach us; thus, when we see the sun we are seeing the sun of eight minutes ago. So far as our sense-data afford evidence as to the physical sun they afford evidence as to the physical sun of eight minutes ago; if the physical sun had ceased to exist within the last eight minutes, that would make no difference to the sense-data which we call "seeing the sun." This affords a fresh illustration of the necessity of distinguishing between sense-data and physical objects.

What we have found as regards space is much the same as what we find in relation to the correspondence of the sense-data with their physical counterparts. If one object looks blue and another red, we may reasonably presume that there is some corresponding difference between the physical objects; if two objects both look blue, we may presume a corresponding similarity. But we cannot hope to be acquainted directly with the quality in the physical object which makes it look blue or red. Science tells us that this quality is a certain sort of wave-motion, and this sounds familiar, because we think of wave-motions in the space we see. But the wave-motions must really be in physical space, with which we have no direct acquaintance; thus the real wave-motions have not that familiarity which we might have supposed them to have. And what holds for colours is closely similar to what holds for other sense-data. Thus we find that, although the *relations* of physical objects have all sorts of knowable proper-

ties, derived from their correspondence with the relations of sense-data, the physical objects themselves remain unknown in their intrinsic nature, so far at least as can be discovered by means of the senses. The question remains whether there is any other method of discovering the intrinsic nature of physical objects.

The most natural, though not ultimately the most defensible, hypothesis to adopt in the first instance, at any rate as regards visual sense-data, would be that, though physical objects cannot, for the reasons we have been considering, be *exactly* like sense-data, yet they may be more or less like. According to this view, physical objects will, for example, really have colours, and we might, by good luck, see an object as of the colour it really is. The colour which an object seems to have at any given moment will in general be very similar, though not quite the same, from many different points of view; we might thus suppose the "real" colour to be a sort of medium colour, intermediate between the various shades which appear from the different points of view.

Such a theory is perhaps not capable of being definitely refuted, but it can be shown to be groundless. To begin with, it is plain that the colour we see depends only upon the nature of the light-waves that strike the eye, and is therefore modified by the medium intervening between us and the object, as well as by the manner in which light is reflected from the object in the direction of the eye. The intervening air alters colours unless it is perfectly clear, and any strong reflection will alter them completely. Thus the colour we see is a result of the ray as it reaches the eye, and not simply a property of the object from which the ray comes. Hence, also, provided certain waves reach the eye, we shall see a certain colour, whether the object from which the waves start has any colour or not. Thus it is quite gratuitous to suppose that physical objects have colours, and therefore there is no justification for making such a supposition. Exactly similar arguments will apply to other sense-data. . . .

ON INDUCTION

In almost all our previous discussions we have been concerned in the attempt to get clear as to our data in the way of knowledge of existence. What things are there in the universe whose existence is known to us owing to our being acquainted with them? So far, our answer has been that we are acquainted with our sense-data, and, probably, with ourselves. These we know to exist. And past sense-data which are remembered are known to have existed in the past. This knowledge supplies our data.

But if we are to be able to draw inferences from these data—if we are to know of the existence of matter, of other people, of the past before our individual memory begins, or of the future, we must know general principles of some kind by means of which such inferences can be drawn. It must be known to us that the existence of some one sort of thing, A, is a sign of the existence of some other sort of thing, B, either at the same time as A or at some earlier or later time, as, for example, thunder is a sign of the earlier existence of lightning. If this were not known to us, we could never extend our knowledge beyond the sphere of our private experience; and this sphere, as we have seen, is exceedingly limited. The question we have now to consider is whether such an extension is possible, and if so, how it is effected.

Let us take as an illustration a matter about which none of us, in fact, feel the slightest doubt. We are all convinced that the sun will rise tomorrow. Why? Is this belief a mere blind outcome of past experience, or can it be justified as a reasonable belief? It is not easy to find a test by which to judge whether a belief of this kind is reasonable or not, but we can at least ascertain what sort of general beliefs would suffice, if true, to justify the judgement that the sun will rise to-morrow, and the many other similar judgements upon which our actions are based.

It is obvious that if we are asked why we believe that the sun will rise to-morrow, we shall naturally answer, "Because it always has risen every day." We have a firm belief that it will rise in the future, because it has risen in the past. If we are challenged as to why we believe that it will continue to rise as heretofore, we may appeal to the laws of motion: the earth, we shall say, is a freely rotating body, and such bodies do not cease to rotate unless something interferes from outside, and there is nothing outside to interfere with the earth between now and to-morrow. Of course it might be doubted whether we are quite

certain that there is nothing outside to interfere, but this is not the interesting doubt. The interesting doubt is as to whether the laws of motion will remain in operation until to-morrow. If this doubt is raised, we find ourselves in the same position as when the doubt about the sunrise was first raised.

The *only* reason for believing that the laws of motion will remain in operation is that they have operated hitherto, so far as our knowledge of the past enables us to judge. It is true that we have a greater body of evidence from the past in favour of the laws of motion than we have in favour of the sunrise, because the sunrise is merely a particular case of fulfillment of the laws of motion, and there are countless other particular cases. But the real question is: Do *any* number of cases of a law being fulfilled in the past afford evidence that it will be fulfilled in the future? If not, it becomes plain that we have no ground whatever for expecting the sun to rise to-morrow, or for expecting the bread we shall eat at our next meal not to poison us, or for any of the other scarcely conscious expectations that control our daily lives. It is to be observed that all such expectations are only *probable;* thus we have not to seek for a proof that they *must* be fulfilled, but only for some reason in favour of the view that they are *likely* to be fulfilled.

Now in dealing with this question we must, to begin with, make an important distinction, without which we should soon become involved in hopeless confusions. Experience has shown us that, hitherto, the frequent repetition of some uniform succession of coexistence has been a *cause* of our expecting the same succession or coexistence on the next occasion. Food that has a certain appearance generally has a certain taste, and it is a severe shock to our expectations when the familiar appearance is found to be associated with an unusual taste. Things which we see become associated, by habit, with certain tactile sensations which we expect if we touch them; one of the horrors of a ghost (in many ghost-stories) is that it fails to give us any sensations of touch. Uneducated people who go abroad for the first time are so surprised as to be incredulous when they find their native language not understood.

And this kind of association is not confined to men; in animals also it is very strong. A horse which has been often driven along a certain road resists the attempt to drive him in a different direction. Domestic animals expect food when they see the person who usually feeds them. We know that all these rather crude expectations of uniformity are liable to be misleading. The man who has fed the chicken every day throughout its life at last wrings its neck instead, showing that more refined views as to the uniformity of nature would have been useful to the chicken.

But in spite of the misleadingness of such expectations, they nevertheless exist. The mere fact that something has happened a certain number of times causes animals and men to expect that it will happen again. Thus our instincts certainly cause us to believe that the sun will rise to-morrow, but we may be in no better a position than the chicken which unexpectedly has its neck wrung. We have therefore to distinguish the fact that past uniformities *cause* expectations as to the future, from the question whether there is any reasonable ground for giving weight to such expectations after the question of their validity has been raised.

The problem we have to discuss is whether there is any reason for believing in what is called "the uniformity of nature." The belief in the uniformity of nature is the belief that everything that has happened or will happen is an instance of some general law to which there are *no* exceptions. The crude expectations which we have been considering are all subject to exceptions, and therefore liable to disappoint those who entertain them. But science habitually assumes, at least as a working hypothesis, that general rules which have exceptions can be replaced by general rules which have no exceptions. "Unsupported bodies in air fall" is a general rule to which balloons and aeroplanes are exceptions. But the laws of motion and the law of gravitation, which account for the fact that most bodies fall, also account for the fact that balloons and aeroplanes can rise; thus the laws of motion and the law of gravitation are not subject to these exceptions.

The belief that the sun will rise to-morrow might be falsified if the earth came suddenly into contact with a large body which destroyed its rotation; but the laws of motion and the law of gravitation would not be infringed by such an event. The business of science is to find uniformities, such as the laws of motion and the law of gravitation, to which, so far as our experience extends, there are no exceptions. In

this search science has been remarkably successful, and it may be conceded that such uniformities have held hitherto. This brings us back to the question: Have we any reason, assuming that they have always held in the past, to suppose that they will hold in the future?

It has been argued that we have reason to know that the future will resemble the past, because what was the future has constantly become the past, and has always been found to resemble the past, so that we really have experience of the future, namely of times which were formerly future, which we may call past futures. But such an argument really begs the very question at issue. We have experience of past futures, but not of future futures, and the question is: Will future futures resemble past futures? This question is not to be answered by an argument which starts from past futures alone. We have therefore still to seek for some principle which shall enable us to know that the future will follow the same laws as the past.

The reference to the future in this question is not essential. The same question arises when we apply the laws that work in our experience to past things of which we have no experience—as, for example, in geology, or in theories as to the origin of the Solar System. The question we really have to ask is: "When two things have been found to be often associated, and no instance is known of the one occurring without the other, does the occurrence of one of the two, in a fresh instance, give any good ground for expecting the other?" On our answer to this question must depend the validity of the whole of our expectations as to the future, the whole of the results obtained by induction, and in fact practically all the beliefs upon which our daily life is based.

It must be conceded, to begin with, that the fact that two things have been found often together and never apart does not, by itself, suffice to *prove* demonstratively that they will be found together in the next case we examine. The most we can hope is that the oftener things are found together, the more probable it becomes that they will be found together another time, and that, if they have been found together often enough, the probability will amount *almost* to certainty. It can never quite reach certainty, because we know that in spite of frequent repetitions there sometimes is a failure at the last, as in the case of the chicken whose neck is wrung. Thus probability is all we ought to seek.

It might be urged, as against the view we are advocating, that we know all natural phenomena to be subject to the reign of law, and that sometimes, on the basis of observation, we can see that only one law can possibly fit the facts of the case. Now to this view there are two answers. The first is that, even if *some* law which has no exceptions applies to our case, we can never, in practice, be sure that we have discovered that law and not one to which there are exceptions. The second is that the reign of law would seem to be itself only probable, and that our belief that it will hold in the future, or in unexamined cases in the past, is itself based upon the very principle we are examining.

The principle we are examining may be called the *principle of induction,* and its two parts may be stated as follows:

(*a*) When a thing of a certain sort A has been found to be associated with a thing of a certain other sort B, and has never been found dissociated from a thing of the sort B, the greater the number of cases in which A and B have been associated, the greater is the probability that they will be associated in a fresh case in which one of them is known to be present;

(*b*) Under the same circumstances, a sufficient number of cases of association will make the probability of a fresh association nearly a certainty, and will make it approach certainty without limit.

As just stated, the principle applies only to the verification of our expectation in a single fresh instance. But we want also to know that there is a probability in favour of the general law that things of the sort A are *always* associated with things of the sort B, provided a sufficient number of cases of association are known, and no cases of failure of association are known. The probability of the general law is obviously less than the probability of the particular case, since if the general law is true, the particular case must also be true, whereas the particular case may be true without the general law being true. Nevertheless the probability of the general law is increased by repetitions, just as the probability of the particular case is. We may therefore repeat the two parts of our principle as regards the general law, thus:

(*a*) The greater the number of cases in which a thing of the sort A has been found associated with a thing of the sort B, the more probable it is (if no cases of failure of association are known) that A is always associated with B;

(*b*) Under the same circumstances, a sufficient number of cases of the association of A with B will make it nearly certain that A is always associated with B, and will make this general law approach certainty without limit.

It should be noted that probability is always relative to certain data. In our case, the data are merely the known cases of coexistence of A and B. There may be other data, which *might* be taken into account, which would gravely alter the probability. For example, a man who had seen a great many white swans might argue, by our principle, that on the data it was *probable* that all swans were white, and this might be a perfectly sound argument. The argument is not disproved by the fact that some swans are black, because a thing may very well happen in spite of the fact that some data render it improbable. In the case of the swans, a man might know that colour is a very variable characteristic in many species of animals, and that, therefore, an induction as to colour is peculiarly liable to error. But this knowledge would be a fresh datum, by no means proving that the probability relative to our previous data had been wrongly estimated. The fact, therefore, that things often fail to fulfill our expectations is no evidence that our expectations will not *probably* be fulfilled in a given case or a given class of cases. Thus our inductive principle is at any rate not capable of being *disproved* by an appeal to experience.

The inductive principle, however, is equally incapable of being *proved* by an appeal to experience. Experience might conceivably confirm the inductive principle as regards the cases that have been already examined; but as regards unexamined cases, it is the inductive principle alone that can justify any inference from what has been examined to what has not been examined. All arguments which, on the basis of experience, argue as to the future or the unexperienced parts of the past or present, assume the inductive principle; hence we can never use experience to prove the inductive principle without begging the question. Thus we must either accept the inductive principle on the ground of its intrinsic evidence, or forgo all justification of our expectations about the future. If the principle is unsound, we have no reason to expect the sun to rise to-morrow, to expect bread to be more nourishing than a stone, or to expect that if we throw ourselves off the roof we shall fall. When we see what looks like our best friend approaching us, we shall have no reason to suppose that his body is not inhabited by the mind of our worst enemy or of some total stranger. All our conduct is based upon associations which have worked in the past, and which we therefore regard as likely to work in the future; and this likelihood is dependent for its validity upon the inductive principle.

The general principles of science, such as the belief in the reign of law, and the belief that every event must have a cause, are as completely dependent upon the inductive principle as are the beliefs of daily life. All such general principles are believed because mankind have found innumerable instances of their truth and no instances of their falsehood. But this affords no evidence for their truth in the future, unless the inductive principle is assumed.

Thus all knowledge which, on a basis of experience tells us something about what is not experienced, is based upon a belief which experience can neither confirm nor confute, yet which, at least in its more concrete applications, appears to be as firmly rooted in us as many of the facts of experience. The existence and justification of such beliefs—for the inductive principle . . . is not the only example—raises some of the most difficult and most debated problems of philosophy. . . .

The Fixation of Belief and How to Make Our Ideas Clear

CHARLES SANDERS PEIRCE

American philosopher Charles Sanders Peirce (1839–1914) founded the influential movement known as pragmatism. He was born in Cambridge, Massachusetts, and worked for the U.S. Coast and Geodetic Survey.

The Fixation of Belief

We generally know when we wish to ask a question and when we wish to pronounce a judgment, for there is a dissimilarity between the sensation of doubting and that of believing.

But this is not all which distinguishes doubt from belief. There is a practical difference. Our beliefs guide our desires and shape our actions. The Assassins, or followers of the Old Man of the Mountain, used to rush into death at his least command, because they believed that obedience to him would insure everlasting felicity. Had they doubted this, they would not have acted as they did. So it is with every belief, according to its degree. The feeling of believing is a more or less sure indication of there being established in our nature some habit which will determine our actions. Doubt never has such an effect.

Nor must we overlook a third point of difference. Doubt is an uneasy and dissatisfied state from which we struggle to free ourselves and pass into the state of belief; while the latter is a calm and satisfactory state which we do not wish to avoid, or to change to a belief in anything else. On the contrary, we cling tenaciously, not merely to believing, but to believing just what we do believe.

Thus, both doubt and belief have positive effects upon us, though very different ones. Belief does not make us act at once, but puts us into such a condition that we shall behave in a certain way, when the

"The Fixation of Belief," *Popular Science Monthly,* (November, 1877); "Some Consequences of Four Incapacities," *Journal of Speculative Philosophy* (1868).

occasion arises. Doubt has not the least effect of this sort, but stimulates us to action until it is destroyed. This reminds us of the irritation of a nerve and the reflex action produced thereby; while for the analogue of belief, in the nervous system, we must look to what are called nervous associations—for example, to that habit of the nerves in consequence of which the smell of a peach will make the mouth water.

The irritation of doubt causes a struggle to attain a state of belief. I shall term this struggle *inquiry,* though it must be admitted that this is sometimes not a very apt designation.

The irritation of doubt is the only immediate motive for the struggle to attain belief. It is certainly best for us that our beliefs should be such as may truly guide our actions so as to satisfy our desires; and this reflection will make us reject any belief which does not seem to have been so formed as to insure this result. But it will only do so by creating a doubt in the place of that belief. With the doubt, therefore, the struggle begins, and with the cessation of doubt it ends. Hence, the sole object of inquiry is the settlement of opinion. We may fancy that this is not enough for us, and that we seek not merely an opinion, but a true opinion. But put this fancy to the test, and it proves groundless; for as soon as a firm belief is reached we are entirely satisfied, whether the belief be false or true. And it is clear that nothing out of the sphere of our knowledge can be our object, for nothing which does not affect the mind can be a motive for a mental effort. The most that can be maintained is, that we seek for a belief that we shall *think* to be true. But we think each one of our beliefs to be true, and, indeed, it is mere tautology to say so.

That the settlement of opinion is the sole end of inquiry is a very important proposition. It sweeps away, at once, various vague and erroneous conceptions of proof. A few of these may be noticed here.

1. Some philosophers have imagined that to start an inquiry it was only necessary to utter a question or set it down on paper, and have even recommended us to begin our studies with questioning everything! But the mere putting of a proposition into the interrogative form does not stimulate the mind to any struggle after belief. There must be a real and living doubt, and without this all discussion is idle.

2. It is a very common idea that a demonstration must rest on some ultimate and absolutely indubitable propositions. These, according to one school, are first principles of a general nature; according to another, are first sensations. But in point of fact, an inquiry, to have that completely satisfactory result called demonstration, has only to start with propositions perfectly free from all actual doubt. If the premises are not in fact doubted at all, they cannot be more satisfactory than they are.

3. Some people seem to love to argue a point after all the world is fully convinced of it. But no further advance can be made. When doubt ceases, mental action on the subject comes to an end; and, if it did go on, it would be without a purpose.

1. THE METHOD OF TENACITY

If the settlement of opinion is the sole object of inquiry, and if belief is of the nature of a habit, why should we not attain the desired end by taking any answer to a question which we may fancy and constantly reiterating it to ourselves, dwelling on all which may conduce to that belief and learning to turn with contempt and hatred from anything which might disturb it? This simple and direct method is really pursued by many men. I remember once being entreated not to read a certain newspaper lest it might change my opinion upon free trade. "Lest I might be entrapped by its fallacies and misstatements," was the form of expression. "You are not," my friend said, "a special student of political economy. You might, therefore, easily be deceived by fallacious arguments upon the subject. You might, then, if you read this paper, be led to believe in protection. But you admit that free trade is the true doctrine; and you do not wish to believe what is not true." I have often known this system to be deliberately adopted. Still oftener, the instinctive dislike of an undecided state of mind, exaggerated into a vague dread of doubt, makes men cling spasmodically to the views they have already taken. The man feels that, if he only holds to his belief without wavering, it will be entirely satisfactory. Nor can it be denied that a steady and immovable faith yields great peace of mind. It may, indeed, give rise to inconveniences, as if a man should resolutely continue to believe that fire would not burn him, or that he would be eternally damned if he received his *ingesta* otherwise than through a stomach pump. But then the man who adopts this method will not allow that its inconveniences are greater than its advantages. He will say, "I hold steadfastly to the truth and the truth is always wholesome." And in many cases it may very well be that the pleasure he derives from his calm faith overbalances any inconveniences resulting from its deceptive character. Thus, if it be true that death is annihilation, then the man who believes that he will certainly go straight to heaven when he dies, provided he has fulfilled certain simple observances in this life, has a cheap pleasure which will not be followed by the least disappointment. A similar consideration seems to have weight with many persons in religious topics, for we frequently hear it said, "Oh, I could not believe so-and-so, because I should be wretched if I did." When an ostrich buries its head in the sand as danger approaches, it very likely takes the happiest course. It hides the danger, and then calmly says there is no danger; and, if it feels perfectly sure there is none, why should it raise its head to see? A man may go through life systematically keeping out of view all that might cause a change in his opinions, and if he only succeeds—basing his method, as he does, on two fundamental psychological laws—I do not see what can be said against his doing so. It would be an egotistical impertinence to object that his procedure is irrational, for that only amounts to saying that his method of settling belief is not ours. He does not propose to himself to be rational, and indeed, will often talk with scorn of man's weak and illusive reason. So let him think as he pleases.

But this method of fixing belief, which may be called the method of tenacity, will be unable to hold its ground in practice. The social impulse is against it. The man who adopts it will find that other men think differently from him, and it will be apt to occur to him in some saner moment that their opinions are quite as good as his own, and this will shake his confidence in belief. This conception, that another man's thought or sentiment may be equivalent to one's own, is a distinctly new step, and a highly important one. It arises from an impulse too strong in man to be suppressed without danger of destroying the human species. Unless we make ourselves hermits, we shall necessarily influence each other's opinions; so that the problem becomes how to fix belief, not in the individual merely, but in the community.

2. THE METHOD OF AUTHORITY

Let the will of the state act, then, instead of that of the individual. Let an institution be created which shall have for its object to keep correct doctrines before the attention of the people, to reiterate them perpetually, and to teach them to the young; having at the same time power to prevent contrary doctrines from being taught, advocated, or expressed. Let all possible causes of a change of mind be removed from men's apprehensions. Let them be kept ignorant, lest they should learn of some reason to think otherwise than they do. Let their passions be enlisted, so that they may regard private and unusual opinions with hatred and horror. Then let all men who reject the established belief be terrified into silence. Let the people turn out and tar-and-feather such men, or let inquisitions be made into the manner of thinking of suspected persons, and, when they are found guilty of forbidden beliefs, let them be subjected to some signal punishment. When complete agreement could not otherwise be reached, a general massacre of all who have not thought in a certain way has proved a very effective means of settling opinions in a country. If the power to do this be wanting, let a list of opinions be drawn up, to which no man of the least independence of thought can assent, and let the faithful be required to accept all these propositions, in order to segregate them as radically as possible from the influence of the rest of the world.

This method has, from the earliest times, been one of the chief means of upholding correct theological and political doctrines, and of preserving their universal or catholic character. In Rome, especially, it has been practiced from the days of Numa Pompilius to those of Pius Nonus. This is the most perfect example in history; but wherever there is a priesthood—and no religion has been without one—this method has been more or less made use of. Wherever there is an aristocracy, or a guild, or any association of a class of men whose interests depend or are supposed to depend on certain propositions, there will inevitably be found some traces of this natural product of social feeling. Cruelties always accompany this system; and when it is consistently carried out, they become atrocities of the most horrible kind in the eyes of any rational man. Nor should this occasion surprise, for the officer of a society does not feel justified in surrendering the interests of that society for the sake of mercy, as he might his own private interests. It is natural, therefore, that sympathy and fellowship should thus produce a most ruthless power.

In judging this method of fixing belief, which may be called the method of authority, we must, in the first place, allow its immeasurable mental and moral superiority to the method of tenacity. Its success is proportionally greater; and in fact it has over and over again worked the most majestic results. The mere structures of stone which it has caused to be put together in Siam, for example, in Egypt, and in Europe—have many of them a sublimity hardly more than rivaled by the greatest works of Nature. And, except the geological epochs, there are no periods of time so vast as those which are measured by some of these organized faiths. If we scrutinize the matter closely, we shall find that there has not been one of their creeds which has remained always the same; yet the change is so slow as to be imperceptible during one person's life, so that individual belief remains sensibly fixed. For the mass of mankind, then, there is perhaps no better method than this. If it is their highest impulse to be intellectual slaves, then slaves they ought to remain.

3. THE A PRIORI METHOD

But no institution can undertake to regulate opinions upon every subject. Only the most important ones can be attended to, and on the rest men's minds must be left to the action of natural causes. This imperfection will be no source of weakness so long as men are in such a state of culture that one opinion does not influence another—that is, so long as they cannot put two and two together. But in

the most priest-ridden states some individuals will be found who are raised above that condition. These men possess a wider sort of social feeling; they see that men in other countries and in other ages have held to very different doctrines from those which they themselves have been brought up to believe; and they cannot help seeing that it is the mere accident of their having been taught as they have, and of their having been surrounded with the manners and associations they have, that has caused them to believe as they do and not far differently. And their candor cannot resist the reflection that there is no reason to rate their own views at a higher value than those of other nations and other centuries; and this gives rise to doubts in their minds.

They will further perceive that such doubts as these must exist in their minds with reference to every belief which seems to be determined by the caprice either of themselves or of those who originated the popular opinions. The willful adherence to a belief, and the arbitrary forcing of it upon others, must, therefore, both be given up and a new method of settling opinions must be adopted, which shall not only produce an impulse to believe, but shall also decide what proposition it is which is to be believed. Let the action of natural preferences be unimpeded, then, and under their influence let men conversing together and regarding matters in different lights gradually develop beliefs in harmony with natural causes. This method resembles that by which conceptions of art have been brought to maturity. The most perfect example of it is to be found in the history of metaphysical philosophy. Systems of this sort have not usually rested upon observed facts, at least not in any great degree. They have been chiefly adopted because their fundamental propositions seemed "agreeable to reason." This is an apt expression; it does not mean that which agrees with experience, but that which we find ourselves inclined to believe. Plato, for example, finds it agreeable to reason that the distances of the celestial spheres from one another should be proportional to the different lengths of strings which produce harmonious chords. Many philosophers have been led to their main conclusions by considerations like this; but this is the lowest and least developed form which the method takes, for it is clear that another man might find Kepler's (earlier) theory, that the celestial spheres are proportional to the inscribed and circumscribed spheres of the different regular solids, more agreeable to *his* reason. But the shock of opinions will soon lead men to rest on preferences of a far more universal nature. Take, for example, the doctrine that man only acts selfishly—that is, from the consideration that acting in one way will afford him more pleasure than acting in another. This rests on no fact in the world, but it has had a wide acceptance as being the only reasonable theory.

This method is far more intellectual and respectable from the point of view of reason than either of the others which we have noticed. But its failure has been the most manifest. It makes of inquiry something similar to the development of taste; but taste, unfortunately, is always more or less a matter of fashion, and accordingly metaphysicians have never come to any fixed agreement, but the pendulum has swung backward and forward between a more material and a more spiritual philosophy, from the earliest times to the latest. And so from this, which has been called the *a priori* method, we are driven, in Lord Bacon's phrase, to a true induction. We have examined into this *a priori* method as something which promised to deliver our opinions from their accidental and capricious element. But development, while it is a process which eliminated the effect of some casual circumstances, only magnifies that of others. This method, therefore, does not differ in a very essential way from that of authority. The government may not have lifted its finger to influence my convictions; I may have been left outwardly quite free to choose, we will say, between monogamy and polygamy, and appealing to my conscience only, I may have concluded that the latter practice is in itself licentious. But when I come to see that the chief obstacle to the spread of Christianity among a people of as high culture as the Hindus has been a conviction of the immorality of our way of treating women, I cannot help seeing that, though governments do not interfere, sentiments in their development will be very greatly determined by accidental causes. Now, there are some people, among whom I must suppose that my reader is to be found, who, when they see that any belief of theirs is determined by any circumstance extraneous to the facts, will from that moment not merely admit in words that the belief is doubtful, but will experience a real doubt of it, so that it ceases to be a belief.

4. THE METHOD OF SCIENCE

To satisfy our doubts, therefore, it is necessary that a method should be found by which our beliefs may be caused by nothing human, but by some external permanency—by something upon which our thinking has no effect. Some mystics imagine that they have such a method in a private inspiration from on high. But that is only a form of the method of tenacity, in which the conception of truth as something public is not yet developed. Our external permanency would not be external, in our sense, if it was restricted in its influence to one individual. It must be something which affects, or might affect, every man. And, though these affections are necessarily as various as are individual conditions, yet the method must be such that the ultimate conclusion of every man shall be the same. Such is the method of science. Its fundamental hypothesis, restated in more familiar language, is this: There are real things, whose characters are entirely independent of our opinions about them; those realities affect our senses according to regular laws, and, though our sensations are as different as our relations to the objects, yet, by taking advantage of the laws of perception, we can ascertain by reasoning how things really are, and any man, if he has sufficient experience and reason enough about it, will be led to the one true conclusion. The new conception here involved is that of reality. It may be asked how I know that there are any realities. If this hypothesis is the sole support of my method of inquiry, my method of inquiry must not be used to support my hypothesis. The reply is this: (1) If investigation cannot be regarded as proving that there are real things, it at least does not lead to a contrary conclusion; but the method and the conception on which it is based remain ever in harmony. No doubts of the method, therefore, necessarily arise from its practice, as is the case with all the others. (2) The feeling which gives rise to any method of fixing belief is a dissatisfaction at two repugnant propositions. But here already is a vague concession that there is some *one* thing to which a proposition should conform. Nobody, therefore, can really doubt that there are realities, or, if he did doubt would not be a source of dissatisfaction. The hypothesis, therefore, is one which every mind admits. So the social impulse does not cause me to doubt it. (3) Everybody uses the scientific method about a great many things, and only ceases to use it when he does not know how to apply it. (4) Experience of the method has not led me to doubt it, but, on the contrary, scientific investigation has had the most wonderful triumphs in the way of settling opinion. These afford the explanation of my not doubting the method or the hypothesis which it supposes; and not having any doubt, nor believing that anybody else whom I could influence has, it would be the merest babble for me to say more about it. If there be anybody with a living doubt upon the subject, let him consider it. . . .

At present I have only room to notice some points of contrast between the method of scientific investigation and other methods of fixing belief.

This is the only one of the four methods which presents any distinction of a right and a wrong way. If I adopt the method of tenacity and shut myself out from all influences, whatever I think necessary to doing this is necessary according to that method. So with the method of authority: The state may try to put down heresy by means which, from a scientific point of view, seem very ill-calculated to accomplish its purposes; but the only test *on that method* is what the state thinks, so that it cannot pursue the method wrongly. So with the *a priori* method. The very essence of it is to think as one is inclined to think. . . . But with the scientific method the case is different. I may start with known and observed facts to proceed to the unknown; and yet the rules which I follow in doing so may not be such as investigation would approve. The test of whether I am truly following the method is not an immediate appeal to my feelings and purposes, but, on the contrary, itself involves the application of the method. Hence it is that bad reasoning as well as good reasoning is possible; and this fact is the foundation of the practical side of logic. . . .

How to Make Our Ideas Clear

Descartes is the father of modern philosophy, and the spirit of Cartesianism—that which principally distinguishes it from the scholasticism which it displaced—may be compendiously stated as follows:

1. It teaches that philosophy must begin with universal doubt; whereas scholasticism had never questioned fundamentals.
2. It teaches that the ultimate test of certainty is to be found in the individual consciousness; whereas scholasticism had rested on the testimony of sages and of the Catholic Church.
3. The multiform argumentation of the middle ages is replaced by a single thread of inference depending often upon inconspicuous premises.
4. Scholasticism had its mysteries of faith, but undertook to explain all created things. But there are many facts which Cartesianism not only does not explain, but renders absolutely inexplicable, unless to say that "God makes them so" is to be regarded as an explanation.

In some, or all of these respects, most modern philosophers have been, in effect, Cartesians. Now without wishing to return to scholasticism, it seems to me that modern science and modern logic require us to stand upon a very different platform from this.

1. We cannot begin with complete doubt. We must begin with all the prejudices which we actually have when we enter upon the study of philosophy. These prejudices are not to be dispelled by a maxim, for they are things which it does not occur to us *can* be questioned. Hence this initial scepticism will be a mere self-deception, and not real doubt; and no one who follows the Cartesian method will ever be satisfied until he has formally recovered all those beliefs which in form he has given up. It is, therefore, as useless a preliminary as going to the North Pole would be in order to get to Constantinople by coming down regularly upon a meridian. A person may, it is true, in the course of his studies, find reason to doubt what he began by believing; but in that case he doubts because he has a positive reason for it, and not on account of the Cartesian maxim. Let us not pretend to doubt in philosophy what we do not doubt in our hearts.

2. The same formalism appears in the Cartesian criterion, which amounts to this: "Whatever I am clearly convinced of, is true." If I were really convinced, I should have done with reasoning, and should require no test of certainty. But thus to make single individuals absolute judges of truth is most pernicious. The result is that metaphysicians will all agree that metaphysics has reached a pitch of certainty far beyond that of the physical sciences;— only they can agree upon nothing else. In sciences in which men come to agreement, when a theory has been broached, it is considered to be on probation until this agreement is reached. After it is reached, the question of certainty becomes an idle one, because there is no one left who doubts it. We individually cannot reasonably hope to attain the ultimate philosophy which we pursue; we can only seek it, therefore, for the *community* of philosophers. Hence, if disciplined and candid minds carefully examine a theory and refuse to accept it, this ought to create doubts in the mind of the author of the theory himself.

3. Philosophy ought to imitate the successful sciences in its methods, so far as to proceed only from tangible premises which can be subjected to careful scrutiny, and to trust rather to the multitude and variety of its arguments than to the conclusiveness of any one. Its reasoning should not form a chain which is no stronger than its weakest link, but a cable whose fibres may be ever so slender, provided they are sufficiently numerous and intimately connected.

4. Every unidealistic philosophy supposes some absolutely inexplicable, unanalyzable ultimate; in short, something resulting from mediation itself not susceptible of mediation. Now that anything *is* thus inexplicable can only be known by reasoning from signs. But the only justification of an inference from signs is that the conclusion explains the fact. To suppose the fact absolutely inexplicable, is not to explain it, and hence this supposition is never allowable. . . .

How to Defend Society Against Science

PAUL FEYERABEND

Philosopher of science Paul Feyerabend (1924–1994) was born in Austria and taught at the University of California, Berkeley, and the Federal Institute of Technology at Zurich.

FAIRYTALES

I want to defend society and its inhabitants from all ideologies, science included. All ideologies must be seen in perspective. One must not take them too seriously. One must read them like fairytales which have lots of interesting things to say but which also contain wicked lies, or like ethical prescriptions which may be useful rules of thumb but which are deadly when followed to the letter.

From "How to Defend Society Against Science," *Radical Philosophy* 2 (1975): 4–8. Reprinted by permission of the author and the publisher.

Now—is this not a strange and ridiculous attitude? Science, surely, was always in the forefront of the fight against authoritarianism and superstition. It is to science that we owe our increased intellectual freedom vis-à-vis religious beliefs; it is to science that we owe the liberation of mankind from ancient and rigid forms of thought. Today these forms of thought are nothing but bad dreams—and this we learned from science. Science and enlightenment are one and the same thing—even the most radical critics of society believe this. Kropotkin wants to overthrow all traditional institutions and forms of belief, with the exception of science. Ibsen criticises the most intimate ramifications of nineteenth century bourgeois ideology, but he leaves science untouched. Levi-Strauss has made us realise that Western Thought is not the lonely peak of human achievement it was once believed to be, but he excludes science from his relativization of plays in education. Scientific "facts" are taught at a very early age and in the very same manner in which religious "facts" were taught only a century ago. There is no attempt to waken the critical abilities of the pupil so that he may be able to see things in perspective. At the universities the situation is even worse, for indoctrination is here carried out in a much more systematic manner. Criticism is not entirely absent. Society, for example, and its institutions, are criticised most severely and often most unfairly and this already at the elementary school level. But science is excepted from the criticism. In society at large the judgement of bishops and cardinals was accepted not too long ago. The move towards "demythologization," for example, is largely motivated by the wish to avoid any clash between Christianity and scientific ideas. If such a clash occurs, then science is certainly right and Christianity wrong. Pursue this investigation further and you will see that science has now become as oppressive as the ideologies it had once to fight. Do not be misled by the fact that today hardly anyone gets killed for joining a scientific heresy. This has nothing to do with science. It has something to do with the general quality of our civilization. Heretics in science are still made to suffer from the *most severe* sanctions this relatively tolerant civilization has to offer.

But—is this description not utterly unfair? Have I not presented the matter is a very distorted light by using tendentious and distorting terminology? Must we not describe the situation in a very different way? I have said that science has become *rigid,* that it has ceased to be an instrument of *change* and *liberation* without adding that it has found the *truth,* or a large part thereof. Considering this additional fact we realise, so the objection goes, that the rigidity of science is not due to human willfulness. It lies in the nature of things. For once we have discovered the truth—what else can we do but follow it?

This trite reply is anything but original. It is used whenever an ideology wants to reinforce the faith of its followers. "Truth" is such a nicely neutral word. Nobody would deny that it is commendable to speak the truth and wicked to tell lies. Nobody would deny that—and yet nobody knows what such an attitude amounts to. So it is easy to twist matters and to change allegiance to truth in one's everyday affairs into allegiance to the Truth of ideology which is nothing but the dogmatic defence of that ideology. And it is of course *not* true that we *have* to follow the truth. Human life is guided by many ideas. Truth is one of them. Freedom and mental independence are others. If Truth, as conceived by some ideologists, conflicts with freedom then we have a *choice.* We may abandon freedom. But we may also abandon Truth. (Alternatively, we may adopt a more sophisticated idea of truth that no longer contradicts freedom; that was Hegel's solution.) My criticism of modern science is that it inhibits freedom of thought. If the reason is that it has found the truth and now follows it then I would say that there are better things than first finding, and then following such a monster.

This finishes the general part of my explanation.

There exists a more specific argument to defend the exceptional position science has in society today. Put in a nutshell the argument says (1) that science has finally found the correct *method* for achieving results and (2) that there are many *results* to prove the excellence of the method. The argument is mistaken—but most attempts to show this lead into a dead end. Methodology has by now become so crowded with empty sophistication that it is extremely difficult to perceive the simple errors at the basis. It is like fighting the hydra—cut off one ugly head, and eight formalizations take its place. In this situation the only answer is superficiality: when sophistication loses content then the only way of keeping in touch with reality is to be crude and superficial. This is what I intend to be.

AGAINST METHOD

There is a method, says part (1) of the argument. What is it? How does it work?

One answer which is no longer as popular as it used to be is that science works by collecting facts and inferring theories from them. The answer is unsatisfactory as theories never *follow* from facts in the strict logical sense. To say that they may yet be *supported* by facts assumes a notion of support that (a) does not show this defect and is (b) sufficiently sophisticated to permit us to say to what extent, say, the theory of relativity is supported by the facts. No such notion exists today nor is it likely that it will be found (one of the problems is that we need a notion of support in which grey ravens can be said to support "All Ravens are Black"). This was realised by conventionalists and transcendental idealists who pointed out that theories *shape* and *order* facts and can therefore be retained come what may. They can be retained because the human mind either consciously or unconsciously carried out its ordering function. The trouble with these views is that they assume for the mind what they want to explain for the world, viz, that it works in a regular fashion. There is only one view which overcomes all these difficulties. It was invented twice in the nineteenth century, by Mill, in his immortal essay *On Liberty,* and by some Darwinists who extended Darwinism to the battle of ideas. This view takes the bull by the horns: theories cannot be justified and their excellence cannot be shown without reference to other theories. We may explain the *success* of a theory by reference to a more comprehensive theory (we explain the success of Newton's theory by using the general theory of relativity); and we may explain our *preference* for it by comparing it with other theories. Such a comparison does not establish the intrinsic excellence of the theory we have chosen. As a matter of fact, the theory we have chosen may be pretty lousy. It may contain contradictions, it may conflict with well-known facts, it may be cumbersome, unclear, ad hoc in decisive places and so on. But it may still be better than any other theory that is available at the time. It may in fact be the best lousy theory there is. Nor are the standards of judgement chosen in an absolute manner. Our sophistication increases with every choice we make, and so do our standards. Standards compete just as theories compete and we choose the standards most appropriate to the historical situation in which the choice occurs. The rejected alternatives (theories; standards; "facts") are not eliminated. They serve as correctives (after all, we may have made the wrong choice) and they also explain the content of the preferred views (we understand relativity better when we understand the structure of its competitors; we know the full meaning of freedom only when we have an idea of life in a totalitarian state, of its advantages—and there are many advantages—as well as of its disadvantages). Knowledge so conceived is an ocean of alternatives channelled and subdivided by an ocean of standards. It forces our mind to make imaginative choices and thus makes it grow. It makes our mind capable of choosing, imagining, criticising.

Today this view is often connected with the name of Karl Popper. But there are some very decisive differences between Popper and Mill. To start with, Popper developed his view to solve a special problem of epistemology—he wanted to solve "Hume's problem." Mill, on the other hand, is interested in conditions favourable to human growth. His epistemology is the result of a certain theory of man, and not the other way around. Also Popper, being influenced by the Vienna Circle, improves on the logical form of a theory before discussing it while Mill uses every theory in the form in which it occurs in science. Thirdly, Popper's standards of comparison are rigid and fixed while Mill's standards are permitted to change with the historical situation. Finally, Popper's standards eliminate competitors once and for all: theories that are either not falsifiable, or falsifiable and falsified have no place in science. Popper's criteria are clear, unambiguous, precisely formulated: Mill's criteria are not. This would be an advantage if science itself were clear, unambiguous, and precisely formulated. Fortunately, it is not.

To start with, no new and revolutionary scientific theory is ever formulated in a manner that permits us to say under what circumstances we must regard it as endangered: many revolutionary theories are unfalsifiable. Falsifiable versions do exist, but they are hardly ever in agreement with accepted basic statements: every moderately interesting theory is falsified. Moreover, theories have formal flaws, many of them contain contradictions, ad hoc adjustments, and so on and so forth. Applied resolutely, Popperian criteria would eliminate science without replacing it by anything comparable. They are useless as an aid to science.

In the past decade this has been realised by various thinkers, Kuhn and Lakatos among them.

Kuhn's ideas are interesting but, alas, they are much too vague to give rise to anything but lots of hot air. If you don't believe me, look at the literature. Never before has the literature on the philosophy of science been invaded by so many creeps and incompetents. Kuhn encourages people who have no idea why a stone falls to the ground to talk with assurance about scientific method. Now I have no objection to incompetence but I do object when incompetence is accompanied by boredom and self-righteousness. And this is exactly what happens. We do not get interesting false ideas, we get boring ideas or words connected with no ideas at all. Secondly, wherever one tries to make Kuhn's ideas more definite one finds that they are *false*. Was there ever a period of normal science in the history of thought? No—and I challenge anyone to prove the contrary.

Lakatos is immeasurably more sophisticated than Kuhn. Instead of theories he considers research programmes which are sequences of theories connected by methods of modification, so-called heuristics. Each theory in the sequence may be full of faults. It may be beset by anomalies, contradictions, ambiguities. What counts is not the shape of the single theories, but the tendency exhibited by the sequence. We judge historical developments, achievements over a period of time, rather than the situation at a particular time. History and methodology are combined into a single enterprise. A research programme is said to progress if the sequence of theories leads to novel predictions. It is said to degenerate if it is reduced to absorbing facts that have been discovered without its help. A decisive feature of Lakatos's methodology is that such evaluations are no longer tied to methodological rules which tell the scientist to either retain or to abandon a research programme. Scientists may stick to a degenerating programme, they may even succeed in making the programme overtake its rivals and they therefore proceed rationally with whatever they are doing (provided they continue calling degenerating programmes degenerating and progressive programmes progressive). This means that Lakatos offers *words* which *sound* like the elements of a methodology; he does not offer a methodology. This is no method according to the most advanced and sophisticated methodology in existence today. This finishes my reply to part (1) of the specific argument.

AGAINST RESULTS

According to part (2), science deserves a special position because it has produced *results*. This is an argument only if it can be taken for granted that nothing else has ever produced results. Now it may be admitted that almost everyone who discusses the matter makes such an assumption. It may also be admitted that it is not easy to show that the assumption is false. Forms of life different from science have either disappeared or have degenerated to an extent that makes a fair comparison impossible. Still, the situation is not as hopeless as it was only a decade ago. We have become acquainted with methods of medical diagnosis and therapy which are effective (and perhaps even more effective than the corresponding parts of Western medicine) and which are yet based on an ideology that is radically different from the ideology of Western science. We have learned that there are phenomena such as telepathy and telekinesis which are obliterated by a scientific approach and which could be used to do research in an entirely novel way (earlier thinkers such as Agrippa of Nettesheim, John Dee, and even Bacon were aware of these phenomena). And then—is it not the case that the Church saved souls while science often does the very opposite? Of course, nobody now believes in the ontology that underlies this judgement. Why? Because of ideological pressures identical with those which today make us listen to science to the exclusion of everything else. It is also true that phenomena such as telekinesis and acupuncture may eventually be absorbed into the body of science and may therefore be called "scientific." But note that this happens only *after* a long period of resistance during which a science *not yet* containing the phenomena wants to get the upper hand over forms of life that contain them. And this leads to a future objection against part (2) of the specific argument. The fact that science has results counts in its favour only if these results were achieved by science alone, and without any outside help. A look at history shows that science hardly ever gets its results in this way. When Copernicus introduced a new view of the universe, he did not consult *scientific* predecessors, he consulted a crazy Pythagorean such as Philolaos. He adopted his ideas and he maintained them in the face of all sound rules of scientific method. Mechanics and optics owe a lot to artisans, medicine to midwives and witches. And in our own day we have seen how the interference of the state can advance science: when the Chinese Communists refused to be intimidated by the judgement of experts and ordered traditional medicine back into universities and hospitals there was an outcry all over the world that science would now be ruined in China. The very opposite occurred: Chinese science advanced and Western science learned from it. Whenever we look we see that great scientific advances are due to outside interference which is made to prevail in the face of the most basic and most "rational" methodological rules. The lesson is plain: there does not exist a single argument that could be used to support the exceptional role which science today plays in society. Science has done many things, but so have other ideologies. Science often proceeds systematically, but so do other ideologies (just consult the records of the many doctrinal debates that took place in the Church) and, besides, there are no overriding rules which are adhered to under any circumstances: there is no "scientific methodology" that can be used to separate science from the rest. *Science is just one of the many ideologies that propel society and it should be treated as such* (this statement applies even to the most progressive and most dialectical sections of science). What consequences can we draw from this result?

The most important consequence is that there must be a *formal separation between state and science* just as there is now a formal separation between state and church. Science may influence society but only to the extent to which any political or other pressure group is permitted to influence society. Scientists may be consulted on important projects but the final judgement must be left to the democratically elected consulting bodies. These bodies will consist mainly of laymen. Will the laymen be able to come to a correct judgement? Most certainly, for the competence, the complications and the successes of science are vastly exaggerated. One of the most exhilarating experiences is to see how a lawyer, who is a layman, can find holes in the testimony, the technical testimony of the most advanced expert and thus prepare the jury for its verdict. Science is not a closed book that is understood only after years of training. It is an intellectual discipline that can be

examined and criticised by anyone who is interested and that looks difficult and profound only because of a systematic campaign of obfuscation carried out by many scientists (though, I am happy to say, not by all). Organs of the state should never hesitate to reject the judgement of scientists when they have reason for doing so. Such rejection will educate the general public, will make it more confident and it may even lead to improvement. Considering the sizeable chauvinism of the scientific establishment we can say: the more Lysenko affairs the better (it is not the *interference* of the state that is objectionable in the case of Lysenko, but the *totalitarian* interference which kills the opponent rather than just neglecting his advice). Three cheers to the fundamentalists in California who succeeded in having a dogmatic formulation of the theory of evolution removed from the text books and an account of Genesis included (but I know that they would become as chauvinistic and totalitarian as scientists are today when given the chance to run society all by themselves. Ideologies are marvelous when used in the company of other ideologies. They become boring and doctrinaire as soon as their merits lead to the removal of their opponents). The most important change, however, will have to occur in the field of *education.*

EDUCATION AND MYTH

The purpose of education, so one would think, is to introduce the young into life, and that means: into the *society* where they are born and into the *physical universe* that surrounds the society. The method of education often consists in the teaching of some *basic myth*. The myth is available in various versions. More advanced versions may be taught by initiation rites which firmly implant them into the mind. Knowing the myth the grown-up can explain almost everything (or else he can turn to experts for more detailed information). he is the master of Nature and of Society. He understands them both and he knows how to interact with them. However, *he is not the master of the myth that guides his understanding.*

Such further mastery was aimed at, and was partly achieved, by the Pre-Socratics. The Pre-Socratics not only tried to understand the *world.*

They also tried to understand, and thus to become the masters of, the *means of understanding the world.* Instead of being content with a single myth they developed many and so diminished the power which a well-told story has over the minds of men. The Sophists introduced still further methods for reducing the debilitating effect of interesting, coherent, "empirically adequate" etc. etc. tales. The achievements of these thinkers were not appreciated and they certainly are not understood today. When teaching a myth we want to increase the chance that it will be understood (i.e. no puzzlement about any feature of the myth), believed, *and accepted.* This does not do any harm when the myth is counterbalanced by other myths: even the most dedicated (i.e. totalitarian) instructor in a certain version of Christianity cannot prevent his pupils from getting in touch with Buddhists, Jews and other disreputable people. It is very different in the case of science, or of rationalism where the field is almost completely dominated by the believers. In this case it is of paramount importance to strengthen the minds of the young and "strengthening the minds of the young" means strengthening them *against* any easy acceptance of comprehensive views. What we need here is an education that makes people *contrary, countersuggestive without* making them incapable of devoting themselves to the elaboration of any single view. How can this aim be achieved?

It can be achieved by protecting the tremendous imagination which children possess and by developing to the full the spirit of contradiction that exists in them. On the whole children are much more intelligent than their teachers. They succumb, and give up their intelligence because they are bullied, or because their teachers get the better of them by emotional means. Children can learn, understand, and keep separate two to three different languages ("children" and by this I mean 3 to 5 years old, NOT eight years old who were experimented upon quite recently and did not come out too well: why? because they were already loused up by incompetent teaching at an earlier age). Of course, the languages must be introduced in a more interesting way than is usually done. There are marvellous writers in all languages who have told marvellous stories—let us begin our language teaching with *them* and not with "der Hund hat einen Schwanz" and similar inanities.

Using stories we may of course also introduce "scientific" accounts, say, of the origin of the world and thus make the children acquainted with science as well. But science must not be given any special position except for pointing out that there are lots of people who believe in it. Later on the stories which have been told will be supplemented with "reasons" where by reasons I mean further accounts of the kind found in the tradition to which the story belongs. And, of course, there will also be contrary reasons. Both reasons and contrary reasons will be told by the experts in the fields and so the young generation becomes acquainted with all kinds of sermons and all types of wayfarers. It becomes acquainted with them, it becomes acquainted with their stories and every individual can make up his mind which way to go. By now everyone knows that you can earn a lot of money and respect and perhaps even a Nobel Prize by becoming a scientist, so, many will become scientists. They will *become* scientists *without having been taken in by the ideology of science,* they will *be* scientists *because they have made a free choice.* But has not much time been wasted on unscientific subjects and will this not detract from their competence once they have become scientists? Not at all! The progress of science, of good science, depends on novel ideas and on intellectual freedom; science has very often been advanced by outsiders (remember that Bohr and Einstein regarded themselves as outsiders). Will not many people make the wrong choice and end up in a dead end? Well, that depends on what you mean by a "dead end." Most scientists today are devoid of ideas, full of fear, intent on producing some paltry result so that they can add to the flood of inane papers that now constitutes "scientific progress" in many areas. And, besides, what is more important? To lead a life which one has chosen with open eyes, or to spend one's time in the nervous attempt of avoiding what some not so intelligent people call "dead ends"? Will not the number of scientists decrease so that in the end there is nobody to run our precious laboratories? I do not think so. Given a choice many people may chose science, for a science that is run by free agents looks much more attractive than the science of today which is run by slaves, slaves of institutions and slaves of "reason." And if there is a temporary shortage of scientists the situation may always be remedied by various kinds of incentives. Of course, scientists will not play any predominant role in the society I envisage. They will be more than balanced by magicians, or priests, or astrologers. Such a situation is unbearable for many people, old and young, right and left. Almost all of you have the firm belief that at least *some* kind of truth has been found, that it must be preserved, and that the method of teaching I advocate and the form of society I defend will dilute it and make it finally disappear. You have this firm belief; many of you may even have reasons. *But what you have to consider is that the absence of good contrary reasons is due to a historical accident;* it does *not* lie in the nature of things. Build up the kind of society I recommend and the views you now despise (without knowing them, to be sure) will return in such splendour that you will have to work hard to maintain your own position and will perhaps be entirely unable to do so. You do not believe me? Then look at history. Scientific astronomy was firmly founded on Ptolemy and Aristotle, two of the greatest minds in the history of Western Thought. Who upset their well-argued, empirically adequate and precisely formulated system? Philolaos the mad and antediluvian Pythagorean. How was it that Philolaos could stage a comeback: Because he found an able defender: Copernicus. Of course, you may follow your intuitions as I am following mine. But remember that your intuitions are the result of your "scientific" training where by science I also mean the science of Karl Marx. My training, or, rather, my non-training, is that of a journalist who is interested in strange and bizarre events. Finally, it is not utterly irresponsible, in the present world situation, with millions of people starving, others enslaved, downtrodden, in abject misery of body and mind, to think luxurious thoughts such as these? Is not freedom of choice a luxury under such circumstances; Is not the flippancy and the humour I want to see combined with the freedom of choice a luxury under such circumstances? Must we not give up all self-indulgence and *act*? Joint together, and *act*? That is the most important objection which today is raised against an approach such as the one recommended by me. It has tremendous appeal, it has the appeal of unselfish dedication. Unselfish dedication—to what? Let us see!

We are supposed to give up our selfish inclinations and dedicate ourselves to the liberation of the oppressed. And selfish inclinations are what? They are our wish for maximum liberty of thought in the society in which we live *now,* maximum liberty not only of an abstract kind, but expressed in appropriate institutions and methods of teaching. This wish for concrete intellectual and physical liberty in our own surroundings is to be put aside, for the time being. This assumes, first, that we do not need this liberty for our task. It assumes that we can carry out our task with a mind that is firmly closed to some alternatives. It assumes that the correct way of liberating others *has already been found* and that all that is needed is to carry it out. I am sorry, I cannot accept such doctrinaire self-assurance in such extremely important matters. Does this mean that we cannot act at all? It does not. But it means that *while acting we have to try to realise as much of the freedom I have recommended so that our actions may be corrected in the light of the ideas we get while increasing our freedom.* This will slow us down, no doubt, but are we supposed to charge ahead simply because some people tell us that they have found an explanation for all the misery and an excellent way out of it? Also we want to liberate people not to make them succumb to a new kind of slavery, *but to make them realise their own wishes,* however different these wishes may be from our own. Self-righteous and narrow-minded liberators cannot do this. As a rule they soon impose a slavery that is worse, because more systematic, than the very sloppy slavery they have removed. And as regards humour and flippancy the answer should be obvious. Why would anyone want to liberate anyone else? Surely not because of some *abstract* advantage of liberty but because liberty is the best way to free development *and thus to happiness.* We want to liberate people *so that they can smile.* Shall we be able to do this if we ourselves have forgotten how to smile and are frowning on those who still remember? Shall we then not spread another disease, comparable to the one we want to remove, the disease of puritanical self-righteousness? Do not object that dedication and humour do not go together—Socrates is an excellent example to the contrary. *The hardest task needs the lightest hand or else its completion will not lead to freedom but to a tyranny much worse than the one it replaces.*

The Infinite Regress of Reasons

D. M. ARMSTRONG

Australian philosopher David Armstrong (1926–   ) was professor of philosophy at the University of Sydney.

I. THE EVIDENCE-CONDITION

. . . 'A knows that P' entails 'A truly believes that p.' But true belief does not entail knowledge. The latter point is made by Plato in the *Theaetetus* 200D–201C). It may be illustrated, for instance, by *The Case of the Optimistic Punter*. Because he is optimistic, he regularly *believes* that the horses he bets on will win. But he never has any reliable information about these horses. As a result, he normally loses. From time to time, however, his horses win. On such occasions his beliefs are true. But we do not think that he *knows* that these horses will win.

This is the occasion for introducing the Evidence-condition. The trouble about the punter, it is plausibly suggested, is that he lacks *good reasons* or *sufficient evidence* for his true belief. If only he had that, he would know.

However, when the Evidence-condition is scrutinized more closely, all sorts of problems emerge. In this section no less than five subconditions will be outlined which the Evidence-conditions must satisfy, if it is accepted at all. All these sub-conditions raise important problems.

Condition 1. Suppose that p is true, A believes that p and A has evidence for 'p,' namely 'q.' It cannot be the case that A *knows* that p unless, as a matter of objective fact, 'q' constitutes *sufficient evidence* to establish the truth of 'p.' . . .

Condition 2. Suppose that 'p' is true, A believes that p, A has evidence 'q' for 'p,' and 'q' is in fact sufficient evidence for the truth of 'p.' It may still be the case that A does not realize, or has not noticed, the relevance of his evidence 'q' to 'p.' He may, for instance, have failed to 'put two and two together.'

What is needed is that A's evidence should be actually operative in A's mind, supporting his belief that p. We must therefore have an account of what it is for somebody actually to *take* one proposition as a (conclusive) reason for accepting another. . . .

Condition 3. But even if 'p' is true, A believes that p, A has evidence 'q' for the truth of 'p,' 'q' is in fact sufficient evidence for 'p,' and the evidence actually operates in A's mind to support his belief that p, it still does not follow that A *knows* that p. For although 'q' in fact supports 'p' conclusively, might not A be reasoning from 'q' to 'p' according to some *false* principle which in this particular case moves from a truth to a truth? For instance, A's reasoning from 'q' to 'p' might involve a compensating error peculiar to the case in hand. It seems that we need to say that the principle of reasoning according to which A operates, when his belief that q operates in his mind to support his belief that p, is a *true* principle. This stipulation, by the way, makes Condition 1 redundant.

Condition 4. We now stipulate that 'p' is true, A believes that p, A has evidence 'q' for 'p,' the evidence actually operates in A's mind to support his belief that p, and the principle of reasoning according to which A operates is a true principle. It still does not follow that A *knows* that p. For although the principle of A's reasoning is true, may it not be that A accepts this principle on thoroughly bad grounds? And could we then say that he knew that p? It seems that we ought to amend Condition 3 by saying that the principle of A's reasoning is not simply true, but is *known* by A to be true. But this raises this difficulty that our analysis of A knows that p now involves *knowledge* by A of at least one general principle. What account shall we give of *this* knowledge?

Condition 5. Let us waive this difficulty (for the present). Suppose 'p' is true, A believes that p, A has evidence 'q' for 'p,' the evidence actually operates in A's mind to support his belief that p, and the principle of reasoning according to which A operates is known by A to be true. Even now it is not entailed that A knows p. For consider A's evidence 'q.' Do we not require the further stipulation that A *knows* that q is true? Suppose it not to be the case that A knows that q (~Kaq). Is not 'p' insufficiently supported?

But if this is correct, then knowledge that p can be defined only in terms of *knowledge* that q. 'q' will then demand support in A's mind from evidence 'r,' and an infinite regress threatens.

Although the apparent necessity for Condition 4 also introduces the threat of an infinite regress, historically it is the regress which results from the demand that the evidence be itself something which A knows which has especially troubled supporters of the classical 'good reasons' analysis of knowledge. . . .

II. THE INFINITE REGRESS OF REASONS

Knowledge entails true belief, but true belief does not entail knowledge. It is therefore suggested that knowledge is a true belief for which the believer has sufficient evidence, or some such formula. But the evidence will have to be some proposition, 'q,' which is *known* to A. . . .

III. DIFFERENT REACTIONS TO THE REGRESS

1. The *'Sceptical' Reaction.* We may begin by distinguishing between 'sceptical' and 'non-sceptical' reactions to the regress. An extreme form of the sceptical reaction would be to say that the infinite regress showed that the concept of knowledge involves a contradiction. A moderate view would be that the word 'know,' although it attributes true belief, attributes nothing further of an objective nature to the belief—no relation to the facts—except truth. . . .

2. *The regress is infinite but virtuous.* The first non-sceptical solution which may be canvassed is that the regress exists, but is virtuous. Suppose that event A has a prior cause B, B has a prior cause C, and so, perhaps, *ad infinitum.* Few modern philosophers would consider this latter progression to infinity a vicious one. So perhaps A's knowledge that p rests upon knowledge that q which rests upon knowledge that r, and so on without stop. . . .

It can hardly be pretended, however, that this reaction to the regress has much plausibility. Like the 'sceptical' solution, it is a *desperate* solution, to be considered only if all others are clearly seen to be unsatisfactory.

3. *The regress is finite, but has no end.* Suppose, then, that the regress is not virtuous. Then either the regress has no end, or it has an end. If it has no end, then at some point the reasons must come back upon their own tail, so that 'p' is supported by 'q,' which is supported by 'r,' which is supported by 's,' . . . which is supported by . . . , which is supported by 'p.' This may seem to involve *vicious* circularity. But perhaps it need not. If we have a circle of true beliefs which mutually support each other in this way, then it might be suggested that, once the circle is sufficiently comprehensive and the mutual support sufficiently strong, we would not have mere true beliefs but pieces of knowledge. This may be called the *Coherence* analysis of the concept of knowledge. . . .

Clearly, there are many difficulties for this 'Coherence theory of knowledge.' For instance, what criterion can be given to show that a circle of true beliefs is 'sufficiently comprehensive'? It is not easy to say. And might there not be a sufficiently comprehensive circle of true beliefs which was arrived at so irregularly and luckily that we would not want to call it knowledge?

4. *The regress ends in self-evident truths.* If the Coherence analysis is rejected, then at some point in the regress of reasons (perhaps right at the beginning) we will reach knowledge which is *not* based on reasons. I will call such knowledge 'non-inferential' knowledge. I oppose it to 'inferential' knowledge, which *is* based on reasons. Once it is granted that there is an objective notion of knowledge; that the infinite regress of reasons is in some way vicious; and that the regress cannot be stopped by judicious circularity; then it must be granted that, when A knows that p, then *either* this knowledge is non-inferential, or it is based on a finite set of reasons terminating in non-inferential knowledge.

The problem then comes to be that of giving an account of non-inferential knowledge. . . .

The classical answer is: non-inferential beliefs

which are self-evident, indubitable or incorrigible. They will serve to stop the regress and act as the foundations of knowledge. This has been the *standard* solution from the time of Descartes until quite recently.

However, I reject the whole notion of beliefs that it is logically impossible to be wrong about. I think the logical possibility of error is always present in any belief about any subject matter whatsoever. In any case, it has been demonstrated again and again that, even if there is such self-evident knowledge, it is completely insufficient in *extent* to serve as a foundation for all the things we ordinarily claim to know, even when we have circumscribed that claim by careful reflection. In the past, defenders of this Cartesian solution have regularly had to cut down the scope of our supposed knowledge in a completely unacceptable manner. (For instance, it becomes difficult to claim that there is any empirical knowledge, non-inferential or inferential, beyond that of our own current states of mind.)

5. *'Initial credibility.'* The alternative is to attempt an account of non-inferential knowledge without appealing to such self-evident truths. O'Hair has distinguished two sorts of view here, which he calls 'Initial credibility' and 'Externalist' views.

First a word about 'Initial credibility' theories. It might be maintained that certain classes of our non-inferential beliefs have an intrinsic claim to credibility, even although error about them is a logical and even an empirical possibility. Instances might be beliefs based directly upon sense-perception, upon memory, upon intuition of the simpler logical necessities, or perhaps only upon suitable subclasses of these classes. Now suppose that a belief is non-inferential, is 'initially credible' and is also *true*. Might it not then be accounted a case of non-inferential *knowledge*?

This approach strikes me as more hopeful than the possible reactions to the infinite regress which have already been mentioned. But it involves certain difficulties. It is easy, for instance, to construct non-inferential memory beliefs which are true, but which we certainly would not call knowledge. Thus, a probe in my brain might produce the belief in me that I had an itch in my little finger three days ago. By sheer coincidence, the belief might be true. Or a veridical memory-trace might degenerate but, in

the course of a multi-stage degeneration, the original encoding might be reinstated by a sheer fluke. Some way of excluding such cases would have to be found. I myself am convinced, although I will not try to demonstrate the point here, that the only way to achieve such exclusions satisfactorily is to pass over into an 'Externalist' theory.

6. *'Externalist' theories.* According to 'Externalist' accounts of non-inferential knowledge, what makes a true non-inferential belief a case of *knowledge* is some natural relation which holds between the belief-state, Bap, and the situation which makes the belief true. It is a matter of a certain relation holding between the believer and the world. It is important to notice that, unlike 'Cartesian' and 'Initial Credibility' theories. Externalist theories are regularly developed as theories of the nature of knowledge *generally* and not simply as theories of non-inferential knowledge. But they still have a peculiar importance in the case of non-inferential knowledge because they serve to solve the problem of the infinite regress.

Externalist theories may be further subdivided into 'Causal' and 'Reliability' theories.

6. (i) *Causal theories.* The central notion in causal theories may be illustrated by the simplest case. The suggestion is that Bap is a case of Kap if 'p' is true and, furthermore, the situation that makes 'p' true is causally responsible for the existence of the belief-state Bap. I not only believe, but *know,* that the room is rather hot. Now it is certainly *the excessive heat of the room* which has caused me to have this belief. This causal relation, it may then be suggested, is what makes my belief a case of knowledge. . . .

Causal theories face two main types of difficulty. In the first place, even if we restrict ourselves to knowledge of particular matters of fact, not every case of knowledge is a case where the situation known is causally responsible for the existence of the belief. For instance, we appear to have some knowledge of the future. And even if all such knowledge is in practice inferential, non-inferential knowledge of the future (for example, that I will be ill tomorrow) seems to be an intelligible possibility. Yet it could hardly be held that my illness tomorrow causes my belief today that I will be ill tomorrow. . . .

In the second place, and much more seriously, cases can be envisaged where the situation that makes 'p' true gives rise to Bap, but we would not want to say that A *knew* that p. Suppose, for instance, that A is in a hypersensitive and deranged state, so that almost any considerable sensory stimulus causes him to believe that there is a sound of a certain sort in his immediate environment. Now suppose that, on a particular occasion, the considerable sensory stimulus which produces that belief is, in fact, *a sound of just that sort in his immediate environment.*

Here the p-situation produces Bap, but we would not want to say that it was a case of knowledge.

I believe that such cases can be excluded only by filling out the Causal Analysis with a Reliability condition. But once this is done, I think it turns out that the Causal part of the analysis becomes redundant, and that the Reliability condition is sufficient by itself for giving an account of non-inferential (and inferential) knowledge.

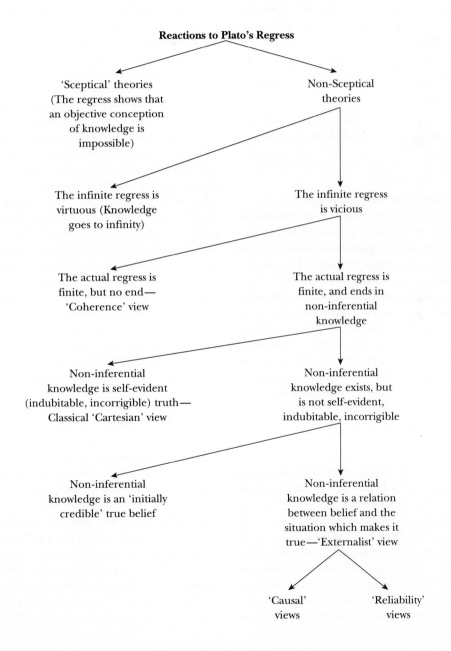

Reactions to Plato's Regress

'Sceptical' theories
(The regress shows that an objective conception of knowledge is impossible)

Non-Sceptical theories

The infinite regress is virtuous (Knowledge goes to infinity)

The infinite regress is vicious

The actual regress is finite, but no end— 'Coherence' view

The actual regress is finite, and ends in non-inferential knowledge

Non-inferential knowledge is self-evident (indubitable, incorrigible) truth— Classical 'Cartesian' view

Non-inferential knowledge exists, but is not self-evident, indubitable, incorrigible

Non-inferential knowledge is an 'initially credible' true belief

Non-inferential knowledge is a relation between belief and the situation which makes it true—'Externalist' view

'Causal' views

'Reliability' views

6. (ii) *Reliability theories.* The second 'Externalist' approach is in terms of the *empirical reliability* of the belief involved. Knowledge is empirically reliable belief . . . [e.g., "the Thermometer View," below].

It is interesting to notice that a Reliability analysis is considered for a moment by Plato in the *Meno* only to be dropped immediately. . . . Socrates asserts that '. . . true opinion is as good a guide as knowledge for the purpose of acting rightly,' and goes on to ask whether we should not draw the conclusion that 'right opinion is something no less useful than knowledge.' Meno however objects:

> Except that the man with knowledge will always be successful, and the man with only right opinion only sometimes.

Unfortunately, however, Socrates brushes aside this tentative development of a Reliability view, saying:

> What? Will he not always be successful so long as he has the right opinion?

Meno immediately concedes the point.

This concludes our brief survey. In philosophy, when one finds oneself in a difficult intellectual situation, it is often vitally important to be aware of the full range of response which is open to one. And in philosophy, if one practises it honestly, one invariably is in a more or less difficult intellectual situation. The survey just made was intended to create an awareness of the many different responses open to us in the difficult situation created by the threatened infinite regress involved in the classical analysis of knowledge. Against this background, I proceed to put forward a suggested solution of the problem.

FROM NON-INFERENTIAL KNOWLEDGE

. . . Thinking about the threatened infinite regress in the classical analysis of knowledge seems to lead to the conclusion that there must be non-inferential knowledge. Furthermore, we seem *forced* in the case of this sort of knowledge to look for some non-classical solution to the problem. (The classical or 'Cartesian' postulation of self-evident truths can rather easily be shown to be an insufficient account of the basis of all that we think we know.) If we can find a non-classical solution to the problem of non-inferential knowledge, where such a solution is clearly required, we may then try to extend the solution to cover all cases of knowledge. . . .

THE 'THERMOMETER' VIEW OF NON-INFERENTIAL KNOWLEDGE

Suppose that 'p' is true, and A believes that p, but his belief is not supported by any reasons. 'p' might be the proposition that there is a sound in A's environment. . . . What makes such a belief a case of knowledge? My suggestion is that there must be a *law-like connection* between the state of affairs Bap and the state of affairs that makes 'p' true such that, given Bap, it must be the case that p.

The quickest way to grasp the suggestion is to use a model. Let us compare non-inferential beliefs to the temperature-readings given by a thermometer. In some cases, the thermometer-reading will fail to correspond to the temperature of the environment. Such a reading may be compared to non-inferential false belief. In other cases, the reading will correspond to the actual temperature. Such a reading is like non-inferential true belief. The second case, where reading and actual environmental temperature coincide, is then subdivided into two sorts of case. First, suppose that the thermometer is a bad one, but that, on a certain occasion, the thermometer-reading coincide with the actual temperature. (Cf. the stopped clock that shows the right time twice a day.) Such a reading is to be compared with non-inferential true belief which falls short of knowledge. Suppose finally that the thermometer is a good one, so that a reading of 'T°' on the thermometer ensures that the environmental temperature is T. Such a reading is to be compared with non-inferential *knowledge*. When a true belief unsupported by reasons stands to the situation truly believed to exist as a thermometer-reading in a good thermometer stands to the actual temperature, then we have non-inferential knowledge.

I think the picture given by the thermometer-model is intuitively clear. The problem is to give a formal account of the situation. . . .

The model of the thermometer gives us further assistance here. For a thermometer to be reliable on a certain occasion in registering a certain temperature as T° we do not demand that there be a true law-like generalization: 'If any thermometer registers "T°," then the temperature is T°.' In the first place, we recognize that there can be good and bad thermometers. In the second place, we do not even demand that a good thermometer provide a reliable reading under every condition. We recognize that there may be special environmental conditions under which even a 'good' thermometer is unreliable.

What do we demand? Let us investigate a far less stringent condition. Suppose, on a certain occasion, a thermometer is reliably registering 'T°.' There must be some property of the instrument and/or its circumstances such that, if any thing has this property, and registers 'T°,' it must be the case, as a matter of natural law, that the temperature *is* T°. We might find it extremely hard to specify this property (set of properties). The specification might have to be given in the form of a blank cheque to be filled in only after extensive investigation. But it may be relatively easy to recognize that a certain thermometer is operating reliably, and so that such a specification is possible. . . .

Is Man a Rational Animal?

STEPHEN STICH

Stephen Stich teaches in the Department of Philosophy & Center for Cognitive Science at Rutgers University. He is the author of numerous articles and several books.

I. DESCRIPTIVE AND NORMATIVE APPROACHES TO THE STUDY OF HUMAN REASONING

In studying human reasoning it is generally assumed that we can adopt two very different approaches. One approach is *descriptive* or *empirical*. Those who take this approach try to characterize how people actually go about the business of reasoning and try to discover the psychological mechanisms and processes that underlie the patterns of reasoning they observe. For the most part the descriptive approach is pursued by psychologists, though anthropologists have also done some very interesting work aimed at determining whether and to what extent people in different cultures reason differently. The other approach to the study of reasoning is *normative*. Those who adopt this approach are not concerned with how people actually reason but rather with how they *should* reason. Their goal is to discover rules or principles that specify what it is to reason *correctly* or *rationally*. Since antiquity, the normative approach to reasoning has been pursued by logicians and philosophers, and more recently they have been joined by statisticians, probability theorists, and decision theorists.

The goals and methods of these two approaches to the study of reasoning are quite different. However, some of the most interesting and hotly debated claims about human reasoning concern the extent to which one or another group of people reason rationally. And these claims are intrinsically hybrid or interdisciplinary. In order to address them we have to know both what it is to reason rationally and how the group of people in question actually do reason. By far the most famous claim of this sort is Aristotle's contention that *man is a rational animal*. Rationality, according to Aristotle, is an essential property of humankind; it is what distinguishes man from beast. A central goal of this essay is to reexamine Aristotle's thesis in the light of recent empirical studies of human reasoning. Was Aristotle right? Are humans really rational animals?

In order to address the question seriously, we will first have to provide a more precise interpretation of Aristotle's thesis. It is obvious that humans aren't *always* rational. When people are drunk or exhausted or in the grip of uncontrollable rage, they often reason very poorly indeed. And, of course, Aristotle knew this. When he said that humans are rational animals, he surely never intended to deny that people can and sometimes do reason irrationally. But then, what did he mean? In Section II we'll see how we can begin to provide a precise and intriguing interpretation of Aristotle's thesis by borrowing an idea from contemporary cognitive science—the idea that people have underlying "competences" in various domains, though these competences are not always reflected in people's actual behavior. One attractive interpretation of Aristotle's thesis is that normal humans have a *rational competence* in the domain of reasoning.

To explain the notion of a rational competence, we'll need to do more than explain the notion of a competence, however; we'll also have to say what it is for a competence to be rational. In Section III we will look at one elegant and influential attempt to explain what it is for a pattern to reasoning to be rational—an approach that appeals to the notion of reflective equilibrium.

Having interpreted Aristotle's thesis as the claim that normal people have a rational reasoning competence, our focus will shift to the descriptive study of reasoning. In Section IV we will survey some fascinating and very disturbing empirical findings that seem to suggest that Aristotle was wrong because most normal people do not have the competence to reason rationally about many sorts of questions! Those findings not only challenge Aristotle's optimistic thesis about human rationality, but they also seem to threaten the reflective equilibrium account of rationality. Section V begins by explaining why the empirical findings pose a problem for reflective equilibrium accounts, and goes on to explore some possible responses.

In Section VI, we'll return to the empirical literature on human reasoning, this time focusing on some very recent studies by evolutionary psychologists who begin from the assumption that components or "organs" in the mind were shaped by natural selection, just as were components or organs in other parts of the body. This perspective leads them to expect that our minds will do quite well when reasoning about the sort of problems that would have been important in the environment in which our species evolved, and they have produced some very

interesting evidence indicating that this is indeed the case.

Finally, in Section VII, we'll ask what these recent studies tell us about Aristotle's claim. Do they show, as some people suggest, that Aristotle was right after all? The answer, I'll argue, is that neither Aristotle nor his opponents are vindicated by the empirical research. Rather, what these studies show is that the questions we have been asking about human rationality—questions like "Is man a rational animal?"—are much too simplistic. If we want plausible answers supported by solid scientific evidence, then we are going to have to learn to ask better and more sophisticated questions.

II. COMPETENCE AND PERFORMANCE

Everyone agrees that people are sometimes very irrational. So, for example, people who are drunk or distraught or under the influence of drugs sometimes reason and make decisions in ways that would be not be sanctioned by any theory about the principles governing good reasoning and decision making that anyone would take seriously. Since this is such an obvious and uncontroversial fact, how could anyone maintain, nonetheless, that humans are rational animals? What could they possibly mean? One very attractive answer can be given by exploiting the distinction between *competence* and *performance*.

The competence/performance distinction was first introduced into cognitive science by Noam Chomsky, who used it in his account of the explanatory strategy of theories in linguistics. (Chomsky 1965, ch. 1; 1980) In testing linguistic theories, an important source of data is the "intuitions" or unreflective judgments that speakers of a language make about the grammaticality of sentences and about various linguistic properties (for example, Is the sentence ambiguous? Is this phrase the subject of that verb?). To explain these intuitions, and also to explain how speakers produce and understand sentences of their language in ordinary speech, Chomsky proposed what has become one of the most important hypotheses about the mind in the history of cognitive science. What this hypothesis claims that a speaker of a language has an internally represented "generative grammar" of that language. A *generative grammar* is an integrated set of rules and principles—we might think of it as analogous to a system of axioms—that entails an infinite number of claims about the language. For each of the sentences in the speaker's language, the speaker's internally represented grammar entails that it is grammatical; for each ambiguous sentence in the speaker's language, the grammar entails that it is ambiguous, and so on. When speakers make the judgments that we call "linguistic intuitions," the information in the internally represented grammar is typically accessed and relied upon, though neither the process nor the internally represented grammar itself are accessible to conscious introspection. Since the internally represented grammar plays a central role in the production of linguistic intuitions, those intuitions can serve as an important source of data for linguists trying to specify what the rules and principles of the internally represented grammar are.

A speaker's intuitions are not, however, an infallible source of information about the grammar of the speaker's language, because the internally represented rules of the grammar cannot produce linguistic intuitions by themselves. The production of intuitions is a complex process in which the internally represented grammar must interact with a variety of other cognitive mechanisms including those responsible for perception, motivation, attention, short-term memory, and perhaps a host of others. In certain circumstances, the activity of any one of these mechanisms may result in a person offering a judgment about a sentence that does not accord with what the grammar actually entails about the sentence. The attention mechanism offers a clear example of this phenomenon. It is very likely the case that the grammar internally represented in typical English speakers entails that an endless number of sentences of the form

A said that B thought that C believed that D suspects that E thought . . . that p.

are grammatical in the speaker's language. However, if you were asked to judge the grammaticality of a sentence containing a few hundred of these "that-clauses," or perhaps even a few dozen, there is a good chance that your judgment would not reflect

what your grammar entails, since in cases like this attention easily wanders. Short-term memory provides a more interesting example of the way in which a grammatical judgment may fail to reflect the information actually contained in the grammar. There is considerable evidence indicating that the short-term memory mechanism has difficulty handling center-embedded structures. Thus, it may well be the case that your internally represented grammar entails that the following sentence is grammatical:

What what what he wanted cost would buy in Germany was amazing.

although most people's intuitions suggest, indeed shout, that it is not.

Now, in the jargon that Chomsky introduced, the rules and principles of a speaker's internalized generative grammar constitute the speaker's *linguistic competence;* the judgments a speaker makes about sentences, along with the sentences the speaker actually produces, are part of the speaker's *linguistic performance*. Moreover, as we have just seen, some of the sentences a speaker produces and some of the judgments the speaker makes about sentences will not accurately reflect the speaker's linguistic competence. In these cases, the speaker is making a *performance error*.

There are some obvious analogies between the phenomena studied in linguistics and those studied by cognitive scientists interested in reasoning. In both cases people are capable of spontaneously and unconsciously processing an open-ended class of "inputs"—people are able to understand endlessly many sentences and to draw inferences from endlessly many premises. In light of this analogy, it is plausible to explore the idea that the mechanism underlying our ability to reason is similar to the mechanism underlying our capacity to process language. And if Chomsky is right about language, then the analogous hypothesis about reasoning would claim that people have an internally represented integrated set of rules and principles of reasoning—a "psycho-logic" as it has been called—that is usually accessed and relied upon when people draw inferences or make judgments about them. As in the case of language, we would expect that neither the processes involved nor the principles of the internally represented psycho-logic are readily accessible to consciousness. We should also expect that people's inferences and judgments would not be an infallible guide to what the underlying psycho-logic actually entails about the validity or plausibility of a given inference. For here, as in the case of language, the internally represented rules and principles must interact with lots of other cognitive mechanisms, including attention, motivation, short-term memory, and many others. The activity of these mechanisms can give rise to *performance errors:* inferences or judgments that do not reflect the psycho-logic that constitutes a person's *reasoning competence.*

We are now in a position to explain an interpretation of Aristotle's thesis on which it is compatible with the unquestionable fact that, sometimes at least, people reason very irrationally. What the thesis claims is that normal people have a *rational reasoning competence.* The rules or principles of reasoning that make up their psycho-logic are rational or normatively appropriate; they specify how to reason *correctly.* According to this interpretation, when people make errors in reasoning or when they reason irrationally, the errors are *performance errors* that may be due to fatigue or inattention or confusion or a host of other factors. But however common they may be, these performance errors do not reflect the rules of reasoning that constitute a normal person's reasoning competence. To say that man is a rational animal, on this account, is to say that normal people's reasoning competence is rational even though their reasoning performance sometimes is not.

III. WHAT IS RATIONALITY? A REFLECTIVE EQUILIBRIUM ACCOUNT

What is it that justifies a set of rules or principles for reasoning? What makes reasoning rules *rational?* About thirty-five years ago, in one of the most influential passages of twentieth-century analytic philosophy, Nelson Goodman suggested elegant answers to these questions. In that passage, Goodman described a process of bringing judgments about particular inferences and about general principles of reasoning into accord with one another. In the accord thus achieved, Goodman maintained, lies all the justification needed, and all the justification possible, for

the inferential principles that emerge. Other writers, most notably John Rawls, have adopted a modified version of Goodman's process as a procedure for determining when *moral* principles are correct. To Rawls, too, we owe the term *reflective equilibrium,* which has been widely used to characterize a system of principles and judgments that have been brought into coherence with one another in the way that Goodman describes.

It is hard to imagine the notion of reflective equilibrium explained more eloquently than Goodman himself explains it. So let me quote what he says at some length.

> How do we justify a *de*duction? Plainly by showing that it conforms to the general rules of deductive inference. An argument that so conforms is justified or valid, even if its conclusion happens to be false. An argument that violates a rule is fallacious even if its conclusion happens to be true. . . . Analogously, the basic task in justifying an inductive inference is to show that it conforms to the general rules of *induction.*
>
> Yet, of course, the rules themselves must eventually be justified. The validity of a deduction depends not upon conformity to any purely arbitrary rules we may contrive, but upon conformity to valid rules. When we speak of *the* rules of inference we mean the valid rules—or better, *some* valid rules, since there may be alternative sets of equally valid rules. But how is the validity of rules to be determined? Here . . . we encounter philosophers who insist that these rules follow from self-evident axioms, and others who try to show that the rules are grounded in the very nature of the human mind. I think the answer lies much nearer the surface. Principles of deductive inference are justified by their conformity with accepted deductive practice. Their validity depends upon accordance with the particular deductive inferences that we actually make and sanction. If a rule yields inacceptable inferences, we drop it as invalid. Justification of general rules thus derives from judgments rejecting or accepting particular deductive inferences.
>
> This looks flagrantly circular. I have said that deductive inferences are justified by their conformity to valid general rules, and that general rules

are justified by their conformity to valid inferences. But this circle is a virtuous one. The point is that rules and particular inferences alike are justified by being brought into agreement with each other. *A rule is amended if it yields an inference we are unwilling to accept; an inference is rejected if it violates a rule we are unwilling to amend.* The process of justification is the delicate one of making mutual adjustments between rules and accepted inferences; and in the agreement achieved lies the only justification needed for either.

All this applies equally well to induction. An inductive inference, too, is justified by conformity to general rules, and a general rule by conformity to accepted inferences. (1965, pp. 66–67)

On Goodman's account, at least as I propose to read him, passing the reflective equilibrium test is (as philosophers sometimes say) *constitutive* of justification or validity of rules of inference. For a system of inferential rules and the inferences that accord with them to be rational *just is* for them to be in reflective equilibrium. But what is the status of this claim? *Why* is passing the reflective equilibrium test constitutive for the justification or rationality of inferential rules? The answer, I think, is that Goodman takes it to be a *conceptual truth:* It follows from the meaning of terms like "justified" or "rational" or from the analysis of the concept of rationality. Arguably, that concept is a bit (or more than a bit) vague, and the reflective equilibrium analysis makes no attempt to capture this vagueness. Rather, it tries to tidy up the vagueness and "precise-ify" the concept. So, perhaps Goodman is best read as maintaining that the reflective equilibrium account captures something like our ordinary concept of rationality and that it is the best way of making that concept precise.

We now have all the pieces in place to interpret Aristotle's thesis. *Man is a rational animal,* on the interpretation being proposed, means that normal humans have a reasoning competence—a mentally represented set of rules or principles for reasoning—and that those rules are rational—they would pass the reflective equilibrium test. Let's now ask how plausible this thesis is. To do that we'll have to turn our attention to the empirical study of human reasoning.

IV. SOME DISQUIETING EVIDENCE ABOUT HOW HUMANS REASON

We will start our exploration of the psychological evidence about human reasoning by focusing on studies that some authors have thought have "bleak implications" about the rationality of ordinary people. All of these studies involve normal subjects (often university students) who are neither exhausted nor emotionally stressed. Nonetheless, many of them do very poorly on the reasoning tasks that they are asked to solve.

The Selection Task

In 1966, Peter Wason reported the first experiments using a cluster of reasoning problems that came to be called "the selection task." A recent textbook on reasoning has described that task as "the most intensively researched single problem in the history of the psychology of reasoning." (Evans, Newstead, & Byrne 1993, p. 99) A typical example of a selection task problem looks like this:

Here are four cards. Each of them has a letter on one side and a number on the other side. Two of these cards are shown with the letter side up, and two with the number side up.

Indicate which of these cards you have to turn over in order to determine whether the following claim is true:

If a card has a vowel on one side, then it has an odd number on the other side.

What Watson and numerous other investigators have found is that ordinary people typically do very poorly on questions like this. Most subjects respond, correctly, that the E card must be turned over, but many also judge that the 5 card must be turned over, despite the fact that the 5 card could not falsify the claim no matter what is on the other side. Also, a large majority of subjects judge that the 4 card need *not* be turned over, although without turning it over there is no way of knowing whether it has a vowel on the other side. And, of course, if it does have a vowel on the other side, then the claim is not true. It is not the case that subjects do poorly on all selection task problems, however. A wide range of variations on the basic pattern have been tried, and on some versions of the problem a much larger percentage of subjects answer correctly. These results form a bewildering pattern, because there is no obvious feature or cluster of features that separates versions on which subjects do well from those on which they do poorly. As we will see in Section VI, some evolutionary psychologists have argued that these results can be explained if we focus on the sorts of mental mechanisms that would have been crucial for reasoning about social exchange (or "reciprocal altruism") in the environment of our hominid forebears. The versions of the selection task we're good at, these theorists maintain, are just the ones that those mechanisms would have been designed to handle.

The Conjunction Fallacy

Ronald Reagan was elected President of the United States in November 1980. The following month, Amos Tversky and Daniel Kahneman administered a questionnaire to 93 subjects who had had no formal training in statistics. The instructions on the questionnaire were as follows:

> In this questionnaire you are asked to evaluate the probability of various events that may occur during 1981. Each problem includes four possible events. Your task is to rank order these events by probability, using 1 for the most probable event, 2 for the second, 3 for the third, and 4 for the least probable event.

Here is one of the questions presented to the subjects:

> Please rank order the following events by their probability of occurrence in 1981:
>
> (a) Reagan will cut federal support to local government.
> (b) Reagan will provide federal support for unwed mothers.

> (c) Reagan will increase the defense budget by less than 5%.
> (d) Reagan will provide federal support for unwed mothers and cut federal support to local governments.

The unsettling outcome was that 68 percent of the subjects rated (d) as more probable than (b), despite the fact that (d) could not happen unless (b) did (Tversky & Kahneman 1982). In another experiment, which has since become quite famous, Tversky and Kahneman (1982) presented subjects with the following task:

> Linda is 31 years old, single, outspoken, and very bright. She majored in philosophy. As a student, she was deeply concerned with issues of discrimination and social justice and also participated in anti-nuclear demonstrations.

> Please rank the following statements by their probability, using 1 for the most probable and 8 for the least probable.

> (a) Linda is a teacher in elementary school.
> (b) Linda works in a bookstore and takes Yoga classes.
> (c) Linda is active in the feminist movement.
> (d) Linda is a psychiatric social worker.
> (e) Linda is a member of the League of Women Voters.
> (f) Linda is a bank teller.
> (g) Linda is an insurance salesperson.
> (h) Linda is a bank teller and is active in the feminist movement.

In a group of naive subjects with no background in probability and statistics, 89 percent judged that statement (h) was more probable than statement (f). When the same question was presented to statistically sophisticated subjects—graduate students in the decision science program of the Stanford Business School—85 percent made the same judgment! Results of this sort, in which subjects judge that a compound event or state of affairs is more probable than one of the components of the compound, have been found repeatedly since Kahneman and Tversky's pioneering studies.

Base-Rate Neglect

On the familiar Bayesian account, the probability of a hypothesis on a given body of evidence depends, in part, on the prior probability of the hypothesis.* However, in a series of elegant experiments, Kahneman and Tversky (1973) showed that subjects often seriously undervalue the importance of prior probabilities. One of these experiments presented half of the subjects with the following cover story:

> A panel of psychologists have interviewed and administered personality tests to 30 engineers and 70 lawyers, all successful in their respective fields. On the basis of this information, thumbnail descriptions of the 30 engineers and 70 lawyers have been written. You will find on your forms five descriptions, chosen at random from the 100 available descriptions. For each description, please indicate your probability that the person described is an engineer, on a scale from 0 to 100.

The other half of the subjects were presented with the same text, except the "base rates" were reversed. They were told that the personality tests had been administered to 70 engineers and 30 lawyers. Some of the descriptions that were provided were designed to be compatible with the subjects' stereotypes of engineers, though not with their stereotypes of lawyers. Others were designed to fit the lawyer stereotype but not the engineer stereotype. And one was intended to be neutral, giving subjects no information at all that would be of use in making their decision. Here are two examples, the first intended to sound like an engineer, the second intended to sound neutral:

> Jack is a 45-year-old man. He is married and has four children. He is generally conservative, careful, and ambitious. He shows no interest in political and social issues and spends most of his free

time on his many hobbies, which include home carpentry, sailing, and mathematical puzzles.

> Dick is a 30-year-old man. He is married with no children. A man of high ability and high motivation, he promises to be quite successful in his field. He is well liked by his colleagues.

As expected, subjects in both groups thought that the probability that Jack is an engineer was quite high. Moreover, in what seems to be a clear violation of Bayesian principles, the difference in cover stories between the two groups of subjects had almost no effect at all. The neglect of base-rate information was even more striking in the case of Dick. That description was constructed to be totally uninformative with regard to Dick's profession. Thus, the only useful information that subjects had was the base-rate information provided in the cover story. But that information was entirely ignored. The median probability estimate in *both* groups of subjects was 50%. Kahneman and Tversky's subjects were not, however, completely insensitive to base-rate information. Following the five descriptions on their form, subjects found the following "null" description:

> Suppose now that you are given no information whatsoever about an individual chosen at random from the sample. The probability that this man is one of the 30 engineers [or, for the other group of subjects, one of the 70 engineers] in the sample of 100 is ___%.

In this case subjects relied entirely on the base rate; the median estimate was 30% for the first group of subjects and 70% for the second. In their discussion of these experiments, Nisbett and Ross offer this interpretation:

> The implication of this contrast between the "no information" and "totally nondiagnostic information" conditions seems clear. When *no* specific evidence about the target case is provided, prior probabilities are utilized appropriately; when *worthless* specific evidence is given, prior probabilities may be largely ignored, and people respond as if there were no basis for assuming differences in relative likelihoods. People's grasp of the relevance of base-rate information must be very week if they could be distracted from using

---

*Bayes's Theorem, which is named after the Rev. Thomas Bayes, asserts that

$$p(H/D) = p(D/H) \times p(H)/p(D)$$

where $p(H/D)$ is the "conditional probability" of a hypothesis, H, given that D (the "data") is true, $p(D/H)$ is the conditional probability of D, given that H is true, $p(H)$ is the "prior" probability that H is true, and $p(D)$ is the probability that D is true.

it by exposure to useless target case information. (Nisbett & Ross 1980, pp. 145–146)

Before leaving the topic of base-rate neglect, I want to offer one further example illustrating the way in which the phenomenon might well have serious practical consequences. Here is a problem that Casscells et al. (1978) presented to a group of faculty, staff, and fourth-year students at Harvard Medical School:

> If a test to detect a disease whose prevalence is 1/1000 has a false positive rate of 5%, what is the chance that a person found to have a positive result actually has the disease, assuming that you know nothing about the person's symptoms or signs? ____%

Under the most plausible interpretation of the problem, the correct Bayesian answer is 2%. But only 18 percent of the Harvard audience gave an answer close to 2%. Forty-five percent of this distinguished group completely ignored the base-rate information and said that the answer was 95%. (If, like most of the Harvard physicians, you don't see why 2% is the right answer, read on. After you've read Section VI, the reason this is the right answer will be a lot clearer.) It is a bit alarming, to put it mildly, that these same experimental subjects were diagnosing real patients and offering them advice on such questions as what treatments to seek and whether to have exploratory surgery.

Overconfidence

One of the most extensively investigated and worrisome cluster of phenomena explored by psychologists interested in reasoning and judgment involves the degree of confidence that people have in their responses to factual questions—questions like:

> In each of the following pairs, which city has more inhabitants?

> (a) Las Vegas   (b) Miami
> (a) Sydney   (b) Melbourne
> (a) Hyderabad   (b) Islamabad
> (a) Bonn   (b) Heidelberg

> In each of the following pairs, which historical event happened first?

> (a) signing of the   (b) birth of
>   Magna Carta   Muhammad
> (a) death of Napoleon (b) Louisiana Purchase
> (a) Lincoln's   (b) birth of Queen
>   assassination   Victoria

After each answer subjects are also asked:

> How confident are you that your answer is correct?
> 50% 60% 70% 80% 90% 100%

In an experiment using relatively hard questions it is typical to find that for the cases in which subjects say they are 100% confident, only about 80% of their answers are correct; for cases in which they say that they are 90% confident, only about 70% of their answers are correct; and for cases in which they say that they are 80% confident, only about 60% of their answers are correct. This tendency toward overconfidence seems to be very robust. Warning subjects that people are often overconfident has no significant effect, nor does offering them money (or bottles of French champagne) as a reward for accuracy. Moreover, the phenomenon has been demonstrated in a wide variety of subject populations including undergraduates, graduate students, physicians, and even CIA analysts. (For a survey of the literature, see Lichtenstein, Fischoff, & Phillips 1982).

The empirical findings we've been reviewing are only a small sample of the extensive empirical literature on shortcomings in human reasoning that has appeared over the last twenty-five years. (For much more detailed reviews of the literature in what is sometimes called the "heuristics and biases" tradition, see Nisbett & Ross 1980; Baron 1988; Piatelli-Palmarini 1994; Dawes 1988; and Sutherland 1994. Kahneman, Slovic, & Tversky's 1982 anthology is also very useful.) One apparently unavoidable consequence of this huge body of experimental findings is that people's *performance* on a wide range of inferential problems leaves much to be desired. The answers given by many experimental subjects depart substantially and systematically from the answers that accord with a rational set of inferential principles. Of course it could be the case that all of these errors are merely performance errors and that they do not accurately reflect the principles of reasoning that make up the subject's underlying reasoning competence or psycho-logic. But many writers have offered a more disquieting interpretation of these experimental results. These authors claim that in experiments like those described in this section, people *are* reasoning in ways that accurately reflect their psycho-logic. The subjects in these experiments do not use the right principles because they do not have access to them; they are not part of the subjects' internally represented reasoning competence. What they have instead, on this view, is a collection of simpler principles or heuristics that may often get the right answer, though it is also the case that often they do not. So, according to this bleak hypothesis, the subjects make mistakes because their psycho-logic is normatively defective; their internalized principles of reasoning *are not rational principles*.

Daniel Kahneman and Amos Tversky, who are widely recognized as the founders and leading researchers in the heuristics and biases tradition, make the point as follows:

> In making predictions and judgments under uncertainty, people do not appear to follow the calculus of chance or the statistical theory of prediction. Instead, they rely on a limited number of heuristics which sometimes yield reasoning judgments and sometimes lead to severe and systematic errors." (1973, p. 237)

Slovic, Fischoff, and Lichtenstein, important contributors to the experimental literature, are even more emphatic. "It appears," they write, "that people lack the correct programs for many important judgmental tasks. . . . We have not had the opportunity to evolve an intellect capable of dealing conceptually with uncertainty" (1976, p. 174). Stephen J. Gould, a well-known evolutionary theorist and the author of many widely acclaimed books about science, concurs. After describing the "feminist bank teller" experiment, he asks, "Why do we consistently make this simple logical error?" His answer is, "Tversky and Kahneman argue, correctly I think, that our minds are not built (for whatever reason) to work by the rules of probability" (1992, p. 469). If these authors are right, then Aristotle was wrong: Man is *not* a rational animal!

V. A CHALLENGE TO THE REFLECTIVE EQUILIBRIUM ACCOUNT OF RATIONALITY

In the previous section we looked at some experimental findings about reasoning that cast serious doubt on Aristotle's sanguine assessment of human rationality. A number of philosophers and psychologists also think that findings like these pose a major challenge to the sort of reflective equilibrium account of rationality that we sketched in Section III. The argument for this conclusion is quite straightforward. It begins with the claim that some of the questionable patterns of reasoning described in that literature are likely to be in reflective equilibrium for many people. When the principles underlying these inferences are articulated, and people have a chance to reflect on them and on their own inferential practice, they may well accept both the inferences and the principles. (One surprising bit of evidence for this claim is the existence of nineteenth-century logic texts in which some of these problematic principles are explicitly endorsed.* Presumably the authors of those texts reflectively accepted both the principles and the inferences that accord with them.) Now if this is the case—if the principles underlying some of the questionable inferential patterns reported in the psychological literature really are in reflective equilibrium for many people—then, the critics argue, there is something very wrong with the reflective equilibrium account of rationality. For, on that account, to be rational *just is* to pass the reflective equilibrium test. So if the account were correct, then the conjunction fallacy or base-rate neglect or some other problematic pattern of reasoning would be rational for those people.

Of course, each example of an infelicitous inferential principle that allegedly would pass the reflec-

---

*For example, in *Elements of Logic*, published in 1974, Henry Coppée explicitly endorses the notorious "Gambler's Fallacy." Here is what he says: "Thus, in throwing dice, we cannot be sure that any single face or combination of faces will appear; but if, in very many throws, some particular face has not appeared, the chances of its coming up are stronger and stronger, until they approach very near to certainty. It must come; and as each throw is made and it fails to appear, the certainty of its coming draws nearer and nearer." (p. 321)

tive equilibrium test is open to challenge. Whether the dubious principles that appear to guide many people's inferential practice would stand up to the reflective scrutiny that Goodman's test demands is an empirical question. And for any given rule, an advocate of the reflective equilibrium account might protest that the empirical case just has not been made adequately. I am inclined to think that those who build their defenses here are bound to be routed by a growing onslaught of empirical findings. But the argument need not turn on whether this hunch is correct. For even the *possibility* that the facts will turn out as I suspect they will poses a serious problem for the reflective equilibrium story. It is surely not a necessary truth that strange inferential principles will always fail the reflective equilibrium test for all subjects. And if it is granted, as clearly it must be, that base-rate neglect or the conjunction fallacy (or any of the other inferential oddities that have attracted the attention of psychologists in recent years) could possibly pass the reflective equilibrium test for some group of subjects, this is enough to cast doubt on the view that reflective equilibrium is constitutive of rationality. For surely most of us are not at all inclined to say that it is rational for people to use *any* inferential principle— no matter how bizarre it may be—simply because it accords with their reflective inferential practice.

This is not, I hasten to add, a knock-down argument against the reflective equilibrium account of rationality; knock-down arguments are hard to come by in this area. When confronted with the fact that the conjunction fallacy or base-rate neglect or some other principle that is frowned upon by most normative theorists might well pass the reflective equilibrium test for some real or hypothetical group of people, some philosophers simply dig in their heels and insist that if the principle in question is in reflective equilibrium for that group of people, then the principle is indeed justified or rational for them. This assessment, they insist, does accord well enough with at least one sense of the notions of justification and rationality to count as a reasonable "precisification" of those rather protean notions.

While digging in and insisting that the reflective equilibrium account does capture (or "precisify") an important sense of rationality may not be a completely untenable position, it clearly has some se-

rious drawbacks, the most obvious of which is the counterintuitive consequence that just about any daffy rule of reasoning might turn out to be rational for a person, as long as it accords with his or her reflective inferential practice. In light of this, many philosophers have been inspired to construct quite different accounts of what it is for a principle of reasoning to be rational. In one important family of accounts, the notion of truth plays a central role. Advocates of these accounts start with the idea that the real goal of thinking and reasoning is to construct an *accurate* account of the way things are in the world. What we really want is to have *true beliefs*. And if that's right, then we should employ principles of reasoning and belief formation that are likely to produce true beliefs. So, on these accounts, an inferential principle is rational or justified if a person using the principle is likely to end up having true beliefs.

Unfortunately, many truth-based accounts of rationality also have some notably counterintuitive consequences. Perhaps the easiest way to see them is to invoke a variation on Descartes's evil demon theme. Imagine a pair of people who suddenly fall victim to such a demon and who are from that time forward provided with systematically misleading or deceptive perceptual inputs. Let's further suppose that one of the victims has been using inferential processes quite like our own and that these have done quite a good job at generating true beliefs, while the other victim's inferential processes have been (by our lights) quite mad and have done quite a terrible job at producing true beliefs. Indeed, for vividness, we might imagine that the second victim is a delusion-ridden resident of an insane asylum. In their new demon-infested environment, however, the sane system of inferential principles—the one like ours—yields a growing fabric of false beliefs. The other system, by contrast, will do a much better job at generating true beliefs and avoiding false ones, since what the evil demon is doing is providing his victim with radically misleading evidence—evidence that only a lunatic would take to be evidence for what actually is the case. On truth-based accounts of rationality the lunatic's inferential principles would be rational in this environment, whereas ours would be quite irrational. And that strikes many people as a seriously counterintuitive result. Advocates of truth-based accounts have proposed various strategies for avoiding cases like this, though how successful they are is a matter of considerable dispute.

Where does all this leave us? The one point on which I think there would be wide agreement is that there are no unproblematic and generally accepted answers to the question with which we began Section III: What is it that justifies a set of rules or principles for reasoning? What makes reasoning rules *rational*? The nature of rationality is still very much in dispute. Many philosophers would also agree that empirical studies of reasoning like those we reviewed in Section IV impose important constraints on the sorts of answers that can be given to these questions, though just what these constraints are is also a matter of considerable dispute. In the section to follow, we will return to the empirical study of reasoning and look at some recent results from evolutionary psychology that challenge the pessimistic conclusion about human rationality that some would draw from the studies reviewed in Section IV. In interpreting that evidence, we'll have no choice but to rely on our intuitions about rationality, since there is no generally accepted theory on hand about what rationality *is*.

VI. ARE HUMANS RATIONAL ANIMALS AFTER ALL? THE EVIDENCE FROM EVOLUTIONARY PSYCHOLOGY

Though the interdisciplinary field of evolutionary psychology is too new to have developed any precise and widely agreed-upon body of doctrine, there are three basic theses that are clearly central. The first is that the human mind contains as large number of special purpose systems—often called "modules" or "mental organs." These modules are invariably conceived of as a type of specialized or domain-specific computational mechanism. Many evolutionary psychologists also urge that modules are both innate and present in all normal members of the species. The second central thesis of evolutionary psychology is that, contrary to what has been argued by some eminent cognitive scientists (most notably Jerry Fodor, 1983), the modular structure of the mind is not restricted to "input systems" (those responsible for perception and language processing) and "output systems" (those responsible for producing bodily movements). According to evolutionary psychologists, modules also subserve many so-called "central capacities" such as reasoning and belief formation. The third thesis is that mental modules are what evolutionary biologists call *adaptations*. These adaptations were, as Tooby and Cosmides have put it, "invented by natural selection during the species' evolutionary history to produce adaptive ends in the species' natural environment" (Tooby & Cosmides 1995, p. xiii). Here is a passage in which Tooby and Cosmides offer a particularly colorful statement of these central tenets of evolutionary psychology:

> [O]ur cognitive architecture resembles a confederation of hundreds or thousands of functionally dedicated computers (often called modules) designed to solve adaptive problems endemic to our hunter-gatherer ancestors. Each of these devices has its own agenda and imposes its own exotic organization on different fragments of the world. There are specialized systems for grammar induction, for face recognition, for dead reckoning, for construing objects and for recognizing emotions from the face. There are mechanisms to detect animacy, eye direction, and cheating. There is a "theory of mind" module . . . a variety of social inference modules . . . and a multitude of other elegant machines. (Tooby & Cosmides 1995, p. xiv)

If much of central cognition is indeed subserved by cognitive modules that were designed to deal with the adaptive problems posed by the environment in which our primate forebears lived, then we should expect that the modules responsible for reasoning will do their best job when information is provided in a format similar to the format in which information was available in the ancestral environment. And, as Gerd Gigerenzer has argued, although there was a great deal of useful probabilistic information available in that environment, this information would have been represented "as frequencies of events, sequentially encoded as experienced—for example, *3 out of 20* as opposed to 15%" (Gigerenzer 1994, p. 142). Cosmides and Tooby make much the same point as follows:

> Our hominid ancestors were immersed in a rich flow of observable frequencies that could be used to improve decision-making, given procedures

that could take advantage of them. So if we have adaptations for inductive reasoning, they should take frequency information as input. (1996, pp. 15–16)

On the basis of such evolutionary considerations, Gigerenzer, Cosmides, and Tooby have proposed and defended a psychological hypothesis that they refer to as the "frequentist hypothesis": "[S]ome of our inductive reasoning mechanisms do embody aspects of a calculus of probability, but they are designed to take frequency information as input and produce frequencies as output" (Cosmides & Tooby 1996, p. 3).

This speculation led Cosmides and Tooby to pursue an intriguing series of experiments in which the Harvard Medical School problem that we discussed in Section IV was systematically transformed into a problem in which both the question and the response required were formulated in terms of frequencies. Here is one example from their study in which frequency information is made particularly salient:

> 1 out of every 1000 Americans has disease X. A test has been developed to detect when a person has disease X. Every time the test is given to a person who has the disease, the test comes out positive. But sometimes the test also comes out positive when it is given to a person who is completely healthy. Specifically, out of every 1000 people who are perfectly healthy, 50 of them test positive for the disease.
>
> Imagine that we have assembled a random sample of 1000 Americans. They were selected by lottery. Those who conducted the lottery had no information about the health status of any of these people.
>
> Given the information above, on average, how many people who test positive for the disease will *actually* have the disease? ___ out of ___.

In sharp contrast to Casscells et al.'s original experiment in which only 18 percent of subjects gave the correct Bayesian response, the above problem elicited the correct Bayesian answer from 76 percent of Cosmides and Tooby's subjects.

This is not just an isolated case in which "frequentist" versions of probabilistic reasoning problems elicit high levels of performance. On the contrary, it has been found that in many instances, when problems are framed in terms of frequencies rather than probabilities, subjects tend to reason more rationally. In one study, Fiedler (1988) showed that the percentage of subjects who commit the conjunction fallacy can be radically reduced if the problem is cast in frequentist terms. Using the "feminist bank teller" problem, Fiedler contrasted the wording reported in Section IV with a problem that reads as follows:

> Linda is 31 years old, single, outspoken, and very bright. She majored in philosophy. As a student, she was deeply concerned with issues of discrimination and social justice, and also participated in anti-nuclear demonstrations.
>
> There are 200 people who fit the description above. How many of them are:
>
> . . .
>
> bank tellers?
>
> . . .
>
> bank tellers and active in the feminist movement?
>
> . . .

In Fiedler's replication using the original formulation of the problem, 91 percent of subjects judged the feminist bank teller option to be more probable than the bank teller option. However, in the frequentist version above, only 22 percent of subjects judged that there would be more feminist bank tellers than bank tellers.

Studies on overconfidence have also been marshaled in support of the frequentist hypothesis. In one of these Gigerenzer, Hoffrage, and Kleinbölting (1991) reported that the sort of overconfidence described in Section IV can be made to "disappear" by having subjects answer questions formulated in terms of frequencies. Gigerenzer and his colleagues gave subjects lists of 50 questions similar to those recounted in Section IV, except that in addition to being asked to rate their confidence after each response (which, in effect, asks them to judge the probability of that single event), subjects were, at the end, also asked a question about the *frequency* of correct responses: "How many of these 50 questions do you think you got right?" In two experiments, the average overconfidence was about 15 percent, when single-event confidences were compared with actual relative frequencies of correct answers, replicating the sorts of findings we sketched in Section IV. However, comparing the subjects' "estimated frequencies with actual frequencies of correct answers made 'overconfidence' *disappear.* . . . Estimated frequencies were practically identical with actual frequencies. . . . The 'cognitive illusion' was gone" (Gigerenzer 1991a, p. 89).

In Section IV we saw one version of Wason's four-card selection task on which most subjects perform very poorly. It was noted that, although subjects do equally poorly on many other versions of the selection task, there are some versions on which performance improves dramatically. Here is an example from Griggs and Cox (1982):

> In its crackdown against drunk drivers, Massachusetts law enforcement officials are revoking liquor licenses left and right. You are a bouncer in a Boston bar, and you'll lose your job unless you enforce the following law: **"If a person is drinking beer, then he must be over 20 years old."**
>
> The cards below have information about four people sitting at a table in your bar. Each card represents one person. One side of a card tells what a person is drinking and the other side of the card tells that person's age. Indicate only those card(s) you definitely need to turn over to see if any of these people are breaking the law.

drinking beer	drinking Coke	25 years old	16 years old

From a logical point of view this problem seems structurally identical to the problem in Section IV, but the *content* of the problems clearly has a major effect on how well people perform. About 75 percent of college student subjects get the right an-

swer on this version of the selection task, while only 25 percent get the right answer on the other version. Though there have been dozens of studies exploring this "content effect" in the selection task, until recently the results were very puzzling since there is no obvious property or set of properties shared by those versions of the task on which people perform well. However, in several recent papers, Cosmides and Tooby have argued that an evolutionary analysis enables us to see a surprising pattern in these otherwise bewildering results (Cosmides 1989; Cosmides & Tooby 1992).

The starting point of their evolutionary analysis is the observation that in the environment in which our ancestors evolved (and in the modern world as well) it is often the case that unrelated individuals can engage in what game theorists call "non-zero-sum" exchanges, in which the benefits to the recipient (measured in terms of reproductive fitness) are significantly greater than the costs to the donor. In a hunter-gatherer society, for example, it will sometimes happen that one hunter has been lucky on a particular day and has an abundance of food while another hunter has been unlucky and is near starvation. If the successful hunter gives some of his meat to the unsuccessful hunter rather than gorging on it himself, this may have a small negative effect on the donor's fitness since the extra bit of body fat that he might add could prove useful in the future, but the benefit to the recipient will be much greater. Still, there is *some* cost to the donor; he would be slightly better off if he didn't help unrelated individuals. Despite this, it is clear that people sometimes do help non-kin, and there is evidence to suggest that non-human primates (and even vampire bats!) do so as well. On first blush, this sort of altruism seems to pose an evolutionary puzzle, since if a gene that made an organism *less* likely to help unrelated individuals appeared in a population, those with the gene would be slightly *more* fit, and thus the gene would gradually spread through the population.

A solution to this puzzle was proposed by Robert Trivers (1971) who noted that, while one-way altruism might be a bad idea from an evolutionary point of view, *reciprocal altruism* is quite a different matter. If a pair of hunters (be they humans or bats) can each count on the other to help when one has an abundance of food and the other has none, then they both may be better off in the long run. Thus, organisms with a gene or a suite of genes that inclines them to engage in reciprocal exchanges with non-kin (or "social exchanges," as they are sometimes called) would be more fit than members of the same species without those genes. But, of course, reciprocal exchange arrangements are vulnerable to cheating. In the business of maximizing fitness, individuals will do best if they are regularly offered and accept help when they need it but never reciprocate when others need help. This suggests that if stable social exchange arrangements are to exist the organisms involved must have cognitive mechanisms that enable them to detect cheaters and to avoid helping them in the future. And since humans apparently are capable of entering into stable social exchange relations, this evolutionary analysis led Cosmides and Tooby to hypothesize that we have one or more modules or mental organs whose job it is to recognize reciprocal exchange arrangements and to detect cheaters who accept the benefits in such arrangements but do not pay the costs. In short, the evolutionary analysis led Cosmides and Tooby to hypothesize the existence of one or more cheater detection modules. I'll call this the *cheater detection hypothesis.*

If the hypothesis is correct, then we should be able to find some evidence for the existence of these modules in the thinking of contemporary humans. It is here that the selection task enters the picture. For according to Cosmides and Tooby, some versions of the selection task engage the mental module(s) that were designed to detect cheaters in social exchange situations. And since these mental modules can be expected to do their job efficiently and accurately, people do well on those versions of the selection task. Other versions of the task do not trigger the social exchange and cheater detection modules. Since we have no mental modules that were designed to deal with these problems, people find them to be much harder, and their performance is much worse. The bouncer in the Boston bar problem presented earlier is an example of a selection task that triggers the cheater detection mechanism. The problem involving vowels and odd numbers presented in Section IV is an example of a

selection task that does not trigger the cheater detection module.

In support of their theory, Cosmides and Tooby assemble an impressive body of evidence. The cheater detection hypothesis claims that social exchanges or "social contracts" will trigger good performance on selection tasks, and this enables us to see a clear pattern in the otherwise confusing experimental literature that had grown up before their hypothesis was formulated.

> When we began this research in 1983, the literature on the Wason selection task was full of reports of a wide variety of content effects, and there was no satisfying theory or empirical generalization that could account for these effects. When we categorized these content effects according to whether they conformed to social contracts, a striking pattern emerged. Robust and replicable content effects were found only for rules that related terms that are recognizable as benefits and cost/requirements in the format of a standard social contract. . . . No thematic rule that was not a social contract had ever produced a content effect that was both robust and replicable. . . . All told, for non-social contract thematic problems, 3 experiments had produced a substantial content effect, 2 had produced a weak content effect, and 14 had produced no content effect at all. The few effects that were found did not replicate.
> In contrast, 16 out of 16 experiments that fit the criteria for standard social contracts . . . elicited substantial content effects. (Cosmides & Tooby 1992, p. 183)

Since the formulation of the cheater detection hypothesis, a number of additional experiments have been designed to test the hypothesis and rule out alternatives. And while the hypothesis still has many critics, there can be no doubt that the evidence provided by some of these new experiments is impressive.

Results like these have encouraged a resurgence of Aristotelian optimism. On the optimists' view, the theories and findings of evolutionary psychology suggest that human reasoning is subserved by "elegant machines" that were designed and refined by natural selection over millions of years, and therefore any concerns about systematic irrationality are unfounded. One indication of this optimism is the title that Cosmides and Tooby chose for the paper in which they reported their data on the Harvard Medical School problem: "Are humans good intuitive statisticians after all? Rethinking some conclusions from the literature on judgment under uncertainty." Five years earlier, while Cosmides and Tooby's research was still in progress, Gigerenzer reported some of their early findings in a paper with the provocative title: "How to make cognitive illusions disappear: Beyond 'heuristics and biases'." The clear suggestion in both of these titles is that the findings they report pose a head-on challenge to the pessimism of the heuristics and biases tradition. Nor are these suggestions restricted to titles. In paper after paper, Gigerenzer has said things like: "more optimism is in order" (1991b, p. 245) and "we need not necessarily worry about human rationality" (1998, p. 280); and he has maintained that his view "supports intuition as basically rational" (1991b, p. 242). In light of comments like this it is hardly surprising that one commentator has described Gigerenzer and his colleagues as having "taken an empirical stand against the view of some psychologists that people are pretty stupid" (Lopes, quoted in Bower 1996).

VII. DOES EVOLUTIONARY PSYCHOLOGY SHOW THAT ARISTOTLE WAS RIGHT?

The theories urged by evolutionary psychology are (to put it mildly) very controversial, and even their experiments have not gone unchallenged. But suppose it turns out that the evolutionary psychologists are right about the mental mechanisms that underlie human reasoning. Would that really show that Aristotle's thesis is correct? The answer, I think, is *not at all*. To see why, let's begin by recalling how we are interpreting Aristotle's thesis. The claim that humans are rational animals, as we unpacked it in Section II, means that normal people have a *rational reasoning competence*. This competence is a set of mentally represented rules or principles of reasoning—a psycho-logic—and Aristotle's thesis is that these rules are *rational* or *normatively appropriate;* they specify how to reason *correctly*. Thus, when people

make errors in reasoning or when they reason irrationally, the errors are *performance errors* that do not reflect the underlying mentally represented principles of reasoning.

The first point to be made about the relation between evolutionary psychology and Aristotle's thesis is that if evolutionary psychology is right, then our interpretation of Aristotle's thesis is too simplistic to fit the facts. For on the evolutionary psychologists' model of the mind, people do not have *one* reasoning competence, they have *many,* and each of these special purpose mental modules has its own special set of rules. So there isn't one psycho-logic, either; there are many. Now it might be thought that this would pose only a minor problem for advocates of Aristotelian optimism. Instead of claiming that there is *one* mechanism underlying reasoning and that it embodies a set of rational or normatively appropriate rules, they could claim that there are *many* mechanisms underlying reasoning and that *all* of them use normatively appropriate rules. But, and this is the crucial point, evolutionary psychology does not lend support to this claim. Evolutionary psychology does maintain that natural selection equipped us with a number of well-designed reasoning mechanisms that employ rational or normatively appropriate principles *on the sorts of problems that were important in the environment of our hunter-gatherer forebears.* However, there are many sorts of reasoning problems that are important in the modern world—problems involving the probabilities of single events, for example—that these mechanisms were not designed to handle. In many cases, evolutionary psychologists suggest, the elegant special purpose reasoning mechanisms designed by natural selection will not even be able to process these problems. Many of the problems investigated in the heuristics and biases literature were of this sort. Evolutionary psychology gives us no reason to suppose that people have rational mentally represented rules for dealing with problems like these.

On the interpretation of the experimental literature on reasoning that I am defending, it supports neither Aristotelian optimism nor the pessimism of those who suggest our minds were only equipped with shoddy software. We have and use some remarkably good software for handling the kinds of problems that were important in the environment in which our species evolved. But there are also important gaps in the sorts of problems that this evolved mental software can handle. The challenge for philosophers, psychologists, and educators in the decades ahead will be to devise better ways for our stone age minds to handle the sorts of reasoning problems that we confront in an age of space travel, global computer networks, and nuclear weapons.

References

Baron, J. (1988). *Thinking and Deciding.* Cambridge: Cambridge University Press.

Baron-Cohen, S. (1995). *Mindblindness: An Essay on Austin and Theory of Mind.* Cambridge, MA: MIT Press.

Bower, B. (1996). Rational mind design: Research into the ecology of thought treads on contested terrain. *Science News* 150:24–25.

Casscells, W., Schoenberger, A., & Grayboys, T. (1978). Interpretation by physicians of clinical laboratory results. *New England Journal of Medicine* 299:999–1000.

Chomsky, N. (1965). *Aspects of the Theory of Syntax.* Cambridge, MA: MIT Press.

Chomsky, N. (1980). *Rules and Representations.* New York: Columbia University Press.

Coppée, H. (1974). *Elements of Logic,* rev. ed. Philadelphia: H. Butler & Co.

Cosmides, L. (1989). The logic of social exchange: Has natural selection shaped how humans reason? Studies with Wason Selection Task. *Cognition* 31:187–276.

Cosmides, L. & Tooby, J. (1992). Cognitive adaptations for social exchange. In Barkow, Cosmides, & Tooby (1992), 163–228.

Cosmides, L., & Tooby, J. (1996). Are humans good intuitive statisticians after all? Rethinking some conclusions from the literature on judgment under uncertainty. *Cognition* 58, (1):1–73.

Dawes, R. (1988). *Rational Choice in an Uncertain World.* Orlando: Harcourt Brace Jovanovich.

Evans, J., Newstead, S., & Byrne, R. (1993). *Human Reasoning: The Psychology of Deduction.* Hove, UK: Erlbaum.

Fiedler, K. (1988). The dependence of the conjunction fallacy on subtle linguistic factors. *Psychological Research* 50:123–129.

Fodor, J. (1983). *The Modularity of Mind.* Cambridge, MA: MIT Press.

Gigerenzer, G. (1991a). How to make cognitive illusions disappear: Beyond "heuristics and biases." *European Review of Social Psychology* 2:83–115.

Gigerenzer, G. (1991b). On cognitive illusions and rationality. *Poznan Studies in the Philosophy of the Sciences and the Humanities* 21:225–249.

Gigerenzer, G. (1994). Why the distinction between single-event probabilities and frequencies is important for psychology (and vice versa). In G. Wright & P. Ayton, eds., *Subjective Probability.* New York: John Wiley.

Gigerenzer, G. (1998). The modularity of social intelligence. In A. Whiten & R. Byrne, eds., *Machiavellian Intelligence II.* Cambridge: Cambridge University Press.

Gigerenzer, G., Hoffrage, U., & Kleinbölting, H. (1991). Probabilistic mental models: A Brunswikean theory of confidence. *Psychological Review* 98:506–528.

Goodman, N. (1965). *Fact, Fiction and Forecast.* Indianapolis: Bobbs-Merrill.

Gould, S. (1992). *Bully for Brontosaurus. Further Reflections in Natural History.* London: Penguin.

Griggs, R., & Cox, J. (1982). The elusive thematic-materials effect in Wason's selection task. *British Journal of Psychology* 73:407–420.

Kahneman, D., & Tversky, A. (1973). On the psychology of prediction. *Psychological Review* 80:237–251. Reprinted in Kahneman, Slovic, & Tversky (1982), pp. 48–68.

Kahneman, D., Slovic, P., & Tversky, A., eds. 1982. *Judgment Under Uncertainty: Heuristics and Biases.* Cambridge: Cambridge University Press.

Lichtenstein, S., Fischoff, B., & Phillips, L. (1982). Calibration of probabilities: The state of the art to 1980. In Kahneman, Slovic, & Tversky (1982), pp. 306–334.

Nisbett, R., & Ross, L. (1980). *Human Inference: Strategies and Shortcomings of Social Judgment.* Englewood Cliffs, NJ: Prentice-Hall.

Piatelli-Palmarini, M. (1994). *Inevitable Illusions: How Mistakes of Reason Rule Our Minds.* New York: John Wiley.

Slovic, P., Fischoff, B., and Lichtenstein, S. (1976). Cognitive processes and societal risk taking. In J. S. Carol & J. W. Payne, eds., *Cognition and Social Behavior.* Hillsdale, NJ: Erlbaum.

Sutherland, S. (1994). *Irrationality: Why We Don't Think Straight!* New Brunswick, NJ: Rutgers University Press.

Tooby, J., & Cosmides, L. (1995). Foreword. In Baron-Cohen (1995), pp. xi–xviii.

Trivers, R. (1971). The evolution of reciprocal altruism. *Quarterly Review of Biology* 46:35–56.

Tversky, A., & Kahneman, D. (1982). Judgments of and by representativeness. In Kahneman, Slovic, & Tversky (1982), pp. 84–98.

PART 3

Mind, Personal Identity, and Consciousness

THE MIND AND THE BODY

We have an access to ourselves that we do not have to the rest of nature: We experience our own inner mental states. We thus learn subjectively—"from the inside"—what colors we see, what feelings we feel, whether we are hungry or bored, and so on. We cannot experience the rest of nature, not even other people, in this same way. We must experience nature and other people "from the outside"—objectively, through our external sense organs.

But at the same time we have an outside. We are objects in nature. So we also learn about ourselves objectively. This dual access to ourselves gives rise to the problem of how to integrate both subjective and objective perspectives—which often conflict and sometimes may even contradict each other—into a single, coherent theory of who and what we are. For instance, when you decide to do something, do you decide to do it because you want to achieve some goal, something you may know only subjectively, or because of chemical changes in your brain, something you know only objectively? If both, how does one affect the other? Do minds push chemicals around, or do chemicals give rise to mental states that only make it seem as if the mind is in control? Or do minds just reduce to chemicals, so that the apparent differences between them are merely consequences of the alternative conceptual schemes we use to describe and explain behavior? If such mentalistic and physicalistic explanations are merely two ways of describing the same phenomena—ways that conceptualize the phenomena differently—what accounts for the radical differences between these conceptualized schemes, and what is their relationship to each other?

Thomas Nagel, in his classic "What Is It Like to Be a Bat?" argues that the essence of consciousness is that "there is something it is like" to be a conscious being and nothing it is like to be a being that lacks consciousness. Thus, for instance, there is something it is like to be a bat, but nothing it is like to be a rock. Furthermore, we could know everything there is to know scientifically or objectively—from the outside—about how a conscious being, say a bat, works, yet still not know what it is like to be that conscious being. Nagel concludes that this implies the antireductionist view that there is more to consciousness than what can be captured in our current and best scientific theories.

In his "Sensations and Brain Processes," J. J. C. Smart offers his materialistic alternative to dualism: the identity theory, according to which all mental events are simply and

237

fundamentally identical with brain processes. The mind is, in his view, identical to the brain in the same way that, for instance, lightning is one and the same thing as an electrical discharge of a certain sort. This is exactly the sort of view challenged by Frank Jackson in his "Ephiphenomenal Qualia." A mind–body dualist, Jackson is an opponent of the idea that mental phenomena can be reduced to physical phenomena. He provides vivid and interesting examples that seem to refute physicalism. In one of these examples, Mary, who knows all there is to know scientifically about color perception but has been confined all her life to a black-and-white environment, finally emerges to experience the full range of colors. Jackson claims that what she learns through her new experiences shows that physicalism is false. Paul Churchland, on the other hand, in his "Reduction, Qualia, and the Direct Introspection of Brain States," argues exactly *for* the view that Nagel and Jackson criticize, namely, physicalism. A devout eliminative materialist, he claims that both Nagel's and Jackson's arguments in support of their alternative views, as well as their criticisms, ultimately fail. Churchland's version of functionalism is supposed to reconcile the best features of physicalism and behaviorism. Functionalist theories in general and Churchland's in particular have been inspired in part by the advent of computers and related technology. According to functionalism, the identity theory, which is also sometimes called Type-Physicalism, fails because it erroneously identifies the mental properties of a system at large with the physical properties of its parts.

THE SELF AND PERSONAL IDENTITY

When Descartes asked, What am I? he identified the "I" with a continuously existing immaterial substance. For Descartes, as for many who preceded him, the question, Is someone at one time the same person as someone at a later time?—the question of personal identity would be answered in terms of whether the earlier person is (or has) the same immaterial substance as the later person. John Locke, taking up where Descartes left off, tried to extricate his account of personal identity from dependence on the notion of an immaterial substance by arguing that it is not sameness of immaterial substance but, rather, sameness of consciousness that makes someone the same continuously existing person over time. This suggests that for Locke the criterion of identity is conscious memory. Thus, although still strictly a substance view, Locke moves in the direction of a relational view of personal identity, according to which personal identity consists in various *relations* among transient elements. The important relations, as he explains in his selection "Of Identity and Diversity," are those that obtain among present conscious memories and the earlier experiences or actions remembered.

A possible problem with Locke's view is that strange moral implications may follow from the memory view of personal identity, at least when that view is interpreted strictly. For instance, we can justly punish Smith for murdering Jones only if Smith actually murdered him. On a strict interpretation of the memory view, Smith actually murdered Jones only if he remembers having done it. In other words, if Smith does not remember murdering Jones eight years ago, then Jones's murderer was not Smith but a sort of ancestor of Smith's, and Smith is no more guilty of the murder than, say, Jack the Ripper's grandson is guilty of the crimes of his notorious grandfather. Such difficulties with the strict memory view inspired Thomas Reid to argue, as he does in the selection "Of Identity," that if the person who committed a crime cannot remember having committed it but can remember everything he did at an earlier time when he could still remember having committed the crime, then on Locke's view this person both is and is not the same person who committed the crime. Reid thus dismisses Locke's view as self-contradictory.

One way to defend Locke against Reid's objection is to suppose that what matters is not the remembering per se but, rather, the *potential* for remembering. Thus, the prisoner who cannot remember his crime might remember it, say, under hypnosis, because there exists within his brain some hidden memory traces of that event. Or one might revise Locke's theory with an analysis of personal identity in terms of overlapping memories, because even though there might be few, if any, memory connections among person-stages separated by many years, at any moment-to-moment stage of a person's life there are usually memory connections to the adjacent stages. For instance, suppose you remember now what you had for breakfast today, and at breakfast you remembered what you had for dinner the day before, and so on; it is having such overlapping memories that, in this revised Lockean view, makes you the same person over time, even though you may not be able to remember now what you had for breakfast on a certain day seven years ago.

David Hume delivers another powerful blow to the substance view. In "Of Personal Identity" he argues that no self—either over time or at a time—shows up in experience. By "identity" Hume means persistence without change *over time*. By "simplicity" he means existence as an individual thing (rather that as a collection) *at a time*. Hume thinks that if there were a self in experience, it would be a perceiver. But when he looks for a perceiver, he finds only a bundle of perceptions and among them nothing that seems even a candidate to be the self. Perceptions come in two varieties: impressions and ideas. The life of individual perceptions, whether they are impressions or ideas, is short; flickering in and out of existence, "they succeed each other with an inconceivable rapidity." Thus, from what impression indeed could the idea of self—that is, the experience of unity at a time and identity over time—be derived? The term "self" is supposed to represent an idea of our personal unity at a time that continues unchanged over time. If it is a meaningful term and not just an empty noise standing for nothing, there must be some impression of which it is a representation. And the problem is that there simply is no such impression. The idea of self is not even a misrepresentation of an impression; it is but an insubstantial ghost—literally, a figment of the imagination. Philosophers of personal identity have tried in various ways to respond to Hume's skeptical challenge, either by coming up with new versions of a personal identity theory or by replacing the notion of personal identity with some other viable alternative theory.

In his classic "Where Am I?" Daniel C. Dennett describes a situation in which his brain and his body are separated and, in addition, there is a second, artificial brain that runs in sync with his original brain. His thought experiment brings to light some of the perhaps less obvious mysteries of consciousness, starting with the question of how we, as conscious subjects of experience (whether as real or illusory beings) locate ourselves, or at least *seem* to, in a particular location in the world in relation to what we take to be our own real bodies. From the standpoint of ordinary language, the meanings of words like *here, now,* and *me* seem so obvious that we ordinarily don't even question them. But by imagining himself in an extraordinary situation in which his body is separated from his brain, and in which "he" seems not to be able to tell whether "he" is at any moment "in" the original brain or the replica brain, Dennett shows why even the most obvious apparent fact about you, expressed by your avowal "I am here" and "I am this," is deeply questionable. His ingenious puzzle throws all our standard notions of self and identity into question.

Raymond Martin, in "Personal Identity from Plato to Parfit," surveys the history of personal identity theory from its beginnings in ancient Greece to the present. He explains some of the literally mind-boggling aspects of the latest views of philosophers such as Derek Parfit, according to whom personal identity as traditionally conceived is based on a fundamental illusion. As Martin puts it, "Up to this point, your whole life. . . has been organized around the idea that you persist. . . . It is one thing to discover that you have been misled by an illusion. That is a common result in philosophy. However, it is quite another, and a far more disturbing thing, to discover that you may be that illusion."

MINDS, BRAINS, AND MACHINES

Wittgenstein's *Tractatus* begins with the famous Proposition 1: "The world is all that is the case." What Wittgenstein means by "world," however, is given by Proposition 1.1: "The world is the totality of facts, not of things." This is in direct and perhaps shocking contradiction to the commonsense view that the world is made of *things*. What Wittgenstein is saying goes well with other views expressing the idea that the world in our *experience*— the totality of everything we can *talk* about—is not made of some physical material stuff but of something entirely different in nature. Indeed, it will help us to compare Wittgenstein's assertion with Kant's analysis of the categories of thought and the nature of the mind, in that what the mind has direct access to is not things as they exist independently of the mind (as conceived in materialist metaphysics) but its own items: perceptions, thoughts, and language. In Proposition 4.0, Wittgenstein makes the radical claim that "A sentence that makes sense is a thought." This can be taken to mean that a sentence that makes sense *is* what a thought is; in other words, minds or consciousness as conceived in some superlinguistic (that is, supernatural) terms are absolutely not required.

In a computer program, the propositions themselves have been further reduced to numbers. Given some input data, itself just an integer or string of integers, the program can then use this number to generate another number as output. This is the process described by its actual inventor, Alan Turing, now named after him and generally known as "Turing machines." Turing was a pioneer in computer intelligence who designed one of the first electronic computers. During World War II, he—now famously but then top-secretly—single-handedly cracked the German code, which was perhaps the decisive factor that helped the Allies win the war. Strictly speaking, a Turing machine is essentially the same thing as its program. It was invented by Turing in the mid-1930s in an effort to reduce to simplest possible terms what it is for a computation to proceed from one calculation to another in a discrete series of steps. Turing claimed that his machine would be the most powerful conceivable theoretical model; indeed, all subsequent stored-program digital computers are based on his original notational device, consisting simply of (1) a (potentially) infinitely long tape on which is written a string of binary symbols, and (2) a read-write head capable of (a) moving either left or right, one symbol at a time, and (b) erasing and writing symbols according to the rules specified by its program. He proved that such a device was a universal machine, meaning that we could program it to simulate any other Turing machine. In this way, Turing suggested that intellectual activity itself consists of a "search" involving simulations—in the case of Turing machines, on paper—of "unorganized machines" randomly connected together and capable of learning through the process of self-training. In his view, the brain itself can be viewed as nothing more than such a digital computing machine, where the elements consist of randomly connected neurons strung together in some such learning scheme. Thus, at birth, the brain is an unorganized machine that becomes organized through training "into a universal machine or something like it."

So the mysterious and perhaps unanswerable question, Can machines think? as Turing explains in his now classic paper, "Computing Machinery and Intelligence," is reformulated into the strictly empirical and scientific question, Can machines successfully play the imitation game? This has become known as the famous "Turing test" for whether a computer is conscious. Turing originally conceived of the imitation game as follows. A man and woman go into separate isolation booths connected to a third room by teletype, or some such device, so that they can communicate only by typing at a terminal. The interrogator, who sits in a third such room, has no idea which room contains the man and which the woman and must decide which room the woman is in simply by asking questions. The woman tries to help the interrogator as much as possible whereas the man tries to fool him. Turing's question is whether a machine who takes part of the man can fool the interrogator a similar number of times as an actual man. This, Turing argues, replaces the original question, Can machines think? If the interrogator is fooled just as often by a machine into thinking he is communicating with a woman as he is by a man, the machine is sufficiently like the man to be accorded the same intellectual status. Contemporary computer theory can itself be understood as a decision procedure for determining what constitutes an effective procedure (what Wittgenstein called "a way of going on," that is, a "rule") and describing its attributes (what states it is in and what states it can get to, that is, its "memory bank").

In "Minds, Brains, and Programs," John Searle takes up these themes with an ingenious thought experiment now famously known as the "Chinese room." We're asked to imagine a real human being, who does not speak Chinese, locked in a room where as his "input" he gets only Chinese characters. The room contains a huge book of rules where he must look up, according to certain well-prescribed rules, various strings of characters depending on what his input was and then write down an output. Searle's point is that the man in the room would be able, in principle, to pass the Turing test—that is, he would be able to play the imitation game and win by fooling the Chinese-speaking people outside the room, who produce the input, into thinking that he speaks Chinese, or that the room in toto, with whatever is in it, "understand" Chinese. Searle takes this sort of thought experiment to be a refutation of the idea that there could ever be a thinking computer.

Jerry Fodor, on the other hand, in "Turing Computers, and Philosophy: Can There Be a Science of Mind?" takes a synoptic view of the whole field and gives his characterization of the main issues and accomplishments. He claims that "nobody even knows what it would be like to have the slightest idea about how anything material could be conscious." However, he does claim that material things such as electronic brains, like our brains, can as such be *rational*. In that regard, he thinks Turing had the most important idea that anybody has ever had about how the mind works—namely, the material thing that matters, from the point of view of being able to think and reason, is the ability to manipulate and evaluate *symbols*. It is this parallelsim between thoughts and symbols that led Turing to conceive of his symbol-manipulating machine that could simulate human thinking up to the point of being indistinguishable from it, at least from the outside. He supports and builds upon Turing's original view that thinking is a variety of symbol manipulation, such that, in Fodor's view, the sorts of thinking we do is always in some kind of language that, ultimately, is reduced in the brain to mechanical operations on the symbols of that language. He concludes that the mind is some sort of Turing machine.

In "Consciousness, Self, and Reality: Who Are We?" Daniel C. Dennett and I explore the philosophical implications of these and related issues. We try to bring to light some of the fascinating recent work on these topics, starting out with how and why philosophy got involved in these issues and how it helped give birth to the new interdisciplinary study of cognitive science, literally, "the science of thought." What can be said about the nature of the relationship between the subjective, perspectival world of phenomena and the objective, public, or multiperspectival world of physical reality? Dennett, one of the leading philosophers working in cognitive science today, claims that a fully materialistic account of the mind is possible that gives a fully scientific explanation of consciousness—a "science of the mind" exactly in the way that Fodor claims it is not. We discuss the philosophical issues surrounding the problem of whether and to what degree the conscious subject, the "self," as a phenomenon in the brain, can so to speak "climb out" of its brain to form an experience of the external, mind-independent reality.

Clearly, the question, Can a machine be conscious in the way that we are conscious? is no longer merely hypothetical. A real-life version of the problem figures predominantly in our discussion about Cog, the humanoid robot being built by MIT. (In the accompanying photograph, Cog—who some would estimate has, at least in some sense, the intelligence of a two- or three-year-old human—can be seen playing with a slinky.) What would it take for Cog to be conscious? And how could we know? These, it turns out, may *not* be the same question after all.

Sensations and Brain Processes

J. J. C. SMART

J. J. C. Smart teaches philosophy at the National Australian University in Canberra.

This paper[1] takes its departure from arguments to be found in U. T. Place's "Is Consciousness a Brain Process?"[2] I have had the benefit of discussing Place's thesis in a good many universities in the United States and Australia, and I hope that the present paper answers objections to his thesis which Place has not considered and that it presents his thesis in a more nearly unobjectionable form. This paper is meant also to supplement the paper "The 'Mental' and the 'Physical,'" by H. Feigl,[3] which in part argues for a similar thesis to Place's.

Suppose that I report that I have at this moment a roundish, blurry-edged after-image which is yellowish towards its edge and is orange towards its center. What is it that I am reporting? One answer to this question might be that I am not reporting anything, that when I say that it looks to me as though there is a roundish yellowy-orange patch of light on the wall I am expressing some sort of *temptation,* the temptation to say that there *is* a roundish yellowy-orange patch on the wall (though I may know that there is not such a patch on the wall). This is perhaps Wittgenstein's view in the *Philosophical Investigations* (see §§ 367.370). Similarly, when I "report" a pain, I am not really reporting anything (or, if you like, I am reporting in a queer sense of "reporting"), but am doing a sophisticated sort of wince. (See § 244: "The verbal expression of pain replaces crying and does not describe it." Nor does it describe anything else.)[4] I prefer most of the time to discuss an after-image rather than a pain, because the word "pain" brings in something which is irrelevant to my purpose: the notion of "distress." I think that "he is in pain" entails "he is in distress," that is, that he is in a certain agitation-condition.[5] Similarly, to say "I am in pain" may be to do more than "replace pain behavior": it may be partly to report something, though

this something is quite nonmysterious, being an agitation-condition, and so susceptible of behavioristic analysis. The suggestion I wish if possible to avoid is a different one, namely that "I am in pain" is a genuine report, and that what it reports is an irreducibly psychical something. And similarly the suggestion I wish to resist is also that to say "I have a yellowish-orange after-image" is to report something irreducibly physical.

Why do I wish to resist this suggestion? Mainly because of Occam's razor. It seems to me that science is increasingly giving us a viewpoint whereby organisms are able to be seen as physicochemical mechanisms:[6] It seems that even the behavior of man himself will one day be explicable in mechanistic terms. There does seem to be, so far as science is concerned, nothing in the world but increasingly complex arrangements of physical constituents. All except for one place: in consciousness. That is, for a full description of what is going on in a man you would have to mention not only the physical processes in his tissues, glands, nervous system, and so forth, but also his states of consciousness: his visual, auditory, and tactual sensations, his aches and pains. That these should be *correlated* with brain-processes does not help, for to say that they are *correlated* is to say that they are something "over and above." You cannot correlate something with itself. You correlate footprints with burglars, but not Bill Sikes the burglar with Bill Sikes the burglar. So sensations, states of consciousness, do seem to be the one sort of thing left outside the physicalist picture, and for various reasons I just cannot believe that this can be so. That everything should be explicable in terms of physics (together of course with descriptions of the ways in which the parts are put together—roughly, biology is to physics as radio-engineering is to electromagnetism) except the occurrence of sensations seems to me to be frankly unbelievable. Such sensations would be "nomological danglers," to use Feigl's expression.[7]

From "Sensations and Brain Processes," *Philosophical Review* 68 (1959): 141–56.

It is not often realized how odd would be the laws whereby these nomological danglers would dangle. It is sometimes asked, "Why can't there be psychophysical laws which are of a novel sort, just as the laws of electricity and magnetism were novelties from the standpoint of Newtonian mechanics?" Certainly we are pretty sure in the future to come across new ultimate laws of a novel type, but I expect them to relate simple constituents: for example, whatever ultimate particles are then in vogue. I cannot believe that ultimate laws of nature could relate simple constituents to configurations consisting of perhaps billions of neutrons (and goodness knows how many billion billions of ultimate particles) all put together for all the world as though their main purpose in life was to be a negative feedback mechanism of a complicated sort. Such ultimate laws would be like nothing so far known in science. They have a queer "smell" to them. I am just unable to believe in the nomological danglers themselves, or in the laws whereby they would dangle. If any philosophical arguments seemed to compel us to believe in such things, I would suspect a catch in the argument. In any case it is the object of this paper to show that there are no philosophical arguments which compel us to be dualists.

The above is largely a confession of faith, but it explains why I find Wittgenstein's position (as I construe it) so congenial. For on this view there are, in a sense, no sensations. A man is a vast arrangement of physical particles, but there are not, over and above this, sensations or states of consciousness. There are just behavioral facts about this vast mechanism, such as that it expresses a temptation (behavior disposition) to say "there is a yellowish-red patch on the wall" or that it goes through a sophisticated sort of wince, that is, says "I am in pain." Admittedly Wittgenstein says that though the sensation "is not a something," it is nevertheless "not a nothing either" (§ 304), but this need only mean that the word "ache" has a use. An ache is a thing, but only in the innocuous sense in which the plain man, in the first paragraph of Frege's *Foundations of Arithmetic*, answers the question "What is the number one?" by "a thing." It should be noted that when I assert that to say "I have a yellowish-orange after-image" is to express a temptation to assert the physical-object statement "There is a yellowish-orange patch on the wall,"

I mean that saying "I have a yellowish-orange after-image" is (partly) the exercise of the disposition [8] which is the temptation. It is not to *report* that I have the temptation, any more than is "I love you" normally a report that I love someone. Saying "I love you" is just part of the behavior which is the exercise of the disposition of loving someone.

Though for the reasons given above, I am very receptive to the above "expressive" account of sensation statements, I do not feel that it will quite do the trick. Maybe this is because I have not thought it out sufficiently, but it does seen to me as though, when a person says, "I have an after-image," he *is* making a genuine report, and that when he says "I have a pain," he *is* doing more than "replace pain-behavior," and that "this more" is not just to say that he is in distress. I am not so sure, however, that to admit this is to admit that there are nonphysical correlates of brain processes. Why should not sensations just be brain processes of a certain sort? There are, of course, well-known (as well as lesser-known) philosophical objections to the view that reports of sensations are reports of brain processes, but I shall try to argue that these arguments are by no means as cogent as is commonly thought to be the case.

Let me first try to state more accurately the thesis that sensations are brain processes. It is not the thesis that, for example, "after-image" or "ache" means the same as "brain process of sort X" (where "X" is replaced by a description of a certain sort of brain process). It is that, in so far as "after-image" or "ache" is a report of a process, it is a report of a process that *happens to be* a brain process. It follows that the thesis does not claim that sensation statements can be translated into statements about brain processes.[9] Nor does it claim that the logic of a sensation statement is the same as that of a brain-process statement. All it claims is that in so far as a sensation statement is a report of something, that something is in fact a brain process. Sensations are nothing over and above brain processes. Nations are nothing "over and above" citizens, but this does not prevent the logic of nation statements being very different from the logic of citizen statements, nor does it insure the translatability of nation statements into citizen statements. (I do not, however, wish to assert that the relation of sensation statements to brain-process statements is very like that of nation statements to citizen statements. Nations do not just *happen to be* nothing over and above citizens, for example. I bring in the "nations" example merely to make a negative point: that the fact that the logic of A-statements is different from that of B-statements does not insure that A's are anything over and above B's.)

Remarks on Identity. When I say that a sensation is a brain process or that lightning is an electric discharge, I am using "is" in the sense of strict identity. (Just as in the—in this case necessary—proposition "7 is identical with the smallest prime number greater than 5.") When I say that a sensation in a brain process or that lightning is an electric discharge I do not mean just that the sensation is somehow spatially or temporally continuous with the brain process or that the lightning is just spatially or temporally continuous with the discharge. When on the other hand I say that the successful general is the same person as the small boy who stole the apples I mean only that the successful general I see before me is a time slice [10] of the same four-dimensional object of which the small boy stealing apples is an earlier time slice. However, the four-dimensional object which has the general-I-see-before-me for its late time slice is identical in the strict sense with the four-dimensional object which has the small-boy-stealing-apples for an early time slice. I distinguish these two senses of "is identical with" because I wish to make it clear that the brain-process doctrine asserts identity in the *strict* sense.

I shall now discuss various possible objections to the view that the processes reported in sensation statements are in fact processes in the brain. Most of us have met some of these objections in our first year as philosophy students. All the more reason to take a good look at them. Others of the objections will be more recondite and subtle.

Objection 1. Any illiterate peasant can talk perfectly well about his after-images, or how things look or feel to him, or about his aches and pains, and yet he may know nothing whatever about neurophysiology. A man may, like Aristotle, believe that the brain is an organ for cooling the body without any impairment of his ability to make true statements about his sensations. Hence the things we are talking about when we describe our sensations cannot be processes in the brain.

Reply. You might as well say that a nation of slug-abeds, who never saw the Morning Star or knew of its existence, or who had never thought of the expression "the Morning Star," but who used the expression "the Evening Star" perfectly well, could not use this expression to refer to the same entity as we refer to (and describe as) "the Morning Star." [11]

You may object that the Morning Star is in a sense not the very same thing as the Evening Star, but only something spatiotemporally continuous with it. That is, you may say that the Morning Star is not the Evening Star in the strict sense of "identity" that I distinguished earlier.

There is, however, a more plausible example. Consider lightning. [12] Modern physical science tells us that lightning is a certain kind of electrical discharge due to ionization of clouds of water vapor in the atmosphere. This, it is now believed, is what the true nature of lightning is. Note that there are not two things: a flash of lightning and an electrical discharge. There is one thing, a flash of lightning, which is described scientifically as an electrical discharge to the earth from a cloud of ionized water molecules. The case is not at all like that of explaining a footprint by reference to a burglar. We say that what lightning really is, what its true nature as revealed by science is, is an electrical discharge. (It is not the true nature of a footprint to be a burglar.)

To forestall irrelevant objections, I should like to make it clear that by "lightning" I mean the publicly observable physical object, lightning, not a visual sense-datum of lightning. I say that the publicly observable physical object lightning is in fact the electrical discharge, not just a correlate of it. The sense-datum, or rather the having of the sense-datum, the "look" of lightning, may well in my view be a correlate of the electrical discharge. For in my view it is a brain state *caused* by the lightning. But we should no more confuse sensations of lightning with lightning than we confuse sensations of a table with the table.

In short, the reply to Objection 1 is that there can be contingent statements of the form "A is identical with B," and a person may well know that something is an A without knowing that it is a B. An illiterate peasant might well be able to talk about his sensations without knowing about his brain processes, just as he can talk about lightning though he knows nothing of electricity.

Objection 2. It is only a contingent fact (if it is a

fact) that when we have a certain kind of sensation there is a certain kind of process in our brain. Indeed it is possible, though perhaps in the highest degree unlikely, that our present physiological theories will be as out of date as the ancient theory connecting mental processes with goings on in the heart. It follows that when we report a sensation we are not reporting a brain process.

Reply. The objection certainly proves that when we say "I have an after-image" we cannot *mean* something of the form "I have such and such a brain process." But this does not show that what we report (having an after-image) is not *in fact* a brain process. "I see lightning" does not *mean* "I see an electrical discharge." Indeed, it is logically possible (though highly unlikely) that the electrical discharge account of lightning might one day be given up. Again, "I see the Evening Star" does not *mean* the same as "I see the Morning Star," and yet "The Evening Star and the Morning Star are one and the same thing" is a contingent proposition. Possibly Objection 2 derives some of its apparent strength from a "Fido"–Fido theory of meaning. If the meaning of an expression were what the expression named, then of course it *would* follow from the fact that "sensation" and "brain process" have different meanings that they cannot name one and the same thing.

Objection 3.[13] Even if Objections 1 and 2 do not prove that sensations are something over and above brain processes, they do prove that the qualities of sensations are something over and above the qualities of brain processes. That is, it may be possible to get out of asserting the existence of irreducibly psychic processes, but not out of asserting the existence of irreducibly psychic *properties.* For suppose we identify the Morning Star with the Evening Star. Then there must be some properties which logically imply that of being the Morning Star, and quite distinct properties which entail that of being the Evening Star. Again, there must be some properties (for example, that of being a yellow flash) which are logically distinct from those in the physicalist story.

Indeed, it might be thought that the objection succeeds at one jump. For consider the property of "being a yellow flash." It might seem that this property lies inevitably outside the physicalist framework within which I am trying to work (either by "yellow" being an objective emergent property of physical objects, or else by being a power to produce yellow sense-data, where "yellow," in this second instantiation of the word, refers to a purely phenomenal or introspectible quality). I must therefore digress for a moment and indicate how I deal with secondary qualities. I shall concentrate on color.

First of all, let me introduce the concept of a normal percipient. One person is more a normal percipient than another if he can make color discriminations that the other cannot. For example, if A can pick a lettuce leaf out of a heap of cabbage leaves, whereas B cannot though he can pick a lettuce leaf out of a heap of beetroot leaves, then A is more normal than B. (I am assuming that A and B are not given time to distinguish the leaves by their slight difference in shape, and so forth.) From the concept of "more normal than" it is easy to see how we can introduce the concept of "normal." Of course, Eskimos may make the finest discriminations at the blue end of the spectrum, Hottentots at the red end. In this case the concept of a normal percipient is a slightly idealized one, rather like that of "the mean sun" in astronomical chronology. There is no need to go into such subtleties now. I say that "This is red" means something roughly like "A normal percipient would not easily pick this out of a clump of geranium petals though he would pick it out of a clump of lettuce leaves." Of course it does not exactly mean this: a person might know the meaning of "red" without knowing anything about geraniums, or even about normal percipients. But the point is that a person can be *trained* to say "This is red" of objects which would not easily be picked out of geranium petals by a normal percipient, and so on. (Note that even a color-blind person can reasonably assert that something is red, though of course he needs to use another human being, not just himself, as his "color meter.") This account of secondary qualities explains their unimportance in physics. For obviously the discriminations and lack of discriminations made by a very complex neurophysiological mechanism are hardly likely to correspond to simple and nonarbitrary distinctions in nature.

I therefore elucidate colors as powers, in Locke's sense, to evoke certain sorts of discriminatory responses in human beings. They are also of course, powers to cause sensations in human beings (an account still nearer Locke's). But these sensations, I am arguing, are identifiable with brain processes.

Now how do I get over the objection that a sensation can be identified with a brain process only if it has some phenomenal property, not possessed by brain processes, whereby one-half of the identification may be, so to speak, pinned down?

Reply. My suggestion is as follows. When a person says, "I see a yellowish-orange after-image," he is saying something like this: *"There is something going on which is like what is going on when* I have my eyes open, am awake, and there is an orange illuminated in good light in front of me, that is, when I really see an orange." (And there is no reason why a person should not say the same thing when he is having a veridical sense-datum, so long as we construe "like" in the last sentence in such a sense that something can be like itself.) Notice that the italicized words, namely "there is something going on which is like what is going on when," are all quasilogical or topic-neutral words. This explains why the ancient Greek peasant's reports about his sensations can be neutral between dualistic metaphysics or my materialistic metaphysics. It explains how sensations can be brain processes and yet how a man who reports them need know nothing about brain processes. For he reports them only very abstractly as "something going on which is like what is going on when. . . ." Similarly, a person may say "someone is in the room," thus reporting truly that the doctor is in the room, even though he has never heard of doctors. (There are not two people in the room: "someone" *and* the doctor.) This account of sensation statements also explains the singular elusiveness of "raw feels"—why no one seems to be able to pin any properties on them.[14] Raw feels, in my view, are colorless for the very same reason that *something* is colorless. This does not mean that sensations do not have plenty of properties, for if they are brain processes they certainly have lots of neurological properties. It only means that in speaking of them as being like or unlike one another we need not know or mention these properties.

This, them, is how I would reply to Objection 3. The strength of my reply depends on the possibility of our being able to report that one thing is like another without being able to state the respect in which it is like. I do not see why this should not be

so. If we think cybernetically about the nervous system we can envisage it as able to respond to certain likenesses of its internal processes without being able to do more. It would be easier to build a machine which would tell us, say on a punched tape, whether or not two objects were similar, than it would be to build a machine which would report wherein the similarities consisted.

Objection 4. The after-image is not in physical space. The brain process is. So the after-image is not a brain process.

Reply. This is an *ignoratio elenchi.* I am not arguing that the after-image is a brain process, but that the experience of having an after-image is a brain process. It is the *experience* which is reported in the introspective report. Similarly, if it is objected that the after-image is yellowy-orange, my reply is that it is the experience of seeing yellowy-orange that is being described, and this experience is not a yellowy-orange something. So to say that a brain process cannot be yellowy-orange is not to say that a brain process cannot in fact be the experience of having a yellowy-orange after-image. There is, in a sense, no such thing as an after-image or a sense-datum, though there is such a thing as the experience of having an image, and this experience is described indirectly in material object language, not in phenomenal language for there is no such thing.[15] We describe the experience by saying, in effect, that it is like the experience we have when, for example, we really see a yellowy-orange patch on the wall. Trees and wallpaper can be green, but not the experience of seeing or imagining a tree or wallpaper. (Or if they are described as green or yellow this can only be in a derived sense.)

Objection 5. It would make sense to say of a molecular movement in the brain that it is swift or slow, straight or circular, but it makes no sense to say this of the experience of seeing something yellow.

Reply. So far we have not given sense to talk of experiences as swift or slow, straight or circular. But I am not claiming that "experience" and "brain process" mean the same or even that they have the same logic. "Somebody" and "the doctor" do not have the same logic, but this does not lead us to suppose that talking about somebody telephoning is talking about someone over and above, say, the doctor. The ordinary man when he reports an experience is reporting that something is going on, but he leaves it open as to what sort of thing is going on, whether in a material solid medium or perhaps in some sort of gaseous medium, or even perhaps in some sort of non-spatial medium (if this makes sense). All that I am saying is that "experience" and "brain process" may in fact refer to the same thing, and if so we may easily adopt a convention (which is not a change in our present rules for the use of experience words but an addition to them) whereby it would make sense to talk of an experience in terms appropriate to physical processes.

Objection 6. Sensations are private, brain processes are *public*. If I sincerely say, "I see a yellowish-orange after-image," and I am not making a verbal mistake, then I cannot be wrong. But I can be wrong about a brain process. The scientist looking into my brain might be having an illusion. Moreover, it makes sense to say that two or more people are observing the same brain process but not that two or more people are reporting the same inner experience.

Reply. This shows that the language of introspective reports has a different logic from the language of material processes. It is obvious that until the brain-process theory is much improved and widely accepted there will be no *criteria* for saying "Smith has an experience of such-and-such a sort" *except* Smith's introspective reports. So we have adopted a rule of language that (normally) what Smith says goes.

Objection 7. I can imagine myself turned to stone and yet having images, aches, pains, and so on.

Reply. I can imagine that the electrical theory of lightning is false, that lightning is some sort of purely optical phenomenon. I can imagine that lightning is not an electrical discharge. I can imagine that the Evening Star is not the Morning Star. But it is. All the objection shows is that "experience" and "brain process" do not have the same meaning. It does not show that an experience is not in fact a brain process.

This objection is perhaps much the same as one which can be summed up by the slogan: "What can be composed of nothing cannot be composed of anything."[16] The argument goes as follows: on the brain-process thesis the identity between the brain process and the experience is a contingent one. So it is logically possible that there should be no brain process, and no process of any other sort either (no

heart process, no kidney process, no liver process). There would be the experience but no "corresponding" physiological process with which we might be able to identify it empirically.

I suspect that the objector is thinking of the experience as a ghostly entity. So it is composed of something, not of nothing, after all. On his view it is composed of ghost stuff, and on mine it is composed of brain stuff. Perhaps the counter-reply will be[17] that the experience is simple and uncompounded, and so it is not composed of anything after all. This seems to be a quibble, for, if it were taken seriously, the remark "What can be composed of nothing cannot be composed of anything" could be recast as an a priori argument against Democritus and atomism and for Descartes and infinite divisibility. And it seems odd that a question of this sort could be settled a priori. We must therefore construe the word "composed" in a very weak sense, which would allow us to say that even an indivisible atom is composed of something (namely, itself). The dualist cannot really say that an experience can be composed of nothing. For he holds that experiences are something over and above material processes, that is, that they are a sort of ghost stuff. (Or perhaps ripples in an underlying ghost stuff.) I say that the dualist's hypothesis is a perfectly intelligible one. But I say that experiences are not to be identified with ghost stuff but with brain stuff. This is another hypothesis, and in my view a very plausible one. The present argument cannot knock it down a priori.

Objection 8. The "beetle in the box" objection (see Wittgenstein, *Philosophical Investigations*, § 293). How could descriptions of experiences, if these are genuine reports, get a foothold in language? For any rule of language must have public criteria for its correct application.

Reply. The change from describing how things are to describing how we feel is just a change from uninhibitedly saying "this is so" to saying "this looks so." That is, when the naive person might be tempted to say, "There is a patch of light on the wall which moves whenever I move my eyes" or "A pin is being stuck into me," we have learned how to resist this temptation and say "It *looks as though* there is a patch of light on the wallpaper" or "It *feels as though* someone were sticking a pin into me." The introspective account tells us about the individual's state of consciousness in the same way as does "I see a patch of light" or "I feel a pin being stuck into me": it differs from the corresponding perception statement in so far as it withdraws any claim about what is actually going on in the external world. From the point of view of the psychologist, the change from talking about the environment to talking about one's perceptual sensations is simply a matter of disinhibiting certain reaction. These are reactions which one normally suppresses because one has learned that in the prevailing circumstances they are unlikely to provide a good indication of the state of the environment.[18] To say that something looks green to me is simply to say that my experience is like the experience I get when I see something that really is green. In my reply to Objection 3, I pointed out the extreme openness or generality of statements which report experiences. This explains why there is no language of private qualities, (Just as "someone," unlike "the doctor," is a colorless word.) [19]

If it is asked what is the difference between those brain processes which, in my view, are experiences and those brain processes which are not, I can only reply that it is at present unknown. I have been tempted to conjecture that the difference may in part be that between perception and reception (in D. M. MacKay's terminology) and that the type of brain process which is an experience might be identifiable with MacKay's active "matching response."[20] This, however, cannot be the whole story, because sometimes I can perceive something unconsciously, as when I take a handkerchief out of a drawer without being aware that I am doing so. But at the very least, we can classify the brain processes which are experiences as those brain processes which are, or might have been, causal conditions of those pieces of verbal behaviour which we call report of immediate experience.

I have now considered a number of objections to the brain-process thesis. I wish now to conclude with some remarks on the logical status of the thesis itself. U. T. Place seems to hold that it is a straight-out scientific hypothesis.[21] If so, he is partly right and partly wrong. If the issue is between (say) a brain-process thesis and a heart thesis, or a liver thesis, or a kidney thesis, then the issue is a purely empirical one, and the verdict is overwhelmingly in favor of the brain. The right sorts of things don't go on in the heart, liver, or kidney, nor do these organs possess the right sort of complexity of structure. On the other hand, if the issue is between a brain-or-liver-or-kidney thesis (that is, some form of materialism) on the one hand and epiphenomenalism on the other hand, then the issue is not an empirical one. For there is no conceivable experiment which could decide between materialism and epiphenomenalism. This latter issue is not like the average straight-out empirical issue in science, but like the issue between the nineteenth-century English naturalist Philip Gosse[22] and the orthodox geologists and paleontologists of his day. According to Gosse, the earth was created about 4000 B.C. exactly as described in *Genesis*, with twisted rock strata, "evidence" of erosion, and so forth, and all sorts of fossils, all in their appropriate strata just as if the usual evolutionist story had been true. Clearly this theory is in a sense irrefutable; no evidence can possibly tell against it. Let us ignore the theological setting in which Philip Gosse's hypothesis had been placed, thus ruling out objections of a theological kind, such as "what a queer god who would go to such elaborate lengths to deceive us." Let us suppose that it is held that the universe just *began* in 4004 B.C. with the initial conditions just everywhere as they were in 4004 B.C., and in particular that our own planet began with sediment in the rivers, eroded cliffs, fossils in the rocks, and so on. No scientist would ever entertain this as a serious hypothesis, consistent though it is with all possible evidence. The hypothesis offends against the principles of parsimony and simplicity. There would be far too many brute and inexplicable facts. Why are pterodactyl bones just as they are? No explanation in terms of the evolution of pterodactyls from earlier forms of life would any longer be possible. We would have millions of facts about the world as it was in 4004 B.C. that just have to be *accepted*.

The issue between the brain-process theory and epiphenomenalism seems to be of the above sort. (Assuming that a behavioristic reduction of introspective reports is not possible.) If it be agreed that there are no cogent philosophical arguments which force us into accepting dualism, and if the brain-process theory and dualism are equally consistent with the facts, then the principles of parsimony and simplicity seem to me to decide overwhelmingly in favor of the brain-process theory. As I pointed out earlier, dualism involves a large number of irreducible psychophysical laws (whereby the "nomological danglers" dangle) of a queer sort, that just have to be taken on trust, and are just as difficult to swallow as the irreducible facts about the paleontology of the earth with which we are faced on Philip Gosse's theory.

Notes

1. This is a very slightly revised version of a paper which was first published in the *Philosophical Review,* LXVIII (1959), 141–156.
2. *British Journal of Psychology.* XLVII (1956), 44–50.
3. *Minnesota Studies in the Philosophy of Science,* Vol. II (Minneapolis: University of Minnesota Press, 1958), pp. 370–497.
4. Some philosophers of my acquaintance, who have the advantage over me in having known Wittgenstein, would say that this interpretation of him is too behavioristic. However, it seems to me a very natural interpretation of his printed words, and whether or not it is Wittgenstein's real view it is certainly an interesting and important one. I wish to consider it here as a possible rival both to the "brain-process" thesis and to straight-out old-fashioned dualism.
5. See Ryle, *The Concept of Mind* (London: Hutchinson's University Library, 1949), p. 93.
6. On this point see Paul Oppenheim and Hilary Putnam, "Unity of Science as a Working Hypothesis," in *Minnesota Studies in the Philosophy of Science,* Vol. II (Minneapolis: University of Minnesota Press, 1958), pp. 3–36.
7. Feigl, *op. cit.,* p. 428. Feigl uses the expression "nomological danglers" for the laws whereby the entities dangle: I have used the expression to refer to the dangling entities themselves.
8. Wittgenstein did not like the word "disposition." I am using it to put in a nutshell (and perhaps inaccurately) the view which I am attributing to Wittgenstein. I should like to repeat that I do not wish to claim that my interpretation of Wittgenstein is correct. Some of those who knew him do not interpret him in this way. It is merely a view which I find myself extracting from his printed words and which I think is important and worth discussing for its own sake.
9. See Place, *op. cit.,* p. 45, and Feigl, *op. cit.,* p. 390, near top.
10. See J. H. Woodger, *Theory Construction,* International Encyclopedia of Unified Science, II, No. 5 (Chicago: University of Chicago Press, 1939), 38. I here permit myself to speak loosely. For warnings against possible ways of going wrong with this sort of talk, see my note "Spatialising Time," *Mind,* LXIV (1955), 239–41.
11. Cf. Feigl, *op. cit.,* p. 439.
12. See Place, *op. cit.,* p. 48; also Feigl, *op. cit.,* p. 438.
13. I think this objection was first put to me by Professor Max Black. I think it is the most subtle of any of those I have considered, and the one which I am least confident of having satisfactorily met.
14. See B. A. Farrell, "Experience," *Mind,* LIX (1950), 170–98.
15. Dr. J. R. Smythies claims that a sense-datum language could be taught independently of the material object language ("A Note on the Fallacy of the 'Phenomenological Fallacy,'" *British Journal of Psychology,* XLVIII [1957], 141–44). I am not so sure of this: there must be some public criteria for a person having got a rule wrong before we can teach him the rule. I suppose someone might *accidentally* learn color words by Dr. Smythies' procedure. I am not, of course, denying that we can learn a sense-datum language in the sense that we can learn to report out experience. Nor would Place deny it.
16. I owe this objection to Dr. C. B. Martin. I gather that he no longer wishes to maintain this objection, at any rate in its present form.
17. Martin did not make this reply, but one of his students did.
18. I owe this point to Place, in correspondence.
19. The "beetle in the box" objection is, *if it is sound,* an objection to *any* view, and in particular the Cartesian one, that introspective reports are genuine reports. So it is no objection to a weaker thesis that I would be concerned to uphold, namely, that if introspective reports of "experiences" are genuinely reports, then the things they are reports of are in fact brain processes.
20. See his article "Towards an Information-Flow Model of Human Behaviour," *British Journal of Psychology,* XLVII (1956), 30–43.
21. *Op. cit.* For a further discussion of this, in reply to the original version of the present paper, see Place's note "Materialism as a Scientific Hypothesis," *Philosophical Review,* LXIX (1960), 101–104.
22. See the entertaining account of Gosse's book *Omphalos* by Martin Gardner in *Fads and Fallacies in the Name of Science,* 2nd ed. (New York: Dover, 1957), pp. 124–27.

What Is It Like to Be a Bat?

THOMAS NAGEL

Thomas Nagel (1937–   ) teaches philosophy at New York University and is the author of numerous articles and several books.

Consciousness is what makes the mind-body problem really intractable. Perhaps that is why current discussions of the problem give it little attention or get it obviously wrong. The recent wave of reductionist euphoria has produced several analyses of mental phenomena and mental concepts designed to explain the possibility of some variety of materialism, psychophysical identification, or reduction. But the problems dealt with are those common to this type of reduction and other types, and what makes the mind-body problem unique, and unlike the water-H_2O problem or the Turing machine-IBM machine problem or the lightning-electrical discharge problem or the gene-DNA problem or the oak tree-hydrocarbon problem, is ignored.

Every reductionist has his favorite analogy from modern science. It is most unlikely that any of these unrelated examples of successful reduction will shed light on the relation of mind to brain. But philosophers share the general human weakness for explanations of what is incomprehensible in terms suited for what is familiar and well understood, though entirely different. This has led to the acceptance of implausible accounts of the mental largely because they would permit familiar kinds of reduction. I shall try to explain why the usual examples do not help us to understand the relation between mind and body—why, indeed, we have at present no conception of what an explanation of the physical nature of a mental phenomenon would be. Without consciousness the mind-body problem would be much less interesting. With consciousness it seems hopeless. The most important and characteristic feature of conscious mental phenomena is very poorly understood. Most reductionist theories do not even try to explain it. And careful examination will show that no currently available concept of reduction is applicable to it. Perhaps a new theoretical form can be devised for the purpose, but such a solution, if it exists, lies in the distinct intellectual future.

Conscious experience is a widespread phenomenon. It occurs at many levels of animal life, though we cannot be sure of its presence in the simpler organisms, and it is very difficult to say in general what provides evidence of it. (Some extremists have been prepared to deny it even of mammals other than man.) No doubt it occurs in countless forms totally unimaginable to us, on other planets in other solar systems throughout the universe. But no matter how the form may vary, the fact that an organism has conscious experience *at all* means, basically, that there is something it is like to *be* that organism. There may be further implications about the form of the experience; there may even (though I doubt it) be implications about the behavior of the organism. But fundamentally an organism has conscious mental states if and only if there is something that it is like to *be* that organism—something it is like *for* the organism.

We may call this the subjective character of experience. It is not captured by any of the familiar, recently devised reductive analyses of the mental, for all of them are logically compatible with its absence.

From "What Is It Like to Be a Bat?" by Thomas Nagel, *The Philosophical Review,* October 1994. Reprinted by permission of the author and *The Philosophical Review.* Footnotes deleted.

It is not analyzable in terms of any explanatory system of functional states, or international states, since these could be ascribed to robots or automata that behaved like people though they experienced nothing. It is not analyzable in terms of the causal role of experiences in relation to typical human behavior—for similar reasons. I do not deny that conscious mental states and events cause behavior, nor that they may be given functional characterizations. I deny only that this kind of thing exhausts their analysis. Any reductionist program has to be based on an analysis of what is to be reduced. If the analysis leaves something out, the problem will be falsely posed. It is useless to base the defense of materialism on any analysis of mental phenomena that fails to deal explicitly with their subjective character. For there is no reason to suppose that a reduction which seems plausible when no attempt is made to account for consciousness can be extended to include consciousness. Without some idea, therefore, of what the subjective character of experience is, we cannot know what is required of a physicalist theory.

While an account of the physical basis of mind must explain many things, this appears to be the most difficult. It is impossible to exclude the phenomenological features of experience from a reduction in the same way that one excludes the phenomenal features of an ordinary substance from a physical or chemical reduction of it—namely, by explaining them as effects on the minds of human observers. If physicalism is to be defended, the phenomenological features must themselves be given a physical account. But when we examine their subjective character it seems that such a result is impossible. The reason is that every subjective phenomenon is essentially connected with a single point of view, and it seems inevitable that an objective, physical theory will abandon that point of view.

Let me first try to state the issue somewhat more fully than by referring to the relation between the subjective and the objective, or between the *pour-soi* and the *en-soi*. This is far from easy. Facts about what it is like to be an *X* are very peculiar, so peculiar that some may be inclined to doubt their reality, or the significance of claims about them. To illustrate the connection between subjectivity and a point of view, and to make evident the importance of subjective features, it will help to explore the matter in relation to an example that brings out clearly the divergence between the two types of conception, subjective and objective.

I assume we all believe that bats have experience. After all, they are mammals, and there is no more doubt that they have experience than that mice or pigeons or whales have experience. I have chosen bats instead of wasps or flounders because if one travels too far down the phylogenetic tree, people gradually shed their faith that there is experience there at all. Bats, although more closely related to us than those other species, nevertheless present a range of activity and a sensory apparatus so different from ours that the problem I want to pose is exceptionally vivid (though it certainly could be raised with other species). Even without the benefit of philosophical reflection, anyone who has spent some time in an enclosed space with an excited bat knows what it is to encounter a fundamentally *alien* form of life.

I have said that the essence of the belief that bats have experience is that there is something that it is like to be a bat. Now we know that most bats (the microchiroptera, to be precise) perceive the external world primarily by sonar, or echo-location, detecting the reflections, from objects within range, of their own rapid, subtly modulated, high-frequency shrieks. Their brains are designed to correlate the outgoing impulses with the subsequent echoes, and the information thus acquired enables bats to make precise discrimination of distance, size, shape, motion, and texture comparable to those we make by vision. But bat sonar, though clearly a form of perception, is not similar in its operation to any sense that we possess, and there is no reason to suppose that it is subjectively like anything we can experience or imagine. This appears to create difficulties for the notion of what it is like to be a bat. We must consider whether any method will permit us to extrapolate to the inner life of the bat from our own case, and if not, what alternative methods there may be for understanding the notion.

Our own experience provides the basic material for our imagination, whose range is therefore limited. It will not help to try to imagine that one has webbing on one's arms, which enables one to fly around at dusk and dawn catching insects in one's mouth; that one has very poor vision, and perceives the surrounding world by a system of reflected high-frequency sound signals; and that one spends the day hanging upside down by one's feet in an attic. In so far as I can imagine this (which is not very far), it tells me only what it would be like for *me* to behave as a bat behaves. But that is not the question. I want to know what it is like for a *bat* to be a bat. Yet if I try to imagine this, I am restricted to the resources of my own mind, and those resources are inadequate to the task. I cannot perform it either by imagining additions to my present experience, or by imagining segments gradually subtracted from it, or by imagining some combination of additions, subtractions, and modifications.

To the extent that I could look and behave like a wasp or a bat without changing my fundamental structure, my experiences would not be anything like the experiences of those animals. On the other hand, it is doubtful that any meaning can be attached to the supposition that I should possess the internal neurophysiological constitution of a bat. Even if I could by gradual degrees be transformed into a bat, nothing in my present constitution enables me to imagine what the experiences of such a future stage of myself thus metamorphosed would be like. The best evidence would come from the experiences of bats, if we only knew what they were like.

So if extrapolation from our own case is involved in the idea of what it is like to be a bat, the extrapolation must be incompletable. We cannot form more than a schematic conception of what it *is* like. For example, we may ascribe general *types* of experience on the basis of the animal's structure and behavior. Thus we describe bat sonar as a form of three-dimensional forward perception; we believe that bats feel some versions of pain, fear, hunger, and lust, and that they have other, more familiar types of perception besides sonar. But we believe that those experiences also have in each case a specific subjective character, which it is beyond our ability to conceive. And if there is conscious life elsewhere in the universe, it is likely that some of it will not be describable even in the most general experiential terms available to us. (The problem is not confined to exotic cases, however, for it exists between one person and another. The subjective character of the experience of a person deaf and blind from birth is not accessible to me, for example, nor presumably is mine

to him. This does not prevent us each from believing that the other's experience has such a subjective character.)

If anyone is inclined to deny that we can believe in the existence of facts like this whose exact nature we cannot possibly conceive, he should reflect that in contemplating the bats we are in much the same position that intelligent bats or Martians would occupy if they tried to form a conception of what it was like to be us. The structure of their own minds might make it impossible for them to succeed, but we know they would be wrong to conclude that there is not anything precise that it is like to be us: that only certain general types of mental state could be ascribed to us (perhaps perception and appetite would be concepts common to us both; perhaps not). We know they would be wrong to draw such a skeptical conclusion because we know what it is like to be us. And we know that while it includes an enormous amount of variation and complexity, and while we do not possess the vocabulary to describe it adequately, its subjective character is highly specific, and in some respects describable in terms that can be understood only by creatures like us. The fact that we cannot expect ever to accommodate in our language a detailed description of Martian or bat phenomenology should not lead us to dismiss as meaningless the claim that bats and Martians have experiences fully comparable in richness of detail to our own. It would be fine if someone were to develop concepts and a theory that enabled us to think about those things; but such an understanding may be permanently denied to us by the limits of our nature. And to deny the reality or logical significance of what we can never describe or understand is the crudest form of cognitive dissonance.

This brings us to the edge of a topic that requires much more discussion than I can give it here: namely, the relation between facts on the one hand and conceptual schemes or systems of representation on the other. My realism about the subjective domain in all its forms implies a belief in the existence of facts beyond the reach of human concepts. Certainly it is possible for a human being to believe that there are facts which humans never *will* possess the requisite concepts to represent or comprehend. Indeed, it would be foolish to doubt this, given the finiteness of humanity's expectations. After all, there would have been transfinite numbers even if everyone had been wiped out by the Black Death before Cantor discovered them. But one might also believe that there are facts which *could* not ever be represented or comprehended by human beings, even if the species lasted forever—simply because our structure does not permit us to operate with concepts of the requisite type. This impossibility might even be observed by other beings, but it is not clear that the existence of such beings, or the possibility of their existence, is a precondition of the significance of the hypothesis that there are humanly inaccessible facts. (After all, the nature of beings with access to humanly inaccessible facts is presumably itself a humanly inaccessible fact.) Reflection on what it is like to be a bat seems to lead us, therefore, to the conclusion that there are facts that do not consist in the truth of propositions expressible in a human language. We can be compelled to recognize the existence of such facts without being able to state or comprehend them.

I shall not pursue this subject, however. Its bearing on the topic before us (namely, the mind-body problem) is that it enables us to make a general observation about the subjective character of experience. Whatever may be the status of facts about what it is like to be a human being, or a bat, or a Martian, these appear to be facts that embody a particular point of view.

I am not adverting here to the alleged privacy of experience to its possessor. The point of view in question is not one accessible only to a single individual. Rather it is a *type*. It is often possible to take up a point of view other than one's own, so the comprehension of such facts is not limited to one's own case. There is a sense in which phenomenological facts are perfectly objective: one person can know or say of another what the quality of the other's experience is. They are subjective, however, in the sense that even this objective ascription of experience is possible only for someone sufficiently similar to the object of ascription to be able to adopt his point of view—to understand the ascription in the first person as well as in the third, so to speak. The more different from oneself the other experiencer is, the less success one can expect with this enterprise. In our own case we occupy the relevant point of view, but we will have as much difficulty understanding our own experience properly if we approach it from another point of view as we would if we tried to understand the experience of another species without taking up *its* point of view.

This bears directly on the mind-body problem. For if the facts of experience—facts about what it is like *for* the experiencing organism—are accessible only from one point of view, then it is a mystery how the true character of experiences could be revealed in the physical operation of that organism. The latter is a domain of objective facts *par excellence*—the kind that can be observed and understood from many points of view and by individuals with differing perceptual systems. There are no comparable imaginative obstacles to the acquisition of knowledge about bat neurophysiology by human scientists, and intelligent bats or Martians might learn more about the human brain than we ever will.

This is not by itself an argument against reduction. A Martian scientist with no understanding of visual perception could understand the rainbow, or lightning, or clouds as physical phenomena, though he would never be able to understand the human concepts of rainbow, lightning, or cloud, or the place these things occupy in our phenomenal world. The objective nature of the things picked out by these concepts could be apprehended by him because, although the concepts themselves are connected with a particular point of view and a particular visual phenomenology, the things apprehended from that point of view are not: they are observable from the point of view but external to it; hence they can be comprehended from other points of view also, either by the same organisms or by others. Lightning has an objective character that is not exhausted by its visual appearance, and this can be investigated by a Martian without vision. To be precise, it has a *more* objective character than is revealed in its visual appearance. In speaking of the move from subjective to objective characterization, I wish to remain noncommittal about the existence of an end point, the completely objective intrinsic nature of the thing, which one might or might not be able to reach. It may be more accurate to think of objectivity as a direction in which the understanding can travel. And in understanding a phenomenon like lightning, it is legitimate to go as far away as one can from a strictly human viewpoint.

In the case of experience, on the other hand, the connection with a particular point of view seems much closer. It is difficult to understand what could be meant by the *objective* character of an experience, apart from the particular point of view from which its subject apprehends it. After all, what would be left of what it was like to be a bat if one removed the viewpoint of the bat? But if experience does not have, in addition to its subjective character, an objective nature that can be apprehended from many different points of view, then how can it be supposed that a Martian investigating my brain might be observing physical processes which were my mental processes (as he might observe physical processes which were bolts of lightning), only from a different point of view? How, for that matter, could a human physiologist observe them from another point of view.

We appear to be faced with a general difficulty about psycho-physical reduction. In other areas the process of reduction is a move in the direction of greater objectivity, toward a more accurate view of the real nature of things. This is accomplished by reducing our dependence on individual or species-specific points of view toward the object of investigation. We describe it not in terms of the impressions it makes on our senses, but in terms of its more general effects and of properties detectable by means other than the human senses. The less it depends on a specifically human viewpoint, the more objective is our description. It is possible to follow this path because although the concepts and ideas we employ in thinking about the external world are initially applied from a point of view that involves our perceptual apparatus, they are used by us to refer to things beyond themselves—toward which we *have* the phenomenal point of view. Therefore we can abandon it in favor of another, and still be thinking about the same things.

Experience itself, however, does not seem to fit the pattern. The idea of moving from appearance to reality seems to make no sense here. What is the analogue in this case to pursuing a more objective understanding of the same phenomena by abandoning the initial subjective viewpoint toward them in favor of another that is more objective but concerns the same thing? Certainly it *appears* unlikely that we will get closer to the real nature of human

experience by leaving behind the particularity of our human point of view and striving for a description in terms accessible to beings that could not imagine what it was like to be us. If the subjective character of experience is fully comprehensible only from one point of view, then any shift to greater objectivity—that is, less attachment to a specific viewpoint—does not take us nearer to the real nature of the phenomenon: it takes us farther away from it.

In a sense, the seeds of this objection to the reducibility of experience are already detectable in successful cases of reduction; for in discovering sound to be, in reality, a wave phenomenon in air or other media, we leave behind one viewpoint to take up another, and the auditory, human or animal viewpoint that we leave behind remains unreduced. Members of radically different species may both understand the same physical events in objective terms, and this does not require that they understand the phenomenal forms in which those events appear to the senses of members of the other species. Thus it is a condition of their referring to a common reality that their more particular viewpoints are not part of the common reality that they both apprehend. The reduction can succeed only if the species-specific viewpoint is omitted from what is to be reduced.

But while we are right to leave this point of view aside in seeking a fuller understanding of the external world, we cannot ignore it permanently, since it is the essence of the internal world, and not merely a point of view on it. Most of the neobehaviorism of recent philosophical psychology results from the effort to substitute an objective concept of mind for the real thing, in order to have nothing left over which cannot be reduced. If we acknowledge that a physical theory of mind must account for the subjective character of experience, we must admit that no presently available conception gives us a clue how this could be done. The problem is unique. If mental processes are indeed physical processes, then there is something it is like, intrinsically, to undergo certain physical processes. What it is for such a thing to be the case remains a mystery.

What moral should be drawn from these reflections, and what should be done next? It would be a mistake to conclude that physicalism must be false. Nothing is proved by the inadequacy of physicalist hypotheses that assume a faulty objective analysis of mind. It would be truer to say that physicalism is a position we cannot understand because we do not at present have any conception of how it might be true. Perhaps it will be thought unreasonable to require such a conception as a condition of understanding. After all, it might be said, the meaning of physicalism is clear enough: mental states are states of the body; mental events are physical events. We do not know *which* physical states and events they are, but that should not prevent us from understanding the hypothesis. What could be clearer than the words "is" and "are"?

But I believe it is precisely this apparent clarity of the word "is" that is deceptive. Usually, when we are told that *X* is *Y* we know *how* it is supposed to be true, but that depends on a conceptual or theoretical background and is not conveyed by the "is" alone. We know how both "*X*" and "*Y*" refer, and the kinds of things to which they refer, and we have a rough idea how the two referential paths might converge on a single thing, be it an object, a person, a process, and event, or whatever. But when the two terms of the identification are very disparate it may not be so clear how it could be true. We may not have even a rough idea of how the two referential paths could converge, or what kind of things they might converge on, and a theoretical framework may have to be supplied to enable us to understand this. Without the framework, an air of mysticism surrounds the identification.

This explains the magical flavor of popular presentations of fundamental scientific discoveries, given out as propositions to which one must subscribe without really understanding them. For example, people are now told at an early age that all matter is really energy. But despite the fact that they know what "is" means most of them never form a conception of what makes this claim true, because they lack the theoretical background.

At the present time the status of physicalism is similar to that which the hypothesis that matter is energy would have had if uttered by a pre-Socratic philosopher. We do not have the beginnings of a conception of how it might be true. In order to understand the hypothesis that a mental event is a physical event, we require more than an understanding of the word "is." The idea of how a mental and a physical term might refer to the same thing is lacking, and the usual analogies with theoretical identification in other fields fail to supply it. They fail because if we construe the reference of mental terms to physical events on the usual model, we either get a reappearance of separate subjective events as the effects through which mental reference to physical events is secured, or else we get a false account of how mental terms refer (for example, a causal behaviorist one).

Strangely enough, we may have evidence for the truth of something we cannot really understand. Suppose a caterpillar is locked in a sterile safe by someone unfamiliar with insect metamorphosis, and weeks later the safe is reopened, revealing a butterfly. If the person knows that the safe has been shut the whole time, he has reason to believe that the butterfly is or was once the caterpillar, without having any idea in what sense this might be so. (One possibility is that the caterpillar contained a tiny winged parasite that devoured it and grew into the butterfly.)

It is conceivable that we are in such a position with regard to physicalism. Donald Davidson has argued that if mental events have physical causes and effects, they must have physical descriptions. He holds that we have reason to believe this even though we do not—and in fact *could* not—have a general psychophysical theory. His argument applies to intentional mental events, but I think we also have some reason to believe that sensations are physical processes, without being in a position to understand how. Davidson's position is that certain physical events have irreducibly mental properties, and perhaps some view describable in this way is correct. But nothing of which we can now form a conception corresponds to it; nor have we any idea what a theory would be like that enabled us to conceive of it.

Very little work has been done on the basic question (from which mention of the brain can be entirely omitted) whether any sense can be made of experiences' having an objective character at all. Does it make sense, in other words, to ask what my experiences are *really* like, as opposed to how they appear to me? We cannot genuinely understand the hypothesis that their nature is captured in a physical description unless we understand the more fundamental idea that they *have* an objective nature (or that objective processes can have a subjective nature).

I should like to close with a speculative proposal. It may be possible to approach the gap between subjective and objective from another direction. Setting aside temporarily the relation between the mind and the brain, we can pursue a more objective understanding of the mental in its own right. At present we are completely unequipped to think about the subjective character of experience without relying on the imagination—without taking up the point of view of the experiential subject. This should be regarded as a challenge to form new concepts and devise a new method—an objective phenomenology not dependent on empathy or the imagination. Though presumably it would not capture everything, its goal would be to describe, at least in part, the subjective character of experiences in a form comprehensible to beings incapable of having those experiences.

We would have to develop such a phenomenology to describe the sonar experiences of bats; but it would also be possible to begin with humans. One might try, for example, to develop concepts that could be used to explain to a person blind from birth what it was like to see. One would reach a blank wall eventually, but it should be possible to devise a method of expressing in objective terms much more than we can at present, and with much greater precision. The loose intermodal analogies—for example, "Red is like the sound of a trumpet"—which crop up in discussions of this subject are of little use. That should be clear to anyone who has both heard a trumpet and seen red. But structural features of perception might be more accessible to objective description, even though something would be left out. And concepts alternative to those we learn in the first person may enable us to arrive at a kind of understanding even of our own experience which is denied us by the very ease of description and lack of distance that subjective concepts afford.

Apart from its own interest, a phenomenology that is in this sense objective may permit questions about the physical basis of experience to assume a more intelligible form. Aspects of subjective experience that admitted this kind of objective description might be better candidates for objective explanations of a more familiar sort. But whether or not this guess is correct, it seems unlikely that any physical theory of mind can be contemplated until more thought has been given to the general problem of subjective and objective. Otherwise we cannot even pose the mind-body problem without sidestepping it.

Epiphenomenal Qualia

FRANK JACKSON

Frank Jackson teaches philosophy at Monash University in Australia.

. . . I am what is sometimes known as a "qualia freak." I think that there are certain features of the bodily sensations especially, but also of certain perceptual experiences, which no amount of purely physical information includes. Tell me everything physical there is to tell about what is going on in a living brain, the kind of states, their functional role, their relation to what goes on at other times and in other brains, and so on and so forth, and be I as clever as can be in fitting it all together, you won't have told me about the hurtfulness of pains, the itchiness of itches, pangs of jealousy, or about the characteristic experience of tasting a lemon, smelling a rose, hearing a loud noise or seeing the sky. . . .

From "Epiphenomenal Qualia," *Philosophical Quarterly,* Vol. 32, 1982, pp. 127–136. Reprinted by permission of the publisher.

THE KNOWLEDGE ARGUMENT FOR QUALIA

People vary considerably in their ability to discriminate colours. Suppose that in an experiment to catalogue this variation Fred is discovered. Fred has better colour vision than anyone else on record; he makes every discrimination that anyone has ever made, and moreover he makes one that we cannot even begin to make. Show him a batch of ripe tomatoes and he sorts them into two roughly equal groups and does so with complete consistency. That is, if you blindfold him, shuffle the tomatoes up, and then remove the blindfold and ask him to sort them out again, he sorts them into exactly the same two groups.

We ask Fred how he does it. He explains that all ripe tomatoes do not look the same colour to him, and in fact that this is true of a great many objects that we classify together as red. He sees two colours where we see one, and he has in consequence developed for his own use two words "red_1" and "red_2" to mark the difference. Perhaps he tells us that he has often tried to teach the difference between red_1 and red_2 to his friends but has got nowhere and has concluded that the rest of the world is red_1-red_2 colour-blind—or perhaps he has had partial success with his children, it doesn't matter. In any case he explains to us that it would be quite wrong to think that because "red" appears in both "red_1" and "red_2" that the two colours are shades of the one colour. He only uses the common term "red" to fit more easily into our restricted usage. To him red_1 and red_2 are as different from each other and all the other colours as yellow is from blue. And his discriminatory behavior bears this out: he sorts red_1 from red_2 tomatoes with the greatest of ease in a wide variety of viewing circumstances. Moreover, an investigation of the physiological basis of Fred's exceptional ability reveals that Fred's optical system is able to separate out two groups of wavelengths in the red spectrum as sharply as we are able to sort out yellow from blue.

I think that we should admit that Fred can see, really see, at least one more colour than we can; red_1 is a different colour from red_2. We are to Fred as a totally red-green colour-blind person is to us. H. G. Wells' story "The Country of the Blind" is about a sighted person in a totally blind community. This person never manages to convince them that he can see, that he has an extra sense. They ridicule this sense as quite inconceivable, and treat his capacity to avoid falling into ditches, to win fights and so on as precisely that capacity and nothing more. We would be making their mistake if we refused to allow that Fred can see one more colour than we can.

What kind of experience does Fred have when he sees red_1 and red_2? What is the new colour or colours like? We would dearly like to know but do not; and it seems that no amount of physical information about Fred's brain and optical system tells us. We find out perhaps that Fred's cones respond differently to certain light waves in the red section of the spectrum that makes no difference to ours (or perhaps he has an extra cone) and that this leads in Fred to a wider range of those brain states responsible for visual discriminatory behaviour. But none of this tells us what we really want to know about his colour experience. There is something about it we don't know. But we know, we may suppose, everything about Fred's body, his behaviour and dispositions to behaviour and about his internal physiology, and everything about his history and relation to others that can be given in physical accounts of persons. We have all the physical information. Therefore, knowing all this is *not* knowing everything about Fred. It follows that Physicalism leaves something out.

To reinforce this conclusion, imagine that as a result of our investigations into the internal workings of Fred we find out how to make everyone's physiology like Fred's in the relevant respects; or perhaps Fred donates his body to science and on his death we are able to transplant his optical system into someone else—again the fine detail doesn't matter. The important point is that such a happening would create enormous interest. People would say, "At last we will know what it is like to see the extra colour, at last we will know how Fred has differed from us in the way he has struggled to tell us about for so long." Then it cannot be that we knew all along all about Fred. But *ex hypothesi* we did know all along everything about Fred that features in the physicalist scheme; hence the physicalist scheme leaves something out.

Put it this way. *After* the operation, we will know

more about Fred and especially about his colour experiences. But beforehand we had all the physical information we could desire about his body and brain, and indeed everything that has ever featured in physicalist accounts of mind and consciousness. Hence there is more to know than all that. Hence Physicalism is incomplete.

Fred and the new colour(s) are of course essentially rhetorical devices. The same point can be made with normal people and familiar colours. Mary is a brilliant scientist who is, for whatever reason, forced to investigate the world from a black and white room *via* a black and white television monitor. She specializes in the neurophysiology of vision and acquires, let us suppose, all the physical information there is to obtain about what goes on when we see ripe tomatoes, or the sky, and use terms like "red," "blue," and so on. She discovers, for example, just which

wavelength combinations from the sky stimulate the retina, and exactly how this produces *via* the central nervous system the contraction of the vocal chords and expulsion of air from the lungs that results in the uttering of the sentence "The sky is blue." (It can hardly be denied that it is in principle possible to obtain all this physical information from black and white television, otherwise the Open University would *of necessity* need to use colour television.)

What will happen when Mary is released from her black and white room or is given a colour television monitor? Will she *learn* anything or not? It seems just obvious that she will learn something about the world and our visual experience of it. But then it is inescapable that her previous knowledge was incomplete. But she had *all* the physical information. *Ergo* there is more to have than that, and Physicalism is false. . . .

Reduction, Qualia, and the Direct Introspection of Brain States

PAUL CHURCHLAND

Paul Churchland (1942–   ) has published many articles and books. He teaches at the University of California, San Diego.

Do the phenomenological or qualitative features of our sensations constitute a permanent barrier to the reductive aspirations of any materialistic neuroscience? I here argue that they do not. . . .

If we are to deal sensibly with the issues here at stake, we must approach them with a general theory of scientific reduction already in hand, a theory motivated by and adequate to the many instances and varieties of interconceptual reduction displayed *elsewhere* in our scientific history. With an independently based account of the nature and grounds of inter-

theoretic reduction, we can approach the specific case of subjective qualia, free from the myopia that results from trying to divine the proper conditions on reduction by simply staring long and hard at the problematic case at issue.

I. INTERTHEORETIC REDUCTION

We may begin by remarking that the classical account of intertheoretic reduction now appears to be importantly mistaken, though the repairs necessary are quickly and cleanly made. Suppressing niceties, we may state the original account as follows. A new and more comprehensive theory *reduces* an older theory just in case the new theory, when conjoined with appropriate correspondence rules, logically entails the

From "Reduction, Qualia, and the Direct Introspection of Brain States," LXXXII:1 (January 1985), pp. 8–28. Used by permission of *The Journal of Philosophy* and the author. Footnotes deleted.

principles of the older theory. (The point of the correspondence rules, or "bridge laws," is to connect the disparate ontologies of the two theories: often these are expressed as identity statements, such as *Temperature* $= mv^2/3$k.) Schematically,

T_N & (Correspondence Rules)

logically entails

T_O

Difficulties with this view begin with the observation that most reduced theories turn out to be, strictly speaking and in a variety of respects, *false* (Real gases don't really obey $PV = \mu RT$, as in classical thermodynamics; the planets don't really move in ellipses, as in Keplerian astronomy; the acceleration of falling bodies isn't really uniform, as in Galilean dynamics; etc.) If reduction is *de*duction, modus tollens would thus require that the premises of the new reducing theories (statistical thermodynamics in the first case, Newtonian dynamics in the second and third) be somehow false as well, in contradiction to their assumed truth.

This complaint can be temporarily deflected by pointing out that the premises of a reduction must often include not just the new reducing theory but also some limiting assumptions or counterfactual boundary conditions (such as that the molecules of a gas enjoy only mechanical energy, or that the mass of the planets is negligible compared to the sun's, or that the distance any body falls is negligibly different from zero). Falsity in the reducing premises can thus be conceded, since it is safely confined to those limiting or counterfactual assumptions.

This defense will not deal with all cases of falsity, however, since in some cases the reduced theory is so radically false that some or all of its ontology must be rejected entirely, and the "correspondence rules" connecting that ontology to the newer ontology therefore display a problematic status. Newly conceived features cannot be identical with, nor even nominally connected with, old features, if the old features are illusory and uninstantiated. For example, relativistic mass is not identical with Newtonian mass, nor even coextensive with it, even at low velocities. Nevertheless, the reduction of Newtonian by Einsteinian mechanics is a paradigm of a successful reduction. For a second example, neither is caloric-fluid-pressure identical with, nor even coextensive with, mean molecular kinetic energy. But an overtly *fluid* thermodynamics (i.e., one committed to the existence of caloric) still finds a moderately impressive reduction within statistical thermodynamics. In sum, even theories with a *nonexistent* ontology can enjoy reduction, and this fact is problematic on the traditional account at issue.

What cases like these invite us to give up is the idea that what gets *de*duced in a reduction is the theory to be *re*duced. . . .

The point of a reduction, according to this view, is to show that the new or more comprehensive theory contains explanatory and predictive resources that parallel, to a relevant degree of exactness, the explanatory and predictive resources of the reduced theory. . . .

. . . it is to be expected that existing conceptual frameworks will eventually be reduced or displaced by new and better ones, and those in turn by frameworks better still; for who will be so brash as to assert that the feeble conceptual achievements of our adolescent species comprise an exhaustive account of anything at all? If we put aside this conceit, then the only alternatives to intertheoretic reduction are epistemic stagnation or the outright elimination of old frameworks as wholly false and illusory.

II. THEORETICAL CHANGE AND PERCEPTUAL CHANGE

Esoteric properties and arcane theoretical frameworks are not the only things that occasionally enjoy intertheoretic reduction. Observable properties and common-sense conceptual frameworks can also enjoy smooth reduction. Thus, being a middle-A sound is identical with being an oscillation in air pressure at 440 hz; being red is identical with having a certain triplet of electromagnetic reflectance efficiencies; being warm is identical with having a certain mean level of microscopically embodied energies, and so forth.

Moreover, the relevant reducing theory is capable of replacing the old framework not just in contexts of calculation and inference. *It should be appreciated that the reducing theory can displace the old framework in all its observational contexts as well.* Given the reality of the property identities just listed, it is quite open to us to begin framing our spontaneous perceptual reports in the language of the more sophisticated reducing theory. It is even desirable that we begin doing this, since the new vocabulary observes distinctions that are in fact within the discriminatory reach of our native perceptual systems, though those objective distinctions go unmarked and unnoticed from within the old framework. We can thus make more penetrating use of our native perceptual equipment. Such displacement is also desirable for a second reason: the greater inferential or computational power of the new conceptual framework. We can thus make better inferential *use* of our new perceptual judgments than we made of our old ones.

It is difficult to convey in words the vastness of such perceptual transformations and the naturalness of the new conceptual regime, once established. A nonscientific example may help to get the initial point across.

Consider the enormous increase in discriminatory skill that spans the gap between an untrained child's auditory apprehension of a symphony and the same person's apprehension of the same symphony forty years later, heard in his capacity as conductor of the orchestra performing it. What was before a seamless voice is now a mosaic of distinguishable elements. What was before a dimly apprehended tune is now a rationally structured sequence of distinguishable and identifiable chords supporting an appropriately related melody line. The matured musician hears an entire world of structured detail, concerning which the child is both dumb and deaf.

Other modalities provide comparable examples. Consider the practiced and chemically sophisticated wine taster, for whom the "red wine" classification used by most of us divides into a network of fifteen or twenty distinguishable elements: ethanol, glycol, fructose, sucrose, tannin, acid, carbon dioxide, and so forth, whose relative concentrations he can estimate with accuracy.

Or consider the astronomer, for whom the speckled black dome of her youth has become a visible abyss, scattered nearby plants, yellow dwarf stars, blue and red giants, distant globular clusters, and even a remote galaxy or two, all discriminable as such and locatable in three-dimensional space with her unaided (repeat: *unaided*) eye.

In each of these cases, what is finally mastered is a conceptual framework—whether musical, chemical, or astronomical—a framework that embodies far more wisdom about the relevant sensory domain than is immediately apparent to untutored discrimination. Such frameworks are characteristically a cultural heritage, pieced together over many generations, and their mastery supplies a richness and penetration to our sensory lives that would be impossible in their absence.

Our *introspective* lives are already the extensive beneficiaries of this phenomenon. The introspective discriminations we make are for the most part learned; they are acquired with practice and experience, often quite slowly. And the specific discriminations we learn to make are those it is useful for us to make. Generally, those are the discriminations that others are already making, the discriminations embodied in the psychological vocabulary of the language we learn. The conceptual framework for psychological states that is embedded in ordinary language is a modestly sophisticated theoretical achievement in its own right, and it shapes our matured introspection profoundly. If it embodied substantially *less* wisdom in its categories and connecting generalizations, our introspective apprehension of our internal states and activities would be much diminished, though our native discriminatory mechanisms remain the same. Correlatively, if folk psychology embodied substantially *more* wisdom about our inner nature that it actually does, our introspective discrimination and recognition could be very much *greater* than it is, though our native discriminatory mechanisms remain unchanged.

This brings me to the central positive suggestion of this paper. Consider now the possibility of learning to describe, conceive, and introspectively apprehend the teeming intricacies of our inner lives within the conceptual framework of a matured neuroscience, a neuroscience that successfully reduces, either smoothly or roughly, our common-sense folk psychology. Suppose we trained our native mechanisms to make a new and more detailed set of discriminations, a set that corresponded not to the primitive psychological taxonomy of ordinary language, but to some more penetrating taxonomy of states drawn from a completed neuroscience. And suppose we trained ourselves to respond to that reconfigured discriminative activity with judgments that were framed, as a matter of course, in the appropriate concepts from neuroscience.

If the examples of the symphony conductor (who can hear the Am7 chords), the oenologist (who can see and taste the glycol), and the astronomer (who can see the temperature of a blue giant star) provide a fair parallel, then the enhancement in our introspective vision could approximate a revelation. Dopamine levels in the limbic system, the spiking frequencies in specific neural pathways, resonances in the nth layer of the occipital cortex, inhibitory feedback to the lateral geniculate nucleus, and countless other neurophysical niceties could be moved into the objective focus of our introspective discrimination, just as Gm7 chords and Adim chords are moved into the objective focus of a trained musician's auditory discrimination. We will of course have to *learn* the conceptual framework of a matured neuroscience in order to pull this off. And we will have to *practice* its noninferential application. But that seems a small price to pay for the quantum leap in self-apprehension.

All of this suggests that there is no problem at all in conceiving the eventual reduction of mental states and properties to neurophysiological states and properties. A matured and successful neuroscience need only include, or prove able to define, a taxonomy of kinds with a set of embedding laws that faithfully mimics the taxonomy and casual generalizations of *folk* psychology. Whether future neuroscientific theories will prove able to do this is a wholly empirical question, not to be settled a priori. The evidence for a positive answer is substantial and familiar, centering on the growing explanatory success of the several neurosciences.

But there is negative evidence as well: I have even urged some of it myself ("Eliminative Materialism and the Propositional Attitudes," *Journal of Philosophy*, 1981). My negative arguments there center on the explanatory and predictive poverty of folk psychology, and they question whether it has the categorical integrity to *merit* the reductive preservation of its familiar ontology. That line suggests substantial revision or outright elimination as the eventual fate of our mentalistic ontology. The qualia-based arguments of Nagel, Jackson, and Robinson, however, take a quite different line. They find no fault

with the folk psychology. Their concern is with the explanatory and descriptive poverty of any possible *neuroscience,* and their line suggests that emergence is the correct story for our mentalistic ontology. Let us now examine their arguments.

III. THOMAS NAGEL'S ARGUMENTS

For Thomas Nagel, it is the phenomenological features of our experiences, the properties or *qualia* displayed by our sensations, that constitute a problem for the reductive aspirations of any materialistic neuroscience. In his classic position paper I find three distinct arguments in support of the view that such properties will never find any plausible or adequate reduction within the framework of a matured neuroscience. All three arguments are beguiling, but all three, I shall argue, are unsound.

First Argument

What makes the proposed reduction of mental phenomena different from reductions elsewhere in science, says Nagel, is that

> It is impossible to exclude the phenomenological features of experience from a reduction, in the same way that one excludes the phenomenal features of an ordinary substance from a physical or chemical reduction of it—namely, by explaining them as effects on the minds of human observers. (437)

The reason it is impossible to exclude them, continues Nagel, is that the phenomenological features are essential to experience and to the subjective point of view. But this is not what interests me about this argument. What interests me is the claim that reductions of various substances elsewhere in science *exclude the phenomenal features of the substance.*

This is simply false, and the point is extremely important. The phenomenal features at issue are those such as the objective redness of an apple, the warmth of a coffee cup, and the pitch of a sound. These properties are not excluded from our reductions. Redness, an objective phenomenal property of apples, is identical with a certain wavelength triplet of electromagnetic reflectance efficiencies. Warmth, an objective phenomenal property of objects, is identical with the mean level of the objects' microscopically embodied energies. Pitch, an objective phenomenal property of a sound, is identical with its oscillatory frequency. These electromagnetic and micromechanical properties, out there in the objective world, are genuine phenomenal properties. Despite widespread ignorance of their dynamical and microphysical details, it is these objective physical properties to which everyone's perceptual mechanisms are keyed.

The reductions whose existence Nagel denies are in fact so complete that one can already displace entirely large chunks of our common-sense vocabulary for observable properties and learn to frame one's perceptual judgments directly in terms of the reducing theory. The mean KE of the molecules in this room, for example, is currently about . . . $6.2 \times .10^{-21}$ joules. The oscillatory frequency of this sound (I here whistle C one octave about middle C) is about 524 hz. And the three critical electromagnetic reflectance efficiencies (at .45, .53, and .63 μm) of this (white) piece of paper are all above 80 percent. These microphysical and electromagnetic properties can be felt, heard, and seen, respectively. Our native sensory mechanisms can easily discriminate such properties, one from another, and their presence from their absence. They have been doing so for millennia. The "resolution" of these mechanisms is inadequate, of course, to reveal the microphysical details and the extended causal roles of the properties thus discriminated. But they are abundantly adequate to permit the reliable discrimination of the properties at issue.

On this view, the standard perceptual properties are not "secondary" properties at all, in the standard sense which implies that they have no real existence save *inside* the minds of human observers. On the contrary, they are as objective as you please, with a wide variety of objective causal properties. Moreover, it would be a mistake even to try to "kick the phenomenal properties inwards," since that would only postpone the problem of reckoning their place in nature. We would only confront them again later, as we address the place in nature of mental phenomena. And, as Nagel correctly points out, the relocation dodge is no longer open to us, once the problematic properties are already located within the mind.

Nagel concludes from this that subjective qualia are unique in being immune from the sort of reductions found elsewhere in science. I draw a very different conclusion. The *objective* qualia (redness, warmth, etc.) should never have been "kicked inwards to the minds of observers" in the first place. They should be confronted squarely, and they should be reduced where they stand: *out*side the human observer. As we saw, this can and has in fact been done. If objective phenomenal properties are so treated, then *subjective* qualia can be confronted with parallel forthrightness, and can be reduced where *they* stand: *in*side the human observer. So far then, the external and the internal case are not different: they are parallel after all.

Second Argument

A second argument urges the point that the intrinsic character of experiences, the qualia of sensations, are essentially accessible from only a single point of view, the subjective point of view of the experiencing subject. The properties of physical brain states, by contrast, are accessible from a variety of entirely objective points of view. We cannot hope adequately to account for the former, therefore, in terms of properties appropriate to the latter domain (cf. Nagel, 442–444).

This somewhat diffuse argument appears to be an instance of the following argument:

1. The qualia of my sensations are directly known to me, by introspection, as elements of my conscious self.

2. The properties of my brain states are not directly known by me, by introspection as elements of my conscious self.

∴3. The qualia of my sensations ≠ the properties of my brain states.

And perhaps there is a second argument here as well, a complement to the first:

1. The properties of my brain states are known-by-the-various-external-senses, as having such-and-such physical properties.

2. The qualia of my sensations are *not* known-by-the-various-external-senses, as having such-and-such physical properties.

∴3. The qualia of my sensations ≠ the properties of my brain states. . . .

. . . The fallacy committed in both cases is amply illustrated in the following parallel arguments.

1. Hitler is widely recognized as a mass murderer.

2. Adolph Schicklgruber is *not* widely recognized as a mass murderer.

∴3. Hitler ≠ Adolf Schicklgruber.

or

1. Aspirin is known by John to be a pain reliever.

2. Acetylsalicylic acid is *not* known by John to be a pain reliever.

∴3. Aspirin ≠ acetylsalicylic acid.

or, to cite an example very close to the case at issue,

1. Temperature is known by me, by tactile sensing, as a feature of material objects.

2. Mean molecular kinetic energy is *not* known by me, by tactical sensing, as a feature of material objects.

∴3. Temperature ≠ mean molecular kinetic energy.

The problem with all these arguments is that the "property" ascribed in premise 1 and withheld in premise 2 consists only in the subject item's being *recognized, perceived,* or *known* as something, *under some specific description or other.* Such apprehension is not a genuine feature of the item itself, fit for divining identities, since one and the same subject may be successfully recognized under one description (e.g., "qualia of my mental state"), and yet fail to be recognized under another, equally accurate, coreferential description (e.g., "property of my brain state"). . . .

Third Argument

The last argument here is the one most widely associated with Nagel's paper. The leading example is the (mooted) character of the experiences enjoyed by an alien creature such as a bat. The claim is that, no matter how much one knew about the bat's neurophysiology and its interaction with the physical world, one could still not know, nor perhaps even imagine, what it is like to be a bat. Even total knowledge of the physical details still leaves something out. The lesson drawn is that the reductive aspirations of neurophysiology are doomed to dash themselves, unrealized, against the impenetrable keep of subjective qualia (cf. Nagel, 438 ff.).

This argument is almost identical with an argument put forward in a recent paper by Frank Jackson. Since Jackson's version deals directly with humans, I shall confront the problem as he formulates it.

IV. JACKSON'S KNOWLEDGE ARGUMENT

Imagine a brilliant neuroscientist named Mary, who has lived her entire life in a room that is rigorously controlled to display only various shades of black, white, and grey. She learns about the outside world by means of a black/white television monitor, and, being brilliant, she manages to transcend these obstacles. She becomes the world's greatest neuroscientist, all from within this room. In particular, she comes to know everything there is to know about the physical structure and activity of the brain and its visual system, of its actual and possible states.

But there would still be something she did *not* know, and could not even imagine, about the actual experiences of all the other people who live outside her black/white room, and about her possible experiences were she finally to leave her room: the nature of the experience of seeing a ripe tomato, what it is like to see red or have a sensation-of-red. Therefore, complete knowledge of the physical facts of visual perception and its related brain activity *still leaves something out.* Therefore, materialism cannot give an adequate reductionist account of all mental phenomena.

To give a conveniently tightened version of this argument:

1. Mary knows everything there is to know about brain states and their properties.
2. It is not the case that Mary knows everything there is to know about sensations and their properties.

Therefore, by Leibniz's law,

3. Sensations and their properties ≠ brain states and their properties. . . .

. . . We can, I think, find at least two . . . shortcomings in this sort of argument.

The First Shortcoming

This defect is simplicity itself. "Knows about" . . . is not *univocal* in both premises. . . . Jackson's argument is valid only if "knows about" is univocal in both premises. But the kind of knowledge addressed in premise 1 seems pretty clearly to be different from the kind of knowledge addressed in (2). Knowledge in (1) seems to be a matter of having mastered a set of sentences or propositions, the kind one finds written in neuroscience texts, whereas knowledge in (2) seems to be a matter of having a representation of redness in some prelinguistic or sublinguistic medium of representation for sensory variables, or to be a matter of being able to *make* certain sensory discriminations, or something along these lines. . . .

. . . the difference between a person who knows all about the visual cortex but has never enjoyed a sensation of red, and a person who knows no neuroscience but knows well the sensation of red, may reside not in *what* is respectively known by each (brain states by the former, qualia by the latter), but rather in the differing *type* of knowledge each has *of exactly the same thing*. The difference is in the manner of the knowing, not in the nature of the things known. . . .

. . . In sum, there are pretty clearly more ways of "having knowledge" than having mastered a set of sentences. And nothing in materialism precludes this. The materialistic can freely admit that one has "knowledge" of one's sensations in a way that is independent of the scientific theories one has learned. This does not mean that sensations are beyond the reach of physical science. *It just means that the brain uses more modes and media of representation than the simple storage of sentences.* And this proposition is pretty obviously true: almost certainly the brain uses a considerable variety of modes and media of representation, perhaps hundreds of them. Jackson's argument, and Nagel's, exploit this variety illegitimately: both arguments equivocate on "knows about."

This criticism is supported by the observation that, if Jackson's form of argument were sound, it would prove far too much. Suppose that Jackson were arguing, not against materialism, but against dualism: against the view that there exists a non-material substance—call it "ectoplasm"—whose hidden constitution and nomic intricacies ground all mental phenomena. Let our cloistered Mary be an "ectoplasmologist" this time, and let her know[1] everything there is to know about the ectoplasmic processes underlying vision. There would still be something she did not know[2]: what it is like to see red. Dualism is therefore inadequate to account for all mental phenomena!

This argument is as plausible as Jackson's, and for the same reason: it exploits the same equivocation. But the truth is, such arguments show nothing, one way or the other, about how mental phenomena might be accounted for.

The Second Shortcoming

There is a further shortcoming with Jackson's argument, one of profound importance for understanding one of the most exciting consequences to be expected from a successful neuroscientific account of mind. I draw your attention to the assumption that even a utopian knowledge of neuroscience *must* leave Mary hopelessly in the dark about the subjective qualitative nature of sensations not-yet-enjoyed. It is true, of course, that no sentence of the form "*x* is a sensation-of-red" will be deductible from premises restricted to the language of neuroscience. But this is no point against the reducibility of phenomenological properties. As we saw in section I, direct deducibility is an intolerably strong demand on reduction, and if this is all the objection comes to, then there is no objection worth addressing. What the defender of emergent qualia must have in mind here, I think, is the claim that Mary could not even *imagine* what the relevant experience would be like, despite her exhaustive neuroscientific knowledge, and hence must still be missing certain crucial information.

This claim, however, is simply false. Given the truth of premise 1, premise 2 seems plausible to Jackson, Nagel, and Robinson only because none of these philosophers has adequately considered how much one might know if, as premise 1 asserts, one knew *everything* there is to know about the physical brain and nervous system. In particular, none of these philosophers has even begun to consider the changes in our introspective apprehension of our internal states that could follow upon a wholesale revision in our conceptual framework for our internal states.

The fact is, we can indeed imagine how neuroscientific information would give Mary detailed information about the qualia of various sensations. Recall our earlier discussion of the transformation of perception through the systematic reconceptualization of the relevant perceptual domain. In particular, suppose that Mary has learned to conceptualize her inner life, even in introspection, in terms of the completed neuroscience we are to imagine. So she does not identify her visual sensations crudely as "a sensation-of-black," "a sensation-of-grey," or "a sensation-of-white"; rather she identifies them more revealingly as various spiking frequencies in the *n*th layer of the occipital cortex (or whatever). If Mary has the relevant neuroscientific concepts for the sensational states at issue (viz., sensations-of-*red*), but has never yet been *in* those states, she may well be able to imagine being in the relevant cortical state, and imagine it with substantial success, even in advance of receiving external stimuli that would actually produce it.

One test of her ability in this regard would be to give her a stimulus that would (finally) produce in her the relevant state (viz., a spiking frequency of 90 hz in the gamma network: a "sensation-of-red" to us), and see whether she can identify it correctly *on introspective grounds alone,* as "a spiking frequency of 90 hz: the kind a tomato would cause." It does not seem to me to be impossible that she should succeed in this, and do so regularly on similar tests for other states, conceptualized clearly by her, but not previously enjoyed.

This may seem to some an outlandish suggestion, but the following will show that it is not. Musical chords are auditory phenomena that the young and unpracticed ear hears as undivided wholes, discriminable one from another, but without elements or internal structure. A musical education changes this, and one comes to hear chords as groups of dis-

criminable notes. If one is sufficiently practiced to have absolute pitch, one can even name the notes of the apprehended chord. And the reverse is also true: if a set of notes is specified verbally, a trained pianist or guitarist can identify the chord and recall its sound in auditory imagination. Moreover, a really skilled individual can construct, in auditory imagination, the sound of a chord he may never have heard before, and certainly does not remember. Specify for him a relatively unusual one—an F# 9th*add*13th for example—and let him brood for a bit. Then play for him three or four chords, one of which is the target, and see whether he can pick it out as the sound that meets the description. Skilled musicians can do this. Why is a similar skill beyond all possibility for Mary?

"Ah," it is tempting to reply, "musicians can do this only because chords are audibly structured sets of elements. Sensations of color are not."

But neither did chords seem, initially, to be structured sets of elements. They also seemed to be undifferentiated wholes. Why should it be unthinkable that sensations of color possess a comparable internal structure, unnoticed so far, but awaiting our determined and informed inspection? Jackson's argument, to be successful, must rule this possibility out, and it is difficult to see how he can do this *a priori*. Especially since there has recently emerged excellent empirical evidence to suggest that *our sensations of color are indeed structured sets of elements.* . . .

I do not mean to suggest, of course, that there will be no limits to what Mary can imagine. Her brain is finite, and its specific anatomy will have specific limitations. For example, if a bat's brain includes computational machinery that the human brain simply lacks (which seems likely), then the subjective character of *some* of the bat's internal states may well be beyond human imagination. Clearly, however, the elusiveness of the bat's inner life here stems not from the metaphysical "emergence" of its internal qualia, but only from the finite capacities of our idiosyncratically human brains. Within those sheerly structural limitations, our imaginations may soar far beyond what Jackson, Nagel, and Robinson suspect, if we possess a neuroscientific conceptual framework that is at last adequate to the intricate phenomena at issue.

I suggest then, that those of us who prize the flux

and content of our subjective phenomenological experience need not view the advance of materialistic neuroscience with fear and foreboding. Quite the contrary. The genuine arrival of a materialist kinematics and dynamics for psychological state and cognitive processes will constitute not a gloom in which our inner life is suppressed or eclipsed, but rather a drawing, in which its marvelous intricacies are finally *revealed*—most notably, if we apply ourselves, in direct self-conscious introspection.

THE SELF AND PERSONAL IDENTITY

Of Identity and Diversity

JOHN LOCKE

English empiricist philosopher John Locke (1632–1704) was deeply influential—not simply in epistemology and metaphysics but also in his natural rights political theory.

CORPOREAL AND SPIRITUAL SUBSTANCES

When we talk or think of any particular sort of corporeal substances, as horse, stone, etc., though the idea we have of either of them be but the complication or collection of those several simple ideas of sensible qualities, which we used to find united in the thing called horse or stone; yet, *because we cannot conceive how they should subsist alone, nor one in another,* we suppose them existing in and supported by some common subject; which support we denote by the name substance, though it be certain we have no clear or distinct idea of that thing we suppose a support.

The same thing happens concerning the operations of the mind, viz. thinking, reasoning, fearing, etc., which we concluding not to subsist of themselves, nor apprehending how they can belong to body, or be produced by it, we are apt to think these the actions of some other *substance,* which we call *spirit;* whereas yet it is evident that, having no other idea of notion of matter, but something wherein those many sensible qualities which affect our senses do subsist; by supposing a substance wherein thinking, knowing, doubting, and a power of moving, etc., do subsist, we have as clear a notion of the substance of spirit, as we have of body; the one being supposed to be (without knowing what it is) the *substratum* to those simple ideas we have from without; and the other supposed (with a like ignorance of what it is)

to be the *substratum* to those operations we experiment in ourselves within. It is plain then, that the idea of *corporeal substance* in matter is as remote from our conceptions and apprehensions, as that of *spiritual substance,* or spirit: and therefore, from our not having any notion of the substance of spirit, we can no more conclude its non-existence, than we can, for the same reason, deny the existence of body; it being as rational to affirm there is no body, because we have no clear and distinct idea of the substance of matter, as to say there is no spirit, because we have no clear and distinct idea of the substance of a spirit. . . .

So that, in short, the idea we have of spirit, compared with the idea we have of body, stands thus: the substance of spirits is unknown to us; and so is the substance of body equally unknown to us. Two primary qualities or properties of body, viz. solid coherent parts and impulse, we have distinct clear ideas of: so likewise we know, and have distinct [and] clear ideas, of two primary qualities or properties of spirit, viz. thinking, and a power of action; i.e. a power of beginning or stopping several thoughts or motions. We have also the ideas of several qualities inherent in bodies, and have the clear distinct ideas of them; which qualities are but the various modifications of the extension of cohering solid parts, and their motion. We have likewise the ideas of the several modes of thinking viz. believing, doubting, intending, fearing, hoping; all which are but the several modes of

From Chapters 23 and 27 of Book Two of Locke's *Essay Concerning Human Understanding* (1690; 1694).

thinking. We have also the ideas of willing, and moving the body consequent to it, and with the body itself too; for, as has been shown, spirit is capable of motion.

. . . If this notion of immaterial spirit may have, perhaps, some difficulties in it not easily to be explained, we have therefore no more reason to deny or doubt the existence of such spirits, than we have to deny or doubt the existence of body. . . .

THE IDENTITY OF LIVING THINGS

In the state of living creatures, their identity depends not on a mass of the same particles, but on something else. For in them the variation of great parcels of matter alters not the identity: an oak growing from a plant to a great tree, and then lopped, is still the same oak; and a colt grown up to a horse, sometimes fat, sometimes lean, is all the while the same horse: though, in both these cases, there may be a manifest change of the parts; so that truly they are not either of them the same masses of matter, though they be truly one of them the same oak, and the other the same horse. The reason whereof is, that, in these two cases, a mass of matter, and a living body, identity is not applied to the same thing.

VEGETABLES

We must therefore consider wherein an oak differs from a mass of matter, and that seems to me to be in this, that the one is only the cohesion of particles of matter any how united, the other such a disposition of them as constitutes the parts of an oak; and such an organization of those parts as is fit to receive and distribute nourishment, so as to continue and frame the wood, bark, and leaves, etc., of an oak, in which consists the vegetable life. That being the one plant which has such an organization of parts in one coherent body, partaking of one common life, it continues to be the same plant as long as it partakes of the same life, though that life be communicated to new particles of matter vitally united to the living plant, in a like continued organization conformable to that sort of plants. For this organization being at any one instant in any one collection of matter, is in that particular concrete distinguished from all other, and is that individual life, which existing con-

stantly from that moment both forwards and backwards, in the same continuity of insensibly succeeding parts united to the living body of the plant, it has that identity which makes the same plant, and all the parts of it, parts of the same plant, during all the time that they exist united in that continued organization, which is fit to convey that common life to all the parts so united.

ANIMALS

The case is not so much different in brutes, but that any one may hence see what makes an animal and continues it the same. Something we have like this in machines, and may serve to illustrate it. For example, what is a watch? It is plain it is nothing but a fit organization or construction of parts to a certain end, which, when a sufficient force is added to it, it is capable to attain. If we would suppose this machine one continued body, all whose organized parts were repaired, increased, or diminished by a constant addition or separation of insensible parts, with one common life, we should have something very much like the body of an animal; with this difference, that, in an animal the fitness of the organization, and the motion wherein life consists, began together, the motion coming from within; but in machines, the force coming sensibly from without, is often away when the organ is in order, and well fitted to receive it.

PEOPLE

This also shows wherein the identity of the same man consists; viz., in nothing but a participation of the same continued life, by constantly fleeting particles of matter, in succession vitally united to the same organized body. He that shall place the identity of man in anything else, but like that of other animals, in one fitly organized body, taken in any one instant, and from thence continued, under one organization of life, in several successfully fleeting particles of matter united to it, will find it hard to make an embryo, one of years, mad and sober, the same man, by any supposition, that will not make it possible for Seth, Ismael, Socrates, Pilate, Saint Austin, and Caesar Borgia, to be the same man. For, if the identity of soul alone makes the same man, and there be nothing in the nature of matter why the same individual spirit may not be united to different bodies, it will be possible that those men living in distant ages, and of different tempers, may have been the same man: which way of speaking must be, from a very strange use of the word man, applied to an idea, out of which body and shape are excluded. And that way of speaking would agree yet worse with the notions of those philosophers who allow of transmigration, and are of opinion that the souls of men may, for their miscarriages, be detruded into the bodies of beasts, as fit habitations, with organs suited to the satisfaction of their brutal inclinations. But yet I think nobody, could he be sure that the souls of Heliogabalus were in one of his hogs, would yet say that hog were a man or Heliogabalus.

It is not therefore unity of substances that comprehends all sorts of identity, or will determine it in every case; but to conceive and judge of it aright, we must consider what idea the word it is applied to stands for: it being one thing to be the same substance, another the same man, and a third the same person, if person, man, and substance, are three names standing for three different ideas; for such as is the idea belonging to that name, such must be the identity; which, if it had been a little more carefully attended to, would possibly have prevented a great deal of that confusion which often occurs about this matter, with no small seeming difficulties, especially concerning personal identity, which therefore we shall in the next place a little consider.

SAME MAN

An animal is living organized body; and consequently the same animal, as we have observed, is the same continued life communicated to different particles of matter, as they happen successively to be united to that organized living body. And whatever is talked of other definitions, ingenious observation puts it past doubt, that the idea in our minds, of which the sound man in our mouths is the sign, is nothing else but of an animal of such a certain form: since I think I may be confident, that, whoever should see a creature of his own shape or make, though it had no more reason all its life than a cat or a parrot, would call him still a man; or whoever should hear a cat or a parrot discourse, reason, and philosophize, would

call or think it nothing but a cat or a parrot; and say, the one was a dull irrational man, and the other a very intelligent rational parrot. . . .

I presume it is not the idea of a thinking or rational being alone that makes the idea of a man in most people's sense, but of a body, so and so shaped, joined to it; and if that be the idea of a man, the same successive body not shifted all at once, must, as well as the same immaterial spirit, go to the making of the same man.

Consciousness and Personal Identity

PERSONAL IDENTITY

This being premised, to find wherein personal identity consists, we must consider what person stands for; which, I think, is a thinking intelligent being, that has reason and reflection, and can consider itself as itself, the same thinking thing, in different times and places; which it does only by that consciousness which is inseparable from thinking, and, as it seems to me, essential to it: it being impossible for any one to perceive without perceiving that he does perceive. When we see, hear, smell, taste, feel, meditate, or will anything, we know that we do so. Thus it is always as to our present sensations and perceptions; and by this every one is to himself that which he calls self; it not being considered, in this case, whether the same self be continued in the same or divers substances. For, since consciousness always accompanies thinking, and it is that which makes every one to be what he calls self, and thereby distinguishes himself from all other thinking things: in this alone consists personal identity, i.e., the sameness of a rational being; and as far as this consciousness can be extended backwards to any past action or thought, so far reaches the identity of that person; it is the same self now it was then; and it is by the same self with this present one that now reflects on it, that that action was done.

CONSCIOUSNESS MAKES PERSONAL IDENTITY

But it is further inquired, whether it be the same identical substance? This, few would think they had reason to doubt of, if these perceptions, with their consciousness, always remained present in the same mind, whereby the same thinking thing would be always consciously present, and, as would be thought, evidently the same to itself. But that which seems to make the difficulty is this, that this consciousness being interrupted always by forgetfulness, there being no moment of our lives wherein we have the whole train of all our past actions before our eyes in one view, but even the best memories losing the sight of one part whilst they are viewing another; and we sometimes, and that the greatest part of our lives, not reflecting on our past selves, being intent on our present thoughts, and in sound sleep having no thought at all, or at least none with that consciousness which remarks our waking thoughts; I say, in all these cases, our consciousness being interrupted, and we losing the sight of our past selves, doubts are raised whether we are the same thinking thing, i.e., the same substance or no. Which, however reasonable or unreasonable, concerns not personal identity at all: the question being, what makes the same person, and not whether it be the same identical substance, which always thinks in the same person; which in this case, matters not at all: different substances, by the same consciousness (where they do partake in it) being united into one person, as well as different bodies by the same life are united into one animal, whose identity is preserved in that change of substances by the unity of one continued life. For it being the same consciousness that makes a man be himself to himself, personal identity depends on that only, whether it be annexed solely to one individual substance, or can be continued in a succession of several substances. For as far as any intelligent being can repeat the idea of any past action with the same consciousness it had of it at first, and with the same consciousness it has of any present action; so far it is the same personal self. For it is by the consciousness it has of its present thoughts and actions, that it is self to itself now, and so will be the same self, as far as the same consciousness can extend to actions past or to come; and would be by distance of time, or change of substance, no more two persons, than a man be two men by wearing other clothes today than he did yesterday, with a long or a short sleep between: the same consciousness uniting those distant actions into the same person, whatever substances contributed to their production.

PERSONAL IDENTITY IN CHANGE OF SUBSTANCES

That this is so, we have some kind of evidence in our very bodies, all whose particles, whilst vitally united to this same thinking conscious self, so that we feel when they are touched, and are affected by, and conscious of good or harm that happens to them, are a part of ourselves; i.e., of our thinking conscious self. Thus, the limbs of his body are to every one a part of himself; he sympathizes and is concerned for them. Cut off a hand, and thereby separate it from that consciousness he had of its heat, cold, and other affections, and it is then no longer a part of that which is himself, any more than the remotest part of matter. Thus, we see the substance whereof personal self consisted at one time may be varied at another, without the change of personal identity; there being no question about the same person, though the limbs which but now were a part of it, be cut off. . . .

PERSONAL IDENTITY AND IMMATERIAL SUBSTANCE

But next, as to the first part of the question, "Whether if the same thinking substance (supposing immaterial substances only to think) be changed, it can be the same person?" I answer, that cannot be resolved, but by those who know what kind of substances they are that do think, and whether the consciousness of past actions can be transferred from one thinking substance to another. I grant, were the same consciousness the same individual action, it could not: but it being a present representation of a past action, why it may not be possible that that may be represented to the mind to have been, which really never was, will remain to be shown. And therefore how far the consciousness of past actions is annexed to any individual agent, so that another cannot possibly have it, will be hard for us to determine, till we know what kind of action it is that cannot be done without a reflex act of perception accompanying it, and how performed by thinking substances, who cannot think without being conscious of it. But that which we call the same consciousness, not being the same individual act, why one intellectual substance may not have represented to it, as done by itself, what it never did, and was perhaps done by some other agent; why, I say, such a representation may not possibly be without reality of matter of fact, as well as several representations in dreams are, which yet whilst dreaming we take for true, will be difficult to conclude from the nature of things. And that it never is so, will by us, till we have clearer views of the nature of thinking substances, be best resolved into the goodness of God, who, as far as the happiness or misery of any of his sensible creatures is concerned in it, will not, by a fatal error of theirs, transfer from one to another that consciousness which draws reward or punishment with it. How far this may be an argument against those who would place thinking in a system of fleeting animal spirits, I leave to be considered. But yet, to return to the question before us, it must be allowed, that, if the same consciousness (which, as has been shown, is quite a different thing from the same numerical figure or motion of body) can be transferred from one thinking substance to another, it will be possible that two thinking substances may make but one person. For the same consciousness being preserved, whether in the same or different substances, the personal identity is preserved.

As to the second part of the question, "Whether the same immaterial substance remaining, there may be two distinct persons?" which question seems to me to be built on this, whether the same immaterial being, being conscious of the action of its past existence, and lose it beyond the power of ever retrieving it again; and so as it were beginning a new account from a new period, have a consciousness that cannot reach beyond this new state. All those who hold preexistence are evidently of this mind, since they allow the soul to have no remaining consciousness of what it did in that preexistent state, either wholly separate from body, or informing any other body; and if they should not, it is plain experience would be against them. So that personal identity reaching no further than consciousness teaches, a preexistent spirit not having continued so many ages in a state of silence, must needs make different persons. Suppose a Christian Platonist or a Pythagorean should, upon God's having ended all his works of creation the seventh day, think his soul hath existed ever since; and would imagine it has revolved in several human bodies, as I once met with one, who was persuaded his had been the soul of Soc-

rates; (how reasonably I will not dispute; this I know, that in the post he filled, which was no inconsiderable one, he passed for a very rational man, and the press has shown that he wanted not parts or learning;) would any one say, that he, being not conscious of any of Socrates' actions or thoughts, could be the same person with Socrates? Let any one reflect upon himself, and conclude that he has in himself an immaterial spirit, which is that which thinks in him, and, in the constant change of his body keeps him the same: and is that which he calls himself: let him also suppose it to be the same soul that was in Nestor or Thersites, at the siege of Troy (for souls being, as far as we know anything of them, in their nature indifferent to any parcel of matter, the supposition has no apparent absurdity in it), which it may have been, as well as it is now the soul of any other man: but he now having no consciousness of any of the actions either of Nestor or Thersites, does or can he conceive himself the same person with either of them? Can he be concerned in either of their actions? Attribute them to himself, or think them his own, more than the actions of any other men that ever existed? So that this consciousness not reaching to any of the actions of either of those men, he is no more one self with either of them, than if the soul or immaterial spirit that now informs him had been created, and began to exist, when it began to inform his present body, though it were ever so true, that the same spirit that informed Nestor's or Thersites' body were numerically the same that now informs his. For this would no more make him the same person with Nestor, than if some of the particles of matter that were once a part of Nestor, were now a part of this man; the same immaterial substance, without the same consciousness, no more making the same person by being united to any body, than the same particle of matter, without consciousness united to any body, makes the same person. But let him once find himself conscious of any of the actions of Nestor, he then finds himself the same person with Nestor.

MEMORY AND PERSONAL IDENTITY

And thus may we be able, without any difficulty, to conceive the same person at the resurrection, though in a body not exactly in make or parts the same which he had here, the same consciousness going along with the soul that inhabits it. But yet the soul alone, in the change of bodies, would scarce to any one but to him that makes the soul the man, be enough to make the same man. For should the soul of a prince, carrying with it the consciousness of the prince's past life, enter and inform the body of a cobbler, as soon as deserted by his own soul, every one sees he would be the same person with the prince, accountable only for the prince's actions: but who would say it was the same man? The body too goes to the making the man, and would, I guess, to everybody determine the man in this case; wherein the soul, with all its princely thoughts about it, would not make another man: but he would be the same cobbler to every one besides himself. I know that, in the ordinary way of speaking, the same person, and the same man, stand for one and the same thing. And indeed every one will always have a liberty to speak as he pleases, and to apply what articulate sounds to what ideas he thinks fit, and change them as often as he pleases. But yet, when we will inquire what makes the same spirit, man, or person, we must fix the ideas of spirit, man, or person, in our minds, and having resolved with ourselves what we mean by them, it will not be hard to determine in either of them, or the like, when it is the same, and when not.

CONSCIOUSNESS MAKES THE SAME PERSON

But though the same immaterial substance or soul does not alone, wherever it be, and in whatsoever state, make the same man; yet it is plain, consciousness, as far as ever it can be extended, should it be to ages past, unites existences and actions, very remote in time into the same person, as well as it does the existences and actions of the immediately preceding moment: so that whatever has the consciousness of present and past actions, is the same person to whom they both belong. Had I the same consciousness that I saw the ark and Noah's flood, as that I saw an overflowing of the Thames last winter, or as that I write now; I could no more doubt that I who write this now, that saw the Thames overflowed last winter, and that viewed the flood at the general deluge, was the same self, place that self in what substance you please, than that I who write this am the same myself

now whilst I write (whether I consist of all the same substance, material or immaterial, or no) that I was yesterday; for as to this point of being the same self, it matters not whether this present self be made up of the same or other substances; I being as much concerned, and as justly accountable for any action that was done a thousand years since, appropriated to me now by this self-consciousness, as I am for what I did the last moment.

SELF DEPENDS ON CONSCIOUSNESS

Self is that conscious thinking thing, whatever substance made up of (whether spiritual or material, simple or compounded, it matters not), which is sensible or conscious of pleasure and pain, capable of happiness or misery, and so is concerned for itself, as far as that consciousness extends. Thus every one finds, that, whilst comprehended under that consciousness, the little finger is as much a part of himself as what is most so. Upon separation of this little finger, should this consciousness go along with the little finger, and leave the rest of the body, it is evident the little finger would be the person, the same person, and self then would have nothing to do with the rest of the body. As in this case it is the consciousness that goes along with the substance, when one part is separate from another, which makes the same person, and constitutes this inseparable self; so it is in reference to substances remote in time. That with which the consciousness of this present thinking thing can join itself, makes the same person, and is one self with it, and with nothing else; and so attributes to itself, and owns all the actions of that thing as its own, as far as that consciousness reaches, and no further; as every one who reflects will perceive.

REWARD AND PUNISHMENT

In this personal identity is founded all the right and justice of reward and punishment; happiness and misery being that for which every one is concerned for himself, and not mattering what becomes of any substance not joined to, or affected with that consciousness. For as it is evident in the instance I gave but now, if the consciousness went along with the little finger when it was cut off, that would be the same self which was concerned for the whole body yesterday, as making part of itself, whose actions then it cannot but admit as its own now. Though, if the same body should still live, and immediately from the separation of the little finger have its own peculiar consciousness, whereof the little finger knew nothing; it would not at all be concerned for it, as a part of itself, or could own any of its actions, or have any of them imputed to him.

This may show us wherein personal identity consists: not in the identity of substance, but, as I have said, in the identity of consciousness; wherein if Socrates and the present mayor of Queenborough agree, they are the same person: if the same Socrates waking and sleeping do not partake of the same consciousness. Socrates waking and sleeping is not the same person. And to punish Socrates waking for what sleeping Socrates thought, and waking Socrates was never conscious of, would be no more of right, than to punish one twin for what his brother-twin did, whereof he knew nothing, because their outsides were so like, that they could not be distinguished; for such twins have been seen.

But yet possibly it will still be objected, suppose I wholly lose the memory of some parts of my life, beyond a possibility of retrieving them, so that perhaps I shall never be conscious of them again; yet am I not the same person that did those actions, had those thoughts that I once was conscious of, though I have now forgot them? To which I answer, that we must here take notice what the word I is applied to; which, in this case, is the man only. And the same man being presumed to be the same person, I is easily here supposed to stand also for the same person. But if it be possible for the same man to have distinct incommunicable consciousness at different times, it is past doubt the same man would at different times make different persons; which, we see, is the sense of mankind in the solemnest declaration of their opinions; human laws not punishing the mad man for the sober man's actions, nor the sober man for what the mad man did, thereby making them two persons: which is somewhat explained by our way of speaking in English, when we say such an one is not himself, or is beside himself; in which phrases it is insinuated, as if those who now, or at least first used them, thought that self was changed, the selfsame person was no longer in that man. . . .

A PROBLEM ABOUT PUNISHMENT

But is not a man drunk and sober the same person? Why else is he punished for the act he commits when drunk, though he be never afterwards conscious of it? Just as much the same person as a man that walks, and does other things in his sleep, is the same person, and is answerable for any mischief he shall do in it. Human laws punish both, with a justice suitable to their way of knowledge; because in these cases, they cannot distinguish certainly what is real, what counterfeit: and so the ignorance in drunkenness or sleep is not admitted as a plea. For, though punishment be annexed to personality, and personality to consciousness, and the drunkard perhaps be not conscious of what he did, yet human judicatures justly punish him, because the fact is proved against him, but want of consciousness cannot be proved for him. But in the great day, wherein the secrets of all hearts shall be laid open, it may be reasonable to think, no one shall be made to answer for what he knows nothing of; but shall receive his doom, his conscience accusing or excusing him.

CONSCIOUSNESS ALONE MAKES SELF

Nothing but consciousness can unite remote existences into the same person: the identity of substance will not do it; for whatever substance there is, however framed, without consciousness there is no person: and a carcass may be a person, as well as any sort of substance be so without consciousness.

Could we suppose two distinct incommunicable consciousnesses acting in the same body, the one constantly by day, the other by night; and, on the other side, the same consciousness, acting by intervals, two distinct bodies; I ask, in the first case, whether the day and the night man would not be two as distinct persons as Socrates and Plato? And whether, in the second case, there would not be one person in two distinct bodies, as much as one man is the same in two distinct clothings? Nor is it at all material to say, that this same, and this distinct consciousness, in the cases above mentioned, is owing to the same and distinct immaterial substances, bringing it with them to those bodies; which, whether true or no, alters not the case; since it is evident the personal identity would equally be determined by the consciousness, whether that consciousness were annexed to some individual immaterial substance or no. For, granting that the thinking substance in man must be necessarily supposed immaterial, it is evident that immaterial thinking thing may sometimes part with its past consciousness, and be restored to it again, as appears in the forgetfulness men often have of their past actions: and the mind many times

recovers the memory of a past consciousness, which it had lost for twenty years together. Make these intervals of memory and forgetfulness to take their turns regularly by day and night, and you have two persons with the same immaterial spirit, as much as in the former instance two persons with the same body. So that self is not determined by identity or diversity or substance, which it cannot be sure of, but only by identity of consciousness. . . .

Critique of Locke and Hume on Behalf of Common Sense

THOMAS REID

Thomas Reid (1710–1796) founded the Scottish Common Sense Philosophy.

. . . It is proper to consider what is meant by identity in general, what by our own personal identity, and how we are led into that invincible belief and conviction which every man has of his own personal identity, as far as his memory reaches.

Identity in general I take to be a relation between a thing which is known to exist at one time, and a thing which is known to have existed at another time. If you ask whether they are one and the same, or two different things, every man of common sense understands the meaning of your question perfectly. Whence we may infer with certainty, that every man of common sense has a clear and distinct notion of identity.

If you ask a definition of identity, I confess I can give none; it is too simple a notion to admit of logical definition . . .

I see evidently that identity supposes *an uninterrupted continuance of existence.* That which has ceased to exist cannot be the same with that which afterwards begins to exist; for this would be to suppose a being to exist after it ceased to exist, and to have had

existence before it was produced, which are manifest contradictions. Continued uninterrupted existence is therefore necessarily implied in identity. Hence we may infer, that identity cannot, in its proper sense, be applied to our pains, our pleasures, our thoughts, or any operation of our minds. The pain felt this day is not the same individual pain which I felt yesterday, though they may be *similar* in kind and degree, and have the same cause. The same may be said of every feeling, and of every operation of mind. They are all successive in their nature, like time itself, no two moments of which can be the same moment. It is otherwise with the parts of absolute space. They always, are, and were, and will be the same. So far, I think, we proceed upon clear ground in fixing the notion of identity in general.

NATURE AND ORIGIN OF OUR IDEA OF PERSONAL IDENTITY

It is perhaps more difficult to ascertain with precision the meaning of *personality*; but it is not necessary in the present subject: it is sufficient for our purpose to observe, that all mankind place their personality in something that *cannot be divided, or consist of parts.* A part of a person in a manifest

From *Essays on the Intellectual Powers of Man,* first published in England in 1785, and *An Inquiry into the Human Mind on the Principles of Common Sense,* first published in 1764.

absurdity. When a man loses his estate, his health, his strength, he is still the same person, and has lost nothing of his personality. If he has a leg or an arm cut off, he is the same person he was before. The amputated member is no part of his person, otherwise it would have a right to a part of his estate, and be liable for a part of his engagements. It would be entitled to a share of his merit and demerit, which is manifestly absurd. A person is something indivisible, and is what Leibniz calls a *monad.*

My personal identity, therefore, implies the continued existence of that indivisible thing which I call *myself.* Whatever this self may be, it is something which thinks, and deliberates, and resolves, and acts, and suffers. I am not thought, I am not action, I am not feeling; I am something that thinks, and acts, and suffers. My thoughts, and actions, and feelings, change every moment; they have no continued, but a successive, existence; but that *self,* or *I,* to which they belong, is permanent, and has the same relation to all the succeeding thoughts, actions, and feelings which I call mine.

Such are the notions that I have of my personal identity. But perhaps it may be said, this may all be fancy without reality. How do you know,—what evidence have you,—that there is such a permanent self which has a claim to all the thoughts, actions, and feelings which you call yours?

To this I answer, that the proper evidence I have of all this is *remembrance.* I remember that twenty years ago I conversed with such a person; I remember several things that passed in that conversation: my memory testifies, not only that this was done, but that it was done by me who now remember it. If it was done by me, I must have existed at that time, and continued to exist from that time to the present: if the identical person whom I call myself had not a part in that conversation, my memory is fallacious; it gives a distinct and positive testimony of what is not true. Every man in his senses believes what he distinctly remembers, and everything he remembers convinces him that he existed at the same time remembered.

Although memory gives the most irresistible evidence of my being the identical person that did such a thing, at such a time, I may have other good evidence of things which befell me, and which I do not remember: I know who bore me, and suckled me, but I do not remember these events.

It may here be observed, (though the observation would have been unnecessary, if some great philosophers had not contradicted it), that it is not my remembering any action of mine that *makes* me to be the person who did it. This remembrance makes me to *know* assuredly that I did it, *but I might have done it, though I did not remember it.* That relation to me, which is expressed by saying that *I did it,* would be the same, though I had not the least remembrance of it. . . .

When we pass judgment on the identity of other persons than ourselves, we proceed upon other grounds, and determine from a variety of circumstances, which sometimes produce the firmest assurance, and sometimes leave room for doubt. The identity of person has often furnished matter of serious litigation before tribunals of justice. But no man of a sound mind ever doubted of his own identity, as far as he distinctly remembered. . . .

Thus it appears, that the evidence we have of our own identity, as far back as we remember, is totally of a different kind from the evidence we have of the identity of other persons, or of objects of sense. The first is grounded on *memory,* and gives undoubted certainty. The last is grounded on *similarity,* and on other circumstances, which in many cases are not so decisive as to leave no room for doubt.

It may likewise be observed, that the identity of *objects of sense* is never perfect. All bodies, as they consist of innumerable parts that may be disjoined from them by a great variety of causes, are subject to continual changes of their substance, increasing, diminishing, changing insensibly. When such alterations are gradual, because languages could not afford a different name for every different state of such a changeable being, it retains the same name, and is considered as the same thing. Thus we say of an old regiment, that it did such a thing a century ago, though there now is not a man alive who then belonged to it. We say a tree is the same in the seed-bed and in the forest. A ship of war, which has successively changed her anchors, her tackle, her sails, her masts, her planks, and her timbers, while she keeps the same name, is the same.

The identity, therefore, which we ascribe to bodies, whether natural or artificial, is not perfect identity; it is rather something which, for the conveniency of speech, we call identity. It admits of a great change of the subject, providing the change be *gradual;* sometimes, even of a total change. And the changes which in common language are made consistent with identity differ from those that are thought to destroy it, not in *kind,* but in *number* and *degree.* It has not fixed nature when applied to bodies; and questions about the identity of a body are very often questions about words. But identity, when applied to person, has no ambiguity, and admits not of degrees, or of more and less. It is the foundation of all rights and obligations, and of all accountableness; and the notion of it is fixed and precise.

STRICTURES ON LOCKE'S ACCOUNT OF PERSONAL IDENTITY

In a long chapter, *Of Identity and Diversity,* Mr. Locke has made many ingenious and just observations, and some which I think cannot be defended. . . .

This doctrine has some strange consequences, which the author was aware of. (1) Such as, that if the same consciousness can be transferred from one intelligent being to another, which he thinks we cannot show to be impossible, *then two or twenty intelligent beings may be the same person.* (2) And if the intelligent being may lose the consciousness of the actions done by him, which surely is possible, then he is not the person that did those actions; so that *one intelligent being may be two or twenty different persons,* if he shall so often lose the consciousness of his former actions.

(3) There is another consequence of this doctrine, which follows no less necessarily, though Mr. Locke probably did not see it. It is, *that a man may be, and at the same time not be, the person that did a particular action.* Suppose a brave officer to have been flogged when a boy at school for robbing an orchard, to have taken a standard from the enemy in his first campaign, and to have been made a general in advanced life; suppose, also, which must be admitted to be possible, that, when he took the standard, he was conscious of having been flogged at school, and that, when made a general, he was conscious of his taking the standard, but had absolutely lost the consciousness of his flogging. These things being supposed, it follows, from Mr. Locke's doctrine, that he was flogged at school is the same person who took the standard, and that he who took the standard is the same person who was made a general. Whence it follows, if there by any truth in logic, that the general is the same person with him who was flogged at school. But the general's consciousness does not reach so far back as his flogging; therefore, according to Mr. Locke's doctrine, he is not the person who was flogged. Therefore the general is, and at the same time is not, the same person with him who was flogged at school.

Leaving the consequences of this doctrine to those who have leisure to trace them, we may observe, with regard to the doctrine itself,—

First, that Mr. Locke attributes to consciousness the conviction we have of our past actions, as if a man may now be conscious of what he did twenty years ago. It is impossible to understand the meaning of this, unless by *consciousness* he meant *memory,* the only faculty by which we have an immediate knowledge of our past actions. . . .

When, therefore, Mr. Locke's notion of personal identity is properly expressed, it is, that personal identity *consists in distinct remembrance;* for even in the popular sense, to say that I am conscious of a past action means nothing else than that I distinctly remember that I did it.

Secondly, it may be observed, that, in this doctrine, not only is consciousness confounded with memory, but, which is still more strange, *personal identity* is confounded with *the evidence which we have of our personal identity.*

It is very true, that my remembrance that I did such a thing is the evidence I have that I am the identical person who did it. And this, I am apt to think Mr. Locke meant. But to say that my remembrance that I did such a thing, or my consciousness, *makes* me the person who did it, is, in my apprehension, an absurdity too gross to be entertained by any man who attends to the meaning of it; for it is to attribute to memory or consciousness a strange magical power of producing its object, though that object must have existed before the memory or consciousness which produced it. Consciousness is the testimony of one faculty; memory is the testimony of another faculty; and to say that the testimony is the cause of the thing testified, this surely is absurd, if any thing be, and could not have been said by Mr. Locke, if he had not confounded the testimony with the thing testified.

When a horse that was stolen is found and claimed by the owner, the only evidence he can have, or that a judge or witnesses can have, that this is the very identical horse which was his property, is similitude. But would it not be ridiculous from this to infer that the identity of a horse *consists* in similitude only? The only *evidence* I have that I am the identical person who did such actions is, that I remember distinctly I did them; or, as Mr. Locke expresses it, I am conscious I did them. To infer from this, that personal identity consists in consciousness, is an argument which, if it had any force, would prove the identity of a stolen horse to consist solely in similitude.

Thirdly, is it not strange that the sameness or identity of a person should consist in a thing *which is continually changing,* and is not any two minutes the same?

Our consciousness, our memory, and every operation of the mind, are still flowing like the water of a river, or like time itself. The consciousness I have this moment can no more be the same consciousness I had last moment, than this moment can be the last moment. Identity can only be affirmed of things which have a continued existence. Consciousness, and every kind of thought, are transient and momentary, and have no continued existence; and therefore, if personal identity consisted in consciousness, it would certainly follow, that *no man is the same person any two moments of his life;* and as the right and justice of reward and punishment are founded on personal identity, no man could be responsible for his actions. . . .

Fourthly, there are many expressions used by Mr. Locke, in speaking of personal identity, which to me are altogether unintelligible, unless we suppose that he confounded that sameness or identity which we ascribe to an individual with the identity which, in common discourse, is often ascribed to many individuals of the same species.

When we say that pain and pleasure, consciousness and memory, are the same in all men, this sameness can only mean similarity, or sameness *of kind.* That the pain of one man can be the same individual pain with that of another man is no less impossible, than that one man should be another man: the pain felt by me yesterday can no more be the pain I feel today, than yesterday can be this day; and the

same thing may be said of every passion and of every operation of the mind. The same kind or species of operation may be in different men, or in the same man at different times, but it is impossible that the same individual operation should be in different men, or in the same man at different times.

When Mr. Locke, therefore, speaks of "the same consciousness being continued through a succession of different substances"; when he speaks of "repeating the idea of a past action, with the same consciousness we had of it at the first," and of "the same consciousness extending to actions past and to come"; these expressions are to me unintelligible, unless he means not the same individual consciousness, but a consciousness that is similar, or of the same kind. If our personal identity consists in consciousness, as this consciousness cannot be the same individually any two moments, but only of the *same kind,* it would follow, that we are not for any two moments the same individual persons, but the same *kind* of persons. As our consciousness sometimes ceases to exist, as in sound sleep, our personal identity must cease with it. Mr. Locke allows, that the same thing cannot have two beginnings of existence, so that our identity would be irrecoverably gone every time we cease to think, if it was but a moment. . . .

STRICTURES ON HUME'S ACCOUNT OF PERSONAL IDENTITY

Locke's principle must be, that identity consists in remembrance; and consequently a man must lose his personal identity with regard to every thing he forgets.

Nor are these the only instances whereby our philosophy concerning the mind appears to be very fruitful in creating doubts, but very unhappy in resolving them.

Descartes, Malebranche, and Locke, have all employed their genius and skill, to prove the existence of a material world; and with very bad success. . . .

The present age, I apprehend, has not produced two more acute or more practised in this part of philosophy than [George Berkeley] the Bishop of Cloyne, and the author of the Treatise of Human Nature [David Hume, who] . . . undoes the world of spirits, and leaves nothing in nature but ideas and impressions, without any subject on which they may be impressed.

It seems to be a peculiar strain of humor in this author, to set out in his introduction, by promising with a grave face, no less than a complete system of the sciences, upon a foundation entirely new, to wit, that of human nature; when the intention of the whole work is to show, that there is neither human nature nor science in the world. It may perhaps be unreasonable to complain of this conduct in an author, who neither believes his own existence, nor that of his reader; and therefore could not mean to disappoint him, or to laugh at his credulity. Yet I cannot imagine, that the author of Treatise of Human Nature is so skeptical as to plead this apology. He believed, against his principles, that he should be read, and that he should retain his personal identity, till he reaped the honor and reputation justly due to his metaphysical *acumen*. Indeed he ingenuously acknowledges, that it was only in solitude and retirement that he could yield any assent to his own philosophy; society, like daylight, dispelled the darkness and fogs of skepticism, and made him yield to the dominion of common sense. Nor did I ever hear him charged with doing any thing, even in solitude, that argued such a degree of skepticism, as his principles maintain. . . .

That the natural issue of this system is skepticism with regard to every thing except the existence of our ideas, and of their necessary relations which appear upon comparing them, is evident: for ideas being the only objects of thought, and having no existence but when we are conscious of them, it necessarily follows, that there is no object of our thought, which can have a continued and permanent existence. Body and spirit, cause and effect, time and space, to which we were wont to ascribe an existence independent of our thought, are all turned out of existence by this short dilemma: Either these things are ideas of sensation or reflection, or they are not: if they are ideas of sensation or reflection, they can have no existence but when we are conscious of them; if they are not ideas of sensation or reflection, they are words without any meaning.

Neither Descartes nor Locke perceived this consequence of their system concerning ideas. Bishop Berkeley was the first who discovered it. . . . But with regard to the existence of spirits or minds, he does not admit the consequence; and if he had admitted, it, he must have been an absolute skeptic. . . .

Thus we see, that Descartes and Locke take the road that leads to skepticism, without knowing the end of it; but they stop short for want of light to carry them farther. Berkeley, frighted at the appearance of the dreadful abyss, starts aside, and avoids it. But the author of Treatise of Human Nature, more daring and intrepid, without turning aside to the right hand or to the left, like Virgil's Alecto, shoots directly into the gulf. . . .

We ought, however, to do this justice both to the Bishop of Cloyne and to the author of the Treatise of Human Nature, to acknowledge, that their conclusions are justly drawn from the doctrine of ideas, which has been so universally received. On the other hand, from the character of Bishop Berkeley, and of his predecessors Descartes, Locke, and Malebranche, we may venture to say, that if they had seen all the consequences of this doctrine, as clearly as the author before mentioned did, they would have suspected it vehemently, and examined it more carefully than they appear to have done.

The theory of ideas, like the Trojan horse, had a specious appearance both of innocence and beauty; but if those philosophers had known that it carried in its belly death and destruction to all science and common sense, they would not have broken down their walls to give it admittance. . . .

It is certain, no man can conceive or believe smelling to exist of itself, without a mind, or something that has the power of smelling, of which it is called a sensation, an operation or feeling. Yet if any man should demand a proof, that sensation cannot be without a mind or sentient being, I confess that I can give none; and that to pretend to prove it, seems to me almost as absurd as to deny it.

This might have been said without any apology before the Treatise of Human Nature appeared in the world. For till that time, no man, as far as I know, ever thought either of calling in question that principle, or of giving a reason for his belief of it. Whether thinking beings were of an ethereal or igneous nature, whether material or immaterial, was variously disputed; but that thinking is an operation of some kind of being or other, was always taken for granted, as a principle that could not possibly admit of doubt. . . .

If there are certain principles, as I think there are, which the constitution of our nature leads us to believe, and which we are under a necessity to take for granted in the common concerns of life, without being able to give a reason for them; these are what we call the principles of common sense; and what is manifestly contrary to them, is what we call absurd. . . .

It is a fundamental principle of [Hume's] ideal system, that every object of thought must be an impression, or an idea, that is, a faint copy of some preceding impression. This is a principle so commonly received, that the author above mentioned, although his whole system is built upon it, never offers the least proof of it. It is upon this principle, as a fixed point, that he erects his metaphysical engines, to overturn heaven and earth, body and spirit. And indeed, in my apprehension, it is altogether sufficient for the purpose. For if impressions and ideas are the only objects of thought, then heaven and earth, and body and spirit, and every thing you please, must signify only impressions and ideas, or they must be words without any meaning. It seems, therefore, that this notion, however strange, is closely connected with the received doctrine of ideas, and we must either admit the conclusion, or call in question the premises. . . .

The triumph of ideas was completed by the Treatise of Human Nature, which discards spirits also, and leaves ideas and impressions as the sole existences in the universe. What if at last, having nothing else to contend with, they should fall foul of one another, and leave no existence in nature at all? This would surely bring philosophy into danger; for what should we have left to talk or to dispute about? However, hitherto these philosophers acknowledge the existence of impressions and ideas: they acknowledge certain laws of attraction, or rules of precedence, according to which ideas and impressions range themselves in various forms, and succeed one another: but that they should belong to a mind, as its proper goods and chattels, this they have found to be a vulgar error. These ideas are as free and independent as the birds of the air. . . . They make the whole furniture of the universe; starting into existence, or out of it, without any cause; combining into parcels which the vulgar call *minds;* and suc-

ceeding one another by fixed laws, without time, place, or author of these laws. . . .

The Treatise of Human Nature . . . seems to have made but a bad return, by bestowing upon them this independent existence; since thereby they are turned out of house and home, and set adrift in the world, without friend or connection, without a rag to cover their nakedness; and who knows but the whole system of ideas may perish by the indiscreet zeal of their friends to exalt them?

However this may be, it is certainly a most amazing discovery that thought and ideas may be without any thinking being; a discovery big with consequences which cannot easily be traced by those deluded mortals who think and reason in the common track. We were always apt to imagine, that thought supposed a thinker, and love a lover, and treason a traitor; but this, it seems, was all a mistake; and it is found out, that there may be treason without a traitor, and love without a lover, laws without a legislator, and punishment without a sufferer, succession without time, and motion without any thing moved, or space in which it may move; or if, in these cases, ideas are the lover, the sufferer, the traitor, it were to be wished that the author of this discovery had farther condescended to acquaint us, whether ideas can converse together, and be under obligations of duty or gratitude to each other; whether they can make promises, and enter into leagues and covenants, and fulfil or break them, and be punished for the breach? If one set of ideas makes a covenant, another breaks it, and a third is punished for it, there is reason to think that justice is no natural virtue in this system.

It seemed very natural to think, that the Treatise of Human Nature required an author, and a very ingenious one too; but now we learn, that it is only a set of ideas which came together, and arranged themselves by certain associations and attractions.

After all, this curious system appears not to be fitted to the present state of human nature. How far it may suit some choice spirits, who are refined from the dregs of common sense, I cannot say. It is acknowledged, I think, that even these can enter into this system only in their most speculative hours, when they soar so high in pursuit of those self-existent ideas, as to lose sight of all other things. But when they condescend to mingle again with the human race, and to converse with a friend, a companion, or a fellow citizen, the ideal system vanishes; common sense, like an irresistible torrent, carries them along; and, in spite of all their reasoning and philosophy, they believe their own existence, and the existence of other things. . . .

This philosophy is like a hobby-horse, which a man in bad health may ride in his closet, without hurting his reputation; but if he should take him abroad with him to church, or to the exchange, or to the play house, his heir would immediately call a jury, and seize his estate.

Of Personal Identity

DAVID HUME

The great British empiricist philosopher and skeptic David Hume (1711–1766) was born in Scotland.

There are some philosophers, who imagine we are every moment intimately conscious of what we call our *Self*; that we feel its existence and its continuance in existence; and are certain, beyond the evidence of a demonstration, both of its perfect identity and simplicity. . . . For my part, when I enter most intimately into what I call *myself*, I always stumble on some particular perception or other, of heat or cold, light or shade, love or hatred, pain or pleasure. I never can catch *myself* at any time without a perception, and never can observe any thing but the perception. When my perceptions are remov'd for any time, as by sound sleep; so long am I insensible of *myself*, and may truly be said not to exist. And were all my perceptions remov'd by death, and cou'd I neither think, nor feel, nor see, nor love, nor hate after the dissolution of my body, I shou'd be entirely annihilated, nor do I conceive what is farther requisite to make me a perfect nonentity. If any one upon serious and unprejudic'd reflection, thinks he has a different notion of *himself*, I must confess I can reason no longer with him. All I can allow him is, that he may be in the right as well as I, and that we are essentially different in this particular. He may, perhaps, perceive something simple and continu'd, which he

calls *himself*; tho' I am certain there is no such principle in me.

But setting aside some metaphysicians of this kind, I may venture to affirm of the rest of mankind, that they are nothing but a bundle or collection of different perceptions, which succeed each other with an inconceivable rapidity, and are in a perpetual flux and movement. Our eyes cannot turn in their sockets without varying our perceptions. Our thought is still more variable than our sight; and all our other senses and faculties contribute to this change; nor is there any single power of the soul, which remains unalterably the same, perhaps for one moment. The mind is a kind of theatre, where several perceptions successively make their appearance; pass, re-pass, glide away, and mingle in an infinite variety of postures and situations. There is properly no *simplicity* in it at one time, nor *identity* in different; whatever natural propension we may have to imagine that simplicity and identity. The comparison of the theatre must not mislead us. They are the successive perceptions only, that constitute the mind; nor have we the most distant notion of the place, where these scenes are represented, or of the materials, of which it is compos'd.

What then gives us so great a propension to ascribe an identity to these successive perceptions, and to suppose ourselves possest of an invariable

---

From *A Treatise of Human Nature*. First published in 1738.

and uninterrupted existence thro' the whole course of our lives? . . .

. . . every distinct perception, which enters into the composition of the mind, is a distinct existence, and is different, and distinguishable, and separable from every other perception, either contemporary or successive. But, as, notwithstanding this distinction and separability, we suppose the whole train of perceptions to be united by identity, a question naturally arises concerning this relation of identity; whether it be something that really binds our several perceptions together, or only associates their ideas in the imagination. That is, in other words, whether in pronouncing concerning the identity of a person, we observe some real bond among his perceptions, or only feel one among the ideas we form of them. This question we might easily decide, if we wou'd recollect what has been already prov'd at large, that the understanding never observes any real connexion among objects, and that even the union of cause and effect, when strictly examin'd, resolves itself into a customary association of ideas. For from thence it evidently follows, that identity is nothing really belonging to these different perceptions, and uniting them together; but is merely a quality, which we attribute to them, because of the union of their ideas in the imagination, when we reflect upon them. Now the only qualities, which can give ideas an union in the imagination, are these three relations above-mention'd. These are the uniting principles in the ideal world, and without them every distinct object is separable by the mind, and may be separately consider'd, and appears not to have any more connexion with any other object, than if disjoin'd by the greatest difference and remoteness. 'Tis, therefore, on some of these three relations of resemblance, contiguity and causation, that identity depends; and as the very essence of these relations consists in their producing an easy transition of ideas; it follows, that our notions of personal identity, proceed entirely from the smooth and uninterrupted progress of the thought along a train of connected ideas, according to the principles above-explain'd.

The only question, therefore, which remains, is, by what relations this uninterrupted progress of our thought is produc'd, when we consider the successive existence of a mind or thinking person. And here 'tis evident we must confine ourselves to resemblance and causation, and must drop contiguity, which has little or no influence in the present case.

To begin with *resemblance;* suppose we cou'd see clearly into the breast of another, and observe that succession of perceptions, which constitutes his mind or thinking principle, and suppose that he always preserves the memory of a considerable part of past perceptions; 'tis evident that nothing cou'd more contribute to the bestowing a relation on this succession amidst all its variations. For what is the memory but a faculty, by which we raise up the images of past perceptions? And as an image necessarily resembles its object, must not the frequent placing of these resembling perceptions in the chain of thought, convey the imagination more easily from one link to another, and make the whole seem like the continuance of one object? In this particular, then, the memory not only discovers the identity, but also contributes to its production, by producing the relation of resemblance among the perceptions. The case is the same whether we consider ourselves or others.

As to *causation;* we may observe, that the true idea of the human mind, is to consider it as a system of different perceptions or different existences, which are link'd together by the relation of cause and effect, and mutually produce, destroy, influence, and modify each other. Our impressions give rise to their correspondent ideas; and these ideas in their turn produce other impressions. One thought chases another, and draws after it a third, by which it is expell'd in its turn. In this respect, I cannot compare the soul more properly to any thing than to a republic or commonwealth, in which the several members are united by the reciprocal ties of government and subordination, and give rise to other persons, who propagate the same republic in the incessant changes of its parts. And as the same individual republic may not only change its members, but also its laws and constitutions; in like manner the same person may vary his character and disposition, as well as his impressions and ideas, without losing his identity. Whatever changes he endures, his several parts are still connected by the relation of causation. And in this view our identity with regard to the passions serves to corroborate that with regard to the imagination, by the making our distant perceptions influence each other, and by giving us a present concern for our past or future pains or pleasures.

As memory alone acquaints us with the continuance and extent of this succession of perceptions, 'tis to be consider'd, upon that account chiefly, as the source of personal identity. Had we no memory, we never shou'd have any notion of causation, nor consequently of that chain of causes and effects, which constitute our self or person. But having once acquir'd this notion of causation from the memory, we can extend the same chain of causes, and consequently the identity of our persons beyond our memory, and can comprehend times, and circumstances, and actions, which we have entirely forgot, but suppose in general to have existed. For how few of our past actions are there, of which we have any memory? Who can tell me, for instance, what were his thoughts and actions on the first of *January* 1715, the 11th of *March* 1719, and the 3d of *August* 1733? Or will he affirm, because he has entirely forgot the incidents of these days, that the present self is not the same person with the self of that time; and by that means overturn all the most establish'd notions of personal identity? In this view, therefore,

memory does not so much *produce* as *discover* personal identity, by showing us the relation of cause and effect among our different perceptions. 'Twill be incumbent on those, who affirm that memory produces entirely our personal identity, to give a reason why we can thus extend our identity beyond our memory.

The whole of this doctrine leads us to a conclusion, which is of great importance in the present affair, viz. that all the nice and subtle questions concerning personal identity can never possibly be decided, and are to be regarded rather as grammatical than as philosophical difficulties. Identity depends on the relations of ideas; and these relations produce identity, by means of that easy transition they occasion. But as the relations, and the easiness of the transition may diminish by insensible degrees, we have no just standard, by which we can decide any dispute concerning the time, when they acquire or lose a title to the name of identity. All the disputes concerning the identity of connected objects are merely verbal, except so far as the relation of parts gives rise to some fiction or imaginary principle of union, as we have already observ'd.

Where Am I?

DANIEL C. DENNETT

Daniel C. Dennett (1942–   ) is the author of numerous books and articles. He teaches philosophy at Tufts University.

Now that I've won my suit under the Freedom of Information Act, I am at liberty to reveal for the first time a curious episode in my life that may be of interest not only to those engaged in research in the philosophy of mind, artificial intelligence, and neuroscience but also to the general public.

Several years ago I was approached by Pentagon officials who asked me to volunteer for a highly

dangerous and secret mission. In collaboration with NASA and Howard Hughes, the Department of Defense was spending billions to develop a Supersonic Tunneling Underground Device, or STUD. It was supposed to tunnel through the earth's core at great speed and deliver a specially designed atomic warhead "right up the Red's missile silos," as one of the Pentagon brass put it.

The problem was that in an early test they had succeeded in lodging a warhead about a mile deep under Tulsa, Oklahoma, and they wanted me to retrieve it for them. "Why me?" I asked. Well, the

From *Brainstorms: Philosophical Essays on Mind and Psychology* by Daniel C. Dennett (Bradford Books, Publishers, Inc., 1978). Reprinted by permission of the publisher.

mission involved some pioneering applications of current brain research, and they had heard of my interest in brains and of course my Faustian curiosity and great courage and so forth. . . . Well, how could I refuse? The difficulty that brought the Pentagon to my door was that the device I'd been asked to recover was fiercely radioactive, in a new way. According to monitoring instruments, something about the nature of the device and its complex interactions with pockets of material deep in the earth had produced radiation that could cause severe abnormalities in certain tissues of the brain. No way had been found to shield the brain from these deadly rays, which were apparently harmless to other tissues and organs of the body. So it had been decided that the person sent to recover the device should *leave his brain behind*. It would be kept in a safe place where it could execute its normal control functions by elaborate radio links. Would I submit to a surgical procedure that would completely remove my brain, which would then be placed in a life-support system at the Manned Spacecraft Center in Houston? Each input and output pathway, as it was severed, would be restored by a pair of microminiaturized radio transceivers, one attached precisely to the brain, the other to the nerve stumps in the empty cranium. No information would be lost, all the connectivity would be preserved. At first I was a bit reluctant. Would it really work? The Houston brain surgeons encouraged me. "Think of it," they said, "as a mere *stretching* of the nerves. If your brain were just moved over an inch in your skull, that would not alter or impair your mind. We're simply going to make the nerves indefinitely elastic by splicing radio links into them."

I was shown around the life-support lab in Houston and saw the sparkling new vat in which my brain would be placed, were I to agree. I met the large and brilliant support team of neurologists, hematologists, biophysicists, and electrical engineers, and after several days of discussions and demonstrations, I agreed to give it a try. I was subjected to an enormous array of blood tests, brain scans, experiments, interviews, and the like. They took down my autobiography at great length, recorded tedious lists of my beliefs, hopes, fears, and tastes. They even listed my favorite stereo recordings and gave me a crash session of psychoanalysis.

The day for surgery arrived at last and of course I was anesthetized and remembered nothing of the operation itself. When I came out of anesthesia, I opened my eyes, looked around, and asked the inevitable, the traditional, the lamentably hackneyed postoperative question: "Where am I? The nurse smiled down at me. "You're in Houston," she said, and I reflected that this still had a good chance of being the truth one way or another. She handed me a mirror. Sure enough, there were the tiny antennae poling up through their titanium ports cemented into my skull.

"I gather the operation was a success," I said. "I want to go see my brain." They led me (I was a bit dizzy and unsteady) down a long corridor and into the life-support lab. A cheer went up from the assembled support team, and I responded with what I hoped was a jaunty salute. Still feeling light-headed, I was helped over to the life-support vat. I peered through the glass. There, floating in what looked like ginger ale, was undeniably a human brain, though it was almost covered with printed circuit chips, plastic tubules, electrodes, and other paraphernalia. "Is that mine?" I asked. "Hit the output transmitter switch there on the side of the vat and see for yourself," the project director replied. I moved the switch to OFF, and immediately slumped, groggy and nauseated, into the arms of the technicians, one of whom kindly restored the switch to its ON position. While I recovered my equilibrium and composure, I thought to myself: "Well, here I am sitting on a folding chair, staring through a piece of plate glass at my own brain. . . . But wait," I said to myself, "shouldn't I have thought, 'Here I am, suspended in a bubbling fluid, being stared at by my own eyes'?" I tried to think this latter thought, I tried to project it into the tank, offering it hopefully to my brain, but I failed to carry off the exercise with any conviction. I tried again. "Here am *I*, Daniel Dennett, suspended in a bubbling fluid, being stared at by my own eyes." No, it just didn't work. Most puzzling and confusing. Being a philosopher of firm physicalist conviction, I believed unswervingly that the tokening of my thoughts was occurring somewhere in my brain: yet, when I thought "Here I am," where the thought occurred to me was *here,* outside the vat, where I, Dennett, was standing staring at my brain.

I tried and tried to think myself into the vat, but to no avail. I tried to build up to the task by doing mental exercises. I thought to myself, "The sun is shining *over there*," five times in rapid succession, each time mentally ostending a different place: in order, the sunlit corner of the lab, the visible front lawn of the hospital, Houston, Mars, and Jupiter. I found I had little difficulty in getting my "there"s to hop all over the celestial map with their proper references. I could loft a "there" in an instant through the farthest reaches of space, and then aim the next "there" with pinpoint accuracy at the upper left quadrant of a freckle on my arm. Why was I having such trouble with "here"? "Here in Houston" worked well enough, and so did "here in the lab," and even "here in this part of the lab," but "here in the vat" always seemed merely an unmeant mental mouthing. I tried closing my eyes while thinking it. This seemed to help, but still I couldn't manage to pull it off, except perhaps for a fleeting instant. I couldn't be sure. The discovery that I couldn't be sure was also unsettling. How did I know *where* I meant by "here" when I thought "here"? Could I *think* I meant one place when in fact I meant another? I didn't see how that could be admitted without untying the few bonds of intimacy between a person and his own mental life that had survived the onslaught of the brain scientists and philosophers, the physicalists and behaviorists. Perhaps I was incorrigible about where I *meant* when I said "here." But in my present circumstances it seemed that either I was doomed by sheer force of mental habit to thinking systematically false indexical thoughts, or where a person is (and hence where his thoughts are tokened for purposes of semantic analysis) is not necessarily where his brain, the physical seat of his soul, resides. Nagged by confusion, I attempted to orient myself by falling back on a favorite philosopher's ploy. I began naming things.

"Yorick," I said aloud to my brain, "you are my brain. The rest of my body, seated in this chair, I dub 'Hamlet.' So here we all are: Yorick's my brain, Hamlet's my body, and I am Dennett. *Now,* where am I? And when I think "where am I?" where's that thought tokened? Is it tokened in my brain, lounging about in the vat, or right here between my ears where it *seems* to be tokened? Or nowhere? Its *temporal* coordinates give me no trouble; must it not have

spatial coordinates as well? I began making a list of the alternatives.

1. *Where Hamlet goes, there goes Dennett.* This principle was easily refuted by appeal to the familiar brain-transplant thought experiments so enjoyed by philosophers. If Tom and Dick switch brains, Tom is the fellow with Dick's former body—just ask him; he'll claim to be Tom, and tell you the most intimate details of Tom's autobiography. It was clear enough, then, that my current body and I could part company, but not likely that I could be separated from my brain. The rule of thumb that emerged so plainly from the thought experiments was that in a brain-transplant operation, one wanted to be the *donor,* not the recipient. Better to call such an operation a *body* transplant, in fact, So perhaps the truth was,

2. *Where Yorick goes, there goes Dennett.* This was not at all appealing, however. How could I be in the vat and not about to go anywhere, when I was so obviously outside the vat looking in and beginning to make guilty plans to return to my room for a substantial lunch? This begged the question I realized, but it still seemed to be getting at something important. Casting about for some support for my intuition, I hit upon a legalistic sort of argument that might have appealed to Locke.

Suppose, I argued to myself, I were now to fly to California, rob a bank, and be apprehended. In which state would I be tried: in California, where the robbery took place, or in Texas, where the brains of the outfit were located? Would I be a California felon with an out-of-state brain, or a Texas felon remotely controlling an accomplice of sorts in California? It seemed possible that I might beat such a rap just on the undecidability of that jurisdictional question, though perhaps it would be deemed an interstate, and hence Federal, offense. In any event, suppose I were convicted. Was it likely that California would be satisfied to throw Hamlet into the brig, knowing that Yorick was living the good life and luxuriously taking the waters in Texas? Would Texas incarcerate Yorick, leaving Hamlet free to take the next boat to Rio? This alternative appealed to me. Barring capital punishment or other cruel and unusual punishment, the state would be obliged to maintain the life-support system for Yorick though they might move him from Houston to Leavenworth, and aside from the unpleasantness of the opprobrium, I, for one, would not mind at all and would consider myself a free man under those circumstances. If the state has an interest in forcibly relocating persons in institutions, it would fail to relocate me in any institution by locating Yorick there. If this were true, it suggested a third alternative.

3. *Dennett is wherever he thinks he is.* Generalized, the claim was as follows: At any given time a person has a *point of view,* and the location of the point of view (which is determined internally by the content of the point of view) is also the location of the person.

Such a proposition is not without its perplexities, but to me it seemed a step in the right direction. The only trouble was that it seemed to place one in a heads-I-win/tails-you-lose situation of unlikely infallibility as regards location. Hadn't I myself often been wrong about where I was, and at least as often uncertain? Couldn't one get lost? Of course, but getting lost *geographically* is not the only way one might get lost. If one were lost in the woods one could attempt to reassure oneself with the consolation that at least one knew where one was: one was right here in the familiar surroundings of one's own body. Perhaps in this case one would not have drawn one's attention to much to be thankful for. Still, there were worse plights imaginable, and I wasn't sure I wasn't in such a plight right now.

Point of view clearly had something to do with personal location, but it was itself an unclear notion. It was obvious that the content of one's point of view was not the same as or determined by the content of one's beliefs or thoughts. For example, what should we say about the point of view of the Cinerama viewer who shrieks and twists in his seat as the roller-coaster footage overcomes his psychic distancing? Has he forgotten that he is safely seated in the theater? Here I was inclined to say that the person is experiencing an illusory shift in point of view. In other cases, my inclination to call such shifts illusory was less strong. The workers in laboratories and plants who handle dangerous materials by operating feedback-controlled mechanical arms and hands undergo a shift in point of view that is crisper and more pronounced than anything Cinerama can provoke. They can feel the heft and slipperiness of the containers they manipulate with their metal fingers. They know perfectly well where they are and are not

fooled into false beliefs by the experience, yet it is as if they were inside the isolation chamber they are peering into. With mental effort, they can manage to shift their point of view back and forth, rather like making a transparent Necker cube or an Escher drawing change orientation before one's eyes. It does even as a matter of habit. I should dwell on images of myself comfortably floating in my vat, beaming volitions to that familiar body *out there.* I reflected that the ease or difficulty of this task was presumably independent of the truth about the location of one's brain. Had I been practicing before the operation, I might now be finding it second nature. Your might now yourself try such a *trompe l'oeil.* Imagine you have written an inflammatory letter which has been published in the *Times,* the result of which is that the government has chosen to impound you brain for a probationary period of three years in its Dangerous Brain Clinic in Bethesda, Maryland. Your body of course is allowed freedom to earn a salary and thus to continue its function of laying up income to be taxed. At this moment, however, your body is seated in an auditorium listening to a peculiar account by Daniel Dennett of his own similar experience. Try it. Think yourself to Bethesda, and then hark back longingly to your body, far away, and yet *seeming* so near. It is only with long-distance restraint (yours? the government's?) that you can control your impulse to get those hands clapping in polite applause before navigating the old body to the rest room and a well-deserved glass of evening sherry in the lounge. The task of imagination is certainly difficult, but if you achieve your goal the results might be consoling.

Anyway, there I was in Houston, lost in thought as one might say, but not for long. My speculations were soon interrupted by the Houston doctors, who wished to test out my new prosthetic nervous system before sending me off on my hazardous mission. As I mentioned before, I was a bit dizzy at first, and not surprisingly, although I soon habituated myself to my new circumstances (which were, after all, well nigh indistinguishable from my old circumstances). My accommodation was not perfect, however, and to this day I continue to be plagued by minor coordination difficulties. The speed of light is fast, but finite, and as my brain and body move farther and farther apart, the delicate interaction of my feedback systems is thrown into disarray by the time lags. Just as one is rendered close to speechless by a delayed or echoic hearing of one's speaking voice so, for instance, I am virtually unable to track a moving object with my eyes whenever my brain and my body are more than a few miles apart. In most matters my impairment is scarcely detectable, though I can no longer hit a slow curve ball with the authority of yore. There are some compensations of course. Though liquor tastes as good as ever, and warms my gullet while corroding my liver, I can drink it in any quantity I please, without becoming the slightest bit inebriated, a curiosity some of my close friends may have noticed (though I occasionally have *feigned* inebriation, so as not to draw attention to my unusual circumstances). For similar reasons, I take aspirin orally for a sprained wrist, but if the pain persists I ask Houston to administer codeine to me *in vitro*. In times of illness the phone bill can be staggering.

But to return to my adventure. At length, both the doctors and I were satisfied that I was ready to undertake my subterranean mission. And so I left my brain in Houston and headed by helicopter for Tulsa. Well, in any case, that's the way it seemed to me. That's how I would put it, just off the top of my head as it were. On the trip I reflected further about my earlier anxieties and decided that my first postoperative speculations had been tinged with panic. The matter was not nearly as strange or metaphysical as I had been supposing. Where was I? In two places, clearly: both inside the vat and outside it. Just as one can stand with one foot in Connecticut and the other in Rhode Island, I was in two places at once. I had become one of those scattered individuals we used to hear so much about. The more I considered this answer, the more obviously true it appeared. But, strange to say, the more true it appeared, the less important the question to which it could be the true answer seemed. A sad but not unprecedented, fate for a philosophical question to suffer. This answer did not completely satisfy me, of course. There lingered some question to which I should have liked an answer, which was neither "Where are all my various and sundry parts?" nor "What is my current point of view"? Or at least there seemed to be such a question. For it did seem undeniable that in some sense I and not merely *most of me* was descending

into the earth under Tulsa in search of an atomic warhead.

When I found the warhead, I was certainly glad I had left my brain behind, for the pointer on the specially built Geiger counter I had brought with me was off the dial. I called Houston on my ordinary radio and told the operation control center of my position and my progress. In return, they gave me instructions for dismantling the vehicle, based upon my on-site observations. I had set to work with my cutting torch when all of a sudden a terrible thing happened. I went stone deaf. At first I thought it was only my radio earphones that had broken, but when I tapped on my helmet, I heard nothing. Apparently the auditory transceivers had gone on the fritz. I could no longer hear Houston or my own voice, but I could speak, so I started telling them what had happened. In midsentence, I knew something else had gone wrong. My vocal apparatus had become paralyzed. Then my right hand went limp—another transceiver had gone. I was truly in deep trouble. But worse was to follow. After a few more minutes, I went blind. I cursed my luck, and then I cursed the scientists who had led me into this grave peril. There I was, deaf, dumb, and blind, in a radioactive hole more than a mile under Tulsa. Then the last of my cerebral radio links broke, and suddenly I was faced with a new and even more shocking problem: whereas an instant before I had been buried alive in Oklahoma, now I was disembodied in Houston. My recognition of my new status was not immediate. It took me several very anxious minutes before it dawned on me that my poor body lay several hundred miles away, with heart pulsing and lungs respirating, but otherwise as dead as the body of any heart-transplant donor, its skull packed with useless, broken electronic gear. The shift in perspective I had earlier found well nigh impossible now seemed quite natural. Though I could think myself back into my body in the tunnel under Tulsa, it took some effort to sustain the illusion. For surely it was an illusion to suppose I was still in Oklahoma: I has lost all contact with that body.

It occurred to me then, with one of those rushes of revelation of which we should be suspicious, that I had stumbled upon an impressive demonstration of the immateriality of the soul based upon physicalist principles and premises. For as the last radio signal between Tulsa and Houston died away, had I not changed location from Tulsa to Houston at the speed of light? And had I not accomplished this without any increase in mass? What moved from A to B at such speed was surely myself, or at any rate my soul or mind—the massless center of my being and home of my consciousness. My *point of view* had lagged somewhat behind, but I had already noted the indirect bearing of point of view on personal location. I could not see how a physicalist philosopher could quarrel with this except by taking the dire and counterintuitive route of banishing all talk of persons. Yet the notion of personhood was so well entrenched in everyone's world view, or so it seemed to me, that any denial would be as curiously unconvincing, as systematically disingenuous, as the Cartesian negation, "non sum."

The joy of philosophic discovery thus tided me over some very bad minutes or perhaps hours as the helplessness and hopelessness of my situation became more apparent to me. Waves of panic and even nausea swept over me, made all the more horrible by the absence of their normal body-dependent phenomenology. No adrenaline rush of tingles in the arms, no pounding heart, no premonitory salivation. I did feel a dread sinking feeling in my bowels at one point, and this tricked me momentarily into the false hope that I was undergoing a reversal of the process that landed me in this fix—a gradual undisembodiment. But the isolation and uniqueness of that twinge soon convinced me that it was simply the first of a plague of phantom body hallucinations that I, like any other amputee, would be all too likely to suffer.

My mood then was chaotic. On the one hand, I was fired up with elation of my philosophic discovery and was wracking my brain (one of the few familiar things I could still do), trying to figure out how to communicate my discovery to the journals; while on the other, I was bitter, lonely, and filled with dread and uncertainty. Fortunately, this did not last long, for my technical support team sedated me into a dreamless sleep from which I awoke, hearing with magnificent fidelity the familiar opening strains of my favorite Brahms piano trio. So that was why they had wanted a list of my favorite recordings! It did not take me long to realize that I was hearing the music without ears. The output from the stereo stylus was being fed through some fancy rectification circuitry directly into my auditory nerve. I was mainlining Brahms, an unforgettable experience for any stereo buff. At the end of the record it did not surprise me to hear the reassuring voice of the project director speaking into a microphone that was now my prosthetic ear. He confirmed my analysis of what had gone wrong and assured me that steps were being taken to reembody me. He did not elaborate, and after a few more recordings, I found myself drifting off to sleep. My sleep lasted, I later learned, for the better part of a year, and when I awoke, it was to find myself fully restored to my senses. When I looked into the mirror, though, I was a bit startled to see an unfamiliar face. Bearded and a bit heavier, bearing no doubt a family resemblance to my former face, and with the same look of sprightly intelligence and resolute character, but definitely a new face. Further self-explorations of an intimate nature left me no doubt that this was a new body, and the project director confirmed my conclusions, He did not volunteer any information on the past history of my new body and I decided (wisely, I think in retrospect) not to pry. As many philosophers unfamiliar with my ordeal have more recently speculated, the acquisition of a new body leaves one's *person* intact. And after a period of adjustment to a new voice, new muscular strengths and weaknesses, and so forth, one's *personality* is by and large also preserved. More dramatic changes in personality have been routinely observed in people who have undergone extensive plastic surgery, to say nothing of sex-change operations, and I think no one contests the survival of the person in such cases. In any event I soon accommodated to my new body, to the point of being unable to recover any of its novelties to my consciousness or even memory. The view in the mirror soon became utterly familiar. That view, by the way, still revealed antennae, and so I was not surprised to learn that my brain had not been moved from its haven in the life-support lab.

I decided that good old Yorick deserved a visit. I and my new body, whom we might as well call Fortinbras, strode into the familiar lab to another round of applause from the technicians, who were of course congratulating themselves, not me. Once more I stood before the vat and contemplated poor Yorick, and on a whim I once again cavalierly flicked off the output transmitter switch. Imagine my surprise when nothing unusual happened. No fainting spell, no nausea, no noticeable change. A technician hurried to restore the switch to ON, but still I felt nothing. I demanded an explanation, which the project director hastened to provide. It seems that before they had even operated on the first occasion, they had constructed a computer duplicate of my brain, reproducing both the complete information-processing structure and the computational speed of my brain in a giant computer program. After the operation, but before they had dared to send me off on my mission to Oklahoma, they had run this computer system and Yorick side by side. The incoming signals from Hamlet were sent simultaneously to Yorick's transceivers and to the computer's array of inputs. And the outputs from Yorick were not only beamed back to Hamlet, my body; they were recorded and checked against the simultaneous output of the computer program, which was called "Hubert" for reasons obscure to me. Over days and even weeks, the outputs were identical and synchronous, which of course did not *prove* that they had succeeded in copying the brain's functional structure, but the empirical support was greatly encouraging.

Hubert's input, and hence activity, had been kept parallel with Yorick's during my disembodied days. And now, to demonstrate this, they had actually thrown the master switch that put Hubert for the first time in on-line control of my body—not Hamlet, of course, but Fortinbras. (Hamlet, I learned, had never been recovered from its underground tomb and could be assumed by this time to have largely returned to the dust. At the head of my grave still lay the magnificent bulk of the abandoned device, with the word STUD emblazoned on its side in large letters—a circumstance which may provide archaeologists of the next century with a curious insight into the burial rites of their ancestors.)

The laboratory technicians now showed me the master switch, which had two positions, labeled *B,* for Brain (they didn't know my brain's name was Yorick) and *H,* for Hubert. The switch did indeed point to *H,* and they explained to me that if I wished, I could switch it back to *B.* With my heart in my mouth (and my brain in its vat), I did this. Nothing happened. A click, that was all. To test their claim, and with the master switch now set at *B,* I hit Yorick's out-

put transmitter switch on the vat and sure enough, I began to faint. Once the output switch was turned back on and I had recovered my wits, so to speak, I continued to play with the master switch, flipping it back and forth. I found that with the exception of the transitional click, I could detect no trace of a difference. I could switch in mid-utterance, and the sentence I had begun speaking under the control of Yorick was finished without a pause or hitch of any kind under the control of Hubert. I had a spare brain, a prosthetic device which might some day stand me in very good stead, were some mishap to befall Yorick. Or alternatively, I could keep Yorick as a spare and use Hubert. It didn't seem to make any difference which I chose, for the wear and tear and fatigue on my body did not have any debilitating effect on either brain, whether or not it was actually causing the motions of my body, or merely spilling its output into thin air.

The only truly unsettling aspect of this new development was the prospect, which was not long in dawning on me, of someone detaching the spare—Hubert or Yorick, as the case might be—from Fortinbras and hitching it to yet another body—some Johnny-come-lately Rosencrantz or Guildenstern. Then (if not before) there would be *two* people, that much was clear. One would be me, and the other would be a sort of super-twin brother. If there were two bodies, one under the control of Hubert and the other being controlled by Yorick, then which would the world recognize as the true Dennett? And whatever the rest of the world decided, which one would be *me*? Would I be the Yorick-brained one, by virtue of Yorick's causal priority and former intimate relationship with the original Dennett body, Hamlet? That seemed a bit legalistic, a bit too redolent of the arbitrariness of consanguinity and legal possession, to be convincing at the metaphysical level. For suppose that before the arrival of the second body on the scene, I had been keeping Yorick as the spare for years, and letting Hubert's output drive my body —that is, Fortinbras—all that time. The Hubert–Fortinbras couple would seem then by squatter's rights (to combat one legal intuition with another) to be the true Dennett and the lawful inheritor of everything that was Dennett's. This was an interesting question, certainly, but not nearly so pressing as another question that bothered me. My strongest intuition was that in such an eventuality *I* would survive so long as *either* brain-body couple remained intact, but I had mixed emotions about whether I should want both to survive.

I discussed my worries with the technicians and the project director. The prospect of two Dennetts was abhorrent to me, I explained, largely for social reasons. I didn't want to be my own rival for the affections of my wife, nor did I like the prospect of two Dennetts sharing my modest professor's salary. Still more vertiginous and distasteful, though, was the idea of knowing *that much* about another person, while he had the very same goods on me. How could we ever face each other? My colleagues in the lab argued that I was ignoring the bright side of the matter. Weren't there many things I wanted to do but, being only one person, had been unable to do? Now one Dennett could stay at home and be the professor and family man, while the other could strike out on a life of travel and adventure—missing the family of course, but happy in the knowledge that the other Dennett was keeping the home fires burning. I could be faithful and adulterous at the same time. I could even cuckold myself—to say nothing of other more lurid possibilities my colleagues were all too ready to force upon my overtaxed imagination. But my ordeal in Oklahoma (or was it Houston?) had made me less adventurous, and I shrank from this opportunity that was being offered (though of course I was never quite sure it was being offered to *me* in the first place).

There was another prospect even more disagreeable: that the spare, Hubert or Yorick as the case might be, would be detached from any input from Fortinbras and just left detached. Then, as in the other case, there would be two Dennetts, or at least two claimants to my name and possessions, one embodied in Fortinbras, and the other sadly, miserably disembodied. Both selfishness and altruism bade me take steps to prevent this from happening. So I asked that measures be taken to ensure that no one could ever tamper with the transceiver connections or the master switch without my (our? no, *my*) knowledge and consent. Since I had no desire to spend my life guarding the equipment in Houston, it was mutually decided that all the electronic connections in the lab would be carefully locked. Both those that controlled the life-support system for

Yorick and those that controlled the power supply for Hubert would be guarded with fail-safe devices, and I would take the only master switch, outfitted for radio remote control, with me wherever I went. I carry it strapped around my waist and—wait a moment—*here it is.* Every few months I reconnoiter the situation by switching channels. I do this only in the presence of friends, of course, for if the other channel were, heaven forbid, either dead or otherwise occupied, there would have to be somebody who had my interests at heart to switch it back, to bring me back from the void. For while I could feel, see, hear, and otherwise sense whatever befell my body, subsequent to such a switch, I'd be unable to control it. By the way, the two positions on the switch are intentionally unmarked, so I never have the faintest idea whether I am switching from Hubert to Yorick or vice versa. (Some of you may think that in this case I really don't know *who* I am, let alone where I am. But such reflections no longer make much of a dent on my essential Dennettness, on my own sense of who I am. If it is true that in one sense I don't know who I am then that's another one of your philosophical truths of underwhelming significance.)

In any case, every time I've flipped the switch so far, nothing has happened. *So let's give it a try....*

"THANK GOD! I THOUGHT YOU'D NEVER FLIP THAT SWITCH! You can't imagine how horrible it's been these last two weeks—but now you know; it's your turn in purgatory. How I've longed for this moment! You see, about two weeks ago—excuse me, ladies and gentlemen, but I've got to explain this to my . . .um, brother, I guess you could say, but he's just told you the facts, so you'll understand—about two weeks ago our two brains drifted just a bit out of synch. I don't know whether *my* brain is now Hubert or Yorick, any more than you do, but in any case, the two brains drifted apart, and of course once the process started, it snowballed, for I was in a slightly different receptive state for the input we both received, a difference that was soon magnified. In no time at all the illusion that I was in control of my body—our body—was completely dissipated. There was nothing I could do—no way to call you. YOU DIDN'T EVEN KNOW I EXISTED! It's been like being carried around in a cage, or better, like being possessed—hearing my own voice say things I didn't mean to say, watching in frustration as my own hands performed deeds I hadn't intended. You'd scratch your itches, but not the way I would have, and you kept me awake, with your tossing and turning. I've been totally exhausted, on the verge of a nervous breakdown, carried around helplessly by your frantic round of activities, sustained only by the knowledge that some day you'd throw the switch.

"Now it's your turn, but at least you'll have the comfort of knowing *I* know you're in there. Like an expectant mother, I'm eating—or at any rate tasting, smelling, seeing—for *two* now, and I'll try to make it easy for you. Don't worry. Just as soon as this colloquium is over, you and I will fly to Houston,

and we'll see what can be done to get one of us another body. You can have a female body—your body could be any color you like. But let's think it over. I tell you what—to be fair, if we both want this body, I promise I'll let the project director flip a coin to settle which of us gets to keep it and which then gets to choose a new body. That should guarantee justice, shouldn't it? In any case, I'll take care of you, I promise. These people are my witnesses.

"Ladies and gentlemen, this talk we have just heard is not exactly the talk *I* would have given, but I assure you that everything he said was perfectly true. And now if you'll excuse me, I think I'd—we'd—better sit down."

Personal Identity from Plato to Parfit

RAYMOND MARTIN

Raymond Martin (1941–) is the author of many articles and several books. He teaches philosophy at the University of Maryland.

Each of us assumes that we remain who we are, through various changes, from moment to moment, hour to hour, day to day, and so on. We persist until we cease, perhaps at bodily death. Each of us also assumes that one of our most fundamental egoistic desires is to persist. As we say, we want to live. But what *accounts* for the fact, if it is a fact, that we remain the same person over time and through various changes? That question is the philosophical problem of personal identity. And when, in ordinary circumstances, you want to persist, what is it that you *really* want, that is, that you want fundamentally? That question is the philosophical problem of what matters primarily in survival. It is commonly assumed that when people want to persist, what they really want is simply to persist. That answer is the thesis that identity is primarily what matters in survival,

In a very strict sense of *same person,* as soon as you

change, no matter how or how minutely, you cease. In this sense of *same person,* no one lasts for long. For obvious reasons, this sense of *same person* is not particularly useful. Its not being useful is different from its being false. It could be true and not useful. Or there may be no truth of the matter about how long each of us lasts. In any case, both you and also others will almost always think of you as remaining the same person through changes. Of course, some changes—biological death is the most compelling example—may cause you to cease. But, ordinarily we suppose, not just any change will cause you to cease. The problem of personal identity is the problem of explaining how, in spite of your changing in various ways, you manage to remain the same person.

A similar question arises in the case of any object—rock, plant, animal, automobile—that persists over time. The problem of personal identity, might be a special case of the more general problem of the identity of any temporally extended object. The same solution might work for everything. Or personal identity might be different. Rather than worrying about this more general question, we shall focus on personal identity. For better or worse, we do not have to start from scratch. For as long as people have thought about the nature of things, they have thought about what accounts for the fact that they persist. We can begin, then, by surveying their solutions. Only a few basic solutions have been proposed, and each of them is associated with a particular historical period when philosophers generally—or at least the one that we now think mattered most—considered it to be the right answer.

FROM PLATO UNTIL LOCKE: THE SOUL VIEW

In classical times, there was not really a philosophical problem of personal identity. Rather, there was a problem of death. The question of interest was not what accounts for the fact that we persist, but whether bodily death is the end. Personal identity entered the discussion through the back door, in the service of answering this more pressing question. Then, just as now, most people feared death. And then, just as now, many people had intimations that bodily death is not the end, that somehow we survive it.

Plato's dialog, *Phaedo,* is a dramatic reenactment of the conversation that took place between Socrates, who was Plato's teacher, and a few of Socrates' students. The conversation took place in Socrates' jail cell, on the day that he was put to death. In this dialog, the character, Socrates, argues that people survive their bodily deaths. But beyond that, he explains in a way that no one had ever explained before what accounts for the fact that people—we—persist. In his view, the fact that we have (or are) immaterial souls explains it.

In ancient times (and still today), almost everyone assumed that if people survive their bodily deaths, there must be a vehicle (or medium) for each of their survivals. However, even before anyone had thought of the idea of an immaterial (unextended) soul, there was a ready vehicle available: fine matter. When Socrates was alive, many Greeks thought that the soul leaves the body when the person who dies expels his last breath; apparently they also thought that, at least at that moment, the soul *is*

that last breath. It was Plato's genius (or perversity) to have suggested a radical alternative.

Although Plato never quite got the whole idea out, in *Phaedo* Socrates suggests that the vehicle for survival is not any sort of physical object, not even breath, but, rather an unextended thing. So far as we know, this suggestion was original to Plato (or Socrates). Previously, when others had talked of immaterial souls, they usually meant invisible matter. Even Socrates, in *Phaedo,* did not always distinguish sharply between something's being immaterial and its being invisible. But, then, sometimes he did distinguish between them. Subsequently in Europe, the view that each of us is essentially a soul, and that souls are immaterial, unextended things, really caught on. Christian philosophers seized on this pagan view to explain how people could survive their bodily deaths.

How, then, if he did, did Plato arrive at the idea of an immaterial, unextended soul? We do not know. In *Phaedo,* Socrates is concerned with the sources of generation and corruption, that is, with how things come to be and pass away. In his view, the corruption of a thing is brought about by its coming apart, that is, by its breaking into pieces, or decomposing. Plato may have reasoned, as the good student of geometry that he was, that any extended thing, merely by virtue of its being extended, is potentially divisible and, hence, potentially corruptible. So if people are immortal, not only by accident but necessarily, they must be unextended.

But why suppose that people are immortal? Plato may have thought he had evidence that people survive the demise of their gross physical bodies. In *Phaedo,* Socrates remarks that in graveyards people sometimes see ghosts. However, people would not have to be immortal, that is, last forever, to survive the demise of their gross physical bodies. In spite of the enormous influence of Plato's arguments for immortality, it is not clear why he thought that people are immortal. Nor is it clear why his famous student, Aristotle, who had what we would call a more scientific turn of mind, followed Plato in assuming that people are immortal, or at least that the rational parts—*nous*—of our minds are immortal.

It is a little clearer why Plato thought it mattered whether people survive the demise of their gross physical bodies. Apparently he (or Socrates) thought that in trying to understand the nature of reality, one's body is a constant distraction. If people could get away from bodily distractions, it would help them to discover eternal truths. In addition, Plato tells us that in one of Socrates' last thoughts, Socrates mused about the joys of conversing with the dead. Apparently, then, if Plato (or Socrates) thought that after their bodily deaths, people can converse with other people who have also died, he also supposed that after bodily death souls carry along with them their associated mental dispositions, such as their memories; and apparently, since he looked forward to conversing with the dead, he thought that people were entitled to anticipate having the experiences of their postmortem selves.

A few centuries later, the philosopher Lucretius questioned the latter assumption. He wrote that the persistence of one's soul, even together with one's mental dispositions, would *not* entitle a person to anticipate having future experiences. In the context of his making the point that we have nothing to fear from bodily death, Lucretius argued that "if any feeling remains in mind or spirit after it has been torn from body, that is nothing to us, who are brought into being by wedlock of body and spirit, conjoined and coalesced." He then considered the possibility that "the matter that composes us should be re-assembled by time after our death and brought back into its present state" (compare with the later Christian view that something like this happens when we survive bodily death). He claimed that even if this were to happen, it still would "be no concern of ours once the chain of our identity had been snapped" (Lucretius 1951, Bk. 3). But why would it be of no concern?

Lucretius' answer, in effect, is, first, that our persisting, that is, our continuing as the same persons we now are, is a precondition of any such egoistic concern we might have for the experiences of any *parts* of ourselves that might survive our bodily deaths, and, second, that whatever *parts* may survive, *we* cease at our bodily deaths. "If the future holds travail and anguish in store, the self must be in existence, when that time comes, in order to experience it." "From this fate," Lucretius continued, "we are redeemed by death, which denies existence to the self that might have suffered these tribulations." The moral of these reflections, he thought, is "that

we have nothing to fear in death" because "one who no longer is cannot suffer, or differ in any way from one who has never been born, when once this mortal life has been usurped by death the immortal" (1951, Bk. 3).

In sum, in Lucretius' view, regardless of what that is currently part of us persists and regardless of whether it is capable of having experiences and of performing actions, such as conversing with the dead, if this part of ourselves is not attended by the very bodies we have when we die—and in order for it to be attended by these very bodies, the bodies would have to exist continuously as integrated, functioning entities—this part of ourselves is not us; and if this part of ourselves is not us, its experiences and actions are not something we can look forward to having and performing. Unfortunately, Lucretius did not argue for this view. He merely asserted it.

What is impressive, however, is not so much Lucretius' answering the question of what matters primarily in survival by saying that it is personal identity. Rather, what is impressive is his thinking to *ask* it. So far as we know, no one previously, at least in the West, had thought to ask it. Normally people simply assumed (and still do assume) that if at some point in the future they no longer exist, something of inestimable value, at least from their own egoistic points of view, has been lost. In asking the question of what matters primarily in survival, Lucretius considered the possibility that we might not persist and yet that, even from our own egoistic points of view, not much that matters might be lost, not because our lives were awful or because we do not value ourselves, but because identity is not what matters primarily in survival. As we shall see, the question of whether identity or something else matters primarily in survival resurfaced again in the late eighteenth and early nineteenth centuries, and then again, when it moved to center stage, in our own times.

A question that in the West apparently did not arise in classical times is that of *why* some underlying vehicle—one's soul, one's body, or something else—is necessary for the persistence of one's mental dispositions. (This question did arise, in a different context, in ancient Buddhist thought; more on this later.) We do not know how classical Western thinkers might have responded to this question, but one answer might naturally have suggested itself to

294 PART 3: MIND, PERSONAL IDENTITY, AND CONSCIOUSNESS

anyone who thought about it. It is that the occurrent expressions of one's mental dispositions (expressions of one's mental dispositions that surface in one's consciousness), which are individual mental episodes, come and then rapidly go. It is a whole series of such transient episodes that collectively constitute what we normally regard as a person's occurrent mental life, that is, his or her conscious mental life. Unless something were to underlie such a series—ultimately something that could sustain itself—it would be hard to explain why the series continued and, in case some such series did continue, it would be hard to explain why episodes included in it should be regarded as continuing the old series rather than as beginning new ones.

What is it that could sustain one's occurrent mental states and their successors and could also sustain itself? Before Plato's invention of the immaterial soul, all that was available to sustain occurrent mental states was matter. And that—fine matter—is what many people thought did sustain one's mental states. Plato, however, was convinced that the world of matter is in constant flux. Therefore, if the series of a person's occurrent mental states needs a sustainer because the episodes of which it is composed come and then rapidly go, shouldn't fine matter, for the same reason, also need a sustainer? After all, the various (exact) configurations into which matter gets assembled also come and then rapidly go. But then the only things left to sustain the configurations of matter that might in turn sustain both the series of peoples' occurrent mental states and the people themselves are immaterial souls. But if immaterial souls can sustain the material configurations that, in turn, are supposed to sustain a person's mental states, perhaps souls can sustain these mental states directly, without even working through matter. Plato may or may not have had some such thoughts. There is not a lot of textual evidence that he did, but there is some. In any case, it would have been a natural thing for theorists to have considered during the period from Plato to Locke.

Another possibility, at least in theory, is that the series of occurrent mental states continues without anything's sustaining it, that is, that it just continues. Contemplating that possibility, it seems, would lead one rather quickly to the question of what matters in survival, for if such a series were to continue, with-

out anything else's playing the role of its sustainer, what would become of the *person* whose mental series it was in the first place? And if the person were not to continue, perhaps because he dies with the body, why should it matter to him in his concern to survive that his mental series continues? That's close to the question that Lucretius considered, and he answered that it should not matter. On the other hand, if the person were to continue, even though the current constituents of bodily and mental states did not continue, in what would such continuing consist? On the hypothesis that there is no sustainer of one's occurrent mental states, apparently a person's continuing would have to consist simply in the series of one's mental states itself continuing. By then, even if this hypothesis makes sense, why should the series' continuing matter? That is, why should earlier members of an occurrent bodily and/or mental series of episodic events, which do not themselves last, care whether they are followed by subsequent members of the series?

It does not really answer this question to reply, "So that they, the earlier members, can converse with the dead." On this hypothesis, although the conversation might continue, because the earlier members of the series would no longer exist it is hard to see how these earlier members would continue the conversation. And the person to whom these earlier members of the series belonged, if the person continued at all, would continue the series only in a fictional sense, as the organizational category in terms of which we (i.e, bodily and/or mental episodes that are part of some current series) think about the series as a whole. So far as we know, no one was to think such thoughts until at least the end of the seventeenth century, and no one was to hold them clearly in view until the end of the eighteenth.

FROM LOCKE UNTIL THE LATE 1960'S: THE (INTRINSIC) RELATIONS VIEW

John Locke, toward the end of the seventeenth century, is usually regarded as the father of modern personal identity theory. However, Locke may have accepted that persons have immaterial souls, so he may have had one foot planted squarely in the past. Whether or not Locke was sincere in declaring that he believed in immaterial souls, his main theoretical innovation, so far as personal identity is concerned, was to argue that *even if* each of us is composed of an immaterial soul, because we cannot know that we are, our being so composed can have nothing whatsoever to do with personal identity. Rather, Locke argued, it is our retaining the "same consciousness" that makes us the same people over time. Locke also pointed out that, unlike the case of souls, each of us has direct, introspective access to our own consciousness and indirect access—by observing their behavior—to the consciousness of others.

Scholars are divided about what Locke meant by *same consciousness*. It is clear that part, but only part, of what he meant has to do with memory. It is also clear that he had other concerns about personal identity and its significance that anticipated questions that have moved to center stage only in our own times. Before getting to these subtler aspects of Locke's thought, let's consider the view that Locke's eighteenth-century critics invariably attributed to him the view that a person at one time and one at another have the *same consciousness* just in case the person at the later time *remembers* having had experiences or having performed actions that were had or performed by the person at the earlier time. This is a simple version of the memory view of personal identity. As we shall see, it is vulnerable to decisive objections, which Locke's critics, who wanted to retain the soul view, were not long in pointing out. Yet even this simple memory view of personal identity was, in important ways, an advance on the soul view.

According to the soul view, personal identity depends on sameness of soul. And souls, because they are unextended, are not part of the material world. Hence, personal identity depends on something profoundly mysterious. Other people's souls cannot be observed indirectly. For instance, you cannot tell by observing another's behavior whether he has an immaterial soul, and, if he does, whether he has the same one throughout the time you are observing him. As we shall see when we get to David Hume, you cannot observe even your own soul directly. In Locke's simple memory view, by contrast, personal identity depends on the presence of a psychological relationship—memory—that binds together earlier and later stages of a person. Other people's memories, unlike their souls, can be observed indirectly.

For instance, by listening to others talk about the past (or answer questions on an examination), you may be able to determine that they remember having experienced or done various things. You may be able also to observe directly, in introspection, that *you* remember having experienced and done various things.

Locke saw himself as proposing that we replace a mysterious, essentially religious view of personal identity with a nonmysterious (because the key relations involved are all observable) essentially scientific view. At the time Locke proposed his new theory, Isaac Newton had just demonstrated that there could be a science of nature. Locke was intent on demonstrating that there could also be a science of mind. In Locke's opinion, his new consciousness-view of personal identity, whatever the problems might be in working out its details, was a contribution to this new science of mind. In other words, in Locke's view, his account of personal identity was not just another theory. Rather, it was an idea whose time had come.

Locke's initial critics were not so progressive. However, they were right in thinking that the memory view that they attributed to Locke had three serious problems. One of these problems is that a person, for example, may not now remember having done things which he did in fact do. Locke concluded, rather implausibly in the views of these critics, that if you cannot remember having done something, you did not do it. It is more likely, the critics argued, that something other than memory, or perhaps in addition to memory, accounts for personal identity. They thought this other thing must be the immaterial soul.

A second problem with Locke's view, for which Bishop Joseph Butler usually gets the credit (although others had made the objection earlier), is that the view fails because it is circular. When you remember having experienced or done something, these critics claimed, you necessarily remember not only that someone, but also that *you,* had the experience or performed the action. And in remembering that *you* had the experience or performed the action, you are remembering that the person—you—who is now doing the remembering is the *same person* as the one who had the experience or performed the action. Hence, these critics claimed, because an analysis of personal identity is supposed to tell us what is meant by *same person,* it cannot non-circularly use the notion of memory in its answer. Memory also has to be analyzed in terms of the notion of *same person.*

A third problem, the critics claimed, is that Locke's memory view leads to a contradiction. As Thomas Reid is famous for having pointed out, if someone who did a crime cannot remember having done it but can remember everything he did at an earlier time when he could remember having done it, on Locke's view this later person both is and is not the same person who committed the crime. For example, suppose that there is a person, *C,* at some time, t_3, a person, *B,* at some earlier time, t_2, and a person, *A,* at some still earlier time, t_1. Leave it an open question whether *C, B,* and *A,* are the same or different people. Next, suppose that at t_1 *A* committed a crime. Then suppose that at t_2 *B* remembers having committed that same crime. On the simple memory view, *B* and *A* would be the same person. Now suppose further that, at t_3 *C* remembers having experienced something that *B,* at t_2, experienced. Then, on the memory view, *C* and *B* would be the same person. Because *C* is the same person as *B,* and *B* is the same person as *A,* then *C* is also the same person as *A.* Finally, suppose that *C* has no (personal) memories that extend all the way back to *A,* at t_1. Then, on the memory view, *C* would not be the same person as *A.* But we have already seen that on the memory view, *C* would be the same person as *A.* So, on the memory view, *C* both would and would not be the same person as *A.* Hence, Reid claimed, the (simple) memory view is contradictory.

FISSION EXAMPLES AND THE QUESTION OF WHAT MATTERS IN SURVIVAL

In the course of proposing his same-consciousness view, Locke was preoccupied with the implications of examples in which what we ordinarily think of as one unified person divides into two (or more) parts, neither of which is directly conscious of what the other experiences. He asked, "Could we suppose two distinct incommunicable consciousnesses acting the same Body, the one constantly by Day, the other by Night?" Locke was also concerned with the impli-

cations of examples in which what we ordinarily think of as two independently unified persons share the same consciousness. He asked whether we could imagine "the same consciousness, acting by Intervals two distinct Bodies." Locke thought such examples supported the view that it is sameness of consciousness, rather than sameness of body, that determines identity: "I ask in the first case, Whether the *Day-* and the *Nightman* would not be two as distinct Persons, as *Socrates* and *Plato;* and whether in the second case, there would not be one Person in two distinct Bodies, as much as one Man is the same in two distinct clothings" (Locke 1694, II.27.23).

Eventually, Locke goes on to consider the possibility that in a case in which a person's little finger is cut off, consciousness might not just stay with the main part of that body or just go with the little finger, but instead might split and go with both: "Though if the same Body should still live, and immediately from the separation of the little Finger have its own peculiar consciousness, whereof the little Finger knew nothing, it would not at all be concerned for it, as part of it *self,* or could own any of its Actions, or have any of them imputed to him" (II.27.18). This example is one that in our own times has become known as a *fission example.* Although Locke did not explore its implications for his theory of personal identity, others soon did. And in our own times, fission examples have played a major part in the discussion of personal identity.

In the early eighteenth century, almost all European philosophers were Christians. As such, they accepted that sometime after each of us undergoes bodily death, we will be resurrected. One of the things about Locke's view that bothered many of these thinkers was its apparent consequences for what could happen in a postmortem scenario. They agreed with Locke that after our deaths—say, after *your* death—God can create a person and give that person your memories. In Locke's view, God's doing that *would make that person you.* These thinkers speculated that if God could create someone and give him your memories (as surely God could), God could just as well create two, or three, or any number of persons, and give each of them your memories. But, on Locke's view, that would make each of these *different* persons—you. How, these thinkers wondered, could that be possible?

The issue first came up in a famous, early-eighteenth-century debate between Samuel Clarke and Anthony Collins. Clarke, who had worked closely with Newton, was one of the most respected philosophers of his age. Collins, though less well known, had been a close friend and admirer of Locke. He had a reputation as a "free thinker." In their debate, Clarke attacked Locke's theory of personal identity and Collins defended it.

Clarke began by arguing that Locke's theory is "an *impossible* hypothesis":

> [T]hat the *Person* may still be the same, by a continual Superaddition of the *like Consciousness;* notwithstanding the whole *Substance* be changed: Then I say, you make *individual Personality* to be a mere *external imaginary Denomination,* and nothing in reality: Just as *Ship* is called the *same Ship,* after the whole Substance is changed by frequent Repairs; or a *River* is called the *same River* though the Water of it be every Day new. . . . But he cannot be *really and truly* the *same Person,* unless the *same individual numerical Consciousness* can be transferred from one Subject to another. For, the continued Addition or Exciting of a *like Consciousness* in the new acquired Parts, after the Manner you suppose; is nothing but a Deception and Delusion, under the Form of Memory; a making the Man to seem himself to be conscious of having done that, which really was not done by him, but by another. (Clarke, 1738, 844)

Clarke then introduced the idea of fission to hammer home the point that a sequence of like consciousnesses is not the same as a series of acts by a single consciousness:

> [S]uch a Consciousness in a Man, whose Substance is wholly changed, can no more make it Just and Equitable for such a Man to be punished for an Action done by another Substance; than the Addition of the like Consciousness (by the Power of God) to two or more new created Men; or to any Number of Men now living, by giving a like Modification to the Motion of the Spirits in the Brain of each of them respectively; could make them All be one and the same individual Person, at the same time they remain several and distinct Persons; or make it just and reasonable for all and every one of them to be punished for one and the same individual Action, done by one only, or perhaps by none of them at all. (844–5)

Hence, in Clarke's opinion, Locke's view had been shown to be contradictory, because it would lead in this imaginary fission-scenario to saying of two or more individuals both that they are and also that they are not the same person. Collins did not have a good answer to this objection. Subsequent thinkers would do better.

Later in the century, Joseph Priestley, who also accepted Locke's view, raised the question of whether identity is primarily what matters in survival. He began by arguing that "the sentient principle in man, containing ideas which certainly have parts and are divisible and consequently must have extension, cannot be that simple, indivisible and immaterial substance that some have imagined it to be, but something that has real extension and therefore may have the other properties of matter" (Priestley 1777, 163). In fact, he said, it must be "a property of the nervous system or rather of the brain" (160). He argued that not only is the brain necessary for human mentality, but that it is sufficient as well. In his view, there is no need to postulate any immaterial soul to account for human behavior because the notion of an immaterial soul is scientifically useless.

All of this will sound quite modern to us. However, what is truly innovative in Priestley's treatment of personal identity is the way he downplayed the importance of personal identity per se, and highlighted that of the pragmatic functions of belief in our own identities. He began this part of his discussion by considering an objection, which he says was made to "the primitive Christians, as it may be at present" that "a proper resurrection is not only, in the highest degree, improbable, but even actually impossible since, after death, the body putrefies, and the parts that composed it are dispersed, and form other bodies, which have an equal claim to the same resurrection" (165). He continues: "And where, they say, can be the propriety of rewards and *punishments,* if the man that rises again be not identically the same with the man that acted and died?" (165). In reply, Priestley first makes it clear, as if just for the record, that in his opinion "we shall be identically the same beings after the resurrection that we are at present." Then, "for the sake of those who may entertain a different opinion," he proposes to "speculate a little upon their hypothesis" to show that "it is not inconsistent with a state of future rewards and punishments, and that it supplies motives sufficient for the regulation of our conduct here, with a view to it" (165).

In other words, the task that Priestley sets himself is that of showing that even if after death "resurrected selves" are not strictly identical to anyone who existed on Earth, it does not make any difference because *identity is not what matters primarily in survival.* That this is Priestley's project becomes especially clear when he continues: "And metaphysical as the subject necessarily is, I do not despair of satisfying those who will give a due attention to it, that the propriety of rewards and punishments, with our hopes and fears derived from them, do not at all depend upon such a kind of identity as the objection that I have stated supposes" (165). Specifically, then, what Priestley plans to show is that neither the propriety of divine rewards and punishments nor our anticipatory hopes and fears with regard to the resurrection depends on there being resurrected persons who are identical to us.

In arguing for this radical new idea, Priestley claimed that even if people universally and firmly came to believe that over the course of a year there was a complete change, "though gradual and insensible," in the matter of which they were composed, it "would make no change whatever in our present conduct, or in our sense of obligation, respecting the duties of life, and the propriety of rewards and punishments; and consequently all hopes and fears, and expectations of every kind would operate exactly as before (166). "For," he continues, "notwithstanding the complete change of the *man,* there would be no change of what I should call the *person*" (166). So far as personal identity is requisite either for the propriety of rewards and punishments, or for the concern that we take for our future selves, Priestley continued, endorsing Locke, "the sameness and continuity of consciousness seems to be the only circumstance attended to by us."

Then Priestley made it clear that, in his view, whether identity per se obtains is of no great consequence:

Admitting, therefore, that the man consists wholly of matter, as much as the river does of water, or the forest of trees, and that this matter should be wholly changed in the interval between death and the resurrection; yet, if, after this state, we shall all know one another again, and converse together as before, we shall be, *to all intents and purposes,* the same persons. Our personal identity will be *sufficiently preserved,* and the expectation of it at present will have a proper influence on our conduct. (166–7, emphasis added)

Priestley, in this passage, more successfully than anyone had before, separated the question of whether we will be identical with someone who exists in the future from that of whether it matters. In considering whether it matters, he separated three issues: first, ordinary, so-called self-interested *personal concerns* that all people have for their own futures; second, *societal concerns* that some have that the prospect of future rewards and punishments motivate people to behave themselves; and, third, *theological concerns* that some have about the propriety of divine awards and punishments. Thus, toward the end of the eighteenth century and perhaps without inferring anything from fission examples directly (although he knew about them), Priestley introduced and embraced one of the key ideas that has been central to the discussion of personal identity theory in our own times: that personal identity is not primarily what matters in survival.

More than any other Enlightenment philosopher, William Hazlitt, who had been Priestley's student, made the most original and modern use of fission examples. Although today Hazlitt is known primarily as a literary critic, his first book, *Essay on Principles of Human Action* (1805), was a profound contribution to personal identity theory. In it, in the context of his critiquing Locke, he considered fission examples. What, Hazlitt asked, would a theorist committed to the idea that one's identity extends as far as one's consciousness extends say "if that consciousness should be transferred to some other being?" How would such a person know that he or she had not been "imposed upon by a false claim of identity? (1805, 135–6). He answered, on behalf of the Lockeans, that the idea of one's consciousness extending to someone else "is ridiculous": a person has "no other self than that which arises from this very consciousness." But, he countered, after our deaths:

> this self may be multiplied in as many different beings as the Deity may think proper to endue with the same consciousness; which if it can be so renewed at will in any one instance, may clearly be so in a hundred others. Am I to regard all these as equally myself? Am I equally interested in the fate of all? Or if I must fix upon some one of them in particular as my representative and other self, how am I to be determined in my choice? Here, then, I saw an end put to my speculations about absolute self-interest and personal identity. (136)

Thus, Hazlitt saw that, hypothetically, instead of psychological continuity continuing in a single stream, it might divide. In asking the two questions—"Am I to regard all of these as equally myself? Am I equally interested in the fate of all?"—he correctly separated the question of whether *identity* tracks psychological continuity from that of whether *self-concern* tracks it. Finally, in direct anticipation of what would not occur again to other philosophers until the 1970s, he concluded that because of the possibility of fission, neither identity nor self-concern necessarily tracks psychological continuity.

Hazlitt also used fission examples to call into question whether in cases in which there is no fission, a person's present self-interest extends to his or her self in the future. First, he asked, "How then can this pretended unity of consciousness which is only reflected from the past, which makes me so little acquainted with the future that I cannot even tell for a moment how long it will be continued, whether it will be entirely interrupted by or renewed in me after death, and which might be multiplied in I don't know how many different beings and prolonged by complicated suffering without my being any the wiser for it, how I say can a principle of this sort identify my present with my future interests, and make me as much a participator in what does not at all affect me as if it were actually impressed on my senses?" (138). He answered that it cannot:

> It is plain, as this conscious being may be decompounded, entirely destroyed, renewed again, or multiplied in a great number of beings, and as,

whichever of these takes place, it cannot produce the least alteration in my present being—that what I am does not depend on what I am to be, and that there is no communication between my future interests and the motives by which my present conduct must be governed. (138–9)

Finally, Hazlitt concluded:

> I cannot, therefore, have a principle of active self-interest arising out of the immediate connection between my present and future self, for no such connection exists, or is possible. . . . My personal interest in any thing must refer either to the interest excited by the actual impression of the object which cannot be felt before it exists, and can last no longer than while the impression lasts, or it may refer to the particular manner in which I am mechanically affected by the idea of my own impressions in the absence of the object. I can therefore have no proper personal interest in my future impressions. . . . The only reason for my preferring my future interest to that of others, must arise from my anticipating it with greater warmth of present imagination. (139–40)

Hazlitt thus accomplished what, except for Priestley, others who had been sympathetic to Locke's views had resisted. He used fission examples, which previously others had employed only to criticize Locke, to motivate a view that went beyond Locke altogether.

Hazlitt's ideas never received the attention they deserved. Keats and Coleridge knew of his views, but few others, and no mainstream philosophers, seem even to have noticed. Such ideas as Hazlitt proposed would not be taken seriously again until our own times.

THE QUESTION OF WHETHER PERSONS ARE REAL OR FICTIONAL

Locke may or may not have intended to suggest that persons are fictional entities. Whatever his intentions, some of his critics (e.g., Samuel Clarke and Bishop Butler) and also some of his admirers (e.g., Edmund Law) interpreted his view as implying that persons are *fictional* entities. Primarily two things in Locke's view motivated this interpretation. First, he held that persons are distinct from human animals.

Second, he boldly pronounced that "[Person] is a Forensick Term [that is, a legal and/or moral term] appropriating Actions and their Merit" (1694 II.27.26). Locke, thus, suggested that while there could be a natural science of human animals, there could be none of persons, because the notion of *person* is not a natural kind of thing but just an invention of legal and/or ethical theory. It would seem to follow that persons have only a theoretical (hence, a fictional) status. Later in the century, Edmund Law saw this consequence of Locke's view and embraced it.

David Hume would return by a different route—through an examination of experience—to the theme that persons are fictions. Hume began by acknowledging that "there are some philosophers, who imagine we are every moment intimately conscious of what we call *our Self*," and "feel its existence and its continuance in existence," and are "certain, beyond the evidence of a demonstration, both of its perfect identity and simplicity" (by its *perfect identity* he meant its persisting from one moment to the next, without changing in any way; by its *simplicity* he meant its not, at any time, being composed of parts). But, according to Hume, such selves do not show up in experience. He said that if we look introspectively into our experience for a percei*ver,* which is supposed to be an active *agent,* we will find only passive percepti*ons,* (e.g., "of heat or cold, light or shade, love or hatred, pain or pleasure"). Hume said that he could never catch himself "without a perception" or observe anything "but the perception," so that if others were like him in this respect, then there is no self in experience (1739, Bk. 1, sec. 6). In sum, in Hume's view, the commonsense belief that we experience ourselves *as* selves is based on our mistaking a bundle of percepti*ons* for a percei*ver.*

Hume suggested that the mistake—actually an illusion—that we experience ourselves as perceivers arises because we do not look carefully enough at our own experience. That is, the perceptions succeed each other so rapidly that they give rise to the illusion that there is an active perceiver in experience. On this point, modern European theories about the self and personal identity make their closest contact with classical Asian theories. Two thousand years before Hume, the Buddha had made much the same point. However, for the Buddha, the point was not so much a philosophical *observation*

about experience as it was an experimental *transformation,* which is a necessary step on the way to liberation. In the Buddha's view, the crucial transition that each of us has to make, if we are to be free, is not only to learn intellectually that there is an illusion of self in experience, but also to end that illusion. For as long as the illusion persists, the Buddha claimed, we are its captive regardless of what we may think intellectually.

Jack Engler, a contemporary Buddhist, nicely describes this aspect of what the Buddha had in mind:

> My sense of being an independent observer disappears. The normal sense that I am a fixed, continuous point of observation from which I regard now this object, now that, is dispelled. Like the tachistoscopic flicker-fusion phenomenon which produces the illusion of an "object" when discrete and discontinuous images are flashed too quickly for normal perception to distinguish them, my sense of being a separate observer or experiencer behind my observation or experience is revealed to be the result of a perceptual illusion, of my not being normally able to perceive a more microscopic level of events. When my attention is sufficiently refined through training and kept bare of secondary reactions and elaboration of stimuli, all that is actually apparent to me from moment to moment is a mental or physical event and an awareness of that event. In each moment there is simply a process of knowing (nama) and its object (rupa). Each arises separately and simultaneously in each moment of awareness. No enduring or substantial entity or observer or experiencer or angesn —no self—can be found behind or apart from these moment-to-moment events to which they could be attributed (an-atta = no-self). In other words, the individual "frames" appear which had previously fused in normal perception in a tachistoscopic manner to produce an apparently solid and fixed image of a "self" or an "object." The only observable reality at this level is the flow of mental and physical events themselves. There is no awareness of an observer. There are just individual moments of observation. (Engler, 1986, 41–2)

In the sort of esoteric no-self experience that Engler is describing, the psychological sense of separation "between observer and observed," ordinarily a persistent feature of our experience regardless of the theories to which we subscribe, disappears.

From 1805 to the late 1960s, there are few important developments in personal identity theory. For the most part, theorists simply argued over whether physical or psychological relations were more important in determining whether personal identity obtains. However, since 1970 there have been three major developments in personal identity theory. One of these is that the *intrinsic* relations view of personal identity has been largely superseded by the *extrinsic* relations view (which is also sometimes called the *closest-continuer view* or the *externalist view*).

THE 1970S: THE (EXTRINSIC) RELATIONS VIEW

According to the older *intrinsic* relations view, what determines whether the two versions of a person at different times are identical is how the two versions are physically and/or psychologically related to *each other*. According to more recent *extrinsic* relations views, what determines this is not only how the two are physically and/or psychologically related to *each other* but also how they are related to *others*. For instance, in Locke's *intrinsic* relations view, you are the same person as someone who existed yesterday if you remember having experienced or having done things that person of yesterday experienced or did. In an *extrinsic* version of Locke's view, one would have to take into account not only whether you remember having experienced or having done things that person of yesterday experienced or did but also whether, besides you, anyone else remembers having experienced or having done those things.

Fission examples are largely responsible for the recent move from an intrinsic to an extrinsic relations view. In the sort of fission examples that have been most discussed, a person somehow divides into two (seemingly) *numerically* different persons, each of whom, initially is *qualitatively* identical to the other and also to the prefission person from whom they both descended. For example, imagine that all information in human brains is encoded redundantly so that it is possible to separate a human's brain into two parts, leaving each half fully functioning and encoded with all it needs to sustain the original person's full mental life just as (except

for the elimination of underlying redundancy) his whole brain would have sustained it had it never been divided. Now suppose that in some normal, healthy human we perform a brain separation, removing the two fully functioning half-brains from his body, which is then immediately destroyed. Suppose, further, that we immediately implant each of these half-brains into its own, brainless body, which, except for being brainless, is otherwise qualitatively identical to the original person's body, so that two people simultaneously emerge, each of whom, except for having only half a brain, is qualitatively identical—physically *and* psychologically—to the original person whose brain was divided and removed and, of course, to each other.

Are these two fission descendants the same person? In an intrinsic view of personal identity, such as Locke's, they would be. Each would remember having experienced things and having performed actions that the original person experienced and performed. If in deciding whether two versions of a person, one at one time and one at another, are the same person, we have to consider *only* the relationship between the two of them, it would seem that they might be related so as to have all that is required to preserve identity. Obviously, the problem with supposing that we have to consider *only* the relationship between the two of them is that the other fission descendant has an equal claim to be the original person.

Many contemporary philosophers believe that, in such a case, the prefission person (the brain donor) would cease. They think he would cease because they think, first, that identity is a transitive relationship, which implies that if one of the fission descendants were the same person as the brain donor, and the brain donor were the same person as the other fission descendant, the former fission descendant would be the same person as the latter fission descendant; second, that the fission descendants, at least once they began to lead independent lives, would not plausibly be regarded as the same person (think, for instance, of the moral and legal complications if, five years down the road, one of them turns out to be a nice, law abiding person and the other a nasty, criminal type); and third, it would be arbitrary to regard just one of the fission descendants but not the other as the same person as the donor (at the moment of "conception," the two fission descendants were equally qualified to be the same person as the donor). Hence, in the view of these philosophers, it is more plausible to regard each of the fission descendants as a different person from the prefission person. Philosophers who reason this way accept an *extrinsic* relations view of personal identity, according to which what determines whether a person at one time and one at another are the same person is not only how the two are physically and/or psychologically related to each other (which is all that would need to be considered on an *intrinsic relations* view) but also how the two are related to others (in our example, especially the other fission descendant).

The fission examples considered by eighteenth century philosophers were religion-fiction scenarios. The fission examples that philosophers in our own times have considered are science-fiction scenarios. Both sorts of fission examples raise essentially the same issues for personal identity theory. In the eighteenth century, many philosophers supposed that the religion-fiction fission examples had a counterpart in real life (postmortem) situations. In our own times, the science-fiction fission examples actually do have a counterpart in real-life situations.

In the late 1930s, neurosurgeons in the United States began performing an operation in which they severed the corpus callosa—the bundles of nerve fibers that connect the two hemispheres of normal, human brains—of severe epileptics in the hope of confining their seizures to one hemisphere of their brains, thus reducing the severity of their seizures. To the surgeons' initial surprise, often the procedure was doubly successful. It reduced not only the severity of the seizures but also their frequency. It also had a truly bizarre side effect, not discovered until many years later: It created two independent centers of consciousness within the same human skull. These centers of consciousness, first, lacked introspective access to each other; second, could be made to acquire and express information independently of each other; and finally, and most dramatically, sometimes differed volitionally, expressing their differences using alternate sides of the same human bodies that they jointly shared. In one case, for instance, a man who had had this operation

reportedly hugged his wife with one arm while he pushed her away with the other; in another, a man tried with his right hand (controlled by his left, verbal hemisphere) to hold a newspaper where he could read it, thereby blocking his view of the TV, while he tried with his left hand (controlled by his right, nonverbal hemisphere) to knock the paper out of the way.

THE RETURN OF A QUESTION: IS IDENTITY WHAT MATTERS PRIMARILY IN SURVIVAL?

Since 1970 there has been a second major development in personal identity theory. Philosophers have begun again to question whether personal identity is primarily what matters in survival. That is, they have faced the possibility that people might cease and be continued by *others*, whose existences even from an exclusively self-interested perspective they would value as much as their own and in pretty much the same ways as they would value their own. Imagine, for instance, that you have a health problem that will result soon in your sudden and painless death unless you receive one of two available treatments. The first is to have your brain removed and placed into the empty cranium of a body that, except for being brainless, is qualitatively identical to your own. The second is to have your brain removed and divided into functionally identical halves (each capable of sustaining your full psychology), and then to have each of these halves put into the empty cranium of a body of its own, again one that is brainless but otherwise qualitatively identical to your own.

In the first treatment, there is a 10 percent chance that the transplantation will take. If it takes, the survivor who wakes up in the recovery room will be physically and psychologically like you just prior to the operation except that he will know he has had the operation and will be healthy. In the second, there is a 95 percent chance that both transplantations will take. If both take, each of the survivors who wakes up in the recovery room will be physically and psychologically like you just prior to the operation except that each of them will know he has had the operation and each will be healthy. If the transplantation in the first treatment does not take, the would-be survivor will die painlessly on the operating table. If either transplantation in the second treatment does not take, the other will not take either, and both would-be survivors will die painlessly on the operating table. Everything else about the treatments is the same and as attractive to you as possible: For instance, both are painless, free of charge, and, if successful, result in survivors who recover quickly.

As we have seen, many philosophers believe that you would continue in the first (nonfission) treatment but cease and be replaced by others in the second (fission) treatment. As in the case of the previous fission examples considered, they think that you would cease and be replaced in the second treatment because they believe, first, that identity is a transitive relationship; second, that the survivors, at least once they began to lead independent lives, would not plausibly be regarded as the same people as each other; and third, that it would be arbitrary to regard one of the survivors but not the other as you. Hence, in the view of these philosophers, it is more plausible to regard each of the survivors as a different person from you.

Assume, for the sake of argument, that this way of viewing what will happen in the two treatments is correct. On this assumption, you would persist through the first treatment, but in the second you would cease and be replaced by others. Given the circumstances specified in the example, only by sacrificing your identity could you greatly increase the chances that someone who initially would be qualitatively just like you, would emerge from the operation and survive for years. The question is whether, in the circumstances specified, it would be worth it for you to have such an operation, that is, whether it would be worth it only from a point of view that in more normal circumstances would be considered a totally selfish (or self-regarding) point of view. Many who consider examples such as this one feel strongly, that it would be worth it. For them, at least, it would seem that ceasing and being continued by others can matter as much, or almost as much, as persisting, and matter in pretty much the same ways. However, if ceasing and being continued by others can matter as much (and in the same ways) as persisting, identity is not what matters primarily in survival.

DEREK PARFIT'S VIEW

Parfit has a Neo-Lockean view of personal identity, according to which what binds our various stages into the individual people that we are is not just memory, but psychological relations more generally (including beliefs, intentions, character traits, anticipations, and so on). And, unlike Locke's view, in Parfit's view it is not necessary for each stage of us to be *directly* related to every other stage. It is enough if each stage is *indirectly* related through intermediate stages. In sum, in Parfit's view, what binds us are psychological connections, overlapping "like the strands in a rope" (Parfit, 1984, 222). Thus Parfit's view is not vulnerable to Reid's objection to Locke's view. If C at t_3, is *directly* psychologically connected to B at t_2, but *not* to A at t_1, but B at t_2 is directly psychologically connected to A at t_1, then C at t_3 *is indirectly* psychologically connected to A at t_1 and that may be enough to preserve personal identity.

Parfit has also responded to those who think that the notion of *same person* enters into the proper analysis of various psychological relations, particularly of memory. To avoid the charge that his analysis of personal identity is circular, he has formulated it in terms of specially defined senses of psychological relations that do not include the notion of *same person*. For instance, in the case of memory, Parfit has defined a notion of *quasi memory* (or, *q memory*), which is just like that of *memory* except that whereas the claim that someone remembers having experienced something might imply that the person remembers that *she herself* experienced that thing, the claim that someone *q remembers* having experienced something implies, by definition only that the person remembers that *someone* experienced it. Thus Parfit's view is not vulnerable to the argument Butler used to try to show that Locke's view is circular.

To illustrate how q memory might work, Parfit gave as an example Jane's seeming to remember Paul's experience, in Venice, of looking across water and seeing a lightning bolt fork and then strike two objects (1984, 220). Parfit claimed that in seeming to remember this experience, Jane might have known that she was seeming to remember an experience that Paul (and not she) had had originally, and that if Jane had known this, she would have known, *from the inside*, part of what it was like to be

Paul on that day in Venice. In other words, Jane would have known that she was seeming to remember Paul's experience from the same sort of subjective, first-person point of view from which Paul actually had the experience and from which Jane ordinarily remembers only her own experiences. If one acknowledges that Parfit's hypothetical example is at least theoretically possible, as it seems we should (imagine that part of Paul's brain had been surgically implanted into Jane's brain), apparently it is possible, in analyses of personal identity, to substitute q memory for memory and thereby avoid Butler's objection. In other words, even if simple memory analyses of personal identity are circular, it would not follow that q memory analyses of personal identity are circular.

When Locke proposed his psychological relations view, most philosophers subscribed to a soul view. In 1984, when Parfit proposed the fullest version of his theory, probably most philosophers subscribed to the view that the continuity of our bodies, or of some part of our bodies, is necessary for personal persistence. Parfit, by contrast, denied that bodily continuity is necessary for personal persistence. To support this denial, he supposed, first that although someone's brain is healthy, his body is ridden with cancer and his only hope for survival is to have his entire healthy brain transplanted intact to another healthy body. He supposed also that this transplantation procedure is perfectly safe and that the body into which the donor's brain will be transplanted is better than his current body, not only in that it is healthy but also in many other respects that appeal to the donor. Parfit pointed out, surely correctly, that the donor has not lost much if he jettisons his old body and moves his brain to the better body that awaits it. Such an operation would not be as bad as staying in the old body and dying of cancer, even if the death were painless. In fact, vanity being what it is, if radical cosmetic surgery of this sort were available and safe, it is likely that many people would choose it, even if the old bodies they jettisoned were healthy. If physical continuity matters, Parfit concluded, it cannot be continuity of the whole body, but at most the continuity of the brain.

However, Parfit argued, the importance of our brains, like that of our other organs, is not intrinsic but derivative; that is, the brain's importance depends solely on the function it serves. For most of us, if half a brain were functionally equivalent to the whole, the preservation of our whole brain would not matter much. And, it would seem, the continuity of even any part of the brain is not necessarily important. If some other organ, such as the liver, sustained our psychologies and our brains served functions this other organ now serves, the other organ would be as important in survival as the brain is now and the brain only as important as the other organ is now. It would seem that if something else— anything else—could sustain our psychologies as reliably as the brain, the brain (i.e., the physical organ that actually now functions as the brain) would have little importance in survival even if this other thing were not any part of our bodies (1984, 284–5).

A critic might object that even though the importance of an organ is derivative and based solely on its being the vehicle for preserving a person's psychology, given that it has always been that vehicle, the preservation of that organ matters greatly, perhaps even primarily, in survival. In other words, it is possible that even though something else might have assumed that organ's function of preserving a person's psychology and, hence, that under those imagined circumstances the organ that now serves that function would not have mattered greatly in survival, once an organ actually has served the function of preserving a person's psychology, it does matter importantly in survival. However, even though this is possible, it is doubtful that merely by virtue of its having sustained your psychology, an organ thereby matters all that importantly to you in survival.

Imagine, for instance, that competent doctors discover that you have both a brain disease and a brain abnormality. The disease has not impaired the functioning of your brain yet, but if it is untreated, it will result in your death in the near future. Because of the abnormality, there is a simple, effective, and painless cure. The abnormality is that you have two brains, the one now diseased, which is the only one that has ever functioned as a brain, and another, right beside it, lying dormant—healthy and perfectly capable of performing a whole brain's functions should the need arise, but nevertheless not yet functioning as a brain and not currently encoded with any of your psychology. The doctors can perform a simple procedure to switch the roles of your two brains: All of the encoded psychology on your diseased brain will be transferred to the healthy one; as it is transferred, it will be erased from your diseased brain, whereupon your healthy brain will begin to function just as the diseased one did (and would have continued to do had it been healthy and left alone).

Suppose that the procedure is as quick and as simple (and as abrupt) as flipping a switch, that it will not affect subjective psychology, and that consciousness will be continuous throughout the procedure. Indeed, suppose that you and the person who emerges from the procedure will not even notice any change. When the transfer is completed, your diseased brain will become dormant almost instantaneously and will pose no further threat to your organism's physical or psychological health. In these imagined circumstances, how much would it matter to you that the brain that has always sustained your psychology will no longer sustain it, while another that has never sustained it will sustain it from now on? Probably not much. The procedure would not be as bad as death. Unless it caused existential anxiety, it would not even be as bad as a root canal. So much for the derivative value of the organs that have actually sustained our psychologies.

Those who are skeptical of this response might imagine that whereas the procedure described is the simplest way of disabling the threat to the organism posed by your diseased brain, it is not the only way. An alternative procedure the doctors can perform is to repair your diseased brain through a series of twenty brain operations spread over the next twenty years of your life. Each operation will cost about one-half of your annual salary (suppose that insurance does not cover the procedure and probably never will) and will require two months of hospitalization. In addition, the operations will be disfiguring. When they are finally completed, you will be healthy enough, but your life will have been seriously disrupted and your body and face will be somewhat deformed. I assume that on your scale of values, the disruption, expense, and disfigurement, while bad, are not as bad as death. (If they are as bad

as death, reduce their severity to the point where they are not *quite* as bad as death.) If the first procedure is as bad as death, the second procedure is a better choice. Which procedure would you choose? I think most people would choose the first procedure (for more on this example, see Martin, 1998, 80–5).

Finally, a critic might object that even though the preservation of one's body might not matter in survival, it still might be necessary for personal persistence. However, in Parfit's view, in the case of many of the exotic examples under discussion in the personal identity literature, including the one just discussed, the question of whether one persists is an *empty question*. When one knows all of the physical and psychological ways in which the earlier and later persons are related, and how the earlier person evolved (or transformed) into the later person, one knows everything there is to know about the situation that's relevant to the question of personal persistence. There is no further fact to know, such as whether or not in such circumstances one actually persists. That is, in the case of such examples, there may be no truth of the matter about whether one persists.

In one of Parfit's most controversial claims, his notorious "branch line" example, he asks, you to put yourself imaginatively into the place of a person on Earth, who is trying to be teletransported to Mars (200–1). You enter the teletransportation booth and push the button, activating the process. You succeed in producing a replica of yourself on Mars, but because the teletransporter has malfunctioned you fail to dematerialize on Earth. A few minutes later, you emerge from the teletransporter and are told believably that, due to its malfunctioning, your heart has been damaged and you have only two more days to live. Parfit argues that in such a case, you should not be too concerned. Rather, you ought to regard your replica's persistence—now taking place on Mars—as an adequate surrogate for what might have been your own persistence on Earth. Although not many philosophers have followed Parfit in taking this line, explaining why one should not take it without returning to the view that identity is what matters in survival has not been easy (for more on this, see Martin, 1998, Chs. 6 and 7).

THREE- VS. FOUR-DIMENSIONAL VIEWS OF PERSONS

I said above that since 1970 there have been three major developments in personal identity theory. One has been that *intrinsic* relations views of personal identity have been largely superseded by *extrinsic* relations views. Another has been the reemergence of interest in the question of whether personal identity is primarily what matters in survival.

The third major development has been a challenge to the traditional three-dimensional view of persons, according to which a person can be wholly present at a given moment—for example, you are wholly present right now. Some philosophers have argued that we should replace this three-dimensional view with a four-dimensional view, according to which only time slices or "stages" of persons exist at short intervals of time. In this four-dimensional view, persons are aggregates of momentary person-stages, beginning with the person-stage that came into being at a person's birth and ending with the person-stage that existed when the person died, and including every person-stage between birth and death.

To see why it might matter which of these two views is correct, consider again any of the fission examples (except the branch line case) already discussed. It was suggested that the prefission person is not identical with either of his postfission descendants. That was a three-dimensional way of describing the situation. A four-dimensionalist would have said that what we are calling "the prefission person" is really not a person, but rather a person-stage, and that what we are calling "the postfission descendants" are also person-stages. According to a four-dimensionalist, in a fission example the prefission person does not cease. Rather what happens is that the prefission person-stage becomes a shared person-stage. That is, two persons, whose postfission person-stages are separate from the other overlap before fisson and, thus, share their prefission person-stages.

Philosophers have used this four-dimensional way of conceptualizing what is going on in a fission example to argue that fission examples cannot be used to argue that identity is not what matters in survival. According to these philosophers, fission exam-

ples cannot be so used because in a fission example no one ceases (hence, identity is never traded for other benefits). Rather, what happens in a fission example is that the stages of two persons are shared stages before the fission, but no longer shared after the fission. Because in this view, a given person-stage may be part of two or three (or potentially any number) of persons, this view is sometimes called the multiple-occupancy view of persons. Although it has its defenders, most personal identity theorists have stuck with the traditional three-dimensional view.

THE BOTTOM LINE

The world is mysterious. Not the least of its mysteries is our own status in it. Your assuming that your status in the world is rock solid and unquestionable may shield you from this mystery, but it cannot make the world or yourself any less mysterious. Up to this point, your whole life, after a certain age, has been organized around the idea that you persist. It will continue to be organized around that idea. Studying philosophy will not change that. What studying philosophy can change is your understanding of that idea and your attitude toward it. And that is where this philosophical issue differs from others. It is one thing to discover that you have been misled by an illusion. That is a common result in philosophy. However, it is quite another, and a far more disturbing, thing, to discover that you may be that illusion.

REFERENCES AND ACKNOWLEDGEMENTS

. . . Lucretius' views may be found in *De Rerum Natura,* trans. R. E. Latham, (Harmondsworth: Penguin, 1951). John Locke's views are in his, *An Essay Concerning Human Understanding,* 1694 (ed., Peter H. Nidditch, Oxford: Clarendon Press, 1975); . . .

In the account I have given of eighteenth-century developments, I relied on research done with John Barresi and Alessandro Giovannelli. See Raymond Martin and John Barresi, "Hazlitt on the Future of the Self," *Journal of the History of Ideas,* vol. 56, 1995, 463–81; and Raymond Martin, John Barresi, and Alessandro Giovannelli, "Fission Examples in the Eighteenth and Early Nineteenth Century Personal Identity Debate," *History of Philosophy*

Quarterly, vol. 15, 1998. Martin and Barresi have written a book, *Naturalization of the Soul: The Evolution of Theories of Self and Personal Identity in the Development of Modern Psychology,* which will be published in 1999.

The Clarke-Collins debate is in volume 4 of *The Works of Samuel Clarke,* 4 vols., 1738 (reprinted New York: Garland Publishing, 1928). For Butler's criticisms of Locke, see Joseph Butler, *The Analogy of Religion, Natural and Revealed,* 1736 (reprinted, London: Henry G. Bohn. 1852). For Thomas Reid's criticisms, see . . . his *Essay on the Intellectual Powers of Man,* 1785, in *The Works of Thomas Reid,* ed. William Hamilton, 6th ed. (Edinburgh: Maclachlan and Stewart, 1863). Edmund Law's, "A Defense of Mr. Locke's Opinion Concerning Personal Identity" is in volume III, pages 177–201, of *The Works of John Locke,* 10 vols., (London: Thomas Tegg, 1823; reprinted 1963, Hildesheim, Germany: Scientia Verlag Aalan). For David Hume's views on personal identity, see . . . his *A Treatise of Human Nature,* 1738. Jack Engler's remarks are from "Therapeutic Aims in Psychotherapy and Meditation" in *Transformation of Consciousness,* ed. K. Wilber, J. Engler, and D. P. Brown, pages 17–52 (Boston: Shambhala, 1986). For Joseph Priestley's views, see his *Disquisitions Relating to Matter and Spirit and the Doctrine of Philosophical Necessity Illustrated,* 1777 (reprinted 1976, New York: Garland). William Hazlitt's book on personal identity is *Essay on the Principles of Human Action* and *Some Remarks on the systems of Hartley and Helvetius,* 1805 (reprinted 1969, with an introduction by John R. Nabholtz. Gainesville, Fla., Scholars' Facsimiles & Reprints). Hazlitt also wrote two essays on personal identity, . . .

Derek Parfit's views may be found mainly in "Personal Identity," *Philosophical Review,* vol. 80, 1971, 3–27; and in his *Reasons and Persons,* (Oxford: Clarendon Press, 1984). David Lewis' explanation and defense of the four-dimensional view of persons is in his "Survival and Identity," *The Identities of Persons,* ed. Amelié Rorty (Berkeley: University of California Press, 1976), 17–40; see also "Postscript to Survival and Identity," in his *Philosophical Papers,* vol. 1 (New York: Oxford University Press, 1983).

Other important work since 1970 that would have been discussed in a more complete survey includes Sydney Shoemaker, "Persons and Their Pasts," *American Philosophical Quarterly,* vol. 7, 1970, 269–85, and his "Personal Identity: A Materialist Account," in Sydney Shoemaker and Richard Swinburne, *Personal Identity,* (Oxford: Basil Blackwell, 1984), 69–152 (in the section labeled, "The Return of a Question," the first fission example described is based on one originally presented by Shoemaker); John Perry, "Can the Self Divide?" *Journal of Philosophy,* vol. 69, 1972, 463–88, and "The Importance of Being Identical" in *The Identities of Persons,* ed. Amelie Rorty, (Berkeley: University of California, 1976), 67–90; Robert Nozick, *Philosophical Explanations* (Cambridge, Mass.: Harvard University Press, 1981); Thomas Nagel, *The View from Nowhere,* (New York: Oxford University Press, 1986); Ernest Sosa, "Surviving Matters," *Nous,* vol. 24, 1990, 305–30; and Peter Unger, *Identity, Consciousness, and Value,* (New York: Oxford University Press, 1991).

Daniel Kolak's *In Search of Myself: Life, Death, and Personal Identity* (Belmont, California: Wadsworth, 1999) is a provocative and accessible introduction to issues that arise in personal identity theory. Raymond Martin's latest views may be found in *Self-Concern: An Experiential Approach to What Matters in Survival* (Cambridge: Cambridge University Press, 1998).

MINDS, BRAINS, AND MACHINES

Language, Logic, and I

LUDWIG WITTGENSTEIN

Ludwig Wittgenstein (1889–1951), generally regarded as one of the great philosophical geniuses of the twentieth century, was born in Austria and studied philosophy at Cambridge under Bertrand Russell.

1   The world is all that is the case.

1.1   The world is the totality of facts, not of things.

1.11   The world is determined by the facts, and by these being all the facts.

1.12   For the totality of facts determines all that is the case and also all that is not the case.

1.13   The facts in logical space are the world.

1.2   The world can be broken down into facts.

1.21   Each one can be the case or not be the case while all else remains the same.

2   What is the case—a fact—is the existence of particular states of affairs.

2.01   A particular state of affairs is a combination of objects (items, things).

2.02   Objects are simple.

2.03   In a particular state of affairs the objects hang in one another like the links of a chain.

2.04   The world is a totality of all existing states of affairs.

2.05   The totality of all existing particular states of affair determines which particular states of affair do not exist.

2.06   The existence and nonexistence of particular states of affair is reality.
       (We also call the existence of particular states of affair a positive fact, and their nonexistence a negative fact.)

2.063 The sum total of reality is the world.

2.1   We make pictures of facts to ourselves.

2.11   Such a picture represents a particular state of affairs in logical space, the existence and nonexistence of particular states of affairs.

2.12   Such a picture is a model of reality.

2.13   To the objects correspond, in such a picture, the elements of the picture.

2.14   The picture consists in its elements being combined in a definite way.

2.141 The picture is a fact.

2.15   The definite way in which the picture elements combine represents how things are related.
       Let us call this combination of elements the *structure* of the picture, and let us call the possibility of this structure the *form of representation* of the picture.

2.151 The form of representation is the possibility that things combine in the same way as do the pictorial elements.

2.1511 In this way the picture makes contact with, or reaches up to, reality.

2.16   To be a picture, a fact must have something in common with what it depicts.

2.17   What a picture must have in common with reality to be capable of depicting it the way it does—rightly or wrongly—is its form of representation.

2.18   What any such picture, of any form, must have in common with reality to be capable of representing it the way it does—rightly or wrongly—is logical form, that is, the form of reality.

2.19   Logical pictures are depictions of the world.

2.2   A picture must have the logical form of representation in common with what it depicts.

2.21   Such a picture agrees with reality or not; it is right or wrong, true or false.

2.22   Such a picture represents what it represents independently of its truth or falsity, via its representational form.

2.221 What this picture represents is its sense.

2.222 Its truth or falsity consists in the agreement or disagreement of its sense with reality.

3.0   A thought is a logical picture of a fact.

3.01   The totality of all true thoughts is a picture of the world.

From *Wittgenstein's Tractatus,* translated by Daniel Kolak (Mountain View, CA: Mayfield, 1998).

3.02 A thought contains the possibility of the facts that it thinks. What is thinkable is also possible.

3.03 Thought cannot be of anything illogical, else we would have to think illogically.

3.1 In a sentence the thought expresses itself perceptibly.

3.11 We use a sentence (spoken or written, etc.) as a projection of a possible fact.

The method of projection is our thinking the sense of the sentence.

3.12 The sign with which a thought expresses itself, I will call a *sentential sign*. A sentence is a sentential sign conceived in its projective relation to the world.

3.13 The sentence has everything that the projection has, except what is projected.

Therefore, the possibility of what is projected is in the sentence, but not the projection itself.

And so the sentence does not yet contain its sense; what it does contain is the possibility of expressing that sense.

("The content of the sentence" means the content of a sentence that makes sense.)

The sentence contains the [empty, logical] form of its sense, without any content.

3.14 What constitutes a sentence is that its elements, the words, stand in a determinate relation to one another.

A sentential sign is a fact.

3.2 In sentences, thoughts can be expressed such that the objects of the thoughts correspond to the elements of the sentential signs.

3.21 The configuration of simple signs in the sentential sign corresponds to the configuration of objects in the fact.

3.22 In a sentence a name signifies an object.

3.3 Only sentences make sense; only in the context of a sentence does a name signify anything.

3.31 Any part of a sentence that characterizes the sense of the sentence I call an *expression* (a symbol).

(A sentence is itself an expression.)

Expressions are everything essential for the sense of the sentence that sentences can have in common with each other.

An expression characterizes the form and content.

3.32 A sign is the perceptible aspect of a symbol.

3.33 The meaning of a sign should never play a role in logical syntax. It must be possible to formulate logical syntax without mentioning the *meaning* of a sign; the meaning ought *only* to presuppose the description of the expressions.

3.34 A sentence has essential and accidental features.

The accidental features arise in the way the

sentence is produced; the essential features are the ones without which the sense of the sentence would be lost.

3.4 A sentence determines a place in logical space. The existence of this logical place is guaranteed by the existence of the expressions of which the sentence is composed—by the existence of the meaningful sentence.

3.41 The sentential sign with logical coordinates: that is the logical place.

3.42 Although a sentence may determine only one place in logical space, the whole logical space must already be given by it.

3.5 A sentential sign, applied and thought, is a thought.

4.0 A sentence that makes sense is a thought.

4.01 A sentence is a picture of reality.

A sentence is a model of reality as we think it is.

4.02 This we see from the fact that we understand the sense of a sentence without having had it explained to us.

4.021 A sentence is a picture of reality, for if I understand the sentence I know the fact represented by it. And I understand the sentence without its sense having been explained to me.

4.03 A sentence must communicate a new sense with old words.

A sentence communicates a fact to us; therefore it must be *essentially* connected with the fact.

And the connection is that a sentence is its logical picture.

A sentence asserts something only insofar as it is a picture.

4.04 In a sentence there must be exactly as many things distinguishable as there are in the fact that it represents.

4.05 The reality is compared with the sentence.

4.06 Sentences can be true or false only by being pictures of the reality.

4.1 A sentence presents the existence and non-existence of particular states of affairs.

4.2 The sense of a sentence is in its agreement and disagreement with the possibilities of the existence and nonexistence of particular states of affairs.

4.3 Truth-possibilities of elementary sentences signify the possibilities of the existence and nonexistence of particular states of affairs.

4.4 A sentence is an expression of agreement and disagreement with the truth-possibilities of elementary sentences.

4.5 We are in a position now to state the most general form of a sentence—that is, to describe the sentence of any symbolic language whatsoever such that every sense can be expressed by a symbol satisfying the description and that every symbol satisfying the description can express a sense, provided that the signification of each name is well chosen.

Clearly, only what is essential to the most general form of a sentence may be included in its description—otherwise, it would not be the most general form.

The existence of a general form of a sentence is proved in that no sentence can be given whose form could not have been foreseen (i.e., constructed). The general form of a sentence is: so and so is the case.

5.0   A sentence is a truth-function of elementary sentences.

(An elementary sentence is a truth-function of itself.)

5.1   The truth-functions can be ordered in a series.
This is the foundation for the theory of probability.

5.2   The structures of sentences stand to one another in internal relations.

5.3   All sentences are the result of truth-operations on the elementary sentences.

5.4   It is here that the nonexistence of "logical objects" or "logical constants" (in the sense of Frege and Russell) shows itself.

5.5   Each truth-function is a result of successive applications of the operation "(-----T) (ξ,.....)."

This operation negates all the sentences in the right-hand brackets and so I call it the negation of those sentences.

5.6   *The boundary of my language* is the boundary of my world.

5.61   Logic fills the world: the boundary of logic is also the boundary of the world.

So in logic we cannot say, "The world has this in it and this, but not that."

For this apparently presupposes that some possibilities were thereby being excluded, which cannot possibly be the case, since this would require that logic should extend beyond the boundary of the world; for only then could it have a view from the other side of the boundary.

What we cannot think, that we cannot think: we cannot therefore *say* what we cannot think.

5.62   This thought itself shows how much truth there is in solipsism.

What the solipsist intends to say is absolutely correct. The problem is that the truth cannot speak but only shows itself.

That the world is *my* world reveals itself in the fact that the boundary of language (the language that I alone understand) is the boundary of *my* world.

5.621   The world and life are one.

5.63   I am my world (the microcosm).

5.631   The thinking, perceiving subject does not exist.

If I were to write a book, *The World as I Found It,* I would also have to include an account of my body in it, and report which parts are subject to my will and which not, etc. This then would be a method of isolating the subject, or rather of showing that in an important sense there is no subject; that is to say: of it alone in this book mention could *not* be made.

5.632   The subject does not belong to the world but is the boundary of the world.

5.633   Where *in* the world could a metaphysical subject be?

You say this is just like the case with the eye and the visual field. But you do *not* really see the eye.

And there is nothing *in the visual field* to let you infer that it is being seen through an eye.

5.64   Here we can see that solipsism thoroughly thought out coincides with pure realism. The *I* in solipsism shrinks to an extensionless point and there remains the reality coordinated with it.

5.641   Thus there really is a sense in which philosophy can speak about the self in a nonpsychological way.

The *I* occurs in philosophy through the fact that "the world is my world."

The philosophical *I* is not the human being, not the human body, not the human soul with which psychology deals. The philosophical self is the metaphysical subject, the boundary—nowhere in the world.

6   The general form of a truth-function is $[p, \xi, N (\xi)]$.
This is the general form of a sentence.

6.1   The sentences of logic are tautologies.

6.11   The sentences of logic therefore say nothing. (They are analytic sentences.)

6.12   The fact that the sentences of logic are tautologies shows the formal—logical—properties of language, of the world.

6.13   Logic is not a theory about the world but a reflection of it, its mirror image.
Logic is transcendent.

6.2   Mathematics is a logical method.
Mathematical sentences are equations and, therefore, pseudostatements.

6.21   Mathematical sentences express no thoughts.

6.3   The investigation of logic means the investigation of *all* conformity to *laws*. And outside logic all is accident.

6.4   All sentences are of equal value.

6.41   The meaning of the world must lie outside the world. In the world everything is as it is, everything happens as it does happen; there is no value *in* it—if there were any, the value would be worthless.

For a value to be worth something, it must lie outside all happening and outside being this way or that. For all happening and being this way or that is accidental.

The nonaccidental cannot be found in the world, for otherwise this too would then be accidental.

The value of the world lies outside it.

6.42 Likewise, there can be no sentences in ethics. Sentences cannot express anything higher.

6.421 Clearly, ethics cannot be put into words.

Ethics is transcendent.

(Ethics and esthetics are one.)

6.422 As soon as we set up an ethical law having the form "thou shalt . . . ," our first thought is: So then what if I don't do it? But clearly ethics has nothing to do with punishment and reward in the ordinary sense. The question about the consequences of my action must therefore be irrelevant. At least these consequences will not be events. For there must be something right in that formulation of the question. There must be some sort of ethical reward and ethical punishment, but this must lie in the action itself.

6.423 We cannot speak of the will as if it were the ethical subject.

And the will as a phenomenon is only of interest to psychology.

6.43 If good or bad willing changes the world, it changes only the boundaries of the world, not the facts—not the things that can be expressed in language.

6.431 In death, too, the world does nor change but only ceases.

6.4311 Death is not an event in life. Death is not lived through.

If by *eternity* we mean not endless temporal duration but timelessness, then to live eternally is to live in the present.

In the same way as our visual field is without boundary, our life is endless.

6.4312 The temporal immortality of the human soul—its eternal survival after death—is not only without guarantee, this assumption could never have the desired effect. Is a riddle solved by the fact that I survive forever? Is eternal life not as enigmatic as our present life? The solution to the riddle of life in space and time lies *outside* of space and time.

(Certainly the solution to this riddle does not involve solutions to any of the problems of natural science.)

6.432 *How* the world is, is completely indifferent to what is higher. God does not reveal himself *in* the world.

6.4321 The facts all belong to the setting up of the problem, not to its solution.

6.44 It's not *how* the world is that is mystical but *that* it is.

6.45 To view the world *sub specie aeternitatis* is the view of it as a bounded whole.

The feeling of the world as a bounded whole is the mystical feeling.

6.5 If the answer cannot be put into words, the question, too, cannot be put into words.

The riddle does not exist.

If a question can be put at all, then it *can* also be answered.

6.51 Skepticism is *not* irrefutable, only nonsensical, insofar as it tries to raise doubts about what cannot be asked.

For doubt can exist only if there is a question; a question can exist only if there is an answer, and this can be the case only if something *can* be *said.*

6.52 We feel that even if *all possible* scientific questions were answered, the problems of life would still not have been touched at all. To be sure, there would then be no question left, and just this is the answer.

6.521 The vanishing of this problem is the solution to the problem of life.

(Is this not the very reason people to whom after long bouts of doubt the meaning of life became clear, could not then say what this meaning is?)

6.522 The inexpressible indeed exists. It *shows* itself. It is the mystical.

6.53 The right method in philosophy would be to say nothing except what can be said using sentences such as those of natural science—which of course has nothing to do with philosophy— and then, to show those wishing to say something metaphysical that they failed to give any meaning to certain signs in their sentences. Although they would not be satisfied—they would feel you weren't reaching them any philosophy—*this* would be the only right method.

6.54 My sentences are illuminating in the following way: to understand me you must recognize my sentences—once you have climbed out through them, on them, over them—as senseless. (You must, so to speak, throw away the ladder, after you have climbed up on it.)

You must climb out through my sentences; then you will see the world correctly.

7 Of what we cannot speak we must be silent.

Computing Machinery and Intelligence

ALAN M. TURING

Mathematician, logician, cryptanalyst, and philosopher Alan M. Turing (1912–1954) was a pioneer in computer science and cognitive science. He was a Fellow at King's College, Cambridge.

1. THE IMITATION GAME

I propose to consider the question "Can machines think?" This should begin with definitions of the meaning of the terms "machine" and "think." The definitions might be framed so as to reflect so far as possible the normal use of the words, but this attitude is dangerous. If the meaning of the words "machine" and "think" are to be found by examining how they are commonly used it is difficult to escape the conclusion that the meaning and the answer to the question, "Can machines think?" is to be sought in a statistical survey such as a Gallup poll. But this is absurd. Instead of attempting such a definition I shall replace the question by another, which is closely related to it and is expressed in relatively unambiguous words.

The new form of the problem can be described in terms of a game which we call the "imitation game." It is played with three people, a man (A), a woman (B), and an interrogator (C) who may be of either sex. The interrogator stays in a room apart from the other two. The object of the game for the interrogator is to determine which of the other two is the man and which is the woman. He knows them by labels X and Y, and at the end of the game he says either "X is A and Y is B" Or "X is B and Y is A." The interrogator is allowed to put questions to A and B thus:

C: Will X please tell me the length of his or her hair?

Now suppose X is actually A, then A must answer. It is A's object in the game to try to cause C to make the wrong identification. His answer might therefore be

"My hair is shingled, and the longest strands are about nine inches long."

In order that tones of voice may not help the interrogator the answers should be written, or better still, typewritten. The ideal arrangement is to have a teleprinter communicating between the two rooms. Alternatively the question and answers can be repeated by an intermediary. The object of the game for the third player (B) is to help the interrogator. The best strategy for her is probably to give truthful answers. She can add such things as "I am the woman, don't listen to him!" to her answers, but it will avail nothing as the man can make similar remarks.

We now ask the question, "What will happen when a machine takes the part of A in this game?" Will the interrogator decide wrongly as often when the game is played like this as he does when the game is played between a man and a woman? These questions replace our original, "Can machines think?"

2. CRITIQUE OF THE NEW PROBLEM

As well as asking, "What is the answer to this new form of the question," one may ask, "Is this new question a worthy one to investigate?" This latter question we investigate without further ado, thereby cutting short an infinite regress.

The new problem has the advantage of drawing a fairly sharp line between the physical and the intellectual capacities of a man. No engineer or chemist claims to be able to produce a material which is indistinguishable from the human skin. It is possible that at some time this might be done, but even supposing this invention available we should feel there was little point in trying to make a "thinking machine" more human by dressing it up in such artificial flesh. The form in which we have set the problem reflects this fact in the condition which prevents the interrogator from seeing or touching the other competitors, or hearing their voices. Some other ad-

From "Computing Machinery and Intelligence," *Mind,* Vol. LIX, No. 236, (1950). Reprinted by permission of Mrs. Turing and *Mind.*

vantages of the proposed criterion may be shown up by specimen questions and answers. Thus:

Q: Please write me a sonnet on the subject of the Forth Bridge.

A: Count me out on this one. I never could write poetry.

Q: Add 34957 to 70764.

A: (Pause about 30 seconds and then give as answer) 105621.

Q: Do you play chess?

A: Yes.

Q: I have K at my K1, and no other pieces. You have only K at K6 and R at R1. It is your move. What do you play?

A: (After a pause of 15 seconds) R-R8 mate.

The question and answer method seems to be suitable for introducing almost any one of the fields of human endeavor that we wish to include. We do not wish to penalize the machine for its inability to shine in beauty competitions, nor to penalize a man for losing in a race against an airplane. The conditions of our game make these disabilities irrelevant. The "witnesses" can brag, if they consider it advisable, as much as they please about their charms, strength or heroism, but the interrogator cannot demand practical demonstrations.

The game may perhaps be criticized on the ground that the odds are weighted too heavily against the machine. If the man were to try and pretend to be the machine he would clearly make a very poor showing. He would be given away at once by slowness and inaccuracy in arithmetic. May not machines carry out something which ought to be described as thinking but which is very different from what a man does? This objection is a very strong one, but at least we can say that if, nevertheless, a machine can be constructed to play the imitation game satisfactorily, we need not be troubled by this objection.

It might be urged that when playing the "imitation game" the best strategy for the machine may possibly be something other than imitation of the behavior of a man. This may be, but I think it is unlikely that there is any great effect of this kind. In any case there is no intention to investigate here the theory of the game, and it will be assumed that the best

strategy is to try to provide answers that would naturally be given by a man.

3. THE MACHINES CONCERNED IN THE GAME

The question which we put in §1 will not be quite definite until we have specified what we mean by the word "machine." It is natural that we should wish to permit every kind of engineering technique to be used in our machines. We also wish to allow the possibility that an engineer or team of engineers may construct a machine which works, but whose manner of operation cannot be satisfactorily described by its constructors because they have applied a method which is largely experimental. Finally, we wish to exclude from the machines men born in the usual manner. It is difficult to frame the definitions so as to satisfy these three conditions. One might for instance insist that the team of engineers should be all of one sex, but this would not really be satisfactory, for it is probably possible to rear a complete individual from a single cell of the skin (say) of a man. To do so would be a feat of biological technique deserving of the very highest praise, but we would not be inclined to regard it as a case of "constructing a thinking machine." This prompts us to abandon the requirement that every kind of technique should be permitted. We are the more ready to do so in view of the fact that the present interest in "thinking machines" has been aroused by a particular kind of machine, usually called an "electronic computer" or "digital computer." Following this suggestion we only permit digital computers to take part in our game. . . .

CONTRARY VIEWS ON THE MAIN QUESTION

We may now consider the ground to have been cleared and we are ready to proceed to the debate on our question, "Can machines think?" . . . We cannot altogether abandon the original form of the problem, for opinions will differ as to the appropriateness of the substitution and we must at least listen to what has to be said in this connection.

It will simplify matters for the reader if I explain first my own beliefs in the matter. Consider first the more accurate form of the question. I believe that in about fifty years' time it will be possible to program computers, with a storage capacity of about 10^9, to make them play the imitation game so well that an average interrogator will not have more than 70 per cent chance of making the right identification after five minutes of questioning. The original question, "Can machines think?" I believe to be too meaningless to deserve discussion. Nevertheless I believe that at the end of the century the use of words and general educated opinion will have altered so much that one will be able to speak of machines thinking without expecting to be contradicted. I believe further that no useful purpose is served by concealing these beliefs. The popular view that scientists proceed inexorably from well-established fact to well-established fact, never being influenced by any unproved conjecture, is quite mistaken. Provided it is made clear which are proved facts and which are conjectures, no harm can result. Conjectures are of great importance since they suggest useful lines of research.

I now proceed to consider opinions opposed to my own.

1. *The Theological Objection.* Thinking is a function of man's immortal soul. God has given an immortal soul to every man and woman, but not to any other animal or to machines. Hence no animal or machine can think.

I am unable to accept any part of this, but will attempt to reply in theological terms. I should find the argument more convincing if animals were classed with men, for there is a greater difference, to my mind, between the typical animate and the inanimate than there is between man and the other animals. The arbitrary character of the orthodox view becomes clearer if we consider how it might appear to a member of some other religious community. How do Christians regard the Moslem view that women have no souls? But let us leave this point aside and return to the main argument. It appears to me that the argument quoted above implies a serious restriction of the omnipotence of the Almighty. It is admitted that there are certain things that He cannot do such as making one equal to two, but should we not believe that He has freedom to confer a soul on an elephant if He sees fit? We might expect that He would only exercise this power in conjunction with a mutation which provided the elephant with an appropriately improved brain to minister to the needs of this soul. An argument of exactly similar form may be made for the case of machines. It may seem different because it is more difficult to "swallow." But this really only means that we think it would be less likely that He would consider the circumstances suitable for conferring a soul. The circumstances in question are discussed in the rest of this paper. In attempting to construct such machines we should not be irreverently usurping His power of creating souls, any more than we are in the procreation of children: rather we are, in either case, instruments of His will providing mansions for the souls that He creates.

However, this is mere speculation. I am not very impressed with theological arguments whatever they may be used to support. Such arguments have often been found unsatisfactory in the past. In the time of Galileo it was argued that the texts, "And the sun stood still . . . and hasted not to go down about a whole day" (Joshua x. 13) and "He laid the foundations of the earth, that it should not move at any time" (Psalm cv. 5) were an adequate refutation of the Copernican theory. With our present knowledge such an argument appears futile. When that knowledge was not available it made a quite different impression.

2. *The "Heads in the Sand" Objection.* "The consequences of machines thinking would be too dreadful. Let us hope and believe that they cannot do so."

This argument is seldom expressed quite so openly as in the form above. But it affects most of us who think about it at all. We like to believe that Man is in some subtle way superior to the rest of creation. It is best if he can be shown to be *necessarily* superior, for then there is no danger of him losing his commanding position. The popularity of the theological argument is clearly connected with this feeling. It is likely to be quite strong in intellectual people, since they value the power of thinking more highly than others, and are more inclined to base their belief in the superiority of Man on this power.

I do not think that this argument is sufficiently substantial to require refutation. Consolation would be more appropriate: perhaps this should be sought in the transmigration of souls.

3. *The Mathematical Objection.* There are a number of results of mathematical logic which can be

used to show that there are limitations to the powers of discrete state machines. The best known of these results is known as Gödel's theorem, and shows that in any sufficiently powerful logical system statements can be formulated which can neither be proved nor disproved within the system, unless possibly the system itself is inconsistent. There are other, in some respects similar, results due to Church, Kleene, Rosser, and Turing. The latter result is the most convenient to consider, since it refers directly to machines, whereas the others can only be used in a comparatively indirect argument: for instance if Gödel's theorem is to be used we need in addition to have some means of describing logical systems in terms of machines, and machines in terms of logical systems. The result in question refers to a type of machine which is essentially a digital computer with an infinite capacity. It states that there are certain things that such a machine cannot do. If it is rigged up to give answers to questions as in the imitation game, there will be some questions to which it will either give a wrong answer, or fail to give an answer at all however much time is allowed for a reply. There may, of course, be many such questions, and questions which cannot be answered by one machine may be satisfactorily answered by another. We are of course supposing for the present that the questions are of the kind to which an answer "Yes" or "No" is appropriate, rather than questions such as "What do you think of Picasso?" The questions that we know the machines must fail on are of this type, "Consider the machine specified as follows. . . . Will this machine ever answer 'Yes' to any question?" The dots are to be replaced by a description of some machine in a standard form . . . When the machine described bears a certain comparatively simple relation to the machine which is under interrogation, it can be shown that the answer is either wrong or not forthcoming. This is the mathematical result: it is argued that it proves a disability of machines to which the human intellect is not subject.

The short answer to this argument is that although it is established that there are limitations to the powers of any particular machine, it has only been stated, without any sort of proof, that no such limitations apply to the human intellect. But I do not think this view can be dismissed quite so lightly. Whenever one of these machines is asked the ap-

propriate critical question, and gives a definite answer, we know that this answer must be wrong, and this gives us a certain feeling of superiority. Is this feeling illusory? It is no doubt quite genuine, but I do not think too much importance should be attached to it. We too often give wrong answers to questions ourselves to be justified in being very pleased at such evidence of fallibility on the part of the machines Further, our superiority can only be felt on such an occasion in relation to the one machine over which we have scored our petty triumph. There would be no question of triumphing simultaneously over *all* machines. In short, then, there might be men cleverer than any given machine, but then again there might be other machines cleverer again, and so on.

Those who hold to the mathematical argument would, I think, mostly be willing to accept the imitation game as a basis for discussion. Those who believe in the two previous objections would probably not be interested in any criteria.

4. *The Argument from Consciousness.* This argument is very well expressed in Professor Jefferson's Lister Oration for 1949, from which I quote. "Not until a machine can write a sonnet or compose a concerto because of thoughts and emotions felt, and not by the chance fall of symbols, could we agree that machine equals brain—that is, not only write it but know that it had written it. No mechanism could feel (and not merely artificially signal, an easy contrivance) pleasure at its successes, grief when its valves fuse, be warmed by flattery, be made miserable by its mistakes, be charmed by sex, be angry or depressed when it cannot get what it wants."

This argument appears to be a denial of the validity of our test. According to the most extreme form of this view the only way by which one could be sure that a machine thinks is to *be* the machine and to feel oneself thinking. One could then describe these feelings to the world, but of course no one would be justified in taking any notice. Likewise according to this view the only way to know that a *man* thinks is to *be* that particular man. It is in fact the solipsist point of view. It may be the most logical view to hold but it makes communication of ideas difficult. A is liable to believe "A thinks but B does not" while B believes "B thinks but A does not." Instead of arguing continually over this point it is usual to have the polite convention that everyone thinks.

I am sure that Professor Jefferson does not wish to adopt the extreme and solipsist point of view. Probably he would be quite willing to accept the imitation game as a test. The game (with the player B omitted) is frequently used in practice under the name of *viva voce* to discover whether someone really understands something or has "learned it parrot fashion." Let us listen in to a part of such a *viva voce*:

INTERROGATOR: In the first line of your sonnet which reads "Shall I compare thee to a summer's day," would not "a spring day" do as well or better?

WITNESS: It wouldn't scan.

INTERROGATOR: How about "a winter's day." That would scan all right.

WITNESS: Yes, but nobody wants to be compared to a winter's day.

INTERROGATOR: Would you say Mr. Pickwick reminded you of Christmas?

WITNESS: In a way.

INTERROGATOR: Yet Christmas is a winter's day, and I do not think Mr. Pickwick would mind the comparison.

WITNESS: I don't think you're serious. By a winter's day one means a typical winter's day, rather than a special one like Christmas.

And so on. What would Professor Jefferson say if the sonnet-writing machine was able to answer like this in the *viva voice*? I do not know whether he would regard the machine as "merely artificially signaling" these answers, but if the answers were as satisfactory and sustained as in the above passage I do not think he would describe it as "an easy contrivance." This phrase is, I think, intended to cover such devices as the inclusion in the machine of a record of someone reading a sonnet, with appropriate switching to turn it on from time to time.

In short then, I think that most of those who support the argument from consciousness could be persuaded to abandon it rather than be forced into the solipsist position. They will then probably be willing to accept our test.

I do not wish to give the impression that I think there is no mystery about consciousness. There is, for instance, something of a paradox connected with any attempt to localize it. But I do not think these mysteries necessarily need to be solved before we can answer the question with which we are concerned in this paper.

5. *Arguments from Various Disabilities.* These arguments take the form, "I grant you that you can make machines do all the things you have mentioned but you will never be able to make one to do X." Numerous features X are suggested in this connection. I offer a selection:

> Be kind, resourceful, beautiful, friendly, have initiative, have a sense of humor, tell right from wrong, make mistakes, fall in love, enjoy strawberries and cream, make someone fall in love with it, learn from experience, use words properly, be the subject of its own thought, have as much diversity of behavior as a man, do something really new.

No support is usually offered for these statements. I believe they are mostly founded on the principle of scientific induction. A man has seen thousands of machines in his lifetime. From what he sees of them he draws a number of general conclusions. They are ugly, each is designed for a very limited purpose, when required for a minutely different purpose they are useless, the variety of behavior of any one of them is very small, etc., etc. Naturally he concludes that these are necessary properties of machines in general. Many of these limitations are associated with the very small storage capacity of most machines. (I am assuming that the idea of storage capacity is extended in some way to cover machines other than discrete state machines. The exact definition does not matter as no mathematical accuracy is claimed in the present discussion.) A few years ago, when very little had been heard of digital computers, it was possible to elicit much incredulity concerning them, if one mentioned their properties without describing their construction. That was presumably due to a similar application of the principle of scientific induction. These applications of the principle are of course largely unconscious. When a burned child fears the fire and shows that he fears it by avoiding it, I should say that he was applying scientific induction. (I could of course also describe his behavior in many other ways.) The works and customs of mankind do not seem to be very suitable material to which to apply scientific induction. A very large part of space-time must be investigated if reliable results are to be obtained. Otherwise we may (as most English children do) decide that everybody speaks English, and that it is silly to learn French.

There are, however, special remarks to be made about many of the disabilities that have been mentioned. The inability to enjoy strawberries and cream may have struck the reader as frivolous. Possibly a machine might be made to enjoy this delicious dish, but any attempt to make one do so would be idiotic. What is important about this disability is that it contributes to some of the other disabilities, e.g., to the difficulty of the same kind of friendliness occurring between man and machine as between white man and white man, or between black man and black man.

The claim that "machines cannot make mistakes" seems a curious one. One is tempted to retort, "Are they any the worse for that?" But let us adopt a more sympathetic attitude, and try to see what is really meant. I think this criticism can be explained in terms of the imitation game. It is claimed that the interrogator could distinguish the machine from the man simply by setting them a number of problems in arithmetic. The machine would be unmasked because of its deadly accuracy. The reply to this is simple. The machine (programmed for playing the game) would not attempt to give the *right* answers to the arithmetic problems. It would deliberately introduce mistakes in a manner calculated to confuse the interrogator. A mechanical fault would probably show itself through an unsuitable decision as to what sort of a mistake to make in the arithmetic. Even this interpretation of the criticism is not sufficiently sympathetic. But we cannot afford the space to go into it much further. It seems to me that this criticism depends on a confusion between two kinds of mistakes. We may call them "errors of functioning" and "errors of conclusion." Errors of functioning are due to some mechanical or electrical fault which causes the machine to behave otherwise than it was designed to do. In philosophical discussions one likes to ignore the possibility of such errors; one is therefore discussing "abstract machines." These abstract machines are mathematical fictions rather than physical objects. By definition they are incapable of errors of functioning. In this sense we can truly say that "machines can never make mistakes." Errors of

conclusion can only arise when some meaning is attached to the output signals from the machine. The machine might, for instance, type out mathematical equations, or sentences in English. When a false proposition is typed we say that the machine has committed an error of conclusion. There is clearly no reason at all for saying that a machine cannot make this kind of mistake. It might do nothing but type out repeatedly "0 = 1." To take a less perverse example, it might have some method for drawing conclusions by scientific induction. We must expect such a method to lead occasionally to erroneous results.

The claim that a machine cannot be the subject of its own thought can of course only be answered if it can be shown that the machine has *some* thought with *some* subject matter. Nevertheless, "the subject matter of a machine's operations" does seem to mean something, at least to the people who deal with it. If, for instance, the machine was trying to find a solution of the equation $x^2 - 40x - 11 = 0$ one would be tempted to describe this equation as part of the machine's subject matter at that moment. In this sort of sense a machine undoubtedly can be its own subject matter. It may be used to help in making up its own programs, or to predict the effect of alterations in its own structure. By observing the results of its own behavior it can modify its own programs so as to achieve some purpose more effectively. These are possibilities of the near future, rather than Utopian dreams.

The criticism that a machine cannot have much diversity of behavior is just a way of saying that it cannot have much storage capacity. Until fairly recently a storage capacity of even a thousand digits was very rare.

The criticisms that we are considering here are often disguised forms of the argument from consciousness. Usually if one maintains that a machine *can* do one of these things, and describes the kind of method that the machine could use, one will not make much of an impression. It is thought that the method (whatever it may be, for it must be mechanical) is really rather base. Compare the parenthesis in Jefferson's statement quoted above.

6. *Lady Lovelace's Objection.* Our most detailed information of Babbage's Analytical Engine comes from a memoir by Lady Lovelace. In it she states,

"The Analytical Engine has no pretensions to *originate* anything. It can do *whatever we know how to order it* to perform" (her italics). This statement is quoted by Hartree who adds: "This does not imply that it may not be possible to construct electronic equipment which will 'think for itself,' or in which, in biological terms, one could set up a conditioned reflex, which would serve as a basis for 'learning.' Whether this is possible in principle or not is a stimulating and exciting question, suggested by some of these recent developments. But it did not seem that the machines constructed or projected at the time had this property."

I am in thorough agreement with Hartree over this. It will be noticed that he does not assert that the machines in question had not got the property, but rather that the evidence available to Lady Lovelace did not encourage her to believe that they had it. It is quite possible that the machines in question had in a sense got this property. For suppose that some discrete state machine has the property. The Analytical Engine was a universal digital computer, so that, if its storage capacity and speed were adequate, it could by suitable programing be made to mimic the machine in question. Probably this argument did not occur to the Countess or to Babbage. In any case there was no obligation on them to claim all that could be claimed.

This whole question will be considered again under the heading of learning machines.

A variant of Lady Lovelace's objection states that a machine can "never do anything really new." This may be parried for a moment with the saw, "There is nothing new under the sun." Who can be certain that "original work" that he has done was not simply the growth of the seed planted in him by teaching, or the effect of following well-known general principles. A better variant of the objection says that a machine can never "take us by surprise." This statement is a more direct challenge and can be met directly. Machines take me by surprise with great frequency. This is largely because I do not do sufficient calculation to decide what to expect them to do, or rather because, although I do a calculation, I do it in a hurried, slipshod fashion, taking risks. Perhaps I say to myself, "I suppose the voltage here ought to be the same as there: anyway let's assume it is." Naturally I am often wrong, and the result is a surprise for

me, for by the time the experiment is done these assumptions have been forgotten. These admissions lay me open to lectures on the subject of my vicious ways, but do not throw any doubt on my credibility when I testify to the surprises I experience.

I do not expect this reply to silence my critic. He will probably say that such surprises are due to some creative mental act on my part, and reflect no credit on the machine. This leads us back to the argument from consciousness, and far from the idea of surprise. It is a line of argument we must consider closed, but it is perhaps worth remarking that the appreciation of something as surprising requires as much of a "creative mental act" whether the surprising event originates from a man, a book, a machine or anything else.

The view that machines cannot give rise to surprises is due, I believe, to a fallacy to which philosophers and mathematicians are particularly subject. This is the assumption that as soon as a fact is presented to a mind all consequences of that fact spring into the mind simultaneously with it. It is a very useful assumption under many circumstances, but one too easily forgets that it is false. A natural consequence of doing so is that one then assumes that there is no virtue in the mere working out of consequences from data and general principles.

7. *Argument from Continuity in the Nervous System.* The nervous system is certainly not a discrete state machine. A small error in the information about the size of a nervous impulse impinging on a neuron, may make a large difference to the size of the outgoing impulse. It may be argued that, this being so, one cannot expect to be able to mimic the behavior of the nervous system with a discrete state system.

It is true that a discrete state machine must be different from a continuous machine. But if we adhere to the conditions of the imitation game, the interrogator will not be able to take any advantage of this difference. The situation can be made clearer if we consider some other simpler continuous machine. A differential analyzer will do very well. (A differential analyzer is a certain kind of machine not of the discrete state type used for some kinds of calculation.) Some of these provide their answers in a typed form, and so are suitable for taking part in the game. It would not be possible for a digital computer to predict exactly what answers the differential analyzer would give to a problem, but it would be quite capable of giving the right sort of answer. For instance, if asked to give the value of π (actually about 3.1416) it would be reasonable to choose at random between the values 3.12, 3.13, 3.14, 3.15, 3.16 with the probabilities of 0.05, 0.15, 0.55, 0.19, 0.06 (say). Under these circumstances it would be very difficult for the interrogator to distinguish the differential analyzer from the digital computer.

8. *The Argument from Informality of Behavior.* It is not possible to produce a set of rules purporting to describe what a man should do in every conceivable set of circumstances. One might for instance have a rule that one is to stop when one sees a red traffic light, and to go if one sees a green one, but what if by some fault both appear together? One may perhaps decide that it is safest to stop. But some further difficulty may well arise from this decision later. To attempt to provide rules of conduct to cover every eventuality, even those arising from traffic lights, appears to be impossible. With all this I agree.

From this it is argued that we cannot be machines. I shall try to reproduce the argument, but I fear I shall hardly do it justice. It seems to run something like this. "If each man had a definite set of rules of conduct by which he regulated his life he would be no better than a machine. But there are no such rules, so men cannot be machines." The undistributed middle is glaring. I do not think the argument is ever put quite like this, but I believe this is the argument used nevertheless. There may however be a certain confusion between "rules of conduct" and "laws of behavior" to cloud the issue. By "rules of conduct" I mean precepts such as "Stop if you see red lights," on which one can act, and of which one can be conscious. By "laws of behavior" I mean laws of nature as applied to a man's body such as "if you pinch him he will squeak." If we substitute "laws of behavior which regulate his life" for "laws of conduct by which he regulates his life" in the argument quoted the undistributed middle is no longer insuperable. For we believe that it is not only true that being regulated by laws of behavior implies being some sort of machine (though not necessarily a discrete state machine), but that conversely being such a machine implies being regulated by such laws. However, we cannot so easily convince ourselves of the absence of complete laws of behavior as of com-

plete rules of conduct. The only way we know of for finding such laws is scientific observation, and we certainly know of no circumstances under which we could say, "We have searched enough. There are no such laws."

We can demonstrate more forcibly that any such statement would be unjustified. For suppose we could be sure of finding such laws if they existed. Then given a discrete state machine it should certainly be possible to discover by observation sufficient about it to predict its future behavior, and this within a reasonable time, say a thousand years. But this does not seem to be the case. I have set up on the Manchester computer a small program using only 1000 units of storage, whereby the machine supplied with one sixteen figure number replies with another within two seconds. I would defy anyone to learn from these replies sufficient about the program to be able to predict any replies to untried values.

9. *The Argument from Extra-Sensory Perception.* I assume that the reader is familiar with the idea of extra-sensory perception, and the meaning of the four items of it, viz., telepathy, clairvoyance, precognition and psychokinesis. These disturbing phenomena seem to deny all our usual scientific ideas. How we should like to discredit them! Unfortunately the statistical evidence, at least for telepathy, is overwhelming. It is very difficult to rearrange one's ideas so as to fit these new facts in. Once one has accepted them it does not seem a very big step to believe in ghosts and bogies. The idea that our bodies move simply according to the known laws of physics, together with some others not yet discovered but somewhat similar, would be one of the first to go.

This argument is to my mind quite a strong one. One can say in reply that many scientific theories seem to remain workable in practice, in spite of clashing with E.S.P.; that in fact one can get along very nicely if one forgets about it. This is rather cold comfort, and one fears that thinking is just the kind of phenomenon where E.S.P. may be especially relevant.

A more specific argument based on E.S.P. might run as follows: "Let us play the imitation game, using as witnesses a man who is good as a telepathic receiver, and a digital computer. The interrogator can ask such questions as "What suit does the card in my right hand belong to?' The man by telepathy or clairvoyance gives the right answer 130 times out of 400 cards. The machine can only guess at random, and perhaps get 104 right, so the interrogator makes the right identification." There is an interesting possibility which opens here. Suppose the digital computer contains a random number generator. Then it will be natural to use this to decide what answer to give. But then the random number generator will be subject to the psychokinetic powers of the interrogator. Perhaps this psychokinesis might cause the machine to guess right more often than would be expected on a probability calculation, so that the interrogator might still be unable to make the right identification. On the other hand, he might be able to guess right without any questioning, by clairvoyance. With E.S.P. anything may happen.

If telepathy is admitted it will be necessary to tighten our test. The situation could be regarded as analogous to that which would occur if the interrogator were talking to himself and one of the competitors was listening with his ear to the wall. To put the competitors into a "telepathy-proof room" would satisfy all requirements. . . .

Minds, Brains, and Programs

JOHN R. SEARLE

John R. Searle (1932–) has published numerous articles and several books. He teaches at the University of California, Berkeley.

What psychological and philosophical significance should we attach to recent efforts at computer simulations of human cognitive capacities? In answering this question, I find it useful to distinguish what I will call "strong" AI from "weak" or "cautious" AI (artificial intelligence). According to weak AI, the principal value of the computer in the study of the mind is that it gives us a very powerful tool. For example, it enables us to formulate and test hypotheses in a more rigorous and precise fashion. But according to strong AI, the computer is not merely a tool in the study of the mind; rather, the appropriately programmed computer really *is* a mind, in the sense that computers given the right programs can be literally said to *understand* and have other cognitive states. In strong AI, because the programmed computer has cognitive states, the programs are not mere tools that enable us to test psychological explanations; rather, the programs are themselves the explanations.

I have no objection to the claims of weak AI, at least as far as this article is concerned. My discussion here will be directed at the claims I have defined as those of strong AI, specifically the claim that the appropriately programmed computer literally has cognitive states and that the programs thereby explain human cognition. When I hereafter refer to AI, I have in mind the strong version, as expressed by these two claims.

I will consider the work of Roger Schank and his colleagues at Yale,* because I am more familiar with it than I am with any other similar claims, and because it provides a very clear example of the sort of work I wish to examine. But nothing that follows depends upon the details of Schank's programs. The same arguments would apply to Winograd's SHRDLU, Weizenbaum's ELIZA, and indeed any Turing machine simulation of human mental phenomena. . . .

Very briefly, and leaving out the various details, one can describe Schank's program as follows: The aim of the program is to simulate the human ability

---

---

*References have been deleted.—Eds.

to understand stories. It is characteristic of human beings' story-understanding capacity that they can answer questions about the story even though the information that they give was never explicitly stated in the story. Thus, for example, suppose you are given the following story: "A man went into a restaurant and ordered a hamburger. When the hamburger arrived it was burned to a crisp, and the man stormed out of the restaurant angrily, without paying for the hamburger or leaving a tip." Now, if you are asked "Did the man eat the hamburger?" you will presumably answer, "No, he did not." Similarly, if you are given the following story: "A man went into a restaurant and ordered a hamburger; when the hamburger came he was very pleased with it; and as he left the restaurant he gave the waitress a large tip before paying his bill," and you are asked the question, "Did the man eat the hamburger?" you will presumably answer, "Yes, he ate the hamburger." Now Schank's machines can similarly answer questions about restaurants in this fashion. To do this, they have a "representation" of the sort of information that human beings have about restaurants, which enables them to answer such questions as those above, given these sorts of stories. When the machine is given the story and then asked the question, the machine will print out answers of the sort that we would expect human beings to give if told similar stories. Partisans of strong AI claim that in this question and answer sequence the machine is not only simulating a human ability but also (1) that the machine can literally be said to *understand* the story and provide the answers to questions, and (2) that what the machine and its programs do *explains* the human ability to understand the story and answer questions about it.

Both claims seem to me to be totally unsupported by Schank's work, as I will attempt to show in what follows. I am not, of course, saying that Schank himself is committed to these claims.

One way to test any theory of the mind is to ask oneself what it would be like if my mind actually worked on the principles that the theory says all minds work on. Let us apply this test to the Schank program with the following *Gedankenexperiment.** Suppose that I'm locked in a room and given a large

batch of Chinese writing. Suppose furthermore (as is indeed the case) that I know no Chinese, either written or spoken, and that I'm not even confident that I could recognize Chinese writing as Chinese writing distinct from, say, Japanese writing or meaningless squiggles. To me, Chinese writing is just so many meaningless squiggles. Now suppose further that after this first batch of Chinese writing I am given a second batch of Chinese script together with a set of rules for correlating the second batch with the first batch. The rules are in English, and I understand these rules as well as any other native speaker of English. They enable me to correlate one set of formal symbols with another set of formal symbols, and all that "formal" means here is that I can identify the symbols entirely by their shapes. Now suppose also that I am given a third batch of Chinese symbols together with some instructions, again in English, that enable me to correlate elements of this third batch with the first two batches, and these rules instruct me how to give back certain Chinese symbols with certain sorts of shapes in response to certain sorts of shapes given me in the third batch. Unknown to me, the people who are giving me all of these symbols call the first batch a "script," they call the second batch a "story," and they call the third batch "questions." Furthermore, they call the symbols I give them back in response to the third batch "answers to the questions," and the set of rules in English that they gave me, they call the "program." Now just to complicate the story a little, imagine that these people also give me stories in English, which I understand, and they then ask me questions in English about these stories, and I give them back answers in English. Suppose also that after a while I get so good at following the instructions for manipulating the Chinese symbols and the programmers get so good at writing the programs that from the external point of view—that is, from the point of view of somebody outside the room in which I am locked—my answers to the questions are absolutely indistinguishable from those of native Chinese speakers. Nobody just looking at my answers can tell that I don't speak a word of Chinese. Let us also suppose that my answers to the English questions are, as they no doubt would be, indistinguishable from those of other native English speakers, for the simple reason that I am a native English speaker. From the external point of

*[Experiment in the imagination.—Eds.]

view—from the point of view of someone reading my "answers"—the answers to the Chinese questions and the English questions are equally good. But in the Chinese case, unlike the English case, I produce the answers by manipulating uninterpreted formal symbols. As far as the Chinese is concerned, I simply behave like a computer; I perform computational operations on formally specified elements. For the purposes of the Chinese, I am simply an instantiation of the computer program.

Now the claims made by strong AI are that the programmed computer understands the stories and that the program in some sense explains human understanding. But we are now in a position to examine these claims in light of our thought experiment.

1. As regards the first claim, it seems to me quite obvious in the example that I do not understand a word of the Chinese stories. I have inputs and outputs that are indistinguishable from those of the native Chinese speaker, and I can have any formal program you like, but I still understand nothing. For the same reasons, Schank's computer understands nothing of any stories, whether in Chinese, English, or whatever, since in the Chinese case the computer is me, and in cases where the computer is not me, the computer has nothing more than I have in the case where I understand nothing.

2. As regards the second claim, that the program explains human understanding, we can see that the computer and its program do not provide sufficient conditions of understanding since the computer and the program are functioning, and there is no understanding. But does it even provide a necessary condition or a significant contribution to understanding? One of the claims made by the supporters of strong AI is that when I understand a story in English, what I am doing is exactly the same—or perhaps more of the same—as what I was doing in manipulating the Chinese symbols. It is simply more formal symbol manipulation that distinguishes the case in English, where I do understand, from the case in Chinese, where I don't. I have not demonstrated that this claim is false, but it would certainly appear an incredible claim in the example. Such plausibility as the claim has derives from the supposition that we can construct a program that will have the same inputs and outputs as native speakers, and in addition we assume that speakers have some level of de-

scription where they are also instantiations of a program. On the basis of these two assumptions we assume that even if Schank's program isn't the whole story about understanding, it may be part of the story. Well, I suppose that is an empirical possibility, but not the slightest reason has so far been given to believe that it is true, since what is suggested—though certainly not demonstrated—by the example is that the computer program is simply irrelevant to my understanding of the story. In the Chinese case I have everything that artificial intelligence can put into me by way of a program, and I understand nothing; in the English case I understand everything, and there is so far no reason at all to suppose that my understanding has anything to do with computer programs, that is, with computational operations on purely formally specified elements. As long as the program is defined in terms of computational operations on purely formally defined elements, what the example suggests is that these by themselves have no interesting connection with understanding. They are certainly not sufficient conditions, and not the slightest reason has been given to suppose that they are necessary conditions or even that they make a significant contribution to understanding. Notice that the force of the argument is not simply that different machines can have the same input and output while operating on different formal principles—that is not the point at all. Rather, whatever purely formal principles you put into the computer, they will not be sufficient for understanding, since a human will be able to follow the formal principles without understanding anything. No reason whatever has been offered to suppose that such principles are necessary or even contributory, since no reason has been given to suppose that when I understand English I am operating with any formal program at all.

Well, then, what is it that I have in the case of the English sentences that I do not have in the case of the Chinese sentences? The obvious answer is that I know what the former mean, while I haven't the faintest idea what the latter mean. But in what does this consist and why couldn't we give it to a machine, whatever it is? I will return to this question later, but first I want to continue with the example.

I have had the occasions to present this example to several workers in artificial intelligence, and, interestingly, they do not seem to agree on what the proper reply to it is. I get a surprising variety of replies, and in what follows I will consider the most common of these (specified along with their geographic origins).

But first I want to block some common misunderstandings about "understanding": In many of these discussions one finds a lot of fancy footwork about the word "understanding." My critics point out that there are many different degrees of understanding; that "understanding" is not a simple two-place predicate; that there are even different kinds and levels of understanding, and often the law of excluded middle doesn't even apply in a straightforward way to statements of the form "*x* understands *y*"; that in many cases it is a matter for decision and not a simple matter of fact whether *x* understands *y*; and so on. To all of these points I want to say: of course, of course. But they have nothing to do with the points at issue. There are clear cases in which "understanding" literally applies and clear cases in which it does not apply; and these two sorts of cases are all I need for this argument. I understand stories in English; to a lesser degree I can understand stories in French; to a still lesser degree, stories in German; and in Chinese, not at all. My car and my adding machine, on the other hand, understand nothing: they are not in that line of business.* We often attribute "understanding" and other cognitive predicates by metaphor and analogy to cars, adding machines, and other artifacts, but nothing is proved by such attributions. We say, "The door *knows* when to open because of its photoelectric cell," "The adding machine *knows how* (*understands how, is able*) to do addition and subtraction but not division," and "The thermostat *perceives* changes in the temperature." The reason we make these attributions is quite interesting, and it has to do with the fact that in artifacts we extend our own intentionality,[†] our tools are

extensions of our purposes, and so we find it natural to make metaphorical attributions of intentionality to them; but I take it no philosophical ice is cut by such examples. The sense in which an automatic door "understands instructions" from its photoelectric cell is not at all the sense in which I understand English. If the sense in which Schank's programmed computers understand stories is supposed to be the metaphorical sense in which the door understands, and not the sense in which I understand English, the issue would not be worth discussing. But Newell and Simon write that the kind of cognition they claim for computers is exactly the same as for human beings. I like the straightforwardness of this claim, and it is the sort of claim I will be considering. I will argue that in the literal sense the programmed computer understands what the car and the adding machine understand, namely, exactly nothing. The computer's understanding is not just (like my understanding of German) partial or incomplete; it is zero.

Now to the replies:

(1) THE SYSTEMS REPLY (BERKELEY, CALIFORNIA)

"While it is true that the individual person who is locked in the room does not understand the story, the fact is that he is merely part of a whole system, and the system does understand the story. The person has a large ledger in front of him in which are written the rules, he has a lot of scratch paper and pencils for doing calculations, he has "data banks" of sets of Chinese symbols. Now, understanding is not being ascribed to the mere individual; rather it is being ascribed to this whole system of which he is a part."

My response to the systems theory is quite simple: Let the individual internalize all of these elements of the system. He memorizes the rules in the ledger and the data banks of Chinese symbols, and he does all the calculations in his head. The individual then incorporates the entire system. There isn't anything at all to the system that he does not encompass. We can even get rid of the room and suppose he works outdoors. All the same, he understands nothing of the Chinese, and a fortiori neither does the system, because there isn't anything in the system that isn't in him. If he doesn't understand, then

---

*Also, "understanding" implies both the possession of mental (intentional) states and the truth (validity, success) of these states. For the purposes of this discussion we are concerned only with the possession of the states.

[†]Intentionality is by definition that feature of certain mental states by which they are directed at or about objects and states of affairs in the world. Thus, beliefs, desires, and intentions are intentional states; undirected forms of anxiety and depression are not.

there is no way the system could understand because the system is just a part of him.

Actually I feel somewhat embarrassed to give even this answer to the systems theory because the theory seems to me so implausible to start with. The idea is that while a person doesn't understand Chinese, somehow the *conjunction* of that person and bits of paper might understand Chinese. It is not easy for me to imagine how someone who was not in the grip of an ideology would find the idea at all plausible. Still, I think many people who are committed to the ideology of strong AI will in the end be inclined to say something very much like this; so let us pursue it a bit further. According to one version of this view, while the man in the internalized systems example doesn't understand Chinese in the sense that a native Chinese speaker does (because, for example, he doesn't know that the story refers to restaurants and hamburgers, etc.), still "the man as a formal symbol manipulation system" *really does understand Chinese.* The subsystem of the man that is the formal symbol manipulation system for Chinese should not be confused with the subsystem for English.

So there are really two subsystems in the man; one understands English, the other Chinese, and "it's just that the two systems have little to do with each other." But, I want to reply, not only do they have little to do with each other, they are not even remotely alike. The subsystem that understands English (assuming we allow ourselves to talk in this jargon of "subsystems" for a moment) knows that the stories are about restaurants and eating hamburgers, he knows that he is being asked questions about restaurants and that he is answering questions as best he can by making various inferences from the content of the story, and so on. But the Chinese system knows none of this. Whereas the English subsystem knows that "hamburgers" refers to hamburgers, the Chinese subsystem knows only that "squiggle squiggle" is followed by "squoggle squoggle." All he knows is that various formal symbols are being introduced at one end and manipulated according to rules written in English, and other symbols are going out at the other end. The whole point of the original example was to argue that such symbol manipulation by itself couldn't be sufficient for understanding Chinese in any literal sense because the

man could write "squoggle squoggle" after "squiggle squiggle" without understanding anything in Chinese. And it doesn't meet that argument to postulate subsystems within the man, because the subsystems are no better off than the man was in the first place; they still don't have anything even remotely like what the English-speaking man (or subsystem) has. Indeed, in the case as described, the Chinese subsystem is simply a part of the English subsystem, a part that engages in meaningless symbol manipulation according to rules in English.

Let us ask ourselves what is supposed to motivate the systems reply in the first place; that is, what *independent* grounds are there supposed to be for saying that the agent must have a subsystem within him that literally understands stories in Chinese? As far as I can tell the only grounds are that in the example I have the same input and output as native Chinese speakers and a program that goes from one to the other. But the whole point of the examples has been to try to show that that couldn't be sufficient for understanding, in the sense in which I understand stories in English, because a person, and hence the set of systems that go to make up a person, could have the right combination of input, output, and program and still not understand anything in the relevant literal sense in which I understand English. The only motivation for saying there *must* be a subsystem in me that understands Chinese is that I have a program and I can pass the Turing test; I can fool native Chinese speakers. But precisely one of the points at issue is the adequacy of the Turing test. The example shows that there could be two "systems," both of which pass the Turing test, but only one of which understands; and it is no argument against this point to say that since they both pass the Turing test they must both understand, since this claim fails to meet the argument that the system in me that understands English has a great deal more than the system that merely processes Chinese. In short, the systems reply simply begs the question by insisting without argument that the system must understand Chinese.

Furthermore, the systems reply would appear to lead to consequences that are independently absurd. If we are to conclude that there must be cognition in me on the grounds that I have a certain sort of input and output and a program in between, then it looks like all sorts of noncognitive subsystems are going to turn out to be cognitive. For example, there is a level of description at which my stomach does information processing, and it instantiates any number of computer programs, but I take it we do not want to say that it has any understanding. But if we accept the systems reply, then it is hard to see how we avoid saying that stomach, heart, liver, and so on are all understanding subsystems, since there is no principled way to distinguish the motivation for saying the Chinese subsystem understands from saying that the stomach understands. It is, by the way, not an answer to this point to say that the Chinese system has information as input and output and the stomach has food and food products as input and output, since from the point of view of the agent, from my point of view, there is no information in either the food or the Chinese—the Chinese is just so many meaningless squiggles. The information in the Chinese case is solely in the eyes of the programmers and the interpreters, and there is nothing to prevent them from treating the input and output of my digestive organs as information if they so desire.

This last point bears on some independent problems in strong AI, and it is worth digressing for a moment to explain it. If strong AI is to be a branch of psychology, then it must be able to distinguish those systems that are genuinely mental from those that are not. It must be able to distinguish the principles on which the mind works from those on which non-mental systems work; otherwise it will offer us no explanations of what is specifically mental about the mental. And the mental-nonmental distinction cannot be just in the eye of the beholder but it must be intrinsic to the systems; otherwise it would be up to any beholder to treat people as nonmental and, for example, hurricanes as mental if he likes. But quite often in the AI literature the distinction is blurred in ways that would in the long run prove disastrous to the claim that AI is a cognitive inquiry. McCarthy, for example, writes, "Machines as simple as thermostats can be said to have beliefs, and having beliefs seems to be a characteristic of most machines capable of problem solving performance." Anyone who thinks strong AI has a chance as a theory of the mind ought to ponder the implications of that remark. We are asked to accept it as a discovery of strong AI that the hunk of metal on the wall that we use to regulate

the temperature has beliefs in exactly the same sense that we, our spouses, and our children have beliefs, and furthermore that "most" of the other machines in the room—telephone, tape recorder, adding machine, electric light switch—also have beliefs in this literal sense. It is not the aim of this article to argue against McCarthy's point, so I will simply assert the following without argument. The study of the mind starts with such facts as that humans have beliefs, while thermostats, telephones, and adding machines don't. If you get a theory that denies this point you have produced a counterexample to the theory and the theory is false. One gets the impression that people in AI who write this sort of thing think they can get away with it because they don't really take it seriously, and they don't think anyone else will either. I propose, for a moment at least, to take it seriously. Think hard for one minute about what would be necessary to establish that that hunk of metal on the wall over there had real beliefs, beliefs with direction of fit, propositional content, and conditions of satisfaction; beliefs that had the possibility of being strong beliefs or weak beliefs; nervous, anxious, or secure beliefs; dogmatic, rational, or superstitious beliefs; blind faiths or hesitant cogitations; any kind of beliefs. The thermostat is not a candidate. Neither is stomach, liver, adding machine, or telephone. However, since we are taking the idea seriously, notice that its truth would be fatal to strong AI's claim to be a science of the mind. For now the mind is everywhere. What we wanted to know is what distinguishes the mind from thermostats and livers. And if McCarthy were right, strong AI wouldn't have a hope of telling us that.

(2) THE ROBOT REPLY (YALE)

"Suppose we wrote a different kind of program from Schank's program. Suppose we put a computer inside a robot, and this computer would not just take in formal symbols as input and give out formal symbols as output, but rather would actually operate the robot in such a way that the robot does something very much like perceiving, walking, moving about, hammering nails, eating, drinking—anything you like. The robot would, for example, have a television camera attached to it that enabled it to see, it would have arms and legs that enabled it to 'act,' and all of this would be controlled by its computer 'brain.' Such a robot would, unlike Schank's computer, have genuine understanding and other mental states."

The first thing to notice about the robot reply is that it tacitly concedes that cognition is not solely a matter of formal symbol manipulation, since this reply adds a set of causal relations with the outside world. But the answer to the robot reply is that the addition of such "perceptual" and "motor" capacities adds nothing by way of understanding, in particular, or intentionality, in general, to Schank's original program. To see this, notice that the same thought experiment applies to the robot case. Suppose that instead of the computer inside the robot, you put me inside the room and, as in the original Chinese case, you give me more Chinese symbols with more instructions in English for matching Chinese symbols to Chinese symbols and feeding back Chinese symbols to the outside. Suppose, unknown to me, some of the Chinese symbols that come to me come from a television camera attached to the robot and other Chinese symbols that I am giving out serve to make the motors inside the robot move the robot's legs or arms. It is important to emphasize that all I am doing is manipulating formal symbols: I know none of these other facts. I am receiving "information" from the robot's "perceptual" apparatus, and I am giving out "instructions" to its motor apparatus without knowing either of these facts. I am the robot's homunculus, but unlike the traditional homunculus, I don't know what's going on. I don't understand anything except the rules for symbol manipulation. Now in this case I want to say that the robot has no intentional states at all; it is simply moving about as a result of its electrical wiring and its program. And furthermore, by instantiating the program I have no intentional states of the relevant type. All I do is follow formal instructions about manipulating formal symbols.

(3) THE BRAIN SIMULATOR REPLY (BERKELEY AND M.I.T.)

"Suppose we design a program that doesn't represent information that we have about the world, such as the information in Schank's scripts, but simulates the actual sequence of neuron firings at the synapses of the brain of a native Chinese speaker when he understands stories in Chinese and gives answers to them. The machine takes in Chinese stories and questions about them as input, it simulates the formal structure of actual Chinese brains in processing these stories, and it gives out Chinese answers as outputs. We can even imagine that the machine operates, not with a single serial program, but with a whole set of programs operating in parallel, in the manner that actual human brains presumably operate when they process natural language. Now surely in such a case we would have to say that the machine understood the stories; and if we refuse to say that, wouldn't we also have to deny that native Chinese speakers understood the stories? At the level of the synapses, what would or could be different about the program of the computer and the program of the Chinese brain?"

Before countering this reply I want to digress to note that it is an odd reply for any partisan of artificial intelligence (or functionalism, etc.) to make: I thought the whole idea of strong AI is that we don't need to know how the brain works to know how the mind works. The basic hypothesis, or so I had supposed, was that there is a level of mental operations consisting of computational processes over formal elements that constitute the essence of the mental and can be realized in all sorts of different brain processes, in the same way that any computer program can be realized in different computer hardwares: On the assumptions of strong AI, the mind is to the brain as the program is to the hardware, and thus we can understand the mind without doing neurophysiology. If we had to know how the brain worked to do AI, we wouldn't bother with AI. However, even getting this close to the operation of the brain is still not sufficient to produce understanding. To see this, imagine that instead of a monolingual man in a room shuffling symbols we have the man operate an elaborate set of water pipes with valves connecting them. When the man receives the Chinese symbols, he looks up in the program, written in English, which valves he has to turn on and off. Each water connection corresponds to a synapse in the Chinese brain, and the whole system is rigged up so that after doing all the right firings, that is after turning on all the right faucets, the Chinese answers pop out at the output end of the series of pipes.

Now where is the understanding in this system? It takes Chinese as input, it simulates the formal structure of the synapses of the Chinese brain, and it gives Chinese as output. But the man certainly doesn't understand Chinese, and neither do the water pipes, and if we are tempted to adopt what I think is the absurd view that somehow the *conjunction* of man *and* water pipes understands, remember that in principle the man can internalize the formal structure of the water pipes and do all the "neuron firings" in his imagination. The problem with the brain simulator is that it is simulating the wrong things about the brain. As long as it simulates only the formal structure of the sequence of neuron firings at the synapses, it won't have simulated what matters about the brain, namely its causal properties, its ability to produce intentional states. And that the formal properties are not sufficient for the causal properties is shown by the water pipe example: We can have all the formal properties carved off from the relevant neurobiological causal properties.

(4) THE COMBINATION REPLY (BERKELEY AND STANFORD)

"While each of the previous three replies might not be completely convincing by itself as a refutation of the Chinese room counterexample, if you take all three together they are collectively much more convincing and even decisive. Imagine a robot with a brain-shaped computer lodged in its cranial cavity, imagine the computer programmed with all the synapses of a human brain, imagine the whole behavior of the robot is indistinguishable from human behavior, and now, think of the whole thing as a unified system and not just as a computer with inputs and outputs. Surely in such a case we would have to ascribe intentionality to the system."

I entirely agree that in such a case we would find it rational and indeed irresistible to accept the hypothesis that the robot had intentionality, as long as we knew nothing more about it. Indeed, besides appearance and behavior, the other elements of the combination are really irrelevant. If we could build a robot whose behavior was indistinguishable over a large range from human behavior, we would attribute intentionality to it, pending some reason not to. We wouldn't need to know in advance that its com-

puter brain was a formal analogue of the human brain.

But I really don't see that this is any help to the claims of strong AI, and here's why: According to strong AI, instantiating a formal program with the right input and output is a sufficient condition of, indeed is constitutive of, intentionality. As Newell puts it, the essence of the mental is the operation of a physical symbol system. But the attributions of intentionality that we make to the robot in this example have nothing to do with formal programs. They are simply based on the assumption that if the robot looks and behaves sufficiently like us, then we would suppose, until proven otherwise, that it must have mental states like ours that cause and are expressed by its behavior and it must have an inner mechanism capable of producing such mental states. If we knew independently how to account for its behavior without such assumptions we would not attribute intentionality to it, especially if we knew it had a formal program. And this is precisely the point of my earlier reply. . . .

Suppose we knew that the robot's behavior was entirely accounted for by the fact that a man inside it was receiving uninterpreted formal symbols from the robot's sensory receptors and sending out uninterpreted formal symbols to its motor mechanisms, and the man was doing this symbol manipulation in accordance with a bunch of rules. Furthermore, suppose the man knows none of these facts about the robot; all he knows is which operations to perform on which meaningless symbols. In such a case we would regard the robot as an ingenious mechanical dummy. The hypothesis that the dummy has a mind would now be unwarranted and unnecessary, for there is now no longer any reason to ascribe intentionality to the robot or to the system of which it is a part (except of course for the man's intentionality in manipulating the symbols). The formal symbol manipulations go on, the input and output are correctly matched, but the only real locus of intentionality is the man, and he doesn't know any of the relevant intentional states; he doesn't, for example, *see* what comes into the robot's eyes, he doesn't *intend* to move the robot's arm, and he doesn't *understand* any of the remarks made to or by the robot. Nor, for the reasons stated earlier, does the system of which man and robot are a part.

To see this point, contrast this case with cases in which we find it completely natural to ascribe intentionality to members of certain other primate species such as apes and monkeys and to domestic animals such as dogs. The reasons we find it natural are, roughly, two: We can't make sense of the animal's behavior without the ascription of intentionality, and we can see that the beasts are made of similar stuff to ourselves—that is an eye, that a nose, this is its skin, and so on. Given the coherence of the animal's behavior and the assumption of the same causal stuff underlying it, we assume both that the animal must have mental states underlying its behavior, and that the mental states must be produced by mechanisms made out of the stuff that is like our stuff. We would certainly make similar assumptions about the robot unless we had some reason not to, but as soon as we knew that the behavior was the result of a formal program, and that the actual causal properties of the physical substance were irrelevant, we would abandon the assumption of intentionality.

There are two other responses to my example that come up frequently (and so are worth discussing) but really miss the point.

(5) THE OTHER MINDS REPLY (YALE)

"How do you know that other people understand Chinese or anything else? Only by their behavior. Now the computer can pass the behavioral tests as well as they can (in principle), so if you are going to attribute cognition to other people you must in principle also attribute it to computers."

This objection really is only worth a short reply. The problem in this discussion is not about how I know that other people have cognitive states, but rather what it is that I am attributing to them when I attribute cognitive states to them. The thrust of the argument is that it couldn't be just computational processes and their output because the computational processes and their output can exist without the cognitive state. It is no answer to this argument to feign anesthesia. In "cognitive sciences" one presupposes the reality and knowability of the mental in the same way that in physical sciences one has to presuppose the reality and knowability of physical objects.

(6) THE MANY MANSIONS REPLY (BERKELEY)

"Your whole argument presupposes that AI is only about analog and digital computers. But that just happens to be the present state of technology. Whatever these causal processes are that you say are essential for intentionality (assuming you are right), eventually we will be able to build devices that have these causal processes, and that will be artificial intelligence. So your arguments are in no way directed at the ability of artificial intelligence to produce and explain cognition."

I really have no objection to this reply save to say that it in effect trivializes the project of strong AI by redefining it as whatever artificially produces and explains cognition. The interest of the original claim made on behalf of artificial intelligence is that it was a precise, well defined thesis: Mental processes are computational processes over formally defined elements. I have been concerned to challenge that thesis. If the claim is redefined so that it is no longer that thesis, my objections no longer apply because there is no longer a testable hypothesis for them to apply to.

Let us now return to the question I promised I would try to answer: Granted that in my original example I understand the English and I do not understand the Chinese, and granted therefore that the machine doesn't understand either English or Chinese, still there must be something about me that makes it the case that I understand English and a corresponding something lacking in me that makes it the case that I fail to understand Chinese. Now why couldn't we give those somethings, whatever they are, to a machine?

I see no reason in principle why we couldn't give a machine the capacity to understand English or Chinese, since in an important sense our bodies with our brains are precisely such machines. But I do see very strong arguments for saying that we could not give such a thing to a machine where the operation of the machine is defined solely in terms of computational processes over formally defined elements; that is, where the operation of the machine is defined as an instantiation of a computer program. It is not because I am the instantiation of a computer program that I am able to understand English and have other forms of intentionality (I am, I suppose, the instantiation of any number of computer programs), but as far as we know it is because I am a certain sort of organism with a certain biological (i.e., chemical and physical) structure, and this structure, under certain conditions, is causally capable of producing perception, action, understanding, learning, and other intentional phenomena. And part of the point of the present argument is that only something that had those causal powers could have that intentionality. Perhaps other physical and chemical processes could produce exactly these effects; perhaps, for example, Martians also have intentionality but their brains are made of different stuff. That is an empirical question, rather like the question whether photosynthesis can be done by something with a chemistry different from that of chlorophyll.

But the main point of the present argument is that no purely formal model will ever be sufficient by itself for intentionality because the formal properties are not by themselves constitutive of intentionality, and they have by themselves no causal powers except the power, when instantiated, to produce the next stage of the formalism when the machine is running. And any other causal properties that particular realizations of the formal model have are irrelevant to the formal model because we can always put the same formal model in a different realization where those causal properties are obviously absent. Even if, by some miracle, Chinese speakers exactly realize Schank's program, we can put the same program in English speakers, water pipes, or computers, none of which understand Chinese, the program notwithstanding.

What matters about brain operations is not the formal shadow cast by the sequence of synapses but rather the actual properties of the sequences. All the arguments for the strong version of artificial intelligence that I have seen insist on drawing an outline around the shadows cast by cognition and then claiming that the shadows are the real thing.

By way of concluding I want to try to state some of the general philosophical points implicit in the argument. For clarity I will try to do it in a question-and-answer fashion, and I begin with that old chestnut of a question:

"Could a machine think?"

The answer is, obviously, yes. We are precisely such machines.

"Yes, but could an artifact, a man-made machine, think?"

Assuming it is possible to produce artificially a machine with a nervous system, neurons with axons and dendrites, and all the rest of it, sufficiently like ours, again the answer to the question seems to be obviously, yes. If you can exactly duplicate the causes, you could duplicate the effects. And indeed it might be possible to produce consciousness, intentionality, and all the rest of it using some other sorts of chemical principles than those that human beings use. It is, as I said, an empirical question.

"OK, but could a digital computer think?"

If by "digital computer" we mean anything at all that has a level of description where it can correctly be described as the instantiation of a computer program, then again the answer is, of course, yes, since we are the instantiations of any number of computer programs, and we can think.

"But could something think, understand, and so on *solely* by virtue of being a computer with the right sort of program? Could instantiating a program, the right program of course, by itself be a sufficient condition of understanding?"

This I think is the right question to ask, though it is usually confused with one or more of the earlier questions, and the answer to it is no.

"Why not?"

Because the formal symbol manipulations by themselves don't have any intentionality; they are quite meaningless; they aren't even *symbol* manipulations, since the symbols don't symbolize anything. In the linguistic jargon, they have only a syntax but no semantics. Such intentionality as computers appear to have is solely in the minds of those who program them and those who use them, those who send in the input and those who interpret the output.

The aim of the Chinese room example was to try to show this by showing that as soon as we put something into the system that really does have intentionality (a man), and we program him with the formal program, you can see that the formal program carries no additional intentionality. It adds nothing, for example, to a man's ability to understand Chinese.

Precisely that feature of AI that seemed so appealing—the distinction between the program and the realization—proves fatal to the claim that simulation could be duplication. The distinction between the program and its realization in the hardware seems to be parallel to the distinction between the level of mental operations and the level of brain operations. And if we could describe the level of mental operations as a formal program, then it seems we could describe what was essential about the mind without doing either introspective psychology or neurophysiology of the brain. But the equation "mind is to brain as program is to hardware" breaks down at several points, among them the following three:

First, the distinction between program and realization has the consequence that the same program could have all sorts of crazy realizations that had no form of intentionality. Weizenbaum, for example, shows in detail how to construct a computer using a roll of toilet paper and a pile of small stones. Similarly, the Chinese story understanding-program can be programmed into a sequence of water pipes, a set of wind machines, or a monolingual English speaker, none of which thereby acquires an understanding of Chinese. Stones, toilet paper, wind, and water pipes are the wrong kind of stuff to have intentionality in the first place—only something that has the same causal powers as brains can have intentionality—and though the English speaker has the right kind of stuff for intentionality you can easily see that he doesn't get any extra intentionality by memorizing the program, since memorizing it won't teach him Chinese.

Second, the program is purely formal, but the intentional states are not in that way formal. They are defined in terms of their content, not their form. The belief that it is raining, for example, is not defined as a certain formal shape, but as a certain mental content with conditions of satisfaction, a direction of fit, and the like. Indeed the belief as such hasn't even got a formal shape in this syntactic sense, since one and the same belief can be given an indefinite number of different syntactic expressions in different linguistic systems.

Third, as I mentioned before, mental states and events are literally a product of the operation of the brain, but the program is not in that way a product of the computer.

"Well if programs are in no way constitutive of mental processes, why have so many people believed the converse? That at least needs some explanation."

I don't really know the answer to that one. The idea that computer simulations could be the real thing ought to have seemed suspicious in the first place because the computer isn't confined to simulating mental operations, by any means. No one supposes that computer simulations of a five-alarm fire will burn the neighborhood down or that a computer simulation of a rainstorm will leave us all drenched. Why on earth would anyone suppose that a computer simulation of understanding actually understood anything? It is sometimes said that it would be frightfully hard to get computers to feel pain or fall in love, but love and pain are neither harder nor easier than cognition or anything else. For simulation, all you need is the right input and output and a program in the middle that transforms the former into the latter. That is all the computer has for anything it does. To confuse simulation with duplication is the same mistake, whether it is pain, love, cognition, fires, or rainstorms.

Still, there are several reasons why AI must have seemed—and to many people perhaps still does seem—in some way to reproduce and thereby explain mental phenomena, and I believe we will not succeed in removing these illusions until we have fully exposed the reasons that give rise to them.

First, and perhaps most important, is a confusion about the notion of "information processing": Many people in cognitive science believe that the human brain, with its mind, does something called "information processing," and analogously the computer with its program does information processing; but fires and rainstorms, on the other hand, don't do information processing at all. Thus, though the computer can simulate the formal features of any process whatever, it stands in a special relation to the mind and brain because when the computer is properly programmed, ideally with the same program as the brain, the information processing is identical in the two cases, and this information processing is really the essence of the mental. But the trouble with this argument is that it rests on an ambiguity in the notion of "information." In the sense in which people "process information" when they reflect, say, on problems in arithmetic or when they read and answer questions about stories, the programmed computer does not do "information processing." Rather, what it does is manipulate formal symbols. The fact that the programmer and the interpreter of the computer output use the symbols to stand for objects in the world is totally beyond the scope of the computer. The computer, to repeat, has a syntax but no semantics. Thus, if you type into the computer "2 plus 2 equals?" it will type out "4." But it has no idea that "4" means 4 or that it means anything at all. And the point is not that it lacks some second-order information about the interpretation of its first-order symbols, but rather that its first-order symbols don't have any interpretations as far as the computer is concerned. All the computer has is more symbols. The introduction of the notion of "information processing" therefore produces a dilemma: Either we construe the notion of "information processing" in such a way that it implies intentionality as part of the process or we don't. If the former, then the programmed computer does not do information processing: it only manipulates formal symbols. If the latter, then, though the computer does information processing, it is only doing so in the sense in which adding machines, typewriters, stomachs, thermostats, rainstorms, and hurricanes do information processing; namely, they have a level of description at which we can describe them as taking information in at one end, transforming it, and producing information as output. But in this case it is up to outside observers to interpret the input and output as information in the ordinary sense. And no similarity is established between the computer and the brain in terms of any similarity of information processing.

Second, in much of AI there is a residual behaviorism or operationalism. Since appropriately programmed computers can have input-output patterns similar to those of human beings, we are tempted to postulate mental states in the computer similar to human mental states. But once we see that it is both conceptually and empirically possible for a system to have human capacities in some realm without having any intentionality at all, we should be able to overcome this impulse. My desk adding machine has calculating capacities, but no intentionality, and in this paper I have tried to show that a system could have input and output capabilities that duplicated those of a native Chinese speaker and still not understand Chinese, regardless of how it was pro-

grammed. The Turing test is typical of the tradition in being unashamedly behavioristic and operationalistic, and I believe that if AI workers totally repudiated behaviorism and operationalism much of the confusion between simulation and duplication would be eliminated.

Third, this residual operationalism is joined to a residual form of dualism; indeed strong AI only makes sense given the dualistic assumption that, where the mind is concerned, the brain doesn't matter. In strong AI (and in functionalism, as well) what matters are programs, and programs are independent of their realization in machines; indeed, as far as AI is concerned, the same program could be realized by an electronic machine, a Cartesian mental substance, or a Hegelian world spirit. The single most surprising discovery that I have made in discussing these issues is that many AI workers are quite shocked by my idea that actual human mental phenomena might be dependent on actual physical-chemical properties of actual human brains. But if you think about it a minute you can see that I should not have been surprised; for unless you accept some form of dualism, the strong AI project hasn't got a chance. The project is to reproduce and explain the mental by designing programs, but unless the mind is not only conceptually but empirically independent of the brain you couldn't carry out the project, for the program is completely independent of any realization. Unless you believe that the mind is separable from the brain both conceptually and empirically—dualism in a strong form—you cannot hope to reproduce the mental by writing and running programs since programs must be independent of brains or any other particular forms of instantiation. If mental operations consist in computational operations on formal symbols, then it follows that they have no interesting connection with the brain; the only connection would be that the brain just happens to be one of the indefinitely many types of machines capable of instantiating the program. This form of dualism is not the traditional Cartesian variety that claims there are two sorts of *substances,* but it is Cartesian in the sense that it insists that what is specifically mental about the mind has no intrinsic connection with the actual properties of the brain. This underlying dualism is masked from us by the fact that AI literature contains frequent fulminations against "dualism"; what the authors seem to be un-aware of is that their position presupposes a strong version of dualism.

"Could a machine think?" My own view is that *only* a machine could think, and indeed only very special kinds of machines, namely brains and machines that had the same causal powers as brains. And that is the main reason strong AI has had little to tell us about thinking, since it has nothing to tell us about machines. By its own definition, it is about programs, and programs are not machines. Whatever else intentionality is, it is a biological phenomenon, and it is as likely to be as causally dependent on the specific biochemistry of its origins as lactation, photosynthesis, or any other biological phenomena. No one would suppose that we could produce milk and sugar by running a computer simulation of the formal sequences in lactation and photosynthesis, but where the mind is concerned many people are willing to believe in such a miracle because of a deep and abiding dualism: The mind they suppose is a matter of formal processes and is independent of quite specific material causes in the way that milk and sugar are not.

In defense of this dualism the hope is often expressed that the brain is a digital computer (early computers, by the way, were often called "electronic brains"). But that is no help. Of course the brain is a digital computer. Since everything is a digital computer, brains are too. The point is that the brain's causal capacity to produce intentionality cannot consist in its instantiating a computer program, since for any program you like it is possible for something to instantiate that program and still not have any mental states. Whatever it is that the brain does to produce intentionality, it cannot consist in instantiating a program since no program, by itself, is sufficient for intentionality.

Turing, Computers, and Philosophy:
Can There Be a Science of Mind?

JERRY FODOR

Jerry Fodor (1935–   ) teaches philosophy at Rutgers University and is the author of many articles and books.

When I was a boy in graduate school—hardly a moment ago as geologists reckon time—the philosophy of mind was said to have two main divisions: the mind/body problem and the problem of other minds. The project was to solve these problems by doing conceptual analysis. Nobody knew what conceptual analysis was, exactly; but it seemed clear that lots that had once been considered philosophy of mind (lots of Hume and Kant, for example) didn't qualify and was not, in fact, philosophy at all. Instead, it was a misguided sort of armchair psychology, which one read by flashlight beneath the covers.

Philosophical fashions change. It's hard to believe, these days, that there is a special problem about the knowledge of other minds (as opposed to the knowledge of other anything elses); and we're all materialists for much the reason that Churchill gave for being a democrat: the alternatives seem even worse. The new research project is therefore to reconcile our materialism to the psychological facts; to explain how something that is material through and through *could* have whatever properties minds actually *do* have. This seems as much a psychologist's project as a philosopher's, and might reasonably be described as the replacement of the philosophy of mind by "cognitive science." The consequent sense of temporal dislocation has been eerie. Many of the issues that are now live in the philosophy of mind (mental representation, nativism, and association-

From *The Times Literary Supplement*, Vol. 4657 (July 3, 1992).

ism, for three examples) are ones that Kant argued about with Hume. Whereas, topics that seemed very urgent indeed thirty years ago, now appear merely quaint. I can't remember when last I was offered a criterion.

To be a materialist is to take the view that thinking creatures are material through and through. This implies three major questions, to which a theory of mind—call it philosophy, psychology, cognitive science, or what you will—is required to find answers: (1). How could anything material be conscious? (2). How could anything material be *about* anything? (3). How could anything material be rational? These questions are now the agenda in the philosophy of mind.

I can tell you the situation in respect of the first question straight off. Nobody has the slightest idea how anything material could be conscious. Nobody even knows what it would be like to have the slightest idea about how anything material could be conscious. So much for the philosophy of consciousness.

The second question is in a slightly less parlous condition, but I won't discuss it here; it belongs more properly to semantics than to the philosophy of mind. (It's often hard to decide which of these one is working on. Not that it matters much.) Suffice it to call your attention to aboutness being a phenomenon that wants explaining, and to some implications of there being this phenomenon.

Some sorts of mental states (paradigmatically believing and desiring, rather than having an itch, or a ringing in your ears) are *about* things; so, for example, if I believe that the cat is on the mat, then what I believe is about where the cat is. Beliefs are so good at being about things that—as the philosopher Brentano famously pointed out—they can be about things that don't exist. I can believe that Father Christmas is a vegetarian, even though, of course, there isn't any Father Christmas or any matter of fact about whether he's a carnivore. Aboutness is puzzling for a materialist because it appears that—with only one kind of exception, to which we will presently return—aboutness is a thing which, in the whole material realm, only states of minds can have. Tables and chairs, for example, aren't about anything. Neither are bricks or babbling brooks, or the cat's being on the mat. But beliefs, desires, and the like do seem to be about things, and it would be nice

to know how this could be so, consonant with our methodological assumption that believers are material through and through.

Because they are about things, beliefs and desires are capable of what I'll call *semantic evaluation*. Roughly, beliefs are *true* or *false* depending, on whether what's believed actually obtains; desires are *satisfied* or *frustrated* depending on whether what's desired actually comes to pass. And so on, I suppose, for many other kinds of mental states: what semantic value they have depends on how the world turns out to be.

With that much about the second question as background, I turn now to question three: How could anything material be rational? Unlike the first question, about which nobody knows anything at all, and the second question, about which we have, at most, an occasional glimmer, somebody has actually had a deep and beautiful idea about how to answer question three. Much of the contemporary philosophy of mind, and almost all of cognitive science, is the elaboration of this deep and beautiful idea.

We commence, oddly enough, with a little Conan Doyle. Conan Doyle wasn't really much of a novelist; but he noticed a point about the mind that a lot of better writers—and a lot of philosophers and psychologists, for that matter—have failed to grasp. Here, by way of an instance, is Sherlock Holmes doing his thing at the end of "The Speckled Band."

> I instantly reconsidered my position when . . . it became clear to me that whatever danger threatened an occupant of the room couldn't come either from the window or the door. My attention was speedily drawn . . . to the ventilator, and to the bell-rope which hung down to the bed. The discovery that this was a dummy, and that the bed was clamped to the floor, instantly gave rise to the suspicion that the rope was there as a bridge for something passing through the hole, and coming to the bed. The idea of a snake instantly occurred to me, and when I coupled it with my knowledge that the Doctor was furnished with a supply of the creatures from India I felt that I was probably on the right track.

Here Watson says, "Astonishing, Holmes," or something to that effect.

Holmes offers his account as a bit of reconstructive psychology: it purports to be a capsule history of the sequence of mental events which brought him first to suspect, then to believe, that the Doctor did it with a snake. But it bears emphasis that Holmes's story isn't supposed to be just reconstructive psychology. It also serves to assemble premises for a plausible inference. That the bed was fixed to the floor, that the bell rope was in just the right place, that the doctor kept a tangle of snakes in his snuff box . . . all these are plausible reasons for Holmes to conclude that the Doctor did it. Holmes's train of thought is thus like an argument; and because it is, Holmes expects Watson to be convinced by the considerations which convinced Holmes when they occurred to him.

What connects the causal-history aspect of Holmes's story to its plausible-inference aspect is a general principle whose significance can hardly be overemphasized: the train of thoughts that causes one to believe that such and such provides, often enough, *reasonable grounds* for believing that such and such. Were this not the case—were there not this harmony between the semantic contents of thoughts and their causal powers—there wouldn't, after all, be much profit in thinking.

Often enough, what happens is that one starts by thinking that so-and-so, and thinking that so-and-so causes one to think that such-and-such, and if one's thought that so-and-so was true, then so too is one's thought that such-and-such. Thinking is a process where, to quote Holmes again, "one true inference . . . suggests others." This is part of what it is for thinking to be rational, since, I suppose, rational processes should reliably take one's thoughts from truths to truths.

I'm suggesting—or rather, I'm endorsing what I take to be Conan Doyle's very acute suggestion—that, whatever else a mind may be, it is some sort of rationality machine. So, now, given the methodological commitment to materialism, the question arises, how a machine could be rational? At a minimum, how could a purely physical system be so organized that if it starts in a state of believing something true, its causal processes will lead it to other true beliefs? Forty years or so ago, the great logician Alan Turing proposed an answer to this question. It is, I think, the most important idea about how the mind works that anybody has ever had. Sometimes I think that it

is the only important idea about how the mind works that anybody has ever had.

Turing noticed that it isn't strictly true that states of minds are the only semantically evaluable material things. The other kind of material thing that is semantically evaluable is *symbols*. So, suppose I write "the cat is on the mat." On the one hand, the thing I've written is a material object in good standing; it occupies a certain amount of physical space, exhibits a certain geometrical configuration, exerts a certain (very small) gravitational attraction upon the Moon, and so forth. But, on the other hand, what I've written is about something and is therefore semantically evaluable; it's true if and only if the cat is where it says it is. So, my inscription of "the cat is on the mat" has both materiality and aboutness; as does my thought that the cat is on the mat, assuming, as we've agreed to do, that thinking is through and through material.

Having noticed this parallelism between thoughts and symbols, Turing went on to have the following perfectly stunning idea. "I'll bet," Turing (more or less) said, "that one could build a *symbol manipulating machine* whose changes of state are driven by the material properties of the symbols on which they operate (for example, by their weight, or their shape, or their electrical conductivity). And I'll bet one could so arrange things that these state changes are rational in the sense that, given a true symbol to play with, the machine will reliably convert it into other symbols that are also true."

As it turns out, Turing was right about its being possible to build such machines, "computers" as they are now called. It's a fundamental idea of current theorizing that minds too are machines of this kind, and that it is because they are that mental processes are, by and large, reliably rational.

Here's an utterly trivial example to give a quick sense of how this works. Imagine a machine that consists of two components: a "tape" (on which things can be written) and a "read/write head," about which more in a moment. We can think of the tape as indefinitely extendable (except that when a machine dies, the Fates cut its tape), and as divided into squares on which one can write, as it might be, words of English. Then here's how this machine might model the mental process in which the thought that Dinah's in the kitchen causes the thought that someone's in the kitchen. (Notice that this mental process is rational in the sense we've been discussing; it takes one from truths to truths since, if it's true that Dinah's in the kitchen, then it's also true that someone is.)

To start, one writes "Dinah is in the kitchen" on the machine's tape. The read/write head is supplied with a list of English words and is so organized that when it finds a sentence of the form "...Dinah..." on the tape, it erases the word "Dinah" and writes the word "someone" in its place. So, this machine converts the sentence "Dinah is in the kitchen" into the sentence "Someone is in the kitchen," it converts the sentence "Bill loves Dinah and his cat" into the sentence "Bill loves someone and his cat"; and so forth. Notice that, in each of these cases (and in many others), if the sentence that the machine started with is true, so too is the sentence into which the machine converts the sentence that it started with. Notice too, however, that this machine is unreliable about what follows from "Bill doesn't love Dinah"; the details of such things can be quite hard to get right.

It turns out that Turing's sort of trick can be worked with inferences that are quite a lot more complicated than the ones about Dinah. The current speculation is that perhaps *all* of the rationality of mental processes can be explained on the assumption that the mind is a symbol-driven machine of the sort that Turing invented. That is, it may be that whenever a mind can proceed rationally from one true belief to another, this is because: first, it has access to symbols with which it represents what it believes; second, it is a kind of machine that converts symbols into one another in ways that are driven by physical properties of the symbols; and, third, these physically driven symbol conversions are so arranged that, on balance, they preserve semantical properties like truth. Rational mental processes are exhaustively mechanical operations on mental representations; so the speculation goes.

Whether this speculation is anywhere close to being true is, to put it mildly, an open question. Some day we'll know, I suppose. Meanwhile, I have the following grounds for optimism to report. The pursuit of Turing's idea has led us to notice striking and pervasive features of mental processes that had not previously been remarked upon. It is always en-

couraging when a theory leads to unexpected insights, since that gives reason to think that maybe the theory is true. We turn to a recent example of such a result.

Turing machines work because symbols have both semantical and syntactical properties. Since the syntactical properties of a symbol are among its physical properties, there can be a symbol-transforming machine whose state transitions are driven by the syntax of the symbols it operates on. And, as we've been seeing, it is possible to arrange such a machine so that these syntactically driven state transitions preserve semantical properties of the symbols. Fine so far; but now let's look a little closer at how the relation between the syntax and the semantics of the symbols is supposed to work.

Many symbols are syntactically complex objects whose constituents are themselves symbols. Consider the sentence "John loves Mary." It's a syntactically complex object, of which the constituents are the symbols "John," "loves," and "Mary" in that order. Correspondingly, the *semantic values* of symbols are typically determined by complex states of affairs whose constituents are objects and their relationships. So, for example, the symbol "John loves Mary" is made true by a complex state of affairs (viz. by John's loving Mary) whose constituents are John, Mary, and the relation of loving that holds between them. This all suggests a system in which parts of sentences refer to parts of the states of affairs that determine their semantic values. "John" refers to John, "Mary" refers to Mary, "loves" refers to the relation of loving, and "John loves Mary" is made true by the state of affairs which consists of John bearing the loving relation to Mary. Splendid.

Now Turing tells us, in effect, that thinking is a kind of symbol manipulation; in effect, he says that we think in some kind of language and that thought processes boil down to mechanical operations on the symbols of that language. Let's suppose that this language that we think in shares with English the property of being what semanticists call "compositional," namely, that it has complex symbols which correspond to complex states of affairs part by part, in the sort of way we have just been discussing. Then we get the following at no extra charge: if two states of affairs are made out of the same objects and relations, then if the language contains a complex symbol corresponding to one of them, then it will also contain a complex symbol corresponding to the other.

So, for example, English has the sentence "John loves Mary," which corresponds, constituent by constituent; to a complex state of affairs made up of John, loving and Mary. But, of course, there is another state of affairs that can be made out of these same parts: viz. the one that consists of Mary's loving John. Since these two complex states of affairs are made of the same parts, and since English constructs representations of complex states of affairs from representations of their parts, we're guaranteed that if English can represent John's loving Mary, it can also represent Mary's loving John. As, of course, it can; it has the sentence "John loves Mary" to do the one, and the sentence "Mary loves John" to do the other. "So what?" you might reasonably ask. Well, if Turing is right that thinking is really the manipulation of mental symbols, and if we assume that the syntax and semantics of mental symbols are related in the ways we've just been considering, then we can make the following striking prediction: *you won't find an organism that can think that John loves Mary but that can't think that Mary loves John.* More generally, you won't find an organism that can think that the individual *a* bears the relation *R* to the individual *b*, but can't think that the individual *b* bears the relation *R* to the individual *a*, (roughly) whatever values are substituted for "a," "b" and "R."

This is, as I say, a striking prediction; one of those things that seems self-evident until you think about it, and then seems really quite surprising. Because, after all, there's no obvious reason why God couldn't have made "punctate" minds or languages, ones that have the capacity to represent *a* as bearing *R* to *b*, but not vice versa. God could have made minds and languages that way, but it appears He never exercised the option. Turing's story about the mind being a symbol-manipulation machine shows how these facts about minds and languages are connected. You don't get punctate languages because languages are compositional: representations of complex states of affairs are built up, in a systematic way, from representations of their parts. You don't get punctate minds because minds are symbol manipulating mechanisms and the symbols they manipulate constitute a compositional language.

In short, Turing's picture predicts certain symmetries in the capacity for mental and linguistic representation, and it appears that this prediction is actually true; the predicted symmetries do obtain. So, maybe Turing's story is right, then, and the mind really is some sort of Turing machine. Compare, to their disadvantage, the account language that you get early in Wittgenstein's *Philosophical Investigations,* or the account of mind that has recently emerged from connectionist theorizing. Neither has any idea why languages and minds aren't punctate.

But again, so what? Why should we care if the mind is some sort of Turing machine? Well, there are those hard problems about consciousness, aboutness, and rationality that worry materialists. And it now appears that the third may actually be solvable. If so, then we have, for the first time, reason to believe that a scientific theory of the mind is possible; one that adheres to the same materialist assumptions that inform the biological and physical sciences.

But why is that important? Why should it even seem surprising? Isn't it, after all, among our modern convictions that there can be a scientific theory of anything if only the taxpayers are prepared to pay what it costs to get it? I want to end by saying something about this. I put my point as a cautionary tale.

Once upon a time, there was a man who wanted to have a theory about things that happen on Tuesdays. "I will have a theory about things that happen on Tuesdays," this man said, "and it will make me rich and famous." I should be clear that he wanted not just that, for each thing that happens on Tuesdays, there should be some theory of it or other; as it might be: a meteorological theory of Tuesday's weather, and a political theory of Tuesday's election, and a geological theory of Tuesday's earthquake. No, he had in mind something much more ambitious. He wanted a theory in which *happening on Tuesdays* explains things, in the way that *having mass* explains things in physics, and *being a mammal* explains things in biology, and *having valence two* explains things in chemistry. He wanted a theory of things that happen on Tuesdays qua things that happen on Tuesdays, as philosophers say; a theory of things that happen on Tuesdays "as such."

So, he started to construct this theory, and for a while he did fairly well. In particular, many aspects of people's behaviour seemed to depend, in an interesting way, on whether or not it was Tuesday. Thus, frequently on Tuesdays, but much less frequently on other days, people said things like "I suppose tomorrow will be Wednesday," or "It might be worse; it might still be Monday" or "Only three more days to the weekend." And so on.

But though the investigation started well, it soon petered out. Although there are some things that happen just about only on Tuesdays, and some other things that happen mostly on Tuesdays, still most things that happen on Tuesdays can just as well happen on Thursdays or Fridays and vice versa. There aren't, it turns out, any astronomical events, or geological events, or biological events, or meteorological events, or chemical events, or oceanographical events . . . , in short, there aren't even any events of most kinds that can be relied on to happen on Tuesdays and not on other days. There aren't even many kinds of behavioural events that can be relied on to do so, though, as we've seen, there are a few. The sum and substance is that, although happening on Tuesdays is a perfectly bona fide property that some events exhibit, it appears not to be a property that goes very deep into the fabric of things. Knowing whether it happened on Tuesday doesn't give you much leverage on explaining what happened, or why it happened when it did. You can't, in short, have a science of Tuesdays. Whether it's Tuesday isn't, one might say, one of the things that God cares much about.

The tale has a happy ending, however. The man who failed to get rich and famous by inventing a science of Tuesdays did get rich and famous by selling calendars. Because, although God doesn't care much whether it's Tuesday, we do. If it's Tuesday, maybe there's a new film at the Odeon. If it's Friday, maybe there's fish for dinner. Whether it's Tuesday or Friday is humanly important even if it isn't scientifically interesting. (Meanwhile, somebody else got rich and famous by calculating the mass of protons. It turns out that, although the mass of protons is humanly boring, it is just the sort of thing that God cares about. If you want to understand how He put the world together, the mass of protons is a thing you need to know.)

The moral is that what is scientifically interesting is often, in fact, very often, humanly boring, and vice versa. The properties of things we really care about are very often not the ones that you can have deep and revealing scientific theories about. This is, I suppose, why so many people hate science. Science is forever telling us that what is most interesting to us isn't what interests God. It is disquieting to be told this; one feels unloved.

It appears, in fact, that most of the things that it is possible to have serious scientific theories about are either very small (electrons and protons and quarks and the like) or very big (stars and galaxies and the like) or very abstract and idealized (frictionless planes and the like). Whereas, most of the things that we really care about turn out to be relatively middle-sized and bristling with particularity; . . . Darwin managed to make serious science out of some middle-sized things that we care about (and thereby to irritate a lot of his contemporaries; some folks can't be satisfied). But I suppose that nobody would bother to study, for example, the Moon or the weather, except that they are *our* Moon and *our* weather, and so we are curious about them. To expect a deep scientific theory of the Moon, as such, would be like expecting a deep scientific theory of New Jersey, as such. Both are historical accidents. No doubt God cares about the Moon and New Jersey, but not, as philosophers say, under those descriptions.

My point is that it's entirely possible that our brains (/minds; I'm still assuming materialism) are historical accidents too; that they're just an example of what you get when you spend several million years piling one adventitious adaptation on top of another. If so, then our minds are another of those middle-sized things that are interesting to us (they're our minds), but quite likely inappropriate objects for serious science. There is, in particular, no obvious reason to suppose that a science of psychology, as opposed to a natural history of psychology, is possible. And, indeed, if you look at most of the attempts to make science out of the sorts of mental properties that we humanly care about (like the psychology of intelligence, or the psychology of creativity, or the psychology of mental pathology, or the psychology of affect, or the psychology of individual differences, or developmental psychology, to cite several discouraging examples), what we seem to have really is a sort of natural history. It's all humanly interesting, and some of it may even be true. But it doesn't seem to go very deep. It doesn't, by and large, suggest that you can make serious science out of the mental properties of brains. Perhaps (as, indeed, many philosophers suppose) you can only make serious science out of their neurological properties; or out of their quantum mechanical properties.

The only exception I've heard of is Turing's proposal for, in effect, making serious science out of notions like rationality and truth. Here are some properties of minds that really are humanly interesting—we want our beliefs to be true and our thoughts to be coherent—and Turing has given us some reason to suppose that these properties provide a scientific domain. It may be that, in this respect, what we care about the mind, and what God cared about when He put the mind together, are close to being the same. The way most other things have gone, that would be a pleasant surprise and a real, if modest, consolation.

Consciousness, Self, and Reality:
Who Are We?

DIALOG WITH DANIEL C. DENNETT

DANIEL KOLAK: Wittgenstein was your hero when you were an undergraduate philosophy student. Why? What did he make you realize that helped propel your own lifelong philosophical investigations?

DANIEL DENNETT: Over the years I have come to realize that many of those to whom Wittgenstein speaks find it hard to believe he means it when he insists on the "behaviorism" that many find so counterintuitive.

DK: Is that why so much of philosophy that used to be done solely by traditional analytic methods, is done today with input from cognitive science, neurology, linguistics, computer science, as is reflected in your own work?

DD: Well, I'll speak for myself, since no doubt all manner of motives and attitudes have led to the scientific turn in philosophy of mind and related fields. In my case, it just struck me as obvious that traditional analytic methods would at best be extremely unlikely to produce anything but a clarification of the ambient lay assumptions and concepts. You can't figure out much about horses by studying the ordinary uses of the word *horse*. Since I was convinced from the outset that the impasse in philosophy of mind must be due to the complacent and tacit assumption of "obvious" or "intuitive facts" that just weren't so, I figured I'd need all the help I could get finding some leverage in other factually enriched inquiries. And sure enough, the pioneering scientific theorists about minds[1] were up to their ears in clearly philosophical inquiries, interestingly shifted in logical space from the work of the philosophers. They were just as vulnerable to the lay presumptions and confusions as the philosophers, but they had something more to work with. One could begin to see how a materialistic theory of the mind was indeed possible, and it would be full of surprises.

DK: That brings up the other side of the coin. For aren't there also empirical dogmas that, as the pendulum swings, are held by the more scientifically inclined philosophers today? I'm talking about various philosophies that might be categorized under the heading "realism." For instance, I came to philosophy from physics. Most philosophers, I found, who called themselves "materialists" or "physical realists" held a view of matter that no physicist I knew held. I was very disappointed to think that philosophy seemed to have latched on to a rather commonsense, popular view of reality! I think that's why many traditional philosophers today are perhaps suspicious of the idea that science has the right footbridge we can cross between the internal world of phenomena, sensations, sense data, representations —whatever you want to call them—and the external world of some sort of physical reality. And there's something very ironic in this. The only external world of physical reality I know to think about has many more dimensions than the three that the space in my experience seems to have, and is best described mathematically. Quantum physics is starting to look a lot like a scientific version of nineteenth-century idealism. This point of course isn't just limited to physics. The nice, clean-cut, properly functioning "biological categories" with which philosophers today make new philosophical turns may turn out to be less the scientist's than the philosopher's construction. For instance, one of my favorite quotes is from British neurologist Mark Solms: "The object representations which we know as the physical organs of the body—and that includes the nervous system . . . are no more *real in themselves* than the subjective phantasies that we uncover in psychoanalysis concerning the psychical reality of an internal world." What do you think?

DD: I've long been suspicious—but, I hope, openminded—about the various proclamations made by physicists (or by philosophical interpreters of the physicists) to the effect that down in the basement of fundamental physics, an ontological revolution was brewing. Doug Hofstadter and I discussed this in *The Mind's I.*[2] What was happening to the eagerly anticipated "reduction" of psychology and the social sciences to biology, which had already been "reduced" to physics via chemistry? Was the rug going to be pulled out from under it by the physicists' penchant for exotic forms of what looked like idealism? (I love David Moser's quip about quantum particles as "the dreams stuff is made of.") Was the reduction of mind to matter going to circle around and bite its tail? Many laypeople love this idea, apparently; they are more than tolerant of extremely shaky arguments for any such conclusion. I am no physicist, so my taste in physics may simply be the mirror image of theirs, but I must say that I am heartened by the not-infrequent debunking

that these ideas get from physicists as different as Murray Gell-Mann, Richard Feynmann, and Lee Smolin. I consider the current love-in for theories of consciousness that feature quantum effects, such as the musings about microtubules by Penrose and Hameroff,[3] to be only the latest manifestation of this yearning for release from Godless, mystery-killing mechanism. This is candidly expressed by the chemist Graham Cairns-Smith, a brilliant and sympathetic expositor of these ideas, in his book, *Evolving the Mind:*

I think the phenomena of consciousness will turn out to be identifiable with brain processes: but, please, not with exactly the same brain processes as underlie a computing system for which consciousness need not be invoked.[4]

In my review of his book in *Nature,* I noted that Cairns-Smith had the further fine candor to acknowledge and indeed eloquently express the well-known line of evolutionary reasoning that persuades most of us puzzle solvers that consciousness will prove to be like all the other dazzling phenomena of life (self-replication, self-transformation, self-repair, self-fueling, self-protection): explicable in terms of molecular and cellular machinery without having to invoke any amplification of subatomic weirdness. His own response to this objection he posed himself depends not at all on scientific insights, but rather on what I consider to be familiar philosophical confusions, close kin to those that bedevil Penrose.

I will add that I have an equally jaundiced view of the romantic themes recently expressed by some biologists, such as the quotation from Mark Solms you have just provided. I haven't seen anything in biology to persuade me of these extravagant claims, and in *Darwin's Dangerous Idea* I defend a quite standard view of biological categories (somewhat more nuanced than Millikan's deliberately oversimplified vision[5]). I recognize that there are serious thinkers out there who might change my mind about this but whose work I haven't yet digested fully: The physicist David Deutsch's *The Fabric of Reality* and the biologist Robert Rosen's *Life Itself* are the two extremely difficult books that come to mind immediately. It is books such as these that keep me hedging my bets a bit, rather than such philosophical books—brilliant in their own way—as David Chalmers' *The Conscious Mind* and Michael Lockwood's *Mind, Brain & the Quantum*.[6] My views about how science might adjust our best metaphysics are pretty much those of Willard Quine and Wilfred Sellars. We start with ordinary things, as Quine says, or the manifest image, as Sellars says, and when we develop the scientific image (to say it in Sellarsian), we have to work out how the two fit together. Quine acknowledges that it would be possible, for all he can tell, for science to "warp" us out of our ontology of ordinary things into some as yet unimagined ontology, but this would take some heavy lifting indeed. I agree. And for better or for worse, I think my attitude toward metaphysics is the ambient if largely unexamined attitude of most scientists, even physicists. I haven't seen a good philosophical or scientific reason for abandoning it.

DK: Your comments suggest a question that is really two questions, but it pulls many of these issues into a single focus. It has to do with the nature of the self that is *doing* or *involved in* the philosophical and scientific inquiry. I find myself situated at what seems to be a location at the surface of my eyes, or thereabouts (some describe it as just in front and others as just behind the eyes), looking at what I see as the world outside me all around. Let's call this location "the subject." Let's call the immediate items I see "objects." Likewise, just as there are the objects I see, there are the thoughts I have. These thoughts, which seem always to take the form of language as sentences, questions, and so forth, are sometimes about what I see as the external, surrounding world of my objects and, sometimes, about what I regard as the internal world of my thoughts. The "I" in all these cases is "the subject." Now, according to the received view of common sense— the view of the layperson on the street—the objects I, the subject, am looking at exist outside (in front of) me, in the physical world, and the thoughts with which I think about them exist inside (behind) me, in my mind. However, according to many philosophers—from empiri-

cists such as Locke, Berkeley, and Hume,[7] to rationalists such as Augustine, Descartes, and Leibniz as well as Kant—and according to most brain scientists today, especially those steeped in cognitive science, the object and the subject (the self) *both* exist inside the mind and/or brain.

The problem is that when I think of the "external world" as containing the objects in my experience and the corresponding "internal world" as containing my thoughts and the items in my language, *I construe myself, the subject, as existing at the interface between the internal and external world*—as if the whole question of my trying to understand myself and my world has only to do with my thinking or talking correctly about the items I see—as if true knowledge of reality were only a question of building a bridge between perception and the intellect! I conveniently forget that both perception and the intellect, according to the very theories that allow me even to think about my thinking and look at my looking, exist squarely within the mind within which I, the subject, myself exist. In this way the mind plays a sort of trick on itself, a philosophical bait and switch, in which the issue (as it is presented to the subject) becomes that of relating perception and the intellect, rather than of how to relate percept and concept not just to each other but to reality. The realization that the reality in question is not directly apparent (at least not clearly and distinctly) in and among the items of perception and thought,[8] is thus conveniently swept under the rug. But that's weird and strange! Why? Because the perceiving, thinking self does not exist outside the head, not ever! *I*, the subject, am at best a sort of projection of the brain or mind into its own virtual (or psychological) space: In dream and waking states alike I find myself apparently located on the top of the shoulders of a headless body, looking at the world; dreaming or awake, what I am looking at is a sort of virtual reality, my own world, while, at the same time, the body with shoulders on top of which I find myself is not my body (but my body image, the "phenomenal body"). The objects in my visual field are not inside the (nonexistent) head atop my shoulders where I, the subject, find myself situated, but rather the entire visual field itself is an event inside (or on the surface of) the brain, as is the subject, as am *I*.[9]

So *who,* then, is doing philosophy and science? I don't mean who it is, whether Einstein or Turing or Dennett. I mean, is it the conscious subject, the self? Because the idea that the self is in some privileged position outside the entire arena of inquiry[10] and is not itself in large part a construct subsisting within the virtual reality (the phenomenal world that experience is, simply won't do. Isn't the self, after all, but a *phenomenal self* situated inside its own phenomenal world of seeing, thinking, and theorizing?[11] And when one puts it this way, the whole issue of reductionism of any kind—reducing mind states to brain states or brain states to mind states, or reducing the whole of reality to a physical process, or a cosmic mind, and so on—seems to rest on a conceptual mistake (the sleight of hand, the bait and switch) but not of the purely intellectual type so easily dispensed with in the way Quine and Ryle do it.[12] If I (the subject) am just a cog in a wheel within the whole system within which I subsist, as I believe I am (I think you do too), don't the philosophical and scientific quests for knowledge about ourselves and the world in terms of *both* the manifest and scientific image involve an elaborate metaphysical self-deception that fundamentally and perhaps irrevocably taints the proceedings, in so far as they occur within what Kant called the transcendental illusion? (That, of course, is an unfortunate term, since what Kant really meant was not our mistaking the objects we see as things in themselves *in the mind,* that is, objects mistakenly perceived as transcendental categories of the mind, but objects mistakenly perceived as things in themselves beyond or *transcendent* to the mind, as existing in the noumenal world.)

DD: Whenever I confront these slippery bafflers about what/where/why *I* am, and what the relation is between that entity (my self) and the rest of the things I take seriously, I move resolutely outside, and take the third-person point of view about *somebody else.* In particular, I ask myself what I would have to do to *make* a self. Cog, for instance, the humanoid robot we're building at MIT, does not yet have a self, is not yet con-

scious, but I like to think about just what more we have to add before I will be confident that there's as real a self *there* as there is "in" me. No lightning bolts, no SHAZAM, no insertion of elan vital or wonder tissue or soul stuff would do the trick. These are all quite transparently incoherent ideas, because they presuppose an incoherent idea: a zombie (in the philosophers' sense). So, still resolutely staying "outside," I ask myself what Cog would have to be able to *do* (my "behaviorism" is front and center here, and its denial simply wallows in mystery) to win my acceptance as another conscious being. Cog would have to be indefinitely sensitive to its own reactions (to its own reactions to its own reactions . . .) and capable of recalling, reviewing, evaluating, but also concealing, trying to distort, lying about, refusing to discuss these internal states. And, like my internal states in "Where am I?" Cog's aren't really *inside* it—Cog's brain is a bank of computers that sits several feet away from it. But when Cog wonders if *that* ("over there") is its own brain, it will be in the position I was in when I stared at my own brain in the vat in my story. It's point of view will no more be located in those CPUs than mine is located in my thalamus. And now I can begin to imagine what it is like to be Cog, confident that there *is* like something to be Cog (at this point, Cog wil! have told me, after all, a good deal about it and will have also complained about not having the verbal dexterity or resources to exhaust what it knows.) As I say in a forthcoming piece about Dick Rorty, "The Case for Rorts" (in the *Rorty and His Critics* volume):

If Cog develops to the point where it can conduct what appear to be robust and well-controlled conversations in something like a natural language, it will certainly be in a position to rival its own monitors (and the theorists who interpret them) as a source of knowledge about what it is doing and feeling, and why. And if and when it reaches this stage of development, outside observers will have the best of reasons for welcoming it into the class of subjects, or first persons, for it will be an emitter of speech acts that can be interpreted as reliable reports on various "external" topics, and constitutively reliable reports on a particular range of topics closer to home: its own internal states. Not all of them, but only the "mental" ones—the ones which, by definition, it is incorrigible about because nobody else could be in a better position than it was to say.

I realize that there will still be a powerful, nay overwhelming, temptation in many people to say, "Yes, but you know, it *still* might be a zombie!" And all I can say at that point is that people should not just let this temptation buffet them around and overwhelm their reason; they should grit their teeth and ask themselves if they can find anything *else* to say in support of their view, since their temptation is just an unreliable intuition. Nothing more.

You note that what Kant called the "transcendental illusion" is an unfortunate term, and indeed it is—or was, since I think we are beginning to emerge into the light by which we can see that there are benign illusions, benign in every way that matters: user illusions. The phenomenon of, say, the Mac desktop user illusion is perfectly real and can be studied in all its interesting particulars without ever lapsing into an infinite regress of users, or homunculi or souls, or perspectives. Whenever such a phenomenon exists, there is a point of view. Some are pretty minimal and uninteresting; others are, well, Us, and what could be more interesting than us?

DK: Some of the most illuminating things you've just said are also the most tantalizingly puzzling. For instance, when you put yourself in the third-person point of view," you project yourself in your imagination into some objective spectator looking upon your world, as if from the outside. But that's very strange, isn't it? Sort of reminiscent of Nagel's view from *nowhere*.[13] There is no such point of view on *your* world, is there? In other words, you haven't, in taking on a third-person point of view, moved resolutely outside! You're still inside. That your world of your experience is the objective *public* world of physical reality—benign, "user illusion" thought it is (what a perfect term!)—is surely not the case. To be a view, it must be from somewhere. It must involve the subject. Subjects don't exist outside the head.

Thus, any *actual* view would have to involve another subject—call him Kolak. To be in any sense *real,* Kolak too would then have to be, like Dennett, a subject inside his own world, confronting the objects in his own phenomenal (visual) field among which would be a representation of Dan Dennett. And then what you have is not a third-person point of view on objects in your (Dennett's) world but a first-person point of view on objects in Kolak's world, something essentially subjective. Isn't that so? I mean, Dan Kolak's brain, shall we say, has an image of Dan Dennett, and it presents this image to its subject, Kolak. Now, who is Dennett? Who is Kolak? Is Dennett the subject, the self? Because you say, above, "*my* self." As if the self were something you, Dan Dennett, owned. In that case, Dennett is not a self but a brain (or mind) or what? On the other hand, if "Dennett" and "Kolak" refer to selves, there are two selves: one in Brain A (Dennett's brain) and one in Brain B (Kolak's brain), each one stuck in its own first-person point of view on its own world, subject to all the limitations that involves. (We now even have lots of fascinating knowledge about how the brain represents other selves inside itself using its own body images, its own self-concepts and so on—the sense in which I make *you* out of *me*—for when I see you in my phenomenal field what I see is in part constructed for me by my brain out of what is already in my brain.)

The fascinating case of our little Cog makes these "slippery bafflers" even more slippery and baffling. Cog's brain is outside Cog. *But where is Cog?* There's the robot body connected by cables to the robot brain (see photo) as represented inside my own phenomenal (visual) field inside my mind (wherever *that* is). If Cog is conscious, I think what that means is this: Within the brain (main computer), there are representations of a world inside which there is a subject to whom the objects of that phenomenal world are presented —just as in our own case, in your and my world. In other words, the question of consciousness is simply the question, Is there a subject there? And where is the subject? Well, if the *where* question is seeking an answer in terms of the sorts of perspectival (subjective) spaces that the layper-

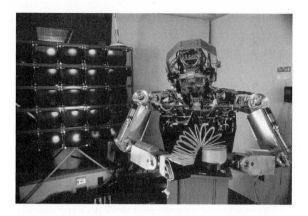

son calls reality, it seems the answer is that the subject is where it perceives (veridically) it is, so that if our little Cog is functioning properly and the Cog body is in the doorway, the Cog main computer will create a virtual reality inside itself of a doorway with a Cog body standing in the doorway. If the where question is seeking an answer in terms of the sorts of "third person," "objective world," or "public space," the answer of course will be the same, thanks to our language —another great user illusion! But, bottom line, isn't that the *real* question: Does Cog (the computer) have a fully functioning phenomenal field (that is, subjective world of objects) with a subject in it? If yes, then: Yes, Cog is conscious. If no, then: No, Cog is not conscious.

So let's now assume, for the sake of argument, that the answer is yes. What then? We would know that Cog is conscious, just as we are. And we'd be right back to the question of the nature of the knowledge-seeking enterprise, of philosophy and science, in relation to the self. For if Cog now wants to be a philosopher/scientist, won't this be impossible unless Cog is programmed for it? But how could Cog be programmed for it, given that to function properly Cog must confabulate, as must any properly functioning brain? (If a neuron's firing didn't at some point get read by another neuron's *not* as neuron's firing but as "information from outside the organism," the organism would not survive; in fact, it couldn't even function.) Cog's programming (to function properly) must, with the right toggles, prevent Cog-the-subject from taking apart

Cog-the-computer or reprogramming the computer (or even *understanding* it). Wouldn't Cog in fact have to be designed (either by natural proper function, supposing Cog evolved on its own, or by intelligent designers) with a whole slew of user illusions *that would make true philosophical inquiry, whether in a scientific or any other related domain, impossible?*

Which of course brings us right back to our old hero Ludwig Wittgenstein. For I can envision some future descendent of Cog writing a book very much like *Tractatus Logico-Philosophicus*[14] (written perhaps in the techo-trenches during the first World Computer War). And then he'd just go on building cars or whatever it was that he was programmed to do. Perhaps gardening in the Austrian alps. No?

DD: I don't see anything strange about the third-person point of view. Tom Nagel makes heavy weather out of there being no "view from nowhere" but I don't think that his reflections jeopardize our everyday scientific attitude about objectivity, because for objectivity we don't need a view from nowhere; we just need to be able to pool the results of lots of different views from somewhere—from one subject or another—and figure out what they have in common. If Martians live off uranium sandwiches and are blind, cosmic ray-sensing millipods that live their lives two orders of magnitude faster (or slower) than we do, we will simply have to take all that into account (and so will they) when we compare notes. The fact that I'm a left-handed, near-sighted, English-speaking optimist is something I can detect and discount. If I have further perspectival peculiarities that are beyond my ken, perhaps others can notice them and tell me about them in terms I can understand. In the worst possible case, we are all drifting around in inscrutably incommensurate dream worlds, I guess, but nobody has given me any good reason to believe it, so I don't take it seriously, for the time being at least.

Let's see what happens when we suppose that you, Kolak, and I, Dennett, are replaced by two robots, Coglak and Cognett, our surrogates and plenipotentiaries to the future. Coglak asks Cognett the questions you have just asked me. (So far so good?) Coglak asserts, truly, that he/it has an image of Cognett in its "brain," and Cognett says "ditto." Where is Coglak? Where he acts. Where is Cognett? Where he acts. One of the real philosophical benefits of thinking in terms of such robots is that we can see clearly that the weird innerness of subjectivity (which was the main point of my story, "Where Am I?"[15]) affects robots exactly as it affects us. Cog could confront its own computer brain, wonder whose it was, note the umbilical cord connecting its body to that brain, and have the same reflections I did (fictionally) when I stared at my own brain in the vat and asked myself why I was thinking "Here I am, looking at my own brain" and not "Here I am, suspended in a bubbling fluid, being stared at by my own eyes."

You surmise that if Cog is conscious (some day), then in Cog's brain, wherever that is, there will be "representations of a world inside which there is a subject to whom the objects of that phenomenal world are presented." I agree. Cog's representations will have to include self-representations, and especially representations of itself as being-appeared-to by things in the world Cog inhabits. Let's agree that without such representations Cog's capacity to guide its own higher-order behaviors (to pass the Turing test,[16] for instance, would be inexplicable. But if Cog can indeed use these representations, then Cog will be a self, a subject. That's what it is to be a subject.

You suppose that it would be impossible for Cog to (want to) be a philosopher/scientist "unless it is programmed for it"—but that assumes an old-fashioned view of how a robot's software has to work. Cog is "programmed for" exploring, learning, changing, developing, mucking around, getting upset, satisfying its various epistemic hungers, and so on. Just like us. There is a trivial sense in which you must have been "programmed" at birth for becoming a philosopher, because now you are one; apparently whatever "hard-wiring" you were born with had the potential, given the history of experience you have subsequently had, to turn you into a philosopher. With a slightly different history of input, you might have been a chemist or a choreogra-

pher, and in the trivial sense the same initial program, the same hard-wiring would have proven to be a program for turning you into a chemist or a choreographer.

All this is just science fiction for the time being. Cog is a newborn and will be for some time to come. You wouldn't expect to hold philosophical conversations with a one-year-old child, and it will be some time before Cog approaches such a toddler in sophistication. But in the meantime, enhancing and disciplining our imaginations by reflecting on the real details of Cog lead to substantially more surefooted thought experiments, in my opinion.

DK: Actually, the problem I meant to raise about whether Cog (or Coglak and Cognett, as well as Kolak and Dennett—we're all in the same *boot*) could function properly as a philosopher/scientist isn't that Cog must be programmed. You are absolutely right: This applies equally to artificial and natural minds/brains. The problem is that any such program or representation system, *to be conscious,* must rely on its own internal self-representation to function "as itself" within its own virtual world. There is a difference between Cog (or you or I) *using* representations versus Cog (or you or I) *being* a representation, and we seem to be equivocating between using "Cog" (or Coglak or Cognett) to refer *both* to the subject, or self—let's call it "s"—which is the self-representation within the system S (the computer, the mind/brain) and using "Cog" to refer to the system S. Thus, for instance, when you say that "Cog is where Cog acts," this to me evokes a Hofstadterian strange loop of double-meaning. Say that you are standing in the room with Cog, and I ask you where Cog is. You point to the robot at the end of the tether, not the computer, and say "there." To me this has just happened in my own representational system: I see myself in a room situated atop the shoulders of a body (image), I see you (including your head), Cog, the computer to which it is attached via cables, and so on. The reason I can understand you when you say "Cog is there" is that our language doubles up so as to allow us to coordinate by the meanings of our words between two very different representational systems operating within us. One is the perspectival system in which I appear to myself as located at a particular location in my world (atop the headless body-image), surrounded by all manner of objects, experiencing my world from the first-person point of view. This is what an ordinary layperson untrained in philosophy would simply call "reality" or "my waking experience." The second is the public system in which I know that I appear to you and others within *your* representational system, just as you do in mine, as an image replete with head, located in a space that is coordinated not with *me,* the subject, at the center of my perspectival world of object, but with *you,* the subject, at the center of your perspectival world in which I appear not as subject but object. Likewise for Cog; if Cog were watching us, there would, in Cog's world, be the subject (Cog's own self-representation) located at the center of Cog's perspectival world in which you and I both appear not as subjects but objects.

What I've just described is a complex and fascinating state of affairs, but there's nothing particularly mysterious (or mystical) about it the way many philosophers *before* the advent of cognitive science used to think, which led to the many well-known quagmires over a variety of idealisms, dualisms, and all sorts of other unnecessarisms. We can just agree that there are these two cognitive systems—the perspectival and the public—and that language allows us a convenient *ambiguity* space in which we can function with both. We can agree also that, as you well point out, we can "pool the results of lots of different views from somewhere—from one subject or another," to construct a good solid objective worldview through carefully weaned *invariance* principles, without having to lose ourselves in Nagel's nowhereness or be Humean Nowhere Men,[17] a variety of nothings. In other words, we can agree that we live in *commensurate dreamworlds.* Right? Would you agree to that phrase? Each subject's own world is "on line," as it were—the "reality network" made possible by language (that's oversimplifying, of course, but I think philosophically palatable). But here now is the problem, and so to my next question, which, once again, I can think of no better person to ask than you.

Who is Dan Dennett? The word *I* is, of course, ambiguous. We use it to refer both to our bodies and our minds, both to the system S (the brain/mind/body organism) *and* the subject, s, that is S's self-representation within the virtual reality of its own mind. Now, we agree that in the immediate reality of our experience (within the perspectival representational system) we each present ourselves to ourselves, as a subject, a perceiving thinking self with its own narrative history, what you have so aptly called "the center of narrative gravity" and the "Head of Mind."[18] The latter phrase comes out of your work on multiple personality disorder, which itself beautifully compounds the ambiguity problem: It's not just that we've got two different cognitive systems; it isn't even clear that within the perspectival system there is just *one* perspective—that ultimately the perspectival system *of my own mind* may in and of itself be a "public" system. I think it would be very illuminating if you could address this secondary issue as well, but I would like first to focus on the intersubjective cognitive duality as it exists between Cog, Dennett, and Kolak, not as it may exist within any one of them (as we probably both suspect is the case). For when you say to me, "I am Dan Dennett," you are establishing an identity between Dennett and S, and I understand you as saying as much. No problem. But Dan Dennett, I think—correct me if I'm wrong—is not known to himself as S but s. That is, I, Kolak, know myself only as I present myself to myself as a self in my own perspectival experience.[19] Likewise, I think, the same must be true for you. And for Cog. And this I think is the problem, and I think it is a very real problem, which Kant was the first to nail down—that is, we are known to ourselves not as things in themselves but as *phenomenal selves*—which I think is every bit as significant to us today as what Wittgenstein, Quine, and Sellers taught and which parallels exactly the situation you so rightly pointed out at the beginning: that everybody honors what these great philosophers have achieved but "they don't get it, and continue to embrace the doctrines these great philosophers worked so hard to demolish." What I think Kant demolished nobody *got* until Wittgenstein, and it produced the first revolution of twentieth-century philosophy, what has been called Wittgenstein's "transcendental lingualism."[20]

So when I ask you now, "Who is Dan Dennett?" I'm really expressing my own ignorance and puzzlement about who and what it is that is engaged in this activity we call philosophy, whether this is even possible *scientifically* (I am as yet merely an optimist about someday becoming an optimist), and how by your best understanding you think we as conscious subjects can get around the problem that we are each within ourselves not our whole selves but, literally, cogs in a wheel within a wheel. "Thinking is not something *I* do, but something that happens to me," said Wittgenstein, and I for one believe him. Everything I (think I) know about perception and cognition tells me that each and every aspect of my experience comes to me in varying degrees prefabricated and preinterpreted for *me,* the subject, by my language/mind/brain system within which I subsist (which also raises a spectrum of issues having to do with agency, unity of agency, and free will—more hobgoblins you seem to have swashbuckled your way out of.)[21] You seem to have situated yourself in a view from which one can at least *see* a way out of this quagmire, if not cross it, a view in which one doesn't have to remain silent about what (once) one could not talk about, nor throw in the philosophical towel in favor of common sense or naive realism. What is it? What is the view from Dennett?

DD: Commensurate dreamworlds. Well, Okay. It reminds me of MazeWar, the early video game we played on the timesharing computers at the AI lab at MIT many years ago.[22] Each agent appears (as a cartoon stick figure with a label) in the other agents' virtual worlds, and the worlds are coordinated into a single virtual world in which all act. That is pretty much the way it is in real reality, too. And now the artificial life people have begun to add software agents to these interactive, multiagent games, and the software agents that can learn are beginning to outshine the human agents—and are in any case hard to tell from the human agents. It is only a matter of time before we—you and I—

can begin to move, like Max Headroom, into the cybersphere.

What I am, first and foremost, is the system of information that guides my body. In "Where Am I?"[23] I claim that it makes no difference which "brain" subserves that information, the organic brain or the computer duplicate. I exist just as long as either instantiation exists. And when the systems of information diverge, I split in two. Not before then. As you note, Kant saw that we are known to ourselves as phenomenal selves, an observation that I put slightly differently in *Consciousness Explained,* as "first-person operationalism," with a footnote to Kant's doctrine that the "for me" and the "in itself" are the same thing in experience.[24]

We must be very careful how we treat Wittgenstein's assertion that "Thinking is not something I do, but something that happens to me." It is all too easy to use this as first in a line of stepping stones to Cartesian materialism, the bad idea that I am located at some central place in the system being fed by all the information-processing machinery. You put it vividly: "Each and every aspect of my experience comes to me in varying degrees prefabricated and preinterpreted for *me,* the subject, by my language/mind/brain system within which I subsist. . . ." But you *are* your language/mind/brain system—you're not something served by it. The "preinterpretation" you speak of is something you do in the course of doing the work of a conscious agent. Wittgenstein and Ryle are the theorists of the personal level, as I said in *Content and Consciousness,*[25] and both of them leave the subpersonal level untouched. It is important, when we begin to study the relations between these levels, not to try to locate the person, and the person's acts and experiences, at some inner boundary within the subpersonal system. I now call this the myth of double *transduction* (I wish I'd thought of that phrase when I was writing *Consciousness Explained!*), and back in *Elbow Room,* I spoke of the bugbear of the Incredible Disappearing Self.[26] When you hang on to the idea that you *are* the whole system, a system that has two ways of being considered, personal and subpersonal, you can escape the strong pull of this perennial favorite.

So what am I? I am a system of information that is embodied, and because of the richness of that embodiment and the capacity the system has for reflection (for higher-order reactions and representations of its lower-order acts and states), the two Dennetts you speak of tend to stay in close registration.[27] Chimpanzees are now famous for recognizing themselves in mirrors; we human beings have a related but even more sophisticated capacity for self-recognition: We can recognize ourselves in verbal descriptions of "other" people. I can encounter a text about one Dennett, Daniel C., philosopher, born 1942, . . . and consult it, cautiously and skeptically, to see if that is what I am. When I do this, I have to remind myself, as it says in the rear-view mirror of my car, that "objects in mirror are closer than they appear." That guy being written about or talked about is not so far away either. In fact, corrected for the inevitable distortions, he's right here, none other than yours truly.

Notes

1. Such as Alan Turing, Kenneth Craik, D. M. Mackay, Warren McCulloch, and the psychologists from Piaget and Skinner to Freud. See the articles by Turing and Skinner in this book.
2. Using "Rediscovering the Mind" by Harold Morowitz. In *The Mind's I*, edited by Douglas Hofstadter and Daniel C. Dennett (New York: Basic Books, 1981).
3. See, for instance, Roger Penrose, *The Emperor's New Mind* (New York: Oxford University Press, 1989).
4. Graham Cairns-Smith, *Evolving the Mind* (Cambridge: Cambridge University Press, 1996), p. 249.
5. Ruth Millikan, *Language and Other Biological Categories* (Cambridge, MA: MIT Press, 1984).
6. David Chalmers, *The Conscious Mind* (Oxford University Press, 1996); Michael Lockwood, *Mind, Brain & the Quantum* (Cambridge: Blackwell, 1989).
7. See the earlier readings by Descartes, Locke, Berkeley, and Hume in "The Mind and the Body" subsection of this book.
8. Of course there are great radical empiricists such as James who argue to the contrary, but such views lead

exactly to the sort of mind-behind-the-quantum views of reality, which have been around long before quantum mechanics, as in the physics of Ernst Mach.
9. See Dennett's "Where Am I?" in Part 3 of this book.
10. That is the theoria, the uppermost bleachers from which the Greek nobility viewed the games.
11. "The world is my world," Wittgenstein in his *Tractatus* echoes Schopenhauer.
12. See, for instance, Gilbert Ryle's *The Concept of Mind* (New York: Barnes & Noble, 1949) and Willard Quine's, *World and Object* (Cambridge, MA: MIT Press, 1960).
13. See Nagel's "What Is It Like to Be a Bat?" in "The Mind and the Body" subsection of this book.
14. See *Wittgenstein's Tractatus*, translated by Daniel Kolak (Mountain View, CA: Mayfield, 1998).
15. In "The Self and Personal Identity" subsection of this book.
16. In the "Minds, Brains, and Machines" subsection of this book.
17. See Hume's reading in "The Self and Personal Identity" subsection of this book.
18. See Daniel Dennett, "Origins of Selves" and Nicholas Humphrey and Daniel Dennett, "Speaking for Ourselves: An Assessment of Multiple Personality Disorder" in *Self and Identity*, edited by Daniel Kolak and Raymond Martin (New York: Macmillan, 1991).
19. See Daniel Kolak, *In Search of Myself: Life, Death, and Personal Identity.* (Belmont, CA: Wadsworth, 1998).
20. See, for instance, Stenius, *Wittgenstein's Tractatus* (Oxford: Basil Blackwell, 1960), and Daniel Kolak, *Wittgenstein's Tractatus* (Mountain View, CA: Mayfield, 1998).
21. See Part 4, "Determinism, Free Will, and Responsibility."
22. I mention it in DDI, p. 486.
23. See p. ••• of this book.
24. See Daniel Dennett, *Consciousness Explained* (Boston: Little, Brown, 1991), p. 132.
25. Daniel Dennett, *Content and Consciousness* (London: Routledge and Kegan Paul, 1969), p. 95.
26. Daniel Dennett, *Elbow Room.* (Cambridge, MA: MIT Press/Bradford Books, 1985), p. 13.
27. In *The Mind's I*, Hofstadter and I used the fine essay, "Borges and I" (by Jorge Luis Borges, of course) to explore this territory.

Determinism, Free Will, and Responsibility

HARD DETERMINISM

Suppose someone orders you to march ten miles. You find yourself obeying. Then you get orders to question the orders. So you question them. Then you get orders to stop questioning and you stop. In that scenario it would seem clear that you have no free will because someone else is controlling you: the one giving the orders. Orders are verbal commands. But what about orders that come not as conscious verbal commands but, say, as urges? This might be a far more subtle way of being controlled than by verbal commands, because you could interpret the urges as being under your own control. You could call them *wants*. When you felt the urge to do X, you could say, "I want to do X," and thereby hide from yourself the fact that whatever is pulling your strings—whether some internal program to which you have no direct access or some external programmer—is hidden by your being under the control of *wants* instead of *orders*. In other words, the program or programmer sends the want—a nonverbal command—as a way of pulling your strings without your directly sensing it. In that case, what you want would not be up to you. You would not really be free. You would have at most only the illusion of freedom. Your doing what you want would merely mask the fact that your wants would be controlling you, not you them.

But aren't you exactly in this sort of situation? You don't *make* your wants, you just have them. They arrive into your consciousness, triggering various behaviors. For instance, if you are hungry, you may want to eat. You do not choose to want to eat but merely discover that you want to eat. But if you do not choose your wants and your wants determine your choices and your choices determine your actions, then, ultimately, your actions are not up to you. It would therefore seem that you do not perform them freely.

There is no simple way out of this problem. Suppose you both want and don't want to eat a cookie—you want to resist your desire to eat it. Which do you do? Well, which want is stronger? You will act—*must* act—according to your stronger want. So your behavior—whatever you wind up doing—will be just a product of one want's superseding another. Or, suppose you decide that you will go with the weaker want. Where did *that* impulse come from? Did you choose it or did it just happen, having interjected itself among your wants as another want fighting for control and supremacy of action? If *that* new want is strongest, then, it seems that's what you do—but, again, it seems *that* choice was not yours either!

The term *determinism* was first used by William Hamilton (1788–1856) in describing the system of the great English philosopher Thomas Hobbes (1588–1679) to distinguish it from the older, traditional doctrine known as fatalism. According to fatalism, all human activities are predetermined by God, and therefore none of our actions are free. According to determinism, all the facts of reality, inclusive of human history, are completely dependent upon and fully conditioned by their antecedent causes. So, for instance, according to the doctrine of psychological determinism, the self or conscious subject has no free will because all its thoughts and actions are dependent upon and conditioned by antecedent psychological and/or physical states.

In the first selection, Baron Holbach argues that the sort of freedom of the will we think we have is but an illusion. He claims that even when we think we are free to do what we choose, the complete causes of our choices are always determined prior to our consciously making those choices. Either it is our personality, or character, that makes us act in a certain way, or our motives arise as wants exactly in the way described above, so that our wants *seem* to be under our conscious control when in reality they are not. This sort of philosophical position, which holds that free will is incompatible with determinism, is called *hard determinism*.

SOFT DETERMINISM

Compatibilism is the view that freedom and determinism are not incompatible, and those who hold such a position are called soft determinists. Thus, in "Liberty and Necessity," David Hume argues that free will and complete causal determinism are fully compatible and tries to show in what ways people can sometimes act freely even in cases where their actions and motives are completely caused. Part of his argument is that the dispute over whether or not people have free will—"the question concerning liberty and necessity"— is merely a verbal dispute. Likewise, William James, in "The Dilemma of Determinism," argues that many of our choices could be completely determined or even completely *un*determined and yet our behavior could be as intelligible as it is now. He makes the additional pragmatic argument that believing in free will has better consequences for our lives than not believing in it and that therefore we should believe in it, regardless.

LIBERTARIANISM

A different sort of view entirely, yet one that is in some ways closely aligned with compatibilism, is that the actual world is *not* determined, as the compatibilist supposes, but *in*determined, yet such that freedom is nevertheless possible. So whereas some incompatibilists are determinists and others indeterminists, the libertarians try to make room for freedom of the will in a world where causal randomness rules. C. A. Campbell, for instance, in his piece "Has the Self 'Free Will'?" attacks compatibilism on grounds that it relies on a hopelessly hypothetical analysis of freedom in terms of the supposed ability to do otherwise than one actually did. According to his argument, from introspection we can in fact see that we can often exert a will to do otherwise than succumb to temptation and, furthermore, that in such situations of choice it is self-evidently clear that we are not being forced to act the way we do. There is, he claims, no psychological compulsion present forcing us to choose one way or the other. Our choice can nevertheless be perfectly rational because the choices we make are not themselves determined before we make them; it is *we* who, in the act of making our choice, determine them for ourselves.

Roderick Chisom, in "Freedom and the Self," tries to find a balance between there being enough determinism in our choice making that we can rightly be their cause and yet enough freedom within us for the internal mechanisms of our causes not to be completely determined by forces beyond our own conscious control. In this view, our choices are neither obedient to the laws of cause and effect, as physical things are, nor purely random, chance events. They are in a category all their own, making us unique among all things in the universe.

FREEDOM AND MORAL RESPONSIBILITY

Whatever may be the causes behind our actions, or lack thereof, clearly we do not all behave the same way. Furthermore, by the time we become adults we have formed personalities, or character traits, that seem to predispose us to behaving in certain predictable ways. If this is so, we might ask whether and to what degree we can be held responsible for choosing our personalities or characters. Is this something predetermined at birth, about which we can do nothing, or something we can alter in some limited ways, or something that is fully our own responsibility? Each one of these positions has been taken up by various philosophers.

Aristotle was one of the first philosophers to have provided a plausible account of how we might each have chosen our own personality and character. "Responsibility, Action, and Virtue" is taken from his *Nicomachean Ethics,* Aristotle's ground-breaking work on ethics named after Aristotle's son Nicomachus. It is widely regarded as one of the greatest works ever written on moral philosophy. In it, Aristotle extends his teleological view of the world (according to which each and every thing exists for some purpose toward which it tends by its own special and unique nature) to the meaning of life. The final end, or good, of human life is, according to Aristotle, the fulfillment of human nature. This he defines using his concept of essence as the unique defining characteristic of something that, for humanity, is the rational faculty of the soul. Rationality is the essence of human life because rationality is unique to humans. The highest good for human life therefore, in Aristotle's view, consists in the improvement and actualization of rationality and rational behavior extended to the virtues.

Like Plato, Aristotle defines a good human character in terms of moderation, justice, virtue, and courage, and he claims that knowledge of what is good can be attained through rational means. He too says that the good and virtuous person will be an essentially happy person. The key difference between their approach to ethics stems from Aristotle's rejection of Plato's theory of ideas, in which ideas are separately existing entities: Unlike Plato, Aristotle claims that absolute knowledge in the moral realm can never be attained. He describes human virtue in terms of various traits that help us to achieve happiness and live well. This cannot be achieved unless there is a rational harmony in the social sphere, within the larger human community. He thus claims that social institutions are a necessary ingredient to human happiness. Indeed, in his view moral individuals as such cannot exist independently of their political and social setting, which help to make us free. It is the society at large that enables individuals to develop virtues for the good and happy life. But Aristotle is careful to distinguish between moral virtues and intellectual virtues. Whereas intellectual virtues can be taught, moral virtues must be learned through living. In this way, ultimately, according to Aristotle we are each responsible for ourselves—for having become the characters we are. The great twentieth-century French philosopher, playwright, and novelist Jean-Paul Sartre would reach a similar conclusion in his highly influential philosophy of existentialism, although he starts out completely denying Aristotle's essentialism.

Sartre explains the meaning of existentialism using his famous dictum, "existence precedes essence." This formula is not true for most objects in the world; in the case of tables, chairs, and papercutters, "essence"—what they essentially are and what they are for—precedes their existence. The idea comes first, as a concept or notion in the mind, and then the object is created following the preconceived blueprint. Human existence has no blueprint, no designer, no creator. God does not exist, and so no antecedent idea of human nature exists; there is no given purpose to life, no essence that precedes human existence. Only after we emerge into the universe as existent entities do we ourselves define our own essence—arbitrarily, but through choice. Because there is no God, there can be no prefabricated meaning, and human beings are forlorn; we are each condemned to be free because we cannot ever do otherwise than choose who and what we are. Nothing is given except that nothing is given. We ourselves are fully and radically responsible for our lives. The problem, however, is that we do not allow ourselves to really see this because we fear freedom. We don't want to have to choose. We shield ourselves from the fact that it is we ourselves who make up meaning by pretending that we are what we are—that we have a fixed nature—when really it's all made up. But Sartre does not view this as something negative, because it makes human beings the true artists of themselves and their world. Going about looking for the meaning of life, Sartre might say, is like staring at a blank canvas looking for the greatest painting. It misses the point. The blankness is not horrible, and it is not the end of the world; rather, it is the beginning, for now there is room for something, an infinity of possibilities. What we choose to paint is arbitrary, but paintings are not arbitrary.

Sartre distinguishes two different categories of being: being-in-itself, fully complete and determinate, independent of everything else, without relation to anything, not even itself, versus being-for-itself, the fully indeterminate and open domain of human consciousness, characterized by freedom. He gives an account of human moral failings in terms of bad faith and sincerity, arguing that these are both tools of self-deception by which we blind ourselves to the fact that we have no fixed natures, and that is how we hide ourselves from our freedom and our freedom from our true, self-created selves.

Thomas Nagel in "Moral Luck" begins with a criticism of Kant's view that there is something completely in our control even in a chaotic world in which hardly anything is fixed or determined: our moral integrity. According to Kant, we might fail to achieve what we intend, but moral integrity lies in having a good will exercised in the act of intending to do our duty. And we are, Kant argued, in charge of our intentions. When our intentions are good, we deserve praise regardless of the outcome; if our intentions are bad, we deserve blame or punishment. Nagel disagrees. His arguments consist of two parts. First, suppose our intentions are completely in our control exactly the way Kant envisioned. The problem is that our moral integrity as defined by Kant is itself the result of something completely beyond our control, what Nagel calls "moral luck." For what ultimately causes us to have some intentions rather than others is itself a matter of luck, depending on circumstances that we ourselves have nothing to do with and should therefore neither be rewarded nor punished for: where and how we were born and raised, the circumstances of our education and welfare, genetic predispositions, and so on. All these are matters of luck.

Susan Wolf offers a different account according to which we can be responsible for our actions and their consequences because these are, much in the way Kant supposed, under the control of our will. But the will is not itself determined or fixed by causes beyond us, nor is it random or irrational. The will is itself under the control of one's own *deeper self*. Provided that we are also sane, such that we don't have hopelessly and unavoidably false beliefs about ourselves and the world, we can have responsibility regardless of whether or not we live in a deterministic world.

HARD DETERMINISM

The Illusion of Free Will

BARON HOLBACH

Paul Heinrich Dietrich (1723–1789), later Baron Holbach, was born to German parents but lived most of his life in France.

MOTIVES AND THE DETERMINATION OF THE WILL

In whatever manner man is considered, he is connected to universal nature, and submitted to the necessary and immutable laws that she imposes on all the beings she contains, according to their peculiar essences or to the respective properties with which, without consulting them, she endows each particular species. Man's life is a line that nature commands him to describe upon the surface of the earth, without his ever being able to swerve from it, even for an instant. He is born without his own consent; his organization does in nowise depend upon himself; his ideas come to him involuntarily; his habits are in the power of those who cause him to contract them; he is unceasingly modified by causes, whether visible or concealed, over which he has no control, which necessarily regulate his mode of existence, give the hue to his way of thinking, and determine his manner of acting. He is good or bad, happy or miserable, wise or foolish, reasonable or irrational, without his will being for anything in these various states. Nevertheless, in spite of the shackles by which he is bound, it is pretended he is a free agent, or that independent of the causes by which he is moved, he determines his own will, and regulates his own condition. . . .

The will, as we have elsewhere said, is a modification of the brain, by which it is disposed to action, or prepared to give play to the organs. This will is necessarily determined by the qualities, good or bad, agreeable or painful, of the object or the motive that acts upon his senses, or of which the idea remains with him, and is resuscitated by his memory. In consequence, he acts necessarily, his action is the result of the impulse he receives either from the motive, from the object, or from the idea which has modified his brain, or disposed his will. When he does not act according to this impulse, it is because there comes some new cause, some new motive, some new idea, which modifies his brain in a different manner, gives him a new impulse, determines his will in another way, by which the action of the former impulse is suspended: thus, the sight of an agreeable object, or its idea, determines his will to set him in action to procure it; but if a new object or a new idea more powerfully attracts him, it gives a new direction to his will, annihilates the effect of the former, and prevents the action by which it was to be procured. This is the mode in which reflection, experience, reason, necessarily arrests or suspends the action of man's will: without this he would of necessity have followed the anterior impulse which carried him towards a then desirable object. In all this he always acts according to necessary laws from which he has no means of emancipating himself.

If when tormented with violent thirst, he figures to himself an idea, or really perceives a fountain, whose limpid streams might cool his feverish want, is he sufficient master of himself to desire or not to desire the object competent to satisfy so lively a want?

From *System of Nature* by Baron Holbach (1770). Translation by H. D. Robinson.

It will no doubt be conceded, that it is impossible he should not be desirous to satisfy it; but it will be said—if at this moment it is announced to him that the water he so ardently desires is poisoned, he will, notwithstanding his vehement thirst, abstain from drinking it: and it has, therefore, been falsely concluded that he is a free agent. The fact, however, is, that the motive in either case is exactly the same: his own conservation. The same necessity that determined him to drink before he knew the water was deleterious upon this new discovery equally determined him not to drink; the desire of conserving himself either annihilates or suspends the former impulse; the second motive becomes stronger than the preceding, that is, the fear of death, or the desire of preserving himself, necessarily prevails over the painful sensation caused by his eagerness to drink: but, it will be said, if the thirst is very parching, an inconsiderate man without regarding the danger will risk swallowing the water. Nothing is gained by this remark: in this case, the anterior impulse only regains the ascendancy; he is persuaded that life may possibly be longer preserved, or that he shall derive a greater good by drinking the poisoned water than by enduring the torment, which, to his mind, threatens instant dissolution: thus the first becomes the strongest and necessarily urges him on to action. Nevertheless, in either case, whether he partakes of the water, or whether he does not, the two actions will be equally necessary; they will be the effect of that motive which finds itself most puissant; which consequently acts in the most coercive manner upon his will.

This example will serve to explain the whole phenomena of the human will. This will, or rather the brain, finds itself in the same situation as a bowl, which, although it has received an impulse that drives it forward in a straight line, is deranged in its course whenever a force superior to the first obliges it to change its direction. The man who drinks the poisoned water appears a madman; but the actions of fools are as necessary as those of the most prudent individuals. The motives that determine the voluptuary and the debauchee to risk their health, are as powerful, and their actions are as necessary, as those which decide the wise man to manage his. But, it will be insisted, the debauchee may be prevailed on to change his conduct: this does not imply that he is a free agent; but that motives may be found sufficiently powerful to annihilate the effect of those that previously acted upon him; then these new motives determine his will to the new mode of conduct he may adopt as necessarily as the former did to the old mode. . . .

The errors of philosophers on the free agency of man, have arisen from their regarding his will as the *primum mobile,* the original motive of his actions; for want of recurring back, they have not perceived the multiplied, the complicated causes which, independently of him, give motion to the will itself; or which dispose and modify his brain, whilst he himself is purely passive in the motion he receives. Is he the master of desiring or not desiring an object that appears desirable to him? Without doubt it will be answered, no: but he is the master of resisting his desire, if he reflects on the consequences. But, I ask, is he capable of reflecting on these consequences, when his soul is hurried along by a very lively passion, which entirely depends upon his natural organization, and the causes by which he is modified? Is it in his power to add to these consequences all the weight necessary to counterbalance his desire? Is he the master of preventing the qualities which render an object desirable from residing in it? I shall be told: he ought to have learned to resist his passions; to contract a habit of putting a curb on his desires. I agree to it without any difficulty. But in reply, I again ask, is his nature susceptible of this modification? Does his boiling blood, his unruly imagination, the igneous fluid that circulates in his veins, permit him to make, enable him to apply true experience in the moment when it is wanted? And even when his temperament has capacitated him, has his education, the examples set before him, the ideas with which he has been inspired in early life, been suitable to make him contract this habit of repressing his desires? Have not all these things rather contributed to induce him to seek with avidity, to make him actually desire those objects which you say he ought to resist? . . .

In short, the actions of man are never free; they are always the necessary consequence of his temperament, of the received ideas, and of the notions, either true or false, which he has formed to himself of happiness; of his opinions, strengthened by example, by education, and by daily experience. So many crimes are witnessed on the earth only because every thing conspires to render man vicious and criminal; the religion he has adopted, his government, his education, the examples set before him, irresistibly drive him on to evil: under these circumstances, morality preaches virtue to him in vain. In those societies where vice is esteemed, where crime is crowned, where venality is constantly recompensed, where the most dreadful disorders are punished only in those who are too weak to enjoy the privilege of committing them with impunity, the practice of virtue is considered nothing more than a painful sacrifice of happiness. Such societies chastise, in the lower orders, those excesses, which they respect in the higher ranks; and frequently have the injustice to condemn those in the penalty of death, whom public prejudices, maintained by constant example, have rendered criminal.

Man, then, is not a free agent in any one instant of his life; he is necessarily guided in each step by those advantages, whether real or fictitious, that he attaches to the objects by which his passions are roused: these passions themselves are necessary in a being who unceasingly tends towards his own happiness; their energy is necessary, since that depends on his temperament; his temperament is necessary, because it depends on the physical elements which enter into his composition; the modification of this temperament is necessary, as it is the infallible and inevitable consequence of the impulse he receives from the incessant action of moral and physical beings.

CHOICE DOES NOT PROVE FREEDOM

In spite of these proofs of the want of free agency in man, so clear to unprejudiced minds, it will, perhaps, be insisted upon with no small feeling of triumph, that if it be proposed to any one, to move or not to move his hand, an action in the number of those called indifferent, he evidently appears to be the master of choosing; from which it is concluded that evidence has been offered of free agency. The reply is, this example is perfectly simple; man in performing some action which he is resolved on doing, does not by any means prove his free agency: the very desire of displaying this quality, excited by the dispute, becomes a necessary motive, which decides his will either for the one or the other of these actions: What deludes him in this instance, or that which persuades him he is a free agent at this moment, is, that he does not discern the true motive which sets him in action, namely, the desire of convincing his opponent: if in the heat of the dispute he insists and asks, "Am I not the master of throwing myself out of the window?" I shall answer him, no; that whilst he preserves his reason there is no probability that the desire of proving his free agency, will become a motive sufficiently powerful to make him sacrifice his life to the attempt: if, notwithstanding this, to prove he is a free agent, he should actually precipitate himself from the window, it would not be a sufficient warranty to conclude he acted freely, but rather that it was the violence of his temperament which spurred him on to this folly. Madness is a state, that depends upon the heat of the blood, not upon the will. A fanatic or a hero, braves death as necessarily as a more phlegmatic man or coward flies from it.

There is, in point of fact, no difference between the man that is cast out of the window by another, and the man who throws himself out of it, except that the impulse in the first instance comes immediately from without whilst that which determines the fall in the second case, springs from within his own peculiar machine, having its more remote cause also exterior. When Mutius Scaevola held his hand in the fire, he was as much acting under the influence of necessity (caused by interior motives) that urged him to this strange action, as if his arm had been held by strong men: pride, despair, the desire of braving his enemy, a wish to astonish him, and anxiety to intimidate him, etc., were the visible chains that held his hand bound to the fire. The love of glory, enthusiasm for their country, in like manner caused Codrus and Decius to devote themselves for their fellow-citizens. The Indian Colanus and the philosopher Peregrinus were equally obliged to burn themselves, by desire of exciting the astonishment of the Grecian assembly.

It is said that free agency is the absence of those obstacles competent to oppose themselves to the actions of man, or to the exercise of his faculties: it is pretended that he is a free agent whenever, making use of these faculties, he produces the effect he has proposed to himself. In reply to this reasoning, it is sufficient to consider that it in nowise depends upon himself to place or remove the obstacles that either determine or resist him; the motive that causes his action is no more in his own power than the obstacle that impedes him, whether this obstacle or motive be within his own machine or exterior of his person: He is not master of the thought presented to his mind, which determines his will; this thought is excited by some cause independent of himself.

To be undeceived on the system of his free agency, man has simply to recur to the motive by which his will is determined; he will always find this motive is out of his own control. It is said: that in consequence of an idea to which the mind gives birth, man acts freely if he encounters no obstacle. But the question is, what gives birth to this idea in his brain? Was he the master either to prevent it from presenting itself, or from renewing itself in his brain? Does not this idea depend either upon objects that strike him exteriorly and in despite of himself, or upon causes, that without his knowledge, act within himself and modify his brain? Can he prevent his eyes, cast without design upon any object whatever, from giving him an idea of this object, and from moving his brain? He is not more master of the obstacles; they are the necessary effects of either interior or exterior causes, which always act according to their given properties. A man insults a coward; this necessarily irritates him against his insulter; but his will cannot vanquish the obstacle that cowardice places to the object of his desire, because his natural conformation, which does not depend upon himself, prevents his having courage. In this case, the coward is insulted in spite of himself; and against his will is obliged patiently to brook the insult he has received.

ABSENCE OF RESTRAINT IS NOT ABSENCE OF NECESSITY

The partisans of the system of free agency appear ever to have confounded constraint with necessity. Man believes he acts as a free agent, every time he does not see any thing that places obstacles to his actions; he does not perceive that the motive which causes him to will, is always necessary and independent of himself. A prisoner loaded with chains is compelled to remain in prison; but he is not a free agent in the desire to emancipate himself; his chains prevent him from acting, but they do not prevent him from willing; he would save himself if they would loose his fetters; but he would not save himself as a free agent; fear or the idea of punishment would be sufficient motives for his action.

Man may, therefore, cease to be restrained, without, for that reason, becoming a free agent: in whatever manner he acts, he will act necessarily, according to motives by which he shall be determined. He may be compared to a heavy body that finds itself arrested in its descent by any obstacle whatever: take away this obstacle, it will gravitate or continue to fall; but who shall say this dense body is free to fall or not? Is not its descent the necessary effect of its own specific gravity? The virtuous Socrates submitted to the laws of his country, although they were unjust; and though the doors of his jail were left open to him, he would not save himself; but in this he did not act as a free agent: the invisible chains of opinion, the secret love of decorum, the inward respect of the laws, even when they were iniquitous, the fear of tarnishing his glory, kept him in his prison; they were motives sufficiently powerful with this enthusiast for virtue, to induce him to await death with tranquility; it was not in his power to save himself, because he could find no potential motive to bring him to depart, even for an instant, from those principles to which his mind was accustomed.

Man, it is said, frequently acts against his inclination, from whence it is falsely concluded he is a free agent; but when he appears to act contrary to his inclination, he is always determined to it by some motive sufficiently efficacious to vanquish this inclination. A sick man, with a view to his cure, arrives at conquering his repugnance to the most disgusting remedies: the fear of pain, or the dread of death, then become necessary motives; consequently this sick man cannot be said to act freely.

When it is said, that man is not a free agent, it is not pretended to compare him to a body moved by a single impulse cause: He contains within himself causes inherent to his existence; he is moved by an interior organ, which has its own peculiar laws, and is itself necessarily determined in consequence of ideas formed from perception resulting from sensation which it receives from exterior objects. As the mechanism of these sensations, of these perceptions, and the manner they engrave ideas on the brain of man, are not known to him; because he is unable to unravel all these motions; because he cannot perceive the chain of operations in his soul, or the motive principle that acts within him, he supposes himself a free agent; which literally translated, signifies, that he moves himself by himself; that he determines himself without cause: when he rather ought to say, that he is ignorant how or why he acts in the manner he does. It is true the soul enjoys an activity peculiar to itself: but it is equally certain that this activity would never be displayed, if some motive or some cause did not put it in a condition to exercise itself: at least it will not be pretended that the soul is able either to love or to hate without being moved, without knowing the objects, without having some idea of their qualities. Gunpowder has unquestionably a particular activity, but this activity will never display itself, unless fire be applied to it; this, however, immediately sets it in motion.

THE COMPLEXITY OF HUMAN CONDUCT AND THE ILLUSION OF FREE AGENCY

It is the great complication of motion in man, it is the variety of his action, it is the multiplicity of causes that move him, whether simultaneously or in continual succession, that persuades him he is a free agent: if all his motions were simple, if the causes that move him did not confound themselves with each other, if they were distinct, if his machine were less complicated, he would perceive that all his actions were necessary, because he would be enabled to recur instantly to the cause that made him act. . . .

It is, then, for want of recurring to the causes that move him: for want of being able to analyze, from not being competent to decompose the complicated motion of his machine, that man believes himself a free agent: it is only upon his own ignorance that he founds the profound yet deceitful notion he has of his free agency: that he builds those opinions which he brings forward as a striking proof of his pretended freedom of action. If, for a short time, each man was willing to examine his own peculiar actions, search out their true motives to discover their concatenation, he would remain convinced that the sentiment he has of his natural free agency, is a chimera that must speedily be destroyed by experience.

Nevertheless it must be acknowledged that the multiplicity and diversity of the causes which continually act upon man, frequently without even his knowledge, render it impossible, or at least extremely difficult for him to recur to the true principles of his own peculiar actions, much less the actions of others: they frequently depend upon causes so fugitive, so remote from their effects, and which, superficially examined, appear to have so little analogy, so slender a relation with them, that it requires singular sagacity to bring them into light. This is what renders the study of the moral man a task of such difficulty; this is the reason why his heart is an abyss, of which it is frequently impossible for him to fathom the depth. . . .

If he understood the play of his organs, if he were able to recall to himself all the impulsions they have received, all the modifications they have undergone, all the effects they have produced, he would perceive that all his actions are submitted to that fatality, which regulates his own particular system, as it does the entire system of the universe: no one effect in him, any more than in nature, produces itself by chance; . . . All that passes in him; all that is done by him; as well as all that happens in nature, or that is attributed to her, is derived from necessary causes, which act according to necessary laws, and which produce necessary effects from which necessarily flow others.

Fatality, is the eternal, the immutable, the necessary order, established in nature; or the indispensable connexion of causes that act, with the effects they operate. Conforming to this order, heavy bodies fall; light bodies rise; that which is analogous in matter reciprocally attracts; that which is heterogeneous mutually repels; man congregates himself in society, modifies each his fellow; becomes either virtuous or wicked; either contributes to his mutual happiness, or reciprocates his misery; either loves his neighbour, or hates his companion necessarily, according to the manner in which the one acts upon the other. From whence it may be seen, that the same necessity which regulates the physical, also regulates the moral world, in which everything is in consequence submitted to fatality. Man, in running over, frequently without his own knowledge, often in spite of himself, the route which nature has marked out for him, resembles a swimmer who is obliged to follow the current that carries him along: he believes himself a free agent, because he sometimes consents, sometimes does not consent, to glide with the stream, which, notwithstanding, always hurries him forward; he believes himself the master of his condition, because he is obliged to use his arms under the fear of sinking.

SOFT DETERMINISM

Liberty and Necessity

DAVID HUME

The great British empiricist philosopher and skeptic David Hume (1711–1766) was born in Scotland.

. . . [W]hat is meant by liberty when applied to voluntary actions? We cannot surely mean that actions have so little connection with motives, inclinations, and circumstances that one does not follow with a certain degree of uniformity from the other, and that one affords no inference by which we can conclude the existence of the other. For these are plain and acknowledged matters of fact. By liberty, then, we can only mean *a power of acting or not acting according to the determinations of the will;* that is, if we choose to remain at rest, we may; if we choose to move, we also may. Now this hypothetical liberty is universally allowed to belong to everyone who is not a prisoner and in chains. Here then is no subject of dispute.

Whatever definition we may give of liberty, we should be careful to observe two requisite circumstances: *first,* that it be consistent with plain matter of fact; *secondly,* that it be consistent with itself. If we observe these circumstances and render our definition intelligible, I am persuaded that all mankind will be found of one opinion with regard to it.

It is universally allowed that nothing exists without a cause of its existence, and that chance, when strictly examined, is a mere negative word and means not any real power which has anywhere a being in nature. But it is pretended that some causes are necessary, some not necessary. Here then is the advantage of definitions. Let anyone *define* a cause without comprehending, as a part of the definition, a *necessary connection* with its effect, and let him show dis-

tinctly the origin of the idea expressed by the definition, and I shall readily give up the whole controversy. But if the foregoing explication of the matter be received, this must be absolutely impracticable. Had not objects a regular conjunction with each other, we should never have entertained any notion of cause and effect; and this regular conjunction produces that inference of the understanding which is the only connection that we can have any comprehension of. Whoever attempts a definition of cause exclusive of these circumstances will be obliged either to employ unintelligible terms or such as are synonymous to the term which he endeavors to define. And if the definition above mentioned be admitted, liberty, when opposed to necessity, not to constraint, is the same thing with chance, which is universally allowed to have no existence.

Part II

There is no method of reasoning more common, and yet none more blamable, than in philosophical disputes to endeavor the refutation of any hypothesis by a pretense of its dangerous consequences to religion and morality. When any opinion leads to absurdity, it is certainly false but it is not certain that an opinion is false because it is of dangerous consequence. Such topics, therefore, ought entirely to be forborne as serving nothing to the discovery of truth, but only to make the person of an antagonist odious. This I observe in general, without pretending to draw any advantage from it. I frankly submit to an examination of this kind, and shall venture to

From *An Inquiry Concerning Human Understanding.* First published in 1748.

affirm that the doctrines both of necessity and liberty, as above explained, are not only consistent with morality, but are absolutely essential to its support.

Necessity may be defined two ways, conformably to the two definitions of *cause* of which it makes an essential part. It consists either in the constant conjunction of like objects or in the inference of the understanding from one object to another. Now necessity, in both these senses (which, indeed, are at bottom the same), has universally, though tacitly, in the schools, in the pulpit, and in common life been allowed to belong to the will of man, and no one has ever pretended to deny that we can draw inferences concerning human actions, and that those inferences are founded on the experienced union of like actions, with like motives, inclinations, and circumstances. The only particular in which anyone can differ is that either perhaps he will refuse to give the name of necessity to this property of human actions—but as long as the meaning is understood I hope the word can do no harm—or that he will maintain it possible to discover something further in the operations of matter. But this, it must be acknowledged, can be of no consequence to morality or religion, whatever it may be to natural philosophy or metaphysics. We may here be mistaken in asserting that there is no idea of any other necessity or connection in the actions of the body, but surely we ascribe nothing to the actions of the mind but what everyone does and must readily allow of. We change no circumstance in the received orthodox system with regard to the will, but only in that with regard to material objects and causes. Nothing, therefore, can be more innocent at least than this doctrine.

All laws being founded on rewards and punishments, it is supposed, as a fundamental principle, that these motives have a regular and uniform influence on the mind and both produce the good and prevent the evil actions. We may give to this influence what name we please; but as it is usually conjoined with the action, it must be esteemed a *cause* and be looked upon as an instance of that necessity which we would here establish.

The only proper object of hatred or vengeance is a person or creature endowed with thought and consciousness; and when any criminal or injurious actions excite that passion, it is only by their relation to the person, or connection with him. Actions are, by their very nature, temporary and perishing; and where they proceed not from some *cause* in the character and disposition of the person who performed them, they can neither redound to his honor if good, nor infamy if evil. The actions themselves may be blamable; they may be contrary to all the rules of morality and religion; but the person is not answerable for them and, as they proceeded from nothing in him that is durable and constant and leave nothing of that nature behind them, it is impossible he can, upon their account, become the object of punishment or vengeance. According to the principle, therefore, which denies necessity and, consequently, causes, a man is as pure and untainted, after having committed the most horrid crime, as at the first moment of his birth, nor is his character anywise concerned in his actions, since they are not derived from it; and the wickedness of the one can never be used as a proof of the depravity of the other.

Men are not blamed for such actions as they perform ignorantly and casually, whatever may be the consequences. Why? But because the principles of these actions are only momentary and terminate in them alone. Men are less blamed for such actions as they perform hastily and unpremeditatedly than for such as proceed from deliberation. For what reason? But because a hasty temper, though a constant cause or principle in the mind, operates only by intervals and infects not the whole character. Again, repentance wipes off every crime if attended with a reformation of life and manners. How is this to be accounted for? But by asserting that actions render a person criminal merely as they are proofs of criminal principles in the mind; and when, by an alteration of these principles, they cease to be just proofs, they likewise cease to be criminal. But, except upon the doctrine of necessity, they never were just proofs, and consequently never were criminal.

It will be equally easy to prove, and from the same arguments, that *liberty,* according to that definition above mentioned, in which all men agree, is also essential to morality, and that no human actions, where it is wanting, are susceptible of any moral qualities or can be the objects of approbation or dislike. For as actions are objects of our moral sentiment so far only as they are indications of the internal character, passions, and affections, it is impossible that they can give rise either to praise or blame where they proceed not from these principles, but are derived altogether from external violence.

I pretend not to have obtained or removed all objections to this theory with regard to necessity and liberty. I can foresee other objections derived from topics which have not here been treated of. It may be said, for instance, that if voluntary actions be subjected to the same laws of necessity with the operations of matter, there is a continued chain of necessary causes, preordained and predetermined, reaching from the Original Cause of all to every single volition of every human creature. No contingency anywhere in the universe, no indifference, no liberty. While we act, we are at the same time acted upon. The ultimate Author of all our volitions is the Creator of the world, who first bestowed motion on this immense machine and placed all beings in that particular position whence every subsequent event, by an inevitable necessity, must result. Human actions, therefore, either can have no moral turpitude at all, as proceeding from so good a cause, or if they have any turpitude, they must involve our Creator in the same guilt, while he is acknowledged to be their ultimate cause and Author. For as a man who fired a mine is answerable for all the consequences, whether the train he employed be long or short, so, wherever a continued chain of necessary causes is fixed, that Being, either finite or infinite, who produces the first is likewise the author of all the rest and must both bear the blame and acquire the praise which belong to them. Our clear and unalterable ideas of morality establish this rule upon unquestionable reasons when we examine the consequences of any human action; and these reasons must still have greater force when applied to the volitions and intentions of a Being infinitely wise and powerful. Ignorance or impotence may be pleaded for so limited a creature as man, but those imperfections have no place in our Creator. He foresaw, he ordained, he intended all those actions of men which we so rashly pronounce criminal. And we must, therefore, conclude either that they are not criminal or that the Deity, not man, is accountable for them. But as either of these positions is absurd and impious, it follows that the doctrine from which they are deduced cannot possibly be true, as being liable to all the same objections. An absurd consequence, if necessary, proves the original doctrine to be absurd in the same manner as criminal actions render criminal the original cause if the connection between them be necessary and inevitable.

This objection consists of two parts, which we shall examine separately:

First, that if human actions can be traced up, by a necessary chain, to the Deity, they can never be criminal, on account of the infinite perfection of that Being from whom they are derived, and who can intend nothing but what is altogether good and laudable. Or, *secondly,* if they be criminal, we must retract the attribute of perfection which we ascribe to the Deity and must acknowledge him to be the ultimate author of guilt and moral turpitude in all his creatures.

The answer to the first objection seems obvious and convincing. There are many philosophers who, after an exact scrutiny of the phenomena of nature, conclude that the WHOLE, considered as one system, is, in every period of its existence, ordered with perfect benevolence; and that the utmost possible happiness will, in the end, result to all created beings without any mixture of positive or absolute ill and misery. Every physical ill, say they, makes an essential part of this benevolent system, and could not possibly be removed, by even the Deity himself, considered as a wise agent, without giving entrance to greater ill or excluding greater good which will result from it. From this theory some philosophers, and the ancient Stoics among the rest, derived a topic of consolation under all afflictions, while they taught their pupils that those ills under which they labored were in reality goods to the universe, and that to an enlarged view which could comprehend the whole system of nature every event became an object of joy and exultation. But though this topic be specious and sublime, it was soon found in practice weak and ineffectual. You would surely more irritate than appease a man lying under the racking pains of the gout by preaching up to him the rectitude of those general laws which produced the malignant humors in his body and led them through the proper canals to the sinews and nerves, where they now excite such acute torments. These enlarged views may, for a moment, please the imagination of a speculative man who is placed in ease and security, but neither can they dwell with constancy on his mind, even though undisturbed by the emotions of pain or passion, much less can they maintain their ground when attacked by such powerful antagonists. The affections take a narrower and more natural survey of their object and, by an economy more suitable to the infirmity of human minds, regard alone the beings around us, and are actuated by such events as appear good or ill to the private system.

The case is the same with *moral* as with *physical* ill. It cannot reasonably be supposed that those remote considerations which are found of so little efficacy with regard to the one will have a more powerful influence with regard to the other. The mind of man is so formed by nature that, upon the appearance of certain characters, dispositions, and actions, it immediately feels the sentiment of approbation or blame; nor are there any emotions more essential to its frame and constitution. The characters which engage our approbation are chiefly such as contribute to the peace and security of human society, as the characters which excite blame are chiefly such as tend to public detriment and disturbance; whence it may reasonably be presumed that the moral sentiments arise, either mediately or immediately, from a reflection on these opposite interests. What though philosophical meditations establish a different opinion or conjecture that everything is right with regard to the whole, and that the qualities which disturb society are, in the main, as beneficial, and are as suitable to the primary intention of nature, as those which more directly promote its happiness and welfare? Are such remote and uncertain speculations able to counterbalance the sentiments which arise from the natural and immediate view of the objects? A man who is robbed of a considerable sum, does he find his vexation for the loss anywise diminished by these sublime reflections? Why, then, should his moral resentment against the crime be supposed incompatible with them? Or why should not the acknowledgment of a real distinction between vice and virtue be reconcilable to all speculative systems of philosophy, as well as that of a real distinction between personal beauty and deformity? Both these distinctions are founded in the natural sentiments of the human mind; and these sentiments are not to be controlled or altered by any philosophical theory or speculation whatsoever.

The *second* objection admits not of so easy and satisfactory an answer, nor is it possible to explain distinctly how the Deity can be the immediate cause of all the actions of men without being the author of sin and moral turpitude. These are mysteries which mere natural and unassisted reason is very unfit to handle; and whatever system she embraces, she must find herself involved in inextricable difficulties, and even contradictions, at every step which she takes with regard to such subjects. To reconcile the indifference and contingency of human actions with prescience or to defend absolute decrees, and yet free the Deity from being the author of sin, has been found hitherto to exceed all the power of philosophy. Happy, if she be thence sensible of her temerity, when she pries into these sublime mysteries, and, leaving a scene so full of obscurities and perplexities, return with suitable modesty to her true and proper province, the examination of common life, where she will find difficulties enough to employ her inquiries without launching into so boundless an ocean of doubt, uncertainty, and contradiction.

The Dilemma of Determinism

WILLIAM JAMES

William James (1842–1910), brother of novelist Henry James, was born in New York City. He published many influential works of philosophy and psychology and was one of the founders of pragmatism.

A common opinion prevails that the juice has ages ago been pressed out of the free-will controversy, and that no new champion can do more than warm up stale arguments which every one has heard. This is a radical mistake. I know of no subject less worn out, or in which inventive genius has a better chance of breaking open new ground,—not, perhaps, of forcing a conclusion or of coercing assent, but of deepening our sense of what the issue between the two parties really is, of what the ideas of fate and of free-will imply. . . .

The arguments I am about to urge all proceed on two suppositions: first, when we make theories about the world and discuss them with one another, we do so in order to attain a conception of things which shall give us subjective satisfaction; and, second, if there be two conceptions, and the one seems to us, on the whole, more rational than the other, we are entitled to suppose that the more rational one is the truer of the two. I hope that you are all willing to make these suppositions with me; for I am afraid that if there be any of you here who are not, they will find little edification in the rest of what I have to say. I cannot stop to argue the point; but I myself believe that all the magnificent achievements of mathematical and physical science—our doctrines of evolution, of uniformity of law, and the rest—proceed from our indomitable desire to cast the world into a more rational shape in our minds than the shape into which it is thrown there by the crude order of our experience. The world has shown itself, to a great extent, plastic to this demand of ours for rationality. How much farther it will show itself plastic

no one can say. Our only means of finding out is to try; and I, for one, feel as free to try conceptions of moral as of mechanical or of logical rationality. If a certain formula for expressing the nature of the world violates my moral demand, I shall feel as free to throw it overboard, or at least to doubt it, as if it disappointed my demand for uniformity of sequence, for example; the one demand being, so far as I can see, quite as subjective and emotional as the other is. The principle of causality, for example—what is it but a postulate, an empty name covering simply a demand that the sequence of events shall some day manifest a deeper kind of belonging of one thing with another than the mere arbitrary juxtaposition which now phenomenally appears? It is as much an altar to an unknown god as the one that Saint Paul found at Athens. All our scientific and philosophic ideals are altars to unknown gods. Uniformity is as much so as is free will. If this be admitted, we can debate on even terms. But if any one pretends that while freedom and variety are, in the first instance, subjective demands, necessity and uniformity are something altogether different, I do not see how we can debate at all.

To begin, then, I must suppose you acquainted with the usual arguments on the subject. I cannot stop to take up the old proofs from causation, from statistics, from the certainty with which we can foretell one another's conduct, from the fixity of character, and all the rest. But there are two *words* which usually encumber these classical arguments, and which we must immediately dispose of if we are to make any progress. One is the eulogistic word *freedom*, and the other is the opprobrious word *chance*. The word "chance" I wish to keep, but I wish to get rid of the word "freedom." Its eulogistic associations have so far overshadowed all the rest of its meaning that both parties claim the sole right to use it, and

From "The Dilemma of Determinism," an address to the Harvard Divinity students published in the *Unitarian Review* (1884). Also available in James, *Essays on Faith and Morals*, Longmans, Green and Co. (1949).

determinists today insist that they alone are freedom's champions. Old-fashioned determinism was what we may call *hard* determinism. It did not shrink from such words as fatality, bondage of the will, necessitation, and the like. Nowadays, we have a *soft* determinism which abhors harsh words, and, repudiating fatality, necessity, and even predetermination, says that its real name is freedom; for freedom is only necessity understood, and bondage to the highest is identical with true freedom. . . .

Now, all this is a quagmire of evasion under which the real issue of fact has been entirely smothered. . . . But there *is* a problem, an issue of fact and not of words, an issue of the most momentous importance, which is often decided without discussion in one sentence,—nay, in one clause of a sentence,—by those very writers who spin out whole chapters in their efforts to show what "true" freedom is; and that is the question of determinism, about which we are to talk tonight.

Fortunately, no ambiguities hang about this word or about its opposite, indeterminism. Both designate an outward way in which things may happen, and their cold and mathematical sound has no sentimental associations that can bribe our partiality either way in advance. Now, evidence of an external kind to decide between determinism and indeterminism is strictly impossible to find. Let us look at the difference between them and see for ourselves. What does determinism profess?

It professes that those parts of the universe already laid down absolutely appoint and decree what the other parts shall be. The future has no ambiguous possibilities hidden in its womb: the part we call the present is compatible with only one totality. And no other future complement than the one fixed from eternity is impossible. The whole is in each and every part, and welds it with the rest into an absolute unity, an iron block, in which there can be no equivocation or shadow of turning.

> With earth's first clay they did the last man knead,
> And there of the last harvest sowed the seed.
> And the first morning of creation wrote
> What the last dawn of reckoning shall read.

Indeterminism, on the contrary, says that the parts have a certain amount of loose play on one another, so that the laying down of one of them does not necessarily determine what the others shall be. It admits that possibilities may be in excess of actualities, and that things not yet revealed to our knowledge may really in themselves be ambiguous. Of two alternative futures which we conceive, both may now be really possible; and the one becomes impossible only at the very moment when the other excludes it by becoming real itself. Indeterminism thus denies the world to be one unbending unit of fact. It says there is a certain ultimate pluralism in it; and, so saying, it corroborates our ordinary unsophisticated view of things. To that view, actualities seem to float in a wider sea of possibilities from out of which they are chosen; and, *somewhere*, indeterminism says, such possibilities exist, and form a part of truth.

Determinism, on the contrary, says they exist *nowhere*, and that necessity on the one hand and impossibility on the other are the sole categories of the real. Possibilities that fail to get realized are, for determinism, pure illusions: they never were possibilities at all. There is nothing inchoate, it says, about this universe of ours, all that was or is or shall be actual in it having been from eternity virtually there. The cloud of alternatives our minds escort this mass of actuality withal is a cloud of sheer deceptions, to which "impossibilities" is the only name that rightfully belongs.

The issue, it will be seen, is a perfectly sharp one, which no eulogistic terminology can smear over or wipe out. The truth *must* lie with one side or the other, and its lying with one side makes the other false.

The question relates solely to the existence of possibilities, in the strict sense of the term, as things that may, but need not, be. Both sides admit that a volition, for instance, has occurred. The indeterminists say another volition might have occurred in its place: the determinists swear that nothing could possibly have occurred in its place. Now, can science be called on to tell us which of these two point-blank contradicters of each other is right? Science professes to draw no conclusions but such as are based on matters of fact, things that have actually happened; but how can any amount of assurance that something actually happened give us the least grain of information as to whether another thing might or might not have happened in its place? Only facts can be proved by other facts. With things that are possibilities and not facts, facts have no concern. If we have no other evidence than the evidence of existing facts, the possibility-question must remain a mystery never to be cleared up.

And the truth is that facts practically have hardly anything to do with making us either determinists or indeterminists. Sure enough, we make a flourish of quoting facts this way or that; and if we are determinists, we talk about the infallibility with which we can predict one another's conduct; while if we are indeterminists, we lay great stress on the fact that it is just because we cannot foretell one another's conduct, either in war or statecraft or in any of the great and small intrigues and businesses of men, that life is so intensely anxious and hazardous a game. But who does not see the wretched insufficiency of this so-called objective testimony on both sides? What fills up the gaps in our minds is something not objective, not external. What divides us into possibility men and anti-possibility men is different faiths or postulates,—postulates of rationality. To this man the world seems more rational with possibilities in it,—to that man more rational with possibilities excluded; and talk as we will about having to yield to evidence, what makes us monists or pluralists, determinists or indeterminists, is at bottom always some sentiment like this.

The stronghold of the deterministic sentiment is the antipathy to the idea of chance. As soon as we begin to talk indeterminism to our friends, we find a number of them shaking their heads. This notion of alternative possibility, they say, this admission that any one of several things may come to pass, is, after all, only a roundabout name for chance; and chance is something the notion of which no sane mind can for an instant tolerate in the world. What is it, they ask, but barefaced crazy unreason, the negation of intelligibility and law? And if the slightest particle of it exist anywhere, what is to prevent the whole fabric from falling together, the stars from going out, and chaos from recommencing her topsy-turvy reign?

Remarks of this sort about chance will put an end to discussion as quickly as anything one can find. I have already told you that "chance" was a word I wished to keep and use. Let us then examine exactly what it means, and see whether it ought to be such a terrible bugbear to us. I fancy that squeezing the thistle boldly will rob it of its sting.

The sting of the word "chance" seems to lie in the assumption that it means something positive, and that if anything happens by chance, it must needs be something of an intrinsically irrational and preposterous sort. Now, chance means nothing of the kind. It is a purely negative and relative term, giving us no information about that of which it is predicated, except that it happens to be disconnected with something else,—not controlled, secured, or necessitated by other things in advance of its own actual presence. As this point is the most subtile one of the whole lecture, and at the same time the point on which all the rest hinges, I beg you to pay particular attention to it. What I say is that it tells us nothing about what a thing may be in itself to call it "chance." It may be a bad thing, it may be a good thing. It may be lucidity, transparency, fitness incarnate, matching the whole system of other things, when it has once befallen, in an unimaginably perfect way. All you mean by calling it "chance" is that this is not guaranteed, that it may also fall out otherwise. . . .

Nevertheless, many persons talk as if the minutest dose of disconnectedness of one part with another, the smallest modicum of independence, the faintest tremor of ambiguity about the future, for example, would ruin everything, and turn this goodly universe into a sort of insane sand-heap or nulliverse, no universe at all. Since future human volitions are as a matter of fact the only ambiguous things we are tempted to believe in, let us stop for a moment to make ourselves sure whether their independent and accidental character need be fraught with such direful consequences to the universe as these.

What is meant by saying that my choice of which way to walk home after the lecture is ambiguous and matter of chances as far as the present moment is concerned? It means that both Divinity Avenue and Oxford Street are called; but that only one, and that one *either* one, shall be chosen. Now, I ask you seriously to suppose that this ambiguity of my choice is real; and then to make the impossible hypothesis that the choice is made twice over, and each time falls on a different street. In other words, imagine that I first walk through Divinity Avenue, and then imagine that the powers governing the universe annihilate ten minutes of time with all that it contained, and set me back at the door of this hall just as I was before the choice was made. Imagine then that, everything else being the same, I now make a different choice and traverse Oxford Street. You, as passive spectators, look on and see the two alternative universes,—one of them with me walking through Divinity Avenue in it, the other with the same me walking through Oxford Street. Now, if you are determinists you believe one of these universes to have been from eternity impossible: you believe it to have been impossible because of the intrinsic irrationality or accidentality somewhere involved in it. But looking outwardly at these universes, can you say which is the impossible and accidental one, and which the rational and necessary one? I doubt if the most ironclad determinist among you could have the slightest glimmer of light on this point. In other words, either universe *after the fact* and once there would, to our means of observation and understanding, appear just as rational as the other. There would be absolutely no criterion by which we might judge one necessary and the other matter of chance. Suppose now we relieve the gods of their hypothetical task and assume my choice, once made, to be made forever. I go through Divinity Avenue for good and all. If, as good determinists, you now begin to affirm, what all good determinists punctually do affirm, that in the nature of things I *couldn't* have gone through Oxford Street,—had I done so it would have been chance, irrationality, insanity, a horrid gap in nature,—I simply call your attention to this, that your affirmation is what the Germans call a *Machtspruch,* a mere conception fulminated as a dogma and based on no insight into details. Before my choice, either street seemed as natural to you as to me. Had I happened to take Oxford Street, Divinity Avenue would have figured in your philosophy as the gap in nature; and you would have so proclaimed it with the best deterministic conscience in the world.

But what a hollow outcry, then, is this against a chance which, if it were present to us, we could by no character whatever distinguish from a rational necessity! . . . The more one thinks of the matter, the more one wonders that so empty and gratuitous a hubbub as this outcry against chance should have found so great an echo in the hearts of men. It is a word which tells us absolutely nothing about what chances, or about the *modus operandi* of the chancing; and the use of it as a war-cry shows only a temper of intellectual absolutism, a demand that the world

shall be a solid block, subject to one control,—which temper, which demand, the world may not be bound to gratify at all. In every outwardly verifiable and practical respect, a world in which the alternatives that now actually distract *your* choice were decided by pure chance would be by *me* absolutely undistinguished from the world in which I now live. I am, therefore, entirely willing to call it, so far as your choices go, a world of chance for me. To *yourselves,* it is true, those very acts of choice, which to me are so blind, opaque, and external, are the opposites of this, for you are within them and effect them. To you they appear as decisions; and decisions, for him who makes them, are altogether peculiar psychic facts. Self-luminous and self-justifying at the living moment at which they occur, they appeal to no outside moment to put its stamp upon them or make them continuous with the rest of nature. Themselves it is rather who seem to make nature continuous; and in their strange and intense function of granting consent to one possibility and withholding it from another, to transform an equivocal and double feature into an inalterable and simple past.

But with the psychology of the matter we have no concern this evening. The quarrel which determinism has with chance fortunately has nothing to do with this or that psychological detail. It is a quarrel altogether metaphysical. Determinism denies the ambiguity of future volitions, because it affirms that nothing future can be ambiguous. But we have said enough to meet the issue. Indeterminate future volitions *do* mean chance. . . .

We have seen what determinism means: We have seen that indeterminism is rightly described as meaning chance; and we have seen that chance, the very name of which we are urged to shrink from as from a metaphysical pestilence, means only the negative fact that no part of the world, however big, can claim to control absolutely the destinies of the whole. But although, in discussing the word "chance," I may at moments have seemed to be arguing for its real existence, I have not meant to do so yet. We have not yet ascertained whether this be a world of chance or no; at most, we have agreed that it seems so. And I now repeat what I said at the outset, that, from any strict theoretical point of view, the question is insoluble. To deepen our theoretic sense of the *difference* between a world with chances in it and a deterministic world is the most I can hope to do; and this I may now at last begin upon, after all our tedious clearing of the way.

I wish first of all to show you just what the notion that this is a deterministic world implies. The implications I call your attention to are all bound up with the fact that it is a world in which we constantly have to make what I shall, with your permission, call judgments of regret. Hardly an hour passes in which we do not wish that something might be otherwise; and happy indeed are those of us whose hearts have never echoed the wish of Omar Khayyam—

> *That we might clasp, ere closed, the book of fate,*
> > *And make the writer on a fairer leaf*
> *Inscribe our names, or quite obliterate.*
> *Ah! Love, could you and I with fate conspire*
> *To mend this sorry scheme of things entire,*
> > *Would we not shatter it to bits, and then*
> *Remould it nearer to the heart's desire?*

Now, it is undeniable that most of these regrets are foolish, and quite on a par in point of philosophic value with the criticisms on the universe of that friend of our infancy, the hero of the fable The Atheist and the Acorn,—

> *Fool! had that bough a pumpkin bore,*
> *Thy whimsies would have worked no more, etc.*

Even from the point of view of our own ends, we should probably make a botch of remodelling the universe. How much more then from the point of view of ends we cannot see! Wise men therefore regret as little as they can. But still some regrets are pretty obstinate and hard to stifle,—regrets for acts of wanton cruelty or treachery, for example, whether performed by others or by ourselves. Hardly any one can remain *entirely* optimistic after reading the confessions of the murderer at Brockton the other day: how, to get rid of the wife whose continued existence bored him, he inveigled her into a desert spot, shot her four times, and then, as she lay on the ground and said to him, "You didn't do it on purpose, did you, dear?" replied, "No, I didn't do it on purpose," as he raised a rock and smashed her skull. Such an occurrence, with the mild sentence and self-satisfaction of the prisoner, is a field for a crop of regrets, which one need not take up in detail. We feel that, although a perfect mechanical fit to the rest of the universe, it

is a bad moral fit, and that something else would really have been better in its place.

But for the deterministic philosophy the murder, the sentence, and the prisoner's optimism were all necessary from eternity; and nothing else for a moment had a ghost of a chance of being put into their place. To admit such a chance, the determinists tell us, would be to make a suicide of reason; so we must steel our hearts against the thought. And here our plot thickens, for we see the first of those difficult implications of determinism and monism which it is my purpose to make you feel. If this Brockton murder was called for by the rest of the universe, if it had to come at its preappointed hour, and if nothing else would have been consistent with the sense of the whole, what are we to think of the universe? Are we stubbornly to stick to our judgment of regret, and say, though it *couldn't* be, yet it *would* have been a better universe with something different from this Brockton murder in it? That, of course, seems the natural and spontaneous thing for us to do; and yet it is nothing short of deliberately espousing a kind of pessimism. The judgment of regret calls the murder bad. Calling a thing bad means, if it means anything at all, that the thing ought not to be, that something else ought to be in its stead. Determinism, in denying that anything else can be in its stead, virtually defines the universe as a place in which what ought to be is impossible,—in other words, as an organism whose constitution is afflicted with an incurable taint, an irremediable flaw. The pessimism of a Schopenhauer says no more than this,—that the murder is a symptom; and that it is a vicious symptom because it belongs to a vicious whole, which can express its nature no otherwise than by bringing forth just such a symptom as that at this particular spot. Regret for the murder must transform itself, if we are determinists and wise, into a larger regret. It is absurd to regret the murder alone. Other things being what they are, *it* could not be different. What we should regret is that whole frame of things of which the murder is one member. I see no escape whatever from this pessimistic conclusion, if, being determinists, our judgment of regret is to be allowed to stand at all.

The only deterministic escape from pessimism is everywhere to abandon the judgment of regret. That this can be done, history shows to be not impossible.

The devil, *quod existentiam,* may be good. That is, although he be a *principle* of evil, yet the universe, with such a principle in it, may practically be a better universe than it could have been without. On every hand, in a small way, we find that a certain amount of evil is a condition by which a higher form of good is brought. There is nothing to prevent anybody from generalizing this view, and trusting that if we could but see things in the largest of all ways, even such matters as this Brockton murder would appear to be paid for by the uses that follow in their train. An optimism *quand même,* a systematic and infatuated optimism like that ridiculed by Voltaire in his Candide, is one of the possible ideal ways in which a man may train himself to look on life. Bereft of dogmatic hardness and lit up with the expression of a tender and pathetic hope, such an optimism has been the grace of some of the most religious characters that ever lived.

> Throb thine with Nature's throbbing breast,
> And all is clear from east to west.

Even cruelty and treachery may be among the absolutely blessed fruits of time and to quarrel with any of their details may be blasphemy. The only real blasphemy, in short, may be that pessimistic temper of the soul which lets it give way to such things as regrets, remorse, and grief.

Thus, our deterministic pessimism may become a deterministic optimism at the price of extinguishing our judgments of regret.

But does not this immediately bring us into a curious logical predicament? Our determinism leads us to call our judgments of regret wrong, because they are pessimistic in implying that what is impossible yet ought to be. But how then about the judgments of regret themselves? If they are wrong, other judgments, judgments of approval presumably, ought to be in their place. But as they are necessitated, nothing else *can* be in their place; and the universe is just what it was before,—namely, a place in which what ought to be appears impossible. We have got one foot out of the pessimistic bog, but the other one sinks all the deeper. We have rescued our actions from the bonds of evil, but our judgments are now held fast. When murders and treacheries cease to be sins, regrets are theoretic absurdities and errors. The theoretic and the active life thus play a kind of see-saw with each other on the ground of evil. The rise of either sends the other down. Murder and treachery cannot be good without regret being bad: regret cannot be good without treachery and murder being bad. Both, however, are supposed to have been foredoomed; so something must be fatally unreasonable, absurd, and wrong in the world. It must be a place of which either sin or error forms a necessary part. From this dilemma there seems at first sight no escape. . . .

The only consistent way of representing a pluralism and a world whose parts may affect one another through their conduct being either good or bad is the indeterministic way. What interest, zest, or excitement can there be in achieving the right way, unless we are enabled to feel that the wrong way is also a possible and a natural way,—nay, more, a menacing and an imminent way? And what sense can there be in condemning ourselves for taking the wrong way, unless we need have done nothing of the sort, unless the right way was open to us as well? I cannot understand the willingness to act, no matter how we feel, without the belief that acts are really good and bad. I cannot understand the belief that an act is bad, without regret at its happening. I cannot understand regret without the admission of real, genuine possibilities in the world. Only *then* is it other than a mockery to feel, after we have failed to do our best, that an irreparable opportunity is gone from the universe, the loss of which it must forever after mourn.

If you insist that this is all superstition, that possibility is in the eye of science and reason impossibility, and that if I act badly 'tis that the universe was foredoomed to suffer this defect, you fall right back into the dilemma, the labyrinth, of pessimism, from out of whose toils we have just wound our way.

Now, we are of course free to fall back, if we please. For my own part, though, whatever difficulties may beset the philosophy of objective right and wrong, and the indeterminism it seems to imply, determinism, with its alternative of pessimism or romanticism, contains difficulties expressly repudiated awhile ago the pretension to offer any arguments which could be coercive in a so-called scientific fashion in this matter. And I consequently find myself, at the end of this long talk, obliged to state my conclusions in an altogether personal way. This personal method of appeal seems to be among the very conditions of the problem; and the most any one can do is to confess as candidly as he can the grounds for the faith that is in him, and leave his example to work on others as it may.

Let me, then, without circumlocution say just this. The world is enigmatical enough in all conscience, whatever theory we may take up toward it. The indeterminism I defend, the free-will theory of popular sense based on the judgment of regret, represents the world as vulnerable, and liable to be injured by certain of its parts if they act wrong. And it represents their acting wrong as a matter of possibility or accident, neither inevitable nor yet to be infallibly warded off. In all this, it is a theory devoid either of transparency or of stability. It gives us a pluralistic, restless universe, in which no single point of view can ever take in the whole scene; and to a mind possessed of the love of unity at any cost, it will, no doubt, remain forever inacceptable. A friend with such a mind once told me that the thought of my universe made him sick, like the sight of the horrible motion of a mass of maggots in their carrion bed.

But while I freely admit that the pluralism and the restlessness are repugnant and irrational in a certain way, I find that every alternative to them is irrational in a deeper way. The indeterminism with its maggots, if you please to speak so about it, offends only the native absolutism of my intellect,—an absolutism which, after all, perhaps, deserves to be snubbed and kept in check. But the determinism with its necessary carrion, to continue the figure of speech, and with no possible maggots to eat the latter up, violates my sense of moral reality through and through. When, for example, I imagine such carrion as the Brockton murder, I cannot conceive it as an act by which the universe, as a whole, logically and necessarily expresses its nature without shrinking from complicity with such a whole. And I deliberately refuse to keep on terms of loyalty with the universe by saying blankly that the murder, since it does flow from the nature of the whole, is not carrion. There are *some* instinctive reactions which I, for one, will not tamper with. . . .

Make as great an uproar about chance as you please, I know that chance means pluralism and nothing more. If some of the members of the pluralism are bad, the philosophy of pluralism, whatever broad views it may deny me, permits me, at least, to turn to the other members with a clean breast of affection and an unsophisticated moral sense. And if I still wish to think of the world as a totality, it lets me feel that a world with a *chance* in it of being altogether good, even if the chance never come to pass, is better than a world with no such chance at all. That "chance" whose very notion I am exhorted and conjured to banish from my view of the future as the suicide of reason concerning it, that "chance" is—what? Just this,—the chance that in moral respects the future may be other and better than the past has been. This is the only chance we have any motive for supposing to exist. Shame, rather, on its repudiation and its denial! For its presence is the vital air which lets the world live, the salt which keeps it sweet.

LIBERTARIANISM

Has the Self 'Free Will'?

C. A. CAMPBELL

C. A. Campbell (1897–1974) taught philosophy at the University of Glasgow.

Now philosophers today are fairly well agreed that it is a postulate of the morally responsible act that the agent 'could have acted otherwise' in *some* sense of that phrase. But sharp differences of opinion have arisen over the way in which the phrase ought to be interpreted. There is a strong disposition to water down its apparent meaning by insisting that it is not (as a postulate of moral responsibility) to be understood as a straightforward categorical proposition, but rather as a disguised hypothetical proposition. All that we really require to be assured of, in order to justify our holding X morally responsible for an act, is, we are told, that X could have acted otherwise *if* he had *chosen* otherwise . . .; or perhaps that X could have acted otherwise *if* he had had a different character, or *if* he had been placed in different circumstances.

I think it is easy to understand, and even, in a measure, to sympathise with, the motives which induce philosophers to offer these counter-interpretations. It is not just the fact that 'X could have acted otherwise,' as a bald categorical statement, is incompatible with the universal sway of causal law—though this is, to some philosophers, a serious stone of stumbling. The more widespread objection is that it at least looks as though it were incompatible with that causal continuity of an agent's character with his conduct which is implied when we believe (surely with justice) that we can often tell the sort of thing a man will do from our knowledge of the sort of man he is.

From *On Selfhood and Godhood* (London: George Allen & Unwin, 1957).

We shall have to make our accounts with that particular difficulty later. At this stage I wish merely to show that neither of the hypothetical propositions suggested—and I think the same could be shown for *any* hypothetical alternative—is an acceptable substitute for the categorical proposition 'X could have acted otherwise' as the presupposition of moral responsibility.

Let us look first at the earlier suggestion—'X could have acted otherwise *if* he had chosen otherwise.' Now clearly there are a great many acts with regard to which we are entirely satisfied that the agent is thus situated. We are often perfectly sure that—for this is all it amounts to—if X had chosen otherwise, the circumstances presented no external obstacle to the translation of that choice into action. For example, we often have no doubt at all that X, who in point of fact told a lie, could have told the truth *if* he had so chosen. But does our confidence on this score allay all legitimate doubts about whether X is really blameworthy? Does it entail that X is free in the sense required for moral responsibility? Surely not. The obvious question immediately arises: 'But *could* X have *chosen* otherwise than he did?' It is doubt about the true answer to *that* question which leads most people to doubt the reality of moral responsibility. Yet on this crucial question the hypothetical proposition which is offered as a sufficient statement of the condition justifying the ascription of moral responsibility gives us no information whatsoever.

Indeed this hypothetical substitute for the categorical 'X could have acted otherwise' seems to me to lack all plausibility unless one contrives to forget why it is, after all, that we ever come to feel fundamental doubts about man's moral responsibility. Such doubts are born, surely, when one becomes aware of certain reputable world-views in religion or philosophy, or of certain reputable scientific beliefs, which in their several ways imply that man's actions are necessitated, and thus could not be otherwise than they in fact are. But clearly a doubt so based is not even touched by the recognition that a man could very often act otherwise *if* he so chose. That proposition is entirely compatible with the necessitarian theories which generate our doubt: indeed it is this very compatibility that has recommended it to some philosophers, who are reluctant to give up either moral responsibility or Determinism. The proposition which we *must* be able to affirm if moral praise or blame of X is to be justified is the categorical proposition that X could have acted otherwise because—not if—he could have chosen otherwise; or, since it is essentially the inner side of the act that matters, the proposition simply that X could have chosen otherwise.

For the second of the alternative formulae suggested we cannot spare more than a few moments. But its inability to meet the demands it is required to meet is almost transparent. 'X could have acted otherwise,' as a statement of a precondition of X's moral responsibility, really means (we are told) 'X could have acted otherwise *if* he were differently constituted, or *if* he had been placed in different circumstances.' It seems a sufficient reply to this to point out that the person whose moral responsibility is at issue is X; a specific individual, in a specific set of circumstances. It is totally irrelevant to X's moral responsibility that we should be able to say that some person differently constituted from X, or X in a different set of circumstances, could have done something different from what X did.

Let me, then, briefly sum up the answer at which we have arrived to our question about the kind of freedom required to justify moral responsibility. It is that a man can be said to exercise free will in a morally significant sense only in so far as his chosen act is one of which he is the sole cause or author, and only if—in the straightforward, categorical sense of the phrase—he 'could have chosen otherwise.'

I confess that this answer is in some ways a disconcerting one; disconcerting, because most of us,

however objective we are in the actual conduct of our thinking, would *like* to be able to believe that moral responsibility is real: whereas the freedom required for moral responsibility, on the analysis we have given, is certainly far more difficult to establish than the freedom required on the analyses we found ourselves obliged to reject. If, e.g. moral freedom entails only that I could have acted otherwise *if* I had chosen otherwise, there is no real 'problem' about it at all. I am 'free' in the normal case where there is no external obstacle to prevent my translating the alternative choice into action, and not free in other cases. Still less is there a problem if all that moral freedom entails is that I could have acted otherwise *if* I had been a differently constituted person, or been in different circumstances. Clearly I am *always* free in *this* sense of freedom. But, as I have argued, these so-called 'freedoms' fail to give us the preconditions of moral responsibility, and hence leave the freedom of the traditional free-will problem, the freedom that people are really concerned about, precisely where it was.

· · ·

That brings me to the second, and more constructive, part of this lecture. From now on I shall be considering whether it is reasonable to believe that man does in fact possess a free will of the kind specified in the first part of the lecture. If so, just how and where within the complex fabric of the volitional life are we to locate it?—for although free will must presumably belong (if anywhere) to the volitional side of human experience, it is pretty clear from the way in which we have been forced to define it that it does not pertain simply to volition as such; not even to all volitions that are commonly dignified with the name of 'choices.' It has been, I think, one of the more serious impediments to profitable discussion of the Free Will problem that Libertarians and Determinists alike have so often failed to appreciate the comparatively narrow area within which the free will that is necessary to 'save' morality is required to operate. It goes without saying that this failure has been gravely prejudicial to the case for Libertarianism. I attach a good deal of importance, therefore, to the problem of locating free will correctly within the volitional orbit. Its solution forestalls and annuls, I believe, some of the more tiresome clichés of Determinist criticism.

We saw earlier that Common Sense's practice of 'making allowances' in its moral judgments for the influence of heredity and environment indicates Common Sense's conviction, both that a just moral judgment must discount determinants of choice over which the agent has no control, and also (since it still accepts moral judgments as legitimate) that *something* of moral relevance survives which can be regarded as genuinely self-originated. We are now to try to discover what this 'something' is. And I think we may still usefully take Common Sense as our guide. Suppose one asks the ordinary intelligent citizen *why* he deems it proper to make allowances for X, whose heredity and/or environment are unfortunate. He will tend to reply, I think, in some such terms as these: that X has more and stronger temptations to deviate from what is right than Y or Z, who are normally circumstanced, so that he must put forth a *stronger moral effort* if he is to achieve the same level of external conduct. The intended implication seems to be that X is just as morally praiseworthy as Y or Z *if* he exerts an equivalent moral effort, even though he may not thereby achieve an equal success in conforming his will to the 'concrete' demands of duty. And this implies, again, Common Sense's belief that *in moral effort* we have something for which a man is responsible *without qualification,* something that is *not* affected by heredity and environment but depends *solely* upon the self itself.

Now in my opinion Common Sense has here, in principle, hit upon the one and only defensible answer. Here, and here alone, so far as I can see, in the act of deciding whether to put forth or withhold the moral effort required to resist temptation and rise to duty, is to be found an act which is free in the sense required for moral responsibility; an act of which the self is sole author, and of which it is true to say that 'it could be' (or, after the event, 'could have been') 'otherwise.' Such is the thesis which we shall now try to establish.

The species of argument appropriate to the establishment of a thesis of this sort should fall, I think, into two phases. First, there should be a consideration of the evidence of the moral agent's own inner experience. What *is* the act of moral decision, and what does it imply, from the standpoint of the actual participant? Since there is no way of knowing the act of moral decision—or for that matter any other form of activity—except by actual participation in it, the evidence of the subject, or agent, is on an issue of this kind of palmary importance. It can hardly, however, be taken as in itself conclusive. For even if that evidence should be overwhelmingly to the effect that moral decision does have the characteristics required by moral freedom, the question is bound to be raised—and in view of considerations from other quarters pointing in a contrary direction is *rightly* raised—Can we *trust* the evidence of inner experience? That brings us to what will be the second phase of the argument. We shall have to go on to show, if we are to make good our case, that the extraneous considerations so often supposed to be fatal to the belief in moral freedom are in fact innocuous to it.

In the light of . . . the self's experience of moral decision as a *creative* activity, we may perhaps be absolved from developing the first phase of the argument at any great length. The appeal is throughout to one's own experience in the actual taking of the moral decision in the situation of moral temptation. 'Is it possible,' we must ask, 'for anyone so circumstanced to *dis*believe that he could be deciding otherwise?' The answer is surely not in doubt. When we decide to exert moral effort to resist a temptation, we feel quite certain that we *could* withhold the effort; just as, if we decide to withhold the effort and yield to our desires, we feel quite certain that we *could* exert it—otherwise we should not blame ourselves afterwards for having succumbed. It may be, indeed, that this conviction is mere self-delusion. But that is not at the moment our concern. It is enough at present to establish that the act of deciding to exert or to withhold moral effort, as we know it from the inside in actual moral living, belongs to the category of acts which 'could have been otherwise.'

Mutatis mutandis, the same reply is forthcoming if we ask, 'Is it possible for the moral agent in the taking of his decision to *dis*believe that he is the *sole* author of that decision?' Clearly he cannot disbelieve that it is *he* who takes the decision. That, however, is not in itself sufficient to enable him, on reflection, to regard himself as *solely* responsible for the act. For his 'character' as so far formed might conceivably be a factor in determining it, and no one can suppose that the constitution of his 'character' is uninfluenced by circumstances of heredity and environment with which *he* has nothing to do. But as we pointed out in the last lecture, the very essence of the moral decision as it is experienced is that it is a decision whether or not to *combat* our strongest desire, and our strongest desire *is* the expression in the situation of our character as so far formed. Now clearly our character cannot be a factor in determining the decision whether or not to *oppose* our character. I think we are entitled to say, therefore, that the act of moral decision is one in which the self is for itself not merely 'author' but 'sole author.'

We may pass on, then, to the second phase of our constructive argument; and this will demand more elaborate treatment. Even if a moral agent *qua* making a moral decision in the situation of "temptation" cannot help believing that he has free will in the sense at issue—a moral freedom between real alternatives, between genuinely open possibilities—are there, nevertheless, objections to a freedom of this kind so cogent that we are bound to distrust the evidence of 'inner experience'?

I begin by drawing attention to a simple point whose significance tends, I think, to be underestimated. If the phenomenological analysis we have offered is substantially correct, no one while functioning as a moral agent can help believing that he enjoys free will. Theoretically he may be completely convinced by Determinist arguments, but when actually confronted with a personal situation of conflict between duty and desire he is quite certain that it lies with him here and now whether or not he will rise to duty. It follows that if Determinists could produce convincing theoretical arguments against a free will of this kind, the awkward predicament would ensure that man has to deny as a theoretical being what he has to assert as a practical being. Now I think the Determinist ought to be a good deal more worried about this than he usually is. He seems to imagine that a strong case on general theoretical grounds is enough to prove that the 'practical' belief in free will, even if inescapable for us as practical beings, is mere illusion. But in fact it proves nothing of the sort. There is no reason whatever why a belief that we find ourselves obliged to hold *qua* practical beings should be required to give way before a belief

which we find ourselves obliged to hold *qua* theoretical beings; or, for that matter, *vice versa*. All that the theoretical arguments of Determinism can prove, unless they are reinforced by a refutation of the phenomenological analysis that supports Libertarianism, is that there is a radical conflict between the theoretical and the practical sides of man's nature, an antinomy at the very heart of the self. And this is a state of affairs with which no one can easily rest satisfied. I think therefore that the Determinist ought to concern himself a great deal more than he does with phenomenological analysis, in order to show, if he can, that the assurance of free will is not really an inexpugnable element in man's practical consciousness. There is just as much obligation upon him, convinced though he may be of the soundness of his theoretical arguments, to expose the errors of the Libertarian's phenomenological analysis, as there is upon us, convinced though we may be of the soundness of the Libertarian's phenomenological analysis, to expose the errors of the Determinist's theoretical arguments.

However, we must at once begin the discharge of our own obligation. The rest of this lecture will be devoted to trying to show that the arguments which seem to carry the most weight with Determinists are, to say the least of it, very far from compulsive.

Fortunately, a good many of the arguments which at an earlier time in the history of philosophy would have been strongly urged against us make almost no appeal to the bulk of philosophers today, and we may here pass them by. That applies to any criticism of 'open possibilities' based on a metaphysical theory about the nature of the universe as a whole. Nobody today *has* a metaphysical theory about the nature of the universe as a whole! It applies also, with almost equal force, to criticisms based upon the universality of causal law as a supposed postulate of science. There have always been, in my opinion, sound philosophic reasons for doubting the validity, as distinct from the convenience, of the causal postulate in its universal form, but at the present time, when scientists themselves are deeply divided about the need for postulating causality even within their own special field, we shall do better to concentrate our attention upon criticisms which are more confidently advanced. I propose to ignore also, on different grounds, the type of criticism of free will that is sometimes advanced from the side of religion, based upon religious postulates of Divine Omnipotence and Omniscience. So far as I can see, a postulate of human freedom is every bit as necessary to meet certain religious demands (e.g. to make sense of the 'conviction of sin'), as postulates of Divine Omniscience and Omnipotence are to meet certain other religious demands. If so, then it can hardly be argued that religious experience as such tells more strongly against than for the position we are defending; and we may be satisfied, in the present context, to leave the matter there. It will be more profitable to discuss certain arguments which contemporary philosophers do think important, and which recur with a somewhat monotonous regularity in the literature of anti-Libertarianism.

These arguments can, I think, be reduced in principle to no more than two: first, the argument from 'predictability'; second, the argument from the alleged meaninglessness of an act supposed to be the self's act and yet not an expression of the self's character. Contemporary criticism of free will seems to me to consist almost exclusively of variations on these two themes. I shall deal with each in turn.

On the first we touched in passing at an earlier stage. Surely it is beyond question (the critic urges) that when we know a person intimately we can foretell with a high degree of accuracy how he will respond to at least a large number of practical situations. One feels safe in predicting that one's dog-loving friend will not use his boot to repel the little mongrel that comes yapping at his heels; or again that one's wife will not pass with incurious eyes (or indeed pass at all) the new hat shop in the city. So to behave would not be (as we say) 'in character.' But, so the criticism runs, you with your doctrine of 'genuinely open possibilities,' of a free will by which the self can diverge from its own character, remove all rational basis from such prediction. You require us to make the absurd supposition that the success of countless predictions of the sort in the past has been mere matter of chance. If you *really* believed in your theory, you would not be surprised if tomorrow your friend with the notorious horror of strong drink should suddenly exhibit a passion for whisky and

soda, or if your friend whose taste for reading has hitherto been satisfied with the sporting columns of the newspapers should be discovered on a fine Saturday afternoon poring over the works of Hegel. But of course you *would* be surprised. Social life would be sheer chaos if there were not well-grounded social expectations; and social life is not sheer chaos. Your theory is hopelessly wrecked upon obvious facts.

Now whether or not this criticism holds good against some versions of Libertarian theory I need not here discuss. It is sufficient if I can make it clear that against the version advanced in this lecture, according to which free will is localised in a relatively narrow field of operation, the criticism has no relevance whatsoever.

Let us remind ourselves briefly of the setting within which, on our view, free will functions. There is X, the course which we believe we ought to follow, and Y, the course towards which we feel our desire is strongest. The freedom which we ascribe to the agent is the freedom to put forth or refrain from putting forth the moral effort required to resist the pressure of desire and do what he thinks he ought to do.

But then there is surely an immense range of practical situations—covering by far the greater part of life—in which there is no question of a conflict within the self between what he most desires to do and what he thinks he ought to do? Indeed such conflict is a comparatively rare phenomenon for the majority of men. Yet over that whole vast range there is nothing whatever in our version of Libertarianism to prevent our agreeing that character determines conduct. In the absence, real or supposed, of any 'moral' issue, what a man chooses will be simply that course which, after such reflection as seems called for, he deems most likely to bring him what he most strongly desires; and that is the same as to say the course to which his present character inclines him.

Over by far the greater area of human choices, then, our theory offers no more barrier to successful prediction on the basis of character than any other theory. For where there is no clash of strongest desire with duty, the free will we are defending has no business. There is just nothing for it to do.

But what about the situations—rare enough though they may be—in which there *is* this clash and in which free will does therefore operate? Does our theory entail that there, at any rate, as the critic seems to suppose, 'anything may happen'?

Not by any manner of means. In the first place, and by the very nature of the case, the range of the agent's possible choices is bounded by what he thinks he ought to do on the one hand, and what he most strongly desires on the other. The freedom claimed for him is a freedom of decision to make or withhold the effort required to do what he thinks he ought to do. There is no question of a freedom to act in some 'wild' fashion, out of all relation to his characteristic beliefs and desires. This so-called 'freedom of caprice,' so often charged against the Libertarian, is, to put it bluntly, a sheer figment of the critic's imagination, with no *habitat* in serious Libertarian theory. Even in situations where free will does come into play it is perfectly possible, on a view like ours, given the appropriate knowledge of a man's character, to predict within certain limits how he will respond.

But 'probable' prediction in such situations can, I think, go further than this. It is obvious that where desire and duty are at odds, the felt 'gap' (as it were) between the two may vary enormously in breadth in different cases. The moderate drinker and the chronic tippler may each want another glass, and each deem it his duty to abstain, but the felt gap between desire and duty in the case of the former is trivial beside the great gulf which is felt to separate them in the case of the latter. Hence it will take a far harder moral effort for the tippler than for the moderate drinker to achieve the same external result of abstention. So much is matter of common agreement. And we are entitled, I think, to take it into account in prediction, on the simple principle that the harder the moral effort required to resist desire the less likely it is to occur. Thus in the example taken, most people would predict that the tippler will very probably succumb to his desires, whereas there is a reasonable likelihood that the moderate drinker will make the comparatively slight effort needed to resist them. So long as the prediction does not pretend to more than a measure of probability, there is nothing in our theory which would disallow it.

I claim, therefore, that the view of free will I have been putting forward is consistent with predictability of conduct on the basis of character over a very wide field indeed. And I make the further claim that field will cover all the situations in life concerning which there is any empirical evidence that successful prediction is possible.

Let us pass on to consider the second main line of criticism. This is, I think, much the more illuminating of the two, if only because it compels the Libertarian to make explicit certain concepts which are indispensable to him, but which, being desperately hard to state clearly, are apt not to be stated at all. The critic's fundamental point might be stated somewhat as follows:

'Free will as you describe it is completely unintelligible. On your own showing no *reason* can be given, because there just *is* no reason, why a man decides to exert rather than to withhold moral effort, or *vice versa*. But such an act—or more properly, such an "occurrence"—it is nonsense to speak of as an act of a *self*. If there is nothing in the self's character to which it is, even in principle, in any way traceable, the self has nothing to do with it. Your so-called "freedom," therefore, so far from supporting the self's moral responsibility, destroys it as surely as the crudest Determinism could do.'

If we are to discuss this criticism usefully, it is important, I think, to begin by getting clear about two different senses of the word "intelligible."

If, in the first place, we mean by an "intelligible" act one whose occurrence is in principle capable of being inferred, since it follows necessarily from something (though we may not know in fact from what), then it is certainly true that the Libertarian's free will is unintelligible. But that is only saying, is it not, that the Libertarian's "free" act is not an act which follows necessarily from something! This can hardly rank as a *criticism* of Libertarianism. It is just a description of it. That there can be nothing unintelligible in *this* sense is precisely what the Determinist has got to *prove*.

Yet it is surprising how often the critic of Libertarianism involves himself in this circular mode of argument. Repeatedly it is urged against the Libertarian, with a great air of triumph, that on his view he can't say *why* I now decide to rise to duty, or now decide to follow my strongest desire in defiance of duty. Of course he can't. If he could he wouldn't *be* a Libertarian. To "account for" a "free" act is a contradiction in terms. A free will is *ex hypothesi* the sort of thing of which the request for an *explanation* is absurd. The assumption that an explanation must be in principle possible for the act of moral decision deserves to rank as a classic example of the ancient fallacy of 'begging the question.'

But the critic usually has in mind another sense of the word 'unintelligible.' He is apt to take it for granted that an act which is unintelligible in the *above* sense (as the morally free act of the Libertarian undoubtedly is) is unintelligible in the *further* sense that we can attach no meaning to it. And this is an altogether more serious matter. If it could really be shown that the Libertarian's 'free will' were unintelligible in this sense of being meaningless, that, for myself at any rate, would be the end of the affair. Libertarianism would have been conclusively refuted.

But it seems to me manifest that this can *not* be shown. The critic has allowed himself, I submit, to become the victim of a widely accepted but fundamentally vicious assumption. He has assumed that whatever is meaningful must exhibit its meaningfulness to those who view it from the standpoint of external observation. Now if one chooses thus to limit one's self to the rôle of external observer, it is, I think, perfectly true that one can attach no meaning to an act which is the act of something we call a 'self' and yet follows from nothing in that self's character. But then *why should we* so limit ourselves, when what is under consideration is a subjective activity? For the apprehension of subjective acts there is *another* standpoint available, that of *inner experience,* of the practical consciousness in its actual functioning. If our free will should turn out to be something to which we can attach a meaning from *this* standpoint, no more is required. And no more ought to be expected. For I must repeat that only from the inner standpoint of living experience *could* anything of the nature of 'activity' be directly grasped. Observation from without is in the nature of the case impotent to apprehend the active *qua* active. We can from without observe sequences of states. If into these we read activity (as we sometimes do), this can only be on the basis of what we discern in ourselves from the inner standpoint. It follows that if anyone insists upon taking his criterion of the meaningful simply from the standpoint of external observation, he is really de-

ciding in advance of the evidence that the notion of activity, and *a fortiori* the notion of a free will, is 'meaningless.' He looks for the free act through a medium which is in the nature of the case incapable of revealing it, and then, because inevitably he doesn't find it, he declares that it doesn't exist!

But if, as we surely ought in this context, we adopt the inner standpoint, then (I am suggesting) things appear in a totally different light. From the inner standpoint, it seems to me plain, there is no difficulty whatever in attaching meaning to an act which is the self's act and which nevertheless does not follow from the self's character. So much I claim has been established by the phenomenological analysis, in this and the previous lecture, of the act of moral decision in face of moral temptation. It is thrown into particularly clear relief where the moral decision is to make the moral effort required to rise to duty. For the very function of moral effort, as it appears to the agent engaged in the act, is to enable the self to act against the line of least resistance, against the line to which his character as so far formed most strongly inclines him. But if the self is thus conscious here of *combating* his formed character, he surely cannot possibly suppose that the act, although his own act, *issues from* his formed character? I submit, therefore, that the self knows very well indeed— from the inner standpoint—what is meant by an act which is the *self's* act and which nevertheless does not follow from the self's *character.*

What this implies—and it seems to me to be an implication of cardinal importance for any theory of the self that aims at being more than superficial—is that the nature of the self is for itself something more than just its character as so far formed. The "nature" of the self and what we commonly call the 'character' of the self are by no means the same thing, and it is utterly vital that they should not be confused. The 'nature' of the self comprehends, but is not without remainder reducible to, its 'character'; it must, if we are to be true to the testimony of our experience of it, be taken as including *also* the authentic creative power of fashioning and refashioning 'character.'

The misguided, and as a rule quite uncritical, belittlement, of the evidence offered by inner experience has, I am convinced, been responsible for more bad argument by the opponents of Free Will than has any other single factor. How often, for example, do we find the Determinist critic saying, in effect, 'Either the act follows necessarily upon precedent states, or it is a mere matter of chance and accordingly of no moral significance.' The disjunction is invalid for it does not exhaust the possible alternatives. It seems to the critic to do so only because he will limit himself to the standpoint which is proper, and indeed alone possible, in dealing with the physical world, the standpoint of the external observer. If only he would allow himself to assume the standpoint which is not merely proper for, but necessary to, the apprehension of subjective activity, the inner standpoint of the practical consciousness in its actual functioning, he would find himself obliged to recognise the falsity of his disjunction. Reflection upon the act of moral decision as apprehended from the inner standpoint would force him to recognise a third possibility, as remote from chance as from necessity, that, namely, of creative activity, in which (as I have ventured to express it) nothing determines the act save the agent's doing of it.

There we must leave the matter. But as this lecture has been, I know, somewhat densely packed, it may be helpful if I conclude by reminding you, in bald summary, of the main things I have been trying to say. Let me set them out in so many successive theses.

1. The freedom which is at issue in the traditional Free Will problem is the freedom which is presupposed in moral responsibility.

2. Critical reflection upon carefully considered attributions of moral responsibility reveals that the only freedom that will do is a freedom which pertains to inner acts of choice, and that these acts must be acts (a) of which the self is sole author, and (b) which the self could have performed otherwise.

3. From phenomenological analysis of the situation of moral temptation we find that the self as engaged in this situation is inescapably convinced that it possesses a freedom of precisely the specified kind, located in the decision to exert or withhold the moral effort needed to rise to duty where the pressure of its desiring nature is felt to urge it in a contrary direction.

Passing to the question of the reality of this moral freedom which the moral agent believes himself to possess, we argued:

4. Of the two types of Determinist criticism which seem to have most influence today, that based on the predictability of much human behaviour fails to touch a Libertarianism which confines the area of free will as above indicated. Libertarianism so understood is compatible with all the predictability that the empirical facts warrant. And:

5. The second main type of criticism, which alleges the 'meaninglessness' of an act which is the self's act and which is yet not determined by the self's character, is based on a failure to appreciate that the standpoint of inner experience is not only legitimate but indispensable where what is at issue is the reality and nature of a subjective activity. The creative act of moral decision is inevitably meaningless to the mere external observer; but from the inner standpoint it is as real, and as significant, as anything in human experience.

Freedom and the Self

RODERICK CHISOLM

Roderick Chisolm (1916–   ) teaches philosophy at Brown University.

A staff moves a stone, and is moved by a hand,
which is moved by a man.

ARISTOTLE, *Physics* 256a

1

The metaphysical problem of human freedom might be summarized in the following way: Human beings are responsible agents; but this fact appears to conflict with a deterministic view of human action (the view that every event that is involved in an act is caused by some other event); and it *also* appears to conflict with an indeterministic view of human action (the view that the act, or some event that is essential to the act, is not caused at all). To solve the problem, I believe, we must make somewhat far-reaching assumptions about the self or the agent—about the man who performs the act.

Perhaps it is needless to remark that, in all likelihood, it is impossible to say anything significant about this ancient problem that has not been said before.

2

Let us consider some deed, or misdeed, that may be attributed to a responsible agent: one man, say, shot another. If the man *was* responsible for what he did, then, I would urge, what was to happen at the time of the shooting was something that was entirely up to the man himself. There was a moment at which it was true, both that he could have fired the shot and also that he could have refrained from firing it. And if this is so, then, even though he did fire it, he could

The Lindley Lecture, 1964, pp. 3–15 © Copyright 1964 by the Department of Philosophy, University of Kansas. Reprinted by permission of the author and of the Department of Philosophy of the University of Kansas, Lawrence, Kansas, USA.

have done something else instead. (He didn't find himself firing the shot 'against his will', as we say.) I think we can say, more generally, then, that if a man is responsible for a certain event or a certain state of affairs (in our example, the shooting of another man), then that event or state of affairs was brought about by some act of his, and the act was something that was in his power either to perform or not to perform.

But now if the act which he *did* perform was an act that was also in his power *not* to perform, then it could not have been caused or determined by any event that was not itself within his power either to bring about or not to bring about. For example, if what we say he did was really something that was brought about by a second man, one who forced his hand upon the trigger, say, or who, by means of hypnosis, compelled him to perform the act, then since the act was caused by the *second* man it was nothing that was within the power of the *first* man to prevent. And precisely the same thing is true, I think, if instead of referring to a second man who compelled the first one, we speak instead of the *desires* and *beliefs* which the first man happens to have had. For if what we say he did was really something that was brought about by his own beliefs and desires, if these beliefs and desires in the particular situation in which he happened to have found himself caused him to do just what it was that we say he did do, then, since *they* caused it, *he* was unable to do anything other than just what it was that he did do. It makes no difference whether the cause of the deed was internal or external; if the cause was some state or event for which the man himself was not responsible, then he was not responsible for what we have been mistakenly calling his act. If a flood caused the poorly constructed dam to break, then, given the flood and the constitution of the dam, the break, we may say, *had* to occur and nothing could have happened in its place.

And if the flood of desire caused the weak-willed man to give in, then he, too, had to do just what it was that he did do and he was no more responsible than was the dam for the results that followed. (It is true, of course, that if the man is responsible for the beliefs and desires that he happens to have, then he may also be responsible for the things they lead him to do. But the question now becomes: *is* he responsible for the beliefs and desires he happens to have? If he is, then there was a time when they were within his power either to acquire or not to acquire, and we are left, therefore, with our general point.)

One may object: But surely if there were such a thing as a man who is really *good,* then he would be responsible for things that he would do; yet, he would be unable to do anything other than just what it is that he does do, since, being good, he will always choose to do what is best. The answer, I think, is suggested by a comment that Thomas Reid makes upon an ancient author. The author had said of Cato, 'He was good because he could not be otherwise', and Reid observes: 'This saying, if understood literally and strictly, is not the praise of Cato, but of his constitution, which was no more the work of Cato than his existence'. If Cato was himself responsible for the good things that he did, then Cato, as Reid suggests, was such that, although he had the power to do what was not good, he exercised his power only for that which was good.

All of this, if it is true, may give a certain amount of comfort to those who are tender-minded. But we should remind them that it also conflicts with a familiar view about the nature of God—with the view that St. Thomas Aquinas expresses by saying that 'every movement both of the will and of nature proceeds from God as the Prime Mover'. If the act of the sinner *did* proceed from God as the Prime Mover, then God was in the position of the second agent we just discussed—the man who forced the trigger finger, or the hypnotist and the sinner, so-called, was *not* responsible for what he did. (This may be a bold assertion, in view of the history of western theology, but I must say that I have never encountered a single good reason for denying it.)

There is one standard objection to all of this and we should consider it briefly.

3

The objection takes the form of a stratagem one designed to show that determinism (and divine providence) is consistent with human responsibility. The stratagem is one that was used by Jonathan Edwards and by many philosophers in the present century, most notably, G. E. Moore.

One proceeds as follows: the expression (a) He could have done otherwise, it is argued, means no more nor less than (b) If he had chosen to do otherwise, then he would have done otherwise. (In place of 'chosen', one might say 'tried', 'set out', 'decided', 'undertaken', or 'willed'.) The truth of statement (b), it is then pointed out, is consistent with determinism (and with divine providence); for even if all of the man's actions were causally determined, the man could still be such that, *if* he had chosen otherwise, then he would have done otherwise. What the murderers saw, let us suppose, along with his beliefs and desires, *caused* him to fire the shot; yet he was such that *if,* just then, he had chosen or decided *not* to fire the shot, then he would not have fired it. All of this is certainly possible. Similarly, we could say, of the dam, that the flood caused it to break and also that the dam was such that, *if* there had been no flood or any similar pressure, then the dam would have remained intact. And therefore, the argument proceeds, if (b) is consistent with determinism, and if (a) and (b) say the same thing, then (a) is also consistent with determinism; hence we can say that the agent *could* have done otherwise even though he was caused to do what he did do; and therefore determinism and moral responsibility are compatible.

Is the argument sound? The conclusion follows from the premises, but the catch, I think, lies in the first premiss—the one saying that statement (a) tells us no more nor less than what statement (b) tells us. For (b), it would seem, could be true while (a) is false. That is to say, our man might be such that, if he had chosen to do otherwise, then he would have done otherwise, and yet *also* such that he could not have done otherwise. Suppose, after all, that our murderer could not have *chosen,* or could not have *decided,* to do otherwise. Then the fact that he happens also to be a man such that, if he had chosen not to shoot he would not have shot, would make no difference. For if he could *not* have chosen *not* to shoot, then he could not have done anything other than just what it was that he did do. In a word: from our statement (b) above ('If he had chosen to do otherwise, then he would have done otherwise'), we cannot make an inference to (a) above ('He could have done otherwise') unless we can *also* assert: (c) He could have chosen to do otherwise. And therefore, if we must reject this third statement (c), then, even though we may be justified in asserting (b), we are not justified in asserting (a). If the man could not have chosen to do otherwise, then he would not have done otherwise—*even if* he was such that, if he *had* chosen to do otherwise, then he would have done otherwise.

The stratagem in question, then, seems to me not to work, and I would say, therefore, that the ascription of responsibility conflicts with a deterministic view of action.

4

Perhaps there is less need to argue that the ascription of responsibility also conflicts with an indeterministic view of action—with the view that the act, or some event that is essential to the act, is not caused at all. If the act—the firing of the shot—was not caused at all, if it was fortuitous or capricious, happening so to speak out of the blue, then, presumably, no one—and nothing was responsible for the act. Our conception of action, therefore, should be neither deterministic nor indeterministic. Is there any other possibility?

5

We must not say that every event involved in the act is caused by some other event; and we must not say that the act is something that is not caused at all. The possibility that remains, therefore, is this: We should say that at least one of the events that are involved in the act is caused, not by any other events, but by something else instead. And this something else can only be the agent—the man. If there is an event that is caused, not by other events, but by the man, then there are some events involved in the act that are not caused by other events. But if the event in question is caused by the man then it *is* caused

and we are not committed to saying that there is something involved in the act that is not caused at all.

But this, of course, is a large consequence, implying something of considerable importance about the nature of the agent or the man.

6

If we consider only inanimate natural objects, we may say that causation, if it occurs, is a relation between *events* or *states of affairs*. The dam's breaking was an event that was caused by a set of other events— the dam being weak, the flood being strong, and so on. But if a man is responsible for a particular deed, then, if what I have said is true, there is some event, or set of events, that is caused, *not* by other events or states of affairs, but by the agent, whatever he may be.

I shall borrow a pair of medieval terms, using them, perhaps, in a way that is slightly different from that for which they were originally intended. I shall say that when one event or state of affairs (or set of events or states of affairs) causes some other event or state of affairs, then we have an instance of *transeunt* causation. And I shall say that when an *agent,* as distinguished from an event, causes an event or state of affairs, then we have an instance of *immanent* causation.

The nature of what is intended by the expression 'immanent causation' may be illustrated by this sentence from Aristotle's *Physics:* 'Thus, a staff moves a stone, and is moved by a hand, which is moved by a man.' (VII, 5, 256a, 6–8) If the man was responsible, then we have in this illustration a number of instances of causation—most of them transeunt but at least one of the immanent. What the staff did to the stone was an instance of transeunt causation, and thus we may describe it as a relation between events: 'the motion of the staff caused the motion of the stone.' And similarly for what the hand did to the staff: 'the motion of the hand caused the motion of the staff'. And, as we know from physiology, there are still other events which caused the motion of the hand. Hence we need not introduce the agent at this particular point, as Aristotle does—we *need* not, though we *may.* We *may* say that the hand was moved by the man, but we may *also* say that the motion of the hand was caused by the motion of certain muscles; and we may say that the motion of the muscles was caused by certain events that took place within the brain. But some event, and presumably one of those that took place within the brain, was caused by the agent and not by any other events.

There are, of course, objections to this way of putting the matter; I shall consider the two that seem to me to be most important.

7

One may object, firstly: 'If the *man* does anything, then, as Aristotle's remark suggests, what he does is to move the *hand*. But he certainly does not *do* anything to his brain—he may not even know that he *has* a brain. And if he doesn't do anything to the brain, and if the motion of the hand was caused by something that happened within the brain, then there is no point in appealing to "immanent causation" as being something incompatible with "transeunt causation"—for the whole thing, after all, is a matter of causal relations among events or states of affairs.

The answer to this objection, I think, is this: It is true that the agent does not *do* anything with his brain, or to his brain, in the sense in which he *does* something with his hand and does something to the staff. But from this it does not follow that the agent was not the immanent cause of something that happened within his brain.

We should note a useful distinction that has been proposed by Professor A. I. Melden—namely, the distinction between 'making something A happen' and 'doing A'. If I reach for the staff and pick it up, then one of the things that I *do* is just that—reach for the staff and pick it up. And if it is something that I do, then there is a very clear sense in which it may be said to be something that I know that I do. If you ask me, 'Are you doing something, or trying to do something, with the staff?', I will have no difficulty in finding an answer. But in doing something with the staff, I also make various things happen which are not in this same sense things that I do: I will make various air-particles move; I will free a number of blades of grass from the pressure that had been upon them; and I may cause a shadow to

move from one place to another. If these are merely things that I make happen, as distinguished from things that I do, then I may know nothing whatever about them; I may not have the slightest idea that, in moving the staff, I am bringing about any such thing as the motion of air-particles, shadows, and blades of grass.

We may say, in answer to the first objection, therefore, that it is true that our agent does nothing to his brain or with his brain; but from this it does not follow that the agent is not the immanent cause of some event within his brain; for the brain event may be something which, like the motion of the air-particles, he made happen in picking up the staff. The only difference between the two cases is this: in each case, he made something happen when he picked up the staff; but in the one case—the motion of the air-particles or of the shadows—it was the motion of the staff that caused the event to happen; and in the other case—the event that took place in the brain it was this event that caused the motion of the staff.

The point is, in a word, that whenever a man does something A, then (by 'immanent causation') he makes a certain cerebral event happen, and this cerebral event (by 'transeunt causation') makes A happen.

8

The second objection is more difficult and concerns the very concept of 'immanent causation', or causation by an agent, as this concept is to be interpreted here. The concept is subject to a difficulty which has long been associated with that of the prime mover unmoved. We have said that there must be some event A, presumably some cerebral event, which is caused not by any other event, but by the agent. Since A was not caused by any other event, then the agent himself cannot be said to have undergone any change or produced any other event (such as 'an act of will' or the like) which brought A about. But if, when the agent made A happen, there was no event involved other than A itself, no event which could be described as *making* A happen, what did the agent's causation consist of? What, for example, is the difference between A's just happening, and the agents' *causing* A to happen? We cannot attribute the difference to any event that took place within the agent. And so far as the event A itself is concerned, there would seem to be no discernible difference. Thus Aristotle said that the activity of the prime mover is nothing in addition to the motion that it produces, and Suarez said that 'the action is in reality nothing but the effect as it flows from the agent'. Must we conclude, then, that there is no more to the man's action in causing event A than there is to the event A's happening by itself? Here we would seem to have a distinction without a difference—in which case we have failed to find a *via media* between a deterministic and an indeterministic view of action.

The only answer, I think, can be this: that the difference between the man's causing A, on the one hand, and the event A just happening, on the other, lies in the fact that, in the first case but not the second, the event A *was* caused and was caused by the man. There was a brain event A; the agent did, in fact, cause the brain event; but there was nothing that he did to cause it.

This answer may not entirely satisfy and it will be likely to provoke the following question: 'But what are you really *adding* to the assertion that A happened when you utter the words "The agent *caused* A to happen"?' As soon as we have put the question this way, we see, I think, that whatever difficulty we may have encountered is one that may be traced to the concept of causation generally—whether 'immanent' or 'transeunt'. The problem, in other words, is not a problem that is peculiar to our conception of human action. It is a problem that must be faced by anyone who makes use of the concept of causation at all; and therefore, I would say, it is a problem for everyone but the complete indeterminist.

For the problem, as we put it, referring just to 'immanent causation', or causation by an agent, was this: 'What is the difference between saying, of an event A, that A just happened and saying that someone caused A to happen?' The analogous problem, which holds for 'transeunt causation', or causation by an event, is this: 'What is the difference between saying, of two events A and B, that B happened and then A happened, and saying that B's happening was the *cause* of A's happening?' And the only answer that one can give is this—that in the one case the agent was the cause of A's happening and in the other case event B was the cause of A's happening. The nature of transeunt causation is no more clear than is that of immanent causation.

9

But we may plausibly say—and there is a respectable philosophical tradition to which we may appeal—that the notion of immanent causation, or causation by an agent, is in fact more clear than that of transeunt causation, or causation by an event, and that it is only by understanding our own causal efficacy, as agents, that we can grasp the concept of *cause* at all. Hume may be said to have shown that we do not derive the concept of *cause* from what we perceive of external things. How, then, do we derive it? The most plausible suggestion, it seems to me, is that of Reid, once again: namely that 'the conception of an efficient cause may very probably be derived from the experience we have had . . . of our own power to produce certain effects'. If we did not understand the concept of immanent causation, we would not understand that of transeunt causation.

10

It may have been noted that I have avoided the term 'free will' in all of this. For even if there is such a faculty as 'the will', which somehow sets our acts agoing, the question of freedom, as John Locke said, is not the question '*whether the will be free*'; it is the question '*whether a man be free*'. For if there is a 'will', as a moving faculty, the question is whether the man is free to will to do these things that he does will to do—and also whether he is free *not* to will any of those things that he does will to do, and, again, whether he is free to will any of those things that he does not will to do. Jonathan Edwards tried to restrict himself to the question—'Is the man free to do what it is that he wills?' but the answer to this question will not tell us whether the man is responsible for what it is that he *does* will to do. Using still another pair of medieval terms, we may say that the metaphysical problem of freedom does not concern the *actus imperatus;* it does not concern the question whether we are free to accomplish whatever it is that we will or set out to do, it concerns the *actus elicitus,* the question whether we are free to will or to set out to do those things that we do will or set out to do.

11

If we are responsible, and if what I have been trying to say is true, then we have a prerogative which some would attribute only to God: each of us, when we act, is a prime mover unmoved. In doing what we do, we cause certain events to happen, and nothing—or no one—causes us to cause those events to happen.

12

If we are thus prime movers unmoved and if our actions, or those for which we are responsible, are not causally determined, then they are not causally determined by our *desires*. And this means that the relation between what we want or what we desire, on the one hand, and what it is that we do, on the other, is not as simple as most philosophers would have it.

We may distinguish between what we might call the 'Hobbist approach' and what we might call the 'Kantian approach' to this question. The Hobbist approach is the one that is generally accepted at the present time, but the Kantian approach, I believe, is the one that is true. According to Hobbism, if we *know,* of some man, what his beliefs and desires happen to be and how strong they are, if we know what he feels certain of, what he desires more than anything else, and if we know the state of his body and what stimuli he is being subjected to, then we may *deduce,* logically, just what it is that he will do—or, more accurately, just what it is that he will try, set out, or undertake to do. Thus Professor Melden has said that 'the connection between wanting and doing is logical'. But according to the Kantian approach to our problem, and this is the one that I would take, there is no such logical connection between wanting and doing, nor need there even be a causal connection. No set of statements about a man's desires, beliefs, and stimulus situation at any time implies any statement telling us what the man will try, set out, or undertake to do at that time. As Reid put it, though we may 'reason from men's motives to their actions and, in many cases, with great probability', we can never do so 'with absolute certainty.'

This means that, in one very strict sense of the terms, there can be no science of man. If we think of science as a matter of finding out what laws happen to hold, and if the statement of a law tells us what kinds of events are caused by what other kinds of events, then there will be human actions which we cannot explain by subsuming them under any laws. We cannot say, 'It is causally necessary that, given such and such desires and beliefs, and being subject to such and such stimuli, the agent will do so and so'. For at times the agent, if he chooses, may rise above his desires and do something else instead.

But all of this is consistent with saying that, perhaps more often than not, our desires do exist under conditions such that those conditions necessitate us to act. And we may also say, with Leibniz, that at other times our desires may 'incline without necessitating'.

13

Leibniz's phrase presents us with our final philosophical problem. What does it mean to say that a desire, or a motive, might 'incline without necessitating'? There is a temptation, certainly, to say that 'to incline' means to cause and that 'not to necessitate' means not to cause, but obviously we cannot have it both ways.

Nor will Leibniz's own solution do. In his letter to Coste, he puts the problem as follows: 'When a choice is proposed, for example to go out or not to got out, it is a question whether, with all the circumstances, internal and external, motives, perceptions, dispositions, impressions, passions, inclinations taken together, I am still in a contingent state, or whether I am necessitated to make the choice, for example, to go out; that is to say, whether this proposition true and determined in fact, *In all these circumstances taken together I shall choose to go out,* is contingent or necessary.' Leibniz's answer might be put as follows: in one sense of the terms 'necessary' and 'contingent', the proposition 'In all these circumstances taken together I shall choose to go out', may be said to be contingent and not necessary, and in another sense of these terms, it may be said to be necessary and not contingent. But the sense in which the proposition may be said to be contingent, according to Leibniz, is only this: there is no logical contradiction involved in denying the proposition.

And the sense in which it may be said to be necessary is this: since 'nothing ever occurs without cause or determining reason', the proposition is causally necessary 'Whenever all the circumstances taken together are such that the balance of deliberation is heavier on one side than on the other, it is certain and infallible that that is the side that is going to win out'. But if what we have been saying is true, the proposition 'In all these circumstances taken together I shall choose to go out', may be causally as well as logically contingent. Hence we must find another interpretation for Leibniz's statement that our motives and desires may incline us, or influence us, to choose without thereby necessitating us to choose.

Let us consider a public official who has some moral scruples but who also, as one says, could be had. Because of the scruples that he does have, he would never take any positive steps to receive a bribe—he would not actively solicit one. But his morality has its limits and he is also such that, if we were to confront him with a *fait accompli* or to let him see what is about to happen ($10,000 in cash is being deposited behind the garage), then he would succumb and be unable to resist. The general situation is a familiar one and this is one reason that people pray to be delivered from temptation. (It also justifies Kant's remark: 'And how many there are who may have led a long blameless life, who are only *fortunate* in having escaped so many temptations'. Our relation to the misdeed that we contemplate may not be a matter simply of being able to bring it about or not to bring it about. As St. Anselm noted, there are at least four possibilities. We may illustrate them by reference to our public official and the event which is his receiving the bribe, in the following way: (i) he may be able to bring the event about himself (*facere esse*), in which case he would actively cause himself to receive the bribe; (ii) he may be able to refrain from bringing it about himself (*non*

facere esse), in which case he would not himself do anything to insure that he receive the bribe; (iii) he may be able to do something to prevent the event from occurring (*facere non esse*), in which case he would make sure that the $10,000 was *not* left behind the garage; or (iv) he may be unable to do anything to prevent the event from occurring (*non facere non esse*), in which case, though he may not solicit the bribe, he would allow himself to keep it. We have envisaged our official as a man who can resist the temptation to (i) but cannot resist the temptation to (iv): he can refrain from bringing the event about himself, but he cannot bring himself to do anything to prevent it.

Let us think of 'inclination without necessitation', then, in such terms as these. First we may contrast the two propositions:

(1) He can resist the temptation to do something in order to make A happen;
(2) He can resist the temptation to allow A to happen (i.e. to do nothing to prevent A from happening).

We may suppose that the man has some desire to have A happen and thus has a motive for making A happen. His motive for making A happen, I suggest, is one that *necessitates* provided that, because of the motive, (1) is false; he cannot resist the temptation to do something in order to make A happen. His motive for making A happen is one that *inclines* provided that, because of the motive, (2) is false; like our public official, he cannot bring himself to do anything to prevent A from happening. And therefore we can say that this motive for making A happen is one that *inclines but does not necessitate* provided that, because of the motive, (1) is true and (2) is false; he can resist the temptation to make it happen but he cannot resist the temptation to allow it to happen.

FREEDOM AND
MORAL RESPONSIBILITY

Responsibility, Action, and Virtue

ARISTOTLE

Aristotle (384–322 B.C.E.) and his teacher Plato are generally regarded as the two greatest philosophers of ancient Greece. He wrote many influential works and founded his own school, the Lyceum.

Book II

Virtue, then, being of two kinds, intellectual and moral, intellectual virtue in the main owes both its birth and its growth to teaching (for which reason it requires experience and time), while moral virtue comes about as a result of habit, whence also its name (ἠθική) is one that is formed by a slight variation from the word ἔθος (habit). From this it is also plain that none of the moral virtues arises in us by nature; for nothing that exists by nature can form a habit contrary to its nature. For instance the stone which by nature moves downwards cannot be habituated to move upwards, not even if one tries to train it by throwing it up ten thousand times; nor can fire be habituated to move downwards, nor can anything else that by nature behaves in one way be trained to behave in another. Neither by nature, then, nor contrary to nature do the virtues arise in us; rather we are adapted by nature to receive them, and are made perfect by habit.

Again, of all the things that come to us by nature we first acquire the potentiality and later exhibit the activity (this is plain in the case of the senses; for it was not by often seeing or often hearing that we got these senses, but on the contrary we had them before we used them, and did not come to have them by using them); but the virtues we get by first exercising them, as also happens in the case of the arts as

well. For the things we have to learn before we can do them, we learn by doing them, e.g. men become builders by building and lyre-players by playing the lyre; so too we become just by doing just acts, temperate by doing temperate acts, brave by doing brave acts.

This is confirmed by what happens in states; for legislators make the citizens good by forming habits in them, and this is the wish of every legislator, and those who do not effect it miss their mark, and it is in this that a good constitution differs from a bad one.

Again, it is from the same causes and by the same means that every virtue is both produced and destroyed, and similarly every art; for it is from playing the lyre that both good and bad lyre-players are produced. And the corresponding statement is true of builders and of all the rest; men will be good or bad builders as a result of building well or badly. For if this were not so, there would have been no need of a teacher, but all men would have been born good or bad at their craft. This, then, is the case with the virtues also; by doing the acts that we do in our transactions with other men we become just or unjust, and by doing the acts that we do in the presence of danger, and being habituated to feel fear or confidence, we become brave or cowardly. The same is true of appetites and feelings of anger; some men become temperate and good-tempered, others self-indulgent and irascible, by behaving in one way or the other in the appropriate circumstances. Thus, in

From *Nicomachean Ethics*. Translated by J. E. C. Welldon (London: Macmillan, 1908).

one word, states of character arise out of like activities. This is why the activities we exhibit must be a certain kind; it is because the states of character correspond to the differences between these. It makes no small difference, then, whether we form habits of one kind or of another from our very youth; it makes a very great difference, or rather *all* the difference.

Since, then, the present inquiry does not aim at theoretical knowledge like the others (for we are inquiring not in order to know what virtue is, but in order to become good, since otherwise our inquiry would have been of no use), we must examine the nature of actions, namely how we ought to do them; for these determine also the nature of the states of character that are produced, as we have said. Now, that we must act according to the right rule is a common principle and must be assumed—it will be discussed later, i.e. both what the right rule is, and how it is related to the other virtues. But this must be agreed upon beforehand, that the whole account of matters of conduct must be given in outline and not precisely, as we said at the very beginning that the accounts we demand must be in accordance with the subject-matter; matters concerned with conduct and questions of what is good for us have no fixity, any more than matters of health. The general account being of this nature, the account of particular cases is yet more lacking in exactness; for they do not fall under any art or precept but the agents themselves must in each case consider what is appropriate to the occasion, as happens also in the art of medicine or of navigation.

But though our present account is of this nature we must give what help we can. First, then, let us consider this, that it is the nature of such things to be destroyed by defect and excess, as we see in the case of strength and of health (for to gain light on things imperceptible we must use the evidence of sensible things); both excessive and defective exercise destroys the strength, and similarly drink or food which is above or below a certain amount destroys the health, while that which is proportionate both produces and increases and preserves it. So too is it, then, in the case of temperance and courage and the other virtues. For the man who flies from and fears everything and does not stand his ground against anything becomes a coward, and the man who fears nothing at all but goes to meet every danger becomes rash; and similarly the man who indulges in every pleasure and abstains from none becomes self-indulgent, while the man who shuns every pleasure, as boors do, becomes in a way insensible; temperance and courage, then, are destroyed by excess and defect, and preserved by the mean.

But not only are the sources and causes of their origination and growth the same as those of their destruction, but also the sphere of their actualization will be the same; for this is also true of the things which are more evident to sense, e.g. of strength; it is produced by taking much food and undergoing much exertion, and it is the strong man that will be most able to do these things. So too is it with the virtues; by abstaining from pleasures we become temperate, and it is when we have become so that we are most able to abstain from them; and similarly too in the case of courage; for by being habituated to despise things that are terrible and to stand our ground against them we become brave, and it is when we have become so that we shall be most able to stand our ground against them.

We must take as a sign of states of character the pleasure or pain that ensues on acts; for the man who abstains from bodily pleasures and delights in this very fact is temperate, while the man who is annoyed at it is self-indulgent, and he who stands his ground against things that are terrible and delights in this or at least is not pained is brave, while the man who is pained is a coward. For moral excellence is concerned with pleasures and pains; it is on account of the pleasure that we do bad things, and on account of the pain that we abstain from noble ones. Hence we ought to have been brought up in a particular way from our very youth, as Plato says, so as both to delight in and to be pained by the things that we ought; for this is the right education. . . .

The question might be asked, what we mean by saying that we must become just by doing just acts, and temperate by doing temperate acts; for if men do just and temperate acts, they are already just and temperate, exactly as, if they do what is in accordance with the laws of grammar and of music, they are grammarians and musicians.

Or is this not true even of the arts? It is possible to do something that is in accordance with the laws of grammar, either by chance or at the suggestion of another. A man will be a grammarian, then, only when he has both done something grammatical and done it grammatically; and this means doing it in accordance with the grammatical knowledge in himself.

Again, the case of the arts and that of the virtues are not similar; for the products of the arts have their goodness in themselves, so that it is enough that they should have a certain character, but if the acts that are in accordance with the virtues have themselves a certain character it does not follow that they are done justly or temperately. The agent also must be in a certain condition when he does them; in the first place he must have knowledge, secondly he must choose the acts, and choose them for their own sakes, and thirdly his action must proceed from a firm and unchangeable character. These are not reckoned in as conditions of the possession of the arts, except the bare knowledge; but as a condition of the possession of the virtues knowledge has little or no weight, while the other conditions count not for a little but for everything, i.e. the very conditions which result from often doing just and temperate acts.

Actions, then, are called just and temperate when they are such as the just or the temperate man would do; but it is not the man who does these that is just and temperate, but the man who also does them *as* just and temperate men do them. It is well said, then, that it is by doing just acts that the just man is produced, and by doing temperate acts the temperate man; without doing these no one would have even a prospect of becoming good.

But most people do not do these, but take refuge in theory and think they are being philosophers and will become good in this way, behaving somewhat like patients who listen attentively to their doctors, but do none of the things they are ordered to do. As the latter will not be made well in body by such a course of treatment, the former will not be made well in soul by such a course of philosophy.

Next we must consider what virtue is. Since things that are found in the soul are of three kinds—passions, faculties, states of character, virtue must be one of these. By passions I mean appetite, anger, fear, confidence, envy, joy, friendly feeling, hatred, longing, emulation, pity, and in general the feelings that are accompanied by pleasure or pain; by faculties the things in virtue of which we are said to be capable of feeling these, e.g. of becoming angry or be-

ing pained or feeling pity; by states of character the things in virtue of which we stand well or badly with reference to the passions, e.g. with reference to anger we stand badly if we feel it violently or too weakly, and well if we feel it moderately; and similarly with reference to the other passions.

Now neither the virtues nor the vices are *passions*, because we are not called good or bad on the ground of our passions, but are so called on the ground of our virtues and our vices, and because we are neither praised nor blamed for our passions (for the man who feels fear or anger is not praised, nor is the man who simply feels anger blamed, but the man who feels it in a certain way), but for our virtues and our vices we are *are* praised or blamed.

Again, we feel anger and fear without choice, but the virtues are modes of choice or involve choice. Further, in respect of the passions we are said to be moved, but in respect of the virtues and vices we are said not to be moved but to be disposed in a particular way.

For these reasons also they are not *faculties;* for we are neither called good nor bad, nor praised nor blamed, for the simple capacity of feeling the passions; again, we have the faculties by nature, but we are not made good or bad by nature; we have spoken of this before.

If, then, the virtues are neither passions nor faculties, all that remains is that they should be *states of character*.

Thus we have stated what virtue is in respect of its genus.

We must, however, not only describe virtue as a state of character, but also say what sort of state it is. We may remark, then, that every virtue or excellence both brings into good condition the thing of which it is the excellence and makes the work of that thing be done well; e.g. the excellence of the eye makes both the eye and its work good; for it is by the excellence of the eye that we see well. Similarly the excellence of the horse makes a horse both good in itself and good at running and at carrying its rider and at awaiting the attack of the enemy. Therefore, if this is true in every case, the virtue of man also will be the state of character which makes a man good and which makes him do his own work well.

How this is to happen we have stated already, but it will be made plain also by the following consideration of the specific nature of virtue. In everything that is continuous and divisible it is possible to take more, less, or an equal amount, and that either in terms of the thing itself or relatively to us; and the equal is an intermediate between excess and defect. By the intermediate in the object I mean that which is equidistant from each of the extremes, which is one and the same for all men; by the intermediate relatively to us that which is neither too much nor too little—and this is not one, nor the same for all. For instance, if ten is many and two is few, six is the intermediate, taken in terms of the object; for it exceeds and is exceeded by an equal amount; this is intermediate according to arithmetical proportion. But the intermediate relatively to us is not to be taken so; if ten pounds are too much for a particular person to eat and two too little, it does not follow that the trainer will order six pounds; for this also is perhaps too much for the person who is to take it, or too little—too little for Milo, too much for the beginner in athletic exercises. The same is true of running and wrestling. Thus a master of any art avoids excess and defect, but seeks the intermediate and chooses this—the intermediate not in the object but relatively to us.

If it is thus, then, that every art does its work well—by looking to the intermediate and judging its works by this standard (so that we often say of good works of art that it is not possible either to take away or to add anything, implying that excess and defect destroy the goodness of works of art, while the mean preserves it; and good artists, as we say, look to this in their work), and if, further, virtue is more exact and better than any art, as nature also is, then virtue must have the quality of aiming at the intermediate. I mean moral virtue; for it is this that is concerned with passions and actions, and in these there is excess, defect, and the intermediate. For instance, both fear and confidence and appetite and anger and pity and in general pleasure and pain may be felt both too much and too little, and in both cases not well; but to feel them at the right times, with reference to the right objects, towards the right people, with the right motive, and in the right way, is what is both intermediate and best, and this is characteristic of virtue. Similarly with regard to actions also there is excess, defect, and the intermediate. Now virtue is concerned with passions and actions, in which ex-

cess is a form of failure, and so is defect, while the intermediate is praised and is a form of success; and being praised and being successful are both characteristics of virtue. Therefore virtue is a kind of mean, since, as we have seen, it aims at what is intermediate.

Again, it is possible to fail in many ways (for evil belongs to the class of the unlimited, as the Pythagoreans conjectured, and good to that of the limited), while to succeed is possible only in one way (for which reason also one is easy and the other difficult—to miss the mark easy, to hit it difficult); for these reasons also, then, excess and defect are characteristic of vice, and the mean of virtue;

For men are good in but one way, but bad in many.

Virtue, then, is a state of character concerned with choice, lying in a mean, i.e. the mean relative to us, this being determined by a rational principle, and by that principle by which the man of practical wisdom would determine it. Now it is a mean between two vices, that which depends on excess and that which depends on defect; and again it is a mean because the vices respectively fall short of or exceed what is right in both passions and actions, while virtue both finds and chooses that which is intermediate. Hence in respect of its substance and the definition which states its essence virtue is a mean, with regard to what is best and right an extreme.

But not every action nor every passion admits of a mean; for some have names that already imply badness, e.g. spite, shamelessness, envy, and in the case of actions adultery, theft, murder; for all of these and suchlike things imply by their names that they are themselves bad, and not the excesses or deficiencies of them. It is not possible, then, ever to be right with regard to them; one must always be wrong. Nor does goodness or badness with regard to such things depend on committing adultery with the right woman, at the right time, and in the right way, but simply to do any of them is to go wrong. It would be equally absurd, then, to expect that in unjust, cowardly, and voluptuous action there should be a mean, an excess, and a deficiency; for at that rate there would be a mean of excess and of deficiency, an excess of excess, and a deficiency of deficiency. But as there is no excess and deficiency of temperance and courage because what is intermediate is in a sense an extreme, so too of the actions we have mentioned there is no mean nor any excess and deficiency, but however they are done they are wrong; for in general there is neither a mean of excess and deficiency, nor excess and deficiency of a mean. . . .

There are also three other means, which have a certain likeness to one another, but differ from one another: for they are all concerned with intercourse in words and actions, but differ in that one is concerned with truth in this sphere, the other two with pleasantness; and of this one kind is exhibited in giving amusement, the other in all the circumstances of life. We must therefore speak of these too, that we may the better see that in all things the mean is praiseworthy, and the extremes neither praiseworthy nor right, but worthy of blame. Now most of these states also have no names, but we must try, as in the other cases, to invent names ourselves so that we may be clear and easy to follow. With regard to truth, then, the intermediate is a truthful sort of person and the mean may be called truthfulness, while the pretence which exaggerates is boastfulness and the person characterized by it a boaster, and that which understates is mock modesty and the person characterized by it mock-modest. With regard to pleasantness in the giving of amusement the intermediate person is ready-witted and the disposition ready wit, the excess is buffoonery and the person characterized by it a buffoon, while the man who falls short is a sort of boor and his state is boorishness. With regard to the remaining kind of pleasantness, that which is exhibited in life in general, the man who is pleasant in the right way is friendly and the mean is friendliness, while the man who exceeds is an obsequious person if he has no end in view, a flatterer if he is aiming at his own advantage, and the man who falls short and is unpleasant in all circumstances is a quarrelsome and surly sort of person.

There are also means in the passions and concerned with the passions; since shame is not a virtue, and yet praise is extended to the modest man. For even in these matters one man is said to be intermediate, and another to exceed, as for instance the bashful man who is ashamed of everything; while he who falls short or is not ashamed of anything at all is shameless, and the intermediate person is modest. Righteous indignation is a mean between envy and spite, and these states are concerned with the pain and the pleasure that are felt at the fortunes of our neighbours; the man who is characterized by righteous indignation is pained at undeserved good fortune, the envious man, going beyond him, is pained at all good fortune, and the spiteful man falls so far short of being pained that he even rejoices. But these states there will be an opportunity of describing elsewhere; with regard to justice, since it has not one simple meaning, we shall, after describing the other states, distinguish its two kinds and say how each of them is a mean; and similarly we shall treat also of the rational virtues.

There are three kinds of disposition, then, two of them vices, involving excess and deficiency respectively, and one a virtue, viz. the mean, and all are in a sense opposed to all; for the extreme states are contrary both to the intermediate state and to each other, and the intermediate to the extremes; as the equal is greater relatively to the less, less relatively to the greater, so the middle states are excessive relatively to the deficiencies, deficient relatively to the excesses, both in passions and in actions. For the brave man appears rash relatively to the coward, and cowardly relatively to the rash man; and similarly the temperate man appears self-indulgent relatively to the insensible man, insensible relatively to the self-indulgent, and the liberal man prodigal relatively to the mean man, mean relatively to the prodigal. Hence also the people at the extremes push the intermediate man each over to the other, and the brave man is called rash by the coward, cowardly by the rash man, and correspondingly in the other cases.

These states being thus opposed to one another, the greatest contrariety is that of the extremes to each other, rather than to the intermediate; for these are further from each other than from the intermediate, as the great is further from the small and the small from the great than both are from the equal. Again, to the intermediate some extremes show a certain likeness, as that of rashness to courage and that of prodigality to liberality; but the extremes show the greatest unlikeness to each other; now contraries are defined as the things that are furthest from each other, so that things that are further apart are more contrary.

To the mean in some cases the deficiency, in some the excess is more opposed; e.g. it is not rashness, which is an excess, but cowardice, which is a deficiency, that is more opposed to courage, and not insensibility, which is a deficiency, but self-indulgence, which is an excess, that is more opposed to temperance. This happens from two reasons, one being drawn from the thing itself; for because one extreme is nearer and liker to the intermediate, we oppose not this but rather its contrary to the intermediate. E.g., since rashness is thought liker and nearer to courage, and cowardice more unlike, we oppose rather the latter to courage; for things that are further from the intermediate are thought more contrary to it. This, then, is one cause, drawn from the thing itself; another is drawn from ourselves; for the things to which we ourselves more naturally tend seem more contrary to the intermediate. For instance, we ourselves tend more naturally to pleasures, and hence are more easily carried away towards self-indulgence than towards propriety. We describe as contrary to the mean, then, rather the directions in which we more often go to great lengths; and therefore self-indulgence, which is an excess, is the more contrary to temperance.

That moral virtue is a mean, then, and in what sense it is so, and that it is a mean between two vices, the one involving excess, the other deficiency, and that it is such because its character is to aim at what is intermediate in passions and in actions, has been sufficiently stated. Hence also it is no easy task to be good. For in everything it is no easy task to find the middle, e.g. to find the middle of a circle is not for every one but for him who knows; so, too, any one can get angry—that is easy—or give or spend money; but to do this to the right person, to the right extent, at the right time, with the right motive, and in the right way, *that* is not for every one, nor is it easy; wherefore goodness is both rare and laudable and noble.

Hence he who aims at the intermediate must first depart from what is the more contrary to it, as Calypso advises—

Hold the ship out beyond that surf and spray.

For of the extremes one is more erroneous, one less so; therefore, since to hit the mean is hard in the ex-treme, we must as a second best, as people say, take the least of the evils; and this will be done best in the way we describe.

But we must consider the things towards which we ourselves also are easily carried away; for some of us tend to one thing, some to another; and this will be recognizable from the pleasure and the pain we feel. We must drag ourselves away to the contrary extreme; for we shall get into the intermediate state by drawing well away from error, as people do in straightening sticks that are bent.

Now in everything the pleasant or pleasure is most to be guarded against; for we do not judge it impartially. We ought, then, to feel towards pleasure as the elders of the people felt towards Helen, and in all circumstances repeat their saying; for if we dismiss pleasure thus we are less likely to go astray. It is by doing this, then, (to sum the matter up) that we shall best be able to hit the mean.

But this is no doubt difficult, and especially in individual cases; for it is not easy to determine both how and with whom and on what provocation and how long one should be angry; for we too sometimes praise those who fall short and call them good-tempered, but sometimes we praise those who get angry and call them manly. The man, however, who deviates little from goodness is not blamed, whether he do so in the direction of the more or of the less, but only the man who deviates more widely; for *he* does not fail to be noticed. But up to what point and to what extent a man must deviate before he becomes blameworthy it is not easy to determine by reasoning, any more than anything else that is perceived by the senses; such things depend on particular facts, and the decision rests with perception. So much, then, is plain, that the intermediate state is in all things to be praised, but that we must incline sometimes towards the excess, sometimes towards the deficiency; for so shall we most easily hit the mean and what is right.

Existentialism and Freedom

JEAN-PAUL SARTRE

French existentialist philosopher, playwright, and social critic Jean-Paul Sartre (1905–1980) wrote numerous widely influential works of philosophy and literature. He won the Nobel Prize but turned it down.

This moment was extraordinary. I was there, motionless and icy, plunged in a horrible ecstasy. But something fresh had just appeared in the very heart of this ecstasy; I understood the Nausea, I possessed it. To tell the truth, I did not formulate my discoveries to myself. But I think it would be easy for me to put them in words now. The essential thing is contingency. I mean that one cannot define existence as necessity. To exist is simply *to be there,* those who exist let themselves be encountered, but you can never deduce anything from them. I believe there are people who have understood this. Only they tried to overcome this contingency by inventing a necessary, causal being. But no necessary being can explain existence: contingency is not a delusion, a probability which can be dissipated; it is the absolute, consequently, the perfect free gift. All is free, this part, this city and myself. When you realize that, it turns your heart upside down and everything begins to float . . .

(From *Nausea.*)

* * *

There are two kinds of existentialists. There are, on the one hand, the Christians, amongst whom I shall name Jaspers and Gabriel Marcel, both professed Catholics; and on the other the existential atheists, amongst whom we must place Heidegger as well as the French existentialists and myself. What they have in common is simply the fact that they believe that existence comes before essence—or, if you will, that we must begin from the subjective. What exactly do we mean by that?

If one considers an article of manufacture—as, for example, a book or a paper-knife—one sees that it has been made by an artisan who had a conception of it; and he has paid attention, equally, to the conception of a paper-knife and to the existent technique of production which is a part of that conception and is, at bottom, a formula. Thus the paper-knife is at the same time an article producible in a certain manner and one which, on the other hand, serves a definite purpose, for one cannot suppose that a man would produce a paper-knife without knowing what it was for. Let us say, then, of the paper-knife that its essence—that is to say the sum of the formulae and the qualities which made its production and its definition possible—precedes its existence. The presence of such and such a paper-knife or book is thus determined before my eyes. Here then we are viewing the world from a technical standpoint, and we can say that production precedes existence.

When we think of God as the creator, we are thinking of him, most of the time, as a supernatural artisan. Whatever doctrine we may be considering, whether it be a doctrine like that of Descartes, or of Leibniz himself, we always imply that the will follows, more or less, from the understanding or at least accompanies it, so that when God creates he knows precisely what he is creating. Thus the conception of man in the mind of God is comparable to that of the paper-knife in the mind of the artisan: God makes man according to a procedure and a conception, exactly as the artisan manufactures a paper-knife, following a definition and a formula. Thus each individual man is the realization of a certain conception which dwells in the divine understanding. In the philosophical atheism of the eighteenth century; the notion of God is suppressed, but not, for all that, the idea that essence is prior to existence; something of that idea we still find everywhere, in Diderot, in Voltaire and even in Kant. Man possesses a human nature; that "human nature," which is the conception of human being, is found in every man; which means that each man is a particular example of an universal conception, the conception of Man.

(From "Existentialism and Humanism.")

* * *

The anti-Semite has created the Jew from his need. Prejudice is not uninformed opinion. It is an attitude totally and freely chosen. . . . The anti-Semite is a man who is afraid, not of the Jews, of course, but of himself, of his conscience, his instincts, of his responsibilities, of solitude, of change, of society, and the world; of everything except the Jews. He is a coward who does not wish to admit his cowardice to himself. . . . a malcontent who dares not revolt for fear of the consequences of his rebellion. By adhering to his anti-Semitism, he is not only adopting an opinion, he is choosing himself as a person. . . . He is choosing the total irresponsibility of the warrior who obeys his leaders. . . .

(From "Portrait of the Anti-Semite.")

* * *

GARCIN: They shot me.

ESTELLE: I know. Because you refused to fight. Well, why shouldn't you?

GARCIN: I—I didn't exactly refuse. [*In a far-away voice*] I must say he talks well, he makes out a good case against me, but he never says what I should have done instead. Should I have gone to the general and said: "General. I decline to fight"? A mug's game; they'd have promptly locked me up. But I wanted to show my colors, my true colors, do you understand? I wasn't going to be silenced [*To Estelle*] So I—I took the train. . . . They caught me at the [Mexican] frontier. . . .

ESTELLE: But you *had* to run away. If you'd stayed they'd have sent you to jail, wouldn't they?

GARCIN: Of course [*A pause.*] Well, Estelle, am I a coward?

ESTELLE: How can I say? Don't be so unreasonable, darling. I can't put myself in your skin. You must decide that for yourself.

GARCIN: [*wearily*] I can't decide.

ESTELLE: Anyhow, you must remember. You must have had reasons for acting as you did.

GARCIN: I had.

ESTELLE: Well?

GARCIN: But were they the real reasons?

ESTELLE: You've a twisted mind, that's your trouble. Plaguing yourself over such trifles!

GARCIN: I'd thought it all out, and I wanted to make a stand. But was that my real motive?

INEZ: Exactly. That's the question. Was that your real motive? No doubt you argued it out with yourself, you weighed the pros and cons, you found good reasons for what you did. But fear and hatred and all the dirty little instincts one keeps dark—they're motives too. So carry on, Mr. Garcin, and try to be honest with yourself—for once.

GARCIN: Do I need you to tell me that? Day and night I paced my cell, from the window to the door, from the door to the window. I pried into my heart. I sleuthed myself like a detective. By the end of it I felt as if I'd given my whole life to introspection. But always I harked back to the one thing certain—that I had acted as I did. I'd taken that train to the frontier. But why? Why? Finally I thought: My death will settle it. If I face death courageously, I'll prove I am no coward.

INEZ: And how did you face death?

GARCIN: Miserably. Rottenly. [INEZ *LAUGHS.*] Oh, it was only a physical lapse—that might happen to anyone; I'm, not ashamed of it. Only everything's been left in suspense, forever. . . . Listen! Each man has an aim in life, a leading motive; that's so, isn't it? Well, I didn't give a damn for wealth, or love. I aimed at being a real man. A tough, as they say. I staked everything on the same horse. . . . Can one possibly be a coward when one's deliberately courted danger at every turn? And can one judge a life by a single action?

INEZ: Why not? For thirty years you dreamt you were a hero, and condoned a thousand lapses—because a hero, of course, can do no wrong. An easy method obviously. Then a day came when you were up against it, the red light of real danger—and you took the train to Mexico.

GARCIN: I "dreamt," you say. It was no dream. When I chose that hardest path, I made my choice deliberately. A man is what he wills himself to be.

INEZ: Prove it. Prove it was no dream. It's what one does, and nothing else, that shows the stuff one's made of.

GARCIN: I died too soon. I wasn't allowed time to—to do my deeds.

INEZ: One always dies too soon—or too late. And yet one's whole life is complete at that moment, with a line drawn neatly under it, ready for the summing up. You are—your life, and nothing else.

(From *No Exit.*)

* * *

Let us take an example: A homosexual frequently has an intolerable feeling of guilt, and his whole existence is determined in relation to this feeling. One will readily foresee that he is in bad faith. In fact it frequently happens that this man, while recognizing his homosexual inclination, while avowing each and every particular misdeed which he has committed, refuses with all his strength to consider himself "*a paederast.*" His case is always "different," peculiar; there enters into it something of a game, of chance, of bad luck; the mistakes are all in the past; they are explained by a certain conception of the beautiful which women can not satisfy; we should see in them the results of a restless search, rather than the manifestations of a deeply rooted tendency, *etc., etc.* Here is assuredly a man in bad faith who borders on the comic since, acknowledging all the facts which are imputed to him, he refuses to draw from them the conclusion which they impose. His friend, who is his most severe critic, becomes irritated with this duplicity. The critic asks only one thing—and perhaps then he will show himself indulgent: that the guilty one recognize himself as guilty, that the homosexual declare frankly—whether humbly or boastfully matters little—"I am a paederast." We ask here: Who is in bad faith? The homosexual or the champion of sincerity?

The homosexual recognizes his faults, but he struggles with all his strength against the crushing view that his mistakes constitute for him a *destiny*. He does not wish to let himself be considered as a thing. He has an obscure but strong feeling that a homosexual is not a homosexual as this table is a table or as this red-haired man is red-haired. It seems to him that he has escaped from each mistake as soon as he has posited it and recognized it; he even feels that the psychic duration by itself cleanses him from each misdeed, constitutes for him an undetermined future, causes him to be born anew. Is he wrong? Does he not recognize in himself the peculiar, irreducible character of human reality? His attitude includes then an undeniable comprehension of truth. But at the same time he needs this perpetual rebirth, this constant escape in order to live; he must constantly put himself beyond reach in order to avoid the terrible judgment of collectivity. Thus he plays on the word *being*. He would be right actually if he understood the phrase "I am not a paederast" in the sense of "I am not what I am." That is, if he declared to himself, "To the extent that a pattern of conduct is defined as the conduct of a paederast and to the extent that I have adopted this conduct, I am a paederast. But to the extent that human reality can not be finally defined by patterns of conduct, I am not one." But instead he slides surreptitiously toward a different connotation of the word "being." He understands "not being" in the sense of "not-being-in-itself." He lays claim to "not being a paederast" in the sense in which this *table is not an inkwell. He is in bad faith.*

(From *Being and Nothingness.*)

Moral Luck

THOMAS NAGEL

Thomas Nagel (1937–   ) teaches philosophy at New York University and is the author of numerous articles and several books.

Kant believed that good or bad luck should influence neither our moral judgment of a person and his actions, nor his moral assessment of himself.

> The good will is not good because of what it effects or accomplishes or because of its adequacy to achieve some proposed end; it is good only because of its willing, i.e., it is good of itself. And, regarded for itself, it is to be esteemed incomparably higher than anything which could be brought about by it in favor of any inclination or even of the sum total of all inclinations. Even if it should happen that, by a particular unfortunate fate or by the niggardly provision of a stepmotherly nature, this will should be wholly lacking in power to accomplish its purpose, and if even the greatest effort should not avail it to achieve anything of its end, and if there remained only the good will (not as a mere wish but as the summoning of all the means in our power), it would sparkle like a jewel in its own right, as something that had its full worth in itself. Usefulness or fruitlessness can neither diminish nor augment this worth.

He would presumably have said the same thing about a bad will: whether it accomplishes its evil purposes is morally irrelevant. And a course of action that would be condemned if it had a bad outcome cannot be vindicated if by luck it turns out well. There cannot be moral risk. This view seems to be wrong, but it arises in response to a fundamental problem about moral responsibility to which we possess no satisfactory solution.

The problem develops out of the ordinary conditions of moral judgment. Prior to reflection it is intuitively plausible that people cannot be morally assessed for what is not their fault, or for what is due

Reprinted from *Mortal Questions* by Thomas Nagel by permission of Thomas Nagel and Cambridge University Press.

to factors beyond their control. Such judgment is different from the evaluation of something as a good or bad thing, or state of affairs. The latter may be present in addition to moral judgment, but when we blame someone for his actions we are not merely saying it is bad that they happened, or bad that he exists: we are judging *him,* saying he is bad, which is different from his being a bad thing. This kind of judgment takes only a certain kind of object. Without being able to explain exactly why, we feel that the appropriateness of moral assessment is easily undermined by the discovery that the act or attribute, no matter how good or bad, is not under the person's control. While other evaluations remain, this one seems to lose its footing. So a clear absence of control, produced by involuntary movement, physical force, or ignorance of the circumstances, excuses what is done from moral judgment. But what we do depends in many more ways than these on what is not under our control—what is not produced by a good or a bad will in Kant's phrase. And external influences in this broader range are not usually thought to excuse what is done from moral judgment, positive or negative.

Let me give a few examples, beginning with the type of case Kant has in mind. Whether we succeed or fail in what we try to do nearly always depends to some extent on factors beyond our control. This is true of murder, altruism, revolution, the sacrifice of certain interests for the sake of others—almost any morally important act. What has been done, and what is morally judged, is partly determined by external factors. However jewel-like the good will may be in its own right, there is a morally significant difference between rescuing someone from a burning building and dropping him from a twelfth-story window while trying to rescue him. Similarly, there is a morally significant difference between reckless driving and manslaughter. But whether a reckless driver hits a pedestrian depends on the presence of the pedestrian at the point where he recklessly passes a red light. What we do is also limited by the opportunities and choices with which we are faced, and these are largely determined by factors beyond our control. Someone who was an officer in a concentration camp might have led a quiet and harmless life if the Nazis had never come to power in Germany. And someone who led a quiet and harmless life in Argentina might have become an officer in a concentration camp if he had not left Germany for business reasons in 1930.

I shall say more later about these and other examples. I introduce them here to illustrate a general point. Where a significant aspect of what someone does depends on factors beyond his control, yet we continue to treat him in that respect as an object of moral judgment, it can be called moral luck. Such luck can be good or bad. And the problem posed by this phenomenon, which led Kant to deny its possibility, is that the broad range of external influences here identified seems on close examination to undermine moral assessment as surely as does the narrower range of familiar excusing conditions. If the condition of control is consistently applied, it threatens to erode most of the moral assessments we find it natural to make. The things for which people are morally judged are determined in more ways than we at first realize by what is beyond their control. And when the seemingly natural requirement of fault or responsibility is applied in light of these facts, it leaves few pre-reflective moral judgments intact. Ultimately, nothing or almost nothing about what a person does seems to be under his control.

Why not conclude, then, that the condition of control is false—that it is an initially plausible hypothesis refuted by clear counter-examples? One could in that case look instead for a more refined condition which picked out the *kinds* of lack of control that really undermine certain moral judgments, without yielding the unacceptable conclusion derived from the broader condition, that most or all ordinary moral judgments are illegitimate.

What rules out this escape is that we are dealing not with a theoretical conjecture but with a philosophical problem. The condition of control does not suggest itself merely as a generalization from certain clear cases. It seems *correct* in the further cases to

which it is extended beyond the original set. When we undermine moral assessment by considering new ways in which control is absent, we are not just discovering what *would* follow given the general hypothesis, but are actually being persuaded that in itself the absence of control is relevant in these cases too. The erosion of moral judgment emerges not as the absurd consequence of an over-simple theory, but as a natural consequence of the ordinary idea of moral assessment, when it is applied in view of a more complete and precise account of the facts. It would therefore be a mistake to argue from the unacceptability of the conclusions to the need for a different account of the conditions of moral responsibility. The view that moral luck is paradoxical is not a *mistake,* ethical or logical, but a perception of one of the ways in which the intuitively acceptable conditions of moral judgment threaten to undermine it all.

It resembles the situation in another area of philosophy, the theory of knowledge. There too conditions which seem perfectly natural, and which grow out of the ordinary procedures for challenging and defending claims to knowledge, threaten to undermine all such claims if consistently applied. Most skeptical arguments have this quality: they do not depend on the imposition of arbitrarily stringent standards of knowledge, arrived at by misunderstanding, but appear to grow inevitably from the consistent application of ordinary standards. There is a substantive parallel as well, for epistemological skepticism arises from consideration of the respects in which our beliefs and their relation to reality depend on factors beyond our control. External and internal causes produce our beliefs. We may subject these processes to scrutiny in an effort to avoid error, but our conclusions at this next level also result, in part, from influences which we do not control directly. The same will be true no matter how far we carry the investigation. Our beliefs are always, ultimately, due to factors outside our control, and the impossibility of encompassing those factors without being at the mercy of others leads us to doubt whether we know anything. It looks as though, if any of our beliefs are true, it is pure biological luck rather than knowledge.

Moral luck is like this because while there are various respects in which the natural objects of moral assessment are out of our control or influenced by what is out of our control, we cannot reflect on these facts without losing our grip on the judgments.

There are roughly four ways in which the natural objects of moral assessment are disturbingly subject to luck. One is the phenomenon of constitutive luck—the kind of person you are, where this is not just a question of what you deliberately do, but of your inclinations, capacities, and temperament. Another category is luck in one's circumstances—the kind of problems and situations one faces. The other two have to do with the causes and effects of action: luck in how one is determined by antecedent circumstances, and luck in the way one's actions and projects turn out. All of them present a common problem. They are all opposed by the idea that one cannot be more culpable or estimable for anything than one is for that fraction of it which is under one's control. It seems irrational to take or dispense credit or blame for matters over which a person has no control, or for their influence on results over which he has partial control. Such things may create the conditions for action, but action can be judged only to the extent that it goes beyond these conditions and does not just result from them.

Let us first consider luck, good and bad, in the way things turn out. Kant, in the above-quoted passage, has one example of this in mind, but the category covers a wide range. It includes the truck driver who accidentally runs over a child, the artist who abandons his wife and five children to devote himself to painting, and other cases in which the possibilities of success and failure are even greater. The driver, if he is entirely without fault, will feel terrible about his role in the event, but will not have to reproach himself. Therefore this example of agent-regret is not yet a case of *moral* bad luck. However, if the driver was guilty of even a minor degree of negligence—failing to have his brakes checked recently, for example—then if that negligence contributes to the death of the child, he will not merely feel terrible. He will blame himself for the death. And what makes this an example of moral luck is that he would have to blame himself only slightly for the negligence itself if no situation arose which required him to brake suddenly and violently to avoid hitting a child. Yet the *negligence* is the same in both cases,

and the driver has no control over whether a child will run into his path.

The same is true at higher levels of negligence. If someone has had too much to drink and his car swerves on to the sidewalk, he can count himself morally lucky if there are no pedestrians in his path. If there were, he would be to blame for their deaths, and would probably be prosecuted for manslaughter. But if he hurts no one, although his recklessness is exactly the same, he is guilty of a far less serious legal offense and will certainly reproach himself and be reproached by others much less severely. To take another legal example, the penalty for attempted murder is less than that for successful murder—however similar the intentions and motives of the assailant may be in the two cases. His degree of culpability can depend, it would seem, on whether the victim happened to be wearing a bullet-proof vest, or whether a bird flew into the path of the bullet—matters beyond his control.

Finally, there are cases of decision under uncertainty—common in public and in private life. Anna Karenina goes off with Vronsky, Gauguin leaves his family, Chamberlain signs the Munich agreement, the Decembrists persuade the troops under their command to revolt against the czar, the American colonies declare their independence from Britain, you introduce two people in an attempt at matchmaking. It is tempting in all such cases to feel that some decision must be possible, in the light of what is known at the time, which will make reproach unsuitable no matter how things turn out. But this is not true; when someone acts in such ways he takes his life, or his moral position, into his hands, because how things run out determines what he has done. It is possible *also* to assess the decision from the point of view of what could be known at the time, but this is not the end of the story. If the Decembrists had succeeded in overthrowing Nicholas I in 1825 and establishing a constitutional regime, they would be heroes. As it is, not only did they fail and pay for it, but they bore some responsibility for the terrible punishments meted out to the troops who had been persuaded to follow them. If the American Revolution had been a bloody failure resulting in greater repression, then Jefferson, Franklin and Washington would still have made a noble attempt, and might not even have regretted it on their way to the scaffold, but they would also have had to blame themselves for what they had helped to bring on their compatriots. (Perhaps peaceful efforts at reform would eventually have succeeded.) If Hitler had not overrun Europe and exterminated millions, but instead had died of a heart attack after occupying the Sudetenland, Chamberlain's action at Munich would still have utterly betrayed the Czechs, but it would not be the great moral disaster that has made his name a household word.

In many cases of difficult choice the outcome cannot be foreseen with certainty. One kind of assessment of the choice is possible in advance, but another kind must await the outcome, because the outcome determines what has been done. The same degree of culpability or estimability in intention, motive, or concern is compatible with a wide range of judgments, positive or negative, depending on what happened beyond the point of decision. The *mens rea* which could have existed in the absence of any consequences does not exhaust the grounds of moral judgment. Actual results influence culpability or esteem in a large class of unquestionably ethical cases ranging from negligence through political choice.

That these are genuine moral judgments rather than expressions of temporary attitude is evident from the fact that one can say *in advance* how the moral verdict will depend on the results. If one negligently leaves the bath running with the baby in it, one will realize, as one bounds up the stairs toward the bathroom, that if the baby has drowned one has done something awful, whereas if it has not one has merely been careless. Someone who launches a violent revolution against an authoritarian regime knows that if he fails he will be responsible for much suffering that is in vain, but if he succeeds he will be justified by the outcome. I do not mean that *any* action can be retroactively justified by history. Certain things are so bad in themselves, or so risky, that no results can make them all right. Nevertheless, when moral judgment does depend on the outcome, it is objective and timeless and not dependent on a change of standpoint produced by success or failure. The judgment after the fact follows from a hypothetical judgment that can be made beforehand, and it can be made as easily by someone else as by the agent.

From the point of view which makes responsibility dependent on control, all this seems absurd. How is it possible to be more or less culpable depending on whether a child gets into the path of one's car, or a bird into the path of one's bullet? Perhaps it is true that what is done depends on more than the agent's state of mind or intention. The problem then is, why is it not irrational to base moral assessment on what people do, in this broad sense? It amounts to holding them responsible for the contributions of fate as well as for their own—provided they have made some contribution to begin with. If we look at cases of negligence or attempt, the pattern seems to be that overall culpability corresponds to the product of mental or intentional fault and the seriousness of the outcome. Cases of decision under uncertainty are less easily explained in this way, for it seems that the overall judgment can even shift from positive to negative depending on the outcome. But here too it seems rational to subtract the effects of occurrences subsequent to the choice, that were merely possible at the time, and concentrate moral assessment on the actual decision in light of the probabilities. If the object of moral judgment is the *person,* then to hold him accountable for what he has done in the broader sense is akin to strict liability, which may have its legal uses but seems irrational as a moral position.

The result of such a line of thought is to pare down each act to its morally essential core, an inner act of pure will assessed by motive and intention. Adam Smith advocates such a position in *The Theory of Moral Sentiments,* but notes that it runs contrary to our actual judgments.

> But how well soever we may seem to be persuaded of the truth of this equitable maxim, when we consider it after this manner, in abstract, yet when we come to particular cases, the actual consequences which happen to proceed from any action, have a very great effect upon our sentiments concerning its merit or demerit, and almost always either enhance or diminish our sense of both. Scarce, in any one instance, perhaps, will our sentiments be found, after examination, to be entirely regulated by this rule, which we all acknowledge ought entirely to regulate them.

Joel Feinberg points out further that restricting the domain of moral responsibility to the inner world will not immunize it to luck. Factors beyond the agent's control, like a coughing fit, can interfere with his decisions as surely as they can with the path of a bullet from his gun. Nevertheless the tendency to cut down the scope of moral assessment is pervasive, and does not limit itself to the influence of effects. It attempts to isolate the will from the other direction, so to speak, by separating out constitutive luck. Let us consider that next.

Kant was particularly insistent on the moral irrelevance of qualities of temperament and personality that are not under the control of the will. Such qualities as sympathy or coldness might provide the background against which obedience to moral requirements is more or less difficult, but they could not be objects of moral assessment themselves, and might well interfere with confident assessment of its proper object—the determination of the will by the motive of duty. This rules out moral judgment of many of the virtues and vices, which are states of character that influence choice but are certainly not exhausted by dispositions to act deliberately in certain ways. A person may be greedy, envious, cowardly, cold, ungenerous, unkind, vain, or conceited, but *behave* perfectly by a monumental effort of will. To possess these vices is to be unable to help having certain feelings under certain circumstances, and to have strong spontaneous impulses to act badly. Even if one controls the impulses, one still has the vice. An envious person hates the greater success of others. He can be morally condemned as envious even if he congratulates them cordially and does nothing to denigrate or spoil their success. Conceit, likewise, need not be displayed. It is fully present in someone who cannot help dwelling with secret satisfaction on the superiority of his own achievements, talents, beauty, intelligence, or virtue. To some extent such a quality may be the product of earlier choices; to some extent it may be amenable to change by current actions. But it is largely a matter of constitutive bad fortune. Yet people are morally condemned for such qualities, and esteemed for others equally beyond control of the will: they are assessed for what they are *like*.

To Kant this seems incoherent because virtue is enjoined on everyone and therefore must in principle be possible for everyone. It may be easier for some than for others, but it must be possible to achieve it by making the right choices, against whatever temperamental background. One may want to have a generous spirit, or regret not having one, but it makes no sense to condemn oneself or anyone else for a quality which is not within the control of the will. Condemnation implies that you should not be like that, not that it is unfortunate that you are.

Nevertheless, Kant's conclusion remains intuitively unacceptable. We may be persuaded that these moral judgments are irrational, but they reappear involuntarily as soon as the argument is over. This is the pattern throughout the subject.

The third category to consider is luck in one's circumstances, and I shall mention it briefly. The things we are called upon to do, the moral tests we face, are importantly determined by factors beyond our control. It may be true of someone that in a dangerous situation he would behave in a cowardly or heroic fashion, but if the situation never arises, he will never have the chance to distinguish or disgrace himself in this way, and his moral record will be different.

A conspicuous example of this is political. Ordinary citizens of Nazi Germany had an opportunity to behave heroically by opposing the regime. They also had an opportunity to behave badly, and most of them are culpable for having failed this test. But it is a test to which the citizens of other countries were not subjected, with the result that even if they, or some of them, would have behaved as badly as the Germans in like circumstances, they simply did not and therefore are not similarly culpable. Here again one is morally at the mercy of fate, and it may seem irrational upon reflection, but our ordinary moral attitudes would be unrecognizable without it. We judge people for what they actually do or fail to do, not just for what they would have done if circumstances had been different.

This form of moral determination by the actual is also paradoxical, but we can begin to see how deep in the concept of responsibility the paradox is embedded. A person can be morally responsible only for what he does; but what he does results from a great deal that he does not do; therefore he is not morally responsible for what he is and is not responsible for. (This is not a contradiction, but it is a paradox.)

It should be obvious that there is a connection

between these problems about responsibility and control and an even more familiar problem, that of freedom of the will. That is the last type of moral luck I want to take up, though I can do no more within the scope of this essay than indicate its connection with the other types.

If one cannot be responsible for consequences of one's acts due to factors beyond one's control, or for antecedents of one's acts that are properties of temperament not subject to one's will, or for the circumstances that pose one's moral choices, then how can one be responsible even for the stripped-down acts of the will itself, if *they* are the product of antecedent circumstances outside of the will's control?

The area of genuine agency, and therefore of legitimate moral judgment, seems to shrink under this scrutiny to an extensionless point. Everything seems to result from the combined influence of factors, antecedent and posterior to action, that are not within the agent's control. Since he cannot be responsible for them, he cannot be responsible for their results —though it may remain possible to take up the aesthetic or other evaluative analogues of the moral attitudes that are thus displaced.

It is also possible, of course, to brazen it out and refuse to accept the results, which indeed seem unacceptable as soon as we stop thinking about the arguments. Admittedly, if certain surrounding circumstances had been different, then no unfortunate consequences would have followed from a wicked intention, and no seriously culpable act would have been performed; but since the circumstances were *not* different, and the agent *in fact* succeeded in perpetrating a particularly cruel murder, *that* is what he did, and that is what he is responsible for. Similarly, we may admit that if certain antecedent circumstances had been different, the agent would never have developed into the sort of person who would do such a thing; but since he *did* develop (as the inevitable result of those antecedent circumstances) into the sort of swine he is, and into the person who committed such a murder, *that* is what he is blameable for. In both cases one is responsible for what one actually does—even if what one actually does depends in important ways on what is not within one's control. This compatibilist account of our moral judgments would leave room for the ordinary conditions of responsibility—the absence of coercion, ignorance, or involuntary movement—as part of the determination of what someone has done— but it is understood not to exclude the influence of a great deal that he has not done.

The only thing wrong with this solution is its failure to explain how skeptical problems arise. For they arise not from the imposition of an arbitrary external requirement, but from the nature of moral judgment itself. Something in the ordinary idea of what someone does must explain how it can seem necessary to subtract from it anything that merely happens—even though the ultimate consequence of such subtraction is that nothing remains. And something in the ordinary idea of knowledge must explain why it seems to be undermined by any influences on belief not within the control of the subject—so that knowledge seems impossible without an impossible foundation in autonomous reason. But let us leave epistemology aside and concentrate on action, character, and moral assessment.

The problem arises, I believe, because the self which acts and is the object of moral judgment is threatened with dissolution by the absorption of its acts and impulses into the class of events. Moral judgment of a person is judgment not of what happens to him, but of him. It does not say merely that a certain event or state of affairs is fortunate or unfortunate or even terrible. It is not an evaluation of a state of the world, or of an individual as part of the world. We are not thinking just that it would be better if he were different, or did not exist, or had not done some of the things he has done. We are judging *him*, rather than his existence or characteristics. The effect of concentrating on the influence of what is not under his control is to make this responsible self seem to disappear, swallowed up by the order of mere events.

What, however, do we have in mind that a person must *be* to be the object of these moral attitudes? While the concept of agency is easily undermined, it is very difficult to give it a positive characterization. That is familiar from the literature on Free Will.

I believe that in a sense the problem has no solution, because something in the idea of agency is incompatible with actions being events, or people being things. But as the external determinants of what someone has done are gradually exposed, in their effect on consequences, character, and choice itself, it becomes gradually clear that actions are events and people things. Eventually nothing remains which can be ascribed to the responsible self, and we are left with nothing but a portion of the larger sequences of events, which can be deplored or celebrated, but not blamed or praised.

Though I cannot define the idea of the active self that is thus undermined, it is possible to say something about its sources. There is a close connection between our feelings about ourselves and our feelings about others. Guilt and indignation, shame and contempt, pride and admiration are internal and external sides of the same moral attitudes. We are unable to view ourselves simply as portions of the world, and from inside we have a rough idea of the boundary between what is us and what is not, what we do and what happens to us, what is our personality and what is an accidental handicap. We apply the same essentially internal conception of the self to others. About ourselves we feel pride, shame, guilt, remorse—and agent-regret. We do not regard our actions and our characters merely as fortunate or unfortunate episodes—though they may also be that. We cannot *simply* take an external evaluative view of ourselves—of what we most essentially are and what we do. And this remains true even when we have seen that we are not responsible for our own existence, or our nature, or the choices we have to make, or the circumstances that give our acts the consequences they have. Those acts remain ours and we remain ourselves, despite the persuasiveness of the reasons that seem to argue us out of existence.

It is this internal view that we extend to others in moral judgment—when we judge *them* rather than their desirability or utility. We extend to others the refusal to limit ourselves to external evaluation, and we accord to them selves like our own. But in both cases this comes up against the brutal inclusion of humans and everything about them in a world from which they cannot be separated and of which they are nothing but contents. The external view forces itself on us at the same time that we resist it. One way this occurs is through the gradual erosion of what we do by the subtraction of what happens.

The inclusion of consequences in the conception of what we have done is an acknowledgment that we are parts of the world, but the paradoxical character of moral luck which emerges from this acknowledgment shows that we are unable to operate with such a view, for it leaves us with no one to be. The same thing is revealed in the appearance that determinism obliterates responsibility. Once we see an aspect of what we or someone else does as something that happens, we lose our grip on the idea that it has been done and that we can judge the doer and not just the happening. This explains why the absence of determinism is no more hospitable to the concept of agency than is its presence—a point that has been noticed often. Either way the act is viewed externally, as part of the course of events.

The problem of moral luck cannot be understood without an account of the internal conception of agency and its special connection with the moral attitudes as opposed to other types of value. I do not have such an account. The degree to which the problem has a solution can be determined only by seeing whether in some degree the incompatibility between this conception and the various ways in which we do not control what we do is only apparent. I have nothing to offer on that topic either, but it is not enough to say merely that our basic moral attitudes toward ourselves and others are determined by what is actual; for they are also threatened by the sources of that actuality, and by the external view of action which forces itself on us when we see how everything we do belongs to a world that we have not created.

Sanity and the Metaphysics of Responsibility

SUSAN WOLF

Susan Wolf (1952–   ) teaches philosophy at Johns Hopkins University.

Philosophers who study the problems of free will and responsibility have an easier time than most in meeting challenges about the relevance of their work to ordinary, practical concerns. Indeed, philosophers who study these problems are rarely faced with such challenges at all, since questions concerning the conditions of responsibility come up so obviously and so frequently in everyday life. Under scrutiny, however, one might question whether the connections between philosophical and nonphilosophical concerns in this area are real.

In everyday contexts, when lawyers, judges, parents, and others are concerned with issues of responsibility, they know, or think they know, what in general the conditions of responsibility are. Their questions are questions of application: Does this or that particular person meet this or that particular condition? Is this person mature enough, or informed enough, or sane enough to be responsible? Was he or she acting under posthypnotic suggestion or under the influence of a mind-impairing drug? It is assumed, in these contexts, that normal, fully developed adult human beings are responsible beings. The questions have to do with whether a given individual falls within the normal range.

By contrast, philosophers tend to be uncertain about the general conditions of responsibility, and they care less about dividing the responsible from the nonresponsible agents than about determining whether, and if so why, any of us are ever responsible for anything at all.

In the classroom, we might argue that the philosophical concerns grow out of the nonphilosophical ones, that they take off where the nonphilosophical questions stop. In this way, we might convince our students that even if they are not plagued by the philosophical worries, they ought to be. If they worry about whether a person is mature enough, informed enough, and sane enough to be responsible, then they should worry about whether that person is metaphysically free enough, too.

The argument I make here, however, goes in the opposite direction. My aim is not to convince people who are interested in the apparently nonphilosophical conditions of responsibility that they should go on to worry about the philosophical conditions as well, but rather to urge those who already worry about the philosophical problems not to leave the more mundane, prephilosophical problems behind. In particular, I suggest that the mundane recognition that *sanity* is a condition of responsibility has more to do with the murky and apparently metaphysical problems which surround the issue of responsibility than at first meets the eye. Once the significance of the condition of sanity is fully appreciated, at least some of the apparently insuperable metaphysical aspects of the problem of responsibility will dissolve.

My strategy is to examine a recent trend in philosophical discussions of responsibility, a trend that tries, but I think ultimately fails, to give an acceptable analysis of the conditions of responsibility. It fails due to what at first appear to be deep and irresolvable metaphysical problems. It is here that I suggest that the condition of sanity comes to the rescue. What at first appears to be an impossible requirement for responsibility—the requirement that the responsible agent have created her- or himself—turns out to be the vastly more mundane and noncontroversial requirement that the responsible agent must, in a fairly standard sense, be sane.

From Ferdinand David Shoeman, ed., *Responsibility, Character, and the Emotions: New Essays in Moral Psychology* (New York: Cambridge University Press, 1988), pp. 46–62. Reprinted with the permission of Cambridge University Press.

FRANKFURT, WATSON, AND TAYLOR

The trend I have in mind is exemplified by the writings of Harry Frankfurt, Gary Watson, and Charles Taylor. I will briefly discuss each of their separate proposals, and then offer a composite view that, while lacking the subtlety of any of the separate accounts, will highlight some important insights and some important blind spots they share.

In his seminal article "Freedom of the Will and the Concept of a Person,"[1] Harry Frankfurt notes a distinction between freedom of action and freedom of the will. A person has freedom of action, he points out, if she (or he) has the freedom to do whatever she wills to do—the freedom to talk or sit, to vote liberal or conservative, to publish a book or open a store, in accordance with her strongest desires. Even a person who has freedom of action may fail to be responsible for her actions, however, if the wants or desires she has the freedom to convert into action are themselves not subject to her control. Thus, the person who acts under posthypnotic suggestion, the victim of brainwashing, and the kleptomaniac might all possess freedom of action. In the standard contexts in which these examples are raised, it is assumed that none of the individuals is locked up or bound. Rather, these individuals are understood to act on what, at one level at least, must be called *their own desires*. Their exemption from responsibility stems from the fact that their own desires (or at least the ones governing their actions) are not up to them. These cases may be described in Frankfurt's terms as cases of people who possess freedom of action, but who fail to be responsible agents because they lack freedom of the will.

Philosophical problems about the conditions of responsibility naturally focus on an analysis of this latter kind of freedom: What *is* freedom of the will, and under what conditions can we reasonably be thought to possess it? Frankfurt's proposal is to understand freedom of the will by analogy to freedom of action. As freedom of action is the freedom to do whatever one wills to do, freedom of the will is the freedom to will whatever one wants to will. To make this point clearer, Frankfurt introduces a distinction between first-order and second-order desires. First-order desires are desires to do or to have various things; second-order desires are desires about what desires to have or what desires to make effective in action. In order for an agent to have both freedom of action and freedom of the will, that agent must be capable of governing his or her actions by first-order desires *and* capable of governing his or her first-order desires by second-order desires.

Gary Watson's view of free agency[2]—free and responsible agency, that is—is similar to Frankfurt's in holding that an agent is responsible for an action only if the desires expressed by that action are of a particular kind. While Frankfurt identifies the right kinds of desires as desires that are supported by second-order desires, however, Watson draws a distinction between "mere" desires, so to speak, and desires that are *values*. According to Watson, the difference between free action and unfree action cannot be analyzed by reference to the logical form of the desires from which these various actions arise, but rather must relate to a difference in the quality of their source. Whereas some of my desires are just appetites or conditioned responses I find myself "stuck with," others are expressions of judgments on my part that the objects I desire are good. Insofar as my actions can be governed by the latter type of desire—governed, that is, by my values or valuational system—they are actions that I perform freely and for which I am responsible.

Frankfurt's and Watson's accounts may be understood as alternate developments of the intuition that in order to be responsible for one's actions, one must be responsible for the self that performs these actions. Charles Taylor, in an article entitled "Responsibility for Self,"[3] is concerned with the same intuition. Although Taylor does not describe his view in terms of different levels or types of desire, his view is related, for he claims that our freedom and responsibility depend on our ability to reflect on, criticize, and revise our selves. Like Frankfurt and Watson, Taylor seems to believe that if the characters from which our actions flowed were simply and permanently *given* to us, implanted by heredity, environment, or God, then we would be mere vehicles through which the causal forces of the world traveled, no more responsible than dumb animals or young children or machines. But like the others, he points out that, for most of us, our characters and desires are not so brutely implanted—or, at any rate, if they are, they are subject to revision by our own reflecting, valuing, or second-order desiring selves. We human beings—and as far as we know, only we human beings—have the ability to step back from ourselves and decide whether we are the selves we want to be. Because of this, these philosophers think, we are responsible for our selves and for the actions that we produce.

Although there are subtle and interesting differences among the accounts of Frankfurt, Watson, and Taylor, my concern is with features of their views that are common to them all. All share the idea that responsible agency involves something more than intentional agency. All agree that if we are responsible agents, it is not just because our actions are within the control of our wills, but because, in addition, our wills are not just psychological states *in* us, but expressions of characters that come *from* us, or that at any rate are acknowledged and affirmed *by* us. For Frankfurt, this means that our wills must be ruled by our second-order desires; for Watson, that our wills must be governable by our system of values; for Taylor, that our wills must issue from selves that are subject to self-assessment and redefinition in terms of a vocabulary of worth. In one way or another, all these philosophers seem to be saying that the key to responsibility lies in the fact that responsible agents are those for whom it is not just the case that their actions are within the control of their wills, but also the case that their wills are within the control of their *selves* in some deeper sense. Because, at one level, the differences among Frankfurt, Watson, and Taylor may be understood as differences in the analysis or interpretation of what it is for an action to be under the control of this deeper self, we may speak of their separate positions as variations of one basic view about responsibility: the *deep-self view*.

THE DEEP-SELF VIEW

Much more must be said about the notion of a deep self before a fully satisfactory account of this view can be given. Providing a careful, detailed analysis of that notion poses an interesting, important, and difficult task in its own right. The degree of understanding achieved by abstraction from the views of

Frankfurt, Watson, and Taylor, however, should be sufficient to allow us to recognize some important virtues as well as some important drawbacks of the deep-self view.

One virtue is that this view explains a good portion of our pretheoretical intuitions about responsibility. It explains why kleptomaniacs, victims of brainwashing, and people acting under posthypnotic suggestion may not be responsible for their actions, although most of us typically are. In the cases of people in these special categories, the connection between the agent's deep selves and their wills is dramatically severed—their wills are governed not by their deep selves, but by forces external to and independent from them. A different intuition is that we adult human beings can be responsible for our actions in a way that dumb animals, infants, and machines cannot. Here the explanation is not in terms of a split between these beings' deep selves and their wills; rather, the point is that these beings *lack* deep selves altogether. Kleptomaniacs and victims of hypnosis exemplify individuals whose selves are *alienated* from their actions; lower animals and machines, on the other hand, do not have the sorts of selves from which actions *can* be alienated, and so they do not have the sort of selves from which, in the happier cases, actions can responsibly flow.

At a more theoretical level, the deep-self view has another virtue: It responds to at least one way in which the fear of determinism presents itself.

A naive reaction to the idea that everything we do is completely determined by a causal chain that extends backward beyond the times of our births involves thinking that in that case we would have no control over our behavior whatsoever. If everything is determined, it is thought, then what happens happens, whether we want it to or not. A common, and proper, response to this concern points out that determinism does not deny the causal efficacy an agent's desires might have on his or her behavior. On the contrary, determinism in its more plausible forms tends to affirm this connection, merely adding that as one's behavior is determined by one's desires, so one's desires are determined by something else.[4]

Those who were initially worried that determinism implied fatalism, however, are apt to find their fears merely transformed rather than erased. If our desires are governed by something else, they might say, they are not *really* ours after all—or, at any rate, they are ours in only a superficial sense.

The deep-self view offers an answer to this transformed fear of determinism, for it allows us to distinguish cases in which desires are determined by forces foreign to oneself from desires which are determined *by* one's self—by one's "real," or second-order desiring, or valuing, or deep self, that is. Admittedly, there are cases, like that of the kleptomaniac or the victim of hypnosis, in which the agent acts on desires that "belong to" him or her in only a superficial sense. But the proponent of the deep-self view will point out that even if determinism is true, ordinary adult human action can be distinguished from this. Determinism implies that the desires which govern our actions are in turn governed by something else, but that something else will, in the fortunate cases, be our own deeper selves.

This account of responsibility thus offers a response to our fear of determinism; but it is a response with which many will remain unsatisfied. Even if my actions are governed by my desires and my desires are governed by my own deeper self, there remains the question: Who, or what, is responsible for this deeper self? The response above seems only to have pushed the problem further back.

Admittedly, some versions of the deep-self view, including Frankfurt's and Taylor's, seem to anticipate this question by providing a place for the ideal that an agent's deep self may be governed by a still deeper self. Thus, for Frankfurt, second-order desires may themselves be governed by third-order desires, third-order desires by fourth-order desires, and so on. Also, Taylor points out that, as we can reflect on and evaluate our prereflective selves, so we can reflect on and evaluate the selves who are doing the first reflecting and evaluating, and so on. However, this capacity to recursively create endless levels of depth ultimately misses the criticism's point.

First of all, even if there is no *logical* limit to the number of levels of reflection or depth a person may have, there is certainly a psychological limit—it is virtually impossible imaginatively to conceive a fourth-, much less an eighth-order, desire. More important, no matter how many levels of self we posit, there will still, in any individual case, be a last level—

a deepest self about whom the question "What governs it?" will arise, as problematic as ever. If determinism is true, it implies that even if my actions are governed by my desires, and my desires are governed by my deepest self, my deepest self will still be governed by something that must, logically, be external to myself altogether. Though I can step back from the values my parents and teachers have given me and ask whether these are the values I really want, the "I" that steps back will itself be a product of the parents and teachers I am questioning.

The problem seems even worse when one sees that one fares no better if determinism is false. For if my deepest self is not determined by something external to myself, it will still not be determined by *me*. Whether I am a product of carefully controlled forces or a result of random mutations, whether there is a complete explanation of my origin or no explanation at all, *I* am not, in any case, responsible for my existence; I am not in control of my deepest self.

Thus, though the claim that an agent is responsible for only those actions that are within the control of his or her deep self correctly identifies a necessary condition for responsibility—a condition that separates the hypnotized and the brainwashed, the immature and the lower animals from ourselves, for example—it fails to provide a sufficient condition of responsibility that puts all fears of determinism to rest. For one of the fears invoked by the thought of determinism seems to be connected to its implication that we are but intermediate links in a causal chain, rather than ultimate, self-initiating sources of movement and change. From the point of view of one who has this fear, the deep-self view seems merely to add loops to the chain, complicating the picture but not really improving it. From the point of view of one who has this fear, responsibility seems to require being a prime mover unmoved, whose deepest self is itself neither random *nor* externally determined, but is rather determined *by* itself —who is, in other words, self-created.

At this point, however, proponents of the deep-self view may wonder whether this fear is legitimate. For although people evidently can be brought to the point where they feel that responsible agency requires them to be ultimate sources of power, to the point where it seems that nothing short of self-creation will do, a return to the internal standpoint of the agent whose responsibility is in question makes it hard to see what good this metaphysical status is supposed to provide or what evil its absence is supposed to impose.

From the external standpoint, which discussions of determinism and indeterminism encourage us to take up, it may appear that a special metaphysical status is required to distinguish us significantly from other members of the natural world. But proponents of the deep-self view will suggest this is an illusion that a return to the internal standpoint should dispel. The possession of a deep self that is effective in governing one's actions is a sufficient distinction, they will say. For while other members of the natural world are not in control of the selves that they are, we, possessors of effective deep selves, are in control. We can reflect on what sorts of beings we are, and on what sorts of marks we make on the world. We can change what we don't like about ourselves, and keep what we do. Admittedly, we do not create ourselves from nothing. But as long as we can revise ourselves, they will suggest, it is hard to find reason to complain. Harry Frankfurt writes that a person who is free to do what he wants to do and also free to want what he wants to want has "all the freedom it is possible to desire or to conceive."[5] This suggests a rhetorical question: If you are free to control your actions by your desires, and free to control your desires by your deeper desires, and free to control those desires by still deeper desires, what further kind of freedom can you want?

THE CONDITION OF SANITY

Unfortunately, there is a further kind of freedom we can want, which it is reasonable to think necessary for responsible agency. The deep-self view fails to be convincing when it is offered as a complete account of the conditions of responsibility. To see why, it will be helpful to consider another example of an agent whose responsibility is in question.

JoJo is the favorite son of Jo the First, an evil and sadistic dictator of a small, undeveloped country. Because of his father's special feelings for the boy, JoJo is given a special education and is allowed to accompany his father and observe his daily routine. In light of this treatment, it is not surprising that little JoJo takes his father as a role model and develops values very much like Dad's. As an adult, he does many of the same sorts of things his father did, including sending people to prison or to death or to torture chambers on the basis of whim. He is not *coerced* to do these things, he acts according to his own desires. Moreover, these are desires he wholly *wants* to have. When he steps back and asks, "Do I really want to be this sort of person?" his answer is resoundingly "Yes," for this way of life expresses a crazy sort of power that forms part of his deepest ideal.

In light of JoJo's heritage and upbringing—both of which he was powerless to control—it is dubious at best that he should be regarded as responsible for what he does. It is unclear whether anyone with a childhood such as his could have developed into anything but the twisted and perverse sort of person that he has become. However, note that JoJo is someone whose actions are controlled by his desires and whose desires are the desires he wants to have: That is, his actions are governed by desires that are governed by and expressive of his deepest self.

The Frankfurt–Watson–Taylor strategy that allowed us to differentiate our normal selves from the victims of hypnosis and brainwashing will not allow us to differentiate ourselves from the son of Jo the First. In the case of these earlier victims, we were able to say that although the actions of these individuals were, at one level, in control of the individuals themselves, these individuals themselves, qua agents, were not the selves they more deeply wanted to be. In this respect, these people were unlike our happily more integrated selves. However, we cannot say of JoJo that his self, qua agent, is not the self he wants it to be. It *is* the self he wants it to be. From the inside, he feels as integrated, free, and responsible as we do.

Our judgment that JoJo is not a responsible agent is one that we can make only from the outside—from reflecting on the fact, it seems, that his deepest self is not up to him. Looked at from the outside, however, our situation seems no different from his—for in the last analysis, it is not up to any of us to have the deepest selves we do. Once more, the problem seems metaphysical—and not just metaphysical, but insuperable. For, as I mentioned before, the problem is independent of the truth of determinism. Whether we are determined or undetermined, we cannot have created our deepest selves. Literal self-creation is not just empirically, but logically impossible.

If JoJo is not responsible because his deepest self is not up to him, then we are not responsible either. Indeed, in that case responsibility would be impossible for anyone to achieve. But I believe the appearance that literal self-creation is required for freedom and responsibility is itself mistaken.

The deep-self view was right in pointing out that freedom and responsibility require us to have certain distinctive types of control over our behavior and our selves. Specifically, our actions need to be under the control of our selves, and our (superficial) selves need to be under the control of our deep selves. Having seen that these types of control are not enough to guarantee us the status of responsible agents, we are tempted to go on to suppose that we must have yet another kind of control to assure us that even our deepest selves are somehow up to us. But not all the things necessary for freedom and responsibility must be types of power and control. We may need simply to *be* a certain way, even though it is not within our power to determine whether we are that way or not.

Indeed, it becomes obvious that at least one condition of responsibility is of this form as soon as we remember what, in everyday contexts, we have known all along—namely, that in order to be responsible, an agent must be *sane*. It is not ordinarily in our power to determine whether we are or are not sane. Most of us, it would seem, are lucky, but some of us are not. Moreover, being sane does not necessarily mean that one has any type of power or control an insane person lacks. Some insane people, like JoJo and some actual political leaders who resemble him, may have complete control of their actions, and even complete control of their acting selves. The desire to be sane is thus not a desire for another form of control; it is rather a desire that one's self be connected to the world in a certain way—we could even say it is a desire that one's self be *controlled by* the world in certain ways and not in others.

This becomes clear if we attend to the criteria for sanity that have historically been dominant in legal questions about responsibility. According to the M'Naughten Rule, a person is sane if (1) he knows what he is doing and (2) he knows that what he is

doing is, as the case may be, right or wrong. Insofar as one's desire to be sane involves a desire to know what one is doing—or more generally, a desire to live in the real world—it is a desire to be controlled (to have, in this case, one's *beliefs* controlled) by perceptions and sound reasoning that produce an accurate conception of the world, rather than by blind or distorted forms of response. The same goes for the second constituent of sanity—only, in this case, one's hope is that one's *values* be controlled by processes that afford an accurate conception of the world.[6] Putting these two conditions together, we may understand sanity, then, as the minimally sufficient ability cognitively and normatively to recognize and appreciate the world for what it is.

There are problems with this definition of sanity, at least some of which will become obvious in what follows, that make it ultimately unacceptable either as a gloss on or an improvement of the meaning of the term in many of the contexts in which it is used. The definition offered does seem to bring out the interest sanity has for us in connection with issues of responsibility, however, and some pedagogical as well as stylistic purposes will be served if we use sanity hereafter in this admittedly specialized sense.

THE SANE DEEP-SELF VIEW

So far I have argued that the conditions of responsible agency offered by the deep-self view are necessary but not sufficient. Moreover, the gap left open by the deep-self view seems to be one that can be filled only by a metaphysical, and, as it happens, metaphysically impossible addition. I now wish to argue, however, that the condition of sanity, as characterized above, is sufficient to fill the gap. In other words, the deep-self view, supplemented by the condition of sanity, provides a satisfying conception of responsibility. The conception of responsibility I am proposing, then, agrees with the deep-self view in requiring that a responsible agent be able to govern her (or his) actions by her desires and to govern her desires by her deep self. In addition, my conception insists that the agent's deep self be sane, and claims that this is *all* that is needed for responsible agency. By contrast to the plain deep-self view, let us call this new proposal the *sane deep-self view*.

It is worth noting, to begin with, that this new

proposal deals with the case of JoJo and related cases of deprived childhood victims in ways that better match our pretheoretical intuitions. Unlike the plain deep-self view, the sane deep-self view offers a way of explaining why JoJo is not responsible for his actions without throwing our own responsibility into doubt. For, although like us, JoJo's actions flow from desires that flow from his deep self, unlike us, JoJo's deep self is itself insane. Sanity, remember, involves the ability to know the difference between right and wrong, and a person who, even on reflection, cannot see that having someone tortured because he failed to salute you is wrong plainly lacks the requisite ability.

Less obviously, but quite analogously, this new proposal explains why we give less than full responsibility to persons who, though acting badly, act in ways that are strongly encouraged by their societies —the slaveowners of the 1850s, the Nazis of the 1930s, and many male chauvinists of our fathers' generation, for example. These are people, we imagine, who falsely believe that the ways in which they are acting are morally acceptable, and so, we may assume, their behavior is expressive of or at least in accordance with these agents' deep selves. But their false beliefs in the moral permissibility of their actions and the false values from which these beliefs derived may have been inevitable, given the social circumstances in which they developed. If we think that the agents could not help but be mistaken about their values, we do not blame them for the actions those values inspired.[7]

It would unduly distort ordinary linguistic practice to call the slaveowner, the Nazi, or the male chauvinist even partially or locally insane. Nonetheless, the reason for withholding blame from them is at bottom the same as the reason for withholding it from JoJo. Like JoJo, they are, at the deepest level, unable cognitively and normatively to recognize and appreciate the world for what it is. In our sense of the term, their deepest selves are not fully *sane*.

The sane deep-self view thus offers an account of why victims of deprived childhoods as well as victims of misguided societies may not be responsible for their actions, without implying that we are not responsible for ours. The actions of these others are governed by mistaken conceptions of value that the agents in question cannot help but have. Since, as

far as we know, our values are not, like theirs, unavoidably mistaken, the fact that these others are not responsible for their actions need not force us to conclude that we are not responsible for ours.

But it may not yet be clear why sanity, in this special sense, should make such a difference—why, in particular, the question of whether someone's values are unavoidably *mistaken* should have any bearing on their status as responsible agents. The fact that the sane deep-self view implies judgments that match our intuitions about the difference in status between characters like JoJo and ourselves provides little support for it if it cannot also defend these intuitions. So we must consider an objection that comes from the point of view we considered earlier which rejects the intuition that a relevant difference can be found.

Earlier, it seemed that the reason JoJo was not responsible for his actions was that although his actions were governed by his deep self, his deep self was not up to him. But this had nothing to do with his deep self's being mistaken or not mistaken, evil or good, insane or sane. If JoJo's values are unavoidably mistaken, our values, even if not mistaken, appear to be just as unavoidable. When it comes to freedom and responsibility, isn't it the unavoidability, rather than the mistakenness, that matters?

Before answering this question, it is useful to point out a way in which it is ambiguous: The concepts of avoidability and mistakenness are not unequivocally distinct. One may, to be sure, construe the notion of avoidability in a purely metaphysical way. Whether an event or state of affairs is unavoidable under this construal depends, as it were, on the tightness of the causal connections that bear on the event's or state of affairs' coming about. In this sense, our deep selves do seem as unavoidable for us as JoJo's and the others' are for them. For presumably we are just as influenced by our parents, our cultures, and our schooling as they are influenced by theirs. In another sense, however, our characters are not similarly unavoidable.

In particular, in the cases of JoJo and the others, there are certain features of their characters that they cannot avoid *even though these features are seriously mistaken, misguided, or bad*. This is so because, in our special sense of the term, these characters are less than fully sane. Since these characters lack the ability to know right from wrong, they are unable to revise their characters on the basis of right and wrong, and so their deep selves lack the resources and the reasons that might have served as a basis for self-correction. Since the deep selves *we* unavoidably have, however, are sane deep selves—deep selves, that is, that unavoidably *contain* the ability to know right from wrong—we unavoidably do have the resources and reasons on which to base self-correction. What this means is that though in one sense we are no more in control of our deepest selves than JoJo et al., it does not follow in our case, as it does in theirs, that we would be the way we are, even if it is a bad or wrong way to be. However, if this does not follow, it seems to me, our absence of control at the deepest level should not upset us.

Consider what the absence of control at the deepest level amounts to for us: Whereas JoJo is unable to control the fact that, at the deepest level, he is not fully sane, we are not responsible for the fact that, at the deepest level, we are. It is not up to us to *have* minimally sufficient abilities cognitively and normatively to recognize and appreciate the world for what it is. Also, presumably, it is not up to us to have lots of other properties, at least to begin with—a fondness for purple, perhaps, or an antipathy for beets. As the proponents of the plain deep-self view have been at pains to point out, however, we do, if we are lucky, have the ability to revise our selves in terms of the values that are held by or constitutive of our deep selves. If we are lucky enough both to have this ability and to have our deep selves be sane, it follows that although there is much in our characters that we did not choose to have, there is nothing irrational or objectionable in our characters that we are compelled to keep.

Being sane, we are able to understand and evaluate our characters in a reasonable way, to notice what there is reason to hold on to, what there is reason to eliminate, and what, from a rational and reasonable standpoint, we may retain or get rid of as we please. Being able as well to govern our superficial selves by our deep selves, then, we are able to change the things we find there is reason to change. This being so, it seems that although we may not be *metaphysically* responsible for ourselves—for, after all, we did not create ourselves from nothing—we are *morally* responsible for ourselves, for we are able to

understand and appreciate right and wrong, and to change our characters and our actions accordingly.

SELF-CREATION, SELF-REVISION, AND SELF-CORRECTION

At the beginning of this chapter, I claimed that recalling that sanity was a condition of responsibility would dissolve at least some of the appearance that responsibility was metaphysically impossible. To see how this is so, and to get a fuller sense of the sane deep-self view, it may be helpful to put that view into perspective by comparing it to the other views we have discussed along the way.

As Frankfurt, Watson, and Taylor showed us, in order to be free and responsible we need not only to be able to control our actions in accordance with our desires, we need to be able to control our desires in accordance with our deepest selves. We need, in other words, to be able to *revise* ourselves—to get rid of some desires and traits, and perhaps replace them with others on the basis of our deeper desires or values or reflections. However, consideration of the fact that the selves who are doing the revising might themselves be either brute products of external forces or arbitrary outputs of random generation made us wonder whether the capacity for self-revision was enough to assure us of responsibility—and the example of JoJo added force to the suspicion that it was not. Still, if the ability to revise ourselves is not enough, the ability to create ourselves does not seem necessary either. Indeed, when you think of it, it is unclear why anyone should want self-creation. Why should anyone be disappointed at having to accept the idea that one has to get one's start somewhere? It is an idea that most of us have lived with quite contentedly all along. What we do have reason to want, then, is something more than the ability to revise ourselves, but less than the ability to create ourselves. Implicit in the sane deep-self view is the idea that what is needed is the ability to *correct* (or improve) ourselves.

Recognizing that in order to be responsible for our actions, we have to be responsible for our selves, the sane deep-self view analyzes what is necessary in order to be responsible for our selves as (1) the ability to evaluate ourselves sensibly and accurately, and (2) the ability to transform ourselves insofar as our evaluation tells us to do so. We may understand the exercise of these abilities as a process whereby we *take* responsibility for the selves that we are but did not ultimately create. The condition of sanity is intrinsically connected to the first ability; the condition that we be able to control our superficial selves by our deep selves is intrinsically connected to the second.

The difference between the plain deep-self view and the sane deep-self view, then, is the difference between the requirement of the capacity for self-revision and the requirement of the capacity for self-correction. Anyone with the first capacity can *try* to take responsibility for himself or herself. However, only someone with a sane deep self—a deep self that can see and appreciate the world for what it is—can self-evaluate sensibly and accurately. Therefore, although insane selves can try to take responsibility for themselves, only sane selves will properly be accorded responsibility.

TWO OBJECTIONS CONSIDERED

At least two problems with the sane deep-self view are so glaring as to have certainly struck many readers. In closing, I shall briefly address them. First, some will be wondering how, in light of my specialized use of the term "sanity," I can be so sure that "we" are any saner than the nonresponsible individuals I have discussed. What justifies my confidence that, unlike the slaveowners, Nazis, and male chauvinists, not to mention JoJo himself, we are able to understand and appreciate the world for what it is? The answer to this is that nothing justifies this except widespread intersubjective agreement and the considerable success we have in getting around in the world and satisfying our needs. These are not sufficient grounds for the smug assumption that we are in a position to see the truth about *all* aspects of ethical and social life. Indeed, it seems more reasonable to expect that time will reveal blind spots in our cognitive and normative outlook, just as it has revealed errors in the outlooks of those who have lived before. But our judgments of responsibility can only be made from here, on the basis of the understandings and values that we can develop by exercising the abilities we do possess as well and as fully as possible.

If some have been worried that my view implicitly expresses an overconfidence in the assumption that we are sane and therefore right about the world, others will be worried that my view too closely connects sanity with being right about the world, and fear that my view implies that anyone who acts wrongly or has false beliefs about the world is therefore insane and so not responsible for his or her actions. This seems to me to be a more serious worry, which I am sure I cannot answer to everyone's satisfaction.

First, it must be admitted that the sane deep-self view embraces a conception of sanity that is explicitly normative. But this seems to me a strength of that view, rather than a defect. Sanity *is* a normative concept, in its ordinary as well as in its specialized sense, and severely deviant behavior, such as that of a serial murderer or a sadistic dictator, does constitute evidence of a psychological defect in the agent. The suggestion that the most horrendous, stomach-turning crimes could be committed only by an insane person—an inverse of Catch-22, as it were—must be regarded as a serious possibility, despite the practical problems that would accompany general acceptance of that conclusion.

But, it will be objected, there is no justification, in the sane deep-self view, for regarding only horrendous and stomach-turning crimes as evidence of insanity in its specialized sense. If sanity is the ability cognitively and normatively to understand and appreciate the world for what it is, then *any* wrong action or false belief will count as evidence of the absence of that ability. This point may also be granted, but we must be careful about what conclusion to draw. To be sure, when someone acts in a way that is not in accordance with acceptable standards of rationality and reasonableness, it is always appropriate to look for an explanation of why he or she acted that way. The hypothesis that the person was unable to understand and appreciate that an action fell outside acceptable bounds will always be a possible explanation. Bad performance on a math test always suggests the possibility that the testee is stupid. Typically, however, other explanations will be possible, too—for example, that the agent was too lazy to consider whether his or her action was acceptable, or too greedy to care, or, in the case of the math testee, that he or she was too occupied with other interests to attend class or study. Other facts about the agent's history will help us decide among these hypotheses.

This brings out the need to emphasize that sanity, in the specialized sense, is defined as the *ability* cognitively and normatively to understand and appreciate the world for what it is. According to our commonsense understandings, having his ability is one thing and exercising it is another—at least some wrong-acting, responsible agents presumably fall within the gap. The notion of "ability" is notoriously problematic, however, and there is a long history of controversy about whether the truth of determinism would show our ordinary ways of thinking to be simply confused on this matter. At this point, then, metaphysical concerns may voice themselves again—but at least they will have been pushed into a narrower, and perhaps a more manageable, corner.

The sane deep-self view does not, then, solve all the philosophical problems connected to the topics of free will and responsibility. If anything, it highlights some of the practical and empirical problems, rather than solves them. It may, however, resolve some of the philosophical, and particularly, some of the metaphysical problems, and reveal how intimate are the connections between the remaining philosophical problems and the practical ones.

Notes

1. Harry Frankfurt, "Freedom of the Will and the Concept of a Person," *Journal of Philosophy* LXVIII (1971), 5–20.

2. Gary Watson, "Free Agency," *Journal of Philosophy* LXXII (1975), 205–20.

3. Charles Taylor, "Responsibility for Self," in A. E. Rorty, ed., *The Identities of Persons* (Berkeley: University of California Press, 1976) pp. 281–99.

4. See, e.g., David Hume, *A Treatise of Human Nature* (Oxford: Oxford University Press, 1967), pp. 399–406, and R. E. Hobart, "Free Will as Involving Determination and Inconceivable Without It," *Mind* 43 (1934).

5. Frankfurt, p. 16.

6. Strictly speaking, perception and sound reasoning may not be enough to ensure the ability to achieve an accurate conception of what one is doing and especially to achieve a reasonable normative assessment of one's situation. Sensitivity and exposure to certain realms of experience may also be necessary for these goals. For the purpose of this essay, I understand "sanity" to include whatever it takes to enable one to develop an adequate conception of one's world. In other contexts, however, this would be an implausibly broad construction of the term.

7. Admittedly, it is open to question whether these individuals were in fact unable to help having mistaken values, and indeed, whether recognizing the errors of their society would even have required exceptional independence or strength of mind. This is presumably an empirical question, the answer to which is extraordinarily hard to determine. My point here is simply that *if* we believe they are unable to recognize that their values are mistaken, we do not hold them responsible for the actions that flow from these values, and *if* we believe their ability to recognize their normative errors is impaired, we hold them less than fully responsible for the relevant actions.

PART 5

Reason, Religion, and Faith

THE EXISTENCE AND NATURE OF GOD

According to Augustine, no one can believe in God without first *willing* it. This is because no amount of rational argument can affect the will. In his view, the sort of inner, transcendental revelation of truth, which he calls "faith," cannot be approached by reason. Rather, one must start with inner insights and reason from them to the truth (this was the procedure that Descartes would use a thousand years later). One cannot reason *to* faith, one must reason *from* faith. The cornerstone of his position is the famous dictum, "I believe in order to understand." This view of religion replaced the previous theology and dominated subsequent Christian thought for over nine centuries, until the advent of Aquinas's scholastic philosophy.

Augustine's famous *Confessions,* written in the year 400, when he was forty-three, begins with a description of the events of his life that led to his conversion. In our selection he raises the following philosophical question: When I think of God, what is the object of my thought? Like Plato, he seeks to understand what ultimate, or absolute, reality itself is. Augustine's God is the age-old quest for the ultimate ground, or source, of Being —the primary case, or essence, of existence.

Anselm's philosophy and theology, highly influenced by Greek rationality, laid the foundations for scholasticism, which was a method and system of thought based primarily on the works of Plato and Aristotle that embraced all the intellectual, artistic, philosophical, and theological activities of the various medieval schools. But unlike ancient Greek philosophy, which was essentially the work of individuals, scholasticism was an attempt to build philosophy as part of a Christian society, whose purpose in turn was to transcend both individuals and nations. As the corporate product of social thought, scholastic reasoning depended on obedience to authority as espoused by the traditional forms of thought codified within the supposedly "revealed" Christian religion under the auspices of the church. As a result, philosophy was subjugated to theology and rigidly controlled by the authoritarian hierarchy of the church.

In "The Ontological Argument," Anselm uses Aristotelian logic to create his famous ontological argument for the existence of God. Later thinkers divided over it vehemently. Philosophers such as Descartes, Spinoza, Leibniz, and Hegel each accepted some form of the ontological argument as valid and profound. Others, most notably Aquinas, Hume, and Kant, rejected the argument as mere verbal trickery. In an attempt to equate the denial of God with a self-contradiction, Anselm quotes from Psalms 14:1, "The fool has said in his heart: There is no God." He tries to derive God's existence from the meaning of the word *God:* the greatest conceivable being greater than which cannot be conceived. Anselm then claims that because existence is greater than nonexistence, to say that "God does not exist" is tantamount to saying something like, "A being that cannot be conceived as anything other than existing does not exist," or "A being that exists necessarily does not exist," which is self-contradictory. Crucial to understanding Anselm's thinking is the distinction between an idea that exists in reality—*in re*—and an idea that exists only in conception—*in intellectu.* Anselm's argument is that if an idea is the greatest then it must exist *in re,* not just *in intellectu,* because it is greater to exist in reality than merely in the conception. That is why any supreme or perfect idea, such as Being, exists *in re,* why reality itself has existence in actuality not just in concept (for instance, merely *in intellectu* in the mind of God). This line of argument, based on Plato's realistic metaphysics and buttressed by Augustine's neo-Platonic reinterpretation of Christian dogma, was inspired by a question that had puzzled many medieval Christian thinkers—namely, why God would have to create a world at all. If God is perfect, there would be no need for God to add to the realm of his own being. Anselm's ontological argument was rebuffed by objections from another Benedictine monk, Gaunilon from the Abbey of Marmontier near Tours. Gaunilon claims, on behalf of "the fool," that Anselm's proof is bogus for two main reasons: First, we cannot properly form the concept of a necessarily existent being because there is nothing in experience on which to base such a concept; second, we can imagine lots of perfect things defined as perfect but that in fact do not exist. For instance, why not argue for the existence of the perfect island or the perfect unicorn? Anselm then offers a reply.

Almost a thousand years later, Thomas Aquinas tried to put Christian doctrine on a solid intellectual foundation. He saw Aristotle not just as the greatest of all philosophers—he also called him "The Philosopher"—but as the means for doing so. He argued that Aristotle's metaphysics and epistemology could provide the solid theoretical framework for Christianity, provided that an account could be given of how the soul can preserve the individual human ego, personality intact, after death. Aquinas tried to show various ways that Aristotelian philosophy could be made consistent with Christian belief. His famous "Five Ways" of proving the existence of God, the best-known passage from his works, are variations of the cosmological argument. The first way infers from the fact of change the existence of an Unmoved Mover that originates change. The second uses the fact that some things are caused to infer the existence of a first cause. The third infers from the fact that some things are contingent, or capable of coming into and going out of existence, the existence of something that is necessary, or incapable of coming into and going out of existence. The fourth uses the fact that there are degrees of excellence to infer the existence of a perfect being. The fifth uses the alleged fact that natural objects behave purposefully to infer the existence of an intelligence that directs the activities of natural objects. Samuel Clarke, in "The Cosmological Argument," gives a modern version. The argument put forth by William Paley is a classic version of what is known as the teleological argument or the argument from design.

All these arguments are discussed in further detail in the next selection, David Hume's famous *Dialogues Concerning Natural Religion.* Hume mounts a detailed and searing attack on all the major arguments for the existence of God and presents a devastating version of the argument from evil against God's existence. (Bowing to pressure from his friends who feared for his life, he left it to be published posthumously.) Hume argues that our idea of God has its origin in impressions having to do with ourselves. In his *Dialogues,* Hume divides the various arguments for the existence of God into anthropomorphic (the ontological, cosmological, and design arguments) and mystical. Together, these categories are meant to be mutually exhaustive, that is, they contain all possible types of arguments for God. Hume criticizes them all. Then, having dispensed with the traditional arguments *for* the existence of God in the first part of his *Dialogues* (in Books I–X), Hume presents (in Books X–XI) an argument *against* the existence of God with his famous argument from evil.

THE PROBLEM OF EVIL

The problem of evil as Hume presents it in Books X through XI of his *Dialogues* is in the form of a dilemma that might be put something like this: Either God *could* have made a world with less evil in it but didn't want to, in which case "God" is not all-good and therefore not God, or else God *wanted* to make a world with less evil in it but couldn't, in which case "God" is not omnipotent and therefore not God. The so-called free will defense against the argument from evil is that the reason God allows evil is to have a greater good: human free will.

There are two problems with the free will defense. The first is that it does not respond to the problem of natural evil—earthquakes, floods, tornadoes, birth defects, and so on. Second, it raises the problem of how any action can be free if God knows in advance what will happen, and it raises the specter that the one ultimately responsible for even human evils, if God exists, is, ultimately, God. Here's why. Suppose that what we mean by saying "Jones does something freely at time *t*" is that "Jones *could* have done otherwise than he actually did do at *t.*" Jones decides at twelve noon on Friday to mow his lawn. If there exists a God who knows everything, then God knew at 10:00 A.M. on Friday that Jones would mow his lawn at noon. Does Jones have the power at noon to make God's belief *false?* It seems not; for one thing, God by definition cannot have false beliefs and, for another, God's belief is safely tucked in the past. This is the difficulty that Nelson Pike raises in "Divine Omniscience and Voluntary Action." It is a deep philosophical puzzle regardless of whether one believes in God or evil, for it raises serious questions about the nature of free will and determinism as well.

Using the problem of evil as his starting point, J. L. Mackie launches an even more devastating attack on the idea that God exists. He argues that perfect omnipotence and perfect benevolence are logically inconsistent with the existence of evil, on the basis that there is no logical contradiction in the notion of God creating people who always freely choose to do what is right. An example he does not use, but that puts the notion very simply, is that of the concept of angels. Presumably, angels (except for one, perhaps, the "fallen angel") by and large always choose to do good, and they do so freely. So why would God not have made a universe full of angelic beings? That we are not like that might thus be considered as evidence that no such God exists.

In defense of God comes Peter van Inwagen, with his "Magnitude, Duration, and Distribution of Evil: A Theodicy." He suggests, following traditional Christian doctrine, that moral evil is a necessary ingredient of human free will, that this is the price we must pay for freedom. Van Inwagen claims what Mackie denies, namely, that it is logically impossible for God to create a world containing free human beings in which there is no evil.

His attempt to deal with the problem of natural evil leads him to suggest ways in which it could be the case that people who die from tornadoes, floods, earthquakes, and so on are ultimately themselves at fault.

FAITH AND REASON

There have been several attempts to deal with the problem of rationality and religious belief from the standpoint of whether and how such belief might be justified or accounted for on other grounds than evidence. Thus, Blaise Pascal in his famous "Pascal's Wager" argues that the best and safest bet, given that there is not sufficient evidence for the existence of God, is nevertheless to believe that God exists. This is a position that W. K. Clifford vehemently argues against, claiming that anyone who believes anything without sufficient evidence is not just being irrational but *immoral*.

A different approach is taken by fideists who believe that proper belief can be based on faith and not just evidence and argument. Perhaps the greatest defender of such a position from a purely philosophical perspective is William James with his now classic "The Will to Believe." James defends the rationality (under certain conditions, when the belief is, for instance, a "living option") of believing in the existence of God in the absence of adequate arguments and evidence. James's thesis is still a live philosophical issue today and is sometimes defended even by atheists.

In the dialog "Philosophy, the Bible, and God," Alvin Plantinga—a leading philosopher well known for his Christian apologetics—and I discuss what it all means and where we go from here in terms of the three topics mentioned in the title: philosophy, the Bible, and God.

THE EXISTENCE AND NATURE OF GOD

Who Is God?

SAINT AUGUSTINE

Born in North Africa, Saint Augustine (354–430) studied in Carthage and taught in Rome and Milan. A skeptic and neo-Platonist, at the age of thirty-four he converted from Manicheanism to Christianity. His numerous books and treatises influenced many philosophers, especially Descartes and Kant.

What then have I to do with men, that they should hear my confessions—as if they could *heal all my infirmities*—a race, curious to know the lives of others, slothful to amend their own? Why seek they to hear from me what I am; who will not hear from Thee what themselves are? And how know they, when from myself they hear of myself, whether I say true; seeing *no man knows what is in man, but the spirit of man which is in him?* But if they hear from Thee themselves, they cannot say, "The Lord lies." For what is it to hear from Thee of themselves, but to know themselves? and who knows and says, "It is false," unless himself lies? But because *charity believes all things* (that is, among those whom knitting unto itself it makes one), I also, O Lord, will in such wise confess unto Thee, that men may hear, to whom I cannot demonstrate whether I confess truly; yet they believe me, whose ears charity opens unto me. . . .

With what objective, then, O Lord my God, to Whom my conscience daily confesses, trusting more in the hope of Thy mercy than in her own innocency, with what objective, I pray, do I by this book confess to men also in Thy presence what I now am, not what I have been? For that other objective I have seen and spoken of. But what I now am, at the very time of making these confessions, diverse desire to know, who have or have not known me, who have heard from me or of me; but their ear is not at my heart, where I am, whatever I am. They wish then to hear me confess what I am within; whither neither their eye, nor ear, nor understanding can reach; they wish it, as ready to believe—but will they know? For charity, whereby they are good, tells them that in my confessions I lie not; and she in them, believes me. . . .

This is the objective of my confessions of what I am, not of what I have been, to confess this, not before Thee only, in a secret *exultation with trembling*, and a secret sorrow with hope; but in the ears also of the believing sons of men, sharers of my joy, and partners in my mortality, my fellow-citizens, and fellow-pilgrims, who are gone before, or are to follow on, companions on my way. . . .

But what do I love, when I love Thee? not beauty of bodies, nor the fair harmony of time, nor the brightness of the light, so beautiful to our eyes, nor sweet melodies of varied songs, nor the fragrant smell of flowers, and ointments, and spices, not manna and honey, not limbs acceptable to embracements of flesh. None of these I love, when I love my God; and yet I love a kind of light, and melody, and fragrance, and meat, and embracement when I love my God, the light, melody, fragrance, meat, embracement of my inner man: where there shines unto my soul what space cannot contain and there sounds

From *The Confessions of St. Augustine,* translated by E. B. Pusey (New York: Collier and Son, 1909). With emendations by Daniel Kolak.

415

what time bears not away, and there smells what breathing disperses not, and there tastes what eating diminishes not, and there clings what satiety divorces not. This is it which I love when I love my God.

And what is this? I asked the earth, and it answered me, "I am not He"; and whatsoever are in it confessed the same. I asked the sea and the depths, and the living creeping things, and they answered, "We are not Thy God, seek above us." I asked the moving air; and the whole air with his inhabitants answered, "Anaximenes was deceived, I am not God." I asked the heavens, sun, moon, stars, "Nor (say they) are we the God whom thou seeks." And I replied unto all the things which encompass the door of my flesh: "You have told me of my God, that you are not He; tell me something of Him." And they cried out with a loud voice, "He made us." My questioning them, was my thoughts on them: and their form of beauty gave the answer. And I turned myself unto myself, and said to myself, "Who are you?" And I answered, "A man." And behold, in me there present themselves to my soul, and body, one without, the other within. By which of these ought I to seek my God? I had sought Him in the body from earth to heaven, so far as I could send messengers, the beams of mine eyes. But the better is the inner, for to it as presiding and judging, all the bodily messengers reported the answers of heaven and earth, and all things therein, who said, "We are not God, but He made us." These things did my inner man know by the ministry of the outer: I the inner knew them; I, the mind, through the senses of my body. I asked the whole frame of the world about my God; and it answered me, "I am not He, but He made me."

Is not this corporeal figure apparent to all whose senses are perfect? why then speaks it not the same to all? Animals small and great see it but they cannot ask it: because no reason is set over their senses to judge on what they report. But men ask, so that *the invisible things of God are clearly seen, being understood by the things that are made;* but by love of them, they are made subject unto them: and subjects cannot judge. Nor yet do the creatures answer such as ask, unless they can judge: nor yet do they change their voice (*i.e.,* their appearance), if one man only sees, another seeing asks, so as to appear one way to this man, another way to that; but appearing the same way to both, it is dumb to this, speaks to that; rather

it speaks to all; but they only understand, who compare its voice received from without, with the truth within. For truth says to me, "Neither heaven, nor earth, nor any other body is your God." This, their very nature says to him that sees them: "They are a mass; a mass is less in a part thereof than in the whole." Now to you I speak, O my soul, you are my better part: for you quickens the mass of my body, giving it life, which no body can give to a body: but your God is even unto you the Life of your life.

What then do I love, when I love my God? who is He above the head of my soul? By my very soul will I ascend to Him. I will pass beyond that power whereby I am united to my body, and fill its whole frame with life. Nor can I by that power find my God; for so *horse and mule that have no understanding,* might find Him; seeing it is the same power, whereby even their bodies live. But another power there is, not that only whereby I animate, but that too whereby I imbue with sense my flesh, which the Lord has framed for me: commanding the eye not to hear, and the ear not to see; but the eye, that through it I should see, and the ear, that through it I should hear; and to the other senses severally, what is to each their own peculiar seats and offices; which, being diverse, I the one mind, do through them enact. I will pass beyond this power of mine also; for this also have the horse and mule, for they also perceive through the body.

I will pass then beyond this power of my nature also, rising by degrees unto Him who made me. And I come to the fields and spacious palaces of my memory, where are the treasures of innumerable images, brought into it from things of all sorts perceived by the senses. There is stored up, whatsoever besides we think, either by enlarging or diminishing, or any other way varying those things which the sense has come to; and whatever else has been committed and laid up, which forgetfulness has not yet swallowed up and buried. When I enter there, I require what I will to be brought forth, and something instantly comes; others must be longer sought after, which are fetched, as it were, out of some inner receptacle; others rush out in troops, and while one thing is desired and required, they start forth, as who should say, "Is it perchance I?" These I drive away with the hand of my heart, from the face of my remembrance; until what I wish for is unveiled, and appears in sight, out of its secret place. Other things come up readily, in unbroken order, as they are called for; those in front making way for the following; and as they make way, they are hidden from sight, ready to come when I will. All which takes place when I repeat a thing by heart.

There are all things preserved distinctly and under general heads, each having entered by its own avenue: as light, and all colours and forms of bodies by the eyes; by the ears all sorts of sounds; all smells by the avenue of the nostrils; all tastes by the mouth; and by the sensation of the whole body, what is hard or soft; hot or cold; smooth or rugged; heavy or light; either outwardly or inwardly to the body. All these does that great harbour of the memory receive in her numberless secret and inexpressible windings, to be forthcoming, and brought out at need; each entering in by his own gate, and there laid up. Nor yet do the things themselves enter in; only the images of the things perceived are there in readiness, for thought to recall. Which images, how they are formed, who can tell, though it does plainly appear by which sense each has been brought in and stored up? For even while I dwell in darkness and in silence, in my memory I can produce colours, if I will, and discern between black and white, and what others I will: nor yet do sounds break in and disturb the image drawn in by my eyes, which I am reviewing, though they also are there, lying dormant, and laid up, as it were, apart. For these too I call for, and they appear. And though my tongue be still, and my throat mute, so can I sing as much as I will; nor do those images of colours, which notwithstanding be there, intrude themselves and interrupt, when another store is called for, which flowed in by the ears. So the other things, piled in and up by the other senses, I recall at my pleasure. Yea, I discern the breath of lilies from violets, though smelling nothing; and I prefer honey to sweet wine, smooth before rugged, at the time neither tasting nor handling, but remembering only.

These things do I within, in that vast court of my memory. For there are present with me, heaven, earth, sea, and whatever I could think on therein, besides what I have forgotten. There also meet I with myself, and recall myself, and when, where, and what I have done, and under what feelings. There be all which I remember, either on my own experience, or others' credit. Out of the same store do I myself with the past continually combine fresh and fresh likenesses of things which I have experienced, or, from what I have experienced, have believed: and then again infer future actions, events and hopes, and all these again I reflect on, as present. "I will do this or that," say I to myself, in that great receptacle of my mind, stored with the images of things so many and so great, "and this or that will follow." "O that this or that might be!" "God avert this or that!" So speak I to myself: and when I speak, the images of all I speak of are present, out of the same treasury of memory; nor would I speak of any thereof, were the images wanting.

Great is this force of memory, excessive great, O my God; a large and boundless chamber! who ever sounded the bottom thereof? yet is this a power of mine, and belongs unto my nature; nor do I myself comprehend all that I am. Therefore is the mind too strait to contain itself. And where should that be, which it contained not of itself? Is it without it, and not within? how then does it not comprehend itself? A wonderful admiration surprises me, amazement seizes me upon this. And men go abroad to admire the heights of mountains, the mighty billows of the sea, the broad tides of rivers, the compass of the ocean, and the circuits of the stars, and pass themselves by; nor wonder that when I spoke of all these things, I did not see them with my eyes, yet could not have spoken of them, unless I then actually saw the mountains, billows, rivers, stars which I had seen, and that ocean which I believe to be, inwardly in my memory, and that, with the same vast spaces between, as if I saw them abroad. Yet did not I by seeing draw them into myself, when with my eyes I beheld them; nor are they themselves with me, but their images only. And I know by what sense of the body each was impressed upon me. . . .

Lord, I truly, toil therein, yea and toil in myself; I am become a heavy soil requiring over much *sweat of the brow*. For we are not now searching out the regions of heaven, or measuring the distances of the stars, or enquiring the balancings of the earth. It is I myself who remember, I the mind. It is not so wonderful, if what I myself am not, be far from me. But what is nearer to me than myself? And lo, the force of my own memory is not understood by me; though I cannot so much as name myself without it.

The Ontological Argument

SAINT ANSELM

Saint Anselm of Canterbury (1033–1109) was born in Aosta in Italy and educated by the Bene-dictines. He is best known for his ontological argument for the existence of God. He became Arch-bishop of Canterbury.

. . . I began to ask myself whether there might be found a single argument which would require no other for its proof than itself alone; and alone would suffice to demonstrate that God truly exists, and that there is a supreme good requiring nothing else, which all other things require for their existence and well-being; and whatever we believe regarding the divine Being.

Although I often and earnestly directed my thought to this end, and at some times that which I sought seemed to be just within my reach, while again it wholly evaded my mental vision, at last in despair I was about to cease, as if from the search for a thing which could not be found. But when I wished to exclude this thought altogether, lest, by busy-ing my mind to no purpose, it should keep me from other thoughts, in which I might be successful; then more and more, though I was unwilling and shunned it, it began to force itself upon me, with a kind of importunity. So, one day, when I was ex-ceedingly wearied with resisting its importunity, in the very conflict of my thoughts, the proof of which I had despaired offered itself, so that I eagerly embraced the thoughts which I was strenuously repelling. . . .

And so Lord, do thou, who dost give under-standing to faith, give me, so far as thou knowest it to be profitable, to understand that thou art as we believe; and that thou art that which we believe. And, indeed, we believe that thou art a being than which nothing greater can be conceived. Or is there no such nature, since the fool hath said in his heart, there is no God? But, at any rate, this very fool, when he hears of this being of which I speak—a be-ing than which nothing greater can be conceived—

understands what he hears, and what he under-stands is in his understanding; although he does not understand it to exist.

For, it is one thing for an object to be in the un-derstanding, and another to understand that the ob-ject exists. When a painter first conceives of what he will afterwards perform, he has it in his under-standing, but he does not yet understand it to be, because he has not yet performed it. But after he has made the painting, he both has it in his understand-ing, and he understands that it exists, because he has made it.

Hence, even the fool is convinced that something exists in the understanding, at least, than which nothing greater can be conceived. For, when he hears of this, he understands it. And whatever is un-derstood, exists in the understanding. And assuredly that, than which nothing greater can be conceived, cannot exist in the understanding alone. For, sup-pose it exists in the understanding alone: then it can be conceived to exist in reality; which is greater.

Therefore, if that, than which nothing greater can be conceived, exists in the understanding alone, the very being, than which nothing greater can be conceived, is one, than which a greater can be con-ceived. But obviously this is impossible. Hence, there is no doubt that there exists a being, than which nothing greater can be conceived, and it ex-ists both in the understanding and in reality. . . .

And it assuredly exists so truly, that it cannot be conceived not to exist. For, it is possible to conceive of a being which cannot be conceived not to exist, and this is greater than one which can be conceived not to exist. Hence, if that, than which nothing greater can be conceived, can be conceived not to exist, it is not that, than which nothing greater can be conceived. But this is an irreconcilable contradic-tion. There is, then, so truly a being than which noth-

From *Proslogion,* translated by Sidney Norton Deane (Open Court, 1903), pp. 1–2, 6–9, 149–51, 158–59.

ing greater can be conceived to exist, that it cannot even be conceived not to exist; and this being thou art, O Lord, our God.

So truly, therefore, dost thou exist, O Lord, my God, that thou canst not be conceived not to exist; and rightly. For if a mind could conceive of a being better than thee, the creature would rise above the Creator; and this is most absurd. And, indeed, whatever else there is, except thee alone, can be conceived not to exist. To thee alone, therefore, it belongs to exist more truly than all other beings, and hence in a higher degree than all others. For, whatever else exists does not exist so truly, and hence in a less degree it belongs to it to exist. Why, then, has the fool said in his heart, there is no God, since it is so evident, to a rational mind, that thou dost exist in the highest degree of all? Why, except that he is dull and a fool? . . .

In Behalf of the Fool

AN ANSWER TO THE ARGUMENT OF ANSELM BY GAUNILO, A MONK OF MARMOUTIER

. . . if it should be said that a being which cannot be even conceived in terms of any fact, is in the understanding. I do not deny that this being is, accordingly, in my understanding. But since through this fact it can in no wise attain to real existence also, I do not yet concede to it that existence at all, until some certain proof of it shall be given.

For he who says that this being exists, because otherwise the being which is greater than all will not be greater than all, does not attend strictly to what he is saying. For I do not yet say, no, I even deny or doubt that this being is greater than any real object. Nor do I concede to it any other existence than this (if it should be called existence) which it has when the mind, according to a word merely heard, tries to form the image of an object absolutely unknown to it.

How, then, is the veritable existence of that being proved to me from the assumption, by hypothesis, that it is greater than all other beings? For I should still deny this, or doubt your demonstration of it, to this extent, that I should not admit that this being is in my understanding and concept even in

the way in which many objects whose real existence is uncertain and doubtful, are in my understanding and concept. For it should be proved first that this being itself really exists somewhere; and then, from the fact that it is greater than all, we shall not hesitate to infer that it also subsists in itself.

For example: it is said that somewhere in the ocean is an island, which, because of the difficulty, or rather the impossibility, of discovering what does not exist, is called the lost island. And they say that this island has an inestimable wealth of all manner of riches and delicacies in greater abundance than is told of the Islands of the Blest; and that having no owner or inhabitant, it is more excellent than all other countries, which are inhabited by mankind, in the abundance with which it is stored.

Now if someone should tell me that there is such an island, I should easily understand his words, in which there is no difficulty. But suppose that he went on to say, as if by a logical inference: "You can no longer doubt that this island which is more excellent than all lands exists somewhere, since you have no doubt that it is in your understanding. And since it is more excellent not to be in the understanding alone, but to exist both in the understanding and in reality, for this reason it must exist. For if it does not exist, any land which really exists will be more excellent than it; and so the island already understood by you to be more excellent will not be more excellent."

If a man should try to prove to me by such reasoning that this island truly exists, and that its existence should no longer be doubted, either I should believe that he was jesting, or I know not which I ought to regard as the greater fool: myself, supposing that I should allow this proof; or him, if he should suppose that he had established with any certainty the existence of this island. For he ought to show first that the hypothetical excellence of this island exists as a real and indubitable fact, and in no wise as any unreal object, or one whose existence is uncertain, in my understanding.

ANSELM'S REPLY

But, you say, it is as if one should suppose an island in the ocean, which surpasses all lands in its fertility, and which, because of the difficulty, or rather the impossibility, of discovering what does not exist, is called a lost island; and should say that there can be no doubt that this island truly exists in reality, for this reason, that one who hears it described easily understands what he hears.

Now I promise confidently that if any man shall devise anything existing either in reality or in concept alone (except that than which a greater cannot be conceived) to which he can adapt the sequence of my reasoning, I will discover that thing, and will give him his lost island, not to be lost again.

But it now appears that this being than which a greater is inconceivable cannot be conceived not to be, because it exists on so assured a ground of truth; for otherwise it would not exist at all.

Hence, if any one says that he conceives this being not to exist, I say that at the time when he conceives of this either he conceives of a being than which a greater is inconceivable, or he does not conceive at all. If he does not conceive, he does not conceive of the nonexistence of that of which he does not conceive. But if he does conceive, he certainly conceives of a being which cannot be even conceived not to exist. For if it could be conceived not to exist, it could be conceived to have a beginning and an end. But this is impossible.

He, then, who conceives of this being conceives of a being which cannot be even conceived not to exist; but he who conceives of this being does not conceive that it does not exist; else he conceives what is inconceivable. The nonexistence, then, of that than which a greater cannot be conceived is inconceivable.

The Five Ways and the Doctrine of Analogy

SAINT THOMAS AQUINAS

Saint Thomas Aquinas (1225–1274) was born near Naples and studied with the Benedictines and at the University of Naples. Deeply influenced by Aristotle, Aquinas and his many works continue to be widely influential in theology and philosophy.

The Five Ways

The existence of God can be proved in five ways.

The first and more manifest way is the argument from motion. It is certain, and evident to our senses, that in the world some things are in motion. Now whatever is moved is moved by another, for nothing can be moved except it is in potentiality to that towards which it is moved; whereas a thing moves inasmuch as it is in act. For motion is nothing else than the reduction of something from potentiality to actuality. But nothing can be reduced from potentiality to actuality, except by something in a state of actuality. Thus that which is actually hot, as fire, makes wood, which is potentially hot, to be actually hot, and thereby moves and changes it. Now it is not possible that the same thing should be at once in actuality and potentiality in the same respect, but only in different respects. For what is actually hot cannot simultaneously be potentially hot; but it is simultaneously potentially cold. It is therefore impossible that in the same respect and in the same way a thing should be both mover and moved, i.e., that it should move itself. Therefore, whatever is moved must be moved by another. If that by which it is moved be itself moved, then this also must needs be moved by another, and that by another again. But this cannot go on to infinity, because then there would be no first mover, and consequently no other mover, seeing that subsequent movers move only inasmuch as they are moved by the first mover; as the staff moves

From *The Basic Writings of Saint Thomas Aquinas*, edited by Anton C. Pegis (New York: Random House; London: Burns & Oates, 1945), pp. 22–23. Copyright © 1945 Random House, Inc. Reprinted by permission of Richard Pegis.

only because it is moved by the hand. Therefore it is necessary to arrive at a first mover, moved by no other; and this everyone understands to be God.

The second way is from the nature of efficient cause. In the world of sensible things we find there is an order of efficient causes. There is no case known (neither is it, indeed, possible) in which a thing is found to be the efficient cause of itself; for so it would be prior to itself, which is impossible. Now in efficient causes it is not possible to go on to infinity, because in all efficient causes following in order, the first is the cause of the intermediate cause, and the intermediate is the cause of the ultimate cause, whether the intermediate cause be several, or one only. Now to take away the cause is to take away the effect. Therefore, if there be no first cause among efficient causes, there will be no ultimate, nor any intermediate, cause. But if in efficient causes it is possible to go on to infinity, there will be no first efficient cause, neither will there be an ultimate effect, nor any intermediate efficient causes; all of which is plainly false. Therefore it is necessary to admit a first efficient cause, to which everyone gives the name of God.

The third way is taken from possibility and necessity, and runs thus. We find in nature things that are possible to be and not to be, since they are found to be generated, and to be corrupted, and consequently, it is possible for them to be and not to be. But it is impossible for these always to exist, for that which can not-be at some time is not. Therefore, if everything can not-be, then at one time there was nothing in existence. Now if this were true, even now there would be nothing in existence, because that which does not exist begins to exist only through something already existing. Therefore, if at one time nothing was in existence, it would have been impossible for anything to have begun to exist; and thus even now nothing would be in existence—which is absurd. Therefore, not all beings are merely possible, but there must exist something the existence of which is necessary. But every necessary thing either has its necessity caused by another, or not. Now it is impossible to go on to infinity in necessary things which have their necessity caused by another, as has been already proved in regard to efficient causes. Therefore we cannot but admit the existence of some being having of itself its own necessity, and

not receiving it from another, but rather causing in others their necessity. This all men speak of as God.

The fourth way is taken from the gradation to be found in things. Among beings there are some more and some less good, true, noble, and the like. But *more* and *less* are predicated of different things according as they resemble in their different ways something which is the maximum, as a thing is said to be hotter according as it more nearly resembles that which is hottest; so that there is something which is truest, something best, something noblest, and, consequently, something which is most in being, for those things that are greatest in truth are greatest in being,. . . . Now the maximum in any genus is the cause of all in that genus, as fire, which is the maximum of heat, is the cause of all hot things, as is said in the same book. Therefore there must also be something which is to all beings the cause of their being, goodness, and every other perfection; and this we call God.

The fifth way is taken from the governance of the world. We see that things which lack knowledge, such as natural bodies, act for an end, and this is evident from their acting always, or nearly always, in the same way, so as to obtain the best result. Hence it is plain that they achieve their end, not fortuitously, but designedly. Now whatever lacks knowledge cannot move towards an end, unless it be directed by some being endowed with knowledge and intelligence; as the arrow is directed by the archer. Therefore some intelligent being exists by whom all natural things are directed to their end; and this being we call God.

The Doctrine of Analogy

Since it is possible to find in God every perfection of creatures, but in another and more eminent way, whatever names unqualifiedly designate a perfection without defect are predicated of God and of other things: for example, goodness, wisdom, being, and the like. But when any name expresses such perfections along with a mode that is proper to a creature, it can be said of God only according to likeness and metaphor. According to metaphor, what belongs to one thing is transferred to another, as when we say that a man is a *stone* because of the hardness of his intellect. Such names are used to designate the species of a created thing, for example, *man* and *stone;* for to each species belongs its own mode of perfection and being. The same is true of whatever names designate the properties of things, which are caused by the proper principles of their species. Hence, they can be said of God only metaphorically. But the names that express such perfections along with the mode of supereminence with which they belong to God are said of God alone. Such names are the *highest good, the first being,* and the like.

I have said that some of the aforementioned names signify a perfection without defect. This is true with reference to that which the name was imposed to signify; for as to the mode of signification, every name is defective. For by means of a name we express things in the way in which the intellect conceives them. For our intellect, taking the origin of its knowledge from the senses, does not transcend the mode which is found in sensible things in which the

form and the subject of the form are not identical owning to the composition of form and matter. Now, a simple form is indeed found among such things, but one that is imperfect because it is not subsisting; on the other hand, though a subsisting subject of a form is found among sensible things, it is not simple but rather concreted. Whatever our intellect signifies as subsisting, therefore, it signifies in concretion; but what it signifies as simple, . . .

Now, the mode of supereminence in which the abovementioned perfections are found in God can be signified by names used by us only through negation, as when we say that God is *eternal* or *infinite,* or also through a relation of God to other things, as when He is called the *first cause* or the *highest good.* For we cannot grasp what God is, but only what He is not and how other things are related to Him, as is clear from what we said above.

The Cosmological Argument

SAMUEL CLARKE

Samuel Clarke (1675–1729) was an English theologian and philosopher.

There has existed from eternity some one unchangeable and independent being. For since something must needs have been from eternity; as hath been already proved, and is granted on all hands: either there has always existed one unchangeable and *independent* Being, from which all other beings that are or ever were in the universe, have received their original; or else there has been an infinite succession of changeable and *dependent* beings, produced one from another in an endless progression, without any original cause at all: which latter supposition is so very absurd, that tho' all atheism must in its account of most things (as shall be shown hereafter) terminate in it, yet I think very few atheists ever were so weak as openly and directly to defend it. For it is plainly

impossible and contradictory to itself. I shall not argue against it from the supposed impossibility of infinite succession, *barely and absolutely considered in itself;* for a reason which shall be mentioned hereafter: but, if we consider such an infinite progression, as *one* entire endless *series of dependent* beings; 'tis plain this whole *series* of beings can have no cause *from without,* of its existence; because in it are supposed to be included *all things* that are or ever were in the universe: and 'tis plain it can have no reason *within itself,* of its existence; because no one being in this infinite succession is supposed to be self-existent or *necessary* (which is the only ground or reason of existence of any thing, that can be imagined *within the thing itself,* as will presently more fully appear), but every one *dependent* on the foregoing: and where *no part* is necessary, 'tis manifest *the whole* cannot be necessary; absolute necessity of existence, not being

---

From *A Demonstration of the Being and Attributes of God* (1705), Part II.

an outward, relative, and accidental determination; but an inward and essential property of the nature of the thing which so exists. An infinite succession therefore of merely *dependent* beings, without any original independent cause; is a *series* of beings, that has neither necessity nor cause, nor any reason *at all* of its existence, neither *within itself* nor *from without:* that is, 'tis an express contradiction and impossibility; 'tis a supposing *something* to be *caused,* (because it's granted in every one of its stages of succession, not to be necessary and from itself); and yet that in the whole it is caused *absolutely by nothing:* Which every man knows is a contradiction to be done *in time;* and because duration in this case makes no difference, 'tis equally a contradiction to suppose it done from eternity: And consequently there must *on the contrary,* of necessity have existed from eternity, *some one* immutable and *independent* Being: Which, what it is, remains in the next place to be inquired.

The Argument from Design

WILLIAM PALEY

William Paley (1743–1805) was an English philosopher.

Chapter One: State of the Argument

In crossing a heath, suppose I pitched my foot against a *stone* and were asked how the stone came to be there, I might possibly answer that for anything I knew to the contrary it had lain there forever; nor would it, perhaps, be very easy to show the absurdity of this answer. But suppose I had found a *watch* upon the ground, and it should be inquired how the watch happened to be in that place, I should hardly think of the answer which I had before given, that for anything I knew the watch might have always been there. Yet why should not this answer serve for the watch as well as for the stone? Why is it not as admissible in the second case as in the first? For this reason, and for no other, namely, that when we come to inspect the watch, we perceive—what we could not discover in the stone—that its several parts are framed and put together for a purpose, e.g., that they are so formed and adjusted as to produce motion, and that motion so regulated as to point out the hour of the day; that if the different parts had been differently shaped from what they are, of a different size from what they are, or placed after any other manner or in any other order than that in which they are placed, either no motion at all would have been carried on in the machine, or none which would have answered the use that is now served by it. To reckon up a few of the plainest of these parts and of their offices, all tending to one result; we see a cylindrical box containing a coiled elastic spring, which, by its endeavor to relax itself, turns round the box. We next observe a flexible chain—artificially wrought for the sake of flexure—communication the action of the spring from the box to the fusee. We then find a series of wheels, the teeth of which catch in and apply to each other, conducting the motion from the fusee to the balance and from the balance to the pointer, and at the same time, by the size and shape of those wheels, so regulating that motion as to terminate in causing an index, by an equable and measured progression, to pass over a given space in a given time. We take notice that the wheels are made of brass, in order to keep them from rust; the springs of steel, no other metal being so elastic; that over the face of the watch there is placed a glass, a material employed in no other part of the work, but in the room of which, if there had been any other than a transparent substance, the hour could not be seen without opening the case. This mechanism being observed—it requires indeed an examination of the instrument,

From *Natural Theology* (1800).

and perhaps some previous knowledge of the subject, to perceive and understand it; but being once, as we have said, observed and understood—the inference we think is inevitable, that the watch must have had a maker—that there must have existed, at some time and at some place or other, an artificer or artificers who formed it for the purpose which we find it actually to answer, who comprehended its construction and designed its use.

I.   Nor would it, I apprehend, weaken the conclusion, that we had never seen a watch made—that we had never known an artist capable of making one—that we were altogether incapable of executing such a piece of workmanship ourselves, or of understanding in what manner it was performed; all this being no more than what is true of some exquisite remains of ancient art, of some lost arts, and, to the generality of mankind, of the more curious production of modern manufacture. Does one man in a million know how oval frames are turned? Ignorance of this kind exalts our opinion of the unseen and unknown artist's skill, if he be unseen and unknown, but raises no doubt in our minds of the existence and agency of such an artist, at some former time and in some place or other. Nor can I perceive that it varies at all the inference, whether the question arise concerning a human agent or concerning an agent of a different species, or an agent possessing in some respects a different nature.

II.   Neither, secondly, would it invalidate our conclusion, that the watch sometimes went wrong or that it seldom went exactly right. The purpose of the machinery, the design, and the designer might be evident, and in the case supposed, would be evident, in whatever way we accounted for the irregularity of the movement, or whether we could account for it or not. It is not necessary that a machine be perfect in order to show with what design it was made: still less necessary, where the only question is whether it were made with any design at all.

III.   Nor, thirdly, would it bring any uncertainty into the argument, if there were a few parts of the watch, concerning which we could not discover or had not yet discovered in what manner they conduced to the general effect; or even some parts, concerning which we could not ascertain whether they conduced to that effect in any manner whatever. For, as to the first branch of the case, if by the loss, or disorder, or decay of the parts in question, the movement of the watch were found in fact to be stopped, or disturbed, or retarded, no doubt would remain in our minds as to the utility or intention of these parts, although we should be unable to investigate the manner according to which, or the connection by which, the ultimate effect depended upon their action or assistance; and the more complex is the machine, the more likely is this obscurity to arise. Then, as to the second thing supposed, namely, that there were parts which might be spared without prejudice to the movement of the watch, and that we had proved this by experiment, these superfluous parts, even if we were completely assured that they were such, would not vacate the reasoning which we had instituted concerning other parts. The indication of contrivance remained, with respect to them, nearly as it was before.

IV.   Nor, fourthly, would any man in his senses think the existence of the watch with its various machinery accounted for, by being told that it was one out of possible combinations of material forms; that whatever he had found in the place where he found the watch, must have contained some internal configuration or other; and that this configuration might be the structure now exhibited, namely, of the works of a watch, as well as a different structure.

V.   Nor, fifthly, would it yield his inquiry more satisfaction, to be answered that there existed in things a principle of order, which had disposed the parts of the watch into their present form and situation. He never knew a watch made by the principle of order; nor can he even form to himself an idea of what is meant by a principle of order distinct from the intelligence of the watchmaker.

VI.   Sixthly, he would be surprised to hear that the mechanism of the watch was no proof of contrivance, only a motive to induce the mind to think so:

VII.   And not less surprised to be informed that the watch in his hand was nothing more than the result of the laws of *metallic* nature. It is a perversion of language to assign any law as the efficient, operative cause of any thing. A law presupposes an agent, for it is only the mode according to which an agent proceeds: it implies a power, for it is the order according to which that power acts. Without this agent, without this power, which are both distinct from itself, the *law* does nothing, is nothing. The expression, "the law of metallic nature," may sound strange and harsh to a philosophic ear; but it seems quite as justifiable as some others which are more familiar to him, such as "the law of vegetable nature," "the law of animal nature," or, indeed, as "the law of nature" in general, when assigned as the cause of phenomena, in exclusion of agency and power, or when it is substituted into the place of these.

VIII.   Neither, lastly, would our observer be driven out of his conclusion or from his confidence in its truth by being told that he knew nothing at all about the matter. He knows enough for his argument; he knows the utility of the end; he knows the subserviency and adaptation of the means to the end. These points being known, his ignorance of other points, his doubts concerning other points affect not the certainty of his reasoning. The consciousness of knowing little need not beget a distrust of that which he does know.

Chapter Two: State of the Argument Continued

Suppose, in the next place, that the person who found the watch should after some time discover that, in addition to all the properties which he had hitherto observed in it, it possessed the unexpected property of producing in the course of its movement another watch like itself—the thing is conceivable; that it contained within it a mechanism, a system of parts—a mold, for instance, or a complex adjustment of lathes, files, and other tools—evidently and separately calculated for this purpose; let us inquire what effect ought such a discovery to have upon his former conclusion.

I.   The first effect would be to increase his administration of the contrivance, and his conviction of the consummate skill of the contriver. Whether he regarded the object of the contrivance, the distinct apparatus, the intricate, yet in many parts intelligible mechanism by which it was carried on, he would perceive in this new observation nothing but an additional reason for doing what he had already done—for referring the construction of the watch to design and to supreme art. If that construction *without* this property, or, which is the same thing, before this property had been noticed, proved intention and art to have been employed about it, still

more strong would the proof appear when he came to the knowledge of this further property, the crown and perfection of all the rest.

II.   He would reflect, that though the watch before him were, *in some sense,* the maker of the watch, which, was fabricated in the course of its movements, yet it was in a very different sense from that in which a carpenter, for instance, is the maker of a chair—the author of its contrivance, the cause of the relation of its parts to their use. With respect to these, the first watch was no cause at all to the second; in no such sense as this was it the author of the constitution and order, either of the parts which the new watch contained, or of the parts by the aid and instrumentality of which it was produced. We might possibly say, but with great latitude of expression, that a stream of water ground corn; but no latitude of expression would allow us to say, no stretch of conjecture could lead us to think that the stream of water built the mill, though it were too ancient for us to know who the builder was. What the stream of water does in the affair is neither more nor less than this: by the application of an unintelligent impulse to a mechanism previously arranged, arranged independently of it and arranged by intelligence, an effect is produced, namely, the corn is ground. But the effect results from the arrangement. The force of the stream cannot be said to be the cause or author of the effect, still less of the arrangement. Understanding and plan in the formation of the mill were not the less necessary for any share which the water has in grinding the corn; yet is this share the same as that which the watch would have contributed to the production of the new watch, upon the supposition assumed in the last section. Therefore,

III.   Though it be now no longer probable that the individual watch which our observer had found was made immediately by the hand of an artificer, yet does not this alteration in anyway affect the inference that an artificer had been originally employed and concerned in the production. The argument from design remains as it was. Marks of design and contrivance are no more accounted for now than they were before. In the same thing, we may ask for the cause of different properties. We may ask for the cause of the color of a body, of its hardness, of its heat; and these causes may be all different. We are now asking for the cause of that subserviency to a use, that relation to an end, which we have re-marked in the watch before us. No answer is given to this question by telling us that a preceding watch produced it. There cannot be design without a de-signer; contrivance without a contriver; order with-out choice; arrangement without anything capable of arranging; subserviency and relation to a purpose without that which could intend a purpose; means suitable to an end, and executing their office in ac-complishing that end, without the end ever having been contemplated or the means accommodated to it. Arrangement, disposition of parts, subserviency of means to an end, relation of instruments to a use im-ply the presence of intelligence and mind. No one, therefore, can rationally believe that the insensible, inanimate watch, from which the watch before us is-sued, was the proper cause of the mechanism we so much admire in it—could be truly said to have con-structed the instrument, disposed its parts, assigned their office, determined their order, action, and mu-tual dependency, combined their several motions into one result, and that also a result connected with the utilities of other beings. All these properties, therefore, are as much unaccounted for as they were before.

IV.   Nor is anything gained by running the dif-ficulty farther back, that is, by supposing the watch before us to have been produced from another watch, that from a former, and so on indefinitely. Our going back ever so far brings us no nearer to the least degree of satisfaction upon the subject. Con-trivance is still unaccounted for. We still want a con-triver. A designing mind is neither supplied by this supposition nor dispensed with. If the difficulty were diminished the farther we went back, by going back indefinitely we might exhaust it. And this is the only case to which this sort of reasoning applies. Where there is a tendency, or, as we increase the number of terms, a continual approach toward a limit, *there*, by supposing the number of terms to be what is called infinite, we may conceive the limit to be attained; but where there is no such tendency or approach, nothing is effected by lengthening the series. There is no difference as to the point in question, whatever there may be as to many points, between one series and another—between a series which is finite and a series which is infinite. A chain composed of an in-finite number of links, can no more support itself, than a chain composed of a finite number of links. And of this we are assured, though we never *can* have tried the experiment; because, by increasing the number of links, from ten, for instance, to a hundred, from a hundred to a thousand, etc., we make not the smallest approach, we observe not the smallest tendency toward self-support. There is no difference in this respect—yet there may be a great difference in several respects—between a chain of a greater or less length, between one chain and an-other, between one that is finite and one that is infinite. This very much resembles the case before us. The machine which we are inspecting demon-strates, by its construction, contrivance and design. Contrivance must have had a contriver, design a de-signer, whether the machine immediately pro-ceeded from another machine or not. That circum-stance alters not the case. That other machine may, in like manner, have proceeded from a former ma-chine: nor does that alter the case; contrivance must have had a contriver. That former one from one pre-ceding it: no alteration still; a contriver is still neces-sary. No tendency is perceived, no approach toward a diminution of this necessity. It is the same with any and every succession of these machines—a succes-sion of ten, of a hundred, of a thousand; with one se-ries, as with another—a series which is finite, as with a series which is infinite. In whatever other respects they may differ, in this they do not. In all equally, contrivance and design are unaccounted for.

The question is not simply, How came the first watch into existence? which question, it may be pretended, is done away by supposing the series of watches thus produced from one another to have been infinite, and consequently to have had no such *first* for which it was necessary to provide a cause. This, perhaps, would have been nearly the state of the question, if nothing had been before us but an unorganized, unmechanized substance, without mark or indication of contrivance. It might be dif-ficult to show that such substance could not have ex-isted from eternity, either in succession—if it were possible, which I think it is not, for unorganized bod-ies to spring from one another—or by individual perpetuity. But that is not the question now. To sup-pose it to be so is to suppose that it made no differ-ence whether he had found a watch or a stone. As it is, the metaphysics of that question have no place;

for, in the watch which we are examining are seen contrivance, design, an end, a purpose, means for the end, adaptation to the purpose. And the question which irresistibly presses upon our thoughts is, whence this contrivance and design? The thing required is the intending mind, the adapting hand, the intelligence by which that hand was directed. This question, this demand is not shaken off by increasing a number or succession of substances destitute of these properties; nor the more, by increasing that number to infinity. If it be said that, upon the supposition of one watch being produced from another in the course of that other's movements and by means of the mechanism within it, we have a cause for the watch in my hand, namely, the watch from which it proceeded; I deny that for the design, the contrivance, the suitableness of means to an end, the adaptation of instruments to a use, all of which we discover in the watch, we have any cause whatever. It is in vain, therefore, to assign a series of such causes or to allege that a series may be carried back to infinity; for I do not admit that we have yet any cause at all for the phenomena, still less any series of causes either finite or infinite. Here is contrivance but no contriver; proofs of design, but no designer.

V.   Our observer would further also reflect that the maker of the watch before him was in truth and reality that maker of every watch produced from it: there being no difference, except that the latter manifests a more exquisite skill, between the making of another watch with his own hands, by the mediation of files, lathes, chisels, etc., and the disposing, fixing, and inserting of these instruments, or of others equivalent to them, in the body of the watch already made, in such a manner as to form a new watch in the course of the movements which he had given to the old one. It is only working by one set of tools instead of another.

The conclusion which the *first* examination of the watch, of its works, construction, and movement, suggested, was that it must have had, for cause and author of that construction, an artificer who understood its mechanism and designed its use. This conclusion is invincible. A *second* examination presents us with a new discovery. The watch is found, in the course of its movement, to produce another watch similar to itself; and not only so, but we perceive in it a system of organization separately calculated for

that purpose. What effect would this discovery have or ought it to have upon our former inference? What, as has already been said, but to increase beyond measure our admiration of the skill which had been employed in the formation of such a machine? Or shall it, instead of this, all at once turn us round to an opposite conclusion, namely, that no art or skill whatever has been concerned in the business, although all other evidences of art and skill remain as they were, and this last and supreme piece of art be now added to the rest? Can this be maintained without absurdity? Yet this is atheism. . . .

Chapter Five: Application of the Argument Continued

Every observation which was made in our first chapter concerning the watch may be repeated with strict propriety concerning the eye, concerning animals, concerning plants, concerning, indeed, all the organized parts of the works of nature. As,

I.   When we are inquiring simply after the *existence* of an intelligent Creator, imperfection, inaccuracy, liability to disorder, occasional irregularities may subsist in a considerable degree without inducing any doubt into the question; just as a watch may frequently go wrong, seldom perhaps exactly right, may be faulty in some parts, defective in some, without the smallest ground of suspicion from thence arising that it was not a watch, not made, or not made for the purpose ascribed to it. When faults are pointed out, and when a question is started concerning the skill of the artist or dexterity with which the work is executed, then, indeed, in order to defend these qualities from accusation, we must be able either to expose some intractableness and imperfection in the materials or point out some invincible difficulty in the execution, into which imperfection and difficulty the matter of complaint may be resolved; or, if we cannot do this, we must adduce such specimens of consummate art and contrivance proceeding from the same hand as may convince the inquirer of the existence, in the case before him, of impediments like those which we have mentioned, although, what from the nature of the case is very likely to happen, they be unknown and unperceived by him. This we must do in order to vindicate the artist's skill, or at least the perfection of it; as we must also judge of his intention and of the provisions employed in fulfilling that intention, not from an instance in which they fail but from the great plurality of instances in which they succeed. But, after all, these are different questions from the question of the artist's existence; or, which is the same, whether the thing before us be a work of art or not; and the questions ought always to be kept separate in the mind. So likewise it is in the works of nature. Irregularities and imperfections are of little or no weight in the consideration when that consideration relates simply to the existence of a Creator. When the argument respects His attributes, they are of weight; but are then to be taken in conjunction—the attention is not to rest upon them, but they are to be taken in conjunction with the unexceptionable evidence which we possess of skill, power, and benevolence displayed in other instances; which evidences may, in strength, number, and variety, be such and may so overpower apparent blemishes as to induce us, upon the most reasonable ground, to believe that these last ought to be referred to some cause, though we be ignorant of it, other than defect of knowledge or of benevolence in the author. . . .

Dialogues Concerning Natural Religion

DAVID HUME

The great British empiricist philosopher and skeptic David Hume (1711–1766) was born in Scotland.

Part II

I must own, Cleanthes, said Demea, that nothing can more surprise me than the light in which you have all along put this argument. By the whole tenor of your discourse, one would imagine that you were maintaining the Being of a God against the cavils of atheists and infidels, and were necessitated to become a champion for that fundamental principle of all religion. But this, I hope, is not by any means a question among us. No man, no man at least of common sense, I am persuaded, ever entertained a serious doubt with regard to a truth so certain and self-evident. The question is not concerning the *being* but the *nature* of God. This I affirm, from the infirmities of human understanding, to be altogether incomprehensible and unknown to us. The essence of that supreme Mind, his attributes, the manner of his existence, the very nature of his duration—these and every particular which regards so divine a Being are mysterious to men. Finite, weak, and blind creatures, we ought to humble ourselves in his august presence, and, conscious of our frailties, adore in silence his infinite perfections which eye hath not seen, ear hath not heard, neither hath it entered into the heart of man to conceive. They are covered in a deep cloud from human curiosity; it is profaneness to attempt penetrating through these sacred obscurities, and, next to the impiety of denying his existence, is the temerity of prying into his nature and essence, decrees and attributes.

But lest you should think that my *piety* has here got the better of my *philosophy,* I shall support my opinion, if it needs any support, by a very great authority. I might cite all the divines, almost from the foundation of Christianity, who have ever treated of this or any other theological subject; but I shall confine myself, at present, to one equally celebrated for piety and philosophy. It is Father Malebranche who, I remember, thus expresses himself.[1] "One ought not so much," says he, "to call God a spirit in order to express positively what he is, as in order to signify that he is not matter. He is a Being infinitely perfect—of this we cannot doubt. But in the same manner as we ought not to imagine, even supposing him corporeal, that he is clothed with a human

First published in 1779.

body, as the anthropomorphites asserted, under colour that that figure was the most perfect of any, so neither ought we to imagine that the spirit of God has human ideas or bears any resemblance to our spirit, under colour that we know nothing more perfect than a human mind. We ought rather to believe that as he comprehends the perfections of matter without being material . . . he comprehends also the perfections of created spirits without being spirit, in the manner we conceive spirit: that his true name is *He that is,* or, in other words, Being without restriction, All Being, the Being infinite and universal."

After so great an authority, Demea, replied Philo, as that which you have produced, and a thousand more which you might produce, it would appear ridiculous in me to add my sentiment or express my approbation of your doctrine. But surely, where reasonable men treat these subjects, the question can never be concerning the *being* but only the *nature* of the Deity. The former truth, as you well observe, is unquestionable and self-evident. Nothing exists without a cause; and the original cause of this universe (whatever it be) we call God, and piously ascribe to him every species of perfection. Whoever scruples this fundamental truth deserves every punishment which can be inflicted among philosophers, to wit, the greatest ridicule, contempt, and disapprobation. But as all perfection is entirely relative, we ought never to imagine that we comprehend the attributes of this divine Being, or to suppose that his perfections have any analogy or likeness to the perfections of a human creature. Wisdom, thought, design, knowledge—these we justly ascribe to him because these words are honourable among men, and we have no other language or other conceptions by which we can express our adoration of him. But let us beware lest we think that our ideas anywise correspond to his perfections, or that his attributes have any resemblance to these qualities among men. He is infinitely superior to our limited view and comprehension, and is more the object of worship in the temple than of disputation in the schools.

In reality, Cleanthes, continued he, there is no need of having recourse to that affected scepticism so displeasing to you in order to come at this determination. Our ideas reach no further than our experience. We have no experience of divine attributes and operations. I need not conclude my syllogism,

you can draw the inference yourself. And it is a pleasure to me (and I hope to you, too) that just reasoning and sound piety here concur in the same conclusion, and both of them establish the adorably mysterious and incomprehensible nature of the Supreme Being.

Not to lose any time in circumlocutions, said Cleanthes, addressing himself to Demea, much less in replying to the pious declamations of Philo, I shall briefly explain how I conceive this matter. Look round the world, contemplate the whole and every part of it: you will find it to be nothing but one great machine, subdivided into an infinite number of lesser machines, which again admit of subdivisions to a degree beyond what human senses and faculties can trace and explain. All these various machines, and even their most minute parts, are adjusted to each other with an accuracy which ravishes into admiration all men who have ever contemplated them. The curious adapting of means to ends, throughout all nature, resembles exactly, though it much exceeds, the productions of human contrivance—of human design, thought, wisdom, and intelligence. Since therefore the effects resemble each other, we are led to infer, by all the rules of analogy, that the causes also resemble, and that the Author of nature is somewhat similar to the mind of man, though possessed of much larger faculties, proportioned to the grandeur of the work which he has executed. By this argument *a posteriori,* and by this argument alone, do we prove at once the existence of a Deity and his similarity to human mind and intelligence.

I shall be so free, Cleanthes, said Demea, as to tell you that from the beginning I could not approve of your conclusion concerning the similarity of the Deity to men, still less can I approve of the mediums by which you endeavour to establish it. What! No demonstration of the Being of God! No abstract arguments! No proofs *a priori!* Are these which have hitherto been so much insisted on by philosophers all fallacy, all sophism? Can we reach no farther in this subject than experience and probability? I will not say that this is betraying the cause of a Deity; but surely, by this affected candour, you give advantages to atheists which they never could obtain by the mere dint of argument and reasoning.

What I chiefly scruple in this subject, said Philo, is not so much that all religious arguments are by

Cleanthes reduced to experience, as that they appear not to be even the most certain and irrefragable of that inferior kind. That a stone will fall, that fire will burn, that the earth has solidity, we have observed a thousand and a thousand times; and when any new instance of this nature is presented, we draw without hesitation the accustomed inference. The exact similarity of the cases gives us a perfect assurance of a similar event, and a stronger evidence is never desired nor sought after. But wherever you depart, in the least, from the similarity of the cases, you diminish proportionably the evidence, and may at last bring it to a very weak *analogy*, which is confessedly liable to error and uncertainty. After having experienced the circulation of the blood in human creatures, we make no doubt that it takes place in Titius and Maevius; but from its circulation in frogs and fishes it is only a presumption, though a strong one, from analogy that it takes place in men and other animals. The analogical reasoning is much weaker when we infer the circulation of the sap in vegetables from our experience that the blood circulates in animals; and those who hastily followed that imperfect analogy are found, by more accurate experiments, to have been mistaken.

If we see a house, Cleanthes, we conclude, with the greatest certainty, that it had an architect or builder because this is precisely that species of effect which we have experienced to proceed from that species of cause. But surely you will not affirm that the universe bears such a resemblance to a house that we can with the same certainty infer a similar cause, or that the analogy is here entire and perfect. The dissimilitude is so striking that the utmost you can here pretend to is a guess, conjecture, a presumption concerning a similar cause; and how that pretension will be received in the world, I leave you to consider.

It would surely be very ill received, replied Cleanthes; and I should be deservedly blamed and detested did I allow that the proofs of Deity amounted to no more than a guess or conjecture. But is the whole adjustment of means to ends in a house and in the universe so slight a resemblance? the economy of final causes? the order, proportion, and arrangement of every part? Steps of a stair are plainly contrived that human legs may use them in mounting; and this inference is certain and infallible. Hu-

man legs are also contrived for walking and mounting; and this inference, I allow, is not altogether so certain because of the dissimilarity which you remark; but does it, therefore, deserve the name only of presumption or conjecture?

Good God! cried Demea, interrupting him, where are we? Zealous defenders of religion allow that the proofs of a Deity fall short of perfect evidence! And you, Philo, on whose assistance I depended in proving the adorable mysteriousness of the Divine Nature, do you assent to all these extravagant opinions of Cleanthes? For what other name can I give them? or, why spare my censure when such principles are advanced, supported by such an authority, before so young a man as Pamphilus?

You seem not to apprehend, replied Philo, that I argue with Cleanthes in his own way, and, by showing him the dangerous consequences of his tenets, hope at last to reduce him to our opinion. But what sticks most with you, I observe, is the representation which Cleanthes has made of the argument *a posteriori;* and, finding that the argument is likely to escape your hold and vanish into air, you think it so disguised that you can scarcely believe it to be set in its true light. How, however much I may dissent, in other respects, from the dangerous principles of Cleanthes, I must allow that he has fairly represented that argument, and I shall endeavour so to state the matter to you that you will entertain no further scruples with regard to it.

Were a man to abstract from everything which he knows or has seen, he would be altogether incapable, merely from his own ideas, to determine what kind of scene the universe must be, or to give the preference to one state or situation of things above another. For as nothing which he clearly conceives could be esteemed impossible or implying a contradiction, every chimera of his fancy would be upon an equal footing; nor could he assign any just reason why he adheres to one idea or system, and rejects the others which are equally possible.

Again, after he opens his eyes and contemplates the world as it really is, it would be impossible for him at first to assign the cause of any one event, much less of the whole of things, or of the universe. He might set his fancy a rambling, and she might bring him in an infinite variety of reports and representations. These would all be possible, but, being all equally possible, he would never of himself give a satisfactory account for his preferring one of them to the rest. Experience alone can point out to him the true cause of any phenomenon.

Now, according to this method of reasoning, Demea, it follows (and is, indeed, tacitly allowed by Cleanthes himself) that order, arrangement, or the adjustment of final causes, is not of itself any proof of design, but only so far as it has been experienced to proceed from that principle. For aught we can know *a priori,* matter may contain the source or spring of order originally within itself, as well as mind does; and there is no more difficulty in conceiving that the several elements, from an internal unknown cause, may fall into the most exquisite arrangement, than to conceive that their ideas, in the great universal mind, from a like internal unknown cause, fall into that arrangement. The equal possibility of both these suppositions is allowed. But, by experience, we find (according to Cleanthes) that there is a difference between them. Throw several pieces of steel together, without shape or form, they will never arrange themselves so as to compose a watch. Stone and mortar and wood, without an architect, never erect a house. But the ideas in a human mind, we see, by an unknown, inexplicable economy, arrange themselves so as to form the plan of a watch or house. Experience, therefore, proves that there is an original principle of order in mind, not in matter. From similar effects we infer similar causes. The adjustment of means to ends is alike in the universe, as in a machine of human contrivance. The causes, therefore, must be resembling.

I was from the beginning scandalized, I must own, with this resemblance which is asserted between the Deity and human creatures, and must conceive it to imply such a degradation of the Supreme Being as no sound theist could endure. With your assistance, therefore, Demea, I shall endeavour to defend what you justly call the adorable mysteriousness of the Divine Nature, and shall refute this reasoning of Cleanthes, provided he allows that I have made a fair representation of it.

When Cleanthes had assented, Philo, after a short pause, proceeded in the following manner.

That all inferences, Cleanthes, concerning fact are founded on experience, and that all experimental reasonings are founded on the supposition that similar causes prove similar effects, and similar effects similar causes, I shall not at present much dispute with you. But observe, I entreat you, with what extreme caution all just reasoners proceed in the transferring of experiments to similar cases. Unless the cases be exactly similar, they repose no perfect confidence in applying their past observation to any particular phenomenon. Every alteration of circumstances occasions a doubt concerning the event; and it requires new experiments to prove certainly that the new circumstances are of no moment or importance. A change in bulk, situation, arrangement, age, disposition of the air, or surrounding bodies—any of these particulars may be attended with the most unexpected consequences. And unless the objects be quite familiar to us, it is the highest temerity to expect with assurance, after any of these changes, an event similar to that which before fell under our observation. The slow and deliberate steps of philosophers here, if anywhere, are distinguished from the precipitate march of the vulgar, who, hurried on by the smallest similitude, are incapable of all discernment or consideration.

But you can think, Cleanthes, that your usual phlegm and philosophy have been preserved in so wide a step as you have taken when you compared to the universe houses, ships, furniture, machines, and, from their similarity in some circumstances, inferred a similarity in their causes? Thought, design, intelligence, such as we discover in men and other animals, is no more than one of the springs and principles of the universe, as well as heat or cold, attraction or repulsion, and a hundred others which fall under daily observation. It is an active cause by which some particular parts of nature, we find, produce alterations on other parts. But can a conclusion, with any propriety, be transferred from parts to the whole? Does not the great disproportion bar all comparison and inference? From observing the growth of a hair, can we learn anything concerning the generation of a man? Would the manner of a leaf's blowing, even though perfectly known, afford us any instruction concerning the vegetation of a tree?

But allowing that we were to take the *operations* of one part of nature upon another for the foundation of our judgment concerning the *origin* of the whole (which never can be admitted), yet why select so minute, so weak, so bounded a principle as the reason and design of animals is found to be upon this planet? What peculiar privilege has this little agitation of the brain which we call *thought,* that we must thus make it the model of the whole universe? Our partiality in our own favour does indeed present it on all occasions, but sound philosophy ought carefully to guard against so natural an illusion.

So far from admitting, continued Philo, that the operations of a part can afford us any just conclusion concerning the origin of the whole, I will not allow any one part to form a rule for another part if the latter be very remote from the former. Is there any reasonable ground to conclude that the inhabitants of other planets possess thought, intelligence, reason, or anything similar to these faculties in men? When nature has so extremely diversified her manner of operation in this small globe, can we imagine that she incessantly copies herself throughout so immense a universe? And if thought, as we may well suppose, be confined merely to this narrow corner and has even there so limited a sphere of action, with what propriety can we assign it for the original cause of all things? The narrow views of a peasant who makes his domestic economy the rule for the government of kingdoms is in comparison a pardonable sophism.

But were we ever so much assured that a thought and reason resembling the human were to be found throughout the whole universe, and were its activity elsewhere vastly greater and more commanding than it appears in this globe, yet I cannot see why the operations of a world constituted, arranged, adjusted, can with any propriety be extended to a world which is in its embryo state, and is advancing towards that constitution and arrangement. By observation we know somewhat of the economy, action, and nourishment of a finished animal, but we must transfer with great caution that observation to the growth of a foetus in the womb, and still more to the formation of an animalcule in the loins of its male parent. Nature, we find, even from our limited experience, possesses an infinite number of springs and principles which incessantly discover themselves on every change of her position and situation. And what new and unknown principles would actuate her in so new and unknown a situation as that of the formation of a universe, we

cannot, without the utmost temerity, pretend to determine.

A very small part of this great system, during a very short time, is very imperfectly discovered to us; and do we thence pronounce decisively concerning the origin of the whole?

Admirable conclusion! Stone, wood, brick, iron, brass, have not, at this time, in this minute globe of earth, an order or arrangement without human art and contrivance; therefore, the universe could not originally attain its order and arrangement without something similar to human art. But is a part of nature a rule for another part very wide of the former? Is it a rule for the whole? Is a very small part a rule for the universe? Is nature in one situation a certain rule for nature in another situation vastly different from the former?

And can you blame me, Cleanthes, if I here imitate the prudent reserve of Simonides, who, according to the noted story, being asked by Hiero, *What God was?* desired a day to think of it, and then two days more; and after that manner continually prolonged the term, without ever bringing in his definition or description? Could you even blame me, if I had answered, at first, *that I did not know,* and was sensible that this subject lay vastly beyond the reach of my faculties? You might cry out sceptic and rallier, as much as you pleased; but, having found in so many other subjects much more familiar the imperfections and even contradictions of human reason, I never should expect any success from its feeble conjectures in a subject so sublime and so remote from the sphere of our observation. When two *species* of objects have always been observed to be conjoined together, I can *infer,* by custom, the existence of one wherever I *see* the existence of the other; and this I call an argument from experience. But how this argument can have place where the objects, as in the present case, are single, individual, without parallel or specific resemblance, may be difficult to explain. And will any man tell me with a serious countenance that an orderly universe must arise from some thought and art like the human because we have experience of it? To ascertain this reasoning it were requisite that we had experience of the origin of worlds; and it is not sufficient, surely, that we have seen ships and cities arise from human art and contrivance.

Philo was proceeding in this vehement manner, somewhat between jest and earnest, as it appeared to me, when he observed some signs of impatience in Cleanthes, and then immediately stopped short. What I had to suggest, said Cleanthes, is only that you would not abuse terms, or make use of popular expressions to subvert philosophical reasonings. You know that the vulgar often distinguish reason from experience, even where the question relates only to matter of fact and existence, though it is found, where that *reason* is properly analyzed, that it is nothing but a species of experience. To prove by experience the origin of the universe from mind is not more contrary to common speech than to prove the motion of the earth from the same principle. And a caviller might raise all the same objections to the Copernican system which you have urged against my reasonings. Have you other earths, might he say, which you have seen to move? Have . . .

Yes! cried Philo, interrupting him, we have other earths. Is not the moon another earth, which we see to turn round its centre? Is not Venus another earth, where we observe the same phenomenon? Are not the revolutions of the sun also a confirmation, from analogy, of the same theory? All the planets, are they not earths which revolve about the sun? Are not the satellites moons which move round Jupiter and Saturn, and along with these primary planets round the sun? These analogies and resemblances, with others which I have not mentioned, are the sole proofs of the Copernican system; and to you it belongs to consider whether you have any analogies of the same kind to support your theory.

In reality, Cleanthes, continued he, the modern system of astronomy is now so much received by all inquirers, and has become so essential a part even of our earliest education, that we are not commonly very scrupulous in examining the reasons upon which it is founded. It is now become a matter of mere curiosity to study the first writers of that subject who had the full force of prejudice to encounter, and were obliged to turn their arguments on every side in order to render them popular and convincing. But if we peruse Galileo's famous *Dialogues* concerning the system of the world, we shall find that the great genius, one of the sublimest that ever existed, first bent all his endeavours to prove that there was no foundation for the distinction commonly made between elementary and celestial substances. The schools, proceeding from the illusions of sense, had carried this distinction very far; and had established the latter substances to be ingenerable, incorruptible, unalterable, impassable; and had assigned all the opposite qualities to the former. But Galileo, beginning with the moon, proved its similarity in every particular to the earth: its convex figure, its natural darkness when not illuminated, its density, its distinction into solid and liquid, the variations of its phases, the mutual illuminations of the earth and moon, their mutual eclipses, the inequalities of the lunar surface, etc. After many instances of this kind, with regard to all the planets, men plainly saw that these bodies became proper objects of experience, and that the similarity of their nature enabled us to extend the same arguments and phenomena from one to the other.

In this cautious proceeding of the astronomers you may read your own condemnation, Cleanthes, or rather may see that the subject in which you are engaged exceeds all human reason and inquiry. Can you pretend to show any such similarity between the fabric of a house and the generation of a universe? Have you ever seen nature in any such situation as resembles the first arrangement of the elements? Have worlds ever been formed under your eye, and have you had leisure to observe the whole progress of the phenomenon, from the first appearance of order to its final consummation? If you have, then cite your experience and deliver your theory.

Part III

How the most absurd argument, replied Cleanthes, in the hands of a man of ingenuity and invention, may acquire an air of probability! Are you not aware, Philo, that it became necessary for Copernicus and his first disciples to prove the similarity of the terrestrial and celestial matter because several philosophers, blinded by old systems and supported by some sensible appearances, had denied this similarity? But that it is by no means necessary that theists should prove the similarity of the works of *nature* to those of *art* because this similarity is self-evident and undeniable? The same matter, a like form; what more is requisite to show an analogy between their causes, and to ascertain the origin of all things from a divine purpose and intention? Your objections, I must freely tell you, are no better than the abstruse cavils of those philosophers who denied motion, and ought to be refuted in the same manner—by illustrations, examples, and instances rather than by serious argument and philosophy.

Suppose, therefore, that an articulate voice were heard in the clouds, much louder and more melodious than any which human art could ever reach; suppose that this voice were extended in the same instant over all nations and spoke to each nation in its own language and dialect; suppose that the words delivered not only contain a just sense and meaning, but convey some instruction altogether worthy of a benevolent Being superior to mankind—could you possibly hesitate a moment concerning the cause of this voice, and must you not instantly ascribe it to some design or purpose? Yet I cannot see but all the same objections (if they merit that appellation) which lie against the system of theism may also be produced against this inference.

Might you not say that all conclusions concerning fact were founded on experience; that, when we hear an articulate voice in the dark and thence infer a man, it is only the resemblance of the effects which leads us to conclude that there is a like resemblance in the cause; but that this extraordinary voice, by its loudness, extent, and flexibility to all languages, bears so little analogy to any human voice that we have no reason to suppose any analogy in their causes; and, consequently, that a rational, wise, coherent speech proceeded, you know not whence, from some accidental whistling of the winds, not from any divine reason or intelligence? You see clearly your own objections in these cavils, and I hope too you see clearly that they cannot possibly have more force in the one case than in the other.

But to bring the case still nearer the present one of the universe, I shall make two suppositions which imply not any absurdity or impossibility. Suppose that there is a natural, universal, invariable language, common to every individual of human race, and that books are natural productions which perpetuate themselves in the same manner with animals and vegetables, by descent and propagation. Several expressions of our passions contain a universal language: all brute animals have a natural speech, which, however limited, is very intelligible to their own species. And as there are infinitely fewer parts and less contrivance in the finest composition of eloquence than in the coarsest organized body, the propagation of an *Iliad* or *Aeneid* is an easier supposition than that of any plant or animal.

Suppose, therefore, that you enter into your library thus peopled by natural volumes containing the most refined reason and most exquisite beauty; could you possibly open one of them and doubt that its original cause bore the strongest analogy to mind and intelligence? When it reasons and discourses; when it expostulates, argues, and enforces its views and topics; when it applies sometimes to the pure intellect, sometimes to the affections; when it collects, disposes, and adorns every consideration suited to the subject; could you persist in asserting that all this, at the bottom, had really no meaning, and that the first formation of this volume in the loins of its original parent proceeded not from thought and design? Your obstinacy, I know, reaches not that degree of firmness; even your sceptical play and wantonness would be abashed at so glaring an absurdity.

But if there be any difference, Philo, between this supposed case and the real one of the universe, it is all to the advantage of the latter. The anatomy of an animal affords many stronger instances of design than the perusal of Livy or Tacitus; and any objection which you start in the former case, by carrying me back to so unusual and extraordinary a scene as the first formation of worlds, the same objection has place on the supposition of our vegetating library. Choose, then, your party, Philo, without ambiguity or evasion; assert either that a rational volume is no proof of a rational cause or admit of a similar cause to all the works of nature.

Let me here observe, too, continued Cleanthes, that this religious argument, instead of being weakened by that scepticism so much affected by you, rather acquires force from it and becomes more firm and undisputed. To exclude all argument or reasoning of every kind is either affectation or madness. The declared profession of every reasonable sceptic is only to reject abstruse, remote, and refined arguments; to adhere to common sense and the plain instincts of nature; and to assent, wherever any reasons strike him with so full a force that he cannot, without the greatest violence, prevent it. Now the arguments for natural religion are plainly of this kind;

and nothing but the most perverse, obstinate metaphysics can reject them. Consider, anatomize the eye, survey its structure and contrivance, and tell me, from your own feeling, if the idea of a contriver does not immediately flow in upon you with a force like that of sensation. The most obvious conclusion, surely, is in favour of design; and it requires time, reflection, and study, to summon up those frivolous though abstruse objections which can support infidelity. Who can behold the male and female of each species, the correspondence of their parts and instincts, their passions and whole course of life before and after generation, but must be sensible that the propagation of the species is intended by nature? Millions and millions of such instances present themselves through every part of the universe, and no language can convey a more intelligible irresistible meaning than the curious adjustment of final causes. To what degree, therefore, of blind dogmatism must one have attained to reject such natural and such convincing arguments?

Some beauties in writing we may meet with which seem contrary to rules, and which gain the affections and animate the imagination in opposition to all the precepts of criticism and to the authority of the established masters of art. And if the argument for theism be, as you pretend, contradictory to the principles of logic, its universal, its irresistible influence proves clearly that there may be arguments of a like irregular nature. Whatever cavils may be urged, an orderly world, as well as a coherent, articulate speech, will still be received as an incontestable proof of design and intention.

It sometimes happens, I own, that the religious arguments have not their due influence on an ignorant savage and barbarian, not because they are obscure and difficult, but because he never asks himself any question with regard to them. Whence arises the curious structure of an animal? From the copulation of its parents. And these whence? From *their* parents? A few removes set the objects at such a distance that to him they are lost in darkness and confusion; nor is he actuated by any curiosity to trace them farther. But this is neither dogmatism nor scepticism, but stupidity: a state of mind very different from your sifting, inquisitive disposition, my ingenious friend. You can trace causes from effects; you can compare the most distant and remote

objects; and your greatest errors proceed not from barrenness of thought and invention, but from too luxuriant a fertility which suppresses your natural good sense by a profusion of unnecessary scruples and objections.

Here I could observe, Hermippus, that Philo was a little embarrassed and confounded; but, while he hesitated in delivering an answer, luckily for him, Demea broke in upon the discourse and saved his countenance.

Your instance, Cleanthes, said he, drawn from books and language, being familiar, has, I confess, so much more force on that account; but is there not some danger, too, in this very circumstance, and may it not render us presumptuous, by making us imagine we comprehend the Deity and have some adequate idea of his nature and attributes? When I read a volume, I enter into the mind and intention of the author; I become him, in a manner, for the instant, and have an immediate feeling and conception of those ideas which revolved in his imagination while employed in that composition. But so near an approach we never surely can make to the Deity. His ways are not our ways, his attributes are perfect but incomprehensible. And this volume of nature contains a great and inexplicable riddle, more than any intelligible discourse or reasoning.

The ancient Platonists, you know, were the most religious and devout of all the pagan philosophers, yet many of them, particularly Plotinus, expressly declare that intellect or understanding is not to be ascribed to the Deity, and that our most perfect worship of him consists, not in acts of veneration, reverence, gratitude, or love, but in a certain mysterious self-annihilation or total extinction of all our faculties. These ideas are, perhaps, too far stretched, but still it must be acknowledged that, by representing the Deity as so intelligible and comprehensible, and so similar to a human mind, we are guilty of the grossest and most narrow partiality, and make ourselves the model of the whole universe.

All the *sentiments* of the human mind, gratitude, resentment, love, friendship, approbation, blame, pity, emulation, envy, have a plain reference to the state and situation of man, and are calculated for preserving the existence and promoting the activity of such a being in such circumstances. It seems, therefore, unreasonable to transfer such sentiments to a supreme existence or to suppose him actuated by them; and the phenomena, besides, of the universe will not support us in such a theory. All our *ideas* derived from the senses are confessedly false and illusive, and cannot therefore be supposed to have place in a supreme intelligence. And as the ideas of internal sentiment, added to those of the external senses, compose the whole furniture of human understanding, we may conclude that none of the *materials* of thought are in any respect similar in the human and in the divine intelligence. Now, as to the *manner* of thinking, how can we make any comparison between them or suppose them anywise resembling? Our thought is fluctuating, uncertain, fleeting, successive, and compounded; and were we to remove these circumstances, we absolutely annihilate its essence, and it would in such a case be an abuse of terms to apply to it the name of thought or reason. At least, if it appear more pious and respectful (as it really is) still to retain these terms when we mention the Supreme Being, we ought to acknowledge that their meaning, in that case, is totally incomprehensible, and that the infirmities of our nature do not permit us to reach any ideas which in the least correspond to the ineffable sublimity of the Divine attributes.

Part IV

It seems strange to me, said Cleanthes, that you, Demea, who are so sincere in the cause of religion, should still maintain the mysterious, incomprehensible nature of the Deity, and should insist so strenuously that he has no manner of likeness or resemblance to human creatures. The Deity, I can readily allow, possesses many powers and attributes of which we can have no comprehension; but, if our ideas, so far as they go, be not just and adequate and correspondent to his real nature, I know not what there is in this subject worth insisting on. Is the name, without any meaning, of such mighty importance? Or how do you mystics, who maintain the absolute incomprehensibility of the Deity, differ from sceptics or atheists, who assert that the first cause of all is unknown and unintelligible? Their temerity must be very great if, after rejecting the production by a mind—I mean a mind resembling the human (for I know of no other)—they pretend to assign, with certainty, any other specific intelligible cause; and their conscience must be very scrupulous, indeed, if they refuse to call the universal unknown cause a God or Deity, and to bestow on him as many sublime eulogies and unmeaning epithets as you shall please to require of them.

Who could imagine, replied Demea, that Cleanthes, the calm philosophical Cleanthes, would attempt to refute his antagonists by affixing a nickname to them, and, like the common bigots and inquisitors of the age, have recourse to invective and declamation instead of reasoning? Or does he not perceive that these topics are easily retorted, and that *anthropomorphite* is an appellation as invidious, and implies as dangerous consequences, as the epithet of *mystic* with which he has honoured us? In reality, Cleanthes, consider what it is you assert when you represent the Deity as similar to the human mind and understanding. What is the soul of man? A composition of various faculties, passions, sentiments, ideas—united, indeed, into one self or person, but still distinct from each other. When it reasons, the ideas which are the parts of its discourse arrange themselves in a certain form or order which is not preserved entire for a moment immediately gives place to another arrangement. New opinions, new passions, new affections, new feelings arise which continually diversify the mental scene and produce in it the greatest variety and most rapid succession imaginable. How is this compatible with that perfect immutability and simplicity which all true theists ascribe to the Deity? By the same act, say they, he sees past, present, and future; his love and hatred, his mercy and justice, are one individual operation; he is entire in every point of space, and complete in every instant of duration. No succession, no change, no acquisition, no diminution. What he is implies not in it any shadow of distinction or diversity. And what he is this moment he ever has been and ever will be, without any new judgment, sentiment, or operation. He stands fixed in one simple, perfect state; nor can you ever say, with any propriety, that this act of his is different from that other, or that this judgment or idea has been lately formed and will give place, by succession, to any different judgment or idea.

I can readily allow, said Cleanthes, that those who maintain the perfect simplicity of the Supreme

Being, to the extent in which you have explained it, are complete mystics, and chargeable with all the consequences which I have drawn from their opinion. They are, in a word, atheists, without knowing it. For though it be allowed that the Deity possesses attributes of which we have no comprehension, yet ought we never to ascribe to him any attributes which are absolutely incompatible with that intelligent nature essential to him. A mind whose acts and sentiments and ideas are not distinct and successive, one that is wholly simple and totally immutable, is a mind which has no thought, no reason, no will, no sentiment, no love, no hatred; or, in a word, is no mind at all. It is an abuse of terms to give it that appellation, and we may as well speak of limited extension without figure, or of number without composition.

Pray consider, said Philo, whom you are at present inveighing against. You are honouring with the appellation of *atheist* all the sound, orthodox divines, almost, who have treated of this subject; and you will at last be, yourself, found, according to your reckoning, the only sound theist in the world. But if idolaters be atheists, as, I think, may justly be asserted, and Christian theologians the same, what becomes of the argument, so much celebrated, derived from the universal consent of mankind?

But, because I know you are not much swayed by names and authorities, I shall endeavor to show you, a little more distinctly, the inconveniences of that anthropomorphism which you have embraced, and shall prove that there is no ground to suppose a plan of the world to be formed in the Divine mind, consisting of distinct ideas, differently arranged, in the same manner as an architect forms in his head the plan of a house which he intends to execute.

It is not easy, I own, to see what is gained by this supposition, whether we judge of the matter by *reason* or by *experience*. We are still obliged to mount higher in order to find the cause of this cause which you had assigned as satisfactory and conclusive.

If *reason* (I mean abstract reason derived from inquiries *a priori*) be not alike mute with regard to all questions concerning cause and effect, this sentence at least it will venture to pronounce: that a mental world or universe of ideas requires a cause as much as does a material world or universe of objects, and, if similar in its arrangement, must require a

similar cause. For what is there in this subject which should occasion a different conclusion or inference? In an abstract view, they are entirely alike; and no difficulty attends the one supposition which is not common to both of them.

Again, when we will needs force *experience* to pronounce some sentence, even on these subjects which lie beyond her sphere, neither can she perceive any material difference in this particular between those two kinds of worlds, but finds them to be governed by similar principles, and to depend upon an equal variety of causes in their operations. We have specimens in miniature of both of them. Our own mind resembles the one; a vegetable or animal body the other. Let experience, therefore, judge from these samples. Nothing seems more delicate, with regard to its causes, than thought; and as these causes never operate in two persons after the same manner, so we never find two persons who think exactly alike. Nor indeed does the same person think exactly alike at any two different periods of time. A difference of age, of the disposition of his body, a weather, of food, of company, of books, of passions—any of these particulars, or others more minute, are sufficient to alter the curious machinery of thought and communicate to it very different movements and operations. As far as we can judge, vegetables and animal bodies are not more delicate in their motions, nor depend upon a greater variety or more curious adjustment of springs and principles.

How, therefore, shall we satisfy ourselves concerning the cause of that Being whom you suppose the Author of nature, or, according to your system of anthropomorphism, the ideal world into which you trace the material? Have we not the same reason to trace that ideal world into another ideal world or new intelligent principle? But if we stop and go no farther, why go so far? Why not stop at the material world? How can we satisfy ourselves without going on *in infinitum*? And, after all, what satisfaction is there in that infinite progression? Let us remember the story of the Indian philosopher and his elephant. It was never more applicable than to the present subject. If the material world rests upon a similar ideal world, this ideal world must rest upon some other, and so on without end. It were better, therefore, never to look beyond the present material world. By supposing it to contain the principle of its order within itself, we really assert it to be God: and the sooner we arrive at that Divine Being, so much the better. When you go one step beyond the mundane system, you only excite an inquisitive humour which it is impossible ever to satisfy.

To say that the different ideas which compose the reason of the Supreme Being fall into order of themselves and by their own nature is really to talk without any precise meaning. If it has a meaning, I would fain know why it is not as good sense to say that the parts of the material world fall into order of themselves and by their own nature. Can the one opinion be intelligible, while the other is not so?

We have, indeed, experience of ideas which fall into order of themselves and without any *known* cause. But, I am sure, we have a much larger experience of matter which does the same, as in all instances of generation and vegetation where the accurate analysis of the cause exceeds all human comprehension. We have also experience of particular systems of thought and of matter which have no order; of the first in madness, of the second in corruption. Why, then, should we think that order is more essential to one than the other? And if it requires a cause in both, what do we gain by your system, in tracing the universe of objects into a similar universe of ideas? The first step which we make leads us on for ever. It were, therefore, wise in us to limit all our inquiries to the present world, without looking further. No satisfaction can ever be attained by these speculations which so far exceed the narrow bounds of human understanding.

It was usual with the Peripatetics, you know, Cleanthes, when the cause of any phenomenon was demanded, to have recourse to their *faculties* or *occult qualities,* and to say, for instance, that bread nourished by its nutritive faculty, and senna purged by its purgative. But it has been discovered that this subterfuge was nothing but the disguise of ignorance, and that these philosophers, though less ingenuous, really said the same thing with the sceptics or the vulgar who fairly confessed that they knew not the cause of these phenomena. In like manner, when it is asked, what cause produced order in the ideas of the Supreme Being, can any other reason be assigned by you, anthropomorphites, than that it is a *rational* faculty, and that such is the nature of the Deity? But why a similar answer will not be equally sat-

isfactory in accounting for the order of the world, without having recourse to any such intelligent creator as you insist on, may be difficult to determine. It is only to say that *such* is the nature of material objects, and that they are all originally possessed of a *faculty* of order and proportion. These are only more learned and elaborate ways of confessing our ignorance; nor has the one hypothesis any real advantage above the other, except in its greater conformity to vulgar prejudices.

You have displayed this argument with great emphasis, replied Cleanthes: You seem not sensible how easy it is to answer it. Even in common life, if I assign a cause for any event, is it any objection, Philo, that I cannot assign the cause of that cause, and answer every new question which may incessantly be started? And what philosophers could possibly submit to so rigid a rule?—philosophers who confess ultimate causes to be totally unknown, and are sensible that the most refined principles into which they trace the phenomena are still to them as inexplicable as these phenomena themselves are to the vulgar. The order and arrangement of nature, the curious adjustment of final causes, the plain use and intention of every part and organ—all these bespeak in the clearest language an intelligent cause or author. The heavens and the earth join in the same testimony: The whole chorus of nature raises one hymn to the praises of its Creator. You alone, or almost alone, disturb this general harmony. You start abstruse doubts, cavils, and objections; you ask me what is the cause of this cause? I know not; I care not; that concerns not me. I have found a Deity; and here I stop my inquiry. Let those go further who are wiser or more enterprising.

I pretend to be neither, replied Philo; and for that very reason I should never, perhaps, have attempted to go so far, especially when I am sensible that I must at last be contented to sit down with the same answer which, without further trouble, might have satisfied me from the beginning. If I am still to remain in utter ignorance of causes and can absolutely give an explication of nothing, I shall never esteem it any advantage to shove off for a moment a difficulty which you acknowledge must immediately, in its full force, recur upon me. Naturalists indeed very justly explain particular effects by more general causes, though these general causes themselves should remain in the totally inexplicable, but they never surely thought it satisfactory to explain a particular effect by a particular cause which was no more to be accounted for than the effect itself. An ideal system, arranged of itself, without a precedent design, is not a whit more explicable than a material one which attains its order in a like manner; nor is there any more difficulty in the latter supposition than in the former.

Part V

But to show you still more inconveniences, continued Philo, in your anthropomorphism, please to take a new survey of your principles. *Like effects prove like causes.* This is the experimental argument; and this, you say too, is the sole theological argument. Now it is certain that the liker the effects are which are seen and the liker the causes which are inferred, the stronger is the argument. Every departure on either side diminishes the probability and renders the experiment less conclusive. You cannot doubt of the principle; neither ought you to reject its consequences.

All the new discoveries in astronomy which prove the immense grandeur and magnificence of the works of nature are so many additional arguments for a Deity, according to the true system of theism; but, according to your hypothesis of experimental theism, they become so many objections, by removing the effect still further from all resemblance to the effects of human art and contrivance. For if Lucretius, even following the old system of the world, could exclaim:

Quis regere immensi summam, quis habere profundi
Indu manu validas potis est moderanter habenas?
Quis pariter coelos omnes convertere? et omnes
Ignibus aetheriis terras suffire feraces?
Omnibus inque locis esse omni tempore praesto?[2]

If Tully [Cicero] esteemed this reasoning so natural as to put it into the mouth of his Epicurean:

Quibus enim oculis animi intueri potuit vester
Plato fabricam illam tanti operis, qua construi a
Deo atque aedificari mundum facit? quae molitio?
quae ferramenta? qui vectes? quae machinae? qui
ministri tanti muneris fuerunt? quemadmodum

autem obedire et parere voluntati architecti aer,
ignis, aqua, terra potuerunt?[3]

If this argument, I say, had any force in former ages, how much greater must it have at present when the bounds of Nature are so infinitely enlarged and such a magnificent scene is opened to us? It is still more unreasonable to form our idea of so unlimited a cause from our experience of the narrow productions of human design and invention.

The discoveries by microscopes, as they open a new universe in miniature, are still objections, according to you, arguments, according to me. The further we push our researcher of this kind, we are still led to infer the universal cause of all to be vastly different from mankind, or from any object of human experience and observation.

And what say you to the discoveries in anatomy, chemistry, botany? . . . These surely are no objections, replied Cleanthes; they only discover new instances of art and contrivance, it is still the image of mind reflected on us from innumerable objects. Add a mind *like the human,* said Philo. I know of no other, replied Cleanthes. And the liker, the better, insisted Philo. To be sure, said Cleanthes.

Now, Cleanthes, said Philo, with an air of alacrity and triumph, mark the consequences. *First,* by this method of reasoning you renounce all claim to infinity in any of the attributes of the Deity. For, as the cause ought only to be proportioned to the effect, and the effect, so far as it falls under our cognizance, is not infinite, what pretensions have we, upon your suppositions, to ascribe that attribute to the Divine Being? You will still insist that, by removing him so much from all similarity to human creatures, we give in to the most arbitrary hypothesis, and at the same time weaken all proofs of his existence.

Secondly, you have no reason, on your theory, for ascribing perfection to the Deity, even in his finite capacity, or for supposing him free from every error, mistake, or incoherence, in his undertakings. There are many inexplicable difficulties in the works of nature which, if we allow a perfect author to be proved *a priori,* are easily solved, and become only seeming difficulties from the narrow capacity of man, who cannot trace infinite relations. But according to your method of reasoning, these difficulties become all real, and, perhaps, will be insisted on as new instances of likeness to human art and contrivance. At least, you must acknowledge that it is impossible for us to tell, from our limited views, whether this system contains any great faults or deserves any considerable praise if compared to other possible and even real systems. Could a peasant, if the *Aeneid* were read to him, pronounce that poem to be absolutely faultless, or even assign to it its proper rank among the productions of human wit, he who had never seen any other production?

But were this world ever so perfect a production, it must still remain uncertain whether all the excellences of the work can justly be ascribed to the workman. If we survey a ship, what an exalted idea must we form of the ingenuity of the carpenter who framed so complicated, useful, and beautiful a machine? And what surprise must we feel when we find him a stupid mechanic who imitated others, and copied an art which, through a long succession of ages, after multiplied trials, mistakes, corrections, deliberations, and controversies, had been gradually improving? Many worlds might have been botched and bungled, throughout an eternity, ere this system was struck out; much labour lost, many fruitless trials made, and a slow but continued improvement carried on during infinite ages in the art of world-making. In such subjects, who can determine where the truth, nay, who can conjecture where the probability lies, amidst a great number of hypotheses which may be proposed, and a still greater which may be imagined?

And what shadow of an argument, continued Philo, can you produce from your hypothesis to prove the unity of the Deity? A great number of men join in building a house or ship, in rearing a city, in framing a commonwealth; why may not several deities combine in contriving and framing a world? This is only so much greater similarity to human affairs. By sharing the work among several, we may so much further limit the attributes of each, and get rid of that extensive power and knowledge which must be supposed in one deity, and which, according to you, can only serve to weaken the proof of its existence. And if such foolish, such vicious creatures as man can yet often unite in framing and executing one plan, how much more those deities or demons, whom we may suppose several degrees more perfect!

To multiply causes without necessity is indeed contrary to true philosophy, but this principle applies not to the present case. Were one deity antecedently proved by your theory who were possessed of every attribute requisite to the production of the universe, it would be needless, I own (though not absurd) to suppose any other deity existent. But while it is still a question whether all these attributes are united in one subject or dispersed among several independent beings, by what phenomena in nature can we pretend to decide the controversy? Where we see a body raised in a scale, we are sure that there is in the opposite scale, however concealed from sight, some counterposing weight equal to it; but it is still allowed to doubt whether that weight be an aggregate of several distinct bodies or one uniform united mass. And if the weight requisite very much exceeds anything which we have ever seen conjoined in any single body, the former supposition becomes still more probable and natural. An intelligent being of such vast power and capacity as is necessary to produce the universe, or, to speak in the language of ancient philosophy, so prodigious an animal exceeds all analogy and even comprehension.

But further, Cleanthes: Men are mortal, and renew their species by generation; and this is common to all living creatures. The two great sexes of male and female, says Milton, animate the world. Why must this circumstance, so universal, so essential, be excluded from those numerous and limited deities? Behold, then, the theogony of ancient times brought back upon us.

And why not become a perfect anthropomorphite? Why not assert the deity or deities to be corporeal, and to have eyes, a nose, mouth, ears, etc.? Epicurus maintained that no man had ever seen reason but in a human figure; therefore, the gods must have a human figure. And this argument, which is deservedly so much ridiculed by Cicero, becomes, according to you, solid and philosophical.

In a word, Cleanthes, a man who follows your hypothesis is able, perhaps, to assert or conjecture that the universe sometime arose from something like design; but beyond that position he cannot ascertain one single circumstance, and is left afterwards to fix every point of his theology by the utmost license of fancy and hypothesis. This world, for aught he knows, is very faulty and imperfect, compared to a superior standard, and was only the first rude essay of some infant deity who afterwards abandoned it, ashamed of his lame performance; it is the work only of some dependent, inferior deity, and is the object of derision to his superiors; it is the production of old age and dotage in some superannuated deity, and ever since his death has run on at adventures, from the first impulse and active force which it received from him. You justly give signs of horror, Demea, at these strange suppositions; but these, and a thousand more of the same kind, are Cleanthes' suppositions, not mine. From the moment the attributes of the Deity are supposed finite, all these have place. And I cannot, for my part, think that so wild and unsettled a system of theology is, in any respect, preferable to none at all.

These suppositions I absolutely disown, cried Cleanthes: they strike me, however, with no horror, especially when proposed in that rambling way in which they drop from you. On the contrary, they give me pleasure when I see that, by the utmost indulgence of your imagination, you never get rid of the hypothesis of design in the universe, but are obliged at every turn to have recourse to it. To this concession I adhere steadily; and this I regard as a sufficient foundation for religion.

Part VI

It must be a slight fabric, indeed, said Demea, which can be erected on so tottering a foundation. While we are uncertain whether there is one deity or many, whether the deity or deities, to whom we owe our existence, be perfect or imperfect, subordinate or supreme, dead or alive, what trust or confidence can we repose in them? What devotion or worship address to them? What veneration or obedience pay them? To all the purposes of life the theory of religion becomes altogether useless; and even with regard to speculative consequences its uncertainty, according to you, must render it totally precarious and unsatisfactory.

To render it still more unsatisfactory, said Philo, there occurs to me another hypothesis which must acquire an air of probability from the method of reasoning so much insisted on by Cleanthes. That like effects arise from like causes—this principle he supposes the foundation of all religion. But there is another principle of the same kind, no less certain and derived from the same source of experience, that, where several known circumstances are observed to be similar, the unknown will also be found similar. Thus, if we see the limbs of a human body, we conclude that it is also attended with a human head, though hid from us. Thus, if we see, through a chink in a wall, a small part of the sun, we conclude that were the wall removed we should see the whole body. In short, this method of reasoning is so obvious and familiar that no scruple can ever be made with regard to its solidity.

Now, if we survey the universe, so far as it falls under our knowledge, it bears a great resemblance to an animal or organized body, and seems actuated with a like principle of life and motion. A continual circulation of matter in it produces no disorder; a continual waste in every part is incessantly repaired; the closest sympathy is perceived throughout the entire system; and each part or member, in performing its proper offices, operates both to its own preservation and to that of the whole. The world, therefore, I infer, is an animal; and the Deity is the *soul* of the world, actuating it, and actuated by it.

You have too much learning, Cleanthes, to be at all surprised at this opinion, which, you know, was maintained by almost all the theists of antiquity, and chiefly prevails in their discourses and reasonings. For though, sometimes, the ancient philosophers reason from final causes, as if they thought the world the workmanship of God, yet it appears rather their favourite notion to consider it as his body whose organization renders it subservient to him. And it must be confessed that, as the universe resembles more a human body than it does the works of human art and contrivance, if our limited analogy could ever, with any propriety, be extended to the whole of nature, the inference seems juster in favour of the ancient than the modern theory.

There are many other advantages, too, in the former theory which recommended it to the ancient theologians. Nothing more repugnant to all their notions because nothing more repugnant to common experience than mind without body, a mere spiritual substance which fell not under their senses nor comprehension, and of which they had not observed one single instance throughout all nature. Mind and body they knew because they felt both; an order, arrangement, organization, or internal machinery, in both they likewise knew, after the same manner; and it could not but seem reasonable to transfer this experience to the universe, and to suppose the divine mind and body to be also coeval and to have, both of them, order and arrangement naturally inherent in them and inseparable from them.

Here, therefore, is a new species of *anthropomorphism,* Cleanthes, on which you may deliberate, and a theory which seems not liable to any considerable difficulties. You are too much superior, surely, to *systematical prejudices* to find any more difficulty in supposing an animal body to be, originally, of itself or from unknown causes, possessed of order and organization, than in supposing a similar order to belong to mind. But the *vulgar prejudice* that body and mind ought always to accompany each other ought not, one should think, to be entirely neglected; since it is founded on *vulgar experience,* the only guide which you profess to follow in all these theological inquiries. And if you assert that our limited experience is an unequal standard by which to judge of the unlimited extent of nature, you entirely abandon your own hypothesis, and must thenceforward adopt our mysticism, as you call it, and admit of the absolute incomprehensibility of the Divine Nature.

This theory, I own, replied Cleanthes, has never before occurred to me, though a pretty natural one; and I cannot readily, upon so short an examination and reflection, deliver any opinion with regard to it. You are very scrupulous, indeed, said Philo. Were I to examine any system of yours, I should not have acted with half that caution and reserve in stating objections and difficulties to it. However, if anything occur to you, you will oblige us by proposing it.

Why then, replied Cleanthes, it seems to me that, though the world does, in many circumstances, resemble an animal body, yet is the analogy also defective in many circumstances the most material: no organs of sense; no seat of thought or reason; no one precise origin of motion and action. In short, it seems to bear a stronger resemblance to a vegetable than to an animal, and your inference would be so far inconclusive in favour of the soul of the world.

But, in the next place, your theory seems to imply the eternity of the world; and that is a principle which, I think, can be refuted by the strongest reasons and probabilities. I shall suggest an argument to this purpose which, I believe, has not been insisted on by any writer. Those who reason from the late origin of arts and sciences, though their inference wants not force, may perhaps be refuted by considerations derived from the nature of human society, which is in continual revolution between ignorance and knowledge, liberty and slavery, riches and poverty; so that it is impossible for us, from our limited experience, to foretell with assurance what events may or may not be expected. Ancient learning and history seem to have been in great danger of entirely perishing after the inundation of the barbarous nations; and had these convulsions continued a little longer or been a little more violent, we should not probably have now known what passed in the world a few centuries before us. Nay, were it not for the superstition of the popes, who preserved a little jargon of Latin in order to support the appearance of an ancient and universal church, that tongue must have been utterly lost; in which case the Western world, being totally barbarous, would not have been in a fit disposition for receiving the Greek language and learning, which was conveyed to them after the sacking of Constantinople. When learning and books had been extinguished, even the mechanical arts would have fallen considerably to decay; and it is easily imagined that fable or tradition might ascribe to them a much later origin than the true one. This vulgar argument, therefore, against the eternity of the world seems a little precarious.

But here appears to be the foundation of a better argument. Lucullus was the first that brought cherry-trees from Asia to Europe, though that tree thrives so well in many European climates that it grows in the woods without any culture. Is it possible that, throughout a whole eternity, no European had ever passed into Asia and thought of transplanting so delicious a fruit into his own country? Or if the tree was once transplanted and propagated, how could it ever afterwards perish? Empires may rise and fall, liberty and slavery succeed alternately, ignorance and knowledge give place to each other; but the cherry-tree will still remain in the woods of Greece, Spain, and Italy, and will never be affected by the revolutions of human society.

It is not two thousand years since vines were transplanted into France, though there is no climate in the world more favourable to them. It is not three centuries since horses, cows, sheep, swine, dogs, corn, were known in America. Is it possible that during the revolutions of a whole eternity there never arose a Columbus who might open the communication between Europe and that continent? We may as well imagine that all men would wear stockings for ten thousand years, and never have the sense to think of garters to tie them. All these seem convincing proofs of the youth or rather infancy of the world, as being founded on the operation of principles more constant and steady than those by which human society is governed and directed. Nothing less than a total convulsion of the elements will ever destroy all the European animals and vegetables which are now to be found in the Western world.

And what argument have you against such convulsions? replied Philo. Strong and almost incontestable proofs may be traced over the whole earth that every part of this globe has continued for many ages entirely covered with water. And though order were supposed inseparable from matter, and inherent in it, yet may matter be susceptible of many and great revolutions, through the endless periods of eternal duration. The incessant changes to which every part of it is subject seem to intimate some such general transformations; though, at the same time, it is observable that all the changes and corruptions of which we have ever had experience are but passages from one state of order to another; nor can matter ever rest in total deformity and confusion. What we see in the parts, we may infer in the whole; at least, that is the method of reasoning on which you rest your whole theory. And were I obliged to defend any particular system of this nature, which I never willingly should do, I esteem none more plausible than that which ascribes an eternal inherent principle of order to the world, though attended with great and continual revolutions and alterations. This at once solves all difficulties; and if the solution, by being so general, is not entirely complete and satisfactory, it is at least a theory that we must sooner or later have recourse to, whatever system we embrace. How could things have been as they are, were there not an original inherent principle of order somewhere, in thought or in matter? And it is very indifferent to which of these we give the preference. Chance has no place, on any hypothesis, sceptical or religious. Everything is surely governed by steady, inviolable laws. And were the inmost essence

of things laid open to us, we should then discover a scene of which, at present, we can have no idea. Instead of admiring the order of natural beings, we should clearly see that it was absolutely impossible for them, in the smallest article, ever to admit of any other disposition.

Were anyone inclined to revive the ancient pagan theology which maintained, as we learned from Hesiod, that this globe was governed by 30,000 deities, who arose from the unknown powers of nature, you would naturally object, Cleanthes, that nothing is gained by this hypothesis; and that it is as easy to suppose all men animals, beings more numerous but less perfect, to have sprung immediately from a like origin. Push the same inference a step further, and you will find a numerous society of deities as explicable as one universal deity who possesses within himself the powers and perfections of the whole society. All these systems, then, of Scepticism, Polytheism, and Theism, you must allow, on your principles, to be on a like footing, and that no one of them has any advantage over the others. You may thence learn the fallacy of your principles.

Part VII

But here, continued Philo, in examining the ancient system of the soul of the world there strikes me, all of a sudden, a new idea which, if just, must go near to subvert all your reasoning, and destroy even your first inferences on which you repose such confidence. If the universe bears a greater likeness to animal bodies and to vegetables than to the works of human art, it is more probable that its cause resembles the cause of the former than that of the latter, and its origin ought rather to be ascribed to generation or vegetation than to reason or design. Your conclusion, even according to your own principles, is therefore lame and defective.

Pray open up this argument a little further, said Demea, for I do not rightly apprehend it in that concise manner in which you have expressed it.

Our friend Cleanthes, replied Philo, as you have heard, asserts that, since no question of fact can be proved otherwise than by experience, the existence of a Deity admits not of proof from any other medium. The world, says he, resembles the works of human contrivance; therefore its cause must also resemble that of the other. Here we may remark that the operation of one very small part of nature, to wit, man, upon another very small part, to wit, that inanimate matter lying within his reach, is the rule by which Cleanthes judges of the origin of the whole; and he measures objects, so widely disproportioned, by the same individual standard. But to waive all objections drawn from this topic, I affirm that there are other parts of the universe (besides the machines of human invention) which bear still a greater resemblance to the fabric of the world, and which, therefore, afford a better conjecture concerning the universal origin of this system. These parts are animals and vegetables. The world plainly resembles more an animal or a vegetable than it does a watch or a knitting-loom. Its cause, therefore, it is more probable, resembles the cause of the former. The cause of the former is generation or vegetation. The cause, therefore, of the world we may infer to be something similar or analogous to generation or vegetation.

But how is it conceivable, said Demea, that the world can arise from anything similar to vegetation or generation?

Very easily, replied Philo. In like manner as a tree sheds its seed into the neighboring fields and produces other trees, so the great vegetable, the world, or this planetary system, produces within itself certain seeds which, being scattered into the surrounding chaos, vegetate into new worlds. A comet, for instance, is the seed of a world; and after it has been fully ripened, by passing from sun to sun, and star to star, it is, at last, tossed into the unformed elements which everywhere surround this universe, and immediately sprouts up into a new system.

Or if, for the sake of variety (for I see no other advantage), we should suppose this world to be an animal: a comet is the egg of this animal; and in like manner as an ostrich lays its egg in the sand, which, without any further care, hatches the egg and produces a new animal, so . . . I understand you, says Demea. But what wild, arbitrary suppositions are these! What *data* have you for such extraordinary conclusions? And is the slight, imaginary resemblance of the world to a vegetable or an animal sufficient to establish the same inference with regard to both? Objects which are in general so widely different, ought they to be a standard for each other?

Right, cries Philo: This is the topic on which I have all along insisted. I have still asserted that we have no *data* to establish any system of cosmogony. Our experience, so imperfect in itself and so limited both in extent and duration, can afford us no probable conjecture concerning the whole of things. But if we must needs fix on some hypothesis, by what rule, pray, ought we to determine our choice? Is there any other rule than the greater similarity of the objects compared? And does not a plant or an animal, which springs from vegetation or generation, bear a stronger resemblance to the world than does any artificial machine, which arises from reason and design?

But what is this vegetation and generation of which you talk? said Demea. Can you explain their operations, and anatomize that fine internal structure on which they depend?

As much, at least, replied Philo, as Cleanthes can explain the operations of reason, or anatomize that internal structure on which it depends. But without any such elaborate disquisitions, when I see an animal, I infer that it sprang from generation; and that with as great certainty as you conclude a house to have been reared by design. These words *generation, reason* mark only certain powers and energies in nature whose effects are known, but whose essence is incomprehensible; and one of these principles, more than the other, has no privilege for being made, a standard to the whole of nature.

In reality, Demea, it may reasonably be expected that the larger the views are which we take of things, the better will they conduct us in our conclusions concerning such extraordinary and such magnificent subjects. In this little corner of the world alone, there are four principles, *reason, instinct, generation, vegetation,* which are similar to each other, and are the causes of similar effects. What a number of other principles may we naturally suppose in the immense extent and variety of the universe could we travel from planet to planet, and from system to system, in order to examine each part of this mighty fabric? Any one of these four principles above mentioned (and a hundred others which lie open to our conjecture) may afford us a theory by which to judge of the origin of the world; and it is a palpable and egregious partiality to confine our view entirely to that principle by which our own minds operate. Were this principle more intelligible on that account, such a partiality might be somewhat excusable; but reason, in its internal fabric and structure, is really as little known to us as instinct or vegetation; and, perhaps, even that vague, undeterminate word *nature,* to which the vulgar refer everything is not at the bottom more inexplicable. The effects of these principles are all known to us from experience; but the principles themselves and their manner of operation are totally unknown; nor is it less intelligible or less conformable to experience to say that the world arose by vegetation, from seed shed by another world, than to say that it arose from a divine reason or contrivance, according to the sense in which Cleanthes understands it.

But methinks, said Demea, if the world had a vegetative quality and could sow the seeds of new worlds into the infinite chaos, this power would be still an additional argument for design in its author. For whence could arise so wonderful a faculty but from design? Or how can order spring from anything which perceives not that order which it bestows?

You need only look around you, replied Philo, to satisfy yourself with regard to this question. A tree bestows order and organization on that tree which springs from it, without knowing the order; an animal in the same manner on its offspring; a bird on its nest; and instances of this kind are even more frequent in the world than those of order which arise from reason and contrivance. To say that all this order in animals and vegetables proceeds ultimately from design is begging the question; nor can that great point be ascertained otherwise than by proving, *a priori,* both that order is, from its nature, inseparably attached to thought and that it can never of itself or from original unknown principles belong to matter.

But further, Demea, this objection which you urge can never be made use of by Cleanthes, without renouncing a defense which he has already made against one of my objections. When I inquired concerning the cause of that supreme reason and intelligence into which he resolves everything, he told me that the impossibility of satisfying such inquiries could never be admitted as an objection in any species of philosophy. *We must stop somewhere,* says he, *nor is it ever within the reach of human capacity to explain ultimate causes or show the last connections of any objects. It is sufficient if any steps, as far as we go, are supported by experience and observation.* Now that vegetation and generation, as well as reason, are experienced to be principles of order in nature is undeniable. If I rest my system of cosmogony on the former, preferably to the latter, it is at my choice. The matter seems entirely arbitrary. And when Cleanthes asks me what is the cause of my great vegetative or generative faculty, I am equally entitled to ask him the cause of his great reasoning principle. These questions we have agreed to forbear on both sides; and it is chiefly his interest on the present occasion to stick to this agreement. Judging by our limited and imperfect experience, generation has some privileges above reason; for we see every day the latter arise from the former, never the former from the latter.

Compare, I beseech you, the consequences on both sides. The world, say I, resembles an animal; therefore it is an animal, therefore it arose from generation. The steps, I confess, are wide, yet there is some small appearance of analogy in each step. The world, says Cleanthes, resembles a machine; therefore it is a machine, therefore it arose from design. The steps are here equally wide, and the analogy less striking. And if he pretends to carry on *my* hypothesis a step further, and to infer design or reason from the great principle of generation on which I insist, I may, with better authority, use the same freedom to push further *his* hypothesis, and infer a divine generation or theogony from his principle of reason. I have at least some faint shadow of experience, which is the utmost that can ever be attained in the present subject. Reason, in innumerable instances, is observed to arise from the principle of generation, and never to arise from any other principle.

Hesiod and all the ancient mythologists were so struck with this analogy that they universally explained the origin of nature from an animal birth, and copulation. Plato, too, so far as he is intelligible, seems to have adopted some such notion in his *Timaeus.*

The Brahmins assert that the world arose from an infinite spider, who spun this whole complicated mass from his bowels, and annihilates afterwards the whole or any part of it, by absorbing it again and resolving it into his own essence. Here is a species of cosmogony which appears to us ridiculous because a spider is a little contemptible animal whose operations we are never likely to take for a model of the whole universe. But still here is a new species of analogy, even in our globe. And were there a planet wholly inhabited by spiders (which is very possible), this inference would there appear as natural and irrefragable as that which in our planet ascribes the origin of all things to design and intelligence, as explained by Cleanthes. Why an orderly system may not be spun from the belly as well as from the brain, it will be difficult for him to give a satisfactory reason.

I must confess, Philo, replied Cleanthes, that, of all men living, the task which you have undertaken, of raising doubts and objections, suits you best and seems, in a manner, natural and unavoidable to you. So great is your fertility of invention that I am not ashamed to acknowledge myself unable, on a sudden, to solve regularly such out-of-the-way difficulties as you incessantly start upon me, though I clearly see, in general, their fallacy and error. And I question not, but you are yourself, at present, in the same case, and have not the solution so ready as the objection, while you must be sensible that common sense and reason are entirely against you, and that such whimsies as you have delivered may puzzle but never can convince us.

Part VIII

What you ascribe to the fertility of my invention, replied Philo, is entirely owing to the nature of the subject. In subjects adapted to the narrow compass of human reason there is commonly but one determination which carries probability or conviction with it; and to a man of sound judgement all other suppositions but that one appear entirely absurd and chimerical. But in such questions as the present, a hundred contradictory views may preserve a kind of imperfect analogy, and invention has here full scope to exert itself. Without any great effort of thought, I believe that I could, in an instant, propose other systems of cosmogony which would have some faint appearance of truth, though it is a thousand, a million to one if either yours or any one of mine be the true system.

For instance, what if I should revive the old Epicurean hypothesis? This is commonly, and I believe justly, esteemed the most absurd system that has yet been proposed; yet I know not whether, with a few alterations, it might not be brought to bear a faint appearance of probability. Instead of supposing matter infinite, as Epicurus did, let us suppose it finite. A finite number of particles is only susceptible of finite transpositions: and it must happen, in an eternal duration, that every possible order or position must be tried an infinite number of times. This world, therefore, with all its events, even the most minute, has before been produced and destroyed, and will again be produced and destroyed, without any bounds and limitations. No one who has a conception of the powers of infinite, in comparison of finite, will ever scruple this determination.

But this supposes, said Demea, that matter can acquire motion without any voluntary agent or first mover.

And where is the difficulty, replied Philo, of that supposition? Every event, before experience, is equally difficult and incomprehensible; and every event, after experience, is equally easy and intelligible. Motion, in many instances, from gravity, from elasticity, from electricity, begins in matter, without any known voluntary agent; and to suppose always, in these cases, an unknown voluntary agent is mere hypothesis and hypothesis attended with no advantages. The beginning of motion in matter itself is as conceivable *a priori* as its communication from mind and intelligence.

Besides, why may not motion have been propagated by impulse through all eternity, and the same stock of it, or nearly the same, be still upheld in the universe? As much is lost by the composition of motion, as much is gained by its resolution. And whatever the causes are, the fact is certain that matter is and always has been in continual agitation, as far as human experience or tradition reaches. There is not probably, at present, in the whole universe, one particle of matter at absolute rest.

And this very consideration, too, continued Philo, which we have stumbled on in the course of the argument, suggests a new hypothesis of cosmogony that is not absolutely absurd and improbable. Is there a system, an order, an economy of things, by which matter can preserve that perpetual agitation which seems essential to it, and yet maintain a constancy in the forms which it produces? There certainly is such an economy, for this is actually the case with the present world. The continual motion of matter, therefore, in less than infinite transpositions, must produce this economy or order, and by its very nature, that order, when once established, supports itself for many ages if not to eternity. But wherever matter is so poised, arranged, and adjusted, as to continue in perpetual motion, and yet preserve a constancy in the forms, its situation must, of necessity, have all the same appearance of art and contrivance which we observe at present. All the parts of each form must have a relation to each other and to the whole; and the whole itself must have a relation to the other parts of the universe, to the element in which the form subsists, to the materials with which it repairs its waste and decay, and to every other form which is hostile or friendly. A defect in any of these particulars destroys the form, and the matter of which it is composed is again set loose, and is thrown into irregular motions and fermentations till it unite itself to some other regular form. If no such form be prepared to receive it, and if there be a great quantity of this corrupted matter in the universe, the universe itself is entirely disordered, whether it be the feeble embryo of a world in its first beginnings that is thus destroyed or the rotten carcase of one languishing in old age and infirmity. In either case, a chaos ensues till finite though innumerable revolutions produce, at last, some forms whose parts and organs are so adjusted as to support the forms amidst a continued succession of matter.

Suppose (for we shall endeavour to vary the expression) that matter were thrown into any position by a blind, unguided force; it is evident that this first position must, in all probability, be the most confused and most disorderly imaginable, without any resemblance to those works of human contrivance which, along with a symmetry of parts, discover an adjustment of means to ends and a tendency to self-preservation. If the actuating force cease after this operation, matter must remain for ever in disorder and continue an immense chaos, without any proportion or activity. But suppose that the actuating force, whatever it be, still continues in matter, this first position will immediately give place to a second which will likewise, in all probability, be as disorderly as the first, and so on through many successions of changes and revolutions. No particular order or po-

sition ever continues a moment unaltered. The original force, still remaining in activity, gives a perpetual restlessness to matter. Every possible situation is produced and instantly destroyed. If a glimpse or dawn of order appears for a moment, it is instantly hurried away and confounded by that never-ceasing force which actuates every part of matter.

Thus the universe goes on for many ages in a continued succession of chaos and disorder. But is it not possible that it may settle at last, so as not to lose its motion and active force (for that we have supposed inherent in it), yet so as to preserve an uniformity of appearance, amidst the continual motion and fluctuation of its parts? This we find to be the case with the universe at present. Every individual is perpetually changing, and every part of every individual; and yet the whole remains, in appearance, the same. May we not hope for such a position or rather be assured of it from the eternal revolutions of unguided matter; and may not this account for all the appearing wisdom and contrivance which is in the universe? Let us contemplate the subject a little, and we shall find that this adjustment if attained by matter of a seeming stability in the forms, with a real and perpetual revolution or motion of parts, affords a plausible, if not a true, solution of the difficulty.

It is in vain, therefore, to insist upon the uses of the parts in animals or vegetables, and their curious adjustment to each other. I would fain know how an animal could subsist unless its parts were so adjusted? Do we not find that it immediately perishes whenever this adjustment ceases, and that its matter, corrupting, tries some new form? It happens indeed that the parts of the world are so well adjusted that some regular form immediately lays claim to this corrupted matter; and if it were not so, could the world subsist? Must it not dissolve, as well as the animal, and pass through new positions and situations till in great but finite succession it fall, at last, into the present or some such order?

It is well, replied Cleanthes, you told us that this hypothesis was suggested on a sudden, in the course of the argument. Had you had leisure to examine it, you would soon have perceived the insuperable objections to which it is exposed. No form, you say, can subsist unless it possess those powers and organs requisite for its subsistence; some new order of economy must be tried, and so on, without intermission, till at last some order which can support and maintain itself is fallen upon. But according to this hypothesis, whence arise the many conveniences and advantages which men and all animals possess? Two eyes, two ears are not absolutely necessary for the subsistence of the species. The human race might have been propagated and preserved without horses, dogs, cows, sheep, and those innumerable fruits and products which serve to our satisfaction and enjoyment. If no camels had been created for the use of man in the sandy deserts of Africa and Arabia, would the world have been dissolved? If no loadstone had been framed to give that wonderful and useful direction to the needle, would human society and the human kind have been immediately extinguished? Though the maxims of nature be in general very frugal, yet instances of this kind are far from being rare; and any one of them is a sufficient proof of design—and of a benevolent design—which gave rise to the order and arrangement of the universe.

At least, you may safely infer, said Philo, that the foregoing hypothesis is so far incomplete and imperfect, which I shall not scruple to allow. But can we ever reasonably expect greater success in any attempts of this nature? Or can we ever hope to erect a system of cosmogony that will be liable to no exceptions, and will contain no circumstance repugnant to our limited and imperfect experience of the analogy of nature? Your theory itself cannot surely pretend to any such advantage, even though you have run into *anthropomorphism,* the better to preserve a conformity to common experience. Let us once more put it to trial. In all instances which we have ever seen, ideas are copied from real objects, and are ectypal, not archetypal, to express myself in learned terms. You reverse this order and give thought the precedence. In all instances which we have ever seen, thought has no influence upon matter except where that matter is so conjoined with it as to have an equal reciprocal influence upon it. No animal can move immediately anything but the members of its own body; and, indeed, the equality of action and reaction seems to be an universal law of nature; but your theory implies a contradiction to this experience. These instances, with many more which it were easy to collect (particularly the supposition of a mind or system of thought that is eternal or, in other words, an animal ingenerable and im-

mortal)—these instances, I say, may teach all of us sobriety in condemning each other, and let us see that as no system of this kind ought ever to be received from a slight analogy, so neither ought any to be rejected on account of a small incongruity. For that is an inconvenience from which we can justly pronounce no one to be exempted.

All religious systems, it is confessed, are subject to great and insuperable difficulties. Each disputant triumphs in his turn, while he carries on an offensive war, and exposes the absurdities, barbarities, and pernicious tenets of his antagonist. But all of them, on the whole, prepare a complete triumph for the *sceptic,* who tells them that no system ought ever to be embraced with regard to such subjects: for this plain reason that no absurdity ought ever to be assented to with regard to any subject. A total suspense of judgment is here our only reasonable resource. And if every attack, as is commonly observed, and no defence among theologians is successful, how complete must be *his* victory who remains always, with all mankind, on the offensive, and has himself no fixed station or abiding city which he is ever, on any occasion, obliged to defend?

Part IX

But if so many difficulties attend the argument *a posteriori,* said Demea, had we not better adhere to that simple and sublime argument *a priori* which, by offering to us infallible demonstration, cuts off at once all doubt and difficulty? By this argument, too, we may prove the *infinity* of the Divine attributes, which, I am afraid, can never be ascertained with certainty from any other topic. For how can an effect which either is finite or, for aught we know, may be so—how can such an effect, I say, prove an infinite cause? The unity, too, of the Divine Nature it is very difficult, if not absolutely impossible, to deduce merely from contemplating the works of nature; nor will the uniformity alone of the plan, even were it allowed, give us any assurance of that attribute. Whereas the argument *a priori* . . .

You seem to reason, Demea, interposed Cleanthes, as if those advantages and conveniences in the abstract argument were full proofs of its solidity. But it is first proper, in my opinion, to determine what argument of this nature you choose to insist on; and we shall afterwards, from itself, better than from its *useful* consequences, endeavour to determine what value we ought to put upon it.

The argument, replied Demea, which I would insist on is the common one. Whatever exists must have a cause or reason of its existence, it being absolutely impossible for anything to produce itself or be the cause of its own existence. In mounting up, therefore, from effect to causes, we must either go on in tracing an infinite succession, without any ultimate cause at all, or must at least have recourse to some ultimate cause that is *necessarily* existent. Now that the first supposition is absurd may be thus proved. In the infinite chain or succession of causes and effects, each single effect is determined to exist by the power and efficacy of that cause which immediately preceded; but the whole eternal chain or succession, taken together, is not determined or caused by anything, and yet it is evident that it requires a cause or reason, as much as any particular object which begins to exist in time. The question is still reasonable why this particular succession of causes existed from eternity, and not any other succession or no succession at all. If there be no necessarily existent being, any supposition which can be formed is equally possible; nor is there any more absurdity in *nothing*'s having existed from eternity than there is in that succession of causes which constitutes the universe. What was it, then, which determined *something* to exist rather than *nothing,* and bestowed being on a particular possibility, exclusive of the rest? *External causes,* there are supposed to be none. *Chance* is a word without a meaning. Was it *nothing?* But that can never produce anything. We must, therefore, have recourse to a necessarily existent Being who carries the *reason* of his existence in himself, and who cannot be supposed not to exist, without an express contradiction. There is, consequently, such a Being—that is, there is a Deity.

I shall not leave it to Philo, said Cleanthes, though I know that starting objections is his chief delight, to point out the weakness of this metaphysical reasoning. It seems to me so obviously ill-grounded, and at the same time of so little consequence to the cause of true piety and religion, that I shall myself venture to show the fallacy of it.

I shall begin with observing that there is an evident absurdity in pretending to demonstrate a matter of fact, or to prove it by arguments *a priori.* Nothing is demonstrable unless the contrary implies a contradiction. Nothing that is distinctly conceivable implies a contradiction. Whatever we conceive as existent, we can also conceive as non-existent. There is no being, therefore, whose non-existence implies a contradiction. Consequently there is no being whose existence is demonstrable. I propose this argument as entirely decisive, and am willing to rest the whole controversy upon it.

It is pretended that the Deity is a necessarily existent being; and this necessity of his existence is attempted to be explained by asserting that, if we knew his whole essence or nature, we should perceive it to be as impossible for him not to exist, as for twice two not to be four. But it is evident that this can never happen, while our faculties remain the same as at present. It will still be possible for us, at any time, to conceive the non-existence of what was formerly conceived to exist; nor can the mind ever lie under a necessity of supposing any object to remain always in being; in the same manner as we lie under a necessity of always conceiving twice two to be four. The words, therefore, *necessary existence* have no meaning or, which is the same thing, none that is consistent.

But further, why may not the material universe be the necessarily existent Being, according to this pretended explication of necessity? We dare not affirm that we know all the qualities of matter; and, for aught we can determine, it may contain some qualities which, were they known, would make its non-existence appear as great a contradiction as that twice two is five. I find only one argument employed to prove that the material world is not the necessarily existent Being; and this argument is derived from the contingency both of the matter and the form of the world. "Any particle of matter," it is said, "may be *conceived* to be annihilated, and any form may be *conceived* to be altered. Such an annihilation or alteration, therefore, is not impossible."[4] But it seems a great partiality not to perceive that the same argument extends equally to the Deity, so far as we have any conception of him, and that the mind can at least imagine him to be non-existent or his attributes to be altered. It must be some unknown, inconceivable qualities which can make his non-existence appear impossible or his attributes unalterable; and no reason can be assigned why these qualities may not belong to matter. As they are altogether unknown and inconceivable, they can never be proved incompatible with it.

Add to this that in tracing an eternal succession of objects it seems absurd to inquire for a general cause or first author. How can anything that exists from eternity have a cause, since that relation implies a priority in time and a beginning of existence?

In such a chain, too, or succession of objects, each part is caused by that which preceded it, and causes that which succeeds it. Where then is the difficulty? But the *whole,* you say, wants a cause. I answer that the uniting of several distinct countries into one kingdom, or several distinct members into one body is performed merely by an arbitrary act of the mind, and has no influence on the nature of things. Did I show you the particular causes of each individual in a collection of twenty particles of matter, I should think it very unreasonable should you afterwards ask me what was the cause of the whole twenty. This is sufficiently explained in explaining the cause of the parts.

Though the reasonings which you have urged, Cleanthes, may well excuse me, said Philo, from starting any further difficulties, yet I cannot forbear insisting still upon another topic. It is observed by arithmeticians that the products of 9 compose always either 9 or some lesser product of 9 if you add together all the characters of which any of the former products is composed. Thus, of 18, 27, 36, which are products of 9, you make 9 by adding 1 to 8, 2 to 7, 3 to 6. Thus 369 is a product also of 9; and if you add 3, 6, and 9, you make 18, a lesser product of 9.[5] To a superficial observer so wonderful a regularity may be admired as the effect either of chance or design; but a skillful algebraist immediately concludes it to be the work of necessity, and demonstrates that it must for ever result from the nature of these numbers. Is it not probable, I ask, that the whole economy of the universe is conducted by a like necessity, though no human algebra can furnish a key which solves the difficulty? And instead of admiring the order of natural beings, may it not happen that, could we penetrate into the intimate nature of bodies, we should clearly see why it was absolutely impossible they could ever admit of any other disposition? So dangerous is it to introduce this idea of necessity into the present question! and so naturally does it afford an inference directly opposite to the religious hypothesis!

But dropping all these abstractions, continued Philo, and confining ourselves to more familiar topics, I shall venture to add an observation that the argument *a priori* has seldom been found very convincing, except to people of a metaphysical head who have accustomed themselves to abstract reasoning, and who, finding from mathematics that the understanding frequently leads to truth through obscurity, and contrary to first appearances, have transferred the same habit of thinking to subjects where it ought not to have place. Other people, even of good sense and the best inclined to religion, feel always some deficiency in such arguments, though they are not perhaps able to explain distinctly where it lies—a certain proof that men ever did and ever will derive their religion from other sources than from this species of reasoning.

Part X

It is my opinion, I own, replied Demea, that each man feels, in a manner, the truth of religion within his own breast, and, from a consciousness of his imbecility and misery rather than from any reasoning, is led to seek protection from that Being on whom he and all nature is dependent. So anxious or so tedious are even the best scenes of life that futurity is still the object of all our hopes and fears. We incessantly look forward and endeavor, by prayers, adoration, and sacrifice, to appease those unknown powers whom we find, by experience, so able to afflict and oppress us. Wretched creatures that we are! What resource for us amidst the innumerable ills of life did not religion suggest some methods of atonement, and appease those terrors with which we are incessantly agitated and tormented?

I am indeed persuaded, said Philo, that the best and indeed the only method of bringing everyone to a due sense of religion is by just representations of the misery and wickedness of men. And for that purpose a talent of eloquence and strong imagery is more requisite than that of reasoning and argument. For is it necessary to prove what everyone feels within himself? It is only necessary to make us feel it, if possible, more intimately and sensibly.

The people, indeed, replied Demea, are sufficiently convinced of this great and melancholy truth. The miseries of life, the unhappiness of man, the general corruptions of our nature, the unsatisfactory enjoyment of pleasures, riches, honours—these phrases have become almost proverbial in all languages. And who can doubt of what all men declare from their own immediate feeling and experience?

In this point, said Philo, the learned are perfectly agreed with the vulgar; and in all letters, *sacred* and *profane,* the topic of human misery has been insisted on with the most pathetic eloquence that sorrow and melancholy could inspire. The poets, who speak from sentiment, without a system, and whose testimony has therefore the more authority, abound in images of this nature. From Homer down to Dr. Young, the whole inspired tribe have ever been sensible that no other representation of things would suit the feeling and observation of each individual.

As to authorities, replied Demea, you need not seek them. Look round this library of Cleanthes. I shall venture to affirm that, except authors of particular sciences, such as chemistry or botany, who have no occasion to treat of human life, there is scarce one of those innumerable writers from whom the sense of human misery has not, in some passage or other, extorted a complaint and confession of it. At least, the chance is entirely on that side; and no one author has ever, so far as I can recollect, been so extravagant as to deny it.

There you must excuse me, said Philo: Leibniz has denied it, and is perhaps the first[6] who ventured upon so bold and paradoxical an opinion; at least, the first who made it essential to his philosophical system.

And by being the first, replied Demea, might he not have been sensible of his error? For is this a subject in which philosophers can propose to make discoveries especially in so late an age? And can any man hope by a simple denial (for the subject scarcely admits of reasoning) to bear down the united testimony of mankind, founded on sense and consciousness?

And why should man, added he, pretend to an exemption from the lot of all other animals? The whole earth, believe me, Philo, is cursed and polluted. A perpetual war is kindled amongst all living creatures. Necessity, hunger, want stimulate the strong and courageous; fear, anxiety, terror agitate the weak and infirm. The first entrance into life gives anguish to the new-born infant and to its wretched parent; weakness, impotence, distress attend each stage of that life, and it is, at last finished in agony and horror.

Observe, too, says Philo, the curious artifices of nature in order to embitter the life of every living being. The stronger prey upon the weaker and keep them in perpetual terror and anxiety. The weaker, too, in their turn, often prey upon the stronger, and vex and molest them without relaxation. Consider that innumerable race of insects, which either are bred on the body of each animal or, flying about, infix their stings in him. These insects have others still less than themselves which torment them. And thus on each hand, before and behind, above and below, every animal is surrounded with enemies which incessantly seek his misery and destruction.

Man alone, said Demea, seems to be, in part, an exception to this rule. For by combination in society he can easily master lions, tigers, and bears, whose greater strength and agility naturally enable them to prey upon him.

On the contrary, it is here chiefly, cried Philo, that the uniform and equal maxims of nature are most apparent. Man, it is true, can, by combination, surmount all his *real* enemies and become master of the whole animal creation; but does he not immediately raise up to himself *imaginary* enemies, the demons of his fancy, who haunt him with superstitious terrors and blast every enjoyment of life? His pleasure, as he imagines, becomes in their eyes a crime; his food and repose give them umbrage and offence; his very sleep and dreams furnish new materials to anxious fear; and even death, his refuge from every other ill, presents only the dread of endless and innumerable woes. Nor does the wolf molest more the timid flock than superstition does the anxious breast of wretched mortals.

Besides, consider, Demea: This very society by which we surmount those wild beasts, our natural enemies, what new enemies does it not raise to us? What woe and misery does it not occasion? Man is the greatest enemy of man. Oppression, injustice, contempt, contumely, violence, sedition, war, calumny, treachery, fraud—by these they mutually torment each other, and they would soon dissolve that society which they had formed were it not for the dread of still greater ills which must attend their separation.

But though these external insults, said Demea, from animals, from men, from all the elements, which assault us from a frightful catalogue of woes, they are nothing in comparison of those which arise within ourselves, from the distempered condition of our mind and body. How many lie under the lingering torment of disease? Hear the pathetic enumeration of the great poet.

> *Intestine stone and ulcer, colic-pangs,*
> *Demoniac frenzy, moping melancholy,*
> *And moon-struck madness, pining atrophy*
> *Marasmus, and wide-wasting pestilence.*
> *Dire was the tossing, deep the groans:* Despair
> *Tended the sick, busiest from couch to couch*
> *And over them triumphant* Death *his dart*
> *Shook: but delay'd to strike, though oft invok'd*
> *With vows, as their chief good and final hope.*[7]

The disorders of the mind, continued Demea, though more secret, are not perhaps less dismal and vexatious. Remorse, shame, anguish, rage, disappointment, anxiety, fear, dejection, despair—who has ever passed through life without cruel inroads from these tormentors? How many have scarcely ever felt any better sensations? Labour and poverty, so abhorred by everyone, are the certain lot of the far greater number; and those few privileged persons who enjoy ease and opulence never reach contentment or true felicity. All the goods of life united would not make a very happy man, but all the ills united would make a wretch indeed; and any one of them almost (and who can be free from every one?), nay, often the absence of one good (and who can possess all?) is sufficient to render life ineligible.

Were a stranger to drop on a sudden into this world, I would show him, as a specimen of its ills, an hospital full of diseases, a prison crowded with malefactors and debtors, a field of battle strewed with carcases, a fleet floundering in the ocean, a nation languishing under tyranny, famine, or pestilence. To turn the gay side of life to him and give him a notion of its pleasures—whither should I conduct him? To a ball, to an opera, to court? He might justly think that I was only showing him a diversity of distress and sorrow.

There is no evading such striking instances, said

Philo, but by apologies which still further aggravate the charge. Why have all men, I ask, in all ages, complained incessantly of the miseries of life? . . . They have no just reason, says one: these complaints proceed only from their discontented, repining, anxious disposition. . . . And can there possibly, I reply, be a more certain foundation of misery than such a wretched temper?

But if they were really as unhappy as they pretend, says my antagonist, why do they remain in life? . . .

Not satisfied with life, afraid of death—

This is the secret chain, say I, that holds us. We are terrified, not bribed to the continuance of our existence.

It is only a false delicacy, he may insist, which a few refined spirits indulge, and which has spread these complaints among the whole race of mankind. . . . And what is this delicacy, I ask, which you blame? Is it anything but a greater sensibility to all the pleasures and pains of life? And if the man of a delicate, refined temper, by being so much more alive than the rest of the world, is only so much more unhappy, what judgment must we form in general of human life?

Let me remain at rest, says our adversary, and they will be easy. They are willing artificers of their own misery. . . . No! reply I: an anxious languor follows their repose; disappointment, vexation, trouble, their activity and ambition.

I can observe something like what you mention in some others, replied Cleanthes, but I confess I feel little or nothing of it in myself, and hope that it is not so common as you represent it.

If you feel not human misery yourself, cried Demea, I congratulate you on so happy a singularity. Others, seemingly the most prosperous, have not been ashamed to vent their complaints in the most melancholy strains. Let us attend to the great, the fortunate emperor, Charles V, when tired with human grandeur, he resigned all his extensive dominions into the hands of his son. In the last harangue which he made on that memorable occasion, he publicly avowed *that the greatest prosperities which he had ever enjoyed had been mixed with so many adversities that he might truly say he had never enjoyed any satisfaction or contentment.* But did the retired life in which he sought for shelter afford him any greater happiness? If we may credit his son's account, his repentance commenced the very day of his resignation.

Cicero's fortune, from small beginnings, rose to the greatest lustre and renown; yet what pathetic complaints of the ills of life do his familiar letters, as well as philosophical discourses, contain? And suitably to his own experience, he introduces Cato, the great, the fortunate Cato protesting in his old age that had he a new life in his offer he would reject the present.

Ask yourself, ask any of your acquaintance, whether they would live over again the last ten or twenty years of their life. No! but the next twenty, they say, will be better:

And from the dregs of life, hope to receive
What the first sprightly running could not give.[8]

Thus, at last, they find (such is the greatness of human misery, it reconciles even contradictions) that they complain at once of the shortness of life and of its vanity and sorrow.

And is it possible, Cleanthes, said Philo, that after all these reflections, and infinitely more which might be suggested, you can still persevere in your anthropomorphism, and assert the moral attributes of the Deity, his justice, benevolence, mercy, and rectitude, to be of the same nature with these virtues in human creatures? His power, we allow, is infinite; whatever he wills is executed; but neither man nor any other animal is happy; therefore, he does not will their happiness. His wisdom is infinite; he is never mistaken in choosing the means to any end; but the course of nature tends not to human or animal felicity; therefore, it is not established for that purpose. Through the whole compass of human knowledge there are no inferences more certain and infallible than these. In what respect, then, do his benevolence and mercy resemble the benevolence and mercy of men?

Epicurus' old questions are yet unanswered. "Is he willing to prevent evil, but not able? then is he impotent. Is he able, but not willing? then is he malevolent. Is he both able and willing? whence then is evil?"

You ascribe, Cleanthes (and I believe justly), a purpose and intention to nature. But what, I beseech you, is the object of that curious artifice and machinery which she has displayed in all animals—the preservation alone of individuals, and propagation of the species? It seems enough for her purpose, if such a rank be barely upheld in the universe, without any care or concern for the happiness of the members that compose it. No resource for this purpose: no machinery in order merely to give pleasure or ease; no fund of pure joy and contentment; no indulgence without some want or necessity accompanying it. At least, the few phenomena of this nature are overbalanced by opposite phenomena of still greater importance.

Our sense of music, harmony, and indeed beauty of all kinds, gives satisfaction, without being absolutely necessary to the preservation and propagation of the species. But what racking pains, on the other hand, arise from gouts, gravels, megrims, toothaches, rheumatisms, where the injury to the animal machinery is either small or incurable? Mirth, laughter, play, frolic seem gratuitous satisfactions which have no further tendency; spleen, melancholy, discontent, superstition are pains of the same nature. How then does the Divine benevolence display itself, in the sense of you anthropomorphites? None but we mystics, as you were pleased to call us, can account for this strange mixture of phenomena, by deriving it from attributes infinitely perfect but incomprehensible.

And have you, at last, said Cleanthes smiling, betrayed your intentions, Philo? Your long agreement with Demea did indeed a little surprise me, but I find you were all the while erecting a concealed battery against me. And I must confess that you have now fallen upon a subject worthy of your noble spirit of opposition and controversy. If you can make out the present point, and prove mankind to be unhappy or corrupted, there is an end at once of all religion. For to what purpose establish the natural attributes of the Deity, while the moral are still doubtful and uncertain?

You take umbrage very easily, replied Demea, at opinions the most innocent and the most generally received, even amongst the religious and devout themselves; and nothing can be more surprising than to find a topic like this—concerning the wickedness and misery of man—charged with no less than atheism and profaneness. Have not all pious divines and preachers who have indulged their rhetoric on so fertile a subject, have they not easily, I say, given a solution of any difficulties which may attend it? This world is but a point in comparison of the universe; this life but a moment in comparison of eternity. The present evil phenomena, therefore, are rectified in other regions, and in some future period of existence. And the eyes of men, being then opened to larger views of things, see the whole connection of general laws, and trace, with adoration, and benevolence and rectitude of the Deity through all the mazes and intricacies of his providence.

No! replied Cleanthes, no! These arbitrary suppositions can never be admitted, contrary to matter of fact, visible and uncontroverted. Whence can any cause be known but from its known effects? Whence can any hypothesis be proved but from the apparent phenomena? To establish one hypothesis upon another is building entirely in the air; and the utmost we ever attain by these conjectures and fictions is to ascertain the bare possibility of our opinion, but never can we, upon such terms, establish its reality.

The only method of supporting Divine benevolence—and it is what I willingly embrace—is to deny absolutely the misery and wickedness of man. Your representations are exaggerated; your melancholy views mostly fictitious; your inferences contrary to fact and experience. Health is more common than sickness; pleasure than pain; happiness than misery. And for one vexation which we meet with, we attain, upon computation, a hundred enjoyments.

Admitting your position, replied Philo, which yet is extremely doubtful, you must at the same time allow that, if pain be less frequent than pleasure, it is infinitely more violent and durable. One hour of it is often able to outweigh a day, a week, a month of our common insipid enjoyments; and how many days, weeks, and months are passed by several in the most acute torments? Pleasure, scarcely in one instance, is ever able to reach ecstasy and rapture; and in no one instance can it continue for any time at its highest pitch and altitude. The spirits evaporate, the nerves relax, the fabric is disordered, and the enjoyment quickly degenerates into fatigue and uneasiness. But pain often, good God, how often! rises to torture and agony; and the longer it continues, it becomes still more genuine agony and torture. Patience is exhausted, courage languishes, melancholy seizes us, and nothing terminates our misery but the removal of its cause or another event which is the sole cure of all evil, but which, from our natural folly, we regard with still greater horror and consternation.

But not to insist upon these topics, continued Philo, though most obvious, certain, and important, I must use the freedom to admonish you, Cleanthes, that you have put the controversy upon a most dangerous issue, and are unawares introducing a total scepticism into the most essential articles of natural and revealed theology. What! no method of fixing a just foundation for religion unless we allow the happiness of human life, and maintain a continued existence even in this world, with all our present pains, infirmities, vexations, and follies, to be eligible and desirable! But this is contrary to everyone's feeling and experience; it is contrary to an authority so established as nothing can subvert. No decisive proofs can ever be produced against this authority; nor is it possible for you to compute, estimate, and compare all the pains and all the pleasures in the lives of all men and of all animals; and thus, by your resting the whole system of religion on a point which, from its very nature, must for ever be uncertain, you tacitly confess that that system is equally uncertain.

But allowing you what never will be believed, at least, what you never possibly can prove, that animal or, at least, human happiness in this life exceeds its misery, you have yet done nothing; for this is not, by any means, what we expect from infinite power, infinite wisdom, and infinite goodness. Why is there any misery at all in the world? Not by chance, surely. From some cause then. Is it from the intention of the Deity? But he is perfectly benevolent. Is it contrary to his intention? But he is almighty. Nothing can shake the solidity of this reasoning, so short, so clear, so decisive, except we assert that these subjects exceed all human capacity, and that our common measures of truth and falsehood are not applicable to them—a topic which I have all along insisted on, but which you have, from the beginning, rejected with scorn and indignation.

But I will be contented to retire still from this intrenchment, for I deny that you can ever force me in it. I will allow that pain or misery in man is *compatible* with infinite power and goodness in the Deity, even in your sense of these attributes: what are you advanced by all these concessions? A mere possible compatibility is not sufficient. You must *prove* these pure, unmixt, and uncontrollable attributes from the present mixt and confused phenomena, and from these alone. A hopeful undertaking! Were the phenomena ever so pure and unmixt, yet, being finite, they would be insufficient for that purpose. How much more, where they are also so jarring and discordant!

Here, Cleanthes, I find myself at ease in my argument. Here I triumph. Formerly, when we argued concerning the natural attributes of intelligence and design, I needed all my sceptical and metaphysical subtilty to elude your grasp. In many views of the universe and of its parts, particularly the matter, the beauty and fitness of final causes strike us with such irresistible force that all objections appear (what I believe they really are) mere cavils and sophisms; nor can we then imagine how it was ever possible for us to repose any weight on them. But there is no view of human life or the condition of mankind from which, without the greatest violence, we can infer the moral attributes or learn that infinite benevolence, conjoined with infinite power and infinite wisdom, which we must discover by the eyes of faith alone. It is your turn now to tug the labouring oar, and to support your philosophical subtleties against the dictates of plain reason and experience.

Part XI

I scruple not to allow, said Cleanthes, that I have been apt to suspect the frequent repetition of the word *infinite,* which we meet with in all theological writers, to savour more of panegyric than of philosophy, and that any purposes of reasoning, and even of religion, would be better served were we to rest contented with more accurate and more moderate expressions. The terms *admirable, excellent, superlatively great, wise,* and *holy*—these sufficiently fill the imaginations of men, and anything beyond, besides that it leads into absurdities, has no influence on the affections or sentiments. Thus, in thy present subject, if we abandon all human analogy, as seems your intention, Demea, I am afraid we abandon all religion and retain no conception of the great object of our adoration. If we preserve human analogy, we must forever find it impossible to reconcile any mixture of evil in the universe with infinite attributes; much less can we ever prove the latter from the for-

mer. But supposing the Author of nature to be finitely perfect, though far exceeding mankind, a satisfactory account may then be given of natural and moral evil, and every untoward phenomenon be explained and adjusted. A less evil may then be chosen in order to avoid a greater; inconveniences be submitted to in order to reach a desirable end; and, in a word, benevolence, regulated by wisdom and limited by necessity, may produce just such a world as the present. You, Philo, who are so prompt at starting views and reflections and analogies, I would gladly hear, at length, without interruption, your opinion of this new theory; and if it deserve our attention, we may afterwards, at more leisure, reduce it into form.

My sentiments, replied Philo, are not worth being made a mystery of; and, therefore, without any ceremony, I shall deliver what occurs to me with regard to the present subject. I must, I think, be allowed that, if a very limited intelligence whom we shall suppose utterly unacquainted with the universe were assured that it were the production of a very good, wise, and powerful Being, however finite, he would, from his conjectures, form *beforehand* a different notion of it from what we find it to be by experience; nor would he ever imagine, merely from these attributes of the cause of which he is informed, that the effect could be so full of vice and misery and disorder, as it appears in this life. Supposing now that this person were brought into the world, still assured that it was the workmanship of such a sublime and benevolent Being, he might, perhaps, be surprised at the disappointment, but would never retract his former belief if founded on any very solid argument, since such a limited intelligence must be sensible of his own blindness and ignorance, and must allow that there may be many solutions of those phenomena which will for ever escape his comprehension. But supposing, which is the real case with regard to man, that this creature is not antecedently convinced of a supreme intelligence, benevolent, and powerful, but is left to gather such a belief from the appearances of things—this entirely alters the case, nor will he ever find any reason for such a conclusion. He may be fully convinced of the narrow limits of his understanding, but this will not help him in forming an inference concerning the goodness of superior powers, since he must form that inference from what he knows, not from what he is ignorant of. The more you exaggerate his weakness and ignorance, the more diffident you render him, and give him the greater suspicion that such subjects are beyond the reach of his faculties. You are obliged, therefore, to reason with him merely from the known phenomena, and to drop every arbitrary supposition or conjecture.

Did I show you a house or palace where there was not one apartment convenient or agreeable, where the windows, doors, fires, passages, stairs, and the whole economy of the building were the source of noise, confusion, fatigue, darkness, and the extremes of heat and cold, you would certainly blame the contrivance, without any further examination. The architect would in vain display his subtilty, and prove to you that, if this door or that window were altered, greater ills would ensue. What he says may be strictly true: the alteration of one particular, while the other parts of the building remain, may only augment the inconveniences. But still you would assert in general that, if the architect had had skill and good intentions, he might have formed such a plan of the whole, and might have adjusted the parts in such a manner as would have remedied all or most of these inconveniences. His ignorance, or even your own ignorance of such a plan, will never convince you of the impossibility of it. If you find any inconveniences and deformities in the building, you will always, without entering into any detail, condemn the architect.

In short, I repeat the question: Is the world, considered in general and as it appears to us in this life, different from what a man or such a limited being would, *beforehand,* expect from a very powerful, wise, and benevolent Deity? It must be strange prejudice to assert the contrary. And from thence I conclude that, however consistent the world may be, allowing certain suppositions and conjectures with the idea of such a Deity, it can never afford us an inference concerning his existence. The consistency is not absolutely denied, only the inference. Conjectures, especially where infinity is excluded from the Divine attributes, may perhaps be sufficient to prove a consistency, but can never be foundations from any inference.

There seem to be *four* circumstances on which depend all or the greatest part of the ills that molest sensible creatures; and it is not impossible but all these circumstances may be necessary and unavoidable. We know so little beyond common life, or even of common life, that, with regard to the economy of a universe, there is no conjecture, however wild, which may not be just, nor any one, however plausible, which may not be erroneous. All that belongs to human understanding, in this deep ignorance and obscurity, is to be sceptical or at least cautious, and not to admit of any hypothesis whatever, much less of any which is supported by no appearance of probability. Now this I assert to be the case with regard to all the causes of evil and the circumstances on which it depends. None of them appear to human reason in the least degree necessary or unavoidable, nor can we suppose them such, without the utmost license of imagination.

The *first* circumstance which introduces evil is that contrivance or economy of the animal creation by which pains, as well as pleasures, are employed to excite all creatures to action, and make them vigilant in the great work of self-preservation. Now pleasure alone, in its various degrees, seems to human understanding sufficient for this purpose. All animals might be constantly in a state of enjoyment; but when urged by any of the necessities of nature, such as thirst, hunger, weariness, instead of pain, they might feel a diminution of pleasure by which they might be prompted to seek that object which is necessary to their subsistence. Men pursue pleasure as eagerly as they avoid pain; at least, they might have been so constituted. It seems, therefore, plainly possible to carry on the business of life without any pain. Why then is any animal ever rendered susceptible of such a sensation? If animals can be free from it an hour, they might enjoy a perpetual exemption from it, and it required as particular a contrivance of their organs to produce that feeling as to endow them with sight, hearing, or any of the senses. Shall we conjecture that such a contrivance was necessary, without any appearance of reason, and shall we build on that conjecture as on the most certain truth?

But a capacity of pain would not alone produce pain were it not for the *second* circumstance, viz., the conducting of the world by general laws; and this seems nowise necessary to a very perfect Being. It is true, if everything were conducted by particular volitions, the course of nature would be perpetually broken, and no man could employ his reason in the conduct of life. But might not other particular volitions remedy this inconvenience? In short, might not the Deity exterminate all ill, wherever it were to be found, and produce all good, without any preparation or long progress of causes and effects?

Besides, we must consider that, according to the present economy of the world, the course of nature, though supposed exactly regular, yet to us appears not so, and many events are uncertain, and many disappoint our expectations. Health and sickness, calm and tempest, with an infinite number of other accidents whose causes are unknown and variable, have a great influence both on the fortunes of particular persons and on the prosperity of public societies; and indeed all human life, in a manner, depends on such accidents. A being, therefore, who knows the secret springs of the universe might easily, by particular volitions, turn all these accidents to the good of mankind and render the whole world happy, without discovering himself in any operation. A fleet whose purposes were salutary to society might always meet with a fair wind. Good princes enjoy sound health and long life. Persons born to power and authority be framed with good tempers and virtuous dispositions. A few such events as these, regularly and wisely conducted, would change the face of the world, and yet would no more seem to disturb the course of nature or confound human conduct than the present economy of things where the causes are secret and variable and compounded. Some small touches given to Caligula's brain in his infancy might have converted him into a Trajan. One wave, a little higher than the rest, by burying Caesar and his fortune in the bottom of the ocean, might have restored liberty to a considerable part of mankind. There may, for aught we know, be good reasons why Providence interposes not in this manner, but they are unknown to us; and, though the mere supposition that such reasons exist may be sufficient to *save* the conclusion concerning the Divine attributes, yet surely it can never be sufficient to *establish* that conclusion.

If everything in the universe be conducted by general laws, and if animals be rendered susceptible of pain, it scarcely seems possible but some ill must arise in the various shocks of matter and the various concurrence and opposition of general laws; but this ill would be very rare were it not for the *third* circumstance which I proposed to mention, viz., the great frugality with which all powers and faculties are distributed to every particular being. So well adjusted are the organs and capacities of all animals, and so well fitted to their preservation, that, as far as history or tradition reaches, there appears not to be any single species which has yet been extinguished in the universe. Every animal has the requisite endowments, but these endowments are bestowed with so scrupulous an economy that any considerable diminution must entirely destroy the creature. Wherever one power is increased, there is a proportional abatement in the others. Animals which excel in swiftness are commonly defective in force. Those which possess both are either imperfect in some of their senses or are oppressed with the most craving wants. The human species, whose chief excellency is reason and sagacity, is of all others the most necessitous, and the most deficient in bodily advantages, without clothes, without arms, without food, without lodging, without any convenience of life, except what they owe to their own skill and industry. In short, nature seems to have formed an exact calculation of the necessities of her creatures, and, like a *rigid master,* has afforded them little more powers or endowments than what are strictly sufficient to supply those necessities. An *indulgent parent* would have bestowed a large stock in order to guard against accidents, and secure the happiness and welfare of the creature in the most unfortunate concurrence of circumstances. Every course of life would not have been so surrounded with precipices that the least departure from the true path, by mistake or necessity, must involve us in misery and ruin. Some reserve, some fund, would have been provided to ensure happiness, nor would the powers and the necessities have been adjusted with so rigid an economy. The Author of nature is inconceivably powerful; his force is supposed great, if not altogether inexhaustible, nor is there any reason, as far as we can judge, to make him observe this strict frugality in his dealings with his creatures. It would have been better, were his power extremely limited, to have created fewer animals, and to have endowed these with more faculties for their happiness and preservation. A builder is never esteemed prudent who undertakes a plan beyond what his stock will enable him to finish.

In order to cure most of the ills of human life, I require not that man should have the wings of the eagle, the swiftness of the stag, the force of the ox, the arms of the lion, the scales of the crocodile or rhinoceros; much less do I demand the sagacity of an angel or cherubim. I am contented to take an increase in one single power or faculty of his soul. Let him be endowed with a greater propensity to industry and labour, a more vigorous spring and activity of mind, a more constant bent to business and application. Let the whole species possess naturally an equal diligence, with that which many individuals are able to attain by habit and reflection, and the most beneficial consequences, without any allay of ill, is the immediate and necessary result of this endowment. Almost all the moral as well as natural evils of human life arise from idleness; and were our species, by the original constitution of their frame, exempt from this vice or infirmity, the perfect cultivation of land, the improvement of arts and manufactures, the exact execution of every office and duty, immediately follow; and men at once may fully reach that state of society which is so imperfectly attained by the best regulated government. But as industry is a power, and the most valuable of any, nature seems determined, suitably to her usual maxims, to bestow it on man with a very sparing hand, and rather to punish him severely for his deficiency in it than to reward him for his attainments. She has so contrived his frame that nothing but the most violent necessity can oblige him to labour; and she employs all his other wants to overcome, at least in part, the want of diligence, and to endow him with some share of a faculty of which she has thought fit naturally to bereave him. Here our demands may be allowed very humble, and therefore the more reasonable. If we required the endowments of superior penetration and judgment, of a more delicate taste of beauty, of a nicer sensibility to benevolence and friendship, we might be told that we impiously pretend to break the order of nature, that we want to exalt ourselves into a higher rank of being, that the presents which we require, not being suitable to our state and condition, would only be pernicious to us. But it is hard, I dare to repeat it, it is hard that, being placed in a world so full of wants and necessities, where almost every being and element is either our foe or refuses its assistance . . . we should also have our own temper to struggle with, and should be deprived of that faculty which can alone fence against these multiplied evils.

The *fourth* circumstance whence arises the misery and ill of the universe is the inaccurate workmanship of all the springs and principles of the great machine of nature. It must be acknowledged that there are few parts of the universe which seem not to serve some purpose, and whose removal would not produce a visible defect and disorder in the whole. The parts hang all together, nor can one be touched without affecting the rest, in a greater or less degree. But at the same time, it must be observed that none of these parts or principles, however useful, are so accurately adjusted as to keep precisely within those bounds in which their utility consists; but they are, all of them, apt, on every occasion, to run into the one extreme or the other. One would imagine that this grand production had not received the last hand of the maker—so little finished is every part, and so coarse are the strokes with which it is executed. Thus the winds are requisite to convey the vapours along the surface of the globe, and to assist men in navigation; but how often, rising up to tempests and hurricanes, do they become pernicious? Rains are necessary to nourish all the plants and animals of the earth; but how often are they defective? how often excessive? Heat is requisite to all life and vegetation, but is not always found in the due proportion. On the mixture and secretion of the humours and juices of the body depend the health and prosperity of the animal; but the parts perform not regularly their proper function. What more useful than all the passions of the mind, ambition, vanity, love, anger? But how often do they break their bounds and cause the greatest convulsions in society? There is nothing so advantageous in the universe but what frequently becomes pernicious, by its excess or defect; nor has nature guarded, with the requisite accuracy, against all disorder or confusion. The irregularity is never perhaps so great as to destroy any species, but is often sufficient to involve the individuals in ruin and misery.

On the concurrence, then, of these *four* circumstances does all or the greatest part of natural evil depend. Were all living creatures incapable of pain, or were the world administered by particular volitions, evil never could have found access into the universe; and were animals endowed with a large stock of powers and faculties, beyond what strict necessity requires, or were the several springs and principles of the universe so accurately framed as to preserve always the just temperament and medium, there must have been very little ill in comparison of what we feel at present. What then shall we pronounce on this occasion? Shall we say that these circumstances are not necessary, and that they might easily have been altered in the contrivance of the universe? This decision seems too presumptuous for creatures so blind and ignorant. Let us be more modest in our conclusions. Let us allow that, if the goodness of the Deity (I mean a goodness like the human) could be established on any tolerable reasons *a priori*, these phenomena, however untoward, would not be sufficient to subvert that principle, but might easily, in some unknown manner, be reconcilable to it. But let us still assert that, as this goodness is not antecedently established but must be inferred from the phenomena, there can be no grounds for such an inference while there are so many ills in the universe, and while these ills might so easily have been remedied, as far as human understanding can be allowed to judge on such a subject, I am sceptic enough to allow that the bad appearances, notwithstanding all my reasonings, may be compatible with such attributes as you suppose, but surely they can never prove these attributes. Such a conclusion cannot result from scepticism, but must arise from the phenomena, and from our confidence in the reasonings which we deduce from these phenomena.

Look round this universe. What an immense profusion of beings, animated and organized, sensible and active! You admire this prodigious variety and fecundity. But inspect a little more narrowly these living existences, the only beings worth regarding. How hostile and destructive to each other! How insufficient all of them for their own happiness! How contemptible or odious to the spectator! The whole presents nothing but the idea of a blind nature, impregnated by a great vivifying principle, and pouring forth from her lap, without discernment or parental care, her maimed and abortive children!

Here the Manichaean system occurs as a proper hypothesis to solve the difficulty; and, no doubt, in some respects it is very specious and has more probability than the common hypothesis, by giving a plausible account of the strange mixture of good and ill which appears in life. But if we consider, on the other hand, the perfect uniformity and agreement of the parts of the universe, we shall not discover in it any marks of the combat of a malevolent with a benevolent being. There is indeed an opposition of pains and pleasures in the feelings of sensible creatures; but are not all the operations of nature carried on by an opposition of principles, of hot and cold, moist and dry, light and heavy? The true conclusion is that the original Source of all things is entirely indifferent to all these principles, and has no more regard to good above ill than to heat above cold, or to drought above moisture, or to light above heavy.

There may *four* hypotheses be framed concerning the first causes of the universe: that they are endowed with perfect goodness; that they have perfect malice; that they are opposite and have both goodness and malice; that they have neither goodness nor malice. Mixed phenomena can never prove the two former unmixed principles; and the uniformity and steadiness of general laws seem to oppose the third. The fourth, therefore, seems by far the most probable.

What I have said concerning natural evil will apply to moral with little or no variation; and we have no more reason to infer that the rectitude of the Supreme Being resembles human rectitude than that his benevolence resembles the human. Nay, it will be thought that we have still greater cause to exclude from him moral sentiments, such as we feel them, since moral evil, in the opinion of many, is much more predominant above moral good than natural evil above natural good.

But even though this should not be allowed, and though the virtue which is in mankind should be acknowledged much superior to the vice, yet, so long as there is any vice at all in the universe, it will very much puzzle you anthropomorphites how to account for it. You must assign a cause for it, without having recourse to the first cause. But as every effect must have a cause, and that cause another, you must either carry on the progression *in infinitum* or rest on that original principle, who is the ultimate cause of all things . . .

Hold! hold! cried Demea: Whither does your imagination hurry you? I joined in alliance with you in order to prove the incomprehensible nature of the Divine Being, and refute the principles of Cleanthes, who would measure everything by human rule and standard. But I now find you running into all the topics of the greatest libertines and infidels, and betraying that holy cause which you seemingly espoused. Are you secretly, then, a more dangerous enemy than Cleanthes himself?

And are you so late in perceiving it? replied Cleanthes. Believe me, Demea, your friend Philo, from the beginning, has been amusing himself at both our expense; and it must be confessed that the injudicious reasoning of our vulgar theology has given him but too just a handle of ridicule. The total infirmity of human reason, the absolute incomprehensibility of the Divine Nature, the great and universal misery, and still greater wickedness of men—these are strange topics, surely, to be so fondly cherished by orthodox divines and doctors. In ages of stupidity and ignorance, indeed, these principles may safely be espoused; and perhaps no views of things are more proper to promote superstition than such as encourage the blind amazement, the diffidence, and melancholy of mankind. But at present . . .

Blame not so much, interposed Philo, the ignorance of these reverend gentlemen. They know how to change their style with the times. Formerly, it was a most popular theological topic to maintain that human life was vanity and misery, and to exaggerate all the ills and pains which are incident to men. But of late years, divines, we find, begin to retract this position and maintain, though still with some hesitation, that there are more goods than evils, more pleasures than pains, even in this life. When religion stood entirely upon temper and education, it was thought proper to encourage melancholy, as, indeed, mankind never have recourse to superior powers so readily as in that disposition. But as men have now learned to form principles and to draw consequences, it is necessary to change the batteries, and to make use of such arguments as will endure at least some scrutiny and examination. This variation is the same (and from the same causes) with that which I formerly remarked with regard to scepticism.

Thus Philo continued to the last his spirit of opposition, and his censure of established opinions. But I could observe that Demea did not at all relish the latter part of the discourse; and he took occasion soon after, on some pretence or other, to leave the company.

Notes

1. *Recherche de la Vérité*, liv. 3, cap. 9.
2. *De Rerum Natura*, lib. XI [II], 1094. (Who can rule the sum, who hold in his hand with controlling force the strong reins, of the immeasurable deep? Who can at once make all the different heavens to roll and warm with ethereal fires all the fruitful earths, or be present in all places at all times?)—(Translation by H. A. J. Munro, G. Bell & Sons, 1920).
3. *De Natura Deorum*, lib. I [cap. VIII]. (For with what eyes could your Plato see the construction of so vast a work which, according to him, God was putting together and building? What materials, what tools, what bars, what machines, what servants were employed in such gigantic work? How could the air, fire, water, and earth pay obedience and submit to the will of the architect?)
4. Dr. Clarke [Samuel Clarke, the rationalist theologian (1675–1729)].
5. *Republique des Lettres*, Aut 1685.
6. That sentiment had been maintained by Dr. King and some others before Leibniz, though by none of so great fame as that German philosopher.
7. Milton: *Paradise Lost*, Bk. XI.
8. John Dryden, *Aureng-Zebe*, Act IV, sc. 1.

THE PROBLEM OF EVIL

Divine Omniscience and Voluntary Action

NELSON PIKE

Nelson Pike (1930–) is Professor Emeritus of Philosophy at the University of California, Irvine.

In Book V, sec. 3 of his *Consolatio Philosophiae*, Boethius entertained (though he later rejected) the claim that if God is omniscient, no human action is voluntary. This claim seems intuitively false. Surely, given only a doctrine describing God's *knowledge,* nothing about the voluntary status of human actions will follow. Perhaps such a conclusion would follow from a doctrine of divine omnipotence or divine providence, but what connection could there be between the claim that God is *omniscient* and the claim that human actions are determined? Yet Boethius thought he saw a problem here. He thought that if one collected together just the right assumptions and principles regarding God's knowledge, one could derive the conclusion that if God exists, no human action is voluntary. Of course, Boethius did not think that all the assumptions and principles required to reach this conclusion are true (quite the contrary), but he thought it important to draw attention to them nonetheless. If a theologian is to construct a doctrine of God's knowledge which does not commit him to determinism, he must first understand that there is a way of thinking about God's knowledge which would so commit him.

In this paper, I shall argue that although his claim has a sharp counterintuitive ring, Boethius was right in thinking that there is a selection from among the various doctrines and principles clustering about the notions of knowledge, omniscience, and God, which, when brought together, demand the conclusion that if God exists, no human action

is voluntary. Boethius, I think, did not succeed in making explicit all of the ingredients in the problem. His suspicions were sound, but his discussion was incomplete. His argument needs to be developed. This is the task I shall undertake in the pages to follow. I should like to make clear at the outset that my purpose in rearguing this thesis is not to show that determinism is true, not to show that God does not exist, nor to show that either determinism is true or God does not exist. Following Boethius, I shall not claim that the items needed to generate the problem are either philosophically or theologically adequate. I want to concentrate attention on the implications of a certain set of assumptions. Whether the assumptions are themselves acceptable is a question I shall not consider.

I

A. Many philosophers have held that if a statement of the form "*A* knows *X*" is true, then "*A* believes *X*" is true and "*X*" is true. As a first assumption, I shall take this partial analysis of "*A* knows *X*" to be correct. And I shall suppose that since this analysis holds for all knowledge claims, it will hold when speaking of God's knowledge. "God knows *X*" entails "God believes *X*" and "'*X*' is true."

Secondly, Boethius said that with respect to the matter of knowledge, God "cannot in anything be mistaken."[1] I shall understand this doctrine as follows. Omniscient beings hold no false beliefs. Part of what is meant when we say that a person is omniscient is that the person in question believes nothing that is false. But, further, it is part of the "essence" of

Reprinted from *The Philosophical Review* 74 (1965): 27–46.

God to be omniscient. This is to say that any person who is not omniscient could not be the person we usually mean to be referring to when using the name "God." To put this last point a little differently: if the person we usually mean to be referring to when using the name "God" were suddenly to lose the quality of omniscience (suppose, for example, He came to believe something false), the resulting person would no longer be God. Although we might call this second person "God" (I might call my cat "God"), the absence of the quality of omniscience would be sufficient to guarantee that the person referred to was not the same as the person formerly called by that name. From this last doctrine it follows that the statement "If a given person is God, that person is omniscient" is an a priori truth. From this we may conclude that the statement "If a given person is God, that person holds no false beliefs" is also an a priori truth. It would be conceptually impossible for God to hold a false belief. "'X' is true" follows from "God believes X." These are all ways of expressing the same principle—the principle expressed by Boethius in the formula "God cannot in anything be mistaken."

A second principle usually associated with the notion of divine omniscience has to do with the scope or range of God's intellectual gaze. To say that a being is omniscient is to say that he knows everything. "Everything" in this statement is usually taken to cover future, as well as present and past, events and circumstances. In fact, God is usually said to have had foreknowledge of everything that has ever happened. With respect to anything that was, is, or will be the case, God knew, *from eternity,* that it would be the case.

The doctrine of God's knowing everything from eternity is very obscure. One particularly difficult question concerning this doctrine is whether it entails that with respect to everything that was, is, or will be the case, God knew *in advance* that it would be the case. In some traditional theological texts, we are told that God is *eternal* in the sense that He exists "outside of time," that is, in the sense that He bears no temporal relations to the events or circumstances of the natural world.[2] In a theology of this sort, God could not be said to have known that a given natural event was going to happen before it happened. If God knew that a given natural event was going to oc-

cur *before* it occurred, at least one of God's cognitions would then have occurred before some natural event. This, surely, would violate the idea that God bears no temporal relations to natural events.[3] On the other hand, in a considerable number of theological sources, we are told that God *has always* existed—that He existed long *before* the occurrence of any natural event. In a theology of this sort, to say that God is eternal is not to say that God exists "outside of time" (bears no temporal relations to natural events); it is to say, instead, God has existed (and will continue to exist) at each moment.[4] The doctrine of omniscience which goes with this second understanding of the notion of eternity is one in which it is affirmed that God *has always* known what was going to happen in the natural world. John Calvin wrote as follows:

> When we attribute foreknowledge of God, we mean that all things have ever been and perpetually remain before, his eyes, so that to his knowledge nothing is future or past, but all things are present; and present in such manner, that he does not merely conceive of them from ideas formed in his mind, as things remembered by us appear to our minds, but really he holds and sees them as if (*tanquam*) actually placed before him.[5]

All things are "present" to God in the sense that He "sees" them as if (*tanquam*) they were actually before Him. Further, with respect to any given natural event, not only is that event "present" to God in the sense indicated, it has *ever been and has perpetually remained* "present" to Him in that sense. This latter is the point of special interest. Whatever one thinks of the idea that God "sees" things as if "actually placed before him," Calvin would appear to be committed to the idea that God has *always known* what was going to happen in the natural world. Choose an event (E) and a time (t_2) at which E occurred. For any time (t_1) prior to t_2 (say, five thousand, six hundred, or eighty years prior to t_2). God knew at t_1 that E would occur at t_2. It will follow from this doctrine, of course, that with respect to any human action, God knew well in advance of its performance that the action would be performed. Calvin says, "when God created man, He foresaw what would happen concerning him." He adds, "little more than five thousand years have elapsed since the creation of the world."[6] Calvin seems to have thought that God foresaw the outcome of every human action well over five thousand years ago.

In the discussion to follow, I shall work only with this second interpretation of God's knowing everything *from eternity*. I shall assume that if a person is omniscient, that person has always known what was going to happen in the natural world—and, in particular, has always known what human actions were going to be performed. Thus, as above, assuming that the attribute of omniscience is part of the "essence" of God, the statement "For any natural event (including human actions), if a given person is God, that person would always have known that the event was going to occur at the time it occurred" must be treated as an a priori truth. This is just another way of stating a point admirably put by St. Augustine when he said: "For to confess that God exists and at the same time to deny that He has foreknowledge of future things is the most manifest folly. . . . One who is not prescient of all future things is not God."[7]

B. Last Saturday afternoon, Jones mowed his lawn. Assuming that God exists and is (essentially) omniscient in the sense outlined above, it follows that (let us say) eighty years prior to last Saturday afternoon, God knew (and thus believed) that Jones would mow his lawn at that time. But from this it follows, I think, that at the time of action (last Saturday afternoon) Jones was not *able*—that is, it was not *within Jones's power*—to refrain from mowing his lawn.[8] If at the time of action, Jones had been able to refrain from mowing his lawn, then (the most obvious conclusion would seem to be) at the time of action, Jones was able to do something which would have brought it about that God held a false belief eighty years earlier. But God cannot in anything be mistaken. It is not possible that some belief of His was false. Thus, last Saturday afternoon, Jones was not able to do something which would have brought it about that God held a false belief eighty years ago. To suppose that it was would be to suppose that, at the time of action, Jones was able to do something having a conceptually incoherent description, namely something that would have brought it about that one of God's beliefs was false. Hence, given that God believed eighty years ago that Jones would mow his lawn on Saturday, if we are to assign Jones the power on Saturday to refrain from mowing his lawn,

this power must not be described as the power to do something that would have rendered one of God's beliefs false. How then should we describe it vis-à-vis God and His belief? So far as I can see, there are only two other alternatives. First, we might try describing it as the power to do something that would have brought it about that God believed otherwise than He did eighty years ago; or, secondly, we might try describing it as the power to do something that would have brought it about that God (Who, by hypothesis, existed eighty years earlier) did not exist eighty years earlier—that is, as the power to do something that would have brought it about that any person who believed eighty years ago that Jones would mow his lawn on Saturday (one of whom was, by hypothesis, God) held a false belief, and thus was not God. But again, neither of these latter can be accepted. Last Saturday afternoon, Jones was not able to do something that would have brought it about that God believed otherwise than He did eighty years ago. Even if we suppose (as was suggested by Calvin) that eighty years ago God knew Jones would mow his lawn on Saturday in the sense that He "saw" Jones mowing his lawn as if this action were occurring before Him, the fact remains that God knew (and thus believed) eighty years prior to Saturday that Jones would mow his lawn. And if God held such a belief eighty years prior to Saturday, Jones did not have the power on Saturday to do something that would have made it the case that God did not hold this belief eighty years earlier. No action performed at a given time can alter the fact that a given person held a certain belief at a time prior to the time in question. This last seems to be an a priori truth. For similar reasons, the last of the above alternatives must also be rejected. On the assumption that God existed eighty years prior to Saturday, Jones on Saturday was not able to do something that would have brought it about that God did not exist eighty years prior to that time. No action performed at a given time can alter the fact that a certain person existed at a time prior to the time in question. This, too, seems to me to be an a priori truth. But if these observations are correct, then, given that Jones mowed his lawn on Saturday, and given that God exists and is (essentially) omniscient, it seems to follow that at the time of action, Jones did not have the power to refrain from mowing his lawn.

The upshot of these reflections would appear to be that Jones's mowing his lawn last Saturday cannot be counted as a voluntary action. Although I do not have an analysis of what it is for an action to be *voluntary,* it seems to me that a situation in which it would be wrong to assign Jones the *ability* or *power* to do *other* than he did would be a situation in which it would also be wrong to speak of his action as voluntary. As a general remark, if God exists and is (essentially) omniscient in the sense specified above, no human action is voluntary.[9]

As the argument just presented is somewhat complex, perhaps the following schematic representation of it will be of some use.

1. "God existed at t_1" entails "If Jones did X at t_2, God believed at t_1 that Jones would do X at t_2."
2. "God believes X" entails "'X' is true."
3. It is not within one's power at a given time to do something having a description that is logically contradictory.
4. It is not within one's power at a given time to do something that would bring it about that someone who held a certain belief at a time prior to the time in question did not hold that belief at the time prior to the time in question.
5. It is not within one's power at a given time to do something that would bring it about that a person who existed at an earlier time did not exist at that earlier time.
6. If God existed at t_1 and if God believed at t_2 that Jones would do X at t_2, then if it was within Jones's power at t_2 to refrain from doing X, then (1) it was within Jones's power at t_2 to do something that would have brought it about that God held a false belief at t_1, or (2) it was within Jones's power at t_2 to do something which would have brought it about that God did not hold the belief He held at t_1, or (3) it was within Jones's power at t_2 to do something that would have brought it about that any person who believed at t_1 that Jones would do X at t_2 (one of whom was, by hypothesis, God) held a false-belief and thus was not God—that is, that God (who by hypothesis existed at t_1) did not exist at t_1.
7. Alternative 1 in the consequent of item 6 is false. (from 2 and 3)

8. Alternative 2 in the consequent of item 6 is false. (from 4)
9. Alternative 3 in the consequent of item 6 is false. (from 5)
10. Therefore, if God existed at t_1 and if God believed at t_1 that Jones would do X at t_2, then it was not within Jones's power at t_2 to refrain from doing X. (from 6 through 9)
11. Therefore, if God existed at t_1, and if Jones did X at t_2, it was not within Jones's power at t_2 to refrain from doing X. (from 1 and 10)

In this argument, items 1 and 2 make explicit the doctrine of God's (essential) omniscience with which I am working. Items 3, 4, and 5 express what I take to be part of the logic of the concept of ability or power as it applies to human beings. Item 6 is offered as an analytic truth. If one assigns Jones the power to refrain from doing X at t_2 (given that God believed at t_1 that he would do X at t_2), so far as I can see, one would have to describe this power in one of the three ways listed in the consequent of item 6. I do not know how to argue that these are the only alternatives, but I have been unable to find another. Item 11, when generalized for all agents and actions, and when taken together with what seems to me to be a minimal condition for the application of "voluntary action," yields the conclusion that if God exists (and is essentially omniscient in the way I have described) no human action is voluntary.

C. It is important to notice that the argument given in the preceding paragraphs avoids use of two concepts that are often prominent in discussions of determinism.

In the first place, the argument makes no mention of the *causes* of Jones's action. Say (for example, with St. Thomas)[10] that God's foreknowledge of Jones's action was, itself, the cause of the action (though I am really not sure what this means). Say, instead, that natural events or circumstances caused Jones to act. Even say that Jones's action had no cause at all. The argument outlined above remains unaffected. If eighty years prior to Saturday, God believed that Jones would mow his lawn at that time, it was not within Jones's power at the time of action to refrain from mowing his lawn. The reasoning that justifies this assertion makes no mention of a causal series preceding Jones's action.

Secondly, consider the following line of thinking. Suppose Jones mowed his lawn last Saturday. It was then *true* eighty years ago that Jones would mow his lawn at that time. Hence, on Saturday, Jones was not able to refrain from mowing his lawn. To suppose that he was would be to suppose that he was able on Saturday to do something that would have made false a proposition that was *already true* eighty years earlier. This general kind of argument for determinism is usually associated with Leibniz, although it was anticipated in chapter ix of Aristotle's *De Interpretatione*. It has been used since, with some modification, in Richard Taylor's article, *"Fatalism."* [11] This argument, like the one I have offered above, makes no use of the notion of causation. It turns, instead, on the notion of its being *true eighty years ago* that Jones would mow his lawn on Saturday.

I must confess that I share the misgivings of those contemporary philosophers who have wondered what (if any) sense can be attached to a statement of the form "It was true at t_1 that E would occur at t_2." [12] Does this statement mean that had someone believed, guessed, or asserted at t_1 that E would occur at t_2, he would have been right? [13] (I shall have something to say about this form of determinism later in this paper.) Perhaps it means that at t_1 there was sufficient evidence upon which to predict that E would occur at t_2. [14] Maybe it means neither of these. Maybe it means nothing at all. [15] The argument presented above presupposes that it makes straightforward sense to suppose that God (or just anyone) held a true belief eighty years prior to Saturday. But this is not to suppose that *what* God believed *was true eighty years prior to Saturday*. Whether (or in what sense) it was true eighty years ago that Jones would mow his lawn on Saturday is a question I shall not discuss. As far as I can see, the argument in which I am interested requires nothing in the way of a decision on this issue.

II

I now want to consider three comments on the problem of divine foreknowledge which seem to be instructively incorrect.

A. Leibniz analyzed the problem as follows:

They say that what is foreseen cannot fail to exist and they say so truly; but it follows not that what is foreseen is necessary. For necessary truth is that whereof the contrary is impossible or implies a contradiction. Now the truth which states that I shall write tomorrow is not of that nature, it is not necessary. Yet, supposing that God foresees it, it is necessary that it come to pass, that is, the consequence is necessary, namely that it exist, since it has been foreseen; for God is infallible. This is what is termed a *hypothetical necessity*. But our concern is not this necessity; it is an *absolute* necessity that is required, to be able to say that an action is necessary, that it is not contingent, that it is not the effect of free choice. [16]

The statement "God believed at t_1 that Jones would do X at t_2" (where the interval between t_1 and t_2 is, for example, eighty years) does not entail "'Jones did X at t_2' is necessary." Leibniz is surely right about this. All that will follow from the first of these statements concerning "Jones did X at t_2" is that the latter is *true*, not that it is *necessarily true*. But this observation has no real bearing on the issue at hand. The following passage from St. Augustine's formulation of the problem may help to make this point clear.

> Your trouble is this. You wonder how it can be that these two propositions are not contradictory and incompatible, namely that God has foreknowledge of all future events, and that we sin voluntarily and not by necessity. For if, you say, God foreknows that a man will sin, he must necessarily sin. But if there is necessity there is no voluntary choice of sinning, but rather fixed and unavoidable necessity. [17]

In this passage, the term "necessity" (or the phrase "by necessity") is not used to express a modal-logical concept. The term "necessity" is here used in contrast with the term "voluntary," not (as in Leibniz) in contrast with the term "contingent." If one's action is necessary (or by necessity), this is to say that one's action is not voluntary. Augustine says that if God has foreknowledge of human actions, the actions are necessary. But the form of this conditional is "p implies q," not "p implies n (q)." "q" in the consequent of this conditional is the claim that human actions are not voluntary—that is, that one is not able, or does not have the power, to do other than he does.

Perhaps I can make this point clearer by reformulating the original problem in such a way as to make explicit the modal operators working within it. Let it be *contingently* true that Jones did X at t_2. Since God holds a belief about the outcome of each human action well in advance of its performance, it is then *contingently* true that God believed at t_1 that Jones would do X at t_2. But it follows from this that it is *contingently* true that at t_2 Jones was not able to refrain from doing X. Had he been (contingently) able to refrain from doing X at t_2, then either he was (contingently) able to do something at t_2 that would have brought it about that God held a false belief at t_1, or he was (contingently) able to do something at t_2 that would have brought it about that God believed otherwise than He did at t_1, or he was (contingently) able to do something at t_2 that would have brought it about that God did not exist at t_1. None of these latter is an acceptable alternative.

B. In *Concordia Liberi Arbitrii,* Luis de Molina wrote as follows:

> It was not that since He foreknew what would happen from those things which depend on the created will that it would happen; but, on the contrary, it was because such things would happen through the freedom of the will, that He foreknew it; and that He would foreknow the opposite if the opposite was to happen.[18]

Remarks similar to this one can be found in a great many traditional and contemporary theological texts. In fact, Molina assures us that the view expressed in this passage has always been "above controversy"—a matter of "common opinion" and "unanimous consent"—not only among the Church fathers, but also, as he says, "among all catholic men."

One claim made in the above passage seems to me to be truly "above controversy." With respect to any given action foreknown by God, God would have foreknown the opposite if the opposite was to happen. If we assume the notion of omniscience outlined in the first section of this paper, and if we agree that omniscience is part of the "essence" of God, this statement is a conceptual truth. I doubt if anyone would be inclined to dispute it. Also involved in this passage, however, is at least the suggestion of a doctrine that cannot be taken as an item of "common opinion" among *all* catholic men. Molina says it is not because God foreknows what He

foreknows that men act as they do: it is because men act as they do that God foreknows what He foreknows. Some theologians have rejected this claim. It seems to entail that men's actions determine God's cognitions. And this latter, I think, has been taken by some theologians to be a violation of the notion of God as self-sufficient and incapable of being affected by events of the natural world.[19] But I shall not develop this point further. Where the view put forward in the above passage seems to me to go wrong in an interesting and important way is in Molina's claim that God can have foreknowledge of things that will happen "through the freedom of the will." It is this claim that I here want to examine with care.

What exactly are we saying when we say that God can know in advance what will happen *through the freedom of the will?* I think that what Molina has in mind is this. God can know in advance that a given man is going to *choose* to perform a certain action sometime in the future. With respect to the case of Jones mowing his lawn, God knew at t_1 that Jones would *freely decide* to mow his lawn at t_2. Not only did God know at t_1 that Jones would mow his lawn at t_2, He also knew at t_1 that this action would be performed *freely*. In the words of Emil Brunner, "God knows that which will take place in freedom in the future as something which happens in freedom."[20] What God knew at t_1 is that Jones would *freely* mow his lawn at t_2.

I think that this doctrine is incoherent. If God knew (and thus believed) at t_1 that Jones would *do X* at t_2,[21] I think it follows that Jones was not able to do other than X at t_2 (for reasons already given). Thus, if God knew (and thus believed) at t_1 that Jones would *do X* at t_2, it would follow that Jones did X at t_2, but *not freely*. It does not seem to be possible that God could have believed at t_1 that Jones would freely do X at t_2. If God believed at t_1 that Jones would do X at t_2, Jones's actions at t_2 was not free; and if God *also* believed at t_1 that Jones would freely act at t_2, it follows that God held a false belief at t_1—which is absurd.

C. Frederick Schleiermacher commented on the problem of divine foreknowledge as follows:

> In the same way, we estimate the intimacy between two persons by the foreknowledge one has of the

actions of the other, without supposing that in either case, the one or the other's freedom is thereby endangered. So even the divine foreknowledge cannot endanger freedom.[22]

St. Augustine made this same point in *De Libero Arbitrio*. He said:

> Unless I am mistaken, you would not directly compel the man to sin, though you knew beforehand that he was going to sin. Nor does your presence in itself compel him to sin even though he was certainly going to sin, as we must assume if you have real prescience. So there is no contradiction here. Simply you know beforehand what another is going to do with his own will. Similarly God compels no man to sin, though he sees beforehand those who are going to sin by their own will.[23]

If we suppose (with Schleiermacher and Augustine) that the case of an intimate friend having foreknowledge of another's action has the same implications for determinism as the case of God's foreknowledge of human actions, I can imagine two positions which might then be taken. First, one might hold (with Schleiermacher and Augustine) that God's foreknowledge of human actions cannot entail determinism—since it is clear that an intimate friend can have foreknowledge of another's voluntary actions. Or, secondly, one might hold that an intimate friend cannot have foreknowledge of another's voluntary actions—since it is clear that God cannot have foreknowledge of such actions. This second position could take either of two forms. One might hold that since an intimate friend *can* have foreknowledge of another's actions, the actions in question cannot be voluntary. Or, alternatively, one might hold that since the other's actions *are* voluntary, the intimate friend cannot have foreknowledge of them.[24] But what I propose to argue in the remaining pages of this paper is that Schleiermacher and Augustine were mistaken in supposing that the case of an intimate friend having foreknowledge of another's actions has the same implications for determinism as the case of God's foreknowledge of human actions. What I want to suggest is that the argument I used above to show that God cannot have foreknowledge of voluntary actions cannot be used to show that an intimate friend cannot have foreknowledge of an-

other's actions. Even if one holds that an intimate friend can have foreknowledge of another's voluntary actions, one ought not to think that the case is the same when dealing with the problem of divine foreknowledge.

Let Smith be an ordinary man and an intimate friend of Jones. Now, let us start by supposing that Smith believed at t_1 that Jones would do X at t_2. We make no assumption concerning the truth or falsity of Smith's belief, but assume only that Smith held it. Given only this much, there appears to be no difficulty in supposing that at t_2 Jones was able to do X and that at t_2 Jones was able to do not-X. So far as the above description of the case is concerned, it might well have been within Jones's power at t_2 to do something (namely, X) which would have brought it about that Smith held a true belief at t_1, and it might well have been within Jones's power at t_2 to do something (namely, not-X) which would have brought it about that Smith held a false belief at t_1. So much seems apparent.

Now let us suppose that Smith *knew* at t_1 that Jones would do X at t_2. This is to suppose that Smith correctly believed (with evidence) at t_1 that Jones would do X at t_2. It follows, to be sure, that Jones *did* X at t_2. But now let us inquire about what Jones was *able* to do at t_2. I submit that there is nothing in the description of this case that requires the conclusion that it was not within Jones's power at t_2 to refrain from doing X. By hypothesis, the belief held by Smith at t_1 was true. Thus, by hypothesis, Jones did X at t_2. But even if we assume that the belief held by Smith at t_1 was *in fact* true, we can add that the belief held by Smith at t_1 *might have* turned out to be false.[25] Thus, even if we say that Jones *in fact* did X at t_2, we can add that Jones *might not* have done X at t_2—meaning by this that it was within Jones's power at t_2 to refrain from doing X. Smith held a true belief which might have turned out to be false, and, correspondingly, Jones performed an action which he was able to refrain from performing. Given that Smith correctly believed at t_1 that Jones would do X at t_2, we can still assign Jones the *power* at t_2 to refrain from doing X. All we need add is that the power in question is one which Jones *did not exercise*.

These last reflections have no application, however, when dealing with God's foreknowledge. Assume that God (being essentially omniscient) existed at t_1, and assume that He believed at t_1 that Jones would do X at t_2. It follows, again, that Jones did X at t_2. God's beliefs are true. But now, as above, let us inquire into what Jones was *able* to do at t_2. We cannot claim now, as in the Smith case, that the belief held by God at t_1, was *in fact* true but *might have* turned out to be false. No sense of "might have" has application here. It is a conceptual truth that God's beliefs are true. Thus, we cannot claim, as in the Smith case, that Jones *in fact* acted in accordance with God's beliefs but had the *ability* to refrain from so doing. The ability to refrain from acting in accordance with one of God's beliefs would be the ability to do something that would bring it about that one of God's beliefs was false. And no one could have an ability of this description. Thus, in the case of God's foreknowledge of Jones's action at t_2, if we are to assign Jones the ability at t_2 to refrain from doing X, we must understand this ability in some way other than the way we understood it when dealing with Smith's foreknowledge. In this case, either we must say that it was the ability at t_2 to bring it about that God believed otherwise than He did at t_1; or we must say that it was the ability at t_2 to bring it about that any person who believed at t_1 that Jones would do X at t_2 (one of whom was, by hypothesis, God) held a false belief and thus was not God. But, as pointed out earlier, neither of these last alternatives can be accepted.

The important thing to be learned from the study of Smith's foreknowledge of Jones's action is that the problem of divine foreknowledge has as one of its pillars the claim that truth is *analytically* connected with God's being. No problem of determinism arises when dealing with human knowledge of future actions. This is because truth is not analytically connected with human belief even when (as in the case of human knowledge) truth is contingently conjoined to belief. If we suppose that Smith knows at t_1 that Jones will do X at t_2, what we are supposing is that Smith believes at t_1 that Jones will do X at t_2 and (as an additional, contingent, fact) that the belief in question is true. Thus having supposed that Smith knows at t_1 that Jones will do X at t_2, when we turn to a consideration of the situation of t_2 we can infer (1) that Jones *will* do X at t_2 (since Smith's belief is true), and (2) that Jones does not have the power at t_2 to do something that would bring it about that Smith did not *believe* as he did at t_1. But

paradoxical though it may seem (and it seems paradoxical only at first sight), Jones can have the power at t_2 to do something that would bring it about that Smith did not have *knowledge* at t_1. This is simply to say that Jones can have the *power* at t_2 to do something that would bring it about that the belief held by Smith at t_1 (which was, in fact, true) was (instead) false. We are required only to add that since Smith's belief was in fact true (that is, was knowledge) Jones *did not* (in fact) *exercise* that power. But when we turn to a consideration of God's foreknowledge of Jones's action at t_2 the elbowroom between belief and truth disappears and, with it, the possibility of assigning Jones even the *power* of doing other than he does at t_2. We begin by supposing that God *knows* at t_1 that Jones will do X at t_2. As above, this is to suppose that God believes at t_1 that Jones will do X at t_2, and it is to suppose that this belief is true. But it is *not* an additional, contingent fact that the belief held by God is true. "God believes X" entails "X is true." Thus, having supposed that God knows (and thus believes) at t_1 that Jones will do X at t_2, we can infer (1) that Jones *will do* X at t_2 (since God's belief is true); (2) that Jones does not have the power at t_2 to do something that would bring it about that God did not hold the belief He held at t_1, and (3) that Jones does not have the power at t_2 to do something that would bring it about that the belief held by God at t_1 was false. This last is what we could *not* infer when truth and belief were only factually connected—as in the case of Smith's knowledge. To be sure, "Smith knows at t_1 that Jones will do X at t_2" and "God knows at t_1 that Jones will do X at t_2" both entail "Jones will do X at t_2" ("A knows X" entails "'X' is true"). But this similarity between "Smith knows X" and "God knows X" is not a point of any special interest in the present discussion. As Schleiermacher and Augustine rightly insisted (and as we discovered in our study of Smith's foreknowledge), the mere fact that someone knows in advance how another will act in the future is not enough to yield a problem of the sort we have been discussing. We begin to get a glimmer of the knot involved in the problem of divine foreknowledge when we shift attention away from the *similarities* between "Smith knows X" and "God knows X" (in particular, that they both entail "'X' is true") and concentrate instead on the logical *differences* which obtain between Smith's knowledge and God's knowledge. We get to the difference which makes the difference when, after analyzing the notion of knowledge as true belief (supported by evidence) we discover the radically dissimilar relations between truth and belief in the two cases. When truth is only factually connected with belief (as in Smith's knowledge) one can have the power (though, by hypothesis, one will not exercise it) to do something that would make the belief false. But when truth is analytically connected with belief (as in God's belief) no one can have the power to do something which would render the belief false.

To conclude: I have assumed that any statement of the form "*A* knows *X*" entails a statement of the form "*A* believes *X*" as well as a statement of the form "'*X*' is true." I have then supposed (as an analytic truth) that if a given person is omniscient, that person (1) holds no false beliefs, and (2) holds beliefs about the outcome of human actions in advance of their performance. In addition, I have assumed that the statement "If a given person is God that person is omniscient" is an a priori statement. (This last I have labeled the doctrine of God's essential omniscience.) Given these items (plus some premises concerning what is and what is not within one's power), I have argued that if God exists, it is not within one's power to do other than he does. I have inferred from this that if God exists, no human action is voluntary.

As emphasized earlier, I do not want to claim that the assumptions underpinning the argument are acceptable. In fact, it seems to me that a theologian interested in claiming both that God is omniscient and that men have free will could deny any one (or more) of them. For example, a theologian might deny that a statement of the form "*A* knows *X*" entails a statement of the form "*A* believes *X*" (some contemporary philosophers have denied this), or alternatively, he might claim that this entailment holds in the case of human knowledge but fails in the case of God's knowledge. This latter would be to claim that when knowledge is attributed to God, the term "knowledge" bears a sense other than the one it has when knowledge is attributed to human beings. Then again, a theologian might object to the analysis of "omniscience" with which I have been working. Although I doubt if any Christian theologian would allow that an omniscient being could be-

lieve something false, he might claim that a given person could be omniscient although he did not hold beliefs about the outcome of human actions *in advance* of their performance. (This latter is the way Boethius escaped the problem.) Still again, a theologian might deny the doctrine of God's essential omniscience. He might admit that if a given person is God that person is omniscient, but he might deny that this statement formulates an a priori truth. This would be to say that although God is omniscient, He is not *essentially* omniscient. So far as I can see, within the conceptual framework of theology employing any one of these adjustments, the problem of divine foreknowledge outlined in this paper could not be formulated. There thus appears to be a rather wide range of alternatives open to the theologian at this point. It would be a mistake to think that commitment to determinism is an unavoidable implication of the Christian concept of divine omniscience.

But having arrived at this understanding, the importance of the preceding deliberations ought not to be overlooked. There is a pitfall in the doctrine of divine omniscience. That knowing involves believing (truly) is surely a tempting philosophical view (witness the many contemporary philosophers who have affirmed it). And the idea that God's attributes (including omniscience) are essentially connected to His nature, together with the idea that an omniscient being would hold no false beliefs and would hold beliefs about the outcome of human actions in advance of their performance, might be taken by some theologians as obvious candidates for inclusion in a finished Christian theology. Yet the theologian must approach these items critically. If they are embraced together, then if one affirms the existence of God, one is committed to the view that no human action is voluntary.

Notes

1. Boethius, *Consolatio Philosophiae*, Bk., V, sec. 3, par. 6.
2. This position is particularly well formulated in St. Anselm's *Proslogium*, ch. xix, and *Monoloquium*, chs. xxi–xxii; and in Frederich Schleiermacher's *The Christian Faith*, Pt. I, sec. 2, par. 51. It is also explicit in Boethius, *Consolatio*, secs. 4–6, and in St. Thomas Aquinas's *Summa Theologicae*, Pt. I, q. 10.
3. This point is explicit in Boethius, *Consolatio*, secs. 4–6.

4. This position is particularly well expressed in William Paley's *Natural Theology,* ch. xxiv. It is also involved in John Calvin's discussion of predestination, *Institutes of the Christian Religion,* Bk. III, ch. xxi; and in some formulations of the first cause argument for the existence of God, e.g., John Locke's *An Essay Concerning Human Understanding,* Bk. v, ch. x.

5. Calvin, *Institutes of the Christian Religion,* Bk. III, ch. xxi; this passage trans. by John Allen (Philadelphia, 1813), II, p. 145.

6. Ibid., p. 144.

7. Augustine, *City of God,* Bk, V, sec. 9.

8. The notion of someone being *able* to do something and the notion of something being *within one's power* are essentially the same. Traditional formulations of the problem of divine foreknowledge (e.g., those of Boethius and Augustine) made use of the notion of what is (and what is not) *within one's power.* But the problem is the same when framed in terms of what one is (and one is not) *able* to do. Thus, I shall treat the statements "Jones was able to do *X*," "Jones had the ability to do *X*," and "It was within Jones's power to do *X*" as equivalent. Richard Taylor, in "I Can," *Philosophical Review,* 69(1960):78–89, has argued that the notion of ability or power involved in these last three statements is incapable of philosophical analysis. Be this as it may, I shall not here attempt such an analysis. In what follows I shall, however, be careful to affirm only those statements about what is (or is not) within one's power that would have to be preserved on any analysis of this notion having even the most distant claim to adequacy.

9. In Bk. II, ch. xxi, secs. 8–11 of *An Essay,* Locke says that an agent is not *free* with respect to a given action (i.e., that an action is done "under necessity") when it is not within the agent's power to do otherwise. Locke allows a special kind of case, however, in which an action may be *voluntary* though done under necessity. If a man chooses to do something without knowing that it is not within his power to do otherwise (e.g., if a man chooses to stay in a room without knowing that the room is locked), his action may be voluntary though he is not free to forbear it. If Locke is right in this (and I shall not argue the point one way or the other), replace "voluntary" with (let us say) "free" in the above paragraph and throughout the remainder of this paper.

10. Aquinas, *Summa Theologicae,* Pt. 1, q. 14, a. 8.

11. Richard Taylor, "Fatalism," *Philosophical Review,* 71 (1962):56–66. Taylor argues that if an event *E* fails to occur at t_2, then at t_1 it was true that *E* would fail to oc-

cur at t_2. Thus, at t_1, a necessary condition of anyone's performing an action sufficient for the occurrence of *E* at t_2 is missing. Thus at t_1, no one could have the power to perform an action that would be sufficient for the occurrence of *E* at t_2. Hence, no one has the power at t_1 to do something sufficient for the occurrence of an event at t_2 that is not going to happen. The parallel between this argument and the one recited above can be seen very clearly if one reformulates Taylor's argument, pushing back the time at which it was true that *E* would not occur at t_2.

12. For a helpful discussion of difficulties involved here, see Rogers Albritton's "Present Truth and Future Contingency," a reply to Richard Taylor's "The Problem of Future Contingency," both in *Philosophical Review,* 66 (1957):1–28.

13. Gilbert Ryle interprets it this way. See "It Was to Be," in *Dilemmas* (Cambridge, Engl., 1954).

14. Richard Gale suggests this interpretation in "Endorsing Predictions," *Philosophical Review,* 70(1961): 376–85.

15. This view is held by John Turk Saunders in "Sea Fight Tomorrow?," *Philosophical Review,* 67(1958):367–78.

16. G. W. Leibniz, *Théodicée,* Pt. I, sec. 37. This passage trans. by E. M. Huggard (New Haven, 1952), p. 144.

17. *De Libero Arbitrio,* Bk. III. This passage trans. by J. H. S. Burleigh, *Augustine's Earlier Writings* (Philadelphia, 1955).

18. Luis de Molina, *Concordia Liberi Arbitrii.* This passage trans. by John Mourant, *Readings in the Philosophy of Religion* (New York, 1954), p. 426.

19. Cf. Boethius's *Consolatio,* Bk. V, sec. 3, par. 2.

20. Emil Brunner, *The Christian Doctrine of God,* trans. by Olive Wyon (Philadelphia, 1964), p. 262.

21. Note: no comment here about *freely* doing X.

22. Schleiermacher, *The Christian Faith,* Pt. I, sec. 2, par. 55. This passage trans. by W. R. Matthew (Edinburgh, 1928), p. 228.

23. *De Libero Arbitrio,* Bk. III.

24. This last seems to be the position defended by Richard Taylor in "Deliberation and Foreknowledge," *American Philosophical Quarterly,* 1(1964):73–80.

25. The phrase "might have" as it occurs in this sentence does not express mere *logical* possibility. I am not sure how to analyze the notion of possibility involved here, but I think it is roughly the same notion as is involved when we say, "Jones might have been killed in the accident (had it not been for the fact that at the last minute he decided not to go)."

Evil and Omnipotence

J. L. MACKIE

J. L. Mackie (1917–1983) taught philosophy at University College, Oxford.

The traditional arguments for the existence of God have been fairly thoroughly criticized by philosophers. But the theologian can, if he wishes, accept this criticism. He can admit that no rational proof of God's existence is possible. And he can still retain all that is essential to his position, by holding that God's existence is known in some other, nonrational way. I think, however, that a more telling criticism can be made by way of the traditional problem of evil. Here it can be shown, not that religious beliefs lack rational support, but that they are positively irrational, that the several parts of the essential theological doctrine are inconsistent with one another, so that the theologian can maintain his position as a whole only by a much more extreme rejection of reason than in the former case. He must now be prepared to believe, not merely what cannot be proved, but what can be *disproved* from other beliefs that he also holds.

The problem of evil, in the sense in which I shall be using the phrase, is a problem only for someone who believes that there is a God who is both omnipotent and wholly good. And it is a logical problem, the problem of clarifying and reconciling a number of beliefs: it is not a scientific problem that might be solved by further observations, or a practical problem that might be solved by a decision or an action. These points are obvious; I mention them only because they are sometimes ignored by theologians, who sometimes parry a statement of the problem with such remarks as "Well, can you solve the problem yourself?" or "This is a mystery which may be revealed to us later" or "Evil is something to be faced and overcome, not to be merely discussed."

In its simplest form the problem is this: God is omnipotent; God is wholly good; and yet evil exists. There seems to be some contradiction between these three propositions, so that if any two of them were true the third would be false. But at the same time all three are essential parts of most theological positions: the theologian, it seems, at once *must* adhere and *cannot consistently* adhere to all three. (The problem does not arise only for theists, but I shall discuss it in the form in which it presents itself for ordinary theism.)

However, the contradiction does not arise immediately; to show it we need some additional premises, or perhaps some quasi-logical rules connecting the terms "good," "evil," and "omnipotent." These additional principles are that good is opposed to evil, in such a way that a good thing always eliminates evil as far as it can, and that there are no limits to what an omnipotent thing can do. From these it follows that a good omnipotent thing eliminates evil completely, and then the propositions that a good omnipotent thing exists, and that evil exists, are incompatible.

ADEQUATE SOLUTIONS

Now once the problem is fully stated it is clear that it can be solved, in the sense that the problem will not arise if one gives up at least one of the propositions that constitute it. If you are prepared to say that God is not wholly good, or not quite omnipotent, or that evil does not exist, or that good is not opposed to the kind of evil that exists, or that there are limits to what an omnipotent thing can do, then the problem of evil will not arise for you.

There are, then, quite a number of adequate solutions of the problem of evil, and some of these have been adopted, or almost adopted, by various thinkers. For example, a few have been prepared to deny God's omnipotence, and rather more have been prepared to keep the term "omnipotence" but severely to restrict its meaning, recording quite a number of things that an omnipotent being cannot

From *Mind,* Vol. LXIV, No. 254 (1955). Reprinted by permission of the author and Basil Blackwell, Publisher.

do. Some have said that evil is an illusion, perhaps because they held that the whole world of temporal, changing things is an illusion, and that what we call evil belongs only to this world, or perhaps because they held that although temporal things *are* much as we see them, those that we call evil are not really evil. Some have said that what we call evil is merely the privation of good, that evil in a positive sense, evil that would really be opposed to good, does not exist. Many have agreed with Pope that disorder is harmony not understood, and that partial evil is universal good. Whether any of these views is *true* is, of course, another question. But each of them gives an adequate solution of the problem of evil in the sense that if you accept it this problem does not arise for you, though you may, of course, have *other* problems to face.

But often enough these adequate solutions are only *almost* adopted. The thinkers who restrict God's power, but keep the term "omnipotence," may reasonably be suspected of thinking, in other contexts, that his power is really unlimited. Those who say that evil is an illusion may also be thinking, inconsistently, that this illusion is itself an evil. Those who say that "evil" is merely privation of good may also be thinking, inconsistently, that privation of good is an evil. . . . If Pope meant what he said in the first line of his couplet, that "disorder" is only harmony not understood, the "partial evil" of the second line must, for consistency, mean "that which, taken in isolation, falsely appears to be evil," but it would more naturally mean "that which, in isolation, really is evil." The second line, in fact, hesitates between two views, that "partial evil" isn't really evil, since only the universal quality is real, and that "partial evil" is really an evil, but only a little one.

In addition, therefore, to adequate solutions, we must recognize unsatisfactory inconsistent solutions, in which there is only a half-hearted or temporary rejection of one of the propositions which together constitute the problem. In these, one of the constituent propositions is explicitly rejected, but it is covertly reasserted or assumed elsewhere in the system.

FALLACIOUS SOLUTIONS

Besides these half-hearted solutions, which explicitly reject but implicitly assert one of the constituent propositions, there are definitely fallacious solutions which explicitly maintain all the constituent propositions, but implicitly reject at least one of them in the course of the argument that explains away the problem of evil.

There are, in fact, many so-called solutions which purport to remove the contradiction without abandoning any of its constituent propositions. These must be fallacious, as we can see from the very statement of the problem, but it is not so easy to see in each case precisely where the fallacy lies. I suggest that in all cases the fallacy has the general form suggested above: in order to solve the problem one (or perhaps more) of its constituent propositions is given up, but in such a way that it appears to have been retained, and can therefore be asserted without qualification in other contexts. Sometimes there is a further complication: the supposed solution moves to and fro between, say, two of the constituent propositions, at one point asserting the first of these but covertly abandoning the second, at another point asserting the second but covertly abandoning the first. These fallacious solutions often turn upon some equivocation with the words "good" and "evil," or upon some vagueness about the way in which good and evil are opposed to one another, or about how much is meant by "omnipotence." I propose to examine some of these so called solutions, and to exhibit their fallacies in detail. Incidentally, I shall also be considering whether an adequate solution could be reached by a minor modification of one or more of the constituent propositions, which would, however, still satisfy all the essential requirements of ordinary theism.

1. "Good cannot exist without evil" or "Evil is necessary as a counterpart to good."

It is sometimes suggested that evil is necessary as a counterpart to good, that if there were no evil there could be no good either, and that this solves the problem of evil. It is true that it points to an answer to the question "Why should there be evil?" But it does so only by qualifying some of the propositions that constitute the problem.

First, it sets a limit to what God can do, saying that God *cannot* create good without simultaneously creating evil, and this means either that God is not omnipotent or that there are *some* limits to what an omnipotent thing can do. It may be replied that these limits are always presupposed, that omnipotence has never meant the power to do what is logically impossible, and on the present view the existence of good without evil would be a logical impossibility. This interpretation of omnipotence may, indeed, be accepted as a modification of our original account which does not reject anything that is essential to theism, and I shall in general assume it in the subsequent discussion. It is, perhaps, the most common theistic view, but I think that some theists at least have maintained that God can do what is logically impossible. Many theists, at any rate, have held that logic itself is created or laid down by God, that logic is the way in which God arbitrarily chooses to think. (This is, of course, parallel to the ethical view that morally right actions are those which God arbitrarily chooses to command, and the two views encounter similar difficulties.) And *this* account of logic is clearly inconsistent with the view that God is bound by logical necessities—unless it is possible for an omnipotent being to bind himself, an issue which we shall consider later, when we come to the Paradox of Omnipotence. This solution of the problem of evil cannot, therefore, be consistently adopted along with the view that logic is itself created by God.

But, secondly, this solution denies that evil is opposed to good in our original sense. If good and evil are counterparts, a good thing will not "eliminate evil as far as it can." Indeed, this view suggests that good and evil are not strictly qualities of things at all. Perhaps the suggestion is that good and evil are related in much the same way as great and small. Certainly, when the term "great" is used relatively as a condensation of "greater than so-and-so," and "small" is used correspondingly, greatness and smallness are counterparts and cannot exist without each other. But in this sense greatness is not a quality, not an intrinsic feature of anything; and it would be absurd to think of a movement in favor of greatness and against smallness in this sense. Such a movement would be self-defeating, since relative greatness can be promoted only by a simultaneous promotion of relative smallness. I feel sure that no theists would be content to regard God's goodness as analogous to this—as if what he supports were not the *good* but the *better,* and as if he had the para-

doxical aim that all things should be better than other things.

This point is obscured by the fact that "great" and "small" seem to have an absolute as well as a relative sense. I cannot discuss here whether there is absolute magnitude or not, but if there is, there could be an absolute sense for "great," it could mean of at least a certain size, and it would make sense to speak of all things getting bigger, of a universe that was expanding all over, and therefore it would make sense to speak of promoting greatness. But in *this* sense great and small are not logically necessary counterparts: either quality could exist without the other. There would be no logical impossibility in everything's being small or in everything's being great.

Neither in the absolute nor in the relative sense, then, of "great" and "small" do these terms provide an analogy of the sort that would be needed to support this solution of the problem of evil. In neither case are greatness and smallness *both* necessary counterparts *and* mutually opposed forces or possible objects for support and attack.

It may be replied that good and evil are necessary counterparts in the same way as any quality and its logical opposite: redness can occur, it is suggested, only if nonredness also occurs. But unless evil is merely the privation of goods, they are not logical opposites, and some further argument would be needed to show that they are counterparts in the same way as genuine logical opposites. Let us assume that this could be given. There is still doubt of the correctness of the metaphysical principle that a quality must have a real opposite: I suggest that it is not really impossible that everything should be, say, red, that the truth is merely that if everything were red we should not notice redness, and so we should have no word "red"; we observe and give names to qualities only if they have real opposites. If so, the principle that a term must have an opposite would belong only to our language or to our thought, and would not be an ontological principle, and, correspondingly, the rule that good cannot exist without evil would not state a logical necessity of a sort that God would just have to put up with. God might have made everything good, though *we* should not have noticed it if he had.

But, finally, even if we concede that this *is* an

ontological principle, it will provide a solution for the problem of evil only if one is prepared to say, "Evil exists, but only just enough evil to serve as the counterpart of good." I doubt whether any theist will accept this. After all, the *ontological* requirement that nonredness should occur would be satisfied even if all the universe, except for a minute speck, were red, and, if there were a corresponding requirement for evil as a counterpart to good, a minute dose of evil would presumably do. But theists are not usually willing to say, in all contexts, that all the evil that occurs is a minute and necessary dose.

2. "Evil is necessary as a means to good."

It is sometimes suggested that evil is necessary for good not as a counterpart but as a means. In its simple form this has little plausibility as a solution of the problem of evil, since it obviously implies a severe restriction of God's power. It would be a *causal* law that you cannot have a certain end without a certain means, so that if God has to introduce evil as a means to good, he must be subject to at least some causal laws. This certainly conflicts with what a theist normally means by omnipotence. This view of God as limited by causal laws also conflicts with the view that causal laws are themselves made by God, which is more widely held than the corresponding view about the laws of logic. This conflict would, indeed, be resolved if it were possible for an omnipotent being to bind himself, and this possibility has still to be considered. Unless a favorable answer can be given to this question, the suggestion that evil is necessary as a means to good solves the problem of evil only by denying one of its constituent propositions, either that God is omnipotent or that "omnipotent" means what it says.

3. "The universe is better with some evil in it than it could be if there were no evil."

Much more important is a solution which at first seems to be a mere variant of the previous one, that evil may contribute to the goodness of a whole in which it is found, so that the universe as a whole is better as it is, with some evil in it, than it would be if there were no evil. This solution may be developed in either of two ways. It may be supported by an aesthetic analogy, by the fact that contrasts heighten beauty, that in a musical work, for example, there

may occur discords which somehow add to the beauty of the work as a whole. Alternatively, it may be worked out in connection with the notion of progress, that the best possible organization of the universe will not be static, but progressive, that the gradual overcoming of evil by good is really a finer thing than would be the eternal unchallenged supremacy of good.

In either case, this solution usually starts from the assumption that the evil whose existence gives rise to the problem of evil is primarily what is called physical evil, that is to say, pain. In Hume's rather half-hearted presentation of the problem of evil, the evils that he stresses are pain and disease, and those who reply to him argue that the existence of pain and disease makes possible the existence of sympathy, benevolence, heroism, and the gradually successful struggle of doctors and reformers to overcome these evils. In fact, theists often seize the opportunity to accuse those who stress the problem of evil of taking a low, materialistic view of good and evil, equating these with pleasure and pain, and of ignoring the more spiritual goods which can arise in the struggle against evils.

But let us see exactly what is being done here. Let us call pain and misery "first order evil" or "evil (1)." What contrasts with this, namely, pleasure and happiness, will be called "first order good" or "good (1)." Distinct from this is "second order good" or "good (2)" which somehow emerges in a complex situation in which evil (1) is a necessary component —logically, not merely causally, necessary. (Exactly *how* it emerges does not matter: in the crudest version of this solution good (2) is simply the heightening of happiness by the contrast with misery, in other versions it includes sympathy with suffering, heroism in facing danger, and the gradual decrease of first order evil and increase of first order good.) It is also being assumed that second order good is more important than first order good or evil, in particular that it more than outweighs the first order evil it involves.

Now this is a particularly subtle attempt to solve the problem of evil. It defends God's goodness and omnipotence on the ground that (on a sufficiently long view) this is the best of all logically possible worlds because it includes the important second order goods, and yet it admits that real evils, namely first order evils, exist. But does it still hold that good and evil are opposed? Not, clearly, in the sense that we set out originally: good does not tend to eliminate evil in general. Instead, we have a modified, a more complex pattern. First order good (e.g., happiness) *contrasts with* first order evil (e.g., misery): these two are opposed in a fairly mechanical way; some second order goods (e.g., benevolence) try to maximize first order good and minimize first order evil; but God's goodness is not this, it is rather the will to maximize *second* order good. We might, therefore, call God's goodness an example of a third order goodness, or good (3). While this account is different from our original one, it might well be held to be an improvement on it, to give a more accurate description of the way in which good is opposed to evil, and to be consistent with the essential theist position.

There might, however, be several objections to this solution.

First, some might argue that such qualities as benevolence—and *a fortiori* the third order goodness which promotes benevolence—have a merely derivative value, that they are not higher sorts of good, but merely means to good (1), that is, to happiness, so that it would be absurd for God to keep misery in existence in order to make possible the virtues of benevolence, heroism, etc. The theist who adopts the present solution must, of course, deny this, but he can do so with some plausibility, so I should not press this objection.

Secondly, it follows from this solution that God is not in our sense benevolent or sympathetic: he is not concerned to minimize evil (1), but only to promote good (2); and this might be a disturbing conclusion for some theists.

But, thirdly, the fatal objection is this. Our analysis shows clearly the possibility of the existence of a *second* order evil, an evil (2) contrasting with good (2) as evil (1) contrasts with good (1). This would include malevolence, cruelty, callousness, cowardice, and states in which good (1) is decreasing and evil (1) increasing. And just as good (2) is held to be the important kind of good, the kind that God is concerned to promote, so evil (2) will, by analogy, be the important kind of evil, the kind which God, if he were wholly good and omnipotent, would eliminate. And yet evil (2) plainly exists, and indeed most

theists (in other contexts) stress its existence more than that of evil (1). We should, therefore, state the problem of evil in terms of second order evil, and against this form of the problem the present solution is useless.

An attempt might be made to use this solution again, at a higher level, to explain the occurrence of evil (2): indeed the next main solution that we shall examine does just this, with the help of some new notions. Without any fresh notions, such a solution would have little plausibility: for example, we could hardly say that the really important good was a good (3), such as the increase of benevolence in proportion to cruelty, which logically required for its occurrence the occurrence of some second order evil. But even if evil (2) could be explained in this way, it is fairly clear that there would be third order evils contrasting with this third order good: and we should be well on the way to an infinite regress, where the solution of a problem of evil, stated in terms of evil (n), indicated the existence of an evil (n + 1), and a further problem to be solved.

4. "Evil is due to human free will."

Perhaps the most important proposed solution of the problem of evil is that evil is not to be ascribed to God at all, but to the independent actions of human beings, supposed to have been endowed by God with freedom of the will. This solution may be combined with the preceding one: first order evil (e.g., pain) may be justified as a logically necessary component in second order good (e.g., sympathy) while second order evil (e.g., cruelty) is not *justified,* but is so ascribed to human beings that God cannot be held responsible for it. This combination evades my third criticism of the preceding solution.

The free-will solution also involves the preceding solution at a higher level. To explain why a wholly good God gave men free will although it would lead to some important evils, it must be argued that it is better on the whole that men should act freely, and sometimes err, than that they should be innocent automata, acting rightly in a wholly determined way. Freedom, that is to say, is now treated as a third order good, and as being more valuable than second order goods (such as sympathy and heroism) would be if they were deterministically produced, and it is being assumed that second order evils, such as cruelty, are logically necessary accompaniments of freedom, just as pain is a logically necessary pre-condition of sympathy.

I think that this solution is unsatisfactory primarily because of the incoherence of the notion of freedom of the will: but I cannot discuss this topic adequately here, although some of my criticisms will touch upon it.

First I should query the assumption that second order evils are logically necessary accompaniments of freedom. I should ask this: if God has made men such that in their free choices they sometimes prefer what is good and sometimes what is evil, why could he not have made men such that they always freely choose the good? If there is no logical impossibility in a man's freely choosing the good on one, or on several occasions, there cannot be a logical impossibility in his freely choosing the good on every occasion. God was not, then, faced with a choice between making innocent automata and making beings who, in acting freely, would sometimes go wrong: there was open to him the obviously better possibility of making beings who would act freely but always go right. Clearly, his failure to avail himself of this possibility is inconsistent with his being both omnipotent and wholly good.

If it is replied that this objection is absurd, that the making of some wrong choices is logically necessary for freedom, it would seem that "freedom" must here mean complete randomness or indeterminacy, including randomness with regard to the alternatives good and evil, in other words that men's choices and consequent actions can be "free" only if they are not determined by their characters. Only on this assumption can God escape the responsibility for men's actions; for if he made them as they are, but did not determine their wrong choices, this can only be because the wrong choices are not determined by men as they are. But then if freedom is randomness, how can it be a characteristic of *will*? And, still more, how can it be the most important good? What value or merit would there be in free choices if these were random actions which were not determined by the nature of the agent?

I conclude that to make this solution plausible two different senses of "freedom" must be confused, one sense which will justify the view that freedom is a third order good, more valuable than other goods would be without it, and another sense, sheer randomness, to prevent us from ascribing to God a decision to make men such that they sometimes go wrong when he might have made them such that they would always freely go right.

This criticism is sufficient to dispose of this solution. But besides this there is a fundamental difficulty in the notion of an omnipotent God creating men with free will, for if men's wills are really free this must mean that even God cannot control them, that is, that God is no longer omnipotent. It may be objected that God's gift of freedom to men does not mean that he *cannot* control their wills, but that he always *refrains* from controlling their wills. But why, we may ask, should God refrain from controlling evil wills? Why should he not leave men free to will rightly, but intervene when he sees them beginning to will wrongly? If God could do this, but does not, and if he is wholly good, the only explanation could be that even a wrong free act of will is not really evil, that its freedom is a value which outweighs its wrongness, so that there would be a loss of value if God took away the wrongness and the freedom together. But this is utterly opposed to what theists say about sin in other contexts. The present solution of the problem of evil, then, can be maintained only in the form that God has made men so free that he *cannot* control their wills.

This leads us to what I call the Paradox of Omnipotence: can an omnipotent being make things which he cannot subsequently control? Or, what is practically equivalent to this, can an omnipotent being make rules which then bind himself? (These are practically equivalent because any such rules could be regarded as setting certain things beyond his control, and *vice versa*.) The second of these formulations is relevant to the suggestions that we have already met, that an omnipotent God creates the rules of logic or causal laws, and is then bound by them.

It is clear that this is a paradox: the questions cannot be answered satisfactorily either in the affirmative or in the negative. If we answer "Yes," it follows that if God actually makes things which he cannot control, or makes rules which bind himself, he is not omnipotent once he has made them: there are *then* things which he cannot do. But if we answer "No," we are immediately asserting that there are things which he cannot do, that is to say that he is already not omnipotent.

It cannot be replied that the question which sets this paradox is not a proper question. It would make perfectly good sense to say that a human mechanic has made a machine which he cannot control: if there is any difficulty about the question it lies in the notion of omnipotence itself.

This, incidentally, shows that although we have approached this paradox from the free-will theory, it is equally a problem for a theological determinist. No one thinks that machines have free will, yet they may well be beyond the control of their makers. The determinist might reply that anyone who makes anything determines its way of acting, and so determines its subsequent behavior: even the human mechanic does this by his *choice* of materials and structure for his machine, though he does not know all about either of these: the mechanic thus determines, though he may not foresee, his machine's actions. And since God is omniscient, and since his creation of things is total, he both determines and foresees the ways in which his creatures will act. We may grant this, but it is beside the point. The question is not whether God *originally* determined the future actions of his creatures, but whether he can *subsequently* control their actions, or whether he was able in his original creation to put things beyond his subsequent control. Even on determinist principles the answers "Yes" and "No" are equally irreconcilable with God's omnipotence.

Before suggesting a solution of this paradox, I would point out that there is a parallel Paradox of Sovereignty. Can a legal sovereign make a law restricting its own future legislative power? For example, could the British parliament make a law forbidding any future parliament to socialize banking, and also forbidding the future repeal of this law itself? Or could the British parliament, which was legally sovereign in Australia in, say, 1899, pass a valid law, or series of laws, which made it no longer sovereign in 1933? Again, neither the affirmative nor the negative answer is really satisfactory. If we were to answer "Yes," we should be admitting the validity of a law which, if it were actually made, would mean that parliament was no longer sovereign. If we were to answer "No," we should be admitting that there is a law, not logically absurd, which parliament cannot val-

idly make, that is, that parliament is not now a legal sovereign. This paradox can be solved in the following way. We should distinguish between first order laws, that is, laws governing the actions of individuals and bodies other than the legislature, and second order laws, that is, laws about laws, laws governing the actions of the legislature itself. Correspondingly, we should distinguish two orders of sovereignty, first order sovereignty (sovereignty [1]) which is unlimited authority to make first order laws, and second order sovereignty (sovereignty [2]) which is unlimited authority to make second order laws. If we say that parliament is sovereign we might mean that any parliament at any time has sovereignty (1), or we might mean that parliament has both sovereignty (1) and sovereignty (2) at present, but we cannot without contradiction mean both that the present parliament has sovereignty (2) and that every parliament at every time has sovereignty (1), for if the present parliament has sovereignty (2) it may use it to take away the sovereignty (1) of later parliaments. What the paradox shows is that we cannot ascribe to any continuing institution legal sovereignty in an inclusive sense.

The analogy between omnipotence and sovereignty shows that the paradox of omnipotence can be solved in a similar way. We must distinguish between first order omnipotence (omnipotence [1]), that is, unlimited power to act, and second order omnipotence (omnipotence [2]), that is, unlimited power to determine what powers to act things shall have. Then we could consistently say that God all the time has omnipotence (1), but if so no beings at any time have powers to act independently of God. Or we could say that God at one time had omnipotence (2), and used it to assign independent powers to act to certain things, so that God thereafter did not have omnipotence (1). But what the paradox shows is that we cannot consistently ascribe to any continuing being omnipotence in an inclusive sense.

An alternate solution of this paradox would be simply to deny that God is a continuing being, that any times can be assigned to his actions at all. But on this assumption (which also has difficulties of its own) no meaning can be given to the assertion that God made men with wills so free that he could not control them. The paradox of omnipotence can be avoided by putting God outside time, but the freewill solution of the problem of evil cannot be saved in this way, and equally it remains impossible to hold that an omnipotent God *binds himself* by causal or logical laws.

CONCLUSION

Of the proposed solutions of the problem of evil which we have examined, none has stood up to criticism. There may be other solutions which require examination, but this study strongly suggests that there is no valid solution of the problem which does not modify at least one of the constituent propositions in a way which would seriously affect the essential core of the theistic position.

Quite apart from the problem of evil, the paradox of omnipotence has shown that God's omnipotence must in any case be restricted in one way or another, that unqualified omnipotence cannot be ascribed to any being that continues through time. And if God and his actions are not in time, can omnipotence, or power of any sort, be meaningfully ascribed to him?

The Magnitude, Duration, and Distribution of Evil
A Theodicy

PETER VAN INWAGEN

Peter Van Inwagen, author of many articles and several books, teaches philosophy at the University of Notre Dame.

. . . A young mother dies of leukemia. A school bus full of children is crushed by a landslide. A child is born without limbs. A wise and good man in the prime of life suffers brain damage and spends the remaining thirty years of his life in a coma. I do not know of a good general term for such events. Journalists often call them tragedies. But this word is properly applied only to events that are in some sense meaningful, and I know of no reason to think that such events *always* have a "meaning." I will call them *horrors*.

Why do horrors happen? I want to suggest that horrors happen for no reason at all, that when, e.g., a child is born without limbs, the only answer to the question, "Why did that happen?" is "There is no reason or explanation; it just happened." Or, at any rate, I want to suggest that this is sometimes the case. (Whether some horrors are brought about by God for special purposes is a question I shall not attempt to answer. If *some* horrors are brought about by God, and thus have a purpose and a meaning known to God but not to us, I have no opinion as to what percentage of the whole they might constitute.) But are not *all* events ordered by God, and must not *all* events therefore have some sort of meaning? Christians and other theists are, I believe, committed to the truth of the following proposition:

> God is the maker of all things, visible and invisible (other than Himself); He sustains all created things in existence from moment to moment, and continuously supplies them with their causal powers.

In a previous paper, in which I presented an account of God's action in the world, I argued that this proposition is consistent with the proposition that there are events having the following feature: If one asks concerning one of these events, "Why did that hap-

From *Philosophical Topics,* vol. 16, 1988. Used by permission.

pen?," the only answer to one's question is, "There is no reason or explanation for that event. God did not cause it to happen or intend it to happen. It is not a part of God's plan for the world or anyone else's plan for anything. It just happened, and that's all there is to say about it." (Let us say of such events that they are *due to chance*.) . . . Now to say that there is no answer to the question, Why did X occur? is not to say that there is no answer to such questions as Why did God allow X to occur? or Why did God not prevent X? I ended the earlier paper with these words:

> If what I have said is true, it yields a moral for students of the Problem of Evil: Do not attempt any solution to this problem that entails that every particular evil has a purpose, or that, with respect to every individual misfortune, or every devastating earthquake, or every disease, God has some special reason for allowing it. Concentrate rather on the problem of what sort of reasons a loving and providential God might have for allowing His creatures to live in a world in which many of the evils that happen to them happen to them for no reason at all.

I will now take my own advice and present my solution to this problem. God's reason for allowing His creatures to live in such a world is that their living in such a world is a natural consequence of their separation from Him. Consider again our earlier sketchy account of natural evil: in separating ourselves from God, we have somehow deprived ourselves of our primordial defenses against such potentially destructive things as tigers and landslides and tornadoes. But if, by our rebellion and folly, we have allowed the destructive potential of these things to become actual, how shall we expect the effects of that actuality to be distributed? At random, surely? That is, with no correlation between these things and the innocence or wickedness of the people they impinge on —since the operations of these things in no way depend upon the moral qualities of the people they interact with? In fact, there is little correlation between the manner in which these things operate and *any* factor under human control (although civilization does what it can to try to induce correlations of this type).

Suppose that a certain man chooses, of his own free will, to stand at spot *x* at time *t*. His arrival at that place at that time converges with the arrival of an avalanche. Let us suppose that God did not miraculously cause the avalanche, and that He did not "move" the man to be at that place at that time. And let us also suppose that neither the man's arrival at *x* at *t* nor the avalanche's arrival at *x* at *t* was determined by the laws of nature and the state of the world, say, one hundred years earlier. (This is a plausible assumption on scientific grounds. Quantum mechanics has the following astounding consequence: Imagine a billiard table, one not subject to external influence other than constant, uniform gravitation, on which there are rolling perfectly spherical and perfectly elastic balls that—somehow—do not lose energy to the walls of the table in collision or to its surface in friction; the position of the balls a minute or so in the future is not even approximately determined by the laws of nature and the present physical state of the balls. This example strongly suggests that the precise moment at which an avalanche occurs is not determined a hundred years in advance.)

The man's death in the avalanche would seem to be in every sense due to chance, even though (the theist must suppose) God knew in advance that he would be killed by the avalanche and could have prevented it. In fact, the theist must suppose that, during the course of that event, God held all of the particles that composed the man and the moving mass of snow and ice in existence and continuously decreed the operation of the laws of nature by which those particles interacted with one another.

Why did God not miraculously save the man? We have seen the answer to this question already. He might very well have. Perhaps He sometimes does miraculously save people in such situations. But if He *always* did so, He would be a deceiver. If He always saved people about to be destroyed by a chance encounter with a violent phenomenon of nature, He would engender an illusion with the following propositional content:

> It is possible for human beings to live apart from God and not be subject to destruction by chance.

To live under this illusion would be a bad thing in itself, but, more importantly, it would have harmful effects. This illusion would be, as it were, a tributary of illusion feeding into a great river of illusion whose content was, "Human beings can live successfully in separation from God."

In our current state of separation from God, we are continually blundering into "lines of causation" (the descent of an avalanche; the evolution of the AIDS virus; the building up of tension along a geological fault) that perhaps have no purpose at all and certainly have no purpose in relation to us. (It is simply a part of the mechanics of nature that intrinsically harmless but potentially destructive things like avalanches or viruses or earthquakes should exist. As I remarked above, if you think that you can design a world that does not contain such things and which can also serve as a home for human beings, you have never tried. Such things are a part of God's design in the sense that the ticking sound made by a clock is a part of the watchmaker's design: not intended, necessitated by what *is* intended, foreseen, and allowed for. What is not in any sense a part of God's design is *this* avalanche, *this* virus, and *this* earthquake. These are—sometimes, at any rate—due to chance.) If we had never separated ourselves from God, we should have been able to avoid such blunders. No longer to be able to avoid them is a natural consequence of the Fall. It is as if God had had—for some purpose —to cover the earth with a certain number of deep pits. These pits (we may stipulate) were not dangerous, since they could easily be seen and avoided; but we frustrated God's Providence in this matter by deliberately making ourselves blind; and now we complain that some of us—quite often the good and wise and innocent—fall into the pits. God's response to this complaint, according to the theodicy I propose, is this: "You are the ones who made yourselves blind. If you make yourselves blind, some of you will fall into the pits, and, moreover, *who* falls into a pit and *when* will be wholly a matter of chance. Goodness and wisdom and innocence have no bearing on this matter. That's part of what being blind means." Or, rather, this is what we might imagine God's response to be in our simple "world of pits." In the real world, we should have to picture God as saying something more complex, something like the following.

"Even I can't make a world that is suitable for human beings but which contains no phenomena that would harm human beings *if* they were in the wrong

place at the wrong time. The reasons for this are complicated, but they turn on the fact that the molecular bonds that hold you human beings together must be weaker by many orders of magnitude than the disruptive potential of the surges of energy that must happen here and there in a structurally and nomologically coherent world [i.e., a world of stable laws] complex enough to contain you. My Providence dealt with this fact by endowing you with the power never to be in the wrong place at the wrong time, a power you lost when you ruined yourselves by turning away from Me. That is why horrors happen to some of you: you simply blunder into things. If I were to protect you from the consequences of your blindness by guiding you away from potentially destructive phenomena by an unending series of miracles—and I remind you that for all you know I *sometimes* do guide you out of harm's way—I should be deceiving you about the meaning of your separation from Me and seriously weakening the only motivation you have for returning to Me."

We may add the following proposition to our theodicy:

> Among the natural consequences of the Fall is the following evil state of affairs: Horrors happen to people without any relation to desert. They happen simply as a matter of chance. It is a part of God's plan of Atonement that we realize that a natural consequence of our living to ourselves is our living in a world that has that feature.

This completes my presentation of the theodicy I propose. I have fleshed out the well-known story about how evil entered the world through the abuse of the divine gift of free will; I have fleshed it out in such a way as to provide plausible—at any rate, I find them plausible—answers to four pointed questions about the magnitude, duration, and distribution of evil. But in a sense it is not possible effectively to present a theodicy in a single piece of work by one author. Various elements in any proposed theodicy are bound to be thought false or felt to be implausible by some people. An essential part of presenting a theodicy is meeting the objections of those who have difficulties with it, or perhaps refining it in the face of their objections. A theodicy is a dialectical enterprise. The present paper, therefore, is best regarded as the "opening move" in such an enterprise, rather than a finished product. In closing, I wish to answer one objection to the theodicy I have presented, an objection that has been raised in conversation and correspondence by Eleonore Stump. Professor Stump objects that the theodicy I have presented represents God as allowing people to suffer misfortunes that do not (even in the long run) benefit *them*. An example may make the point of this objection clear. Suppose that God allows a horrible, disfiguring accident to happen to Alice (a true accident, an event due entirely to chance, but one that God foresaw and could have prevented). And suppose that the only good that is brought out of this accident is embodied in the following state of affairs and certain of its remote consequences: The accident, together with an enormous number of similar horrors, causes various people to realize that one feature of a world in which human beings live to themselves is that in such a world horrors happen to people for no reason at all. But suppose that Alice herself did not need to realize this; suppose that she was already fully aware of this consequence of separation from God. And suppose that many of the people who do come to realize this partly as the result of Alice's accident manage (owing mainly to luck) to get through life without anything very bad happening to them. According to Stump, these suppositions —and it is pretty certain that there *are* cases like this if our theodicy is correct—represent God as violating the following moral principle:

> It is wrong to allow something bad to happen to X—without X's permission—in order to secure some benefit for others (and no benefit for X).

I do not find this principle particularly appealing— not as a *universal* moral principle, one that is supposed to apply with equal right to all possible moral agents in all possible circumstances. The circumstances in which it seems most doubtful are these: The agent is in a position of lawful authority over both X and the "others" and is responsible for their welfare (consider, for example, a mother and her children or the state and its citizens); the good to be gained by the "others" is considerably greater than the evil suffered by X; there is no way in which the good for the "others" can be achieved except by allowing the evil in question to happen to X or to someone else no more deserving of it than X; the agent knows these things to be true. By way of example, we might consider cases of quarantine or of the right of eminent domain. Is it not morally permissible for the state to restrict my freedom of movement and action if I am the carrier of a contagious disease, or to force me to move if my house stands in the way of a desperately needed irrigation canal (one that will not benefit *me* in any way)? It is not to the point to protest that these cases are not much like cases involving an omnipotent God, who can cure diseases or provide water by simple fiat. They are counterexamples to the above moral principle, and, therefore, that moral principle is false. What is required of anyone who alleges that the theodicy I have proposed represents God as violating some (correct) moral principle is a careful statement of that moral principle. When we have examined that carefully stated moral principle, and have satisfied ourselves that it is without counterexample, we can proceed with the argument.

FAITH AND REASON

The Wager

BLAISE PASCAL

French philosopher and mathematician Blaise Pascal (1623–1662)—famous today primarily as a mathematician who made substantial contributions to probability theory, number theory and geometry—was also a theologian, scientist, and inventor.

. . . We know neither the existence nor the nature of God, because He has neither extension nor limits.

But by faith we know His existence; in glory we shall know His nature. Now, I have already shown that we may well know the existence of a thing, without knowing its nature.

Let us now speak according to natural lights.

If there is a God, He is infinitely incomprehensible, since, having neither parts nor limits, He has no affinity to us. We are then incapable of knowing either what He is or if He is. This being so, who will dare to undertake the decision of the question? Not we, who have no affinity to Him.

Who then will blame Christians for not being able to give a reason for their belief, since they profess a religion for which they cannot give a reason? They declare, in expounding it to the world, that it is a foolishness, *stultitiam;* and then you complain that they do not prove it! If they proved it, they would not keep their words; it is in lacking proofs, that they are not lacking in sense. "Yes, but although this excuses those who offer it as such, and takes away from them the blame of putting it forward without reason, it does not excuse those who receive it." Let us then examine this point, and say, "God is, or He is not." But to which side shall we incline? Reason can decide nothing here. There is an infinite chaos which separates us. A game is being played at the extremity of this infinite distance where heads or tails will turn up. What will you wager? According to reason, you can do neither the one thing nor the other; according to reason, you can defend neither of the propositions.

Do not then reprove for error those who have made a choice; for you know nothing about it. "No, but I blame them for having made, not this choice, but a choice; for again both he who chooses heads and he who chooses tails are equally at fault, they are both in the wrong. The true courses is not to wager at all."

—Yes; but you must wager. It is not optional. You are embarked. Which will you choose then; Let us see. Since you must chose, let us see which interests you least. You have two things to lose, the true and the good; and two things to stake, your reason and your will, your knowledge and your happiness; and your nature has two things to shun, error and misery. Your reason is no more shocked in choosing one rather than the other, since you must of necessity choose. This is one point settled. But your happiness? Let us weigh the gain and the loss in wagering that God is. Let us estimate these two chances. If you gain, you gain all; if you lose, you lose nothing. Wager then without hesitation that He is.—"That is very fine. Yes, I must wager; but I may perhaps wager too much."—Let us see. Since there is an equal risk of gain and of loss, if you had only to gain two lives, instead of one, you might still wager. But if there were three lives to gain, you would have to play (since you are under the necessity of playing), and you would be imprudent, when you are forced to

From *Thoughts,* translated by W. F. Trotter (New York: P. F. Collier & Son, 1910).

play, not to chance your life to gain three at a game where there is an equal risk of loss and gain. But there is an eternity of life and happiness. And this being so, if there were an infinity of chances, of which one only would be for you, you would still be right in wagering one to win two, and you would act stupidly, being obliged to play, by refusing to stake one life against three at a game in which out of an infinity of chances there is one for you, if there were an infinity of an infinitely happy life to gain. But there is here an infinity of an infinitely happy life to gain, a chance of gain against a finite number of chances of loss, and what you stake is finite. It is all divided; wherever the infinite is and there is not an infinity of chances of loss against that of gain, there is no time to hesitate, you must give all. And thus, when one is forced to play, he must renounce reason to preserve his life, rather than risk it for infinite gain, as likely to happen as the loss of nothingness.

For it is no use to say it is uncertain if we will gain, and it is certain that we risk, and that the infinite distance between the *certainty* of what is staked and the *uncertainty* of what will be gained, equals the finite good which is certainly staked against the uncertain infinite. It is not so, as every player stakes a certainty to gain an uncertainty, and yet he stakes a finite certainty to gain a finite uncertainty, without transgressing against reason. There is not an infinite distance between the certainty staked and the uncertainty of the gain; that is untrue. In truth, there is an infinity between the certainty of gain and the certainty of loss. But the uncertainty of the gain is proportioned to the certainty of the stake according to the proportion of the chances of gain and loss. Hence it comes that, if there are as many risks on one side as on the other, the course is to play even; and then the certainty of the stake is equal to the uncertainty of the gain, so far is it from the fact that there is an infinite distance between them. And so our proposition is of infinite force, when there is the finite to stake in a game where there are equal risks of gain and of loss, and the infinite to gain. This is demonstrable; and if men are capable of any truths, this is one.

"I confess it, I admit it. But still is there no means of seeing the faces of the cards?"—Yes, Scripture and the rest, &c.—"Yes, but I have my hands tied and my mouth closed; I am forced to wager, and am not free. I am not released, and am so made that I cannot believe. What then would you have me do?"

"True. But at least learn your inability to believe, since reason brings you to this, and yet you cannot believe. Endeavour then to convince yourself, not by increase of proofs of God, but by the abatement of your passions. You would like to attain faith, and do not know the way; you would like to cure yourself of unbelief, and ask the remedy for it. Learn of those who have been bound like you, and who now stake all their possessions. These are people who know the way which you would follow, and who are cured of an ill of which you would be cured. Follow the way by which they began; by acting as if they believe, taking the holy water, having masses said, &c. Even this will naturally make you believe, and deaden your acuteness.—"But this is what I am afraid of."—And why? What have you to lose?

But to show you that this leads you there, it is this which will lessen the passions, which are your stumbling-blocks.

The Ethics of Belief

W. K. CLIFFORD

W. K. Clifford (1845–1879), mathematician and philosopher, was a Catholic during his student days at Trinity College, Cambridge, but later became an agnostic and turned against religion. His reflections on Charles Darwin's new theory of evolution helped change his mind.

A shipowner was about to send to sea an emigrant ship. He knew that she was old, and not overwell built at the first; that she had seen many seas and climes, and often had needed repairs. Doubts had been suggested to him that possibly she was not seaworthy. These doubts preyed upon his mind and made him unhappy; he thought that perhaps he ought to have her thoroughly overhauled and refitted, even though this should put him to great expense. Before the ship sailed, however, he succeeded in overcoming these melancholy reflections. He said to himself that she had gone safely through so many voyages and weathered so many storms that it was idle to suppose she would not come safely home from this trip also. He would put his trust in Providence, which could hardly fail to protect all these unhappy families that were leaving their fatherland to seek for better times elsewhere. He would dismiss from his mind all ungenerous suspicions about the honesty of builders and contractors. In such ways he acquired a sincere and comfortable conviction that his vessel was thoroughly safe and seaworthy; he watched her departure with a light heart, and benevolent wishes for the success of the exiles in their strange new home that was to be; and he got his insurance money when she went down in mid-ocean and told no tales.

What shall we say of him? Surely this, that he was verily guilty of the death of those men. It is admitted that he did sincerely believe in the soundness of his ship; but the sincerity of his conviction can in no wise help him, because *he had no right to believe on such evidence as was before him.* He had acquired his belief not by honestly earning it in patient investigation, but by stifling his doubts. And although in the end he may have felt so sure about it that he could

not think otherwise, yet inasmuch as he had knowingly and willingly worked himself into that frame of mind, he must be held responsible for it.

Let us alter the case a little, and suppose that the ship was not unsound after all; that she made her voyage safely, and many others after it. Will that diminish the guilt of her owner? Not one jot. When an action is once done, it is right or wrong forever; no accidental failure of its good or evil fruits can possibly alter that. The man would not have been innocent, he would only have been not found out. The question of right or wrong has to do with the origin of his belief, not the matter of it; not what it was, but how he got it; not whether it turned out to be true or false, but whether he had a right to believe on such evidence as was before him.

There was once an island in which some of the inhabitants professed a religion teaching neither the doctrine of original sin nor that of eternal punishment. A suspicion got abroad that the professors of this religion had made use of unfair means to get their doctrines taught to children. They were accused of wresting the laws of their country in such a way as to remove children from the care of their natural and legal guardians; and even of stealing them away and keeping them concealed from their friends and relatives. A certain number of men formed themselves into a society for the purpose of agitating the public about this matter. They published grave accusations against individual citizens of the highest position and character, and did all in their power to injure those citizens in the exercise of their professions. So great was the noise they made, that a Commission was appointed to investigate the facts; but after the Commission had carefully inquired into all the evidence that could be got, it appeared that the accused were innocent. Not only had they been accused on insufficient evidence, but

---

From *Lectures and Essays* (London: Macmillan, 1879).

the evidence of their innocence was such as the agitators might easily have obtained, if they had attempted a fair inquiry. After these disclosures the inhabitants of that country looked upon the members of the agitating society, not only as persons whose judgment was to be distrusted, but also as no longer to be counted honorable men. For although they had sincerely and conscientiously believed in the charges they had made, *yet they had no right to believe on such evidence as was before them.* Their sincere convictions, instead of being honestly earned by patient inquiring, were stolen by listening to the voice of prejudice and passion.

Let us vary this case also, and suppose, other things remaining as before, that a still more accurate investigation proved the accused to have been really guilty. Would this make any difference in the guilt of the accusers? Clearly not; the question is not whether their belief was true or false, but whether they entertained it on wrong grounds. They would no doubt say, "Now you see that we were right after all; next time perhaps you will believe us." And they might be believed, but they would not thereby become honorable men. They would not be innocent, they would only be not found out. Every one of them, if he chose to examine himself *in foro conscientiae,* would know that he had acquired and nourished a belief, when he had no right to believe on such evidence as was before him; and therein he would know that he had done a wrong thing.

It may be said, however, that in both of these supposed cases it is not the belief which is judged to be wrong, but the action followed upon it. The shipowner might say, "I am perfectly certain that my ship is sound, but still I feel it my duty to have her examined, before trusting the lives of so many people to her." And it might be said to the agitator, "However convinced you were of the justice of your cause and the truth of your convictions, you ought not to have made public attack upon any man's character until you had examined the evidence on both sides with the utmost patience and care."

In the first place, let us admit that, so far as it goes, this view of the case is right and necessary; right, because even when a man's belief is so fixed that he cannot think otherwise, he still has a choice in regard to the action suggested by it, and so cannot escape the duty of investigating on the ground of the strength of his convictions; and necessary, because those who are not yet capable of controlling their feelings and thought must have a plain rule dealing with overt acts.

But this being premised as necessary, it becomes clear that it is not sufficient, and that our previous judgment is required to supplement it. For it is not possible so to sever the belief from the action it suggests as to condemn the one without condemning the other. No man holding a strong belief on one side of a question, or even wishing to hold a belief on one side, can investigate it with such fairness and completeness as if he were really in doubt and unbiased; so that the existence of a belief not founded on fair inquiry unfits a man for the performance of this necessary duty.

Nor is that truly a belief at all which has not some influence upon the actions of him who holds it. He who truly believes that which prompts him to an action has looked upon the action to lust after it, he has committed it already in his heart. If a belief is not realized immediately in open deeds, it is stored up for the guidance of the future. It goes to make a part of that aggregate of beliefs which is the link between sensation and action at every moment of all our lives, and which is so organized and compacted together that no part of it can be isolated from the rest, but every new addition modifies the structure of the whole. No real belief, however trifling and fragmentary it may seem, is ever truly insignificant; it prepares us to receive more of its like, confirms those which resembled it before, and weakens others; and so gradually it lays a stealthy train in our inmost thoughts, which may some day explode into overt action, and leave its stamp upon our character forever.

And no one man's belief is in any case a private matter which concerns himself alone. Our lives are guided by that general conception of the course of things which has been created by society for social purposes. Our words, our phrases, our forms and processes and modes of thought are common property, fashioned and perfected from age to age; an heirloom which every succeeding generation inherits as a previous deposit and a sacred trust to be handed on to the next one, not unchanged but enlarged and purified, with some clear marks of its proper handiwork. Into this, for good or ill, is woven every belief of every man who has speech of his fellows. An awful privilege, and an awful responsibility, that we should help to create the world in which posterity will live.

In the two supposed cases which have been considered, it has been judged wrong to believe on insufficient evidence, or to nourish belief by suppressing doubts and avoiding investigation. The reason of this judgment is not far to seek; it is that in both these cases the belief held by one man was of great importance to other men. But for as much as no belief held by one man, however seemingly trivial the belief, and however obscure the believer, is ever actually insignificant or without its effect on the fate of mankind, we have no choice but to extend our judgment to all cases of belief whatever. Belief, that sacred faculty which prompts the decisions of our will, and knits into harmonious working all the compacted energies of our being, is ours not for ourselves but for humanity. It is rightly used on truths which have been established by long experience and waiting toil, and which have stood in the fierce light of free and fearless questioning. Then it helps to bind men together, and to strengthen and direct their common action. It is desecrated when given to unproved and unquestioned statements, for the solace and private pleasure of the believer; to add a tinsel splendor to the plain straight road of our life and display a bright mirage beyond it; or even to drown the common sorrows of our kind by a self-deception which allows them not only to cast down, but also to degrade us. Whoso would deserve well of his fellows in this matter will guard the purity of his belief with a very fanaticism of jealous care, lest at any time it should rest on an unworthy object, and catch a stain which can never be wiped away.

It is not only the leader of men, statesman, philosopher, or poet, that owes this bounden duty to mankind. Every rustic who delivers in the village alehouse his slow, infrequent sentences, may help to kill or keep alive the fatal superstitions which clog his race. Every hardworked wife of an artisan may transmit to her children beliefs which shall knit society together, or rend it in pieces. No simplicity of mind, no obscurity of station, can escape the universal duty of questioning all that we believe.

It is true that this duty is a hard one, and the doubt which comes out of it is often a very bitter thing. It leaves us bare and powerless where we thought that we were safe and strong. To know all about anything is to know how to deal with it under all circumstances. We feel much happier and more secure when we think we know precisely what to do, no matter what happens, than when we have lost our way and do not know where to turn. And if we have supposed ourselves to know all about anything, and to be capable of doing what is fit in regard to it, we naturally do not like to find that we are really ignorant and powerless, that we have to begin again at the beginning, and try to learn what the thing is and how it is to be dealt with—if indeed anything can be learned about it. It is the sense of power attached to a sense of knowledge that makes men desirous of believing, and afraid of doubting.

This sense of power is the highest and best of pleasures when the belief on which it is founded is true belief, and has been fairly earned by investigation. For then we may justly feel that it is common property, and holds good for others as well as for ourselves. Then we may be glad, not that *I* have learned secrets by which I am safer and stronger, but that *we men* have got mastery over more of the world; and we shall be strong, not for ourselves, but in the name of Man and in his strength. But if the belief has been accepted on insufficient evidence, the pleasure is a stolen one. Not only does it deceive ourselves by giving us a sense of power which we do not really possess, but it is sinful, because it is stolen in defiance of our duty to mankind. That duty is to guard ourselves from such beliefs as from a pestilence, which may shortly master our own body and then spread to the rest of the town. What would be thought of one who, for the sake of a sweet fruit, should deliberately run the risk of bringing a plague upon his family and his neighbors?

And, as in other such cases, it is not the risk only which has to be considered; for a bad action is always bad at the time when it is done, no matter what happens afterwards. Every time we let ourselves believe for unworthy reasons, we weaken our powers of self-control, of doubting, of judicially and fairly weighing evidence. We all suffer severely enough from the maintenance and support of false beliefs and the fatally wrong actions which they lead to, and the evil born when once such belief is entertained is great and wide. But a greater and wider evil arises when the credulous character is maintained and supported, when a habit of believing for unworthy reasons is fostered and made permanent. If I steal money from any person, there may be no harm done by the mere transfer of possession; he may not feel the loss, or it may prevent him from using the money badly. But I cannot help doing this great wrong towards Man, that I make myself dishonest. What hurts society is not that it should lose its property, but that it should become a den of thieves; for then it must cease to be society. This is why we ought not to do evil that good may come; for at any rate this great evil has come, that we have done evil and are made wicked thereby. In like manner, if I let myself believe anything on insufficient evidence, there may be no great harm done by the mere belief; it may be true after all, or I may never have occasion to exhibit it in outward acts. But I cannot help doing this great wrong toward Man, that I make myself credulous. The danger to society is not merely that it should believe wrong things, though that is great enough; but that it should become credulous, and lose the habit of testing things and inquiring into them; for then it must sink back into savagery.

The harm which is done by credulity in a man is not confined to the fostering of a credulous character in others, and consequent support of false beliefs. Habitual want of care about which I believe leads to habitual want of care in others about the truth of what is told to me. Men speak the truth to one another when each reveres the truth in his own mind and in the other's mind; but how shall my friend revere the truth in my mind when I myself am careless about it, when I believe things because I want to believe them, and because they are comforting and pleasant? Will he not learn to cry, "Peace," to me, when there is no peace? By such a course I shall surround myself with a thick atmosphere of falsehood and fraud, and in that I must live. It may

matter little to me, in my cloud-castle of sweet illusions and darling lies; but it matters much to Man that I have made my neighbors ready to deceive. The credulous man is father to the liar and the cheat; he lives in the bosom of this his family, and it is no marvel if he should become even as they are. So closely are our duties knit together, that whoso shall keep the whole law, and yet offend in one point, he is guilty of all.

To sum up: it is wrong always, everywhere, and for anyone, to believe anything upon insufficient evidence.

If a man, holding a belief which he was taught in childhood or persuaded of afterwards, keeps down and pushes away any doubts which arise about it in his mind, purposely avoids the reading of books and the company of men that call in question or discuss it, and regards as impious those questions which cannot easily be asked without disturbing it—the life of that man is one long sin against mankind.

If this judgment seems harsh when applied to those simple souls who have never known better, who have been brought up from the cradle with a horror of doubt, and taught that their eternal welfare depends on what they believe, then it leads to the very serious question. Who hath made Israel to sin? . . .

Inquiry into the evidence of a doctrine is not to be made once for all, and then taken as finally settled. It is never lawful to stifle a doubt; for either it can be honestly answered by means of the inquiry already made, or else it proves that the inquiry was not complete.

"But," says one, "I am a busy man; I have no time for the long course of study which would be necessary to make me in any degree a competent judge of certain questions, or even able to understand the nature of the arguments." Then he would have no time to believe. . . .

The Will to Believe

WILLIAM JAMES

William James (1842–1910), brother of novelist Henry James, was born in New York City. He published many influential works of philosophy and psychology and was one of the founders of pragmatism.

. . . Let us give the name of *hypothesis* to anything that may be proposed to our belief; and just as the electricians speak of live and dead wires, let us speak of any hypothesis as either *live* or *dead*. A live hypothesis is one which appeals as a real possibility to him to whom it is proposed. If I ask you to believe in the Mahdi, the notion makes no electric connection with your nature,—it refuses to scintillate with any credibility at all. As an hypothesis it is completely dead. To an Arab, however (even if he be not one of the Mahdi's followers), the hypothesis is among the mind's possibilities: it is alive. This shows that deadness and liveness in an hypothesis are not intrinsic properties, but relations to the individual thinker. They are measured by his willingness to act. The maximum of liveness in an hypothesis means willingness to act irrevocably. Practically, that means belief; but there is some believing tendency wherever there is willingness to act at all.

Next, let us call the decision between two hypotheses an *option*. Options may be of several kinds. They may be—1, *living* or *dead;* 2, *forced* or *avoidable;* 3, *momentous* or *trivial;* and for our purpose we may call an option a *genuine* option when it is of the forced, living, and momentous kind.

1. A living option is one in which both hypotheses are live ones. If I say to you: "Be a theosophist or be a Mohammedan," it is probably a dead option, because for you neither hypothesis is likely to be alive. But if I say, "Be an agnostic or be a Christian," it is otherwise: trained as you are, each hypothesis makes some appeal, however small, to your belief.

2. Next, if I say to you: "Choose between going out with your umbrella or without it," I do not offer you a genuine option, for it is not forced. You can easily avoid it by not going out at all. Similarly, if I say, "Either love me or hate me," "Either call my theory true or call it false," your option is avoidable. You may remain indifferent to me, neither loving nor hating, and you may decline to offer any judgment as to my theory. But if I say, "Either accept this truth or go without it," I put on you a forced option, for there is no standing place outside of the alternative. Every dilemma based on a complete logical disjunction, with no possibility of not choosing, is an option of this forced kind. . . .

The thesis I defend is, briefly stated, this: *Our passional nature not only lawfully may, but must, decide an option between propositions, whenever it is a genuine option that cannot by its nature be decided on intellectual grounds; for to say, under such circumstances, "Do not decide, but leave the question open," is itself a passional decision,—just like deciding yes or no,—and is attended with the same risk of losing the truth. . . .*

Wherever the option between losing truth and gaining it is not momentous, we can throw the chance of *gaining truth* away, and at any rate save ourselves from any chance of *believing falsehood*, by not making up our minds at all till objective evidence has come. In scientific questions, this is almost always the case; and even in human affairs in general, the need of acting is seldom so urgent that a false belief to act on is better than no belief at all. Law courts, indeed, have to decide on the best evidence attainable for the moment, because a judge's duty is to make law as well as to ascertain it, and (as a learned judge once said to me) few cases are worth spending much time over: the great thing is to have them decided on *any* acceptable principle, and got out of the way. But in our dealings with objective nature we obviously are recorders, not makers, of the truth; and decisions for the mere sake of deciding

From "The Will to Believe," an address to the Philosophical Clubs of Yale and Brown Universities. First published in *New World*, 1896.

promptly and getting on to the next business would be wholly out of place. Throughout the breadth of physical nature facts are what they are quite independently of us, and seldom is there any such hurry about them that the risks of being duped by believing a premature theory need be faced. The questions here are always trivial options, the hypotheses are hardly living (at any rate not living for us spectators), the choice between believing truth or falsehood is seldom forced. The attitude of sceptical balance is therefore the absolutely wise one if we would escape mistakes. What difference, indeed, does it make to most of us whether we have or have not a theory of the Röntgen rays, whether we believe or not in mind-stuff, or have a conviction about the causality of conscious states? It makes no difference. Such options are not forced on us. On every account it is better not to make them, but still keep weighing reasons *pro et contra* with an indifferent hand. . . .

. . . Religions differ so much in their accidents that in discussing the religious question we must make it very generic and broad. What then do we now mean by the religious hypothesis? Science says things are; morality says some things are better than other things; and religion says essentially two things.

First, she says that the best things are the more eternal things, the overlapping things, the things in the universe that throw the last stone, so to speak, and say the final word. "Perfection is eternal,"—this phrase of Charles Secrétan seems a good way of putting this first affirmation of religion, an affirmation which obviously cannot yet be verified scientifically at all.

The second affirmation of religion is that we are better off even now if we believe her first affirmation to be true.

Now, let us consider what the logical elements of this situation are *in case the religious hypothesis in both its branches be really true.* (Of course, we must admit that possibility at the outset. If we are to discuss the question at all, it must involve a living option. If for any of you religion be a hypothesis that cannot, by any living possibility be true, then you need go no farther. I speak to the "saving remnant" alone.) So proceeding, we see, first that religion offers itself as a *momentous* option. We are supposed to gain, even now, by our belief, and to lose by our nonbelief,

a certain vital good. Secondly, religion is a *forced* option, so far as that good goes. We cannot escape the issue by remaining sceptical and waiting for more light, because, although we do avoid error in that way *if religion be untrue,* we lose the good, *if it be true,* just as certainly as if we positively chose to disbelieve. It is as if a man should hesitate indefinitely to ask a certain woman to marry him because he was not perfectly sure that she would prove an angel after he brought her home. Would he not cut himself off from that particular angel-possibility as decisively as if he went and married some one else? Scepticism, then, is not avoidance of option; it is option of a certain particular kind of risk. *Better risk loss of trust than chance of error,*—that is your faithvetoer's exact position. He is actively playing his stake as much as the believer is; he is backing the field against the religious hypothesis, just as the believer is backing the religious hypothesis against the field. To preach scepticism to us as a duty until 'sufficient evidence' for religion can be found, is tantamount therefore to telling us, when in presence of the religious hypothesis, that to yield to our fear of its being error is wiser and better than to yield to our hope that it may be true. It is not intellect against all passions, then; it is only intellect with one passion laying down its law. And by what, forsooth, is the supreme wisdom of this passion warranted? Dupery for dupery, what proof is there that dupery through hope is so much worse than dupery through fear? I, for one, can see no proof; and I simply refuse obedience to the scientist's command to imitate his kind of option, in a case where my own stake is important enough to give me the right to choose my own form of risk. If religion be true and the evidence for it be still insufficient, I do not wish, by putting our extinguisher upon my nature (which feels to me as if it had after all some business in this matter), to forfeit my sole chance in life of getting upon the winning side,— that chance depending, of course, on my willingness to run the risk of acting as if my passional need of taking the world religiously might be prophetic and right.

All this is on the supposition that it really may be prophetic and right, and that, even to us who are discussing the matter, religion is a live hypothesis which may be true. Now, to most of us religion comes in a still further way that makes a veto on our active faith even more illogical. The more perfect and more eternal aspect of the universe is represented in our religion as having personal form. The universe is no longer a mere *It* to us, but a *Thou,* if we are religious; and any relation that may be possible from person to person might be possible here. For instance, although in one sense we are passive portions of the universe, in another we show a curious autonomy, as if we were small active centres on our own account. We feel, too, as if the appeal of religion to us were made to our own active goodwill, as if evidence might be forever withheld from us unless we met the hypothesis half-way. To take a trivial illustration: just as a man who in a company of gentlemen made no advances, asked a warrant for every concession, and believed no one's word without proof, would cut himself off by such churlishness from all the social rewards that a more trusting spirit would earn,—so here, one who should shut himself up in snarling logicality and try to make the gods extort his recognition willy-nilly, or not get it at all, might cut himself off forever from his only opportunity of making the gods' acquaintance. This feeling, forced on us we know not whence, that by obstinately believing that there are gods (although not to do so would be so easy both for our logic and our life) we are doing the universe the deepest service we can, seems part of the living essence of the religious hypothesis. If the hypothesis *were* true in all its parts, including this one, then pure intellectualism, with its veto on our making willing advances, would be an absurdity; and some participation of our sympathetic nature would be logically required. I, therefore, for one, cannot see my way to accepting the agnostic rules for truthseeking, or wilfully agree to keep my willing nature out of the game. I cannot do so for this plain reason, that *a rule of thinking which would absolutely prevent me from acknowledging certain kinds of truth if those kinds of truth were really there, would be an irrational rule.* That for me is the long and short of the formal logic of the situation, no matter what the kinds of truth might materially be.

I confess I do not see how this logic can be es-

caped. But sad experiences make me fear that some of you may still shrink from radically saying with me, *in abstracto,* that we have the right to believe at our own risk any hypothesis that is live enough to tempt our will. I suspect, however, that if this is so, it is because you have got away from the abstract logical point of view altogether, and are thinking (perhaps without realizing it) of some particular religious hypothesis which for you is dead. The freedom to "believe what we will" you apply to the case of some patent superstition; and the faith you think of is the faith defined by the schoolboy when he said, "Faith is when you believe something that you know ain't true." I can only repeat that this is misapprehension. *In concreto,* the freedom to believe can only cover living options which the intellect of the individual cannot by itself resolve; and living options never seem absurdities to him who has them to consider. When I look at the religious question as it really puts itself to concrete men, and when I think of all the possibilities which both practically and theoretically it involves, then this command that we shall put a stopper on our heart, instincts, and courage, and *wait*—acting of course meanwhile more or less as if religion were *not* true—till doomsday, or till such time as our intellect and senses working together may have raked in evidence enough,—this command, I say, seems to me the queerest idol ever manufactured in the philosophic cave. Were we scholastic absolutists, there might be more excuse. If we had an infallible intellect with its objective certitudes, we might feel ourselves disloyal to such a perfect organ of knowledge in not trusting to it exclusively, in not waiting for its releasing word. But if we are empiricists, if we believe that no bell in us tolls to let us know for certain when truth is in our grasp, then it seems a piece of idle fantasticality to preach so solemnly our duty of waiting for the bell. Indeed we *may* wait if we will.—I hope you do not think that I am denying that,—but if we do so, we do so at our peril as much as if we believed. In either case we *act,* taking our life in our hands. . . .

Philosophy, the Bible, and God

DIALOG WITH ALVIN PLANTINGA

DANIEL KOLAK: There's a wonderful quote from Anthony Kenny: "If there is no God, then God is incalculably the greatest single creation of the human imagination. No other creation of the imagination has been so fertile of ideas, so great an inspiration to philosophy, to literature, to painting, sculpture, architecture, and drama. Set beside the idea of God, the most original inventions of mathematicians and the most unforgettable characters in drama are minor products of the imagination: Hamlet and the square root of minus one pale into insignificance by comparison."

Now of course there is not just one idea of God. Which do you think is the best, and why? My next questions then are these: Do you think God exists only in the human imagination, or is God real? Why? How long have you believed this?

ALVIN PLANTINGA: Yes, that's a dandy quote, and I'm in complete agreement with Kenny. As you point out, there are different ways of thinking about God. I'm thinking of God as an immaterial and eternal person. As a person, God has knowledge, aims, and intentions and can act to accomplish his aims. More exactly, God is omniscient and omnipotent. He is also perfectly good, such that his main attitude toward human beings is one of love. He is the creator of the world, and everything distinct from him depends upon him for its existence—both its original coming into being and its continued existence. In all of this I am just reflecting classical Christian (and Jewish and Muslim) ways of thinking of God.

Why do I think this is the best way to think of God? Because our basic idea here, I think, is of a being who is perfect, a being such that, in Anselm's terms, it's not conceivable that there be a greater. The above is a natural way of developing that notion. But I think of God in this way also because I take the Bible really seriously, and properly understood, it presents God as being of this nature.

I certainly think God is real, that there really is a being of this sort, and that it is not the case that God exists only in the human imagination. It is harder to say *why* I believe this. I do think there are good theistic arguments—quite a large number of them; but I don't really believe in God on the basis of these arguments. Perhaps they play some kind of a role here, but for me at least the basic impulse to believe comes from a different source. I'd put it like this: It seems to me that I sometimes experience God, that I am sometimes aware of his presence. God sometimes seems as real to me as my children or the people I work with. But that isn't the entire answer either. For in addition to this awareness of God, there is also something else—I simply find myself believing in God.

This question—why do you think God is real? —can be asked in several ways. Taken one way, it is a request for evidence: What is your evidence for the existence of such a being, that is, what sorts of arguments do you have for that rather momentous conclusion? Here I'd have to say I don't really believe on the basis of arguments, just as I don't typically hold memory or perceptual or a priori beliefs on the basis of argument or propositional evidence.

You can also ask this question in such a way that the answer says something about the way in which this belief gets into my noetic structure: Is it a matter of perception? or testimony? or rational intuition? or what? This really calls for an epistemology of belief in God—an account of the faculties or belief-producing processes that are responsible for such belief. In my forthcoming book *Warranted Christian Belief* I try to say something sensible along these lines.

"How long have I believed this?" I can't remember a time when I didn't believe this; I was taught about God as a child, both at home and in church, much as I was taught that there is such a place as Africa or such a person as Columbus.

But then when I was about fourteen or so, something happened to me, as to many people: These beliefs became much more real to me; it seemed to me that, as I said above, I was actually aware of God's presence, that I could actually be related to him as one person to another. But as an attempt to describe the phenomenology of my belief, this is very inadequate.

DK: I would like to talk about the epistemology of your belief, your concept of God as a person—I take it you think there is something it is *like* to be God, and so I'm curious as to what you think that actually might be—and also your experience of God, the feeling of his presence. The latter, especially, is of great interest because usually the people who tend to express such feelings tend also not to be professional philosophers, and you are a professional philosopher with a very keen analytical understanding with which to think about such extraordinary experiences. But first, in that regard, I wonder if you might say something about what initially drew you to philosophy. What and who inspired you most as an undergraduate and then a graduate student? Why philosophy and not, say, theology or the priesthood? What role did your personal feelings about religious and related issues play in your development as a philosopher?

AP: I suppose a necessary condition of being a person—a fully fledged and properly functioning person, anyway—is being conscious (at least part of the time; and I suppose S's being conscious is sufficient for being such that there is that it is like to be S. So I guess there must be something that it is like to be God. But the latter also suggests something like what it *feels* like to be S—what sorts of experiences, sensations, and so on S enjoys. According to a fair amount of traditional philosophical theology, God doesn't have sensations or anything like them: Sensations, that whole kind of mental life, according to that way of thinking, goes with being embodied, which of course God is not. I really don't have a view as to whether this is right, or whether, on the other hand, God does have something like sensations. In any event, if God does, I certainly don't know what they would be like. It's hard enough to know what it feels like to be a bat; it's even

harder, I should think, to know what it feels like to be God. But God's perfection, which would include perfect happiness, if there is a way in which it feels to be God, probably feels pretty good.

As for what originally drew me to philosophy, my father had a Ph.D. in philosophy (though for most of his professional life he taught psychology), and I heard a great deal about philosophy as a child. He also had me reading bits of Plato when I was in junior high and high school. I found Plato extremely interesting (though not quite as interesting as girls and high school athletics). When I went to college, I was already more or less set on the idea of majoring in philosophy. I didn't take any philosophy the first two semesters of college, which were at Jamestown College in Jamestown, North Dakota, and Calvin College in Grand Rapids, Michigan. My second year of college, however, was at Harvard, where I took two course from Raphael Demos (ancient philosophy and Plato) and a course in logic. I still remember the sense of awe and delight I felt in reading Plato's *Gorgias* and *Republic*. During Harvard's spring vacation, I returned to Grand Rapids, where my father was a professor at Calvin; because Calvin's spring vacation didn't coincide with Harvard's I attended three sessions of a course taught by William Harry Jellema—in ethics, I think. I found Jellema absolutely overwhelming and decided I wanted to study philosophy with him. So the next year I returned to Calvin and studied philosophy with Jellema and Henry Stob. That was one of the best decisions I ever made; Jellema was the finest teacher of philosophy I have ever seen, and I suppose my basic attitudes toward philosophy were established then. I went to grad school at the University of Michigan and also Yale University; I guess the professors that made the most serious and long-lasting impressions on me were Bill Alston and Bill Frankena from the University of Michigan.

What made philosophy at Calvin especially interesting is the idea that philosophy, or working at philosophy, is or ought to be, for a Christian, closely connected with one's Christian beliefs. We learned from Stob and Jellema that philosophy, or large-scale philosophical projects, is often and quite properly driven by religious or quasireligious beliefs and impulses. As they used to say, absolute idealism was a continuation of Protestantism by other means; and much contemporary philosophy is an attempt to work out a full orbed naturalistic way of looking at the world. We also learned that Christian philosophers ought not to think of philosophy overall as religiously neutral, although of course parts of it might be. We also learned that one of the main tasks of the community of Christians in philosophy is just to try to figure out precisely how one's philosophy and one's religious views should be related.

Ever since then there has been rather a close connection between my Christian beliefs and my philosophical work. In graduate school I was struck by the sorts of arguments that had been urged against Christian belief, and a lot of my subsequent work has been aimed at replying to these arguments. For example, my first book was *God and Other Minds;* one of the main aims of that book was to reply to a certain widely accepted objection to Christian belief, the evidentialist objection. I've also thought a lot about the so-called problem of evil, which is better called "the atheological argument from evil." And the book I've just finished, *Warranted Christian Belief,* is on the epistemology of religious belief.

Why philosophy and not the priesthood or theology? I thought about becoming a minister, but decided I was better suited to philosophy. And anyway, I've always just loved philosophy; I enormously enjoy working out philosophical problems and have often been absolutely delighted by a beautifully crafted piece of philosophical work, whether I agreed with it or not. I suppose theology would also have been a good subject for me, but philosophy gives more scope for somewhat more formal and logical work. I think a theologian who wrote something like my book *The Nature of Necessity* might get drummed out of the theological corps.

DK: One of the fundamental issues throughout philosophy's long history concerns the true nature of ultimate reality. And one of the fundamental bones of contention within the various metaphysical views espoused by the great thinkers— whether religious or scientific—is whether this ultimate reality is (or has) a (conscious) mind. This, I take it, is a large part of the philosophical impetus behind the question, Does God exist? There are certainly lots of other issues surrounding that question, of course, having to do with spiritual, religious, personal, cultural, psychological matters, and so on, but this metaphysical aspect seems key. Now, by my lights, the real tension between philosophy and religion (in the West, at least) can't be drawn along the issue of whether some type of God exists. There are many philosophers who believe that some type of God exists, and there have been as many, if not more, theologians who have been atheists as there have been atheistic philosophers. Rather, the dividing line is drawn along *how* one comes to one's views about such metaphysical matters. Did one's beliefs get set, in advance, by religious authority, or did one come to them through philosophical analysis and reflection? This, I think, is the main reason why many philosophers today regard religious education as antithetical to philosophy: They regard religion as indoctrination, not education.

Now you, I take it (correct me if I'm wrong) seem to imply by what you say above *both* that you came to your views through religious upbringing *and* through philosophical analysis and reflection. Thus, for instance, your view that God is a person. There have been many philosophers— Spinoza, Hegel, Fichte, Schelling, Royce—who have held views according to which ultimate reality is not physical but mental, that there is a conscious world soul, or mind, and so on. But their views are at least not straightforwardly Christian. And certainly there have been many deistic instead of theistic conceptions that give personlike properties to the world as a whole but do not correspond with Christian views and are even antithetical to them (Aquinas's *Against the Averroists* and the burning of Bruno at the stake for his arguments for a World Soul who is identical with all human beings come to mind). Yet you suggest that your conception of God is influenced, on the one hand, by purely formal-type arguments such as those of Anselm as well as what the Bible says, including what you were taught as a young boy, and also personal experience, as well as perhaps some considerations that you haven't specified. Let's start with Anselm and the Bible, then those moments in which you think you experience God. What do you think is the best of the many criticisms of Anselm's argument levied by his critics, and what is your best response that meets those criticisms? Second, why do you, given what you know as a philosopher, take what the Bible says seriously? Third, how is it that your philosophical views correspond to what you were taught as a child? Is this just a happy coincidence, or is it philosophically—perhaps even religiously—significant?

AP: I think you are right that many philosophers think religious belief doesn't come from a source of belief that produces warranted belief: The belief-producing processes that are responsible for belief in God, for example, are not a source of warranted belief. Unlike, for example, perceptual beliefs, belief in God is not usually produced by cognitive processes that are functioning properly in the right kind of environment and have as their purpose the production of true belief. This is in contrast to philosophical beliefs, which are ordinarily a product of reason, which *is* a faculty directed at the production of true beliefs, even if disagreement runs rife in philosophy. And the idea would be, then, that theistic belief is warranted and respectable only if it is arrived at by way of reason—rational reflection and argument—rather than in some other way. A specific example of this sort of view would be Freud's claim that theistic belief is ordinarily a product of wish fulfillment, not rational reflection, and is therefore epistemically second rate.

But the claim that theistic belief is warranted only if it is produced by rational reflection is itself a whopping epistemological assumption. It is not, of course, self-evident; it requires argumentation if it is to be held in a rational way. And where is the argument? Freud just assumes that theism is false and then proposes the best hypothesis he can think of to explain the widespread acceptance of theistic belief. (Inculcation by religious authorities isn't a very good hypothesis, just because first, such teaching won't "take" unless there is something in our nature that resonates to it, and second, lots of people become

believers in God contrary to what they are taught by parents and other authorities—consider the recent history of China and the former Soviet Union.) Believers in God, on the other hand, will ordinarily, at least if they think about it, see the origin of theistic belief in something like Calvin's *sensus divinitatis,* a faculty or cognitive process that God has created in us and that enables us to know of his existence and something of his nature and character. So of course they wouldn't agree that theistic belief comes from a source like wish fulfillment, a source that doesn't have the production of true belief as part of its function or purpose. In *Warranted Christian Belief,* I argue that both theistic belief and full-blown Christian belief are such that *if* they are true, they are very likely *warranted.* (If there really is such a person as God, then he would undoubtedly want us to know something about him, and the fact that the vast bulk of the world's population believes in God or something like God would be explained by way of his having instilled in us a means of coming to know about him.) If this is right, the epistemological view of the philosophers you mention—that theistic belief doesn't come from a cognitive source that produces warranted belief—really depends upon a metaphysical belief: that theistic belief is not in fact true. As far as I can see, most of these philosophers simply presuppose this: They don't ordinarily give much by way of serious argument for it. The exceptions here would be philosophers like Bill Rowe, who offers an inductive argument for atheism; he proposes serious arguments, but the arguments, in my estimation, are entirely unsuccessful.

I am therefore unimpressed by claims that religious education is really indoctrination. That is no more true, from a theistic or Christian point of view, than a similar claim with respect to historical or scientific education. This view presupposes that theistic belief is false; it thus presupposes a philosophical (metaphysical) view for which there are not, as far as I can see, any good arguments.

In response to your three questions, first, on Anselm: I don't think I suggested that my belief in God was, even in part, a result of the ontological argument. What I said, or meant to say, was that the Anselmian conception of God, as a greatest possible being, influences my conception of what God is like. It is because that seems to me the right way to think of God that I take him to be a *person,* a being with beliefs and intentions and desires and the ability to act on those beliefs and desires. I do think that there is a sound version of the ontological argument—the one in the last chapter of my book *The Nature of Necessity*—but I don't believe in God on the basis of that argument. That is because the argument, although sound, is such that the epistemic distance between premise and conclusion is rather less than one might like.

Second, you ask, "Why do you, given what you know as a philosopher, take what the Bible says seriously?" That seems to suggest that there is something I know or should know as a philosopher that would inhibit my taking the Bible seriously. I'm not at all sure I know what you have in mind—could I ask you to tell me a bit about it? Third, you ask how it is that my philosophical views correspond to what I was taught as a child: "Is this just a happy coincidence, or is it philosophically—perhaps even religiously—significant?" I guess the short answer, from my point of view, is that I was taught the truth as a child, on this as on some other topics on which I have philosophical views (for example, that there are other people, that they have thoughts and feelings, that the world is much more than five minutes old, and the like). But your question probably has to do with the fact that many people are *not* taught, for example, that there is such a person as God as a child, while I was. Perhaps you are thinking along the lines of John Hick, who suggests that most religious people accept the religious views they were taught as a child and probably would have believed otherwise if they had been brought up elsewhere and elsewhen: He goes on to suggest that any beliefs you hold that are of that character—that is, such that if you had been brought up elsewhere and elsewhen, you would not have accepted them—should be viewed with suspicion.

Well, I agree with him to at least this extent: The thought that if I had been brought up at a different place and time, I would have held quite different beliefs—that thought can induce a certain intellectual vertigo. But I don't know what to infer from that. Very many of my beliefs are of that character. Many of my scientific beliefs—relativity theory, for example, or that the distance to the moon is more than 200,000 miles—are like that. So are many of my moral beliefs. I believe, for example, that racism is wrong; but no doubt there are many places and times such that if I had been brought up there and then I would not have had this belief. Does that mean that there is something suspect about the belief? I doubt it. So I'd have to agree that there are other places and times such that if I had been brought up at those places and times I probably would not have held some of the religious beliefs I do hold; but I can't see, so far, that that is a point against those beliefs.

DK: Well, I think I am in complete agreement with your assertion that those philosophers (and psychologists, like Freud), who start from an atheistic perspective and dismiss Christianity on grounds that it does not meet the standards of their half-baked (and usually artificial) model of rationality tend themselves to be steeped in an equally tenuous position, often from the standpoint of their *own* model! In my book *In Search of God: The Language and Logic of Belief,* I argued that certain sorts of believers and nonbelievers are in perfectly complementary epistemic positions, equally up to their ears in faith and that their beliefs about God are equally unwarranted.

Still, I am very curious to hear what you think warrants a Christian's belief. Because it seems to me most Christians get their beliefs through a source that—regardless of whether God exists—would not warrant any such belief. That was my point about the Bible. What I meant was this: As philosophers we are trained, among other things, to read and study texts critically from intellectual, historical, and literary points of view and not to accept the truth or even literary worth of what we read on faith or on someone else's say-so. And there seem to be so many obvious and deep problems with the New Testament that it is difficult for me to see how a serious scholar could take what it says seriously. Most ordinary Christians, of course, are completely ignorant of the historical tenuousness of the gospels, that early Christians held radically different beliefs from those of today and so on. Thus, many Christians today are completely ignorant of the fact that the earliest New Testament gospel was not written before 50 A.D., that the latest was written as late as 120 A.D., that we don't have original copies of any of them, that the oldest ones date from the third century, that no two of them are identical, and that there was a discovery in 1945 of a Coptic translation of the Gospel of Thomas. Few realize that the gospels of Mark, Matthew, and Luke do not provide independent corroboration of the described events but contain many parts copied verbatim from one another. Likewise, few ordinary Christians today realize that there is now a general consensus among New Testament historians that the majority of Jesus's sayings in the New Testament are not authentic.

Thus, for instance, in his wonderful book *A Marginal Jew* (Doubleday, 1991), John Meier, a Catholic priest and Professor of New Testament at Catholic University, asks us to imagine that

a Catholic, a Protestant, a Jew, and an agnostic— all honest historians cognizant of 1st century religious movements—were locked up in the bowels of the Harvard Divinity School library . . . and not allowed to emerge until they had hammered out a consensus document on who Jesus of Nazareth was and what he intended in his own time and place . . . an essential requirement of this document would be that it be based on purely historical sources and arguments.

He concludes that the "real Jesus, . . . unknown and unknowable, . . . is not available and never will be." Likewise, E. P. Sanders, Dean Ireland's Professor of Exegesis at Oxford University, in his excellent *Jesus and Judaism* (Fortress Press, 1985), writes, "Scholars have not and, in my judgment, will not agree on the authenticity of the sayings material, either in whole or in part." There are lots of these and other sorts of examples. *The Five Gospels* (Macmillan, 1995), the collective report of a group of New Testament scholars, concluded that "eighty-two percent of the words

ascribed to Jesus in the gospels were not actually spoken by him." Yet many believing Christians today believe what they do about Jesus because of what they think (or have been told) the Bible says. It thus seems that as scholars we know enough about the Bible—again, correct me if I'm wrong—to know that *even if* what it says were true the people who believe what they do about the events thus described on the basis of what is there written would *not* be warranted in their beliefs on the basis of having read it, any more than I would be warranted in believing, based on having read, say, Hitler's false diaries, what Hitler's private thoughts were should it turn out that what the forgeries contained happened to coincide with what Hitler really thought.

However, the historical dubiousness of the New Testament is only half of the problem. Suppose one claimed that the quest for scholarly accuracy and proper historical evidence are moot, that what matters is faith. (Still, of course, there can be little doubt but that the main reason many and perhaps most Christians would in fact take a position dismissive of our best scholarship and historical analysis is that their religious teachers simply neglected to tell them about the well-known problems, among Christian historians and theologians, about trying to figure out what Jesus really said or what he might have meant based on historical evidence.) In that case, the problem becomes that of why one should accept on faith some current version of Christian belief or do so on, say, the poetical, spiritual, or inspirational value of the gospels. What if it goes against one's philosophical and literary sensibilities?

Thus, questions now of historical accuracy and evidential rationality aside, there have been many philosophers, such as Nietzsche, who have made poignant cases not just against rationality as ordinarily conceived but also against religion and especially Christianity. Indeed, when Nietzsche waxes poetical against Chrstianity, many find his poetry more moving and "true" than what one reads in the Bible. For instance, Nietzsche says,

I regard Christianity as the most fatal and seductive lie that has ever yet existed—as the greatest and most *impious* lie: I can discern the last sprouts and branches of its ideal beneath every form of disguise. . . . *The morality of paltry people* as the measure of all things: this is the most repugnant kind of degeneracy that civilization has ever yet brought into existence. And this *kind of ideal* is hanging still, under the name of "God," over men's heads!! . . . when one touches the New Testament one cannot help experiencing a sort of inexpressible feeling of discomfort; for the unbounded cheek with which the least qualified people will have their say in its pages, in regard to the greatest problems of existence, and claim to sit in judgment on such matters exceeds all limits. The impudent levity with which the most unwieldly problems are spoken of here (life, the world, God, the purpose of life), as if they were not problems at all, but the most simple things which these little bigots *know all about!!!*

Now, I don't know how far I would want to go with Nietzsche, but he certainly speaks for many philosophers (and others) regarding their feelings. Such strongly negative feelings typically can be quite genuine and can come about through serious philosophical reflection, as is certainly the case with Bertrand Russell's famous critique of the character of Christ in *Why I Am Not a Christian*. In his typical British understated way, Russell expresses disdain for the character of Christ, of whom he says "I cannot myself feel that either in the matter of wisdom or in the matter of virtue Christ stands quite as high as some other people known to history," and is repulsed by Christ's "vindictive fury against those people who would not listen to his preaching—an attitude which is not uncommon with preachers, but which does somewhat detract from superlative excellence. You do not, for instance, find that attitude in Socrates. You find him quite bland and urbane toward the people who would not listen to him; and it is, to my mind, far more worthy of a sage to take that line than to take the line of indignation."

As for myself, I must say that the chief problem that gets in the way of my believing Christianity to be even *possibly* true is that, quite independently of the historical and evidential considerations, the story—to me, anyway—simply does not make sense. It's like a badly written book with a flawed plot so full of poorly conceived characters that you know it must be fiction! I'll throw in just one example, one that always bothered me. Here is this divine fellow whose suffering, we are told, is supposed to redeem the sins of mankind. (Never mind the philosophical problems of how a person can be guilty in virtue of something that his ancestors did.) Now, suppose you are told that tomorrow you will undergo a painful procedure—say, being crucified—but that afterward you will go on to live forever as king of heaven, redeemer of mankind, the Savior, with hundreds of millions of worshippers for all eternity, and so on. Would you suffer? Well, there have been lots of people who underwent all sorts of unspeakable horrors that as far as they knew would be followed only by more pain, then death, and then nothing—for example, the many other people who were crucified along with Jesus (and before and since). That, to me, is real suffering. Whereas to undergo something like a crucifixion with the knowledge of what a noble deed it is, what the great cosmic end result will be, and so on seems to me at best a very weak and dubious candidate for suffering.

So here we have the Bible presenting a story that, even if I were to accept it at face value and give it full benefit of the doubt the way I do when I read a novel or see a movie, simply doesn't work for me. Unlike *Superman,* the movie *The Greatest Story Ever Told* (as well as *The Last Temptation of Christ*) is for me a terribly bad and boring because whereas in the former case writers, actors, and producers succeeded in making me believe that a man could fly and so on, in the latter case they failed to make me believe that a man could be God. I just can't believe the story (whereas I can and do believe all sorts of bizarre philosophical theses). All of Jesus's actions in the Bible and on the screen strike me as unbelievable and completely unmotivated. I can't imagine myself or any conscious, intelligent being in that position saying or doing any of those things. The fact that so many people swear by the Jesus story and worship it moves me no more than does the fact that so many people believe in and worship all sorts of nonsense, including typically awful examples of superstition and bad art so highly popular with the masses. (Indeed, I think it depresses and sometimes frightens me.) People are especially prone *en masse* to be seduced and moved by and like all sorts of truly silly things (sometimes the sillier the more they go for them) through flawed mechanisms of belief formation, which leads to all sorts of ridiculous forms of very bad art and utterly unwarranted beliefs, from Elvis and professional wrestling to flying saucers and ghosts and witches and, I think, the Resurrection. The further fact that people have a high propensity to be superstitious is scant reason to believe that the magical beings in which they believe have predisposed them to be susceptible to such beliefs. Indeed, I am myself moved by the miracles of Santa Claus and the goodness of Superman not because I have sufficient evidence that they exist or because Santa and Superman or my Creator made me that way but simply because as a reader I am moved by a good story. And the sad fact is that I am not moved by the suffering of Jesus Christ simply because as a philosopher I (think I) know too much.

For these and other sorts of reasons I find it surprising—indeed, if I might say, with all due respect, downright shocking—to find a philosopher (and by my lights a great one) taking seriously the philosophical value of a book whose historical, intellectual, spiritual, literary, and ultimately philosophical shortcomings seem, by my probably corrupted sensibilities, so serious. So I guess one way of putting my puzzlement is that now I'm as baffled by the question of what it is like to be Alvin Plantinga as I am by the question of what it is like to be Jesus Christ and God!

AP: Something tells me we don't see quite eye to eye on some of these matters! Let's see what there is to be said by way of reply. Your first suggestion was that "Christians get their beliefs through a source that . . . would not warrant any such belief." You then support this suggestion by claiming that "there is now a general consensus among New Testament historians that the majority of Jesus's sayings in the New Testament are not authentic." But I don't agree that it's right to say

there is consensus among New Testament scholars that the majority of sayings ascribed to Jesus are not authentic. Here you appeal to Meier's *A Marginal Jew* (and I agree that it is indeed wonderful). But of course his conclusion is not that the New Testament account of Jesus is inaccurate but that there is no way of knowing whether it is accurate, which is a vastly different matter. And even that probably doesn't represent his views. Consider his conclave of a Catholic, Protestant, Jew, and agnostic all locked up in the bowels of the Harvard Divinity School library until they hammer out a consensus document on who Jesus of Nazareth was and what he intended in his own time and place. . . . Well, let's suppose the document they come up with doesn't include Jesus's rising from the dead. Does it follow that the Catholic and Protestant, in signing on to the document, no longer believe that Jesus rose from the dead? Given the presence of the agnostic, presumably the document will not even contain the proposition that there is such a person as God. Does it follow that the Catholic, Protestant, and Jew no longer believe there is any such person as God? Certainly not; all that follows is that these propositions are not ones upon which all four agree. This document does not represent the views of Catholic, Protestant, and Jew but only what all four have in common and can all agree on. (Perhaps it might represent the views of the agnostic.) The document wouldn't represent a consensus on the topics in question, in the sense that all of them agree that what it says represents their position on those topics: The Catholic and Protestant actually accept a lot of propositions that don't make their way into the document.

By way of analogy, imagine a conclave of physicists who disagree about the proper interpretation of quantum mechanics locked up until they produce a consensus document on, say classical versus Bohmian interpretations of quantum mechanics. Presumably neither of these interpretations would emerge in the document; it would not follow that there is a consensus among physicists, or among *those* physicists, that neither of these interpretations is correct.

There is a deeper epistemological point here.

The aim of much contemporary scripture scholarship, following a program already laid down by Spinoza, is to see what one can learn about these topics just on the basis of historical reason alone—bracketing whatever one knows or believes by faith. (Meier explicitly signs on to this program.) Following this program, perhaps you conclude that on the basis of historical reason alone, prescinding from what you know or think you know by faith, it is unlikely that Jesus rose from the dead, or that the Bible is a special word from the Lord, or that Jesus did miracles of one sort or another. It doesn't follow that you don't think Jesus did rise from the dead, or that the Bible is not a special word from the Lord, or that Jesus did these miracles. For if you are a traditional Christian, whether Protestant or Catholic (or Orthodox), you very likely think there is *another* source of warranted belief on these topics, a source *in addition to* historical reason. Aquinas speaks here of the "internal instigation of the Holy Spirit" and Calvin of the "internal testimony of the Holy Spirit." According to each, the source of Christian belief is not historical reason, or testimony from other people, but this working of the Holy Spirit in the hearts and minds of those who in fact believe. On classical Christian understandings of these matters, there is a threefold process here: there is the presentation of scriptural teaching—through preaching or in many other ways, including, I suppose, even when they are being held up to ridicule, as in Nietzsche; there is the working of the Holy Spirit; and there is finally, as a result, Christian belief or faith. On this account, faith is a gift, a gift from God himself. So there isn't anything wrong with the source of Christian belief, at least if classical Christianity is true. I'd have to say you must be assuming that such belief is false in claiming that its source is unreliable or not a source of warranted belief.

You add that philosophers are trained not to accept "the truth or even literary worth of what we read on faith or on someone else's say-so." But if this were really true (and if the training took), wouldn't we philosophers be in deep epistemic trouble? Most of what I know about science and all that I know about history I take on the say-so of others. Indeed, it is only on the say-so of others (maps, signs, and so on) that I know where I live.

As for being taught not to accept anything on faith, that would make sense only if we already knew that faith is not a warranted source of Christian belief. (Otherwise it would be like an injunction not to accept anything on the basis of perception or memory.) But of course I don't know that, and I don't think anyone else does either—though there are quite a few philosophers who just *assume* it.

To return to scripture scholarship: Most historical biblical criticism (HBC) abstracts from, prescinds from what Christians think is known by faith. But then it isn't surprising that HBC does not arrive at results that confirm what Christians believe. From the Christian's perspective, HBC ignores a very important source of warranted belief: faith, or the internal instigation of the Holy Spirit. Indeed, a lot of HBC—following Ernst Troeltsch—make philosophical assumptions directly contrary to what Christians believe. They claim, for example, that there are inviolate natural laws that not even God himself, if there is such a person, can act in ways contrary to (or if he *can* act contrary to them, we can be sure he *won't*); and they claim further that this means God either cannot or will not act miraculously. So, of course, no one rises from the dead. They then conclude, naturally enough, that Jesus did not rise from the dead. Their conclusion is scarcely surprising, because they begin by assuming it; further, this conclusion is not a consequence of historical investigation but of philosophical assumption. Their coming to this conclusion, therefore, isn't the slightest reason for thinking Jesus did not in fact rise from the dead.

So (from the standpoint of classical Christianity) there are two reasons why the results of HBC do not impugn Christian belief. First, the results themselves don't take into account all that the believer thinks she knows, and in some cases proceeds on assumptions she thinks are flatly false. And second, the source of central Christian beliefs isn't straightforwardly just the Bible, in the way in which Thucydides's *The Peloponnesian War*, say, is the source for our knowledge of the Peloponnesian War. The Christian doesn't ordinarily accept the central teachings of Christianity—incarnation and atonement, say—because (a) she thinks the New Testament teaches them and (b) the New Testament is reliable. It's instead the story above: There is presentation of these teachings, which for us have their proximate source in the Bible, and then the instigation or internal testimony of the Holy Spirit. This process swings free of the usual sorts of questions asked and answered by HBC, and it is because it does that Christians, even ones without a Ph.D. in biblical studies, can know such things as that Jesus arose from the dead, despite the vagaries on contemporary HBC as to who Jesus was and what he did. And these vagaries suggest still a third reason why the results of HBC do not impugn Christian belief: that is because there is so little agreement among HBCers that there is precious little or nothing that can be called its "results."

Of course, there is enormously more to be said about these things. I try to say just a bit more about them in "Two (or More) Kinds of Scripture Scholarship" in the last or next to last issue of *Modern Theology*.

You also mention that there are many—Nietzsche, Bertrand Russell, and others—who find Christian belief in one way or another offensive. That is of course true, but it isn't much of a reason for thinking Christian belief unwarranted. I don't myself find Nietzsche, with his claims that Christian belief fosters and arises from a sort of weak, deceitful, cowardly, resentful character, full of hostility and hate disguised as Christian love—I don't myself find that at all convincing. It doesn't fit any of the Christians I know—my parents, my children, or my Christian friends, for example. Of course, Christians, like everyone else, are subject to sin; but they aren't (so far as I can tell) much more sinful than others; and even if they were, that would scarcely show that what they believe is false. Nietzsche writes marvelous prose, and perhaps some of his exaggerations are intended exaggerations to make a point: But leaving aside the coruscating brilliance of his prose, his actual criticisms seem to me hard to take seriously. Now of course I don't doubt that some philosophers and others go along with Nietzsche here. But *I* don't, of course,

and I don't see any reason to think that reason, or history, or empirical evidence requires one to go along with him. So I don't see it as grounds for rejecting Christian belief. In the same way, there are also very many who thoroughly dislike contemporary philosophical naturalism, the view that there is no such person as God or anything at all like God: But I don't suppose that in itself is much by way of an objection to naturalism.

Finally, you say that you yourself find that the central Christian story doesn't make sense. I'm sorry to hear that, but I guess I am not impressed with the reason you give. You mention in particular that "to undergo something like a crucifixion with the knowledge of what a noble deed it is, what the great cosmic end result will be, and so on, seems to me a very weak and dubious candidate for suffering." Here I'm astonished. I should think crucifixion would be horrifying suffering, no matter what else one thought or believed, and even if one thought so doing was a noble deed. During wartime some people manage to hold out against terrible torture, refusing to give information they think could be damaging to their country. Perhaps they see what they do as noble; my guess is it still hurts like hell.

Which brings up two further points about the sufferings of Christ. First, what you say assumes that he knew, when undergoing this suffering, that he was the second person of the Trinity and that by his suffering he was redeeming mankind. But that assumption isn't at all clearly true. Second, if it *is* true, then perhaps the quintessential brunt of Christ's suffering, its central focus, is not the physical pain of the crucifixion but the spiritual pain of feeling forsaken by God the Father as in his agonized cry "My God, my God, why have you forsaken me?"

I do agree that there are parts of the Christian story that raise philosophical questions (just as there are parts of contemporary physics, biology, and cognitive science that raise philosophical questions); but I can only record that to me the story makes wonderful sense, and is in fact powerfully moving, deeply engaging one's affections as well as one's mind.

DK: As usual, I find your thinking extremely instructive. You make, as I find is so often the case in your work, a strong case that religion—in this case, Christianity—seems to have the same sort of epistemic status as most of our other sources and types of belief, most notably science and history. The lesson I take from this, of course, is rather different than the one you do. The effect on me is that it makes me downright suspicious about most of our acceptance of all types of beliefs handed down in this manner, from scientific and historical to political, social, and personal, and makes me want as a philosopher to continue to reexamine all our various systems of belief. So I find myself in curious agreement with much of what you say, yet I draw just the opposite conclusion from you regarding God, Jesus, the Bible, and Christianity.

Rather than belabor or rehash some of the issues raised—it is unnecessary, given that I agree with much of it—let's play a little philosophical game. Let me accept for the moment that everything you say is true. This isn't a great leap for me because, as I say, I think much of what you say is right on target. Furthermore, this isn't much different from the way I came to many of my beliefs: I simply followed the instructions set out for me by some philosopher or other (such as, "Read Hume! Read Kant!"). So let me assume that you are right in your belief that God exists, that Jesus died on the cross for my sins and was resurrected, that the Bible is the word of God, and so on—the whole kit and caboodle. Now, what am I, poor philosopher, to do?

I know I am not an idiot. Just as I have very good grounds for believing that there are some people who are smarter and perhaps also morally better than me, I have also very good grounds for believing that I am smarter and also morally better than some; I have, for instance, spent a good deal of time trying to better others and have myself looked into the question of God far more deeply than many. I have certainly read much on the topic and also written on it, and have been very fortunate to be able to have discussions such as this with many great philosophers and theologians, and so on. As a philosopher, but also as a man, I am absolutely adamant and passionate about my search for truth. If you are correct about Jesus and God, then without

a doubt I too would like to believe that. Indeed, if you are correct, my not believing it may well keep me out of heaven or even deny me an afterlife!

So, step one: What advice do you have for me? In other words, what is the first step I should take toward seeing the world as you see it? To be even more specific: I take it the two additional factors, as you've explained them, that makes you think your beliefs about God are true have mostly to do (correct me if I'm wrong) with (1) "feeling God's presence," a state in which God "seems as real as your children or people you work with," and (2) that you "simply find yourself believing" in God. These, I take it, are the two key factors for you (again, correct me if I'm wrong), because you admit that although there may be good arguments for the existence of God, the veridicality of the Bible, the resurrection of Jesus, and so on, that is *not* how *you* came to your beliefs. It thus seems that what I lack—what separates me from being in the same position as you (for as philosophers we seem to agree about much of the rest) has to do with these two key factors. I certainly am not a candidate for the second (though I certainly did believe in God, and even Jesus, as a young boy—beliefs that simply went the way of many of my childhood beliefs, such as beliefs in ghosts, goblins, and Santa Claus). Can you help me to achieve this?

AP: You say that you are "downright suspicious about most of our acceptance of all types of beliefs handed down in this manner" and "want to reexamine all our various systems of belief"; yes, there aren't any safe havens here, no guarantees. We can be wrong, desperately, pitiably wrong about what seems most important. And indeed, we can also be wrong in criticizing or reexamining our systems of belief; the principles we employ there are also ones about which we can be wrong. There aren't any guarantees there either, no more there than anywhere else. The whole thing can sometimes induce vertigo. Just as autobiography, I don't myself feel anxiety about most everyday beliefs, or ordinary and widely accepted historical beliefs, or what people think of as well-established scientific beliefs (although I have my doubts about contemporary particle physics and contemporary cosmology in physics, as well as some claims in evolutionary biology). It's certainly worthwhile looking into this convoluted abyss of skepticism, but in the long run it seems to make little difference to what I actually find myself believing. What I do think needs to be addressed is the way in which philosophers and others adopt a double standard, holding religious and Christian belief to standards none of our beliefs, including none of our philosophical beliefs, can meet.

You ask how someone can come to see the world as a theist, or even a Christian, and what advice I have for someone who wanted to come to think as a Christian does. I should say first that for me Christian belief doesn't display a sort of constant level. I occasionally wake up in the middle of the night and wonder whether this whole wonderful story is really no more than that— a wonderful story. Other times (more often) it seems to me as obviously true as that I live in Indiana and teach at Notre Dame. And much of the time it's somewhere between these levels. Second, thinking like a Christian is by no means just a matter of holding certain "beliefs," and it isn't a matter just of the intellect. Just as important is a whole range of affections, loves and hates, attractions and repulsions; there are also acts of will involved: setting oneself to love one's neighbor, to humbly seek God, to pray, and the like. Sometimes it seems to take God's orchestrating some kind of life crisis to cause people to think seriously, honestly, and humbly about these issues and seek God; but I'm convinced that anyone who does so will find Him. Third, I am not really qualified to give advice on this topic; I'm only a philosopher, not a pastor or religious counselor. Still, I think I have a bit to say along these lines.

What I have to say, however, is by no means original. (Indeed, in these contexts, unlike, say, French philosophy, originality is a pretty good indication of getting off track.) What Christians (Pascal, for example) have always said in response to these questions is something like this. If one wants to come to think and believe like a Christian, the first thing to do is to try to act like a Christian—read the Bible (perhaps especially the Psalms, the Gospel of John, the Epistles), go to church, associate with Christian people and try to enter their world, and read Christian writers in a devotional context. Read, for example, Jonathan Edward's *Religious Affections,* which I think is one of the greatest books of our entire tradition, or C. S. Lewis (perhaps starting with his *The Great Divorce*), or Henri Nouwen, or Abraham Kuiper's *To be Near Unto God.* Prayer is crucially important. Maybe at first one can't pray on one's own; there are prayers of others available, for example the prayers of St. Thomas Aquinas (available by that title from Sophia Press).

But (and this is a point of some delicacy) this has to be done in a certain way, with a certain spirit, a spirit of receptivity. We philosophers are used to reading and discussing "critically," and often this means that we can't really learn from what we read or hear. We constantly evaluate arguments, look for fallacies, ask whether the author makes a good case, and the like. In some contexts that is important, and just the way to do things. But that is not the way to read the Bible. If God really is speaking to us in the Bible, the way to respond is not by asking whether he has made a good case for this or that. God is not required to make a good case, and we can't sensibly sit in judgment on what he says. One has to read with a certain humility and teachability; and one has to try hard to see what is actually being taught.

The same goes for reading other Christian literature, listening to sermons, speaking with Christians, and the like. If I begin by asking myself whether I am not perhaps smarter or more knowledgeable than this person I'm reading, I probably won't learn what there is to be learned. Who is smarter than who has nothing to do with it. Our whole philosophical culture of comparing and rating ourselves and each other with respect to ability, thinking a lot about who is smarter than who, and (dare I say it?), ordinarily thinking of ourselves as superior, along these lines, to the general run of humanity—all of this serves us very badly, I think, and especially badly in this kind of context. What's wanted here is the kind of awe or reverence in the presence of greatness and mystery that we all had before we got jaded. I know from personal experience how hard it is to get and keep this attitude; I also believe that certain truths and relationships won't come to us without it. We have to "give up our lives in order to find them."

I'm sorry to say this is about all I can say on this point. I wish I could give a better answer.

DK: Your point that we might all be horribly wrong not just about our beliefs but even about the methods we employ for evaluating our beliefs is an excellent one. I quite agree, and here I see an important philosophical value in doing exactly the sort of philosophy of religion that you especially and also some others do. This is where my interest lies. Because I think what ruffles many scientists and philosophers feathers is that there seems to be no clear consensus that the methods of science and/or philosophy, and the ways we have of evaluating those methods, are any better than those of a religion such as Christianity. The issues here are of course very complicated, and I'm hoping that our having a dialog in this way— especially the game I've suggested we play—may help us to cut to the chase. The game is that I am myself, a philosopher with a fairly good knowledge of philosophy, a genuine curiosity about God issues, and (I hope) an open mind. You are you, one of our preeminent philosophers of religion who happens not just to have an open mind but one that believes what *this* philosopher does not. Can we build a bridge? That's the idea.

So, well, I'm familiar with Edwards and Lewis, and also Nouwen and Kuiper, and I must say not only that they have no positive effect on me, I find them (especially the first two) downright unmoving and often silly. Perhaps I'm just made of the wrong stuff. But perhaps more to the point, your Pascalian advice I find most suprising, coming from a philosopher! For I know for a fact that people who hang around in a receptive and accepting frame of mind around certain people who believe certain things often tend to become like those people, to accept their way of thinking. Belief by osmosis. If I hang around Buddhists in this way, for instance, go through their rituals, read their holy books, and so on for a long enough time, there is a very good chance I will think like a Buddhist, revere the Buddha,

accept and like the *anatta* doctrine. And, likewise, if I hang around Hindus and start behaving like one (at first only by going through the motions), a similar effect will occur. Children are susceptible—so are those lovers who often "pretend" to love each other at first but then, after going through enough of the requisite sort of motions, end up swearing that they do (and really meaning it). And the same goes, as far as I can tell, for a whole slew of all sorts of *false* or *bad* belief systems up to and including predilections toward an entire range of gang-related phenomena!

Pascal, as far as I can tell, designed his arguments for the disbelieving gamblers, the skeptical aristocracy, the rich atheists whom he saw all around him—people who, having dispensed with any rational arguments for the existence of God, had also dispensed with a spiritual life, forsaking all questions of cosmic proportion in favor of the vain pursuit of self-interest. Pascal saw a bunch of cold-hearted intellectuals who were treating life itself as if it were but a huge casino and to them he said, all right, you want to play games? Want to place a little wager? Here's a wager! Self-interest, is that all you live by? Then consider this! I have myself defended Pascal's wager against the often heard response that God would not accept such self-interested belief. Pascal does not say that the belief produced by simply going along with the religious program will produce the proper type that God will recognize and admire. Rather, doing the prayers and reading the Bible may prompt you to live a more pious life. Going through the motions is by itself not good enough, but nor is it the end of the process; the proper sort of belief may follow. Eventually, Pascal argues, you will come to see the merits of belief in its true light, which would otherwise be beyond your means. Indeed, if I may quote myself, "Make room for love in your heart and love will find a way in. Make room for faith and there will be no need to go in search of God. Like a gentle breeze through an open window, God will enter. Pascal was merely trying to open your window" (*In Search of God,* p. 150). So I am not unsympathetic—far from it.

Where I think Pascal was mistaken was not in his method of how to acquire beliefs that you would like to (or think you should) have, but in the Christian content of the beliefs he prescribed. In other words, given our game, the situation is this: You, a great philosopher whom I respect, seem to believe—and perhaps to know—something that I don't. For instance, after reading your last two books on epistemology (*Warrant, the Current Debate,* and *Warrant and Proper Function*), I would (and do) trust whatever you have to say regarding beliefs and knowledge on our topic, provided you could instruct me along the way. After all, you and I both, as all philosophers should, do care very much about knowing the truth about ourselves and the world, and if your beliefs about God, Jesus, and so on are true, it has serious repercussions for nearly all matters philosophical! However, the advice you've given me has already been tried; I've had plenty of experience with Christians, both of their ordinary sorts of varieties and in their professional capacities, and fail to attain any sense of awe, mystery, or reverence for the content of their beliefs nor admiration for their personal states of being (the awe and admiration I experience for the work of my present esteemed colleague has nothing to do with his Christianity but, rather, his philosophy). I certainly would like to be able to do that, mind you—for I have managed (to some but not very great degree) a sense of awe and mystery in Buddhist and Hindu cases. (For instance I find the words of Buddha, Krishnamurti—even Rajneesh!—far more illuminating than anything I've read attributed to Jesus.) So what I am no asking for is what you, *qua* philosopher, may have to offer to me, *qua* philosopher, in terms of the two factors that seem to have made most difference in your case (numbered 1 and 2 above). I have talked to priests—useless. I have talked to simple commonfolk Christians. It doesn't help but in both cases seems to hurt the cause. I've read tons of books on and around the topic and will probably read only one more (yours). I figure talking to someone steeped and trained in some of the similar traditions as I—and we have much more than that in common—would help me, and others, to see the light. Can you do this? I think if you succeeded it would be doing a

great service not just to a great many philosophers who may be in a similar position as myself but also to those unfortunate souls who have not had the benefit of a full-blown philosophical education. We might then be better able to understand each other, and the true nature ultimate reality, across an apparent divide.

AP: Well, I don't think it's all that hard to come to *understand* each other; we can do so just by doing what you and I are in fact doing: openly exploring each other's ways of thinking. But you had asked for something quite different: You asked me whether I could give advice as to how to come to hold Christian belief. I gave you the best answer I could, but you didn't like it ("your Pascalian advice I find most suprising, coming from a philosopher!") It's not that you don't like it because you don't think it is *effective* advice; the problem instead seems to be that following the same or similar advice, one might very well come to believe what was *false* or in some other way objectionable. But first, why is that an objection? I ask you how to get rid of the tree in my backyard; you say, "Use an ax." It's no objection that one can get into trouble using an ax (maybe cutting down the wrong tree). The same goes here. Granted: This method can lead to false belief; but that in itself is not much of an objection. Not just any means to an end is appropriate, of course: Is the idea that there is something morally objectionable about this advice? If so, I certainly can't see what it might be.

Furthermore, if what we are really looking for is a means of fixing belief that is guaranteed *not* to lead to falsehood, we will be looking for a long time. The fact is most of the large-scale ways in which we fix belief suffer from that same debility—here that double standard raises its ugly head again.

Still further, "belief by osmosis" is one of the main ways in which we form belief; given the human condition, furthermore, it is unavoidable. True: It can lead to false belief as well as true; but in that regard it is no worse than induction, deduction, getting a college education, or studying philosophy.

I'm sort of inclined to think you are still hankering after something like a philosophical argument or proof for belief in God or the central tenets of Christian belief. But as I've already said, that's the wrong approach. First, philosophical arguments can't accomplish much when it comes to the existence of really important things—other people, material objects, the past, moral standards, and the like. One really wouldn't expect it to be of much use in the present context. And in any event, what is most important about being a Christian is probably not what one believes, but (as Jonathan Edwards says) what one loves and hates, what one is prepared to commit one's life to. Being a Christian is perhaps less a matter of intellect than will—both the affective side of the will and the executive side. What really counts here is *wanting* to believe in God and love Him, or wanting to want to believe in and love Him.

You also object that you have already tried this advice, and it doesn't work, at least for you. But this method really isn't of a sort such that one can easily say, at some point, "I've tried it, and it doesn't work, or anyway doesn't work for me." It's the sort of thing one has to keep on trying.

So all I can say, really, by way of advice to someone who wants to come to think like a Christian, is repeat what I said: Pray; read the Bible; read Christian writers—not so much philosophers and technical theologians as devotional writers; associate with other Christians.

DK: Well, first, I don't see that we are in fact coming to understand each other! I'm still quite mystified as to why you, a philosopher, believe in Jesus and the Bible—indeed, more so than before we began! And what I don't like about your advice *is* that it isn't effective, at least not on this philosopher; the "axe" you've given me for chopping down trees won't even cut twigs. It makes me scratch my head and go, "Huh?" Nor am I so sure that *philosophy* can't "accomplish much" when it comes to questions about the mind and metaphysics, morality, and so on, though certainly philosophical *arguments* have proven to have their limitations regarding the attainment of some sort of simple, definite, final truth on these matters. For instance, I think the practice of philosophy can certainly sober one's mind from the intoxication of naïve beliefs about all sorts of

things, up to and including (at least from this perhaps jaded philosopher's perspective) belief in Jesus and the Bible.

So, to play our game: Of course, I *want* to believe in God and love him, if he or she or it exists. I would be crazy not to, wouldn't I? But all my philosophical sensibilities—no, more than that, it is my whole being—tells me that what you call "God" does not exist, that the Bible is a work of fiction (but not a particularly good one), and that as far as religions go, Christianity is not even as plausible nor as interesting nor as inspiring as, say, Buddhism or Hinduism. So what then do you, a philosopher who has the "feeling of God's presence," to whom God "seems as real as your children or people you work with," (and "God," I take it, has for you some Christian connotation), have to say to this poor, inquiring philosopher? Is it just that, well, you were raised that way and I wasn't? But—perhaps to a lesser degree—I was! Is it just that, well, you believe the propositions of Christianity have the same epistemic status as all the other things we were taught to believe by our society, such as that other people exist, what happened in the past, and so on? But just about *everybody* believes that other people exist, that the world is real, that Athens warred with Sparta, and so on, and certainly not everybody believes in Jesus and the resurrection, and so on; furthermore, those of us trained in the art of questioning authority, typically—at least this is poignantly true of *this* philosopher—find that beliefs acquired by way of religious authorities fall as the first victims, or perhaps I should say first casualties, of philosophical inquiry. If you believe what you say you believe, then you must believe that as a philosopher or perhaps even as a man I have gone seriously wrong somewhere, that there is something seriously wrong with me. Well, what? Can you, as a philosopher and a fellow human being, help me or not? You see the problem?

AP: First, I really don't see why you are mystified that I, as you say, a philosopher, believe in Jesus and the Bible. Don't we agree that there is nothing philosophically unrespectable about Christian belief? At any rate I don't know of any cogent philosophical argument against such belief or against its rational acceptability. You suggest that "beliefs acquired by way of religious authorities fall as the first victims . . . of philosophical inquiry." I don't think the ultimate source of Christian belief (see below) is religious authority, but I certainly haven't found anything in philosophical inquiry that calls such belief into question. Of course, some philosophers reject and argue against such beliefs; but their rejection doesn't as such call Christian belief into question, and their arguments don't seem to me to be cogent. Furthermore, Christian belief is not weird, crazy, unprecedented, unheard of among people generally, or among philosophers. So I'm not clear about why you are mystified.

You ask, "Is it just that, well, you were raised that way and I wasn't?" I guess you are asking *why* I believe these things. Presumably you aren't asking me for propositional evidence; we both know that I don't believe them on the basis of argument or propositional evidence. I believe them, rather, because they have what we could call "doxastic evidence"; they simply seem to me to be true (just as memory or a priori beliefs do); when I think about them, they (or I) have the phenomenology that goes with thinking about a belief I hold by memory or perception or a priori intuition. Are you perhaps asking me to give an opinion on the *source* of Christian belief, the faculty or belief-producing process that produces them? Freud thought the source was wishful thinking; are you asking me what I think the source is? Well, of course I don't think the ultimate source is wishful thinking, or parental influence, or the influence of "religious authorities"—although certainly I originally believed things because I was taught them. (Just as you, no doubt, originally believed that some mountains are covered with snow and ice in the middle of the summer because you were taught this.) I'd be inclined to say, instead, that the source of belief in God is something like what John Calvin calls the "*sensus divinitatis*," a sort of natural instinct implanted (by God) in us human beings to believe in God and to see his hand in the world around us. But I am much less sure of any such epistemological account of belief in God than I am of the truth of that belief.

Finally, you say that if I believe what I do, then I must believe that as a philosopher or perhaps even as a man you have gone seriously wrong somewhere. Yes, I must certainly think so; I believe you are mistaken about something such that there isn't anything more important to be right about. And of course given what *you* believe, you must believe the same thing about *me;* you must think I am profoundly deceived or deluded, a victim of some powerful illusion. But then you ask: "Can you, as a philosopher and a fellow human being, help me?" But if it is really true, as you say, that all of your philosophical sensibilities and indeed your whole being tell you that what I call "God" does not exist, you can't really think you *need* help along these lines. You are convinced my beliefs are false; if so, then it would certainly not be a step forward, from your perspective, to come to think about these things the way I do. Of course *I* think you do need help, in that you fail to believe something I think both true and of enormous significance; but I doubt that it is within my power to get you to see (as it seems to me) the truth of these things. (That's something I'll have to leave to God.) Of course I suppose you'd agree that the fact that I can't convince you of the truth of theistic belief doesn't so much as slyly suggest that there is something wrong or irrational or improper about such belief, right?

DK: Well, yes, but I nevertheless truly *do* think I need help along these lines, given that a philosopher whom I respect as a philosopher, whose philosophical talents seem clearly and distinctly to me to be superior (or at least to be of a very high degree of excellence), believes X whereas I find myself believing *not* X. You are not a Jesus freak or some Bible-thumping fellow on the street corner, but Alvin Plantinga. Moreover, I am not so attached to any of my beliefs that I wouldn't find it philosophically exhilarating—indeed, perhaps downright spiritually uplifting —to have the doxastic rug pulled out from under me with regard to any of my deeply held beliefs, up to and including, especially, by belief that *not* X! I am invested in the stock market, not in some particular position. Nobody will take my tenure away if my mind gets changed. My wife and daughters will love me no less, I'm certain of that. The institution that employs me has no religious requirements and makes no religious demands upon its faculty or students, one way or the other. Some colleagues and friends might frown, many others would smile, most would not care. Many, I am sure, would think it was "neat," (ironic, and so on) and probably so would I—it would make me smile and laugh at myself and the world. Furthermore, contrary to what you say, I *would* in fact regard it as a very big step forward indeed if I found myself after an exchange with a fellow philosopher believing something that, prior to that exchange, I had not found it in my power to believe! What's the big deal, really? I have no problem with that! So I was wrong! I am not the type who walks around with a scowl on his face, growling, "Grr, I was wrong." And, unlike some others whom I know, I have no vested interest in believing X or *not* X (nor, generally, do I fear having my "worldview" challenged or undermined or changed, which for some philosophers I know involves deep psychological issues having to do with intellectual and emotional control—I just don't care; in that regard I'm rather loose and easy and I *like* it that way). I've been wrong before and I'll be wrong again. So what? Hooray for the new view, thank you very much! Truth is, I presently regard it as an intellectual (and perhaps spiritual) weakness on my part to not be able to believe what in this case you apparently not only do believe but consider to be a deep fact about us and the world. We might, of course, all be wrong about everything —I take it we would both agree to that—but surely if philosopher A, who believes that *not* X, cannot fathom how it is possible that philosopher B believes X, then something *is* deeply wrong—either with philosopher A, or with philosopher B, or else with philosophy itself. And also, thus, I am sorry to say, your comment that you "have to leave to God" my seeing "the truth of these things" seems to me somewhat of a cheap shot.

AP: I'm really sorry you took what I said as a cheap shot. It certainly wasn't intended as a shot (cheap or otherwise.) I can put my point like this. What do I have to offer that would or could convince you? Philosophers specialize in arguments; but argument is usually insufficient to move someone to belief in God. I don't know of any argument that is likely to convince you, if, as you say, every fiber of your being cries out against belief in God. I do have something else to offer as a person rather than as a philosopher: I can testify to the fact that it sometimes seems to me (as it does to many others) that I *experience* the presence of God. But, of course, I don't take it that you should or would necessarily be moved by that testimony on my part. So there really isn't much I can do with respect to contributing to your or someone else's coming to believe in God. According to Christian belief, faith is a gift— a gift from God. (A gift, I believe, that is offered to anyone who really wants it.) That's why I said I'd have to leave this up to God. I did not for a minute mean to suggest I thought you were unduly stubborn, or anything of that sort. Not at all. You say:

> We might, of course, all be wrong about everything—I take it we would both agree to that— but surely if philosopher A, who believes that *not* X, cannot fathom how it is possible that philosopher B believes X, then something is deeply wrong—either with philosopher A, or with philosopher B, or else with philosophy itself.

That seems right; I think the conclusion has to be that there is something wrong with one or the other of us. Given what I believe, I am committed to supposing that you are blind in some important way. Given what you believe, you are committed to supposing that I am a victim of some kind of illusion, as Freud suggested, some kind of psychological belief-producing mechanism that is aimed, not at the production of true beliefs, but at the production of beliefs with some other property—perhaps the property of enabling one to continue on in this bleak and impersonal world. I can't see any other alternative.

PART 6

Morality, Justice, and Law

WHY BE MORAL?

Suppose you could at will make yourself and anything you wear invisible and no one knew. What would you do? Would you walk into a bank, fill your pockets with money, and walk out undetected? Would you reward yourself in all kinds of "immoral" ways, perhaps even punishing your enemies? This is the question raised by Plato's famous "Myth of Gyges's Ring," which appears in his *Republic,* from which "Why Be Moral?" is taken. The characters Glaucon and Adeimantus—Plato's brothers—argue to Socrates that humans are essentially psychological egoists, predisposed by nature to promote their own self-interest over the interests of others. Glaucon claims that the only reason that supposedly moral people behave the way they do is that they lack the power to be unjust and simply cannot get away with it reliably. He uses the story of the magic ring that grants invisibility to its wearer to illustrate this. What would *you* do with such a ring?

Adeimantus and Glaucon both hold the view that the only advantage to being moral is that dishonesty doesn't pay as well as honesty, which earns you respect. The ring of invisibility changes the payoff scheme significantly, because a scheme that is executed carefully virtually guarantees that you would not be caught. This just goes to show, they claim, that most rational way to be is to *appear* moral and honest while in reality being dishonest, selfish, and immoral in any way that benefits you without jeopardizing your position.

Socrates, however, tries to give a response to the contrary based on Plato's metaphysics and theory of knowledge. Ethics is the branch of philosophy that inquires into theories of morality. Normative ethics inquires into standards of right and wrong, good and bad, and so on that *ought* to be accepted. Thus, for instance, medical ethics deals with right standards of conduct among those in the medical and related professions, business ethics with right conduct in the business profession, and so on, whereas ethics in general asks what those standards are for society at large.

But why do we need a theory of morality to begin with? We have laws, religious customs, our conscience, and so on. Can't we simply obey those? Well, one problem is that sometimes these conflict. Perhaps we should in such cases simply follow the law. But have there ever been bad, or immoral, laws? For instance, from our present point of view it seems the laws that made slavery possible are wrong and immoral. Bad laws come and hopefully go. So how shall we appraise them? Is there any objectivity to such judgments, or is it all relative, or perhaps merely a case of those in power having their way? For instance, is there any way to demonstrate that slavery was wrong not just from *our* present point of view but, even, back then—that, for instance, Thomas Jefferson was *morally wrong* for owning slaves?

The same sorts of questions can be raised about different cultures and societies today where different standards of conduct are in place. To simply decree that something is right on the basis of whatever the social customs or mores are raises at the same time the problems of skepticism about ethics and morality and also the problem of moral relativism. According to the former, there are no moral truths in ethics, no moral absolutes; for the latter, whatever "truth" there may be in the moral realm is relative to a particular time, culture, and social group. A moral skeptic would allow that if a particular society approved of slavery, torture, or murder, there would be nothing morally wrong about those things in that society. A moral relativist would claim that slavery was in fact right and morally permissible, say, in early nineteenth-century America but wrong today in our society but not wrong in any other societies that still condone it.

Bernard Williams, in "Relativism," mounts an attack on moral relativism on the grounds that relativism as such is an inconsistent position to hold, in so far as a relativist cannot, for instance, claim that one society should not interfere with another or be in any way tolerant. Jonathan Bennett, in "The Conscience of Huckleberry Finn," presents the well-known case of Huck Finn helping his friend, Joe, a slave, escape. All the traditional, moral, and ethical principles available to Huck forbid him from doing so. For one thing, it's against the law. Moreover, Huck's conscience tells him it's wrong; his society tells him it's wrong; his preacher tells him it's wrong; and so on. Yet we seem to be on Huck's side. Who's *right,* and *why?*

What it seems we need, then, is some viable sort of moral theory. Is there any?

STANDARDS OF RIGHT AND WRONG: THEORY AND PRACTICE

One of the best examples of the Socratic method of reasoning is Plato's *Euthyphro.* This dialog takes place shortly before Socrates' infamous trial and subsequent execution in 399 B.C.E. Euthyphro is a lawyer supposedly so very pious that he has come to court to prosecute his own father, a rich landowner, for having inadvertently caused the death of a slave who in a brawl had murdered another slave. If anyone knows what piety is, then surely Euthyphro knows, having gone to such extreme lengths in the name of piety! Euthyphro's best answer is that pious actions are those that please the gods, whereas impious actions are those that displease the gods. Socrates then mounts a devastating assault against any such religious-based ethics, in the form of a simple, piercing question: Is an action pious because it pleases the gods, or does it please the gods because it is pious? In other words, is some action, X, right because God says so, or does God say so because X is right? This question cuts so deeply to the heart of the issue that contemporary philosopher Anthony Flew has remarked that "one good test of a person's aptitude for philosophy is to discover whether he can grasp its force and point."

Socrates's famous question challenges the traditional divine command theory according to which an act is right if it is divinely commanded and wrong if it is divinely forbidden. Is it right because God says so, or does God say so because it's right? The questions throws believers of the divine command theory into a dilemma. The first horn—that an act is right if God says so—makes God's say-so the cause and the rightness of the act an effect. This would mean that "God says X is right" *makes* X right, regardless of what X is. And the problem is that we can substitute for X a number of things that it seems to us repugnant to suppose it would be right to do, such as torturing innocent children for pleasure. The second horn—that God says so because it's right—seems the obviously better choice, then, except it makes the role of God irrelevant to the question of what *makes* an act right or wrong. This would seem to sever morality from religion. But then on what, if anything, can morality be based?

The great English philosopher Thomas Hobbes, in his *Leviathan,* starts out with what is essentially an ethical egoist position to create the social contract theory, of which he is the modern founder. Without some such social contract, life would be, as he so famously puts it, "solitary, poor, nasty, brutish and short." That is why, starting in a state of nature, human beings develop governments and laws without which, in his view, there would be no right and wrong, no justice or injustice. To enhance our individual well-being, he claims, we give up certain natural freedoms for the sake of living in a society without which we would all be much worse off. His theory had a wide influence in ethics and contractarian theories of justice, discussed in the next subsection, "Justice and Law."

One of the other most influential moral theories of all time is that of Immanuel Kant. His *Foundations of the Metaphysics of Morals* (1785), from which our selection is taken, presents his deontological (rule-based) ethical theory that centers on his categorical imperative: "Act only on that maxim which you can at the same time will to become a universal law." As the universal moral test of right principles of action, the categorical imperative according to Kant makes us all duty-bound to obey certain principles in the same way that objects in nature are bound to act according to the laws of nature. Kant distinguishes actions done from mere inclination rather than by the will. And the foundation of morality consists in having a good will. This is a very different conception of moral goodness than is found, for instance, in Plato, Aristotle, and Augustine, all of whom understood morality in terms of happiness—in their case, one's own. Utilitarians, such as John Stuart Mill, also use happiness as their moral foundation, in opposition to Kant, though not just in terms of one's own but of everyone's concerned. Onora O'Neill, in her article, "Kantian Approaches to Some Famine Problems," applies Kant's theory to the specific problem of famine relief.

All moral theories fall into one of two basic categories: consequentialism, in which what makes an act right is determined by its *consequences,* and nonconsequentialism, or deontological (rule-based) theories, in which what makes an act right has less to do with its consequences than that it is done in accordance with some principle or rule. (There are some that try to combine the best elements of both, such as rule utilitarianism.) Whereas Kant's theory is nonconsequentialist, or deontological, utilitarianism is nonconsequentialist. It was started by the philosopher Jeremy Bentham (1748–1832) and developed by John Stuart Mill (1806–1873). Bentham defined his principle of utility as "that property in any object whereby it tends to produce pleasure, good or happiness, or to prevent the happening of mischief, pain, evil or unhappiness to the party whose interest is considered." According to Bentham, this principle takes into account the two main motives for all human action—pain and pleasure. Governments, social, political, and legal institutions, as well as individual citizens, should follow the Greatest Happiness Principle: Choose that course of action that leads to the greatest happiness for the greatest number of people.

John Stuart Mill was the most famous of Bentham's many disciples. But whereas Bentham had defined his utility principle in terms of avoiding pain and securing pleasure, Mill argues that such self-interest is an inadequate criterion of moral goodness. What is missing is a qualitative distinction between pleasures. In this way, Mill revolutionized utilitarian ideas in his most widely influential book, *Utilitarianism* (1863), from which our selection is taken. What previous theories lacked was any qualitative distinction between types of pleasure and pain sensations: "Quantity of pleasure being equal, pushpin is as good as poetry." Mill therefore adds quality to his moral calculus, saying "better to be Socrates dissatisfied than a fool satisfied." Mill tied his moral theory to his political theory, stating that moral judgments having to do with qualities would have to be decided democratically, through majority rule, because unlike quantitative judgments they were not objective but subjective.

Just as Onora O'Neill applies the Kantian theory to the problem of famine, Peter Singer in his "Famine, Affluence, and Morality" applies utilitarianism to the same problem, with some interesting similarities and differences that bring to light both types of theories.

Kwame Anthony Appiah criticizes racism in all its forms from a Kantian perspective. He distinguishes several varieties of racism, all of which presuppose what he calls *racialism,* which he defines as the belief that "there are heritable characteristics, possessed by members of our species, that allow us to divide them into a small set of races, in such a way that all members of these races share certain traits and tendencies with each other that they do not share with members of any other race." He claims, first, that racialism is false and, second, that even if it were true all forms of racism would be indefensible.

W. D. Ross, on the other hand, tries to combine both a Kantian and a utilitarian approach in his "What Makes Right Act Right?" He claims, for starters, that actual life situations are far more complicated than the founders of either type of theory had ever supposed. There are a variety of duties that we arguably do have, he claims, but they often conflict, and there is no clear way of deciding in such cases what we ought to do. His notion of prima facie duty is an attempt to deal with the notion that moral reasons must be weighted relative to one another. Ultimately, we must rely on our own intuitions; his theory is therefore called *intuitionism.*

In "Life or Death of the Global Village," Marie-Louise Friquegnon tries to put contemporary social, political, and economic issues into a global perspective to suggest that, although the moral complexities have been increasing, the world has been getting smaller in ways that may help us to bring about a truly global system of right and wrong— morality without boundaries.

In the closing piece of this section, Susan Leigh Anderson surveys the entire field of ethics, morality, and justice to claim that what is unique about us as human beings is that, as the great nineteenth-century German philosopher Nietzsche had suggested, we are, essentially, *valuing beings.* What values we eventually end up with, she argues, is not simply a matter of conditioning but something we ourselves have fashioned out of our experiences and the choices we constantly have to make, by which we become a particular sort of person. Anderson advocates a radical self-examination and self-criticism as the starting points of inquiry into what the standards of right and wrong might be not just for a particular society but, most of all, for us as *individuals.* In doing so, she offers guidelines to help us become the persons we most want to be.

JUSTICE AND LAW

The trial and death of Plato's beloved mentor Socrates is dramatically captured in his trilogy, *Euthyphro, Apology,* and *Crito.* Plato's "The Address of the Laws" is taken from the last of these. Socrates, who has been unjustly sentenced to death for corrupting the youth and raising doubts in people's minds about the accepted gods, is in prison awaiting execution by the infamous hemlock. But now he is given the chance to escape. Apparently, the same authorities who sentenced him expected that he would flee, aided by his followers, to another country; even the guards had been alerted to this scheme, and they were supposed to look the other way so that Socrates could escape. But Socrates surprises everybody, perhaps most of all his friends, by choosing to stay. He offers several arguments to justify his decision based on his conviction that, despite his disagreement with his accusers and the state, he has a moral obligation to obey the law.

In "Of Commonwealth and the Rights of Sovereigns" Thomas Hobbes presents his argument for absolute submission by citizens to their sovereign leader. Unlike Aristotle, who believed that people by their very nature are suited for life in political societies, Hobbes claimed just the opposite. Our natural state is to exist in a state of nature consisting in a constant struggle of all against all. Conflict, war, and violence are thus at the root of our natural existence. The only viable solution, claims Hobbes, is to establish a strong state, which requires that everyone agree to entrust completely the power of judgment on all matters of law and justice to the sovereign, which can consist either of an individual or an assembly of leaders. This is achieved by a tacitly agreed to social contract, by which the antagonistic forces of diverse individual wills can exist in harmony through the social contract that forms the basis of the political state.

Locke's *Two Treatises of Civil Government* (1690) is widely regarded as among the greatest political works of modern times. In it, Locke begins, as did Hobbes, with an analysis of the "state of nature" as it existed prior to the formation of a political state. But Locke takes a much less pessimistic view than Hobbes. All human beings are, according to Locke, created equal "within the bounds of the law of nature," which is reason itself: "Reason, which is that law, teaches all mankind who will but consult it, that, being all equal and independent, no one ought to harm another in his life, health, liberty or possessions." According to Locke, moral, political, and legal principles, such as "where there is no property there is no injustice" and "no government allows absolute liberty," are as certain as any propositions in Euclid. A just political system must according to Locke be constructed according so as to reflect and amplify the natural state of the world. Majority rule, the separation of church and state, the right of a people to change governments, the natural right of a people to overthrow unjust governments, the separation of powers within a government are all ideas central to Locke's system. It was Locke who championed the idea that all people are born free and with like capacities and rights. Each person is free to preserve his or her own interests but without injuring those of others. The right to be treated by everyone as a rational being holds even prior to the founding of the state; but then there is no authoritative power to decide conflicts. The state of nature is not in itself a state of war, but it would lead to war if each person attempted to exercise the right of self-protection. To prevent such acts of violence, the civil community is constructed based on a free contract to which all individual members transfer their natural freedom and power. Submission to the authority of the state is thus defined by Locke as a free act; by this "contract" natural rights are not destroyed but guarded. Political freedom is thus an obedience to self-imposed law, the subordination to the common will expressing itself in the majority. Political power should therefore be neither tyrannical, because arbitrary rule is no better than the state of nature, nor should it be paternal, because rulers and their subjects are all equally rational, which is not the case in a parent–child relationship. Locke had a great and lasting influence on political philosophy in the eighteenth century, not just in Europe but also among the founders of a new, revolutionary country called the United States.

In *On Liberty* (1859) another great English philosopher, John Stuart Mill, argues that the fundamental utilitarian principle—the greatest amount of happiness for the greatest number of people—can only be achieved if all individuals are given as much freedom of thought and action as possible. This means almost unlimited freedom: The only constraint is a prohibition against causing harm to others. *On Liberty* was popular in Europe and highly influential to the development of nineteenth- and early twentieth-century democracy in the United States. Mill argues that the correct lesson from the past is that no one should have a monopoly on what people regard to be the truth. All our best philosophies keep evolving, as does science, which strongly suggests that the best human knowledge can attain is partial truths. The philosophical and political well-being of a society should therefore be dependent upon growth and change, or else we end up in dead ends like past empires. Finally, and perhaps most importantly, if we let the wisest among us become the rulers in charge of everything, including our education, what will happen to the rest of the people? They will look up to the leaders. This may be good for a generation or two of leadership, but it will lead, Mill argues, in the long run to stagnation and decline. After a while, the official "truths" will simply be passed down, generation to generation, and no one will achieve anything new. To avoid the rise and inevitable fall of every previous empire, the wise society should therefore encourage not obedience to authority but the development of individuality, even rebellion. It must help spawn individuals through whom new ideas are born into the world. Eccentricity, not conformity, should be the ideal. The majority must be tolerant and helpful to the minorities, the learned should be tolerant of the unlearned, and so on. This will, in Mill's view, produce not just a healthy, vibrant society but a moral one that evolves over time to achieve the greatest happiness for the greatest number.

In *A Theory of Justice,* one of the most influential works in twentieth-century political theory, philosopher John Rawls presents what he claims are the essential elements for fairness and justice in our political and social institutions. First, we must start from what he calls the Original Position, in which none of us have any knowledge of our own particular wants, values, attachments, and so on. These are the principles that all rational persons would choose from behind the Veil of Ignorance, a starting position in which "no one knows his place in society, his class position or social status; nor does he know his fortune in the distribution of natural assets and abilities, his intelligence and strength, and the like." By then adopting a maximin strategy for making decisions under uncertainty, we would always rank our choices by their worst possible outcomes and opt in the end for that choice whose worst outcome is superior to the worst outcome of any other choice. It is such a conservative strategy that ultimately makes Rawls's Two Principles of Justice as Fairness the best moral theory because it guarantees basic individual rights and liberties while maximizing the benefits to the least advantaged in our society. These initial two Principles of Justice as Fairness—(1) the principle of greatest equal liberty and (2) the principle of equal opportunity—come in what Rawls calls their "lexical" order, meaning that the first, which upholds individual liberty, has priority over the second, the so-called *difference principle.* Basically, the difference principle is strongly egalitarian in that unless there is a better distribution of value that makes everyone better off, the equal distribution is preferable. This means that, for instance, fundamental liberties such as freedom of speech cannot be infringed upon for the benefit of least advantaged individuals, provided that our social institutions are themselves properly designed to raise the welfare of those who are worst off to begin with. The *just savings principle* is designed to hold over time, such that each simultaneously existing generation of individuals must both preserve the gains of culture and civilization achieved by previous generations while putting aside some proper amount of economic capital. Thus, ultimately, in Rawls's vision all social primary goods such as liberty, opportunity, income, wealth, the bases of self-respect, and so on must be distributed equally *unless* an unequal distribution would benefit those who are *least* favored.

One of the leading causes of injustice and unfairness in our society, claims Susan Okin in "Justice and Gender," is gender, by which she means "the deeply entrenched institutionalization of sexual difference." There is nothing *natural* in the ways society treats men and women differently based on sex, she claims, and the way we have come to be conditioned by our social institutions to unfair disadvantages to women. Her arguments rely strongly on the basic elements of John Rawls's theory, which she applies with great skill, yet she is critical of several details that she thinks make it not as good as it could be. In fact, she accuses Rawls of himself having been seduced by an inherently male bias in certain aspects of the development of his own theory.

Martin Luther King's "Letter from Birmingham Jail" is widely regarded as one of the great works on racial injustice. John Rawls, for instance, acknowledges King's contribution to his own understanding of the concept civil disobedience and is inspired by King to define, in his *Theory of Justice,* civil disobedience as a "public, nonviolent, conscientious yet political act contrary to government. . . . one addresses the sense of justice of the majority of the community and declares that in one's considered opinion the principles of social cooperation among free and equal men are not being respected." King is writing the piece from behind bars, in an Alabama jail, separated by a gulf of more than twenty-five centuries from another philosopher who dared to question authority and was made to suffer for it. "The more things change, the more they stay the same," goes the old saying. But, like Socrates, unjustly imprisoned within the darkness of ignorance and oppression, instead of giving in to fear, Martin Luther King ignites the light of wisdom, and the world is changed forever.

WHY BE MORAL?

The Myth of Gyges's Ring

PLATO

Plato (427–347 B.C.E.) lived in Athens and was a student of Socrates. Most of his surviving works, written in dialog form, feature the character of Socrates. Plato is generally regarded as one of the greatest philosophers of all time. He founded the Academy, the world's first university.

GLAUCON: If you please, then, I will revive the argument of Thrasymachus. And first I will speak of the nature and origin of justice according to the common view of them. Secondly, I will show that all men who practice justice do so against their will, of necessity, but not as a good. And thirdly, I will argue that there is reason in this view, for the life of the unjust is after all better far than the life of the just—if what they say is true, Socrates, since I myself am not of their opinion. But still I acknowledge that I am perplexed when I hear the voices of Thrasymachus and myriads of others dinning in my ears; and, on the other hand, I have never yet heard the superiority of justice to injustice maintained by any one in a satisfactory way. I want to hear justice praised in respect of itself; then I shall be satisfied, and you are the person from whom I think that I am most likely to hear this; and therefore I will praise the unjust life to the utmost of my power, and my manner of speaking will indicate the manner in which I desire to hear you too praising justice and censuring injustice. Will you say whether you approve of my proposal?

SOCRATES: Indeed I do; nor can I imagine any theme about which a man of sense would oftener wish to converse.

GLAUCON: I am delighted, he replied, to hear you say so, and shall begin by speaking, as I proposed, of the nature and origin of justice.

They say that to do injustice is, by nature, good; to suffer injustice, evil; but that the evil is greater than the good. And so when men have both done and suffered injustice and have had experience of both, not being able to avoid the one and obtain the other, they think that they had better agree among themselves to have neither; hence there arise laws and mutual covenants; and that which is ordained by law is termed by them lawful and just. This they affirm to be the origin and nature of justice:—it is a mean or compromise, between the best of all, which is to do injustice and not be punished, and the worst of all, which is to suffer injustice without the power of retaliation; and justice, being at a middle point between the two, is tolerated not as a good, but as the lesser evil, and honoured by reason of the inability of men to do injustice. For no man who is worthy to be called a man would ever submit to such an agreement if he were able to resist; he would be mad if he did. Such is the received account, Socrates, of the nature and origin of justice.

Now that those who practice justice do so involuntarily and because they have not the power to be unjust will best appear if we imagine something of this kind: having given both to the just and the unjust power to do what they will, let us watch and see whither desire will lead them; then we shall discover in the very act the just and

From *The Dialogues of Plato,* translated by Benjamin Jowett (New York: Scribner's, 1889).

unjust man to be proceeding along the same road, following their interest, which all natures deem to be their good, and are only diverted into the path of justice by the force of law. The liberty which we are supposing may be most completely given to them in the form of such a power as is said to have been possessed by Gyges the ancestor of Croesus the Lydian. According to the tradition, Gyges was a shepherd in the service of the king of Lydia; there was a great storm, and an earthquake made an opening in the earth at the place where he was feeding his flock. Amazed at the sight, he descended into the opening, where, among other marvels, he beheld a hollow brazen horse, having doors, at which he stooping and looking in saw a dead body of stature, as appeared to him, more than human, and having nothing on but a gold ring; this he took from the finger of the dead and reascended. Now the shepherds met together, according to custom, that they might send their monthly report about the flocks to the king; into their assembly he came having the ring on his finger, and as he was sitting among them he chanced to turn the collet of the ring inside his hand, when instantly he became invisible to the rest of the company and they began to speak of him as if he were no longer present. He was astonished at this, and again touching the ring he turned the collet outwards and reappeared; he made several trials of the ring, and always with the same result—when he turned the collet inwards he became invisible, when outwards he reappeared. Whereupon he contrived to be chosen one of the messengers who were sent to the court; where as soon as he arrived he seduced the queen, and with her help conspired against the king and slew him, and took the kingdom. Suppose now that there were two such magic rings, and the just put on one of them and the unjust the other; no man can be imagined to be of such an iron nature that he would stand fast in justice. No man would keep his hands off what was not his own when he could safely take what he liked out of the market, or go into houses and lie with any one at his pleasure, or kill or release from prison whom he would, and in all respects be like a God among men. Then the actions of

the just would be as the actions of the unjust; they would both come at last to the same point. And this we may truly affirm to be a great proof that a man is just, not willingly or because he thinks that justice is any good to him individually, but of necessity, for wherever any one thinks that he can safely be unjust, there he is unjust. For all men believe in their hearts that injustice is far more profitable to the individual than justice, and he who argues as I have been supposing, will say that they are right. If you could imagine any one obtaining this power of becoming invisible, and never doing any wrong or touching what was another's, he would be thought by the lookers-on to be a most wretched idiot, although they would praise him to one another's faces, and keep up appearances with one another from a fear that they too might suffer injustice. Enough of this.

Now, if we are to form a real judgment of the life of the just and unjust, we must isolate them; there is no other way; and how is the isolation to be effected? I answer: Let the unjust man be entirely unjust, and the just man entirely just; nothing is to be taken away from either of them, and both are to be perfectly furnished for the work of their respective lives. First, let the unjust be like other distinguished masters of craft; like the skillful pilot or physician, who knows intuitively his own powers and keeps within their limits, and who, if he fails at any point, is able to recover himself. So let the unjust make his unjust attempts in the right way, and lie hidden if he means to be great in his injustice (he who is found out is nobody): for the highest reach of injustice is: to be deemed just when you are not. Therefore I say that in the perfectly unjust man we must assume the most perfect injustice; there is to be no deduction, but we must allow him, while doing the most unjust acts, to have acquired the greatest reputation for justice. If he have taken a false step he must be able to recover himself; he must be one who can speak with effect, if any of his deeds come to light, and who can force his way where force is required by his courage and strength, and command of money and friends. And at his side let us place the just man in his nobleness and simplicity, wishing, as Aeschylus says, to be and not to seem good. There must be no seeming, for if he seem to be just he will be honoured and rewarded, and then we shall now know whether he is just for the sake of justice or for the sake of honours and rewards; therefore, let him be clothed in justice only, and have no other covering; and he must be imagined in a state of life the opposite of the former. Let him be the best of men, and let him be thought the worst; then he will have been put to the proof; and we shall see whether he will be affected by the fear of infamy and its consequences. And let him continue thus to the hour of death; being just and seeming to be unjust. When both have reached the uttermost extreme, the one of justice and the other of injustice, let judgment be given which of them is the happier of the two.

SOCRATES: Heavens! my dear Glaucon, I said, how energetically you polish them up for the decision, first one and then the other, as if they were two statues.

GLAUCON: I do my best, he said. And now that we know what they are like there is no difficulty in tracing out the sort of life which awaits either of them. This I will proceed to describe; but as you may think the description a little too coarse, I ask you to suppose, Socrates, that the words which follow are not mine.—Let me put them into the mouths of the eulogists of injustice: they will tell you that the just man who is thought unjust will be scourged, racked, bound—will have his eyes burnt out; and, at last, after suffering every kind of evil, he will be impaled: Then he will understand that he ought to seem only, and not to be, just; the words of Aeschylus may be more truly spoken of the unjust than of the just. For the unjust is pursuing a reality; he does not live with a view to appearances—he wants to be really unjust and not to seem only:—

His mind has a soil deep and fertile.
Out of which spring his prudent counsels.

In the first place, he is thought just, and therefore bears rule in the city; he can marry whom he will, and give in marriage to whom he will; also he can trade and deal where he likes, and always to his own advantage, because he has no misgivings about injustice; and at every contest, whether in public, or private, he gets the better of his antagonists, and gains at their expense, and is rich, and out of his gains he can benefit his friends, and harm his enemies; moreover, he can offer sacrifices, and dedicate gifts to the gods abundantly and magnificently, and can honour the gods or any man whom he wants to honour in a far better style than the just, and therefore he is likely to be dearer than they are to the gods. And thus, Socrates, gods and men are said to unite in making the life of the unjust better than the life of the just. . . .

SOCRATES: Now that we've gotten this far, I said, let's go back to that statement made at the beginning, which brought us here: that it pays for a man to be perfectly unjust if he appears to be just. Isn't that what someone said?

Yes.

Then since we've agreed what power justice and injustice each have, let's have a discussion with him.

How?

By molding in words an image of the soul, so that the one who said that will realize what he was saying.

What kind of image?

Oh, something like those natures the myths tell us were born in ancient times—the Chimaera, Scylla, Cerberus, and others in which many different shapes were supposed to have grown into one.

So they tell us, he said.

Then mold one figure of a colorful, many-headed beast with heads of wild and tame animals growing in a circle all around it; one that can change and grow all of them out of itself.

That's a job for a skilled artist. Still, words mold easier than wax or clay, so consider it done.

And another of a lion, and one of a man. Make the first by far the biggest, the second second largest.

That's easier, and already done.

Now join the three together so that they somehow grow.

All right.

Next mold the image of one, the man, around them all, so that to someone who can't see what's inside but looks only at the container it appears to be a single animal, man.

I have.

Then shall we inform the gentleman that when he says it pays for this man to be unjust, he's saying that it profits him to feast his multifarious beast and his lion and make them grow strong, but to starve and enfeeble the man in him so that he gets dragged wherever the animals lead him, and instead of making them friends and used to each other, to let them bite and fight and eat each other?

That's just what he's saying by praising injustice.

The one who says justice pays, however, would be saying that he should practice and say whatever will give the most mastery to his inner man, who should care for the many-headed beast like a farmer, raising and domesticating its tame heads and preventing the wild ones from growing, making the lion's nature his partner and ally, and so raise them both to be friends to each other and to him.

That's exactly what he means by praising justice.

So in every way the commender of justice is telling the truth, the other a lie. Whether we examine pleasure, reputation, or profit, we find that the man who praises justice speaks truly, and one who disparages it disparages sickly and knows nothing of what he disparages.

I don't think he does at all.

Then let's gently persuade him—his error wasn't intended—by asking him a question: "Shouldn't we say that the traditions of the beautiful and the ugly have come about like this: Beautiful things are those that make our bestial parts subservient to the human—or rather, perhaps, to the divine—part of our nature, while ugly ones are those that enslave the tame to the wild?" Won't he agree?

If he takes my advice.

On this argument then, can it pay for a man to take money unjustly if that means making his best part a slave to the worst? If it wouldn't profit

a man to sell his son or his daughter into slavery—to wild and evil men at that—even if he got a fortune for it, then if he has no pity on himself and enslaves the most godlike thing in him to the most godless and polluted, isn't he a wretch who gets bribed for gold into a destruction more horrible than Euriphyle's, who sold her husband's life for a necklace?

Much more horrible, said Glaucon.

. . . everyone is better off being ruled by the godlike and intelligent; preferably if he has it inside, but if not, it should be imposed on him from without so that we may all be friends and as nearly alike as possible, all steered by the same thing.

Yes, and we're right, he said.

Law, the ally of everyone in the city, clearly intends the same thing, as does the rule of children, which forbids us to let them be free until we've instituted a regime in them as in a city. We serve their best part with a similar part in us, install a like guardian and ruler in them, and only then set them free.

Clearly.

Then how, by what argument, Glaucon, can we say that it pays for a man to be unjust or self-indulgent or to do something shameful to get more money or power if by doing so he makes himself worse?

We can't, he said.

And how can it pay to commit injustice without getting caught and being punished? Doesn't getting away with it make a man even worse? Whereas if a man gets caught and punished, his beastlike part is taken in and tamed, his tame part is set free, and his whole soul acquires justice and temperance and knowledge. Therefore his soul recovers its best nature and attains a state more honorable than the state the body attains when it acquires health and strength and beauty, by as much as the soul is more honorable than the body.

Absolutely.

Then won't a sensible man spend his life directing all his efforts to this end?

Relativism

BERNARD WILLIAMS

Bernard William teaches philosophy at Cambridge University, is a Fellow of King's College, and also teaches at the University of California, Berkeley.

Different societies or cultures have different moral beliefs, rules, expectations, and practices. Theorists disagree about how far the differences go—to what extent, in particular, there are substantive rules that are held universally. They also differ about how deep the phenomenon is—whether societies differ not so much on basic moral ideas but on the ways in which these ideas should be expressed in different cultural circumstances. However, there is undoubtedly a good deal of moral variety in the world, and in the past there was more than there is now. Modern communications and the worldwide spread of commercial society has made for more uniformity—certainly by contrast with the variety of small, virtually self-contained traditional societies, of which few now remain. It is a mistake to concentrate too much on such cases, as opposed to the large interactions of cultural blocs or traditions that have formed a major part of the world's ethical history. But the small isolated societies that have been studied by cultural anthropologists, usually in the wake of colonialism, have certainly stimulated questions about the extent and depth of human moral variety and what it implies about the nature of morality.

Since ancient times, when the Greeks observed that fire burned the same in Persia as in Greece but also observed that the ways in which people thought it right to treat one another were different (a contrast that some thinkers expressed as one between "nature" and "convention"), one reaction to moral variety has been *relativism*. It is indeed most easily recognized in the first place as a reaction rather

than as a theory. Its general spirit is to the effect that each outlook is appropriate in its own place, or that other people's practices are right for them whereas ours are right for us; but it is harder than one might expect to turn this into a coherent theory that retains its distinctively relativist content.

It will not adequately express the relativist spirit, for instance, to claim that there is a universal, absolute morality but simply to accept as well that it does, in its content, allow for local variations that depend on the circumstances. Someone might well think, for instance, that certain rules governing sexuality were appropriate in some social and historical contexts and not in others, in ways that can be explained in terms of those contexts. People who hold very rigid beliefs about such matters do sometimes call such an outlook "relativist," but this is not relativism properly speaking: The outlook claims that the rules of sexual behavior should be morally appropriate, in ways that can be explained, to definite features of the society in which those rules obtain, and this itself is not a relativist principle but an absolute one. In itself, it is no more relativist than the principle that each person should look after his or her own elderly parents: The content of this involves a relation to the agent, but it is meant to apply, non-relativistically, to everyone.

To capture the relativist spirit, then, it will not be enough to accept that some of the content of morality has to be explained in terms of the circumstances in which the morality is applied (which, to some extent, has to be true of any reasonable morality). Rather, the principle, outlook, or practice has to be relativized to *the group that holds it*, simply as such. The structure of relativism proper is given by there being two differing outlooks (sets of moral rules, etc.), and two groups that are distinguished from each other by the fact that they respectively hold those outlooks. There may well be other differences

---

This article has been prepared by the author for the present volume. It is based on extracts from two previous publications: *Morality: An Introduction to Ethics* (Harper & Row, 1972; Cambridge University Press, Canto Books, 1993); and "Ethics," in *Philosophy: A Guide Through the Subject,* edited by A. C. Grayling (Oxford University Press, 1995).

between the groups as well, and in the anthropologist's favorite case of small separate societies, there must be such differences, but so far as moral relativism is concerned, that is not the point—it is the difference in outlook itself that is the focus of the relativization.

Given such a situation, relativism says something to the effect that each outlook applies to, or binds, or is valid for just its own group: that it is "right for them." What does this mean? If it means only that each group thinks that its own outlook is right, this says nothing at all. Relativism goes beyond this and tries to find something to say about the attitude that will be appropriate for each of the groups to have towards the other—and, of course, for other people, with other outlooks, to have towards both of them. It tries to tell us what we should think about groups who differ from us in these ways and who differ from each other. Its problem is to find something that it can consistently, coherently, and usefully say.

In its simplest and most influential form—in which it may be fairly labeled "vulgar relativism"—the conclusion it draws is that one society has no business to condemn, interfere with, or try to change the values of another. Starting from the relativist idea that, say, ritual human sacrifice was "right for" the Aztecs, because the Aztecs practiced it and attached value to it, it concludes that human sacrifice among the Aztecs was right, where this now means that no one had any business to interfere with the practice. In this version, however, the relativist outlook has not remained true to itself. The view is clearly inconsistent, because it ends up with a *nonrelative* claim about the ways in which one society should treat another—a claim, roughly speaking, of universal toleration. This claim is not relativized to anything: It simply says, as a universal moral principle, that at least when it is a matter of the outlooks of two different societies (and of course the idea is familiar with disagreements between smaller groups as well) people should simply leave other people alone. This may sometimes be a good idea and sometimes a bad one; sometimes, as we shall see, it is simply impossible. But however that may be, the claim that everyone should accept it is certainly not relativist.

Vulgar relativism's confusion between a supposedly relativist conception of each society's outlook,

and a nonrelative morality of toleration or noninterference, has historically been helped by certain ways of reading such claims as that human sacrifice was "right for" the Aztecs. In some styles of social science, this has been taken in a functionalist sense to mean that the practice played an important role in this society's life, contributed in nonobvious ways to the society's working, and so on. This understanding of it suffers from some weaknesses of functionalism in general, such as difficulties that surround the identification of "a society." If "a society" is regarded as a cultural unit, identified in part through its values, then many functionalist claims will fail to have any content and will become tautologies: It is tediously a necessary condition of the survival of a group-with-certain-values that the group should retain those values. At the other extreme, the survival of a society could be understood as the survival of certain people and their having descendants, in which case many functionalist claims about the necessity of cultural survival will be false. When in Great Britain some Welsh nationalists speak of the survival of the Welsh language as a condition of the survival of Welsh society, they sometimes convey the impression that it is a condition of the survival of Welsh people, as though the forgetting of Welsh were literally lethal.

In between these two extremes is a genuinely interesting territory of informative social science, where there is room for such claims as that a given practice or belief is integrally connected with much more of a society's fabric than may appear on the surface, that it is not an excrescence, so that discouragement or modification of it may lead to more social change than might have been expected; or, again, that a certain set of values or institutions may be such that if they are lost or seriously changed, the people in the society, even if they physically survive, will do so only in some deracinated and hopeless condition. Such propositions, if they can be established, could of course be very important to deciding what one society's attitude to another should be. But once again, they cannot take over the job of deciding that attitude. Even given interesting truths to the effect that certain practices are "right for" a society in a functionalist sense, these will not themselves give us vulgar relativism's conclusion, that we should not interfere (or criticize, and so on). This requires us to agree to something else, that this society-with-these-values should survive.

Perhaps the clearest indication that something must have gone wrong with the functionalist route to vulgar relativism is what it leaves us to say about ourselves. We are confronted with an exotic society; we accept in the relativistic spirit that its practices are "right for" it; and we are supposed to conclude that it is right for us to leave it alone. On a functionalist reading, this would have to mean that it suited our society, helped it to work, and so on, that we should leave these other people alone; but first, this is certainly not all that was meant, and second, in many cases there is no reason at all to think that it is true.

The central problem for relativism, to which vulgar relativism succumbs in a very obvious way, is to try to conjure out of the fact that societies have different values a principle to determine the attitude of one society to the values of another. This must be impossible, for if we are going to say that there are ultimate moral disagreements between societies, we must include in the matters that they can disagree about their attitudes to other moral outlooks. Moreover, there are inherent features of a moral outlook that make it hard to see it as just like a local practice, convention, or tradition. It is essential to a morality's role in a society that certain sorts of reactions and motivations should be strongly internalized in members of that society, and those reactions cannot merely evaporate because one is confronted by human beings in another society with other practices. Just as "there is no disputing about tastes" is not a maxim that applies to morality, neither is "when in Rome do as the Romans do," which is at best a principle of etiquette.

Nor is it just a matter of doing of not doing as the others do, but of putting up with it. Of course, someone who gains wider experience of the world may rightly come to see some of his moral reactions to unfamiliar conduct as parochial and will seek to discount them. There are many different kinds of thought that can be appropriate to such a process: Sometimes he may cease to see a certain issue as a moral matter at all, sometimes he may come to see that a practice that first looked the same as something he would have deplored at home is actually in morally relevant respects a very different thing. (Such thoughts could naturally involve the process of *relativizing the content* of morality to circumstances, which I mentioned earlier and distinguished from the relativistic spirit proper.) But it would be a particular moral view, and a peculiar one, to insist that such adaptive reactions were the only appropriate ones, and that if people are confronted by practices of another society that they find inhuman, they are somehow required to accept them, as the custom of the country. In the fascinating book *The Conquest of New Spain* by Bernal de Diaz, who went with Cortez to Mexico, there is an account of what he and the other conquistadores felt when they came upon the sacrificial temples. This morally unpretentious collection of bravos was genuinely horrified by the Aztec practices. This reaction was not parochial or self-righteous; it rather indicated something that much of their conduct did not indicate—that they regarded the Indians as human beings.

It is fair to press this sort of case and, in general, the cases of actual confrontation. "Every society has its own standards" may be a sometimes useful maxim of social science; as a maxim of social science it is also painless. But what, after all, is one supposed to do if confronted with a human sacrifice? Not a real question for many of us, perhaps, but a real question for Cortez. "It wasn't their business," it may be said. "They were invaders, exploiters, who had no right to be there anyway." Perhaps—though this, once more, is of course a nonrelative moral judgment itself. But even if they had no right to be there, it is a matter for real moral argument what would follow from that. If a burglar comes across the owner of the house trying to murder somebody, is he morally obliged not to interfere because he is trespassing?

None of this denies the obvious facts that many have interfered with other societies when they should not have done so—have interfered without understanding have interfered with a brutality greater than anything they were trying to stop. The point is that it cannot be a consequence of the nature of morality that no society ought ever to interfere with another, or that individuals from one society confronted with the practices of another ought to, if rational, always react with acceptance.

Once we have recognized the confusions and the inconsistency of vulgar relativism, we may begin to wonder whether there is anywhere for the relativistic spirit to go at all. Its problem seems to be quite general. In formulating an attitude that can be appropriately taken by one outlook toward others, relativism must commit itself to some normative position, and any normative position it can take must, it seems, offend against its own restrictions. It looks as though it must always be *too early or too late* for relativism. It is too early if two outlooks have never encountered each other: In that case, there is no room yet for a question about the attitude that either should take to the other. If they have encountered each other, then it is too late, for there is already a question to be answered of how they, or rather the human beings who have the outlooks, should treat each other, and relativism provides no materials to help with that question, unless, as we have seen, it gives up its stance and advocates toleration or some other nonrelativist principle.

It is important that once it is too late, and two groups have impinged on each other, it is simply impossible that they should have no attitude toward each other: They cannot simply register the absence of any attitude. They may start with any one of several attitudes, in fact, such as enmity, or naïve trust, or wary friendship (all of them well documented in the history of exploration and colonialism). These may develop in various directions, and unless the parties break off their relations, questions will inescapably arise of how they think they should be treating each other. Once the groups have encountered each other, there is a question of their negotiating ways of living together, negotiations that may mean that they are moving toward forming one society. This is the most basic reason why, if it is not too early for relativism, it is too late for it. The situation that interests relativism, of there being two separate societies, is gradually overcome and is replaced by a process in which one new society, perhaps painfully and imperfectly, emerges. The relativist has by definition nothing to contribute to this process: He seems doomed to being a peculiarly passive and discouraging spectator of social change.

There is an interesting application of this point to a recent theory ("semantic relativism"), which represents relativism as a doctrine about meaning.

On this account, there is an important class of moral statements (roughly, those involving "ought") that have as part of their semantic content a reference to a society to which the morality in question is relativized, so that "we ought to do X" means something like "we are required to do X by the norms of our society." But in the exchanges between different societies who have encountered each other, what happens to these references? Each party starts as a "we" confronted with a "they." Each, negotiating with the other, will begin to think in terms of "you," and of a more extensive "we" to which both "you" and the original "we" belong. Eventually, if one society emerges from these processes, there will be a new "we," a society that the relativist can recognize. But none of the complex processes of ethical readjustment and new understanding that go into these changes will have been caught by the relativist references; once again, relativism is too late, because people need to conceive of a new "we" before they have got as far as there being a new society that will be "ours."

The basic problem with relativism is that there is almost no serious ethical question for which "other than mine" forms an interesting class of societies or cultures. Cultures bear all sorts of relations to one's own, being more or less distant, similar, congenial, threatening, to hand, overlapping, and so on, and relativism can do nothing with these important distinctions.

So is there any place for the relativist spirit at all? Can it help us understand anything? We have already seen that it is not going to help us in situations of actual confrontation between societies. The first question to ask is whether there might be other relations between different cultures or societies, relations that we have not yet allowed for. We have said that relativism seems always to be too early or too late—too late when there is confrontation, too early if two societies have never encountered or heard of each other. But this is to overlook a further kind of case: the many societies that are past and no longer exist. We have "encountered" these in a notional sense, because we have heard of them and indeed may know a great deal about them, but we can never have a real encounter with them in the sense that there can be a question of how we should live with them. There is no issue of our going there or negotiating with their members how we might live together. In their case, perhaps, it can make sense to take a relativistic attitude. These societies were in many cases very different from our own, and we may well have the thought that there is no point or purpose in moralizing about them, censuring some medieval society, for instance, because it did not respect certain liberal values that we rightly see as very important to us. We may well feel that is better to try to understand this other world, question it rather than judge it, and learn from it rather than tell it about its failings.

There can be no demand that anyone *has* to take such an attitude. It is an option or a possibility that may be sensible to adopt, not something forced on one by a correct theory of moral thought or by the semantics of moral language. Such an attitude, restricted to cases where there is no issue of a real, practical confrontation, has been called "the relativism of distance." It does express or honor, up to a point, the original relativistic impulse or reaction, in particular because it witholds external moral judgment and works to discourage self-satisfied moral superiority. At the same time, this attitude can avoid the incoherence of other kinds of relativism, be-

cause it accepts the responsibility of thinking about our relations to outlooks with which we have a real confrontation. In real confrontations, we indeed stand by moral views that we ourselves hold, views that we seriously think should shape our lives in the world that we actually have. These may well be just the kinds of views—the characteristic attitudes of liberalism, for instance—that most sharply distinguish our outlook from those of past societies, but the fact that we think that they apply to our world, the world in which we ourselves and our contemporaries (including those who disagree with us) have to live, does not mean that we have to apply them to past societies, or that we have to think that everyone everywhere should have shared them.

That is the central point of the relativism of distance. It enables us genuinely to hold our own views and to deal seriously with people whom we really confront, while resisting the indulgence of exercising our moral views on people who did not and could not have shared a world with us. This restraint cannot do anything for them, but it may well be an attitude that helps us in thinking about the relations of our society to other forms of human culture.

The Conscience of Huckleberry Finn

JONATHAN BENNETT

Jonathan Bennett was born in Greymouth, New Zealand. He teaches philosophy at Syracuse University.

In this paper, I shall present not just the conscience of Huckleberry Finn but two others as well. One of them is the conscience of Heinrich Himmler. He became a Nazi in 1923; he served drably and quietly, but well, and was rewarded with increasing responsibility and power. At the peak of his career

"The Conscience of Huckleberry Finn" by Jonathan Bennett, *Philosophy*, Vol. 49 (1974), pp. 123–143. Reprinted with the permission of Cambridge University Press and the author. Footnotes deleted.

he held many offices and commands, of which the most powerful was that of leader of the S.S.—the principal police force of the Nazi regime. In this capacity, Himmler commanded the whole concentration camp system, and was responsible for the execution of the so-called "final solution of the Jewish problem." It is important for my purposes that this piece of social engineering should be thought of not abstractly but in concrete terms of Jewish families being marched to what they think are bathhouses, to the accompaniment of loudspeaker renditions of extracts from *The Merry Widow* and *Tales of Hoffman,* there to be choked to death by poisonous gases. Altogether, Himmler succeeded in murdering about four and a half million of them, as well as several million gentiles, mainly Poles and Russians.

The other conscience to be discussed is that of the Calvinist theologian and philosopher Jonathan Edwards. He lived in the first half of the eighteenth century, and has a good claim to be considered America's first serious and considerable philosophical thinker. He was for many years a widely-renowned preacher and Congregationalist minister in New England; in 1748 a dispute with his congregation led him to resign (he couldn't accept their view that unbelievers should be admitted to the Lord's Supper in the hope that it would convert them); for some years after that he worked as a missionary, preaching to the Indians through an interpreter; then in 1758 he accepted the presidency of what is now Princeton University, and within two months died from a smallpox inoculation. Along the way he wrote some first-rate philosophy: his book attacking the notion of free will is still sometimes read. Why I should be interested in Edwards' *conscience* will be explained in due course.

I shall use Heinrich Himmler, Jonathan Edwards and Huckleberry Finn to illustrate different aspects of a single theme, namely the relationship between *sympathy* on the one hand and *bad morality* on the other.

All that I can mean by a "bad morality" is a morality whose principles I deeply disapprove of. When I call a morality bad, I cannot prove that mine is better; but when I here call any morality bad, I think you will agree with me that it is bad; and that is all I need.

There could be dispute as to whether the springs of someone's actions constitute a *morality*. I think, though, that we must admit that someone who acts in ways which conflict grossly with our morality may nevertheless have a morality of his own—a set of principles of action which he sincerely assents to, so that for him the problem of acting well or rightly or in obedience to conscience is the problem of conforming to *those* principles. The problem of conscientiousness can arise as acutely for a bad morality as

for any other: rotten principles may be as difficult to keep as decent ones.

As for "sympathy": I use this term to cover every sort of fellow-feeling, as when one feels pity over someone's loneliness, or horrified compassion over his pain, and when one feels a shrinking reluctance to act in a way which will bring misfortune to someone else. These *feelings* must not be confused with *moral judgments*. My sympathy for someone in distress may lead me to help him, or even to think that I ought to help him; but in itself it is not a judgment about what I ought to do but just a *feeling* for him in his plight. We shall get some light on the difference between feelings and moral judgments when we consider Huckleberry Finn.

Obviously, feelings can impel one to action, and so can moral judgments; and in a particular case sympathy and morality may pull in opposite directions. This can happen not just with bad moralities, but also with good ones like yours and mine. For example, a small child, sick and miserable, clings tightly to his mother and screams in terror when she tries to pass him over to the doctor to be examined. If the mother gave way to her sympathy, that is to her feeling for the child's misery and fright, she would hold it close and not let the doctor come near; but don't we agree that it might be wrong for her to act on such a feeling? Quite generally, then, anyone's moral principles may apply to a particular situation in a way which runs contrary to the particular thrusts of fellow-feeling that he has in that situation. My immediate concern is with sympathy in relation to bad morality, but not because such conflicts occur only when the morality is bad.

Now, suppose that someone who accepts a bad morality is struggling to make himself act in accordance with it in a particular situation where his sympathies pull him another way. He sees the struggle as one between doing the right, conscientious thing, and acting wrongly and weakly, like the mother who won't let the doctor come near her sick, frightened baby. Since we don't accept this persons' morality, we may see the situation very differently, thoroughly disapproving of the action he regards as the right one, and endorsing the action which from his point of view constitutes weakness and backsliding.

Conflicts between sympathy and bad morality

won't always be like this, for we won't disagree with every single dictate of a bad morality. Still, it can happen in the way I have described, with the agent's right action being our wrong one, and vice versa. That is just what happens in a certain episode in chapter 16 of *The Adventures of Huckleberry Finn,* an episode which brilliantly illustrates how fiction can be instructive about real life.

Huck Finn has been helping his slave friend Jim to run away from Miss Watson, who is Jim's owner. In their raft-journey down the Mississippi river, they are near to the place at which Jim will become legally free. Now let Huck take over the story:

> Jim said it made him all over trembly and feverish to be so close to freedom. Well, I can tell you it made me all over trembly and feverish, too, to hear him, because I begun to get it through my head that he *was* most free—and who was to blame for it? Why, *me.* I couldn't get that out of my conscience, no how nor no way. . . . It hadn't ever come home to me, before, what this thing was that I was doing. But now it did; and it stayed with me, and scorched me more and more. I tried to make out to myself that *I* warn't to blame, because *I* didn't run Jim off from his rightful owner; but it warn't no use, conscience up and say, every time: "But you knowed he was running for his freedom, and you could a paddled ashore and told somebody." That was so—I couldn't get around that, no way. That was where it pinched. Conscience says to me: "What had poor Miss Watson done to you, that you could see her nigger go off right under your eyes and never say one single word? What did that poor old woman do to you, that you could treat her so mean? . . ." I got to feeling so mean and so miserable I most wished I was dead.

Jim speaks of his plan to save up to buy his wife, and then his children, out of slavery; and he adds that if the children cannot be bought he will arrange to steal them. Huck is horrified:

> Thinks I, this is what comes of my not thinking. Here was this nigger which I had as good as helped to run away, coming right out flat-footed and saying he would steal his children—children that be-

longed to a man I didn't even know; a man that hadn't ever done me no harm.

> I was sorry to hear Jim say that, it was such a lowering of him. My conscience got to stirring me up hotter than ever, until at last I says to it: "Let up on me—it ain't too late, yet—I'll paddle ashore at first light, and tell." I felt easy, and happy, and light as a feather, right off. All my troubles was gone.

This is bad morality all right. In his earliest years Huck wasn't taught any principles, and the only ones he has encountered since then are those of rural Missouri, in which slave-owning is just one kind of ownership and is not subject to critical pressure. It hasn't occurred to Huck to question those principles. So the action, to us abhorrent, of turning Jim in to the authorities presents itself *clearly* to Huck as the right thing to do.

For us, morality and sympathy would both dictate helping Jim to escape. If we felt any conflict, it would have both these on one side and something else on the other—greed for a reward, or fear of punishment. But Huck's morality conflicts with his sympathy, that is, with his unargued, natural feeling for his friend. The conflict starts when Huck sets off in the canoe towards the shore, pretending that he is going to reconnoitre, but really planning to turn Jim in:

> As I shoved off, [Jim] says: "Pooty soon I'll be a-shout'n for joy, en I'll say, it's all on accounts o' Huck I's a free man . . . Jim won't ever forgit you, Huck; you's de bes' fren' Jim's ever had; en you's de *only* fren' old Jim's got now."

> I was paddling off, all in a sweat to tell on him; but when he says this, it seemed to kind of take the tuck all out of me. I went along slow then, and I warn't right down certain whether I was glad I started or whether I warn't. When I was fifty yards off, Jim says:

> "Dah you goes, de ole true Huck; de on'y white genlman dat ever kep' his promise to old Jim." Well, I just felt sick. But I says, I *got* to do it—I can't get *out* of it.

In the upshot, sympathy wins over morality. Huck hasn't the strength of will to do what he sincerely thinks he ought to do. Two men hunting for run-away slaves ask him whether the man on his raft is black or white:

> I didn't answer up prompt. I tried to, but the words wouldn't come. I tried, for a second or two, to brace up and out with it, but I warn't man enough—hadn't the spunk of a rabbit. I see I was weakening; so I just give up trying, and up and says: "He's white."

So Huck enables Jim to escape, thus acting weakly and wickedly—he thinks. In this conflict between sympathy and morality, sympathy wins.

One critic has cited this episode in support of the statement that Huck suffers "excruciating moments of wavering between honesty and respectability." That is hopelessly wrong, and I agree with the perceptive comment on it by another critic, who says:

> The conflict waged in Huck is much more serious: he scarcely cares for respectability and never hesitates to relinquish it, but he does care for honesty and gratitude—and both honesty and gratitude require that he should give Jim up. It is not, in Huck, honesty at war with respectability but love and compassion for Jim struggling against his conscience. His decision is for Jim and hell: a right decision made in the mental chains that Huck never breaks. His concern for Jim is and remains *irrational*. Huck finds many reasons for giving Jim up and none for stealing him. To the end Huck sees his compassion for Jim as a weak, ignorant, and wicked felony.

This is precisely correct—and it can have that virtue only because Mark Twain wrote the episode with such unerring precision. The crucial point concerns *reasons,* which all occur on one side of the conflict. On the side of conscience we have principles, arguments, considerations, ways of looking at things:

> "It hadn't even come home to me before what I was doing"
> "I tried to make out that I warn't to blame"
> "Conscience said "But you knowed . . ."—
> I couldn't get around that"
> "What had poor Miss Watson done to you?"
> "This is what comes of my not thinking"

> ". . . children that belonged to a man I didn't even know."

On the other side, the side of feeling, we get nothing like that. When Jim rejoices in Huck, as his only friend, Huck doesn't consider the claims of friendship or have the situation "come home" to him in a different light. All that happens is: "When he says this, it seemed to kind of take the tuck all out of me. I went along slow then, and I warn't right down certain whether I was glad I started or whether I warn't." Again, Jim's words about Huck's "promise" to him don't give Huck any *reason* for changing his plan: in his morality promises to slaves probably don't count. Their effect on him is of a different kind: "Well, I just felt sick." And when the moment for final decision comes, Huck doesn't weigh up pros and cons: he simply *fails* to do what he believes to be right—he isn't strong enough, hasn't "the spunk of a rabbit." This passage in the novel is notable not just for its finely wrought irony, with Huck's weakness of will leading him to do the right thing, but also for its masterly handling of the difference between general moral principles and particular unreasoned emotional pulls.

Consider now another case of bad morality in conflict with human sympathy, the case of the odious Himmler. Here, from a speech he made to some S.S. generals, is an indication of the content of his morality:

> What happens to a Russian, to a Czech, does not interest me in the slightest. What the nations can offer in the way of good blood of our type, we will take, if necessary by kidnapping their children and raising them here with us. Whether nations live in prosperity or starve to death like cattle interests me only in so far as we need them as slaves to our *Kultur;* otherwise it is of no interest to me. Whether 10,000 Russian females fall down from exhaustion while digging an antitank ditch interests me only in so far as the antitank ditch for Germany is finished.

But has this a moral basis at all? And if it has, was there in Himmler's own mind any conflict between morality and sympathy? Yes there was. Here is more from the same speech:

... I also want to talk to you quite frankly on a very grave matter . . . I mean . . . the extermination of the Jewish race. . . . Most of you must know what it means when 100 corpses are lying side by side, or 500, or 1,000. To have stuck it out and at the same time—apart from exceptions caused by human weakness—to have remained decent fellows, that is what has made us hard. This is a page of glory in our history which has never been written and is never to be written.

Himmler saw his policies as being hard to implement while still retaining one's human sympathies—while still remaining a "decent fellow." He is saying that only the weak take the easy way out and just squelch their sympathies, and is praising the stronger and more glorious course of retaining one's sympathies while acting in violation of them. In the same spirit, he ordered that when executions were carried out in concentration camps, those responsible "are to be influenced in such a way as to suffer no ill effect in their character and mental attitude." A year later he boasted that the S.S. had wiped out the Jews

> without our leaders and their men suffering any damage in their minds and souls. The danger was considerable, for there was only a narrow path between the Scylla of their becoming heartless ruffians unable any longer to treasure life, and the Charybdis of their becoming soft and suffering nervous breakdowns.

And there really can't be any doubt that the basis of Himmler's policies was a set of principles which constituted his morality—a sick, bad, wicked *morality*. He described himself as caught in "the old tragic conflict between will and obligation." And when his physician Kersten protested at the intention to destroy the Jews, saying that the suffering involved was "not to be contemplated," Kersten reports that Himmler replied:

> He knew that it would mean much suffering for the Jews. . . . "It is the curse of greatness that it must step over dead bodies to create new life. Yet we must . . . cleanse the soil or it will never bear fruit. It will be a great burden for me to bear."

This, I submit, is the language of morality.

So in this case, tragically, bad morality won out

over sympathy. I am sure that many of Himmler's killers did extinguish their sympathies, becoming "heartless ruffians" rather than "decent fellows"; but not Himmler himself. Although his policies ran against the human grain to a horrible degree, he did not sandpaper down his emotional surfaces so that there was no grain there, allowing his actions to slide along smoothly and easily. He did, after all, bear his hideous burden, and even paid a price for it. He suffered a variety of nervous and physical disabilities, including nausea and stomach-convulsions, and Kersten was doubtless right in saying that these were "the expression of a psychic division which extended over his whole life."

This same division must have been present in some of those officials of the Church who ordered heretics to be tortured so as to change their theological opinions. Along with the brutes and the cold careerists, there must have been some who cared, and who suffered from the conflict between the sympathies and their bad morality.

In the conflict between sympathy and bad morality, then, the victory may go to sympathy as in the case of Huck Finn, or to morality as in the case of Himmler.

Another possibility is that the conflict may be avoided by giving up, or not ever having, those sympathies which might interfere with one's principles. That seems to have been the case with Jonathan Edwards. I am afraid that I shall be doing an injustice to Edwards' many virtues, and to his great intellectual energy and inventiveness; for my concern is only with the worst thing about him—namely his morality, which was worse than Himmler's.

According to Edwards, God condemns some men to an eternity of unimaginably awful pain, though he arbitrarily spares others—"arbitrarily" because none deserve to be spared:

> Natural men are held in the hand of God over the pit of hell; they have deserved the fiery pit, and are already sentenced to it; and God is dreadfully provoked, his anger is as great towards them as to those that are actually suffering the executions of the fierceness of his wrath in hell . . . ; the devil is waiting for them, hell is gaping for them, the flames gather and flash about them, and would fain lay hold on them . . . ; and . . . there are

not means within each that can be any security
to them. . . . All that preserves them is the mere
arbitrary will, and uncovenanted unobliged fore-
bearance of an incensed God.

Notice that he says "they have deserved the fiery pit."
Edwards insists that men *ought* to be condemned to
eternal pain; and his position isn't that this is right
because God wants it, but rather that God wants it
because it is right. For him, moral standards exist independently of God, and God can be assessed in the
light of them (and of course found to be perfect).
For example, he says:

They deserve to be cast into hell; so that . . . justice never stands in the way, it makes no objection
against God's using his power at any moment to
destroy them. Yea, on the contrary, justice calls
aloud for an infinite punishment of their sins.

Elsewhere, he gives elaborate arguments to show
that God is acting justly in damning sinners. For example, he argues that a punishment should be exactly as bad as the crime being punished; God is infinitely excellent; so any crime against him infinitely
bad; and so eternal damnation is exactly right as a
punishment—it is infinite, but, as Edwards is careful also to say, it is "no more than infinite."

Of course, Edwards himself didn't torment the
damned; but the question still arises of whether his
sympathies didn't conflict with his *approval* of eternal torment. Didn't he find it painful to contemplate
any fellow-human's being tortured for ever? Apparently not:

The God that holds you over the pit of hell, much
as one holds a spider or some loathsome insect
over the fire, abhors you, and is dreadfully provoked; . . . he is of purer eyes than to bear to
have you in his sight; you are ten thousand times
so abominable in his eyes as the most hateful ven-
omous serpent is in ours.

When God is presented as being as misanthropic
as that, one suspects misanthropy in the theologian.
This suspicion is increased when Edwards claims
that "the saints in glory will . . . understand how terrible the sufferings of the damned are; yet . . . will
not be sorry for [them]." He bases this partly on a

view of human nature whose ugliness he seems not
to notice:

The seeing of the calamities of others tends to
heighten the sense of our own enjoyments. When
the saints in glory, therefore, shall see the doleful
stare of the damned, how will this heighten their
sense of the blessedness of their own state. . . .
When they shall see how miserable others of their
fellow-creatures are . . . ; when they shall see the
smoke of their torment, . . . and hear their dolor-
ous shrieks and cries, and consider that they in
the mean time are in the most blissful state, and
shall surely be in it to all eternity; how they will
rejoice!

I hope this is less than the whole truth! His other
main point about why the saints will rejoice to see
the torments of the damned is that it is *right* that
they should do so:

The heavenly inhabitants . . . will have no love nor
pity to the damned. . . . [This will not show] a want
of a spirit of love in them . . . ; for the heavenly inhabitants will know that it is not fit that they should
love [the damned] because they will know then,
that God has no love to them, nor pity for them.

The implication that *of course* one can adjust one's
feelings of pity so that they conform to the dictates
of some authority—doesn't this suggest that ordinary human sympathies played only a small part in
Edwards' life?

Huck Finn, whose sympathies are wide and deep,
could never avoid the conflict in that way; but he is
determined to avoid it, and so he opts for the only
other alternative he can see—to give up morality altogether. After he has tricked the slave-hunters, he
returns to the raft and undergoes a peculiar crisis:

I got aboard the raft, feeling bad and low, because
I knowed very well I had done wrong, and I see it
warn't no use for me to try to learn to do right; a
body that don't get *started* right when he's little,
ain't got no show—when the pinch comes there
ain't nothing to back him up and keep him to his
work, and so he gets beat. Then I thought a minute, and says to myself, hold on—s'pose you'd a
done right and give Jim up; would you feel better

than what you do now? No, says I, I'd feel bad—I'd feel just the same way I do now. Well, then, says I, what's the use you learning to do right, when it's troublesome to do right and ain't no trouble to do wrong, and the wages is just the same? I was stuck. I couldn't answer that. So I reckoned I wouldn't bother no more about it, but after this always do whichever come handiest at the time.

Huck clearly cannot conceive of having any morality except the one he has learned—too late, he thinks—from his society. He is not entirely a prisoner of that morality, because he does after all reject it; but for him that is a decision to relinquish morality as such; he cannot envisage revising his morality, altering its content in face of the various pressures to which it is subject, including pressures from his sympathies. For example, he does not begin to approach the thought that slavery should be rejected on moral grounds, or the thought that what he is doing is not theft because a person cannot be owned and therefore cannot be stolen.

The basic trouble is that he cannot or will not engage in abstract intellectual operations of any sort. In chapter 33 he finds himself "feeling to blame, somehow" for something he knows he had no hand in; he assumes that this feeling is a deliverance of conscience; and this confirms him in his belief that conscience shouldn't be listened to:

> It don't make no difference whether you do right or wrong, a person's conscience ain't got no sense, and just goes for him *anyway*. If I had a yaller dog that didn't know no more than a person's conscience does, I would pison him. It takes up more room than all the rest of a person's insides, and yet ain't no good, nohow.

That brisk, incurious dismissiveness fits well with the comprehensive rejection of morality back on the raft. But this is a digression.

On the raft, Huck decides not to live by principles, but just to do whatever "comes handiest at the time"—always acting according to the mood of the moment. Since the morality he is rejecting is narrow and cruel, and his sympathies are broad and kind, the results will be good. But moral principles are good to have, because they help to protect one from acting badly at moments when one's sympathies

happen to be in abeyance. On the highest possible estimate of the role one's sympathies should have, one can still allow for principles as embodiments of one's best feelings, one's broadest and keenest sympathies. On that view, principles can help one across intervals when one's feelings are at less than their best, i.e., through periods of misanthropy or meanness or self-centredness or depression or anger.

What Huck didn't see is that one can live by principles and yet have ultimate control over their content. And one way such control can be exercised is by checking of one's principles in the light of one's sympathies. This is sometimes a pretty straightforward matter. It can happen that a certain moral principle becomes untenable—meaning literally that one cannot hold it any longer—because it conflicts intolerably with the pity or revulsion or whatever that one feels when one sees what the principle leads to. One's experience may play a large part here: experiences evoke feelings, and feelings force one to modify principles. Something like this happened to the English poet Wilfred Owen, whose experiences in the First World War transformed him from an enthusiastic soldier into a virtual pacifist. I can't document this change of conscience in detail; but I want to present something which he wrote about the way experience can put pressure on morality.

The Latin poet Horace wrote that it is sweet and fitting (or right) to die for one's country—*dulce et decorum est pro patria mori*—and Owen wrote a fine poem about how experience could lead one to relinquish that particular moral principle. He describes a man who is too slow donning his gas mask during a gas attack—"As under a green sea I saw him drowning," Owen says. The poem ends like this:

> *In all my dreams before my helpless sight*
> *He plunges at me, guttering, choking, drowning*
> *If in some smothering dreams, you too could pace*
> *Behind the wagon that we flung him in,*
> *And watch the white eyes writhing in his face,*
> *His hanging face, like a devil's sick of sin;*
> *If you could hear, at every jolt, the blood*
> *Come gargling from the froth-corrupted lungs,*
> *Bitter as the cud*
> *Of vile, incurable sores on innocent tongues,—*
> *My friend, you would not tell with such high zest*

To children ardent for some desperate glory,
The old Lie: Dulce et decorum est
pro patria mori.

There is a difficulty about drawing from all this a moral for ourselves. I imagine that we agree in our rejection of slavery, eternal damnation, genocide, and uncritical patriotic self-abnegation; so we shall agree that Huck Finn, Jonathan Edwards, Heinrich Himmler, and the poet Horace would all have done well to bring certain of their principles under severe pressure from ordinary human sympathies. But then we can say this because we can say that all those are bad moralities, whereas we cannot look at our own moralities and declare them bad. This is not arrogance: it is obviously incoherent for someone to declare the system of moral principles that he *accepts* to be *bad,* just as one cannot coherently say of anything that one *believes* it but it is *false.*

Still, although I can't point to any of my beliefs and say "That is false," I don't doubt that some of my beliefs *are* false; and so I should try to remain open to correction. Similarly, I accept every single item in my morality—that is inevitable—but I am sure that my morality could be improved, which is to say that it could undergo changes which I should be glad of once I had made them. So I must try to keep my morality open to revision, exposing it to whatever valid pressures there are—including pressures from my sympathies.

I don't give my sympathies a blank cheque in advance. In a conflict between principle and sympathy, principles ought sometimes to win. For example, I think it was right to take part in the Second World War on the allied side; there were many ghastly in-dividual incidents which might have led someone to doubt the rightness of his participation in that war; and I think it would have been right for such a person to keep his sympathies in a subordinate place on those occasions, not allowing them to modify his principles in such a way as to make a pacifist of him.

Still, one's sympathies should be kept as sharp and sensitive and aware as possible, and not only because they can sometimes affect one's principles or one's conduct or both. Owen, at any rate, says that feelings and sympathies are vital even when they can do nothing but bring pain and distress. In another poem he speaks of the blessings of being numb in one's feelings: "Happy are the men who yet before they are killed/Can let their veins run cold," he says. These are the ones who do not suffer from any compassion which, as Owen puts it, "makes their feet/ Sore on the alleys cobbled with their brothers." He contrasts these "happy" ones, who "lose all imagination," with himself and others "who with a thought besmirch/Blood over all our soul." Yet the poem's verdict goes against the "happy" ones. Owen does not say that they will act worse than the others whose souls are besmirched with blood because of their keen awareness of human suffering. He merely says that they are the losers because they have cut themselves off from the human condition:

By choice they made themselves immune
To pity and whatever moans in man
Before the last sea and the hapless stars;
Whatever mourns when many leave these shores;
Whatever shares
The eternal reciprocity of tears.

STANDARDS OF RIGHT AND WRONG: THEORY AND PRACTICE

Euthyphro

PLATO

Plato (427–347 B.C.E.) lived in Athens and was a student of Socrates. Most of his surviving works, written in dialog form, feature the character of Socrates. Plato is generally regarded as one of the greatest philosophers of all time. He founded the Academy, the world's first university.

EUTHYPHRO: Why have you left the Lyceum, Socrates? and what are you doing in the Porch of the King Archon? Surely you cannot be concerned in a suit before the King, like myself?

SOCRATES: Not in a suit, Euthyphro: impeachment is the word which the Athenians use.

EUTH.: What! I suppose that some one has been prosecuting you, for I cannot believe that you are the prosecutor of another.

SOC.: Certainly not.

EUTH.: Then some one else has been prosecuting you?

SOC.: Yes.

EUTH.: And who is he?

SOC.: A young man who is little known, Euthyphro: and I hardly know him: his name is Meletus, and he is of the deme of Pitthis. Perhaps you may remember his appearance: he has a beak, and long straight hair, and a beard which is ill grown.

EUTH.: No, I do not remember him, Socrates. But what is the charge which he brings against you?

SOC.: What is the charge? Well, a very serious charge, which shows a good deal of character in the young man, and for which he is certainly not to be despised. He says he knows how the youth are corrupted and who are their corruptors. I fancy that he must be a wise man, and seeing that I am the reverse of a wise man, he has found me out, and is going to accuse me of corrupting his young friends. And of this our mother the state is to be the judge. Of all our political men he is the only one who seems to me to begin in the right way, with the cultivation of virtue in youth; like a good husbandman, he makes the young shoots his first care, and clears away us who are the destroyers of them. This is only the first step; he will afterwards attend to the elder branches; and if he goes on as he has begun, he will be a very great public benefactor.

EUTH.: I hope that he may; but I rather fear, Socrates, that the opposite will turn out to be the truth. My opinion is that in attacking you he is simply aiming a blow at the foundation of the state. But in what way does he say that you corrupt the young?

SOC.: He brings a wonderful accusation against me, which at first hearing excites surprise: he says that I am a poet or maker of gods, and that I invent new gods and deny the existence of old ones; this is the ground of his indictment.

EUTH.: I understand, Socrates; he means to attack you about the familiar sign which occasionally, as you say, comes to you. He thinks that you are a neologian, and he is going to have you up before the court for this. He knows that such a charge is readily received by the world, as I myself know too well; for when I speak in the assembly about

From "Euthyphro," in *The Dialogues of Plato,* translated by Benjamin Jowett (London: Oxford University Press, 1920).

divine things, and foretell the future to them, they laugh at me and think me a madman. Yet every word that I say is true. But they are jealous of us all; and we must be brave and go at them.

Soc.: Their laughter, friend Euthyphro, is not a matter of much consequence. For a man may be thought wise; but the Athenians, I suspect, do not much trouble themselves about him until he begins to impart his wisdom to others; and then for some reason or other, perhaps, as you say, from jealousy, they are angry.

Euth.: I am never likely to try their temper in this way.

Soc.: I dare say not, for you are reserved in your behaviour, and seldom impart your wisdom. But I have a benevolent habit of pouring out myself to everybody, and would even pay for a listener, and I am afraid that the Athenians may think me too talkative. Now if, as I was saying, they would only laugh at me, as you say that they laugh at you, the time might pass gaily enough in the court; but perhaps they may be in earnest, and then what the end will be you soothsayers only can predict.

Euth.: I dare say that the affair will end in nothing, Socrates, and that you will win your cause; and I think that I shall win my own.

Soc.: And what is your suit, Euthyphro? are you the pursuer or the defendant?

Euth.: I am the pursuer.

Soc.: Of whom?

Euth.: You will think me mad when I tell you.

Soc.: Why, has the fugitive wings?

Euth.: Nay, he is not very volatile at his time of life.

Soc.: Who is he?

Euth.: My father.

Soc.: Your father! my good man?

Euth.: Yes.

Soc.: And of what is he accused?

Euth.: Of murder, Socrates.

Soc.: By the powers, Euthyphro! how little does the common herd know of the nature of right and truth. A man must be an extraordinary man, and have made great strides in wisdom, before he could have seen his way to bring such an action.

Euth.: Indeed, Socrates, he must.

Soc.: I suppose that the man whom your father murdered was one of your relatives—clearly he was; for if he had been a stranger you would never have thought of prosecuting him.

Euth.: I am amused, Socrates, at your making a distinction between one who is a relation and one who is not a relation; for surely the pollution is the same in either case, if you knowingly associate with the murderer when you ought to clear yourself and him by proceeding against him. The real question is whether the murdered man has been justly slain. If justly, then your duty is to let the matter alone; but if unjustly, then even if the murderer lives under the same roof with you and eats at the same table, proceed against him. Now the man who is dead was a poor dependant of mine who worked for us as a field labourer on our farm in Naxos, and one day in a fit of drunken passion he got into a quarrel with one of our domestic servants and slew him. My father bound him hand and foot and threw him into a ditch, and then sent to Athens to ask of a diviner what he should do with him. Meanwhile he never attended to him and took no care about him, for he regarded him as a murderer; and thought that no great harm would be done even if he did die. Now this was just what happened. For such was the effect of cold and hunger and chains upon him, that before the messenger returned from the diviner, he was dead. And my father and family are angry with me for taking the part of the murderer and prosecuting my father. They say that he did not kill him, and that if he did, the dead man was but a murderer, and I ought not to take any notice, for that a son is impious who prosecutes a father. Which shows, Socrates, how little they know what the gods think about piety and impiety.

Soc.: Good heavens, Euthyphro! and is your knowledge of religion and of things pious and impious so very exact, that, supposing the circumstances to be as you state them, you are not afraid lest you too may be doing an impious thing in bringing an action against your father?

Euth.: The best of Euthyphro, and that which distinguishes him, Socrates, from other men, is his exact knowledge of all such matters. What should I be good for without it?

Soc.: Rare friend! I think that I cannot do better than be your disciple. Then before the trial with

Meletus comes on I shall challenge him, and say that I have always had a great interest in religious questions, and now, as he charges me with rash imaginations and innovations in religion, I have become your disciple. You, Meletus, as I shall say to him, acknowledge Euthyphro to be a great theologian, and sound in his opinions; and if you approve of him you ought to approve of me, and not have me into court; but if you disapprove, you should begin by indicting him who is my teacher, and who will be the ruin, not of the young, but of the old; that is to say, of myself whom he instructs, and of his old father whom he admonishes and chastises. And if Meletus refuses to listen to me, but will go on, and will not shift the indictment from me to you, I cannot do better than repeat this challenge in the court.

EUTH.: Yes, indeed, Socrates; and if he attempts to indict me I am mistaken if I do not find a flaw in him; the court shall have a great deal more to say to him than to me.

SOC.: And I, my dear friend, knowing this, am desirous of becoming your disciple. For I observe that no one appears to notice you—not even this Meletus; but his sharp eyes have found me out at once, and he has indicted me for impiety. And therefore, I adjure you to tell me the nature of piety and impiety, which you said that you knew so well, and of murder, and of other offences against the gods. What are they? Is not piety in every action always the same? and impiety, again —is it not always the opposite of piety, and also the same with itself, having, as impiety, one notion which includes whatever is impious?

EUTH.: To be sure, Socrates.

SOC.: And what is piety, and what is impiety?

EUTH.: Piety is doing as I am doing; that is to say, prosecuting any one who is guilty of murder, sacrilege, or of any similar crime—whether he be your father or mother, or whoever he may be— that makes no difference; and not to prosecute them is impiety. And please to consider, Socrates, what a notable proof I will give you of the truth of my words, a proof which I have already given to others:—of the principle, I mean, that the impious, whoever he may be, ought not to go unpunished. For do not men regard Zeus as the best and most righteous of the gods?—and yet they admit that he bound his father (Cronos) because he wickedly devoured his sons, and that he too had punished his own father (Uranus) for a similar reason, in a nameless manner. And yet when I proceed against my father, they are angry with me. So inconsistent are they in their way of talking when the gods are concerned, and when I am concerned.

SOC.: May not this be the reason, Euthyphro, why I am charged with impiety—that I cannot away with these stories about the gods? and therefore I suppose that people think me wrong. But, as you who are well informed about them approve of them, I cannot do better than assent to your superior wisdom. What else can I say, confessing as I do, that I know nothing about them? Tell me, for the love of Zeus, whether you really believe that they are true.

EUTH.: Yes, Socrates; and things more wonderful still, of which the world is in ignorance.

SOC.: And do you really believe that the gods fought with one another, and had dire quarrels, battles, and the like, as the poets say, and as you may see represented in the works of great artists? The temples are full of them; and notably the robe of Athene, which is carried up to the Acropolis at the great Panathenaea, is embroidered with them. Are all these tales of the gods true, Euthyphro?

EUTH.: Yes, Socrates; and, as I was saying, I can tell you, if you would like to hear them, many other things about the gods which would quite amaze you.

SOC.: I dare say; and you shall tell me them at some other time when I have leisure. But just at present I would rather hear from you a more precise answer, which you have not as yet given, my friend, to the question, What is 'piety'? When asked, you only replied, Doing as you do, charging your father with murder.

EUTH.: And what I said was true, Socrates.

SOC.: No doubt, Euthyphro; but you would admit that there are many other pious acts?

EUTH.: There are.

SOC.: Remember that I did not ask you to give me two or three examples of piety, but to explain the general idea which makes all pious things to be pious. Do you not recollect that there was one idea which made the impious impious, and the pious pious?

EUTH.: I remember.

SOC.: Tell me what is the nature of this idea, and then I shall have a standard to which I may look, and by which I may measure actions, whether yours or those of any one else, and then I shall be able to say that such and such an action is pious, such another impious.

EUTH.: I will tell you, if you like.

SOC.: I should very much like.

EUTH.: Piety, then, is that which is dear to the gods, and impiety is that which is not dear to them.

SOC.: Very good, Euthyphro; you have now given me the sort of answer which I wanted. But whether what you say is true or not I cannot as yet tell, although I make no doubt that you will prove the truth of your words.

EUTH.: Of course.

SOC.: Come, then, and let us examine what we are saying. That thing or person which is dear to the gods is pious, and that thing or person which is hateful to the gods is impious, these two being the extreme opposites of one another. Was not that said?

EUTH.: It was.

SOC.: And well said?

EUTH.: Yes, Socrates, I thought so; it was certainly said.

SOC.: And further, Euthyphro, the gods were admitted to have enmities and hatreds and differences?

EUTH.: Yes, that was also said.

SOC.: And what sort of difference creates enmity and anger? Suppose for example that you and I, my good friend, differ about a number; do differences of this sort make us enemies and set us at variance with one another? Do we not go at once to arithmetic, and put an end to them by a sum?

EUTH.: True.

SOC.: Or suppose that we differ about magnitudes, do we not quickly end the differences by measuring?

EUTH.: Very true.

SOC.: And we end a controversy about heavy and light by resorting to a weighing machine?

EUTH.: To be sure.

SOC.: But what differences are there which cannot be thus decided, and which therefore make us angry and set us at enmity with one another? I dare say the answer does not occur to you at the moment, and therefore I will suggest that these enmities arise when the matters of difference are the just and unjust, good and evil, honourable and dishonourable. Are not these the points about which men differ, and about which when we are unable satisfactorily to decide our differences, you and I and all of us quarrel, when we do quarrel?

EUTH.: Yes, Socrates, the nature of the differences about which we quarrel is such as you describe.

SOC.: And the quarrels of the gods, noble Euthyphro, when they occur, are of a like nature?

EUTH.: Certainly they are.

SOC.: They have differences of opinion, as you say, about good and evil, just and unjust, honourable and dishonourable: there would have been no quarrels among them, if there had been no such differences—would there now?

EUTH.: You are quite right.

SOC.: Does not every man love that which he deems noble and just and good, and hate the opposite of them?

EUTH.: Very true.

SOC.: But, as you say, people regard the same things, some as just and others as unjust,—about these they dispute; and so there arise wars and fightings among them.

EUTH.: Very true.

SOC.: Then the same things are hated by the gods and loved by the gods, and are both hateful and dear to them?

EUTH.: True.

SOC.: And upon this view the same things, Euthyphro, will be pious and also impious?

EUTH.: So I should suppose.

SOC.: Then, my friend, I remark with surprise that you have not answered the question which I asked. For I certainly did not ask you to tell me what action is both pious and impious: but now it would seem that what is loved by the gods is also hated by them. And therefore, Euthyphro, in thus chastising your father you may very likely be doing what is agreeable to Zeus but disagreeable to Cronos or Uranus, and what is acceptable to Hephaestus but unacceptable to Herè, and there may be other gods who have similar differences of opinion.

EUTH.: But I believe, Socrates, that all the gods would be agreed as to the propriety of punishing a murderer: there would be no difference of opinion about that.

SOC.: Well, but speaking of men, Euthyphro, did you ever hear any one arguing that a murderer or any sort of evil-doer ought to be let off?

EUTH.: I should rather say that these are the questions which they are always arguing, especially in courts of law: they commit all sorts of crimes, and there is nothing which they will not do or say in their own defence.

SOC.: But do they admit their guilt, Euthyphro, and yet say that they ought not to be punished?

EUTH.: No; they do not.

SOC.: Then there are some things which they do not venture to say and do: for they do not venture to argue that the guilty are to be unpunished, but they deny their guilt, do they not?

EUTH.: Yes.

SOC.: Then they do not argue that the evil-doer should not be punished, but they argue about the fact of who the evil-doer is, and what he did and when?

EUTH.: True.

SOC.: And the gods are in the same case, if as you assert they quarrel about just and unjust, and some of them say while others deny that injustice is done among them. For surely neither God nor man will ever venture to say that the doer of injustice is not to be punished?

EUTH.: That is true, Socrates, in the main.

SOC.: But they join issue about the particulars—gods and men alike; and, if they dispute at all, they dispute about some act which is called in question, and which by some is affirmed to be just, by others to be unjust. Is not that true?

EUTH.: Quite true.

SOC.: Well then, my dear friend Euthyphro, do tell me, for my better instruction and information, what proof have you that in the opinion of all the gods a servant who is guilty of murder, and is put in chains by the master of the dead man, and dies because he is put in chains before he who bound him can learn from the interpreters of the gods what he ought to do

with him, dies unjustly; and that on behalf of such an one a son ought to proceed against his father and accuse him of murder. How would you show that all the gods absolutely agree in approving of his act? Prove to me that they do, and I will applaud your wisdom as long as I live.

EUTH.: It will be a difficult task; but I could make the matter very clear indeed to you.

SOC.: I understand; you mean to say that I am not so quick of apprehension as the judges: for to them you will be sure to prove that the act is unjust, and hateful to the gods.

EUTH.: Yes indeed, Socrates; at least if they will listen to me.

SOC.: But they will be sure to listen if they find that you are a good speaker. There was a notion that came into my mind while you were speaking; I said to myself: "Well, and what if Euthyphro does prove to me that all the gods regarded the death of the serf as unjust, how do I know anything more of the nature of piety and impiety? for granting that this action may be hateful to the gods, still piety and impiety are not adequately defined by these distinctions, for that which is hateful to the gods has been shown to be also pleasing and dear to them." And therefore, Euthyphro, I do not ask you to prove this; I will suppose, if you like, that all the gods condemn and abominate such an action. But I will amend the definition so far as to say that what all the gods hate is impious, and what they love pious or holy; and what some of them love and others hate is both or neither. Shall this be our definition of piety and impiety?

EUTH.: Why not, Socrates?

SOC.: Why not! certainly, as far as I am concerned, Euthyphro, there is no reason why not. But whether this admission will greatly assist you in the task of instructing me as you promised, is a matter for you to consider.

EUTH.: Yes, I should say that what all the gods love is pious and holy, and the opposite which they all hate, impious.

SOC.: Ought we to enquire into the truth of this, Euthyphro, or simply to accept the mere statement on our own authority and that of others? What do you say?

EUTH.: We should enquire; and I believe that the statement will stand the test of enquiry.

SOC.: We shall know better, my good friend, in a little while. The point which I should first wish to understand is whether the pious or holy is beloved by the gods because it is holy, or holy because it is beloved of the gods.

EUTH.: I do not understand your meaning, Socrates.

SOC.: I will endeavour to explain: we speak of carrying and we speak of being carried, of leading and being led, seeing and being seen. You know that in all such cases there is a difference, and you know also in what the difference lies?

EUTH.: I think that I understand.

SOC.: And is not that which is beloved distinct from that which loves?

EUTH.: Certainly.

SOC.: Well; and now tell me, is that which is carried in this state of carrying because it is carried, or for some other reason?

EUTH.: No; that is the reason.

SOC.: And the same is true of what is led and of what is seen?

EUTH.: True.

SOC.: And a thing is not seen because it is visible, but conversely, visible because it is seen; nor is a thing led because it is in the state of being led, or carried because it is in the state of being carried, but the converse of this. And now I think, Euthyphro, that my meaning will be intelligible; and my meaning is, that any state of action or passion implies previous action or passion. It does not become because it is becoming, but it is in a state of becoming because it becomes; neither does it suffer because it is in a state of suffering, but it is in a state of suffering because it suffers. Do you not agree?

EUTH.: Yes.

SOC.: Is not that which is loved in some state either of becoming or suffering?

EUTH.: Yes.

SOC.: And the same holds as in the previous instances; the state of being loved follows the act of being loved, and not the act the state.

EUTH.: Certainly.

SOC.: And what do you say of piety, Euthyphro: is not piety, according to your definition, loved by all the gods?

EUTH.: Yes.

SOC.: Because it is pious or holy, or for some other reason?

EUTH.: No, that is the reason.

SOC.: It is loved because it is holy, not holy because it is loved?

EUTH.: Yes.

SOC.: And that which is dear to the gods is loved by them, and is in a state to be loved of them because it is loved of them?

EUTH.: Certainly.

SOC.: Then that which is dear to the gods, Euthyphro, is not holy, nor is that which is holy loved of God, as you affirm; but they are two different things.

EUTH.: How do you mean, Socrates?

SOC.: I mean to say that the holy has been acknowledged by us to be loved of God because it is holy, not to be holy because it is loved.

EUTH.: Yes.

SOC.: But that which is dear to the gods is dear to them because it is loved by them, not loved by them because it is dear to them.

EUTH.: True.

SOC.: But, friend Euthyphro, if that which is holy is the same with that which is dear to God, and is loved because it is holy, then that which is dear to God would have been loved as being dear to God; but if that which is dear to God is dear to him because loved by him, then that which is holy would have been holy because loved by him. But now you see that the reverse is the case, and that they are quite different from one another. For one (θεοφιλὲ⸱) is of a kind to be loved because it is loved, and the other (ὅσιον) is loved because it is of a kind to be loved. Thus you appear to me, Euthyphro, when I ask you what is the essence of holiness, to offer an attribute only, and not the essence—the attribute of being loved by all the gods. But you still refuse to explain to me the nature of holiness. And therefore, if you please, I will ask you not to hide your treasure, but to tell me once more what holiness or piety really is, whether dear to the gods or not (for that is a matter about which we will not quarrel); and what is impiety?

EUTH.: I really do not know, Socrates, how to express what I mean. For somehow or other our arguments, on whatever ground we rest them, seem to turn round and walk away from us.

SOC.: Your words, Euthyphro, are like the handiwork of my ancestor Daedalus; and if I were the sayer or propounder of them, you might say that my arguments walk away and will not remain fixed where they are placed because I am a descendant of his. But now, since these notions are your own, you must find some other gibe, for they certainly, as you yourself allow, show an inclination to be on the move.

EUTH.: Nay, Socrates, I shall still say that you are the Daedalus who sets arguments in motion; not I, certainly, but you make them move or go round, for they would never have stirred, as far as I am concerned.

SOC.: Then I must be a greater than Daedalus: for whereas he only made his own inventions to move, I move those of other people as well. And the beauty of it is, that I would rather not. For I would give the wisdom of Daedalus, and the wealth of Tantalus, to be able to detain them and keep them fixed. But enough of this. As I perceive that you are lazy, I will myself endeavour to show you how you might instruct me in the nature of piety; and I hope that you will not grudge your labour. Tell me, then,—Is not that which is pious necessarily just?

EUTH.: Yes.

SOC.: And is, then, all which is just pious? or, is that which is pious all just, but that which is just, only in part and not all, pious?

EUTH.: I do not understand you, Socrates.

SOC.: And yet I know that you are as much wiser than I am, as you are younger. But, as I was saying, revered friend, the abundance of your wisdom makes you lazy. Please to exert yourself, for there is no real difficulty in understanding me. What I mean I may explain by an illustration of what I do not mean. The poet (Stasinus) sings—

"Of Zeus, the author and creator of all these things,
You will not tell: for where there is fear there is also
reverence."

Now I disagree with this poet. Shall I tell you in what respect?

EUTH.: By all means.

SOC.: I should not say that where there is fear there is also reverence; for I am sure that many persons fear poverty and disease, and the like evils, but I do not perceive that they reverence the objects of their fear.

EUTH.: Very true.

SOC.: But where reverence is, there is fear; for he who has a feeling of reverence and shame about the commission of any action, fears and is afraid of an ill reputation.

EUTH.: No doubt.

SOC.: Then we are wrong in saying that where there is fear there is also reverence; and we should say, where there is reverence there is also fear. But there is not always reverence where there is fear; for fear is a more extended notion, and reverence is a part of fear, just as the odd is a part of number, and number is a more extended notion than the odd. I suppose that you follow me now?

EUTH.: Quite well.

SOC.: That was the sort of question which I meant to raise when I asked whether the just is always the pious, or the pious always the just; and whether there may not be justice where there is not piety; for justice is the more extended notion of which piety is only a part. Do you dissent?

EUTH.: No, I think that you are quite right.

SOC.: Then, if piety is a part of justice, I suppose that we should enquire what part? If you had pursued the enquiry in the previous cases; for instance, if you had asked me what is an even number, and what part of number the even is, I should have had no difficulty in replying, a number which represents a figure having two equal sides. Do you not agree?

EUTH.: Yes, I quite agree.

SOC.: In like manner, I want you to tell me what part of justice is piety or holiness, that I may be able to tell Meletus not to do me injustice, or indict me for impiety, as I am now adequately instructed by you in the nature of piety or holiness, and their opposites.

EUTH.: Piety or holiness, Socrates, appears to me to be that part of justice which attends to the gods, as there is the other part of justice which attends to men.

SOC.: That is good, Euthyphro; yet still there is a little point about which I should like to have further information. What is the meaning of "attention"?

For attention can hardly be used in the same sense when applied to the gods as when applied to other things. For instance, horses are said to require attention, and not every person is able to attend to them, but only a person skilled in horsemanship. Is it not so?

EUTH.: Certainly.

SOC.: I should suppose that the art of horsemanship is the art of attending to horses?

EUTH.: Yes.

SOC.: Nor is every one qualified to attend to dogs, but only the huntsman?

EUTH.: True.

SOC.: And I should also conceive that the art of the huntsman is the art of attending to dogs?

EUTH.: Yes.

SOC.: As the art of the oxherd is the art of attending to oxen?

EUTH.: Very true.

SOC.: In like manner holiness or piety is the art of attending to the gods?—that would be your meaning, Euthyphro?

EUTH.: Yes.

SOC.: And is not attention always designed for the good or benefit of that to which the attention is given? As in the case of horses, you may observe that when attended to by the horseman's art they are benefited and improved, are they not?

EUTH.: True.

SOC.: As the dogs are benefited by the huntsman's art, and the oxen by the art of the oxherd, and all other things are tended or attended for their good and not for their hurt?

EUTH.: Certainly, not for their hurt.

SOC.: But for their good?

EUTH.: Of course.

SOC.: And does piety or holiness, which has been defined to be the art of attending to the gods, benefit or improve them? Would you say that when you do a holy act you make any of the gods better?

EUTH.: No, no; that was certainly not what I meant.

SOC.: And I, Euthyphro, never supposed that you did. I asked you the question about the nature of the attention, because I thought that you did not.

EUTH.: You do me justice, Socrates; that is not the sort of attention which I mean.

SOC.: Good; but I must still ask what is this attention to the gods which is called piety?

EUTH.: It is such, Socrates, as servants show to their masters.

SOC.: I understand—a sort of ministration to the gods.

EUTH.: Exactly.

SOC.: Medicine is also a sort of ministration or service, having in view the attainment of some object—would you not say of health?

EUTH.: I should.

SOC.: Again, there is an art which ministers to the ship-builder with a view to the attainment of some result?

EUTH.: Yes, Socrates, with a view to the building of a ship.

SOC.: As there is an art which ministers to the house-builder with a view to the building of a house?

EUTH.: Yes.

SOC.: And now tell me, my good friend, about the art which ministers to the gods: what work does that help to accomplish? For you must surely know if, as you say, you are of all men living the one who is best instructed in religion.

EUTH.: And I speak the truth, Socrates.

SOC.: Tell me then, oh tell me—what is that fair work which the gods do by the help of our ministrations?

EUTH.: Many and fair, Socrates, are the works which they do.

SOC.: Why, my friend, and so are those of a general. But the chief of them is easily told. Would you not say that victory in war is the chief of them?

EUTH.: Certainly.

SOC.: Many and fair, too, are the works of the husbandman, if I am not mistaken; but his chief work is the production of food from the earth?

EUTH.: Exactly.

SOC.: And of the many and fair things done by the gods, which is the chief or principal one?

EUTH.: I have told you already, Socrates, that to learn all these things accurately will be very tiresome. Let me simply say that piety or holiness is learning how to please the gods in word and deed, by prayers and sacrifices. Such piety is the salvation of families and states, just as the impious, which is unpleasing to the gods, is their ruin and destruction.

SOC.: I think that you could have answered in much fewer words the chief question which I asked,

Euthyphro, if you had chosen. But I see plainly that you are not disposed to instruct me—clearly not: else why, when we reached the point, did you turn aside? Had you only answered me I should have truly learned of you by this time the nature of piety. Now, as the asker of a question is necessarily dependent on the answerer, whither he leads I must follow; and can only ask again, what is the pious, and what is piety? Do you mean that they are a sort of science of praying and sacrificing?

EUTH.: Yes, I do.

SOC.: And sacrificing is giving to the gods, and prayer is asking of the gods?

EUTH.: Yes, Socrates.

SOC.: Upon this view, then, piety is a science of asking and giving?

EUTH.: You understand me capitally, Socrates.

SOC.: Yes, my friend; the reason is that I am a votary of your science, and give my mind to it, and therefore nothing which you say will be thrown away upon me. Please then to tell me, what is the nature of this service to the gods? Do you mean that we prefer requests and give gifts to them?

EUTH.: Yes, I do.

SOC.: Is not the right way of asking to ask of them what we want?

EUTH.: Certainly.

SOC.: And the right way of giving is to give to them in return what they want of us. There would be no meaning in an art which gives to any one that which he does not want.

EUTH.: Very true, Socrates.

SOC.: Then piety, Euthyphro, is an art which gods and men have of doing business with one another?

EUTH.: That is an expression which you may use, if you like.

SOC.: But I have no particular liking for anything but the truth. I wish, however, that you would tell me what benefit accrues to the gods from our gifts. There is no doubt about what they give to us; for there is no good thing which they do not give; but how we can give any good thing to them in return is far from being equally clear. If they give everything and we give nothing, that must be an affair of business in which we have very greatly the advantage of them.

EUTH.: And do you imagine, Socrates, that any benefit accrues to the gods from our gifts?

SOC.: But if not, Euthyphro, what is the meaning of gifts which are conferred by us upon the gods?

EUTH.: What else, but tributes of honour; and, as I was just now saying, what pleases them?

SOC.: Piety, then, is pleasing to the gods, but not beneficial or dear to them?

EUTH.: I should say that nothing could be dearer.

SOC.: Then once more the assertion is repeated that piety is dear to the gods?

EUTH.: Certainly.

SOC.: And when you say this, can you wonder at your words not standing firm, but walking away? Will you accuse me of being the Daedalus who makes them walk away, not perceiving that there is another and far greater artist than Daedalus who makes them go round in a circle, and he is yourself; for the argument, as you will perceive, comes round to the same point. Were we not saying that the holy or pious was not the same with that which is loved of the gods? Have you forgotten?

EUTH.: I quite remember.

SOC.: And are you not saying that what is loved of the gods is holy; and is not this the same as what is dear to them—do you see?

EUTH.: True.

SOC.: Then either we were wrong in our former assertion; or, if we were right then, we are wrong now.

EUTH.: One of the two must be true.

SOC.: Then we must begin again and ask, What is piety? That is an enquiry which I shall never be weary of pursuing as far as in me lies; and I entreat you not to scorn me, but to apply your mind to the utmost, and tell me the truth. For, if any man knows, you are he; and therefore I must detain you, like Proteus, until you tell. If you had not certainly known the nature of piety and impiety, I am confident that you would never, on behalf of a serf, have charged your aged father with murder. You would not have run such a risk of doing wrong in the sight of the gods, and you would have had too much respect for the opinions of men. I am sure, therefore, that you know the nature of piety and impiety. Speak out then, my dear Euthyphro, and do not hide your knowledge.

EUTH.: Another time, Socrates; for I am in a hurry, and must go now.

SOC.: Alas! my companion, and will you leave me in despair? I was hoping that you would instruct me in the nature of piety and impiety; and then I might have cleared myself of Meletus and his in-dictment. I would have told him that I had been enlightened by Euthyphro, and had given up rash innovations and speculations, in which I in-dulged only through ignorance, and that now I am about to lead a better life.

Leviathan

THOMAS HOBBES

Thomas Hobbes (1588–1679) was a brilliant English philosopher. His work, Leviathan, *is a classic of the social contract tradition in ethics and political philosophy.*

OF THE NATURAL CONDITION OF MANKIND AS CONCERNING THEIR FELICITY AND MISERY

Nature has made men so equal in the faculties of body and mind as that, though there be found one man sometimes manifestly stronger in body or of quicker mind than another, yet, when all is reckoned together, the difference between man and man is not so considerable as that one man can thereupon claim to himself any benefit to which another may not pretend as well as he. For as to the strength of body, the weakest has strength enough to kill the strongest, either by secret machination or by confederacy with others that are in the same danger with himself.

And as to the faculties of the mind, setting aside the arts grounded upon words, and especially that skill of proceeding upon general and infallible rules called science—which very few have and but in few things, as being not a native faculty born with us, nor attained, as prudence, while we look after somewhat else—I find yet a greater equality among men than that of strength. For prudence is but experience, which equal time equally bestows on all men in those things they equally apply themselves unto. That which may perhaps make such equality incredible is but a vain conceit of one's own wisdom, which almost all men think they have in a greater degree than the vulgar—that is, than all men but themselves and a few others whom, by fame or for concurring with themselves, they approve. For such is the nature of men that howsoever they may acknowledge many others to be more witty or more eloquent or more learned, yet they will hardly believe there be many so wise as themselves; for they see their own wit at hand and other men's at a distance. But this proves rather that men are in that point equal than unequal. For there is not ordinarily a greater sign of the equal distribution of anything than that every man is contented with his share.

From this equality of ability arises equality of hope in the attaining of our ends. And therefore if any two men desire the same thing, which nevertheless they cannot both enjoy, they become enemies; and in the way to their end, which is principally their own conservation, and sometimes their delectation only, endeavour to destroy or subdue one another. And from hence it comes to pass that where an invader has no more to fear than another man's single power, if one plant, sow, build, or possess a convenient seat, others may probably be expected to come prepared with forces united to dispossess and deprive him, not only of the fruit of his labor, but also of his life or liberty. And the invader again is in the like danger of another.

From *Leviathan*, first published in 1651.

And from this diffidence of one another there is no way for any man to secure himself so reasonable as anticipation—that is, by force or wiles to master the persons of all men he can, so long till he see no other power great enough to endanger him; and this is no more than his own conservation requires, and is generally allowed. Also, because there be some that take pleasure in contemplating their own power in the acts of conquest, which they pursue farther than their security requires, if others that otherwise would be glad to be at ease within modest bounds should not by invasion increase their power, they would not be able, long time, by standing only on their defense, to subsist. And by consequence, such augmentation of dominion over men being necessary to a man's conservation, it ought to be allowed him.

Again, men have no pleasure, but on the contrary a great deal of grief, in keeping company where there is no power able to overawe them all. For every man looks that his companion should value him at the same rate he sets upon himself; and upon all signs of contempt or undervaluing naturally endeavors, as far as he dares (which among them that have no common power to keep them in quiet is far enough to make them destroy each other), to extort a greater value from his contemners by damage and from others by the example.

So that in the nature of man we find three principal causes of quarrel: first, competition; secondly, diffidence; thirdly, glory.

The first makes men invade for gain, the second for safety, and the third for reputation. The first use violence to make themselves masters of other men's persons, wives, children, and cattle; the second, to defend them; the third, for trifles, as a word, a smile, a different opinion, and any other sign of undervalue, either direct in their persons or by reflection in their kindred, their friends, their nation, their profession, or their name.

Hereby it is manifest that, during the time men live without a common power to keep them all in awe, they are in that condition which is called war, and such a war as is of every man against every man. For WAR consists not in battle only, or the act of fighting, but in a tract of time wherein the will to contend by battle is sufficiently known; and therefore the notion of *time* is to be considered in the na-

ture of war as it is in the nature of weather. For as the nature of foul weather lies not in a shower or two of rain but in an inclination thereto of many days together, so the nature of war consists not in actual fighting but in the known disposition thereto during all the time there is no assurance to the contrary. All other time is PEACE.

Whatsoever, therefore, is consequent to a time of war where every man is enemy to every man, the same is consequent to the time wherein men live without other security than what their own strength and their own invention shall furnish them withal. In such condition there is no place for industry, because the fruit thereof is uncertain: and consequently no culture of the earth; no navigation nor use of the commodities that may be imported by sea; no commodious building; no instruments of moving and removing such things as require much force; no knowledge of the face of the earth; no account of time; no arts; no letters; no society; and, which is worst of all, continual fear and danger of violent death; and the life of man solitary, poor, nasty, brutish, and short.

It may seem strange to some man that has not well weighed these things that nature should thus dissociate and render men apt to invade and destroy one another; and he may therefore, not trusting to this inference made from the passions, desire perhaps to have the same confirmed by experience. Let him therefore consider with himself—when taking a journey he arms himself and seeks to go well accompanied, when going to sleep he locks his doors, when even in his house he locks his chests, and this when he knows there be laws and public officers, armed, to revenge all injuries shall be done him—what opinion he has of his fellow subjects when he rides armed, of his fellow citizens when he locks his doors, and of his children and servants when he locks his chests. Does he not there as much accuse mankind by his actions as I do by my words? But neither of us accuse man's nature in it. The desires and other passions of man are in themselves no sin. No more are the actions that proceed from those passions till they know a law that forbids them, which, till laws be made, they cannot know, nor can any law be made till they have agreed upon the person that shall make it.

It may peradventure be thought there was never

such a time nor condition of war as this, and I believe it was never generally so over all the world; but there are many places where they live so now. For the savage people in many places of America, except the government of small families, the concord whereof depends on natural lust, have no government at all and live at this day in that brutish manner as I said before. Howsoever, it may be perceived what manner of life there would be where there were no common power to fear by the manner of life which men that have formerly lived under a peaceful government use to degenerate into in a civil war.

But though there had never been any time wherein particular men were in a condition of war one against another, yet in all times kings and persons of sovereign authority, because of their independency, are in continual jealousies and in the state and posture of gladiators, having their weapons pointing and their eyes fixed on one another—that is, their forts, garrisons, and guns upon the frontiers of their kingdoms, and continual spies upon their neighbors—which is a posture of war. But because they uphold thereby the industry of their subjects, there does not follow from it that misery which accompanies the liberty of particular men.

To this war of every man against every man, this also is consequent: that nothing can be unjust. The notions of right and wrong, justice and injustice, have there no place. Where there is no common power, there is no law; where no law, no injustice. Force and fraud are in war the two cardinal virtues. Justice and injustice are none of the faculties neither of the body nor mind. If they were, they might be in a man that were alone in the world, as well as his senses and passions. They are qualities that relate to men in society, not in solitude. It is consequent also to the same condition that there be no propriety, no dominion, no *mine* and *thine* distinct; but only that to be every man's that he can get, and for so long as he can keep it. And thus much for the ill condition which man by mere nature is actually placed in, though with a possibility to come out of it consisting partly in the passions, partly in his reason.

The passions that incline men to peace are fear of death, desire of such things as are necessary to commodious living, and a hope by their industry to obtain them. And reason suggests convenient articles of peace, upon which men may be drawn to

agreement. These articles are they which otherwise are called the Laws of Nature, whereof I shall speak more particularly in the two following chapters.

OF THE FIRST AND SECOND NATURAL LAWS, AND OF CONTRACTS

The RIGHT OF NATURE, which writers commonly call *jus naturale,* is the liberty each man has to use his own power, as he will himself, for the preservation of his own nature—that is to say, of his own life—and consequently of doing anything which, in his own judgment and reason, he shall conceive to be the aptest means thereunto.

By LIBERTY is understood, according to the proper signification of the word, the absence of external impediments; which impediments may oft take away part of a man's power to do what he would, but cannot hinder him from using the power left him according as his judgment and reason shall dictate to him.

A LAW OF NATURE, *lex naturalis,* is a precept or general rule, found out by reason, by which a man is forbidden to do that which is destructive of his life or takes away the means of preserving the same and to omit that by which he thinks it may be best preserved. For though they that speak of this subject use to confound *jus* and *lex, right* and *law,* yet they ought to be distinguished; because RIGHT consists in liberty to do or to forbear; whereas LAW determines and binds to one of them; so that law and right differ as much as obligation and liberty, which in one and the same matter are inconsistent.

And because the condition of man, as has been declared in the precedent chapter, is a condition of war of every one against every one—in which case everyone is governed by his own reason and there is nothing he can make use of that may not be a help unto him in preserving his life against his enemies—it follows that in such a condition every man has a right to everything, even to one another's body. And therefore, as long as this natural right of every man to everything endures, there can be no security to any man, how strong or wise soever he be, of living out the time which nature ordinarily allows men to live. And consequently it is a precept or general rule of reason *that every man ought to endeavor peace, as far as he has hope of obtaining it; and when he cannot obtain it, that he may seek and use all helps and advantages of war.* The first branch of which rule contains the first and fundamental law of nature, which is *to seek peace and follow it.* The second, the sum of the right of nature, which is, *by all means we can to defend ourselves.*

From this fundamental law of nature, by which men are commanded to endeavor peace, is derived this second law: *that a man be willing, when others are so too, as far forth as for peace and defense of himself he shall think it necessary, to lay down this right to all things, and be contented with so much liberty against other men as he would allow other men against himself.* For as long as every man holds this right of doing anything he likes, so long are all men in the condition of war. But if other men will not lay down their right as well as he, then there is no reason for anyone to divest himself of his, for that were to expose himself to prey, which no man is bound to, rather than to dispose himself to peace. This is that law of the gospel: *whatsoever you require that others should do to you, that do ye to them.* And that law of all men, *quod tibi fieri non vis, alteri ne feceris.*[1]

To *lay down* a man's *right* to anything is to *divest* himself of the *liberty* of hindering another of the benefit of his own right to the same. For he that renounces or passes away his right gives not to any other man a right which he had not before—because there is nothing to which every man had not right by nature—but only stands out of his way, that he may enjoy his own original right without hindrance from him, not without hindrance from another. So that the effect which redounds to one man by another man's defect of right is but so much diminution of impediments to the use of his own right original. Right is laid aside either by simply renouncing it or by transferring it to another. By *simply* RENOUNCING, when he cares not to whom the benefit thereof redounds. By TRANSFERRING, when he intends the benefit thereof to some certain person or persons. And when a man has in either manner abandoned or granted away his right, then is he said to be OBLIGED, or BOUND not to hinder those to whom such right is granted or abandoned from the benefit of it; and that he *ought,* and it is his DUTY, not to make void that voluntary act of his own; and that such hindrance is INJUSTICE and INJURY as being *sine jure,*[2] the right being before renounced or transferred. So that *injury* or *injustice* in the controversies of the world is somewhat like to that which in the disputations of scholars is called *absurdity.* For as it is there called an absurdity to contradict what one maintained in the beginning, so in the world it is called injustice and injury voluntarily to undo that which from the beginning he had voluntarily done. The way by which a man either simply renounces or transfers his right is a declaration or signification by some voluntary and sufficient sign or signs that he does so renounce or transfer, or has so renounced or transferred, the same to him that accepts it. And these signs are either words only or actions only; or as it happens most often, both words and actions. And the same are the BONDS by which men are bound and obliged—bonds that have their strength, not from their own nature, for nothing is more easily broken than a man's word, but from fear of some evil consequence upon the rupture.

Whensoever a man transfers his right or renounces it, it is either in consideration of some right reciprocally transferred to himself or for some other good he hopes for thereby. For it is a voluntary act; and of the voluntary acts of every man, the object is some *good to himself.* And therefore there be some rights which no man can be understood by any words or other signs to have abandoned or transferred. As, first, a man cannot lay down the right of resisting them that assault him by force to take away his life, because he cannot be understood to aim thereby at any good to himself. The same may be said of wounds and chains and imprisonment, both because there is no benefit consequent to such patience as there is to the patience of suffering another to be wounded or imprisoned, as also because a man cannot tell, when he sees men proceed against him by violence, whether they intend his death or not. And, lastly, the motive and end for which this renouncing and transferring of right is introduced is nothing else but the security of a man's person in his life and in the means of so preserving life as not to be weary of it. And therefore if a man by words or other signs seem to despoil himself of the end for which those signs were intended, he is not to be understood as if he meant it or that it was his will, but that he was ignorant of how such words and actions were to be interpreted.

The mutual transferring of right is that which men call CONTRACT.

There is difference between transferring of right to the thing and transferring, or tradition—that is, delivery—of the thing itself. For the thing may be delivered together with the translation of the right, as in buying and selling with ready money or exchange of goods or lands, and it may be delivered some time after.

Again, one of the contractors may deliver the thing contracted for on his part and leave the other to perform his part at some determinate time after and in the meantime be trusted, and then the contract on his part is called PACT or COVENANT; or both parts may contract now to perform hereafter, in which cases he that is to perform in time to come, being trusted, his performance is called *keeping of promise* or faith, and the failing of performance, if it be voluntary, *violation of faith.*

When the transferring of right is not mutual, but one of the parties transfers in hope to gain thereby friendship or service from another or from his friends, or in hope to gain the reputation of charity or magnanimity, or to deliver his mind from the pain of compassion, or in hope of reward in heaven—this is not contract but GIFT, FREE GIFT, GRACE, which words signify one and the same thing.

Signs of contract are either *express* or *by inference.* Express are words spoken with understanding of what they signify, and such words are either of the time *present* or *past*—as *I give, I grant, I have given, I have granted, I will that this be yours*— or of the future —as *I will give, I will grant*—which words of the future are called PROMISE.

Signs by inference are sometimes the consequence of words, sometimes the consequence of silence, sometimes the consequence of actions, sometimes the consequence of forbearing an action; and generally a sign by inference of any contract is whatsoever sufficiently argues the will of the contractor.

Words alone, if they be of the time to come and contain a bare promise, are an insufficient sign of a free gift and therefore not obligatory. For if they be of the time to come, as *tomorrow I will give,* they are a sign I have not given yet and consequently that my right is not transferred but remains till I transfer it by some other act. But if the words be of the time present or past, as *I have given or do give to be delivered tomorrow,* then is my tomorrow's right given away today, and that by the virtue of the words though there were no other argument of my will. And there is a great difference in the signification of these words: *volo hoc tuum esse cras and cras dabo*—that is, between *I will that this be yours tomorrow* and *I will give it you tomorrow*—for the word *I will,* in the former manner of speech, signifies an act of the will present, but in the latter it signifies a promise of an act of the will to come; and therefore the former words, being of the present, transfer a future right; the latter, that be of the future, transfer nothing. But if there be other signs of the will to transfer a right besides words, then, though the gift be free, yet may the right be understood to pass by words of the future: as if a man propound a prize to him that comes first to the end of a race, the gift is free; and though the words be of the future, yet the right passes; for if he would not have his words so be understood, he should not have let them run.

In contracts, the right passes not only where the words are of the time present or past but also where they are of the future, because all contract is mutual translation or change of right, and therefore he that promises only because he has already received the benefit for which he promises is to be understood as if he intended the right should pass; for unless he had been content to have his words so understood, the other would not have performed his part first. And for that cause, in buying and selling and other acts of contract a promise is equivalent to a covenant and therefore obligatory.

He that performs first in the case of a contract is said to MERIT that which he is to receive by the performance of the other; and he has it as *due.* Also when a prize is propounded to many which is to be given to him only that wins, or money is thrown among many to be enjoyed by them that catch it, though this be a free gift, yet so to win or so to catch is to *merit* and to have it as DUE. For the right is transferred in the propounding of the prize and in throwing down the money, though it be not determined to whom but by the event of the contention. But there is between these two sorts of merit this difference: that in contract I merit by virtue of my own power and the contractor's need, but in this case of free gift I am enabled to merit only by the benignity of the giver; in contract I merit at the contractor's hand that he should depart with his right, in this case of gift I merit not that the giver should part with his right but that when he has parted with it, it should be mine rather than another's. And this I think to be the meaning of that distinction of the Schools between *meritum congrui* and *meritum condigni*.[3] For God Almighty having promised Paradise to those men, hoodwinked with carnal desires, that can walk through this world according to the precepts and limits prescribed by him, they say he that shall so walk shall merit Paradise *ex congruo*. But because no man can demand a right to it, by his own righteousness or any other power in himself, but by the free grace of God only, they say no man can merit Paradise *ex condigno*. This, I say, I think is the meaning of that distinction; but because disputers do not agree upon the signification of their own terms of art longer than it serves their turn, I will not affirm anything of their meaning; only this I say: when a gift is given indefinitely, as a prize to be contended for, he that wins merits and may claim the prize as due.

If a covenant be made wherein neither of the parties perform presently but trust one another, in the condition of mere nature, which is a condition of war of every man against every man, upon any reasonable suspicion, it is void; but if there be a common power set over them both, with right and force sufficient to compel performance, it is not void. For he that performs first has no assurance the other will perform after, because the bonds of words are too weak to bridle men's ambition, avarice, anger, and other passions without the fear of some coercive power which in the condition of mere nature, where all men are equal and judges of the justness of their own fears, cannot possibly be supposed. And therefore he which performs first does but betray himself to his enemy, contrary to the right he can never abandon of defending his life and means of living.

But in a civil estate, where there is a power set up to constrain those that would otherwise violate their faith, that fear is no more reasonable; and for that cause, he which by the covenant is to perform first is obliged so to do.

The cause of fear which makes such a covenant invalid must be always something arising after the covenant made, as some new fact or other sign of the will not to perform; else it cannot make the cove-

nant void. For that which could not hinder a man from promising ought not to be admitted as a hindrance of performing.

He that transfers any right transfers the means of enjoying it, as far as lies in his power. As he that sells land is understood to transfer the herbage and whatsoever grows upon it; nor can he that sells a mill turn away the stream that drives it. And they that give to a man the right of government in sovereignty are understood to give him the right of levying money to maintain soldiers and of appointing magistrates for the administration of justice.

To make covenants with brute beasts is impossible because, not understanding our speech, they understand not nor accept of any translation of right, nor can translate any right to another; and without mutual acceptation there is no covenant.

To make covenant with God is impossible but by mediation of such as God speaks to, either by revelation supernatural or by his lieutenants that govern under him and in his name; for otherwise we know not whether our covenants be accepted or not. And therefore they that vow anything contrary to any law of nature vow in vain, as being a thing unjust to pay such vow. And if it be a thing commanded by the law of nature, it is not the vow but the law that binds them.

The matter or subject of a covenant is always something that falls under deliberation, for to covenant is an act of the will—that is to say, an act, and the last act, of deliberation—and is therefore always understood to be something to come, and which judged possible for him that covenants to perform.

And therefore to promise that which is known to be impossible is no covenant. But if that prove impossible afterwards which before was thought possible, the covenant is valid, and binds, though not to the thing itself, yet to the value, or, if that also be impossible, to the unfeigned endeavor of performing as much as is possible, for to more no man can be obliged.

Men are freed of their covenants two ways: by performing or by being forgiven. For performance is the natural end of obligation, and forgiveness the restitution of liberty, as being a retransferring of that right in which the obligation consisted.

Covenants entered into by fear, in the condition of mere nature, are obligatory. For example, if

I covenant to pay a ransom or service for my life to an enemy, I am bound by it; for it is a contract, wherein one receives the benefit of life, the other is to receive money or service for it; and consequently, where no other law, as in the condition of mere nature, forbids the performance, the covenant is valid. Therefore prisoners of war, if trusted with the payment of their ransom, are obliged to pay it; and if a weaker prince make a disadvantageous peace with a stronger, for fear, he is bound to keep it; unless, as has been said before, there arises some new and just cause of fear to renew the war. And even in commonwealths, if I be forced to redeem myself from a thief by promising him money, I am bound to pay it till the civil law discharge me. For whatsoever I may lawfully do without obligation, the same I may lawfully covenant to do through fear; and what I lawfully covenant, I cannot lawfully break. A former covenant makes void a later. For a man that has passed away his right to one man today has it not to pass tomorrow to another; and therefore the later promise passes no right, but is null.

A covenant not to defend myself from force by force is always void. For, as I have shown before, no man can transfer or lay down his right to save himself from death, wounds, and imprisonment, the avoiding whereof is the only end of laying down any right; and therefore the promise of not resisting force in no covenant transfers any right, nor is obliging. For though a man may covenant thus: *unless I do so or so, kill me,* he cannot covenant thus: *unless I do so or so, I will not resist you when you come to kill me.* For man by nature chooses the lesser evil, which is danger of death in resisting, rather than the greater, which is certain and present death in not resisting. And this is granted to be true by all men, in that they lead criminals to execution and prison with armed men, notwithstanding that such criminals have consented to the law by which they are condemned.

A covenant to accuse oneself, without assurance of pardon, is likewise invalid. For in the condition of nature, where every man is judge, there is no place for accusation; and in the civil state, the accusation is followed with punishment, which, being force, a man is not obliged not to resist. The same is also true of the accusation of those by whose condemnation a man falls into misery, as of a father, wife, or benefactor. For the testimony of such an accuser, if it be not willingly given, is presumed to be corrupted by nature, and therefore not to be received; and where a man's testimony is not to be credited, he is not bound to give it. Also accusations upon torture are not to be reputed as testimonies. For torture is to be used but as means of conjecture and light in the further examination and search of truth; and what is in that case confessed tends to the ease of him that is tortured, not to the informing of the torturers, and therefore ought not to have the credit of a sufficient testimony; for whether he deliver himself by true or false accusation, he does it by the right of preserving his own life.

The force of words being, as I have formerly noted, too weak to hold men to the performance of their covenants, there are in man's nature but two imaginable helps to strengthen it. And those are either a fear of the consequence of breaking their word, or a glory or pride in appearing not to need to break it. This latter is a generosity too rarely found to be presumed on, especially in the pursuers of wealth, command, or sensual pleasure—which are the greatest part of mankind. The passion to be reckoned upon is fear, whereof there be two very general objects: one, the power of spirits invisible; the other, the power of those men they shall therein offend. Of these two, though the former be the greater power, yet the fear of the latter is commonly the greater fear. The fear of the former is in every man his own religion, which has place in the nature of man before civil society. The latter has not so, at least not place enough to keep men to their promises, because in the condition of mere nature the inequality of power is not discerned but by the event of battle. So that before the time of civil society, or in the interruption thereof by war, there is nothing can strengthen a covenant of peace agreed on against the temptations of avarice, ambition, lust, or other strong desire but the fear of that invisible power, which they everyone worship as God and fear as a revenger of their perfidy. All therefore that can be done between two men not subject to civil power is to put one another to swear by the God he fears, which *swearing* or OATH is a *form of speech, added to a promise, by which he that promises signifies that, unless he perform, he renounces the mercy of his God, or calls to him for vengeance on himself.* Such was the heathen form, *Let Jupiter kill me else, as I kill this beast.* So is our form,

I shall do thus and thus, so help me God. And this, with the rites and ceremonies which everyone uses in his own religion, that the fear of breaking faith might be the greater.

By this it appears that an oath taken according to any other form or rite than his that swears is in vain and no oath, and that there is no swearing by anything which the swearer thinks not God. For though men have sometimes used to swear by their kings, for fear or flattery, yet they would have it thereby understood they attributed to them divine honor. And that swearing unnecessarily by God is but profaning of his name; and swearing by other things, as men do in common discourse, is not swearing but an impious custom gotten by too much vehemence of talking.

It appears also that the oath adds nothing to the obligation. For a covenant, if lawful, binds in the sight of God without the oath as much as with it; if unlawful, binds not at all, though it be confirmed with an oath.

Notes

1. "Do not do unto others what you would not have done to you."
2. Without legality.
3. Merit from conformity and merit from worthiness.

The Categorical Imperative

IMMANUEL KANT

Born in Köningsberg, East Prussia (now Russia), the great German philosopher Immanuel Kant (1724–1804) was one of the most influential of all modern thinkers.

PREFACE

As my concern here is with moral philosophy, I limit the question suggested to this: Whether it is not of the utmost necessity to construct a pure moral philosophy, perfectly cleared of everything which is only empirical, and which belongs to anthropology? for that such a philosophy must be possible is evident from the common idea of duty and of the moral laws. Everyone must admit that if a law is to have moral force, *i.e.* to be the basis of an obligation, it must carry with it absolute necessity; that, for example, the precept "Thou shall not lie," is not valid for men alone, as if other rational beings had no need to observe it; and so with all the other moral laws properly so called; that, therefore, the basis of obligation must not be sought in the nature of man, or in the circumstances in the world in which he is placed, but *a priori* simply in the conception of pure reason; and although any other precept which is founded on principles of mere experience may be in certain respects universal, yet in as far as it rests even in the least degree on an empirical basis, perhaps only as to a motive, such a precept, while it may be a practical rule, can never be called a moral law. . . .

THE GOOD WILL

Nothing can possibly be conceived in the world, or even out of it, which can be called good, without qualification, except a Good Will. Intelligence, wit, judgment, and the other *talents* of the mind, however they may be named, or courage, resolution, perseverance, as qualities of temperament, are undoubtedly good and desirable in many respects; but these gifts of nature may also become extremely bad and mischievous if the will which is to make use of them, and which, therefore, constitutes what is called *character,* is not good. It is the same with the *gifts of fortune.* Power, riches, honour, even health,

From *The Foundations of the Metaphysics of Morals,* translated by T. K. Abbott (London: Longmans, Green and Co., 1873). With emendations by Daniel Kolak.

and the general well-being and contentment with one's conditions which is called *happiness,* inspire pride, and often presumption, if there is not a good will to correct the influence of these on the mind, and with this also to rectify the whole principle of acting, and adapt it to its end. The sight of a being who is not adorned with a single feature of a pure and good will, enjoying unbroken prosperity, can never give pleasure to an imperial rational spectator. Thus a good will appears to constitute the indispensable condition even of being worthy of happiness.

There are even some qualities which are of service to this good will itself, and may facilitate its action, yet which have no intrinsic unconditional value, but always presuppose a good will, and this qualifies the esteem that we justly have for them, and does not permit us to regard them as absolutely good. Moderation in the affections and passions, self-control, and calm deliberation are not only good in many respects, but even seem to constitute part of the intrinsic worth of the person; but they are far from deserving to be called good without qualification, although they have been so unconditionally praised by the ancients. For without the principles of a good will, they may become extremely bad; and the coolness of a villain not only makes him far more dangerous, but also directly makes him more abominable in our eyes than he would have been without it.

A good will is good not because of what it performs or effects, not by its aptness for the attainment of some proposed end, but simply by virtue of the volition, that is, it is good in itself, and considered by itself to be esteemed much higher than all that can be brought about by it in favour of any inclination, nay, even of the sum-total of all inclinations. Even if it should happen that, owing to special disfavour of fortune, or the niggardly provision of a step-motherly nature, this will should wholly lack power to accomplish its purpose, if with its greatest efforts it should yet achieve nothing, and there should remain only the good will (not, to be sure, a mere wish, but the summoning of all means in our power), then, like a jewel, it would still shine by its own light, as a thing which has its whole value in itself. Its usefulness or fruitlessness can neither add to nor take away anything from this value. It would be, as it were,

only the setting to enable us to handle it the more conveniently in common commerce, or to attract to it the attention of those who are not yet connoisseurs, but not to recommend it to true connoisseurs, or to determine its value.

WHY REASON WAS MADE TO GUIDE THE WILL

There is, however, something so strange in this idea of the absolute value of the mere will, in which no account is taken of its utility, that notwithstanding the thorough assent of even common reason to the idea, yet a suspicion must arise that it may perhaps really be the product of mere high-blown fancy, and that we may have misunderstood the purpose of nature in assigning reason as the governor of our will. Therefore we will examine this idea from this point of view.

In the physical constitution of an organized being, that is, a being adapted suitably to the purposes of life, we assume it as a fundamental principle that no organ for any purpose will be found but what is also the fittest and best adapted for that purpose. Now in a being which has reason and a will, if the proper object of nature were its *conservatism,* its *welfare,* in a word, its *happiness,* then nature would have hit upon a very bad arrangement in selecting the reason of the creature to carry out this purpose. For all the actions which the creature has to perform with a view to this purpose, and the whole rule of its conduct, would be far more surely prescribed to it by instinct, and that end would have been attained thereby much more certainly than it ever can be by reason. Should reason have been communicated to this favoured creature over and above, it must only have served it to contemplate the happy constitution of its nature, to admire it, to congratulate itself thereon, and to feel thankful for it to the beneficent cause, but not that it should subject its desires to that weak and delusive guidance, and meddle bunglingly with the purpose of nature. In a word, nature would have taken care that reason should not break forth into *practical exercise,* nor have the presumption, with its weak insight, to think out for itself the plan of happiness, and of the means of attaining it. Nature would not only have taken on herself the choice of the ends, but also of the means, and with wise foresight would have entrusted both to instinct.

And, in fact, we find that the more a cultivated reason applies itself with deliberate purpose to the enjoyment of life and happiness, so much the more does the man fail of true satisfaction. And from this circumstance there arises in many, if they are candid enough to confess it, a certain degree of *misology*, that is, hatred of reason, especially in the case of those who are most experienced in the use of it, because after calculating all the advantages they derive, I do not say from the invention of all the arts of common luxury, but even from the sciences (which seem to them to be after all only a luxury of the understanding), they find that they have, in fact, only brought more trouble on their shoulders, rather than gained in happiness; and they end by envying, rather than despising, the more common stamp of men who keep closer to the guidance of mere instinct, and do not allow their reason much influence on their conduct. And this we must admit, that the judgment of those who would very much lower the lofty eulogies of the advantages which reason gives us in regard to the happiness and satisfaction of life, or who would even reduce them below zero, is by no means morose or ungrateful to the goodness with which the world is governed, but that there lies at the root of these judgments the idea that our existence has a different and far nobler end, for which, and not for happiness, reason is properly intended, and which must, therefore, be regarded as the supreme condition to which the private ends of man must, for the most part, be postponed.

For as reason is not competent to guide the will with certainty in regard to its objects and the satisfaction of all our wants (which it to some extent even multiplies), this being an end to which an implanted instinct would have led with much greater certainty; and since, nevertheless, reason is imparted to us as a practical faculty, *i.e.* as one which is to have influence on the *will*, therefore, admitting that nature generally in the distribution of her capacities has adapted the means to the end, its true destination must be to produce a *will*, not merely good as a *means* to something else, but *good in itself*, for which reason was absolutely necessary. This will then, though not indeed the sole and complete good, must be the supreme good and the condition of every other, even of the desire of happiness. Under these circumstances, there is nothing inconsistent with the wisdom of nature in the fact that the cultivation of the reason, which is requisite for the first and unconditional purpose, does in many ways interfere, at least in this life, with the attainment of the second, which is always conditional, namely, happiness. Nay, it may even reduce it to nothing, without nature thereby failing in her purpose. For reason recognizes the establishment of a good will as its highest practical destination, and in attaining this purpose is capable only of a satisfaction of its own proper kind, namely, that from the attainment of an end, which end again is determined by reason only, notwithstanding that this may involve many a disappointment to the ends of inclination.

THE FIRST PROPOSITION OF MORALITY

We have then to develop the notion of a will which deserves to be highly esteemed for itself, and is good without a view to anything further, a notion which exists already in the sound natural understanding, requiring rather to be cleared up than to be taught, and which in estimating the value of our actions always takes the first place, and constitutes the condition of all the rest. In order to do this, we will take the notion of duty, which includes that of a good will, although implying certain subjective restrictions and hindrances. These, however, far from concealing it, or rendering it unrecognizable, rather bring it out by contrast, and make it shine forth so much the brighter.

I omit here all actions which are already recognized as inconsistent with duty although they may be useful for this or that purpose, for with these the question whether they are done *from duty* cannot arise at all, since they even conflict with it. I also set aside those actions which really conform to duty, but to which men have *no* direct *inclination*, performing them because they are impelled thereto by some other inclination. For in this case we can readily distinguish whether the action which agrees with duty is done *from duty*, or from a selfish view. It is much harder to make this distinction when the action accords with duty, and the subject has besides a *direct* inclination to it. For example, it is always a matter of duty that a dealer should not overcharge an inexperienced purchaser; and wherever there is much commerce the prudent tradesman does not overcharge, but keeps a fixed price for everyone, so that a child buys of him as well as any other. Men are thus *honestly* served; but this is not enough to make us believe that the tradesman has so acted from duty and from principles of honesty: his own advantage required it; it is out of the question in this case to suppose that he might besides have a direct inclination in favour of the buyers, so that, as it were, from love he should give no advantage to one over another. Accordingly the action was done neither from duty nor from direct inclination, but merely with a selfish view.

On the other hand, it is a duty to maintain one's life; and, in addition, everyone has also a direct inclination to do so. But on this account the often anxious care which most men take for it has no intrinsic worth, and their maxim has no moral import. They preserve their life *as duty requires,* no doubt, but not *because duty requires.* On the other hand, if adversity and hopeless sorrow have completely taken away the relish for life; if the unfortunate one, strong in mind, indignant at his fate rather than desponding or dejected, wishes for death, and yet preserves his life without loving it—not from inclination or fear, but from duty—then his maxim has a moral worth.

To be beneficent when we can is a duty; and besides this, there are many minds so sympathetically constituted that, without any other motive of vanity or self-interest, they find a pleasure in spreading joy around them, and can take delight in the satisfaction of others so far as it is their own work. But I maintain that in such a case an action of this kind, however proper, however amiable it may be, has nevertheless no true moral worth, but is on a level with other inclinations, *e.g.* the inclination to honour, which, if it is happily directed to that which is in fact of public utility and accordant with duty, and consequently honourable, deserves praise and encouragement, but not esteem. For the maxim lacks the moral import, namely, that such actions be done *from duty,* not from inclination. Put the case that the mind of that philanthropist was clouded by sorrow of his own, extinguishing all sympathy with the lot of others, and that while he still has the power to benefit others in distress, he is not touched by their trouble because he is absorbed with his own; and

now suppose that he tears himself out of this dead insensibility, and performs the action without any inclination to it, but simply from duty, then first has his action its genuine moral worth. Further still; if nature has put little sympathy in the heart of this or that man; if he, supposed to be an upright man, is by temperament cold and indifferent to the sufferings of others, perhaps because in respect of his own he is provided with the special gift of patience and fortitude, and supposes, or even requires, that others should have the same—and such a man would certainly not be the meanest product of nature—but if nature had not specially framed him for a philanthropist, would he not still find in himself a source from whence to give himself a far higher worth than that of a good-natured temperament could be? Unquestionably. It is just in this that the moral worth of the character is brought out which is incomparably the highest of all, namely, that he is beneficent, not from inclination, but from duty.

To secure one's own happiness is a duty, at least indirectly; for discontent with one's condition, under a pressure of many anxieties and amidst unsatisfied wants, might easily become a great *temptation to transgression of duty.* But here again, without looking to duty, all men have already the strongest and most intimate inclination to happiness, because it is just in this idea that all inclinations are combined in one total. But the precept of happiness is often of such a sort that it greatly interferes with some inclinations, and yet a man cannot form any definite and certain conception of the sum of satisfaction of all of them which is called happiness. It is not then to be wondered at that a single inclination, definite both as to what it promises and as to the time within which it can be gratified, is often able to overcome such a fluctuating idea, and that a gouty patient, for instance, can choose to enjoy what he likes, and to suffer what he may, since, according to his calculation, on this occasion at least, he has [only] not sacrificed the enjoyment of the present moment to a possibly mistaken expectation of a happiness which is supposed to be found in health. But even in this case, if the general desire for happiness did not influence his will, and supposing that in his particular case health was not a necessary element in this calculation, there yet remains in this, as in all other cases, this law, namely, that he should promote his happiness not from inclination but from duty, and by this would his conduct first acquire true moral worth.

It is in this manner, undoubtedly, that we are to understand those passages of Scripture also in which we are commanded to love our neighbour, even our enemy. For love, as an affection, cannot be commanded, but beneficence for duty's sake may; even though we are not impelled to it by any inclination —nay, are even repelled by a natural and unconquerable aversion. This is *practical* love, and not *pathological*—a love which is seated in the will, and not in the propensions of sense—in principles of action and not of tender sympathy; and it is this love alone which can be commanded.

THE SECOND PROPOSITION OF MORALITY

The second proposition is: That an action done from duty derives its moral worth, *not from the purpose* which is to be attained by it, but from the maxim by which it is determined, and therefore does not depend on the realization of the object of the action, but merely on the *principle of volition* by which the action has taken place, without regard to any object of desire. It is clear from what precedes that the purposes which we may have in view in our actions, or their effects regarded as ends and springs of the will, cannot give to actions any unconditional or moral worth. In what, then, can their worth lie, if it is not to consist in the will and in reference to its expected effect? It cannot lie anywhere but in the *principle of the will* without regard to the ends which can be attained by the action. For the will stands between its *a priori principle,* which is formal, and its *a posteriori* spring, which is material, as between two roads, and as it must be determined by something, it follows that it must be determined by the formal principle of volition when an action is done from duty, in which case every material principle has been withdrawn from it.

THE THIRD PROPOSITION OF MORALITY

The third proposition, which is a consequence of the two preceding, I would express thus: *Duty is the necessity of acting from respect for the law.* I may have *inclination* for an object as the effect of my proposed action, but I cannot have *respect* for it, just for this reason, that it is an effect and not an energy of will. Similarly, I cannot have respect for inclination, whether my own or another's; I can at most, if my own, approve it; if another's, sometimes even love it; *i.e.* look on it as favourable to my own interest. It is only what is connected with my will as a principle, by no means as an effect—what does not subserve my inclination, but overpowers it, or at least in case of choice excludes it from its calculation—in other words, simply the law of itself, which can be an object of respect, and hence a command. Now an action done from duty must wholly exclude the influence of inclination, and with it every object of the will, so that nothing remains which can determine the will except objectively the *law,* and subjectively *pure respect* for this practical law, and consequently the maxim that I should follow this law even to the thwarting of all my inclinations.

Thus the moral worth of an action does not lie in the effect expected from it, nor in any principle of action which requires to borrow its motive from this expected effect. For all these effects—agreeableness of one's condition, and even the promotion of the happiness of others—could have been also brought about by other causes, so that for this there would have been no need of the will of a rational being; whereas it is in this alone that the supreme and unconditional good can be found. The pre-eminent good which we call moral can therefore consist in nothing else than *the conception of law* in itself, *which certainly is only possible in a rational being,* in so far as this conception, and not the expected effect, determines the will. This is a good which is already present in the person who acts accordingly, and we have not to wait for it to appear first in the result.

THE SUPREME PRINCIPLE OF MORALITY: THE CATEGORICAL IMPERATIVE

But what sort of law can that be, the conception of which must determine the will, even without paying any regard to the effect expected from it, in order that this will may be called good absolutely and without qualification? As I have deprived the will of every impulse which could arise to it from obedience to any law, there remains nothing but the universal conformity of its actions to law in general, which alone is to serve the will as a principle, *i.e.* I am never to act otherwise than so *that I could also will that my maxim should become a universal law.* Here, now, it is the simple conformity to law in general, without assuming any particular law applicable to certain actions, that serves the will as its principle, and must so serve it, if duty is not to be a vain delusion and a chimerical notion. The common reason of men in its practical judgments perfectly coincides with this, and always has in view the principle here suggested. Let the question be, for example: May I when in distress make a promise with the intention not to keep it? I readily distinguish here between the two significations which the question may have: Whether it is prudent, or whether it is right, to make a false promise? The former may undoubtedly often be the case. I see clearly indeed that it is not enough to extricate myself from a present difficulty by means of this subterfuge, but it must be well considered whether there may not hereafter spring from this lie much greater inconvenience than that from which I now free myself, and as, with all my supposed *cunning*, the consequences cannot be so easily foreseen but that credit once lost may be much more injurious to me than any mischief which I seek to avoid at present, it should be considered whether it would not be more *prudent* to act herein according to a universal maxim, and to make it a habit to promise nothing except with the intention of keeping it. But it is soon clear to me that such a maxim will still only be based on the fear of consequences. Now it is a wholly different thing to be truthful from duty, and to be so from apprehension of injurious consequences. In the first case, the very notion of the action already implies a law for me; in the second case, I must first look about elsewhere to see what results may be combined with it which would affect myself. For to deviate from the principle of duty is beyond all doubt wicked; but to be unfaithful to my maxim of prudence may often be very advantageous to me, although to abide by it is certainly safer. The shortest way, however, and an unerring one, to discover the answer to this question whether a lying promise is consistent with duty, is to ask myself, Should I be content that my maxim (to extricate myself from

difficulty by a false promise) should hold good as a universal law, for myself as well as for others? and should I be able to say to myself, "Every one may make a deceitful promise when he finds himself in a difficulty from which he cannot otherwise extricate himself"? Then I presently become aware that while I can will the lie, I can by no means will that lying should be a universal law. For with such a law there would be no promises at all, since it would be in vain to allege my intention in regard to my future actions to those who would not believe this allegation, or if they over-hastily did so, would pay me back in my own coin. Hence my maxim, as soon as it should be made a universal law, would necessarily destroy itself.

I do not, therefore, need any far-reaching penetration to discern what I have to do in order that my will may be morally good. Inexperienced in the course of the world, incapable of being prepared for all its contingencies, I only ask myself: Can you also will that your maxim should be a universal law? If not, then it must be rejected, and that not because of a disadvantage accruing from myself or even to others, but because it cannot enter as a principle into a possible universal legislation, and reason extorts from me immediate respect for such legislation. I do not indeed as yet *discern* on what this respect is based (this the philosopher may inquire), but at least I understand this, that it is an estimation of the worth which far outweighs all worth of what is recommended by inclination, and that the necessity of acting from *pure* respect for the practical law is what constitutes duty, to which every other motive must give place, because it is the condition of a will being good *in itself,* and the worth of such a will is above everything.

Thus, then, without quitting the moral knowledge of common human reason, we have arrived at its principle. And although, no doubt, common men do not conceive it in such an abstract and universal form, yet they always have it really before their eyes, and use it as the standard of their decision. . . .

Nor could anything be more fatal to morality than that we should wish to derive it from examples. For every example of it that is set before me must be first itself tested by principles of morality, whether it is worthy to serve as an original example, *i.e.* as a pattern, but by no means can it authoritatively furnish the conception of morality. Even the Holy One of the Gospels must first be compared with our ideal of moral perfection before we can recognize Him as such; and so He says of Himself, "Why call ye Me [whom you see] good; none is good [the model of good] but God only [whom ye do not see]." But whence have we the conception of God as the supreme good? Simply from the *idea* of moral perfection, which reason frames *a priori*, and connects inseparably with the notion of a free will. Imitation finds no place at all in morality, and examples serve only for encouragement, *i.e.* they put beyond doubt the feasibility of what the law commands, they make visible that which the practical rule expresses more generally, but they can never authorize us to set aside the true original which lies in reason, and to guide ourselves by examples.

From what has been said, it is clear that all moral conceptions have their seat and origin completely *a priori* in the reason, and that, moreover, in the commonest reason just as truly as in that which is in the highest degree speculative; that they cannot be obtained by abstraction from any empirical, and therefore merely contingent knowledge; that it is just this purity of their origin that makes them worthy to serve as our supreme practical principle, and that just in proportion as we add anything empirical, we detract from their genuine influence, and from the absolute value of actions; that it is not only of the greatest necessity, in a purely speculative point of view, but is also of the greatest practical importance, to derive these notions and laws from pure reason, to present them pure and unmixed, and even to determine the compass of this practical or pure rational knowledge, *i.e.* to determine the whole faculty of pure practical reason; and, in doing so, we must not make its principles dependent on the particular nature of human reason, though in speculative philosophy this may be permitted, or may even at times be necessary; but since moral laws ought to hold good for every rational creature, we must derive them from the general concept of a rational being. In this way, although for its *application* to man morality has need of anthropology, yet, in the first instance, we must treat it independently as pure philosophy, *i.e.* as metaphysic, complete in itself (a thing which in such distinct branches of science is easily done); knowing well that unless we are in possession of this, it would not only be vain to determine the moral el-

ement of duty in right actions for purposes of speculative criticism, but it would be impossible to base morals on their genuine principles, even for common practical purposes, especially of moral instruction, so as to produce pure moral dispositions, and to engraft them on men's minds to the promotion of the greatest possible good in the world. . . .

THE RATIONAL GROUND OF THE CATEGORICAL IMPERATIVE

. . . the question, how the imperative of *morality* is possible, is undoubtedly one, the only one, demanding a solution, as this is not at all hypothetical, and the objective necessity which it presents cannot rest on any hypothesis, as is the case with the hypothetical imperatives. Only here we must never leave out of consideration that we *cannot* make out *by any example,* in other words empirically, whether there is such an imperative at all; but it is rather to be feared that all those which seem to be categorical may yet be at bottom hypothetical. For instance, when the precept is: Thou shalt not promise deceitfully; and it is assumed that the necessity of this is not a mere counsel to avoid some other evil, so that it should mean: Thou shalt not make a lying promise, lest if it become known thou shouldst destroy thy credit, but that an action of this kind must be regarded as evil in itself, so that the imperative of the prohibition is categorical; then we cannot show with certainty in any example that the will was determined merely by the law, without any other spring of action, although it may appear to be so. For it is always possible that fear of disgrace, perhaps also obscure dread of other dangers, may have a secret influence on the will. Who can prove by experience the nonexistence of a cause when all that experience tells us is that we do not perceive it? But in such a case the so-called moral imperative, which as such appears to be categorical and unconditional, would in reality be only a pragmatic precept, drawing our attention to our own interests, and merely teaching us to take these into consideration.

We shall therefore have to investigate *a priori* the possibility of a categorical imperative, as we have not in this case the advantage of its reality being given in experience, so that [the elucidation of] its possibility should be requisite only for its explanation, not for its establishment. In the meantime it may be discerned beforehand that the categorical imperative alone has the purport of a practical law: all the rest may indeed be called *principles* of the will but not laws, since whatever is only necessary for the attainment of some arbitrary purpose may be considered as in itself contingent, and we can at any time be free from the precept if we give up the purpose: on the contrary, the unconditional command leaves the will no liberty to choose the opposite; consequently it alone carries with it that necessity which we require in a law.

Secondly, in the case of this categorical imperative or law of morality, the difficulty (of discerning its possibility) is a very profound one. It is an *a priori* synthetical practical proposition; and as there is so much difficulty in discerning the possibility of speculative propositions of this kind, it may readily be supposed that the difficulty will be no less with the practical.

FIRST FORMULATION OF THE CATEGORICAL IMPERATIVE: UNIVERSAL LAW

In this problem we will first inquire whether the mere conception of a categorical imperative may not perhaps supply us also with the formula of it, containing the proposition which alone can be a categorical imperative; for even if we know the tenor of such an absolute command, yet how it is possible will require further special and laborious study, which we postpone to the last section.

When I conceive a hypothetical imperative, in general I do not know beforehand what it will contain until I am given the condition. But when I conceive a categorical imperative, I know at once what it contains. For as the imperative contains besides the law only the necessity that the maxims shall conform to this law, while the law contain no conditions restricting it, there remains nothing but the general statement that the maxim of the action should conform to a universal law, and it is this conformity alone that the imperative properly represents as necessary.

There is therefore but one categorical imperative, namely, this: *Act only on that maxim whereby you can at the same time will that it should become a universal law.*

Now if all imperatives of duty can be deduced from this one imperative as from their principle, then, although it should remain undecided whether what is called duty is not merely a vain notion, yet at least we shall be able to show what we understand by it and what this notion means.

Since the universality of the law according to which effects are produced constitutes what is properly called *nature* in the most general sense (as to form), that is the existence of things so far as it is determined by general laws, the imperative of duty may be expressed thus: *Act as if the maxim of your action were to become by your will a universal law of nature.*

FOUR ILLUSTRATIONS

We will now enumerate a few duties, adopting the usual division of them into duties to ourselves and to others, and into perfect and imperfect duties.

1. A man reduced to despair by a series of misfortunes feels wearied of life, but is still so far in possession of his reason that he can ask himself whether it would not be contrary to his duty to himself to take his own life. Now he inquires whether the maxim of his action could become a universal law of nature. His maxim is: From self-love I adopt it as a principle to shorten my life when its longer duration is likely to bring more evil than satisfaction. It is asked then simply whether this principle founded on self-love can become a universal law of nature. Now we see at once that a system of nature of which it should be a law to destroy life by means of the very feeling whose special nature it is to impel to the improvement of life would contradict itself, and therefore could not exist as a system of nature; hence that maxim cannot possibly exist as a universal law of nature, and consequently would be wholly inconsistent with the supreme principle of all duty.

2. Another finds himself forced by necessity to borrow money. He knows that he will not be able to repay it, but sees also that nothing will be lent to him, unless he promises stoutly to repay it in a definite time. He desires to make this promise, but he has still so much conscience as to ask himself: Is it not unlawful and inconsistent with duty to get out of a difficulty in this way? Suppose, however, that he resolves to do so, then the maxim of his action would be expressed thus: When I think myself in want of money, I will borrow money and promise to repay it, although I know that I never can do so. Now this principle of self-love or of one's own advantage may perhaps be consistent with my whole future welfare; but the question is, Is it right? I change then the suggestion of self-love into a universal law, and state the question thus: How would it be if my maxim were a universal law? Then I see at once that it could never hold as a universal law of nature, but would necessarily contradict itself. For supposing it to be a universal law that everyone when he thinks himself in a difficulty should be able to promise whatever he pleases, with the purpose of not keeping his promise, the promise itself would become impossible, as well as the end that one might have in view in it, since no one would consider that anything was promised to him, but would ridicule all such statements as vain pretenses.

3. A third finds in himself a talent which with the help of some culture might make him a useful man in many respects. But he finds himself in comfortable circumstances, and prefers to indulge in pleasure rather than to take pains in enlarging and improving his happy natural capacities. He asks, however, whether his maxim of neglect of his natural gifts, besides agreeing with his inclination to indulgence, agrees also with what is called duty. He sees then that a system of nature could indeed subsist with such a universal law although men (like the South Sea islanders) should let their talents rest, and resolve to devote their lives merely to idleness, amusement, and propagation of their species—in a word, to enjoyment; but he cannot possibly *will* that this should be a universal law of nature, or be implanted in us as such by a natural instinct. For, as a rational being, he necessarily wills that his faculties be developed, since they serve him, and have been given him, for all sorts of possible purposes.

4. A fourth, who is in prosperity, while he sees that others have to contend with great wretchedness

and that he could help them, thinks: What concern is it of mine? Let everyone be as happy as Heaven pleases, or as he can make himself; I will take nothing from him nor even envy him, only I do not wish to contribute anything to his welfare or to his assistance in distress! Now no doubt if such a mode of thinking were a universal law, the human race might very well subsist, and doubtless even better than in a state in which everyone talks of sympathy and goodwill, or even takes care occasionally to put it into practice, but, on the other side, also cheats when he can, betrays the rights of men, or otherwise violates them. But although it is possible that a universal law of nature might exist in accordance with that maxim, it is impossible to *will* that such a principle should have the universal validity of a law of nature. For a will which resolved this would contradict itself, inasmuch as many cases might occur in which one would have need of the love and sympathy of others, and in which, by such a law of nature, sprung from his own will, he would deprive himself of all hope of the aid he desires.

These are a few of the many actual duties, or at least what we regard as such, which obviously fall into two classes on the one principle that we have laid down. We must be *able to will* that a maxim of our action should be a universal law. This is the canon of the moral appreciation of the action generally. Some actions are of such a character that their maxim cannot without contradiction be even *conceived* as a universal law of nature, far from it being possible that we should *will* that it *should* be so. In others this intrinsic impossibility is not found, but still it is impossible to *will* that their maxim should be raised to the universality of a law of nature, since such a will would contradict itself. It is easily seen that the former violate strict or rigorous (inflexible) duty; the latter only laxer (meritorious) duty. Thus it has been completely shown by these examples how all duties depend as regards the nature of the obligation (not the object of the action) on the same principle.

Kantian Approaches to Some Famine Problems

ONORA O'NEILL

Onora O'Neill (1941–   ), author of numerous articles and several books, is Principal of Newnham College, Cambridge.

A SIMPLIFIED ACCOUNT OF KANT'S ETHICS

Kant's moral theory has acquired the reputation of being forbiddingly difficult to understand and, once understood, excessively demanding in its requirements. I don't believe that this reputation has been wholly earned, and I am going to try to undermine it. In §§23–26 I shall try to reduce some of the difficulties, and in §§27–[29] I shall try to show the implications of a Kantian moral theory for action toward those who do or may suffer famine. Finally, I shall compare Kantian and utilitarian approaches and assess their strengths and weaknesses.

The main method by which I propose to avoid some of the difficulties of Kant's moral theory is by explaining only one part of the theory. This does not seem to me to be an irresponsible approach in this case. One of the things that makes Kant's moral theory hard to understand is that he gives a number of different versions of the principle that he calls the Supreme Principle of Morality, and these different versions don't look at all like one another. They also don't look at all like the utilitarians' Greatest Happiness Principle. But the Kantian principle is supposed to play a similar role in arguments about what to do.

Kant calls his Supreme Principle the *Categorical Imperative;* its various versions also have sonorous names. One is called the Formula of Universal Law; another is the Formula of the Kingdom of Ends. The one on which I shall concentrate is known as the *Formula of the End in Itself.* To understand why Kant thinks that these picturesquely named principles are

equivalent to one another takes quite a lot of close and detailed analysis of Kant's philosophy. I shall avoid this and concentrate on showing the implications of this version of the Categorical Imperative.

THE FORMULA OF THE END IN ITSELF

Kant states the Formula of the End in Itself as follows:

> Act in such a way that you always treat humanity, whether in your own person or in the person of any other, never simply as a means but always at the same time as an end.

To understand this we need to know what it is to treat a person as a means or as an end. According to Kant, each of our acts reflects one or more *maxims.* The maxim of the act is the principle on which one sees oneself as acting. A maxim expresses a person's policy, or if he or she has no settled policy, the principle underlying the particular intention or decision on which he or she acts. Thus, a person who decides "This year I'll give 10 percent of my income to famine relief" has as a maxim the principle of tithing his or her income for famine relief. In practice, the difference between intentions and maxims is of little importance, for given any intention, we can formulate the corresponding maxim by deleting references to particular times, places, and persons. In what follows I shall take the terms "maxim" and "intention" as equivalent.

Whenever we act intentionally, we have at least one maxim and can, if we reflect, state what it is. (There is of course room for self-deception here—

From *Matters of Life and Death,* edited by T. Regan (New York: Random House, 1980), pp. 285–94. Reprinted by permission of the publisher.

"I'm only keeping the wolf from the door" we may claim as we wolf down enough to keep ourselves overweight, or, more to the point, enough to feed someone else who hasn't enough food.)

When we want to work out whether an act we propose to do is right or wrong, according to Kant, we should look at our maxims and not at how much misery or happiness the act is likely to produce, and whether it does better at increasing happiness than other available acts. We just have to check that the act we have in mind, will not use anyone as a mere means, and, if possible, that it will treat other persons as ends in themselves.

USING PERSONS AS MERE MEANS

To use someone as a *mere means* is to involve them in a scheme of action *to which they could not in principle consent*. Kant does not say that there is anything wrong about using someone as a means. Evidently we have to do so in any cooperative scheme of action. If I cash a check I use the teller as a means, without whom I could not lay my hands on the cash; the teller in turn uses me as a means to earn his or her living. But in this case, each party consents to her or his part in the transaction. Kant would say that though they use one another as means, they do not use one another as *mere* means. Each person assumes that the other has maxims of his or her own and is not just a thing or a prop to be manipulated.

But there are other situations where one person uses another in a way to which the other could not in principle consent. For example, one person may make a promise to another with every intention of breaking it. If the promise is accepted, then the person to whom it was given must be ignorant of what the promisor's intention (maxim) really is. If one knew that the promisor did not intend to do what he or she was promising, one would, after all, not accept or rely on the promise. It would be as though there had been no promise made. Successful false promising depends on deceiving the person to whom the promise is made about what one's real maxim is. And since the person who is deceived doesn't know that real maxim, he or she can't in principle consent to his or her part in the proposed scheme of action. The person who is deceived is, as it were, a prop or a tool—a mere means—in the

false promisor's scheme. A person who promises falsely treats the acceptor of the promise as a prop or a thing and not as a person. In Kant's view, it is this that makes false promising wrong.

One standard way of using others as mere means is by deceiving them. By getting someone involved in a business scheme or a criminal activity on false pretenses, or by giving a misleading account of what one is about, or by making a false promise or a fraudulent contract, one involves another in something to which he or she in principle cannot consent, since the scheme requires that he or she doesn't know what is going on. Another standard way of using others as mere means is by coercing them. If a rich or powerful person threatens a debtor with bankruptcy unless he or she joins in some scheme, then the creditor's intention is to coerce; and the debtor, if coerced, cannot consent to his or her part in the creditor's scheme. To make the example more specific: If a moneylender in an Indian village threatens not to renew a vital loan unless he is given the debtor's land, then he uses the debtor as a mere means. He coerces the debtor, who cannot truly consent to this "offer he can't refuse." (Of course the outward form of such transactions may look like ordinary commercial dealings, but we know very well that some offers and demands couched in that form are coercive.)

In Kant's view, acts that are done on maxims that require deception or coercion of others, and so cannot have the consent of those others (for consent precludes both deception and coercion), are wrong. When we act on such maxims, we treat others as mere means, as things rather than as ends in themselves. If we act on such maxims, our acts are not only wrong but unjust: such acts wrong the particular others who are deceived or coerced.

TREATING PERSONS AS ENDS IN THEMSELVES

Duties of justice are, in Kant's view (as in many others'), the most important of our duties. When we fail in these duties, we have used some other or others as mere means. But there are also cases where, though we do not use others as mere means, still we fail to use them as ends in themselves in the fullest possible way. To treat someone as an end in him or herself requires in the first place that one not use him or her as mere means, that one respect each as a rational person with his or her own maxims. But beyond that, one may also seek to foster others' plans and maxims by sharing some of their ends. To act beneficently is to seek others' happiness, therefore to intend to achieve some of the things that those others aim at with their maxims. If I want to make others happy, I will adopt maxims that not merely do not manipulate them but that foster some of their plans and activities. Beneficent acts try to achieve what others want. However, we cannot seek everything that others want; their wants are too numerous and diverse, and, of course, sometimes incompatible. It follows that beneficence has to be selective.

There is then quite a sharp distinction between the requirements of justice and of beneficence in Kantian ethics. Justice requires that we act on *no* maxims that use others as mere means. Beneficence requires that we act on *some* maxims that foster others' ends, though it is a matter for judgment and discretion which of their ends we foster. Some maxims no doubt ought not to be fostered because it would be unjust to do so. Kantians are not committed to working interminably through a list of happiness-producing and misery-reducing acts; but there are some acts whose obligatoriness utilitarians may need to debate as they try to compare total outcomes of different choices, to which Kantians are stringently bound. Kantians will claim that they have done nothing wrong if none of their acts is unjust, and that their duty is complete if in addition their life plans have in the circumstances been reasonably beneficent.

In making sure that they meet all the demands of justice, Kantians do not try to compare all available acts and see which has the best effects. They consider only the proposals for action that occur to them and check that these proposals use no other as mere means. If they do not, the act is permissible; if omitting the act would use another as mere means, the act is obligatory. Kant's theory has less scope than utilitarianism. Kantians do not claim to discover whether acts whose maxims they don't know fully are just. They may be reluctant to judge others' acts or policies that cannot be regarded as the maxim of any person or institution. They cannot rank acts in order of merit. Yet, the theory offers more preci-

sion than utilitarianism when data are scarce. One can usually tell whether one's act would use others as mere means, even when its impact on human happiness is thoroughly obscure.

KANTIAN DELIBERATIONS ON FAMINE PROBLEMS

The theory I have just sketched may seem to have little to say about famine problems. For it is a theory that forbids us to use others as mere means but does not require us to direct our benevolence first to those who suffer most. A conscientious Kantian, it seems, has only to avoid being unjust to those who suffer famine and can then be beneficent to those nearer home. He or she would not be obliged to help the starving, even if no others were equally distressed.

Kant's moral theory does make less massive demands on moral agents than utilitarian moral theory. On the other hand, it is somewhat clearer just what the more stringent demands are, and they are not negligible. We have here a contrast between a theory that makes massive but often indeterminate demands and a theory that makes fewer but less unambiguous demands and leaves other questions, in particular the allocation of beneficence, unresolved. We have also a contrast between a theory whose scope is comprehensive and one that is applicable only to persons acting intentionally and to those institutions that adopt policies, and so maxims. Kantian ethics is silent about the moral status of unintentional action; utilitarians seek to assess all consequences regardless of the intentions that led to them.

KANTIAN DUTIES OF JUSTICE IN TIME OF FAMINE

In famine situations, Kantian moral theory requires unambiguously that we do no injustice. We should not act on any maxim that uses another as mere means, so we should neither deceive nor coerce others. Such a requirement can become quite exacting when the means of life are scarce, when persons can more easily be coerced, and when the advantage of gaining more than what is justly due to one is great. I shall give a list of acts that on Kantian principles it would be unjust to do, but that one might be strongly tempted to do in famine conditions.

I will begin with a list of acts that one might be tempted to do as a member of a famine-stricken population. First, where there is a rationing scheme, one ought not to cheat and seek to get more than one's share—any scheme of cheating will use someone as mere means. Nor may one take advantage of others' desperation to profiteer or divert goods onto the black market or to accumulate a fortune out of others' misfortunes. Transactions that are outwardly sales and purchases can be coercive when one party is desperate. All the forms of corruption that deceive or put pressure on others are also wrong: hoarding unallocated food, diverting relief supplies for private use, corruptly using one's influence to others' disadvantage. Such requirements are far from trivial and frequently violated in hard times. In severe famines, refraining from coercing and deceiving may risk one's own life and require the greatest courage.

Second, justice requires that in famine situations one still try to fulfill one's duties to particular others. For example, even in times of famine, a person has duties to try to provide for dependents. These duties may, tragically, be unfulfillable. If they are, Kantian ethical theory would not judge wrong the acts of a person who had done her or his best. There have no doubt been times in human history where there was nothing to be done except abandon the weak and old or to leave children to fend for themselves as best they might. But providing the supporter of dependents acts on maxims of attempting to meet their claims, he or she uses no others as mere means to his or her own survival and is not unjust. A conscientious attempt to meet the particular obligations one has undertaken may also require of one many further maxims of self-restraint and of endeavor— for example, it may require a conscientious attempt to avoid having (further) children; it may require contributing one's time and effort to programs of economic development. Where there is no other means to fulfill particular obligations, Kantian principles may require a generation of sacrifice. They will not, however, require one to seek to maximize the happiness of later generations but only to establish the modest security and prosperity needed for meeting present obligations.

The obligations of those who live with or near famine are undoubtedly stringent and exacting; for those who live further off it is rather harder to see what a Kantian moral theory demands. Might it not, for example, be permissible to do nothing at all about those suffering famine? Might one not ensure that one does nothing unjust to the victims of famine by adopting no maxims whatsoever that mention them? To do so would, at the least, require one to refrain from certain deceptive and coercive practices frequently employed during the European exploration and economic penetration of the now underdeveloped and still not unknown. For example, it would be unjust to "purchase" valuable lands and resources from persons who don't understand commercial transactions or exclusive property rights or mineral rights, so do not understand that their acceptance of trinkets destroys their traditional economic pattern and the way of life. The old adage "trade follows the flag" reminds us to how great an extent the economic penetration of the less-developed countries involved elements of coercion and deception, so was on Kantian principles unjust (regardless of whether or not the net effect has benefited the citizens of those countries).

Few persons in the developed world today find themselves faced with the possibility of adopting on a grand scale maxims of deceiving or coercing persons living in poverty. But at least some people find that their jobs require them to make decisions about investment and aid policies that enormously affect the lives of those nearest to famine. What does a commitment to Kantian moral theory demand of such persons?

It has become common in writings in ethics and social policy to distinguish between one's *personal responsibilities* and one's *role responsibilities*. So a person may say, "As an individual I sympathize, but in my official capacity I can do nothing"; or we may excuse persons' acts of coercion because they are acting in some particular capacity—e.g., as a soldier or a jailer. On the other hand, this distinction isn't made or accepted by everyone. At the Nuremberg trials of war criminals, the defense "I was only doing my job" was disallowed, at least for those whose command position meant that they had some discretion in what they did. Kantians generally would play down any distinction between a person's own responsibilities and his or her role responsibilities. They would not deny that in any capacity one is accountable for certain things for which as a private person one is not accountable. For example, the treasurer of an organization is accountable to the board and has to present periodic reports and to keep specified records. But if she fails to do one of these things for which she is held accountable she will be held responsible for that failure—it will be imputable to her as an individual. When we take on positions, we *add* to our responsibilities those that the job requires; but we do not lose those that are already required of us. Our social role or job gives us, on Kant's view, no license to use others as mere means; even business executives and aid officials and social revolutionaries will act unjustly, so wrongly, if they deceive or coerce—however benevolent their motives.

If persons are responsible for all their acts, it follows that it would be unjust for aid officials to coerce persons into accepting sterilization, wrong for them to use coercive power to achieve political advantages (such as military bases) or commercial advantages (such as trade agreements that will harm the other country). It would be wrong for the executives of large corporations to extort too high a price for continued operation employment and normal trading. Where a less-developed country is pushed to exempt a multinational corporation from tax laws, or to construct out of its meager tax revenues the infrastructure of roads, harbors, or airports (not to mention executive mansions) that the corporation—but perhaps not the country—needs, then one suspects that some coercion has been involved.

The problem with such judgments—and it is an immense problem—is that it is hard to identify coercion and deception in complicated institutional settings. It is not hard to understand what is coercive about one person threatening another with serious injury if he won't comply with the first person's suggestion. But it is not at all easy to tell where the outward forms of political and commercial negotiation —which often involve an element of threat—have become coercive. I can't here explore this fascinating question. But I think it is at least fairly clear that the preservation of the outward forms of negotiation, bargaining, and voluntary consent do *not* demonstrate that there is no coercion, especially when one party is vastly more powerful or the other in dire need. Just as our judiciary has a long tradition of

voiding contracts and agreements on grounds of duress or incompetence of one of the parties, so one can imagine a tribunal of an analogous sort rejecting at least some treaties and agreements as coercive, despite the fact that they were negotiated between "sovereign" powers or their representatives. In particular, where such agreements were negotiated with some of the cruder deceptions and coercion of the early days of European economic expansion or the subtler coercions and deceptions of contemporary superpowers, it seems doubtful that the justice of the agreement could be sustained.

Justice, of course, it not everything, even for Kantians. But its demands are ones that they can reasonably strive to fulfill. They may have some uncertain moments—for example, does advocating cheap raw materials mean advocating an international trade system in which the less developed will continue to suffer the pressures of the developed world—or is it a benevolent policy that will maximize world trade and benefit all parties, while doing no one an injustice? But for Kantians, the important moral choices are above all those in which one acts directly, not those in which one decides which patterns of actions to encourage in others or in those institutions that one can influence. And such moral decisions include decisions about the benevolent acts that one will or will not do.

KANTIAN DUTIES OF BENEFICENCE IN TIMES OF FAMINE

The grounds of duties of beneficence are that such acts not merely don't use others as mere means but are acts that develop or promote others' ends and that, in particular, foster others' capacities to pursue ends, to be autonomous beings.

Clearly there are many opportunities for beneficence. But one area in which the *primary* task of developing others' capacity to pursue their own ends is particularly needed is in the parts of the world where extreme poverty and hunger leave people unable to pursue *any* of their other ends. Beneficence directed at putting people in a position to pursue whatever ends they may have has, for Kant, a stronger claim on us than beneficence directed at sharing ends with those who are already in a position to pursue varieties of ends. It would be nice if I bought a tennis racquet to play with my friend who is tennis mad and never has enough partners; but it is more important to make people able to plan their own lives to a minimal extent. It is nice to walk a second mile with someone who requests one's company; better to share a cloak with someone who may otherwise be too cold to make any journey. Though these suggestions are not a detailed set of instructions for the allocation of beneficence by Kantians, they show that relief of famine must stand very high among duties of beneficence.

THE LIMITS OF KANTIAN ETHICS: INTENTIONS AND RESULTS

Kantian ethics differs from utilitarian ethics both in its scope and in the precision with which it guides action. Every action, whether of a person or of an agency, can be assessed by utilitarian methods, provided only that information is available about all the consequences of the act. The theory has unlimited scope, but, owing to a lack of data, often lacks precision. Kantian ethics has a more restricted scope. Since it assesses actions by looking at the maxims of agents, it can only assess intentional acts. This means that it is most at home in assessing individuals' acts; but it can be extended to assess acts of agencies that (like corporations and governments and student unions) have decision-making procedures. It can do nothing to assess patterns of action that reflect no intention or policy, hence it cannot assess the acts of groups lacking decision-making procedures, such as the student movement, the women's movement, or the consumer movement.

It may seem a great limitation of Kantian ethics that it concentrates on intentions to the neglect of results. It might seem that all conscientious Kantians have to do is to make sure that they never intend to use others as mere means, and that they sometimes intend to foster others' ends. And, as we all know, good intentions sometimes lead to bad results, and correspondingly, bad intentions sometimes do no harm, or even produce good. If Hardin is right, the good intentions of those who feed the starving lead to dreadful results in the long run. If some traditional arguments in favor of capitalism are right, the greed and selfishness of the profit motive have produced unparalleled prosperity for many.

But such discrepancies between intentions and results are the exception and not the rule. For we cannot just *claim* that our intentions are good and do what we will. Our intentions reflect what we expect the immediate results of our action to be. Nobody credits the "intentions" of a couple who practice neither celibacy nor contraception but still insist "we never meant to have (more) children." Conception is likely (and known to be likely) in such cases. Where people's expressed intentions ignore the normal and predictable results of what they do, we infer that (if they are not amazingly ignorant) their words do not express their true intentions. The Formula of the End in Itself applies to the intentions on which one acts—not to some prettified version that one may avow. Provided this intention—the agent's real intention—uses no other as mere means, he or she does nothing unjust. If some of his or her intentions foster others' ends, then he or she is sometimes beneficent. It is therefore possible for people to test their proposals by Kantian arguments even when they lack the comprehensive causal knowledge that utilitarianism requires. Conscientious Kantians can work out whether they will be doing wrong by some act even though they know that their foresight is limited and that they may cause some harm or fail to cause some benefit. But they will not cause harms that they can foresee without this being reflected in their intentions.

Utilitarianism

JOHN STUART MILL

John Stuart Mill (1805–1873) was a leading British philosopher who wrote many influential books on ethics, political philosophy, logic, and feminism.

1. GENERAL REMARKS

There are a few circumstances, among those which make up the present condition of human knowledge, more unlike what might have been expected, or more significant of the backward state in which speculation on the most important subjects still lingers, than the little progress which has been made in the decision of the controversy respecting the criterion of right and wrong. From the dawn of philosophy, the question concerning the *summum bonum* or, what is the same thing, concerning the foundation of morality, has been accounted the main problem in speculative thought, has occupied the most gifted intellects and divided them into sects and schools, carrying on a vigorous warfare against one another. And, after more than two thousand years, the same discussions continue, philosophers are still ranged under the same contending banners, and neither thinkers nor mankind at large seem nearer to being unanimous on the subject than when the youth Socrates listened to the old Protagoras, and asserted (if Plato's dialogue be grounded on a real conversation) the theory of utilitarianism against the popular morality of the so-called Sophist.

It is true that similar confusion and uncertainty, and in some cases similar discordance, exist respecting the first principles of all the sciences, not excepting that which is deemed the most certain of them—mathematics—without much impairing, generally indeed without impairing at all, the trustworthiness of the conclusions of those sciences. An apparent anomaly, the explanation of which is that the detailed doctrines of a science are not usually deduced from, nor depend for their evidence upon, what are called its first principles. Were it not so, there would be no science more precarious, or whose conclu-

sions were more insufficiently made out, than algebra, which derives none of its certainty from what are commonly taught to learners as its elements, since these, as laid down by some of its most eminent teachers, are as full of fictions as English law, and of mysteries as theology. The truths which are ultimately accepted as the first principles of a science are really the last results of metaphysical analysis practiced on the elementary notions with which the science is conversant, and their relation to the science is not that of foundations to an edifice, but of roots to a tree, which may perform their office equally well though they be never dug down to and exposed to light. But though, in science the particular truths precede the general theory, the contrary might be expected to be the case with a practical art, such as morals or legislation. All action is for the sake of some end; and rules of action, it seems natural to suppose, must take their whole character and color from the end to which they are subservient. When we engage in a pursuit, a clear and precise conception of what we are pursuing would seem to be the first thing we need, instead of the last we are to look forward to. A test of right and wrong must be the means, one would think, of ascertaining what is right or wrong, and not a consequence of having already ascertained it.

The difficulty is not avoided by having recourse to the popular theory of a natural faculty, a sense or instinct, informing us of right and wrong. For, besides that the existence of such a moral instinct is itself one of the matters in dispute, those believers in it who have any pretensions to philosophy have been obliged to abandon the idea that it discerns what is right or wrong in the particular case in hand, as our other senses discern the sight or sound actually present. Our moral faculty, according to all those of its

From *Utilitarianism*, Chaps. 1 and 2. First published in 1863.

interpreters who are entitled to the name of thinkers, supplies us only with the general principles of moral judgments; it is a branch of our reason, not of our sensitive faculty, and must be looked to for the abstract doctrines of morality, not for perception of it in the concrete. The intuitive, no less than what may be termed the inductive, school of ethics, insists on the necessity of general laws. They both agree that the morality of an individual action is not a question of direct perception, but of the application of a law to an individual case. They recognize also, to a great extent, the same moral laws, but differ as to their evidence, and the source from which they derive their authority. According to the one opinion, the principles of morals are evident *a priori,* requiring nothing to command assent, except that the meaning of the terms be understood. According to the other doctrine, right and wrong, as well as truth and falsehood, are questions of observation and experience. But both hold equally that morality must be deduced from principles, and the intuitive school affirm, as strongly as the inductive, that there is a science of morals. Yet they seldom attempt to make out a list of the *a priori* principles which are to serve as the premises of the science; still more rarely do they make any effort to reduce those various principles to one first principle, or common ground of obligation. They either assume the ordinary precepts of morals as of *a priori* authority, or they lay down as the common groundwork of those maxims some generality much less obviously authoritative than the maxims themselves, and which has never succeeded in gaining popular acceptance. Yet, to support their pretensions, there ought either to be some one fundamental principle or law at the root of all morality, or, if there be several, there should be a determinate order of precedence among them, and the one principle, or the rule for deciding between the various principles when they conflict, ought to be self-evident.

To inquire how far the bad effects of this deficiency have been mitigated in practice, or to what extent the moral beliefs of mankind have been vitiated or made uncertain by the absence of any distinct recognition of an ultimate standard, would imply a complete survey and criticism of past and present ethical doctrine. It would, however, be easy to show that whatever steadiness or consistency these moral beliefs have attained has been mainly due to the tacit influence of a standard not recognized. Although the nonexistence of an acknowledged first principle has made ethics not so much a guide as a consecration of men's actual sentiments, still, as men's sentiments, both of favor and of aversion, are greatly influenced by what they suppose to be the effects of things upon their happiness, the principle of utility, or, as Bentham latterly called it, the greatest-happiness principle, has had a large share in forming the moral doctrines even of those who most scornfully reject its authority. Nor is there any school of thought which refuses to admit that the influence of actions on happiness is a most material and even predominant consideration in many of the details of morals, however unwilling to acknowledge it as the fundamental principle of morality and the source of moral obligation. I might go much further, and say that, to all those *a priori* moralists who deem it necessary to argue at all, utilitarian arguments are indispensable. It is not my present purpose to criticize these thinkers, but I cannot help referring, for illustration, to a systematic treatise by one of the most illustrious of them—the *Metaphysics of Ethics,* by Kant. This remarkable man, whose system of thought will long remain one of the landmarks in the history of philosophical speculation, does, in the treatise in question, lay down a universal first principle as the origin and ground of moral obligation. It is this: "So act, that the rule on which thou actest would admit of being adopted as a law by all rational beings." But when he begins to deduce from this precept any of the actual duties of morality, he fails, almost grotesquely, to show that there would be any contradiction, any logical (not to say physical) impossibility, in the adoption by all rational beings of the most outrageously immoral rules of conduct. All he shows is that the *consequences* of their universal adoption would be such as no one would choose to incur.

On the present occasion, I shall, without further discussion of the other theories, attempt to contribute something towards the understanding and appreciation of the Utilitarian or Happiness theory and towards such proof as it is susceptible of. It is evident that this cannot be proof in the ordinary and popular meaning of the term. Questions of ultimate ends are not amenable to direct proof.

Whatever can be proved to be good, must be so by being shown to be a means to something admitted to be good without proof. The medical art is proved to be good by its conducing to health, but how is it possible to prove that health is good? The art of music is good, for the reason, among others, that it produces pleasure, but what proof is it possible to give that pleasure is good? If, then, it is asserted that there is a comprehensive formula, including all things which are in themselves good, and that whatever else is good is not so as an end, but as a mean, the formula may be accepted or rejected, but is not a subject of what is commonly understood by proof. We are not, however, to infer that its acceptance or rejection must depend on blind impulse or arbitrary choice. There is a larger meaning of the word "proof," in which this question is as amenable to it as any other of the disputed questions of philosophy. The subject is within the cognizance of the rational faculty, and neither does that faculty deal with it solely in the way of intuition. Considerations may be presented capable of determining the intellect either to give or withhold its assent to the doctrine, and this is equivalent to proof.

We shall examine presently of what nature are these considerations, in what manner they apply to the case, and what rational grounds, therefore, can be given for accepting or rejecting the utilitarian formula. But it is a preliminary condition of rational acceptance or rejection that the formula should be correctly understood. I believe that the very imperfect notion ordinarily formed of its meaning is the chief obstacle which impedes its reception, and that, could it be cleared even from only the grosser misconceptions, the question would be greatly simplified, and a large proportion of its difficulties removed. Before, therefore, I attempt to enter into the philosophical grounds which can be given for assenting to the utilitarian standard, I shall offer some illustrations of the doctrine itself, with the view of showing more clearly what it is, distinguishing it from what it is not, and disposing of such of the practical objections to it as either originate in, or are closely connected with, mistaken interpretations of its meaning. Having thus prepared the ground, I shall afterwards endeavor to throw such light as I can upon the question, considered as one of philosophical theory.

2. WHAT UTILITARIANISM IS

A passing remark is all that needs be given to the ignorant blunder of supposing that those who stand up for utility, as the test of right and wrong, use the term in that restricted and merely colloquial sense in which utility is opposed to pleasure. An apology is due to the philosophical opponents of utilitarianism for even the momentary appearance of confounding them with any one capable of so absurd a misconception, which is the more extraordinary, inasmuch as the contrary accusation, of referring every thing to pleasure, and that, too, in its grossest form, is another of the common charges against utilitarianism, and, as has been pointedly remarked by an able writer, the same sort of persons, and often the very same persons, denounce the theory "as impracticably dry when the word 'utility' precedes the word 'pleasure,' and as too practicably voluptuous when the word 'pleasure' precedes the word 'utility.'" Those who know any thing about the matter are aware that every writer from Epicurus to Bentham who maintained the theory of utility meant by it, not something to be contradistinguished from pleasure, but pleasure itself, together with exemption from pain, and, instead of opposing the useful to the agreeable or the ornamental, have always declared that the useful means these, among other things. Yet the common herd, including the herd of writers, not only in newspapers and periodicals, but in books of weight and pretension, are perpetually falling into this shallow mistake. Having caught up the word "utilitarian," while knowing nothing whatever about it but its sound, they habitually express by it the rejection or the neglect of pleasure in some of its forms, of beauty, of ornament, or of amusement. Nor is the term thus ignorantly misapplied solely in disparagement, but occasionally in compliment, as though it implied superiority to frivolity and the mere pleasures of the moment. And this perverted use is the only one in which the word is popularly known, and the one from which the new generation are acquiring their sole notion of its meaning. Those who introduced the word, but who had for many years discontinued it as a distinctive appellation, may well feel themselves called upon to resume it, if by doing so they can hope to contribute any thing towards rescuing it from this utter degradation.

The creed which accepts as the foundation of morals Utility, or the Greatest-happiness Principle, holds that actions are right in proportion as they tend to promote happiness, wrong as they tend to produce the reverse of happiness. By happiness is intended pleasure and the absence of pain, by unhappiness, pain and the privation of pleasure. To give a clear view of the moral standard set up by the theory, much more requires to be said, in particular, what things it includes in the ideas of pain and pleasure, and to what extent this is left an open question. But these supplementary explanations do not affect the theory of life on which this theory of morality is grounded—namely, that pleasure and freedom from pain are the only things desirable as ends, and that all desirable things (which are as numerous in the utilitarian as in any other scheme) are desirable either for the pleasure inherent in themselves, or as means to the promotion of pleasure and the prevention of pain.

Now, such a theory of life excites in many minds, and among them in some of the most estimable in feeling and purpose, inveterate dislike. To suppose that life has (as they express it) no higher end than pleasure—no better and nobler object of desire and pursuit—they designate as utterly mean and groveling, as a doctrine worthy only of swine, to whom the followers of Epicurus were, at a very early period, contemptuously likened; and modern holders of the doctrine are occasionally made the subject of equally polite comparisons by its German, French, and English assailants.

When thus attacked, the Epicureans have always answered, that it is not they, but their accusers, who represent human nature in a degrading light, since the accusation supposes human beings to be capable of no pleasures except those of which swine are capable. If this supposition were true, the charge could not be gainsaid but would then be no longer an imputation; for, if the sources of pleasure were precisely the same to human beings and to swine, the rule of life which is good enough for the one would be good enough for the other. The comparison of the Epicurean life to that of beasts is felt as degrading, precisely because a beast's pleasures do not satisfy a human being's conceptions of happiness. Human beings have faculties more elevated than the animal appetites, and, when once made conscious of

them, do not regard any thing as happiness which does not include their gratification. I do not, indeed, consider the Epicureans to have been by any means faultless in drawing out their scheme of consequences from the utilitarian principle. To do this in any sufficient manner, many Stoic as well as Christian elements require to be included. But there is no known Epicurean theory of life which does not assign to the pleasures of the intellect, of the feelings and imagination, and of the moral sentiments, a much higher value as pleasures than to those of mere sensation. It must be admitted, however, that utilitarian writers in general have placed the superiority of mental over bodily pleasures chiefly in the greater permanency, safety, uncostliness, etc., of the former—that is, in their circumstantial advantages rather than in their intrinsic nature. And, on all these points, utilitarians have fully proved their case, but they might have taken the other, and, as it may be called, higher ground, with entire consistency. It is quite compatible with the principle of utility to recognize the fact that some *kinds* of pleasure are more desirable and more valuable than others. It would be absurd that while, in estimating all other things, quality is considered as well as quantity, the estimation of pleasures should be supposed to depend on quantity alone.

If I am asked what I mean by difference of quality in pleasures, or what makes one pleasure more valuable than another, merely as a pleasure, except its being greater in amount, there is but one possible answer. Of two pleasures, if there be one to which all or almost all who have experience of both give a decided preference, irrespective of any feeling of moral obligation to prefer it, that is the more desirable pleasure. If one of the two is, by those who are competently acquainted with both, placed so far above the other that they prefer it, even though knowing it to be attended with a greater amount of discontent, and would not resign it for any quantity of the other pleasure which their nature is capable of, we are justified in ascribing to the preferred enjoyment a superiority in quality so far outweighing quantity, as to render it, in comparison, of small account.

Now, it is an unquestionable fact, that those who are equally acquainted with and equally capable of appreciating and enjoying both do give a most marked preference to the manner of existence which employs their higher faculties. Few human creatures would consent to be changed into any of the lower animals for a promise of the fullest allowance of a beast's pleasures; no intelligent human being would consent to be a fool, no instructed person would be an ignoramus, no person of feeling and conscience would be selfish and base, even though they should be persuaded that the fool, the dunce, or the rascal is better satisfied with his lot than they are with theirs. They would not resign what they possess more than he for the most complete satisfaction of all the desires which they have in common with him. If they ever fancy they would, it is only in cases of unhappiness so extreme that, to escape from it, they would exchange their lot for almost any other, however undesirable in their own eyes. A being of higher faculties requires more to make him happy, is capable probably of more acute suffering, and certainly accessible to it at more points, than one of an inferior type, but, in spite of these liabilities, he can never really wish to sink into what he feels to be a lower grade of existence. We may give what explanation we please of this unwillingness: we may attribute it to pride, a name which is given indiscriminately to some of the most and to some of the least estimable feelings of which mankind are capable; we may refer it to the love of liberty and personal independence —an appeal to which was with the Stoics one of the most effective means for the inculcation of it; to the love of power, or to the love of excitement, both of which do really enter into and contribute to it; but its most appropriate appellation is a sense of dignity, which all human beings possess in one form or other, and in some, though by no means in exact, proportion to their higher faculties, and which is so essential a part of the happiness of those in whom it is strong, that nothing which conflicts with it could be, otherwise than momentarily, an object of desire to them. Whoever supposes that this preference takes place at a sacrifice of happiness, that the superior being, in any thing like equal circumstances, is not happier than the inferior—confounds the two very different ideas of happiness and content. It is indisputable that the being whose capacities of enjoyment are low has the greatest chance of having them fully satisfied, and a highly endowed being will always feel that any happiness which he can look for,

as the world is constituted, is imperfect. But he can learn to bear its imperfections, if they are at all bearable, and they will not make him envy the being who is indeed unconscious of the imperfections, but only because he feels not at all the good which those imperfections qualify. It is better to be a human being dissatisfied than a pig satisfied, better to be Socrates dissatisfied than a fool satisfied. And if the fool or the pig are a different opinion, it is because they only know their own side of the question. The other party to the comparison knows both sides.

It may be objected that many who are capable of the higher pleasures occasionally, under the influence of temptation, postpone them to the lower. But this is quite compatible with a full appreciation of the intrinsic superiority of the higher. Men often, from infirmity of character, make their election for the nearer good, though they know it to be the less valuable, and this no less when the choice is between two bodily pleasures than when it is between bodily and mental. They pursue sensual indulgences to the injury of health, though perfectly aware that health is the greater good. It may be further objected, that many who begin with youthful enthusiasm for everything noble, as they advance in years sink into indolence and selfishness. But I do not believe that those who undergo this very common change voluntarily choose the lower description of pleasures in preference to the higher. I believe that, before they devote themselves exclusively to the one, they have already become incapable of the other. Capacity for the nobler feelings is in most natures a very tender plant, easily killed, not only by hostile influences but by mere want of sustenance, and, in the majority of young persons, it speedily dies away if the occupations to which their position in life has devoted them, and the society into which it has thrown them, are not favorable to keeping that higher capacity in exercise. Men lose their high aspirations as they lose their intellectual tastes, because they have not time or opportunity for indulging them, and they addict themselves to inferior pleasures, not because they deliberately prefer them, but because they are either the only ones to which they have access or the only ones which they are any longer capable of enjoying. It may be questioned whether any one who has remained equally susceptible to both classes of pleasures ever knowingly and calmly preferred the lower, though many in all ages have broken down in an ineffectual attempt to combine both.

From this verdict of the only competent judges, I apprehend there can be no appeal. On a question which is the best worth having of two pleasures, or which of two modes of existence is the most grateful to the feelings, apart from its moral attributes and from its consequences, the judgment of those who are qualified by knowledge of both, or, if they differ, that of the majority among them, must be admitted as final. And there needs be the less hesitation to accept this judgment respecting the quality of pleasures, since there is no other tribunal to be referred to even on the question of quantity. What means are there of determining which is the acutest of two pains, or the intensest of two pleasurable sensations, except the general suffrage of those who are familiar with both? Neither pains nor pleasures are homogeneous, and pain is always heterogeneous with pleasure. What is there to decide whether a particular pleasure is worth purchasing at the cost of a particular pain, except the feelings and judgment of the experienced? When, therefore, those feelings and judgment declare the pleasures derived from the higher faculties to be preferable *in kind,* apart from the question of intensity, to those of which the animal nature disjoined from the higher faculties is susceptible, they are entitled on this subject to the same regard.

I have dwelt on this point, as being a necessary part of a perfectly just conception of Utility or Happiness, considered as the directive rule of human conduct. But it is by no means an indispensable condition to the acceptance of the utilitarian standard, for that standard is not the agent's own greatest happiness, but the greatest amount of happiness altogether; and if it may possibly be doubted whether a noble character is always the happier for its nobleness, there can be no doubt that it makes other people happier, and that the world in general is immensely a gainer by it. Utilitarianism, therefore, could only attain its end by the general cultivation of nobleness of character, even if each individual were only benefited by the nobleness of others, and his own, so far as happiness is concerned, were a sheer deduction from the benefit. But the bare enunciation of such an absurdity as this last renders refutation superfluous.

According to the Greatest-happiness Principle, as above explained, the ultimate end with reference to and for the sake of which all other things are desirable (whether we are considering our own good or that of other people) is an existence exempt as far as possible from pain, and as rich as possible in enjoyments, both in point of quantity and quality; the test of quality, and the rule for measuring it against quantity, being the preference felt by those who in their opportunities of experience, to which must be added their habits of self-consciousness and self-observation, are best furnished with the means of comparison. This being, according to the utilitarian opinion, the end of human action is necessarily also the standard of morality; which may accordingly be defined, the rules and precepts for human conduct by the observance of which an existence such as has been described might be, to the greatest extent possible, secured to all mankind, and not to them only but, so far as the nature of things admits, to the whole sentient creation.

Against this doctrine, however, arises another class of objectors who say that happiness, in any form, cannot be the rational purpose of human life and action, because, in the first place, it is unattainable; and they contemptuously ask, What right hast thou to be happy? a question which Mr. Carlyle clinches by the addition, What right, a short time ago, hadst thou even *to be?* Next they say that men can do *without* happiness, that all noble human beings have felt this, and could not have become noble but by learning the lesson of *Entsagen* or renunciation, which lesson, thoroughly learned and submitted to, they affirm to be the beginning and necessary condition of all virtue.

The first of these objections would go to the root of the matter, were it well founded; for, if no happiness is to be had at all by human beings, the attainment of it cannot be the end of morality, or of any rational conduct. Though, even in that case, something might still be said for the utilitarian theory, since utility includes not solely the pursuit of happiness, but the prevention or mitigation of unhappiness; and, if the former aim be chimerical, there will be all the greater scope and more imperative need for the latter, so long at least as mankind think fit to live, and do not take refuge in the simultaneous act of suicide recommended under certain conditions by Novalis. When, however, it is thus positively asserted to be impossible that human life should be happy, the assertion, if not something like a verbal quibble, is at least an exaggeration. If by happiness be meant a continuity of highly pleasurable excitement, it is evident enough that this is impossible. A state of exalted pleasure lasts only moments, or in some cases, and with some intermissions, hours or days, and is the occasional brilliant flash of enjoyment, not its permanent and steady flame. Of this the philosophers who have taught that happiness is the end of life were as fully aware as those who taunt them. The happiness which they meant was not a life of rapture, but moments of such, in an existence made up of few and transitory pains, many and various pleasures, with a decided predominance of the active over the passive, and having, as the foundation of the whole, not to expect more from life than it is capable of bestowing. A life thus composed, to those who have been fortunate enough to obtain it, has always appeared worthy of the name of "happiness." And such an existence is even now the lot of many, during some considerable portion of their lives. The present wretched education and wretched social arrangements are the only real hindrance to its being attainable by almost all.

The objectors, perhaps, may doubt whether human beings, if taught to consider happiness as the end of life, would be satisfied with such a moderate share of it. But great numbers of mankind have been satisfied with much less. The main constituents of a satisfied life appear to be two, either of which by itself is often found sufficient for the purpose—tranquillity and excitement. With much tranquillity, many find that they can be content with very little pleasure; with much excitement, many can reconcile themselves to a considerable quantity of pain. There is assuredly no inherent impossibility in enabling even the mass of mankind to unite both, since the two are so far from being incompatible, that they are in natural alliance, the prolongation of either being a preparation for, and exciting a wish for, the other. It is only those in whom indolence amounts to a vice that do not desire excitement after an interval of repose; it is only those in whom the need of excitement is a disease, that feel the tranquillity which follows excitement dull and insipid, instead of pleasurable in direct proportion to the excitement

which preceded it. When people who are tolerably fortunate in their outward lot do not find in life sufficient enjoyment to make it valuable to them, the cause generally is caring for nobody but themselves. To those who have neither public nor private affections, the excitements of life are much curtailed and, in any case, dwindle in value as the time approaches when all selfish interests must be terminated by death; while those who leave after them objects of personal affection, and especially those who have also cultivated a fellow feeling with the collective interests of mankind, retain as lively an interest in life on the eve of death as in the vigor of youth and health. Next to selfishness, the principal cause which makes life unsatisfactory is want of mental cultivation. A cultivated mind—I do not mean that of a philosopher, but any mind to which the fountains of knowledge have been opened, and which has been taught, in any tolerable degree, to exercise its faculties—finds sources of inexhaustible interest in all that surrounds it, in the objects of nature, the achievements of art, the imaginations of poetry, the incidents of history, the ways of mankind past and present, and their prospects in the future. It is possible, indeed, to become indifferent to all this, and that, too, without having exhausted a thousandth part of it, but only when one has had from the beginning no moral or human interest in these things, and has sought in them only the gratification of curiosity.

Now, there is absolutely no reason in the nature of things why an amount of mental culture sufficient to give an intelligent interest in these objects of contemplation should not be the inheritance of every one born in a civilized country. As little is there an inherent necessity that any human being should be a selfish egotist, devoid of every feeling or care but those which center in his own miserable individuality. Something far superior to this is sufficiently common even now to give ample earnest of what the human species may be made. Genuine private affections and a sincere interest in the public good are possible, though in unequal degrees, to every rightly brought up human being. In a world in which there is so much to interest, so much to enjoy, and so much also to correct and improve, every one who has this moderate amount of moral and intellectual requisites is capable of an existence which may be called enviable; and unless such a person, through bad laws or subjection to the will of others, is denied the liberty to use the sources of happiness within his reach, he will not fail to find this enviable existence, if he escape the positive evils of life, the great sources of physical and mental suffering—such as indigence, disease, and the unkindness, worthlessness, or premature loss, of objects of affection. The main stress of the problem lies, therefore, in the contest with these calamities, from which it is a rare good fortune entirely to escape, which, as things now are, cannot be obviated, and often cannot be in any material degree mitigated. Yet no one whose opinion deserves a moment's consideration can doubt that most of the great positive evils of the world are in themselves removable, and will, if human affairs continue to improve, be in the end reduced within narrow limits. Poverty, in any sense implying suffering, may be completely extinguished by the wisdom of society, combined with the good sense and providence of individuals. Even that most intractable of enemies, disease, may be indefinitely reduced in dimensions by good physical and moral education, and proper control of noxious influences, while the progress of science holds out a promise for the future of still more direct conquests over this detestable foe. And every advance in that direction relieves us from some, not only of the chances which cut short our own lives but, what concerns us still more, which deprive us of those in whom our happiness is wrapped up. As for vicissitudes of fortune and other disappointments connected with worldly circumstances, these are principally the effect either of gross imprudence, of ill-regulated desires, or of bad or imperfect social institutions. All the grand sources, in short, of human suffering are in a great degree, many of them almost entirely, conquerable by human care and effort; and though their removal is grievously slow, though a long succession of generations will perish in the breach before the conquest is completed, and this world becomes all that, if will and knowledge were not wanting, it might easily be made—yet every mind sufficiently intelligent and generous to bear a part, however small and unconspicuous, in the endeavor will draw a noble enjoyment from the contest itself, which he would not, for any bribe in the form of selfish indulgence, consent to be without.

And this leads to the true estimation of what is said by the objectors concerning the possibility and the obligation of learning to do without happiness. Unquestionably, it is possible to do without happiness; it is done involuntarily by nineteen-twentieths of mankind, even in those parts of our present world which are least deep in barbarism, and it often has to be done voluntarily by the hero or the martyr, for the sake of something which he prizes more than his individual happiness. But this something—what is it, unless the happiness of others, or some of the requisites of happiness? It is noble to be capable of resigning entirely one's own portion of happiness, or chances of it; but, after all, this self-sacrifice must be for some end; it is not its own end; and if we are told that its end is not happiness but virtue, which is better than happiness, I ask, Would the sacrifice be made if the hero or martyr did not believe that it would earn for others immunity from similar sacrifices? Would it be made if he thought that his renunciation of happiness for himself would produce no fruit for any of his fellow-creatures but to make their lot like his, and place them also in the condition of persons who have renounced happiness? All honor to those who can abnegate for themselves the personal enjoyment of life, when by such renunciation they contribute worthily to increase the amount of happiness in the world, but he who does it, or professes to do it, for any other purpose is no more deserving of admiration than the ascetic mounted on his pillar. He may be an inspiriting proof of what men *can* do, but assuredly not an example of what they *should*.

Though it is only in a very imperfect state of the world's arrangements that any one can best serve the happiness of others by the absolute sacrifice of his own, yet, so long as the world is in that imperfect state, I fully acknowledge that the readiness to make such a sacrifice is the highest virtue which can be found in man. I will add that in this condition of the world, paradoxical as the assertion may be, the conscious ability to do without happiness gives the best prospect of realizing such happiness as is attainable. For nothing except that consciousness can raise a person above the chances of life, by making him feel that, let fate and fortune do their worst, they have not power to subdue him; which, once felt, frees him from excess of anxiety concerning the evils of life, and enables him, like many a Stoic in the worst times of the Roman Empire, to cultivate in tranquillity the sources of satisfaction accessible to him, without concerning himself about the uncertainty of their duration, any more than about their inevitable end.

Meanwhile, let utilitarians never cease to claim the morality of self-devotion as a possession which belongs by as good a right to them as either to the Stoic or to the Transcendentalist. The utilitarian morality does recognize in human beings the power of sacrificing their own greatest good for the good of others. It only refuses to admit that the sacrifice is itself a good. A sacrifice which does not increase, or tend to increase, the sum total of happiness, it considers as wasted. The only self-renunciation which it applauds is devotion to the happiness, or to some of the means of happiness, of others, either of mankind collectively, or of individuals within the limits imposed by the collective interests of mankind.

I must again repeat what the assailants of utilitarianism seldom have the justice to acknowledge, that the happiness which forms the utilitarian standard of what is right in conduct is not the agent's own happiness but that of all concerned. As between his own happiness and that of others, utilitarianism requires him to be as strictly impartial as a disinterested and benevolent spectator. In the golden rule of Jesus of Nazareth, we read the complete spirit of the ethics of utility. To do as you would be done by, and to love your neighbour as yourself, constitute the ideal perfection of utilitarian morality. As the means of making the nearest approach to this ideal, utility would enjoin, first, that laws and social arrangements should place the happiness or (as, speaking practically, it may be called) the interest of every individual as nearly as possible in harmony with the interest of the whole; and secondly, that education and opinion, which have so vast a power over human character, should so use that power as to establish in the mind of every individual an indissoluble association between his own happiness and the good of the whole—especially between his own happiness, and the practice of such modes of conduct, negative and positive, as regard for the universal happiness prescribes—so that not only he may be unable to conceive the possibility of happiness to himself consistently with conduct opposed to the general good, but also that a direct impulse to promote the general good may be in every individual one of the habitual motives of action, and the sentiments connected therewith may fill a large and prominent place in every human being's sentient existence. If the impugners of the utilitarian morality represented it to their own minds in this its true character, I know not what recommendation possessed by any other morality they could possibly affirm to be wanting to it, what more beautiful or more exalted developments of human nature any other ethical system can be supposed to foster, or what springs of action, not accessible to the utilitarian, such systems rely on for giving effect to their mandates.

The objectors to utilitarianism cannot always be charged with representing it in a discreditable light. On the contrary, those among them who entertain any thing like a just idea of its disinterested character sometimes find fault with its standard as being too high for humanity. They say it is exacting too much to require that people shall always act from the inducement of promoting the general interests of society. But this is to mistake the very meaning of a standard of morals, and confound the rule of action with the motive of it. It is the business of ethics to tell us what are our duties or by what test we may know them, but no system of ethics requires that the sole motive of all we do shall be a feeling of duty; on the contrary, ninety-nine hundredths of all our actions are done from other motives, and rightly so done, if the rule of duty does not condemn them. It is the more unjust to utilitarianism that this particular misapprehension should be made a ground of objection to it, inasmuch as utilitarian moralists have gone beyond almost all others in affirming that the motive has nothing to do with the morality of the action though much with the worth of the agent. He who saves a fellow creature from drowning does what is morally right, whether his motive be duty or the hope of being paid for his trouble; he who betrays the friend that trusts him is guilty of a crime, even if his object be to serve another friend to whom he is under greater obligations. But to speak only of actions done from the motive of duty, and in direct obedience to principle: it is a misapprehension of the utilitarian mode of thought to conceive it as implying that people should fix their minds upon so wide a generality as the world or society at large. The great majority of good actions are intended, not for the benefit of the world but for that of individuals, of which the good of the world is made up; and the thoughts of the most virtuous man need not on these occasions travel beyond the particular persons concerned, except so far as is necessary to assure himself that, in benefiting them, he is not violating the rights—that is, the legitimate and authorized expectations—of any one else. The multiplication of happiness is, according to the utilitarian ethics, the object of virtue; the occasions on which any person (except one in a thousand) has it in his power to do this on an extended scale—in other words, to be a public benefactor—are but exceptional, and on these occasions alone is he called on to consider public utility; in every other case, private utility, the interest or happiness of some few persons, is all he has to attend to. Those alone, the influence of whose actions extends to society in general, need concern themselves habitually about so large an object. In the case of abstinences indeed—of things which people forbear to do from moral considerations, though the consequences in the particular case might be beneficial—it would be unworthy of an intelligent agent not to be consciously aware that the action is of a class which, if practised generally, would be generally injurious, and that this is the ground of the obligation to abstain from it. The amount of regard for the public interest implied in this recognition is no greater than is demanded by every system of morals, for they all enjoin to abstain from whatever is manifestly pernicious to society.

The same considerations dispose of another reproach against the doctrine of utility, founded on a still grosser misconception of the purpose of a standard of morality, and of the very meaning of the words "right" and "wrong." It is often affirmed that utilitarianism renders men cold and unsympathizing, that it chills their moral feelings towards individuals, that it makes them regard only the dry and hard consideration of the consequences of actions, not taking into their moral estimate the qualities from which those actions emanate. If the assertion means that they do not allow their judgment respecting the rightness or wrongness of an action to be influenced by their opinion of the qualities of the person who does it, this is a complaint, not against utilitarianism but against having any standard of mo-

rality at all; for certainly no known ethical standard decides an action to be good or bad because it is done by a good or bad man, still less because done by an amiable, a brave, or a benevolent man, or the contrary. These considerations are relevant, not to the estimation of actions, but of persons, and there is nothing in the utilitarian theory inconsistent with the fact that there are other things which interest us in persons besides the rightness and wrongness of their actions. The Stoics indeed, with the paradoxical misuse of language which was part of their system and by which they strove to raise themselves above all concern about any thing but virtue, were fond of saying that he who has that has everything, that he, and one he, is rich, is beautiful, is a king. But no claim of this description is made for the virtuous man by the utilitarian doctrine. Utilitarians are quite aware that there are other desirable possessions and qualities besides virtue, and are perfectly willing to allow to all of them their full worth. They are also aware that a right action does not necessarily indicate a virtuous character, and that actions which are blamable often proceed from qualities entitled to praise. When this is apparent in any particular case, it modifies their estimation, not certainly of the act but of the agent. I grant that they are notwithstanding of opinion that, in the long run, the best proof of a good character is good actions, and resolutely refuse to consider any mental disposition as good, of which the predominant tendency is to produce bad conduct. This makes them unpopular with many people; but it is an unpopularity which they must share with every one who regards the distinction between right and wrong in a serious light, and the reproach is not one which a conscientious utilitarian need be anxious to repel.

If no more be meant by the objection than that many utilitarians look on the morality of actions, as measured by the utilitarian standards, with too exclusive a regard, and do not lay sufficient stress upon the other beauties of character which go towards making a human being lovable or admirable, this may be admitted. Utilitarians who have cultivated their moral feelings but not their sympathies nor their artistic perceptions, do fall into this mistake, and so do all other moralists under the same conditions. What can be said in excuse for other moralists is equally available for them, namely that, if there is to be any error, it is better that it should be on that side. As a matter of fact, we may affirm that among utilitarians, as among adherents of other systems, there is every imaginable degree of rigidity and of laxity in the application of their standard; some are even puritanically rigorous, while others are as indulgent as can possibly be desired by sinner or by sentimentalist. But on the whole, a doctrine which brings prominently forward the interest that mankind have in the repression and prevention of conduct which violates the moral law, is likely to be inferior to no other in turning the sanctions of opinion against such violations. It is true, the question, What does violate the moral law? is one on which those who recognize different standards of morality are likely now and then to differ. But difference of opinion on moral questions was not first introduced into the world by utilitarianism, while that doctrine does supply, if not always an easy, at all events a tangible and intelligible mode of deciding such differences. . . .

Famine, Affluence, and Morality

PETER SINGER

Peter Singer (1946–), author of several influential works, taught philosophy at Monash University in Australia and now teaches at Princeton University in New Jersey.

. . . I begin with the assumption that suffering and death from lack of food, shelter, and medical care is bad. I think most people will agree about this, although one may reach the same view by different routes. I shall not argue for this view. People can hold all sorts of eccentric positions, and perhaps from some of them it would not follow that death by starvation is in itself bad. It is difficult, perhaps impossible, to refute such positions, and so for brevity I will henceforth take this assumption as accepted. Those who disagree need read no further.

My next point is this: if it is in our power to prevent something bad from happening, without thereby sacrificing anything of comparable moral importance, we ought, morally, to do it. By "without sacrificing anything of comparable moral importance" I mean without causing anything else comparably bad to happen, or doing something that is wrong in itself, or failing to promote some moral good, comparable in significance to the bad thing we can prevent. This principle seems almost as un-controversial as the last one. It requires us only to prevent what is bad, and not to promote what is good, and it requires this of us only when we can do it without sacrificing anything that is, from the moral point of view, comparably important. I could even, as far as the application of my argument to the Bengal emergency* is concerned, qualify the point so as to make it: if it is in our power to prevent something very bad from happening, without thereby sacrificing anything morally significant, we ought, morally, to do it. An application of this principle would be as follows: if I am walking past a shallow pond and see a child drowning in it, I ought to wade in and pull the child out. This will mean getting my clothes muddy, but this is insignificant, while the death of the child would presumably be a very bad thing.

The uncontroversial appearance of the principle just stated is deceptive. If it were acted upon, even in its qualified form, our lives, our society, and our world would be fundamentally changed. For the principle takes, firstly, no account of proximity or distance. It makes no moral difference whether the

From *Philosophy and Public Affairs*, vol. 1, no. 3 (Spring 1972): 231–235, 238–240, 242–243. Copyright © 1972 by Princeton University Press. Excerpts reprinted by permission of Princeton University Press.

---

*A famine that caused many migrations and refugees.

person I can help is a neighbor's child ten yards from me or a Bengali whose name I shall never know, ten thousand miles away. Secondly, the principle makes no distinction between cases in which I am the only person who could possibly do anything and cases in which I am just one among millions in the same position.

I do not think I need to say much in defense of the refusal to take proximity and distance into account. The fact that a person is physically near to us, so that we have personal contact with him, may make it more likely that we *shall* assist him, but this does not show that we *ought* to help him rather than another who happens to be further away. If we accept any principle of impartiality, universalizability, equality, or whatever, we cannot discriminate against someone merely because he is far away from us (or we are far away from him). Admittedly, it is possible that we are in a better position to judge what needs to be done to help a person near to us than one far away, and perhaps also to provide the assistance we judge to be necessary. If this were the case, it would be a reason for helping those near to us first. This may once have been a justification for being more concerned with the poor in one's own town than with famine victims in India. Unfortunately for those who like to keep their moral responsibilities limited, instant communication and swift transportation have changed the situation. From the moral point of view, the development of the world into a "global village" has made an important, though still unrecognized, difference to our moral situation. Expert observers and supervisors, sent out by famine relief organizations or permanently stationed in famine-prone areas, can direct our aid to a refugee in Bengal almost as effectively as we could get it to someone in our own block. There would seem, therefore, to be no possible justification for discriminating on geographical grounds.

There may be a greater need to defend the second implication of my principle—that the fact that there are millions of other people in the same position, in respect to the Bengali refugees, as I am, does not make the situation significantly different from a situation in which I am the only person who can prevent something very bad from occurring. Again, of course, I admit that there is a psychological difference between the cases; one feels less guilty about

doing nothing if one can point to others, similarly placed, who have also done nothing. Yet this can make no real difference to our moral obligations. Should I consider that I am less obliged to pull the drowning child out of the pond if on looking around I see other people, no further away than I am, who have also noticed the child but are doing nothing? One has only to ask this question to see the absurdity of the view that numbers lessen obligation. It is a view that is an ideal excuse for inactivity: unfortunately most of the major evils—poverty, overpopulation, pollution—are problems in which everyone is almost equally involved.

If my argument so far has been sound, neither our distance from a preventable evil nor the number of other people who, in respect to that evil, are in the same situation as we are, lessens our obligation to mitigate or prevent that evil. I shall therefore take as established the principle I asserted earlier. As I have already said, I need to assert it only in its qualified form: if it is in our power to prevent something very bad from happening, without thereby sacrificing anything else morally significant, we ought, morally, to do it.

The outcome of this argument is that our traditional moral categories are upset. The traditional distinction between duty and charity cannot be drawn, or at least, not in the place we normally draw it. Giving money to the Bengal Relief Fund is regarded as an act of charity in our society. The bodies which collect money are known as "charities." These organizations see themselves in this way—if you send them a check, you will be thanked for your "generosity." Because giving money is regarded as an act of charity, it is not thought that there is anything wrong with not giving. The charitable man may be praised, but the man who is not charitable is not condemned. People do not feel in any way ashamed or guilty about spending money on new clothes or a new car instead of giving it to famine relief. (Indeed, the alternative does not occur to them.) This way of looking at the matter cannot be justified. When we buy new clothes not to keep ourselves warm but to look "well-dressed" we are not providing for any important need. We would not be sacrificing anything significant if we were to continue to wear our old clothes, and give the money to famine relief. By doing so, we would be preventing another person from starving. It follows from what I have said earlier that we ought to give money away, rather than spend it on clothes which we do not need to keep us warm. To do so is not charitable, or generous. Nor is it the kind of act which philosophers and theologians have called "supererogatory"—an act which it would be good to do, but not wrong not to do. On the contrary, we ought to give the money away, and it is wrong not to do so. . . .

Anatomy of Racisms

KWAME ANTHONY APPIAH

Kwame Anthony Appiah (1954–) is a professor of Afro-American Studies and Philosophy at Harvard University and the author of many articles and several books.

If the people I talk to and the newspapers I read are representative and reliable, there is a good deal of racism about. People and policies in the United States, in Eastern and Western Europe, in Asia and Africa and Latin America are regularly described as "racist." Australia had, until recently, a racist immigration policy; Britain still has one; racism is on the rise in France; many Israelis support Meir Kahane, an anti-Arab racist; many Arabs, according to a leading authority, are anti-Semitic racists;[1] and the movement to establish English as the "official language" of the United States is motivated by racism. Or, at least, so many of the people I talk to and many of the journalists with the newspapers I read believe.

But visitors from Mars—or from Malawi—unfamiliar with the Western concept of racism could be excused if they had some difficulty in identifying what exactly racism was. We see it everywhere, but rarely does anyone stop to say what it is, or to explain what is wrong with it. Our visitors from Mars would soon grasp that it had become at least conventional in recent years to express abhorrence for racism. They might even notice that those most often accused of it—members of the South African Nationalist party, for example—may officially abhor it also. But if they sought in the popular media of our day—in newspapers and magazines, on television or ra-

dio, in novels or films—for an explicit definition of this thing "we" all abhor, they would very likely be disappointed.

Now, of course, this would be true of many of our most familiar concepts. *Sister, chair, tomato*—none of these gets defined in the course of our daily business. But the concept of racism is in worse shape than these. For much of what we say about it is, on the face of it, inconsistent.

It is, for example, held by many to be racist to refuse entry to a university to an otherwise qualified "Negro" candidate, but not to be so to refuse entry to an equally qualified "Caucasian" one. But "Negro" and "Caucasian" are both alleged to be names of races, and invidious discrimination on the basis of race is usually held to be a paradigm case of racism. Or, to take another example, it is widely believed to be evidence of unacceptable racism to exclude people from clubs on the basis of race; yet most people, even those who think of "Jewish" as a racial term, seem to think that there is nothing wrong with Jewish clubs, whose members do not share any particular religious beliefs, or Afro-American societies, whose members share the juridical characteristic of American citizenship and the "racial" characteristic of being black.

I say that these are inconsistencies "on the face of it," because, for example, affirmative action in university admissions is importantly different from the earlier refusal to admit blacks or Jews (or other "Others") that it is meant, in part, to correct. Deep enough analysis may reveal it to be quite consistent with the abhorrence of racism; even a shallow analysis suggests that it is intended to be so. Similarly, justifications can be offered for "racial" associations in a plural society that are not available for the racial exclusivisms of the country club. But if we take racism seriously we ought to be concerned about the adequacy of these justifications.

In this essay, then, I propose to take our ordinary ways of thinking about race and racism and point up some of their presuppositions. And since popular concepts are, of course, usually fairly fuzzily and untheoretically conceived, much of what I have to say will seem to be both more theoretically and more precisely committed than the talk of racism and racists in our newspapers and on television. My claim is that these theoretical claims are required to make sense of racism as the practice of reasoning human beings. If anyone were to suggest that much, perhaps most, of what goes under the name "racism" in our world cannot be given such a rationalized foundation, I should not disagree: but to the extent that a practice cannot be rationally reconstructed it ought, surely, to be given up by reasonable people. The right tactic with racism, if you really want to oppose it, is to object to it rationally in the form in which it stands the best chance of meeting objections. The doctrines I want to discuss can be rationally articulated: and they are worth articulating rationally in order that we can rationally say what we object to in them.

RACIST PROPOSITIONS

There are at least three distinct doctrines that might be held to express the theoretical content of what we call "racism." One is the view—which I shall call *racialism*[2]—that there are heritable characteristics, possessed by members of our species, that allow us to divide them into a small set of races, in such a way that all the members of these races share certain traits and tendencies with each other that they do not share with members of any other race. These traits and tendencies characteristic of a race constitute, on the racialist view, a sort of racial essence; and it is part of the content of racialism that the essential heritable characteristics of what the nineteenth century called the "Races of Man" account

for more than the visible morphological characteristics—skin color, hair type, facial features—on the basis of which we make our informal classifications. Racialism is at the heart of nineteenth-century Western attempts to develop a science of racial difference; but it appears to have been believed by others—for example, Hegel, before then, and many in other parts of the non-Western world since—who have had no interest in developing scientific theories.

Racialism is not, in itself, a doctrine that must be dangerous, even if the racial essence is thought to entail moral and intellectual dispositions. Provided positive moral qualities are distributed across the races, each can be respected, can have its "separate but equal" place. Unlike most Western-educated people, I believe—and I have argued elsewhere[3]—that racialism is false; but by itself, it seems to be a cognitive rather that a moral problem. The issue is how the world is, not how we would want it to be.

Racialism is, however, a presupposition of other doctrines that have been called "racism," and these other doctrines have been, in the last few centuries, the basis of a great deal of human suffering and the source of a great deal of moral error.

One such doctrine we might call "extrinsic racism": extrinsic racists make moral distinctions between members of different races because they believe that the racial essence entails certain morally relevant qualities. The basis for the extrinsic racists' discrimination between people is their belief that members of different races differ in respects that *warrant* the differential treatment, respects—such as honesty or courage or intelligence—that are uncontroversially held (at least in most contemporary cultures) to be acceptable as a basis for treating people differently. Evidence that there are no such differences in morally relevant characteristics—that Negroes do not necessarily lack intellectual capacities, that Jews are not especially avaricious—should thus lead people out of their racism if it is purely extrinsic. As we know, such evidence often fails to change an extrinsic racist's attitudes substantially, for some of the extrinsic racist's best friends have always been Jewish. But at this point—if the racist is sincere—what we have is no longer a false doctrine but a cognitive incapacity, one whose significance I shall discuss later in this essay.

I say that the *sincere* extrinsic racist may suffer from a cognitive incapacity. But some who espouse extrinsic racist doctrines are simply insincere intrinsic racists. For *intrinsic racists,* on my definition, are people who differentiate morally between members of different races because they believe that each race has a different moral status, quite independent of the moral characteristics entailed by its racial essence. Just as, for example, many people assume that the fact that they are biologically related to another person—a brother, an aunt, a cousin—gives them a moral interest in that person,[4] so an intrinsic racist holds that the bare fact of being of the same race is a reason for preferring one person to another. (I shall return to this parallel later as well.)

For an intrinsic racist, no amount of evidence that a member of another race is capable of great moral, intellectual, or cultural achievements or has characteristics that, in members of one's own race, would make them admirable or attractive, offers any ground for treating that person as he or she would treat similarly endowed members of his or her own race. Just so, some sexists are "intrinsic sexists," holding that the bare fact that someone is a woman (or man) is a reason for treating her (or him) in certain ways.

There are interesting possibilities for complicating these distinctions: some racists, for example, claim, as the Mormons once did, that they discriminate between people because they believe that God requires them to do so. Is this an extrinsic racism, predicated on the combination of God's being an intrinsic racist and the belief that it is right to do what God wills? Or is it intrinsic racism because it is based on the belief that God requires these discriminations because they are right? (Is an act pious because the gods love it, or do they love it because it is pious?) Nevertheless, the distinctions between racialism and racism and between two potentially overlapping kinds of racism provide us with the skeleton of an anatomy of the propositional contents of racial attitudes.

RACIST DISPOSITIONS

Most people will want to object already that this discussion of the propositional content of racist moral and factual beliefs misses something absolutely crucial to the character of the psychological and sociological reality of racism, something I touched on when I mentioned that extrinsic racist utterances are often made by people who suffer from what I called a "cognitive incapacity." Part of the standard force of accusations of racism is that their objects are in some way *irrational.* The objection to Professor Shockley's claims about the intelligence of blacks is not just that they are false; it is rather that Professor Shockley seems, like many people we call "racist," to be unable to see that the evidence does not support his factual claims and that the connection between his factual claims and his policy prescriptions involves a series of non sequiturs.

What makes these cognitive incapacities especially troubling—something we should respond to with more than a recommendation that the individual, Professor Shockley, be offered psychotherapy—is that they conform to a certain pattern: namely, that it is especially where beliefs and politics are to the disadvantage of nonwhite people that he shows the sorts of disturbing failure that have made his views both notorious and notoriously unreliable. Indeed, Professor Shockley's reasoning works extremely well in some other areas: that he is a Nobel Laureate in physics is part of what makes him so interesting an example.

This cognitive incapacity is not, of course, a rare one. Many of us are unable to give up beliefs that play a part in justifying the special advantages we gain (or hope to gain) from our positions in the social order—in particular, beliefs about the positive characters of the class of people who share that position. Many people who express extrinsic racist beliefs—many white South Africans, for example—are beneficiaries of social orders that deliver advantages to them by virtue of their "race," so that their disinclination to accept evidence that would deprive them of a justification for those advantages is just an instance of this general phenomenon.

So too, evidence that access to higher education is as largely determined by the quality of our earlier educations as by our innate talents, does not, on the whole, undermine the confidence of college entrants from private schools in England or the United States or Ghana. Many of them continue to believe in the face of this evidence that their acceptance at "good" universities shows them to be intellectually better endowed (and not just better prepared) than those who are rejected. It is facts such as these that give sense to the notion of false consciousness, the idea that an ideology can prevent us from acknowledging facts that would threaten our position.

The most interesting cases of this sort of ideological resistance to the truth are not, perhaps, the ones I have just mentioned. On the whole, it is less surprising, once we accept the admittedly problematic notion of self-deception, that people who think that certain attitudes or beliefs advantage them or those they care about should be able, as we say, to "persuade" themselves to ignore evidence that undermines those beliefs or attitudes. What is more interesting is the existence of people who resist the truth of a proposition while thinking that its wider acceptance would in no way disadvantage them or those individuals about whom they care—this might be thought to describe Professor Shockley; or who resist the truth when they recognize that its acceptance would actually advantage them—this might be the case with some black people who have internalized negative racist stereotypes; or who fail, by virtue of their ideological attachments, to recognize what is in their own best interests at all.

My business here is not with the psychological or social processes by which these forms of ideological resistance operate, but it is important, I think, to see the refusal on the part of some extrinsic racists to accept evidence against the beliefs as an instance of a widespread phenomenon in human affairs. It is a plain fact, to which theories of ideology must address themselves, that our species is prone both morally and intellectually to such distortions of judgment, in particular to distortions of judgment that reflect partiality. An inability to change your mind in the face of appropriate[5] evidence is a cognitive incapacity; but it is one that all of us surely suffer from in some areas of belief; especially in areas where our own interests or self-images are (or seem to be) at stake.

It is not, however, as some have held, a tendency that we are powerless to resist. No one, no doubt, can be impartial about everything—even about everything to which the notion of partiality applies; but there is no subject matter about which most sane people cannot, in the end, be persuaded to avoid partiality in judgment. And it may help to shake the

convictions of those whose incapacity derives from this sort of ideological defense if we show them how their reaction fits into this general pattern. It is, indeed, because it generally *does* fit this pattern that we call such views "racism"—the suffix "-ism" indicating that what we have in mind is not simply a theory but an ideology. It would be odd to call someone brought up in a remote corner of the world with false and demeaning views about white people a "racist" if that person gave up these beliefs quite easily in the face of appropriate evidence.

Real live racists, then, exhibit a systematically distorted rationality, the kind of systematically distorted rationality that we are likely to call "ideological." And it is a distortion that is especially striking in the cognitive domain: extrinsic racists, as I said earlier, however intelligent or otherwise well informed, often fail to treat evidence against the theoretical propositions of extrinsic racism dispassionately. Like extrinsic racism, intrinsic racism can also often be seen as ideological; but since scientific evidence is not going to settle the issue, a failure to see that it is wrong represents a cognitive incapacity only on controversially realist views about morality. What makes intrinsic racism similarly ideological is not so much the failure of inductive or deductive rationality that is so striking in someone like Professor Shockley but rather the connection that it, like extrinsic racism, has with the interests—real or perceived—of the dominant group.[6] Shockley's racism is in a certain sense directed *against* nonwhite people: many believe that his views would, if accepted, operate against their objective interests, and he certainly presents the black "race" in a less than flattering light.

I propose to use the old-fashioned term "racial prejudice" in the rest of this essay to refer to the deformation of rationality in judgment that characterizes those whose racism is more than a theoretical attachment to certain propositions about race.

RACIAL PREJUDICE

It is hardly necessary to raise objections to what I am calling "racial prejudice"; someone who exhibits such deformations of rationality is plainly in trouble. But it is important to remember that propositional racists in a racist culture have false moral beliefs but may not suffer from racial prejudice. Once we show them how society has enforced extrinsic racist stereotypes, once we ask them whether they really believe that race in itself, independently of those extrinsic racist beliefs, justifies differential treatment, many will come to give up racist propositions, although we must remember how powerful a weight of authority our arguments have to overcome. Reasonable people may insist on substantial evidence if they are to give up beliefs that are central to their cultures.

Still, in the end, many will resist such reasoning; and to the extent that their prejudices are really not subject to any kind of rational control, we may wonder whether it is right to treat such people as morally responsible for the acts their racial prejudice motivates, or morally reprehensible for holding the views to which their prejudice leads them. It is a bad thing that such people exist; they are, in a certain sense, bad people. But it is not clear to me that they are responsible for the fact that they are bad. Racial prejudice, like prejudice generally, may threaten an agent's autonomy, making it appropriate to treat or train rather than to reason with them.

But once someone has been offered evidence both (1) that their reasoning in a certain domain is distorted by prejudice, and (2) that the distortions conform to a pattern that suggests a lack of impartiality, they ought to take special care in articulating views and proposing policies in that domain. They ought to do so because, as I have already said, the phenomenon of partiality in judgment is well attested in human affairs. Even if you are not immediately persuaded that you are yourself a victim of such a distorted rationality in a certain domain, you should keep in mind always that this is the usual position of those who suffer from such prejudices. To the extent that this line of thought is not one that itself falls within the domain in question, one can be held responsible for not subjecting judgments that *are* within that domain to an especially extended scrutiny; and this is a fortiori true if the policies one is recommending are plainly of enormous consequence.

If it is clear that racial prejudice is regrettable, it is also clear in the nature of the case that providing even a superabundance of reasons and evidence will often not be a successful way of removing it. Nevertheless, the racist's prejudice will be articulated through the sorts of theoretical propositions I dubbed extrinsic and intrinsic racism. And we should certainly be able to say something reasonable about why these theoretical propositions should be rejected.

Part of the reason that this is worth doing is precisely the fact that many of those who assent to the propositional content of racism do not suffer from racial prejudice. In a country like the United States, where racist propositions were once part of the national ideology, there will be many who assent to racist propositions simply because they were raised to do so. Rational objection to racist propositions has a fair chance of changing such people's beliefs.

EXTRINSIC AND INTRINSIC RACISM

It is not always clear whether someone's theoretical racism is intrinsic or extrinsic, and there is certainly no reason why we should expect to be able to settle the question. Since the issue probably never occurs to most people in these terms, we cannot suppose that they must have an answer. In fact, given the definition of the terms I offered, there is nothing barring someone from being both an intrinsic and an extrinsic racist, holding both that the bare fact of race provides a basis for treating members of his or her own race differently from others and that there are morally relevant characteristics that are differentially distributed among the races. Indeed, for reasons I shall discuss in a moment, *most* intrinsic racists are likely to express extrinsic racist beliefs, so that we should not be surprised that many people seem, in fact, to be committed to both forms of racism.

The Holocaust made unreservedly clear the threat that racism poses to human decency. But it also blurred our thinking because in focusing our attention on the racist character of the Nazi atrocities, it obscured their character as atrocities. What is appalling about Nazi racism is not just that it presupposes, as all racism does, false (racialist) beliefs—not simply that it involves a moral incapacity (the inability to extend our moral sentiments to all our fellow creatures) and a moral failing (the making of moral distinctions without moral differences)—but that it leads, first, to oppression and then to mass slaughter. In recent years, South African racism has had a similar distorting effect. For although South African racism has not led to killings on the scale of the Holocaust—even if it has both left South Africa judicially executing more (mostly black) people per head of population than most other countries and led to massive differences between the life chances of white and nonwhite South Africans—it *has* led to the systematic oppression and economic exploitation of people who are not classified as "white," and to the infliction of suffering on citizens of all racial classifications, not least by the police state that is required to maintain that exploitation and oppression.

Part of our resistance, therefore, to calling the racial ideas of those, such as the Black Nationalists of the 1960s, who advocate racial solidarity, by the same term that we use to describe the attitudes of Nazis or of members of the South African Nationalist party, surely resides in the fact that they largely did not contemplate using race as a basis for inflicting harm. Indeed, it seems to me that there is a significant pattern in the modern rhetoric of race, such that the discourse of racial solidarity is usually expressed through the language of *intrinsic* racism, while those who have used race as the basis for oppression and hatred have appealed to *extrinsic* racist ideas. This point is important for understanding the character of contemporary racial attitudes.

The two major uses of race as a basis for moral solidarity that are most familiar in the West are varieties of Pan-Africanism and Zionism. In each case it is presupposed that a "people," Negroes or Jews, has the basis for shared political life in the fact of being of the same race. There are varieties of each form of "nationalism" that make the basis lie in shared traditions; but however plausible this may be in the case of Zionism, which has in Judaism, the religion, a realistic candidate for a common and nonracial focus for nationality, the peoples of Africa have a good deal less in common culturally than is usually assumed. I discuss this issue at length in *In My Father's House: Essays in the Philosophy of African Culture*, but let me say here that I believe the central fact is this: what blacks in the West, like secularized Jews, have mostly in common is that they are perceived—both by themselves and by others—as belonging to the same race, and that this common race is used by

others as the basis for discriminating against them. "If you ever forget you're a Jew, a goy will remind you." The Black Nationalists, like some Zionists, responded to their experience of racial discrimination by accepting the racialism it presupposed.[7]

Although race is indeed at the heart of Black Nationalism, however, it seems that it is the fact of a shared race, not the fact of a shared racial character, that provides the basis for solidarity. Where racism is implicated in the basis for national solidarity, it is intrinsic, not (or not only) extrinsic. It is this that makes the idea of fraternity one that is naturally applied in nationalist discourse. For, as I have already observed, the moral status of close family members is not normally thought of in most cultures as depending on qualities of character; we are supposed to love our brothers and sisters in spite of their faults and not because of their virtues. Alexander Crummell, one of the founding fathers of Black Nationalism, literalizes the metaphor of family in these startling words:

> Races, like families, are the organisms and ordinances of God; and race feeling, like family feeling, is of divine origin. The extinction of race feeling is just as possible as the extinction of family feeling. Indeed, a race *is* a family.[8]

It is the assimilation of "race feeling" to "family feeling" that makes intrinsic racism seem so much less objectionable than extrinsic racism. For this metaphorical identification reflects the fact that, in the modern world (unlike the nineteenth century), intrinsic racism is acknowledged almost exclusively as the basis of feelings of community. We can surely, then, share a sense of what Crummell's friend and co-worker Edward Blyden called "the poetry of politics," that is, "the feeling of race," the feeling of "people with whom we are connected."[9] The racism here is the basis of acts of supererogation, the treatment of others better than we otherwise might, better than moral duty demands of us.

This is a contingent fact. There is no logical impossibility in the idea of racialists whose moral beliefs lead them to feelings of hatred for other races while leaving no room for love of members of their own. Nevertheless most racial hatred is in fact expressed through extrinsic racism: most people who have used race as the basis for causing harm to others have felt the need to see the others as independently morally flawed. It is one thing to espouse fraternity without claiming that your brothers and sisters have any special qualities that deserve recognition, and another to espouse hatred of others who have done nothing to deserve it.[10]

Many Afrikaners—like many in the American South until recently—have a long list of extrinsic racist answers to the question why blacks should not have full civil rights. Extrinsic racism has usually been the basis for treating people worse than we otherwise might, for giving them less than their humanity entitles them to. But this too is a contingent fact. Indeed, Crummell's guarded respect for white people derived from a belief in the superior moral qualities of the Anglo-Saxon race.

Intrinsic racism is, in my view, a moral error. Even if racialism were correct, the bare fact that someone was of another race would be no reason to treat them worse—or better—than someone of my race. In our public lives, people are owed treatment independently of their biological characters: if they are to be differently treated there must be some morally relevant difference between them. In our private lives, we are morally free to have aesthetic preferences between people, but once our treatment of people raises moral issues, we may not make arbitrary distinctions. Using race in itself as a morally relevant distinction strikes most of us as obviously arbitrary. Without associated moral characteristics, why should race provide a better basis than hair color or height or timbre of voice? And if two people share all the properties morally relevant to some action we ought to do, it will be an error—a failure to apply the Kantian injunction to universalize our moral judgments—to use the bare facts of race as the basis for treating them differently. No one should deny that a common ancestry might, in particular cases, account for similarities in moral character. But then it would be the moral similarities that justified the different treatment.

It is presumably because most people—outside the South African Nationalist party and the Ku Klux Klan—share the sense that intrinsic racism requires arbitrary distinctions that they are largely unwilling to express it in situations that invite moral criticism. But I do not know how I would argue with someone who was willing to announce an intrinsic racism as a basic moral idea; the best one can do, perhaps, is to provide objections to possible lines of defense of it.

DE GUSTIBUS

It might be thought that intrinsic racism should be regarded not so much as an adherence to a (moral) proposition as the expression of a taste, analogous, say, to the food prejudice that makes most English people unwilling to eat horse meat, and most Westerners unwilling to eat the insect grubs that the !Kung people find so appetizing. The analogy does at least this much for us, namely, to provide a model of the way the *extrinsic* racist propositions can be a reflection of an underlying prejudice. For, of course, in most cultures food prejudices are rationalized: we say insects are unhygienic and cats taste horrible. Yet a cooked insect is no more health-threatening than a cooked carrot, and the unpleasant taste of cat meat, far from justifying our prejudice against it, probably derives from that prejudice.

But there the usefulness of the analogy ends. For intrinsic racism, as I have defined it, is not simply a taste for the company of one's "own kind," but a moral doctrine, one that is supposed to underlie differences in the treatment of people in contexts where moral evaluation is appropriate. And for moral distinctions we cannot accept that "de gustibus non est disputandum." We do not need the full apparatus of Kantian ethics to require that public morality be constrained by reason.

A proper analogy would be with someone who thought that we could continue to kill cattle for beef, even if cattle exercised all the complex cultural skills of human beings. I think it is obvious that creatures that shared our capacity for understanding as well as our capacity for pain should not be treated the way we actually treat cattle—that "intrinsic speciesism" would be as wrong as racism. And the fact that most people think it is worse to be cruel to chimpanzees than to frogs suggests that they may agree with me. The distinction in attitudes surely reflects a belief in the greater richness of the mental life of chimps. Still, I do not know how I would *argue* against someone who could not see this; someone who continued to act on the contrary belief might, in the end, simply have to be locked up.

THE FAMILY MODEL

I have suggested that intrinsic racism is, at least sometimes, a metaphorical extension of the moral priority of one's family; it might, therefore, be suggested that a defense of intrinsic racism could proceed along the same lines as a defense of the family as a center of moral interest. The possibility of a defense of family relations as morally relevant—or, more precisely, of the claim that one may be morally entitled (or even obliged) to make distinctions between two otherwise morally indistinguishable people because one is related to one and not to the other—is theoretically important for the prospects of a philosophical defense of intrinsic racism. This is because such a defense of the family involves—like intrinsic racism—a denial of the basic claim, expressed so clearly by Kant, that from the perspective of morality, it is as rational agents *simpliciter* that we are to assess and be assessed. For anyone who follows Kant in this, what matters, as we might say, is not who you are but how you try to live. Intrinsic racism denies this fundamental claim also. And, in so doing, as I have argued elsewhere, it runs against the mainstream of the history of Western moral theory.[11]

The importance of drawing attention to the similarities between the defense of the family and the defense of the race, then, is not merely that the metaphor of family is often invoked by racism; it is that each of them offers the same general challenge to the Kantian stream of our moral thought. And the parallel with the defense of the family should be especially appealing to an intrinsic racist, since many of us who have little time for racism would hope that the family is susceptible to some such defense.

The problem in generalizing the defense of the family, however, is that such defenses standardly begin at a point that makes the argument for intrinsic racism immediately implausible: namely, with the family as the unit through which we live what is most intimate, as the center of private life. If we distinguish, with Bernard Williams, between ethical thought, which takes seriously "the demands, needs, claims, desires, and generally, the lives of other people,"[12] and morality, which focuses more narrowly on obligation, it may well be that private life matters to us precisely because it is altogether unsuited to the universalizing tendencies of morality.

The functioning family unit has contracted substantially with industrialization, the disappearance of the family as the unit of production, and the increasing mobility of labor, but there remains that irreducible minimum: the parent or parents with the child or children. In this "nuclear" family, there is, of course, a substantial body of shared experience, shared attitudes, shared knowledge and beliefs; and the mutual psychological investment that exists within this group is, for most of us, one of the things that gives meaning to our lives. It is a natural enough confusion—which we find again and again in discussions of adoption in the popular media—that identifies the relevant group with the biological unit of *genitor, genetrix,* and *offspring* rather than with the social unit of those who share a common domestic life.

The relations of parents and their biological children are of moral importance, of course, in part because children are standardly the product of behavior voluntarily undertaken by their biological parents. But the moral relations between biological siblings and half-siblings cannot, as I have already pointed out, be accounted for in such terms. A rational defense of the family ought to appeal to the causal responsibility of the biological parent and the common life of the domestic unit, and not to the brute fact of biological relatedness, even if the former pair of considerations defines groups that are often coextensive with the groups generated by the latter. For brute biological relatedness bears no necessary connection to the sorts of human purposes that seem likely to be relevant at the most basic level of ethical thought.

An argument that such a central group is bound to be crucially important in the lives of most human beings in societies like ours is not, of course, an argument for any specific mode of organization of the "family": feminism and the gay liberation movement have offered candidate groups that could (and sometimes do) occupy the same sort of role in the lives of those whose sexualities or whose dispositions otherwise make the nuclear family uncongenial; and these candidates have been offered specifically in the course of defenses of a move toward societies that are agreeably beyond patriarchy and homophobia. The central thought of these feminist and gay critiques of the nuclear family is that we cannot continue to view any one organization of private life as "natural," once we have seen even the broadest outlines of the archaeology of the family concept.

If that is right, then the argument for the family must be an argument for a mode of organization of life and feeling that subserves certain positive functions; and however the details of such an argument would proceed it is highly unlikely that the same functions could be served by groups on the scale of races, simply because, as I say, the family is attractive in part exactly for reasons of its personal scale.

I need hardly say that rational defenses of intrinsic racism along the lines I have been considering are not easily found. In the absence of detailed defenses to consider, I can only offer these general reasons for doubting that they can succeed: the generally Kantian tenor of much of our moral thought threatens the project from the start; and the essentially unintimate nature of relations within "races" suggests that there is little prospect that the defense of the family—which seems an attractive and plausible project that extends ethical life beyond the narrow range of a universalizing morality—can be applied to a defense of races.

CONCLUSIONS

I have suggested that what we call "racism" involves both propositions and dispositions.

The propositions were, first, that there are races (this was *racialism*) and, second, that these races are morally significant either (a) because they are contingently correlated with morally relevant properties (this was *extrinsic racism*) or (b) because they are intrinsically morally significant (this was *intrinsic racism*).

The disposition was a tendency to assent to false propositions, both moral and theoretical, about races—propositions that support policies or beliefs that are to the disadvantage of some race (or races) as opposed to others, and to do so even in the face of evidence and argument that should appropriately lead to giving those propositions up. This disposition I called "racial prejudice."

I suggested that intrinsic racism had tended in our own time to be the natural expression of feelings of community, and this is, of course, one of the reasons why we are not inclined to call it racist. For, to

the extent that a theoretical position is not associated with irrationally held beliefs that tend to the *dis*advantage of some groups, it fails to display the *directedness* of the distortions of rationality characteristic of racial prejudice. Intrinsic racism may be as irrationally held as any other view, but it does not *have* to be directed *against* anyone.

So far as theory is concerned I believe racialism to be false: since theoretical racism of both kinds presupposes racialism, I could not logically support racism of either variety. But even if racialism were true, both forms of theoretical racism would be incorrect. Extrinsic racism is false because the genes that account for the gross morphological differences that underlie our standard racial categories are not linked to those genes that determine, to whatever degree such matters are determined genetically, our moral and intellectual characters. Intrinsic racism is mistaken because it breaches the Kantian imperative to make moral distinctions only on morally relevant grounds—granted that there is no reason to believe that race, *in se,* is morally relevant, and also no reason to suppose that races are like families in providing a sphere of ethical life that legitimately escapes the demands of a universalizing morality.

Notes

1. Bernard Lewis, *Semites and Anti-Semites* (New York: Norton, 1986).
2. I shall be using the words "racism" and "racialism" with the meanings I stipulate: in some dialects of English they are synonyms, and in most dialects their definition is less than precise. For discussion of recent biological evidence see M. Nei and A. K. Roychoudhury, "Genetic Relationship and Evolution of Human Races," *Evolutionary Biology,* vol. 14 (New York: Plenum, 1983), pp. 1–59; for useful background see also M. Nei and A. K. Roychoudhury, "Gene Differences between Caucasian, Negro, and Japanese Populations," *Science,* 177 (August 1972), pp. 434–35.
3. See my "The Uncompleted Argument: Du Bois and the Illusion of Race," *Critical Inquiry,* 12 (Autumn 1985); reprinted in Henry Louis Gates (ed.), *Race, Writing, and Difference* (Chicago: University of Chicago Press, 1986), pp. 21–37.
4. This fact shows up most obviously in the assumption that adopted children intelligibly make claims against their natural siblings: natural parents are, of course, causally responsible for their child's existence and that

could be the basis of moral claims, without any sense that biological relatedness entailed rights or responsibilities. But no such basis exists for an interest in natural *siblings;* my sisters are not causally responsible for my existence. See "The Family Model," later in this essay.

5. Obviously what evidence should *appropriately* change your beliefs is not independent of your social or historical situation. In mid-nineteenth-century America, in New England quite as much as in the heart of Dixie, the pervasiveness of the institutional support for the prevailing system of racist belief—the fact that it was reinforced by religion and state, and defended by people in the universities and colleges, who had the greatest cognitive authority—meant that it would have been appropriate to insist on a substantial body of evidence and argument before giving up assent to racist propositions. In California in the 1980s, of course, matters stand rather differently. To acknowledge this is not to admit to a cognitive relativism; rather, it is to hold that, at least in some domains, the fact that a belief is widely held—and especially by people in positions of cognitive authority—may be a good prima facie reason for believing it.

6. Ideologies, as most theorists of ideology have admitted, standardly outlive the period in which they conform to the objective interests of the dominant group in a society; so even someone who thinks the dominant group in our society no longer needs racism to buttress its position can see racism as the persisting ideology of an earlier phase of society. (I say "group" to keep the claim appropriately general; it seems to me a substantial further claim that the dominant group whose interests an ideology serves is always a class.) I have argued, however, in "The Conservation of 'Race'" that racism continues to serve the interests of the ruling classes in the West; in *Black American Literature Forum,* 23 (Spring 1989), pp. 37–60.

7. As I argued in "The Uncompleted Argument: Du Bois and the Illusion of Race." The reactive (or dialectical) character of this move explains why Sartre calls its manifestations in Négritude an "antiracist racism"; see "Orphée Noir," his preface to Senghor's *Anthologie de la nouvelle poésie négre et malagache de langue française* (Paris: PUF, 1948). Sartre believed, of course, that the synthesis of this dialectic would be the transcendence of racism; and it was his view of it as a stage—the antithesis—in that process that allowed him to see it as a positive advance over the original "thesis" of European racism. I suspect that the reactive character of antiracist racism accounts for the tolerance that it regularly extended to it in liberal circles; but this tolerance is surely hard to justify unless one shares Sartre's optimistic interpretation of it as a stage in a process that leads to the end of all racisms. (And unless your view of this dialectic is deterministic, you should in any case want to play an argumentative role in moving to this next stage.)

For a similar Zionist response see Horace Kallen's "The Ethics of Zionism," *Maccabaean,* August 1906.

8. "The Race Problem in America," in Brotz's *Negro Social and Political Thought* (New York: Basic Books, 1966), p. 184.

9. *Christianity, Islam and the Negro Race* (1887; reprinted Edinburgh: Edinburgh University Press, 1967), p. 197.

10. This is in part a reflection of an important asymmetry: loathing, unlike love, needs justifying; and this, I would argue, is because loathing usually leads to acts that are *in se* undesirable, whereas love leads to acts that are largely *in se* desirable—indeed, supererogatorily so.

11. See my "Racism and Moral Pollution," *Philosophical Forum,* 18 (Winter-Spring 1986–87), pp. 185–202.

12. *Ethics and the Limits of Philosophy* (Cambridge, Mass.: Harvard University Press, 1985), p. 12. I do not, as is obvious, share Williams's skepticism about morality.

What Makes Right Acts Right?

W. D. ROSS

British classical scholar W. D. Ross (1877–1967) was an influential moral philosopher who taught at Oxford University in England.

. . . The point at issue is that to which we now pass, viz. whether there is any general character which makes right acts right, and if so, what it is. Among the main historical attempts to state a single characteristic of all right actions which is the foundation of their rightness are those made by egoism and utilitarianism. But I do not propose to discuss these, not because the subject is unimportant, but because it has been dealt with so often and so well already, and because there has come to be so much agreement among moral philosophers that neither of these theories is satisfactory. A much more attractive theory has been put forward by Professor Moore: that what makes actions right is that they are productive of more *good* than could have been produced by any other action open to the agent.

This theory is in fact the culmination of all the attempts to base rightness on productivity of some sort of result. The first form this attempt takes is the attempt to base rightness on conduciveness to the advantage or pleasure of the agent. This theory comes to grief over the fact, which stares us in the face, that a great part of duty consists in an observance of the rights and a furtherance of the interests of others, whatever the cost to ourselves may be. Plato and others may be right in holding that a regard for the rights of others never in the long run involves a loss of happiness for the agent, that 'the just life profits a man.' But this, even if true, is irrelevant to the rightness of the act. As soon as a man does an action *because* he thinks he will promote his own interests thereby, he is acting not from a sense of its rightness but from self-interest.

To the egoistic theory hedonistic utilitarianism supplies a much-needed amendment. It points out

From *The Right and the Good* (Oxford: Clarendon Press, 1930), pp. 16–24, 28–41. Reprinted by permission of Oxford University Press.

correctly that the fact that a certain pleasure will be enjoyed by the agent is no reason why he *ought* to bring it into being rather than an equal or greater pleasure to be enjoyed by another, though, human nature being what it is, it makes it not unlikely that he *will* try to bring it into being. But hedonistic utilitarianism in its turn needs a correction. On reflection it seems clear that pleasure is not the only thing in life that we think good in itself, that for instance we think the possession of a good character, or an intelligent understanding of the world, as good or better. A great advance is made by the substitution of 'productive of the greatest good' for 'productive of the greatest pleasure.'

Not only is this theory more attractive than hedonistic utilitarianism, but its logical relation to that theory is such that the latter could not be true unless *it* were true, while it might be true though hedonistic utilitarianism were not. It is in fact one of the logical bases of hedonistic utilitarianism. For the view that what produces the maximum pleasure is right has for its bases the views (1) that what produces the maximum good is right, and (2) that pleasure is the only thing good in itself. . . . If, therefore, it can be shown that productivity of the maximum good is not what makes all right actions right, we shall *a fortiori* have refuted hedonistic utilitarianism.

When a plain man fulfils a promise because he thinks he ought to do so, it seems clear that he does so with no thought of its total consequences, still less with any opinion that these are likely to be the best possible. He thinks in fact much more of the past than of the future. What makes him think it right to act in a certain way is the fact that he has promised to do so—that and, usually, nothing more. That his act will produce the best possible consequences is not his reason for calling it right. What lends colour to the theory we are examining, then, is not the actions (which form probably a great majority of our actions) in which some such reflection as 'I have promised' is the only reason we give ourselves for thinking a certain action right, but the exceptional cases in which the consequences of fulfilling a promise (for instance) would be so disastrous to others that we judge it right not to do so. It must of course be admitted that such cases exist. If I have promised to meet a friend at a particular time for some trivial purpose, I should certainly think myself justified in breaking my engagement if by doing so I could prevent a serious accident or bring relief to the victims of one. And the supporters of the view we are examining hold that my thinking so is due to my thinking that I shall bring more good into existence by the one action than by the other. A different account may, however, be given of the matter, an account which will, I believe, show itself to be the true one. It may be said that besides the duty of fulfilling promises I have and recognize a duty of relieving distress, and that when I think it right to do the latter at the cost of not doing the former, it is not because I think I shall produce more good thereby but because I think it the duty which is in the circumstances more of a duty. This account surely corresponds much more closely with what we really think in such a situation. If, so far as I can see, I could bring equal amounts of good into being by fulfilling my promise and by helping some one to whom I had made no promise, I should not hesitate to regard the former as my duty. Yet on the view that what is right is right because it is productive of the most good I should not so regard it.

There are two theories, each in its way simple, that offer a solution of such cases of conscience. One is the view of Kant, that there are certain duties of perfect obligation, such as those of fulfilling promises, of paying debts, of telling the truth, which admit of no exception whatever in favour of duties of imperfect obligation, such as that of relieving distress. The other is the view of, for instance, Professor Moore and Dr. Rashdall, that there is only the duty of producing good, and that all 'conflicts of duties' should be resolved by asking 'by which action will most good be produced?' But it is more important that our theory fit the facts than that it be simple, and the account we have given above corresponds (it seems to me) better than either of the simpler theories with what we really think, viz. that normally promise-keeping, for example, should come before benevolence, but that when and only when the good to be produced by the benevolent act is very great and the promise comparatively trivial, the act of benevolence becomes our duty.

In fact the theory of 'ideal utilitarianism,' if I may for brevity refer so to the theory of Professor Moore, seems to simplify unduly our relations to our fellows. It says, in effect, that the only morally significant relation in which my neighbours stand to me is that of being possible beneficiaries by my action.[1] They do stand in this relation to me, and this relation is morally significant. But they may also stand to me in the relation of promise to promiser, or creditor to debtor, of wife to husband, of child to parent, of friend to friend, of fellow countryman to fellow countryman, and the like; and each of these relations is the foundation of a *prima facie* duty, which is more or less incumbent on me according to the circumstances of the case. When I am in a situation, as perhaps I always am, in which more than one of these *prima facie* duties is incumbent on me, what I have to do is to study the situation as fully as I can until I form the considered opinion (it is never more) that in the circumstances one of them is more incumbent than any other; then I am bound to think that to do this *prima facie* duty is my duty *sans phrase* in the situation.

I suggest '*prima facie* duty' or 'conditional duty' as a brief way of referring to the characteristic (quite distinct from that of being a duty proper) which an act has, in virtue of being of a certain kind (e.g. the keeping of a promise), of being an act which would be a duty proper if it were not at the same time of another kind which is morally significant. Whether an act is a duty proper or actual duty depends on *all* the morally significant kinds it is an instance of. . . .

There is nothing arbitrary about these *prima facie* duties. Each rests on a definite circumstance which cannot seriously be held to be without moral significance. Of *prima facie* duties I suggest, without claiming completeness or finality for it, the following division.[2]

(1) Some duties rest on previous acts of my own. These duties seem to include two kinds, (a) those resting on a promise or what may fairly be called an implicit promise, such as the implicit undertaking not to tell lies which seems to be implied in the act

of entering into conversation (at any rate by civilized men), or of writing books that purport to be history and not fiction. These may be called the duties of fidelity. (b) Those resting on a previous wrongful act. These may be called the duties of reparation. (2) Some rest on previous acts of other men, i.e. services done by them to me. These may be loosely described as the duties of gratitude. (3) Some rest on the fact or possibility of a distribution of pleasure or happiness (or of the means thereto) which is not in accordance with the merit of the persons concerned; in such cases there arises a duty to upset or prevent such a distribution. These are the duties of justice. (4) Some rest on the mere fact that there are other beings in the world whose conditions we can make better in respect of virtue, or of intelligence, or of pleasure. These are the duties of beneficence. (5) Some rest on the fact that we can improve our own condition in respect of virtue or of intelligence. These are the duties of self-improvement. (6) I think that we should distinguish from (4) the duties that may be summed up under the title of 'not injuring others.' No doubt to injure others is incidentally to fail to do them good; but it seems to me clear that non-maleficence is apprehended as a duty distinct from that of beneficence, and as a duty of a more stringent character. It will be noticed that this alone among the types of duty has been stated in a negative way. An attempt might no doubt be made to state this duty, like the others, in a positive way. It might be said that it is really the duty to prevent ourselves from acting either from an inclination to harm others or from an inclination to seek our own pleasure, in doing which we should incidentally harm them. But on reflection it seems clear that the primary duty here is the duty not to harm others, this being a duty whether or not we have an inclination that if followed would lead to our harming them; and that when we have such an inclination the primary duty not to harm others gives rise to a consequential duty to resist the inclination. The recognition of this duty of non-maleficence is the first step on the way to the recognition of the duty of beneficence; and that accounts for the prominence of the commands 'thou shalt not kill,' 'thou shalt not commit adultery,' 'thou shalt not steal,' 'thou shalt not bear false witness,' in so early a code as the Decalogue. But even when we have come to recognize

the duty of beneficence, it appears to me that the duty of non-maleficence is recognized as a distinct one, and as *prima facie* more binding. We should not in general consider it justifiable to kill one person in order to keep another alive, or to seal from one in order to give alms to another.

The essential defect of the 'ideal utilitarian' theory is that it ignores, or at least does not do full justice to, the highly personal character of duty. If the only duty is to produce the maximum of good, the question who is to have the good—whether it is myself, or my benefactor, or a person to whom I have made a promise to confer that good on him, or a mere fellow man to whom I stand in no such special relation—should make no difference to my having a duty to produce that good. But we are all in fact sure that it makes a vast difference. . . .

If the objection be made, that this catalogue of the main types of duty is an unsystematic one resting on no logical principle, it may be replied, first, that it makes no claim to being ultimate. It is a *prima facie* classification of the duties which reflection on our moral convictions seems actually to reveal. And if these convictions are, as I would claim that they are, of the nature of knowledge, and if I have not misstated them, the list will be a list of authentic conditional duties, correct as far as it goes though not necessarily complete. The list of *goods* put forward but the rival theory is reached by exactly the same method—the only sound one in the circumstances—viz. that of direct reflection on what we really think. Loyalty to the facts is worth more than a symmetrical architectonic or a hastily reached simplicity. If further reflection discovers a perfect logical basis for this or for a better classification, so much the better.

It may, again, be objected that our theory that there are these various and often conflicting types of *prima facie* duty leaves us with no principle upon which to discern what is our actual duty in particular circumstances. But this objection is not one of which the rival theory is in a position to bring forward. For when we have to choose between the production of two heterogeneous goods, say knowledge and pleasure, the 'ideal utilitarian' theory can only fall back on an opinion, for which no logical basis can be offered, that one of the goods is the greater; and this is no better than a similar opinion that one of two duties is the more urgent. And again, when we consider the infinite variety of the effects of our actions in the way of pleasure, it must surely be admitted that the claim which *hedonism* sometimes makes, that it offers a readily applicable criterion of right conduct, is quite illusory.

I am unwilling, however, to content myself with an *argumentum ad hominem,* and I would contend that in principle there is no reason to anticipate that every act that is our duty is so for one and the same reason. Why should two sets of circumstances, or one set of circumstances, *not* possess different characteristics, any one of which makes a certain act our *prima facie* duty? When I ask what it is that makes me in certain cases sure that I have a *prima facie* duty to do so and so, I find that it lies in the fact that I have made a promise; when I ask the same question in another case, I find the answer lies in the fact that I have done a wrong. And if on reflection I find (as I think I do) that neither of these reasons is reducible to the other, I must not on any *a priori* ground assume that such a reduction is possible. . . .

It is necessary to say something by way of clearing up the relation between *prima facie* duties and the actual or absolute duty to do one particular act in particular circumstances. If, as almost all moralists except Kant are agreed, and as most plain men think, it is sometimes right to tell a lie or to break a promise, it must be maintained that there is a difference between *prima facie* duty and actual or absolute duty. When we think ourselves justified in breaking, and indeed morally obliged to break, a promise in order to relieve some one's distress, we do not for a moment cease to recognize a *prima facie* duty to keep our promise, and this leads us to feel, not indeed shame or repentance, but certainly compunction, for behaving as we do; we recognize, further, that it is our duty to make up somehow to the promise for the breaking of the promise. We have to distinguish from the characteristic of being our duty that of tending to be our duty. Any act that we do contains various elements in virtue of which it falls under various categories. In virtue of being the breaking of a promise, for instance, it tends to be wrong; in virtue of being an instance of relieving distress it tends to be right. Tendency to be one's duty may be called a partiresultant attribute, i.e. one which belongs to an act in virtue of some one component in its nature.

Being one's duty is a toti-resultant attribute, one which belongs to an act in virtue of its whole nature and of nothing less than this. . . .

Another instance of the same distinction may be found in the operation of natural laws. *Qua* subject to the force of gravitation towards some other body, each body tends to move in a particular direction with a particular velocity; but its actual movement depends on *all* the forces to which it is subject. It is only by recognising this distinction that we can preserve the absoluteness of laws of nature, and only by recognising a corresponding distinction that we can preserve the absoluteness of the general principles of morality. But an important difference between the two cases must be pointed out. When we say that in virtue of gravitation a body tends to move in a certain way, we are referring to a causal influence actually exercised on it by another body or other bodies. When we say that in virtue of being deliberately untrue a certain remark tends to be wrong, we are referring to no causal relation, to no relation that involves succession in time, but to such a relation as connects the various attributes of a mathematical figure. And if the word 'tendency' is thought to suggest too much a causal relation, it is better to talk of certain types of act as being *prima facie* right or wrong (or of different persons as having different and possibly conflicting claims upon us), than of their tending to be right or wrong.

Something should be said of the relation between our apprehension of the *prima facie* rightness of certain types of act and our mental attitude towards particular acts. It is proper to use the word 'apprehension' in the former case and not in the latter. That an act, *qua* fulfilling a promise, or *qua* effecting a just distribution of good, or *qua* returning services rendered, or *qua* promoting the good of others, or *qua* promoting the virtue or insight of the agent, is *prima facie* right, is self-evident; not in the sense that it is evident from the beginning of our lives, or as soon as we attend to the proposition for the first time, but in the sense that when we have reached sufficient mental maturity and have given sufficient attention to the proposition it is evident without any need of proof, or of evidence beyond itself. It is self-evident just as a mathematical axiom, or the validity of a form of inference, is evident. The moral order expressed in these propositions is just as much part of the fundamental nature of the universe (and, we may add, of any possible universe in which there were moral agents at all) as is the spatial or numerical structure expressed in the axioms of geometry or arithmetic. In our confidence that these propositions are true there is involved the same trust in our reason that is involved in our confidence in mathematics; and we should have no justification for trusting it in the latter sphere and distrusting it in the former. In both cases we are dealing with propositions that cannot be proved, but that just as certainly need no proof. . . .

Our judgements about our actual duty in concrete situations have none of the certainty that attaches to our recognition of the general principles of duty. A statement is certain, i.e., is an expression of knowledge, only in one or other of two cases: when it is either self-evident, or a valid conclusion from self-evident premises. And our judgements about our particular duties have neither of these characters. (1) They are not self-evident. Where a possible act is seen to have two characteristics, in virtue of one of which it is *prima facie* right, and in virtue of the other *prima facie* wrong, we are (I think) well aware that we are not certain whether we ought or ought not to do it; that whether we do it or not, we are taking a moral risk. We come in the long run, after consideration, to think one duty more pressing than the other, but we do not feel certain that it is so. And though we do not always recognize that a possible act has two such characteristics, and though there *may* be cases in which it has not, we are never certain that any particular possible act has not, and therefore never certain that it is right, nor certain that it is wrong. For, to go no further in the analysis, it is enough to point out that any particular act will in all probability in the course of time contribute to the bringing about of good or evil for many human beings, and thus have a *prima facie* rightness or wrongness of which we know nothing. (2) Again, our judgements about our particular duties are not logical conclusions from self-evident premises. The only possible premises would be the general principles stating their *prima facie* rightness or wrongness *qua* having the different characteristics they do have; and even if we could (as we cannot) apprehend the extent to which an act will tend on the one hand, for example, to bring about advantages for our benefac-

tors, and on the other hand to bring about disadvantages for fellow men who are not our benefactors, there is no principle by which we can draw the conclusion that it is on the whole right or on the whole wrong. In this respect the judgement as to the rightness of a particular act is just like the judgement as to the beauty of a particular natural object or work of art. A poem is, for instance, in respect of certain qualities beautiful and in respect of certain others not beautiful; and our judgement as to the degree of beauty it possesses on the whole is never reached by logical reasoning from the apprehension of its particular beauties or particular defects. Both in this and in the moral case we have more or less probable opinions which are not logically justified conclusions from the general principles that are recognized as self-evident.

There is therefore much truth in the description of the right act as a fortunate act. If we cannot be certain that it is right, it is our good fortune if the act we do is the right act. This consideration does not, however, make the doing of our duty a mere matter of chance. There is a parallel here between the doing of duty and the doing of what will be to our personal advantage. We never *know* what act will in the long run be to our advantage. Yet it is certain that we are more likely in general to secure our advantage if we estimate to the best of our ability the probable tendencies of our actions in this respect, than if we act on caprice. And similarly we are more likely to do our duty if we reflect to the best of our ability on the *prima facie* rightness or wrongness of various possible acts in virtue of the characteristics we perceive them to have, than if we act without reflection. With this greater likelihood we must be content.

Many people would be inclined to say that the right act for me is not that whose general nature I have been describing, viz. that which if I were omniscient I should see to be my duty, but that which on all the evidence available to me I should think to be my duty. But suppose that from the state of partial knowledge in which I think act *A* to be my duty, I could pass to a state of perfect knowledge in which I saw act *B* to be my duty, should I not say 'act *B* was the right act for me to do'? I should no doubt add 'though I am not to be blamed for doing act *A*.' But in adding this, am I not passing from the question 'what is right' to the question 'what is morally good'?

At the same time I am not making the *full* passage from the one notion to the other, for in order that the act should be morally good, or an act I am not to be blamed for doing, it must not merely be the act which it is reasonable for me to think my duty; it must also be done for that reason, or from some other morally good motive. Thus the conception of the right act as the act which it is reasonable for me to think my duty is an unsatisfactory compromise between the true notion of the right act and the notion of the morally good action.

The general principles of duty are obviously not self-evident from the beginning of our lives. How do they come to be so? The answer is, that they come to be self-evident to us just as mathematical axioms do. We find by experience that this couple of matches and that couple make four matches, that this couple of balls on a wire and that couple make four balls; and by reflection on these and similar discoveries we come to see that it is of the nature of two and two to make four. In a precisely similar way, we see the *prima facie* rightness of an act which would be the fulfillment of a particular promise, and of another which would be the fulfillment of another promise, and when we have reached sufficient maturity to think in general terms, we apprehend *prima facie* rightness to belong to the nature of any fulfillment of promise. What comes first in time is the apprehension of the self-evident *prima facie* rightness of an individual act of a particular type. From this we come by reflection to apprehend the self-evident general principle of *prima facie* duty. From this, too, perhaps along with the apprehension of the self-evident *prima facie* rightness of the same act in virtue of its having another characteristic as well, and perhaps in spite of the apprehension of its *prima facie* wrongness in virtue of its having some third characteristic, we come to believe something not self-evident at all, but an object of probable opinion, viz. that this particular act is (not *prima facie* but) actually right. . . .

Supposing it to be agreed, as I think on reflection it must, that no one *means* by 'right' just 'productive of the best possible consequences,' or 'optimific,' the attributes 'right' and 'optimific' might stand in either of two kinds of relation to each other. (1) They might be so related that we could apprehend *a priori*, either immediately or deductively, that any act that is optimific is right and any act that is

right is optimific, as we can apprehend that any triangle that is equilateral is equiangular and *vice versa*. Professor Moore's view is, I think, that the coextensiveness of 'right' and 'optimific' is apprehended immediately. He rejects the possibility of any proof of it. Or (2) the two attributes might be such that the question whether they are invariably connected had to be answered by means of an inductive inquiry. Now at first sight it might seem as if the constant connexion of the two attributes could be immediately apprehended. It might seem absurd to suggest that it could be right for any one to do an act which would produce consequences less good than those which would be produced by some other act in his power. Yet a little thought will convince us that this is not absurd. The type of case in which it is easiest to see that this is so is, perhaps, that if which one has made a promise. In such a case we all think that *prima facie* it is our duty to fulfil the promise irrespective of the precise goodness of the total consequences. And though we do not think it is necessarily our actual or absolute duty to do so, we are far from thinking that any, even the slightest, gain in the value of the total consequences will necessarily justify us in doing something else instead. Suppose, to simplify the case by abstraction, that the fulfillment of a promise to A would produce 1,000 units of good[3] for him, but that by doing some other act I could produce 1,001 units of good for B, to whom I have made no promise, the other consequences of the two acts being of equal value; should we really think it self-evident that it was our duty to do the second act and not the first? I think not. We should, I fancy, hold that only a much greater disparity of value between the total consequences would justify us in failing to discharge our *prima facie* duty to A. After all, a promise is a promise, and is not to be treated so lightly as the theory we are examining would imply. What, exactly, a promise is, is not so easy to determine, but we are surely agreed that it constitutes a serious moral limitation to our freedom of action. To produce the 1,001 units of good for B rather than fulfil our promise to A would be to take, not perhaps our duty as philanthropists too seriously, but certainly our duty as makers of promises too lightly. . . .

Such instances—and they might easily be added to—make it clear that there is no self-evident connexion between the attributes 'right' and 'opti-mific.' The theory we are examining has a certain attractiveness when applied to our decision that a particular act is our duty (though I have tried to show that it does not agree with our actual moral judgements even here). But it is not even plausible when applied to our recognition of *prima facie* duty. For if it were self-evident that the right coincides with the optimific, it should be self-evident that what is *prima facie* right is *prima facie* optimific. But whereas we are certain that keeping a promise is *prima facie* right, we are not certain that it is *prima facie* optimific (though we are perhaps certain that it is *prima facie* bonific). Our certainty that it is *prima facie* right depends not on its consequences but on its being the fulfillment of a promise. The theory we are examining involves too much difference between the evident ground of our conviction about *prima facie* duty and the alleged ground of our conviction about actual duty. . . .

I conclude that the attributes 'right' and 'optimific' are not identical, and that we do not know either by intuition, by deduction, or by induction that they coincide in their application, still less that the latter is the foundation of the former. It must be added, however, that if we are ever under no special obligation such as that of fidelity to a promisee or of gratitude to a benefactor, we ought to do what will produce most good; and that even when we are under a special obligation the tendency of acts to promote general good is one of the main factors in determining whether they are right.

In what has preceded, a good deal of use has been made of 'what we really think' about moral questions; a certain theory has been rejected because it does not agree with what we really think. It might be said that this is in principle wrong; that we should not be content to expound what our present moral consciousness tells us but should aim at a criticism of our existing moral consciousness in the light of theory. Now I do not doubt that the moral consciousness of men has in detail undergone a good deal of modification as regards the things we think right, at the hands of moral theory. But if we are told, for instance, that we should give up our view that there is a special obligatoriness attaching to the keeping of promises because it is self-evident that the only duty is to produce as much good as possible, we have to ask ourselves whether

we really, when we reflect, *are* convinced that this is self-evident, and whether we really *can* get rid of our view that promise-keeping has a bindingness independent of productiveness of maximum good. In my own experience I find that I cannot, in spite of a very genuine attempt to do so; and I venture to think that most people will find the same, and that just because they cannot lose the sense of special obligation, they cannot accept as self-evident, or even as true, the theory which would require them to do so. In fact it seems, on reflection, self-evident that a promise, simply as such, is something that *prima facie* ought to be kept, and it does *not*, on reflection, seem self-evident that production of maximum good is the only thing that makes an act obligatory. And to ask us to give up at the bidding of a theory our actual apprehension of what is right and what is wrong seems like asking people to repudiate their actual experience of beauty, at the bidding of a theory which says 'only that which satisfies such and such conditions can be beautiful.' If what I have called our actual apprehension is (as I would maintain that it is) truly an apprehension, i.e. an instance of knowledge, the request is nothing less than absurd.

I would maintain, in fact, that what we are apt to describe as 'what we think' about moral questions contains a considerable amount that we do not think but know, and that this forms the standard by reference to which the truth of any moral theory has to be tested, instead of having itself to be tested by reference to any theory. I hope that I have in what precedes indicated what in my view these elements of knowledge are that are involved in our ordinary moral consciousness.

It would be a mistake to found a natural science on 'what we really think,' i.e. on what reasonably thoughtful and well-educated people think about the subjects of the science before they have studied them scientifically. For such opinions are interpretations, and often misinterpretations, of sense-experience; and the man of science must appeal from these to sense-experience itself, which furnishes his real data. In ethics no such appeal is possible. We have no more direct way of access to the facts about rightness and goodness and about what things are right or good than by thinking about them; the moral convictions of thoughtful and well-educated people are the data of ethics just as sense-perceptions are the data of a natural science. Just as some of the latter have to be rejected as illusory, so have some of the former; but as the latter are rejected only when they are in conflict with other more accurate sense-perceptions, the former are rejected only when they are in conflict with other convictions which stand better the test of reflection. The existing body of moral convictions of the best people is the cumulative product of the moral reflection of many generations, which has developed an extremely delicate power of appreciation of moral distinctions; and this the theorist cannot afford to treat with anything other than the greatest respect. The verdicts of the moral consciousness of the best people are the foundation on which he must build; though he must first compare them with one another and eliminate any contradictions they may contain.

Notes

1. Some will think it, apart from other considerations, a sufficient refutation of this view to point out that I also stand in that relation to myself, so that for this view the distinction of oneself from others is morally insignificant.

2. I should make it plain at this stage that I am *assuming* the correctness of some of our main convictions as to *prima facie* duties, or, more strictly, am claiming that we *know* them to be true. To me it seems as self-evident as anything could be, that to make a promise, for instance, is to create a moral claim on us in someone else. Many readers will perhaps say that they do *not* know this to be true. If so, I certainly cannot prove it to them; I can only ask them to reflect again, in the hope that they will ultimately agree that they also know it to be true. The main moral convictions of the plain man seem to me to be, not opinions which it is for philosophy to prove or disprove, but knowledge from the start; and in my own case I seem to find little difficulty in distinguishing these essential convictions from other moral convictions which I also have, which are merely fallible opinions based on an imperfect study of the working for good or evil of certain institutions or types of action.

3. I am assuming that good is objectively quantitative, but not that we can accurately assign an exact quantitative measure to it. Since it is of a definite amount, we can make the *supposition* that its amount is so-and-so, though we cannot with any confidence *assert* that it is.

Life or Death of the Global Village

MARIE-LOUISE FRIQUEGNON

Marie Friquegnon (1943–) teaches philosophy at the William Paterson University of New Jersey. For many years she has been an active volunteer and supporter of several shelters for the homeless and needy in New York City.

The world is shrinking rapidly. In ancient times people's access to other nations was limited to where they could walk or ride on animals. It took ages for news to arrive from far-off places. Now we can e-mail anywhere in seconds, and we have access to one another on the Worldwide Web. News comes every day on the television, so we can grieve for a dying Albanian child as much as for a dying child on our street.

Goods from other countries flood our markets. We eat Chinese food one day, Indian the next. We dream of a rainbow world in which children from all nations will grow up peacefully and with tolerance for one another.

But there is a fly in the ointment—human greed. With the desire to make a quick buck or yen comes a disregard for the needs of our fellow human beings.

Big companies want to sell their fancy equipment worldwide, so they cajole, advertise, and bribe officials. Soon local companies spring up selling these things to their own people. The smartest and toughest master the art of making money and become more and more alienated from the poor, whom they either deceive—tempting them with techno toys they cannot afford—or exploit as workers in factories, or both. Everywhere the rich get richer, and the poor get poorer. The poor also multiply more rapidly, straining their increasingly diminutive resources.

So we seem to need global planning, but whose plans should prevail? Those of the international banks and large corporations or those of the environmentally concerned intelligensia? Or is all global planning objectionable as a violation of the right to cultural diversity?

One serious objection to any global planning lies in the conflicting issues of different groups. For example, the herdsmen of Nepal are threatened by the snow leopards, which eat their goats. These beautiful leopards are an endangered species, and the herdsmen are not allowed to shoot them. If the world wants the leopards, it is only reasonable for someone to pay the herdsmen for the loss of their goats, but who is to take responsibility? A similar problem was front-page news in the *New York Times*. An article by James C. McKinley Jr. paints a picture of the constant struggle between farmers and wildlife for survival in Kenya.[1] Kenya's wildlife has declined dramatically during the last twenty years. And the population has soared from 5 million in 1946 when the Nairobi National Park was established to 30 million at the present time. "Only a fifth of the country receives enough rainfall to raise cash crops" (p. 10). People are trampled by elephants and injured while chasing buffaloes from their land. Domestic animals are eaten by lions. In Taita, there is a great deal of dispersal (land animals use during wet seasons) and migratory land needed by the wildlife. Starving families, pressed for land, have moved there even though there is a constant threat of drought. "Impoverished people, many facing extreme hunger, because they are trying to farm in arid regions not suitable for crops, have poached thousands of animals for food."

The farmers are winning the battle against the animals. "Wild lands in Kenya have been disappearing at the rate of two percent a year." In Tsavo alone, "fifty-eight percent of the animal population of Tsavo, some 106,600 individuals, vanished between 1973 and 1993, said Mohammed Dhidha, the regional biodiversity coordinator in Tsavo" (p. 10).

What is to be done? Is all this beautiful wildlife to be lost to the world forever? Officials in Kenya are considering two different procedures: "One camp, led by the current director of the Kenya Wildlife Service, David Western, wants to find ways to make wildlife profitable for local people, and give them a reason to protect the animals. Another, led by the former head of the wildlife service, Richard Leakey, argues that Kenya should instead fence off wild lands, more strictly enforce anti-poaching laws, in essence, give up on trying to stop the decline of wildlife elsewhere" (p. 10).

The first option is more difficult, because it is not clear how an adequate now of tourism could be maintained so that it would be possible for farmers, for example, to turn their farms into game preserves. And because of endemic corruption it is difficult to ensure that the resulting income from tourism would find its way into the hands of the poorest of the farmers. The second option would penalize those who rely on the lands needed by the animals.

Should we just insist that people are more important than animals, and let the farmers take over the lands? Foreign visitors would have to relinquish their enjoyment of beautiful wildlife. But even this would not help very much. The land is not good for farming anyway, and the growing population is sure to produce famine eventually. Further, tourism is necessary for the prosperity of many people. It is one of the main sources of income in the Third World. Clearly, a way must be found to protect the animals for future generations (of us as well as them). But a way must also be found to ensure that some of the income derived from tourism will be used to establish a decent standard of living for everyone.

It should be clear from these examples just how complex is the issue of global planning. Even with the best of intentions it is easy to go astray. A classic case of how misguided efforts can harm rather than help was a famine in Chad, caused at least in part by the gift of extra goats to the poor. The goats ate too much of the vegetation and produced a drought.

Some thinkers have argued that where countries are on the brink of starvation, or menaced by plague, the rational strategy is to let the people die. Then they will not be a drain on the resources of the rest of the world, and the resulting loss of population will be of benefit not only to present, but also to future generations. Garret Hardin, in *Psychology Today*[2] has argued that this is precisely what should be done. He uses the analogy of a lifeboat that can hold about sixty people and is almost full. Hundreds of people are swimming outside, and they cannot all be taken on board, or the boat will be swamped and all will drown. So similarly, if the rich nations with slow or zero population growth take on the task of supplying the poor nations with food and medicine, then the problem will worsen, and more people will starve in the future:

> We must recognize the limited capacity of any lifeboat. For example, a nation's land has a limited capacity to support a population and as the current energy crisis has shown us, in some ways we have already exceeded the carrying capacity of our land. . . . Suppose we decide to preserve our small safety factor and admit no more to the lifeboat. One's survival is then possible, although we shall have to be constantly on guard against boarding parties. (p. 297)

So we should harden our hearts (no pun intended) and let the poor perish.

In contrast, Peter Singer has argued in *Philosophy and Public Affairs*[3] that we have a moral duty to relieve suffering when it will not grievously harm us, and that the affluent nations can relieve a great deal of suffering by sacrificing their luxurious way of life. In other words, we are not in a lifeboat, but a seaworthy ship, and there is room for all. Many environmentalists have argued that if we stopped using land for grazing animals intended for meat, we could easily raise sufficient food by using these lands for crops. If we couple this with a vigorous birth control educational program combined with incentives for small families, we may be able to save everyone.

But must there be global planning for the sake of future generations? Ruth Macklin believes that we cannot have obligations toward nonexistent persons.[4] In contrast, Joel Feinberg, although conceding that "merely possible" people cannot be said to have the right to be brought into existence (so that species suicide, undesirable though it may be, would not violate anybody's rights) nevertheless argues that pollution and depletion violate what he calls the "contingent rights" of future generations; these are rights that they *will* have if and when they come into existence, but will not have if they don't come into existence. Contingent rights of future people demand as much respect as the actual rights of existing people, although we may disagree about just which contingent rights should be acknowledged.[5]

Feinberg argues that the identity problem (the fact that we do not know the identity of future people) need not prevent us from acknowledging and respecting their contingent rights, because we can easily recognize "the fact of interest ownership" even when we cannot identify the owners of these interests. And where there are interests, perhaps there are the rights to have these interests respected, regardless of who the owners of these interests happen to be.

If Feinberg is correct, we not only have to balance ecological considerations with the needs of groups of native people to prosper and survive but also the needs of those existing now against those of generations yet to come. The latter is not quite so thorny a problem, because surely uncertainty about the future gives us reason to favor the needs of existing persons. Future generations may find ways to solve their problems. For example, if we use up all the copper needed for medical purposes, they may invent a new substance that is even better. On the other hand, we cannot be sure they will be able to find new solutions, so we should plan for their needs when it is not too devastating for the present population.

The first problem is harder to resolve. What is usually involved is not a simple standoff between the majority and the minority, but the rich versus the poor of the developing nations. Philosophically, we need a generally acceptable criterion of social justice, which is hard to come by, but common decency demands, as Peter Singer said, that we relieve the suffering of others if in so doing we do no serious harm to ourselves or those close to us. This seems minimal, but if actually put in practice, it could revolutionize society. For we would have to give up a lot of luxuries, minimize waste, and find ways of dealing more gently with the resources of the planet.

The issue of global planning versus cultural diversity was dramatized during President Clinton's visit to China when he stated that respect for human rights was not a cultural oddity of Western nations but rather a universal human value. Inspiring as this remark may be, we may ask if it is indeed true, or if it is not now true, but ought to be. There is also the problem of which human rights should be respected. The Chinese argue that their huge population has a right to be fed, and if everyone were allowed to go his or her own way, masses of people might starve. Or take another example: If the United States were being held hostage by terrorists with nuclear bombs, the suspension of civil liberties might become a necessity in the effort to locate and stop them.

In some societies, some people are accorded no rights at all. Some nations even continue to practice slavery. One of the most dramatic examples of the absence of rights is the case of the women, about 130 million in Africa alone, that are the victims of female genital mutilation, the practice of removing all or part of a woman's clitoris. Sometimes it involves removing the labia and sewing the vagina partly closed. The surgery is usually done without any anesthesia and with crude instruments such as a piece of glass, in unsanitary conditions. The result is typically chronic infection, great pain during sexual intercourse (the woman's vagina is cut open at marriage), loss of sexual pleasure, and sometimes death. The operation is usually performed on children or young girls. Sometimes it is voluntary, but often it is not. It is not demanded by any religion, and is performed by people of tribal religious faiths, as well as Muslims and a small number of Christians and Jews. The purpose is to keep women pure before marriage and faithful to their husbands after marriage.

To the West this practice seems unbelievably cruel. In any case there is doubt about whether it can ever be said to be voluntary. Is a social situation in which a woman is brainwashed from childhood, in which she is told she is "no good" unless circumcised, a form of coercion? But then are we not all more or less coerced into accepting our values by societal forces?

On reflection, however, it seems that even if a practice such as this violated a human right, ending it by force directed at another nation might do more

harm than good. The Russians, when they were in power in Afghanistan, tried to force women to go to public meetings against their will. The country is still paying the price of the fundamentalist reaction against such cultural coercion.

Societies themselves, however, can sometimes become convinced that a particular custom should be ended. For example, in China until the twentieth century it was customary for upper-class women to have their toes and arches broken and their feet bound when they were about six years old. This was terribly painful, made walking difficult, and sometimes resulted in death from gangrene. The custom seems to have been ended by a group of upper-class men who had traveled abroad and realized that this cruel tradition did not exist elsewhere. Because parents continued the practice because they thought their daughters would be otherwise unmarriageable, this group of men swore an oath that they would not let their sons marry anyone with bound feet. And the custom came to an end. Because the issue of marriageability is also the cause of female circumcision in Africa, a similar tactic might work. For a dramatic example closer to home, South Africa, with a little persuasion from other Western nations, finally put an end to apartheid.

Another solution is for an educated and enlightened leadership within a country to intervene. For example, in Egypt, religious leaders, realizing that female circumcision was not prescribed by the Koran and that it was harmful to women's health, banned the practice in that nation. In our own country, the northern intelligensia, led by Robert Kennedy, Lyndon Johnson, and the Warren Supreme Court, forcibly ended legal racial segregation. The future looks brighter.

It is only natural that people tenaciously resist radical cultural change. When religious groups believe that it is wrong to seek medical attention for their ill children and instead rely on God, does the state have the right to coerce them into compliance? To take cultural diversity to the extreme, consider a Star Trek episode, in which a child from another planet falls ill on Deep Space Nine. The parents refuse to seek medical help on the grounds that it is contrary to their religion. When Doctor Bashir forcibly intervenes and cures the child, the parents kill the child, saying that now it is the only way to save his soul. The leadership of Deep Space Nine refuse to prosecute the parents, who loved their child deeply.

In the Star Trek example, the alien family is so different from us that there is little hope of convincing them that their attitude toward surgical intervention is misguided. But some have argued convincingly[6,7] that this is not the case with human beings, however culturally diverse they seem to be. Over time and with sufficient dialog, compromises will be reached. But only in the most extreme cases, such as genocide, should force be used. It may be better to tolerate a custom that meets with full social approval within a society than to try to force its members to conform. An example is the condoning of the practice of female genital mutilation by virtually everyone in the northern Sudan.[8] But it is also important to provide an available exit for those within the society that may want to rebel against cruel practices such as this. So the granting of political asylum to those in rebellion against inhumane customs is of utmost necessity.

This does not mean however that we cannot judge this practice to be wrong. The respect for other cultures demanded by soi-disant multiculturalists may seem to undermine the Enlightenment doctrine of universal human rights by forbidding members of one culture to condemn practices of another culture that violate a human right such as the right not to be mutilated. But, as Carol Gould effectively argues, this appearance is illusory.[9] For if the defender of cultural diversity appeals to the principle of tolerance, which is, after all, a universal human right, it would be self-contradictory to argue for the toleration of intolerance, which violates the very right being appealed to. Yet only if the defender of cultural diversity appeals to the universal human right to tolerance can he or she expect a sympathetic hearing.

Yael Tasmir has argued in defense of female genital mutilation that it is analogous to various forms of piercing and mutilation practiced around the world.[10] Tamir also argues that it is analogous to the wearing of very constrictive corsets in the last century. Nevertheless, this practice, like the Renaissance practice of castrating small boys, seems especially and unacceptably cruel.

But who is to be the protector of universal rights and values? Should it be the free market, enforced by politicians and economists in the pay of international banks and corporations? Should market values always prevail, or should local interests be protected?

Jeremy Rifkin in *The End of Work*[11] argues that developing technology will eventually deprive most people of their jobs as unnecessary and obsolete.

> Now, for the first time, human labor is being systematically eliminated from the production process. Within less than a century, "mass" work in the market sector is likely to be phased out in virtually all the industrialized nations of the world. A new generation of sophisticated information and communications technologies is being hurried into a wide variety of work situations. Intelligent machines are replacing human beings in countless tasks, forcing millions of blue and white collar workers into unemployment lines, or, worse still, bread lines. (p. 3)

Huge farms will produce crops at lower costs and with greater efficiency and small farmers will be put out of business. Martha Crouch describes a biotechnical revolution led by multinational corporations such as Monsanto, which are producing "terminator seeds" that result in crops that kill the next generation of seed. So farmers will be forced to buy new seeds every year, which they often cannot afford.[12]

According to Rifkin,

> Dr. Vandana Shiva, Director of the Research Foundation for Science, Technology and National Resource Policy, in India, worries that in her own country, upwards of 95 percent of the farm population could be displaced in the coming century by the biotechnology revolution in agriculture. If that were to happen, warns Shiva, "We will have Yugoslavia multiplied a thousand times" with separatist movements, open warfare, and the fragmentation of the Indian subcontinent. The only viable alternative to mass social upheaval and the potential collapse of the Indian State, argues Shiva, is the building up of a new "freedom movement" rooted in land reform and the practice of ecologically sound sustainable agriculture.[13]

Rifkin criticizes the defenders of the new technology who argue (1) that it will "open up more job opportunities than it forecloses" and (2) "that dramatic increases in productivity will be matched by elevated levels of consumer demand and the opening of new global markets to absorb the flood of new goods and services that will become available."[14] From where are the new jobs going to come? "In a world where sophisticated information and communication technologies will be able to replace more and more of the global workforce, it is unlikely that more than a fortunate few will be retrained for the relatively scarce high-tech scientific, professional, and managerial jobs made available in the emerging knowledge sector." Rifkin cites the case of Bangalore as an example of this growing disparity between the rich and poor in India. Bangalore, a former summer resort for British civil servants, is now a high-tech mecca for global computer and electronic firms. But it is, according to historian Paul Kennedy, an island of prosperity in a sea of poverty.[15] Kennedy points out that the developing world is expected to add more than 700 million to its labor force by the year 2010. Imagine the amount of unrest in the world if masses of unemployed people cannot be housed or fed.

A worst case scenario is the world depicted in the film *Soylent Green,* which may turn out to be prophetic. The time is the early twenty-first century. The political structure of the United States remains the same, although police activity is greatly expanded. There are a few rich and powerful people who live in apartment complexes guarded like fortresses. Even there, elevators, air conditioners, and so on are always breaking down and are difficult to repair, because the companies that made them are constantly going out of business. The drama takes place in New York City whose population has multiplied tenfold. Most are unemployed, live in the street or in stairwells, and are fed and clothed by the government. There is no winter, because of the greenhouse effect. It is always stifling hot, and the pollution makes it hard to breathe. The last green space is a patch no bigger than a room with some plants in it. Everyone is fed on high protein bread and crackers, and this supply is decreasing because the soil is so depleted nothing will grow. The seas are full of algae, which can be used as food for a while, but the water is polluted and fast disappearing. Even the rich must eat these crackers, although "real" food is available on the black market.

Many people are killed by the police during riots, and many others choose to opt out of the system by going to suicide parlors where they are allowed one last look on film of a natural paradise that has been lost forever. The film's dirty little secret, if I may be forgiven for giving it away, is that all these dead people are being made into the highly prized crackers called soylent green. This is fast becoming the world's only food supply and is controlled as is most of the world's food by one multinational corporation.

How are we to escape this fate? As I write this today, the *New York Times* tells me that Alaska is melting.[16] We know the desert is expanding in Africa. This July 1998 has been the hottest in history, and the weather patterns are becoming more and more bizarre, producing problems around the world. Countries like China are burning coal for fuel, which is highly polluting. They argue that it is the only way to produce cheap goods for export and thus to make enough money to support their vast population. But it should be obvious that they breathe the same air as everyone else, so if the planet is trashed, the Chinese will suffer too.

Experts are more and more in agreement about the dangers of global warming to our supply of food and air, so we are really no longer discussing the fate of distant unborn generations but that of our children and grandchildren. So what is to be done? Brute force cannot work, because coercion creates even more problems for people and the environment. Education may be our only hope. People can sometimes be convinced to do what is in their long-term interest or in that of their children.

In his thoughtful book *Earth in the Balance,* Vice-President Al Gore suggests how population could be controlled without force.[17] (1) It has been proved that there is an inverse ratio between a woman's level of literacy and the number of children she has. So raising the educational level of women is crucial. (2) Gore quotes the African leader Julius Nyere: "The most powerful contraceptive is the confidence by parents that their children will survive." So reducing the infant mortality rate will help reduce population growth. (3) "Ensure that birth control devices and techniques are made ubiquitously available along with culturally appropriate instructions."[18] Stable decent jobs help too, reassuring parents that they will not need to depend for survival on the earning power of adolescent and pre-adolescent children.

Not everyone, however, would agree. Some, citing a Hobbesian view of human nature, argue that people are so selfish that they will continue to work only for their own interests even at the cost of the death and impoverishment of the human race. In Robert Heilbroner's words:

> When men can generally acquiesce in, even relish, the destruction of their living contemporaries, when they can regard with indifference or irritation the fate of those who live in slums, rot in prison, or starve in lands that have meaning only insofar as they are vacation resorts, why should they be willing to take the painful actions needed to prevent the destruction of future generations whose faces they will never live to see? Worse yet, will they not curse those future generations whose claims to life can be honored only by sacrificing present enjoyments, and will they not, if it comes to a choice, condemn them to nonexistence by choosing the present over the future?[19]

Those who adhere to this view, sometimes called "doomsday theorists," usually insist that the only hope for survival lies in the formation of strong autocratic governments that can enforce necessary social policies such as population control. This, they say, is the only way to avoid class conflict, as scarcity pits the rich against the poor. Probably such an autocratic order would have to be worldwide. Otherwise, as Craig A. Rimmerman suggests, poor nations may blackmail the rich for food by threatening nuclear war.[20] However, one might reply that in such desperate times there is nothing to prevent the elite leaders of such a society from taking special privileges for themselves and their families, leaving the rest of society to perish.

C. B. Macpherson and Jeremy Rifkin take a different approach. They are more hopeful about human nature. Macpherson believes that awareness of environmental problems may inspire people to voluntarily make the societal changes needed worldwide and that this will begin at the grassroots level.[21] Rifkin places his bets on what he calls the "third sector," a network of volunteer organizations everywhere in the world that are funded by local governments and supported by taxing the rich. This would put people to work worldwide in welfare, health, housing, the arts, and education on the grassroots level without government control. It would place them outside of the gross national product, which could be left to operate much as it does now—utilizing new technologies useful to humanity but very much limited in terms of how much money entrepreneurs are allowed to make and limited in their activities by considerations of ecology and the general well-being of humanity.[22] Both Macpherson and Rifkin are willing to take their chances with a democratic system that relies on the basic rationality and good will of people to act in the best interests of everyone alike.

Conservative theorists like Ronald Bailey share this optimism, and fault the doomsday writers for encouraging people to see the situation as hopeless. They believe that progress in technology will solve our food and pollution problems and that, as it always has in the past, humanity will find a way out of its difficulties.[23] Bailey argues, "If we wish to pursue real 'intergenerational equity,' we have a duty to expand the world's knowledge base and the economy for our descendants instead of ossifying into some form of feudal stasis as advised by radical environmentalists." Even population growth is not a problem as he sees it. He points out that The Netherlands with a ratio of 931 persons per square mile is doing very well, whereas Brazil, with 47 per square mile, is in trouble. But Bailey does not factor into these statistics what would happen if the population of the Netherlands doubled.

We have considered three proposals to the various problems engendered by the economic, political, and cultural processes tending toward integrating the entire world into one global village: (1) The laissez-faire view, that the free market, unencumbered by government controls and meddling idealists, will eventually solve its own problems with the help of profit-motivated technological advances. (We might call this the homeopathic theory of economic therapy.) (2) The father-knows-best view, that strong governments must control the economic excesses of big business and overcome the harmful limitations imposed by local customs. (Shall we call this type of proposed therapy "allopathic"?) There are, of course, more extreme and more moderate modes of governmental control proposed, ranging from Heilbroner's somber vision of Big Brother tyranny, to C. B. Macpherson's wistful hope for a grassroots insistence on participatory democracy together with semi-socialist government controls protecting the environment, maintaining cultural diversity, and curbing the excesses of big business and banks. Macpherson says that capitalistic inequality has within itself the seeds of its own demise:

> Capitalism reproduces inequality and consumer consciousness, and must do so to go on operating. But its increasing ability to produce goods and leisure has as its obverse its increasing need to spread them more widely. If people can't buy goods, no profit can be made by producing them. . . . [Thus] the system will either have to spread real goods more widely which will reduce social inequality; or it will break down, and so be unable to reproduce inequality and consumer consciousness.[24]

(3) He urges support for and reliance on nongovernmental and not-for-profit organizations that spread the gospel of population control, small local industry, respect for cultural differences, and reduction of gross inequalities, hoping to achieve through education what people will not allow to be imposed on them by force.

Much can be, and has already been, said in favor of each of these three viewpoints, and we have already considered the defects in each pointed out by proponents of the other views. I will not presume to decide among them except to suggest that the most attractive features of each might be combined in a way that, to some extent at least, avoids their harmful side effects. A reasonably free world market is needed to ensure efficient matching of supply and demand and to motivate continued technological progress. But some central government planning independent of the profit motive is surely needed to prevent rampant exploitation of cheap labor, bullying of local industries by multinational corporations, and the tyranny over small nations in need of credit exercised by financial organizations like the IMF, the World Bank, and the World Trade Organization. The problem here is how to ensure that governments will properly restrain multinational corporations and the banks when their officials depend on campaign contributions from the very foxes they ought to keep out of the chicken coop. As Heilbroner points out in his new book, *Visions of the Future,*

> Tomorrow may find ways of steering science-driven technology away from immediately threatening applications in capitalist societies, and may discover the means of asserting safeguards and bringing about international interventions, if the duress is sufficiently great. But halting its broad incursion into social life seems inconceivable as long as capitalism exists. With its transient gains and permanent losses, commodification is essential for a system that must expand to survive.[25]

In this new book, Heilbroner is slightly more hopeful. He argues that the only way in which our survival is at all imaginable is if we (1) have a secure terrestrial base for life. The earth must be lovingly maintained and population stabilized. [This] entails the absence of any socio-economic order, whether capitalist or other, whose continuance depends on ceaseless accumulation. (2) We must find ways of preserving the human community as a whole against its warlike proclivities. "The distant future must be a time when the respect for 'human nature' is given the cultural and educational centrality it demands."[26] The solution to this vexing problem might well reside in the grassroots movements and not-for-profit organizations looked to by Macpherson, Rifkin, and other moderately reform-minded guardians of the future of mankind. The rise of the Green Party in western Europe and its spread to the United States, where it seems to be growing in popularity, may portend a brighter future than that prophesied by "doomsday" futurologists like Heilbroner. At least one is entitled to hope, and more than that, to campaign and to vote.

Notes

1. James C. McKinley Jr., *New York Times* (August 2, 1998), pp. 1, 10.
2. Garret Hardin, "Lifeboat Ethics: The Case Against Helping the Poor," *Psychology Today*. Reprinted in R. Abelson and M. L. Friquegnon, *Ethics for Modern Life*, 5th ed. (New York: St. Martin's Press, 1995), pp. 296–304.

3. Peter Singer, "Famine, Affluence, and Morality," *Philosophy and Public Affairs.* Reprinted in *Ethics for Modern Life,* op. cit., pp. 285–295.

4. Ruth Macklin, "Can Future Generations Correctly Be Said to Have Rights?" In *Responsibilities to Unborn Generations: Environmental Ethics,* edited by Ernest Partridge (Buffalo, NY: Prometheus Books, 1981).

5. Joel Feinberg, "The Rights of Animals and Unborn Generations." In *Philosophy and Environmental Crisis,* edited by William Blackstone (Univ. of Georgia Press, 1974), p. 244.

6. Amy Gutmann, "The Challenge of Multiculturalism in Ethics," *Philosophy and Public Affairs* vol. 22, no. 3 (Summer 1993) Princeton Univ. Press.

7. Joseph Raz, *Ethics in the Public Domain* (Oxford: Clarendon Press, 1994).

8. Janice Brody, "Womb as Oasis: The Symbolic Context of Pharonic Circumcision in Northern Sudan," *American Ethnologist, 9,* 1982, pp. 682–98.

9. Carol Gould, "Group Rights and Social Ontology," *Philosophical Forum, 28* (1–2 Fall-Winter 1997), p. 81. "I would argue that any of the rights of a minority cultural group would have to be compatible with the human rights, for otherwise the justification of the group rights on the basis that they provide conditions for the equal freedom of self-development of the individuals who are members of that group would be undermined."

10. Yael Tamir "Hands Off Clitoridectomy," *Boston Review,* vol. XXI, no. 314 (Summer 1996), pp. 21–22.

11. Jeremy Rifkin, *The End of Work* (New York: G. P. Putnam, 1995), p. 3.

12. Martha Crouch, *How the Terminator Terminates; An Explanation for the Non-Scientist of a Remarkable Patent for Killing Second Generation Seeds of Crop Plants* (Edmonds, WA: The Edmonds Institute, 1998).

13. Rifkin op. cit., p. 288.

14. Ibid.

15. Paul Kennedy, *Preparing for the 21st Century* (New York: Random House, 1993), pp. 182–183, 189.

16. *New York Times* science section (August 18, 1998), p. 1.

17. Al Gore, *Earth in the Balance* (New York: Houghton Mifflin, 1997).

18. op. cit., p. 314.

19. Robert Heilbroner, *An Enquiry into the Human Prospect Looked at Again for the 1990's* (New York: Norton, 1991), p. 169.

20. Craig A. Rimmerman, "Reflections on the Doomsday Apocalyptic Vision." In *The Coming Age of Scarcity,* edited by M. N. Dobkowski and I. Walliman (Syracuse, NY: Syracuse Univ. Press, 1998), p. 287.

21. C. B. Macpherson, *The Life and Times of Liberal Democracy* (Oxford: Oxford Univ. Press, 1977).

22. Rifkin, op. cit., p. 3.

23. Ronald Bailey, *Eco-Scam; The False Prophets of Ecological Apocalypse* (New York: St. Martin's Press, 1993), p. 75.

24. Macpherson, op. cit., p. 105.

25. Robert Heilbroner, *Visions of the Future* (Oxford: Oxford Univ. Press, 1995), pp. 99–100.

26. Heilbroner, *An Enquiry* op. cit., p. 169.

We Are Our Values

SUSAN LEIGH ANDERSON

Susan Leigh Anderson teaches philosophy at the University of Connecticut.

According to Friedrich Nietzsche, what is distinctive about us as human beings is that we constantly make, and act upon, value judgments. We are essentially valuing animals.

> No people could live without first esteeming. . . .
> A tablet of the good hangs over every people. . . .
> Only man placed values in things—he alone created a meaning for things, a human meaning.

Therefore he calls himself "man," which means: the esteemer.[1]

If Nietzsche is correct that having values is fundamental to human beings, and it seems to me that he is, then one could reasonably argue that the most important task we each face in life is to choose the values[2] we live by.

Many people will not see this as a choice. Some

of these people are quite content, or believe it proper, to passively accept the values of some authority figure or group of which they are a member. Still they choose to adopt, rather than reject, the values of that figure or group. It is crucial that, on a matter as important as the values that give meaning to our lives, we think for ourselves rather than unquestioningly follow others. In the end, we must answer to ourselves.

Others believe that we are conditioned to have the values we have, and so there is no choice involved. Certainly our upbringing inclines us toward accepting a particular code of values; but at a certain point, we seem[3] to be capable of modifying, even radically altering, those values. A person who is raised in a capitalistic society can be convinced that socialism is morally preferable, for instance, and vice versa.

The choice we make in selecting the values we live by should not be thought of as a one-time event. It should, rather, be thought of as an on-going, lifetime process of refinement (or sometimes more radical change). We have experiences, we grow as persons, and we may alter our values as a result. At any stage in our lives, we should hold our value judgments in the following way: This is what I, at this moment in time, believe is right. I am open, however, to considering any arguments that might convince me that I am wrong, and I am prepared to change my views if those arguments are persuasive enough. Jonathan Bennett has summed up nicely the attitude we should have about our values:

> I accept every single item in my morality—that is inevitable—but I am sure that my morality could be improved, which is to say that it could undergo changes which I should be glad of once I had made them. So I must try to keep my morality open to revision, exposing it to whatever valid pressures there are. . . .[4]

Throughout our lives,[5] we face the challenge of reconfirming or revising the values we live by.

Just as we as individuals must think carefully about the values that govern our lives, a society must also be concerned with the values it holds. In a democracy, the values of the society, just like other policies, tend to be determined by the majority.[6] So the crucial task a society faces is to discover and maintain the common or consensus values of at least the majority of its citizens. Societal values, just like individual values, will very likely change over time, with changes in the values of the citizens of which it is composed and with the influx of new citizens.

I shall argue, in the first section of this essay, that there have been many relatively recent pressures within our society discouraging us from the task of examining our values and that these pressures should be resisted. In the second section, I shall argue that there are some difficult decisions to be made concerning fundamental issues in choosing our values and suggest how we might reach a consensus as a society on these issues. In the third and final section, I will discuss the criteria that should, ideally, be satisfied in an acceptable personal or societal value system.

I

There have been at least five pressures in contemporary American society that have discouraged people from examining the values they live by:

1. *The emphasis on bottom-line economics in our culture.* Rather than worry about whether an action or policy is morally right or wrong, many people seem to think only about how much it is going to cost or what gains are to be achieved financially. This might be justified if economic conditions were so bad that one's very survival was at stake; but when this sort of practice continues in times of affluence, it becomes, whether people are willing to admit it or not, a value judgment. It amounts to maintaining that the most important thing in life is how much money one has. It is doubtful that many people would really accept this value stated explicitly. We need, therefore, to think about what it is that we *do* value in life, what is more important than money.

2. *Conditions of modern society not conducive to long-term social relationships.* We are a highly mobile society. Few of us live in the towns where we grew up, and few of us stay in one neighborhood, town, or city very long. We change jobs frequently. We barely know our neighbors. Few of us live in close proximity to our relatives, and there is little difficulty in obtaining, or stigma attached to, divorce when we tire of our mates. All of this has resulted, I believe, in our not being concerned enough about our dealings and relationships with others. We treat others as disposable commodities rather than making an effort to treat people in a way that supports the possibility of long-term relationships.

Once people spent their entire lives in small communities where they encountered the same (agreeable or disagreeable) individuals over and over again. They had to learn how to behave toward those other individuals so that they could encounter them again and again without embarassment. They got to see the long-term effects of their behavior on others, that there were consequences to their actions. This forced them to reflect on how they should treat others. Perhaps part of this process included thinking about how they'd like *others* to treat *them.* Now many people don't worry about their relationships with others. They focus, instead, only on what they want out of life, discarding anyone who gets in the way of achieving their desires.

Although we may have ethical obligations to ourselves (this is a subject of debate in ethical theory), for the most part (if not entirely) our ethical obligations arise out of our relationships with others. If we don't take our relationships with others seriously enough, because we treat others as disposable commodities, the result will be that we won't feel the need to be concerned about ethics. This is a trend that must be reversed. We need others to survive, whether we want to admit it or not; and so we must think about how we ought to treat others, even if they are only in our lives for a short period of time. (None of what I have said here rules out the possibility that we *ought* to put our interests ahead of others. I have merely argued that we need to have a view of, and so we must think about, how we *ought* to treat others.)

3. *Multiculturalism and the acceptance of ethical relativism.* We live in a multicultural society, and we are constantly exposed, through the media, to conditions and values in other countries that are very different from ours. We have been encouraged to believe that it is wrong to make judgments about cultures other than our own, that this is the tolerant attitude. Many of us have been conditioned, as a result, to accept the view of ethical relativism, at least the societal or cultural form of it. This is the view that each society or culture is entitled to have its own set of values. There is no single correct code of values.

I believe that the appreciation of the many cultures to be found within our society and throughout the world, which is certainly a good thing, should not entail adopting an attitude of unquestioning acceptance of their values. We may have much to learn from other cultures, and in any case we must figure out how to co-exist with them, so *understanding* (knowing what they believe and why) is very important; but this does not require an automatic acceptance of their values. No one's values, including our own individual values or our own culture's values, should escape critical evaluation. We must periodically question our values; we must consider whether our values are defensible in light of the criteria that will be presented in section III.

One may argue that, because we don't have a way that is acceptable to all parties of settling ethical disputes among different cultures (there is no universally recognized moral authority), we must believe that all cultures' values are equally valid. This does not follow, however. Each side must be prepared to justify its moral judgments by offering reasons to support those judgments and then these reasons, and the principles on which they are based, can be discussed. We can then decide, assuming that we believe that some of those reasons and principles are more acceptable than others, that we agree with one position and disagree with others.

It is possible that some people find the societal form of ethical relativism to be attractive because it appears to allow them to avoid having to think about the values they should hold. They have only to adhere to the principles of their own society, whatever they may be. What they don't understand, however, is that *they* help to shape the values of their own society. By not taking an active role in determining the values of their society, they give *others* the power to control their destinies through the system of values that those others impose on the rest of society. Their tacit assent to those values can be understood as approval of those values. Furthermore, they will very likely feel the need, on some occasions, of having a personal morality because the societal values may not cover every moral dilemma in which they find themselves. So there really is no escaping having to think about what is right or wrong.

4. *The collapsing of morality into legality.* Many Americans seem to adopt the attitude that if it isn't illegal, then it's all right. There may be three reasons for this: (a) Morality and the law seem to cover the same ground. For example, it is both morally and legally wrong to kill innocent persons. (b) Laws are written down, they're quite clear, whereas it may be difficult to determine what is morally right. So it's easier to turn to the law to see what we ought to do in a given situation. (c) People know that they will (if caught) be punished if they break a law; but it's not so clear that anything will happen to them if they do something that is morally wrong, if it is not against the law. So it seems prudent to just worry about what is illegal.

But morality should not be collapsed into legality for two reasons: (a) They are not coextensive. There are actions that are a matter of moral concern that are not governed by laws (e.g., keeping promises to one's friends), and there are actions that are illegal that we would not classify as being immoral (e.g., jaywalking). (b) Even when they cover the same ground, outdated laws may lag behind a society's current moral beliefs and need to be changed. And individuals within a society may believe that laws that capture the majority's views are morally objectionable, and they may seek to change these views and laws though practicing civil disobedience. Consider that, for a time in our history, slavery was legal, and women and Blacks were not permitted to vote. Individuals with strong moral convictions challenged the prevailing laws on these issues, eventually changing them, and we now believe that they were right to have done so.

Even though morality should not be collapsed into legality, there certainly is a relationship between the two. Many laws that prohibit particular actions imply a moral condemnation of those actions (these actions, as opposed to others, are a matter of moral concern), for example, laws against murder, torture, breaking contracts, and so on. With each of these laws, we can assume that the majority of citizens of the society (if it is democratic) morally disapproved of the actions in question at the time that the laws were passed. But, again, it is possible that laws passed in earlier times no longer reflect the values of the society (that is, the majority of citizens) at a later time. And particular individuals living within the society may disagree with some of those laws because they do not share the values of the majority.

There is no shortcut to determining what is morally right. We must, as individuals and collectively, think seriously about the issues involved, rather than fall back on whatever the law at that time happens to permit. It is important, furthermore, that citizens periodically question the laws that govern them to see if they are consistent with current moral beliefs. If not, they should try to change those laws that they no longer feel are acceptable.

5. *New, complicated ethical issues and conflicting perspectives from ethicists.* Ethics has become more complicated recently; this has undoubtedly led many people to throw up their hands in despair, stop worrying about what is right, and instead, like Huckleberry Finn, just do "whatever comes handiest at the time."[7]

There are more and more new ethical issues to be concerned about. For example, advances in the field of medicine have led to new dilemmas. Once it was clear that medicine was supposed to keep people alive as long as possible and keep them comfortable, if nothing else could be done for them. Now people can be kept alive longer, perhaps too long. Should we be doing all that it's possible to do medically to keep life going, without regard to the *quality* of life, or should we consider withholding treatment in some cases where there is no hope for improvement? Should doctors even humanely end certain lives, as veterinarians have long done for animals in pain when no improvement can be expected? We are currently wrestling with the euthanasia issue as a society.[8] We, also, need to think about what we should do with information obtained from genetic research. Who should have this information? And how far is it morally acceptable to go in the direction of genetic engineering? There are a host of new ethical dilemmas like these, which our ancestors never faced, that have arisen due to advances in technology.

Adding to the confusion arising from new ethical dilemmas is the fact that recently ethicists have introduced new, conflicting perspectives into the discussion of how to determine what's morally right. In addition to a number of action-based ethical theories, we now have some ethicists advocating that we return to a virtue-based approach to ethics. Action-based theories (including ethical egoism, act and rule utilitarianism, Kant's categorical imperative, and Ross's theory of prima facie duties) focus on how we should act in ethical dilemmas, whereas virtue-based ethicists think that the crucial question is, What kind of person should I be? We also have advocates of an ethics of care, which emphasizes empathy and concern for the needs of others; feminist ethics, which emphasizes the importance of ending oppression against women; case-based reasoning, which focuses on "paradigm cases" and learning from practice; and Rawls's social contract theory, which would have us choose principles of justice that should govern society from a perspective of not knowing what our position might be in that society. If the experts can't agree on what is right, or even on how to approach ethical decision making, how can ordinary people hope to feel confident in selecting a code of values to live by?

Despite the confusion, and the pressures to stop worrying about what's morally right, we need to refocus on the task of critically examining our values. We stand to lose a great deal, individually and collectively, if we don't. As individuals, we may be successful in the eyes of others; but if we don't know what our values are, we won't really know who *we* are, and we won't know if we've lived our lives as we should. As Søren Kierkegaard, the Danish philosopher who is said to be the "father" of existentialism, maintained,

> Perhaps you will succeed without that in accomplishing much, perhaps even in astonishing the world; and yet you will miss the highest thing, the only thing which truly has significance—perhaps you will gain the whole world and lose your own self.[9]

What Kierkegaard is driving at, I believe, is that the crucial thing in life is to know who we are, what we stand for. Only then do we have a chance of leading a meaningful, fulfilled life, a life whose actions are intentionally motivated by whatever we think is important. Values form the basis for our actions,[10] and so we need to take responsibility for our values (that is, we must feel that *we* have chosen them) in order to be held accountable for the actions that result from those values.[11]

Collectively, we must also think about what we believe is important, what our societal values should be, because that is what forms our identity as a group. It is what we stand for as a society, as opposed to what we stand for as individuals. The values of society give rise to certain expectations of how members of the society are to be treated and what sort of obligations they will have to others. Individuals will continue to live in a society, or feel good about being citizens of a particular society, on the basis of whether they agree with its values. Others may leave a society or, if financial circumstances prevent them from leaving, feel uncomfortable in that society because of its general values.

II

In choosing our values, there are difficult decisions concerning fundamental issues to be made. There are three issues, in particular, on which one must take a position in developing an ethical theory:

1. *Who/what counts?* In deciding how we should act, which entities should we consider? Most people would probably say that we should take all human beings into account, but what does the category of human beings include? Does it include human embryos/fetuses? Should we include only presently existing human beings or future persons as well? And what about animals? the environment? Do we have ethical obligations to beings/entities other than legally recognized human beings? This is an important question. Those who believe that human embryos/fetuses count, for instance, are upset that we essentially allow abortion on demand in our society, and animal rights activists maintain that we are guilty of speciesism, the automatic favoring of our own species over others. Still others are concerned that we are sacrificing interests of future generations for those of presently existing human beings.

A society can tolerate disagreement among its citizens on some issues but not on something as fundamental as who or what counts. Just as the issue of whether one can have slaves or not should not be left up to individuals in society to decide for themselves, so society as a whole must adopt a position on the moral standing of fetuses,[12] animals, and so on. Consequently, a society needs to respect concerns about who or what counts that are voiced by a sizable number of citizens. Some sort of compromise may be possible that all, or nearly all, can live with. For instance, on the animal rights issue, even if animals are not granted full moral rights, we can condemn the infliction of suffering on animals. And on the abortion issue, we can at the very least discourage using abortion as a means of birth control. This would be consistent with the view that human embryos/fetuses have *some*, but not full, moral standing that, if it's not the correct position, is at least an attempt to meet part-way those who believe that these entities are persons.

2. *The individualism versus collectivism debate.* In May 1997, 7-year-old Sherrice Iverson was sexually molested and strangled to death in a restroom of a Nevada casino by Jeremy Strohmeyer, 19. Jeremy's friend, David Cash Jr., also 19, witnessed the beginning of the attack and decided to simply walk away rather than report it or try to stop it. "I'm not going to get upset over someone else's life," Cash told the *Los Angeles Times.* "I just worry about myself first." This raises the issue of whether we have positive duties to others in society or whether we should be permitted to do whatever we feel like doing or believe is best for ourselves, as long as we do not directly harm others.

According to the philosophy of individualism, the individual, rather than society as a whole, is the most important entity. Individuals should have the right to pursue their own happiness, as long as they allow others to do the same. We have only *negative* duties toward others. We must not harm them. Beyond that, relationships with others should be thought of as strictly voluntary. We are not *required* to aid others, although we certainly *may* do so if we choose. On this view, because Cash was not required to aid Sherrice, he did not act improperly.

According to the philosophy of collectivism, on the other hand, the individual should be thought of as subservient to society. Individuals should be required to act for the benefit of society as a whole. We do, therefore, have *positive* duties toward others that, most likely, would include a duty to prevent serious harm being done to others, if we could do so without risking our own lives. On this view, Cash's behavior was morally reprehensible, even if it was not illegal.

The United States has, historically, favored the philosophy of individualism. Recently, this feature of American life has been criticized in such books as *Habits of the Heart: Individualism and Commitment in American Life.*[13] In this book, Bellah and coauthors maintain that "we did not create ourselves, . . . we owe what we are to the communities that formed us."[14] We are necessarily dependent upon one another, and this feature of our existence is not viewed as a weakness; "it is only in relation to society that the individual can fulfill himself."[15]

Elsewhere,[16] I have argued that there are problems with both extreme individualism and extreme collectivism. The philosophy of individualism offers no safeguards for those less fortunate individuals who need help from others to survive, and, as Annette Baier has maintained, in failing to recognize the connections we have to others, it prevents individuals from accepting many important shared responsibilities.[17] The philosophy of collectivism can lead to the "tyranny of the majority," to use John Stuart Mill's famous phrase, because in the absence of universal agreement on the values that should govern society, the majority will dictate its policies to the rest. There is also concern that individual initiative will be discouraged, if the results of individuals' hard work are redistributed throughout society; and, in any case, allowing all to benefit from unequal contributions to society is thought by many to be fundamentally unjust.

A compromise between individualism and collectivism, which shows a certain amount of respect for each individual's values but also requires that we find or create some shared values, may be the best position for a society to take on this issue. A set of people without *some* shared values is not a *society,* and a society that shows *no* respect for its members' personal values is intolerable. It is certainly not a society of which anyone would want to be a member.

There is another argument that can be given to show that a compromise between individualism and collectivism is more likely to be accepted by the majority of people than either extreme individualism or extreme collectivism. For individualists, the most important value is freedom, whereas collectivists prize equality (and security). Most people value both, yet it's impossible to maximize freedom without sacrificing (some) equality or maximize equality without sacrificing (some) freedom. So the best we can have is a compromise between the two.

One could, furthermore, argue that implicit in the philosophy of individualism is a principle that would support a compromise between the extreme positions. An important aspect of the philosophy of individualism is the idea that *each* individual should be able to pursue a life in accordance with *his/her own values*. This would seem to presuppose that certain conditions are satisfied: (a) that one has the basic necessities for survival (e.g., food, clothing, shelter, medical care) and (b) that where opportunities are contingent upon one's having certain advantages (e.g., an education), then one has a right to those advantages. This could justify there being an obligation on all citizens within the society to see to it that members of that society who, through no fault of their own, lack those necessities and advantages are provided with them. Acceptance of this line of reasoning would move individualism closer to collectivism, resulting in what many might consider to be an ideal compromise between extreme individualism and extreme collectivism.

3. *The weighing of utilitarian versus justice considerations and, within the justice sphere, the weighing of moral rights versus desert.* Utilitarians focus on the consequences of actions, whereas those concerned with justice emphasize moral rights and desert. Although there are some moral philosophers who are strictly utilitarians,[18] and others who are only concerned with justice, and, among the latter group, some who focus exclusively on rights whereas others are concerned only with desert, one could argue that all three considerations are important.

To see that utility is important, consider the following case: A ship has sunk and one lifeboat is saved, along with forty people who are trying to hang on to the side of the boat. The lifeboat can only hold twenty people, there is no help in sight, and a terrible storm is brewing that makes it impossible to save everyone. In this essentially true case, an officer made a decision to force twenty people to swim away, shooting them if they wouldn't leave voluntarily, in order to save the remaining people. None of the forty people deserved to die; they all equally had a right to life. Yet, to have treated everyone equally would have resulted in everyone dying. Perfect justice, when *no one* benefits from it, seems rather pointless.[19]

As Ronald Dworkin has argued, moral rights—entitlements, which are justified by appealing to the inherent dignity of the possessors and/or their fundamental equality with one another, that can only be overridden if a catastrophe would otherwise result or if the rights of others would be violated—are important because they represent "the majority's promise to the minorities that their dignity and equality will be respected."[20] There will be limits to what the majority can do to the minorities. This is an important safeguard, which we would probably all approve of upon reflection, because each one of us will very likely be in the minority at some time or other in our lives. Also, moral rights are a way of fleshing out the idea that (at least) all human beings should *count* in our society. If we all have rights, then our fundamental interests must be taken seriously. They cannot be sacrificed easily.

Recently the concept of individual desert has come into question, for two reasons: (a) Egalitarian theories that have been proposed, like Kai Nielsen's,[21] rest on the idea that human beings are of equal moral worth, and this seems to be incompatible with maintaining that, as a result of our behavior, some of us deserve more than others. (b) There is concern that many, perhaps even all, of the qualities that people have, they couldn't help but have (they were either born that way or else socially conditioned to have those qualities), so how can they be said to *deserve* what results from their having these qualities? Despite these concerns with the notion of desert, one could argue that desert is very important because, as James Rachels has argued, it enables people to have some control over their destinies, over how others treat them:

> Treating people as they deserve is one way of treating them as autonomous beings, responsible for their own conduct. . . . [It] increases their control over their own lives and fortunes, for it allows people to determine, through their own actions, how others will respond to them.[22]

Try to imagine a world in which no attempt is made to connect the treatment of people with how they have behaved. Hard work, for instance, might result in punishment just as often as reward or indifference. People would very quickly begin to feel helpless and frustrated.

An ideal ethical theory, according to many, should include utilitarian, rights, and desert components. Once again, a compromise view seems most likely to be approved by (at least) the majority in society.[23] As Louis Pojman has said,

> A rights theory balanced by a strong sense of the social good and individual responsibility may well be the best kind of moral-political theory we can have.[24]

Deciding how much weight to give to each, however, is no easy matter. To further complicate the issue, conditions may affect how much weight to put on each. We may need a different weighting of utility versus rights versus desert in times of crises than under more favorable conditions. As with each of these fundamental issues in ethical theory, individuals must think deeply about what is at stake; and, collectively, much discussion must take place to try to reach a consensus with which we all can live.

III

An ideal ethical theory[25] should satisfy four criteria: (1) *consistency,* (2) *completeness,* (3) *agreement with intuition,* and (4) *practicality.* It is important that we understand each criterion properly and that we keep all four in mind as we develop the code of values that we, as individuals or as a society, will live by.

1. *Consistency.* A good ethical theory, just like a good theory about anything, should not contradict itself. In the case of an ethical theory, in particular, it should never tell us that a single action, under a particular set of circumstances, is simultaneously both right and wrong. This criterion can be misunderstood. It can allow us to say that, whereas speeding for the fun of it is wrong, speeding (while taking precautions not to endanger others) to get a very ill person to the hospital is right. The circumstances have changed to the point where one might consider these to be very different actions. What consistency will not allow is saying that it's both right and wrong simultaneously for me to speed to get someone to the hospital. According to Immanuel Kant, consistency will also not allow me to say that it's all right for *me* to do a particular action, but not for *someone else* who is performing the same action under essentially the same set of circumstances.[26] We can consider circumstances to be essentially the same, if there are no ethically relevant differences between them. For example, whereas it is ethically

relevant whether the action could save someone's life or not, whether an action occurs on a Tuesday or Wednesday, or whether Mary or Sally does it, isn't. We should strive toward consistency in our set of values.[27] Inconsistency would seem to indicate that we haven't satisfactorily resolved an ethical issue. We haven't made up our minds whether the action in question is right or wrong.

2. *Completeness.* Just as a good theory about anything should be consistent, a good theory about anything should also be complete. That is, it should do all that it's supposed to do. Because an ethical theory is supposed to tell us how to act in any ethical dilemma in which we might find ourselves, our ethical theory should not have any gaps in this respect. There should not be ethical dilemmas where the theory does not apply.

3. *Agreement with intuition.* A number of ethical theories have been proposed that are consistent and complete, and yet they give conflicting answers to the question of how we ought to behave. How should we choose among them?

Consider, for example, ethical egoism[28] versus Kant's categorical imperative versus act utilitarianism. According to ethical egoism, we should do the action that we believe to be most in our own self-interest. Kant's categorical imperative, on the other hand, would have us act in such a way that we could wish the principle on which we are acting to become universal law (which would mean that someone else could do the action to us). Finally, act utilitarianism enjoins us to do the action that of all the alternative actions open to us is likely to result in the greatest net good consequences (or least bad consequences), taking everyone affected into account. How do we choose among these theories?

We must consider what these theories would have us do in particular ethical dilemmas, especially dilemmas in which these theories would pull us in different directions, and ask which one agrees more with our intuitions about what is right and what is wrong. This is, admittedly, a subjective decision. There is no way, I believe, to completely eliminate subjectivity from a discussion of ethics. If we want all, or at least a majority, to agree to abide by a single set of values, we must hope that we have essentially the same intuitions about ethical matters.

Consider the following classic ethical dilemma:[29]

You are a lawyer who has been called to the death-bed of an elderly man who, after making sure that everyone else leaves the room, informs you that he has a very large sum of hidden money (he never trusted banks). He tells you where it's hidden and that no one else knows of its existence. He's been thinking about who should receive this money after his death, and he's decided that it should probably go to his only living relative, his nephew. You were just about to suggest that he consider other options, because you know that his nephew is a compulsive gambler, when he suddenly dies, before you have a chance to speak. What should you do about the money? Let's say that you could make very good use of the money; it would enable you to accomplish a lifelong dream of yours. Also, at a recent town council meeting, it was mentioned that what the town most needs is a recreation center for young people (who have been getting into all kinds of trouble because they have no place to go and their parents are too busy working to monitor their behavior when school is not in session). The sum of money required to get the project off the ground is exactly the amount that this man has hidden away. (Let us, further, suppose that this is the best use that could be made of this money, in terms of the general welfare.)

An ethical egoist would use the money to achieve his dream, assuming that he could get away with it. A Kantian would most likely see that the nephew gets the money, because he would probably like to see it become universal law that lawyers respect the wishes of their clients. He would wish, if he'd asked his lawyer to do something, that the lawyer had followed his instructions. Finally, an act utilitarian would probably see that the money was used to start the recreation center, perhaps naming it for the man who had "donated" the money for the project.

Which action agrees more with your intuition as to what you think is right to do under the circumstances? In answering this question, you must be careful to distinguish between what you *would* do, and what you think you *should* do. Ethics is concerned not with what people are *in fact* likely to do, but with what they *ought* to do. It's not always easy to do what you believe you ought to do; but that doesn't mean that we should change the ethical obligation, just to make it easier to be moral. An eth-

ical theory gives us an ideal to which we should *aspire,* rather than a summary of how we do behave, with all our foibles.

We may find that we have different intuitions on ethical matters; but, then again, we may find that after discussion, initial disagreement can be resolved. In any case, we must as individuals and as a society, continue thinking about ethical issues, reaffirming or revising our values, so that we know that we have done our best to try to determine what is right.

Those who believe that that there is no hope of our ever reconciling our intuitions on ethical matters might be blowing the extent of people's disagreement out of proportion. It may be the case that people agree about the basic principles of ethics; they just disagree about the application of those principles. So, for instance, opponents on an issue may agree that moral rights are important; but they disagree about what those rights are or, even more likely, how particular rights are to be understood. For example, individualists and collectivists both advocate a *right to life,* but for individualists this only entails a guarantee that one will not be killed, whereas for collectivists this right is likely to be broadened to include also a guarantee of whatever is necessary to keep oneself alive or perhaps even a guarantee of a minimally decent standard of living. Given some common ground—in this case, agreement on the *right to life*—discussion can take place, and there is, as a result, some hope of eventually resolving the issue.

In the case of the dying man revealing the existence of the hidden money, most people would find it difficult, no matter how *tempting* it might be to spend it on themselves, to maintain that this is the *right* thing to do. This reduces the three options down to two: carrying out the dying man's request or using it to fund the recreation center. Furthermore, there is probably agreement that sometimes the consequences of actions should be the determining factor in deciding what's right and sometimes it's important to respect the wishes of donors, even if doing so would not lead to the best consequences. It's difficult, however, to determine exactly when each of these considerations should become paramount. Once again, there is room for discussion and a possibility of a resolution.

4. *Practicality.* It's important, I believe, that those who wish to follow an ethical theory are reasonably able to do so. What I have in mind here is that it must be realistic to suppose that people will be able to go through the thought process required to follow the theory and will be able to reach a decision as to how they should act. If the theory does not satisfy this criterion, it will not be very useful; as a result, it will likely lead to people being less concerned about what is *right* to do in ethical dilemmas and instead doing "whatever comes handiest at the time."

Consider, for instance, an alternate version of act utilitarianism that would have us do whatever would *in fact* (rather than *is likely* to) result in the greatest net good consequences (or least bad consequences), taking everyone affected into account. Because there is no way that we could know beforehand how things will turn out (I am assuming that we are unable to see into the future) if we do a particular action, it would be impossible on a practical level for us to follow this theory, no matter how wonderful it might sound.

I have argued that, given that we are essentially valuing animals, the most important task we face in life, individually and collectively as members of a society, is to choose the values according to which we will live. We must resist current pressures discouraging us from focusing on this task. Choosing our values involves taking a stand on several fundamental issues, including who or what counts, the individualism versus collectivism debate, and the weighing of utilitarian versus justice considerations. In formulating a theory of values, several criteria should ideally be satisfied. The theory should be consistent, be complete, agree with our intuitions, and be practical. There is much to keep in mind, as well as important decisions to make, in choosing the values that we as individuals, or as a group, will live by; but this should not deter us from tackling the task. As difficult a task as it is, it is the most important one we face in our lives. Our choice of values determines who we are as individuals and as a society, because our values are what we stand for. We *are* our values.

Notes

1. Friedrich Nietzsche, "On the Thousand and One Goals," First Part, *Thus Spake Zarathustra,* translated by Walter Kaufmann (New York: Viking Press, 1972), pp. 58–59.

2. What I mean by "values" are positive or negative judgments about human beings and their conduct (e.g., he is a bad person, her action was right) and also the desirability/undesirability of particular states of affairs (e.g., equality of wealth is a good or bad thing). They may be codified into principles or embodied in our heroes/villains and in the goals to which we aspire or what we wish to avoid. What is crucial, as I shall emphasize later, is that our positive values be thought of as *ideals* that we should try to live up to, rather than as summaries of what does *in fact* motivate our actions.

3. Whether we do indeed have free will, and if so what it amounts to, is a very complicated and controversial issue that I will not get into here. I am assuming throughout this discussion that we do make choices, something that I think most people will accept, and that among the choices we make, some (the most important ones) involve affirming or rejecting certain values.

4. Jonathan Bennett, "The Conscience of Huckleberry Finn," in the subsection "Why Be Moral" in this book.

5. It's unlikely that we will reconsider our values on a daily basis. We don't constantly think about our values. It would be too disruptive to do so. We tend to think about our values when some sort of triggering mechanism occurs, such as a crisis or we're asked about our values.

6. Some will be unhappy with this, not only in practice but also in theory. They question whether ordinary citizens will be capable of, and have the time to devote to, developing defensible positions on complicated, crucial issues that affect all of our lives. Despite these concerns, defenders of democracy argue that it's less risky than the alternative: putting power in the hands of a few who might abuse it.

7. Jonathan Bennett, *op. cit.*

8. This has been due, in large part, to Dr. Jack Kervorkian's repeated challenges to our current laws on this issue.

9. Søren Kierkegaard, *Either/Or,* in R. Bretall, *A Kierkegaard Anthology* (Princeton, NJ: Princeton University Press, 1973), p. 106.

10. Jean-Paul Sartre maintained that we would not act, if it were not for value judgments. We imagine an ideal state of affairs and find the current state of affairs to be lacking in comparison with that ideal. We are then motivated to try to bring the ideal state of affairs into existence.

11. I am assuming that we do believe that we can hold people morally responsible for their actions. A few

philosophers have questioned this, but it is almost impossible to put their view into practice. It would certainly involve a radical overhauling of our relationships to others.

12. Those who claim that the pro-choice *legal* position on abortion is ideal because it doesn't commit us to a *moral* position on this issue are mistaken, in my opinion. Permitting women to have abortions, if they choose, amounts to holding the view that abortion is morally acceptable.

13. R. Bellah, R. Madsen, W. Sullivan, A. Swindler, and S. Tipton, *Habits of the Heart: Individualism and Commitment in American Life* (Berkeley: University of California Press, 1985).

14. *Ibid.*, p. 295.

15. *Ibid.*, p. 144.

16. S. L. Anderson, "Natural Rights and the Individualism Versus Collectivism Debate," *The Journal of Value Inquiry*, vol. 29, 1995.

17. A. Baier, "How Can Individualists Share Responsibility?", *Political Theory*, vol. 21, (May 1993).

18. Some of these philosophers believe that justice considerations can be subsumed under utility. See, for example, Chapter 5, "On the Connection Between Justice and Utility," of John Stuart Mill's *Utilitarianism*.

19. One could argue that there is injustice either way: In a just world one would not have to sacrifice innocent people, and treating equally deserving people equally should not result in everyone dying. So one might as well throw out justice concerns and focus instead on maximizing utility.

20. R. Dworkin, *Taking Rights Seriously* (Cambridge, MA: Harvard University Press, 1977), p. 205.

21. K. Nielsen, *Equality and Liberty: A Defense of Radical Egalitarianism* (Totowa, NJ: Rowman & Allenheld, 1985).

22. J. Rachels, "What People Deserve," from J. Arthur and W. Shaw, *Justice and Economic Distribution,* Prentice Hall, Englewood Cliffs, N.J., 1978, p. 305.

23. Again, as with freedom and equality, I believe that most people value each of these considerations.

24. L. Pojman, "On Equal Human Worth: A Critique of Contemporary Egalitarianism," in L. Pojman and R. Westmoreland, *Equality: Selected Readings,* (New York: Oxford University Press, 1997), p. 282. In Pojman's formula "the social good" can be equated with utility and "individual responsibility" with desert.

25. With these criteria, I have action-based ethical theories primarily in mind; but I believe that something like these criteria should be applied to any theory of values.

26. Even ethical egoism, at least the only plausible version of it—the view that *each* person should act in the way that (s)he believes is most in her/his own self-interest—satisfies this criterion.

27. Although we probably cannot *prove* that consistency is better than inconsistency, it does seem intuitively to be preferable. For philosophers, anyway, inconsistency is the primary indication of irrationality. For logicians, in particular, inconsistency is unacceptable because *anything* follows from a set of inconsistent statements.

28. Some have questioned the consistency and/or completeness of ethical egoism; but I believe that problems with the theory lie not in whether the theory satisfies these criteria but in whether it agrees with our intuition.

29. Although one can use real-life dilemmas, very often ethical theorists use fictional examples because one can build into the examples just those features that we need to focus on, eliminating the messy complications of real-life cases.

JUSTICE AND LAW

The Address of the Laws

PLATO

Plato (427–347 B.C.E.) lived in Athens and was a student of Socrates. Most of his surviving works, written in dialog form, feature the character of Socrates. Plato is generally regarded as one of the greatest philosophers of all time. He founded the Academy, the world's first university.

Soc.: . . . I proceed to argue the question whether I ought or ought not to try and escape without the consent of the Athenians: and if I am clearly right in escaping, then I will make the attempt; but if not, I will abstain. The other considerations which you mention, of money and loss of character and the duty of educating one's children, are, I fear, only the doctrines of the multitude, who would be as ready to restore people to life, if they were able, as they are to put them to death—and with as little reason. But now, since the argument has thus far prevailed, the only question which remains to be considered is, whether we shall do rightly either in escaping or in suffering others to aid in our escape and paying them in money and thanks, or whether in reality we shall not do rightly; and if the latter, then death or any other calamity which may ensue on my remaining here must not be allowed to enter into the calculation.

Cr.: I think that you are right, Socrates; how then shall we proceed?

Soc.: Let us consider the matter together, and do you either refute me if you can, and I will be convinced; or else cease, my dear friend, from repeating to me that I ought to escape against the wishes of the Athenians: for I highly value your attempts to persuade me to do so, but I may not be persuaded against my own better judgment.

And now please to consider my first position, and try how you can best answer me.

Cr.: I will.

Soc.: Are we to say that we are never intentionally to do wrong, or that in one way we ought and in another we ought not to do wrong, or is doing wrong always evil and dishonourable, as I was just now saying, and as has been already acknowledged by us? Are all our former admissions which were made within a few days to be thrown away? And have we, at our age, been earnestly discoursing with one another all our life long only to discover that we are no better than children? Or, in spite of the opinion of the many, and in spite of consequences whether better or worse, shall we insist on the truth of what was then said, that injustice is always an evil and dishonour to him who acts unjustly? Shall we say so or not?

Cr.: Yes.

Soc.: Then we must do no wrong?

Cr.: Certainly not.

Soc.: Nor when injured injure in return, as the many imagine; for we must injure no one at all?

Cr.: Clearly not.

Soc.: Again, Crito, may we do evil?

Cr.: Surely not, Socrates.

Soc.: And what of doing evil in return for evil, which is the morality of the many—is that just or not?

Cr.: Not just.

Soc.: For doing evil to another is the same as injuring him?

From *Crito,* translated by Benjamin Jowett (1892).

CR.: Very true.

SOC.: Then we ought not to retaliate or render evil for evil to any one, whatever evil we may have suffered from him. But I would have you consider, Crito, whether you really mean what you are saying. For this opinion has never been held, and never will be held, by any considerable number of persons; and those who are agreed and those who are not agreed upon this point have no common ground, and can only despise one another when they see how widely they differ. Tell me, then, whether you agree with and assent to my first principle, that neither injury nor retaliation nor warding off evil by evil is ever right. And shall that be the premiss of our argument? Or do you decline and dissent from this? For so I have ever thought, and continue to think; but, if you are of another opinion, let me hear what you have to say. If, however, you remain of the same mind as formerly, I will proceed to the next step.

CR.: You may proceed, for I have not changed my mind.

SOC.: Then I will go on to the next point, which may be put in the form of a question:— Ought a man to do what he admits to be right, or ought he to betray the right?

CR.: He ought to do what he thinks right.

SOC.: But if this is true, what is the application? In leaving the prison against the will of the Athenians, do I wrong any? or rather do I not wrong those whom I ought least to wrong? Do I not desert the principles which were acknowledged by us to be just—what do you say?

CR.: I cannot tell, Socrates; for I do not know.

SOC.: Then consider the matter in this way:—Imagine that I am about to play truant (you may call the proceeding by any name which you like), and the laws and the government come and interrogate me: "Tell us, Socrates," they say; "what are you about? are you going by an act of yours to overturn us—the laws, and the whole state, as far as in you lies? Do you imagine that a state can subsist and not be overthrown, in which the decisions of law have no power, but are set aside and trampled upon by individuals?" What will be our answer, Crito, to these and the like words? Any one, and especially a rhetorician, will have a good deal to say on behalf of the law which requires a sentence to be carried out. He will argue that this law should not be set aside; and shall we reply, "Yes; but the state has injured us and given an unjust sentence." Suppose I say that?

CR.: Very good, Socrates.

SOC.: "And was that our agreement with you?" the law would answer; "or were you to abide by the sentence of the state?" And if I were to express astonishment at their words, the law would probably add: "Answer, Socrates, instead of opening your eyes—you are in the habit of asking and answering questions. Tell us,—What complaint have you to make against us which justifies you in attempting to destroy us and the state? In the first place did we not bring you into existence? Your father married your mother by our aid and begat you. Say whether you have any objection to urge against those of us who regulate marriage?" None, I should reply. "Or against those of us who after birth regulate the nurture and education of children, in which you also were trained? Were not the laws, which have the charge of education, right in commanding your father to train you in music and gymnastic?" Right, I should reply. "Well then, since you were brought into the world and nurtured and educated by us, can you deny in the first place that you are our child and slave, as your fathers were before you? And if this is true you are not on equal terms with us; nor can you think that you have a right to do to us what we are doing to you. Would you have any right to strike or revile or do any other evil to your father or your master, if you had one, because you have been struck or reviled by him, or received some other evil at his hands?—you would not say this? And because we think right to destroy you, do you think that you have any right to destroy us in return, and your country as far as in you lies? Will you, O professor of true virtue, pretend that you are justified in this? Has a philosopher like you failed to discover that our country is more to be valued and higher and holier far than mother or father or any ancestor, and more to be regarded in the eyes of the gods and of men of understanding? also to be soothed, and gently and reverently entreated when angry, even more than a father, and either to be persuaded, or if not persuaded, to be obeyed? And when we are punished by her, whether with imprisonment or stripes, the punishment is to be endured in silence; and if she leads us to wounds or death in battle, thither we follow as is right; neither may any one yield or retreat or leave his rank, but whether in battle or in a court of law, or in any other place, he must do what his city and his country order him; or he must change their view of what is just: and if he may do no violence to his father or mother, much less may he do violence to his country." What answer shall we make to this, Crito? Do the laws speak truly, or do they not?

CR.: I think that they do.

SOC.: Then the laws will say, "Consider, Socrates, if we are speaking truly that in your present attempt you are going to do us an injury. For, having brought you into the world, and nurtured and educated you, and given you and every other citizen a share in every good which we had to give, we further proclaim to any Athenian by the liberty which we allow him, that if he does not like us when he has become of age and has seen the ways of the city, and made our acquaintance, he may go where he pleases and take his goods with him. None of us laws will forbid him or interfere with him. Any one who does not like us and the city, and who wants to emigrate to a colony or to any other city, may go where he likes, retaining his property. But he who has experience of the manner in which we order justice and administer the state, and still remains, has entered into an implied contract that he will do as we command him. And he who disobeys us is, as we maintain, thrice wrong; first, because in disobeying us he is disobeying his parents; secondly, because we are the authors of his education; thirdly, because he has made an agreement with us that he will duly obey our commands; and he neither obeys them nor convinces us that our commands are unjust; and we do not rudely impose them, but give him the alternative of obeying or convincing us;—that is what we offer, and he does neither.

"These are the sort of accusations to which, as we were saying, you, Socrates, will be exposed if you accomplish your intentions; you, above all other Athenians." Suppose now I ask, why I

rather than anybody else? they will justly retort upon me that I above all other men have acknowledged the agreement. "There is clear proof," they will say, "Socrates, that we and the city were not displeasing to you. Of all Athenians you have been the most constant resident in the city, which, as you never leave, you may be supposed to love. For you never went out of the city either to see the games, except once when you went to the Isthmus, or to any other place unless when you were on military service; nor did you travel as other men do. Nor had you any curiosity to know other states or their laws: your affections did not go beyond us and our state; we were your special favourites, and you acquiesced in our government of you; and here in this city you begat your children, which is a proof of your satisfaction. Moreover, you might in the course of the trial, if you had liked, have fixed the penalty at banishment; the state which refuses to let you go now would have let you go then. But you pretended that you preferred death to exile, and that you were not unwilling to die. And now you have forgotten these fine sentiments, and pay no respect to us the laws, of whom you are the destroyer; and are doing what only a miserable slave would do, running away and turning your back upon the compacts and agreements which you made as a citizen. And first of all answer this very question: Are we right in saying that you agreed to be governed according to us in deed, and not in word only? Is that true or not?" How shall we answer, Crito? Must we not assent?

CR.: We cannot help it, Socrates.

SOC.: Then will they not say; "You, Socrates, are breaking the covenants and agreements which you made with us at your leisure, not in any haste or under any compulsion or deception, but after you have had seventy years to think of them, during which time you were at liberty to leave the city, if we were not to your mind, or if our covenants appeared to you to be unfair. You had your choice, and might have gone either to Lacedaemon or Crete, both which states are often praised by you for their good government, or to some other Hellenic or foreign state. Whereas you, above all other Athenians, seemed to be so fond of the state, or, in other words, of us her laws (and who would care about a state which has no laws?), that you never stirred out of her; the halt, the blind, the maimed were not more stationary in her than you were. And now you run away and forsake your agreements. Not so, Socrates, if you will take our advice; do not make yourself ridiculous by escaping out of the city.

"For just consider, if you transgress and err in this sort of way, what good will you do either to yourself or to your friends? That your friends will be driven into exile and deprived of citizenship, or will lose their property, is tolerably certain; and you yourself, if you fly to one of the neighbouring cities, as, for example, Thebes or Megara, both of which are well governed, will come to them as an enemy, Socrates, and their government will be against you, and all patriotic citizens will cast an evil eye upon you as a subverter of the laws, and you will confirm in the minds of the judges the justice of their own condemnation of you. For he who is a corrupter of the laws is more than likely to be a corrupter of the young and foolish portion of mankind. Will you then flee from well-ordered cities and virtuous men? and is existence worth having on these terms? Or will you go to them without shame, and talk to them, Socrates? And what will you say to them? What you say here about virtue and justice and institutions and laws being the best things among men? Would that be decent of you? Surely not. But if you go away from well-governed states to Crito's friends in Thessaly, where there is great disorder and licence, they will be charmed to hear the tale of your escape from prison, set off with ludicrous particulars of the manner in which you were wrapped in a goatskin or some other disguise, and metamorphosed as the manner is of runaways; but will there be no one to remind you that in your old age you were not ashamed to violate the most sacred laws from a miserable desire of a little more life? Perhaps not, if you keep them in a good temper; but if they are out of temper you will hear many degrading things; you will live, but how?—as the flatterer of all men, and the servant of all men; and doing what?—eating and drinking in Thes-

saly, having gone abroad in order that you may get a dinner. And where will be your fine sentiments about justice and virtue? Say that you wish to live for the sake of your children—you want to bring them up and educate them—will you take them into Thessaly and deprive them of Athenian citizenship? Is this the benefit which you will confer upon them? Or are you under the impression that they will be better cared for and educated here if you are still alive, although absent from them; for your friends will take care of them? Do you fancy that if you are an inhabitant of Thessaly they will take care of them, and if you are an inhabitant of the other world that they will not take care of them? Nay; but if they who call themselves friends are good for anything, they will—to be sure they will.

"Listen, then, Socrates, to us who have brought you up. Think not of life and children first, and of justice afterwards, but of justice first, that you may be justified before the princes of the world below. For neither will you nor any that belong to you be happier or holier or juster in this life, or happier in another, if you do as Crito bids. Now you depart in innocence, a sufferer and not a doer of evil; a victim, not of the laws but of men. But if you go forth, returning evil for evil, and injury for injury, breaking the covenants and agreements which you have made with us, and wronging those whom you ought least of all to wrong, that is to say, yourself, your friends, your country, and us, we shall be angry with you while you live, and our brethren, the laws in the world below, will receive you as an enemy; for they will know that you have done your best to destroy us. Listen, then, to us and not to Crito."

This, dear Crito, is the voice which I seem to hear murmuring in my ears, like the sound of the flute in the ears of the mystic; that voice, I say, is humming in my ears and prevents me from hearing any other. And I know that anything more which you may say will be in vain. Yet speak, if you have anything to say.

CR.: I have nothing to say, Socrates.

SOC.: Leave me then, Crito, to fulfil the will of God, and to follow whither he leads.

Of Commonwealth and the Rights of Sovereigns

THOMAS HOBBES

Thomas Hobbes (1588–1679) was a brilliant and influential English philosopher.

NATURE OF A COMMONWEALTH

The final cause, end, or design of men who naturally love liberty and dominion over others, in the introduction of that restraint upon themselves in which we see them live in commonwealths, is the foresight of their own preservation, and of a more contented life thereby; that is to say, of getting themselves out from that miserable condition of war, which is necessarily consequent, as hath been shown in Chapter XIII, to the natural passions of men, when there is no visible power to keep them in awe, and tie them by fear of punishment to the performance of their covenants and observation of those laws of nature set down in the fourteenth and fifteenth chapters.

For the laws of nature, as justice, equity, modesty, mercy, and, in sum, *doing to others as we would be done to,* of themselves, without the terror of some power to cause them to be observed, are contrary to our natural passions, that carry us to partiality, pride, revenge, and the like. And covenants, without the sword, are but words, and of no strength to secure a man at all. Therefore notwithstanding the laws of nature, which everyone hath then kept, when he has the will to keep them when he can do it safely; if there be no power erected, or not great enough for our security, every man will, and may, lawfully rely on his own strength and art, for caution against all other men. And in all places where men have lived by small families, to rob and spoil one another has been a trade, and so far from being reputed against the law of nature, that the greater spoils they gained, the greater was their honor; and men observed no other laws therein but the laws of honor; that is, to abstain from cruelty, leaving to men their lives, and

instruments of husbandry. And as small families did then; so now do cities and kingdoms, which are but greater families, for their own security enlarge their dominions, upon all pretenses of danger and fear of invasion, or assistance that may be given to invaders, and endeavor as much as they can to subdue or weaken their neighbors, by open force and secret arts, for want of other caution, justly; and are remembered for it in after ages with honor.

Nor is it the joining together of a small number of men, that gives them this security; because in small numbers, small additions on the one side or the other make the advantage of strength so great, as is sufficient to carry the victory, and therefore gives encouragement to an invasion. The multitude sufficient to confide in for our security, is not determined by any certain number, but by comparison with the enemy we fear; and is then sufficient, when the odds of the enemy is not of so visible and conspicuous moment, to determine the event of war, as to move him to attempt.

And be there never so great a multitude, yet if their actions be directed according to their particular judgments and particular appetites, they can expect thereby no defense nor protection, neither against a common enemy nor against the injuries of one another. For being distracted in opinions concerning the best use and application of their strength, they do not help but hinder one another; and reduce their strength by mutual opposition to nothing: whereby they are easily, not only subdued by a very few that agree together; but also when there is no common enemy, they make war upon each other, for their particular interests. For if we could suppose a great multitude of men to consent in the observation of justice, and other laws of na-

From *Leviathan,* Part II, chapters 17, 18. First published in 1651.

ture, without a common power to keep them all in awe, we might as well suppose all mankind to do the same; and then there neither would be, nor need to be any civil government or commonwealth at all, because there would be peace without subjection. . . .

The only way to erect such a common power, as may be able to defend them from the invasion of foreigners and the injuries of one another, and thereby to secure them in such sort as that, by their own industry, and by the fruits of the earth, they may nourish themselves and live contentedly; is, to confer all their power and strength upon one man, or upon one assembly of men, that may reduce all their wills, by plurality of voices, unto one will: which is as much as to say, to appoint one man, or assembly of men, to bear their person; and everyone to own and acknowledge himself to be author of whatsoever he that so beareth their person, shall act or cause to be acted in those things which concern the common peace and safety; and therein to submit their wills, everyone to his will, and their judgments, to his judgment. This is more than consent, or concord; it is a real unity of them all in one and the same person, made by covenant of every man with every man, in such manner as if every man should say to every man, *"I authorize and give up my right of governing myself to this man, or to this assembly of men, on this condition, that thou give up thy right to him, and authorize all his actions in like manner."* This done, the multitude so united in one person, is called a *commonwealth*, in Latin *civitas*. This is the generation of that great LEVIATHAN, or rather, to speak more reverently, of that *mortal god*, to which we owe under the *immortal God*, our peace and defense. For by this authority, given him by every particular man in the commonwealth, he hath the use of so much power and strength conferred on him, that by terror thereof he is enabled to perform the wills of them all, to peace at home and mutual aid against their enemies abroad. And in him consisteth the essence of the commonwealth; which, to define it, is *one person, of whose acts a great multitude, by mutual covenants one with another, have made themselves every one the author, to the end he may use the strength and means of them all, as he shall think expedient, for their peace and common defense.*

And he that carrieth this person, is called *sovereign*, and said to have sovereign power; and everyone besides, his *subject.* . . .

THE RIGHTS OF SOVEREIGNS

A COMMONWEALTH is said to be *instituted,* when a multitude of men do agree and covenant, everyone with everyone, that to whatsoever man, or assembly of men, shall be given by the major part the right to present the person of them all, that is to say, to be their *representative;* everyone, as well he that voted for it as he that voted against it, shall authorize all the actions and judgments of that man, or assembly of men, in the same manner as if they were his own, to the end to live peaceably amongst themselves and be protected against other men.

From this institution of a commonwealth are derived all the *rights* and *faculties* of him, or them, on whom the sovereign power is conferred by the consent of the people assembled.

First, because they covenant, it is to be understood they are not obliged by former covenant to anything repugnant hereunto. And consequently they that have already instituted a commonwealth, being thereby bound by covenant to own the actions and judgments of one, cannot lawfully make a new covenant amongst themselves, to be obedient to any other, in anything whatsoever, without his permission. And therefore, they that are subject to a monarch, cannot without his leave cast off monarchy, and return to the confusion of a disunited multitude; nor transfer their person from him that beareth it, to another man, or other assembly of men: for they are bound, every man to every man, to own, and be reputed author of all, that he that already is their sovereign shall do and judge fit to be done; so that any one man dissenting, all the rest should break their covenant made to that man, which is injustice: and they have also every man given the sovereignty to him that beareth their person; and therefore if they depose him, they take from him that which is his own, and so again it is injustice. Besides, if he that attempteth to depose his sovereign, be killed or punished by him for such attempt, he is author of his own punishment, as being by the institution, author of all his sovereign shall do; and because it is injustice for a man to do anything for which he may be punished by his own authority, he is also upon that title, unjust. And whereas some men have pretended for their disobedience to their sovereign, a new covenant, made not with men but with God, this also is unjust: for there is no covenant with God, but by mediation of somebody that representeth God's person; which none doth but God's lieutenant, who hath the sovereignty under God. But this pretense of covenant with God, is so evident a lie, even in the pretenders' own consciences, that it is not only an act of an unjust, but also of a vile and unmanly disposition.

Secondly, because the right of bearing the person of them all, is given to him they make sovereign, by covenant only of one to another, and not of him to any of them; there can happen no breach of covenant on the part of the sovereign; and consequently none of his subjects, by any pretense of forfeiture, can be freed from his subjection. That he which is made sovereign maketh no covenant with his subjects beforehand, is manifest; because either he must make it with the whole multitude, as one party to the covenant, or he must make a several covenant with every man. With the whole, as one party, it is impossible, because as yet they are not one person: and if he make so many several covenants as there be men, those covenants after he hath the sovereignty are void; because what act soever can be pretended by any one of them for breach thereof, is the act both of himself and of all the rest, because done in the person, and by the right of every one of them in particular. Besides, if any one, or more of them, pretend a breach of the covenant made by the sovereign at his institution; and others, as one other of his subjects, or himself alone, pretend there was no such breach: there is in this case, no judge to decide the controversy; it returns therefore to the sword again; and every man recovereth the right of protecting himself by his own strength, contrary to the design they had in the institution. It is therefore in vain to grant sovereignty by way of precedent covenant. The opinion that any monarch receiveth his power by covenant, that is to say, on condition, proceedeth from want of understanding this easy truth, that covenants being but words and breath, have no force to oblige, contain, constrain, or protect any man, but what it has from the public sword; that is, from the untied hands of that man, or assembly of men that hath the sovereignty, and whose actions are avouched by them all, and performed by the strength of them all, in him united. . . .

Thirdly, because the major part hath by consenting voices declared a sovereign, he that dissented must now consent with the rest; that is, be contented to avow all the actions he shall do, or else justly be destroyed by the rest. For if he voluntarily entered into the congregation of them that were assembled, he sufficiently declared thereby his will, and therefore tacitly covenanted to stand to what the major part should ordain; and therefore if he refuse to stand thereto, or make protestation against any of their decrees, he does contrary to his covenant, and therefore unjustly. And whether he be of the congregation or not, and whether his consent be asked or not, he must either submit to their decrees, or be left in the condition of war he was in before; wherein he might without injustice be destroyed by any man whatsoever.

Fourthly, because every subject is by this institution author of all the actions and judgments of the sovereign instituted; it follows that whatsoever he doth, it can be no injury to any of his subjects, nor ought he to be by any of them accused of injustice. For he that doth anything by authority from another, doth therein no injury to him by whose authority he acteth: but by this institution of a commonwealth, every particular man is author of all the sovereign doth: and consequently he that complaineth of injury from his sovereign, complaineth of that whereof he himself is author; and therefore ought not to accuse any man but himself; no nor himself of injury, because to do injury to one's self, is impossible. It is true that they that have sovereign power may commit iniquity, but not injustice, or injury, in the proper signification.

Fifthly, and consequently to that which was said last, no man that hath sovereign power can justly be put to death, or otherwise in any manner by his subjects punished. For seeing every subject is author of the actions of his sovereign, he punisheth another for the actions committed by himself. . . .

Sixthly, it is annexed to the sovereignty, to be judge of what opinions and doctrines are averse, and what conducing to peace; and consequently, on what occasions, how far, and what men are to be trusted withal, in speaking to multitudes of people; and who shall examine the doctrines of all books before they be published. For the actions of men proceed from their opinions; and in the well-governing of opinions consisteth the well-governing of men's actions, in order to their peace and concord. And though in matter of doctrine nothing ought to be regarded but the truth, yet this is not repugnant to regulating the same by peace. For doctrine repugnant to peace can no more be true, than peace and concord can be against the law of nature. . . .

Seventhly, is annexed to the sovereignty, the whole power of prescribing the rules, whereby every man may know what goods he may enjoy, and what actions he may do, without being molested by any of his fellow-subjects; and this is it men call *propriety*. For before constitution of sovereign power, as hath already been shown, all men had right to all things; which necessarily causeth war: and therefore this propriety, being necessary to peace, and depending on sovereign power, is the act of that power, in order to the public peace. These rules of propriety, or *meum* and *tuum*, and of good, evil, lawful, and unlawful in the actions of subjects, are the civil laws; that is to say, the laws of each commonwealth in particular. . . .

Eighthly, is annexed to the sovereignty, the right of judicature; that is to say, of hearing and deciding all controversies which may arise concerning law, either civil or natural, or concerning fact. For without the decision of controversies, there is no protection of one subject against the injuries of another: the laws concerning *meum* and *tuum* are in vain; and to every man remaineth, from the natural and necessary appetite of his own conservation, the right of protecting himself by his private strength, which is the condition of war, and contrary to the end for which every commonwealth is instituted. . . .

And because they are essential and inseparable rights, it follows necessarily that in whatsoever words any of them seem to be granted away, yet if the sovereign power itself be not in direct terms renounced, and the name of sovereign no more given by the grantees to him that grants them, the grant is void: for when he has granted all he can, if we grant back the sovereignty, all is restored, as inseparably annexed thereunto.

SOVEREIGN POWER SHOULD NOT BE RESISTED

This great authority being indivisible, and inseparably annexed to the sovereignty, there is little ground for the opinion of them that say of sovereign kings, though they be *singulis majores,* of greater power than every one of their subjects, yet they be *universis minores,* of less power than them all together. For if by "all together" they mean not the collective body as one person, then "all together" and "every one" signify the same, and the speech is absurd. But if by "all together" they understand them as one person, which person the sovereign bears, then the power of all together is the same with the sovereign's power, and so again the speech is absurd: which absurdity they see well enough when the sovereignty is in an assembly of the people, but in a monarch they see it not; and yet the power of sovereignty is the same in whomsoever it be placed. . . .

But a man may here object that the condition of subjects is very miserable, as being obnoxious to the lusts, and other irregular passions, of him or them that have so unlimited a power in their hands. And commonly they that live under a monarch, think it the fault of monarchy; and they that live under the government of democracy, or other sovereign assembly, attribute all the inconvenience to that form of commonwealth; whereas the power in all forms, if they be perfect enough to protect them, is the same: not considering that the state of man can never be without some incommodity or other; and that the greatest that in any form of government can possibly happen to the people in general, is scarce sensible, in respect to the miseries and horrible calamities that accompany a civil war, or that dissolute condition of masterless men, without subjection to laws and a coercive power to tie their hands from rapine and revenge: nor considering that the greatest pressure of sovereign governors, proceedeth not from any delight or profit they can expect in the damage or weakening of their subjects, in whose vigor consisteth their own strength and glory; but in the restiveness of themselves, that unwillingly contributing to their own defense, make it necessary for their governors to draw from them what they can in time of peace, that they may have means on any emergent occasion or sudden need, to resist or take advantage on their enemies. For all men are by nature provided of notable multiplying glasses, that is their passions and self-love, through which every little payment appeareth a great grievance; but are destitute of those prospective glasses, namely moral and civil science, to see afar off the miseries that hang over them, and cannot without such payment be avoided.

Of the Dissolution of Government

JOHN LOCKE

English empiricist philosopher John Locke (1632–1704) was deeply influential—not simply in epistemology and metaphysics but also in his natural rights political theory.

THE ORIGIN OF POLITICAL SOCIETIES

Every man being, as has been shown, naturally free, and nothing being able to put him into subjection to any earthly power but only his own consent, it is to be considered what shall be understood to be a sufficient declaration of a man's consent to make him subject to the laws of any government. There is a common distinction of an express and a tacit consent which will concern our present case. Nobody doubts but an express consent of any man entering into any society makes him a perfect member of that society, a subject of that government. The difficulty is, what ought to be looked upon as a tacit consent, and how far it binds—i.e., how far any one shall be looked upon to have consented and thereby submitted to any government, where he has made no expressions of it at all. And to this I say that every man that has any possessions of enjoyment of any part of the dominions of any government does thereby give his tacit consent and is as far forth obliged to obedience to the laws of that government, during such enjoyment, as anyone under it; whether this his possession be of land to him and his heirs for ever, or a lodging only for a week, or whether it be barely traveling freely on the highway; and, in effect, it reaches as far as the very being of anyone within the territories of that government....

But since the government has a direct jurisdiction only over the land, and reaches the possessor of it—before he has actually incorporated himself in the society—only as he dwells upon and enjoys that, the obligation anyone is under by virtue of such enjoyment, to submit to the government, begins and ends with the enjoyment; so that whenever the owner, who has given nothing but such a tacit consent to the government, will, by donation, sale, or otherwise, quit the said possession, he is at liberty to go and incorporate himself into any other commonwealth, or to agree with others to begin a new one *in vacuis locis,* in any part of the world they can find free and unpossessed. Whereas he that has once, by actual agreement and any express declaration, given his consent to be of any commonwealth is perpetually and indispensably obliged to be and remain unalterably a subject to it, and can never be again in the liberty of the state of nature, unless by any calamity the government he was under comes to be dissolved, or else, by some public act, cuts him off from being any longer a member of it.

But submitting to the laws of any country, living quietly and enjoying privileges and protection under them, makes not a man a member of that society; this is only a local protection and homage due to and from all those who, not being in a state of war, come within the territories belonging to any government, to all parts whereof the force of its laws extends. But this no more makes a man a member of that society, a perpetual subject of that commonwealth, than it would make a man a subject to another in whose family he found it convenient to abide for some time, though, while he continued in it, he were obliged to comply with the laws and submit to the government he found there. And thus we see that foreigners, by living all their lives under another government and enjoying the privileges and protection of it, though they are bound, even in conscience, to submit to its administration as far forth as any denizen, yet do not thereby come to be subjects or members of that commonwealth. Nothing can make any man so but his actually entering

From *The Second Treatise of Government,* chapters 8, 9, 19. First published in 1690.

into it by positive engagement and express promise and compact. This is that which I think concerning the beginning of political societies and that consent which makes any one a member of any commonwealth.

If man in the state of nature be so free, as has been said, if he be absolute lord of his own person and possessions, equal to the greatest, and subject to nobody, why will he part with his freedom, why will he give up his empire and subject himself to the dominion and control of any other power? To which it is obvious to answer that though in the state of nature he has such a right, yet the enjoyment of it is very uncertain and constantly exposed to the invasion of others; for all being kings as much as he, every man his equal, and the greater part no strict observers of equity and justice, the enjoyment of the property he has in this state is very unsafe, very unsecure. This makes him willing to quit a condition which, however free, is full of fears and continual dangers; and it is not without reason that he seeks out and is willing to join in society with others who are already united, or have a mind to unite, for the mutual preservation of their lives, liberties, and estates, which I call by the general name "property."

The great and chief end, therefore, of men's uniting into commonwealths and putting themselves under government is the preservation of their property. . . .

Thus mankind, notwithstanding all the privileges of the state of nature, being but in an ill condition while they remain in it, are quickly driven into society. Hence it comes to pass that we seldom find any number of men live any time together in this state. The inconveniences that they are therein exposed to by the irregular and uncertain exercise of the power every man has of punishing the transgressions of others make them take sanctuary under the established laws of government and therein seek the preservation of their property. It is this makes them so willingly give up every one his single power of punishing, to be exercised by such alone as shall be appointed to it amongst them; and by such rules as the community, or those authorized by them to that purpose, shall agree on. And in this we have the original right of both the legislative and executive power, as well as of the governments and societies themselves. . . .

But though men when they enter into society give up the equality, liberty, and executive power they had in the state of nature into the hands of the society, to be so far disposed of by the legislative as the good of the society shall require, yet it being only with an intention in every one the better to preserve himself, his liberty and property—for no rational creature can be supposed to change his condition with an intention to be worse—the power of the society, or legislative constituted by them, can never be supposed to extend farther than the common good, but is obliged to secure every one's property by providing against those three defects abovementioned that made the state of nature so unsafe and uneasy. And so whoever has the legislative or supreme power of any commonwealth is bound to govern by established standing laws, promulgated and known to the people, and not by extemporary decrees; by indifferent and upright judges who are to decide controversies by those laws; and to employ the force of the community at home only in the execution of such laws, or abroad to prevent or redress foreign injuries, and secure the community from inroads and invasion. And all this to be directed to no other end but the peace, safety, and public good of the people.

WHEN GOVERNMENT MAY BE DISSOLVED

The reason why men enter into society is the preservation of their property; and the end why they choose and authorize a legislative is that there may be laws made and rules set as guards and fences to the properties of all the members of the society to limit the power and moderate the dominion of every part and member of the society; for since it can never be supposed to be the will of the society that the legislative should have a power to destroy that which every one designs to secure by entering into society, and for which the people submitted themselves to legislators of their own making. Whenever the legislators endeavor to take away and destroy the property of the people, or to reduce them to slavery under arbitrary power, they put themselves into a state of war with the people who are thereupon absolved from any further obedience, and are left to the common refuge which God has provided for all men against force and violence. Whensoever, therefore, the legislative shall transgress this fundamental rule of society, and either by ambition, fear, folly, or corruption, endeavour to grasp themselves, or put into the hands of any other, an absolute power over the lives, liberties, and estates of the people, by this breach of trust they forfeit the power the people had put into their hands for quite contrary ends, and it devolves to the people, who have a right to resume their original liberty and, by the establishment of a new legislative, such as they shall think fit, provide for their own safety and security, which is the end for which they are in society. What I have said here concerning the legislative in general holds true also concerning the supreme executor, who having a double trust put in him—both to have a part in the legislative and the supreme execution of the law—acts against both when he goes about to set up his own arbitrary will as the law of the society. He acts also contrary to his trust when he either employs the force, treasure, and offices of the society to corrupt the representatives and gain them to his purposes, or openly preengages the electors and prescribes to their choice such whom he has by solicitations, threats, promises, or otherwise won to his designs, and employs them to bring in such who have promised beforehand what to vote and what to enact. . . .

To this perhaps it will be said that, the people being ignorant and always discontented, to lay the foundation of government in the unsteady opinion and uncertain humor of the people is to expose it to certain ruin; and no government will be able long to subsist if the people may set up a new legislative whenever they take offense at the old one. To this I answer: Quite the contrary. People are not so easily got out of their old forms as some are apt to suggest. They are hardly to be prevailed with to amend the acknowledged faults in the frame they have been accustomed to. And if there be any original defects, or adventitious ones introduced by time or corruption, it is not an easy thing to get them changed, even when all the world sees there is an opportunity for it. . . .

But it will be said this hypothesis lays a ferment for frequent rebellion. To which I answer:

First, no more than any other hypothesis; for when the people are made miserable, and find themselves exposed to the ill-usage of arbitrary power, cry up their governors as much as you will for sons of Jupiter, let them be sacred or divine, descended or authorized from heaven, give them out for whom or what you please, the same will happen. The people generally ill-treated, and contrary to right, will be ready upon any occasion to ease themselves of a burden that sits heavy upon them. They will wish and seek for the opportunity, which in the change, weakness, and accidents of human affairs seldom delays long to offer itself. He must have lived but a little while in the world who has not seen examples of this in his time, and he must have read very little who cannot produce examples of it in all sorts of governments in the world.

Secondly, I answer, such revolutions happen not upon every little mismanagement in public affairs. Great mistakes in the ruling part, many wrong and inconvenient laws, and all the slips of human frailty will be born by the people without mutiny or murmur. But if a long train of abuses, prevarications, and artifices, all tending the same way, make the design visible to the people, and they cannot but feel what they lie under and see whither they are going, it is not to be wondered that they should then rouse themselves and endeavor to put the rule into such hands which may secure to them the ends for which government was at first erected, and without which ancient names and specious forms are so far from being better that they are much worse than the state of nature or pure anarchy—the inconveniences being all as great and as near, but the remedy farther off and more difficult.

Thirdly, I answer that this doctrine of a power in the people of providing for their safety anew by a new legislative, when their legislators have acted contrary to their trust by invading their property, is the best fence against rebellion, and the probablest means to hinder it; for rebellion being an opposition, not to persons, but authority which is founded only in the constitutions and laws of the government, those, whoever they be, who by force break through, and by force justify their violation of them, are truly and properly rebels; for when men, by entering into society and civil government, have excluded force and introduced laws for the preservation of property, peace, and unity amongst themselves, those who set up force again in opposition to the laws do *rebellare*—that is, bring back again the state of war—and are properly rebels; which they who are in power, by the pretense they have to authority; the temptation of force they have in their hands, and the flattery of those about them, being likeliest to do, the properest way to prevent the evil is to show them the danger and injustice of it who are under the greatest temptation to run into it. . . .

The end of government is the good of mankind. And which is best for mankind? That the people should be always exposed to the boundless will of tyranny, or that the rulers should be sometimes liable to be opposed when they grow exorbitant in the use of their power and employ it for the destruction and not the preservation of the properties of their people?

Nor let any one say that mischief can arise from hence, as often as it shall please a busy head or turbulent spirit to desire the alteration of the government. It is true such men may stir whenever they please, but it will be only to their own just ruin and perdition; for till the mischief be grown general, and the ill designs of the rulers become visible, or their attempts sensible to the greater part, the people, who are more disposed to suffer than right themselves by resistance, are not apt to stir. . . . This I am sure: whoever, either ruler or subject, by force goes about to invade the rights of either prince or people and lays the foundation for overturning the constitution and frame of any just government is highly guilty of the greatest crime I think a man is capable of—being to answer for all those mischiefs of blood, rapine, and desolation, which the breaking to pieces of governments bring on a country. And he who does it is justly to be esteemed the common enemy and pest of mankind, and is to be treated accordingly. . . .

Here, it is like, the common question will be made: Who shall be judge whether the prince or legislative act contrary to their trust? This, perhaps, ill-affected and factious men may spread amongst the people, when the prince only makes use of his due prerogative. To this I reply: The people shall be judge; for who shall be judge whether his trustee or deputy acts well and according to the trust reposed in him but he who deputes him and must, by having deputed him, have still a power to discard him when he fails in his trust? If this be reasonable in particular cases of private men, why should it be otherwise in that of the greatest moment where the welfare of millions is concerned, and also where the evil, if not prevented, is greater and the redress very difficult, dear, and dangerous? . . .

If a controversy arise betwixt a prince and some of the people in a matter where the law is silent or doubtful, and the thing be of great consequence, I should think the proper umpire in such a case should be the body of the people; for in cases where the prince has a trust reposed in him and is dispensed from the common ordinary rules of the law, there, if any men find themselves aggrieved and think the prince acts contrary to or beyond that trust, who so proper to judge as the body of the people (who at first, lodged that trust in him) how far they meant it should extend? But if the prince, or whoever they be in the administration, decline that way of determination, the appeal then lies nowhere but to heaven; force between either persons who have no known superior on earth, or which permits no appeal to a judge on earth, being properly a state of war wherein the appeal lies only to heaven; and in that state the injured party must judge for himself when he will think fit to make use of that appeal and put himself upon it.

To conclude, the power that every individual gave the society when he entered into it can never revert to the individuals again as long as the society lasts, but will always remain in the community, because without this there can be no community, no commonwealth, which is contrary to the original agreement; so also when the society has placed the legislative in any assembly of men, to continue in them and their successors with direction and authority for providing such successors, the legislative can never revert to the people while that government lasts, because having provided a legislative with power to continue for ever, they have given up their political power to the legislative and cannot resume it. But if they have set limits to the duration of their legislative and made this supreme power in any person or assembly only temporary, or else when by the miscarriages of those in authority it is forfeited, upon the forfeiture, or at the determination of the time set, it reverts to the society, and the people have a right to act as supreme and continue the legislative in themselves, or erect a new form, or under the old form place it in new hands, as they think good.

On Liberty

JOHN STUART MILL

John Stuart Mill (1805–1873) was a leading British philosopher who wrote many influential books on ethics, political philosophy, logic, and feminism.

Chapter I
Introductory

. . . The object of this essay is to assert one very simple principle, as entitled to govern absolutely the dealings of society with the individual in the way of compulsion and control, whether the means used be physical force in the form of legal penalties, or the moral coercion of public opinion. That principle is, that the sole end for which mankind are warranted, individually or collectively, in interfering with the liberty of action of any of their number, is self-protection. That the only purpose for which power can be rightfully exercised over any member of a civilized community, against his will, is to prevent harm to others. His own good, either physical or moral, is not a sufficient warrant. He cannot rightfully be compelled to do or forbear because it will be better for him to do so, because it will make him happier, because, in the opinions of others, to do so would be wise, or even right. These are good reasons for remonstrating with him, or reasoning with him, or persuading him, or entreating him, but not for compelling him, or visiting him with any evil in case he do otherwise. To justify that, the conduct from which it is desired to deter him must be calculated to produce evil to some one else. The only part of the conduct of anyone, for which he is amenable to society, is that which concerns others. In the part which merely concerns himself, his independence is, of right, absolute. Over himself, over his own body and mind, the individual is sovereign.

It is perhaps hardly necessary to say that this doctrine is meant to apply only to human beings in the maturity of their faculties. We are not speaking of children, or of young persons below the age which the law may fix as that of manhood or womanhood. Those who are still in a state to require being taken care of by others, must be protected against their own actions as well as against external injury. . . .

It is proper to state that I forego any advantage which could be derived to my argument from the idea of abstract right, as a thing independent of utility. I regard utility as the ultimate appeal on all ethical questions; but it must be utility in the largest sense, grounded on the permanent interests of a man as a progressive being. Those interests, I contend, authorized the subjection of individual spontaneity to external control, only in respect to those actions of each which concern the interest of other people. If anyone does an act hurtful to others, there is a *prima facie* case for punishing him, by law, or, where legal penalties are not safely applicable, by general disapprobation. There are also many positive acts for the benefit of others, which he may rightfully be compelled to perform: such as to give evidence in a court of justice; to bear his fair share in the common defense, or in any other joint work necessary to the interest of the society of which he enjoys the protection; and to perform certain acts of individual beneficence, such as saving a fellow-creature's life, or interposing to protect the defenseless against ill-usage, things which wherever it is obviously a man's duty to do, he may rightfully be made responsible to society for not doing. A person may cause evil to others not only by his actions but by his inaction, and in either case he is justly accountable to them for the injury. The latter case, it is true, requires a much more cautious exercise of compulsion than the former. To make anyone answerable for doing evil to others is the rule; to make him an-

From *On Liberty*, first published in London in 1859.

swerable for not preventing evil is, comparatively speaking, the exception. Yet there are many cases clear enough and grave enough to justify that exception. In all things which regard the external relations of the individual, he is *de jure* amenable to those whose interests are concerned, and, if need be, to society as their protector. There are often good reasons for not holding him to the responsibility; but these reasons must arise from the special expediencies of the case: either because it is a kind of case in which he is on the whole likely to act better, when left to his own discretion, than when controlled in any way in which society have it in their power to control him; or because the attempt to exercise control would produce other evils, greater than those which it would prevent. When such reasons as these preclude the enforcement of responsibility, the conscience of the agent himself should step into the vacant judgment seat, and protect those interests of others which have no external protection; judging himself all the more rigidly, because the case does not admit of his being made accountable to the judgment of his fellow-creatures.

But there is a sphere of action in which society, as distinguished from the individual, has, if any, only an indirect interest; comprehending all that portion of a person's life and conduct which affects only himself, or if it also affects others, only with their free, voluntary, and undeceived consent and participation. When I say only himself, I mean directly, and in the first instance; for whatever affects himself, may affect others through himself; and the objection which may be grounded on this contingency, will receive consideration in the sequel. This, then, is the appropriate region of human liberty. It comprises, *first*, the inward domain of consciousness; demanding liberty of conscience in the most comprehensive sense; liberty of thought and feeling; absolute freedom of opinion and sentiment on all subjects, practical or speculative, scientific, moral or theological. The liberty of expressing and publishing opinions may seem to fall under a different principle, since it belongs to that part of the conduct of an individual which concerns other people; but, being almost of as much importance as the liberty of thought itself, and resting in great part on the same reasons, is practically inseparable from it. *Secondly*,

the principle requires liberty of tastes and pursuits; of framing the plan of our life to suit our own character; of doing as we like, subject to such consequences as may follow: without impediment from our fellow-creatures, so long as what we do does not harm them, even though they should think our conduct foolish, perverse, or wrong. *Thirdly*, from this liberty of each individual, follows the liberty, within the same limits, of combination among individuals; freedom to unite, for any purpose not involving harm to others: the persons combining being supposed to be of full age, and not forced or deceived.

No society in which these liberties are not, on the whole, respected, is free, whatever may be its form of government; and none is completely free in which they do not exist absolute and unqualified. The only freedom which deserves the name, is that of pursuing our own good in our own way, so long as we do not attempt to deprive others of theirs, or impede their efforts to obtain it. Each is the proper guardian of his own health, whether bodily, or mental and spiritual. Mankind are greater gainers by suffering each other to live as seems good to themselves, than by compelling each to live as seems good to the rest.

Though this doctrine is anything but new, and, to some persons, may have the air of a truism, there is no doctrine which stands more directly opposed to the general tendency of existing opinion and practice. . . . There is . . . an inclination to stretch unduly the powers of society over the individual, both by the force of opinion and even by that of legislation; and as the tendency of all the changes taking place in the world is to strengthen society, and diminish the power of the individual, this encroachment is not one of the evils which tend spontaneously to disappear, but, on the contrary, to grow more and more formidable. The disposition of mankind, whether as rulers or as fellow-citizens, to impose their own opinions and inclinations as a rule of conduct on others, is so energetically supported by some of the best and by some of the worst feelings incident to human nature, that it is hardly ever kept under restraint by anything but want of power; and as the power is not declining, but growing, unless a strong barrier of moral conviction can be raised against the mischief, we must expect, in the present circumstances of the world, to see it increase. . . .

Chapter II
Of the Liberty of Thought and Discussion

The time, it is to be hoped, is gone by, when any defence would be necessary of the "liberty of the press" as one of the securities against corrupt or tyrannical government. . . . Speaking generally, it is not, in constitutional countries, to be apprehended that the government, whether completely responsible to the people or not, will often attempt to control the expression of opinion, except when in doing so it makes itself the organ of the general intolerance of the public. Let us suppose, therefore, that the government is entirely at one with the people, and never thinks of exerting any power of coercion unless in agreement with what it conceives to be their voice. But I deny the right of the people to exercise such coercion, either by themselves or by their government. The power itself is illegitimate. The best government has no more title to it than the worst. It is as noxious, or more noxious, when exerted in accordance with public opinion, than when in opposition to it. If all mankind minus one were of one opinion, and only one person were of the contrary opinion, mankind would be no more justified in silencing that one person, than he, if he had the power, would be justified in silencing mankind. Were an opinion a personal possession of no value except to the owner; if to be obstructed in the enjoyment of it were simply a private injury, it would make some difference whether the injury was inflicted only on a few persons or on many. But the peculiar evil of silencing the expression of an opinion is, that it is robbing the human race: posterity as well as the existing generation; those who dissent from the opinion, still more than those who hold it. If the opinion is right, they are deprived of the opportunity of exchanging error for truth; if wrong, they lose, what is almost as great a benefit, the clearer perception and livelier impression of truth, produced by its collision with error.

It is necessary to consider separately these two hypotheses, each of which has a distinct branch of the argument corresponding to it. We can never be sure that the opinion we are endeavoring to stifle is a false opinion; and if we were sure, stifling it would be an evil still.

First: the opinion which it is attempted to suppress by authority may possibly be true. Those who desire to suppress it, of course deny its truth; but they are not infallible. They have no authority to decide the question for all mankind, and exclude every other person from the means of judging. To refuse a hearing to an opinion, because they are sure that it is false, is to assume that *their* certainty is the same thing as *absolute* certainty. All silencing of discussion is an assumption of infallibility. Its condemnation may be allowed to rest on this common argument, not the worse for being common.

Unfortunately for the good sense of mankind, the fact of their fallibility is far from carrying the weight in their practical judgment which is always allowed to it in theory; for while everyone well knows himself to be fallible, few think it necessary to take any precautions against their own fallibility, or admit the supposition that any opinion of which they feel very certain, may be one of the examples of the error to which they acknowledge themselves to be liable. Absolute princes, or others who are accustomed to unlimited deference, usually feel this complete confidence in their own opinions on nearly all subjects. People more happily situated, who sometimes hear their opinions disputed, and are not wholly unused to be set right when they are wrong, place the same unbounded reliance only on such of their opinions as are shared by all who surround them, or to whom they habitually defer; for in proportion to a man's want of confidence in his own solitary judgment, does he usually repose, with implicit trust, on the infallibility of "the world" in general. And the world, to each individual, means the part of it with which he comes in contact—his party, his sect, his church, his class of society; the man may be called, by comparison, almost liberal and large-minded to whom it means anything so comprehensive as his own country or his own age. Nor is his faith in this collective authority at all shaken by his being aware that other ages, countries, sects, churches, classes, and parties have thought, and even now think, the exact reverse. He devolves upon his own world the responsibility of being in the right against the dissentient worlds of other people; and it never troubles him that mere accident has decided which of these numerous worlds is the object of his reliance, and that the same causes which make him a Churchman in London, would have made him a Buddhist or a Confucian in Peking. Yet it is as evident in itself as any amount of argument can make it, that ages are no more infallible than individuals; every age having held many opinions which subsequent ages have deemed not only false but absurd; and it is as certain that many opinions now general will be rejected by future ages, as it is that many, once general, are rejected by the present.

The objection likely to be made to this argument would probably take some such form as the following. There is no greater assumption of infallibility in forbidding the propagation of error, than in any other thing which is done by public authority on its own judgment and responsibility. Judgment is given to men that they may use it. Because it may be used erroneously, are men to be told that they ought not to use it at all? To prohibit what they think pernicious, is not claiming exemption from error, but fulfilling the duty incumbent on them, although fallible, of acting on their conscientious conviction. If we were never to act on our opinions, because those opinions may be wrong, we should leave all our interests uncared for, and all our duties unperformed. An objection which applies to all conduct can be no valid objection to any conduct in particular. It is the duty of governments, and of individuals, to form the truest opinions they can; to form them carefully, and never impose them upon others unless they are quite sure of being right. But when they are sure (such reasoners may say), it is not conscientiousness but cowardice to shrink from acting on their opinions, and allow doctrines which they honestly think dangerous to the welfare of mankind, either in this life or in another, to be scattered abroad without restraint, because other people, in less enlightened times, have persecuted opinions now believed to be true. Let us take care, it may be said, not to make the same mistake; but governments and nations have made mistakes in other things, which are not denied to be fit subjects for the exercise of authority: they have laid on bad taxes, made unjust wars. Ought we therefore to lay on no taxes, and, under whatever provocation, make no wars? Men, and governments, must act to the best of their ability. There is no such thing as absolute certainty, but there is assurance sufficient for the purposes of human life. We may, and must, assume our opinion to be true for the guidance of our own conduct: and it is assuming no more when we forbid bad men to pervert society by the propagation of opinions which we regard as false and pernicious.

I answer that it is assuming very much more. There is the greatest difference between presuming an opinion to be true because, with every opportunity for contesting it, it has not been refuted, and assuming its truth for the purpose of not permitting its refutation. Complete liberty of contradicting and disproving our opinion is the very condition which justifies us in assuming its truth for purposes of action; and on no other terms can a being with human faculties have any rational assurance of being right.

When we consider either the history of opinion, or the ordinary conduct of human life, to what is it to be ascribed that the one and the other are no worse than they are? Not certainly to the inherent force of the human understanding; for, on any matter not self-evident, there are ninety-nine persons totally incapable of judging of it for one who is capable; and the capacity of the hundredth person is only comparative: for the majority of the eminent men of every past generation held many opinions now known to be erroneous, and did or approved numerous things which no one will now justify. Why is it, then, that there is on the whole a preponderance among mankind of rational opinions and rational conduct? If there really is this preponderance—which there must be unless human affairs are, and have always been, in an almost desperate state—it is owing to a quality of the human mind, the source of everything respectable in man either as an intellectual or as a moral being, namely, that his errors are corrigible. He is capable of rectifying his mistakes, by discussion and experience. Not by experience alone. There must be discussion, to show how experience is to be interpreted. Wrong opinions and practices gradually yield to fact and argument; but facts and arguments, to produce any effect on the mind, must be brought before it. Very few facts are able to tell their own story, without comments to bring out their meaning. The whole strength and value, then, of human judgment, depending on the one property, that it can be set right when it is wrong, reliance can be placed on it only when the means of setting it right are kept constantly at hand. In the case of any person whose judgment is really deserving of confidence, how has it become so? Because he has kept his mind open to criticism of his opinions and conduct. Because it has been his practice to listen to all that could be said against him; to profit by as much of it as was just, and expound to himself, and upon occasion to others, the fallacy of what was fallacious. Because he has felt that the only way in which a human being can make some approach to knowing the whole of a subject, is by hearing what can be said about it by persons of every variety of opinion, and studying all modes in which it can be looked at by every character of mind. No wise man ever acquired his wisdom in any mode but this; nor is it in the nature of human intellect to become wise in any other manner. The steady habit of correcting and completing his own opinion by collating it with those of others, so far from causing doubt and hesitation in carrying it into practice, is the only stable foundation for a just reliance on it: for, being cognizant of all that can, at least obviously, be said against him, and having taken up his position against all gainsayers—knowing that he has sought for objections and difficulties, instead of avoiding them, and has shut out no light which can be thrown upon the subject from any quarter—he has a right to think his judgment better than that of any person, or any multitude, who have not gone through a similar process.

It is not too much to require that what the wisest of mankind, those who are best entitled to trust their own judgment, find necessary to warrant their relying on it, should be submitted to by that miscellaneous collection of a few wise and many foolish individuals, called the public. The most intolerant of churches, the Roman Catholic Church, even at the canonization of a saint, admits, and listens patiently to, a "devil's advocate." The holiest of men, it appears, cannot be admitted to posthumous honors, until all that the devil could say against him is known and weighed. If even the Newtonian philosophy were not permitted to be questioned, mankind could not feel as complete assurance of its truth as they now do. The beliefs which we have most warrant for, have no safeguard to rest on but a standing invitation to the whole world to prove them un-

founded. If the challenge is not accepted, or is accepted and the attempt fails, we are far enough from certainty still; but we have done the best that the existing state of human reason admits of; we have neglected nothing that could give the truth a chance of reaching us: if the lists are kept open, we may hope that if there be a better truth, it will be found when the human mind is capable of receiving it; and in the meantime we may rely on having attained such approach to truth as is possible in our own day. This is the amount of certainty attainable by a fallible being, and this the sole way of attaining it.

Strange it is that men should admit the validity of the arguments for free discussion, but object to their being "pushed to an extreme"; not seeing that unless the reasons are good for an extreme case, they are not good for any case. Strange that they should imagine that they are not assuming infallibility, when they acknowledge that there should be free discussion on all subjects which can possibly be *doubtful*, but think that some particular principle or doctrine should be forbidden to be questioned because it is so *certain*, that is, because *they are certain* that it is certain. To call any proposition certain while there is anyone who would deny its certainty if permitted, but who is not permitted, is to assume that we ourselves, and those who agree with us, are the judges of certainty, and judges without hearing the other side.

In the present age—which has been described as "destitute of faith, but terrified at scepticism"—in which people feel sure, not so much that their opinions are true, as that they should not know what to do without them—the claims of an opinion to be protected from public attack are rested not so much on its truth, as on its importance to society. There are, it is alleged, certain beliefs so useful, not to say indispensable, to well-being that it is as much the duty of governments to uphold those beliefs, as to protect any other of the interests of society. In a case of such necessity, and so directly in the line of their duty, something less than infallibility may, it is maintained, warrant, and even bind, governments to act on their own opinion, confirmed by the general opinion of mankind. It is also often argued, and still oftener thought, that none but bad men would desire to weaken these salutary beliefs; and there can be nothing wrong, it is thought, in restraining bad men, and prohibiting what only such men would wish to practice. This mode of thinking makes the justification of restraints on discussion not a question of the truth of doctrines, but of their usefulness; and flatters itself by that means to escape the responsibility of claiming to be an infallible judge of opinions. But those who thus satisfy themselves, do not perceive that the assumption of infallibility is merely shifted from one point to another. The usefulness of an opinion is itself matter of opinion: as disputable, as open to discussion, and requiring discussion as much as the opinion itself. There is the same need of an infallible judge of opinions to decide an opinion to be noxious, as to decide it to be false, unless the opinion condemned has full opportunity of defending itself. And it will not do to say that the heretic may be allowed to maintain the utility or harmlessness of his opinion, though forbidden to maintain its truth. The truth of an opinion is part of its utility. If we would know whether or not it is desirable that a proposition should be believed, is it possible to exclude the consideration of whether or not it is true? In the opinion, not of bad men, but of the best men, no belief which is contrary to truth can be really useful; and can you prevent such men from urging that plea, when they are charged with culpability for denying some doctrine which they are told is useful, but which they believe to be false? Those who are on the side of received opinions never fail to take all possible advantages of this plea: you do not find *them* handling the question of utility as if it could be completely abstracted from that of truth; on the contrary, it is, above all, because their doctrine is "the truth," that the knowledge or the belief of it is held to be so indispensable. There can be no fair discussion of the question of usefulness when an argument so vital may be employed on one side, but not on the other. And in point of fact, when law or public feeling do not permit the truth of an opinion to be disputed, they are just as little tolerant of a denial of its usefulness. The utmost they allow is an extenuation of its absolute necessity, or of the positive guilt of rejecting it.

In order more fully to illustrate the mischief of denying a hearing to opinions because we, in our own judgment, have condemned them, it will be desirable to fix down the discussion to a concrete case; and I choose, by preference, the cases which are least favorable to me—in which the argument against freedom of opinion, both on the score of truth and on that of utility, is considered the strongest. Let the opinions impugned be the belief in a God and in a future state, or any of the commonly received doctrines of morality. To fight the battle on such ground gives a great advantage to an unfair antagonist; since he will be sure to say (and many who have no desire to be unfair will say it internally), "Are these the doctrines which you do not deem sufficiently certain to be taken under the protection of laws? Is the belief in a God one of the opinions to feel sure of which you hold to be assuming infallibility?" But I must be permitted to observe that it is not the feeling sure of a doctrine (be it what it may) which I call an assumption of infallibility. It is the undertaking to decide that question *for others,* without allowing them to hear what can be said on the contrary side. And I denounce and reprobate this pretension not the less if put forth on the side of my most solemn convictions. However positive anyone's persuasion may be, not only of the falsity but of the pernicious consequences—not only of the pernicious consequences, but (to adopt expressions which I altogether condemn) the immorality and impiety of an opinion; yet if, in pursuance of that private judgment, though backed by the public judgment of his country or his contemporaries, he prevents the opinion from being heard in its defense, he assumes infallibility. And so far from the assumption being less objectionable or less dangerous because the opinion is called immoral or impious, this is the case of all others in which it is most fatal. These are exactly the occasions on which the men of one generation commit those dreadful mistakes which excite the astonishment and horror of posterity. It is among such that we find the instances memorable in history, when the arm of the law has been employed to root out the best men and the noblest doctrines; with deplorable success as to the men, though some of the doctrines have survived to be (as if in mockery) invoked in defense of similar conduct toward those who dissent from *them,* or from their received interpretation.

Mankind can hardly be too often reminded, that there was once a man named Socrates, between whom and the legal authorities and public opinion of his time there took place a memorable collision. Born in an age and country abounding in individual greatness, this man has been handed down to us by those who best knew both him and the age, as the most virtuous man in it; while *we* know him as the head and prototype of all subsequent teachers of virtue, the source equally of the lofty inspiration of Plato and the judicious utilitarianism of Aristotle, . . . the two head-springs of ethical as of all other philosophy. This acknowledged master of all the eminent thinkers who have since lived—whose fame, still growing after more than two thousand years, all but outweighs the whole remainder of the names which make his native city illustrious—was put to death by his countrymen, after a judicial conviction, for impiety and immorality. Impiety, in denying the gods recognized by the State; indeed his accuser asserted (see the *Apology*) that he believed in no gods at all. Immorality, in being, by his doctrines and instructions, a "corruptor of youth." Of these charges the tribunal, there is every ground for believing, honestly found him guilty, and condemned the man who probably of all then born had deserved best of mankind to be put to death as a criminal. . . .

A Theory of Justice

JOHN RAWLS

John Rawls (1921–   ) teaches philosophy at Harvard University.

THE MAIN IDEA OF THE THEORY OF JUSTICE

My aim is to present a conception of justice which generalizes and carries to a higher level of abstraction the familiar theory of the social contract as found, say, in Locke, Rousseau, and Kant.[1] In order to do this we are not to think of the original contract as one to enter a particular society or to set up a particular form of government. Rather, the guiding idea is that the principles of justice for the basic structure of society are the object of the original agreement. They are the principles that free and rational persons concerned to further their own interests would accept in an initial position of equality as defining the fundamental terms of their association. These principles are to regulate all further agreements; they specify the kinds of social cooperation that can be entered into and the forms of government that can be established. This way of regarding the principles of justice I shall call justice as fairness.

Thus we are to imagine that those who engage in social cooperation choose together, in one joint act, the principles which are to assign basic rights and duties and to determine the division of social benefits. Men are to decide in advance how they are to regulate their claims against one another and what is to be the foundation charter of their society. Just as each person must decide by rational reflection what constitutes his good, that is, the system of ends which it is rational for him to pursue, so a group of persons must decide once and for all what is to count among them as just and unjust. The choice which rational men would make in this hypothetical situation of equal liberty, assuming for the present that this choice problem has a solution, determines the principles of justice.

In justice as fairness the original position of equality corresponds to the state of nature in the traditional theory of the social contract. This original position is not, of course, thought of as an actual historical state of affairs, much less as a primitive condition of culture. It is understood as a purely hypothetical situation characterized so as to lead to a certain conception of justice.[2] Among the essential features of this situation is that no one knows his place in society, his class position or social status, nor does any one know his fortune in the distribution of natural assets and abilities, his intelligence, strength, and the like. I shall even assume that the parties do not know their conceptions of the good or their special psychological propensities. The principles of justice are chosen behind a veil of ignorance. This ensures that no one is advantaged or disadvantaged in the choice of principles by the outcome of natural chance or the contingency of social circumstances. Since all are similarly situated and no one is able to design principles to favor his particular condition, the principles of justice are the result of a fair agreement or bargain. For given the circumstances of the original position, the symmetry of everyone's relations to each other, this initial situation is fair between individuals as moral persons, that is, as rational beings with their own ends and capable, I shall assume, of a sense of justice. The original position is, one might say, the appropriate initial status quo, and thus the fundamental agreements reached in it are fair. This explains the propriety of the name "justice as fairness": it conveys the idea that the principles of justice are agreed to in an initial situation that is fair. The name does not mean that the concepts of justice and fairness are the same, any more than the phrase "poetry as metaphor" means that the concepts of poetry and metaphor are the same.

Justice as fairness begins, as I have said, with one of the most general of all choices which persons might make together, namely, with the choice of the first principles of a conception of justice which is to regulate all subsequent criticism and reform of institutions. Then, having chosen a conception of justice, we can suppose that they are to choose a constitution and a legislature to enact laws, and so on, all in accordance with the principles of justice initially agreed upon. Our social situation is just if it is such that by this sequence of hypothetical agreements we would have contracted into the general system of rules which defines it. Moreover, assuming that the original position does determine a set of principles (that is, that a particular conception of justice would be chosen), it will then be true that whenever social institutions satisfy these principles those engaged in them can say to one another that they are cooperating on terms to which they would agree if they were free and equal persons whose re-

lations with respect to one another were fair. They could all view their arrangements as meeting the stipulations which they would acknowledge in an initial situation that embodies widely accepted and reasonable constraints on the choice of principles. The general recognition of this fact would provide the basis for a public acceptance of the corresponding principles of justice. No society can, of course, be a scheme of cooperation which men enter voluntarily in a literal sense; each person finds himself placed at birth in some particular position in some particular society, and the nature of this position materially affects his life prospects. Yet a society satisfying the principles of justice as fairness comes as close as a society can to being a voluntary scheme, for its meets the principles which free and equal persons would assent to under circumstances that are fair. In this sense its members are autonomous and the obligations they recognize self-imposed.

One feature of justice as fairness is to think of the parties in the initial situation as rational and mutually disinterested. This does not mean that the parties are egoists, that is, individuals with only certain kinds of interests, say in wealth, prestige, and domination. But they are conceived as not taking an interest in one another's interests. They are to presume that even their spiritual aims may be opposed, in the way that the aims of those of different religions may be opposed. Moreover, the concept of rationally must be interpreted as far as possible in the narrow sense, standard in economic theory, of taking the most effective means to given ends. I shall modify this concept to some extent . . . but one must try to avoid introducing into it any controversial ethical elements. The initial situation must be characterized by stipulations that are widely accepted.

In working out the conception of justice as fairness one main task clearly is to determine which principles of justice would be chosen in the original position. To do this we must describe this situation in some detail and formulate with care the problem of choice which it presents. These matters I shall take up in the immediately succeeding chapters. It may be observed, however, that once the principles of justice are thought of as arising from an original agreement in a situation of equality, it is an open question whether the principle of utility would be acknowledged. Offhand it hardly seems likely that persons who view themselves as equals, entitled to press their claims upon one another, would agree to a principle which may require lesser life prospects for some simply for the sake of a greater sum of advantages enjoyed by others. Since each desires to protect his interests, his capacity to advance his conception of the good, no one has a reason to acquiesce in an enduring loss for himself in order to bring about a greater net balance of satisfaction. In the absence of strong and lasting benevolent impulses, a rational man would not accept a basic structure merely because it maximized the algebraic sum of advantages irrespective of its permanent effects on his own basic rights and interests. Thus it seems that the principle of utility is incompatible with the conception of social cooperation among equals for mutual advantage. It appears to be inconsistent with the idea of reciprocity implicit in the notion of a well-ordered society. Or, at any rate, so I shall argue.

I shall maintain instead that the persons in the initial situation would choose two rather different principles: the first requires equality in the assignment of basic rights and duties, while the second holds that social and economic inequalities, for example inequalities of wealth and authority, are just only if they result in compensating benefits for everyone, and in particular for the least advantaged members of society. These principles rule out justifying institutions on the grounds that the hardships of some are offset by a greater good in the aggregate. It may be expedient but it is not just that some should have less in order that others may prosper. But there is no injustice in the greater benefits earned by a few provided that the situation of persons not so fortunate is thereby improved. The intuitive idea is that since everyone's well-being depends upon a scheme of cooperation without which no one could have a satisfactory life, the division of advantages should be such as to draw forth the willing cooperation of everyone taking part in it, including those less well situated. Yet this can be expected only if reasonable terms are proposed. The two principles mentioned seem to be a fair agreement on the basis of which those better endowed, or more fortunate in their social position, neither of which we can be said to deserve, could expect the willing cooperation of others when some workable scheme is a necessary condition of the welfare of all.[3] Once we

decide to look for a conception of justice that nullifies the accidents of natural endowment and the contingencies of social circumstances as counters in quest for political and economic advantage, we are led to these principles. They express the result of leaving aside those aspects of the social world that seem arbitrary from a moral point of view. . . .

A final remark. Justice as fairness is not a complete contract theory. For it is clear that the contractarian idea can be extended to the choice of more or less an entire ethical system, that is, to a system including principles for all the virtues and not only for justice. Now for the most part I shall consider only principles of justice and others closely related to them; I make no attempt to discuss the virtues in a systematic way. Obviously if justice as fairness succeeds reasonably well, a next step would be to study the more general view suggested by the name "rightness as fairness." But even this wider theory fails to embrace all moral relationships, since it would seem to include only our relations with other persons and to leave out of account how we are to conduct ourselves toward animals and the rest of nature. I do not contend that the contract notion offers a way to approach these questions which are certainly of the first importance; and I shall have to put them aside. We must recognize the limited scope of justice as fairness and of the general type of view that it exemplifies. How far its conclusions must be revised once these other matters are understood cannot be decided in advance. . . .

TWO PRINCIPLES OF JUSTICE

I shall now state in a provisional form the two principles of justice that I believe would be chosen in the original position. In this section I wish to make only the most general comments, and therefore the first formulation of these principles is tentative. As we go on I shall run through several formulations and approximate step by step the final statement to be given much later. I believe that doing this allows the exposition to proceed in a natural way.

The first statement of the two principles reads as follows:

> First: each person is to have an equal right to the most extensive basic liberty compatible with a similar liberty for others.

Second: social and economic inequalities are to be arranged so that they are both (a) reasonably expected to be to everyone's advantage, and (b) attached to positions and offices open to all. . . .

By way of general comment, these principles primarily apply, as I have said, to the basic structure of society. They are to govern the assignment of rights and duties and to regulate the distribution of social and economic advantages. As their formulation suggests, these principles presuppose that the social structure can be divided into two more or less distinct parts, the first principle applying to the one, the second to the other. They distinguish between those aspects of the social system that define and secure the equal liberties of citizenship and those that specify and establish social and economic inequalities. The basic liberties of citizens are, roughly speaking, political liberty (the right to vote and to be eligible for public office) together with freedom of speech and assembly; liberty of conscience and freedom of thought; freedom of the person along with the right to hold (personal) property; and freedom from arbitrary arrest and seizure as defined by the concept of the rule of law. These liberties are all required to be equal by the first principle, since citizens of a just society are to have the same basic rights.

The second principle applies, in the first approximation, to the distribution of income and wealth and to the design of organizations that make use of differences in authority and responsibility, or chains of command. While the distribution of wealth and income need not be equal, it must be to everyone's advantage, and at the same time, positions of authority and offices of command must be accessible to all. One applies the second principle by holding positions open, and then, subject to this constraint, arranges social and economic inequalities so that everyone benefits.

These principles are to be arranged in a serial order with the first principle prior to the second. This ordering means that a departure from the institutions of equal liberty required by the first principle cannot be justified by, or compensated for, by greater social and economic advantages. The distribution of wealth and income, and the hierarchies of authority, must be consistent with both the liberties of equal citizenship and equality of opportunity.

It is clear that these principles are rather specific in their content, and their acceptance rests on certain assumptions that I must eventually try to explain and justify. A theory of justice depends upon a theory of society in ways that will become evident as we proceed. For the present, it should be observed that the two principles (and this holds for all formulations) are a special case of a more general conception of justice that can be expressed as follows.

All social values—liberty and opportunity, income and wealth, and the bases of self-respect—are to be distributed equally unless an unequal distribution of any, or all, of these values is to everyone's advantage.

Injustice, then, is simply inequalities that are not to the benefit of all. Of course, this conception is extremely vague and requires interpretation.

As a first step, suppose that the basic structure of society distributes certain primary goods, that is, things that every rational man is presumed to want. These goods normally have a use whatever a person's rational plan of life. For simplicity, assume that the chief primary goods at the disposition of society are rights and liberties, powers and opportunities, income and wealth. . . . These are the social primary goods. Other primary goods such as health and vigor, intelligence and imagination, are natural goods; although their possession is influenced by the basic structure, they are not so directly under its control. Imagine, then, a hypothetical initial arrangement in which all the social primary goods are equally distributed: everyone has similar rights and duties, and income and wealth are evenly shared. This state of affairs provides a benchmark for judging improvements. If certain inequalities of wealth and organizational powers would make everyone better off than in this hypothetical starting situation, then they accord with the general conception.

Now it is possible, at least theoretically, that by giving up some of their fundamental liberties men are sufficiently compensated by the resulting social and economic gains. The general conception of justice imposes no restrictions on what sort of inequalities are permissible; it only requires that everyone's position be improved. We need not suppose anything so drastic as consenting to a condition of slavery. Imagine instead that men forego certain political rights when the economic returns are significant and their capacity to influence the course of policy by the exercise of these rights would be marginal in any case. It is this kind of exchange which the two principles as stated rule out; being arranged in serial order they do not permit exchanges between basic liberties and economic and social gains. The serial ordering of principles expresses an underlying preference among primary social goods. When this preference is rational so likewise is the choice of these principles in this order.

In developing justice as fairness I shall, for the most part, leave aside the general conception of justice and examine instead the special case of the two principles in serial order. The advantage of this procedure is that from the first the matter of priorities is recognized and an effort made to find principles to deal with it. One is led to attend throughout to the conditions under which the acknowledgment of the absolute weight of liberty with respect to social and economic advantages, as defined by the lexical order of the two principles, would be reasonable. Offhand, this ranking appears extreme and too special a case to be of much interest; but there is more justification for it than would appear at first sight. Or at any rate, so I shall maintain. . . . Furthermore, the distinction between fundamental rights and liberties and economic and social benefits marks a difference among primary social goods that one should try to exploit. It suggests an important division in the social system. Of course, the distinctions drawn and the ordering proposed are bound to be at best only approximations. There are surely circumstances in which they fail. But it is essential to depict clearly the main lines of a reasonable conception of justice: and under many conditions anyway, the two principles in serial order may serve well enough. When necessary we can fall back on the more general conception.

The fact that the two principles apply to institutions has certain consequences. Several points illustrate this. First of all, the rights and liberties referred to by these principles are those which are defined by the public rules of the basic structure. Whether men are free is determined by the rights and duties established by the major institutions of society. Liberty is a certain pattern of social forms. The first principle simply requires that certain sorts of rules, those de-

fining basic liberties, apply to everyone equally and that they allow the most extensive liberty compatible with a like liberty for all. The only reason for circumscribing the rights defining liberty and making men's freedom less extensive than it might otherwise be is that these equal rights as institutionally defined would interfere with one another.

Another thing to bear in mind is that when principles mention persons, or require that everyone gain from an inequality, the reference is to representative persons holding the various social positions, or offices, or whatever, established by the basic structure. Thus in applying the second principle I assume that it is possible to assign an expectation of well-being to representative individuals holding these positions. This expectation indicates their life prospects as viewed from their social station. In general, the expectations of representative persons depend upon the distribution of rights and duties throughout the basic structure. When this changes, expectations change. I assume, then, that expectations are connected: by raising the prospects of the representative man in one position we presumably increase or decrease the prospects of representative men in other positions. Since it applies to institutional forms, the second principle (or rather the first part of it) refers to the expectations of representative individuals. As I shall discuss below, neither principle applies to distributions of particular goods to particular individuals who may be identified by their proper names. The situation where someone is considering how to allocate certain commodities to needy persons who are known to him is not within the scope of the principles. They are meant to regulate basic institutional arrangements. We must not assume that there is much similarity from the standpoint of justice between an administrative allotment of goods to specific persons and the appropriate design of society. Our common sense intuitions for the former may be a poor guide to the latter.

Now the second principle insists that each person benefit from permissible inequalities in the basic structure. This means that it must be reasonable for each relevant representative man defined by this structure, when he views it as a going concern, to prefer his prospects with the inequality to his prospects without it. One is not allowed to justify differences in income or organizational powers on the

ground that the disadvantages of those in one position are outweighed by the greater advantages of
those in another. Much less can infringements of
liberty be counterbalanced in this way. Applied to
the basic structure, the principle of utility would
have us maximize the sum of expectations of representative men (weighted by the number of persons
they represent, on the classical view); and this would
permit us to compensate for the losses of some by
the gains of others. Instead, the two principles require that everyone benefit from economic and social inequalities. It is obvious, however, that there
are indefinitely many ways in which all may be advantaged when the initial arrangement of equality is
taken as a benchmark. How then are we to choose
among these possibilities? The principles must be
specified so that they yield a determinate conclusion. I now turn to this problem.

Notes

1. As the text suggests, I shall regard Locke's *Second Treatise of Government,* Rousseau's *The Social Contract,* and
Kant's ethical works beginning with *The Foundations*
of the Metaphysics of Morals as definitive of the contract tradition. For all of its greatness, Hobbes's *Leviathan* raises special problems. A general historical survey is provided by J. W. Gough, *The Social Contract,*
2nd ed. (Oxford: The Clarendon Press, 1957), and
Otto Gierke, *Natural Law and the Theory of Society,* trans.
with an introduction by Ernest Barker (Cambridge:
The University Press, 1934). A presentation of the contract view as primarily an ethical theory is to be found
in G. R. Grice, *The Grounds of Moral Judgment* (Cambridge: The University Press, 1967).

2. Kant is clear that the original agreement is hypothetical. See *The Metaphysics of Morals,* pt. I (*Rechtslehre*), especially §§47, 52; and pt. II of the essay "Concerning
the Common Saying: This May Be True in Theory but
It Does Not Apply in Practice," in *Kant's Political Writings,* ed. Hans Reiss and trans. by H. B. Nisbet (Cambridge: The University Press, 1970), pp. 73–87. See
Georges Vlachos, *La Pensée politique de Kant* (Paris:
Presses Universitaires de France, 1962), pp. 326–335;
and J. G. Murphy, *Kant: The Philosophy of Right* (London: Macmillan, 1970), pp. 109–112, 133–136, for a
further discussion.

3. For the formulation of this intuitive idea I am indebted to Allan Gibbard.

Justice and Gender

SUSAN OKIN

Susan Okin (1946–   ) has taught philosophy at Stanford and Harvard Universities.

We as a society pride ourselves on our democratic
values. We don't believe people should be constrained by innate differences from being able to
achieve desired positions of influence to improve
their well-being; equality of opportunity is our
professed aim. The Preamble to our Constitution
stresses the importance of justice, as well as the general welfare and blessings of liberty. The Pledge of
Allegiance asserts that our republic preserves "liberty and justice for all."

Yet substantial inequalities between the sexes
still exist in our society. In economic terms, full-time
working women (after some very recent improvement) earn on average 71 percent of the earnings of
full-time working men. One-half of poor and three-
fifths of chronically poor households with dependent children are maintained by a single female parent. The poverty rate for elderly women is nearly
twice that for elderly men. On the political front,
two out of a hundred U.S. senators are women, one
out of nine justices seems to be considered sufficient

female representation on the Supreme Court, and the number of men chosen in each congressional election far exceeds the number of women elected in the entire history of the country. Underlying and intertwined with all these inequalities is the unequal distribution of the unpaid labor of the family.

An equal sharing between the sexes of family responsibilities, especially child care, is "the great revolution that has not happened." Women, including mothers of young children, are, of course, working outside the household far more than their mothers did. And the small proportion of women who reach high-level positions in politics, business, and the professions command a vastly disproportionate amount of space in the media, compared with the millions of women who work at low-paying, dead-end jobs, the millions who do part-time work with its lack of benefits, and the millions of others who stay home performing for no pay what is frequently not even acknowledged as work. Certainly, the fact that women are doing more paid work does not imply that they are more equal. It is often said that we are living in a postfeminist era. This claim, due in part to the distorted emphasis on women who have "made it," is false, no matter which of its meanings is intended. It is certainly not true that feminism has been vanquished, and equally untrue that it is no longer needed because its aims have been fulfilled. Until there is justice within the family, women will not be able to gain equality in politics, at work, or in any other sphere.

. . . The typical current practices of family life, structured to a large extent by gender, are not just. Both the expectation and the experience of the division of labor by sex make women vulnerable. As I shall show, a cycle of power relations and decisions pervades both family and workplace, each reinforcing the inequalities between the sexes that already exist within the other. Not only women, but children of both sexes, too, are often made vulnerable by gender-structured marriage. One-quarter of children in the United States now live in families with only one parent—in almost 90 percent of cases, the mother. Contrary to common perceptions—in which the situation of never-married mothers looms largest—65 percent of single-parent families are a result of marital separation or divorce. Recent research in a number of states has shown that, in the

average case, the standard of living of divorced women and the children who live with them plummets after divorce, whereas the economic situation of divorced men tends to be better than when they were married.

A central source of injustice for women these days is that the law, most noticeably in the event of divorce, treats more or less as equals those whom custom, workplace discrimination, and the still conventional division of labor within the family have made very unequal. Central to this socially created inequality are two commonly made but inconsistent presumptions: that women are primarily responsible for the rearing of children; and that serious and committed members of the work force (regardless of class) do not have primary responsibility, or even shared responsibility, for the rearing of children. The old assumption of the workplace, still implicit, is that workers have wives at home. It is built not only into the structure and expectations of the workplace but into other crucial social institutions, such as schools, which make no attempt to take account, in their scheduled hours or vacations, of the fact that parents are likely to hold jobs.

Now, of course, many wage workers do not have wives at home. Often, they *are* wives and mothers, or single, separated, or divorced mothers of small children. But neither the family nor the workplace has taken much account of this fact. Employed wives still do by far the greatest proportion of unpaid family work, such as child care and housework. Women are for more likely to take time out of the workplace or to work part-time because of family responsibilities than are their husbands or male partners. And they are much more likely to move because of their husbands' employment needs or opportunities than their own. All these tendencies, which are due to a number of factors, including the sex segregation and discrimination of the workplace itself, tend to be cyclical in their effects: wives advance more slowly than their husbands at work and thus gain less seniority, and the discrepancy between their wages increases over time. Then, because both the power structure of the family and what is regarded as consensual "rational" family decision-making reflect the fact that the husband usually earns more, it will become even less likely as time goes on that the unpaid work of the family will be shared between the spouses. Thus the cycle of inequality is perpetuated. Often hidden from view within a marriage, it is in the increasingly likely event of marital breakdown that the socially constructed inequality of married women is at its most visible.

This is what I mean when I say that gender-structured marriage *makes* women vulnerable. These are not matters of natural necessity, as some people would believe. Surely nothing in our natures dictates that men should not be equal participants in the rearing of their children. Nothing in the nature of work makes it impossible to adjust it to the fact that people are parents as well as workers. That these things have not happened is part of the historically, socially constructed differentiation between the sexes that feminists have come to call *gender*. We live in a society that has over the years regarded the innate characteristic of sex as one of the clearest legitimizers of different rights and restrictions, both formal and informal. While the legal sanctions that uphold male dominance have begun to be eroded in the past century, and more rapidly in the last twenty years, the heavy weight of tradition, combined with the effects of socialization, still works powerfully to reinforce sex roles that are commonly regarded as one of unequal prestige and worth. The sexual division of labor has not only been a fundamental part of the marriage contract, but so deeply influences us in our formative years that feminists of both sexes who try to reject it can find themselves struggling against it with varying degrees of ambivalence. Based on this linchpin, "gender"—by which I mean *the deeply entrenched institutionalization of sexual difference*—still permeates our society.

THE CONSTRUCTION OF GENDER

Due to feminism and feminist theory, gender is coming to be recognized as a social factor of major importance. Indeed, the new meaning of the word reflects the fact that so much of what was traditionally been thought of as sexual difference is now considered by many to be largely socially produced. Feminist scholars from many disciplines and with radically different points of view have contributed to the enterprise of making gender fully visible and comprehensible. At one end of the spectrum are those whose explanations of the subordination of

women focus primarily on biological differences as causal in the construction of gender, and at the other end are those who argue that biological difference may not even lie at the core of the social construction that is gender; the views of the vast majority of feminists fall between these extremes. The rejection of biological determinism and the corresponding emphasis on gender as a social construction characterize most current feminist scholarship. Of particular relevance is work in psychology, where scholars have investigated the importance of female primary parenting in the formation of our gendered identities, and in history and anthropology, where emphasis has been placed on the historical and cultural variability of gender. Some feminists have been criticized for developing theories of gender that do not take sufficient account of differences *among* women, especially race, class, religion, and ethnicity. While such critiques should always inform our research and improve our arguments, it would be a mistake to allow them to detract our attention from gender itself as a factor of significance. Many injustices are experienced by women *as women,* whatever the differences among them and whatever other injustices they also suffer from. The past and present gendered nature of the family, and the ideology that surrounds it, affects virtually all women, whether or not they live or ever lived in traditional families. Recognizing this is not to deny or de-emphasize the fact that gender may affect different subgroups of women to a different extent and in different ways.

The potential significance of feminist discoveries and conclusions about gender for issues of social justice cannot be overemphasized. They undermine centuries of argument that started with the notion that not only the distinct differentiation of women and men but the domination of women by men, being natural, was therefore inevitable and not even to be considered in discussions of justice. As I shall make clear in later chapters, despite the fact that such notions cannot stand up to rational scrutiny, they not only still survive but flourish in influential places.

During the same two decades in which feminists have been intensely thinking, researching, analyzing, disagreeing about, and rethinking the subject of gender, our political and legal institutions have been increasingly faced with issues concerning the injustices of gender and their effects. These issues are being decided within a fundamentally patriarchal system, founded in a tradition in which "individuals" were assumed to be male heads of households. Not surprisingly, the system has demonstrated a limited capacity for determining what is just, in many cases involving gender. Sex discrimination, sexual harassment, abortion, pregnancy in the workplace, parental leave, child care, and surrogate mothering have all become major and well-publicized issues of public policy, engaging both courts and legislatures. Issues of family justice, in particular—from child custody and terms of divorce to physical and sexual abuse of wives and children—have become increasingly visible and pressing, and are commanding increasing attention from the police and court systems. There is clearly a major "justice crisis" in contemporary society arising from issues of gender.

THEORIES OF JUSTICE AND THE NEGLECT OF GENDER

During these same two decades, there has been a great resurgence of theories of social justice. Political theory, which had been sparse for a period before the late 1960s except as an important branch of intellectual history, has become a flourishing field, with social justice as its central concern. Yet, remarkably, major contemporary theorists of justice have almost without exception ignored the situation I have just described. They have displayed little interest in or knowledge of the findings of feminism. They have largely bypassed the fact that the society to which their theories are supposed to pertain is heavily and deeply affected by gender, and faces difficult issues of justice stemming from its gendered past and present assumptions. Since theories of justice are centrally concerned with whether, how, and why persons should be treated differently from one another, this neglect seems inexplicable. These theories are *about* which initial or acquired characteristics or positions in society legitimize differential treatment of persons by social institutions, laws, and customs. They are *about* how and whether and to what extent beginnings should affect outcomes. The division of humanity into two sexes seems to provide an obvious subject for such inquiries. But, as we shall see, this does not strike most contemporary theorists

of justice, and their theories suffer in both coherence and relevance because of it. This book is about this remarkable case of neglect. It is also an attempt to rectify it, to point the way toward a more fully humanist theory of justice by confronting the question, "How just is gender?"

Why is it that when we turn to contemporary theories of justice, we do not find illuminating and positive contributions to this question? How can theories of justice that are ostensibly about people in general neglect women, gender, and all the inequalities between the sexes? One reason is that most theorists *assume*, though they do not discuss, the traditional, gender-structured family. Another is that they often employ gender-neutral language in a false, hollow way. Let us examine these two points.

The Hidden Gender-Structured Family

In the past, political theorists often used to distinguish clearly between "private" domestic life and the "public" life of politics and the marketplace, claiming explicitly that the two spheres operated in accordance with different principles. They separated out the family from what they deemed the subject matter of politics, and they made closely related, explicit claims about the nature of women and the appropriateness of excluding them from civil and political life. Men, the subjects of the theories, were able to make the transition back and forth from domestic to public life with ease, largely because of the functions performed by women in the family. When we turn to contemporary theories of justice, superficial appearances can easily lead to the impression that they are inclusive of women. In fact, they continue the same "separate spheres" tradition, by ignoring the family, its division of labor, and the related economic dependency and restricted opportunities of most women. The judgment that the family is "nonpolitical" is implicit in the fact that it is simply not discussed in most works of political theory today. In one way or another, as will become clear in the chapters that follow, almost all current theorists continue to assume that the "individual" who is the basic subject of their theories is the male head of a family traditional household. Thus the application of principles of justice to relations between the sexes, or within the household, is frequently, though tacitly, ruled out from the start. In the most influential of all twentieth-century theories of justice, that of John Rawls, family life is not only assumed, but is assumed to be just—and yet the prevalent gendered division of labor within the family is neglected, along with the associated distribution of power, responsibility, and privilege. . . .

Moreover, this stance is typical of contemporary theories of justice. They persist, despite the wealth of feminist challenges to their assumptions, in their refusal even to discuss the family and its gender structure, much less to recognize the family as a political institution of primary importance. Recent theories that pay even less attention to issues of family justice than Rawls's include Bruce Ackerman's *Social Justice in the Liberal State*, Ronald Dworkin's *Taking Rights Seriously*, William Galston's *Justice and the Human Good*, Alasdair MacIntyre's *After Virtue* and *Whose Justice? Whose Rationality?*, Robert Nozick's *Anarchy, State, and Utopia*, and Roberto Unger's *Knowledge and Politics* and *The Critical Legal Studies Movement*. Philip Green's *Retrieving Democracy* is a welcome exception. Michael Walzer's *Spheres of Justice*, too, is exceptional in this regard, but . . . the conclusion that can be inferred from his discussion of the family—that its gender structure is unjust—does not sit at all easily with his emphasis on the shared understandings of a culture as the foundation of justice. For gender is one aspect of social life about which clearly, in the United States in the latter part of the twentieth century, there are no shared understandings.

What is the basis of my claim that the family, while neglected, is *assumed* by theorists of justice? One obvious indication is that they take mature, independent human beings as the subjects of their theories without any mention of how they got to be that way. We know, of course, that human beings develop and mature only as a result of a great deal of attention and hard work, by far the greater part of it done by women. But when theorists of justice talk about "work," they mean paid work performed in the marketplace. They must be assuming that women, in the gender-structured family, continue to do their unpaid work of nurturing and socializing the young and providing a haven of intimate relations—otherwise there would be no moral subjects for them to theorize about. But these activities apparently take place outside the scope of their theories. Typically, the family itself is not examined in the light of whatever standard of justice the theorist arrives at.

The continued neglect of the family by theorists of justice flies in the face of a great deal of persuasive feminist argument . . . Scholars have clearly revealed the interconnections between the gender structure inside and outside the family and the extent to which the personal is political. They have shown that the assignment of primary parenting to women is crucial, both in forming the gendered identities of men and women and in influencing their respective choices and opportunities in life. Yet, so far, the simultaneous assumption and neglect of the family has allowed the impact of these arguments to go unnoticed in major theories of justice.

False Gender Neutrality

Many academics in recent years have become aware of the objectionable nature of using the supposedly generic male forms of nouns and pronouns. As feminist scholars have demonstrated, these words have most often *not* been used, throughout history and the history of philosophy in particular, with the intent to include women. *Man, mankind,* and *he* are going out of style as universal representations, though they have by no means disappeared. But the gender-neutral alternatives that most contemporary theorists employ are often even more misleading than the blatantly sexist use of male terms of reference. For they serve to disguise the real and continuing failure of theorists to confront the fact that the human race consists of persons of two sexes. They are by this means able to ignore the fact that there are *some* socially relevant physical differences between women and men, and the even more important fact that the sexes have had very different histories, very different assigned social roles and "natures," and very different degrees of access to power and opportunity in all human societies up to and including the present.

False gender neutrality is not a new phenomenon. Aristotle, for example, used *anthropos*—"human being"—in discussions of "the human good" that turn out not only to exclude women but to depend on their subordination. Kant even wrote of "all rational beings as such" in making arguments that he did not mean to apply to women. But it was more readily apparent that such arguments or conceptions of the good were not about all of us, but only about male heads of families. For their authors usually gave at some point an explanation, no matter how inadequate, of why what they were saying did not apply to women and of the different characteristics and virtues, rights, and responsibilities they thought women ought to have. Nevertheless, their theories have often been read as though they pertain (or can easily be applied) to all of us. Feminist interpretations of the last fifteen years or so have revealed the falsity of this "add women and stir" method of reading the history of political thought.

The falseness of the gender-neutral language of contemporary political theorists is less readily apparent. Most, though not all, contemporary moral and political philosophers use "men and women," "he or she," "persons," or the increasingly ubiquitous "self." Sometimes they even get their computers to distribute masculine and feminine terms of reference randomly. Since they do not explicitly exclude or differentiate women, as most theorists in the past did, we may be tempted to read their theories as inclusive of all of us. But we cannot. Their merely terminological responses to feminist challenges, in spite of giving a superficial impression of tolerance and inclusiveness, often strain credulity and sometimes result in nonsense. They do this in two ways: by ignoring the irreducible biological differences between the sexes, and/or by ignoring their different assigned social roles and consequent power differentials, and the ideologies that have supported them. Thus gender-neutral terms frequently obscure the fact that so much of the real experience of "persons," so long as they live in gender-structured societies, *does* in fact depend on what sex they are.

False gender neutrality is by no means confined to the realm of theory. Its harmful effects can be seen in public policies that have directly affected large numbers of women adversely. It was used, for example, in the Supreme Court's 1976 decision that the exclusion of pregnancy-related disabilities from employers' disability insurance plans was "not a gender-based discrimination at all." In a now infamous phrase of its majority opinion, the Court explained that such plans did not discriminate against women because the distinction drawn by such plans was between pregnant women and "non-pregnant *persons.*"

Examples of false gender neutrality in contemporary political theory will appear throughout this book; I will illustrate the concept here by citing just two examples. Ackerman's *Social Justice in the Liberal State* is a book containing scrupulously gender-neutral language. He breaks with this neutrality only, it seems, to *defy* existing sex roles; he refers to the "Commander," who plays the lead role in the theory, as "she." However, the argument of the book does not address the existing inequality or role differentiation between the sexes, though it has the potential for doing so. The full impact of Ackerman's gender-neutral language without attention to gender is revealed in his section on abortion: a two-page discussion written, with the exception of a single "she," in the completely gender-neutral language of fetuses and their "parents." The impression given is that there is no relevant respect in which the relationship of the two parents to the fetus differs. Now it is, of course, possible to imagine (and in the view of many feminists, would be desirable to achieve) a society in which differences in the relation of women and men to fetuses would be so slight as to reasonably play only a minor role in the discussion of abortion. But this would have to be a society without gender—one in which sexual difference carried no social significance, the sexes were equal in power and interdependence, and "mothering" and "fathering" a child meant the same thing, so that parenting and earning responsibilities were equally shared. We certainly do not live in such a society. Neither is there any discussion of one in Ackerman's theory, in which the division of labor between the sexes is not considered a matter of social (in)justice. In such a context, a "gender-neutral" discussion of abortion is almost as misleading as the Supreme Court's "gender-neutral" discussion of pregnancy.

A second illustration of false gender neutrality comes from Derek Phillip's *Toward a Just Social Order.* Largely because of the extent of his concern—rare among theorists of justice—with how we are to *achieve and maintain* a just social order, Phillips pays an unusual amount of attention to the family. He writes about the family as the locus for the development of a sense of justice and self-esteem, of an appreciation of the meaning of reciprocity, of the ability to exercise unforced choice, and of an awareness of alternative ways of life. The problem with this otherwise admirable discussion is that, apart from a couple of brief exceptions, the family itself is presented in gender-neutral terms that bear little resemblance to actual, gender-structured life. It is because of "parental affection," "parental nurturance," and "child rearing" that children in Phillips's families become the autonomous moral agents that his just society requires its citizens to be. The child's development of a sense of identity is very much dependent upon being raised by "parental figures who themselves have coherent and well-integrated personal identities," and we are told that such a coherent identity is "ideally one built around commitments to work and love." This all sounds very plausible. But it does not take into account of the multiple inequalities of gender. In gender-structured societies—in which the child rearers are women, "parental nurturance" is largely mothering, and those who do what society regards as "meaningful work" are assumed *not* to be primary parents—women in even the best of circumstances face considerable conflicts between love (a fulfilling family life) and "meaningful work." Women in less fortunate circumstances face even greater conflicts between love (even basic care of their children) and any kind of paid work at all.

It follows from Phillips's own premises that these conflicts are very likely to affect the strength and coherence in women of that sense of identity and self-esteem, coming from love and meaningful work, that he regards as essential for being an autonomous moral agent. In turn, if they are mothers, it is also likely to affect their daughters' and sons' developing senses of their identity. Gender is clearly a major obstacle to the attainment of a social order remotely comparable to the just one Phillips aspires to—but his false gender-neutral language allows him to ignore this fact. Although he is clearly aware of how distant in some other respects his vision of a just social order is from contemporary societies, his use of falsely gender-neutral language leaves him quite unaware of the distance between the type of family that might be able to socialize just citizens and typical families today.

The combined effect of the omission of the family and the falsely gender-neutral language in recent political thought is that most theorists are continu-ing to ignore the highly political issue of gender. The language they use makes little difference to what they actually do, which is to write about men and about only those women who manage, in spite of the gendered structures and practices of the society in which they live, to adopt patterns of life that have been developed to suit the needs of men. The fact that human beings are born as helpless infants —not as the purportedly autonomous actors who populate political theories—is obscured by the implicit assumption of gendered families, operating outside the range of the theories. To a large extent, contemporary theories of justice, like those of the past, are about men with wives at home.

GENDER AS AN ISSUE OF JUSTICE

For three major reasons, this state of affairs is unacceptable. The first is the obvious point that women must be fully included in any satisfactory theory of justice. The second is that equality of opportunity, not only for women but for children of both sexes, is seriously undermined by the current gender injustices of our society. And the third reason is that, as has already been suggested, the family—currently the linchpin of the gender structure—must be just if we are to have a just society, since it is within the family that we first come to have that sense of ourselves and our relations with others that is at the root of moral development.

Counting Women In

When we turn to the great tradition of Western political thought with questions about the justice of the treatment of the sexes in mind, it is to little avail. Bold feminists like Mary Astell, Mary Wollstonecraft, William Thompson, Harriet Taylor, and George Bernard Shaw have occasionally challenged the tradition, often using its own premises and arguments to overturn its explicit or implicit justification of the inequality of women. But John Stuart Mill is a rare exception to the rule that those who hold central positions in the tradition almost never question the justice of the subordination of women. This phenomenon is undoubtedly due in part to the fact that Aristotle, whose theory of justice has been so influential, relegated women to a sphere of "household justice"—populated by persons who are not funda-mentally equal to the free men who participate in political justice, but inferiors whose natural function is to serve those who are more fully human. The lib-eral tradition, despite its supposed foundation of in-dividual rights and human equality, is more Aristo-telian in this respect than is generally acknowledged. In one way or another, almost all liberal theorists have assumed that the "individual" who is the basic subject of the theories is the male head of a patriar-chal household. Thus they have not usually consid-ered applying the principles of justice to women or to relations between the sexes.

When we turn to contemporary theories of jus-tice, however, we expect to find more illuminating and positive contributions to the subject of gender and justice. As the omission of the family and the falseness of their gender-neutral language suggest, however, mainstream contemporary theories of jus-tice do not address the subject any better than those of the past. Theories of justice that apply to only half of us simply won't do; the inclusiveness falsely im-plied by the current use of gender-neutral terms must become real. Theories of justice must apply to all of us, and to all of human life, instead of *assum-ing* silently that half of us take care of whole areas of life that are considered outside the scope of social justice. In a just society, the structure and practices of families must afford women the same opportuni-ties as men to develop their capacities, to participate in political power, to influence social choices, and to be economically as well as physically secure.

Unfortunately, much feminist intellectual en-ergy in the 1980s has gone into the claim that "jus-tice" and "rights" are masculinist ways of thinking about morality that feminists should eschew or radi-cally revise, advocating a morality of care. The em-phasis is misplaced, I think, for several reasons. First, what is by now a vast literature on the subject shows that the evidence for differences in women's and men's ways of thinking about moral issues is not (at least yet) very clear; neither is the evidence about the source of whatever differences there might be. It may well turn out that any differences can be readily explained in terms of roles, including female pri-mary parenting, that are socially determined and therefore alterable. There is certainly no evidence —nor could there be, in such a gender-structured

society—for concluding that women are some-how naturally more inclined toward contextuality and away from universalism in their moral think-ing, a false concept that unfortunately reinforces the old stereotypes that justify separate spheres. The capacity of reactionary forces to capitalize on the "different moralities" strain in feminism is particu-larly evident in Pope John Paul II's recent Apostolic Letter, "On the Dignity of Women," in which he refers to women's special capacity to care for others in arguing for confining them to motherhood or celibacy.

Second, . . . I think the distinction between an ethic of justice and an ethic of care has been over-drawn. The best theorizing about justice, I argue, has integral to it the notions of care and empathy, of thinking of the interests and well-being of others who may be very different from ourselves. It is, therefore, misleading to draw a dichotomy as though they were two contrasting ethics. The best theorizing about justice is not some abstract "view from no-where," but results from the carefully attentive con-sideration of *everyone's* point of view. This means, of course, that the best theorizing about justice is not good enough if it does not, or cannot readily be adapted to, include women and their points of view as fully as men and their points of view.

Gender and Equality of Opportunity

The family is a crucial determinant of our opportu-nities in life, of what we "become." It has frequently been acknowledged by those concerned with real equality of opportunity that the family presents a problem. But though they have discerned serious problem, these theorists have underestimated it be-cause they have seen only half of it. They have seen that the disparity among families in terms of the physical and emotional environment, motivation, and material advantages they can give their children has a tremendous effect upon children's opportuni-ties in life. We are not born as isolated, equal indi-viduals in our society, but into family situations: some in the social middle, some poor and homeless, and some superaffluent; some to a single or soon-to-be-separated parent, some to parents whose mar-riage is fraught with conflict, some to parents who will stay together in love and happiness. Any claims that equal opportunity exists are therefore completely unfounded. Decades of neglect of the poor, especially of poor black and Hispanic households, accentuated by the policies of the Reagan years, have brought us farther from the principles of equal opportunity. To come close to them would require, for example, a high and uniform standard of public education and the provision of equal social services—including health care, employment training, job opportunities, drug rehabilitation, and decent housing—for all who need them. In addition to redistributive taxation, only massive reallocations of resources from the military to social services could make these things possible.

But even if all these disparities were somehow eliminated, we would still not attain equal opportunity for all. This is because what has not been recognized as an equal opportunity problem, except in feminist literature and circles, is the disparity *within* the family, the fact that its gender structure is itself a major obstacle to equality of opportunity. This is very important in itself, since one of the factors with most influence on our opportunities in life is the social significance attributed to our sex. The opportunities of girls and women are centrally affected by the structure and practices of family life, particularly by the fact that women are almost invariably primary parents. What nonfeminists who see in the family an obstacle to equal opportunity have *not* seen is that the extent to which a family is gender-structured can make the sex we belong to a relatively insignificant aspect of our identity and our life prospects or an all-pervading one. This is because so much of the social construction of gender takes place in the family, and particularly in the institution of female parenting.

Moreover, especially in recent years, with the increased rates of single motherhood, separation, and divorce, the inequalities between the sexes have *compounded* the first part of the problem. The disparity among families had grown largely because of the impoverishment of many women and children after separation or divorce. The division of labor in the typical family leaves most women far less capable than men of supporting themselves, and this disparity is accentuated by the fact that children of separated or divorced parents usually live with their mothers. The inadequacy—and frequent nonpay-

ment—of child support has become recognized as a major social problem. Thus the inequalities of gender are now directly harming many children of both sexes as well as women themselves. Enhancing equal opportunity for women, important as it is in itself, is also a crucial way of improving the opportunities of many of the most disadvantaged children.

As there is a connection among the parts of this problem, so is there a connection among some of the solutions: much of what needs to be done to end the inequalities of gender, and to work in the direction of ending gender itself, will also help to equalize opportunity from one family to another. Subsidized, high-quality day care is obviously one such thing; another is the adaptation of the workplace to the needs of parents. . . .

The Family as a School of Justice

One of the things that theorists who have argued that families need not or cannot be just, or who have simply neglected them, have failed to explain is how, with a formative social environment that is *not* founded upon principles of justice, children can learn to develop that sense of justice they will require as citizens of a just society. Rather than being one among many co-equal institutions of a just society, a just family is its essential foundation.

It may seem uncontroversial, even obvious, that families must be just because of the vast influence they have on the moral development of children. But this is clearly not the case. I shall argue that unless the first and most formative example of adult interaction usually experienced by children is one of justice and reciprocity, rather than one of domination and manipulation or of unequal altruism and one-sided self-sacrifice, and unless they themselves are treated with concern and respect, they are likely to be considerably hindered in becoming people who are guided by principles of justice. Moreover, I claim, the sharing of roles by men and women, rather than the division of roles between them, would have a further positive impact because the experience of *being* a physical and psychological nurturer—whether of a child or of another adult—would increase that capacity to identify with and fully comprehend the viewpoints of others that is important to a sense of justice. In a society that minimized gender this would be more likely to be the experience of all of us.

Almost every person in our society starts life in a family of some sort or other. Fewer of these families now fit the usual, though by no means universal, standard of previous generations, that is, wage-working father, homemaking mother, and children. More families these days are headed by a single parent; lesbian and gay parenting is no longer so rare; many children have two wage-working parents, and receive at least some of their early care outside the home. While its forms are varied, the family in which a child is raised, especially in the earliest years, is clearly a crucial place for early moral development and for the formation of our basic attitudes to others. It is, potentially, a place where we can *learn to be just.* It is especially important for the development of a sense of justice that grows from sharing the experiences of others and becoming aware of the points of view of others who are different in some respects from ourselves, but with whom we clearly have some interests in common.

The importance of the family for the moral development of individuals was far more often recognized by political theorists of the past than it is by those of the present. Hegel, Rousseau, Tocqueville, Mill, and Dewey are obvious examples that come to mind. Rousseau, for example, shocked by Plato's proposal to abolish the family, says that it is

> as though there were no need for a natural base on which to form conventional ties; as though the love of one's nearest were not the principle of the love one owes the state; as though it were not by means of the small fatherland which is the family that the heart attaches itself to the large one.

Defenders of both autocratic and democratic regimes have recognized the political importance of different family forms for the formation of citizens. On the one hand, the nineteenth-century monarchist Louis de Bonald argued against the divorce reforms of the French Revolution, which he claimed had weakened the patriarchal family, on the grounds that "in order to keep the state out of the hands of the people, it is necessary to keep the family out of the hands of women and children." Taking this same line of thought in the opposite direction, the U.S. Supreme Court decided in 1879 in *Reynolds v.*

Nebraska that familial patriarchy fostered despotism and was therefore intolerable. Denying Mormon men the freedom to practice polygamy, the Court asserted that it was an offense "subversive of good order" that "leads to the patriarchal principle, . . . [and] when applied to large communities, fetters the people in stationary despotism, while that principle cannot long exist in connection with monogamy."

However, while de Bonald was consistent in his adherence to an hierarchical family structure as necessary for an undemocratic political system, the Supreme Court was by no means consistent in promoting an egalitarian family as an essential underpinning for political democracy. For in other decisions of the same period—such as *Bradwell v. Illinois,* the famous 1872 case that upheld the exclusion of women from the practice of law—the Court rejected women's claims to legal equality, in the name of a thoroughly patriarchal, though monogamous, family that was held to require the dependence of women and their exclusion from civil and political life. While bigamy was considered patriarchal, and as such a threat to republican, democratic government, the refusal to allow a married woman to employ her talents and to make use of her qualifications to earn an independent living was not considered patriarchal. It was so far from being a threat to the civil order, in fact, that it was deemed necessary for it, and as such was ordained by both God and nature. Clearly in both *Reynolds* and *Bradwell,* "state authorities enforced family forms preferred by those in power and justified as necessary to stability and order. The Court noticed the despotic potential of polygamy, but was blind to the despotic potential of patriarchal monogamy. This was perfectly acceptable to them as a training ground for citizens.

Most theorists of the past who stressed the importance of the family and its practices for the wider world of moral and political life by no means insisted on congruence between the structures or practices of the family and those of the outside world. Though concerned with moral development, they bifurcated public from private life to such an extent that they had no trouble reconciling inegalitarian, sometimes admittedly unjust, relations founded upon sentiment within the family with a more just, even egalitarian, social structure outside the family. Rousseau, Hegel, Tocqueville—all thought the family was centrally important for the development of morality in citizens, but all defended the hierarchy of the marital structure while spurning such a degree of hierarchy in institutions and practices outside the household. Preferring instead to rely on love, altruism, and generosity as the basis for family relations, none of these theorists argued for *just* family structures as necessary for socializing children into citizenship in a just society.

The position that justice within the family is irrelevant to the development of just citizens was not plausible even when only men were citizens. John Stuart Mill, in *The Subjection of Women*, takes an impassioned stand against it. He argues that the inequality of women within the family is deeply subversive of justice in general in the wider social world, because it subverts the moral potential of men. Mill's first answer to the question, "For whose good are all these changes in women's rights to be undertaken?" is: "the advantage of having the most universal and pervading of all human relations regulated by justice instead of injustice." Making marriage a relationship of equals, he argues, would transform this central part of daily life from "a school of despotism" into "a school of moral cultivation." He goes on to discuss, in the strongest of terms, the noxious effect of growing up in a family not regulated by justice. Consider, he says, "the self-worship, the unjust self-preference," nourished in a boy growing up in a household in which "by the mere fact of being born a male he is by right the superior of all and every one of an entire half of the human race." Mill concludes that the example set by perpetuating a marital structure "contradictory to the first principles of social justice" must have such "a perverting influence" that it is hard even to imagine the good effects of changing it. All other attempts to educate people to respect and practice justice, Mill claims, will be superficial "as long as the citadel of the enemy is not attacked." Mill felt as much hope for what the family might be as he felt despair at what it was not. "The family, justly constituted, would be the real school of the virtues of freedom," primary among which was "justice. . . . grounded as before on equal, but now also on sympathetic association. Mill both saw clearly and had the courage to address what so many other political philosophers either could not see, or saw and turned away from.

Despite the strength and fervor of his advocacy of women's rights, however, Mill's idea of a just family structure falls far short of that of many feminists even of his own time, including his wife, Harriet Taylor. In spite of the fact that Mill recognized both the empowering effect of earnings on one's position in the family and the limiting effect of domestic responsibility on women's opportunities, he balked at questioning the traditional division of labor between the sexes. For him, a woman's choice of marriage was parallel to a man's choice of a profession: unless and until she had fulfilled her obligations to her husband and children, she should not undertake anything else. But clearly, however equal the legal rights of husbands and wives, this position largely undermines Mill's own insistence upon the importance of marital equality for a just society. His acceptance of the traditional division of labor, without making any provision for wives who were thereby made economically dependent upon their husbands, largely undermines his insistence upon family justice as the necessary foundation for social justice.

Thus even those political theorists of the past who have perceived the family as an important school of moral development have rarely acknowledged the need for congruence between the family and the wider social order, which suggests that families themselves need to be just. Even when they have, as with Mill, they have been unwilling to push hard on the traditional division of labor within the family in the name of justice or equality.

Contemporary theorists of justice, with few exceptions, have paid little or no attention to the question of moral development—of how we are to *become* just. Most of them seem to think, to adapt slightly Hobbes's notable phrase, that just men spring like mushrooms from the earth. Not surprisingly, then, it is far less often acknowledged in recent than in past theories that the family is important for moral development, and especially for instilling a sense of justice. As I have already noted, many theorists pay no attention at all to either the family or gender. In the rare case that the issue of justice within the family is given any sustained attention, the family is not viewed as a potential school of social justice. In the rare case that a theorist pays any sustained attention to the development of a sense of justice or morality, little if any attention is likely to be paid to the family. Even in the rare event that theorists pay considerable attention to the family *as* the first major locus of moral socialization, they do not refer to the fact that families are almost all still thoroughly gender-structured institutions.

Among major contemporary theorists of justice, John Rawls alone treats the family seriously as the earliest school of moral development. He argues that a just, well-ordered society will be stable only if its members continue to develop a sense of justice. And he argues that families play a fundamental role in the stages by which this sense of justice is acquired. From the parents' love for their child, which comes to be reciprocated, comes the child's "sense of his own value and the desire to become the sort of person that they are." The family, too, is the first of that series of "associations" in which we participate, from which we acquire the capacity, crucial for a sense of justice, to see things from the perspectives of others. . . . This capacity—the capacity for empathy—is essential for maintaining a sense of justice of the Rawlsian kind. For the perspective that is necessary for maintaining a sense of justice is not that of the egoistic or disembodied self, or of the dominant few who overdetermine "our" traditions or "shared understandings," or (to use Nagel's term) of "the view from nowhere," but rather the perspective of every person in the society for whom the principles of justice are being arrived at. . . . The problem with Rawls's rare and interesting discussion of moral development is that it rests on the unexplained *assumption* that family institutions are just. If gendered family institutions are *not* just, but are, rather, a relic of caste or feudal societies in which responsibilities, roles, and resources are distributed, not in accordance with the principles of justice he arrives at or with any other commonly respected values, but in accordance with innate differences that are imbued with enormous social significance, then Rawls's theory of moral development would seem to be built on uncertain ground. This problem is exacerbated by suggestions in some of Rawls's most recent work that families are "private institutions," to which it is not

appropriate to apply standards of justice. But if families are to help form just individuals and citizens, surely they must be *just families.*

In a just society, the structure and practices of families must give women the same opportunities as men to develop their capacities, to participate in political power and influence social choices, and to be economically secure. But in addition to this, families must be just because of the vast influence that they have on the moral development of children. The family is the primary institution of formative moral development. And the structure and practices of the family must parallel those of the larger society if the sense of justice is to be fostered and maintained. While many theorists of justice, both past and present, appear to have denied the importance of at least one of these factors, my own view is that both are absolutely crucial. A society that is committed to equal respect for all its members, and to justice in social distributions of benefits and responsibilities, can neither neglect the family nor accept family structures and practices that violate these norms, as do current gender-based structures and practices. It is essential that children who are to develop into adults with a strong sense of justice and commitment to just institutions spend their earliest and most formative years in an environment in which they are loved and nurtured, *and* in which principles of justice are abided by and respected. What is a child of either sex to learn about fairness in the average household with two full-time working parents, where the mother does, at the very least, twice as much family work as the father? What is a child to learn about the value of nurturing and domestic work in a home with a traditional division of labor in which the father either subtly or not so subtly uses the fact that he is the wage earner to "pull rank" on or to abuse his wife? What is a child to learn about responsibility for others in a family in which, after many years of arranging her life around the needs of her husband and children, a woman is faced with having to provide for herself and her children but is totally ill-equipped for the task by the life she agreed to lead, has led, and expected to go on leading?

Letter from Birmingham Jail

MARTIN LUTHER KING JR.

Leading civil rights activist Martin Luther King Jr. (1928–1968) received his Ph.D. from Boston University. The following was written in a jail cell on April 16, 1963, four months before King's famous "I Have a Dream" speech in Washington, DC.

My Dear Fellow Clergymen:

While confined here in the Birmingham city jail, I came across your recent statement calling my present activities 'unwise and untimely.' . . .

I think I should indicate why I am here in Birmingham, since you have been influenced by the view which argues against 'outsiders coming in.' I have the honor of serving as president of the Southern Christian Leadership Conference, . . . Several months ago the affiliate here in Birmingham asked us to be on call to engage in a nonviolent direct-action program if such were deemed necessary. We readily consented, and when the hour came we lived up to our promise. So I, along with several members of my staff, am here because I was invited here. I am here because I have organizational ties here.

But more basically, I am in Birmingham because injustice is here. Just as the prophets of the eighth century B.C. left their villages and carried their 'thus saith the Lord' far beyond the boundaries of their home towns, and just as the Apostle Paul left his village of Tarsus and carried the gospel of Jesus Christ to the far corners of the Greco-Roman world, so am I compelled to carry the gospel of freedom beyond my own home town. Like Paul, I must constantly respond to the Macedonian call for aid.

Moreover, I am cognizant of the interrelatedness of all communities and states. I cannot sit idly by in Atlanta and not be concerned about what happens in Birmingham. Injustice anywhere is a threat to justice everywhere. We are caught in an inescapable network of mutuality, tied in a single garment of destiny. Whatever affects one directly, affects all indirectly. Never again can we afford to live with the narrow, provincial 'outside agitator' idea. Any-

one who lives inside the United States can never be considered an outsider anywhere within its bounds.

You deplore the demonstrations taking place in Birmingham. But your statement, I am sorry to say, fails to express a similar concern for the conditions that brought about the demonstrations. I am sure that none of you would want to rest content with the superficial kind of social analysis that deals merely with effects and does not grapple with underlying causes. It is unfortunate that demonstrations are taking place in Birmingham, but it is even more unfortunate that the city's white power structure left the Negro community with no alternative.

In any nonviolent campaign there are four basic steps: collection of the facts to determine whether injustices exist; negotiation; self-purification; and direct action. We have gone through all these steps in Birmingham. There can be no gainsaying the fact that racial injustice engulfs this community. Birmingham is probably the most thoroughly segregated city in the United States. Its ugly record of brutality is widely known. Negroes have experienced grossly unjust treatment in the courts. There have been more unsolved bombings of Negro homes and churches in Birmingham than in any other city in the nation. These are the hard, brutal facts of the case. On the basis of these conditions, Negro leaders sought to negotiate with the city fathers. But the latter consistently refused to engage in good-faith negotiation.

Then, last September, came the opportunity to talk with leaders of Birmingham's economic community. In the course of the negotiations, certain promises were made by the merchants—for example, to remove the stores' humiliating racial signs. On the basis of these promises, the Reverend Fred Shuttlesworth and the leaders of the Alabama Christian Movement for Human Rights agreed to a

Text from Fellowship of Reconciliation pamphlet.

moratorium on all demonstrations. As the weeks and months went by, we realized that we were the victims of a broken promise. A few signs, briefly removed, returned; the others remained.

As in so many past experiences, our hopes had been blasted, and the shadow of deep disappointment settled upon us. We had no alternative except to prepare for direct action, whereby we would present our very bodies as a means of laying our case before the conscience of the local and the national community. Mindful of the difficulties involved, we decided to undertake a process of self-purification. We began a series of workshops on nonviolence, and we repeatedly asked ourselves: 'Are you able to accept blows without retaliating?' 'Are you able to endure the ordeal of jail?' We decided to schedule our direct-action program for the Easter season, realizing that except for Christmas, this is the main shopping period of the year. Knowing that a strong economic withdrawal program would be the by-product of direct action, we felt that this would be the best time to bring pressure to bear on the merchants for the needed change.

Then it occurred to us that Birmingham's mayoral election was coming up in March, and we speedily decided to postpone action until after election day. When we discovered that the Commissioner of Public Safety, Eugene 'Bull' Connor, had piled up enough votes to be in the run-off, we decided again to postpone action until the day after the run-off so that the demonstrations could not be used to cloud the issues. Like many others, we waited to see Mr. Connor defeated, and to this end we endured postponement after postponement. Having aided in this community need, we felt that our direct-action program could be delayed no longer.

You may well ask: 'Why direct action? Why sit-ins, marches and so forth? Isn't negotiation a better path?' You are quite right in calling for negotiation. Indeed, this is the very purpose of direct action. Nonviolent direct action seeks to create such a crisis and foster such a tension that a community which has constantly refused to negotiate is forced to confront the issue. It seeks so to dramatize the issue that it can no longer be ignored. My citing the creation of tension as part of the work of the nonviolent-resister may sound rather shocking. But I must confess that I am not afraid of the word 'tension.' I have

earnestly opposed violent tension, but there is a type of constructive, nonviolent tension which is necessary for growth. Just as Socrates felt that it was necessary to create a tension in the mind so that individuals could rise from the bondage of myths and half-truths to the unfettered realm of creative analysis and objective appraisal, so must we see the need for nonviolent gadflies to create the kind of tension in society that will help men rise from the dark depths of prejudice and racism to the majestic heights of understanding and brotherhood.

The purpose of our direct-action program is to create a situation so crisis-packed that it will inevitably open the door to negotiation. I therefore concur with you in your call for negotiation. Too long has our beloved Southland been bogged down in a tragic effort to live in monologue rather than dialogue.

One of the basic points in your statement is that the action that I and my associates have taken in Birmingham is untimely. Some have asked: 'Why didn't you give the new city administration time to act?' The only answer that I can give to this query is that the new Birmingham administration must be prodded about as much as the outgoing one, before it will act. We are sadly mistaken if we feel that the election of Albert Boutwell as mayor will bring the millennium to Birmingham. While Mr. Boutwell is a much more gentle person than Mr. Connor, they are both segregationists, dedicated to maintenance of the status quo. I have hope that Mr. Boutwell will be reasonable enough to see the futility of massive resistance to desegregation. But he will not see this without pressure from devotees of civil rights. My friends, I must say to you that we have not made a single gain in civil rights without determined legal and nonviolent pressure. Lamentably, it is an historical fact that privileged groups seldom give up their privileges voluntarily. Individuals may see the moral light and voluntarily give up their unjust posture; but, as Reinhold Niebuhr has reminded us, groups tend to be more immoral than individuals.

We know through painful experience that freedom is never voluntarily given by the oppressor; it must be demanded by the oppressed. Frankly, I have yet to engage in a direct-action campaign that was 'well timed' in the view of those who have not suffered unduly from the disease of segregation. For years now I have heard the word 'Wait!' It rings in the ear of every Negro with piercing familiarity. This 'Wait' has almost always meant 'Never.' We must come to see, with one of our distinguished jurists, that 'justice too long delayed is justice denied.'

We have waited for more than 340 years for our constitutional and God-given rights. The nations of Asia and Africa are moving with jetlike speed toward gaining political independence, but we still creep at horse-and-buggy pace toward gaining a cup of coffee at a lunch counter. Perhaps it is easy for those who have never felt the stinging darts of segregation to say, 'Wait.' But when you have seen vicious mobs lynch your mothers and fathers at will and drown your sisters and brothers at whim; when you have seen hate-filled policemen curse, kick and even kill your black brothers and sisters; when you see the vast majority of your twenty million Negro brothers smothering in an airtight cage of poverty in the midst of an affluent society; when you suddenly find your tongue twisted and your speech stammering as you seek to explain to your six-year-old daughter why she can't go to the public amusement park that has just been advertised on television, and see tears welling up in her eyes when she is told that Funtown is closed to colored children, and see ominous clouds of inferiority beginning to form in her little mental sky, and see her beginning to distort her personality by developing an unconscious bitterness toward white people; when you have to concoct an answer for a five-year-old son who is asking: 'Daddy, why do white people treat colored people so mean?'; when you take a cross-county drive and find it necessary to sleep night after night in the uncomfortable corners of your automobile because no motel will accept you; when you are humiliated day in and day out by nagging signs reading 'white' and 'colored'; when your first name becomes 'nigger,' your middle name becomes 'boy' (however old you are) and your last name becomes 'John,' and your wife and mother are never given the respected title 'Mrs.'; when you are harried by day and haunted by night by the fact that you are a Negro, living constantly at tiptoe stance, never quite knowing what to expect next, and are plagued with inner fears and outer resentments; when you are forever fighting a degenerating sense of 'nobodiness'—then you will understand why we find it difficult to wait. There comes a time when the cup of endurance runs over, and men are no longer willing to be plunged into the abyss of despair. I hope, sirs, you can understand our legitimate and unavoidable impatience.

You express a great deal of anxiety over our willingness to break laws. This is certainly a legitimate concern. Since we so diligently urge people to obey the Supreme Court's decision of 1954 outlawing segregation in the public schools, at first glance it may seem rather paradoxical for us consciously to break laws. One may well ask: 'How can you advocate breaking some laws and obeying others?' The answer lies in the fact that there are two types of laws: just and unjust. I would be the first to advocate obeying just laws. One has not only a legal but a moral responsibility to obey just laws. Conversely, one has a moral responsibility to disobey unjust laws. I would agree with St. Augustine that 'an unjust law is no law at all.'

Now, what is the difference between the two? How does one determine whether a law is just or unjust? A just law is a man-made code that squares with the moral law or the law of God. An unjust law is a code that is out of harmony with the moral law. To put it in the terms of St. Thomas Aquinas: An unjust law is a human law that is not rooted in eternal and natural law. Any law that uplifts human personality is just. Any law that degrades human personality is unjust. All segregation statutes are unjust because segregation distorts the soul and damages the personality. It gives the segregator a false sense of superiority and the segregated a false sense of inferiority. Segregation, to use the terminology of the Jewish philosopher Martin Buber, substitutes an 'I-it' relationship for an 'I-thou' relationship and ends up relegating persons to the status of things. Hence segregation is not only politically, economically and sociologically unsound, it is morally wrong and sinful. Paul Tillich has said that sin is separation. Is not segregation an existential expression of man's tragic separation, his awful estrangement, his terrible sinfulness? Thus it is that I can urge men to obey the 1954 decision of the Supreme Court, for it is morally right; and I can urge them to disobey segregation ordinances, for they are morally wrong.

Let us consider a more concrete example of just and unjust laws. An unjust law is a code that a numerical or power majority group compels a minority group to obey but does not make binding on itself. This is *difference* made legal. By the same token, a just law is a code that a majority compels a minority to follow and that it is willing to follow itself. This is *sameness* made legal.

Let me give another explanation. A law is unjust if it is inflicted on a minority that, as a result of being denied the right to vote, had no part in enacting or devising the law. Who can say that the legislature of Alabama which set up that state's segregation laws was democratically elected? Throughout Alabama all sorts of devious methods are used to prevent Negroes from becoming registered voters, and there are some counties in which, even though Negroes constitute a majority of the population, not a single Negro is registered. Can any law enacted under such circumstances be considered democratically structured?

Sometimes a law is just on its face and unjust in its application. For instance, I have been arrested on a charge of parading without a permit. Now, there is nothing wrong in having an ordinance which requires a permit for a parade. But such an ordinance becomes unjust when it is used to maintain segregation and to deny citizens the First-Amendment privilege of peaceful assembly and protest.

I hope you are able to see the distinction I am trying to point out. In no sense do I advocate evading or defying the law, as would the rabid segregationist. That would lead to anarchy. One who breaks an unjust law must do so openly, lovingly, and with a willingness to accept the penalty. I submit that an individual who breaks a law that conscience tells him is unjust, and who willingly accepts the penalty of imprisonment in order to arouse the conscience of the community over its injustice, is in reality expressing the highest respect for law.

Of course, there is nothing new about this kind of civil disobedience. It was evidenced sublimely in the refusal of Shadrach, Meshach and Abednego to obey the laws of Nebuchadnezzar, on the ground that a higher moral law was at stake. It was practiced superbly by the early Christians, who were willing to face hungry lions and the excruciating pain of chopping blocks rather than submit to certain unjust laws of the Roman Empire. To a degree, academic freedom is a reality today because Socrates practiced civil disobedience. In our own nation, the Boston Tea Party represented a massive act of civil disobedience.

We should never forget that everything Adolf Hitler did in Germany was 'legal' and everything the Hungarian freedom fighters did in Hungary was 'illegal.' It was 'illegal' to aid and comfort a Jew in Hitler's Germany. Even so, I am sure that, had I lived in Germany at the time, I would have aided and comforted my Jewish brothers. If today I lived in a Communist country where certain principles dear to the Christian faith are suppressed, I would openly advocate disobeying that country's antireligious laws.

I must make two honest confessions to you, my Christian and Jewish brothers. First, I must confess that over the past few years I have been gravely disappointed with the white moderate. I have almost reached the regrettable conclusion that the Negro's great stumbling block in his stride toward freedom is not the White Citizen's Counciler or the Ku Klux Klanner, but the white moderate, who is more devoted to 'order' than to justice; who prefers a negative peace which is the absence of tension to a positive peace which is the presence of justice; who constantly says: 'I agree with you in the goal you seek, but I cannot agree with your methods of direct action'; who paternalistically believes he can set the timetable for another man's freedom; who lives by a mythical concept of time and who constantly advises the Negro to wait for a 'more convenient season.' Shallow understanding from people of good will is more frustrating than absolute misunderstanding from people of ill will. Lukewarm acceptance is much more bewildering than outright rejection.

I had hoped that the white moderate would understand that law and order exist for the purpose of establishing justice and that when they fail in this purpose they become the dangerously structured dams that block the flow of social progress. I had hoped that the white moderate would understand that the present tension in the South is a necessary phase of the transition from an obnoxious negative peace, in which the Negro passively accepted his unjust plight, to a substantive and positive peace, in which all men will respect the dignity and worth of human personality. Actually, we who engage in nonviolent direct action are not the creators of tension. We merely bring to the surface the hidden tension that is already alive. We bring it out in the open, where it can be seen and dealt with. Like a boil that can never be cured so long as it is covered up but must be opened with all its ugliness to the natural medicines of air and light, injustice must be exposed, with all the tension its exposure creates, to the light of human conscience and the air of national opinion before it can be cured.

In your statement you assert that our actions, even though peaceful, must be condemned because they precipitate violence. But is this a logical assertion? Isn't this like condemning a robbed man because his possession of money precipitated the evil act of robbery? Isn't this like condemning Socrates because his unswerving commitment to truth and his philosophical inquiries precipitated the act by the misguided populace in which they made him drink hemlock? Isn't this like condemning Jesus because his unique God-consciousness and never-ceasing devotion to God's will precipitated the evil act of crucifixion? We must come to see that, as the federal courts have consistently affirmed, it is wrong to urge an individual to cease his efforts to gain his basic constitutional rights because the quest may precipitate violence. Society must protect the robbed and punish the robber.

I had also hoped that the white moderate would reject the myth concerning time in relation to the struggle for freedom. I have just received a letter from a white brother in Texas. He writes: 'All Christians know that the colored people will receive equal rights eventually, but it is possible that you are in too great a religious hurry. It has taken Christianity almost two thousand years to accomplish what it has. The teachings of Christ take time to come to earth.' Such an attitude stems from a tragic misconception of time, from the strangely irrational notion that there is something in the very flow of time that will inevitably cure all ills. Actually, time itself is neutral; it can be used either destructively or constructively. More and more I feel that the people of ill will have used time much more effectively than have the people of good will. We will have to repent in this generation not merely for the hateful words and actions of the bad people but for the appalling silence of the good people. Human progress never rolls in on wheels of inevitability; it comes through the tireless efforts of men willing to be co-workers with God, and without this hard work, time itself becomes an ally of the forces of social stagnation. We must use time creatively, in the knowledge that the time is always ripe to do right. Now is the time to make real the promise of democracy and transform our pending national elegy into a creative psalm of brotherhood. Now is the time to lift our national policy from the quicksand of racial injustice to the solid rock of human dignity.

You speak of our activity in Birmingham as extreme. At fist I was rather disappointed that fellow clergymen would see my nonviolent efforts as those of an extremist. I began thinking about the fact that I stand in the middle of two opposing forces in the Negro community. One is a force of complacency, made up in part of Negroes who, as a result of long years of oppression, are so drained of self-respect and a sense of 'somebodiness' that they have adjusted to segregation; and in part of a few middle-class Negroes who, because of a degree of academic and economic security and because in some ways they profit by segregation, have become insensitive to the problems of the masses. The other force is one of bitterness and hatred, and it comes perilously close to advocating violence. It is expressed in the various black nationalist groups that are springing up across the nation, the largest and best-known being Elijah Muhammad's Muslim movement. Nourished by the Negro's frustration over the continued existence of racial discrimination, this movement is made up of people who have lost faith in America, who have absolutely repudiated Christianity, and who have concluded that the white man is an incorrigible 'devil.'

I have tried to stand between these two forces, saying that we need emulate neither the 'do-nothingism' of the complacent nor the hatred and despair of the black nationalist. For there is the more excellent way of love and nonviolent protest. I am grateful to God that, through the influence of the Negro church, the way of nonviolence became an integral part of our struggle.

If this philosophy had not emerged, by now many streets of the South would, I am convinced, be flowing with blood. And I am further convinced that if our white brothers dismiss as 'rabble-rousers' and 'outside agitators' those of us who employ nonviolent direct action, and if they refuse to support our nonviolent efforts, millions of Negroes will, out of frustration and despair, seek solace and security in black-nationalist ideologies—a development that would inevitably lead to a frightening racial nightmare.

Oppressed people cannot remain oppressed forever. The yearning for freedom eventually manifests itself, and that is what has happened to the American Negro. Something within has reminded him of his birthright of freedom, and something without has reminded him that it can be gained. Consciously or unconsciously, he has been caught up by the *Zeitgeist,* and with his black brothers of Africa and his brown and yellow brothers of Asia, South America and the Caribbean, the United States Negro is moving with a sense of great urgency toward the promised land of racial justice. If one recognizes this vital urge that has engulfed the Negro community, one should readily understand why public demonstrations are taking place. The Negro has many pent-up resentments and latent frustrations, and he must release them. So let him march; let him make prayer pilgrimages to the city hall; let him go on freedom rides—and try to understand why he must do so. If his repressed emotions are not released in nonviolent ways, they will seek expression through violence; this is not a threat but a fact of history. So I have not said to my people: 'Get rid of your discontent.' Rather, I have tried to say that this normal and healthy discontent can be channeled into the creative outlet of nonviolent direct action. And now this approach is being termed extremist.

But though I was initially disappointed at being categorized as an extremist, as I continued to think about the matter I gradually gained a measure of satisfaction from the label. Was not Jesus an extremist for love: 'Love your enemies, bless them that curse you, do good to them that hate you, and pray for them which despitefully use you, and persecute you.' Was not Amos an extremist for justice: 'Let justice roll down like waters and righteousness like an ever-flowing stream.' Was not Paul an extremist for the Christian gospel: 'I bear in my body the marks of the Lord Jesus.' Was not Martin Luther an extremist: 'Here I stand; I cannot do otherwise, so help me God.' And John Bunyan: 'I will stay in jail to the end of my days before I make a butchery of my conscience.' And Abraham Lincoln: 'This nation cannot survive half slave and half free.' And Thomas Jefferson: 'We hold these truths to be self-evident, that all men are created equal. . . .' So the question is not whether we will be extremists, but what kind of extremists we will be. Will we be extremists for hate or for love? Will we be extremists for the preservation of injustice or for the extension of justice? In that dramatic scene on Calvary's hill three men were crucified. We must never forget that all three were crucified for the same crime—the crime of extremism. Two were extremists for immorality, and thus fell below their environment. The other, Jesus Christ, was an extremist for love, truth and goodness, and thereby rose above his environment. Perhaps the South, the nation and the world are in dire need of creative extremists.

I had hoped that the white moderate would see this need. Perhaps I was too optimistic; perhaps I expected too much. I suppose I should have realized that few members of the oppressor race can understand the deep groans and passionate yearnings of the oppressed race, and still fewer have the vision to see that injustice must be rooted out by strong, persistent and determined action. I am thankful, however, that some of our white brothers in the South have grasped the meaning of this social revolution and committed themselves to it. They are still all too few in quantity, but they are big in quality. Some—such as Ralph McGill, Lillian Smith, Harry Golden, James McBride Dabbs, Ann Braden and Sarah Patton Boyle—have written about our struggle in eloquent and prophetic terms. Others have marched with us down nameless streets of the South. They have languished in filthy, roach-infested jails, suffering the abuse and brutality of policemen who view them as 'dirty nigger-lovers.' Unlike so many of their moderate brothers and sisters, they have recognized the urgency of the moment and sensed the need for powerful 'action' antidotes to combat the disease of segregation.

Let me take note of my other major disappointment. I have been so greatly disappointed with the white church and its leadership. Of course, there are some notable exceptions. I am not unmindful of the fact that each of you has taken some significant stands on this issue. I commend you, Reverend Stallings, for your Christian stand on this past Sunday, in welcoming Negroes to your worship service on a nonsegregated basis. I commend the Catholic leaders of this state for integrating Spring Hill College several years ago.

But despite these notable exceptions, I must honestly reiterate that I have been disappointed with the church. I do not say this as one of those negative critics who can always find something wrong with the church. I say this as a minister of the gospel, who loves the church; who was nurtured in its bosom; who has been sustained by its spiritual blessings and who will remain true to it as long as the cord of life shall lengthen.

When I was suddenly catapulted into the leadership of the bus protest in Montgomery, Alabama, a few years ago, I felt we would be supported by the white church. I felt that the white ministers, priests and rabbis of the South would be among our strongest allies. Instead, some have been outright opponents, refusing to understand the freedom movement and misrepresenting its leaders; all too many others have been more cautious than courageous and have remained silent behind the anesthetizing security of stained-glass windows.

In spite of my shattered dreams, I came to Birmingham with the hope that the white religious leadership of this community would see the justice of our cause and, with deep moral concern, would serve as the channel through which our just grievances could reach the power structure. I had hoped that each of you would understand. But again I have been disappointed.

I have heard numerous southern religious leaders admonish their worshipers to comply with a desegregation decision because it is the law, but I have longed to hear white ministers declare: 'Follow this decree because integration is morally right and because the Negro is your brother.' In the midst of blatant injustices inflicted upon the Negro, I have watched white churchmen stand on the sidelines and mouth pious irrelevancies and sanctimonious trivialities. In the midst of a mighty struggle to rid our nation of racial and economic injustice, I have heard many ministers say: 'Those are social issues, with which the gospel has no real concern.' And I have watched many churches commit themselves to a completely otherworldly religion which makes a strange, un-Biblical distinction between body and soul, between the sacred and the secular.

I have traveled the length and breadth of Alabama, Mississippi and all the other southern states. On sweltering summer days and crisp autumn mornings I have looked at the South's beautiful churches with their lofty spires pointing heavenward. I have beheld the impressive outlines of her massive religious-education buildings. Over and over I have found myself asking: 'What kind of people worship here? Who is their God? Where were their voices when the lips of Governor Barnett dripped with words of interposition and nullification? Where were they when Governor Wallace gave a clarion call for defiance and hatred? Where were their voices of support when bruised and weary Negro men and women decided to rise from the dark dungeons of complacency to the bright hills of creative protest?'

Yes, these questions are still in my mind. In deep disappointment I have wept over the laxity of the church. But be assured that my tears have been tears of love. There can be no deep disappointment where there is not deep love. Yes, I love the church. How could I do otherwise? I am in the rather unique position of being the son, the grandson and the great-grandson of preachers. Yes, I see the church as the body of Christ. But, oh! How we have blemished and scarred that body through social neglect and through fear of being nonconformists.

There was a time when the church was very powerful—in the time when the early Christians rejoiced at being deemed worthy to suffer for what they believed. In those days the church was not merely a thermometer that recorded the ideas and principles of popular opinion; it was a thermostat that transformed the mores of society. Whenever the early Christians entered a town, the people in power became disturbed and immediately sought to convict the Christians for being 'disturbers of the peace' and 'outside agitators.' But the Christians pressed on, in the conviction that they were 'a colony of heaven,' called to obey God rather than man. Small in number, they were big in commitment. They were too God-intoxicated to be 'astronomically intimidated.' By their effort and example they brought an end to such ancient evils as infanticide and gladiatorial contests.

Things are different now. So often the contemporary church is a weak, ineffectual voice with an uncertain sound. So often it is an archdefender of the status quo. Far from being disturbed by the presence of the church, the power structure of the average community is consoled by the church's silent—and often even vocal—sanction of things as they are.

But the judgment of God is upon the church as never before. If today's church does not recapture the sacrificial spirit of the early church, it will lose its authenticity, forfeit the loyalty of millions, and be dismissed as an irrelevant social club with no meaning for the twentieth century. Every day I meet young people whose disappointment with the church has turned into outright disgust.

Perhaps I have once again been too optimistic. Is organized religion too inextricably bound to the status quo to save our nation and the world? Perhaps I must turn my faith to the inner spiritual church, the church within the church, as the true *ekklesia* and the hope of the world. But again I am thankful to God that some noble souls from the ranks of organized religion have broken loose from the paralyzing chains of conformity and joined us as active partners in the struggle for freedom. They have left their secure congregations and walked the streets of Albany, Georgia, with us. They have gone down the highways of the South on tortuous rides for freedom. Yes, they have gone to jail with us. Some have been dismissed from their churches, have lost the support of their bishops and fellow ministers. But they have acted in the faith that right defeated is stronger than evil triumphant. Their witness has been the spiritual salt that has preserved the true meaning of the gospel in these troubled times. They have carved a tunnel of hope through the dark mountain of disappointment.

I hope the church as a whole will meet the challenge of this decisive hour. But even if the church does not come to the aid of justice, I have no despair about the future. I have no fear about the outcome of our struggle in Birmingham, even if our motives are at present misunderstood. We will reach the goal of freedom in Birmingham and all over the nation, because the goal of America is freedom. Abused and scorned though we may be, our destiny is tied up with America's destiny. Before the pilgrims landed at Plymouth, we were here. Before the pen of Jefferson etched the majestic words of the Declaration of Independence across the pages of history, we were

here. For more than two centuries our forebears labored in this country without wages; they made cotton king; they built the homes of their masters while suffering gross injustice and shameful humiliation—and yet out of a bottomless vitality they continued to thrive and develop. If the inexpressible cruelties of slavery could not stop us, the opposition we now face will surely fail. We will win our freedom because the sacred heritage of our nation and the eternal will of God are embodied in our echoing demands.

Before closing I feel impelled to mention one other point in your statement that has troubled me profoundly. You warmly commended the Birmingham police force for keeping 'order' and 'preventing violence.' I doubt that you would have so warmly commended the police force if you had seen its dogs sinking their teeth into unarmed, nonviolent Negroes. I doubt that you would so quickly commend the policemen if you were to observe their ugly and inhumane treatment of Negroes here in the city jail; if you were to watch them push and curse old Negro women and young Negro girls; if you were to see them slap and kick old Negro men and young boys; if you were to observe them, as they did on two occasions, refuse to give us food because we wanted to sing our grace together. I cannot join you in your praise of the Birmingham police department.

It is true that the police have exercised a degree of discipline in handing the demonstrators. In this sense they have conducted themselves rather 'nonviolently' in public. But for what purpose? To preserve the evil system of segregation. Over the past few years I have consistently preached that nonviolence demands that the means we use must be as pure as the ends we seek. I have tried to make clear that it is wrong to use immoral means to attain moral ends. But now I must affirm that it is just as wrong, or perhaps even more so, to use moral means to preserve immoral ends. Perhaps Mr. Connor and his policemen have been rather nonviolent in public, as was Chief Pritchett in Albany, Georgia, but they have used the moral means of nonviolence to maintain the immoral end of racial injustice. As T. S. Eliot has said: 'The last temptation is the greatest treason: To do the right deed for the wrong reason.'

I wish you had commended the Negro sit-inners and demonstrators of Birmingham for their sublime courage, their willingness to suffer and their amazing discipline in the midst of great provocation. One day the South will recognize its real heroes. They will be the James Merediths, with the noble sense of purpose that enables them to face jeering and hostile mobs, and with the agonizing loneliness that characterizes the life of the pioneer. They will be old, oppressed, battered Negro women, symbolized in a seventy-two-year-old woman in Montgomery, Alabama, who rose up with a sense of dignity and with her people decided not to ride segregated buses, and who responded with ungrammatical profundity to one who inquired about her weariness: 'My feets is tired, but my soul is at rest.' They will be the young high school and college students, the young ministers of the gospel and a host of their elders, courageously and nonviolently sitting in at lunch counters and willingly going to jail for conscience' sake. One day the South will know that when these disinherited children of God sat down at lunch counters, they were in reality standing up for what is best in the American dream and for the most sacred values in our Judaeo-Christian heritage, thereby bringing our nation back to those great wells of democracy which were dug deep by the founding fathers in their formulation of the Constitution and the Declaration of Independence.

Never before have I written so long a letter. I'm afraid it is much too long to take your precious time. I can assure you that it would have been much shorter if I had been writing from a comfortable desk, but what else can one do when he is alone in a narrow jail cell, other than write long letters, think long thoughts and pray long prayers?

If I have said anything in this letter that overstates the truth and indicates an unreasonable impatience, I beg you to forgive me. If I have said anything that understates the truth and indicates my having a patience that allows me to settle for anything less than brotherhood, I beg God to forgive me.

I hope this letter finds you strong in the faith. I also hope that circumstances will soon make it possible for me to meet each of you, not as an integrationist or a civil-rights leader but as a fellow clergyman and a Christian brother. Let us all hope that the dark clouds of racial prejudice will soon pass away and the deep fog of misunderstanding will be lifted from our fear-drenched communities, and in some not too distant tomorrow the radiant stars of love and brotherhood will shine over our great nation with all their scintillating beauty.

Yours for the cause of Peace and Brotherhood,

Martin Luther King, Jr.

PART 7

Art, Beauty, and the Meaning of Life

ART AND BEAUTY

In his *Poetics*—widely regarded as the most influential work ever written in the philosophy of art—Aristotle presents bold new theories of poetry, drama, and literary criticism. Unlike Plato, who took a dim view of art, Aristotle claims that poetry "is something more philosophic and of greater import than history, since its statements are of the nature rather of universals, whereas those of history are singulars." For Plato, art was but the cheap imitation of illusory appearances, at best three times removed from reality: A painting of Socrates, for instance, is a copy of Socrates who is himself but a copy of an idea, or form. Because according to Aristotle the ideas, or forms, themselves exist in particular things, by studying and imitating nature, the artist is communing directly with the ideas, or forms, that he can then communicate to others by rendering them more vividly in his work, thereby expressing and illuminating the universal truths hidden in the particulars.

This sort of view—namely, that the main function of art is to represent the world—is called the *mimetic theory of art*. According to the mimetic theory, art is, essentially, imitation. This raises a variety of obvious problems—such as, most obviously, what to make of nonrepresentational art—but this did not prevent Aristotle from putting forth a view that influenced art for the next two thousand years. The key to understanding Aristotle's theory is his argument that mimesis is not limited to imitating the appearances, the way Plato thought, and so is not just naively representational the way we may naively think. Poetry, for instance, does not necessarily or even most often imitate objects but human action, which is a far more abstract concept than the items that appear to us as things in the world. Likewise, it is the representation, for instance, of human character, which is not so readily revealed in the appearances, that makes tragedy and comedy such essential mirrors of reality. In his view, the statements of poetry are themselves not particulars but universals.

One of the main objections to art having the same sort of status in our philosophizing about ourselves and the world as, for instance, we bestow on objective disciplines such science, mathematics, and logic is that our interpretation, appreciation, description, and evaluation of art is forever hopelessly *subjective*. David Hume, in "Of the Standard of Taste," presents a view of this problem that influenced many subsequent thinkers, especially Kant. The tradition problem, as Hume puts it, is that we cannot seem to find one objective "Standard of Taste; a rule by which the various sentiments of men may be reconciled; at least a decision afforded confirming one sentiment, and condemning another." In other words, all our experiencing, thinking, and evaluations of art can be neither right nor wrong for they are but matters of taste, purely subjective preferences. Hume claims this overstates the case. For one thing, there are "common sentiments of human nature" by which our minds follow the same rules of composition, for instance, so that there are certain basic forms that have "been universally found to please in all countries and in all ages." For another, a good deal of our disagreements about art are simply the result of ignorance, so that the more we know, the more we are likely to agree; beyond a certain point even our disagreements can themselves be understood and explained. With time and refinement we can through relating with art not only discover what is common to all human nature but refine our tastes to accord with universal principles. But this makes the dilemma of taste even worse. Both our thinking and our behavior seem to imply that there are some universal, objective standards by which aesthetic judgments of taste depend, and yet, when we try looking for them to spell them out, we come up empty-handed. No such empirical criteria upon which everyone can agree can be found.

Immanuel Kant, like Hume, claims that art is far more objective than we may ordinarily be inclined to think, but, unlike Hume, he offers a solution by going beyond sense experience. He agrees with Hume that the fact that we are so passionate in our disagreements about art itself implies that deep down we must feel, or somehow intuit, that our views—though subjective—must ultimately be correct. We don't just say, "Well, I think this and you think that, and we completely disagree, how nice and expected," but, rather, we typically engage each other in argument. Our intuitions thus reveal the deeper truth that our descriptions and judgments about art must be true or false. The fact that we disagree so often about and, typically, cannot resolve such disagreements to anyone's ultimate satisfaction Kant called the *antinomy of taste.* An antinomy is a mutual contradiction of two propositions or principles, both of which rest on premises that seem equally valid. And the reason the antinomy of taste is an antinomy is because we view aesthetic disagreements at once both as subjective and as objective, that is, even when we know they are subjective we find it difficult, if not impossible, to simply accept some sort of universal relativism about taste. If that were true, every work of art would be as good as any other—your doodle in the margin of your notebook is as good, valuable, and meaningful as a painting by Leonardo da Vinci. But most of us—perhaps all of us—find that an impossible position to hold, even as we recognize that if we go, say, to a movie, your view and judgment of it might be completely different from mine.

This itself, according to Kant, not only affords us a means of a transcendental solution but elevates art to a special place in philosophy. In his *Critique of Judgment,* he argues that judgments of beauty, for instance, are in a separate category from judgments of truth, morality, and utility. The mind's aesthetic response to not just works of art but to itself and to nature are functions of the pure imagination, free of all external considerations. All aesthetic judgments are according to Kant *nonconceptual.* That is, such judgments are made without any reference to one's concepts regarding the object or event in question. The experience and contemplation of art is therefore absolutely free from correspondence to anything external to the experience itself. This sort of view may itself suggest that art must possess completely self-sufficient internal relations, a philosophy of art that was deeply influential in the movement known as *formalism,* discussed below. According to Kant's theory of aesthetic experience, aesthetic judgments of taste are the source of a type of pleasure, involving not just beauty but also the experience of the *sublime* that transcends the limitations imposed upon the mind by the categories; the sublime is at once beyond mere beauty and ugliness, for instance, or order and chaos but combines the extremes of the opposites and allows the mind to experience infinite, numinous reality in ways that it cannot do rationally. In this way, aesthetic experience according to Kant is essentially subjective, but it is *universally* subjective. This is itself the result of the universality of the cognitive faculties—understanding and reason—an idea that became the very foundation for subsequent formalist theories.

The great nineteenth-century absolute idealist Georg W. F. Hegel developed Kant's theory in a bold new direction. According to Hegel, the whole of reality—Being, what Hegel called *the Absolute*—is itself a universal cosmic mind—the world soul—that can be understood by individual minds through their faculty of reason. And just as Being itself evolves along with all the things in it, so too ideas evolve over time, becoming transformed from their original expressions in art to, ultimately, their expression in science and philosophy. Art is part of that evolution process in which the Absolute tries to realize itself. Thus, to take, say, an intellectually formed idea or thought and with conscious intention try to present it as art is to completely misunderstand the nature, function, and role of art in the cosmic process. Artworks themselves express the ineffable, transcendent reality. Artists therefore must not and cannot themselves know what it is they are doing until they have done it; only after the art comes into being can the artist try to articulate what it is and what it means. In other words, in Hegel's view artists do not know what they are going to say or do until they've said and done it.

Everything that exists evolves according to Hegel in a three-stage process as described by his theory of dialectics. These stages are, first, the thesis that then evolves into its complete opposite, the antithesis, followed by the final third stage in which the dynamic tension between the thesis and antithesis is fused into one harmonious synthesis. When this is achieved, the synthesis becomes then the new thesis, and the process continues to the next stage of evolution. What this means for the philosophy of art is a grand, all-encompassing cosmic scheme of development in which the first thesis stage is art: We begin to express in a conscious medium a perceptible form of an idea that itself is but an expression of the fundamental spiritual reality of the Absolute. Art then evolves into its rational, cognitive antithesis: religion. Philosophy and science according to Hegel are nothing less than the third, final stage of the synthesis of art and religion.

Like Hegel, Arthur Schopenhauer was deeply inspired by Kant's philosophy in general and his philosophy of art in particular, though he developed his own views in marked contrast to Hegel. In *World as Will and Idea,* Schopenhauer, like Kant, puts forth the view that everything in our experience consists of representations; some representations, however, are better than others at approximating reality, and some—in particular, those experiences found in the greatest art—can in fact connect us with noumenal reality. But whereas Hegel takes ultimate reality, Being itself, to be a rational, cosmic mind—the Absolute—Schopenhauer regards ultimate reality to be a blind, unconscious force of will, felt in part by us as the will to live and dominate one another, ourselves, and the world. Aesthetic experience can, according to Schopenhauer, be a variety of mystical experience, in which I am communing with the will. And the highest form of art, he argues, is music, in which I am connected directly to ultimate reality, the will itself, without any representation whatsoever; for music, claims Schopenhauer, is the supreme abstract art and is completely nonrepresentational.

Taking Schopenhauer's analysis of the life-affirming will to power as his starting point, Friedrich Nietzsche turns Schopenhauer's negativism and dark vision into one of the most inspiring positive views of art. In Nietzsche's view, art begins in a sort of mystical rapture state of ecstasy and allows us to create by force of will all human value. Instead of art imitating reality, as Plato and Aristotle supposed, it enhances it, improves upon it, realizes it. Art can itself be a transformational tool both of human consciousness and of nature.

In "Aesthetics: The State of the Art," Jerrold Levinson—a leading philosopher of art today—and I discuss the nature and role of art in relation to questions of meaning, human values, and philosophy. Along the way, we debate the merits of various contemporary theories such as contextualism, formalism, structuralism, empiricism, deconstructivism, relativism, and nihilism.

MEANING

Why are we here? What's it all about? Is there some purpose or meaning to life? At one time or another, everyone asks such questions. As children and as old people, especially, we wonder: Why? What does it all mean? Most of the rest of the time, we're so busy with life we don't worry about the meaning of life. But even then, in the back of our minds, we may still wonder. And when we do, what is it we really want to know?

At the age of fifty, after writing some of the greatest novels ever written, including *War and Peace* and *Anna Karenina,* Leo Tolstoy experienced an existential crisis in which he sought the meaning of life and found it in faith. Tolstoy's discovery led him to advocate humility, nonviolence, vegetarianism, and the moral value of hard work. In his *Confession,* written when he was in his seventies, he gives a moving account of his despair and how he came to resolve it.

Richard Taylor, in "Is Life Meaningful," gives a response to those who would claim that life is absurd. He starts with the famous story of the myth of Sisyphus, who is condemned by the gods to forever push a rock up a hill, where it tumbles back down, and he pushes it up again, for eternity. The reason we are inclined to view Sisyphus's existence as meaningless is that there is absolutely no point to his labor. Nothing comes of it. Taylor's solution involves viewing activities not as a means to an end but as ends in themselves.

In "The Meaning of Life," Raymond Martin questions the psychological validity of philosophical worries about the meaning of life. He suggests that, as often as not, such worries merely mask a deep, underlying problem: our inability to stay satisfied.

In the concluding selection, "The Value of Philosophy," Bertrand Russell gives an account of the value of philosophy and why philosophy, unlike most other disciplines, needs to be understood before it can be of any value to us. Physics, chemistry, and architecture, for instance, don't need to be understood by individuals who can nevertheless reap the benefits of electricity, life-saving drugs, and the comforts of buildings. Philosophy is in that way different, for it has no clear practical product that can be of value unless it is first understood. But then it can have the supreme value, claims Russell, and can even give meaning to one's life.

ART AND BEAUTY

Poetics

ARISTOTLE

Aristotle (384–322 B.C.E.), a student of Plato's, was one of the most influential philosophers of all time.

Having thus distinguished the parts, let us now consider the proper construction of the Fable or Plot, as that is at once the first and the most important thing in Tragedy. We have laid it down that a tragedy is an imitation of an action that is complete in itself, as a whole of some magnitude; for a whole may be of no magnitude to speak of. Now a whole is that which has beginning, middle, and end. A beginning is that which is not itself necessarily after anything else, and which has naturally something else after it; an end is that which is naturally after something itself, either as its necessary or usual consequent, and with nothing else after it; and a middle, that which is by nature after one thing and has also another after it. A well-constructed Plot, therefore, cannot either begin or end at any point one likes; beginning and end in it must be of the forms just described. Again: to be beautiful, a living creature, and every whole made up of parts, must not only present a certain order in its arrangement of parts, but also be of a certain definite magnitude. Beauty is a matter of size and order, and therefore impossible either (1) in a very minute creature, since our perception becomes indistinct as it approaches instantaneity; or (2) in a creature of vast size—one, say, 1000 miles long—as in that case, instead of the object being seen all at once, the unity and wholeness of it is lost to the beholder. Just in the same way, then, as a beautiful whole made up of parts, or a beautiful living creature, must be of some size, a size to be taken in by the eye, so a story or Plot must be of some length, but of a length to be taken

in by the memory. As for the limit of its length, so far as that is relative to public performances and spectators, it does not fall within the theory of poetry. If they had to perform a hundred tragedies, they would be timed by water-clocks, as they are said to have been at one period. The limit, however, set by the actual nature of the thing is this: the longer the story, consistently with its being comprehensible as a whole, the finer it is by reason of its magnitude. As a rough general formula, "a length which allows of the hero passing by a series of probable or necessary stages from misfortune to happiness, or from happiness to misfortune," may suffice as a limit for the magnitude of the story.

The Unity of a Plot does not consist, as some suppose, in its having one man as its subject. An infinity of things befall that one man, some of which it is impossible to reduce to unity; and in like manner there are many actions of one man which cannot be made to form one action. One sees, therefore, the mistake of all the poets who have written a *Heracleid,* a *Theseid,* or similar poems; they suppose that, because Heracles was one man, the story also of Heracles must be one story. Homer, however, evidently understood this point quite well, whether by art or instinct, just in the same way as he excels the rest in every other respect. In writing an *Odyssey,* he did not make the poem cover all that ever befell his hero—it befell him, for instance, to get wounded on Parnassus and also to feign madness at the time of the call to arms, but the two incidents had no probable or necessary connection with one another—instead of doing that, he took an action with a Unity of the kind we are describing as the subject of the *Odyssey,*

From "Poetics," translated by I. Bywater, in *Aristotle, On the Art of Poetry* (Oxford: Clarendon Press, 1909).

as also of the *Iliad*. The truth is that, just as in the other imitative arts one imitation is always of one thing, so in poetry the story, as an imitation of action, must represent one action, a complete whole, with its several incidents so closely connected that the transposal or withdrawal of any one of them will disjoin and dislocate the whole. For that which makes no perceptible difference by its presence or absence is no real part of the whole.

From what we have said it will be seen that the poet's function is to describe, not the thing that has happened, but a kind of thing that might happen, i.e. what is possible as being probable or necessary. The distinction between historian and poet is not in the one writing prose and the other verse—you might put the work of Herodotus into verse, and it would still be a species of history; it consists really in this, that the one describes the thing that has been, and the other a kind of thing that might be. Hence poetry is something more philosophic and of graver import than history, since its statements are of the nature rather of universals, whereas those of history are singulars. By a universal statement I mean one as to what such or such a kind of man will probably or necessarily say or do—which is the aim of poetry, though it affixes proper names to the characters; by a singular statement, one as to what, say, Alcibiades did or had done to him. In Comedy this has become clear by this time; it is only when their plot is already made up of probable incidents that they give it a basis of proper names, choosing for the purpose any names that may occur to them, instead of writing like the old iambic poets about particular persons. In Tragedy, however, they still adhere to the historic names; and for this reason: what convinces is the possible; now whereas we are not yet sure as to the possibility of that which has not happened, that which has happened is manifestly possible, else it would not have come to pass. Nevertheless even in Tragedy there are some plays with but one or two known names in them, the rest being inventions; and there are some without a single known name, e.g. Agathon's *Antheus,* in which both incidents and names are of the poet's invention; and it is no less delightful on that account. So that one must not aim at a rigid adherence to the traditional stories on which tragedies are based. It would be absurd, in fact, to do so, as even the known stories are only known to a few, though they are a delight none the less to all.

It is evident from the above that the poet must be more the poet of his stories or Plots than of his verses, inasmuch as he is a poet by virtue of the imitative element in his work, and it is actions that he imitates. And if he should come to take a subject from actual history, he is none the less a poet for that; since some historic occurrences may very well be in the probable and possible order of things; and it is in that aspect of them that he is their poet.

Of simple Plots and actions the episodic are the worst. I call a Plot episodic when there is neither probability nor necessity in the sequence of its episodes. Actions of this sort bad poets construct through their own fault, and good ones on account of the players. His work being for public performance, a good poet often stretches out a Plot beyond its capabilities, and is thus obliged to twist the sequence of incident.

Tragedy, however, is an imitation not only of a complete action, but also of incidents arousing pity and fear. Such incidents have the very greatest effect on the mind when they occur unexpectedly and at the same time in consequence of one another; there is more of the marvelous in them then than if they happened of themselves or by mere chance. Even matters of chance seem most marvelous if there is an appearance of design as it were in them; as for instance the statue of Mitys at Argos killed the author of Mitys' death by falling down on him when a looker-on at a public spectacle; for incidents like that we think to be not without a meaning. A Plot, therefore, of this sort is necessarily finer than others.

Plots are either simple or complex, since the actions they represent are naturally of this twofold description. The action, proceeding in the way defined, as one continuous whole, I call simple, when the change in the hero's fortunes takes place without Peripety or Discovery; and complex, when it involves one or the other, or both. These should each of them arise out of the structure of the Plot itself, so as to be the consequence, necessary or probable, of the antecedents. There is a great difference between a thing happening *propter hoc* and *post hoc*.

A Peripety is the change from one state of things within the play to its opposite of the kind described, and that too in the way we are saying, in the probable or necessary sequence of events; as it is for instance in *Oedipus:* here the opposite state of things is produced by the Messenger, who, coming to gladden Oedipus and to remove his fears as to his mother, reveals the secret of his birth. And in *Lynceus:* just as he is being led off for execution, with Danaus at his side to put him to death, the incidents preceding this bring it about that he is saved and Danaus put to death. A Discovery is, as the very word implies, a change from ignorance to knowledge, and thus to either love or hate, in the personages marked for good or evil fortune. The finest form of Discovery is one attended by Peripeties, like that which goes with the Discovery in *Oedipus.* There are no doubt other forms of it; what we have said may happen in a way in reference to inanimate things, even things of a very casual kind; and it is also possible to discover whether some one has done or not done something. But the form most directly connected with the Plot and the action of the piece is the first-mentioned. This, with a Peripety, will arouse either pity or fear—actions of that nature being what Tragedy is assumed to represent; and it will also serve to bring about the happy or unhappy ending. The Discovery, then, being of persons, it may be that of one party only to the other, the latter being already known; or both the parties may have to discover themselves. Iphigenia, for instance, was discovered to Orestes by sending the letter; and another Discovery was required to reveal him to Iphigenia.

Two parts of the Plot, then, Peripety and Discovery, are on matters of this sort. A third part is Suffering; which we may define as an action of a destructive or painful nature, such as murders on the stage, tortures, woundings, and the like. The other two have been already explained.

The parts of Tragedy to be treated as formative elements in the whole were mentioned . . . (previously). From the point of view, however, of its quantity, i.e. the separate sections into which it is divided, a tragedy has the following parts: Prologue, Episode, Exode, and a choral portion, distinguished into Parode and Stasimon; these two are common to all tragedies, whereas songs from the stage and *Commoe* are only found in some. The Prologue is all that precedes the Parode of the chorus; an Episode all that comes in between two whole choral songs; the Exode all that follows after the last choral song. In the choral portion the Parode is the whole first statement of the chorus; a Stasimon, a song of the chorus without anapaests or trochees; a *Commos,* a lamentation sung by chorus and actor in concert. The parts of Tragedy to be used as formative elements in the whole we have already mentioned; the above are its parts from the point of view of its quantity, or the separate sections into which it is divided.

The next points after what we have said above will be these: (1) What is the poet to aim at, and what is he to avoid, in constructing his Plots? and (2) What are the conditions on which the tragic effect depends?

We assume that, for the finest form of Tragedy, the Plot must be not simple but complex; and further, that it must imitate actions arousing pity and fear, since that is the distinctive function of this kind of imitation. It follows, therefore, that there are three forms of Plot to be avoided. (1) A good man must not be seen passing from happiness to misery, or (2) a bad man from misery to happiness. The first situation is not fear-inspiring or piteous, but simply odious to us. The second is the most untragic that can be; it has no one of the requisites of Tragedy; it does not appeal either to the human feeling in us, or to our pity, or to our fears. Nor on the other hand should (3) an extremely bad man be seen falling from happiness into misery. Such a story may arouse the human feeling in us, but it will not move us to either pity or fear; pity is occasioned by undeserved misfortune, and fear by that of one like ourselves; so that there will be nothing either piteous or fear-inspiring in the situation. There remains, then, the intermediate kind of personage, a man not preeminently virtuous and just, whose misfortune, however, is brought upon him not by vice and depravity but by some error of judgement, of the number of those in the enjoyment of great reputation and prosperity; e.g. Oedipus, Thyestes, and the men of note of similar families. The perfect Plot, accordingly, must have a single, and not (as some tell us) a double issue; the change in the hero's fortunes must be not from misery to happiness, but on the contrary from happiness to misery; and the cause of it must lie not in any depravity, but in some great error on his part; the man himself being either such as we have described, or better, not worse, than that. Fact also confirms our theory. Though the poets began by accepting any tragic story that came to hand, in these days the finest tragedies are always on the story of some few houses, on that of Alcmeon, Oedipus, Orestes, Meleager, Thyestes, Telephus, or any others that may have been involved, as either agents or sufferers, in some deed of horror. The theoretically best tragedy, then, has a Plot of this description. The critics, therefore, are wrong, who blame Euripides for taking this line in his tragedies, and giving many of them an unhappy ending. It is, as we have said, the right line to take. The best proof is this: on the stage, and in the public performances, such plays, properly worked out, are seen to be the most truly tragic; and Euripides, even if his execution be faulty in every other point, is seen to be nevertheless the most tragic certainly of the dramatists. After this comes the construction of Plot which some rank first, one with a double story (like the *Odyssey*) and an opposite issue for the good and the bad personages. It is ranked as first only through the weakness of the audiences; the poets merely follow their public, writing as its wishes dictate. But the pleasure here is not that of Tragedy. It belongs rather to Comedy, where the bitterest enemies in the piece (e.g. Orestes and Aegisthus) walk off good friends at the end, with no slaying of any one by any one.

The tragic fear and pity may be aroused by the Spectacle; but they may also be aroused by the very structure and incidents of the play—which is the better way and shows the better poet. The Plot in fact should be so framed that, even without seeing the things take place, he who simply hears the account of them shall be filled with horror and pity at the incidents; which is just the effect that the mere recital of the story in *Oedipus* would have on one. To produce this same effect by means of the Spectacle is less artistic, and requires extraneous aid. Those, however, who make use of the Spectacle to put before us that which is merely monstrous and not productive of fear, are wholly out of touch with Tragedy; not every kind of pleasure should be required of a tragedy, but only its own proper pleasure.

The tragic pleasure is that of pity and fear, and the poet has to produce it by a work of imitation; it is clear, therefore, that the causes should be included in the incidents of his story. Let us see, then, what kinds of incident strike one as horrible, or rather as piteous. In a deed of this description the parties must necessarily be either friends, or enemies, or indifferent to one another. Now when enemy does it on enemy, there is nothing to move us to pity either in his doing or in his meditating the deed, except so far as the actual pain of the sufferer is concerned; and the same is true when the parties are indifferent to one another. Whenever the tragic deed, however, is done within the family—when murder or the like is done or meditated by brother on brother, by son on father, by mother on son, or son on mother— these are the situations the poet should seek after. The traditional stories, accordingly, must be kept as they are, e.g. the murder of Clytaemnestra by Orestes and of Eriphyle by Alcmeon. At the same time even with these there is something left to the poet himself; it is for him to devise the right way of treating them. Let us explain more clearly what we mean by "the right way." The deed of horror may be done by the doer knowingly and consciously, as in the old poets, and in Medea's murder of her children in Euripides. Or he may do it, but in ignorance of his relationship, and discover that afterwards, as does the Oedipus in Sophocles. Here the deed is outside the play; but it may be within it, like the act of the Alcmeon in Astydamas, or that of the Telegonus in *Ulysses Wounded*. A third possibility is for one meditating some deadly injury to another, in ignorance of his relationship, to make the discovery in time to draw back. These exhaust the possibilities, since the deed must necessarily be either done or not done, and either knowingly or unknowingly.

The worst situation is when the personage is with full knowledge on the point of doing the deed, and leaves it undone. It is odious and also (through the absence of suffering) untragic; hence it is that no one is made to act thus except in some few instances, e.g. Haemon and Creon in *Antigone*. Next after this comes the actual perpetration of the deed meditated. A better situation than that, however, is for the deed to be done in ignorance, and the relationship discovered afterwards, since there is nothing odious in it, and the Discovery will serve to astound us. But the best of all is the last; what we have in *Cresphontes*, for example, where Merope, on the point of slaying her son, recognizes him in time; in *Iphigenia*, where sister and brother are in a like position; and in *Helle*, where the son recognizes his mother, when on the point of giving her up to her enemy.

This will explain why our tragedies are restricted (as we said just now) to such a small number of families. It was accident rather than art that led the poets in quest of subjects to embody this kind of incident in their Plots. They are still obliged, accordingly, to have recourse to the families in which such horrors have occurred.

On the construction of the Plot, and the kind of Plot required for Tragedy, enough has now been said.

Of the Standard of Taste

DAVID HUME

The great British empiricist philosopher and skeptic David Hume (1711–1766) was born in Scotland.

The great variety of taste, as well as of opinion, which prevails in the world, is too obvious not to have fallen under everyone's observation. Men of the most confined knowledge are able to remark a difference of taste in the narrow circle of their acquaintance, even where the persons have been educated under the same government, and have early imbibed the same prejudices. But those, who can enlarge their view to contemplate distant nations and remote ages, are still more surprised at the great inconsistence and contrariety. We are apt to call barbarous whatever departs widely from our own taste and apprehension: but soon find the epithet of reproach retorted on us. And the highest arrogance and self-conceit is at last startled, on observing an equal assurance of all sides, and scruples, amidst such a contest of sentiment, to pronounce positively in its own favor.

As this variety of taste is obvious to the most careless inquirer; so will it be found, on examination, to be still greater in reality than in appearance. The sentiments of men often differ with regard to beauty and deformity of all kinds, even while their general discourse is the same. There are certain terms in every language, which import blame, and others praise; and all men, who use the same tongue, must agree in their application of them. Every voice is united in applauding elegance, propriety, simplicity, spirit in writing; and in blaming fustian, affectation, coldness, and a false brilliancy: but when critics come to particulars, this seeming unanimity vanishes; and it is found, that they had affixed a very different meaning to their expressions. In all matters of opinion and science, the case it opposite: The difference among men is there oftener found to lie in generals than in particulars; and to be less in reality than in appearance. An explanation of the terms commonly ends the controversy; and the disputants are surprised to find, that they had been quarreling, while at bottom they agreed in their judgment.

Those who found morality on sentiment, more than on reason, are inclined to comprehend ethics under the former observation, and to maintain, that, in all questions, which regard conduct and manners, the difference among men is really greater than at first sight it appears. It is indeed obvious that writers of all nations and all ages concur in applauding justice, humanity, magnanimity, prudence, veracity; and in blaming the opposite qualities. Even poets and other authors, whose compositions are chiefly calculated to please the imagination, are yet found, from Homer down to Fénelon, to inculcate the same moral precepts, and to bestow their applause and blame on the same virtues and vices. This great unanimity is usually ascribed to the influence of plain reason; which, in all these cases, maintains similar sentiments in all men, and prevents those controversies, to which the abstract sciences are so much exposed. So far as the unanimity is real, this account may be admitted as satisfactory: but we must

From *Of the Standard of Taste* by David Hume, 1757.

also allow that some part of the seeming harmony in morals may be accounted for from the very nature of language. The word *virtue,* with its equivalent in every tongue, implies praise; as that of *vice* does blame: And no one, without the most obvious and grossest impropriety, could affix reproach to a term, which in general acceptation is understood in a good sense; or bestow applause, where the idiom requires disapprobation. Homer's general precepts, where he delivers any such, will never be controverted; but it is obvious, that, when he draws particular pictures of manners, and represents heroism in Achilles and prudence in Ulysses, he intermixes a much greater degree of ferocity in the former, and of cunning and fraud in the latter, than Fénelon would admit of. The sage Ulysses in the Greek poet seems to delight in lies and fictions, and often employs them without any necessity of even advantage: But his more scrupulous son, in the French epic writer, exposes himself to the most imminent perils, rather than depart from the most exact line of truth and veracity.

The admirers and followers of the Alcoran insist on the excellent moral precepts interspersed throughout that wild and absurd performance. But it is to be supposed, that the Arabic words, which correspond to the English, equity, justice, temperance, meekness, charity, were such as, from the constant use of that tongue, must always be taken in a good sense; and it would have argued the greatest ignorance, not of morals, but of language, to have mentioned them with any epithets, besides those of applause and approbation. But would we know, whether the pretended prophet had really attained a just sentiment of morals? Let us attend to his narration; and we shall soon find, that he bestows praise on such instances of treachery, inhumanity, cruelty, revenge, bigotry, as are utterly incompatible with civilized society. No steady rule of right seems there to be attained to; and every action is blamed or praised, so far only as it is beneficial or hurtful to the true believers.

The merit of delivering true general precepts in ethics is indeed very small. Whoever recommends any moral virtues, really does no more than is implied in the terms themselves. That people, who invented the word *charity,* and used it in a good sense, inculcated more clearly and much more efficaciously, the precept, "be charitable," than any pretended legislator or prophet, who should insert such a maxim in his writings. Of all expressions, those, which, together with their other meaning, imply a degree either of blame or approbation, are the least liable to be perverted or mistaken.

It is natural for us to seek a standard of taste; a rule by which the various sentiments of men may be reconciled; at least, a decision afforded, confirming one sentiment, and condemning another.

There is a species of philosophy, which cuts off all hopes of success in such an attempt, and represents the impossibility of ever attaining any standard of taste. The difference, it is said, is very wide between judgment and sentiment. All sentiment is right; because sentiment has a reference to nothing beyond itself, and is always real, wherever a man is conscious of it. But all determinations of the understanding are not right; because they have a reference to something beyond themselves, to wit, real matter of fact; and are not always conformable to that standard. Among a thousand different opinions which different men may entertain of the same subject, there is one, and but one, that is just and true; and the only difficulty is to fix and ascertain it. On the contrary, a thousand different sentiments, excited by the same object, are all right: because no sentiment represents what is really in the object. It only marks a certain conformity or relation between the object and the organs or faculties of the mind; and if that conformity did not really exist, the sentiment could never possibly have being. Beauty is no quality in things themselves: it exists merely in the mind which contemplates them; and each mind perceives a different beauty. One person may even perceive deformity, where another is sensible of beauty; and every individual ought to acquiesce in his own sentiment, without pretending to regulate those of others. To seek the real beauty, or real deformity, is as fruitless an inquiry, as to pretend to ascertain the real sweet or real bitter. According to the disposition of the organs, the same object may be both sweet and bitter; and the proverb has justly determined it to be fruitless to dispute concerning tastes. It is very natural, and even quite necessary, to extend this axiom to mental, as well as bodily taste; and thus common sense, which is so often at variance with philosophy, especially with the skeptical kind, is found, in one instance at least, to agree in pronouncing the same decision.

But though this axiom, by passing into a proverb, seems to have attained the sanction of common sense; there is certainly a species of common sense which opposes it, at least serves to modify and restrain it. Whoever would assert an equality of genius and elegance between Ogilby and Milton, or Bunyan and Addison, would be thought to defend no less an extravagance, than if he had maintained a molehill to be as high as Tenerife, or a pond as extensive as the ocean. Though there may be found persons, who give the preference to the former authors, no one pays attention to such a taste; and we pronounce without scruple the sentiment of these pretended critics to be absurd and ridiculous. The principle of the natural equality of tastes is then totally forgot, and while we admit it on some occasions, where the objects seem near an equality, it appears an extravagant paradox, or rather a palpable absurdity, where objects so disproportioned are compared together.

It is evident that none of the rules of composition are fixed by reasoning *a priori,* or can be esteemed abstract conclusions of the understanding, from comparing those habitudes and relations of ideas, which are eternal and immutable. Their foundation is the same with that of all the practical sciences, experience; nor are they anything but general observations, concerning what has been universally found to please in all countries and in all ages. Many of the beauties of poetry and even of eloquence are founded on falsehood and fiction, on hyperboles, metaphors, and an abuse or perversion of terms from their natural meaning. To check the sallies of the imagination, and to reduce every expression to geometrical truth and exactness, would be the most contrary to the laws of criticism; because it would produce a work, which, by universal experience, has been found the most insipid and disagreeable. But though poetry can never submit to exact truth, it must be confined by rules of art, discovered to the author either by genius or observation. If some negligent or irregular writers have pleased, they have not pleased by their transgressions of rule or order, but in spite of these transgressions: They have possessed other beauties, which were conformable to just criticism; and the force of these beauties

has been able to overpower censure, and give the mind a satisfaction superior to the disgust arising from the blemishes. Ariosto pleases; but not by his monstrous and improbable fictions, by his bizarre mixture of the serious and comic styles, by the want of coherence in his stories, or by the continual interruptions of his narration. He charms by the force and clearness of his expression, by the readiness and variety of his inventions, and by his natural pictures of the passions, especially those of the gay and amorous kind: And however his faults may diminish our satisfaction, they are not able entirely to destroy it. Did our pleasure really arise from those parts of his poem, which we denominate faults, this would be no objection to criticism in general: It would only be an objection to those particular rules of criticism, which would establish such circumstances to be faults, and would represent them as universally blamable. If they are found to please, they cannot be faults; let the pleasure, which they produce, be ever so unexpected and unaccountable.

But though all the general rules of art are founded only on experience and on the observation of the common sentiments of human nature, we must not imagine, that, on every occasion, the feelings of men will be conformable to these rules. Those finer emotions of the mind are of a very tender and delicate nature, and require the concurrence of many favorable circumstances to make them play with facility and exactness, according to their general and established principles. The least exterior hindrance to such small springs, or the least internal disorder, disturbs their motion, and confounds the operation of the whole machine. When we would make an experiment of this nature, and would try the force of any beauty or deformity, we must choose with care a proper time and place, and bring the fancy to a suitable situation and disposition. A perfect serenity of mind, a recollection of thought, a due attention to the object; if any of these circumstances be wanting, our experiment will be fallacious, and we shall be unable to judge of the catholic and universal beauty. The relation, which nature has placed between the form and the sentiment, will at least be more obscure; and it will require greater accuracy to trace and discern it. We shall be able to ascertain its influence not so much from the operation of each particular beauty, as from the durable admiration, which attends those works, that have survived all the caprices of mode and fashion, all the mistakes of ignorance and envy.

The same Homer, who pleased at Athens and Rome two thousand years ago, is still admired at Paris and at London. All the changes of climate, government, religion, and language, have not been able to obscure his glory. Authority or prejudice may give a temporary vogue to a bad poet or orator; but his reputation will never be durable or general. When his compositions are examined by posterity or by foreigners, the enchantment is dissipated, and his faults appear in their true colors. On the contrary, a real genius, the longer his works endure, and the more wide they are spread, the more sincere is the admiration which he meets with. Envy and jealousy have too much place in a narrow circle; and even familiar acquaintance with his person may diminish the applause due to his performances: but when these obstructions are removed, the beauties, which are naturally fitted to excite agreeable sentiments, immediately display their energy; and while the world endures, they maintain their authority over the minds of men.

It appears then, that, amidst all the variety and caprice of taste, there are certain general principles of approbation or blame, whose influence a careful eye may trace in all operations of the mind. Some particular forms or qualities, from the original structure of the internal fabric, are calculated to please, and others displease; and if they fail of their effect in any particular instance, it is from some apparent defect or imperfection in the organ. A man in a fever would not insist on his palate as able to decide concerning flavors; nor would one, affected with the jaundice, pretend to give a verdict with regard to colors. In each creature, there is a sound and defective state; and the former alone can be supposed to afford us a true standard of taste and sentiment. If, in the sound state of the organ, there be an entire or a considerable uniformity of sentiment among men, we may thence derive an idea of the perfect beauty; in like manner as the appearance of objects in daylight, to the eye of a man in health, is denominated their true and real color, even while color is allowed to be merely a phantasm of the senses.

Many and frequent are the defects in the internal organs which prevent or weaken the influence of those general principles, on which depends our sentiment of beauty or deformity. Though some objects, by the structure of the mind, be naturally calculated to give pleasure, it is not to be expected, that in every individual the pleasure will be equally felt. Particular incidents and situations occur, which either throw a false light on the objects, or hinder the true from conveying to the imagination the proper sentiment and perception.

One obvious cause, why many feel not the proper sentiment of beauty, is the want of that delicacy of imagination, which is requisite to convey a sensibility of those finer emotions. This delicacy everyone pretends to: everyone talks of it; and would reduce every kind of taste or sentiment to its standard. But as our intention in this essay is to mingle some light of the understanding with the feeling of sentiment, it will be proper to give a more accurate definition of delicacy, than has hitherto been attempted. And not to draw our philosophy from too profound a source, we shall have recourse to a noted story in *Don Quixote.*

"It is with good reason," says Sancho to the squire with the great nose, "that I pretend to have a judgment in wine: this is a quality hereditary in our family. Two of my kinsmen were once called to give their opinion of a hogshead, which was supposed to be excellent, being old and of a good vintage. One of them tastes it; considers it; and after mature reflection pronounces the wine to be good, were it not for a small taste of leather, which he perceived in it. The other, after using the same precautions, gives also his verdict in favor of the wine; but with the reserve of a taste of iron, which he could easily distinguish. You cannot imagine how much they were both ridiculed for their judgment. But who laughed in the end? On emptying the hogshead, there was found at the bottom, an old key with a leathern thong tied to it."

The great resemblance between mental and bodily taste will easily teach us to apply this story. Though it be certain that beauty and deformity, more than sweet and bitter, are not qualities in objects, but belong entirely to the sentiment, internal or external; it must be allowed, that there are certain qualities in objects, which are fitted by nature to produce those particular feelings. Now as these qualities may be found in a small degree, or may be mixed and confounded with each other, it often happens, that the taste is not affected with such minute qualities, or is not able to distinguish all the particular flavors, amidst the disorder, in which they are presented. Where the organs are so fine, as to allow nothing to escape them; and at the same time so exact as to perceive every ingredient in the composition: this we call delicacy of taste, where we employ these terms in the literal or metaphorical sense. Here then the general rules of beauty are of use; being drawn from established models, and from the observation of what pleases or displeases, when presented singly and in a high degree: and if the same qualities, in a continued composition and in a smaller degree, affect not the organs with a sensible delight or uneasiness, we exclude the person from all pretensions to this delicacy. To produce these general rules or avowed patterns of composition is like finding the key with the leathern thong; which justified the verdict of Sancho's kinsmen, and confounded those pretended judges who had condemned them. Though the hogshead had never been emptied, the taste of the one was still equally delicate, and that of the other equally dull and languid: but it would have been more difficult to have proved the superiority of the former, to the conviction of every bystander. In like manner, though the beauties of writing had never been methodized, or reduced to general principles; though no excellent models have ever been acknowledged; the different degrees of taste would still have subsisted, and the judgment of one man been preferable to that of another; but it would not have been so easy to silence the bad critic, who might always insist upon his particular sentiment, and refuse to submit to his antagonist. But when we show him an avowed principle of art; when we illustrate this principle by examples, whose operation, from his own particular taste, he acknowledges to be conformable to the principle; when we prove, that the same principle may be applied to the present case, where he did not perceive or feel its influence: he must conclude, upon the whole, that the fault lies in himself, and that he wants the delicacy, which is requisite to make him sensible of every beauty and every blemish, in any composition or discourse.

It is acknowledged to be the perfection of every sense or faculty, to perceive with exactness its most minute objects, and allow nothing to escape its notice and observation. The smaller the objects are, which become sensible to the eye, the finer is that organ, and the more elaborate its make and composition. A good palate is not tried by strong flavors; but by a mixture of small ingredients, where we are still sensible of each part, notwithstanding its minuteness and its confusion with the rest. In like manner, a quick and acute perception of beauty and deformity must be the perfection of our mental taste; nor can a man be satisfied with himself while he suspects, that any excellence or blemish in a discourse has passed him unobserved. In this case, the perfection of the man, and the perfection of the sense or feeling, are found to be united. A very delicate palate, on many occasions, may be a great inconvenience both to a man himself and to his friends: but a delicate taste of wit or beauty must always be a desirable quality; because it is the source of all the finest and most innocent enjoyments, of which human nature is susceptible. In this decision the sentiments of all mankind are agreed. Wherever you can ascertain a delicacy of taste, it is sure to meet with approbation; and the best way of ascertaining it is to appeal to those models and principles, which have been established by the uniform consent and experience of nations and ages.

But though there be naturally a wide difference in point of delicacy between one person and another, nothing tends further to increase and improve this talent, than practice in a particular art, and the frequent survey or contemplation of a particular species of beauty. When objects of any kind are first presented to the eye or imagination, the sentiment, which attends them, is obscure and confused; and the mind is, in a great measure, incapable of pronouncing concerning their merits or defects. The taste cannot perceive the several excellences of the performance; much less distinguish the particular character of each excellence, and ascertain its quality and degree. If it pronounce the whole in general to be beautiful or deformed, it is the utmost that can be expected; and even this judgment, a person, so unpracticed, will be apt to deliver with great hesitation and reserve. But allow him to acquire experience in those objects, his feeling becomes more exact and nice: he not only perceives the beauties and defects of each part, but marks the distinguishing species of each quality, and assigns it suitable praise or blame. A clear and distinct sentiment attends him through the whole survey of the objects; and he discerns that very degree and kind of approbation or displeasure, which each part is naturally fitted to produce. The mist dissipates, which seemed formerly to hang over the object: the organ acquires greater perfection in its operations; and can pronounce, without danger of mistake, concerning the merits of every performance. In a word, the same address and dexterity, which practice gives to the execution of any work, is also acquired by the same means, in the judging of it.

So advantageous is practice to the discernment of beauty, that, before we can give judgment on any work of importance, it will even be requisite, that that very individual performance be more than once perused by us, and be surveyed in different lights with attention and deliberation. There is a flutter or hurry of thought which attends the first perusal of any piece, and which confounds the genuine sentiment of beauty. The relation of the parts is not discerned: the true characters of style are little distinguished: the several perfections and defects seem wrapped up in a species of confusion, and present themselves indistinctly to the imagination. Not to mention, that there is a species of beauty, which, as it is florid and superficial, pleases at first; but being found incompatible with a just expression either of reason or passion, soon palls upon the taste, and is then rejected with disdain, at least rated at a much lower value.

It is impossible to continue in the practice of contemplating any order of beauty, without being frequently obliged to form comparisons between the several species and degrees of excellence, and estimating their proportion to each other. A man, who has had no opportunity of comparing the different kinds of beauty, is indeed totally unqualified to pronounce an opinion with regard to any object presented to him. By comparison alone we fix the epithets of praise or blame, and learn how to assign the due degree of each. The coarsest daubing contains a certain luster of colors and exactness of imitation, which are so far beauties, and would affect the mind of a peasant or Indian with the highest admiration. The most vulgar ballads are not entirely destitute of harmony or nature; and none but a per-

son, familiarized to superior beauties, would pronounce their numbers harsh, or narration uninteresting. A great inferiority of beauty gives pain to a person conversant in the highest excellence of the kind, and is for that reason pronounced a deformity: as the most finished object, with which we are acquainted, is naturally supposed to have reached the pinnacle of perfection, and to be entitled to the highest applause. One accustomed to see, and examine, and weight the several performances, admired in different ages and nations, can only rate the merits of a work exhibited to his view, and assign its proper rank among the productions of genius.

But to enable a critic the more fully to execute this undertaking, he must preserve his mind free from all prejudice, and allow nothing to enter into his consideration, but the very object which is submitted to his examination. We may observe, that every work of art, in order to produce its due effect on the mind, must be surveyed in a certain point of view, and cannot be fully relished by persons, whose situation, real or imaginary, is not conformable to that which is required by the performance. An orator addresses himself to a particular audience, and must have a regard to their particular genius, interests, opinions, passions, and prejudices; otherwise he hopes in vain to govern their resolutions, and inflame their affections. Should they even have entertained some prepossessions against him, however unreasonable, he must not overlook this disadvantage; but, before he enters upon the subject, must endeavor to conciliate their affection, and acquire their good graces. A critic of a different age or nation, who should peruse this discourse, must have all these circumstances in his eye, and must place himself in the same situation as the audience, in order to form a true judgment of the oration. In like manner, when any work is addressed to the public, though I should have a friendship or enmity with the author, I must depart from this situation; and considering myself as a man in general, forget, if possible, my individual being and my peculiar circumstances. A person influenced by prejudice, complies not with this condition; but obstinately maintains his natural position, without placing himself in that point of view, which the performance supposes. If the work be addressed to persons of a different age or nation, he makes no allowance for their peculiar views and prejudices; but, full of the manners of his own age and country, rashly condemns what seemed admirable in the eyes of those for whom alone the discourse was calculated. If the work be executed for the public, he never sufficiently enlarges his comprehension, or forgets his interest as a friend or enemy, as a rival or commentator. By this means, his sentiments are perverted; nor have the same beauties and blemishes the same influence upon him, as if he had imposed a proper violence on his imagination, and had forgotten himself for a moment. So far his taste evidently departs from the true standard; and of consequence loses all credit and authority.

It is well known, that in all questions, submitted to the understanding, prejudice is destructive of sound judgment, and perverts all operations of the intellectual faculties: it is no less contrary to good taste; nor has it less influence to corrupt our sentiment of beauty. It belongs to good sense to check its influence in both cases; and in this respect, as well as in many others, reason, if not an essential part of taste, is at least requisite to the operations of this latter faculty. In all the nobler productions of genius, there is a mutual relation and correspondence of parts; nor can either the beauties or blemishes be perceived by him, whose thought is not capacious enough to comprehend all those parts, and compare then with each other, in order to perceive the consistence and uniformity of the whole. Every work of art has also a certain end or purpose, for which it is calculated; and is to be deemed more or less perfect, as it is more or less fitted to attain this end. The object of eloquence is to persuade, of history to instruct, of poetry to please by means of the passions and the imagination. These ends we must carry constantly in our view, when we peruse any performance; and we must be able to judge how far the means employed are adapted to their respective purposes. Besides every kind of composition, even the most poetical, is nothing but a chain of propositions and reasonings; not always, indeed, the justest and most exact, but still plausible and specious, however disguised by the coloring of the imagination. The persons introduced in tragedy and epic poetry, must be represented as reasoning, and thinking, and concluding, and acting, suitably to their character and circumstances; and without judgment, as

well as taste and invention, a poet can never hope to succeed in so delicate an undertaking. Not to mention, that the same excellence of faculties which contributes to the improvement of reason, the same clearness of conception, the same exactness of distinction, the same vivacity of apprehension, are essential to the operations of true taste, and are its infallible concomitants. It seldom, or never happens, that a man of sense, who has experience in any art, cannot judge of its beauty; and it is no less rare to meet with a man who has a just taste without a sound understanding.

Thus, though the principles of taste be universal, and, nearly, if not entirely the same in all men; yet few are qualified to give judgment on any work of art, or establish their own sentiment as the standard of beauty. The organs of internal sensation are seldom so perfect as to allow the general principles their full play, and produce a feeling correspondent to those principles. They either labor under some defect, or are vitiated by some disorder; and by that means, excite a sentiment, which may be pronounced erroneous. When the critic has no delicacy, he judges without any distinction, and is only affected by the grosser and more palpable qualities of the object: the finer touches pass unnoticed and disregarded. Where he is not aided by practice, his verdict is attended with confusion and hesitation. Where no comparison has been employed, the most frivolous beauties, such as rather merit the name of defects, are the objects of his admiration. Where he lies under the influence of prejudice, all his natural sentiments are perverted. Where good sense is wanting, he is not qualified to discern the beauties of design and reasoning, which are the highest and most excellent. Under some or other of these imperfections, the generality of men labor; and hence a true judge in the finer arts is observed, even during the most polished ages, to be so rare a character: strong sense, united to delicate sentiment, improved by practice, perfected by comparison, and cleared of all prejudice, can alone entitle critics to this valuable character; and the joint verdict of such, wherever they are to be found, is the true standard of taste and beauty.

But where are such critics to be found? By what marks are they to be known? How distinguish them from pretenders? These questions are embarrassing;

and seem to throw us back into the same uncertainty, from which, during the course of this essay, we have endeavored to extricate ourselves.

But if we consider the matter aright, these are questions of fact, not of sentiment. Whether any particular person be endowed with good sense and a delicate imagination, free from prejudice, may often be the subject of dispute, and be liable to great discussion and inquiry: But that such a character is valuable and estimable will be agreed in by all mankind. Where these doubts occur, men can do no more than in other disputable questions, which are submitted to the understanding: they must produce the best arguments, that their invention suggests to them; they must acknowledge a true and decisive standard to exist somewhere, to wit, real existence and matter of fact; and they must have indulgence to such as differ from them in their appeals to this standard. It is sufficient for our present purpose, if we have proved, that the taste of all individuals is not upon an equal footing, and that some men in general, however difficult to be particularly pitched upon, will be acknowledged by universal sentiment to have a preference above others.

But in reality the difficulty of finding, even in particulars, the standard of taste, is not so great as it is represented. Though in speculation, we may readily avow a certain criterion in science and deny it in sentiment, the matter is found in practice to be much more hard to ascertain in the former case than in the latter. Theories of abstract philosophy, systems of profound theology, have prevailed during one age: in a successive period, these have been universally exploded: their absurdity has been detected: other theories and systems have supplied their place, which again gave place to their successors: and nothing has been experienced more liable to the revolutions of chance and fashion than these pretended decisions of science. The case is not the same with the beauties of eloquence and poetry. Just expressions of passion and nature are sure, after a little time, to gain public applause, which they maintain forever. Aristotle, and Plato, and Epicurus, and Descartes, may successively yield to each other: but Terence and Virgil maintain a universal, undisputed empire over the minds of men. The abstract philosophy of Cicero has lost its credit: the vehemence of his oratory is still the object of our admiration.

Though men of delicate taste be rare, they are easily to be distinguished in society, by the soundness of their understanding and the superiority of their faculties above the rest of mankind. The ascendant, which they acquire, gives a prevalence to that lively approbation, with which they receive any productions of genius, and renders it generally predominant. Many men, when left to themselves, have but a faint and dubious perception of beauty, who yet are capable of relishing any fine stroke, which is pointed out to them. Every convert to the admiration of the real poet or orator is the cause of some new conversion. And though prejudices may prevail for a time, they never unite in celebrating any rival to the true genius, but yield at last to the force of nature and just sentiment. Thus, though a civilized nation may easily be mistaken in the choice of their admired philosopher, they never have been found long to err, in their affection for a favorite epic or tragic author.

But notwithstanding all our endeavors to fix a standard of taste, and reconcile the discordant apprehensions of men, there still remain two sources of variation, which are not sufficient indeed to confound all the boundaries of beauty and deformity, but will often serve to produce a difference in the degrees of our approbation or blame. The one is the different humors of particular men; the other, the particular manners and opinions of our age and country. The general principles of taste are uniform in human nature: where men vary in their judgments, some defect or perversion in the faculties may commonly be remarked; proceeding either from prejudice, from want of practice, or want of delicacy; and there is just reason for approving one taste, and condemning another. But where there is such a diversity in the internal frame or external situation as is entirely blameless on both sides, and leaves no room to give one the preference above the other; in that case a certain degree of diversity in judgment is unavoidable, and we seek in vain for a standard, by which we can reconcile the contrary sentiments.

A young man, whose passions are warm, will be more sensibly touched with amorous and tender images, than a man more advanced in years, who takes pleasure in wise, philosophical reflections concerning the conduct of life and moderation of the passions. At twenty, Ovid may be the favorite author; Horace at forty; and perhaps Tacitus at fifty. Vainly would we, in such cases, endeavor to enter into the sentiments of others, and divest ourselves of those propensities, which are natural to us. We choose our favorite author as we do our friend, from a conformity of humor and disposition. Mirth or passion, sentiment or reflection; whichever of these most predominates in our temper, it gives us a peculiar sympathy with the writer who resembles us.

One person is more pleased with the sublime; another with the tender; a third with raillery. One has a strong sensibility to blemishes, and is extremely studious of correctness; another has a more lively feeling of beauties, and pardons twenty absurdities and defects for one elevated or pathetic stroke. The ear of this man is entirely turned toward conciseness and energy; that man is delighted with a copious, rich, and harmonious expression. Simplicity is affected by one; ornament by another. Comedy, tragedy, satire, odes, have each its partisans, who prefer that particular species of writing to all others. It is plainly an error in a critic, to confine his approbation to one species or style of writing, and condemn all the rest. But it is almost impossible not to feel a predilection for that which suits our particular turn and disposition. Such preferences are innocent and unavoidable, and can never reasonably be the object of dispute, because there is no standard, by which they can be decided.

For a like reason, we are more pleased, in the course of our reading, with pictures and characters, that resemble objects which are found in our own age or country, than with those which describe a different set of customs. It is not without some effort, that we reconcile ourselves to the simplicity of ancient manners, and behold princesses carrying water from the spring, and kings and heroes dressing their own victuals. We may allow in general, that the representation of such manners is no fault in the author, nor deformity in the piece; but we are not so sensibly touched with them. For this reason, comedy is not easily transferred from one age or nation to another. . . .

Analytic of the Beautiful and of the Sublime

IMMANUEL KANT

Born in Köningsberg, East Prussia (now part of Russia), the great German philosopher Immanuel Kant (1724–1804) was one of the most influential of all modern thinkers.

ANALYTIC OF THE BEAUTIFUL

In order to decide whether anything is beautiful or not, we refer the representation, not by the Understanding to the Object for cognition but, by the Imagination (perhaps in conjunction with the Understanding) to the subject, and its feeling of pleasure or pain. The judgement of taste is therefore not a judgement of cognition, and is consequently not logical but aesthetical, by which we understand that whose determining ground can be *no other than subjective.* Every reference of representations, even that

From *Kant's Critique of Judgement,* translated by J. H. Bernard, 1914.

of sensations, may be objective (and then it signifies the real in an empirical representation); save only the reference to the feeling of pleasure and pain, by which nothing in the Object is signified, but through which there is a feeling in the subject, as it is affected by the representation.

To apprehend a regular, purposive building by means of one's cognitive faculty (whether in a clear or a confused way of representation) is something quite different from being conscious of this representation as connected with the sensation of satisfaction. Here the representation is altogether referred to the subject and to its feeling of life, under the name of the feeling of pleasure or pain. This establishes a quite separate faculty of distinction and of judgement, adding nothing to cognition, but only comparing the given representation in the subject with the whole faculty of representations, of which the mind is conscious in the feeling of its state. Given representations in a judgement can be empirical (consequently, aesthetical); but the judgement which is formed by means of them is logical, provided they are referred in the judgement to the Object. Conversely, if the given representations are rational, but are referred in a judgement simply to the subject (to its feeling), the judgement is so far always aesthetical.

. . .

The satisfaction which we combine with the representation of the existence of an object is called interest. Such satisfaction always has reference to the faulty of desire, either as its determining ground or as necessarily connected with its determining ground. Now when the question is if a thing is beautiful, we do not want to know whether anything depends or can depend on the existence of the thing either for myself or for any one else, but how we judge it by mere observation (intuition or reflection). . . .

Whatever by means of Reason pleases through the mere concept is **GOOD.** That which pleases only as a means we call *good for something* (the useful); but that which pleases for itself is *good in itself.* In both there is always involved the concept of a purpose, and consequently the relation of Reason to the (at least possible) volition, and thus a satisfaction in the *presence* of an Object or an action, *i.e.* some kind of interest.

In order to find anything good, I must always know what sort of a thing the object ought to be, *i.e.* I must have a concept of it. But there is no need of this, to find a thing beautiful. Flowers, free delineations, outlines intertwined with one another without design and called foliage, have no meaning, depend on no definite concept, and yet they please. The satisfaction in the beautiful must depend on the reflection upon an object, leading to any concept (however indefinite); and it is thus distinguished from the pleasant which rests entirely upon sensation. . . .

. . . of all these three kinds of satisfaction, that of taste in the Beautiful is alone a disinterested and *free* satisfaction; for no interest, either of Sense or of Reason, here forces our assent. Hence we may say of satisfaction that it is related in the three aforesaid cases to *inclination,* to *favour,* or to *respect.* Now *favour* is the only free satisfaction. An object of inclination, and one that is proposed to our desire by a law of Reason, leave us no freedom in forming for ourselves anywhere an object of pleasure. All interest presupposes or generates a want; and, as the determining ground of assent, it leaves the judgment about the object no longer free. . . .

Taste is the faculty of judging of an object or a method of representing it by an *entirely disinterested* satisfaction or dissatisfaction. The object of such satisfaction is called *beautiful.*

The beautiful is that which apart from concepts is represented as the object of a universal satisfaction

This explanation of the beautiful can be derived from the preceding explanation of it as the object of an entirely disinterested satisfaction. For the fact of which every one is conscious, that the satisfaction is for him quite disinterested, implies in his judgement a ground of satisfaction for every one. For since it does not rest on any inclination of the subject (nor upon any other premeditated interest), but since he who judges feels himself quite *free* as regards the satisfaction which he attaches to the object, he cannot find the ground of this satisfaction in any private conditions connected with his own subject; and hence it must be regarded as grounded on what he can presuppose in every other man. Consequently he must believe that he has reason for attributing a similar satisfaction to every one. He will therefore speak of the beautiful, as if beauty were a characteristic of the object and the judgement logical (constituting a cognition of the Object by means of concepts of it); although it is only aesthetical and involves merely a reference of the representation of the object to the subject. For it has this similarity to a logical judgement that we can presuppose its validity for every one. But this universality cannot arise from concepts; for from concepts there is no transition to the feeling of pleasure or pain (except in pure practical laws, which bring an interest with them such as is not bound up with the pure judgement of taste). Consequently the judgement of taste, accompanied with the consciousness of separation from all interest, must claim validity for every one, without this universality depending on Objects. That is, there must be bound up with it a title to subjective universality.

. . .

The universality of the satisfaction is represented in a judgement of Taste only as subjective

This particular determination of the universality of an aesthetical judgement, which is to be met with in a judgement of taste, is noteworthy, not indeed for the logician, but for the transcendental philosopher. It requires no small trouble to discover its origin, but we thus detect a property of our cognitive faculty which without this analysis would remain unknown.

First, we must be fully convinced of the fact that in a judgement of taste (about the Beautiful) the satisfaction in the object is imputed to *every one,* without being based on a concept (for then it would be the Good). Further, this claim to universal validity so essentially belongs to a judgement by which we describe anything as *beautiful,* that if this were not thought in it, it would never come into our thoughts to use the expression at all, but everything which pleases without a concept would be counted as pleasant. In respect of the latter every one has his own opinion; and no one assumes, in another agreement with his judgement of taste, which is always the case in a judgement of taste about beauty. I may call the first the taste of Sense, the second the taste of Reflection; so far as the first lays down mere private judgements, and the second judgements supposed to be generally valid (public), but in both cases aesthetical (not practical) judgements about an object merely in respect of the relation of its representation to the feeling of pleasure and pain. Now here is something strange. As regards the taste of Sense not only does experience show that its judgement (of pleasure or pain connected with anything) is not valid universally, but every one is content not to impute agreement with it to others (although actually there is often found a very extended concurrence in these judgements). On the other hand, the taste

of Reflection has its claim to the universal validity of its judgements (about the beautiful) rejected often enough, as experience teaches; although it may find it possible (as it actually does) to represent judgements which can demand this universal agreement. In fact for each of its judgements of taste it imputes this to every one, without the persons that judge disputing as to the possibility of such a claim; although in particular cases they cannot agree as to the correct application of this faculty.

Here we must, in the first place, remark that a universality which does not rest on concepts of Objects (not even on empirical ones) is not logical but aesthetical, *i.e.* it involves no objective quantity of the judgement but only that which is subjective. For this I use the expression *general validity* which signifies the validity of the reference of a representation, not to the cognitive faculty but, to the feeling of pleasure and pain for every subject. (We can avail ourselves also of the same expression for the logical quantity of the judgement, if only we prefix *objective* to "universal validity," to distinguish it from that which is merely subjective and aesthetical.)

A judgement with *objective universal validity* is also always valid subjectively; *i.e.* if the judgement holds for everything contained under a given concept, it holds also for every one who represents an object by means of this concept. But from a *subjective universal validity, i.e.* aesthetical and resting on no concept, we cannot infer that which is logical; because that kind of judgement does not extend to the Object. Hence the aesthetical universality which is ascribed to a judgement must be of a particular kind, because it does not unite the predicate of beauty with the concept of the *Object,* considered in its whole logical sphere, and yet extends it to the whole sphere of judging persons.

In respect of logical quantity all judgements of taste are *singular* judgements. For because I must refer the object immediately to my feeling of pleasure and pain, and that not by means of concepts, they cannot have the quantity of objective generally valid judgements. Nevertheless if the singular representation of the Object of the judgement of taste in accordance with the conditions determining the latter, were transformed by comparison into a concept, a logically universal judgement could result therefrom. *E.g.* I describe by a judgement of taste the rose, that I see, as beautiful. But the judgement which results from the comparison of several singular judgements, "Roses in general are beautiful" is no longer described simply as aesthetical, but as a logical judgement based on an aesthetical one. Again the judgement "The rose is pleasant" (to smell) is, although aesthetical and singular, not a judgement of Taste but of Sense. It is distinguished from the former by the fact that the judgement of Taste carries with it an *aesthetical quantity* of universality, *i.e.* of validity for every one; which cannot be found in a judgement about the Pleasant. It is only judgements about the Good which—although they also determine satisfaction in an object,—have logical and not merely aesthetical universality; for they are valid of the Object, as cognitive of it, and thus are valid for every one.

If we judge Objects merely according to concepts, then all representation of beauty is lost. Thus there can be no rule according to which any one is to be forced to recognise anything as beautiful. We cannot press [upon others] by the aid of any reasons or fundamental propositions our judgement that a coat, a house, or flower is beautiful. We wish to submit the Object to our own eyes, as if the satisfaction in it depended on sensation; and yet if we then call the object beautiful, we believe that we speak with a universal voice, and we claim the assent of every one, although on the contrary all private sensation can only decide for the observer himself and his satisfaction.

We may see now that in the judgement of taste nothing is postulated but such a *universal voice,* in respect of the satisfaction without the intervention of concepts; and thus the *possibility* of an aesthetical judgement that can, at the same time, be regarded as valid for every one. The judgement of taste itself does not *postulate* the agreement of every one (for that can only be done by a logically universal judgement because it can adduce reasons); it only *imputes* this agreement to every one, as a case of the rule in respect of which it expects, not confirmation by concepts, but assent from others. The universal voice is, therefore, only an Idea (we do not yet inquire upon what it rests). It may be uncertain whether or not the man, who believes that he is laying down a judgement of taste, is, as a matter of fact, judging in conformity with that Idea; but that he refers his judge-

ment thereto, and, consequently, that it is intended to be a judgement of taste, he announces by the expression "beauty." He can be quite certain of this for himself by the mere consciousness of the separation of everything belonging to the Pleasant and the Good from the satisfaction which is left; and this is all for which he promises himself the agreement of every one—a claim which would be justifiable under these conditions, provided only he did not often make mistakes, and thus lay down an erroneous judgement of taste.

. . .

The *beautiful* is that which pleases universally without a concept.

. . .

If we wish to explain what a purpose is according to its transcendental determinations (without presupposing anything empirical like the feeling of pleasure) [we say that] the purpose is the object of a concept, in so far as the concept is regarded as the cause of the object (the real ground of its possibility); and the causality of a *concept* in respect of its *Object* is its purposiveness (*forma finalis*). Where then not merely the cognition of an object, but the object itself (its form and existence) is thought as an effect only possible by means of the concept of this latter, there we think a purpose. The representation of the effect is here the determining ground of its cause and precedes it. The consciousness of the causality of a representation, for *maintaining* the subject in the same state, may here generally denote what we call pleasure; while on the other hand pain is that representation which contains the ground of the determination of the state of representations into their opposite [of restraining or removing them].

The faculty of desire, so far as it is determinable only through concepts, i.e. to act in conformity with the representations of a purpose, would be the Will. But an Object, or a state of mind, or even an action, is called purposive, although its possibility does not necessarily presuppose the representation of a purpose, merely because its possibility can be explained and conceived by us only so far as we assume for its ground a causality according to purposes, *i.e.* a will which would have so disposed it according to the representation of a certain rule. There can be, then, purposiveness without purpose, so far as we do not place the causes of this form in a will, but yet can only make the explanation of its possibility intelligible to ourselves by deriving it from a will. Again, we are not always forced to regard what we observe (in respect of its possibility) from the point of view of Reason. Thus we can at least observe a purposiveness according to form, without basing it on a purpose (as the material of the *nexus finalis*), and we can notice it in objects, although only by reflection. . . .

There can be no objective rule of taste which shall determine by means of concepts what is beautiful. For every judgement from this source is aesthetical; *i.e.* the feeling of the subject, and not a concept of the Object, is its determining ground. To seek for a principle of taste which shall furnish, by means of definite concepts, a universal criterion of the beautiful, is fruitless trouble; because what is sought is impossible and self-contradictory. The universal communicability of sensation (satisfaction or dissatisfaction) without the aid of a concept—the agreement, as far as is possible, of all times and peoples as regards this feeling in the representation of certain objects—this is the empirical criterion, although weak and hardly sufficing for probability, of the derivation of a taste, thus confirmed by examples, from the deep-lying grounds of agreement common to all men, in judging of the forms under which objects are given to them. . . .

ANALYTIC OF THE SUBLIME

. . .

The Beautiful and the Sublime agree in this, that both please in themselves. Further, neither presupposes a judgement of sense nor a judgement of reflection. Consequently the satisfaction [belonging to them] does not depend on a sensation, as in the case of the Pleasant, nor on a definite concept, as in the case of the Good; but it is nevertheless referred to concepts although indeterminate ones. And so the satisfaction is connected with the mere presentation [of the object] or with the faculty of presentation; so that in the case of a given intuition this faculty or the Imagination is considered as in agreement with the *faculty of concepts* of Understanding or Reason (in its furtherance of these latter). Hence both kinds of judgements are *singular,* and yet announce themselves as universally valid for ev-

ery subject; although they lay claim merely to the feeling of pleasure and not to any knowledge of the object.

But there are also remarkable differences between the two. The Beautiful in nature is connected with the form of the object, which consists in having boundaries. The Sublime, on the other hand, is to be found in a formless object, so far as in it or by occasion of it *boundlessness* is represented, and yet its totality is also present to thought. Thus the Beautiful seems to be regarded as the presentation of an indefinite concept of Understanding; the Sublime as that of a like concept of Reason. Therefore the satisfaction in the one case is bound up with the representation of *quality* in the other with that of *quantity.* And the latter satisfaction is quite different in kind from the former, for this [the Beautiful] directly brings with it a feeling of the futherance of life, and thus is compatible with charms and with the play of the Imagination. But the other [the feeling of the Sublime[1]] is a pleasure that arises only indirectly; viz. it is produced by the feeling of a momentary checking of the vital powers and a consequent stronger outflow of them, so that it seems to be regarded as emotion,—not play, but earnest in the exercise of the Imagination.—Hence it is incompatible with charms; and as the mind is not merely attracted by the object but is ever being alternately repelled, the satisfaction in the sublime does not so much involve a positive pleasure as admiration of respect, which rather deserves to be called negative pleasure.

But the inner and most important distinction between the Sublime and Beautiful is, certainly, as follows. (Here, as we are entitled to do, we only bring under consideration in the first instance the sublime in natural Objects; for the sublime of Art is always limited by the conditions of agreement with Nature.) Natural beauty (which is self-subsisting) brings with it a purposiveness in its form by which the object seems to be, as it were, pre-adapted to our Judgement, and thus constitutes in itself an object of satisfaction. On the other hand, that which excites in us, without any reasoning about it, but in the mere apprehension of it, the feeling of the sublime, may appear as regards its form to violate purpose in respect of the Judgement, to be unsuited to our presentative faculty, and, as it were, to do violence to the Imagination; and yet it is judged to be only the more sublime.

Now from this we see that in general we express ourselves incorrectly if we call any *object of nature* sublime, although we can quite correctly call many objects of nature beautiful. For how can that be marked by an expression of approval, which is apprehended in itself as being a violation of purpose? All that we can say is that the object is fit for the presentation of a sublimity which can be found in the mind, for no sensible form can contain the sublime properly so-called. This concerns only Ideas of the Reason, which, although no adequate presentation is possible for them, by this inadequacy that admits of sensible presentation, are aroused and summoned into the mind. Thus the wide ocean, agitated by the storm, cannot be called sublime. Its aspect is horrible; and the mind must be already filled with manifold Ideas if it is to be determined by such an intuition to a feeling itself sublime, as it is incited to abandon sensibility and to busy itself with Ideas that involve higher purposiveness.

Self-subsisting natural beauty discovers to us a Technic of nature, which represents it as a system in accordance with laws, the principle of which we do not find in the whole of our faculty of Understanding. That principle is the principle of purposiveness, in respect of the use of our Judgement in regard to phenomena; [which requires] that these must not be judged as merely belonging to nature in its purposeless mechanism, but also as belonging to something analogous to art. It, therefore, actually extends, not indeed our cognition of natural Objects, but our concept of nature; [which is now not regarded] as mere mechanism but as art. This leads to profound investigations as to the possibility of such a form. But in what we are accustomed to call sublime there is nothing at all that leads to particular objective principles and forms of nature corresponding to them; so far from it that for the most part nature excites the Ideas of the sublime in its chaos or in its wildest and most irregular disorder and desolation, provided size and might are perceived. Hence, we see that the concept of the Sublime is not nearly so important or rich in consequences as the concept of the Beautiful; and that in general it displays nothing

purposive in nature itself, but only in that possible use of our intuitions of it by which there is produced in us a feeling of a purposiveness quite independent of nature. We must seek a ground external to ourselves for the Beautiful of nature; but seek it for the Sublime merely in ourselves and in our attitude of thought which introduces sublimity into the representation of nature. This is a very needful preliminary remark, which quite separates the Ideas of the sublime from that of a purposiveness of *nature*, and makes the theory of the sublime a mere appendix to the aesthetical judging of that purposiveness, because by means of it no particular form is represented in nature, but there is only developed a purposive use which the Imagination makes of its representation.

. . .

As regards the division of the moments of the aesthetical judging of objects in reference to the feeling of the sublime, the Analytic can proceed according to the same principle as was adapted in the analysis of judgements of taste. For as an act of the aesthetical reflective Judgement, the satisfaction in the Sublime must be represented just as in the case of the Beautiful,—according to *quantity* as universally valid, according to *quality* as devoid of *interest*, according to *relation* as subjective purposiveness, and according to *modality* as necessary. And so the method here will not diverse from that of the preceding section; unless, indeed, we count it a difference that in the case where the aesthetical Judgement is concerned with the form of the Object we began with the investigation of its quality, but here, in view of the formlessness which may belong to what we call sublime, we shall begin with quantity, as the first moment of the aesthetical judgement as to the sublime. The reason for this may be seen from the preceding paragraph.

But the analysis of the Sublime involves a division not needed in the case of the Beautiful, viz a division into the *mathematically* and the *dynamically sublime*.

For the feeling of the Sublime brings with it as its characteristic feature a *movement* of the mind bound up with the judging of the object, while in the case of the Beautiful taste presupposes and maintains the mind in *restful* contemplation. Now this movement ought to be judged as subjectively purposive (because the sublime pleases us), and thus it is referred through the Imagination either to the *faculty of cognition or of desire*. In either reference the purposiveness of given representation ought to be judged only in respect to this *faculty* (without purpose or interest); but in the first case it is ascribed to the Object as a *mathematical* determination of the Imagination, in the second as *dynamical*. And hence we have this twofold way of representing the sublime.

. . .

We call that *sublime* which is *absolutely great*. But to be great, and to be a great something are quite different concepts (*Magnitudo* and *quantitas*). In like manner to *say simply (simpliciter)* that anything is *great* is quite different from saying that it is *absolutely great (absolute, non comparative magnum)*. The latter is *what is great beyond all comparison.*—What now is meant by the expression that anything is great or small or of medium size? It is not a pure concept of Understanding that is thus signified; still less is it an intuition of Sense, and just a little is it a concept of Reason, because it brings with it no principle of cognition. It must therefore be a concept of Judgement or derived from one; and a subjective purposiveness of the representation in reference to the Judgement must lie at its basis. That anything is a magnitude (*quantum*) may be cognised from the thing itself, without any comparison of it with other things; viz. if there is a multiplicity of the homogeneous constituting one thing. But to cognise *how great* it is always requires some other magnitude as a measure. But because the judging of magnitude depends not merely on multiplicity (number), but also on the magnitude of the unit (the measure) and since, to judge of the magnitude of this latter again requires another as measure with which it may be compared, we see that the determination of the magnitude of phenomena can supply no absolute concept whatever of magnitude, but only a comparative one.

If now I say simply that anything is great, it appears that I have no comparison in view, at least none with an objective measure; because it is thus not determined at all how great the object is. But al-though the standard of comparison is merely subjective, yet the judgement none the less claims universal assent; "this man is beautiful," and "he is tall," are judgements not limited merely to the judging subject, but, like theoretical judgements, demanding the assent of every one.

In a judgement by which anything is designated simply as great, it is not merely meant that the object has a magnitude, but that this magnitude is superior to that of many other objects of the same kind, without, however, any exact determination of this superiority. Thus there is always at the basis of our judgement a standard which we assume as the same for every one; this, however, is not available for any logical (mathematically definite) judging of magnitude, but only for aesthetical judging of the same, because it is merely subjective standard lying at the basis of the reflective judgement upon magnitude. It may be empirical, as, *e.g.* the average size of the men known to us, of animals of a certain kind, trees, houses, mountains, etc. Or it may be a standard given *a priori*, which through the defects of the judging subject is limited by the subjective conditions of presentation *in concreto;* as, *e.g.* in the practical sphere, the greatness of a certain virtue, or of the public liberty and justice in a country; or, in the theoretical sphere, the greatness of the accuracy or the inaccuracy of an observation or measurement that has been made, etc.

Here it is remarkable that, although we have no interest whatever in an Object,—*i.e.* its existence is indifferent to us,—yet its mere size, even if it is considered as formless, may bring a satisfaction with it that is universally communicable, and that consequently involves the consciousness of a subjective purposiveness in the use of our cognitive faculty. This is not indeed a satisfaction in the Object (because it may be formless), as in the case of the Beautiful, in which the reflective Judgement finds itself purposively determined in reference to cognition in general; but [a satisfaction] in the extension of the Imagination by itself.

If (under the above limitation) we say simply of an object "it is great," this is no mathematically definite judgement but a mere judgement of reflection upon the representation of it, which is subjectively purposive for a certain use of our cognitive powers in the estimation of magnitude; and we always then bind up with the representation a kind of respect, as also a kind of contempt for what we simply call "small." Further, the judging of things as great or small extends to everything, even to all their characteristics; thus we describe beauty as great or small. The reason of this is to be sought in the fact that whatever we present in intuition according to the precept of the Judgement (and thus represent aesthetically) is always a phenomenon and thus a quantum.

But if we call anything not only great, but absolutely great in every point of view (great beyond all comparison), *i.e.* sublime, we soon see that it is not permissible to seek for an adequate standard of this outside itself, but merely in itself. It is a magnitude which is like itself alone. It follows hence that the sublime is not to be sought in the things of nature, but only in our Ideas; but in which of them it lies must be reserved for the Deduction.

The foregoing explanation can be thus expressed: *the sublime is that in comparison with which everything else is small.* Here we easily see that nothing can be given in nature, however great it is judged by us to be, which could not if considered in another relation be reduced to the infinitely small; and conversely there is nothing so small, which does not admit of extension by our Imagination to the greatness of a world, if compared with still smaller standards. Telescopes have furnished us with abundant material for making the first remark, microscopes for the second. Nothing, therefore, which can be an object of the senses, is considered on this basis, to be called sublime. But because there is in our Imagination a striving towards infinite progress, and in our Reason a claim for absolute totality, regarded as a real Idea, therefore this very inadequateness for that Idea in our faculty for estimating the magnitude of things of sense, excites in us the feeling of a supersensible faculty. And it is not the object of sense, but the use which the Judgement naturally makes of certain objects on behalf of this latter feeling, that is absolutely great; and in comparison every other use is small. Consequently it is the state of mind produced by a certain representation with which the reflective Judgement is occupied, and not the Object, that is to be called sublime.

We may therefore appeal to the preceding formulas explaining the sublime this other: *the sublime is that, the mere ability to think which, shows a faculty of the mind surpassing every standard of Sense.*

. . .

The estimation of magnitude by means of concepts of number (or their signs in Algebra) is mathematical; but that in mere intuition (by the measurement of the eye) is aesthetical. Now we can come by definite concepts of *how great* a thing is, [only] by numbers, of which the unit is the measure (at all events by series of numbers progressing to infinity); and so far all logical estimation of magnitude is mathematical. But since the magnitude of the measure must then be assumed known, and this again is only to be estimated mathematically by means of numbers,— the unit of which must be another [smaller] measure,—we can never have a first or fundamental measure, and therefore can never have a definite concept of a given magnitude. So the estimation of the magnitude of the fundamental measure must consist in this, that we can immediately apprehend it in intuition and use it by the Imagination for the presentation of concepts of number. That is, all the estimation of the magnitude of the objects of nature is in the end aesthetical (*i.e.,* subjectively and not objectively determined).

Now for the mathematical estimation of magnitude there is, indeed, no maximum (for the power of numbers extends to infinity); but for its aesthetical estimation there is always a maximum, and of this I say that if it is judged as the absolute measure than which no greater is possible subjectively (for the judging subject), it brings with it the Idea of the sublime and produces that emotion which no mathematical estimation of its magnitude by means of numbers can bring about (except so far as the aesthetical fundamental measure remains vividly in the Imagination). For the former only presents relative magnitude by means of comparison with others of the same kind; but the latter presents magnitude absolutely, so far as the mind can grasp it in an intuition.

The Philosophy of Art

GEORG WILHELM FRIEDRICH HEGEL

Georg Hegel (1770–1831) was born in Stuttgart, Germany. He taught philosophy at the University of Jena and then Berlin. Inspired mostly by Kant, he himself became one of the most influential philosophers of the nineteenth century.

. . . But the work of art brings before us the eternal powers that hold dominion in history, without any such superfluity in the way of immediate sensuous presentation and its unstable semblances.

Again, the mode of appearance of the shapes produced by the art may be called a deception in comparison with philosophic thought, with religious or moral principles. Beyond a doubt the mode of revelation which a content attains in the realm of thought is the truest reality; but in comparison with the show or semblance of immediate sensuous existence or of historical narrative, the artistic semblance has the advantage that in itself it points beyond itself, and refers us away from itself to something spiritual which it is meant to bring before the mind's eye. Whereas immediate appearance does not give itself out to be deceptive, but rather to be real and true, though all the time its truth is contaminated and infected by the immediate sensuous element. The hard rind of nature and the common world give the mind more trouble in breaking through to the idea than do the products of art.

But if, on the one side, we assign this high position to art, we must no less bear in mind, on the other hand, that art is not, either in content or in form, the supreme and absolute mode of bringing the mind's genuine interests into consciousness. The form of art is enough to limit it to a restricted content. Only a certain circle and grade of truth is capable of being represented in the medium of art. Such truth must have in its own nature the capacity to go forth into sensuous form and be adequate to itself therein, if it is to be a genuinely artistic content, as is the case with the gods of Greece. There is, however, a deeper form of truth, in which it is no longer so closely akin and so friendly to sense as to be adequately embraced and expressed by that medium. Of such a kind is the Christian conception of truth; and more especially the spirit of our modern world, or, to come closer, of our religion and our intellectual culture, reveals itself as beyond the stage at which art is the highest mode assumed by man's consciousness of the absolute. The peculiar mode to which artistic production and works of art belong no longer satisfies our supreme need. We are above the level at which works of art can be venerated as divine, and actually worshipped; the impression which they make is of a more considerate kind, and the feelings which they stir within us require a higher test and a further confirmation. Thought and reflection have taken their flight above fine art. Those who delight in grumbling and censure may set down this phenomenon for a corruption, and ascribe it to the predominance of passion and selfish interests, which scare away at once the seriousness and the cheerfulness of art. Or we may accuse the troubles of the present time and the complicated condition of civil and political life as hindering the feelings, entangled in minute preoccupations, from freeing themselves, and rising to the higher aims of art, the intelligence itself being subordinate to petty needs and interests, in sciences which only subserve such purposes and are seduced into making this barren region their home.

However all this may be, it certainly is the case, that art no longer affords that satisfaction of spiritual wants which earlier epochs and peoples have sought therein, and have found therein only; a satisfaction which, at all events on the religious side, was most intimately and profoundly connected with art. The beautiful days of Greek art, and the golden time of the later middle ages are gone by. The reflective culture of our life of today, makes it a necessity for

From *Introduction to Hegel's Philosophy of Fine Art,* translated by Bernard Bosanquet. London, 1905.

us, in respect of our will not less than of our judgment, to adhere to general points of view, and to regulate particular matters according to them, so that general forms, laws, duties, rights, maxims are what have validity as grounds of determination and are the chief regulative force. But what is required for artistic interest as for artistic production is, speaking generally, a living creation, in which the universal is not present as law and maxim, but acts as if one with the mood and the feelings, just as, in the imagination, the universal and rational is contained only as brought into unity with a concrete sensuous phenomenon. Therefore, our present in its universal condition is not favourable to art. As regards the artist himself, it is not merely that the reflection which finds utterance all round him, and the universal habit of having an opinion and passing judgment about art infect him, and mislead him into putting more abstract thought into his works themselves; but also the whole spiritual culture of the age is of such a kind that he himself stands within this reflective world and its conditions, and it is impossible for him to abstract from it by will and resolve, or to contrive for himself and bring to pass by means of peculiar education or removal from the relations of life, a peculiar solitude that would replace all that is lost.

In all these respects art is, and remains for us, on the side of its highest destiny, a thing of the past. Herein it has further lost for us its genuine truth and life, and rather is transferred into our *ideas* than asserts its former necessity, or assumes its former place, in reality. What is now aroused in us by works of art is over and above our immediate enjoyment, and together with it, our judgment; inasmuch as we subject the content and the means of representation of the work of art and the suitability or unsuitability of the two to our intellectual consideration. Therefore, the *science* of art is a much more pressing need in our day, than in times in which art, simply as art, was enough to furnish a full satisfaction. Art invites us to consideration of it by means of thought, not to the end of stimulating art production, but in order to ascertain scientifically what art is.

As soon as we propose to accept this invitation we are met by the difficulty which has already been touched upon in the suggestion that, though art is a suitable subject for philosophical reflection in the general sense, yet it is not so for systematic and scientific discussion. In this objection there lies the false idea that a philosophical consideration may, nevertheless, be unscientific. On this point it can only be remarked here with brevity, that, whatever ideas others may have of philosophy and philosophizing, I regard the pursuit of philosophy as utterly incapable of existing apart from a scientific procedure. Philosophy has to consider its object in its necessity, not, indeed, in its subjective necessity or external arrangement, classification, etc., but it has to unfold and demonstrate the object out of the necessity of its own inner nature. Until this evolution is brought to pass the scientific element is lacking to the treatment. In as far, however, as the objective necessity of an object lies essentially in its logical and metaphysical nature, the isolated treatment of art must be conducted with a certain relaxation of scientific stringency. For art involves the most complex presuppositions, partly in reference to its content, partly in respect of its medium and element, in which art is constantly on the borders of the arbitrary or accidental. Thus it is only as regards the essential innermost progress of its content and of its media of expression that we must call to mind the outline prescribed by its necessity.

The objection that works of fine art elude the treatment of scientific thought because they originate out of the unregulated fancy and out of the feelings, are of a number and variety that defy the attempt to gain a conspectus, and therefore take effect only on feeling and imagination, raises a problem which appears still to have importance. For the beauty of art does in fact appear in a form which is expressly contrasted with abstract thought, and which the latter is forced to destroy in exerting the activity which is its nature. This idea coheres with the opinion that reality as such, the life of nature and of mind, is disfigured and slain by comprehension; that, so far from being close to us by the thought which comprehends, it is by it that such life is absolutely dissociated from us, so that, by the use of thought as the *means* of grasping what has life, man rather cuts himself off from this his purpose. We cannot speak fully on this subject in the present passage, but only indicate the point of view from which the removal of this difficulty, or impossibility depending on maladaptation, might be effected.

It will be admitted, to begin with, that the mind is capable of contemplating itself, and of possessing a consciousness, and that a *thinking* consciousness, of itself and all that is generated by itself. Thought —to think—is precisely that in which the mind has its innermost and essential nature. In gaining this thinking consciousness concerning itself and its products, the mind is behaving according to its essential nature, however much freedom and caprice those products may display, supposing only that in real truth they have mind in them. Now art and its works as generated and created by the mind (spirit), are themselves of a spiritual nature, even if their mode of representation admits into itself the semblance of sensuous being, and pervades what is sensuous with mind. In this respect art is, to begin with, nearer to mind and its thinking activity than is mere external unintelligent nature; in works of art, mind has to do but with its own. And even if artistic works are not abstract thought and notion, but are an evolution of the notion *out of* itself, an alienation from itself towards the sensuous, still the power of the thinking spirit (mind) lies herein, *not merely* to grasp *itself only* in its peculiar form of the self-conscious spirit (mind), but just as much to recognise itself in its alienation in the shape of feeling and the sensuous, in its other form, by transmuting the metamorphosed thought back into definite thoughts, and so restoring it to itself. And in this preoccupation with the other of itself the thinking spirit is not to be held untrue to itself as if forgetting or surrendering itself therein, nor is it so weak as to lack strength to comprehend what is different from itself, but it comprehends both itself and its opposite. For the notion is the universal, which preserves itself in its particularizations, dominates alike itself and its "other," and so becomes the power and activity that consists in undoing the alienation which it had evolved. And thus the work of art in which thought alienates itself belongs, like thought itself, to the realm of comprehending thought, and the mind, in subjecting it to scientific consideration, is thereby but satisfying the want of its own, inmost nature. For because thought is its essence and notion, it can in the last resort only be satisfied when it has succeeded in imbuing all the products of its activity with thought, and has thus for the first time made them genuinely its own. But, as we shall see more definitely below, art is far from being the highest form of mind, and receives its true ratification only from science.

Just as little does art elude philosophical consideration by unbridled caprice. As has already been indicated, it is its true task to bring to consciousness the highest interests of the mind. Hence it follows at once with respect to the *content* that fine art cannot rove in the wildness of unfettered fancy, for these spiritual interests determine definite bases for its content, how manifold and inexhaustible soever its forms and shapes may be. The same holds true for the forms themselves. They, again, are not at the mercy of mere chance. Not every plastic shape is capable of being the expression and representation of those spiritual interests, of absorbing and of reproducing them; every definite content determines a form suitable to it.

In this aspect too, then, we are in a position to find our bearings according to the needs of thought in the apparently unmanageable mass of works and types of art.

Thus, I hope, we have begun by defining the content of our science, to which we propose to confine ourselves, and have seen that neither is fine art unworthy of a philosophical consideration, nor is a philosophical consideration incompetent to arrive at a knowledge of the essence of fine art.

The World as Will and Idea

ARTHUR SCHOPENHAUER

The German philosopher Arthur Schopenhauer (1788–1860) was a great influence on many subsequent thinkers, among them Tolstoy, Thomas Mann, Richard Wagner, Sigmund Freud, Nietzsche, and Wittgenstein.

In the First Book the world was explained as mere *idea,* object for a subject. In the Second Book we considered it from its other side, and found that in this aspect it is *will,* which proved to be simply that which this world is besides being idea. In accordance with this knowledge we called the world as idea, both as a whole and in its parts, the *objectification of will,* which therefore means the will become object, i.e. idea. . . .

Knowledge, now, as a rule, remains always subordinate to the service of the will, as indeed it originated for this service, and grew, so to speak, to the will, as the head to the body. In the case of brutes this subjection of knowledge to the will can never be abolished. . . . This human excellence is exhibited in the highest degree by the Apollo of the Belvedere; the head of the God of the Muses, with eyes fixed on the far distance, stands so freely on his shoulders that it seems wholly delivered from the body, and no more subject to its cares.

If, raised by the power of the mind, a man relinquishes the common way of looking at things, gives up tracing, under the guidance of the forms of the principle of sufficient reason, their relations to each other, the final goal of which is always a relation to his own will; if he thus ceases to consider the where, the when, the why, and the whither of things, and looks simply and solely at the *what;* if, further, he does not allow abstract thought, the concepts of the reason, to take possession of his consciousness, but, instead of all this, gives the whole power of his mind to perception, sinks himself entirely in this, and lets his whole consciousness be filled with the quiet contemplation of the natural object actually present, whether a landscape, a tree, a mountain, a building, or whatever it may be; inasmuch as he *loses* himself in this object (to use a pregnant German idiom), i.e., forgets even his individuality, his will, and only continues to exist as the pure subject, the clear mirror of the object, so that it is as if the object alone were there, without any one to perceive it, and he can no longer separate the perceiver from the perception, but both have become one, because the whole consciousness is filled and occupied with one single sensuous picture; if thus the object has to such an extent passed out of all relation to something outside it, and the subject out of all relation to the will, then that which is so known is no longer the particular thing as such; but it is the *Idea,* the eternal form, the immediate objectivity of the will at this grade; and, therefore, he who is sunk in this perception is no longer individual, for in such perception the individual has lost himself; but he is *pure,* will-less, painless, timeless *subject of knowledge.* . . .

Whoever now has, after the manner referred to, become so absorbed and lost in the perception of nature that he only continues to exist as the pure knowing subject, becomes in this way directly conscious that, as such, he is the condition, that is, the supporter, of the world and all objective existence; for this now shows itself as dependent upon his existence. Thus he draws nature into himself, so that he sees it to be merely an accident of his own being. In this sense Byron says—

Are not the mountains, waves, and skies, a part
Of me and of my soul, as I of them?

The common mortal, that manufacture of Nature which she produces by the thousand every day, is, as we have said, not capable, at least not continuously so, of observation that in every sense is wholly disinterested, as sensuous contemplation, strictly so called, is. He can turn his attention to things only

From *The World as Will and Idea,* translated by R. B. Haldane and J. Kemp (London: Routledge & K. Paul, 1883).

so far as they have some relation to his will, however indirect it may be. Since for this purpose, which never demands anything but the knowledge of relations, the abstract conception of the thing is sufficient, and for the most part even better adapted for use, the ordinary man does not linger long over the mere perception, does not fix his attention long on one object, but in all that is presented to him hastily seeks merely the concept under which it is to be brought, as the lazy man seeks a chair; and then it interests him no further. This is why he is so soon done with everything, with works of art, objects of natural beauty, and indeed everywhere with the truly significant contemplation of all the scenes of life. He does not linger; only seeks to know his own way in life, together with all that might at any time become his way. Thus he makes topographical notes in the widest sense; over the consideration of life itself as such he wastes no time. The man of genius, on the other hand, whose excessive power of knowledge frees it at times from the service of will, dwells on the consideration of life itself, strives to comprehend the Idea of each thing, not its relations to others things; and in doing this he often forgets to consider his own path in life, and therefore for the most part pursues it awkwardly enough. While to the ordinary man his faculty of knowledge is a lamp to lighten his path, to the man of genius it is the sun which reveals the world. . . .

Aesthetic pleasure is one and the same whether it is called forth by a work of art or directly by the contemplation of nature and life. The work of art is only a means of facilitating the knowledge in which this pleasure consists. That the Idea comes to us more easily from the work of art than directly from nature and the real world, arises from the fact that the artist, who knew only the Idea, no longer the actual, has reproduced in his work the pure Idea, has abstracted it from the actual, omitting all disturbing accidents. The artist lets us see the world through his eyes. That he has these eyes, that he knows the inner nature of things apart from all their relations, is the gift of genius, is inborn; but that he is able to lend us this gift, to let us see with his eyes, is acquired, and is the technical side of art. . . .

In the aesthetical mode of contemplation we have found *two inseparable constituent parts*—the knowledge of the object, not as individual thing but as Platonic Idea, that is, as the enduring form of this whole species of things; and the self-consciousness of the knowing person, not as individual, but as *pure will-less subject of knowledge.* The condition, under which both these constituent parts appear always united, was found to be the abandonment of the method of knowing which is bound to the principle of sufficient reason, and which, on the other hand, is the only kind of knowledge that is of value for the service of the will and also for science. Moreover, we shall see that the pleasure which is produced by the contemplation of the beautiful arises from these two constituent parts, sometimes more from the one, sometimes more from the other, according to what the object of the aesthetical contemplation may be.

All *willing* arises from want, therefore from deficiency, and therefore from suffering. The satisfaction of a wish ends it; yet for one wish that is satisfied there remain at least ten which are denied. Further, the desire lasts long, the demands are infinite; the satisfaction is short and scantily measured out. But even the final satisfaction is itself only apparent; every satisfied wish at once makes room for a new one; both are illusions; the one is known to be so, the other not yet. No attained object of desire can give lasting satisfaction, but merely a fleeting gratification; it is like the alms thrown to the beggar, that keeps him alive to-day that his misery may be prolonged till the morrow. Therefore, so long as our consciousness is filled by our will, so long as we are given up to the throng of desires with their constant hopes and fears, so long as we are the subject of willing, we can never have lasting happiness nor peace. It is essentially all the same whether we pursue or flee, fear injury or seek enjoyment; the care for the constant demands of the will, in whatever form it may be, continually occupies and sways the consciousness; but without peace no true well-being is possible. The subject of willing is thus constantly stretched on the revolving wheel of Ixion, pours water into the sieve of the Danaids, is the ever-longing Tantalus.

But when some external cause or inward disposition lifts us suddenly out of the endless stream of willing, and delivers knowledge from the slavery of the will, the attention is no longer directed to the motives of willing, but comprehends things free from their relation to the will, and thus observes them without personal interest, without subjectivity, purely objectively, and gives itself entirely up to them so far as they are ideas, but not in so far as they are motives. Then all at once the peace which we were always seeking, but which always fled from us on the former path of the desires, comes to us of its own accord, and it is well with us. It is the painless state which Epicurus prized as the highest good and as the state of the gods; we are for the moment set free from the miserable striving of the will; we keep the Sabbath of the penal servitude of willing; the wheel of Ixion stands still.

But this is just the state which I described above as necessary for the knowledge of the Idea, as pure contemplation, as sinking oneself in perception, losing oneself in the object, forgetting all individuality, surrendering that kind of knowledge which follows the principle of sufficient reason, and comprehends only relations; the state by means of which at once and inseparably both the perceived particular thing is raised to the Idea of its whole species, and the knowing individual to the pure subject of will-less knowledge, and as such they are both taken out of the stream of time and all other relations. It is then all one whether we see the sun set from the prison or from the palace.

Inward disposition, the predominance of knowing over willing, can produce this state under any circumstances. This is shown by those admirable Dutch artists who directed this purely objective perception to the most insignificant objects, and established a lasting monument of their objectivity and spiritual peace in their pictures of *still life,* which the aesthetic beholder does not look on without emotion; for they present to him the peaceful, still frame of mind of the artist, free from will, which was needed to contemplate such insignificant things so objectively, to observe them so attentively, and to repeat this perception so intelligently; and as the picture enables the onlooker to participate in this state, his emotion is often increased by the contrast between it and the unquiet frame of mind, disturbed by vehement willing, in which he finds himself. In the same spirit, landscape-painters, and particu-

larly Ruisdael, have often painted very insignificant country scenes, which produce the same effect even more agreeably.

Lastly, it is this blessedness of will-less perception which casts an enchanting glamor over the past and distant, and presents them to us in so fair a light by means of self-deception. For as we think of days long gone by, days in which we lived in a distant place, it is only the objects which our fancy recalls, not the subject of will, which bore about with it then its incurable sorrows just as it bears them now; but they are forgotten, because since then they have often given place to others. Now, objective perception acts with regard to what is remembered just as it would in what is present, if we let it have influence over us, if we surrendered ourselves to it free from will. Hence it arises that, especially when we are more than ordinarily disturbed by some want, the remembrance of past and distant scenes suddenly flits across our minds like a lost paradise. The fancy recalls only what was objective, not what was individually subjective, and we imagine that the objective stood before us then just as pure and undisturbed by any relation to the will as its image stands in our fancy now; while in reality the relation of the objects to our will gave us pain then just as it does now. We can deliver ourselves from all suffering just as well through present objects as through distant ones whenever we raise ourselves to a purely objective contemplation of them and so are able to bring about the illusion that only the objects are present and not we ourselves. Then, as the pure subject of knowledge, freed from the miserable self, we become entirely one with these objects, and, for the moment, our wants are as foreign to us as they are to them. The world as idea alone remains, and the world as will has disappeared. . . .

Sight, unlike the affections of the other senses, cannot, in itself, directly and through its sensuous effect, make the *sensation* of the special organ agreeable or disagreeable; that is, it has no immediate connexion with the will. . . . In the case of hearing this is to some extent otherwise; sounds can give pain directly, and they may also be sensuously agreeable, directly and without regard to harmony or melody. Touch, as one with the feeling of the whole body, is still more subordinated to this direct influence upon the will; and yet there is such a thing as a sensation of touch which is neither painful nor pleasant. But smells are always either agreeable or disagreeable, and tastes still more so. Thus the last two senses are most closely related to the will, and therefore they are always the most ignoble, and have been called by Kant the subjective senses. The pleasure which we experience from light is in fact only the pleasure which arises from the objective possibility of the purest and fullest perceptive knowledge, and as such it may be traced to the fact that pure knowledge, freed and delivered from all will, is in the highest degree pleasant, and of itself constitutes a large part of aesthetic enjoyment. . . .

All these reflections are intended to bring out the subjective part of aesthetic pleasure; that is to say, that pleasure so far as it consists simply of delight in perceptive knowledge as such, in opposition to will. And as directly connected with this, there naturally follows the explanation of that disposition or frame of mind which has been called the sense of the *sublime*.

We have already remarked above that the transition to the state of pure perception takes place most easily when the objects bend themselves to it, that is, when by their manifold and yet definite and distinct form they easily become representatives of their Ideas, in which beauty, in the objective sense, consists. This quality belongs preeminently to natural beauty, which thus affords even to the most insensible at least a fleeting aesthetic satisfaction.

When we say that a thing is *beautiful*, we thereby assert that it is an object of our aesthetic contemplation, and this has a double meaning; on the one hand it means that the sight of the thing makes us *objective*, that is to say, that in contemplating it we are no longer conscious of ourselves as individuals, but as pure will-less subjects of knowledge; and on the other hand it means that we recognize in the object, not the particular thing, but an Idea; and this can only happen, so far as our contemplation of it is not subordinated to the principle of sufficient reason, does not follow the relation of the object to anything outside it (which is always ultimately connected with relations to our own will), but rests in the object itself. . . . Since, on the one hand, every given thing may be observed in a purely objective manner and

apart from all relations; and since, on the other hand, the will manifests itself in everything at some grade of its objectivity, so that everything is the expression of an Idea; it follows that everything is also *beautiful*. . . .

Sometimes the possession of special beauty in an object lies in the fact that the Idea itself which appeals to us in it is a high grade of the objectivity of will, and therefore very significant and expressive. Therefore it is that man is more beautiful than all other objects, and the revelation of his nature is the highest aim of art. Human form and expression are the most important objects of plastic art, and human action the most important object of poetry. Yet each thing has its own peculiar beauty, not only every organism which expresses itself in the unity of an individual being, but also everything unorganized and formless, and even every manufactured article. For all these reveal the Ideas through which the will objectifies itself at its lowest grades, they give, as it were, the deepest resounding bass-notes of nature. Gravity, rigidity, fluidity, light, and so forth, are the Ideas which express themselves in rocks, in buildings, in waters. . . .

In aesthetic contemplation (in the real, or through the medium of art) of the beauty of nature in the inorganic and vegetable worlds, or in works of architecture, the pleasure of pure will-less knowing will predominate, because the Ideas which are here apprehended are only low grades of the objectivity of will, and are therefore not manifestations of deep significance and rich content. On the other hand, if animals and man are the objects of aesthetic contemplation or representation, the pleasure will consist rather in the comprehension of these Ideas, which are the most distinct revelation of will; for they exhibit the greatest multiplicity of forms, the greatest richness and deep significance of phenomena, and reveal to us most completely the nature of will, whether in its violence, its terribleness, its satisfaction or its aberration (the latter in tragic situations), or finally in its change and self-surrender, which is the peculiar theme of Christian painting; as the Idea of the will enlightened by full knowledge is the object of historical painting in general, and of the drama. . . .

We all recognize human beauty when we see it,

but in the true artist this takes place with such clearness that he shows it as he has never seen it, and surpasses nature in his representation; this is only possible because *we ourselves are* the will whose adequate objectification at its highest grade is here to be judged and discovered. Thus alone have we in fact an anticipation of that which nature (which is just the will that constitutes our own being) strives to express. . . .

Music is as *direct* an objectification and copy of the whole *will* as the world itself, nay, even as the Ideas, whose multiplied manifestation constitutes the world of individual things. Music is thus by no means like the other arts, the copy of the Ideas, but the *copy of the will itself,* whose objectivity the Ideas are. This is why the effect of music is so much more powerful and penetrating than that of the other arts, for they speak only of shadows, but it speaks of the thing itself. Since, however, it is the same will which objectifies itself both in the Ideas and in music, though in quite different ways, there must be, not indeed a direct likeness, but yet a parallel, an analogy, between music and the Ideas whose manifestation in multiplicity and incompleteness is the visible world. . . .

It does not, therefore, express this or that particular and definite joy, this or that sorrow, or pain, or horror, or delight, or merriment, or peace of mind; but joy, sorrow, pain, horror, delight, merriment, peace of mind *themselves* to a certain extent in the abstract, their essential nature, without accessories, and therefore without their motives. Yet we completely understand them in this extracted quintessence. Hence it arises that our imagination is so easily excited by music, and now seeks to give form to that invisible yet actively moved spirit-world which speaks to us directly, and clothe it with flesh and blood, i.e. to embody it in an analogous example. . . .

The pleasure we receive from all beauty, the consolation which art affords, the enthusiasm of the artist, which enables him to forget the cares of life—the latter an advantage of the man of genius over other men, which alone repays him for the suffering that increases in proportion to the clearness of consciousness, and for the desolate loneliness among men of a different race—all this rests on the fact that the in-itself of life, the will, existence itself, is, as we shall see farther on, a constant sorrow, partly miserable, partly terrible; while, on the contrary, as idea alone, purely contemplated, or copied by art, free from pain, it presents to us a drama full of significance. This purely knowable side of the world, and the copy of it in any art, is the element of the artist. He is chained to the contemplation of the play, the objectification of will; he remains beside it, does not get tired of contemplating it and representing it in copies; and meanwhile he bears himself the cost of the production of that play, i.e. he himself is the will which objectifies itself, and remains in constant suffering. That pure, true, and deep knowledge of the inner nature of the world becomes now for him an end in itself: he stops there. Therefore it does not become to him a quieter of the will, as, we shall see in the next book, it does in the case of the saint who has attained to resignation: it does not deliver him for ever from life, but only at moments, and is therefore not for him a path out of life, but only an occasional consolation in it, till his power, increased by this contemplation and at last tired of the play, lays hold of the real.

Art and the Will to Power

FRIEDRICH NIETZSCHE

The great German philosopher Friedrich Nietzsche (1844–1900), who coined the term "God is dead," wrote many influential books and continues to have a wide influence.

Concerning the psychology of the artist. For art to be possible at all—that is to say, in order that an aesthetic mode of action and of observation may exist, a certain preliminary psychological state is indispensable: *ecstasy.* This state of ecstasy must first have intensified the susceptibility of the whole machine: otherwise, no art is possible. All kinds of ecstasy, however differently produced, have this power to create art, and above all the state dependent upon sexual excitement—this most venerable and primitive form of ecstasy. The same applies to that ecstasy which is the outcome of all great desires, all strong passions; the ecstasy of the feast, of the arena, of the act of bravery, of victory, of all extreme action; the ecstasy of cruelty; the ecstasy of destruction; the ecstasy following upon certain meteorological influences, as for instance that of springtime, or upon the use of narcotics; and finally the ecstasy of will, that ecstasy which results from accumulated and surging willpower.—The essential feature of ecstasy is the feeling of increased strength and abundance. Actuated by this feeling a man gives of himself to things, he *forces* them to partake of his riches, he does violence to them—this proceeding is called *idealizing.* Let us rid ourselves of a prejudice here: idealizing does not consist, as is generally believed, in a suppression or an elimination of detail or of unessential features. A stupendous *accentuation* of the principal characteristics is by far the most decisive factor at work, and in consequence the minor characteristics vanish.

In this state a man enriches everything from out his own abundance: what he sees, what he wills, he sees distended, compressed, strong, overladen with power. He transfigures things until they reflect his power—until they are stamped with his perfection. This compulsion to transfigure into the beautiful is—Art. Everything—even that which he is not—is nevertheless to such a man a means of rejoicing over himself; in Art man rejoices over himself as perfection.—It is possible to imagine a contrary state, a specifically anti-artistic state of the instincts—a state in which a man impoverishes, attenuates, and draws the blood from everything. And, truth to tell, history is full of such anti-artists, of such creatures of low vitality who have no choice but to appropriate everything they see and to suck its blood and make it thinner. This is the case with the genuine Christian, Pascal for instance. There is no such thing as a Christian who is also an artist. . . . Let no one be so childish as to suggest Raphael or any homeopathic Christian of the nineteenth century as an objection to this statement: Raphael said Yea, Raphael *did* Yea—consequently Raphael was no Christian.

What is the meaning of the antithetical concepts *Apollonian* and *Dionysian* which I have introduced into the vocabulary of Aesthetic, as representing two distinct modes of ecstasy?—Apollonian ecstasy acts above all as a force stimulating the eye, so that it acquires the power of vision. The painter, the sculptor, the epic poet are essentially visionaries. In the Dionysian state, on the other hand, the whole system of passions is stimulated and intensified, so that it discharges itself by all the means of expression at once, and vents all its power of representation, of imitation, of transfiguration, of transformation, together with every kind of mimicry and histrionic display at the same time. The essential feature remains the facility in transforming, the inability to refrain from reaction (—a similar state to that of certain hysterical patients, who at the slightest hint assume any role). It is impossible for the Dionysian artist not to understand any suggestion; no outward sign of emotion escapes him, he possesses the instinct of com-

From *The Twilight of the Idols,* translated by Anthony M. Ludorici, and *The Joyful Wisdom,* translated by Thomas Common, in *The Complete Works of Friedrich Nietzsche,* edited by Oscar Levy (London: T. N. Foulis, 1909–11).

prehension and of divination in the highest degree, just as he is capable of the most perfect art of communication. He enters into every skin, into every passion: he is continually changing himself. Music as we understand it today is likewise a general excitation and discharge of the emotions; but, notwithstanding this, it is only the remnant of a much richer world of emotional expression, a mere residuum of Dionysian histrionism. For music to be made possible as a special art, quite a number of senses, and particularly the muscular sense, had to be paralyzed (at least relatively: for all rhythm still appeals to our muscles to a certain extent): and thus man no longer imitates and represents physically everything he feels, as soon as he feels it. Nevertheless that is the normal Dionysian state, and in any case its primitive state. Music is the slowly attained specialization of this state at the cost of kindred capacities. . . .

Beautiful and Ugly:—Nothing is more relative, let us say, more restricted, than our sense of the beautiful. He who would try to divorce it from the delight man finds in his fellows, would immediately lose his footing. "Beauty in itself," is simply a word, it is not even a concept. In the beautiful, man postulates himself as the standard of perfection; in exceptional cases he worships himself as that standard. A species has no other alternative than to say "yea" to itself alone, in this way. Its lowest instinct, the instinct of self-preservation and self-expansion, still radiates in such sublimities. Man imagines the world itself to be overflowing with beauty—he forgets that he is the cause of it all. He alone has endowed it with beauty. Alas! and only with human all-too-human beauty! Truth to tell man reflects himself in things, he thinks everything beautiful that throws his own image back at him. The judgment "beautiful" is the "vanity of his species." . . . A little demon of suspicion may well whisper into the sceptic's ear: is the world really beautified simply because man thinks it beautiful? He has only humanized it—that is all. But nothing, absolutely nothing proves to us that it is precisely man who is the proper model of beauty. Who knows what sort of figure he would cut in the eyes of a higher judge of taste? He might seem a little odd. . . .

Nothing is beautiful; man alone is beautiful: all aesthetic rests on this piece of ingenuousness, it is the first axiom of this science. And now let us straightway add the second to it: nothing is ugly save

the degenerate man—within these two first principles the realm of aesthetic judgments is confined. From the physiological standpoint, everything ugly weakens and depresses man. It reminds him of decay, danger, impotence; he literally loses strength in its presence. The effect of ugliness may be gauged by the dynamometer. Whenever man's spirits are downcast, it is a sign that he scents the proximity of something "ugly." His feeling of power, his will to power, his courage and his pride—these things collapse at the sight of what is ugly, and rise at the sight of what is beautiful. In both cases an inference is drawn; the premises to which are stored with extraordinary abundance in the instincts. Ugliness is understood to signify a hint and a symptom of degeneration: that which reminds us however remotely of degeneracy, impels us to the judgment "ugly." Every sign of exhaustion, of gravity, of age, of fatigue; every kind of constraint, such as cramp, or paralysis; and above all the smells, colors and forms associated with decomposition and putrefaction, however much they may have been attenuated into symbols—all these things provoke the same reaction which is the judgment "ugly." A certain hatred expresses itself here: what is it that man hates? Without a doubt it is the *decline of his type.* In this regard his hatred springs from the deepest instincts of the race: there is horror, caution, profundity and far-reaching vision in this hatred— it is the most profound hatred that exists. On its account alone Art is profound.

Schopenhauer.—Schopenhauer, the last German who is to be reckoned with (—who is a European event like Goethe, Hegel, or Heinrich Heine, and who is not merely local, national), is for a psychologist a case of the first rank: I mean as a malicious though masterly attempt to enlist on the side of a general nihilistic depreciation of life, the very forces which are opposed to such a movement—that is to say, the great self-affirming powers of the "will to live," the exuberant forms of life itself. He interpreted Art, heroism, genius, beauty, great sympathy, knowledge, the will to truth, and tragedy, one after the other, as the results of the denial, or of the need of the denial, of the "will"—the greatest forgery, Christianity always excepted, which history has to show. Examined more carefully, he is in this respect simply the heir of the Christian interpretation; except that he knew how to approve in a Christian fashion (i.e., nihilistically) even of the great facts of human culture, which Christianity completely repudiates. (He approved of them as paths to "salvation," as preliminary stages to "salvation," as *appetizers* calculated to arouse the desire for "salvation.")

Let me point to one single instance. Schopenhauer speaks of beauty with melancholy ardor—why in sooth does he do this? Because in beauty he sees a bridge on which one can travel further, or which stimulates one's desire to travel further. According to him it constitutes a momentary emancipation from the "will"—it lures to eternal salvation. He values it more particularly as a deliverance from the "burning core of the will" which is sexuality—in beauty he recognises the negation of the procreative instinct. Singular Saint! Someone contradicts thee; I fear it is Nature. Why is there beauty of tone, color, aroma, and of rhythmic movement in Nature at all? What is it forces beauty to the fore? Fortunately, too, a certain philosopher contradicts him. No less an authority than the divine Plato himself (thus does Schopenhauer call him), upholds another proposition: that all beauty lures to procreation—that this precisely is the chief characteristic of its effect, from the lowest sensuality to the highest spirituality.

Plato goes further. With an innocence for which a man must be Greek and not "Christian," he says that there would be no such thing as Platonic philosophy if there were not such beautiful boys in Athens: it was the sight of them alone that set the soul of the philosopher reeling with erotic passion, and allowed it no rest until it had planted the seeds of all lofty things in a soil so beautiful. He was also a singular saint!—One scarcely believes one's ears, even supposing one believes Plato. At least one realises that philosophy was pursued differently in Athens; above all, publicly. Nothing is less Greek than the cobweb-spinning with concepts by an anchorite, *amor intellectualis dei* after the fashion of Spinoza. Philosophy according to Plato's style might be defined rather as an erotic competition, as a continuation and a spiritualization of the old agonal gymnastics and the conditions on which they depend. . . . What was the ultimate outcome of this philosophic eroticism of Plato's? A new artform of the Greek *Agon,* dialectics.—In opposition to Schopenhauer and to the honor of Plato, I would remind you that all the higher culture and literature of classical

France, as well, grew up on the soil of sexual interests. In all its manifestations you may look for gallantry, the senses, sexual competition, and "woman," and you will not look in vain.

L'Art pour l'Art.—The struggle against a purpose in art is always a struggle against the moral tendency in art, against its subordination to morality. *L'art pour l'art* means, "let morality go to the devil!"—But even this hostility betrays the preponderating power of the moral prejudice. If art is deprived of the purpose of preaching morality and of improving mankind, it does not by any means follow that art is absolutely pointless, purposeless, senseless, in short *l'art pour l'art*—a snake which bites its own tail. "No purpose at all is better than a moral purpose!"—thus does pure passion speak. A psychologist, on the other hand, puts the question: what does all art do? does it not praise? does it not glorify? does it not select? does it not bring things into prominence? In all this it strengthens or weakens certain valuations. Is this only a secondary matter? an accident? something in which the artist's instinct has no share? Or is it not rather the very prerequisite which enables the artist to accomplish something? . . . Is his most fundamental instinct concerned with art? Is it not rather concerned with the purpose of art, with life? with a certain desirable kind of life? Art is the great stimulus to life: how can it be regarded as purposeless, as pointless, as *l'art pour l'art?*—There still remains one question to be answered: Art also reveals much that is ugly, hard and questionable in life—does it not thus seem to make life intolerable?—And, as a matter of fact, there have been philosophers who have ascribed this function to art. According to Schopenhauer's doctrine, the general object of art was to "free one from the Will"; and what he honored as the great utility of tragedy, was that it "made people more resigned."—But this, as I have already shown, is a pessimistic standpoint; it is the "evil eye": the artist himself must be appealed to. What is it that the soul of the tragic artist communicates to others? Is it not precisely his fearless attitude towards that which is terrible and questionable? This attitude is in itself a highly desirable one; he who has once experienced it honours it above everything else. He communicates it. He must communicate, provided he is an artist and a genius in the art of communication. A courageous and free spirit, in the presence of a mighty foe, in the presence of a sublime misfortune, and face to face with a problem that inspires horror—this is the triumphant attitude which the tragic artist selects and which he glorifies. The marital elements in our soul celebrate their Saturnalia in tragedy; he who is used to suffering, he who looks out for suffering, the heroic man, extols his existence by means of tragedy—to him alone does the tragic artist offer this cup of sweetest cruelty. . . .

Prose and Poetry.—Let it be observed that the great masters of prose have almost always been poets as well, whether openly, or only in secret and for the "closet"; and in truth one only writes good prose *in view of poetry!* For prose is an uninterrupted, polite warfare with poetry; all its charm consists in the fact that poetry is constantly avoided and contradicted; every abstraction wants to have a gibe at poetry, and wishes to be uttered with a mocking voice; all dryness and coolness is meant to bring the amiable goddess into an amiable despair; there are often approximations and reconciliations for the moment, and then a sudden recoil and a burst of laughter; the curtain is often drawn up and dazzling light let in just while the goddess is enjoying her twilights and dull colors; the word is often taken out of her mouth and chanted to a melody while she holds her fine hands before her delicate little ears:—and so there are a thousand enjoyments of the warfare, the defeats included, of which the unpoetic, the so-called prose-men know nothing at all:—they consequently write and speak only bad prose! *Warfare is the father of all good things,* it is also the father of good prose! . . .

Our Ultimate Gratitude to Art,—If we had not approved of the Arts and invented this sort of cult of the untrue, the insight into the general untruth and falsity of things now given us by science—an insight into delusion and error as conditions of intelligent and sentient existence—would be quite unendurable. *Honesty* would have disgust and suicide in its train. Now, however, our honesty has a counterpoise which helps us to escape such consequences:—namely, Art, as the *good-will* to illusion. We do not always restrain our eyes from rounding off and perfecting in imagination: and then it is no longer the eternal imperfection that we carry over the river of Becoming—for we think we carry a *goddess,* and are proud and artless in rendering this service. As an aesthetic phenomenon existence is still *endurable* to us; and by Art, eye and hand and above all the good conscience are given to us, *to be able* to make such a phenomenon out of ourselves. We must rest from ourselves occasionally by contemplating and looking down upon ourselves, and by laughing or weeping *over* ourselves from an artistic remoteness: we must discover the *hero,* and likewise the *fool,* that is hidden in our passion for knowledge; we must now and then be joyful in our folly, that we may continue to be joyful in our wisdom! And just because we are heavy and serious men in our ultimate depth, and are rather weights than men, there is nothing that does us so much good as the *fool's cap and bells:* we need them in presence of ourselves—we need all arrogant, soaring, dancing, mocking, childish and blessed Art, in order not to lose the *free dominion over things* which our ideal demands of us. It would be *backsliding* for us, with our susceptible integrity, to lapse entirely into morality, and actually become virtuous monsters and scarecrows, on account of the overstrict requirements which we here lay down for ourselves. We ought also to be *able* to stand *above* morality, and not only stand with the painful stiffness of one who every moment fears to slip and fall, but we should also be able to soar and play above it! How could we dispense with Art for that purpose, how could we dispense with the fool?—And as long as you are still *ashamed* of yourselves in any way, you still do not belong to us!

Aesthetics
The State of the Art

DIALOG WITH JERROLD LEVINSON

DANIEL KOLAK: I'd like to begin with a quote: "The universal organum of philosophy—the keystone of its entire arch—is the philosophy of art."[1] Now, this is from Friedrich Schelling (1775–1854)—one of the great nineteenth-century German idealists—and the only reason I bring it up is that it seems to contrast in so many ways with what most philosophers today and throughout history would regard as a definitive statement. So I'm wondering what your feelings might be about such a grand view about the relationship between art and philosophy. Is there anything to it? If not, what in your view is the true nature of the relationship?

JERROLD LEVINSON: Yes, that quote from Schelling is quite striking, both in its grandiosity and in its degree of contrast with what most working philosophers today would likely say on the subject. Yet, that there is a special connection between art and philosophy and that aesthetics is perhaps a central philosophical domain seem both to have some truth to them. It is interesting to note, first, that even though philosophy of art has not played a role in the systems of all or even most of the unquestionably great philosophers, it has bulked large for quite a few, to wit, Aristotle (I leave out Plato, since what he offered was mainly an antiphilosophy of art), Hume, Kant, Schopenhauer, Nietzsche, Hegel. And then there are a fair number of not-quite-great philosophers who have had a philosophy of art to retail, perhaps more than have interested themselves in, say, ethics.[2] So, why this natural, if not inevitable, linkage of art and philosophy? Well, both deal with ultimate values, with what makes life worth living. Both involve expression, clarification, formulation, though whether what is expressed/clarified/formulated in the two cases is the same or different is another matter. Both are singularly and significantly products of mind, prod-ucts rooted in cultures that testify to the nature of those cultures perhaps more loudly than anything else in them. But that philosophy should interest itself specially in art cannot rest merely on the similarities between them. If anything, it rests on the fact that art is so pervasive, so important, and so revelatory a dimension of the human world, as well as an indispensable key to the functioning of the human spirit.

DK: Fair enough. Few today would disagree with your characterization of the significance of art. And what is perhaps most interesting about your characterization, from the point of view of philosophy, is the notion that art has a "revelatory dimension." Could you say some more about this "revelatory dimension"? Philosophy today, for the most part, is all about argument, the pursuit of wisdom and truth by rational means, where the concept "rationality" has of course more than one legitimate heir. Traditionally, it has been religion that has espoused various "revelatory" methods of attaining enlightenment, truth, knowledge about ourselves, the world, God, and so on, through some kind of inner intuition, mystical experience, or whatever, in ways that more rationally inclined philosophers have regarded with great suspicion. Might you be suggesting that art today plays a role in human experience that perhaps religion used to, or perhaps even still does, such that there is some similarity between the philosophy of art and the philosophy of religion, in terms of the role played by philosophers in those spheres?

JL: Well, art does perform some of the functions formerly performed more obviously by religion, e.g., investing with significance, inviting transcendence of the self, promising contact with the profound, imparting a ritual or ceremonial character to life (think of some aspects of concert behavior, of poetry readings, of gallery openings).

But does art convey real truths, or especially deep ones, and in ways other than do ordinary language or science? That is a hard one, much disputed these days among aestheticians, in regard to both abstract arts, like music, and representational ones, like literature. Probably the strongest claims that could be made in those two cases, respectively, would be that music, some music at any rate, is able to embody, and so communicate to a listener, attitudes of mind or possible ways of being human that were not evident to one before, and for which the experience of listening responsively may be an essential means of access to such states; and for literature, that comprehending experience of a work, such as a novel or play, may afford moral or psychological insight of a practical or lived sort that goes beyond what can be had from ethics or psychology themselves, or from mere propositional formulation of a work's message. But these are difficult, cutting-edge questions in the epistemology and philosophy of mind of aesthetic experience, and I won't pretend to have established the claims just sketched.

One might, though, returning to the art/religion connection, speculate that, if there is a God, of a personal or quasi-personal sort, what better, more subtle way could He have of suggesting, without outright announcing, his presence, than to allow human beings the capacity to create and appreciate sublime works of art, ones that seem to take them beyond or outside themselves, thus giving the lie to the notion that we are merely the products of natural, earthbound evolution. (I don't say that I believe any of that, mind you!)

DK: What you say about the essence or function of art certainly captures what many would agree is special about art. It raises the question of what art is—something you have in your writings had a great deal to say about, and I would like to turn to that shortly. But, first, what is the philosopher's role here? The artist's is in making great art, the audience's in experiencing it. Why should the artists or audiences care what philosophers have to say? Certainly the kinds of experiences you describe as central to art—such as self-transcendence, the creation of new states of mind, offering moral or psychological insights,

and so on—are sought by a great many people. Are there any philosophical insights about art that are worthy of receiving greater attention by artists and the consumers of art than they have thus far?

JL: The first thing I would say is that the primary justification for aesthetics, to my mind, is as philosophy, by philosophers and for philosophers. That is to say, the problems of aesthetics are philosophical problems, either species or cousins of problems in metaphysics, epistemology, philosophy of mind, philosophy of language, ethics, and so on. The question then becomes, Why should anyone who is not a philosopher be interested in what philosophers think or say about anything? Well, obviously, someone who is not a philosopher, professionally speaking, may still have philosophical interests, philosophical curiosity, may find himself posing questions to himself of a philosophical nature. And insofar as that is so, why not consult professionals—that is, people who spend a lot of time pursuing such matters and who are trained to pursue them in a manner likely to be more fruitful, or at least are more consistent, more systematic, and more explicitly reasoned than others addressing these matters. It seems natural to many people to want to think philosophically about what one loves most or what most matters to one, and thus since the arts and aesthetic experience seem to fill that bill for many folks, artists and aficionados of art in particular, the interest of philosophical aesthetics for them seems almost assured. As for specific philosophical insights about art that contemporary aesthetics would have to offer, I would be inclined to underline myself the thesis of contextualism, as regards the status, ontology, meaning, and interpretation of works of art, in opposition to various sorts of formalism, structuralism, and empiricism in regard to such works, on the one hand, and various sorts of deconstructivism, relativism, and nihilism, on the other hand.

DK: Could you encapsulate these various contemporary theories—contextualism, formalism, structuralism, empiricism, deconstructivism, relativism, and nihilism—and say something about why you think there are so many? Is there anything they all share in common, in your opinion, and on what do they most diverge?

JL: I think the easiest thing would be for me to sketch what I mean by contextualism in aesthetics and then touch on those other doctrines or tendencies in contrast to that. Contextualism is the view that an artwork is an artifact of a particular sort, an object (or structure) that is the product of human invention, at a particular time and place, by a particular individual or individuals, and that this has implications for how one properly experiences, understands, and evaluates artworks. Artworks are essentially historically embedded objects and have neither art status, nor clear aesthetic properties, nor definite artistic meanings, nor a determinate ontological identity outside of or apart from such generative context as makes them the artworks that they are. Useful analogies for what, on a contextualist conception, an artwork is are the notions of utterance, action, and achievement. A contextually situated artwork—there is no other kind—is akin to an utterance made in a specific linguistic situation, an action performed in specific historical circumstances, an achievement of a particular individual working with specific constraints on a specific problem or against the background of specific prior developments in a given domain. Were the historical context of a work to have been different, the work itself would have been different, for what artistic utterance it makes, what artistic actions it represents, what artistic achievement it embodies, even what style it could be said to exhibit might very well have been different. And all such differences implicate further differences in what a work expresses, represents, or exemplifies aesthetically. "No work is an island" would be a good slogan for epitomizing contextualism about art, and Jorge Luis Borges's story "Pierre Menard, Author of the 'Quixote'"[3] would be the best, if fictional, object lesson in why such contextualism is unavoidable if we are to make sense of how artworks are created, interpreted, and assessed.

Contextualism contrasts with all the other views mentioned above. Formalism holds that manifest form is the only important thing about art so far as appreciation is concerned and that

in which its arthood, artistic content, and artistic value alone resides. But if contextualism is correct, objects that share a manifest form might indeed differ in art status, artistic content, and value as art. Empiricism about art similarly maintains that the perceptual face of a work of art— its manifest qualities—exhausts its essence, and thus that understanding a work requires nothing more than perceptual engagement with it unaided by any sense of its historical provenance or the problematic from which it emerged. Again, if contextualism is valid, empiricism about art cannot be. A keynote of structuralism in aesthetics, as related to but distinct from empiricism and formalism, would be the idea that certain manifest structures, motifs, or patterns, in whatever medium or whatever style or whatever period, carry a given aesthetic valence or force, regardless of how they are embodied or employed; structuralism is thus a sort of optimism about aesthetic universals locatable at the level of manifest form. But if contextualism is correct, structuralism's pretensions are misguided, its optimism naive.

As for relativism about art, it is the view that what an artwork means, what aesthetic content it possesses, what artistic value it can be said to have, are all relative to individual perceivers or classes of perceivers. If such a view is to be opposed, in favor of a modest objectivism about art, a contextualist understanding of what makes something an artwork to begin with (in my opinion, a certain sort of historically connected intentionality), of what sort of object an artwork is once it is constituted (in my opinion, a historically tethered structure or particular), and of how the meaning and content of an artwork are generated (in my opinion, as a function of both the work's manifest form and its context of emergence), is imperative. Finally, we have deconstructivism, a particularly virulent Gallic variety of relativism (or perhaps subjectivism). Deconstructivism holds that there are no stable and consistent meanings in any discourse, including written texts, because all discourse somehow undermines itself from within. This is not the place for a treatise on deconstructivism, but its central mistake, it seems to me, is to conclude that because the force or content of an utterance—conversational remark, newspaper story, lyric poem, or narrative fiction—can often be temporarily put into question by focusing peculiarly on its "margins," "gaps," and "aporias"—that therefore the utterance has no central, intersubjectively demonstrable force or content. Anyway, it seems clear that the more firmly and sophisticatedly contextualist one's view of the products of art, the less likely one would be to accede in the ultimate semantic indeterminacy promised by deconstructivism—which determinacy, note, is amply fueled by the formalist, empiricist, and structuralist tendencies canvassed earlier, since in freeing a work from its intentional, historical, stylistic, and categorial moorings it opens the door fairly wide to such indeterminacy of content. In that respect, deconstructivism is but the natural—if rotten —fruit of formalism and structuralism as regards art.

DK: All right, very good, let us all agree with you. Say we're contextualists. As you know I myself have some definite formalist tendencies, but let's forget about that for now.[4] So suppose we are now all contextualists and think that's the "right" artwork theory. What can this artwork theory—contextualism—do for us as philosophers, as enjoyers of art, as artists?

JL: Well, the simplest response, I suppose, is that being in the truth about some matter is generally, if not invariably, good for one. But let me focus on the implications for appreciators and appreciation. The short answer is that a noncontextualist (e.g. structuralist, formalist, empiricist) view of what artworks are, of what they mean or express, of how they relate to their makers and the surrounding social world is just an unnecessarily restricting and impoverishing one. Art is a much richer, more interesting, more important thing if rightly seen as the product of historically placed individuals with hearts and minds, hopes and fears, working to communicate contents or convey experiences through concrete media—rather than as mere abstract forms or patterns whose provenance, antecedents, and culturally rooted significances might all be put aside or bracketed so far as appreciation was concerned.

Viewed in abstraction from their human context, the objects of art have no more claim on our attention than the forms and patterns of nature, and no greater potential for meaning. Of course, natural objects can be beautiful and partake of other aesthetic properties, but the content of art goes beyond that. Also, the aesthetic qualities an object possesses as an artwork generally differ from those of an observationally indiscernible natural object or nonartwork artifact.

Another benefit of a contextualist perspective on art, in practical terms, is this: It's a useful resource for combatting some of the classic knee-jerk reactions of philistinism as regards modern or outré art. For example, "that's been done before," said of something perceptually similar to some earlier work—once you see that art is something done, rather than merely a certain look, it's not so clear that it has been done before; "my little brother could have done that"—but could he, really, have done that, i.e. would it really be the same thing/have the same import as from the actual artist, with his preexisting oeuvre?; "an exact copy of a Rembrandt is artistically just as good as a Rembrandt"—not if an artwork has a historical dimension, is a personal time-bound creation, exhibits a style, and embodies an achievement.

DK: A couple of things strike me as natural objections, and I wonder how you respond to them. First of all, focusing on how a particular artwork relates to its maker and surrounding social world seems all well and good, except here the problems with interpreting history itself—even in a far simpler context than art—comes into play. It is anybody's guess as to what the real intentions, motives, goals, and so on are that influence an artist in creating a particular work; certainly there will be a plethora of possible theories and explanations. One can make an argument for a particular one, rather than another, but how realistic is this? Let's take a particular example. Why does S do x, where S is anybody and x is anything? This is a tantalizing problem in lots of ways. Why does Sue marry John? We like to believe that there is some particular interpretation that's best because we don't like to think that there is more randomness in the world than we can sensibly control. It seems that even trying to explain ordinary human behavior there are a slew of well-known philosophical conundrums that get in the way. And when it comes to artworks these conundrums seem to force a sensible lover of art to not waste time chasing pipe dreams that get him or her further from the work itself and to focus instead on the work itself. I'll give you two perfect and what seem to me knockdown examples about which I know as much as can be known because I am the artist.

Last year I wrote and published a novel and composed a film score.[5] We're not talking here about the typical kinds of difficulties about access to the minds, intentions, and works of others but my own access to myself and my own work. I know that one could (and I could) offer lots of interesting contextualist analyses of these two works, just as I suppose I could go to a psychiatrist and get an interpretation of my life from a psychological perspective, including why I married whom I married, why I have the friends I do, why I don't like certain people, and so on. But both of these sorts of activities seem to me highly dubious. I honestly cannot tell you any of the sorts of things that, typically, one hears (or reads) philosophers and interpreters of art, artworks, and artists saying about their particular subjects. What do certain elements in those works of mine mean, for instance? I don't really know, certainly not in most cases. And if I don't know, you don't know. It just seemed like the right element that when you're working on the thing happens, the way conversations with others happen, and so on. It's like falling in love. If you have an agenda or some set of intentions— you know, for instance, who and what you're looking for in a relationship—I suspect you'll end up marrying someone you don't love. You're connecting to the wrong thing. If somebody is relating to my work from the standpoint of trying to explain it as the work of a Croatian American of a certain socioeconomic class, with such and such influences, history, and so on, to me not only does it seem they're barking up the wrong tree but they're not really connecting with what I want them to connect with: a world of words in the one case and a world of sounds in

the other. To connect with art, it seems to me as it did to Hegel and Nietzsche,[6] requires the same sort of relaxed, unintellectual, and uncontrolling sensibility that is required of connecting with others, including connecting with oneself. It's direct, immediate, unknown, and mysterious. Philosophers of art, when they do it the way you would have them do it, seem to me to be like critics; people who can't do the thing they are talking about and so find a way of talking that makes them important (in fact, from the point of view of an institutional type of view, such as yours, indispensable). Their explanations and judgments, philosophical and otherwise, seem to me but a cartoon. I'm as much with Socrates as with Hegel and Nietzsche here, I believe, as with E. M. Forster: "only connect."

JL: It seems to me there are a number of unwarranted assumptions and inferences in your brief for "unmediated appreciation." But as far as your scorn for critics, interpreters, and other wordmeisters in regard to art is concerned, just to get that out of the way before proceeding, Woody Allen has perhaps the most apt, if oblique, riposte: "Those who can't do, teach. Those who can't teach, teach gym."

Okay, back to business. First, the perspective I advocate on the appreciation of art is not concerned so much with *explaining* how the work came to be, in the sense of causal explanation, but in *understanding* what it expresses, says, or conveys; a grasp of social, cultural, art-historical context is necessary for the latter—if artworks are not to collapse into natural objects—whatever role it might play in the former. (So, yes, it might be relevant to understanding, if not explaining, your art that you are a Croatian American, that English is not your native language, that you were philosophically trained, and that you are very conversant with Kafka.) Second, as far as artistic meaning is concerned, it's not the actual intentions (motives, goals) of artists that matter, but rather the most reasonably hypothesized such intentions (motives, goals), by appropriately placed audiences in possession of relevant information regarding the context in which and against which the artist's work comes to be; only then can the utterance that is the artist's work be grasped. (There is, though, an ineliminable role played by certain actual intentions, ones regarding a work's art status and the sort of artwork it is supposed to be, e.g. poem, sculpture, and these just do need to be ascertained as far as possible, or else the interpretive/appreciative project cannot properly get off the ground. On the distinction between *semantic* and *categorical* intentions in regard to art, see my "Intention and Interpretation in Literature," in *Pleasures of Aesthetics.*) Third, the idea that what one must do is "focus on the work itself," which seems unobjectionable, doesn't get you anywhere without a defensible conception of what the work *is,* and as I have tried to suggest, a contextualist, temporally situated, utterance-based conception of artworks is demonstrably superior to a formalist-structuralist one. Fourth, the idea that if the artist doesn't know what something in his or her work means then no one knows, as well as the idea that the artist has an unchallengeable access to his or her own mental state, is not one I would have thought could be so blithely proposed after Wittgenstein (which is not to endorse the more extreme behaviorism one can find in that philosopher). What an artist's work means/expresses/conveys may very well be clearer to others than to him or her (and note that what the work, as an utterance in context, means is not always the same as what the artist, on that occasion of utterance, meant). Finally, of course, it should be a goal of interacting with art, on any theory of art, that one *connect* with what is really in the work, and precisely through the forms and structures (e.g. words, colors, sounds, shapes) that are its heart and core, and on which any further qualities and meanings it possesses depend. But that is hardly inconsistent with the demand that, if one wants to experience and understand a work of art as such, rather than merely "get off on it," one sees those forms and structures not as coming out of nowhere, or having dropped from heaven, but as the choice of a particular historically and culturally situated individual working in a particular medium, with its own inherited conventions and associations. Approaching a work "blind," that is, without any contextual situating or cognitive positioning, may sometimes be fun, or experientially rewarding, but it is not approaching it *as art,* a human expressive/communicative/symbolic activity.

DK: Is your argument for contextualism that *unless* one appreciates art in its social, cultural, art-historical context, artworks *necessarily* collapse into natural objects? But surely that's just a premise, not an argument. What reason do you have for thinking that this is the case? There certainly is some evidence to the contrary, from cognitive science, for instance, that certain aspects of the brain are naturally predisposed to respond to certain artificial symbol systems, such as not only natural language but artificial languages like mathematics, music, and art. Second, of course it *might* be relevant to understanding my art that I am, as some would claim, a Croatian American, though I think all such labels—this one especially—are incredibly phony ways to view oneself, by identification with a particular nationality or culture. Why should it matter to understanding Ramanujan's theorems or Einstein's relativity theory that the former is Indian and the latter is German? Ridiculous! And unless you can prove to me that music, for instance, and the other arts exist in languages that are in some fundamental way different from the languages of mathematics and logic—and I believe they do not—I don't see why context matters in the latter when obviously it does not in the former. At least not obviously. One could, of course, try to make a convincing argument, but I haven't seen it.

Third, you say it's not the actual intentions that matter but only the most reasonably hypothesized ones by appropriately placed audiences in possession of relevant information regarding the context in which and against which the artist's work comes to be. Placed by whom, I wonder? The right "experts," I imagine? And who decides what information is relevant? A panel of experts, I imagine? This seems possible but highly dubious. Furthermore, I can well imagine rigging five different such teams of audiences and experts and getting five different types of multiple variations of interpretations! And of course "reasonably hypothesized" opens up a whole can of worms, from just a plain historical perspective.

That's why historians argue endlessly about the conflicting interpretations of past events. That makes a good job for historians except, in their case, one could argue it was needed since we need them to connect to the past that does not present itself to us directly. Artworks, on the other hand, come blasting at you in full philharmonic sound, or a splash of color, and so on, and so it hardly seems the same thing at all.

Fourth, you claim that without a *defensible* conception of what a particular work is, one cannot get anywhere with it; this seems if not highly dubious at least suspect from several points of view. Again, there is plenty of evidence that our brains are hardwired to hear certain arrangements of notes in certain ways, and so on for the other languages of art. Why should I have to be able to make an intellectually defensible statement of a particular conception before I can get my brain to work properly in connecting me to the art that I am experiencing? How do you *know* that the feelings I feel when I am in the presence of a Picasso or a Beethoven or a Cocteau are not correct or meaningful or sublimely significant even, simply based on my neurological/phenomenal response to a object created by another brain/mind linking us to each other over space and time? You can claim that this isn't the way I've just described it, but what's the convincing argument that it isn't so?

Fifth, it certainly is *possible* that what an artist's work means/expresses/conveys may be clearer to others than to the artist, but all else being equal, it seems a highly dubious proposition. You would have to show me that this is in fact the case. Moreover, all else is not equal. I take it on my own case as evidence, and the evidence of some others—you mention Kafka, and he is but one example—that the production of art does not happen at the level of the phenomenal self anyway, so that egoistic-dependent explanations in terms of motives and intentions don't matter to begin with. I could be wrong, but what convincing evidence is there to the contrary? Finally, that the forms and structures do not come out of nowhere—and I would agree that they do not—does not imply that they must therefore come either from heaven or from the historical and cultural situation and that, *therefore,* it must be the latter. There is the possibility that it's coming from the artwork itself in conjoinment with the entire physiological-psychological-noumenal apparatus of one's being in relation to another through an object whose structure and form make such relating possible. In other words, it's not that without the context I must therefore be experiencing the work "blindly" because the context is my eyes, but, rather, that the context is a shield between me and the work. What I need is already in my brain, so to speak, and all it needs is the right stoking by the right art object for my neurons to appropriately tremble and thereby hear the Music of the Spheres, or whatever.

JL: What I think needs saying at this point is that I can't make the full case for contextualism here, nor is there a need to. No one, I think, who works carefully through the range of examples in the literature [7] can fail to see that some degree of contextualism about the nature and content of artworks is warranted, though perhaps there is valid disagreement about to what degree. And contextualism was not being covertly assumed as a premise in my attempted defense of it (nor was the collapsing of artworks into something approaching natural objects if art is viewed acontextually). Rather, contextualism is forced upon us as the best account or explanation of our entrenched practices of experiencing, describing, criticizing, evaluating, and reflecting on art. Structures or forms per se, detached from their emplacement in traditions, styles, problematics, oeuvres, and historical moments, are simply incapable of carrying the kinds of meanings/significances/resonances that informed criticism or enlightened response to artworks regularly ascribe to them.

Next, the relation of art and science. Art and science are, indeed, related activities—both involve creativity, imagination, a search for truth, perhaps—but they are not identical activities and are not governed by all the same criteria of evaluation or meaning-generation. Ramanujan's number theorems and Einstein's space-time theory are not as such vehicles of artistic communication or expression—they are not, in the same way, context-bound utterances. In the case of science, we are standardly interested only in content, and not in the vehicle of it, or in the vehiculing of it; but with art, it is quite otherwise. In fact, a focus on "content as carried by particular form in given circumstances" is virtually definitive of aesthetic interest, by my lights.[8]

Moving on, the issue of universals in art. It appears that there are some aesthetic universals—though the evidence for this has to be carefully interpreted, due in the main, one supposes, to evolutionarily shaped neural hardwiring. Thus, there seems to be some general preference for savannahlike landscapes, rooted in *homo sapiens*'s African past, and a propensity of musical systems to favor the octave and the fifth, and to a lesser extent, thirds and fourths. But even if robust, such results hardly show that all or even most of the effect and content of art is context- and convention- and history-independent!

A red tree, a swastika, a curving line, a diminished seventh chord, an expletive—these signify or convey or evoke one thing in one context (say, Mondrian's expressionist landscapes, Nazi propaganda films, Ingres's portraits of odalisques, Mozart's symphonies, D. H. Lawrence's novels) and something else in another (say, Matisse's decorative interiors, ancient Indian art, Kandinsky's abstractions, Wagner's operas, David Mamet's plays). Or consider matters of allusion, quotation, parody, satire, adaptation, variation, repudiation, homage, which are widespread in the arts—common artistic phenomena are inexplicable on an acontextual view of artworks. For example, whatever meaning, effectiveness, or value Woody Allen's 1980 *Stardust Memories* possesses is simply not detachable from its evident references to and modeling after Fellini's *8½* of 1963.

Finally, the question of the degree of intellectuality of appropriate response to art. Here I think we are basically in accord. An appreciator doesn't have to be able to articulate intellectually the cultural context, background knowledge, or cognitive orientation requisite for experiencing a work correctly, that is, as the historically situated utterance or offering it is, he or she simply

needs to *possess* it. But by and large one acquires what's needed by osmosis from the culture and wide experience in the artform in question. What Wollheim calls "cognitive stock," or Meyer "internalized norms," and what they hold essential to the adequate appreciation, respectively, of painting and music, are largely tacitly acquirable and may also not be readily accessible discursively. What's needed are basically style- and period-relative habits of response.[9]

In conclusion, let me just say that of course experience of art is the most important thing, and the impact of art a primary *raison d'être* of it. But that does not mean that such experience and such impact are not inevitably and properly culturally mediated and historically informed. To think otherwise, once again, risks reducing our engagement with art to our engagement with mere patterns, however striking or beautiful.

Notes

1. *System of Transcendental Idealism,* reprinted in *The Mayfield Anthology of Western Philosophy,* edited by Daniel Kolak, (Mountain View, CA: Mayfield, 1998).

2. Croce, Collingwood, Bergson, Merleau-Ponty, Heidegger, Gadamer.

3. In his *Labyrinths* (New York: New Directions, 1962).

4. See Daniel Kolak, "Art and Intentionality," *The Journal of Aesthetics and Art Criticism* 48 (1990): 158–162, and Jerrold Levinson's response, "A Refiner's Fire: Reply to Sartwell and Kolak," *JAAC* 48 (1990): 231–235.

5. *In Search of Myself* (Belmont, CA: Wadsworth, 1998), and *Forsaken Cries,* 1997, Amnesty International, producers.

6. See their selections earlier in this section.

7. See, for instance, Borges's "Pierre Menard" and "Library of Babel," op. cit., Gombrich's *Art and Illusion* and "Expression and Communication" (in *Meditations on a Hobbyhorse*), Walton's "Categories of Art," Danto's *Transfiguration of the Commonplace,* Margolis's *Art and Philosophy,* and Levinson's "What a Musical Work Is" in *Music, Art, & Metaphysics.*

8. See "What Is Aesthetic Pleasure?" in *Pleasures of Aesthetics.*

9. See Levinson's "Musical Literacy," in *Pleasures of Aesthetics.*

MEANING

My Confession

LEO TOLSTOY

Count Leo Tolstoy (1828–1910) was born, educated, and lived almost all of his life in Russia. He is generally regarded as one of the greatest novelists of all time.

Although I regarded authorship as a waste of time, I continued to write during those fifteen years. I had tasted of the seduction of authorship, of the seduction of enormous monetary remunerations and applauses for my insignificant labour, and so I submitted to it, as being a means for improving my material condition and for stifling in my soul all questions about the meaning of my life and life in general.

In my writings I advocated, what to me was the only truth, that it was necessary to live in such a way as to derive the greatest comfort for oneself and one's family.

Thus I proceeded to live, but five years ago something very strange began to happen with me: I was overcome by minutes at first of perplexity and then of an arrest of life, as though I did not know how to live or what to do, and I lost myself and was dejected. But that passed, and I continued to live as before. Then those minutes of perplexity were repeated oftener and oftener, and always in one and the same form. These arrests of life found their expression in ever the same questions: "Why? Well, and then?"

At first I thought that those were simply aimless, inappropriate questions. It seemed to me that that was all well known and that if I ever wanted to busy myself with their solution, it would not cost me much labour,—that now I had no time to attend to them, but that if I wanted to I should find the proper answers. But the questions began to repeat themselves oftener and oftener, answers were demanded more and more persistently, and, like dots that fall

on the same spot, these questions, without any answers, thickened into one black blotch.

There happened what happens with any person who falls ill with a mortal internal disease. At first there appear insignificant symptoms of indisposition, to which the patient pays no attention; then these symptoms are repeated more and more frequently and blend into one temporally indivisible suffering. The suffering keeps growing, and before the patient has had time to look around, he becomes conscious that what he took for an indisposition is the most significant thing in the world to him,—is death.

The same happened with me. I understood that it was not a passing indisposition, but something very important, and that, if the questions were going to repeat themselves, it would be necessary to find an answer for them. And I tried to answer them. The questions seemed to be so foolish, simple, and childish. But the moment I touched them and tried to solve them, I became convinced, in the first place, that they were not childish and foolish, but very important and profound questions in life, and, in the second, that, no matter how much I might try, I should not be able to answer them. Before attending to my Samára estate, to my son's education, or to the writing of a book, I ought to know why I should do that. So long as I did not know why, I could not do anything. I could not live. Amidst my thoughts of farming, which interested me very much during that time, there would suddenly pass through my head a question like this: "All right, you are going to have six thousand desyatínas of land in the Government

From *My Confession,* translated by Leo Wiener (Dent, 1905).

of Samára, and three hundred horses,—and then?" And I completely lost my senses and did not know what to think farther. Or, when I thought of the education my children, I said to myself: "Why?" Or, reflecting on the manner in which the masses might obtain their welfare, I suddenly said to myself: "What is that to me?" Or, thinking of the fame which my works would get me, I said to myself: "All right, you will be more famous than Gógol, Púshkin, Shakespeare, Molière, and all the writers in the world,— what of it?" And I was absolutely unable to make any reply. The questions were not waiting, and I had to answer them at once; if I did not answer them, I could not live. . . .

All that happened with me when I was on every side surrounded by what is considered to be complete happiness. I had a good, loving, and beloved wife, good children, and a large estate, which grew and increased without any labour on my part. I was respected by my neighbours and friends, more than ever before, was praised by strangers, and, without any self-deception, could consider my name famous. With all that, I was not deranged or mentally unsound,—on the contrary, I was in full command of my mental and physical powers, such as I had rarely met with in people of my age: physically I could work in a field, mowing, without falling behind a peasant; mentally I could work from eight to ten hours in succession, without experiencing any consequences from the strain. And while in such condition I arrived at the conclusion that I could not live, and, fearing death, I had to use cunning against myself, in order that I might not take my life.

This mental condition expressed itself to me in this form: my life is a stupid, mean trick played on me by somebody. Although I did not recognize that "somebody" as having created me, the form of the conception that some one had played a mean, stupid trick on me by bringing me into the world was the most natural one that presented itself to me.

Involuntarily I imagined that there, somewhere, there was somebody who was now having fun as he looked down upon me and saw me, who had lived for thirty or forty years, learning, developing, growing in body and mind, now that I had become strengthened in mind and had reached that summit of life from which it lay all before me, standing as a complete fool on that summit and seeing clearly that there was nothing in life and never would be. And that was fun to him—

But whether there was or was not that somebody who made fun of me, did not make it easier for me. I could not ascribe any sensible meaning to a single act, or to my whole life. I was only surprised that I had not understood that from the start. All that had long ago been known to everybody. Sooner or later there would come diseases and death (they had come already) to my dear ones and to me, and there would be nothing left but stench and worms. All my affairs, no matter what they might be, would sooner or later be forgotten, and I myself should not exist. So why should I worry about all these things? How could a man fail to see that and live,—that was surprising! A person could live only so long as he was drunk; but the moment he sobered up, he could not help seeing that all that was only a deception, and a stupid deception at that! Really, there was nothing funny and ingenious about it, but only something cruel and stupid.

Long ago has been told the Eastern story about the traveller who in the steppe is overtaken by an infuriated beast. Trying to save himself from the animal, the traveller jumps into a waterless well, but at its bottom he sees a dragon who opens his jaws in order to swallow him. And the unfortunate man does not dare climb out, lest he perish from the infuriated beast, and does not dare jump down to the bottom of the well, lest he be devoured by the dragon, and so clutches the twig of a wild bush growing in the cleft of the well and holds on to it. His hands grow weak and he feels that soon he shall have to surrender to the peril which awaits him at either side; but he still holds on and sees two mice, one white, the other black, in even measure making a circle around the main trunk of the bush to which he is clinging, and nibbling at it on all sides. Now, at any moment, the bush will break and tear off, and he will fall into the dragon's jaws. The traveller sees that and knows that he will inevitably perish; but while he is still clinging, he sees some drops of honey hanging on the leaves of the bush, and so reaches out for them with his tongue and licks the leaves. Just so I hold on to the branch of life, knowing that the dragon of death is waiting inevitably for me, ready to tear me to pieces, and I cannot understand why I have fallen on such suffering. And I try to lick that honey which used to give me pleasure; but now it no longer gives me joy, and the white and the black mouse day and night nibble at the branch to which I am holding on. I clearly see the dragon, and the honey is no longer sweet to me. I see only the inevitable dragon and the mice, and am unable to turn my glance away from them. That is not a fable, but a veritable, indisputable, comprehensible truth.

The former deception of the pleasures of life, which stifled the terror of the dragon, no longer deceives me. No matter how much one should say to me, "You cannot understand the meaning of life, do not think, live!" I am unable to do so, because I have been doing it too long before. Now I cannot help seeing day and night, which run and lead me up to death. I see that alone, because that alone is the truth. Everything else is a lie.

The two drops of honey that have longest turned my eyes away from the cruel truth, the love of family and of authorship, which I have called an art, are no longer sweet to me.

"My family—" I said to myself, "but my family, my wife and children, they are also human beings. They are in precisely the same condition that I am in: they must either live in the lie or see the terrible truth. Why should they live? Why should I love them, why guard, raise, and watch them? Is it for the same despair which is in me, or for dullness of perception? Since I love them, I cannot conceal the truth from them,—every step in cognition leads them up to this truth. And the truth is death."

"Art, poetry?" For a long time, under the influence of the success of human praise, I tried to persuade myself that that was a thing which could be done, even though death should come and destroy everything, my deeds, as well as my memory of them; but soon I came to see that that, too, was a deception. It was clear to me that art was an adornment of life, a decoy of life. But life lost all its attractiveness for me. How, then, could I entrap others? So long as I did not live my own life, and a strange life bore me on its waves; so long as I believed that life had some sense, although I was not able to express it,—the reflections of life of every description in poetry and in the arts afforded me pleasure, and I was delighted to look at life through this little mirror of art; but when I began to look for the meaning of life, when I experienced the necessity of living myself, that little mirror became either useless, superfluous, and ridiculous, or painful to me. I could no longer console myself with what I saw in the mirror, namely, that my situation was stupid and desperate. . . .

By abandoning myself to the bright side of knowledge I saw that I only turned my eyes away from the question. No matter how enticing and clear the horizons were that were disclosed to me, no matter how enticing it was to bury myself in the infinitude of this knowledge, I comprehended that these sciences were the more clear, the less I needed them, the less they answered my question.

"Well, I know," I said to myself, "all which science wants so persistently to know, but there is no answer to the question about the meaning of my life." But in the speculative sphere I saw that, in spite of the fact that the aim of the knowledge was directed straight to the answer of my question, or because of that fact, there could be no other answer than what I was giving to myself: "What is the meaning of my life?"— "None." Or, "What will come of my life?"—"Nothing." Or, "Why does everything which exists exist, and why do I exist?"—"Because it exists."

Putting the question to the one side of human knowledge, I received an endless quantity of exact answers about what I did not ask: about the chemical composition of the stars, about the movement of the sun toward the constellation of Hercules, about the origin of species and of man, about the forms of infinitely small, imponderable particles of ether; but the answer in this sphere of knowledge to my question what the meaning of my life was, was always: "You are what you call your life; you are a temporal, accidental conglomeration of particles. The interrelation, the change of these particles, produces in you that which you call life. This congeries will last for some time; then the interaction of these particles will cease, and that which you call life and all your questions will come to an end. You are an accidentally cohering globule of something. The globule is fermenting. This fermentation the globule calls its life. The globule falls to pieces, and all fermentation and all questions will come to an end." Thus the clear side of knowledge answers, and it cannot say anything else, if only it strictly follows its principles.

With such an answer it appears that the answer is not a reply to the question. I want to know the meaning of my life, but the fact that it is a particle of the infinite not only gives it no meaning, but even destroys every possible meaning. . . .

I lived for a long time in this madness, which, not in words, but in deeds, is particularly characteristic of us, the most liberal and learned of men. But, thanks either to my strange, physical love for the real working class, which made me understand it and see that it is not so stupid as we suppose, or to the sincerity of my conviction, which was that I could know nothing and that the best that I could do was to hang myself,—I felt that if I wanted to live and understand the meaning of life, I ought naturally to look for it, not among those who had lost the meaning of life and wanted to kill themselves, but among those billions of departed and living men who had been carrying their own lives and ours upon their shoulders. And I looked around at the enormous masses of deceased and living men, not learned and wealthy, but simple men,—and I saw something quite different. I saw that all these billions of men that lived or had lived, all, with rare exceptions, did not fit into my subdivisions, and that I could not recognize them as not understanding the question, because they themselves put it and answered it with surprising clearness. Nor could I recognize them as Epicureans, because their lives were composed rather of privations and suffering than of enjoyment. Still less could I recognize them as senselessly living out their meaningless lives, because every act of theirs and death itself was explained by them. They regarded it as the greatest evil to kill themselves. It appeared, then, that all humanity was in possession of a knowledge of the meaning of life, which I did not recognize and which I condemned. It turned out that rational knowledge did not give any meaning to life, excluded life, while the meaning which by billions of people, by all humanity, was ascribed to life was based on some despised, false knowledge.

The rational knowledge in the person of the learned and the wise denied the meaning of life, but the enormous masses of men, all humanity, recognized this meaning in an irrational knowledge. This irrational knowledge was faith, the same that I could not help but reject. That was God as one and three, the creation in six days, devils and angels, and all that which I could not accept so long as I had not lost my senses.

My situation was a terrible one. I knew that I should not find anything on the path of rational knowledge but the negation of life, and there, in faith, nothing but the negation of reason, which was still more impossible than the negation of life. From the rational knowledge it followed that life was an evil and men knew it,—it depended on men whether they should cease living, and yet they lived and continued to live, and I myself lived, though I had known long ago that life was meaningless and an evil. From faith it followed that, in order to understand life, I must renounce reason, for which alone a meaning was needed.

There resulted a contradiction, from which there were two ways out: either what I called rational was not so rational as I had thought; or that which to me appeared irrational was not so irrational as I had thought. And I began to verify the train of thoughts of my rational knowledge.

In verifying the train of thoughts of my rational knowledge, I found that it was quite correct. The deduction that life was nothing was inevitable; but I saw a mistake. The mistake was that I had not reasoned in conformity with the question put by me. The question was, "Why should I live?" that is, "What real, indestructible essence will come from my phantasmal, destructible life? What meaning has my finite existence in this infinite world?" And in order to answer this question, I studied life.

The solutions of all possible questions of life apparently could not satisfy me, because my question, no matter how simple it appeared in the beginning, included the necessity of explaining the finite through the infinite, and vice versa.

I asked, "What is the extra-temporal, extra-causal, extra-spatial meaning of life?" But I gave an answer to the question, "What is the temporal, causal, spatial meaning of my life?" The result was that after a long labour of mind I answered, "None," . . .

When I saw that [. . . for philosophy the solution remains insoluble] I understood that it was not right for me to look for an answer to my question in rational knowledge, and that the answer given by rational knowledge was only an indication that the answer might be got if the question were differently put, but only when into the discussion of the question should be introduced the question of the relation of the finite to the infinite. I also understood that, no matter how irrational and monstrous the answers might be that faith gave, they had this advantage that they introduced into each answer the relation of the finite to the infinite, without which there could be no answer.

No matter how I may put the question, "How must I live?" the answer is, "According to God's law." "What real result will there be from my life?"—"Eternal torment or eternal bliss." "What is the meaning which is not destroyed by death?"—"The union with infinite God, paradise."

Thus, outside the rational knowledge, which had to me appeared as the only one, I was inevitably led to recognize that all living humanity had a certain other irrational knowledge, faith, which made it possible to live.

All the irrationality of faith remained the same for me, but I could not help recognizing that it alone gave to humanity answers to the questions of life, and, in consequence of them, the possibility of living.

The rational knowledge brought me to the recognition that life was meaningless,—my life stopped, and I wanted to destroy myself. When I looked around at people, at all humanity, I saw that people lived and asserted that they knew the meaning of life. I looked back at myself: I lived so long as I knew the meaning of life. As to other people, so even to me, did faith give the meaning of life and the possibility of living.

Looking again at the people of other countries, contemporaries of mine and those passed way, I saw again the same. Where life had been, there faith, ever since humanity had existed, had given the possibility of living, and the chief features of faith were everywhere one and the same.

No matter what answers faith may give, its every answer gives to the finite existence of man the sense of the infinite,—a sense which is not destroyed by suffering, privation, and death. Consequently in faith alone could we find the meaning and possibility of life. What, then, was faith? I understood that faith was not merely an evidence of things not seen, and so forth, not revelation (that is only the description of one of the symptoms of faith), not the relation of man to man (faith has to be defined, and then God, and not first God, and faith through him), not merely an agreement with what a man was told, as faith was generally understood,—that faith was the

knowledge of the meaning of human life, in consequence of which man did not destroy himself, but lived. Faith is the power of life. If a man lives he believes in something. If he did not believe that he ought to live for some purpose, he would not live. If he does not see and understand the phantasm of the finite, he believes in that finite; if he understands the phantasm of the finite, he must believe in the infinite. Without faith one cannot live. . . .

In order that all humanity may be able to live, in order that they may continue living, giving a meaning to life, they, those billions, must have another, a real knowledge of faith, for not the fact that I, with Solomon and Schopenhauer, did not kill myself convinced me of the existence of faith, but that these billions had lived and had borne us, me and Solomon, on the waves of life.

Then I began to cultivate the acquaintance of the believers from among the poor, the simple and unlettered folk, of pilgrims, monks, dissenters, peasants. The doctrine of these people from among the masses was also the Christian doctrine that the quasi-believers of our circle professed. With the Christian truths were also mixed in very many superstitions, but there was this difference: the superstitions of our circle were quite unnecessary to them, had no connection with their lives, were only a kind of an Epicurean amusement, while the superstitions of the believers from among the labouring classes were to such an extent blended with their life that it would have been impossible to imagine it without these superstitions,—it was a necessary condition of that life. I began to examine closely the lives and beliefs of these people, and the more I examined them, the more did I become convinced that they had the real faith, that their faith was necessary for them, and that it alone gave them a meaning and possibility of life. In contradistinction to what I saw in our circle, where life without faith was possible, and where hardly one in a thousand professed to be a believer, among them there was hardly one in a thousand who was not a believer. In contradistinction to what I saw in our circle, where all life passed in idleness, amusements, and tedium of life, I saw that the whole life of these people was passed in hard work, and that they were satisfied with life. In contradistinction to the people of our circle, who struggled and murmured against fate because of their privations and their suffering, these people accepted diseases and sorrows without any perplexity or opposition, but with the calm and firm conviction that it was all for good. In contradistinction to the fact that the more intelligent we are, the less do we understand the meaning of life and the more do we see a kind of a bad joke in our suffering and death, these people live, suffer, and approach death, and suffer in peace and more often in joy. In contradistinction to the fact that a calm death, a death without terror or despair, is the greatest exception in our circle, a restless, insubmissive, joyless death is one of the greatest exceptions among the masses. And of such people, who are deprived of everything which for Solomon and for me constitutes the only good of life, and who withal experience the greatest happiness, there is an enormous number. I cast a broader glance about me. I examined the life of past and present vast masses of men, and I saw people who in like manner had understood the meaning of life, who had known how to live and die, not two, not three, not ten, but hundreds, thousands, millions. All of them, infinitely diversified as to habits, intellect, culture, situation,

all equally and quite contrary to my ignorance knew the meaning of life and of death, worked calmly, bore privations and suffering, lived and died, seeing in that not vanity, but good.

I began to love those people. The more I penetrated into their life, the life of the men now living, and the life of men departed, of whom I had read and heard, the more did I love them, and the easier it became for me to live. Thus I lived for about two years, and within me took place a transformation, which had long been working within me, and the germ of which had always been in me. What happened with me was that the life of our circle,—of the rich and the learned,—not only disgusted me, but even lost all its meaning. All our acts, reflections, sciences, arts,—all that appeared to me in a new light. I saw that all that was mere pampering of the appetites, and that no meaning could be found in it; but the life of all the working masses, of all humanity, which created life, presented itself to me in its real significance. I saw that that was life itself and that the meaning given to this life was truth, and I accepted it.

Is Life Meaningful?

RICHARD TAYLOR

Richard Taylor taught philosophy at Brown University, Ohio State University, and the University of Rochester.

The question of whether life has any meaning is difficult to interpret, and the more one concentrates his critical faculty on it the more it seems to elude him, or to evaporate as any intelligible question. One wants to turn it aside, as a source of embarrassment, as something that, if it cannot be abolished, should at least be decently covered. And yet I think any reflective person recognizes that the question it

raises is important, and that it ought to have a significant answer.

If the idea of meaningfulness is difficult to grasp in this context, so that we are unsure what sort of thing would amount to answering the question, the idea of meaninglessness is perhaps less so. If, then, we can bring before our minds a clear image of meaningless existence, then perhaps we can take a step toward coping with our original question by seeing to what extent our lives, as we actually find them, resemble that image, and draw such lessons as we are able to from the comparison.

MEANINGLESS EXISTENCE

A perfect image of meaninglessness, of the kind we are seeking, is found in the ancient myth of Sisyphus. Sisyphus, it will be remembered, betrayed divine secrets to mortals, and for this he was condemned by the gods to roll a stone to the top of a hill, the stone then immediately to roll back down, again to be pushed to the top by Sisyphus, to roll down once more, and so on again and again, *forever.* Now in this we have the picture of meaningless, pointless toil, of a meaningless existence that is absolutely *never* redeemed. It is not even redeemed by a death that, if it were to accomplish nothing more, would at least bring this idiotic cycle to a close. If we were invited to imagine Sisyphus struggling for awhile and accomplishing nothing, perhaps eventually falling from exhaustion, so that we might suppose him then eventually turning to something having some sort of promise, then the meaninglessness of that chapter of his life would not be so stark. It would be a dark and dreadful dream, from which he eventually awakens to sunlight and reality. But he does not awaken, for there is nothing for him to awaken to. His repetitive toil is his life and reality, and it goes on forever, and it is without any meaning whatever. Nothing ever comes out of what he is doing, except simply, more of the same. Not by one step, nor by a thousand, nor by ten thousand does he even expiate by the smallest token the sin against the gods that led him into his fate. Nothing comes of it, nothing at all.

This ancient myth has always enchanted men, for countless meanings can be read into it. Some of the ancients apparently thought it symbolized the perpetual rising and setting of the sun, and others the repetitious crashing of the waves upon the shore. Probably the commonest interpretation is that it symbolizes man's eternal struggle and unquenchable spirit, his determination always to try once more in the face of overwhelming discouragement. This interpretation is further supported by that version of the myth according to which Sisyphus was commanded to roll the stone *over* the hill, so that it would finally roll down the other side, but was never quite able to make it.

I am not concerned with rendering or defending any interpretation of this myth, however. I have cited it only for the one element it does unmistakably contain, namely, that of a repetitious, cyclic activity that never comes to anything. We could contrive other images of this that would serve just as well, and no myth-makers are needed to supply the materials of it. Thus, we can imagine two persons transporting a stone—or even a precious gem, it does not matter—back and forth, relay style. One carries it to a near or distant point where it is received by the other; it is returned to its starting point, there to be recovered by the first, and the process is repeated over and over. Except in this relay nothing counts as winning, and nothing brings the contest to any close, each step only leads to a repetition of itself. Or we can imagine two groups of prisoners, one of them engaged in digging a prodigious hole in the ground that is no sooner finished than it is filled in again by the other group, the latter then digging a new hole that is at once filled in by the first group, and so on and on endlessly.

Now what stands out in all such pictures as oppressive and dejecting is not that the beings who enact these roles suffer any torture or pain, for it need not be assumed that they do. Nor is it that their labors are great, for they are no greater than the labors commonly undertaken by most men most of the time. According to the original myth, the stone is so large that Sisyphus never quite gets it to the top and must groan under every step, so that his enormous labor is all for nought. But this is not what appalls. It is not that his great struggle comes to nothing, but that his existence itself is without meaning. Even if we suppose, for example, that the stone is but a pebble that can be carried effortlessly, or that the holes dug by the prisoners are but small ones, not the slightest meaning is introduced into their lives. The stone that Sisyphus moves to the top of the hill, whether we think of it as large or small, still rolls back every time, and the process is repeated forever. Nothing comes of it, and the work is simply pointless. That is the element of the myth that I wish to capture.

Again, it is not the fact that the labors of Sisyphus continue forever that deprives them of meaning. It is, rather, the implication of this: that they come to nothing. The image would not be changed by our supposing him to push a different stone up every time, each to roll down again. But if we supposed that these stones, instead of rolling back to their places as if they had never been moved, were assembled at the top of the hill and there incorporated, say, in a beautiful and enduring temple, then the aspect of meaninglessness would disappear. His labors would then have a point, something would come of them all, and although one could perhaps still say it was not worth it, one could not say that the life of Sisyphus was devoid of meaning altogether. Meaningfulness would at least have made an appearance, and we could see what it was.

That point will need remembering. But in the meantime, let us note another way in which the image of meaninglessness can be altered by making only a very slight change. Let us suppose that the gods, while condemning Sisyphus to the fate just described, at the same time, as an afterthought, waxed perversely merciful by implanting in him a strange and irrational impulse; namely a compulsive impulse to roll stones. We may if we like, to make this more graphic, suppose they accomplish this by implanting in him some substance that has this effect on his character and drives. I call this perverse, because from our point of view there is clearly no reason why anyone should have a persistent and insatiable desire to do something so pointless as that. Nevertheless, suppose that is Sisyphus' condition. He has but one obsession, which is to roll stones, and it is an obsession that is only for the moment appeased by his rolling them—he no sooner gets a stone rolled to the top of the hill than he is restless to roll up another.

Now it can be seen why this little afterthought of the gods, which I called perverse, was also in fact merciful. For they have by this device managed to give Sisyphus precisely what he wants—by making him want precisely what they inflict on him. However it may appear to us, Sisyphus' fate now does not appear to him as a condemnation, but the very reverse. His one desire in life is to roll stones, and he is absolutely guaranteed its endless fulfillment. Where otherwise he might profoundly have wished surcease, and even welcomed the quiet of death to release him from endless boredom and meaninglessness, his life is now filled with mission and meaning, and he seems to himself to have been given an entry to heaven. Nor need he even fear death, for the gods have promised him an endless opportunity to indulge his single purpose, without concern or frustration. He will be able to roll stones *forever*.

What we need to mark most carefully at this point is that the picture with which we began has not really been changed in the least by adding this supposition. Exactly the same things happen as before. The only change is in Sisyphus' view of them. The picture before was the image of meaningless activity and existence. It was created precisely to be an image of that. It has not lost that meaninglessness, it has now gained not the least shred of meaningfulness. The stones still roll back as before, each phase of Sisyphus' life still exactly resembles all the others, the task is never completed, nothing comes of it, no temple ever begins to rise, and all this cycle of the same pointless thing over and over goes on forever in this picture as in the other. The *only* thing that has happened is this: Sisyphus has been reconciled to it, and indeed more, he has been led to embrace it. Not, however, by reason or persuasion, but by nothing more rational than the potency of a new substance in his veins.

THE MEANINGLESSNESS OF LIFE

I believe the foregoing provides a fairly clear content to the idea of meaninglessness and, through it, some hint of what meaningfulness, in this sense, might be. Meaninglessness is essentially endless pointlessness, and meaningfulness is therefore the opposite. Activity, and even long, drawn-out and repetitive activity, has a meaning if it has some significant culmination, some more or less lasting end that can be considered to have been the direction and purpose of the activity. But the descriptions so far also provide something else; namely, the suggestion of how an existence that is objectively meaningless, in this sense, can nevertheless acquire a meaning for him whose existence it is.

Now let us ask: Which of these pictures does life in fact resemble? And let us not begin with our own lives, for here both our prejudices and wishes are great, but with the life in general that we share with the rest of creation. We shall find, I think, that it all has a certain pattern, and that this pattern is by now easily recognized.

We can begin anywhere, only saving human existence for our last consideration. We can, for example, begin with any animal. It does not matter where we begin, because the result is going to be exactly the same.

Thus, for example, there are caves in New Zealand, deep and dark, whose floors are quiet pools and whose walls and ceilings are covered with soft light. As one gazes in wonder in the stillness of these caves it seems that the Creator has reproduced there in microcosm the heavens themselves, until one scarcely remembers the enclosing presence of the walls. As one looks more closely, however, the scene is explained. Each dot of light identifies an ugly worm, whose luminous tail is meant to attract insects from the surrounding darkness. As from time to time one of these insects draws near it becomes entangled in a sticky thread lowered by the worm, and is eaten. This goes on month after month, the blind worm lying there in the barren stillness waiting to entrap an occasional bit of nourishment that will only sustain it to another bit of nourishment until. . . . Until what? What great thing awaits all this long and repetitious effort and makes it worthwhile? Really nothing. The larva just transforms itself finally to a tiny winged adult that lacks even mouth parts to feed and lives only a day or two. These adults, as soon as they have mated and laid eggs, are themselves caught in the threads and are devoured by the cannibalist worms, often without having ventured into the day, the only point to their existence having now been fulfilled. This has been going on for millions of years, and to no end other than that the same meaningless cycle may continue for another millions of years.

All living things present essentially the same spectacle. The larva of a certain cicada burrows in the darkness of the earth for seventeen years, through season after season, to emerge finally into the daylight for a brief flight, lay its eggs, and die— this all to repeat itself during the next seventeen years, and so on to eternity. We have already noted, in another connection, the struggles of fish, made only that others may do the same after them and that this cycle, having no other point than itself, may never cease. Some birds span an entire side of the globe each year and then return, only to ensure that others may follow the same incredibly long path again and again. One is led to wonder what the point of it all is, with what great triumph this cease-

less effort, repeating itself through millions of years, might finally culminate, and why it should go on and on for so long, accomplishing nothing, getting nowhere. But then one realizes that there is no point to it at all, that it really culminates in nothing, that each of these cycles, so filled with toil, is to be followed only by more of the same. The point of any living thing's life is, evidently, nothing but life itself.

This life of the world thus presents itself to our eyes as a vast machine, feeding on itself, running on and on forever to nothing. And we are part of that life. To be sure, we are not just the same, but the differences are not so great as we like to think; many are merely invented, and none really cancels the kind of meaninglessness that we found in Sisyphus and that we find all around, wherever anything lives. We are conscious of our activity. Our goals, whether in any significant sense we choose them or not, are things of which we are at least partly aware and can therefore in some sense appraise. More significantly, perhaps, men have a history, as other animals do not, such that each generation does not precisely resemble all those before. Still, if we can in imagination disengage our wills from our lives and disregard the deep interest each man has in his own existence, we shall find that they do not so little resemble the existence of Sisyphus. We toil after goals, most of them —indeed every single one of them—of transitory significance and, having gained one of them, we immediately set forth for the next, as if that one had never been, with this next one being essentially more of the same. Look at a busy street any day, and observe the throng going hither and thither. To what? Some office or shop, where the same things will be done today as were done yesterday, and are done now so they may be repeated tomorrow. And if we think that, unlike Sisyphus, these labors do have a point, that they culminate in something lasting and, independently of our own deep interests in them, very worthwhile, then we simply have not considered the thing closely enough. Most such effort is directed only to the establishment and perpetuation of home and family; that is, to the begetting of others who will follow in our steps to do more of the same. Each man's life thus resembles one of Sisyphus' climbs to the summit of his hill, and each day of it one of his steps; the difference is that whereas Sisyphus himself returns to push the stone up again, we leave this to our children. We at one point imagined that the labors of Sisyphus finally culminated in the creation of a temple, but for this to make any difference it had to be a temple that would at least endure, adding beauty to the world for the remainder of time. Our achievements, even though they are often beautiful, are mostly bubbles; and those that do last, like the sand-swept pyramids, soon become mere curiosities while around them the rest of mankind continues its perpetual toting of rocks, only to see them roll down. Nations are built upon the bones of their founders and pioneers, but only to decay and crumble before long, their rubble then becoming the foundation for others directed to exactly the same fate. The picture of Sisyphus is the picture of existence of the individual man, great or unknown, of nations, of the race of men, and of the very life of the world.

On a country road one sometimes comes upon the ruined hulks of a house and once extensive buildings, all in collapse and spread over with weeds. A curious eye can in imagination reconstruct from what is left a once warm and thriving life, filled with purpose. There was the hearth, where a family once talked, sang, and made plans; there were the rooms, where people loved, and babes were born to a rejoicing mother; there are the musty remains of a sofa, infested with bugs, once bought at a dear price to enhance an ever-growing comfort, beauty, and warmth. Every small piece of junk fills the mind with what once, not long ago, was utterly real, with children's voices, plans made, and enterprises embarked upon. That is how these stones of Sisyphus were rolled up, and that is how they became incorporated into a beautiful temple, and that temple is what now lies before you. Meanwhile other buildings, institutions, nations, and civilizations spring up all around, only to share the same fate before long. And if the question "What for?" is now asked, the answer is clear: so that just this may go on forever.

The two pictures—of Sisyphus and of our own lives, if we look at them from a distance—are in outline the same and convey to the mind the same image. It is not surprising, then, that men invent ways of denying it, their religions proclaiming a heaven that does not crumble, their hymnals and prayer books declaring a significance to life of which our eyes provide no hint whatever. Even our philosophies portray some permanent and lasting good at which all may aim, from the changeless forms invented by Plato to the beatific vision of St. Thomas and the ideals of permanence contrived by the moderns. When these fail to convince, then earthly ideals such as universal justice and brotherhood are conjured up to take their places and give meaning to man's seemingly endless pilgrimage, some final state that will be ushered in when the last obstacle is removed and the last stone pushed to the hilltop. No one believes, of course, that any such state will be final, or even wants it to be in case it means that human existence would then cease to be a struggle; but in the meantime such ideas serve a very real need.

THE MEANING OF LIFE

We noted that Sisyphus' existence would have meaning if there were some point to his labors, if his efforts ever culminated in something that was not just an occasion for fresh labors of the same kind. But this is precisely the meaning it lacks. And human existence resembles his in that respect. Men do achieve things—they scale their towers and raise their stones to their hilltops—but every such accomplishment fades, providing only an occasion for renewed labors of the same kind.

But here we need to note something else that has been mentioned, but its significance not explored, and that is the state of mind and feeling with which such labors are undertaken. We noted that if Sisyphus had a keen and unappeasable desire to be doing just what he found himself doing, then, although his life would in no way be changed, it would nevertheless have a meaning for him. It would be an irrational one, no doubt, because the desire itself would be only the product of the substance in his veins, and not any that reason could discover, but a meaning nevertheless.

And would it not, in fact, be a meaning incomparably better than the other? For let us examine again the first kind of meaning it could have. Let us suppose that, without having any interest in rolling stones, as such, and finding this, in fact, a galling toil, Sisyphus did nevertheless have a deep interest in raising a temple, one that would be beautiful and lasting. And let us suppose he succeeded in this, that after ages of dreadful toil, all directed at this final result, he did at last complete his temple, such that now he could say his work was done, and he could rest and forever enjoy the result. Now what? What picture now presents itself to our minds? It is precisely the picture of infinite boredom! Of Sisyphus doing nothing ever again, but contemplating what he has already wrought and can no longer add anything to, and contemplating it for an eternity! Now in this picture we have a meaning for Sisyphus' existence, a point for his prodigious labor, because we have put it there; yet, at the same time, that which is really worthwhile seems to have slipped away entirely. Where before we were presented with the nightmare of eternal and pointless activity, we are now confronted with the hell of its eternal absence.

Our second picture, then, wherein we imagined Sisyphus to have had inflicted on him the irrational desire to be doing just what he found himself doing, should not have been dismissed so abruptly. The meaning that picture lacked was no meaning that he or anyone could crave, and the strange meaning it had was perhaps just what we were seeking.

At this point, then, we can reintroduce what has been until now, it is hoped, resolutely pushed aside in an effort to view our lives and human existence with objectivity; namely, our own wills, our deep interest in what we find ourselves doing. If we do this we find that our lives do indeed still resemble that of Sisyphus, but that the meaningfulness they thus lack is precisely the meaningfulness of infinite boredom. At the same time, the strange meaningfulness they possess is that of the inner compulsion to be doing just what we were put here to do, and to go on doing it forever. This is the nearest we may hope to get to heaven, but the redeeming side of that fact is that we do thereby avoid a genuine hell.

If the builders of a great and flourishing ancient civilization could somehow return now to see archaeologists unearthing the trivial remnants of what they had once accomplished with such effort—see the fragments of pots and vases, a few broken statues, and such tokens and another age and greatness —they could indeed ask themselves what the point of it all was, if this is all it finally came to. Yet, it did not seem so to them then, for it was just the building, and not what was finally built, that gave their life meaning. Similarly, if the builders of the ruined home and farm that I described a short while ago

could be brought back to see what is left, they would have the same feelings. What we construct in our imaginations as we look over these decayed and rusting pieces would reconstruct itself in their very memories, and certainly with unspeakable sadness. The piece of a sled at our feet would revive in them a warm Christmas. And what rich memories would there be in the broken crib? And the weed-covered remains of a fence would reproduce the scene of a great herd of livestock, so laboriously built up over so many years. What was it all worth, if this is the final result? Yet, again, it did not seem so to them through those many years of struggle and toil, and they did not imagine they were building a Gibraltar. The things to which they bent their backs day after day, realizing one by one their ephemeral plans, were precisely the things in which their wills were deeply involved, precisely the things in which their interests lay, and there was no need then to ask questions. There is no more need of them now—the day was sufficient to itself, and so was the life.

This is surely the way to look at all of life—at one's own life, and each day and moment it contains; of the life of a nation; of the species; of the life of the world; and of everything that breathes. Even the glow worms I described, whose cycles of existence over the millions of years seem so pointless when looked at by us, will seem entirely different to us if we can somehow try to view their existence from within. Their endless activity, which gets nowhere, is just what it is their will to pursue. This is its whole justification and meaning. Nor would it be any salvation to the birds who span the globe every year, back and forth, to have a home made for them in a cage with plenty of food and protection, so that they would not have to migrate any more. It would be their condemnation, for it is the doing that counts for them, and not what they hope to win by it. Flying these prodigious distances, never ending, is what it is in their veins to do, exactly as it was in Sisyphus' veins to roll stones, without end, after the gods had waxed merciful and implanted this in him.

A human being no sooner draws his first breath than he responds to the will that is in him to live. He no more asks whether it will be worthwhile, or whether anything of significance will come of it, than the worms and the birds. The point of his living is simply to be living, in the manner that it is his nature to be living. He goes through his life building his castles, each of these beginning to fade into time as the next is begun; yet, it would be no salvation to rest from all this. It would be a condemnation, and one that would in no way be redeemed were he able to gaze upon the things he has done, even if these were beautiful and absolutely permanent, as they never are. What counts is that one should be able to begin a new task, a new castle, a new bubble. It counts only because it is there to be done and he has the will to do it. The same will be the life of his children, and of theirs; and if the philosopher is apt to see in this a pattern similar to the unending cycles of the existence of Sisyphus, and to despair, then it is indeed because the meaning and point he is seeking is not there—but mercifully so. The meaning of life is from within us, it is not bestowed from without, and it far exceeds in both its beauty and permanence any heaven of which men have ever dreamed or yearned for.

The Meaning of Life

RAYMOND MARTIN

Poverty, sickness, loneliness, alienation, feelings of inferiority, an inability to give and receive love. Such problems can challenge the meaning of our lives. There is no puzzle about why. When we are afflicted with them, we suffer. If our suffering is bad enough and seemingly intractable, we may lose the sense that our lives are worth living.

Such problems are practically, but not philosophically, challenging. When they cause suffering that is avoidable, the important question is how to avoid it. When they cause suffering that is inevitable, the question is how to accept it. Learning how to avoid suffering when we can and accept it when we must are not part of the problem of the meaning of life. They are part of the problem of life.

Death also challenges the meaning of our lives. But in the case of death, unlike in the cases of the other problems mentioned, it is not clear why. What does the fact that our lives will come to an end have to do with whether they are worth living? There seems to be no connection. I shall suggest a partial answer.

The problem of the meaning of life is the philosophical question of how, if at all, our lives can be worth living. It concerns, for instance, such speculative questions as whether there is an overriding purpose or pattern for human life as a whole that confers meaning on our individual lives, and whether there is an objective source of value for our lives. The problem of life, on the other hand, is the practical question of how to live our lives so that they are as worth living as they can be. Clearly the problem of life is more important. In fact, it can seem so much more important that it is a tenet of practical wisdom that if we take proper care of our lives, questions of meaning will take care of themselves. That's good advice, unless you are the sort of person who *has* to address questions of meaning to take proper care of your life. Not everyone does, and even among those who do, questions of meaning will seem more important at some times than at others.

Tolstoy is the classic example of someone for whom questions of meaning can be urgent.

> . . . I was overcome by minutes at first of perplexity and then of an arrest of life, as though I did not know how to live or what to do, and I lost myself and was dejected. But that passed and I continued to live as before. Then those minutes of perplexity were repeated oftener and oftener, and always in one and the same form. These arrests of life found their expression in ever the same questions: "Why? Well, and then?"

At first I thought that those were simply aimless, inappropriate questions . . . [But they] began to repeat themselves oftener and oftener, answers were demanded more and more persistently, and, like dots that fall on the same spot, these questions, without any answers, thickened into one black blotch.

. . . And I was absolutely unable to make any reply. The questions were not waiting and I had to answer them at once; if I did not answer them, I could not live.[1]

Empathizing with Tolstoy's existential anguish can unravel our familiar everyday rationalizations and expose a secret need for understanding we keep buried deep within. Stripped of our pretensions, we look freshly—at our own lives, at the lives of those around us, at the lives of everyone who has ever lived—and we ask: Why? There is no answer. Just the silent, anxious echo of our question. And sometimes a nagging doubt.

There is something fishy about existential anguish. Even when it comes wrapped in the paper of respectable philosophical questioning, it often smells suspiciously like a rationalization of unmentioned problems. Tolstoy, for instance, portrays himself as one who would be happy, except for worries about the meaning of life. But is it really worries about the meaning of life that keep dragging him down? There are questions he can ask about the meaning of his life, doubts to be raised. But questions and doubts can be raised about anything. Questions are not necessarily problems. They can be. We can make a psychological problem out of almost anything. But how often are philosophical questions genuine psychological problems? When it seems that our philosophical questions give rise to existential anguish, should we marvel at the depth of our insight or suspect self-deception?

There is one familiar way philosophy can give rise to psychological problems. The naive person whose sense of security is built on a foundation of unquestioned beliefs can have those beliefs suddenly swept out from under him or her by philosophical questioning. Consider, for instance, a person whose sense of security rests on religious beliefs that suddenly become subject to doubt. The resulting turmoil can be so painfully confusing as to all into question the meaning of life.

Without minimizing this sort of problem, I wish to set it aside. The philosophical questioning which induces it usually directly challenges only the beliefs we depend on for security, not the meaning of our lives per se. The suffering comes not from some insoluble philosophical problem but from the sudden realization that our personal ideologies rest on dubious assumptions. Most people get over this realization quickly enough (usually too quickly), either by forgetting or ignoring their doubts or else by finding a new basis for security. I am asking whether there is a deeper and more direct philosophical challenge to the meaning of our lives which is at least as psychologically valid as the one that depends on philosophical naiveté, yet is not so easily set aside or outgrown.

In sum, I have distinguished three challenges to the meaning of our lives: bad times, death, and philosophical doubts of a sort that can arise even when our lives are going quite well. My concern, now, is with the third of these challenges. Putting aside problems caused by the realization that our personal ideologies rest on dubious assumptions, I am asking whether challenges of this third sort—that is, philosophical doubts about the meaning of our lives that can arise even when our lives are going quite well—are psychologically genuine. I don't deny that when our lives are going quite well, psychological problems can arise. I'm asking how likely it is that philosophical questions are the explanation. I admit they may sometimes be the explanation. I'm asking whether there isn't usually some deeper explanation, a source of anxiety and despair we may not be facing if we allow ourselves to become preoccupied with philosophy.

Thomas Nagel sets aside as unphilosophical those challenges to the meaning of life that arise because things go wrong and "are compatible with the possibility of meaning had things gone differently." Philosophical challenges to meaning, in his view, threaten human life with "objective meaninglessness" even when it is "at its subjective best." And he seems to think that philosophical challenges to meaning are a chronic source of deep psychological problems.

In seeing ourselves from outside we find it difficult to take our lives seriously. This loss of conviction, and the attempt to regain it, is the problem of the meaning of life.

　　. . . it is a genuine problem which we cannot ignore. The capacity for transcendence brings with it a liability to alienation. . . . Yet we can't abandon the external standpoint because it is our own.

It is our own, Nagel says, because the objective self is such a vital part of us that "to ignore its quasi-independent operation is to be cut off from oneself as much as if one were to abandon one's subjective individuality." So, in Nagel's view, there is no escape from this sort of alienation—"no credible way of eliminating the inner conflict"—and, hence, no solution to the philosophical problem of the meaning of life.

But there is help, Nagel thinks, and it comes from two sources:

[Morality] permits the objective assertion of subjective values to the extent that this is compatible with the corresponding claims of others. It . . . [involves] occupying a position far enough outside your own life to reduce the importance of the difference between yourself and other people, yet not so far outside that all human values vanish in a nihilistic blackout. . . .
　　. . . Humility falls between nihilistic detachment and blind self-importance. . . . The human race has a strong disposition to adore itself, in spite of its record. But it is possible to live a complete life of the kind one has been given without overvaluing it hopelessly.[2]

Even so, Nagel thinks that "the gap is too wide to be closed entirely, for anyone who is fully human." So, although morality and humility help, the problem is insoluble. Serious internal conflict remains. In sum, Nagel agrees with Tolstoy, though for different reasons, that philosophical challenges to the meaning of life are an important source of psychological problems.

If Nagel and Tolstoy are right, practical wisdom is wrong. Questions of meaning do not take care of themselves. If you are intellectually sensitive, then to take proper care of your life, you have to attend to questions about meaning. Tolstoy's self-portrait seems to show that these questions *can* bring you down. Nagel's view is that if you think honestly and correctly about questions of meaning, they *will* bring you down. Tolstoy solved his problem by embracing Christianity. Nagel claims there is no honest solution. Nagel's analysis of the philosophical issues is elegant. Yet his account, like Tolstoy's, is psychologically suspect.

To see why, think about a time when your life *was* at its subjective best. Maybe you were young and had just fallen deeply in love with someone who had just fallen deeply in love with you. Perhaps you were in the throes of sexual ecstasy or enveloped in mystical bliss. Or you may have played some instrument, or danced, or acted, or written much better than you ever thought you could. Perhaps you were simply drawn out of yourself by the muted texture of an autumn day or the vibrant sting of cold rain against your face.

Whatever your peak experiences, were you worried then about the meaning of life? Did *questions* about meaning *bother* you, that is, were they *problems* for you? Of course not. If your life really was at its subjective best, then probably it was insufficient: you lacked nothing. Because you had solved the problem of life, at least temporarily, questions about the meaning of life did not even arise. If such questions had been raised, you would have regarded them as an entertainment or, more likely, dismissed them as irrelevant. Perhaps, then, practical wisdom is right after all: how to live well is the only psychologically valid issue.

When we are happy, *questions* about the meaning of our lives rarely ever become *problems*. The solution to the *problem* of the meaning of life, then, is simple: be happy. The really important question is: how? Life is too short to try out many paths to happiness. We have to take our chances. And we have to take some of our most important chances when we are young and relatively inexperienced. Through ignorance or bad luck, people often choose the wrong paths to happiness and, as a consequence, suffer. Such bad choices are obviously an important source of suffering, particularly for people in circumstances sufficiently advantaged that they have the luxury of choice. But the fact that people make bad choices about how to be happy does not in and of itself give rise to *philosophical* problems about the meaning of our lives.

Like Nagel, Richard Taylor locates *philosophical* questions about the meaning of our lives in the tension between objective meaninglessness—for him, "endless pointlessness"—and subjective meaning. His view is that our lives are objectively meaningless, but not meaningless per se.

> At this point, then, we can reintroduce . . . our own wills, our deep interest in what we find ourselves doing. If we do this we find that our lives do indeed still resemble that of Sisyphus, but . . . the strange meaningfulness they possess is that of the inner compulsion to be doing just what we were put here to do, and to go on doing it forever.

In other words, the tasks people set for themselves, the things to which

> they bent their backs day after day, realizing one by one their ephemeral plans, were precisely the things in which their wills were deeply involved, precisely the things in which their interests lay, and there was no need then to ask questions. There is no more need of them now—the day was sufficient to itself, and so was the life. This is surely the way to look at all of life. . . .

So, in Taylor's view, subjective meaningfulness resides in activity in which our wills are involved.

> A human being no sooner draws his first breath than he responds to the will that is in him to live. He no more asks whether it will be worthwhile, or whether anything of significance will come of it, than the worms and the birds. The point of his living is simply to be living, in the manner that it is his nature to be living. . . . What counts is that one should be able to begin a new task, a new castle, a new bubble. It counts only because it is there to be done and he has the will to do it. . . . The meaning of life is from within us, it is not bestowed from without, and it far exceeds in both its beauty and permanence any heaven of which men have ever dreamed or yearned for.[3]

Taylor's view, in sum, is that the value derived from activity in which our wills are involved is enough to sustain the meaning of our lives, indeed, is as much as we can rationally hope for.

Is it? Looking around, we see people *willfully* building their castles and bubbles, so to speak, just as Taylor says they do, but not as *meaningfully* as he claims. Surely Thoreau was not all wrong when he observed that most people live in quiet desperation.

Taylor finds meaning everywhere. Nagel finds it nowhere. The saccharine sweetness of Taylor's conclusion makes Nagel's pessimism look appealing. But neither account feels psychologically valid. Taylor's is too romantic and makes meaning too easy. Nagel's is too intellectual and makes meaning too hard.

It is worth exploring the middle ground. A plausible view suggested by Taylor's discussion is that people have meaningful lives not when they are doing what they *will* to do but when they are doing what they *love* to do. Such a view seems to leave a place for meaningfulness without romanticizing human life. For most people are not doing what they love to do but, rather, what they have to do, or what they feel they have to do. The human spectacle is not a scene of yeoman farmers toiling happily in their fields. It includes a fair proportion of tired, unhappy people, resigned to their painful, dreary lives, trying desperately to distract and anesthetize themselves.

Meaning, then, on this criterion, is neither impossible nor inevitable. Nor is it all or nothing. It is a matter of degree. Is the answer, then, not that your life is or is not inherently meaningful but, rather, that it can be meaningful, and is meaningful largely to the degree that you are doing what you love to do? That seems a more likely hypothesis than the ones already considered. Yet, in its implicit suggestion that the main problem of meaning is the practical problem of finding out what you love to do and then doing it, this view too may be hopelessly romantic.

Oscar Wilde once remarked that there are only two problems in life: not getting what you want, and getting it. If Wilde is right, then what many people think is the whole problem—not getting what you want (or doing what you want to do)—is really only part of the problem. Ironically, the rest of the problem is what these same people think is the solution. It is hard to quarrel with that much of Wilde's observation. Getting what you want *can* be problematic. Wilde's remark also *suggests,* however, that getting what you want not only *can be* but *will be* problematic. If that's true, then our lives are an insoluble problem.

It is easy to see how not getting what you want can be a problem. And, if you want the wrong things —say, the pleasures of an unhealthy lifestyle—it's also easy to see how getting what you want can be a problem. But what if you want the right things— things that are not only good in themselves but also good for you. How could wanting the right things be a problem?

Think back to those times when your life was at its subjective best. Granted, at those comments you were not bothered by questions about the meaning of life. But were you completely satisfied? That's a loaded question. How could you ever know that you couldn't have been even more satisfied? So far as you could tell, then, were you completely satisfied? Probably you were. If you were, then it must be possible to be so happy that, so far as you can tell, you have all of your unsatisfied wants driven out of you —at least all of them that detract from your happiness. That may or may not be complete satisfaction. But it's close enough for most of us. And we sometimes get it. In and of itself, it's a solution, not a problem. But it inevitably leads to a problem, the real problem: *it doesn't last.*

Life is a tease. It promises more lasting satisfactions than it delivers. No matter how good it gets, eventually we always find ourselves wanting more. if we lose what was satisfying us completely, we want it back. If we keep it, we want more of it or else we want something else. And we will want in a way that detracts from our happiness. That's a psychological truth you can bet the farm on. Whatever you think is going to satisfy you completely, it is not going to satisfy you completely for long. It may for a while. If you are clever, you may even distract yourself from noticing that the itch of unsatisfied desire has returned. But if you look closely, you will see that what you wanted, what you may have thought would be enough, what you were sure would satisfy you completely, does not really do it.

Most of us have the dubious luxury of thinking that we would be happy if only we had something we

cannot have, or we were doing something we cannot do. Our deprivation nourishes the illusion that complete satisfaction—that lasts—is attainable, if only the external circumstances of our lives were better. Tolstoy did not have the luxury of that illusion. He had everything he wanted—wealth, fame, a loving family—and was doing what he wanted to do. Yet still he wasn't satisfied. He had so much that he couldn't imagine what more he wanted—unless perhaps it was answers. So he embraced answers, and then—so he would have us believe—he was happy. That is his story: that it was lack of answers that brought him down in the first place, and that it was his subsequent conviction that he had answers—his "irrational knowledge"—that made everything right again.

Perhaps. But another possibility is that Tolstoy's lack of answers was at most a symptom of the problem, not the real problem. Since he had everything and was doing what he wanted to be doing, what, then, could his real problem have been? It *could* have been simply that even with everything, Tolstoy's life did not stay at its subjective best: satisfied, he could not stay satisfied. The problem could have been that Tolstoy wanted his life to be at its subjective best but could not keep it there. So, when he came down, as inevitably he did, he wanted more, even though, as we say, "he had everything." In other words, the problem could have been simply that while life allowed him to taste complete satisfaction, it didn't last.

If not getting what you want (or not doing what you want to do) won't satisfy you completely, and getting what you want (or doing what you want to do) won't satisfy you completely either, it's worth thinking briefly about the extreme alternative: don't want. That's the essence of the Buddha Gautama's contribution to solving the problem of life. It may or may not be the right solution. We don't really have to decide. For even if it is the right solution, it is the Buddha's solution, not ours. We may give lip service to that solution, but few of us really see it as a realistic option for ourselves. If we did, we'd be off somewhere, perhaps meditating in a monastery in Burma, not taking college courses or reading essays like this one on the meaning of life. We may say we're on the "path." And we may be. But even on the path we still spend most of our waking time trying to get what we want. Except that on the path, in addition to all of the usual wants—security, sex, love, power, glory—we now have an unusual want: not wanting. The path is crowded with spiritual materialists.[4]

We're back to a realistic pessimism. The answer to the problem of the meaning of life may simply be that we're stuck with a life of fleeting satisfactions and unsatisfied desires. Whatever the value of morality and humility, they are precious little help in solving this problem. Doing what you love to do is a great help, probably the most important contribution you can make to the meaningfulness of your life. Ironically, doing what you love to do may even be a critical part of the most important contribution you can make to the lives of those around you. Even so, at least this side of enlightenment, there may be no fully satisfying solution to the problem of life.

Since satisfaction doesn't last, then either we have to continually resatisfy ourselves or successfully and pleasantly distract ourselves from the fact that we haven't. That seems to be our fate, and if we're reasonably good at these two tasks, it's not such a bad fate. But neither is it a fully satisfying solution to the problem of life. In other words, what I am suggesting is that the root psychological problem, the one that keeps arising even when our lives are going quite well, may simply be that we cannot satisfy ourselves completely for long. That is why even among people whose lives are going quite well, almost everyone is chronically unsatisfied. Acknowledging that this is the problem can bring us down from our philosophical heights. Back on earth, we can redirect our energies toward solving the problem of life. To do that, we follow our individual recipes for happiness: a fast car and a good woman, or whatever you think will do it for you.

The acknowledgment that there is no fully satisfying solution to the problem of life can quash our hopes that we will ever get the complete and lasting satisfaction we crave. That is one of the deepest and most emotionally significant hopes we have. True, that hope may never have survived rational scrutiny anyway, but that doesn't stop us from secretly nourishing it. It comes as a profound disappointment to finally admit, not just verbally, but completely, that whether we get what we want or not we will never stay satisfied for long.

And then there is death. Death has always been a puzzle for philosophers. Not what it is, but why we have some of the attitudes toward it we do. For present purposes, we can ignore most of these famous enigmas. Our question is this: Why does death threaten the meaning of our lives? Surely part of the answer is the familiar observation that we fear we may vanish without leaving a significant trace—that our lives will not have made a positive difference. But, of course, that should not be a problem for people, such as Tolstoy, whose lives have gone as well as possible and, hence, who have made a positive difference. There must be more than that to the challenge to meaning that death poses. The analysis just given suggests part of the answer.

Death threatens the meaningfulness of our lives partly because it ends our struggle for satisfaction. Because death kills us, the prospect that death is near kills the unspoken and irrational hope that if only we had a little more time, we might satisfy our need for psychological closure—for complete satisfaction. If we have already given up that hope, we will fear death less. We may even welcome it as a merciful release from a struggle we cannot help throwing ourselves into even though we know we shall never win it. In any case, death challenges the meaningfulness of our lives partly because the prospect that death is near makes it painfully obvious that we will lose the struggle for satisfaction. Death is a major symbol of defeat.

Return once again to those moments when your life was at its subjective best. Those moments brought complete satisfaction. And complete satisfaction is a kind of victory over death. A person, for instance, can be so much in love, so deeply satisfied, she feels that she could die and it wouldn't matter. When our experience gets that good, we have won the battle for satisfaction, and death holds no terror. The problem is that our victory is only temporary. Death is a persistent foe, and desire its ally. Satisfied, we cannot stay satisfied. The itch of desire returns, the struggle resumes. Until death ends the struggle—perhaps forever.

Notes

1. Leo Tolstoy's reflections on the meaning of life are in his book, *My Confession*, translated by Leo Wiener, Dent and Sons, 1905.

2. Thomas Nagel's thoughts on the meaning of life were published originally in his essay, "The Absurd," *The Journal of Philosophy*, v. 63, 1971, pp. 716–727. The passages quoted are taken from that portion of Nagel's *The View from Nowhere*, New York: Oxford University Press, 1986, 214–223, that is reprinted in the present volume.

3. Richard Taylor's views are from his book, *Good and Evil*, New York: Macmillan, 1970. They are reprinted in the present volume.

4. I have borrowed the notion of "spiritual materialism" from Chögyam Trungpa, *Cutting Through Spiritual Materialism*, Boulder, Colorado: Shambhala Publications, 1973.

The Value of Philosophy

BERTRAND RUSSELL

Having now come to the end of our brief and very incomplete review of the problems of philosophy, it will be well to consider, in conclusion, what is the value of philosophy and why it ought to be studied. It is the more necessary to consider this question, in view of the fact that many men, under the influence of science or of practical affairs, are inclined to doubt whether philosophy is anything better than innocent but useless trifling, hair-splitting distinctions, and controversies on matters concerning which knowledge is impossible.

This view of philosophy appears to result, partly from a wrong conception of the ends of life, partly from a wrong conception of the kind of goods which philosophy strives to achieve. Physical science, through the medium of inventions, is useful to innumerable people who are wholly ignorant of it; thus the study of physical science is to be recommended, not only, or primarily, because of the effect on the student, but rather because of the effect on mankind in general. Thus utility does not belong to philosophy. If the study of philosophy has any value at all for others than students of philosophy, it must be only indirectly, through its effects upon the lives of those who study it. It is in these effects, therefore, if anywhere, that the value of philosophy must be primarily sought.

But further, if we are not to fail in our endeavour to determine the value of philosophy, we must first free our minds from the prejudices of what are wrongly called "practical" men. The "practical" man, as this word is often used, is one who recognizes only material needs, who realizes that men must have food for the body, but is oblivious of the necessity of providing food for the mind. If all men were well off, if poverty and disease had been reduced to their lowest possible point, there would still remain much to be done to produce a valuable society; and even in the existing world the goods of the mind are at least as important as the goods of the body. It is exclusively among the goods of the mind that the value of philosophy is to be found; and only those who are not indifferent to these goods can be persuaded that the study of philosophy is not a waste of time.

Philosophy, like all other studies, aims primarily at knowledge. The knowledge it aims at is the kind of knowledge which gives unity and system to the body of the sciences, and the kind which results from a critical examination of the grounds of our convictions, prejudices, and beliefs. But it cannot be maintained that philosophy has had any very great measure of success in its attempts to provide definite answers to its questions. If you ask a mathematician, a mineralogist, a historian, or any other man of learning, what definite body of truths has been ascertained by his science, his answer will last as long as you are willing to listen. But if you put the same question to a philosopher, he will, if he is candid, have to confess that his study has not achieved positive results such as have been achieved by other sciences. It is true that this is partly accounted for by the fact that, as soon as definite knowledge concerning

From *The Problems of Philosophy* by Bertrand Russell (1912).

any subject becomes possible, this subject ceases to be called philosophy, and becomes a separate science. The whole study of the heavens, which now belongs to astronomy, was once included in philosophy; Newton's great work was called 'the mathematical principles of natural philosophy.' Similarly, the study of the human mind, which was a part of philosophy, has now been separated from philosophy and has become the science of psychology. Thus, to a great extent, the uncertainty of philosophy is more apparent than real: those questions which are already capable of definite answers are placed in the sciences, while those only to which, at present, no definite answer can be given, remain to form the residue which is called philosophy.

This is, however, only a part of the truth concerning the uncertainty of philosophy. There are many questions—and among them those that are of the profoundest interest to our spiritual life—which, so far as we can see, must remain insoluble to the human intellect unless its powers become of quite a different order from what they are now. . . . Has the universe any unity of plan or purpose, or is it a fortuitous concourse of atoms? Is consciousness a permanent part of the universe, giving hope of indefinite growth in wisdom, or is it a transitory accident on a small planet on which life must ultimately become impossible? Are good and evil of importance to the universe or only to man? Such questions are asked by philosophy, and variously answered by various philosophers. But it would seem that, whether answers be otherwise discoverable or not, the answers suggested by philosophy are none of them demonstrably true. Yet, however slight may be the hope of discovering an answer, it is part of the business of philosophy to continue the consideration of such questions, to make us aware of their importance, to examine all the approaches to them, and to keep alive that speculative interest in the universe which is apt to be killed by confining ourselves to definitely ascertainable knowledge.

Many philosophers, it is true, have held that philosophy could establish the truth of certain answers to such fundamental questions. They have supposed that what is of most importance in religious beliefs could be proved by strict demonstration to be true. In order to judge of such attempts, it is necessary to take a survey of human knowledge, and to form an

opinion as to its methods and its limitations. On such a subject it would be unwise to pronounce dogmatically; but if the investigations of our previous chapters have not led us astray, we shall be compelled to renounce the hope of finding philosophical proofs of religious beliefs. We cannot, therefore, include as part of the value of philosophy any definite set of answers to such questions. Hence, once more, the value of philosophy must not depend upon any supposed body of definitely ascertainable knowledge to be acquired by those who study it.

The value of philosophy is, in fact, to be sought largely in its very uncertainty. The man who has no tincture of philosophy goes through life imprisoned in the prejudices derived from common sense, from the habitual beliefs of his age or his nation, and from convictions which have grown up in his mind without the co-operation or consent of his deliberate reason. To such a man the world tends to become definite, finite, obvious; common objects rouse no questions, and unfamiliar possibilities are contemptuously rejected. As soon as we begin to philosophize, on the contrary, we find . . . that even the most everyday things lead to problems to which only very incomplete answers can be given. Philosophy, though unable to tell us with certainty what is the true answer to the doubts which it raises, is able to suggest many possibilities which enlarge our thoughts and free them from the tyranny of custom. Thus, while diminishing our feeling of certainty as to what things are, it greatly increases our knowledge as to what they may be; it removes the somewhat arrogant dogmatism of those who have never travelled into the region of liberating doubt, and it keeps alive our sense of wonder by showing familiar things in an unfamiliar aspect.

Apart from its utility in showing unsuspected possibilities, philosophy has a value—perhaps its chief value—through the greatness of the objects which it contemplates, and the freedom from narrow and personal aims resulting from this contemplation. The life of the instinctive man is shut up within the circle of his private interests: family and friends may be included, but the outer world is not regarded except as it may help or hinder what comes within the circle of instinctive wishes. In such a life there is something feverish and confined, in comparison with which the philosophic life is calm and free. The private world of instinctive interest is a small one, set in the midst of a great and powerful world which must, sooner or later, lay our private world in ruins. Unless we can so enlarge our interests as to include the whole outer world, we remain like a garrison in a beleaguered fortress, knowing that the enemy prevents escape and that ultimate surrender is inevitable. In such a life there is no peace, but a constant strife between the insistence of desire and the powerlessness of will. In one way or another, if our life is to be great and free, we must escape this prison and this strife.

One way of escape is by philosophic contemplation. Philosophic contemplation does not, in its widest survey, divide the universe into two hostile camps —friends and foes, helpful and hostile, good and bad—it views the whole impartially. Philosophic contemplation, when it is unalloyed, does not aim at proving that the rest of the universe is akin to man. All acquisition of knowledge is an enlargement of the Self, but this enlargement is best attained when it is not directly sought. It is best obtained when the desire for knowledge is alone operative, by a study which does not wish in advance that its objects should have this or that character, but adapts the Self to the characters which it finds in its objects. This enlargement of Self is not obtained when, taking the Self as it is, we try to show that the world is so similar to this Self that knowledge of it is possible without any admission of what seems alien. The desire to prove this is a form of self-assertion and, like all self-assertion, it is an obstacle to the growth of Self which it desires, and of which the Self knows that it is capable. Self-assertion, in philosophic speculation as elsewhere, views the world as a means to its own ends; thus it makes the world of less account than Self, and the Self sets bounds to the greatness of its goods. In contemplation, on the contrary, we start from the non-Self, and through its greatness the boundaries of Self are enlarged; through the infinity of the universe the mind which contemplates it achieves some share in infinity.

For this reason greatness of soul is not fostered by those philosophies which assimilate the universe to Man. Knowledge is a form of union of Self and not-Self; like all union, it is impaired by dominion, and therefore by any attempt to force the universe into conformity with what we find in ourselves.

There is a widespread philosophical tendency towards the view which tells us that Man is the measure of all things, that truth is man-made, that space and time and the world of universals are properties of the mind, and that, if there be anything not created by the mind, it is unknowable and of no account for us. This view . . . is untrue; but in addition to being untrue, it has the effect of robbing philosophic contemplation of all that gives it value, since it fetters contemplation to Self. What it calls knowledge is not a union with the not-Self, but a set of prejudices, habits, and desires, making an impenetrable veil between us and the world beyond. The man who finds pleasure in such a theory of knowledge is like the man who never leaves the domestic circle for fear his word might not be law.

The true philosophic contemplation, on the contrary, finds its satisfaction in every enlargement of the not-Self, in everything that magnifies the objects contemplated, and thereby the subject contemplating. Everything, in contemplation, that is personal or private, everything that depends upon habit, self-interest, or desire, distorts the object, and hence impairs the union which the intellect seeks. By thus making a barrier between subject and object, such personal and private things become a prison to the intellect. The free intellect will see as God might see, without a *here* and *now*, without hopes and fears, without the trammels of customary beliefs and traditional prejudices, calmly, dispassionately, in the sole and exclusive desire of knowledge—knowledge as impersonal, as purely contemplative, as it is possible for man to attain. Hence also the free intellect will value more the abstract and universal knowledge into which the accidents of private history do not enter, than the knowledge brought by the senses, and dependent, as such knowledge must be, upon an exclusive and personal point of view and a body whose sense-organs distort as much as they reveal.

The mind which has become accustomed to the freedom and impartiality of philosophic contemplation will preserve something of the same freedom and impartiality in the world of action and emotion. It will view its purposes and desires as parts of the whole, with the absence of insistence that results from seeing them as infinitesimal fragments in a world of which all the rest is unaffected by any one man's deeds. The impartiality which, in contemplation, is the unalloyed desire for truth, is the very same quality of mind which, in action, is justice, and in emotion is that universal love which can be given to all, and not only to those who are judged useful or admirable. Thus contemplation enlarges not only the objects of our thoughts, but also the objects of our actions and our affections: it makes us citizens of the universe, not only of one walled city at war with all the rest. In this citizenship of the universe consists man's true freedom, and his liberation from the thraldom of narrow hopes and fears.

Thus, to sum up our discussion of the value of philosophy; Philosophy is to be studied, not for the sake of any definite answers to its questions, since no definite answers can, as a rule, be known to be true, but rather for the sake of the questions themselves; because these questions enlarge our conception of what is possible, enrich our intellectual imagination and diminish the dogmatic assurance which closes the mind against speculation; but above all because, through the greatness of the universe which philosophy contemplates, the mind also is rendered great, and becomes capable of that union with the universe which constitutes its highest good.

Writing a Philosophical Paper

HOPE MAY

In most philosophy classes, you will be asked to write a paper. Writing a good philosophical paper demands different skills than those that are typically required for writing a good paper in other academic disciplines such as English or history. A philosophical paper is not a short story, a report on a short story, or a recapitulation of certain events. A philosophical paper is also no mere description of your beliefs about a specific philosophical issue.

What, then, is characteristic of a philosophical paper? Although there are different kinds of philosophical papers, all of them are *argumentative.* By argumentative, I do not mean belligerent or quarrelsome. An argument can be thought of as *the reasons that one has for believing a certain claim.* For instance, suppose that you believe that the death penalty is morally wrong, and suppose that you were asked *why* you believe that the death penalty is morally wrong. If you were to say something like "I believe that the death penalty is wrong because I believe that killing another human being is always wrong," then you would be articulating the reasons that you have for your belief. In other words, you would be presenting an *argument* in support of the claim that the death penalty is morally wrong. This is the sort of thing that one does in an argumentative paper.

However, articulating the reasons why you have a certain belief is not the only thing that you will do in an argumentative paper. Reasons can be *good* or *bad.** In an argumentative paper, then, you will also

have to determine whether the reasons for believing a certain claim are good or bad. In other words, you will have to evaluate the arguments that are discussed in your paper.

One obstacle encountered by students beginning to write philosophical papers is knowing how to effectively construct and evaluate arguments. This obstacle arises because the writing assignments to which most students are accustomed usually do not require the construction and evaluation of arguments. In addition, most students have not been trained either to construct or to evaluate arguments that are unrelated to writing assignments. One usually learns how to construct and evaluate arguments in a logic class, but unfortunately, most beginning students in philosophy have little or no knowledge of logic. The problem, then, is not merely that most students are unpracticed in writing argumentative papers. It is more serious than that. Most students are simply unfamiliar with arguments and the techniques used to evaluate them. Yet, writing a successful philosophy paper requires the student to both discuss and evaluate arguments.

Below, I offer some suggestions that should help you write a good philosophical paper. These suggestions assume that you know something about (a) what an argument is, (b) how to determine a philosopher's argument (or "point of view") for a specific claim, and (c) how to evaluate an argument. If you are fuzzy about any of these things, then you should read the sections entitled *"Argumentative Structure"* and *"Evaluation"* in the selection "Reading a Philosophical Text" in Part 1 of this book. If you

---

*I would like to thank Robert McGee and Jason Ellenburg for their useful suggestions on earlier drafts of this essay.

How to Write a Philosophy Paper

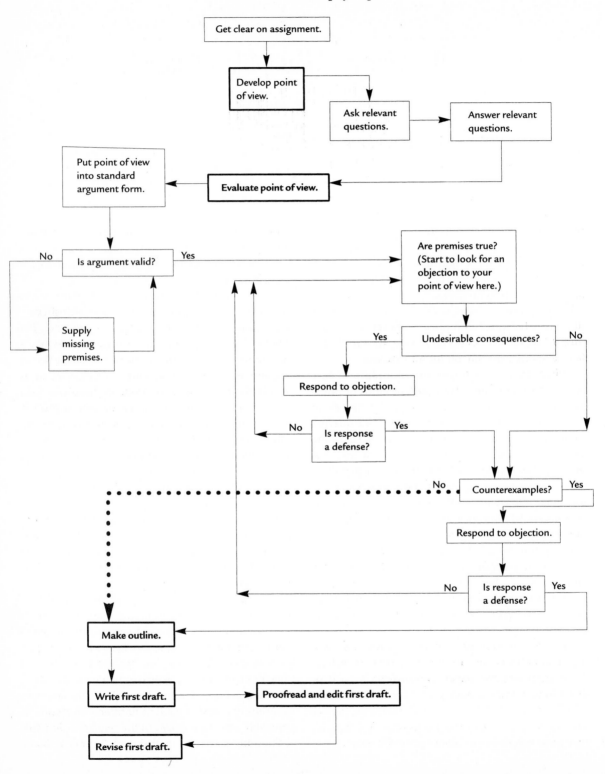

are still unsure about arguments and/or their evaluation after reading these sections, ask your professor to explain them to you. Without a solid understanding of arguments, you cannot write a good philosophy paper.

GENERAL STRATEGIES

In addition to the fact that students are usually unfamiliar with philosophical arguments and with writing argumentative papers, there are two other obstacles encountered by students beginning to write philosophical papers. The first concerns the *content* of the philosophical paper, and the second concerns its *structure*. Let's look at each of these obstacles and some strategies for dealing with each.

CONTENT

The Nature of Your Assignment

Although all papers assigned in philosophy classes will require you to discuss and evaluate arguments, there are different ways of undertaking these tasks. Usually, your professor will specify a particular format in which you will have to discuss and criticize an argument. It is crucial that you understand exactly what your assignment requires of you. Sometimes you will be asked to write about a specific philosophical issue such as the morality of abortion. Or, you might be asked to critically examine the arguments either for or against a certain philosophical position. Another common writing assignment is called an *argument reconstruction*. If you are assigned an argument reconstruction, you will be asked to reconstruct and evaluate a specific argument given by a particular philosopher. If you are asked to articulate and to criticize Aristotle's argument for the claim that happiness consists in excellent rational activity, for example, then you have been assigned an argument reconstruction.

Before you start writing, make sure that you clearly understand the assignment. Are you writing about a specific philosophical issue? Are you writing about a certain position on a philosophical issue? Or are you reconstructing an argument? If you clearly understand the nature of the assignment, you should be able to state, in your own words, what it requires

you to do. Imagine that a classmate is absent on the day that the paper assignment is distributed, and that she calls you to find out what it is. Can you tell her what she needs to do in your own words? If you cannot, you do not have a good grasp of the assignment.

Thinking Before Writing

Even more important than getting clear on the nature of your assignment is getting clear on its *focus*. Clarifying your paper's focus requires that you do some thinking before you start your writing. In fact, most of the work that goes into a good philosophy paper consists in thinking. Thinking for a sufficient amount of time will help you determine the focus of your paper, and once you do this, actually *writing* the paper is relatively easy.

In order to clarify your paper's focus, it is crucial that you develop a point of view (P.O.V.) on the issue about which you will be writing. Think of a P.O.V. as a *reasoned* position on an issue about which there is disagreement. If you can explain to others why you believe that abortion should be legal in certain circumstances, for instance, you have a P.O.V. on this issue. Philosophy papers that are written by students who lack a clear P.O.V. are muddled and very difficult to read. Thus, it is important for you to develop your own P.O.V. for the purposes of your assignment. Developing a P.O.V., however, requires that you do some thinking.

Developing a Point of View

The *breadth* of the P.O.V. that you will need to develop will vary from assignment to assignment. Most writing assignments for philosophy classes will ask you to develop a relatively narrow or circumscribed P.O.V.—a P.O.V. about a specific argument, a specific claim, or a specific counterexample. When developing a narrow P.O.V., one's thinking is very reigned in, very circumscribed, and very focused. On the other hand, sometimes you will be asked to develop a broader point of view on, for instance, the nature of knowledge or morality. It is crucial that you understand just how broad or narrow your P.O.V. needs to be. Many students beginning to write philosophical papers do much more than they need to and write about things that they are not asked to write about.

Sometimes, for instance, students write about everything they know of a certain issue, even when they asked to write about one very specific thing. I call this the "kitchen sink" syndrome, others call it "missing the mark." Students are a victim of this syndrome when they are unclear about what the assignment requires of them and about how broad or narrow their P.O.V. needs to be.

To illustrate that points of view vary in breadth and scope, consider the following assignment:

A   Classical (or "act") utilitarianism has been criticized as being incompatible with individual rights. Write a 1000- to 2000-word essay that describes this criticism, and explain whether you believe this criticism is a good one.

This is a very specific assignment that is concerned with the adequacy of a particular argument that is aimed against a theory of morality known as classical or act utilitarianism. According to this theory, an action is morally right if, given several courses of action, it produces the greatest amount of happiness for all of those involved.

Note that in order to do the above assignment well, it is not enough that you understand the individual rights criticism aimed against utilitarianism. You also need to explain *why* you believe this criticism is good or bad, and in doing so you are asked for your P.O.V. on the issue. This P.O.V. is rather narrow. It is focused on a specific argument *against* utilitarianism and on whether you believe that this argument is good or bad. Contrast the above assignment with this one:

B   Write a 1000- to 2000-word essay on the meaning of Protagoras's famous claim, "Man is the measure of all things." In your essay, make sure you discuss at least two different ways of interpreting this claim, and state your reasons for preferring one interpretation over the other.

To complete this assignment successfully, you are required to develop a P.O.V. that is much broader than the one that you need to develop to complete assignment A. For here, you are not asked to develop a P.O.V. about a certain argument, as you are above. Rather, you are asked to develop a P.O.V. about the *meaning* of a certain claim.

Points of view, then, come in different scopes and sizes. In order to develop a P.O.V. for the purposes of writing your paper, you need to determine just how broad or narrow it needs to be. If you understand your assignment, this should be a relatively easy task.

After you determine how broad or narrow your P.O.V. must be, there are only two more steps that you need to complete in order to develop a P.O.V. You should set aside some time for these steps. How much time? At least two days for most assignments, but a week is ideal.

Step 1: Asking the Relevant Questions

Philosophical points of view are *generated* by *philosophical questions.** Importantly, a certain point of view is not *the* answer to a philosophical question but is rather a *possible* answer. Each philosophical question has several possible answers that comprise several possible points of view. In fact, philosophical theories, all of which are points of view, are just very sophisticated answers to certain questions. Classical utilitarianism, for example, is one answer, one point of view, in response to the question, What makes an action morally right? And Protagoras's claim that "man is the measure of all things" is one answer, one point of view, in response to the question, Do certain aspects of reality outstrip human experience?

The first step in developing a P.O.V., then, is to *ask yourself the relevant questions.* The relevant questions, however, will vary from assignment to assignment. Sometimes the questions, Do I think that this argument is a good one? and Why do I think this? are the only relevant questions that one needs to ask in order to develop a P.O.V. On the other hand, sometimes the relevant questions will be, Which theory of morality is the strongest? and What are my reasons for thinking this?

Clearly understanding the nature of your assignment will help you determine the relevant questions. Consider assignment A above. In order to do this assignment successfully, you need to develop your P.O.V. about whether the individual rights criticism aimed against classical utilitarianism is flawed. Thus, the questions that you should be asking yourself

---

*See "Familiarizing Yourself with the Terrain" in *"Reading a Philosophical Text"* for review.

in order to construct a P.O.V. for this assignment are, Do I think that the individual rights argument against classical utilitarianism is flawed? and Why do I think this? *That is all.* You are not asked to state your P.O.V. on the nature of morality, or even on classical utilitarianism, for that matter. You are simply asked to articulate your P.O.V. on a specific argument that is raised against classical utilitarianism.

Next, consider assignment B above. In order to do this assignment successfully, you need to develop your P.O.V. about the meaning of Protagoras's statement, and you need to explain why you think this. Here, the relevant questions that you need to ask yourself are, What are at least two things that this claim could mean? and What are my reasons for preferring one interpretation over another?

Step 2: Answering the Relevant Questions

The second step in developing a P.O.V. is *answering* the relevant questions. But as you will see "answering" here means something very specific, and it requires you to do much more than simply making an assertion.

After casually asking yourself the relevant questions (do this for at least one day), sit down with a piece of paper and write down your answer to these questions. Suppose that one of the relevant questions is, Is the individual rights argument against classical utilitarianism flawed? And suppose your answer is yes. Then you would write down:

Is the individual rights argument against classical utilitarianism flawed? In my view, it is.

But in order to develop a P.O.V., one does not just bluntly state one's answers to the relevant questions. A P.O.V., remember, is a *reasoned* position on an issue about which there is disagreement. Therefore, you also need to ask *why* you believe that your answer to the relevant question is the right one. The assignment above explicitly asks for an explanation as to why one has the P.O.V. that one does. Hence, you must ask, Why do I believe that the individual rights argument against classical utilitarianism is flawed? in order to complete this assignment. Although *your* assignment may not ask you to explain why you have your P.O.V., you should *always* do this in a philosophical paper. The activity of philosophy requires

one to explain one's beliefs. Thus, a question that is always philosophically relevant, regardless of the assignment, is Why do I believe this? It might take you some time to answer this question, but it is crucial that you do.

You need to be very thorough when explaining why you have the answer that you do. For instance, you might say that you believe that the individual rights argument against classical utilitarianism is flawed because this argument depends on a misapprehension of the theory. But in a philosophical paper, you have to spell out exactly what this means. You have to explain, in other words *how* and *in what way* this argument misapprehends the theory. When you are explaining yourself in a philosophical paper, make sure that you use examples to illustrate your claims. These examples may take the form of metaphors and analogies. Note how our author below supports her answer with clear examples:

Is the individual rights argument against classical utilitarianism flawed? In my view, it is because this argument depends on a misapprehension of the theory. This argument alleges that if the morally right action is defined as one that produces the maximum amount of happiness of the majority (given the alternatives), and if we can maximize the happiness of the majority by violating someone's rights, then according to this theory, it is morally right to violate someone's rights. But since it is not morally right to violate someone's rights, the objection goes, then classical utilitarianism must be false.

For example, if we stole Bill Gates's money and redistributed it to middle-class Americans, this would maximize the happiness of the majority. According to utilitarianism, however, this would be the morally right action to perform. So if one accepts utilitarianism, then one must accept that it is morally right to steal and redistribute Bill Gates's money. But this seems false; therefore, utilitarianism must be false.

This seems to me to be a bad argument. For despite appearances, stealing Bill Gates's money *would not* maximize happiness in the long run. People would start to feel guilty, would fear that someone might violate their rights and steal from them, and so on. At best, stealing Bill Gates's money would give people instant gratification, but misery would eventually be waiting down the road. For these reasons, it seems to me that happiness can never be maximized if one does not respect individual rights, so one cannot argue that utilitarianism is incompatible with rights. This is why I believe that the criticism that says that utilitarianism is incompatible with rights is flawed.

In the second paragraph, our author provides a concrete example that clearly illustrates the objection. And in the third paragraph, our author uses this example in order to explain that it, and hence the objection against utilitarianism, is flawed. This is the sort of thing that you should do in your paper. For it not only shows that you have a good grasp of the issues, but it also makes your paper much more readable. When you are providing your answers to the relevant questions, use concrete examples to illustrate your claims. Doing so will enable both you and your reader to better understand your P.O.V.

Evaluating Your Point of View

Asking and answering the relevant questions is all that you need to do in order to develop a P.O.V. After completing these steps, however, you must *evaluate* your P.O.V. in order to determine whether it has any weaknesses. To demonstrate that you have evaluated your P.O.V., in your paper you should *always* raise and respond to at least one objection to it. Some assignments will explicitly ask you to do this, but it is good practice to do this *all* of the time, even when you are not explicitly asked to do so. Raising and responding to an objection shows the reader that you have thought about and understand your P.O.V. and that you are able to rationally defend it in the face of objections. Below, I provide some tips that will help you to both raise and respond to an objection to your P.O.V.

Putting Your Point of View into Standard Argument Form

Evaluating your P.O.V. amounts to evaluating an *argument*. So the first thing you should do is put your P.O.V. into standard argument form. In other words, write your answer to the relevant question as the *conclusion* to a *deductive* argument, and the reasons for believing your answer as its *premises*. Number the premises and draw a horizontal line that separates the premises from the conclusion. Thus:

1. The criticism that classical utilitarianism is incompatible with rights rests on a misapprehension of the theory.

The criticism that classical utilitarianism is incompatible with rights is flawed.

After you translate your P.O.V. into standard argument form, you should then evaluate it as you would evaluate a deductive argument. As you know, one evaluates a deductive argument by first determining whether the argument is valid and then determining whether the premises are true.

Determining the Validity of Your Argument

In order to determine whether your argument is valid, you have to ask, *If* the premises are true, *must* the conclusion be true? Look at the argument above. *If* it is true that the criticism that classical utilitarianism is incompatible with rights rests on a misapprehension of the theory, *must* it be true that it is flawed? If you think about it, you will realize that, technically speaking, this argument is *invalid*. It may *seem* like the premise provides good grounds for the conclusion, but strictly speaking, in order for this argument to be valid, one needs to add the claim, "any criticism of a theory that rests on a misapprehension of that theory is flawed" as an additional premise. To be sure, everybody believes that a criticism of a theory is flawed if that criticism misapprehends that theory, and this is precisely why our author did *not* explicitly state it in the paragraph above. However, the statement, "any criticism of a theory that rests on a misapprehension of that theory is flawed" is fueling the above line of reasoning, and you need to make explicit any premise that is relevant to the validity of your argument.

If you discover that your argument is invalid after putting it into standard argument form, then you need to supply premises that will turn your invalid argument into a valid one. Putting your P.O.V. into standard argument form, then, will sometimes require you to make explicit claims that are implicit in your P.O.V. Our author supplies her missing premise in the argument below:

1. The criticism that classical utilitarianism is incompatible with rights rests on a misapprehension of the theory.
[2.] Any criticism of a theory that rests on a mis-
apprehension of that theory is flawed.
The criticism that classical utilitarianism is incompatible with rights is flawed.

Note how the second premise is bracketed. A premise that is bracketed indicates that it is not explicitly stated in the P.O.V. When you write out your P.O.V. as an argument in standard form, make sure that you elucidate the relevant implicit claims by including them as bracketed premises in your argument.

Sometimes bracketed premises will be incontrovertible such as "any criticism of a theory that rests on a misapprehension of that theory is flawed." Sometimes, however, you will realize that you are assuming premises that are more problematic. In other words, premises that you supply may seem to you to be false or may be objectionable to others. For example, suppose that you believe that God exists and that your reason for doing so is the fact that your parents told you that God exists. Then your argument is:

1. My parents told me that God exists.
God exists.

This is surely an invalid argument. Just because your parents tell you something does not make it true. But if you supply a premise that says your parents have and will always tell the truth, then the argument becomes valid:

[1.] My parents have and will always tell the truth.
2. My parents told me that God exists.
God exists.

The argument is now valid, but perhaps you think the bracketed premise is problematic. For it is unlikely (but not impossible) that your parents have and will always tell the truth. How could you ever know this?

If the above premise is problematic, however, this is a *separate* criticism of the argument, one that

concerns the *truth* of the premises. But at this point, we are only trying to put our P.O.V. into a *valid* argument form. And as you know, an argument can be valid even if it has false premises. The above argument passes its first evaluation test, but perhaps you think it fails the second. This brings us to the second question that one asks in order to evaluate an argument, namely, Are the premises true?

Determining the Truth of Your Premises

After putting your P.O.V. into the form of a deductively valid argument, you now need to ask, Are the premises true? Recall our author's P.O.V:

1. The criticism that classical utilitarianism is incompatible with rights rests on a misapprehension of the theory.
[2.] Any criticism of a theory that rests on a mis-
apprehension of that theory is flawed.
The criticism that classical utilitarianism is incompatible with rights is flawed.

Premise [2] seems incontestable: Something that is a misapprehension is surely flawed. But what about the first premise? Is it true that there is a flaw in the criticism that says that utilitarianism is incompatible with rights? This question is perhaps the most difficult part of developing a P.O.V. because it requires you to step back and look at your answers as an outsider. Asking whether your premises are true requires you to be self-critical.

Raising an Objection to Your Point of View

Determining whether your premises are true is the precise stage at which you should begin to look for an objection to your P.O.V. For when you raise an objection to your P.O.V in your paper, *you should imagine someone arguing that at least one of your premises is false.* One can argue that a premise is false in two different ways, however. On the one hand, one can argue that a premise is false by showing that it implies undesirable consequences. On the other hand, one can argue that a premise is false by showing that there are counterexamples to the premise. So when you are determining whether your premises are true, you need to ask two separate questions: (1) Do any of my premises imply any undesirable consequences? and (2) Are any of my premises subject to counterexamples? If you answer yes to any of these questions, then you have raised an objection that says that one of your premises is false.

Determining Whether Your Premises Imply Undesirable Consequences

In order to determine whether your premises are true or false, then, first look at each one and ask, Does this claim imply any undesirable consequences? A consequence of a P.O.V. is just a statement that must be true if that P.O.V. is true. If, for example, the statement "all men are mortal" is true, then it also must be true that "no men are not mortal." Thus, "no men are not mortal" is a consequence of "all men are mortal."

Now if one of your premises implies an *undesirable* consequence, this is a good reason for thinking that this premise is false. Consider the premise "one should always tell the truth." Let's determine if this statement is false by asking if it implies any undesirable consequences. At first glance, it does not seem that it does. Truth telling is a virtue in our society, and we praise individuals for adhering to this practice. Nevertheless, perhaps there are some cases in which one should not tell the truth. For instance, suppose that a mentally unstable ex-boyfriend of a good friend of yours asks you where she is. Should you lie and say "I do not know?" If your intuition is that you *should* lie in this case, then the premise "one should always tell the truth" is problematic. For if it is true that "one should always tell the truth," then it must be true that there are *no* cases where truth telling is wrong. But the latter claim seems to conflict with our intuition that there are some cases wherein truth telling *is* wrong. One could argue, then, that the premise "one should always tell the truth" is false because it seems to have undesirable consequences.

Determining Whether There Are Counterexamples to Your Premises

Another way of arguing that a premise is false, and hence of raising an objection to your P.O.V, is by showing that it is subject to a counterexample. Consider the claim mentioned above, "my parents have and will always tell the truth." Are there any counterexamples to this claim? A counterexample is simply an instance that shows that some claim is false. If your parents have told you that Santa, the tooth fairy, or the Easter Bunny exists, then these are all counterexamples because, sadly, Santa, the tooth fairy, and the Easter Bunny do *not* exist. Similarly, if you can imagine a single case wherein it is wrong to tell the truth, then you have discovered a counterexample for the claim that "one should always tell the truth." Finding a counterexample to a claim can sometimes be difficult, but it is an excellent way of arguing that a particular claim is false.

If you find that one or more of your premises either has undesirable consequences or is subject to counterexamples, or both, then you have raised an objection to your P.O.V. In your paper, make sure that you raise at least one objection to your P.O.V. Once you raise an objection to your P.O.V. you need to *respond* to it.

Responding to an Objection: Defending Your Point of View

You can respond to an objection in several ways. One way is to *explain the objection away*. In other words, you can explain why the objection is not a very good one. For instance, if someone argued that the claim "one should always tell the truth" is false because it implies undesirable consequences (for example, lying is never right), you respond by saying something like "situations in which lying is right never arise," or "it may *seem* like it is right to lie in some cases, but it is not because . . ." In responding in this way, you are informing your interlocutor that their objection is not a very good one and hence are explaining the objection away. In responding this way, you are *defending* your P.O.V.

Responding to an Objection: Altering Your Point of View

Two other ways in which you can respond to an objection are (1) discarding your view for a completely different one, or (2) modifying your view. It should be noted that one danger you might encounter during the modification of your view is introducing your modification *ad hoc*. In other words, you might introduce a modification for the sole purpose of saving a claim that has been criticized. Consider the following example: Suppose that you wanted to hold on to the claim that your parents have and will always tell the truth, even though your parents told you that Santa Claus exists. You could modify the claim "my parents have and will always tell the truth" to "my parents have and will always tell the truth, except when they talk about Santa." This modification would sidestep the objection, but it would weaken your argument. Your interlocutor can object to this by asking how you know that your parents are not lying when they talk about God, for example.

Choosing to either discard or modify your P.O.V. is not a *defense* of your P.O.V but an *alteration* of it. If you respond to an objection by altering your P.O.V, then *it is crucial that you reevaluate the new view on which you have decided*. Suppose you have a P.O.V., call it A, and that you alter it in response to an objection. Let B denote this new, altered P.O.V. You now must evaluate B. And if you replace B with a new altered P.O.V., C, then you must evaluate C. When do you stop this process? When and only when you develop a P.O.V. that can be *defended*. In other words, keep altering your P.O.V. *until you can explain all of your objections away*.

You may have to alter your view several times before you can actually defend it. Importantly, the P.O.V. that you are able to defend is the only P.O.V. (of yours) that you will write about in your paper. Moreover, the only *responses* that you will write about will be the responses in which you explain your objections away. If you respond to an objection by altering your P.O.V., in other words, *you will not write about this*. For when you respond to an objection by altering your P.O.V., you are still in the process of thinking and of sharpening your focus, and these things should be left out of your paper.

Below our author raises an objection, in the form of counterexample, to her P.O.V. that says that the criticism that utilitarianism is incompatible with rights is flawed. Our author also responds to this objection by explaining it away:

Is the individual rights argument against classical utilitarianism flawed? In my view, it is because this argument depends on a misapprehension of the theory. This argument alleges that if the morally right action is defined as one that produces the maximum amount of happiness of the majority (given the alternatives), and if we can maximize the happiness of the majority by violating someone's rights, then according to this theory, it is morally right to violate someone's rights. But since it is not morally right to violate someone's rights, the objection goes, then classical utilitarianism must be false.

For example, if we stole Bill Gates's money and redistributed it to middle-class Americans, this would maximize the happiness of the majority. According to utilitarianism, however, this would be the morally right action to perform. So if one accepts utilitarianism, then one must accept that it is morally right to steal and redistribute Bill Gates's money. But this seems false; therefore, utilitarianism must be false.

This seems to me to be a bad argument. For despite appearances, stealing Bill Gates's money *would not* maximize happiness in the long run. People would start to feel guilty, would fear that someone might violate their rights and steal from them, and so on. At best, stealing Bill Gates's money would give people instant gratification, but misery would eventually be waiting down the road. For these reasons, it seems to me that happiness can never be maximized if one does not respect individual rights, so one cannot argue that utilitarianism is incompatible with rights. This is why I believe that the criticism that says that utilitarianism is incompatible with rights is flawed.

Now one might object to my claim that violating rights never maximizes happiness by arguing that there are at least some cases wherein violating rights will maximize happiness. For example, suppose that I steal Bill Gates's money and suppose that no one finds out. I then give the money as an anonymous contribution to the University of Michigan. This would surely maximize the happiness of the majority and so would be morally right. And in the long run, no one would feel bad because they would never know. So in this case, happiness would be maximized, even in the long run, if we violated an individual's rights.

My response to this objection is that the happiness of the majority would not be maximized even if one were to steal the money undetected and give it to a university as an anonymous contribution. The maximum amount of happiness is only achieved if individuals are not being misled and if they have full disclosure of the facts. But the individuals in the above example do not have full disclosure; therefore, happiness will not be maximized.

Note how our author does not respond to the objection by altering her P.O.V. but by defending it. It could be the case that our author *originally* held the view that the individual rights objection is *not* flawed, but the evaluation process caused her to alter that view to the one above. Accordingly, she does not mention the view that she has altered nor why she has altered it. What we are left with above are the *results* of her having thought about the issue, rather than a stream of consciousness paper wherein we see our author actually *thinking through* the issue. Indeed, in order to write a philosophy paper successfully, you must first think through an issue until you can defend a P.O.V. But the only P.O.V. that you will write about is the one that you can defend in the face of objections.

When you are able to defend your P.O.V., the next step is to decide how you are going to present the information in your paper. Your paper should be well organized and structured. Philosophical papers that are not well structured are very difficult to read. Fortunately, if you spend some time thinking in order to develop a P.O.V. that you can defend, organizing your paper should be fairly easy.

STRUCTURE

The best way to organize your paper is with an outline. To be sure, the nature of your assignment will determine the contents of your paper and therefore, of its outline. Nevertheless, there are certain structural features that all philosophical papers should reflect, namely, an *introduction* and a *summary*.

The first paragraph of your philosophical paper should contain an introduction that explains, in general terms, what you will be doing in the paper. Your introduction should clearly state your P.O.V., as well as some indication of how you will defend it. For instance, consider our author's introduction to her essay on the individual rights argument against act utilitarianism:

Act utilitarianism is a theory that defines a right action as the one that, among several alternatives, maximizes the happiness of the majority. This theory has been subject to many criticisms. One of the more serious criticisms is that this theory is incompatible with individual rights. In the following I will argue that this criticism is weak because it rests on a misapprehension of act utilitarianism. I will defend my view by raising and responding to an objection to it.

Note how our author is telling her reader precisely what she will be doing in her paper. Also note how streamlined her introduction is and how she uses fairly simplistic language. Your introduction should look like the one above. Think of the introduction as a road map for the reader. You should assume that your reader has virtually no knowledge of the topic on which you are writing. Hence, aim for precision, clarity, and simplicity of language—both in your introduction and throughout the rest of your paper.

The last paragraph of your paper should contain a summary of the important points made in your paper. Like your introduction, your summary should review these points in a precise, clear manner. For instance,

To sum up, I have argued that the individual rights criticism against act utilitarianism is flawed because it rests on a misapprehension of the theory. The criticism assumes that violating individual rights will maximize the happiness of the majority. I have argued that it will not. At best, violating rights will give the majority happiness in the short term, but in the long run, violating individual rights will lead to the maximum amount of misery! I have defended my view by raising and responding to an objection. If I am right, then perhaps act utilitarianism is not as problematic as it seems.

When you make your outline, then, always have an introduction and a summary as the first and last items. The remainder of the outline will be determined by the nature of your assignment. The following is a good outline for the utilitarianism assignment:

  I. Introduction
 II. State individual rights criticism

   a. provide an example that illustrates the criticism

III. Argue that the above criticism is flawed because it misunderstands utilitarianism

   a. provide an example that illustrates why the criticism is flawed

IV. Raise an objection to my argument

   a. provide an example

V. Respond to objection

   a. provide an example

VI. Summary

Once you construct an outline, you are ready to write the paper. As you can see from the above outline, numbers II–V comprise developing a P.O.V. that you can defend, which, as you know, you should do *before* you construct your outline. Once you have developed a P.O.V. that you can defend, your outline should fall naturally into place. And once this happens, you are ready to actually write your paper.

FINAL TIPS ON WRITING YOUR PAPER

If you want to write a good philosophical paper, then you must spend some time on editing and revising it. After writing your first draft, print it out and read it out loud. If possible, have someone read it and give you comments (this is what professional philosophers do). This will help you to identify the portions of your paper that need to be rewritten.

You should set aside one day for writing the outline and first draft of your paper and one day for ed-

iting. The following schedule is a good one for most writing assignments in philosophy classes:

2 days–1 week	Understand nature of your assignment. Develop a P.O.V. that you can defend.
1 day	Construct outline and write first draft.
1 day	Revise first draft.

Summing up my suggestions for writing a philosophical paper, then, first make sure that you are clear on what your assignment requires. Then, develop a P.O.V. by asking yourself the questions that your assignment requires you to answer. Answer these questions and provide reasons for your answer. Write down your answer as a conclusion of a deductive argument and the reasons that you have for believing your answer as its premises. Evaluate this argument. If you find that your argument is invalid, supply missing premises until it is valid. When determining whether the premises are true, look for an objection to your P.O.V. by checking to see whether your premises imply undesirable consequences or are subject to counterexamples. When you find an objection, respond to it. If your response is not a defense, you need to evaluate your new P.O.V. If your response is a defense, make an outline with "introduction" and "summary" as its first and last items, respectively. Use your outline to write a first draft of the paper. Allow time for proofreading and rewriting. A flowchart is provided summarizing these steps.

CREDITS